Business Law & the Legal Environment

Virginia Tech

6th Edition

Jeffrey F. Beatty | Susan S. Samuelson

CENGAGE
Learning

Australia • Brazil • Japan • Korea • Mexico • Singapore • Spain • United Kingdom • United States

CENGAGE Learning

Business Law & the Legal Environment: Virginia Tech, 6th Edition

Senior Project Development Manager:
Linda deStefano

Market Development Manager:
Heather Kramer

Senior Production/Manufacturing Manager:
Donna M. Brown

Production Editorial Manager:
Kim Fry

Sr. Rights Acquisition Account Manager:
Todd Osborne

Printed in the United States of America

Business Law and the Legal Environment, Standard Edition, 6th Edition
Jeffrey F. Beatty | Susan S. Samuelson

ISBN-13: 978-1-285-89504-8

ISBN-10: 1-285-89504-5

Cengage Learning
5191 Natorp Boulevard
Mason, Ohio 45040
USA

Cengage Learning is a leading provider of customized learning solutions with office locations around the globe, including Singapore, the United Kingdom, Australia, Mexico, Brazil, and Japan. Locate your local office at:
international.cengage.com/region.

Cengage Learning products are represented in Canada by Nelson Education, Ltd.
For your lifelong learning solutions, visit **www.cengage.com/custom.**
Visit our corporate website at **www.cengage.com.**

Brief Contents

Looking for more examples for class? Find all the latest developments on our blog at **bizlawupdate.com**. To be notified when we post updates, just "like" our Facebook page at Beatty Business Law or follow us on Twitter @bizlawupdate.

Note from the Authors

New to This Edition

A New Chapter: Practical Contracts

The contracts chapters in this and other business law texts focus on the *theory* of contract law. And that theory is important. But our students tell us that theory, by itself, is not enough. They need to know how these abstract rules operate in *practice*. They want to understand the structure and content of a standard agreement. Our students ask questions such as: Do I need a written agreement? What do these legal terms *really* mean? Are any important provisions missing? What happens if a provision is unclear? Do I need to hire a lawyer? How can I use a lawyer most effectively? These are the questions that we answer in this new chapter. As an illustration throughout the chapter, we use a real contract between a movie studio and an actor.

Landmark Cases

As a general rule, we want our cases to be as current as possible—reporting on the world as it is now. However, sometimes students can benefit from reading vintage cases that are still good law and also provide a deep understanding of how and why the law has developed as it has. Thus, for example, we have added *Miranda v. Arizona*. Reading this case provides students with a much better understanding of why the Supreme Court created Miranda rights. And this context helps students follow the recent Supreme Court rulings on *Miranda*. Other landmark cases include: *Palsgraf v. Long Island Railroad, Hawkins v. McGee* (the case of the hairy hand), *Hadley v. Baxendale, Griggs v. Duke Power Co.*, and *Chiarella v. United States*.

CPA Material

We have made two changes to the CPA material. First, faculty have told us that they are sometimes pressured to teach the CPA material, even if not really necessary, because students feel cheated if they skip a chapter. To solve this problem, we have created a separate unit entitled **Additional CPA Topics**. In it, we have placed topics that are of primary interest to accounting students: Secured Transactions, Negotiable Instruments, and Accountants' Liability. Certainly all professors have the option of including this material in their courses, but those who want to skip it will now have free rein to do so.

Second, to reflect the changes in the new CPA exam, we have eliminated the chapter on Article 4 of the UCC, entitled Liability for Negotiable Instruments: Banks and Their Customers. We have taken this step for several reasons: (1) this material is no longer covered on the CPA exam, (2) it is not as relevant as it used to be and (3) faculty would like more breathing room in their syllabus. Also, we felt that class time would be better spent on Practical Contracts than on a third day of negotiable instruments.

The New Patent Law

This statute represents the most major change in patent law in our lifetime.

End of Chapter Material

To facilitate student learning and class discussion, we have overhauled the study questions at the end of the chapters. They are now divided into three parts:

1. Multiple Choice Questions. Many instructors use this format in their tests, so it seemed appropriate to provide practice questions. The answers to these multiple choice questions are available to students online.
2. Essay Questions. Students can use these as study questions and professors can also assign them as written homework problems.
3. Discussion Questions. Instructors can use these questions to enhance class discussion. If assigned in advance, students will have a chance to think about the answers before class. This format is familiar to students because business cases often pose discussion questions in advance.

New Material

We have, of course, added substantial new material, with a particular focus on the Internet and social media. For example, there is a discussion in the Securities Law chapter about special issues involving Facebook and LinkedIn. The Employment Law chapter includes a section on social media. The chapter on the Life and Death of a Corporation uses Facebook's charter as an illustration. There are new cases involving eBay and craigslist. In addition, the chapter on Starting a Business includes a new section about Benefit organizations—both Corporations and LLCs.

Staying Current: Our Blog, Facebook and Twitter

Business law changes rapidly. To find out about new developments, visit our blog at bizlawupdate.com. If you "like" our Facebook page at Beatty Business Law or follow us on Twitter @bizlawupdate, you will automatically receive a notification whenever we post to the blog.

The Beatty/Samuelson Difference

It has been 18 years since we began work on the first edition of this textbook. At the time, publishers warned us that our undertaking was risky because there were already so many business law texts. Despite these warnings, we were convinced that there was a market for a business law book that was different from all the others. Our goal was to capture the passion and excitement, the sheer enjoyment, of the law. Business law is notoriously complex, and as authors, we are obsessed with accuracy. Yet this intriguing subject also abounds with human conflict and hard-earned wisdom, forces that can make a law book sparkle.

Now, as the sixth edition goes to press, we look back over the past eighteen years and are touched by unsolicited comments from students, such as these posted on Amazon: "Glad I purchased this. It really helps put the law into perspective and allows me as a leader to make intelligent decisions. Thanks." Or, "I enjoyed learning business law and was happy my college wanted this book. THUMBS UP!" We think of the students who have emailed us to say, "In terms of clarity, comprehensiveness and vividness of style, I think it's probably the best textbook I've ever used in any subject," and "I had no idea business law could be so interesting." Or the faculty who have told us, "Until I read your book I never really understood UCC 2-207" or, "With your book, we have great class discussions." Comments such as these never cease to thrill us and to make us grateful that we persisted in writing a business law text like no other—a book that is precise and authoritative, *yet a pleasure to read.*

Comprehensive. Staying comprehensive means staying current. This sixth edition contains nearly 100 new cases. Almost all were reported within the last two or three years, and many within the last 12 months. We never include a new court opinion merely because it is recent. Yet the law evolves continually, and our willingness to toss out old cases and add important new ones ensures that this book—and its readers—remain on the frontier of legal developments.

Strong Narrative. The law is full of great stories, and we use them. Your students and ours should come to class excited. Look at Chapter 3, on dispute resolution. No tedious list of next steps in litigation, this chapter teaches the subject by tracking a double-indemnity lawsuit. An executive is dead. Did he drown accidentally, obligating the insurance company to pay? Or did the businessman commit suicide, voiding the policy? The student follows the action from the discovery of the body, through each step of the lawsuit, to the final appeal.

Students read stories and remember them. Strong narratives provide a rich context for the remarkable quantity of legal material presented. When students care about the material they are reading, they persevere. We have been delighted to find that they also arrive in class eager to question, discuss, and learn.

Precise. The great joy of using English accurately is the power it gives us to attack and dissect difficult issues, rendering them comprehensible to any lay reader. This text takes on the most complex legal topics of the day, yet it is appropriate for *all college and graduate level students*. Accessible prose goes hand in hand with legal precision. We take great pride in walking our readers through the most serpentine mazes this tough subject can offer. UCC section 2-207, on "battle of forms" conflicts, is hardly sexy material, but it is important. We spotlight the real-world need for section 2-207, and then use pinpoint directions to guide our readers through its many switchbacks, arriving at a full understanding with sanity and good humor intact.

As we explore this extraordinary discipline, we lure readers along with quirky anecdotes and colorful diagrams. However, before the trip is over, we insist that students:

- gauge policy and political considerations,
- grapple with legal and social history,
- spot the nexus between disparate doctrines, and
- confront tough moral choices.

Authoritative. We insist, as you do, on a law book that is indisputably accurate. A professor must teach with assurance, confident that every paragraph is the result of exhaustive research and meticulous presentation. Dozens of tough-minded people spent thousands of hours reviewing this book, and we are delighted with the stamp of approval we have received from trial and appellate judges, working attorneys, scholars, and teachers.

We reject the cloudy definitions and fuzzy explanations that can invade judicial opinions and legal scholarship. To highlight the most important rules, we use bold print, and then follow with vivacious examples written in clear, forceful English. We cheerfully venture into contentious areas, relying on very recent decisions. Can a creditor pierce the veil of an LLC? What are the rights of an LLC member in the absence of an operating agreement? Where there is doubt about the current (or future) status of a doctrine, we say so. In areas of particularly heated debate, we footnote our work: we want you to have absolute trust in this book.

A Book for Students. We have written this book as if we were speaking directly to our students. We provide black letter law, but we also explain concepts in terms that hook students. Every chapter begins with a story, either fictional or real, to illustrate the issues in the chapter and provide context. Over the years, we have learned how much more successfully we can teach when our students are intrigued. No matter what kind of a show we put on in class, *they are only learning when they want to learn.*

Many of our students were not yet born when George H. W. Bush was elected president. They come to college with varying levels of preparation; many now arrive from other countries. We have found that to teach business law most effectively we must provide its context. Only with this background do students grasp the importance and impact of our laws.

At the same time, we enjoy offering "nuts and bolts" information that grab students: how to obtain a free credit report, how scam artists create car accidents in order to file fraudulent insurance claims, how to create a living will. Students respond enthusiastically to this approach. One professor asked a student to compare our book with the one that the class was then using. This was the student's reaction: "I really enjoy reading the [Beatty & Samuelson] textbook, and I have decided that I will give you this memo ASAP, but I am keeping the book until Wednesday so that I may continue reading. Thanks! :-)"

Along with other professors, we have used this text in courses for undergraduates, MBAs, and Executive MBAs, the students ranging in age from 18 to 55. This book works, as some unsolicited comments indicate:

- An undergraduate wrote, "This is the best textbook I have had in college, on any subject."
- A business law professor stated that the "clarity of presentation is superlative. I have never seen the complexity of contract law made this readable."
- An MBA student commented, "I think the textbook is great. The book is relevant, easy to understand, and interesting."
- A state supreme court justice wrote that the book is "a valuable blend of rich scholarship and easy readability. Students and professors should rejoice with this publication."
- A Fortune 500 vice president, enrolled in an Executive MBA program, commented, "I really liked the chapters. They were crisp, organized, and current. The information was easy to understand and enjoyable."
- An undergraduate wrote, "The textbook is awesome. A lot of the time I read more than what is assigned—I just don't want to stop."

Humor. Throughout the text we use humor—judiciously—to lighten and enlighten. Not surprisingly, students have applauded—but is wit appropriate? How dare we employ levity in this venerable discipline? We offer humor because we take law seriously. We revere the law for its ancient traditions, its dazzling intricacy, its relentless though imperfect attempt to give order and decency to our world. Because we are confident of our respect for the law, we are not afraid to employ some levity. Leaden prose masquerading as legal scholarship does no honor to the field.

Humor also helps retention. Research shows that the funnier or more bizarre the example, the longer students will remember it. Students are more likely to remember a contract problem described in an original setting, and from that setting recall the underlying principle. By contrast, one widget is hard to distinguish from another.

Features

We chose the features for our book with great care. Each feature responds to an essential pedagogical goal. Here are some of those goals and the matching feature.

Exam Strategy

GOAL: To help students learn more effectively and to prepare for exams. In developing this feature, we asked ourselves: What do students want? The short answer is—a good grade in the course. How many times a semester does a student ask you, "What can I do to study for the exam?" We are happy to help them study and earn a good grade because that means that they will also be learning.

About six times per chapter, we stop the action and give students a two-minute quiz. In the body of the text, again in the end-of-chapter review, and also in the Instructor's Manual, we present a typical exam question. Here lies the innovation: we guide the student in analyzing the issue. We teach the reader—over and over—how to approach a question: to start with the overarching principle, examine the fine point raised in the question, apply the analysis that courts use, and deduce the right answer. This skill is second nature to lawyers but not to students. Without practice, too many students panic, jumping at a convenient answer, and leaving aside the tools they have spent the course acquiring. Let's change that. Students love the Exam Strategy feature.

You Be The Judge

GOAL: Get them thinking independently. When reading case opinions, students tend to accept the court's "answer." Judges, of course, try to write decisions that appear indisputable, when in reality they may be controversial—or wrong. From time to time we want students to think through the problem and reach their own answer. Virtually every chapter contains a You Be The Judge feature, providing the facts of the case and conflicting appellate arguments. The court's decision, however, appears only in the Instructor's Manual. Because students do not know the result, discussions are more complex and lively.

Devil's Advocate

GOAL: Encourage deeper analysis. In this feature we provide short critical commentary on the decision just reported. We are reminding students that the court's holding is the work of mortals. There is generally a very respectable counter-argument, which at least some people will find more persuasive. Students should consider the opposing view and practice formulating their own positions, independent of the judges' reasoning. A student who concludes, after analyzing alternative views, that the court got it right, understands the holding more comprehensively than one who never considered the other side.

For example, in Chapter 8, on Criminal Law, we include the famous *Ewing* case on cruel and unusual punishment, but follow it with a Devil's Advocate feature arguing against a sentence of 25 years to life in a shoplifting case.

Ethics

GOAL: Make ethics real. We ask ethical questions about cases, legal issues, and commercial practices. Is it fair for one party to void a contract by arguing, months after the fact, that there was no consideration? What is a manager's ethical obligation when asked to provide a reference for a former employee? What is wrong with bribery? What is the ethical obligation of developed nations to dispose of toxic waste from computers? We believe that asking the questions, and encouraging discussion, reminds students that ethics is an essential element of justice, and of a satisfying life.

Cases

GOAL: Let the judges speak. Each case begins with a summary of the facts and a statement of the issue. Next comes a tightly edited version of the decision, in the court's own language, so that students "hear" the law developing in the diverse voices of our many judges. We cite cases using a modified bluebook form. In the principal cases in each chapter, we provide the state or federal citation, the regional citation, and the LEXIS or Westlaw citation. We also give students a brief description of the court. Because many of our cases are so recent, some will have only a LEXIS or Westlaw citation.

End of Chapter Exam Review and Questions

GOAL: Encourage students to practice! At the end of the chapters we provide a list of review points and several additional Exam Strategy exercises in the Question/Strategy/Result format. We also challenge the students with 15 or more problems—Multiple Choice, Essay Questions and Discussion Questions. The questions include the following:

- *You Be The Judge Writing Problem.* The students are given appellate arguments on both sides of the question and must prepare a written opinion.
- *Ethics.* This question highlights the ethical issues of a dispute and calls upon the student to formulate a specific, reasoned response.
- *CPA Questions.* For topics covered by the CPA exam, administered by the American Institute of Certified Public Accountants, the Exam Review includes questions from previous CPA exams.

Answers to all the Multiple Choice questions are available to the students online through www.cengagebrain.com.

Author Transition

Jeffrey Beatty fought an unremitting ten-year battle against a particularly aggressive form of leukemia which, despite his great courage and determination, he ultimately lost. Jeffrey, a gentleman to the core, was an immensely kind, funny, and thoughtful human being, someone who sang and danced, and who earned the respect and affection of colleagues and students alike. In writing these books he wanted students to see and understand the impact of law in their everyday lives as well as its role in supporting human dignity, and what's more, he wanted students to laugh.

Because of the length of Jeffrey's illness, we had ample time to develop an author-transition plan. Through a combination of new and old methods (social media and personal connections), we were able to identify a wonderfully talented group of applicants—graduates of top law schools who had earned myriad teaching and writing prizes. We read two rounds of blind submissions and met with finalists. In the end, we are thrilled to report that Dean Bredeson has joined the Beatty/Samuelson author team. A member of the faculty at the University of Texas McCombs School of Business, Dean is a devoted teacher who has received the school's highest teaching award for the last four years. He is also the author of the text, *Applied Business Ethics*. Dean has a number of qualities that are essential to a textbook writer: a keen insight into explaining complex material in an engaging manner, meticulous attention to detail, an ability to meet deadlines, and a wry sense of humor.

Teaching Materials

For more information about any of these ancillaries, contact your Cengage Learning/South-Western Legal Studies Sales Representative, or visit the Beatty & Samuelson Business Law (Standard Edition) Web site at **www.cengagebrain.com**.

Instructor's Manual. The Instructor's Manual, available on both the IRCD and the Instructor's Support Site at www.cengagebrain.com, includes special features to enhance class discussion and student progress:

- Exam Strategy Problems. If your students would like more of these problems, there is an additional section of Exam Strategy problems in the Instructor's Manual.
- Dialogues. These are a series of questions-and-answers on pivotal cases and topics. The questions provide enough material to teach a full session. In a pinch, you could walk into class with nothing but the manual and use the Dialogues to conduct an exciting class.
- Action learning ideas: interviews, quick research projects, drafting exercises, classroom activities, commercial analyses, and other suggested assignments that get students out of their chairs and into the diverse settings of business law.
- Skits. Various chapters have lively skits that students can perform in class, with no rehearsal, to put legal doctrine in a real-life context.
- A chapter theme and a quote of the day.
- Current Focus. This feature offers updates of text material.
- Additional cases and examples.
- Answers to You Be the Judge cases from the text and to the Exam Review questions found at the end of each chapter.

Test Bank. The test bank offers hundreds of multiple choice, short answer and essay problems and may be obtained online at **www.cengagebrain.com** or on the Instructor's Resource CD.

ExamView Testing Software—Computerized Testing Software. This testing software contains all of the questions in the test bank. This program is an easy-to-use test creation software compatible with Microsoft Windows. Instructors can add or edit questions, instructions, and answers; they can also select questions by previewing them on the screen, selecting them randomly, or selecting them by number. ExamView gives instructors the ability to create and administer quizzes online, whether over the Internet, a local area network (LAN), or a wide area network (WAN). The ExamView testing software is available on the Instructor's Resource CD.

Instructor's Resource CD (IRCD). The IRCD contains the ExamView testing software files, the test bank in Microsoft Word files, the Instructor's Manual in Microsoft Word files, and the Microsoft PowerPoint Lecture Review Slides.

Microsoft PowerPoint Lecture Review Slides. PowerPoint slides are available for use by instructors for enhancing their lectures and to aid students in note taking. Download these slides at **www.cengagebrain.com**. The PowerPoint slides are also available on the IRCD.

CengageNOW. This robust, online course management system gives you more control in less time and delivers better student outcomes—NOW. CengageNOW for *Business Law and the Legal Environment* 6e has been expanded to include six homework types that align with the six levels of Bloom's taxonomy: Knowledge: Chapter Review; Comprehension: Business Law Scenarios; Application: Legal Reasoning; Analysis: IRAC; Synthesis: Exam Strategy; and Evaluation: Business Wisdom. Used together, CengageNOW will ensure that students develop the higher-level thinking skills they need to reach an advanced understanding of the material.

Aplia. Engage, prepare and educate your students with this ideal online learning solution. Aplia's™ business law solution ensures that students stay on top of their coursework with regularly scheduled homework assignments and automatic grading with detailed, immediate feedback on every question. Interactive teaching tools and content further increase engagement and understanding. Aplia™ assignments match the language, style, and structure of *Business Law and the Legal Environment* 6e, allowing your students to apply what they learn in the text directly to their homework.

Business Law CourseMate. Cengage Learning's Business Law CourseMate brings course concepts to life with interactive learning, study, and exam preparation tools—including an e-book–that supports the printed textbook. Designed to address a variety of learning styles, students will have access to flashcards, Learning Objectives, and the Key Terms for quick reviews. A set of auto-gradable, interactive quizzes will allow students to instantly gauge their comprehension of the material. On the instructor's side, all quiz scores and student activity are mapped within a set of intuitive student performance analytical tools called Engagement Tracker, which helps the instructor identify at-risk students. An interactive blog helps connect book concepts to real-world situations happening now.

WebTutor™ for Blackboard® or WebCT®. Jumpstart your course with this interactive, web-based, teaching and learning resource that is designed specifically for *Business Law and the Legal Environment* 6e. Easily blend, add, edit, reorganize, or delete content, including media assets, quizzing, Web links, discussion topics, interactive games and exercises, and more. These tools supplement the classroom experience and ensure students leave with the resources they need to succeed.

Business Law Digital Video Library. This dynamic online video library features over 60 video clips that spark class discussion and clarify core legal principles. The library is organized into four series:

- ***Legal Conflicts in Business*** includes specific modern business and e-commerce scenarios.
- ***Ask the Instructor*** contains straightforward explanations of concepts for student review.
- ***Drama of the Law*** features classic business scenarios that spark classroom participation.
- ***LawFlix*** contains clips from many popular films, including *The Money Pit*, *Midnight Run*, and *Casino*.
- ***Real World Legal*** takes students out of the classroom and into real life situations, encouraging them to consider the legal aspects of decision-making in the business world.
- ***Business Ethics in Action*** challenges students to examine ethical dilemmas in the world of business.

Access to the Business Law Digital Video Library is available as an optional package with each new student text at no additional charge. Students with used books can purchase access to the video clips online. For more information about the Business Law Digital Video Library, visit: **www.cengagebrain.com**.

A Handbook of Basic Law Terms, Black's Law Dictionary Series. This paperback dictionary, prepared by the editor of the popular Black's Law Dictionary, can be packaged for a small additional cost with any new South-Western Legal Studies in Business text.

Student Guide to the Sarbanes-Oxley Act. This brief overview for business students explains the Sarbanes-Oxley Act, what is required of whom, and how it might affect students in their business life. Available as an optional package with the text.

Interaction with the Authors. This is our standard: every professor who adopts this book must have a superior experience. We are available to help in any way we can. Adopters of this text often call us or email us to ask questions, obtain a syllabus, offer suggestions, share pedagogical concerns, or inquire about ancillaries. (And if you would like to share your course syllabus, please send it to us so that we can post it on our blog, bizlawupdate.com.) One of the pleasures of working on this project has been this link to so many colleagues around the country. We value those connections, are eager to respond, and would be happy to hear from you.

Jeffrey F. Beatty

Susan S. Samuelson
Phone: (617) 353-2033
Email: ssamuels@bu.edu

Dean A. Bredeson
Phone: (512) 471-5248
Email: bredeson@mail.utexas.edu

Acknowledgments

We are grateful to the following reviewers who gave such helpful comments on the first six editions:

Joseph Adamo
Cazenovia College

Joy M. Alessi
New York City College of Technology

J. Mark Anderson
Athens State University

John H. Bailey, III
Vanderbilt University

Robert Bird
University of Connecticut

Weldon Blake
Bethune Cookman College

Karl Boedecker
University of San Francisco

Jeff W. Bruns
Bacone College

Martin Carrigan
The University of Findlay

Machiavelli Chao
University of California, Irvine

Amy Chataginer
Mississippi Gulf Coast Community College

Eric Chen
Saint Joseph College

Brad Childs
Belmont University

Wade M. Chumney
Georgia Institute of Technology

George Oscar Darkenwald
South Puget Sound Community College

Raven Davenport
Houston Community College

Philip E. DeMarco
Mission Community College

Laura Dendinger
Wayne State College

Julia Derrick
Brevard Community College

Carol Docan
California State University, Northridge

Kiren Dosanjh
California State University Northridge

Thomas N. Edmonds
Western Michigan University

Rafi Efrat
California State University, Northridge

Jason Royce Fichtner
Drake University

Mary Kay Finn
The University of Akron

Jerrold Fleisher
Dominican College

David Forsyth
Arizona State University

Edward Gac
University of Colorado

Kimberly Ann Goudy
Central Ohio Technical College

Janet Riola Hale
Texas State University

Randall K. Hanson
University of North Carolina at Wilmington

Charles Hartmann
Wright State University

Paul A. Hatchett, Jr.
St. Petersburg College

Thomas Higgins
Illinois Central College

Greg Hughes
Vermont Technical College

Charles J. Hunt, Jr.
Pepperdine University

John Jackson
California State University Fullerton

Charles E. King
Colorado Christian University

Cynthia King
Beaufort County Community College

Richard L. Kohn
Southeast Community College

Samuel Kohn
New York Institute of Technology

Frank J. Kolb, Jr.
Quinnipiac University

Murray S. Levin
University of Kansas

Leslie S. Lukasik
Skagit Valley College, Whidbey Island Campus

Diane MacDonald
Pacific Lutheran University

Greg McCann
Stetson University

Gail K. McCracken
University of Michigan–Dearborn

MarySheila E. McDonald
Philadelphia University

Sharlene McEvoy
Fairfield University

Michael McKinney
East Tennessee State University

Jeff W. Meverden
Fox Valley Technical College

Linda Moran
Santa Rosa Jr. College

James F. Morgan
California State University Chico

Carol L. Nielsen
Bemidji State University

Cliff Olson
Southern Adventist University

Jeffrey Douglas Penley
Catawba Valley Community College

Cynthia Phillips
Moorehead State University

Vivica Pierre
California State University, Long Beach

Stephen R. Prescott
Wake Technical Community College

Mary Rau-Foster
Belmont University

Ian Redpath
Canisius College

Irene K. Rudnick
University of South Carolina, Aiken

Linda Samuels
The University of Akron

Kurt M. Saunders
California State University, Northridge

Minna Schiller
Bellevue Community College

Sean D. K. Scott
St. Petersburg College

Lara Short
Middle Tennessee State University

Yolanda I. Smith
Northern Virginia Community College

Charles Soos
Rutgers School of Business

Alexis Stokes
Texas State University

Susan Marie Taylor
Andrews University

Ben Thompson
Georgia Southern University

Jan Tucker
Western Governors University

Bob Young
University of Nebraska at Kearney

David B. Washington
Augsburg College

Scott White
University of Wisconsin–Platteville

Melanie Williams
California State University, Northridge

Asher Wilson
Central Washington University—Des Moines

Dexter Woods
Ohio Northern University

ABOUT THE AUTHORS

Jeffrey F. Beatty was an Associate Professor of Business Law at the Boston University School of Management. After receiving his B.A. from Sarah Lawrence and his J.D. from Boston University, he practiced with the Greater Boston Legal Services representing indigent clients. At Boston University, he won the Metcalf Cup and Prize, the university's highest teaching award. Professor Beatty also wrote plays and television scripts that were performed in Boston, London, and Amsterdam.

Susan S. Samuelson is a Professor of Business Law at Boston University's School of Management. After earning her A.B. at Harvard University and her J.D. at Harvard Law School, Professor Samuelson practiced with the firm of Choate, Hall and Stewart. She has written many articles on legal issues for scholarly and popular journals, including the *American Business Law Journal*, *Ohio State Law Journal*, *Boston University Law Review*, *Harvard Journal on Legislation*, *National Law Journal*, *Sloan Management Review*, *Inc. Magazine*, *Better Homes and Gardens*, and *Boston Magazine*. At Boston University she won the Broderick Prize for excellence in teaching. Professor Samuelson is the Faculty Director of the Boston University Executive MBA program.

Dean A. Bredeson is a Senior Lecturer at the University of Texas' McCombs School of Business, where he has been on the faculty for 16 years. He also holds a J.D. from the University of Texas. He has previously published *Student Guide to the Sarbanes-Oxley Act* and two textbooks which explore the intersection of law and ethics: *Applied Business Ethics* and *Ethics in the Workplace*. He is a four-time winner of the Lockheed-Martin Award, which is awarded each year to the one member of the faculty at McCombs with the highest student course evaluations in undergraduate courses. He is also among the youngest-ever recipients of the Board of Regents Teaching Award, the UT System's highest teaching honor.

For Jeffrey, best of
colleagues and dearest of
friends.

S.S.S.

UNIT 1

erstock.com

The Legal Environment

CHAPTER 1

INTRODUCTION TO LAW

© r.nagy/Shutterstock.com

Near Campus

Alan Dawson dumped his Calculus II textbook into his backpack. Outside, a light snow began to fall. With a sigh, he left his apartment and headed out into the early December evening.

Halfway to the library, he encountered a group of his friends "Hey, Alan, we're done with finals," said Gary with a flourish. "You should come to Thirsty's with us."

"I can't. I have my Calculus final tomorrow."

"Carrie's going to be there." Gary raised his eyebrows.

"Come on, Dawson! Be a man! Come on!" said the others. Without a word, Alan reversed direction and headed away from the library. His friends cheered loudly.

When he opened the door, he saw Alan rolling around on the floor, groaning.

At Thirsty's Bar

Anna stood behind the bar and watched four bikers enter. They wore jackets with gang insignia, and purple headscarves. One of them approached the bar. "Four Budweisers," he said to Anna.

After gathering her courage, Anna said, "Look, you guys know you can't wear your colors in here."

"What are you gonna do about it, missy?" the biker asked. When she didn't reply, he leaned closer to her. "Four beers."

Anna thought about it for a moment, then gathered four Budweiser longnecks and placed them on the bar. The biker tossed down a $10 bill, took the beers, and joined his three associates at a table.

Anna eyed the telephone on the counter behind her. The owner of Thirsty's had told her to call the cops immediately if she saw any gang colors in there. But the bikers were watching her, and she decided not to make a call right away.

At a back table

"I'm not going home for a few more days," Alan said to Carrie.

"I'm not either. We should do something," Carrie said.

"Yeah," Alan said, trying hard to not seem too excited. "Have you, ah, seen the new DiCaprio movie? We could go see that."

"That would be great."

Alan blissfully made small talk with Carrie, unaware of the bikers or anyone else in the bar.

Eventually, he excused himself and made his way to the restroom.

As he washed his hands, he saw two bikers in the mirror. "Howdy, college boy," one of them said. It was the last thing Alan remembered for awhile.

Twenty minutes later

"Hey, where's Alan?" Gary asked

Carrie said, "I think he went to the restroom."

Frowning, Gary headed back to the men's room. When he opened the door, he saw Alan rolling around on the floor, groaning. His shirt was torn, his face bloody.

"Oh, man, what happened? Are you OK?" Gary asked.

"No," Alan replied.

Gary thumbed 911 on his cell phone.

"Wait a moment," you may be thinking. "Are we reading a chapter on business law or one about biker crimes in a roadside tavern?" Both. Later in the chapter we examine a real case that mirrors the opening scenario. The crime committed against Alan will enable us to explore one of the law's basic principles, negligence. Should a pub owner pay money damages to the victim of gang violence? The owner herself did nothing aggressive. Should she have prevented the harm? Does her failure to stop the assault make her responsible? What begins as a gang incident ends up an issue of commercial liability.

Law is powerful, essential, and fascinating. We hope this book will persuade you of all three ideas. We place great demands on our courts, asking them to make our large, complex, and sometimes violent society into a safer, fairer, more orderly place. Judges must reason their way through countless complex issues.

Three Important Ideas about Law

Power

The strong reach of the law touches nearly everything we do, especially at work. Consider a mid-level manager at Sublime Corp., which manufactures and distributes video games.

During the course of a day's work, she might negotiate a deal with a game developer (contract law). Before signing any deals, she might research whether similar games already exist which might diminish her ability to market the proposed new game (intellectual property law). One of her subordinates might complain about being harassed by a coworker (employment law). Another worker may complain about being required to work long hours (administrative law). And she may consider investing her own money in her company's stock, but she may wonder whether she will get into trouble if she invests based on inside information (securities law).

It is not only as a corporate manager that you will confront the law. As a voter, investor, juror, entrepreneur, and community member, you will influence and be affected by the law. Whenever you take a stance about a legal issue, whether in the corporate office, in the voting booth, or as part of local community groups, you help to create the fabric of our nation. Your views are vital. This book will offer you knowledge and ideas from which to form and continually reassess your legal opinions and values.

Importance

Law is also essential. *Every* society of which we have any historical record has had some system of laws. For example, consider the Visigoths, a nomadic European people who overran much of present-day France and Spain during the fifth and sixth centuries A.D. Their code admirably required judges to be "quick of perception, clear in judgment, and lenient in the infliction of penalties." It detailed dozens of crimes.

Our legal system is largely based upon the English model, but many societies contributed ideas. The Iroquois Native Americans, for example, played a role in the creation of our own government. Five major nations made up the Iroquois group: the Mohawk, Cayuga, Oneida, Onondaga, and Seneca. Each nation governed its own domestic issues. But each nation also elected "sachems" to a League of the Iroquois. The league had authority over any matters that were common to all, such as relations with outsiders. Thus, by the fifteenth century, the Iroquois had solved the problem of *federalism:* how to have two levels of government, each with specified powers. Their system impressed Benjamin Franklin and others and influenced the drafting of our Constitution, with its powers divided between state and federal governments.[1]

Fascination

In 1835, the young French aristocrat Alexis de Tocqueville traveled through the United States, observing the newly democratic people and the qualities that made them unique. One of the things that struck de Tocqueville most forcefully was the American tendency to file suit: "Scarcely any political question arises in the United States that is not resolved, sooner or later, into a judicial question."[2] De Tocqueville got it right: For better or worse, we do expect courts to solve many problems.

Not only do Americans litigate—they watch each other do it. Every television season offers at least one new courtroom drama to a national audience breathless for more cross-examination. Almost all of the states permit live television coverage of real trials. The most heavily viewed event in the history of the medium was the O.J. Simpson murder trial. In most nations, coverage of judicial proceedings is not allowed.[3]

The law is a big part of our lives, and it is wise to know something about it. Within a few weeks, you will probably find yourself following legal events in the news with keener

[1]JackWeatherford, *Indian Givers* (New York: Fawcett Columbine, 1988), pp. 133–150.
[2]Alexis deTocqueville, *Democracy in America* (1835), Vol. 1, Ch. 16.
[3]Regardless of whether we allow cameras, it is an undeniable benefit of the electronic age that we can obtain information quickly. From time to time, we will mention websites of interest. Some of these are for nonprofit groups, while others are commercial sites. We do not endorse or advocate on behalf of any group or company; we simply wish to alert you to what is available.

interest and deeper understanding. In this chapter, we develop the background for our study. We look at where law comes from: its history and its present-day institutions. In the section on jurisprudence, we examine different theories about what "law" really means. And finally we see how courts—and students—analyze a case.

Origins of Our Law

It would be nice if we could look up "the law" in one book, memorize it, and then apply it. But the law is not that simple, and *cannot* be that simple, because it reflects the complexity of contemporary life. In truth, there is no such thing as "the law." Principles and rules of law actually come from *many different* sources. Why is this so? In part because we inherited a complex structure of laws from England.

Additionally, ours is a nation born in revolution and created, in large part, to protect the rights of its people from the government. The Founding Fathers created a national government but insisted that the individual states maintain control in many areas. As a result, each state has its own government with exclusive power over many important areas of our lives. To top it off, the Founders guaranteed many rights to the people alone, ordering national *and* state governments to keep clear. This has worked, but it has caused a multilayered system, with 50 state governments and one federal government all creating and enforcing law.

English Roots

England in the tenth century was a rustic agricultural community with a tiny population and very little law or order. Vikings invaded repeatedly, terrorizing the Anglo-Saxon peoples. Criminals were hard to catch in the heavily forested, sparsely settled nation. The king used a primitive legal system to maintain a tenuous control over his people.

England was divided into shires, and daily administration was carried out by a "shire reeve," later called a sheriff. The shire reeve collected taxes and did what he could to keep peace, apprehending criminals and acting as mediator between feuding families. Two or three times a year, a shire court met; lower courts met more frequently. Today, this method of resolving disputes lives on as mediation, which we will discuss in Chapter 3.

Because there were so few officers to keep the peace, Anglo-Saxon society created an interesting method of ensuring public order. Every freeman belonged to a group of 10 freemen known as a "tithing," headed by a "tithingman." If anyone injured a person outside his tithing or interfered with the king's property, all 10 men of the tithing could be forced to pay. Today, we still use this idea of collective responsibility in business partnerships. All partners are personally responsible for the debts of the partnership. They could potentially lose their homes and all assets because of the irresponsible conduct of one partner. That liability has helped create new forms of business organization, including limited liability companies.

When cases did come before an Anglo-Saxon court, the parties would often be represented either by a clergyman, by a nobleman, or by themselves. There were few professional lawyers. Each party produced "oath helpers," usually 12, who would swear that one version of events was correct. The Anglo-Saxon oath helpers are forerunners of our modern jury of 12 persons.

Medieval tenants in demesne *harrowing, plowing, and seeding a field.*

In 1066, the Normans conquered England. William the Conqueror made a claim never before made in England: that he owned all of the land. The king then granted sections of his lands to his favorite noblemen, as his tenants in chief, creating the system of feudalism. These tenants in chief then granted parts of their land to *tenants in demesne,* who actually occupied a particular estate. Each tenant in demesne owed fidelity to his lord (hence, "landlord"). So what? Just this: land became the most valuable commodity in all of England, and our law still reflects that. One thousand years later, American law still regards land as special. The statute of frauds, which we study in the section on contracts, demands that contracts for the sale or lease of property be in writing. And landlord-tenant law, vital to students and many others, still reflects its ancient roots. Some of a landlord's rights are based on the 1,000-year-old tradition that land is uniquely valuable.

In 1250, Henry de Bracton (d. 1268) wrote a legal treatise that still influences us. *De Legibus et Consuetudinibus Angliae* (*On the Laws and Customs of England*), written in Latin, summarized many of the legal rulings in cases since the Norman Conquest. De Bracton was teaching judges to rule based on previous cases. He was helping to establish the idea of **precedent**. The doctrine of precedent, which developed gradually over centuries, requires that judges decide current cases based on previous rulings. This vital principle is the heart of American common law. Precedent ensures predictability. Suppose a 17-year-old student promises to lease an apartment from a landlord, but then changes her mind. The landlord sues to enforce the lease. The student claims that she cannot be held to the agreement because she is a minor. The judge will look for precedent, that is, older cases dealing with the same issue, and he will find many holding that a contract generally may not be enforced against a minor. That precedent is binding on this case, and the student wins. The accumulation of precedent, based on case after case, makes up the **common law**.

Precedent
The tendency to decide current cases based on previous rulings.

Common law
Judge-made law.

In the end, today's society is dramatically different from that of medieval English society. But interestingly, legal disputes from hundreds of years ago are often quite recognizable today. Some things have changed but others never do.

Here is an actual case from more than six centuries ago, in the court's own language. The plaintiff claims that he asked the defendant to heal his eye with "herbs and other medicines." He says the defendant did it so badly that he blinded the plaintiff in that eye.

The Oculist's Case (1329)

LI MS. Hale 137 (1), fo. 150, Nottingham[4]

Attorney Launde [for defendant]: Sir, you plainly see how [the plaintiff claims] that he had submitted himself to [the defendant's] medicines and his care; and after that he can assign no trespass in his person, inasmuch as he submitted himself to his care: but this action, if he has any, sounds naturally in breach of covenant. We demand [that the case be dismissed].

Excerpts from Judge Denum's Decision: I saw a Newcastle man arraigned before my fellow justice and me for the death of a man. I asked the reason for the indictment, and it was said that he had slain a man under his care, who died within four days afterwards. And because I saw that he was a [doctor] and that he had not done the thing feloniously but [accidentally] I ordered him to be discharged. And suppose a blacksmith, who is a man of skill, injures your horse with a nail, whereby you lose your horse: you shall never have recovery against him. No more shall you here.

Afterwards the plaintiff did not wish to pursue his case any more.

[4]J.Baker and S.Milsom, Sources of English Legal History (London: Butterworth & Co., 1986).

This case from 1329 is an ancient medical malpractice action. Attorney Launde does not deny that his client blinded the plaintiff. He claims that the plaintiff has brought the wrong kind of lawsuit. Launde argues that the plaintiff should have brought a case of "covenant," that is, a lawsuit about a contract.

Judge Denum decides the case on a different principle. He gives judgment to the defendant because the plaintiff voluntarily sought medical care. He implies that the defendant would lose only if he had attacked the plaintiff. As we will see when we study negligence law, this case might have a different outcome today. Note also the informality of the judge's ruling. He rather casually mentions that he came across a related case once before and that he would stand by that outcome. The idea of precedent is just beginning to take hold.

Law in the United States

The colonists brought with them a basic knowledge of English law, some of which they were content to adopt as their own. Other parts, such as religious restrictions, were abhorrent to them. Many had made the dangerous trip to America precisely to escape persecution, and they were not interested in recreating their difficulties in a new land. Finally, some laws were simply irrelevant or unworkable in a world that was socially and geographically so different. American law ever since has been a blend of the ancient principles of English common law and a zeal and determination for change.

During the nineteenth century, the United States changed from a weak, rural nation into one of vast size and potential power. Cities grew, factories appeared, and sweeping movements of social migration changed the population. Changing conditions raised new legal questions. Did workers have a right to form industrial unions? To what extent should a manufacturer be liable if its product injured someone? Could a state government invalidate an employment contract that required 16-hour workdays? Should one company be permitted to dominate an entire industry?

In the twentieth century, the rate of social and technological change increased, creating new legal puzzles. Were some products, such as automobiles, so inherently dangerous that the seller should be responsible for injuries even if no mistakes were made in manufacturing? Who should clean up toxic waste if the company that had caused the pollution no longer existed? If a consumer signed a contract with a billion-dollar corporation, should the agreement be enforced even if the consumer never understood it? New and startling questions arise with great regularity. Before we can begin to examine the answers, we need to understand the sources of contemporary law.

Sources of Contemporary Law

Throughout the text, we will examine countless legal ideas. But binding rules come from many different places. This section describes the significant *categories* of laws in the United States.

United States Constitution

America's greatest legal achievement was the writing of the United States Constitution in 1787. It is the supreme law of the land.[5] Any law that conflicts with it is void. This federal Constitution does three basic things. First, it establishes the national government of the

[5]The Constitution took effect in 1788, when 9 of 13 colonies ratified it. Two more colonies ratified it that year, and the last of the 13 did so in 1789, after the government was already in operation. The complete text of the Constitution appears in Appendix A.

United States, with its three branches. Second, it creates a system of checks and balances among the branches. And third, the Constitution guarantees many basic rights to the American people.

Branches of Government

The Founding Fathers sought a division of government power. They did not want all power centralized in a king or in anyone else. And so, the Constitution divides legal authority into three pieces: legislative, executive, and judicial power.

Legislative power gives the ability to create new laws. In Article I, the Constitution gives this power to the Congress which is comprised of two chambers—a Senate and a House of Representatives. Voters in all 50 states elect representatives who go to Washington, D.C., to serve in the Congress and debate new legal ideas.

The House of Representatives has 435 voting members. A state's voting power is based on its population. Large states (Texas, California, and Florida) send dozens of representatives to the House. Some small states (Wyoming, North Dakota, and Delaware) send only one. The Senate has 100 voting members—two from each state.

Executive power is the authority to enforce laws. Article II of the Constitution establishes the president as commander-in-chief of the armed forces and the head of the executive branch of the federal government.

Judicial power gives the right to interpret laws and determine their validity. Article III places the Supreme Court at the head of the judicial branch of the federal government. Interpretive power is often underrated, but it is often every bit as important at the ability to create laws in the first place. For instance, the Supreme Court ruled that privacy provisions of the Constitution protect a woman's right to abortion, although neither the word "privacy" nor "abortion" appears in the text of the Constitution.[6]

At times, courts void laws altogether. For example, in 1995, the Supreme Court ruled that the *Gun-Free School Zones Act of 1990* was unconstitutional because Congress did not have the authority to pass such a law.[7]

Checks and Balances

Sidney Crosby would score 300 goals per season if checking were not allowed in the National Hockey League. But because opponents are allowed to hit Crosby and the rest of his teammates on the Penguins, he is held to a much more reasonable 50 goals per year.

Political checks work in much the same way. They allow one branch of the government to trip up another.

The authors of the Constitution were not content merely to divide government power three ways. They also wanted to give each part of the government some power over the other two branches. Many people complain about "gridlock" in Washington, but the government is slow and sluggish by design. The Founding Fathers wanted to create a system that, without broad agreement, would tend towards inaction.

The president can veto Congressional legislation. Congress can impeach the president. The Supreme Court can void laws passed by Congress. The president appoints judges to the federal courts, including the Supreme Court, but these nominees do not serve unless approved by the Senate. Congress (with help from the 50 states) can override the Supreme Court by amending the Constitution. The president and the Congress influence the Supreme Court by controlling who is placed on the court in the first place.

Many of these checks and balances will be examined in more detail in Chapter 4.

---

[6] *Roe v. Wade*, 410 U.S. 113 (1973).

[7] *United States v. Alfonso Lopez, Jr.*, 514 U.S. 549 (1995).

Fundamental Rights

The Constitution also grants many of our most basic liberties. For the most part, they are found in the amendments to the Constitution. The First Amendment guarantees the rights of free speech, free press, and the free exercise of religion. The Fourth, Fifth, and Sixth Amendments protect the rights of any person accused of a crime. Other amendments ensure that the government treats all people equally and that it pays for any property it takes from a citizen.

By creating a limited government of three branches and guaranteeing basic liberties to all citizens, the Constitution became one of the most important documents ever written.

Statutes

The second important source of law is statutory law. The Constitution gave to the United States Congress the power to pass laws on various subjects. These laws are called **statutes,** and they can cover absolutely any topic, so long as they do not violate the Constitution.

Statute

A law created by a legislative body.

Almost all statutes are created by the same method. An idea for a new law—on taxes, health care, texting while driving, or any other topic, big or small—is first proposed in the Congress. This idea is called a *bill.* The House and Senate then independently vote on the bill. To pass Congress, the bill must win a simple majority vote in each of these chambers.

If Congress passes a bill, it goes to the White House for the president's approval. If the president signs it, a new statute is created. It is no longer a mere idea; it is the law of the land. If the president refuses to approve, or *vetoes* a bill, it does not become a statute unless Congress overrides the veto. To do that, both the House and the Senate must approve the bill by a two-thirds majority. If this happens, it becomes a statute without the president's signature.

Common Law

Binding legal ideas often come from the courts. Judges generally follow *precedent.* When courts decide a case, they tend to apply the legal rules that other courts have used in similar cases.

The principle that precedent is binding on later cases is called *stare decisis,* which means "let the decision stand." *Stare decisis* makes the law predictable, and this in turn enables businesses and private citizens to plan intelligently.

It is important to note that precedent is binding only on *lower* courts. For example, if the Supreme Court decided a case in one way in 1965, it is under no obligation to follow precedent if the same issue arises in 2015.

Sometimes, this is quite beneficial. In 1896, the Supreme Court decided (unbelievably) that segregation—separating people by race in schools, hotels, public transportation, and other public services—was legal under certain conditions.[8] In 1954, on the exact same issue, the court changed its mind.[9]

In other circumstances, it is more difficult to see the value in breaking with an established rule.

Court Orders

Judges have the authority to issue court orders that place binding obligations on specific people or companies. An injunction, for example, is a court order to stop doing something. A judge might order a stalker to stay more than 500 yards away from an ex-boyfriend or -girlfriend. Lindsey Lohan might be ordered to stop drinking and enter rehab. Courts have the authority to imprison or fine those who violate their orders.

---

[8] *Plessy v. Ferguson*, 163 U.S.537 (1896).

[9] *Brown v. Board of Education of Topeka*, 347 U.S. 483 (1954) .

Administrative Law

In a society as large and diverse as ours, the executive and legislative branches of government cannot oversee all aspects of commerce. Congress passes statutes about air safety, but United States senators do not stand around air traffic towers, serving coffee to keep everyone awake. The executive branch establishes rules concerning how foreign nationals enter the United States, but presidents are reluctant to sit on the dock of the bay, watching the ships come in. Administrative agencies do this day-to-day work.

Most government agencies are created by Congress. Familiar examples are the Environmental Protection Agency (EPA), the Securities and Exchange Commission (SEC), and the Internal Revenue Service (IRS), whose feelings are hurt if it does not hear from you every April 15. Agencies have the power to create laws called *regulations.*

Treaties

The Constitution authorizes the president to make treaties with foreign nations. These must then be ratified by the United States Senate by a two-thirds vote. When they are ratified, they are as binding upon all citizens as any federal statute. In 1994 the Senate ratified the North American Free Trade Agreement (NAFTA) with Mexico and Canada. NAFTA was controversial then and remains so today—but it is the law of the land.

CLASSIFICATIONS

We have seen where law comes from. Now we need to classify the various types of laws. First, we will distinguish between criminal and civil law. Then, we will take a look at the intersection between law and morality.

Criminal and Civil Law

Criminal law
Criminal law prohibits certain behavior.

Civil law
Civil law regulates the rights and duties between parties.

It is a crime to embezzle money from a bank, to steal a car, to sell cocaine. **Criminal law** concerns behavior so threatening that society outlaws it altogether. Most criminal laws are statutes, passed by Congress or a state legislature. The government itself prosecutes the wrongdoer, regardless of what the bank president or car owner wants. A district attorney, paid by the government, brings the case to court. The injured party, for example the owner of the stolen car, is not in charge of the case, although she may appear as a witness. The government will seek to punish the defendant with a prison sentence, a fine, or both. If there is a fine, the money goes to the state, not to the injured party.

Civil law is different, and most of this book is about civil law. **The civil law regulates the rights and duties between parties.** Tracy agrees in writing to lease you a 30,000-square-foot store in her shopping mall. She now has a *legal duty* to make the space available. But then another tenant offers her more money, and she refuses to let you move in. Tracy has violated her duty, but she has not committed a crime. The government will not prosecute the case. It is up to you to file a civil lawsuit. Your case will be based on the common law of contract. You will also seek equitable relief, namely, an injunction ordering Tracy not to lease to anyone else. You should win the suit, and you will get your injunction and some money damages. But Tracy will not go to jail.

Some conduct involves both civil and criminal law. Suppose Tracy is so upset over losing the court case that she becomes drunk and causes a serious car accident. She has committed the crime of driving while intoxicated, and the state will prosecute. Tracy may be fined or imprisoned. She has also committed negligence, and the injured party will file a lawsuit against her, seeking money. We will again see civil and criminal law joined together in the *Pub Zone* case, later in the chapter.

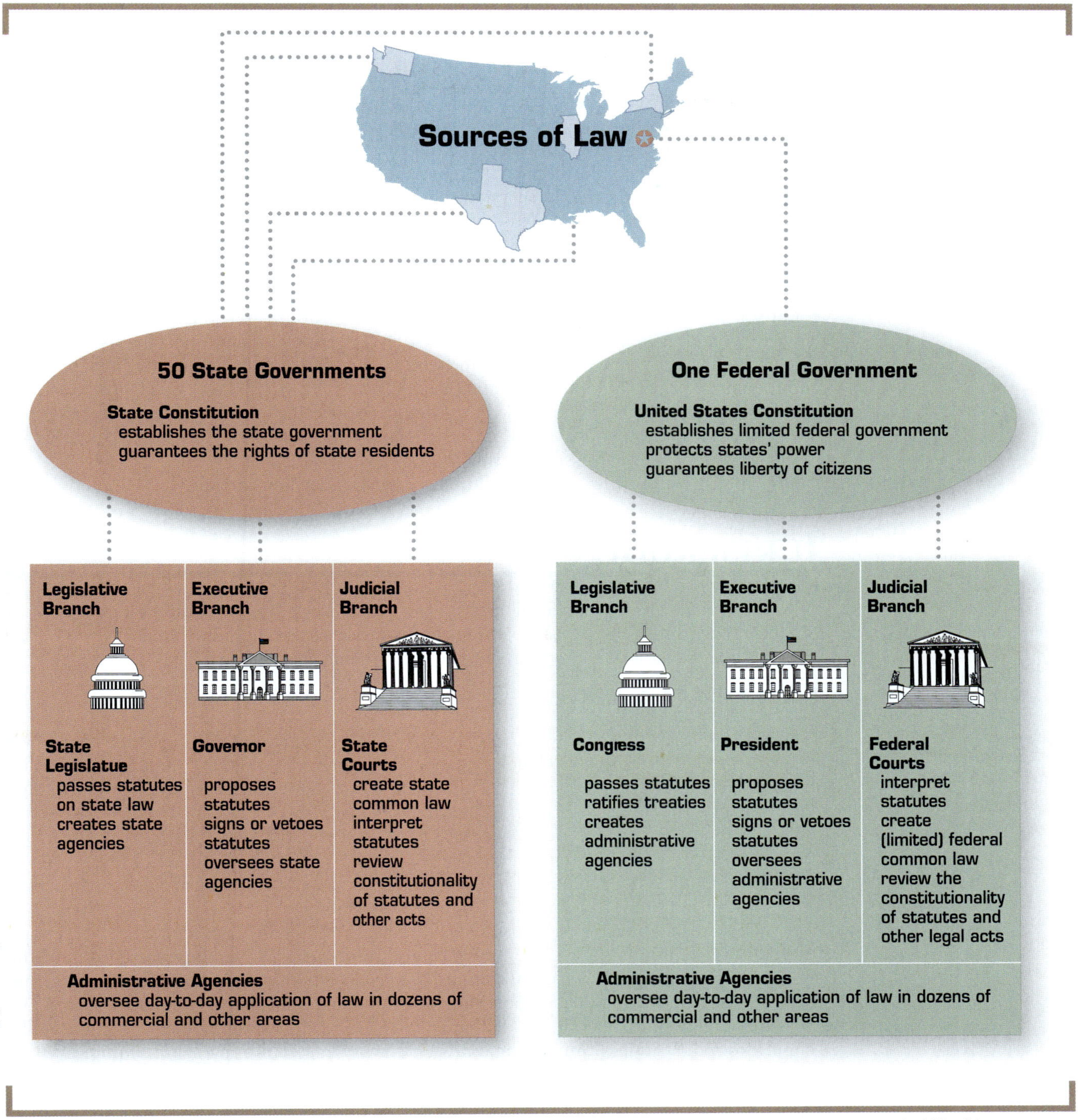

Federal Form of Government. Principles and rules of law come from many sources. The government in Washington creates and enforces law throughout the nation. But 50 state governments exercise great power in local affairs. And citizens enjoy constitutional protection from both state and federal government. The Founding Fathers wanted this balance of power and rights, but the overlapping authority creates legal complexity.

Law and Morality

Law is different from morality, yet the two are obviously linked. There are many instances when the law duplicates what all of us would regard as a moral position. It is negligent to drive too fast in a school district, and few would dispute the moral value of seeking to limit harm to students. And the same holds with contract law: If the owner of land agrees in writing to sell property to a buyer at a stated price, both the buyer and the seller must go through with the deal, and the legal outcome matches our moral expectations.

On the other hand, we have had laws that we now clearly regard as immoral. At the turn of the century, a factory owner could typically fire a worker for any reason at all—including, for example, his religious or political views. It is immoral to fire a worker because she is Jewish—and today the law prohibits it.

Finally, there are legal issues where the morality is less clear. You are walking down a country lane and notice a three-year-old child playing with matches near a barn filled with hay. Are you obligated to intervene? No, says the law, though many think that is preposterous. (See Chapter 4, on common law, for more about this topic.) A company buys property and then discovers, buried under the ground, toxic waste that will cost $300,000 to clean up. The original owner has gone bankrupt. Should the new owner be forced to pay for the cleanup? If the new owner fails to pay for the job, who will? (See Chapter 40, on environmental law, for more discussion on this issue.)

Chapter 2 will further examine the bond between law and morality.

JURISPRUDENCE

Jurisprudence
The philosophy of law.

We have had a glimpse of legal history and a summary of the present-day sources of American law. But what *is* law? That question is the basis of a field known as **jurisprudence**. What is the real nature of law? Can there be such a thing as an "illegal" law?

Legal Positivism

Sovereign
The recognized political power, whom citizens obey.

This philosophy can be simply stated: Law is what the sovereign says it is. The **sovereign** is the recognized political power whom citizens obey, so in the United States, both state and federal governments are sovereign. A legal positivist holds that whatever the sovereign declares to be the law *is* the law, whether it is right or wrong.

The primary criticism of legal positivism is that it seems to leave no room for questions of morality. A law permitting a factory owner to fire a worker because she is Catholic is surely different from a law prohibiting arson. Do citizens in a democracy have a duty to consider such differences? Consider the following example.

Most states allow citizens to pass laws directly at the ballot box, a process called voter referendum. California voters often do this, and during the 1990s, they passed one of the state's most controversial laws. Proposition 187 was designed to curb illegal immigration into the state by eliminating social spending for undocumented aliens. Citizens debated the measure fiercely but passed it by a large margin. One section of the new law forbade public schools from educating illegal immigrants. The law obligated a principal to inquire into the immigration status of all children enrolled in the school and to report undocumented students to immigration authorities. Several San Diego school principals rejected the new rules, stating that they would neither inquire into immigration status nor report undocumented aliens. Their statements produced a heated response. Some San Diego residents castigated the school officials as lawbreakers, claiming that

- A school officer who knowingly disobeyed a law was setting a terrible example for students, who would assume they were free to do the same;
- The principals were advocating permanent residence and a free education for anyone able to evade our immigration laws; and

- The officials were scorning grass-roots democracy by disregarding a law passed by popular referendum.

Others applauded the principals' position, asserting that

- The referendum's rules would transform school officials from educators into border police, forcing them to cross-examine young children and their parents;
- The new law was foolish because it punished innocent children for violations committed by their parents; and
- Our nation has long respected civil disobedience based on humanitarian ideals, and these officials were providing moral leadership to the whole community.

Ultimately, no one had to decide whether to obey Proposition 187. A federal court ruled that only Congress had the power to regulate immigration and that California's attempt was unconstitutional and void. The debate over immigration reform—and ethics—did not end, however. It continues to be a thorny issue.

Natural Law

St. Thomas Aquinas (1225–1274) answered the legal positivists even before they had spoken. In his *Summa Theologica*, he argued that an unjust law is no law at all and need not be obeyed. It is not enough that a sovereign makes a command. The law must have a moral basis.

St. Thomas Aquinas argued that an unjust law is no law at all …

Where do we find the moral basis that would justify a law? Aquinas says that "good is that which all things seek after." Therefore, the fundamental rule of all laws is that "good is to be done and promoted, and evil is to be avoided." This sounds appealing, but also vague. Exactly which laws promote good and which do not? Is it better to have a huge corporation dominate a market or many smaller companies competing? Did the huge company get that way by being better than its competitors? If Wal-Mart moves into a rural area, establishes a mammoth store, and sells inexpensive products, is that "good"? Yes, if you are a consumer who cares only about prices. No, if you are the owner of a Main Street store driven into bankruptcy. Maybe, if you are a resident who values small-town life but wants lower prices.

Legal Realism

Legal realists take a very different tack. They claim it does not matter what is written as law. What counts is who enforces that law and by what process. All of us are biased by issues such as income, education, family background, race, religion, and many other factors. These personal characteristics, they say, determine which contracts will be enforced and which ignored, why some criminals receive harsh sentences while others get off lightly, and so on.

Judge Jones hears a multimillion dollar lawsuit involving an airplane crash. Was the airline negligent? The law is the same everywhere, but legal realists say that Jones's background will determine the outcome. If she spent 20 years representing insurance companies, she will tend to favor the airline. If her law practice consisted of helping the "little guy," she will favor the plaintiff.

Other legal realists argue, more aggressively, that those in power use the machinery of the law to perpetuate their control. The outcome of a given case will be determined by the needs of those with money and political clout. A court puts "window dressing" on a decision, they say, so that society thinks there are principles behind the law. A problem with legal realism, however, is its denial that any lawmaker can overcome personal bias. Yet clearly some do act unselfishly.

SUMMARY OF JURISPRUDENCE	
Legal Positivism	Law is what the sovereign says.
Natural Law	An unjust law is no law at all.
Legal Realism	Who enforces the law counts more than what is in writing.

No one school of jurisprudence is likely to seem perfect. We urge you to keep the different theories in mind as you read cases in the book. Ask yourself which school of thought is the best fit for you.

Working with the Book's Features

In this section, we introduce a few of the book's features and discuss how you can use them effectively. We will start with *cases.*

Analyzing a Case

A law case is the decision a court has made in a civil lawsuit or criminal prosecution. Cases are the heart of the law and an important part of this book. Reading them effectively takes practice. This chapter's opening scenario is fictional, but the following real case involves a similar situation. Who can be held liable for the assault? Let's see.

Kuehn v. Pub Zone

364 N.J. Super. 301, 835 A.2d 692
Superior Court of New Jersey, Appellate Division, 2003

Facts: Maria Kerkoulas owned the Pub Zone bar. She knew that several motorcycle gangs frequented the tavern. From her own experience tending bar, and conversations with city police, she knew that some of the gangs, including the Pagans, were dangerous and prone to attack customers for no reason. Kerkoulas posted a sign prohibiting any motorcycle gangs from entering the bar while wearing "colors," that is, insignia of their gangs. She believed that gangs without their colors were less prone to violence, and experience proved her right.

Rhino, Backdraft, and several other Pagans, all wearing colors, pushed their way past the tavern's bouncer and approached the bar. Although Kerkoulas saw their colors, she allowed them to stay for one drink. They later moved towards the back of the pub, and Kerkoulas believed they were departing. In fact, they followed a customer named Karl Kuehn to the men's room, where without any provocation they savagely beat him. Kuehn was knocked unconscious and suffered brain hemorrhaging, disc herniation, and numerous fractures of facial bones. He was forced to undergo various surgeries, including eye reconstruction.

Although the government prosecuted Rhino and Backdraft for their vicious assault, our case does not concern that prosecution. Kuehn sued the Pub Zone, and that is the case we will read. The jury awarded him $300,000 in damages. However, the trial court judge overruled the jury's verdict. He granted a judgment for the Pub Zone, meaning that the tavern owed nothing. The judge ruled that the pub's owner could not have foreseen the attack on Kuehn, and had no duty to protect him from an outlaw motorcycle gang. Kuehn appealed, and the appeals court's decision follows:

Issue: ***Did the Pub Zone have a duty to protect Kuehn from the Pagans' attack?***

Excerpts from Judge Payne's Decision: Whether a duty exists depends upon an evaluation of a number of factors including the nature of the underlying risk of harm, that is, its foreseeability and severity, the opportunity and ability to exercise care to prevent the harm, the comparative interests of and the relationships between or among the parties, and, ultimately, based on considerations of public policy and fairness, the societal interest in the proposed solution.

Since the possessor [of a business] is not an insurer of the visitor's safety, he is ordinarily under no duty to exercise any care until he knows or has reason to know that the acts of the third person are occurring, or are about to occur. He may, however, know or have reason to know, from past experience, that there is a likelihood of conduct on the part of third persons in general which is likely to endanger the safety of the visitor, even though he has no reason to expect it on the part of any particular individual.

We find the totality of the circumstances presented in this case give rise to a duty on the part of the Pub Zone to have taken reasonable precautions against the danger posed by the Pagans as a group. In this case, there was no reason to suspect any particular Pagan of violent conduct. However, the gang was collectively known to Kerkoulas to engage in random violence. Thus, Kerkoulas had knowledge as the result of past experience and from other sources that there was a likelihood of conduct on the part of third persons in general that was likely to endanger the safety of a patron at some unspecified future time. A duty to take precautions against the endangering conduct thus arose.

We do not regard our recognition of a duty in this case to give rise to either strict or absolute liability on the part of the Pub Zone. To fulfill its duty in this context, the Pub Zone was merely required to employ "reasonable" safety precautions. It already had in place a prohibition against bikers who were wearing their colors, and that prohibition, together with the practice of calling the police when a breach occurred, had been effective in greatly diminishing the occurrence of biker incidents on the premises. The evidence establishes that the prohibition was not enforced on the night at issue, that three Pagans were permitted entry while wearing their colors, and the police were not called. Once entry was achieved, the Pub Zone remained under a duty to exercise reasonable precautions against an attack.

The jury's verdict must therefore be reinstated.

Analysis

Let's take it from the top. The case is called *Kuehn v. Pub Zone.* Karl Kuehn is the **plaintiff**, the person who is suing. The Pub Zone is being sued, and is called the **defendant**. In this example, the plaintiff's name happens to appear first but that is not always true. When a defendant loses a trial and files an appeal, *some* courts reverse the names of the parties.

Plaintiff
The party who is suing.

Defendant
The party being sued.

The next line gives the legal citation, which indicates where to find the case in a law library. We explain in the footnote how to locate a book if you plan to do research.[10]

The *Facts* section provides a background to the lawsuit, written by the authors of this text. The court's own explanation of the facts is often many pages long, and may involve complex matters irrelevant to the subject covered in this book, so we relate only what is necessary. This section will usually include some mention of what happened at the trial

[10]If you want to do legal research, you need to know where to find particular legal decisions. A case citation guides you to the correct volume(s). The full citation of our case is *Kuehn v. Pub Zone*, 364 N.J. Super. 301, 835 A.2d 692. The string of numbers identifies two different books in which you can find the full text of this decision. The first citation is to "N.J. Super," which means the official court reporter of the state of New Jersey. New Jersey, like most states, reports its law cases in a series of numbered volumes. This case appears in volume 364 of the New Jersey Superior Court reporters. If you go to a law library and find that book, you can then turn to page 301 and—*voila!*—you have the case. The decision is also reported in another set of volumes, called the regional reporters. This series of law reports is grouped by geographic region. New Jersey is included in the Atlantic region, so our case appears in reporters dedicated to that region. The "A" stands for Atlantic. After a series of reporters reaches volume 999, a second set begins. Our case appears in volume 835 of the second set of the Atlantic reporters ("A.2d"), at page 692. In addition, most cases are now available online, and your professor or librarian can show you how to find them electronically.

court. Lawsuits always begin in a trial court. The losing party often appeals to a court of appeals, and it is usually an appeals court decision that we are reading. The trial judge ruled in favor of Pub Zone, but later, in the decision we are reading, Kuehn wins.

The *Issue* section is very important. It tells you what the court had to decide—and also why you are reading the case. In giving its decision, a court may digress. If you keep in mind the issue and relate the court's discussion to it, you will not get lost.

Excerpts from Judge Payne's Decision begins the court's discussion. This is called the *holding*, meaning a statement of who wins and who loses. The holding also includes the court's *rationale*, which is the reasoning behind the decision.

The holding that we provide is an edited version of the court's own language. Some judges write clear, forceful prose, others do not. Either way, their words give you an authentic feel for how judges think and rule, so we bring it to you in the original. Occasionally we use brackets [ ] to substitute our language for that of the court, either to condense or to clarify. Notice the brackets in the second paragraph of the Pub Zone decision. Judge Payne explains the point at much greater length, so we have condensed some of his writing into the phrase "of a business."

We omit a great deal. A court's opinion may be 3 pages or it may be 75. We do not use ellipses (...) to indicate these deletions, because there is more taken out than kept in, and we want the text to be clean. When a court quotes an earlier decision verbatim but clearly adopts those words as its own, we generally delete the quotation marks, as well as the citation to the earlier case. If you are curious about the full holding, you can always look it up.

Let us look at a few of Judge Payne's points. The holding begins with a discussion of *duty*. The court explains that whether one person (or bar) owes a duty to protect another depends upon several factors, including whether the harm could be foreseen, how serious the injury could be, and whether there was an opportunity to prevent it.

Judge Payne then points out that the owner of a business is not an insurer of a visitor's safety. Typically, the owner has a duty to a visitor *only* if he has a reason to know that some harm is likely to occur. How would a merchant know that? Based on the character of the business, suggests the judge, or the owner's experience with particular people.

The judge then applies this general rule to the facts of this case. He concludes that the Pub Zone did in fact have a duty to protect Kuehn from the Pagans' attack. Based on Kerkoulas's experience, and warnings received from the police, she knew that the gang was dangerous and should have foreseen that admitting them in their "colors" greatly increased the chance of an attack.

Next, the court points out that it is not requiring the Pub Zone to *guarantee* everyone's safety. The bar was merely obligated to do a *reasonable* job. The prohibition on colors was a good idea, and calling the police had also proven effective. The problem of course was that in this case, Kerkoulas ignored her own rule about gang insignia and failed to call the police.

Based on all the evidence, the jury's finding of liability was reasonable, and its verdict must be reinstated. In other words, Kuehn, who lost at the trial, wins on appeal. What the court has done is to *reverse* the lower court's decision, meaning to turn the loser into the winner. In other cases, we will see an appellate court *remand* the case, meaning to send it back down to the lower court for additional steps. Or the appellate judges could *affirm* the lower court's decision, meaning to leave it unchanged.

Devil's Advocate

Each chapter has several cases. After some of them, a "Devil's Advocate" feature offers you a contrasting view of the legal issue. This is not part of the case, but is instead a suggestion of another perspective on the problem discussed. The authors take no position for or against the court's decision, but merely want you to consider an alternate view, and decide which analysis of the law makes more sense to you—that of the court or the Devil's Advocate. Is the following view persuasive?

Devil's Advocate A court should not force small businesses to guarantee their customers' safety. Two or three violent men, whether motorcycle gang members or frustrated professors, could enter a grocery store or clothing retailer at any time and mindlessly attack innocent visitors. Random attacks are just that—random, unforeseeable. No merchant should be required to anticipate them. Send the criminals to jail, but do not place the burden on honest business people.

Exam Strategy

This feature gives you practice analyzing cases the way lawyers do—and the way *you* must on tests. Law exams are different from most others because you must determine the issue from the facts provided. Too frequently, students faced with a law exam forget that the questions relate to the issues in the text and those discussed in class. Understandably, students new to law may focus on the wrong information in the problem or rely on material learned elsewhere. Exam Strategy teaches you to figure out exactly what issue is at stake, and then analyze it in a logical, consistent manner. Here is an example, relating to the element of "duty," which the court discussed in the Pub Zone case.

EXAM Strategy

Question: The Big Red Traveling (BRT) Carnival is in town. Tony arrives at 8:00 p.m., parks in the lot—and is robbed at gunpoint by a man who beats him and escapes with his money. There are several police officers on the carnival grounds, but no officer is in the parking lot at the time of the robbery. Tony sues, claiming that brighter lighting and more police in the lot would have prevented the robbery. There has never before been any violent crime—robbery, beating, or otherwise—at any BRT carnival. BRT claims it had no duty to protect Tony from this harm. Who is likely to win?

Strategy: Begin by isolating the legal issue. What are the parties disputing? They are debating whether BRT had a duty to protect Tony from an armed robbery, committed by a stranger. Now ask yourself: How do courts decide whether a business has a duty to prevent this kind of harm? The Pub Zone case provides our answer. A business owner is not an ensurer of the visitor's safety. The owner generally has no duty to protect a customer from the criminal act of a third party, unless the owner knows the harm is occurring or could foresee it is about to happen. (In the Pub Zone case, the business owner *knew* of the gang's violent history, and could have foreseen the assault.) Now apply that rule to the facts of this case.

Result: There has never been a violent attack of any kind at a BRT carnival. BRT cannot foresee this robbery, and has no duty to protect against it. The carnival wins.

You Be the Judge

Many cases involve difficult decisions for juries and judges. Often both parties have legitimate, opposing arguments. Most chapters in this book will have a feature called "You Be the Judge," in which we present the facts of a case but not the court's holding.

We offer you two opposing arguments based on the kinds of claims the lawyers made in court. We leave it up to you to debate and decide which position is stronger or to add your own arguments to those given.

The following case is another negligence lawsuit, with issues that overlap those of the Pub Zone case. This time the court confronts a fight that resulted in a death. The victim's distraught family sued the owner of a bar, claiming that one of his employees was partly responsible for the death. Once again, the defendant asked the court to dismiss the case, claiming that he owed no duty to protect the victim—the same argument made by the Pub Zone.

But there is a difference here—this time the defendant owned the bar across the street, not the one where the fight took place. Could he be held legally responsible for the death? You be the judge.

You be the Judge

Soldano v. O'Daniels

141 Cal. App. 3d 443
Court of Appeal of California, 5th Appellate District, 1983

Facts: In the days before cell phones, a fight broke out at Happy Jack's Saloon. A good Samaritan ran across the street to the Circle Inn. He asked the bartender at the Circle Inn to let him use the telephone to call the police, but he refused.

Back at Happy Jack's Saloon, the fight escalated, and a man shot and killed Soldano's father. Soldano sued the owner of the Circle Inn for negligence. He argued that the bartender violated a legal duty when he refused to hand over the inn's telephone and that, as the employer of the bartender, O'Daniels was partially liable for Soldano's father's death.

The lower court dismissed the case, citing the principle that generally, a person does not have a legal responsibility to help another unless he created the dangerous situation in the first place. Soldano appealed.

You Be The Judge: ***Did the bartender have a duty to allow the use of the Circle Inn's telephone?***

Argument for the Defendant: Your honors, my client did not act wrongfully. He did nothing to create the danger. The fight was not even on his property. We sympathize with the plaintiff, but it is the shooter, and perhaps the bar where the fight took place, who are responsible for his father's death. Our client was not involved. Liability can be stretched only so far.

The court would place a great burden on the citizens of California by going against precedent. The Circle Inn is Mr. O'Daniel's private property. If the court imposes potential liability on him in this case, would citizens be forced to open the doors of their homes whenever a stranger claims that there is an emergency? Criminals would delight in their newfound ability to gain access to businesses and residences by simply demanding to use a phone to "call the police."

The law has developed sensibly. People are left to decide for themselves whether to help in a dangerous situation. They are not legally required to place themselves in harm's way.

Argument for the Plaintiff: Your honors, the Circle Inn's bartender had both a moral and a legal duty to allow the use of his establishment's telephone. The Circle Inn may be privately owned, but it is a business and is open to the public. Anyone in the world is invited to stop by and order a drink or a meal. The good Samaritan had every right to be there.

We do not argue that the bartender had an obligation to break up the fight or endanger himself in any way. We simply argue he had a responsibility to stand aside and allow a free call on his restaurant's telephone. Any "burden" on him or on the Circle Inn was incredibly slight. The potential benefits were enormous. The trial court made a mistake in concluding that a person *never* has a duty to help another. Such an interpretation makes for poor public policy.

There is no need to radically change the common law. Residences can be excluded from this ruling. People need not be required to allow telephone-seeking strangers into their homes. This court can simply determine that businesses have a legal duty to allow the placement of emergency calls during normal business hours.

Chapter Conclusion

We depend upon the law to give us a stable nation and economy, a fair society, a safe place to live and work. These worthy goals have occupied ancient kings and twenty-first-century lawmakers alike. But while law is a vital tool for crafting the society we want, there are no easy answers about how to create it. In a democracy, we all participate in the crafting. Legal rules control us, yet *we* create *them*. A working knowledge of the law can help build a successful career—and a solid democracy.

Exam Review

1. **THE FEDERAL SYSTEM** Our federal system of government means that law comes from a national government in Washington, D.C., and from 50 state governments. (p. 7)

2. **LEGAL HISTORY** The history of law foreshadows many current legal issues, including mediation, partnership liability, the jury system, the role of witnesses, the special value placed on land, and the idea of precedent. (pp. 5–6)

3. **PRIMARY SOURCES OF LAW** The primary sources of contemporary law are

- United States Constitution and state constitutions;
- Statutes, which are drafted by legislatures;
- Common law, which is the body of cases decided by judges, as they follow earlier cases, known as precedent;
- Court orders, which place obligations on specific people or companies;
- Administrative law, the rules and decisions made by federal and state administrative agencies; and
- Treaties, agreements between the United States and foreign nations. (p. 7)

Question: The stock market crash of 1929 and the Great Depression that followed were caused in part because so many investors blindly put their money into stocks they knew nothing about. During the 1920s, it was often impossible for an investor to find out what a corporation was planning to do with its money, who was running the corporation, and many other vital things. Congress responded by passing the Securities Act of 1933, which required a corporation to divulge more information about itself before it could seek money for a new stock issue. What kind of law did Congress create?

Strategy: What is the question seeking? The question asks you which *type* of law Congress created when it passed the 1933 Securities Act. What are the primary kinds of law? Administrative law consists of rules passed by agencies. Congress is not a federal agency. Common law is the body of cases decided by judges. Congress is not a judge. Statutes are laws passed by legislatures. Congress is a legislature. (See the "Result" at the end of this section.)

4. **CRIMINAL LAW** Criminal law concerns behavior so threatening to society that it is outlawed altogether. Civil law deals with duties and disputes between parties, not with outlawed behavior. (p. 10)

EXAM Strategy

Question: Bill and Diane are hiking in the woods. Diane walks down a hill to fetch fresh water. Bill meets a stranger, who introduces herself as Katrina. Bill sells a kilo of cocaine to Katrina, who then flashes a badge and mentions how much she enjoys her job at the Drug Enforcement Agency. Diane, heading back to camp with the water, meets Freddy, a motorist whose car has overheated. Freddy is late for a meeting where he expects to make a $30 million profit; he's desperate for water for his car. He promises to pay Diane $500 tomorrow if she will give him the pail of water, which she does. The next day, Bill is in jail and Freddy refuses to pay for Diane's water. Explain the criminal law/civil law distinction and what it means to Bill and Diane. Who will do what to whom, with what results?

Strategy: You are asked to distinguish between criminal and civil law. What is the difference? The criminal law concerns behavior that threatens society and is therefore outlawed. The government prosecutes the defendant. Civil law deals with the rights and duties between parties. One party files a suit against the other. Apply those different standards to these facts. (See the "Result" at the end of this section.)

5. **JURISPRUDENCE** Jurisprudence is concerned with the basic nature of law. Three theories of jurisprudence are

- Legal positivism: The law is what the sovereign says it is.
- Natural law: An unjust law is no law at all.
- Legal realism: Who enforces the law is more important than what the law says. (pp. 12–15)

3. Result: The Securities Act of 1933 is a statute.

4. Result: The government will prosecute Bill for dealing in drugs. If convicted, he will go to prison. The government will take no interest in Diane's dispute. However, if she chooses, she may sue Freddy for $500, the amount he promised her for the water. In that civil lawsuit, a court will decide whether Freddy must pay what he promised; however, even if Freddy loses, he will not go to jail.

Multiple-Choice Questions

1. The United States Constitution is among the finest legal accomplishments in the history of the world. Which of the following influenced Ben Franklin, Thomas Jefferson, and the rest of the Founding Fathers?

(a) English common-law principles

(b) The Iroquois's system of federalism

(c) Both A and B

(d) None of the above

2. Which of the following parts of the modern legal system are "borrowed" from medieval England?

(a) Jury trials

(b) Special rules for selling land

(c) Following precedent

(d) All of the above

3. Union organizers at a hospital wanted to distribute leaflets to potential union members, but hospital rules prohibited leafleting in areas of patient care, hallways, cafeterias, and any areas open to the public. The National Labor Relations Board, a government agency, ruled that these restrictions violated the law and ordered the hospital to permit the activities in the cafeteria and coffee shop. What kind of law was it creating?

(a) A statute

(b) Common law

(c) A constitutional amendment

(d) Administrative regulation

4. If the Congress creates a new statute with the president's support, it must pass the idea by a ____________ majority vote in the House and the Senate. If the president vetoes a proposed statute and the Congress wishes to pass it without his support, the idea must pass by a ____________ majority vote in the House and Senate.

(a) simple; simple

(b) simple; two-thirds

(c) simple; three-fourths

(d) two-thirds; three-fourths

5. What part of the Constitution addresses the most basic liberties?

(a) Article I

(b) Article II

(c) Article III

(d) Amendments

Essay Questions

1. Burglar Bob breaks into Vince Victim's house. Bob steals a flat-screen TV and laptop and does a significant amount of damage to the property before he leaves. Fortunately, Vince has a state-of-the-art security system. It captures excellent images of Bob, who is soon caught by police.

   Assume that two legal actions follow, one civil and one criminal. Who will be responsible for bringing the civil case? What will be the outcome if the jury believes that Bob burgled Vince's house? Who will be responsible for bringing the criminal case? What will be the outcome if the jury believes that Bob burgled Vince's house?

2. As "The Oculist's Case" indicates, the medical profession has faced a large number of lawsuits for centuries. In Texas, a law provides that, so long as a doctor was not reckless and did not intentionally harm a patient, recovery for "pain and suffering" is limited to $750,000. In many other states, no such limit exists. If a patient will suffer a lifetime of pain after a botched operation, for example, he might recover millions in compensation.

   Which rule seems more sensible to you – the "Texas" rule, or the alternative?

3. **YOU BE THE JUDGE WRITING PROBLEM** Should trials be televised? Here are a few arguments to add to those in the chapter. You be the judge. **Arguments against live television coverage:** We have tried this experiment and it has failed. Trials fall into two categories: Those that create great public interest and those that do not. No one watches dull trials, so we do not need to broadcast them. The few that are interesting have all become circuses. Judges and lawyers have shown that they cannot resist the temptation to play to the camera. Trials are supposed to be about justice, not entertainment. If a citizen seriously wants to follow a case, she can do it by reading the daily newspaper. **Arguments for live television coverage:** It is true that some televised trials have been unseemly affairs, but that is the fault of the presiding judges, not the media. Indeed, one of the virtues of television coverage is that millions of people now understand that we have a lot of incompetent people running our courtrooms. The proper response is to train judges to run a tight trial by prohibiting grandstanding by lawyers. Access to accurate information is the foundation on which a democracy is built, and we must not eliminate a source of valuable data just because some judges are ill-trained or otherwise incompetent.

4. Leslie Bergh and his two brothers, Milton and Raymond, formed a partnership to help build a fancy saloon and dance hall in Evanston, Wyoming. Later, Leslie met with his friend and drinking buddy, John Mills, and tricked Mills into investing in the saloon. Leslie did not tell Mills that no one else was investing cash or that the entire enterprise was already bankrupt. Mills mortgaged his home, invested $150,000 in the saloon—and lost every penny of it. Mills sued all three partners for fraud. Milton and Raymond defended on the grounds that they did not commit the fraud; only Leslie did. The defendants lost. Was that fair? By holding them liable, what general idea did the court rely on? What Anglo-Saxon legal custom did the ruling resemble?

5. *Kuehn v. Pub Zone* and *Soldano v. O'Daniels* both involve attacks in a bar. Should they have the same result? If so, in which way—in favor of the injured plaintiffs or owner-defendants? If not, why should they have different outcomes? What are the key facts that lead you to believe as you do?

Discussion Questions

1. Do you believe that there are too many lawsuits in the United States? If so, do you place more blame for the problem on lawyers or on individuals who go to court? Is there anything that would help the problem, or will we always have large numbers of lawsuits?

2. In the 1980s, the Supreme Court ruled that it is legal for protesters to burn the American flag. This activity counts as free speech under the Constitution. If the Court hears a new flag-burning case in this decade, should it consider changing its ruling, or should it follow precedent? Is following past precedent something that seems sensible to you: always, usually, sometimes, rarely, or never?

3. When should a business be held legally responsible for customer safety? Consider the following statements, and circle the appropriate answer:

   a. A business should keep customers safe from its own employees.

      strongly agree   agree   neutral   disagree   strongly disagree

   b. A business should keep customers safe from other customers.

      strongly agree   agree   neutral   disagree   strongly disagree

   c. A business should keep customers safe from themselves. (Example: an intoxicated customer who can no longer walk straight.)

      strongly agree   agree   neutral   disagree   strongly disagree

   d. A business should keep people outside its own establishment safe if it is reasonable to do so.

      strongly agree   agree   neutral   disagree   strongly disagree

4. In his most famous novel, *The Red and the Black*, the French author Stendhal (1783–1842) wrote: "There is no such thing as 'natural law': this expression is nothing but old nonsense. Prior to laws, what is natural is only the strength of the lion, or the need of the creature suffering from hunger or cold, in short, need." What do you think? Does legal positivism or legal realism seem more sensible to you?

5. At the time of this writing, voters are particularly disgruntled. A good many people seem to be disgusted with government. For this question, we intentionally avoid distinguishing between Democrats and Republicans, and we intentionally do not name any particular president. Consider the following statements, and circle the appropriate answer:

   a. I believe that members of Congress usually try to do the right thing for America.

      strongly agree   agree   neutral   disagree   strongly disagree

   b. I believe that presidents usually try to do the right thing for America.

      strongly agree   agree   neutral   disagree   strongly disagree

   c. I believe that Supreme Court justices usually try to do the right thing for America.

      strongly agree   agree   neutral   disagree   strongly disagree

CHAPTER 2

BUSINESS ETHICS AND SOCIAL RESPONSIBILITY

© r.nagy/Shutterstock.com

Three people talk about their temptation to lie:

1. During college, I used drugs—some cocaine, but mostly prescription painkillers. Things got pretty bad. At one point, I would wait outside emergency rooms hoping to buy drugs from people who were leaving. But that was three years ago. I went into rehab and have been clean ever since. I don't even drink. I've applied for a job, but the application asks if I have ever used drugs illegally. I am afraid that if I tell the truth, I will never get a job. What should I say on the application?

I've applied for a job, but the application asks if I have ever used drugs illegally. I am afraid that if I tell the truth, I will never get a job. What should I say?

2. I process payroll at my company, so I know how much everyone earns, including the top executives. This could make for some good gossip, but I have never told anyone about anybody else's salary. Yesterday, the CEO went to my boss to confirm that *she*, my boss, is doing the processing of salaries for top management. It turns out that it is against company policy for me to do it, but my boss handed it off to me anyway. She lied to the CEO and said that she was doing it. Then she begged me not to tell the truth if the CEO checked with me. Now he has called me to go see him. What do I say if he asks about the payroll?

3. I am in charge of a project to redesign a software program that is one of our company's top products. Most of our engineers are French, and I studied the language in college. I enjoy going out with the team in the evenings, and I have become pretty good

friends with everyone. Recently, my boss told me that once the project is finished, all the engineers will be laid off. He joked about how "the French will be fried when they find out." Since they are not U.S. citizens, they will have to leave the country unless they get jobs right away. If I tell them the boss's plan, they will start looking for other jobs and my project could be in the tank. That would be really bad for the company, not to mention a disaster for me. One of the engineers wants to make an offer on a house, so he asked me about his future at the company. What do I say?

INTRODUCTION

This text, for the most part, covers legal ideas. The law dictates how a person *must* behave. This chapter examines **ethics,** or how people *should* behave. It will examine ethical dilemmas that commonly arise in workplaces, and present tools for making decisions when the law does not require or prohibit any particular choice.

Ethics
How people ought to act.

If a person is intent on lying, cheating, and stealing his way through a career, then he is unlikely to be dissuaded by anything in this or any other course. But, for the large majority of people who want to do the right thing, it will be useful to study new ways of approaching difficult problems.

Ethics lies largely beyond the realm of law, so we present a unique feature in this chapter. You will notice that it contains "Ethics Cases" and discussion questions in place of legal cases. It is our hope that these scenarios will generate lively classroom debates on right and wrong. It is important for future leaders to hear a variety of points of view. In your career, you will work with and manage diverse groups of people. If you have insight into how different people perceive ethical issues, you will be better off.

We also hope that hearing these different points of view will help you develop your own Life Principles. These principles are the rules by which you live your life. For example, the opening scenario dealt with lying. It is easy to say, "I will always tell the truth," but many people believe that it is ethically acceptable to lie in certain situations. For example, a large man holding a big knife demands, "Where's Jamie?" You know where Jamie is, but you might be tempted to send the murderer off in the opposite direction and then call the police. At the other end of the spectrum, you could decide that you will lie whenever it seems to be in your best interest. The problem with this approach is that you will soon find that no one trusts you. Where in between these two extremes do your Life Principles fit? Something to think about throughout this chapter (and throughout your life as well). If you develop these Life Principles now, you will be prepared when facing ethical dilemmas in the future.

In this chapter, we will present five basic issues:

1. Why bother to act ethically at all?[1]
2. What is the most important consideration when making an ethical decision? To do the right thing for the right reason, or to do what produces the most favorable results?

[1]Some of the ethics cases and discussion questions featured in this chapter are adapted from *Applied Business Ethics* by Dean A. Bredeson, Cengage Learning, 2011.

3. Should you apply your personal ethics in the workplace, or should you have different ethical values at home and at work?

4. Is the primary role of corporations to make money, or do they have responsibilities to workers, communities, customers, and other "stakeholders"?

5. When, if ever, is lying acceptable?

WHY BOTHER TO ACT ETHICALLY AT ALL?

Ethical decision making generates a range of benefits for employees, companies, and society. Although ethical business practices are not required, the remainder of this chapter makes the case that they are sound.

Society as a Whole Benefits from Ethical Behavior

John Akers, the former chairman of IBM, argues that without ethical behavior, a society cannot be economically competitive. He puts it this way:

> Ethics and competitiveness are inseparable. We compete as a society. No society anywhere will compete very long or successfully with people stabbing each other in the back; with people trying to steal from each other; with everything requiring notarized confirmation because you can't trust the other fellow; with every little squabble ending in litigation; and with government writing reams of regulatory legislation, tying business hand and foot to keep it honest. That is a recipe not only for headaches in running a company, but for a nation to become wasteful, inefficient, and noncompetitive. There is no escaping this fact: the greater the measure of mutual trust and confidence in the ethics of a society, the greater its economic strength.[2]

People Feel Better When They Behave Ethically

Researchers who study happiness find that people expect material goods to make them happier than they actually do. Sure, you enjoy driving that snazzy new car home from the dealership, but afterward your happiness quickly returns to its natural base level. People find themselves on the so-called "hedonic treadmill"—struggling to buy more and more things so they can get that buyer's high, only to discover that they can never buy enough to maintain the thrill. Most people feel that they would be happier if their income were just a little bit higher—no matter how high it is. So what does make people happy in the long run? Good relationships, satisfying work, ties to the community—and all of these are available at no financial cost.

Every businessperson has many opportunities to be dishonest. Consider how one person felt when he resisted temptation:

> Occasionally a customer forgot to send a bill for materials shipped to us for processing.... It would have been so easy to rationalize remaining silent. After all, didn't they deserve to lose because of their inefficiency? However, upon instructing our staff to inform the parties of their errors, I found them eager to do so. They were actually bursting with pride.... Our honesty was beneficial in subtle ways. The "inefficient" customer remained loyal for years.... [O]ur highly moral policy had a marvelously beneficial effect on our employees. Through the years, many an employee visited my office to let me know that they liked working for a "straight" company.[3]

---

[2]David Grier, "Confronting Ethical Dilemmas," unpublished manuscript of remarks at the Royal Bank of Canada, Sept. 19, 1989.

[3]Hugh Aaron, "Doing the Right Thing in Business," *Wall Street Journal,* June 21, 1993, p. A10.

Profitability is generally not what motivates managers to care about ethics. Managers want to feel good about themselves and the decisions they have made; they want to sleep at night. Their decisions—to lay off employees, install safety devices in cars, burn a cleaner fuel—affect people's lives. When two researchers asked businesspeople why they cared about ethics, the answers had little to do with profitability:

> The businesspeople we interviewed set great store on the regard of their family, friends, and the community at large. They valued their reputations, not for some nebulous financial gain but because they took pride in their good names.[4]

Unethical Behavior Can Be Very Costly

Unethical behavior is a risky business strategy—it may lead to disaster. An engaged couple made a reservation, and put down a $1,500 deposit, to hold their wedding reception at a New Hampshire restaurant. Tragically, the bride died four months before the wedding. Invoking the terms of the contract, the restaurant owner refused to return the couple's deposit. In a letter to the groom, he admitted, "Morally, I would of course agree that the deposit should be returned." When newspapers reported this story, customers deserted the restaurant and it was forced into bankruptcy—over a $1,500 disagreement.[5] Unethical behavior does not always damage a business, but it certainly has the potential of destroying a company overnight. So why take the risk?

Even if unethical behavior does not devastate a business, it can cause other, subtler damage. In one survey, a majority of those questioned said that they had witnessed unethical behavior in their workplace and that this behavior had reduced productivity, job stability, and profits. Unethical behavior in an organization creates a cynical, resentful, and unproductive workforce.

Although there is no *guarantee* that ethical behavior pays in the short or long run, there is evidence that the ethical company is more *likely* to win financially. Ethical companies tend to have a better reputation, more creative employees, and higher returns than those that engage in wrongdoing.[6]

But if we decide that we want to behave ethically, how do we know what ethical behavior is?

Utilitarian vs. Deontological Ethics

When making ethical decisions, people sometimes focus on the reason for the decision—they want to do what is right. Thus, if they think it is wrong to lie, then they will tell the truth no matter what the consequence. Other times, people think about the outcome of their actions. They will do whatever it takes to achieve the right result, no matter what. This choice—between doing right and getting the right result—has been the subject of much philosophical debate.

---

[4]Amar Bhide and Howard H.Stevenson, "Why Be Honest If Honesty Doesn't Pay?" *Harvard Business Review*, Sept.-Oct. 1990, pp. 121–29, at 127.

[5]John Milne, "N.H. Restaurant Goes Bankrupt in Wake of Wedding Refund Flap," *Boston Globe,* Sept. 9, 1994, p. 25.

[6]For sources, see "Ethics: A Basic Framework," Harvard Business School case 9-307-059.

Utilitarian Ethics

In 1863, Englishman John Stuart Mill wrote *Utilitarianism*. He was not the first person to write on utilitarian ethics, but his book has best stood the test of time. To Mill, a correct decision was one that tended to maximize overall happiness and minimize overall pain. Risk management and cost-benefit analyses are examples of utilitarian business practices.

Utilitarianism is, in some ways, an almost mathematical approach to ethics. Consider this classic example. If you have two extra baseball tickets and two friends, and if you decide to share the tickets, you might be naturally inclined to give one to each friend. But what if one of your friends likes baseball and the other does not? The transaction might look something like this:

Friend 1: (1 ticket) x (1 unit of happiness per ticket) = 1 unit of happiness produced
Friend 2: (1 ticket) x (0 units of happiness per ticket) = 0 units of happiness produced
Overall happiness generated by the gifts = 1 unit of happiness

A utilitarian might suggest giving both tickets to the friend who would appreciate them. The transaction might then look like this:

Friend 1: (2 tickets) x (1 unit of happiness per ticket) = 2 units of happiness produced
Friend 2: (0 tickets) x (0 units of happiness per ticket) = 0 units of happiness produced
Overall happiness generated by the gifts = 2 units of happiness

The best Hollywood line that reflects utilitarian thinking comes from *Star Trek II: The Wrath of Khan*. Toward the end, Mr. Spock saves the *Enterprise* but in so doing takes a lethal dose of radiation. Captain Kirk cradles the dying Spock and says, "Spock! WHY?" Spock replies, "Because Captain, the needs of the many outweigh the needs of the few (cough) or one."

The critics of utilitarian thought are many. Some argue that it is simply not possible to "measure" happiness in the way that one would measure distance or the passage of time. Others say that utilitarians simply let the ends justify the means, and that they allow for bad behavior so long as the it generates good in the end. A third group argues that utilitarian and other hedonistic philosophies err in equating pleasure with ethical behavior, and pain with wrongful behavior. Caring for an elderly relative with Alzheimer's disease, for example, might generate little pleasure and much pain, but it is still a worthwhile and good endeavor.

Deontological Ethics

Many ethicists believe that utilitarians have it all wrong, and that the *results* of a decision are not as important as the *reason* for which it is made. To a deontological thinker, the ends do not justify the means.

The best-known proponent of the deontological model was 18th-century German philosopher Immanuel Kant. He thought that human beings possessed a unique dignity and that no decision that treated people as commodities could be considered just, even if the decision tended to maximize overall happiness, or profit, or any other quantifiable measure. In his view, a sense of duty or obligation was the best justification for any action. Although not all followers of deontological ethics agree with Kant's specific ideas, most agree that utilitarianism is lacking, and that winning in the end does not automatically make a decision right. Ethical decisions, they argue, are those made for good and moral reasons in the first place, regardless of the outcome.

In the following example, both sides end up better off, but is the operation ethically sound?

◆ Ethics Case: HIV Treatment ◆

Alpha Company has developed a new drug that is an effective treatment for HIV, the virus that causes AIDS. It is not a cure, but it postpones the onset of AIDS indefinitely.

Before this breakthrough, HIV-positive patients were treated with a "cocktail" of medications. Although effective, the combination of drugs required patients to take several pills at a time several times per day. Alpha Company's drug is a single pill that must be taken only twice per day. Because it is more convenient, patients would be less likely to miss doses.

Alpha spent tens of millions of dollars developing the drug, but now that is has been developed, each pill only costs a few dollars to manufacture. Alpha charges $4,150 for a 30-day supply, or about $50,000 per year. The pills generally are not covered by insurance plans. The older "cocktail" of drugs is still available from other drug companies at a much lower cost.

Alpha has a program that makes its drug available at no cost in extreme circumstances, and about 1 percent of the patients taking the drug receive it directly from Alpha at no charge. Alpha has several successful drugs and had earnings of nearly $3 billion last year.

Some activists have called on Alpha to do the following:

- Reduce the price of its drugs for all patients to $35,000 per year. This would be $10,000 above the cost of the older treatment.
- Expand its free drug program to cover 10 percent of the drug's current users.

Questions

1. Should Alpha meet the first demand and reduce its prices across the board? What is a fair price?
2. Should Alpha meet the second demand and expand its free drug program? What guidelines should it use?
3. Justify your answers to Questions 1 and 2 using the ideas presented in this section. Utilitarians might respond to this scenario by saying, "A profitable drug company will stay in business longer, develop more useful medications, and benefit more people in the long run. Alpha is under no ethical obligation to make either policy change." A Kantian thinker might argue, "Alpha has a duty to help people when it is able to do so. It should reduce the price to all patients and provide free drugs to those who need it." Which line of reasoning makes more sense to you?

Applying Personal Ethics in the Workplace

Should you behave in the workplace the way you do at home, or do you have a separate set of ethics for each part of your life? What if your employees behave badly outside of work—should that affect their employment? Consider the following case.

◆ Ethics Case: No Sheen on Sheen ◆

Charlie Sheen, the star of the hit CBS TV show *Two and a Half Men,* has admitted to using large quantities of cocaine. He has been hospitalized with drug overdoses and has been charged with both misdemeanor and felony drug offenses, which have led to probation several times. When asked about entering rehab, he said that only losers go to recovery programs and he could cure himself with his mind. He openly spent tens of thousands of dollars on prostitutes. His second wife filed a restraining order against him, alleging that he had pushed her down the stairs and threatened to kill her. He was also charged with a felony for threatening his third wife. She claims that he held a knife to her throat and said "You better be in fear. If you tell anybody, I'll kill you." Then there was the widely reported incident in the Plaza Hotel in New York City in which the police escorted him to the hospital after he trashed his room and threatened the prostitute whom he had hired—all while his ex-wife and children slept in a room across the hall. Five months later, the police removed his twin sons from his house after their mother obtained a restraining order. On a radio show, Sheen made anti-Semitic comments about his boss, called him a clown and a charlatan, and said that he "violently hated him." This boss was the most successful producer of comedy shows in the business.

Questions

1. If CBS fired Sheen from his TV show, the network would lose tens of millions of dollars. At what point, if any, should CBS have fired him? If not for this, then for what?
2. Would you fire a warehouse worker who behaved this way? How much revenue does an employee have to bring in to be able to buy his way out of bad behavior?
3. What would you say to someone who argues that the goal at work is to make as much money as possible, but at home it is to be a kind and honorable human being?

STAKEHOLDER ETHICS

A fundamental question in business ethics is: *What is the purpose of a corporation?* The answer to this question has changed over time. To begin at the beginning …

In a famous 1919 lawsuit[7], Henry Ford was sued by the Dodge brothers and other major shareholders of Ford Motor Company. The shareholders were upset because Ford paid essentially no dividends, despite fabulous profits. The shareholders complained, especially about Ford's use of corporate profits to support humanitarian and charitable works. The Michigan Supreme Court found in favor of the shareholders because corporation laws at the time required corporate boards to put shareholders first. The Dodge brothers won enough money to start their own car company, which still exists as part of Chrysler.

Companies were legally required to follow the "shareholder model" until the decade after the close of World War II. In the late 1940s and early 1950s, the attitude of many powerful politicians toward corporations changed. Many believed that American companies had contributed mightily to stopping the Nazis, and that without the massive volume of armaments and supplies that American corporations produced, Hitler might well have been victorious. There was a feeling that corporations were an essential part of society.

[7] *Dodge v. Ford*, 170 N.W. 668 (Mich. 1919).

Many politicians wanted corporations to be able to participate more fully in American life. They softened restrictive language in corporation laws so that companies could "do good deeds." Such action was not and is still not required, but it is *allowed*.

Definitions

The Shareholder Model

Noted economist Milton Friedman argued that corporations have two primary responsibilities. First, they must comply with the law. Second, they must make as much money as possible for shareholders. In his view, if shareholder and stakeholder interests conflict, the company should act in the best interests of the shareholders. After all, only shareholders have put their own money on the line. To do otherwise is, according to Friedman, "imposing a tax" on the shareholders.

The Stakeholder Model

The alternative point of view is that corporations should take care of more than shareholders alone. It is not that the owners of a corporation should be ignored—shareholders are included as one of several groups of stakeholders in a firm. But, a company must also look out for (among others) its employees, its customers, and the communities in which it operates. It may even be that companies have an obligation to broader interests such as "society" or "the environment."

The basic notion of stakeholder ethics is that even if a company will make a smaller profit for shareholders, it should nonetheless pay decent wages, support charitable causes, and so forth. A great many Fortune 500 companies put the stakeholder model into practice.

The Debate

Every executive will treat employees well if she believes that doing so will lead to increased profits. Every executive is in favor of donating money to charity if the donation improves the company's image and thereby pays for itself. But such win-win cases are not ethical dilemmas.

In a true dilemma, a company considers an action that would not increase the shareholders' return in any certain or measureable way. In such cases, the shareholder model advises, "Don't spend the shareholders' money." The stakeholder model counsels, "It is often OK to consider the interests of stakeholders other than the owners."

As with most all ethics questions, neither side is "right" in the sense that everyone agrees or that the law requires following either set of ideas. Countless companies follow each of the models.

The remainder of this section examines a company's ethical obligation to three specific stakeholders: employees, customers, and international contractors.

The Organization's Responsibility to Its Employees

Organizations cannot be successful without good workers. In many circumstances, the shareholder and stakeholder models agree that employees should be treated well. Disgruntled workers are likely to be unmotivated and unproductive. But sometimes looking out for employees may not lead to higher profits. In these cases, does an organization have a duty to "take care" of its workers? The shareholder model says no; the stakeholder model takes the opposite view.

Corporate leaders are often faced with difficult decisions when the issue of layoffs arises. Choices can be particularly difficult to navigate when outsourcing is an option. *Outsourcing* refers to cutting jobs at home and relocating operations to another country.

Read the following scenario and critique the CEO's decision making.

◆ Ethics Case: The Storm After the Storm ◆

Yanni is the CEO of Cloud Farm, a company that provides online data centers for Internet companies. Because these data centers are enormous, they are located in rural areas where they are often the main employer. A series of tornados has just destroyed a data center near Farmfield, Arkansas, a town with a population of roughly 5,000 people. Farmfield is a three-hour drive from the nearest city, Little Rock.

Here is the good news: the insurance payout will cover the full cost of rebuilding. Indeed, the payout will be so generous that Cloud Farm could build a bigger and better facility than the one destroyed. The bad news? Data centers are much more expensive to build and operate in the United States than in Africa, Asia, or Latin America. Yanni could take the money from the insurance company and build three data centers overseas. He has asked Adam and Zoe to present the pros and cons of relocating.

Adam says: "If we rebuild overseas, our employees will never find equivalent jobs. We pay $20 an hour, and the other jobs in town are mostly minimum-wage. And remember how some of the guys worked right through Christmas to set up for that new client. They have been loyal to us—we owe them something in return. And it's not just bad for Farmfield or Arkansas, it's bad for the country. We can't continue to ship jobs overseas."

Zoe responds: "That is the government's problem, not ours. We'll pay to retrain the workers, which, frankly, is a generous offer. Our investors get a return of 4 percent; the industry average is closer to 8 percent. If we act like a charity to support Farmfield, we could all lose our jobs. It is our obligation to do what's best for our shareholders—which, in this case, happens to be what's right for us, too."

Questions

1. If you were in Yanni's position, would you rebuild the plant in Arkansas or relocate overseas?
2. Do you agree with Zoe's argument that it is the government's responsibility to create and protect American jobs, and that it is a CEO's job to increase shareholder wealth?
3. Imagine that you personally own $10,000 worth of shares in Cloud Farm. Would you be upset with a decision to rebuild the data center in the United States?
4. If Cloud Farm decides to rebuild in Arkansas, should it pay the workers while the center is being rebuilt? If yes, should it apply to all the workers, or just the high-level ones who might leave if they were not paid?
5. What is your Life Principle on this issue? Would you be willing to risk your job to protect your employees?

An Organization's Responsibility to Its Customers

Customers are another group of essential stakeholders. A corporation must gain and retain loyal buyers if it is to stay in business for long. Treating customers well usually increases profits and helps shareholders.

But when, if ever, does an organization go too far? If a leader "puts customers first" in a way that significantly diminishes the bottom line, has she acted inappropriately? The shareholder model says yes.

After reading the following scenario, assess which option is best.

◆ Ethics Case: Fanning Customer Wrath ◆

Mark is the plant manager at Cooper Fan Company. For six months, he has been angling to ink a deal with Rooms-to-Go, a housewares company. With this contract, company profits would soar and he could hire 75 new workers. It would not hurt his bonus or job security, either. But now the shift foreman at the factory is reporting bad news—an engineer says there may be a problem with the CPRF-300 model, one of Cooper's most popular offerings. With a sinking heart, Mark goes to investigate.

Ann, the engineer, shows Mark the standard remote control. "Notice," she says, "four buttons—Lo, Hi, Off, and Reverse." Mark hits the Lo button, and a ceiling fan just above his head starts to rotate lazily. He pushes Off, and the blades slow to a stop.

"So what's the problem?" Mark asks.

"It's the Reverse button. Most of our models have a switch on top of the fan itself that allows for the fan to spin clockwise or counterclockwise. This way, fans can blow air downward in the summer to cool the room and then draw air upward in the winter to make the same room feel warmer. But that means twice a year, homeowners have to drag out a ladder to change the switch.

"The CPRF-300 solves this problem by putting the Reverse button on the remote control. No ladders, no changing of switches. The problem is that the remote allows the reverse feature to be engaged while the fan is running. Watch."

Ann presses Hi on the remote and waits for the blades to cycle up to speed. When the blades are a blur, she pushes Reverse. There are several rapid clicks and a soft grinding sound as the blades lose speed. The noises stop after a few seconds, the blades slow, come to a stop, change direction, and begin to speed up again.

"If someone does that once or twice, no problem," Ann says. But eventually, the fans all fail. We tested 50 of them—switching back and forth between Hi and Reverse over and over. At somewhere between 75 and 150 reversals, they break. For most of them, it isn't a big problem—they just stop working. Three of them emitted sparks but did nothing else. One of them started a fire. And the last one threw out a half-inch piece of metal from the inner casing. Probably wouldn't kill someone, but it could certainly have put out an eye."

"So who's going to switch back and forth like that 75 times?" Mark asks.

"A kid might want to make a game of it. And, although there have been no reports of any problems, it may be that we are just lucky. So far. The engineers have designed a new fan that solves this problem. But what do we do in the meantime about the 50,000 CPRF-300s that have already been sold?"

Here are Mark's options:

- Recall all the CPRF-300s. Fixing or replacing the fans would probably cost several million dollars. A recall would also jeopardize the Rooms-to-Go contract.
- Never issue a recall. If a fan fails and someone sues, it would probably cost \$20,000 to \$200,000 per incident. But if someone dies in a fire or is disabled by flying debris, then all bets are off. There is no upper limit on a worst-case scenario like that.
- Delay the recall for a month or two, until the Rooms-to-Go contract is resolved one way or the other.

Questions

1. If you were in Mark's position, would you recommend a recall today? How about in two months, after the Rooms-to-Go deal has been completed?
2. Ann's testing showed 6 percent "bad" results (sparks) and 4 percent "really bad" results (fire and thrown metal). Would your answers to Question 1 change if Ann's testing had shown 18 percent "bad" and 12 percent "really bad" results? What if it had shown the same number of "bad" results but zero "really bad" results?
3. What Life Principle are you applying in this situation?

4. Assume that no recall is made, that a fan started a fire and burned a home in your town to the ground, and that a local newspaper identified the ceiling fan as the cause. The newspaper later reports that the Cooper Fan Company knew about the potential problem and did nothing about it. As a consumer, would you consider buying Cooper fans, or would you pass them by even if they were competitive in pricing, appearance, and features?

Organization's Responsibility to Overseas Contract Workers

What are the ethical obligations of a company that uses foreign workers?

Do an American company's ethical obligations end at the border? What ethical duties does an American manager owe to stakeholders in countries where the culture and economic circumstances are very different? Should American companies (and consumers) buy goods that are produced in sweatshop factories?

Industrialization has always been the first stepping stone out of dire poverty—it was in England in centuries past, and it is now in the developing world. Eventually, higher productivity leads to higher wages. In China, factory managers have complained that their employees want to work even longer hours to earn more money. The results in China have been nothing short of remarkable. During the Industrial Revolution in England, per-capita output doubled in 58 years; in China, it took only 10 years.

Industrialization has always been the first stepping stone out of dire poverty.

During the past 50 years, Taiwan and South Korea welcomed sweatshops. During the same period, India resisted what it perceived to be foreign exploitation. Although all three countries started at the same economic level, Taiwan and South Korea today have much lower levels of infant mortality and much higher levels of education than India.[8]

When governments or customers try to force factories in the developing world to pay higher wages, the factory owners typically either relocate to lower-wage countries or mechanize, thereby reducing the need for workers. In either case, the local economy suffers. Companies argue that higher wages lead to increased prices, which in turn drive away customers.

◆ Ethics Case: The Dragon's Den ◆

Ellen is the CEO of a large electronics manufacturer that makes cell phones, among other items. She is reviewing a consultant's report on Quality Dragon Limited, which operates the factory in China where the cell phones are made. She is considering whether to renew the firm's contract for a new three-year term.

The consultant "infiltrated" the Quality Dragon factory by getting a job and working there for a month. Portions of the consultant's report follow.

[8]The data in this and the preceding paragraph are from Nicholas D. Kristof and Sheryl Wu Dunn, "Two Cheers for Sweatshops," *New York Times Magazine*, Sept. 24, 2000, p. 70.

We were awakened at 5 a.m. every day. They always shouted at us and ordered us to hurry. We were fed a poor meal, and were always at our stations by 5:30, although work did not begin until 6. We worked from 6 until 1 p.m. with one 10-minute restroom break at 9 a.m. We were not permitted to talk to coworkers. If we did, even quietly, we were docked pay and the supervisors screamed at us. If we made an assembly error, we lost pay and the supervisors screamed at us. If we yawned, we lost pay and the supervisors screamed at us. If we failed to meet an hourly quota, we lost pay and the supervisors screamed at us.

I drilled holes into the outer casing of your phones at the place where a charger can be plugged in. My quota was to process 120 per hour. The holes had to be perfectly located and perfectly straight. Every 30 seconds, a new one. It was difficult to keep focus. I tried to make fewer than 10 errors per day. One day I made only 4 errors. Another day I made 18. On that day, my supervisor slapped me and docked my entire day's pay.

We had 30 minutes for lunch. The company provides a poor meal. We were permitted to pay for better food at the cafeteria, but it was very expensive. We could speak quietly at lunch.

At 1:30, we went back to work until 8:30. We had another 10-minute break at 4:30. Work was more difficult in the afternoon. The sun warmed the factory. Water was not allowed on the assembly floor. Sometimes, water was available at the restroom break. The supervisors were angrier and less patient after lunch. They called us names that no one should be called. If we missed our quota, we had to work late. This happened several times over the month.

Eventually, we were fed and returned to our dorm. We had 12 men to a room, and we slept in bunk beds that were three bunks high. The room smelled bad, and there were ants.

We worked six days per week. On Sundays, most workers spent much of their day sleeping. The company did provide televisions and chess sets in the recreation building.

I was supposed to earn $150 for the month. But the supervisors always looked for reasons to dock my pay. No one gets full pay. I ended up with $110 at the end of the month. For long-term workers, "take-home pay" is actually lower because there are things they must buy from the factory store. Workers are required to shave, but they have to buy their own razor blades. They also have to buy soap. The company provides a jumpsuit once a year, but workers have to buy socks and underwear.

Life in the factory could be worse, but it is very difficult.

Questions

1. Is the CEO morally required to use her negotiating power to insist upon better treatment of the people who make her company's products? What is your Life Principle?

2. In your opinion, does the treatment described seem reasonable? If not, what parts of the consultant's story indicate to you that workers are being treated wrongfully?

3. Assume that correcting the problems listed below would each result in a 1 percent cost increase for this company. Assume that you are in Ellen's position as CEO. Which of the following items would you insist upon, keeping in mind that each one increases your labor costs?

   - Reducing employees' workdays to a maximum of 12 hours
   - Improving the quality of food served to employees
   - Eliminating the practice of reducing pay for employees who exceed their quota for errors
   - Building additional dorms so that workers sleep with no more than four to a room
   - Prohibiting unpaid or forced overtime

4. As a consumer, are you keenly aware of how much things cost? Would you notice if food prices rose by 5 percent? What about smart phones, computers, and televisions—would a 5 percent increase in the price of these items be noticeable? What if the increase was 2 percent? How much extra would you be willing to pay for your cell phone so that workers could be treated better than the ones in this factory?

When, If Ever, is Lying Acceptable?

Does deception in business amount to lying or bluffing?

We are taught from an early age that we must tell the truth. And usually, honesty is the best policy. The consequences of lying can be severe: students are suspended, employees are fired, and witnesses are convicted of perjury. Sometimes the problems are more subtle but still significant: a loss of trust, a loss of opportunities.

But in some specific circumstances, intentional deception is tolerated, even admired. In sports, for example, athletes spend countless hours perfecting techniques designed to trick opponents. If Peyton Manning looks one way and throws the other, no one is upset even though his intention is to deceive the defensive backs. In other settings, lying is equally acceptable. When poker players bluff their way through lousy hands, we call them "skilled."

But what about in business? Does the presence of *competition* make a difference? Can the ends ever justify the means when it is not a life-and death situation? Consider the following scenario.

◆ Ethics Case: Truth (?) in Borrowing ◆

"Yes," Harold insisted indignantly. "I *am* going to walk in there and give them a file of fake documents. And hope to heaven that I can walk out of there with a $100,000 loan, even if it is fraudulent. What of it? Ethics are all very well when business is good, but now I'm desperate. Without that loan, no payroll and then no business."

"And what happens when you get caught?" his brother demanded. "Don't expect me to come visit you in jail every Sunday."

"Don't worry, they'll never figure it out. I'm only exaggerating the numbers a little, and I've never fudged a single thing in 20 years of banking with them. They won't look too closely. And it's not like the bank is going to lose its money. Orders are already picking up, and they'll come all the way back, just like they did in the last two recessions. I'll pay the bank every penny back—with interest—this time next year. Who gets hurt?"

Questions

1. Rate Harold's plan to lie to his bank to secure the $100,000 loan so that he is able to pay his employees. Is it completely wrongful? Completely justified? Somewhere in between? How does it fit with your Life Principle?

2. Now assume that a year passes, and that business does in fact pick up for Harold's company. He is able to repay the loan in full, with interest. No one is laid off from his company, no one misses a paycheck, and his lie is never caught. Is your assessment of his actions the same? Do the ends at least partially justify the means?

3. What is your Life Principle about telling lies? When is making a misrepresentation acceptable? To protect someone's life or physical safety? To protect a job? To protect another person's feelings? To gain an advantage? When others expect it and may do the same? (Would bluffing in a game of poker be different from cheating on an exam or on your taxes?)
4. What would you say about the three examples in the opening scenario? Do you have the same rule when lying to protect yourself, as opposed to others?

Chapter Conclusion

Even employees who are ethical in their personal lives may find it difficult to uphold their standards at work if those around them behave differently. Managers wonder what they can do to create an ethical environment in their companies. In the end, the surest way to infuse ethics throughout an organization is for top executives to behave ethically themselves. When leaders assess the impact that their decisions will have on stakeholders, they go a long way towards behaving ethically.

Few employees will bother to "do the right thing" unless they observe that their bosses value and support such behavior. To ensure a more ethical world, managers must be an example for others, both within and outside their organizations.

Exam Review

1. **ETHICS** The law dictates how a person *must* behave. Ethics governs how people *should* behave.

2. **LIFE PRINCIPLES** Life Principles are the rules by which you live your life. If you develop these Life Principles now, you will be prepared when facing ethical dilemmas in the future.

3. **WHY BOTHER TO ACT ETHICALLY AT ALL?**
   - Society as a whole benefits from ethical behavior.
   - People feel better when they behave ethically.
   - Unethical behavior can be very costly.
   - Ethical behavior is more likely to pay off.

4. **UTILITARIANISM V. DEONTOLOGICAL ETHICS** Utilitarian thinkers believe that moral actions produce the greatest good for the greatest number. Deontological thinkers such as Immanuel Kant argue that, when assessing whether a decision is the most ethical choice, the end result is immaterial. Kantian thinkers believe that moral choices must be made for sound reasons, and that decisions motivated by a sense of duty or a respect for human dignity are particularly ethical.

5. **PERSONAL VS. WORK ETHICS** Should you apply your personal ethics in the workplace, or should you have different ethical values at home and at work?

6. **PURPOSE OF CORPORATIONS** Is the primary role of corporations to make money, or do companies have responsibilities to workers, communities, customers, and other stakeholders?

7. **ETHICS OVERSEAS** What ethical duties does an American manager owe to stakeholders in countries where the culture and economic circumstances are very different? Should American companies (and consumers) buy goods that are produced in sweatshop factories?

8. **LYING** When, if ever, is lying acceptable?

Multiple-Choice Questions

1. Milton Friedman was a strong believer in the __________ model. He __________ argue that a corporate leader's sole obligation is to make money for the company's owners.
   (a) Shareholder; did
   (b) Shareholder; did not
   (c) Stakeholder; did
   (d) Stakeholder; did not

2. In the 1919 lawsuit *Dodge v. Ford*, the Dodge brothers and other major shareholders sued Henry Ford and his board of directors over nonpayment of dividends. The Michigan Supreme Court sided with __________. Incorporation laws at the time __________ companies to follow the shareholder model.
   (a) Ford; required
   (b) Ford; permitted
   (c) The Dodge brothers; required
   (d) The Dodge brothers; permitted

3. Which of the following historic events led to a significant change in corporation laws, permitting companies to follow the stakeholder model?
   (a) The Great Depression
   (b) World War II
   (c) The election of John F. Kennedy
   (d) The moon landing
   (e) The Supreme Court's decision in *Brown v. Board of Education*

4. Which of the following wrote the book *Utilitarianism* and believed that moral actions should "generate the greatest good for the greatest number"?
   (a) Milton Friedman
   (b) John Stuart Mill
   (c) Immanuel Kant
   (d) None of the above

5. Which of the following believed that the dignity of human beings must be respected, and that the most ethical decisions are made out of a sense of duty or obligation?
   (a) Milton Friedman
   (b) John Stuart Mill
   (c) Immanuel Kant
   (d) None of the above

Essay Questions

1. Executives were considering the possibility of moving their company to a different state. They wanted to determine if employees would be willing to relocate, but they did not want the employees to know the company was contemplating a move because the final decision had not yet been made. Instead of asking the employees directly, the company hired a firm to carry out a telephone survey. When calling the employees, these "pollsters" pretended to be conducting a public opinion poll and identified themselves as working for the new state's Chamber of Commerce. Has this company behaved in an ethical manner? Would there have been a better way to obtain this information?

2. When a fire destroyed the Malden Mills factory in Lawrence, Massachusetts, its 70-year-old owner, Aaron Feuerstein, could have shut down the business, collected the insurance money, and sailed off into retirement. But a layoff of the factory's 3,000 employees would have been a major economic blow to the region. So instead, Feuerstein kept the workers on the payroll while he rebuilt the factory. These actions gained him a national reputation as a business hero. Many consumers promised to buy more of the company's Polartec fabric. In the end, however, the story did not have a fairy-tale ending: five years after the fire, Malden Mills filed bankruptcy papers. The company was not able to pay off the loans it had incurred to keep the business going.

   Did Feuerstein do the right thing?

3. Many socially responsible funds are now available to investors who want to make ethical choices. The Amana Fund buys stocks that comply with Islamic laws. For example, it will not invest in holdings that earn interest, which is prohibited under Islamic law. The Ava Maria Fund is designed for Catholic investors, the Timothy Funds for evangelicals. The Sierra Fund focuses on environmentally friendly investments, while the Women's Equity Fund chooses companies that promote women's interests in the workplace. On average, however, these socially responsible investments earn a lower return than standard index funds that mirror the performance of a stock index, such as the Standard & Poor's 500.

   Are socially responsible funds attractive to you? Do you now, or will you in the future, use them in saving for your own retirement?

4. When James Kilts became CEO of Gillette Co., the consumer products giant had been a mainstay of the Boston community for a hundred years. But the organization was going through hard times: Its stock was trading at less than half its peak price, and some of its storied brands of razors were wilting under intense competitive pressure. In four short years, Kilts turned Gillette around—strengthening its core brands, cutting jobs, and paying off debt. With the company's stock up 61 percent, Kilts had added $20 billion in shareholder value.

Then Kilts suddenly sold Gillette to Procter & Gamble Co. (P&G) for $57 billion. So short was Kilts's stay in Boston that he never moved his family from their home in Rye, New York. The deal was sweet for Gillette shareholders—the company's stock price went up 13 percent in one day. And tasty also for Kilts—his payoff was $153 million, including a $23.9 million reward from P&G for having made the deal and for a "change in control" clause in his employment contract that was worth $12.6 million. In addition, P&G agreed to pay him $8 million a year to serve as vice chairman after the merger. When he retires, his pension will be $1.2 million per year. Moreover, two of his top lieutenants were offered payments totaling $57 million.

Any downside to this deal? Four percent of the Gillette workforce—6,000 employees—were fired. If the payouts to the top three Gillette executives were divided among these 6,000, each unemployed worker would receive $35,000. The loss of this many employees (4,000 of whom lived in New England) had a ripple effect throughout the area's economy. Although Gillette shareholders certainly benefited in the short run from the sale, their profit would have been even greater without this $210 million payout to the executives. Moreover, about half the increase in Gillette revenues during the time that Kilts was running the show were attributable to currency fluctuations. A cheaper dollar increased revenue overseas. If the dollar had moved in the opposite direction, there might not have been any increase in revenue. Indeed, for the first two years after Kilts joined Gillette, the stock price declined. It wasn't until the dollar turned down that the stock price improved.

Do CEOs who receive sweeteners have too strong an incentive to sell their companies? Is it unseemly for them to be paid so much when many employees will lose their jobs?

5. Many of America's largest consumer product companies, such as Wal-Mart, Nike, and Land's End, buy fabric produced in China by Fountain Set Holdings Ltd. Chinese government investigators recently discovered that Fountain Set has contaminated a local river by dumping dye waste into it. What responsibility do U.S. companies have to ensure safe environmental practices by overseas suppliers?

Discussion Questions

1. Darby has been working for 14 months at Holden Associates, a large management consulting firm. She is earning $75,000 a year, which *sounds* good but does not go very far in New York City. It turns out that her peers at competing firms are typically paid 20 percent more and receive larger annual bonuses. Darby works about 60 hours a week—more if she is traveling. A number of times, she has had to reschedule her vacation or cancel personal plans to meet client deadlines. She hopes to go to business school in a year and has already begun the application process.

   Holden has a policy that permits any employee who works as late as 8:00 P.M. to eat dinner at company expense. The employee can also take a taxi home. Darby is in the habit of staying until 8:00 P.M. every night, whether or not her workload requires it. Then she orders enough food for dinner, with leftovers for lunch the next day. She has managed to cut her grocery bill to virtually nothing. Sometimes she invites her boyfriend to join her for dinner. As a student, he is always hungry and broke. Darby often uses the Holden taxi to take them back to his apartment, although the cab fare is twice as high as to her own place.

Sometimes Darby stays late to work on her business school applications. Naturally, she uses Holden equipment to print out and photocopy the finished applications. Darby has also been known to return catalog purchases through the Holden mailroom on the company dime. Many employees do that, and the mailroom workers do not seem to mind.

Is Darby doing anything wrong? How would you behave in these circumstances?

2. H. B. Fuller Co. of St. Paul is a leading manufacturer of industrial glues. Its mission statement says the company "will conduct business legally and ethically." It has endowed a university chair in business ethics and donates 5 percent of its profits to charity. But now it is under attack for selling its shoemakers' glue, Resistol, in Central America. Many homeless children in these countries have become addicted to Resistol's fumes. So widespread is the problem that glue-sniffers in Central America are called *resistoleros*. Glue manufacturers in Europe have added a foul-smelling oil to their glue that discourages abusers. Fuller fears that the smell may also discourage legitimate users. What should Fuller do?

3. According to the Electronic Industries Association, questionable returns have become the toughest problem plaguing the consumer electronics industry. Some consumers purchase electronic equipment to use once or twice for a special occasion and then return it—a radar detector for a weekend getaway or a camcorder to record a wedding. Or a customer might return a cordless telephone because he cannot figure out how it works. The retailer's staff lacks the expertise to help, so they refund the customer's money and ship the phone back to the manufacturer labeled as defective. Excessive and unwarranted returns force manufacturers to repackage and reship perfectly good products, imposing extra costs that squeeze their profits and raise prices to consumers. One retailer returned a cordless telephone that was two years old and had been chewed up by a dog. What ethical obligations do consumers and retailers have in these circumstances?

4. Genentech, Inc., manufactured Protropin, a genetically engineered version of the human growth hormone. This drug's purpose was to enhance the growth of short children. Protropin was an important product for Genentech, accounting for more than one-third of the company's total revenue of $217 million. Although the drug was approved for the treatment of children whose bodies made inadequate quantities of growth hormone, many doctors prescribed it for children with normal amounts of growth hormone who simply happened to be short. There was no firm evidence that the drug actually increased growth for short children with normal growth hormone. Moreover, many people questioned whether it is appropriate to prescribe such a powerful drug for cosmetic reasons, especially when the drug might not work. Nor was there proof that Protropin was safe over the long term. Was Genentech behaving ethically? Should it have discouraged doctors from prescribing the drug to normal, short children?

5. Rapper Ice-T's song "Cop Killer" generated significant controversy when it was released. Among other things, its lyrics anticipate slitting a policeman's throat. Such lyrics have become reasonably common today, but they were much less common 20 years ago.

When "Cop Killer" was recorded, Time Warner, Inc., was struggling with a $15 billion debt and a depressed stock price. Had Time Warner renounced rap albums with harsh themes, its reputation in the music business—and future profits—might have suffered. This damage might even have spilled over into the multimedia market, which was crucial to Time Warner's future.

Did Time Warner do anything wrong when it decided to release "Cop Killer"?

CHAPTER 3

DISPUTE RESOLUTION

Tony Caruso had not returned for dinner, and his wife, Karen, was nervous. She put on some sandals and hurried across the dunes, a half mile to the ocean shore. She soon came upon Tony's dog, Blue, tied to an old picket fence. Tony's shoes and clothing were piled neatly nearby. Karen and friends searched frantically throughout the evening.

A little past midnight, Tony's body washed ashore, his lungs filled with water. A local doctor concluded he had accidentally drowned.

Karen and her friends were not the only ones who were distraught. Tony had been partners with Beth Smiles in an environmental consulting business, Enviro-Vision. They were good friends, and Beth was emotionally devastated. When she was able to focus on business issues, Beth filed an insurance claim with the Coastal Insurance Group. Beth hated to think about Tony's death in financial terms, but she was relieved that the struggling business would receive $2 million on the life insurance policy.

A little past midnight, Tony's body washed ashore, his lungs filled with water.

Several months after filing the claim, Beth received this reply from Coastal: "Under the policy issued to Enviro-Vision, we are conditionally liable in the amount of $1 million in the event of Mr. Caruso's death. If his death is accidental, we are conditionally liable to pay double indemnity of $2 million. But pursuant to section H(5), death by suicide is not covered.

"After a thorough investigation, we have concluded that Anthony Caruso's death was an act of suicide, as defined in section B(11) of the policy. Your claim is denied in its entirety." Beth was furious. She was convinced Tony was incapable of suicide. And her company could not afford the $2 million loss. She decided to consult her lawyer, Chris Pruitt.

Three Fundamental Areas of Law

This case is a fictionalized version of several real cases based on double indemnity insurance policies. In this chapter, we follow Beth's dispute with Coastal from initial interview through appeal, using it to examine three fundamental areas of law: the structure of our court systems, civil lawsuits, and alternative dispute resolution.

When Beth Smiles meets with her lawyer, Chris Pruitt brings a second attorney from his firm, Janet Booker, who is an experienced **litigator**, that is, a lawyer who handles court cases. If they file a lawsuit, Janet will be in charge, so Chris wants her there for the first meeting. Janet probes about Tony's home life, the status of the business, his personal finances, everything. Beth becomes upset that Janet doesn't seem sympathetic, but Chris explains that Janet is doing her job: she needs all the information, good and bad.

Litigation versus Alternative Dispute Resolution

Janet starts thinking about the two methods of dispute resolution: litigation and alternative dispute resolution. **Litigation** refers to lawsuits, the process of filing claims in court, and ultimately going to trial. **Alternative dispute resolution** is any other formal or informal process used to settle disputes without resorting to a trial. It is increasingly popular with corporations and individuals alike because it is generally cheaper and faster than litigation, and we will focus on this topic in the last part of this chapter.

Litigation
The process of filing claims in court and ultimately going to trial.

Alternative dispute resolution
Any other formal or informal process used to settle disputes without resorting to a trial.

Court Systems

The United States has over 50 *systems* of courts. One nationwide system of *federal* courts serves the entire country. In addition, each individual *state*—such as Texas, California, and Florida—has its court system. The state and federal courts are in different buildings, have different judges, and hear different kinds of cases. Each has special powers and certain limitations.

State Courts

The typical state court system forms a pyramid, as Exhibit 3.1 shows. Some states have minor variations on the exhibit. For example, Texas has two top courts: A Supreme Court for civil cases and a Court of Criminal Appeals for criminal cases.

Trial Courts

Almost all cases start in trial courts, which are endlessly portrayed on television and in film. There is one judge, and there will often (but not always) be a jury. This is the only court to hear testimony from witnesses and receive evidence. **Trial courts** determine the facts of a particular dispute and apply to those facts the law given by earlier appellate court decisions.

Trial courts
Determine the facts of a particular dispute and apply to those facts the law given by earlier appellate court decisions.

In the Enviro-Vision dispute, the trial court will decide all important facts that are in dispute. Did Tony Caruso die? Did he drown? Assuming he drowned, was his death accidental or suicide? Once the jury has decided the facts, it will apply the law to those facts. If Tony Caruso died accidentally, contract law provides that Beth Smiles is entitled to double indemnity benefits. If the jury decides he killed himself, Beth gets nothing.

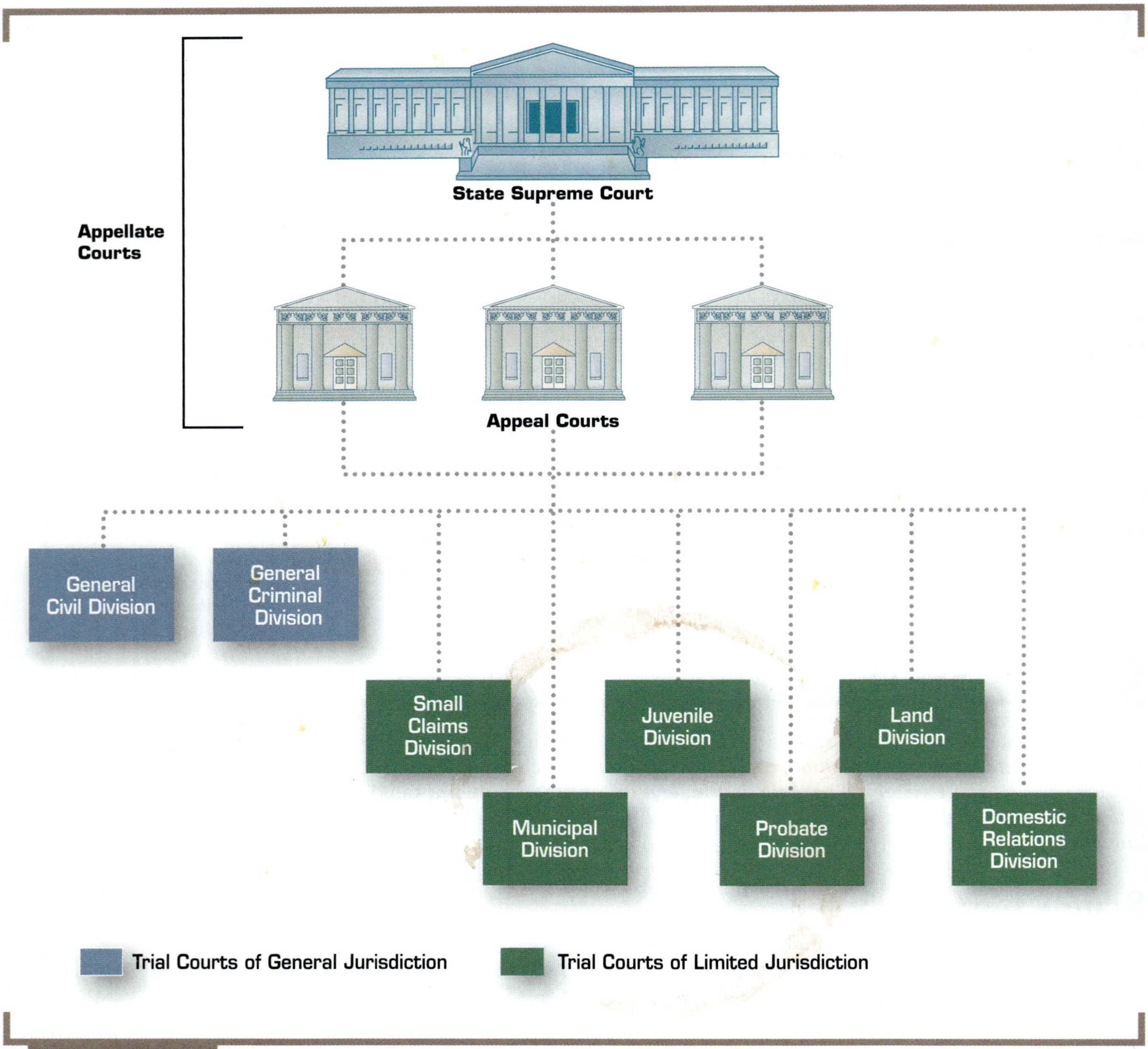

EXHIBIT 3.1 A trial court determines facts, while an appeals court ensures that the lower court correctly applied the law to those facts.

Facts are critical. That may sound obvious, but in a course devoted to legal principles, it is easy to lose track of the key role that factual determinations play in the resolution of any dispute. In the Enviro-Vision case, we will see that one bit of factual evidence goes undetected, with costly consequences.

Jurisdiction
A court's power to hear a case.

Jurisdiction refers to a court's power to hear a case. In state or federal court, a plaintiff may start a lawsuit only in a court that has jurisdiction over that kind of case. Some courts have very limited jurisdiction, while others have the power to hear almost any case.

Subject Matter Jurisdiction

Subject matter jurisdiction means that a court has the authority to hear a particular type of case.

Trial Courts of Limited Jurisdiction. These courts may hear only certain types of cases. Small claims court has jurisdiction only over civil lawsuits involving a maximum of, say, $5,000 (the amount varies from state to state). A juvenile court hears only cases involving minors. Probate court is devoted to settling the estates of deceased persons, though in some states it will hear certain other cases as well.

Trial Courts of General Jurisdiction. Trial courts of general jurisdiction, however, can hear a very broad range of cases. The most important court, for our purposes, is the general civil division. This court may hear virtually any civil lawsuit. In one day it might hear a $450 million shareholders' derivative lawsuit, an employment issue involving freedom of religion, and a foreclosure on a mortgage. Most of the cases we study start in this court.[1] If Enviro-Vision's case against Coastal goes to trial in a state court, it will begin in the trial court of general jurisdiction.

Personal Jurisdiction

In addition to subject matter jurisdiction, courts must also have **personal jurisdiction** over the defendant. Personal jurisdiction is the legal authority to require the defendant to stand trial, pay judgments, and the like. When plaintiffs file lawsuits, defendants sometimes make a *special appearance* to challenge a court's personal jurisdiction. If the court agrees with the defendant's argument, the lawsuit will be dismissed.

Personal jurisdiction generally exists, if:

1. For individuals, the defendant is a resident of the state in which a lawsuit is filed. For companies, the defendant is doing business in that state.
2. The defendant takes a formal step to defend a lawsuit. Most papers filed with a court count as formal steps, but special appearances do not.
3. A **summons** is *served* on a defendant. A summons is the court's written notice that a lawsuit has been filed against the defendant. The summons must be delivered to the defendant when she is physically within the state in which the lawsuit is filed.

For example, Texarkana straddles the Texas/Arkansas border. If a lawsuit is filed in a Texas court, a defendant who lives in Arkansas can be served if, when walking down the street in Texarkana, she steps across the state line into Texas. Corporations are required to hire a registered agent in any state in which they do business. If a registered agent receives a summons, then the corporation is served.

---

[1]Note that the actual name of the court will vary from state to state. In many states it is called *superior court* because it has power superior to the courts of limited jurisdiction. In New York it is called *supreme court* (anything to confuse the layperson); in some states it is called *court of common pleas;* in Oregon and other states it is a *circuit court.* They are all civil trial courts of general jurisdiction. Within this branch, some states are beginning to establish specialized business courts to hear complex commercial disputes. At least one state has created a cybercourt for high-tech cases. Lawyers will argue their cases by teleconference and present evidence via streaming video.

4. A **long-arm statute** applies. If all else fails—the defendant does not reside in the state, does not defend the lawsuit, and has not been served with a summons while in the state—a court still can obtain jurisdiction under long-arm statutes. These statutes typically claim jurisdiction over someone who commits a tort, signs a contract, or conducts "regular business activities" in the state.

As a general rule, courts tend to apply long-arm statutes aggressively, hauling defendants into their courtrooms. However, the due process guarantees in the United States Constitution require fundamental fairness in the application of long-arm statutes. Therefore, courts can claim personal jurisdiction only if a defendant has had *minimum contacts* with a state. In other words, it is unfair to require a defendant to stand trial in another state if he has had no meaningful interaction with that state.

In the following Landmark Case, the Supreme Court explains its views on this important constitutional issue.

Landmark Case

International Shoe Co. v. State of Washington

326 U.S. 310
Supreme Court of the United States, 1945

Facts: Although International Shoe manufactured footwear only in St. Louis, Missouri, it sold its products nationwide. It did not have offices or warehouses in Washington State, but it did send about a dozen salespeople there. The salespeople rented space in hotels and businesses, displayed sample products, and took orders. They were not authorized to collect payments from customers.

When Washington State sought contributions to the state's unemployment fund, International Shoe refused to pay. Washington sued. The company argued that it was not engaged in business in the state, and, therefore, that Washington courts had no jurisdiction over it.

The Supreme Court of Washington ruled that International Shoe did have sufficient contacts with the state to justify a lawsuit there. International Shoe appealed to the United States Supreme Court.

Issue: ***Did International Shoe have sufficient minimum contacts in Washington State to permit jurisdiction there?***

Excerpts from Chief Justice Stone's Decision: Appellant insists that its activities within the state were not sufficient to manifest its "presence" there and that in its absence, the state courts were without jurisdiction, that consequently, it was a denial of due process for the state to subject appellant to suit. Appellant [International Shoe] refers to those cases in which it was said that the mere solicitation of orders for the purchase of goods within a state, to be accepted without the state and filled by shipment of the purchased goods interstate, does not render the corporation seller amenable to suit within the state.

Historically the jurisdiction of courts to render judgment is grounded on their power over the defendant's person. Hence his presence within the territorial jurisdiction of a court was prerequisite to a judgment personally binding him. But now due process requires that [a defendant] have certain minimum contacts with it such that the maintenance of the suit does not offend "traditional notions of fair play and substantial justice."

Since the corporate personality is a fiction, its "presence" without can be manifested only by those activities of the corporation's agent within the state which courts will deem to be sufficient to satisfy the demands of due process.

"Presence" in the state in this sense has never been doubted when the activities of the corporation there have not only been continuous and systematic, but also give rise to the liabilities sued on, even though no consent to be sued or authorization to an agent to accept service of process has been given. Conversely, it has been generally recognized that the casual presence of the corporate agent or even his conduct of single or isolated items of activities in a state in the corporation's behalf are not enough to subject it to suit on causes of action unconnected with the activities there. To require the corporation in such circumstances to defend the suit away from its home or other jurisdiction where it carries on more substantial activities has been thought to lay too great and unreasonable a burden on the corporation to comport with due process.

But to the extent that a corporation exercises the privilege of conducting activities within a state, it enjoys the benefits and protection of the laws of that state. The exercise of that privilege may give rise to obligations.

Applying these standards, the activities carried on in behalf of appellant in the State of Washington were neither irregular nor casual. They were systematic and continuous throughout the years in question. They resulted in a large volume of interstate business, in the course of which appellant received the benefits and protection of the laws of the state, including the right to resort to the courts for the enforcement of its rights. The obligation which is here sued upon arose out of those very activities. It is evident that these operations establish sufficient contacts or ties with the state of the forum to make it reasonable and just, according to our traditional conception of fair play and substantial justice, to permit the state to enforce the obligations which appellant has incurred there.

The state may maintain the present suit to collect the tax.

Affirmed.

Appellate Courts

Appellate courts are entirely different from trial courts. Three or more judges hear the case. There are no juries, ever. These courts do not hear witnesses or take new evidence. They hear appeals of cases already tried below. **Appeals courts** generally accept the facts given to them by trial courts and review the trial record to see if the court made errors of law.

Appeals courts
Have the right to review decisions of trial courts.

Higher courts generally defer to lower courts on factual findings. Juries and trial court judges see all evidence as it is presented, and they are in the best position to evaluate it. An appeals court will accept a factual finding unless there was *no evidence at all* to support it. If the jury decides that Tony Caruso committed suicide, the appeals court will normally accept that fact, even if the appeals judges consider the jury's conclusion dubious. On the other hand, if a jury concluded that Tony had been murdered, an appeals court would overturn that finding if neither side had introduced any evidence of murder during the trial.

An appeals court reviews the trial record to make sure that the lower court correctly applied the law to the facts. If the trial court made an **error of law**, the appeals court may require a new trial. Suppose the jury concludes that Tony Caruso committed suicide but votes to award Enviro-Vision $1 million because it feels sorry for Beth Smiles. That is an error of law: if Tony committed suicide, Beth is entitled to nothing. An appellate court will reverse the decision. Or suppose that the trial judge permitted a friend of Tony's to state that he was certain Tony would never commit suicide. Normally, such opinions are not permissible in trial, and it was a legal error for the judge to allow the jury to hear it.

apellant = files appeal, not okay w/ decision

Court of Appeals. The party that loses at the trial court may appeal to the intermediate court of appeals. The party filing the appeal is the **appellant**. The party opposing the appeal (because it won at trial) is the **appellee**.

Appellant
The party filing the appeal.

Appellee
The party opposing the appeal.

This court allows both sides to submit written arguments on the case, called **briefs**. Each side then appears for oral argument, usually before a panel of three judges. The appellant's lawyer has about 15 minutes to convince the judges that the trial court made serious errors of law, and that the decision should be **reversed**, that is, nullified. The appellee's lawyer has the same time to persuade the court that the trial court acted correctly, and that the result should be **affirmed**, that is, permitted to stand.

Briefs
Written arguments on the case.

Reversed
Nullified.

Affirmed
Permitted to stand.

State Supreme Court. This is the highest court in the state, and it accepts some appeals from the court of appeals. In most states, there is no absolute right to appeal to the Supreme Court. If the high court regards a legal issue as important, it accepts the case. It then takes briefs and hears oral argument just as the appeals court did. If it considers the

apellee = not ok w/ appeal b/c won at trial

matter unimportant, it refuses to hear the case, meaning that the court of appeals' ruling is the final word on the case.[2]

In most states, seven judges, often called *justices,* sit on the Supreme Court. They have the final word on state law.

Federal Courts

As discussed in Chapter 1, federal courts are established by the United States Constitution, which limits what kinds of cases can be brought in any federal court. See Exhibit 3.2. For our purposes, two kinds of civil lawsuits are permitted in federal court: federal question cases and diversity cases.

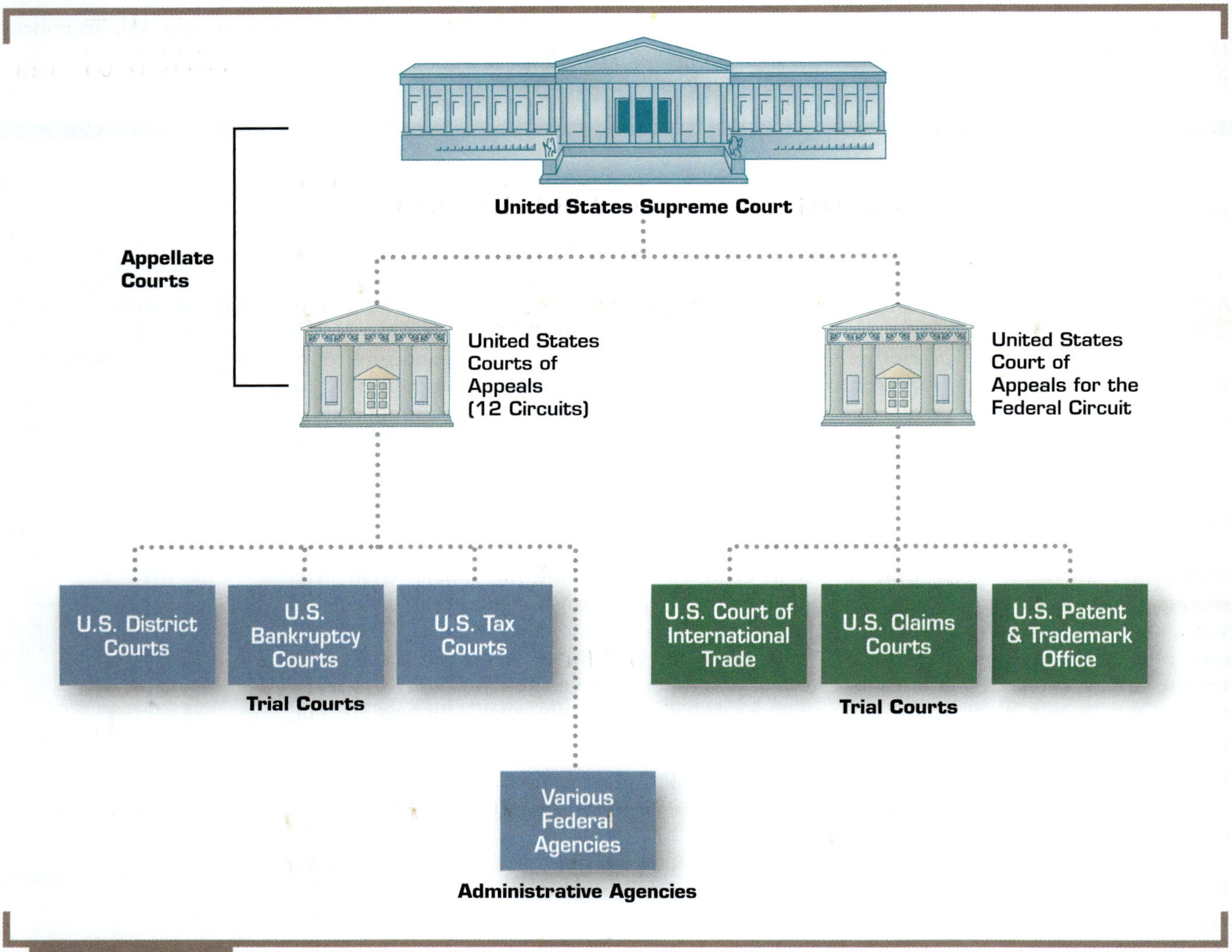

EXHIBIT 3.2

[2] In some states with smaller populations, there is no intermediate appeals court. All appeals from trial courts go directly to the state supreme court.

Federal Question Cases

A claim based on the United States Constitution, a federal statute, or a federal treaty is called a **federal question** case.[3] Federal courts have jurisdiction over these cases. If the Environmental Protection Agency (a part of the federal government) orders Logging Company not to cut in a particular forest, and Logging Company claims that the agency has wrongly deprived it of its property, that suit is based on a federal statute and is thus a federal question. If Little Retailer sues Mega Retailer, claiming that Mega has established a monopoly, that claim is also based on a statute—the Sherman Antitrust Act—and creates federal question jurisdiction. Enviro-Vision's potential suit merely concerns an insurance contract. The federal district court has no federal question jurisdiction over the case.

Federal question
A case in which the claim is based on the United States Constitution, a federal statute, or a federal treaty.

Diversity Cases

Even if no federal law is at issue, federal courts have **diversity jurisdiction** when (1) the plaintiff and defendant are citizens of different states *and* (2) the amount in dispute exceeds $75,000. The theory behind diversity jurisdiction is that courts of one state might be biased against citizens of another state. To ensure fairness, the parties have the option to use a federal court as a neutral playing field.

Diversity jurisdiction
(1) The plaintiff and defendant are citizens of different states *and* (2) the amount in dispute exceeds $75,000.

Enviro-Vision is located in Oregon and Coastal Insurance is incorporated in Georgia.[4] They are citizens of different states and the amount in dispute far exceeds $75,000. Janet could file this case in United States District Court based on diversity jurisdiction.

Trial Courts

United States District Court. This is the primary trial court in the federal system. The nation is divided into about 94 districts, and each has a district court. States with smaller populations have one district. States with larger populations have several; Texas is divided geographically into four districts.

Other Trial Courts. There are other, specialized trial courts in the federal system. Bankruptcy Court, Tax Court, and the United States Court of International Trade all handle name-appropriate cases. The United States Claims Court hears cases brought against the United States, typically on contract disputes. The Foreign Intelligence Surveillance Court is a very specialized, secret court, which oversees requests for surveillance warrants against suspected foreign agents.

Judges. The president of the United States nominates all federal court judges, from district court to Supreme Court. The nominees must be confirmed by the Senate. Once confirmed, federal judges serve for "life in good behavior." Many federal judges literally stay on the job for life. Recently, still-active Judge Wesley Brown of Kansas tied a record as the oldest federal judge in history when he turned 103.

Appellate Courts

United States Courts of Appeals. These are the intermediate courts of appeals. As the map below shows, they are divided into "circuits," which are geographical areas. There are 11 numbered circuits, hearing appeals from district courts. For example, an appeal from the Northern District of Illinois would go to the Court of Appeals for the Seventh Circuit.

A 12th court, the Court of Appeals for the District of Columbia, hears appeals only from the district court of Washington, D.C. This is a particularly powerful court because so many

---

[3] 28 U.S.C. §1331 governs federal question jurisdiction and 28 U.S.C. §1332 covers diversity jurisdiction.

[4] For diversity purposes, a corporation is a citizen of the state in which it is incorporated and the state in which it has its principal place of business.

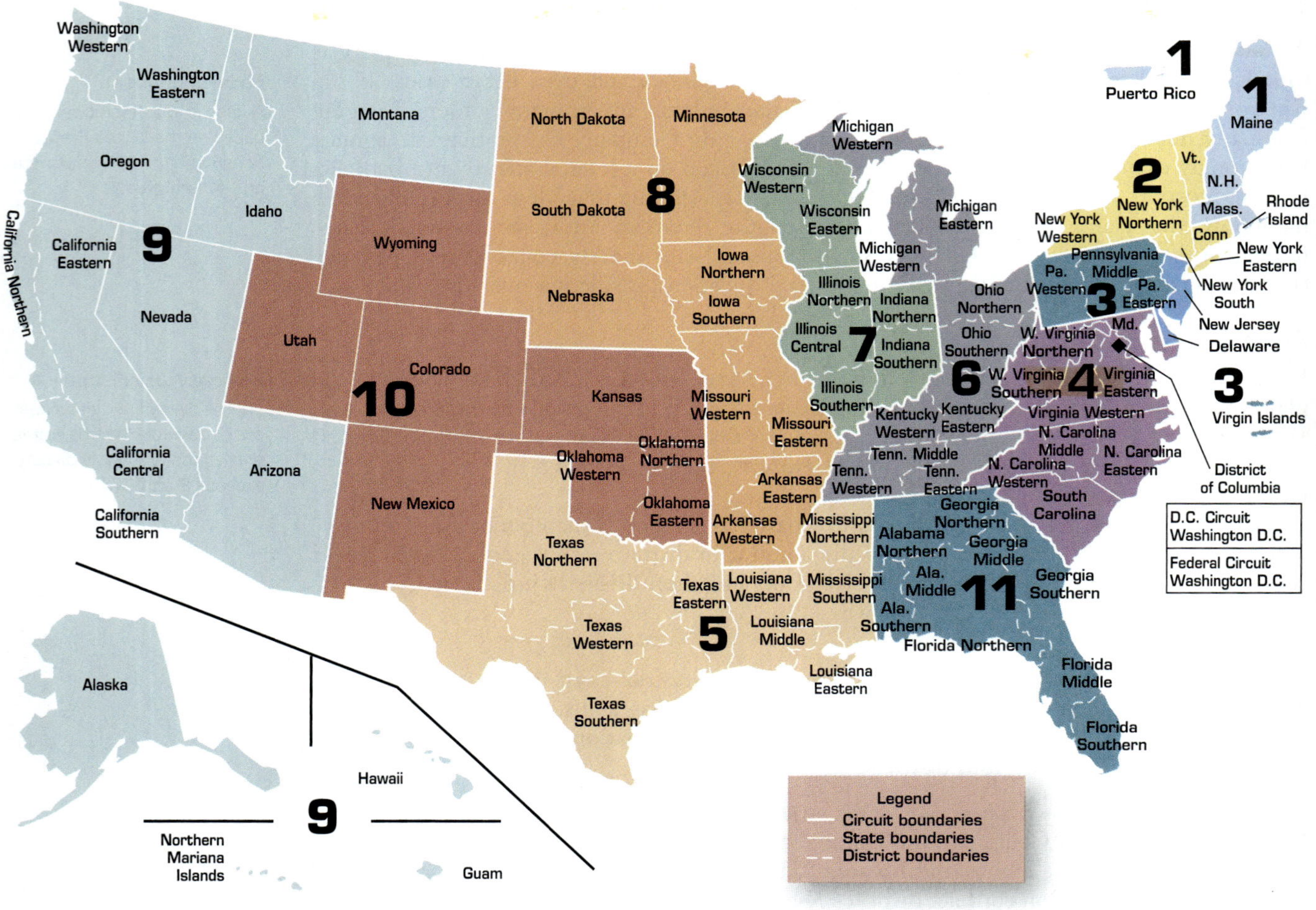

suits about federal statutes begin in the district court for the District of Columbia. Also in Washington is the 13th Court of Appeals, known as the Federal Circuit. It hears appeals from specialized trial courts, as shown in Exhibit 3.2.

Within one circuit there are many circuit judges, up to about 50 judges in the largest circuit, the Ninth. When a case is appealed, three judges hear the appeal, taking briefs and hearing oral arguments.

United States Supreme Court. This is the highest court in the country. There are nine justices on the Court. One justice is the chief justice and the other eight are associate justices. When they decide a case, each justice casts an equal vote. The chief justice's special power comes from his authority to assign opinions to a given justice. The justice assigned to write an opinion has an opportunity to control the precise language and thus to influence the voting by other justices.

The Supreme Court has the power to hear appeals in any federal case and in certain cases that began in state courts. Generally, it is up to the Court whether or not it will accept a case. A party that wants the Supreme Court to review a lower court ruling must file a petition for a **writ of *certiorari***, asking the Court to hear the case. Four of the nine justices must vote in favor of hearing a case before a writ will be granted. The Court receives several thousand requests every year but usually accepts fewer than 100. Most

Writ of certiorari
A petition asking the Supreme Court to hear a case.

cases accepted involve either an important issue of constitutional law or an interpretation of a major federal statute.

EXAM Strategy

Question: Mark has sued Janelle, based on the state common law of negligence. He is testifying in court, explaining how Janelle backed a rented truck out of her driveway and slammed into his Lamborghini, causing $82,000 in damages. Where would this take place?

(a) State appeals court

(b) United States Court of Appeals

(c) State trial court

(d) Federal District Court

(e) Either state trial court or Federal District Court

Strategy: The question asks about trial and appellate courts, and also about state versus federal courts. One issue at a time, please. What are the different functions of trial and appellate courts? *Trial* courts use witnesses, and often juries, to resolve factual disputes. *Appellate* courts never hear witnesses and never have juries. Applying that distinction to these facts tells us whether we are in a trial or appeals court.

Next Issue: *State* trial courts may hear lawsuits on virtually any issue. *Federal District Courts* may only hear two kinds of cases: Federal question (those involving a statute or constitutional provision); or diversity (where the parties are from different states *and* the amount at issue is $75,000 or higher). Apply what we know to the facts here.

Result: We are in a trial court because Mark is testifying. Could we be in Federal District Court? No. The suit is based on state common law. This is not a diversity case because the parties live in the same state. We are in a state trial court.

LITIGATION

Janet Booker decides to file the Enviro-Vision suit in the Oregon trial court. She thinks that a state court judge may take the issue more seriously than a federal district court judge.

Pleadings

The documents that begin a lawsuit are called the **pleadings**. These consist of the complaint, the answer, and sometimes a reply.

Pleadings
The documents that begin a lawsuit, consisting of the complaint, the answer, and sometimes a reply.

Complaint

The plaintiff files in court a **complaint**, which is a short, plain statement of the facts she is alleging and the legal claims she is making. The purpose of the complaint is to inform the defendant of the general nature of the claims and the need to come into court and protect his interests.

Janet Booker files the complaint, as shown below. Since Enviro-Vision is a partnership, she files the suit on behalf of Beth personally.

Complaint
A short, plain statement of the facts alleged and the legal claims made.

STATE OF OREGON
CIRCUIT COURT

Multnomah County — Civil Action No. ________

Elizabeth Smiles,
Plaintiff

JURY TRIAL DEMANDED

v.
Coastal Insurance Company, Inc.,
Defendant

COMPLAINT

Plaintiff Elizabeth Smiles states that:

1. She is a citizen of Multnomah County, Oregon.
2. Defendant Coastal Insurance Company, Inc., is incorporated under the laws of Georgia and has as its usual place of business 148 Thrift Street, Savannah, Georgia.
3. On or about July 5, 2012, plaintiff Smiles ("Smiles"), Defendant Coastal Insurance Co, Inc. ("Coastal") and Anthony Caruso entered into an insurance contract ("the contract"), a copy of which is annexed hereto as Exhibit "A." This contract was signed by all parties or their authorized agents, in Multnomah County, Oregon.
4. The contract obligates Coastal to pay to Smiles the sum of two million dollars ($2 million) if Anthony Caruso should die accidentally.
5. On or about September 20, 2012, Anthony Caruso accidentally drowned and died while swimming.
6. Coastal has refused to pay any sum pursuant to the contract.
7. Coastal has knowingly, willingly and unreasonably refused to honor its obligations under the contract.

WHEREFORE, plaintiff Elizabeth Smiles demands judgment against defendant Coastal for all monies due under the contract; demands triple damages for Coastal's knowing, willing, and unreasonable refusal to honor its obligations; and demands all costs and attorney's fees, with interest.
ELIZABETH SMILES,
By her attorney,
[Signed]
Janet Booker
Pruitt, Booker & Bother
983 Joy Avenue
Portland, OR
October 18, 2012

Service

When she files the complaint in court, Janet gets a summons, which is a paper ordering the defendant to answer the complaint within 20 days. A sheriff or constable then *serves* the two papers by delivering them to the defendant. Coastal's headquarters are in Georgia, so the state of Oregon has required Coastal to specify someone as its agent for receipt of service in Oregon.

Answer

Once the complaint and summons are served, Coastal has 20 days in which to file an answer. Coastal's answer, shown below, is a brief reply to each of the allegations in the complaint. The answer tells the court and the plaintiff exactly what issues are in dispute. Since Coastal admits that the parties entered into the contract that Beth claims they did, there is no need for her to prove that in court. The court can focus its attention on the disputed issue: whether Tony Caruso died accidentally.

STATE OF OREGON
CIRCUIT COURT

Multnomah County — Civil Action No. 09-5626

Elizabeth Smiles,
Plaintiff
v.
Coastal Insurance Company, Inc.,
Defendant

ANSWER

Defendant Coastal Insurance Company, Inc., answers the complaint as follows:

1. Admit.
2. Admit.
3. Admit.
4. Admit.
5. Deny.
6. Admit.
7. Deny.

COASTAL INSURANCE COMPANY, INC.,
By its attorney,
[Signed]
Richard B. Stewart
Kiley, Robbins, Stewart & Glote
333 Victory Boulevard
Portland, OR
October 30, 2012

If the defendant fails to answer in time, the plaintiff will ask for a **default judgment**. In granting a default judgment, the judge accepts every allegation in the complaint as true and renders a decision that the plaintiff wins without a trial.

Default judgment
A decision that the plaintiff wins without a trial because the defendant failed to answer in time.

Recently, two men sued PepsiCo, claiming that the company stole the idea for Aquafina water from them. They argued that they should receive a portion of the profits for every bottle of Aquafina ever sold.

PepsiCo failed to file a timely answer, and the judge entered a default judgment in the amount of $1.26 billion. On appeal, the default judgment was overturned and PepsiCo was able to escape paying the massive sum, but other defendants are sometimes not so lucky.

It is important to respond to courts on time.

Counter-Claim = defendant file lawsuit back at plaintiff

Sometimes a defendant does more than merely answer a complaint and files a **counter-claim**, meaning a second lawsuit by the defendant against the plaintiff. Suppose that after her complaint was filed in court, Beth had written a letter to the newspaper, calling Coastal a bunch of "thieves and scoundrels who spend their days mired in fraud and larceny." Coastal would not have found that amusing. The company's answer would have included a counter-claim against Beth for libel, claiming that she falsely accused the insurer of serious criminal acts. Coastal would have demanded money damages.

Counter-claim
A second lawsuit by the defendant against the plaintiff.

If Coastal counter-claimed, Beth would have to file a **reply**, which is simply an answer to a counter-claim. Beth's reply would be similar to Coastal's answer, admitting or denying the various allegations.

Reply
An answer to a counter-claim.

Class Actions

Suppose Janet uncovers evidence that Coastal denies 80 percent of all life insurance claims, calling them suicide. She could ask the court to permit a **class action**. If the court granted her request, she would represent the entire group of plaintiffs, including those

Class action
One plaintiff represents the entire group of plaintiffs, including those who are unaware of the lawsuit or even unaware they were harmed.

who are unaware of the lawsuit or even unaware they were harmed. Class actions can give the plaintiffs much greater leverage, since the defendant's potential liability is vastly increased. In the back of her mind, Janet has thoughts of a class action, *if* she can uncover evidence that Coastal has used a claim of suicide to deny coverage to a large number of claimants.

Notice how potent a class action can be. From his small town in Maine, Ernie decides to get rich quickly. On the Internet, he advertises "Energy Breakthrough! Cut your heating costs 15 percent for only $25." In response, 100,000 people send him their money, and they receive a photocopied graph, illustrating that if you wear two sweaters instead of one, you will feel 15 percent warmer. Ernie has deceitfully earned $2,500,000 in pure profit. What can the angry homeowners do? Under the laws of fraud and consumer protection, they have a legitimate claim to their $25, and perhaps even to treble damages ($75). But few will sue, because the time and effort required would be greater than the money recovered.

Economists analyze such legal issues in terms of *efficiency*. The laws against Ernie's fraud are clear and well intended, but they will not help in this case because it is too expensive for 100,000 people to litigate such a small claim. The effort would be hugely *inefficient*, both for the homeowners and for society generally. The economic reality may permit Ernie to evade the law's grasp.

That is one reason we have class actions. A dozen or so "heating plan" buyers can all hire the same lawyer. This attorney will file court papers in Maine on behalf of *everyone*, nationwide, who has been swindled by Ernie—including the 99,988 people who have yet to be notified that they are part of the case. Now the con artist, instead of facing a few harmless suits for $25, must respond to a multimillion-dollar claim being handled by an experienced lawyer. Treble damages become menacing: three times $25 times 100,000 is no joke, even to a cynic like Ernie. He may also be forced to pay for the plaintiffs' attorney, as well as all costs of notifying class members and disbursing money to them. With one lawyer representing an entire class, the legal system has become fiercely efficient.

Congress recently passed a statute designed to force large, multi-state class actions out of state courts, into federal. Proponents of the new law complained that state courts often gave excessive verdicts, even for frivolous lawsuits. They said the cases hurt businesses while enriching lawyers. Opponents argued that the new law was designed to shield large corporations from paying for the harm they caused by sending the cases into a federal system that is often hostile to such suits.

Judgment on the Pleadings

Motion
A formal request to the court to take some step or issue an order.

A party can ask the court for a judgment based simply on the pleadings themselves, by filing a motion to dismiss. A **motion** is a formal request to the court that the court take some step or issue some order. During a lawsuit, the parties file many motions. A **motion to dismiss** is a request that the court terminate a case without permitting it to go further. Suppose that a state law requires claims on life insurance contracts to be filed within three years, and Beth files her claim four years after Tony's death. Coastal would move to dismiss based on this late filing. The court might well agree, and Beth would never get into court.

Discovery

Discovery
The pre-trial opportunity for both parties to learn the strengths and weaknesses of the opponent's case.

Few cases are dismissed on the pleadings. Most proceed quickly to the next step. **Discovery** is the critical, pre-trial opportunity for both parties to learn the strengths and weaknesses of the opponent's case.

The theory behind civil litigation is that the best outcome is a negotiated settlement and that parties will move toward agreement if they understand the opponent's case. That is likeliest to occur if both sides have an opportunity to examine most of the evidence the other side will bring to trial. Further, if a case does go all the way to trial, efficient and fair litigation cannot take place in a courtroom filled with surprises. On television dramas, witnesses say astonishing things that amaze the courtroom (and keep viewers hooked through the next commercial). In real trials, the lawyers know in advance the answers to practically all questions asked because discovery has allowed them to see the opponent's documents and question its witnesses. The following are the most important forms of discovery.

Depositions provide a chance for one party's lawyer to question the other party, or a potential witness, under oath.

Interrogatories. These are written questions that the opposing party must answer, in writing, under oath.

Depositions. These provide a chance for one party's lawyer to question the other party, or a potential witness, under oath. The person being questioned is the **deponent**. Lawyers for both parties are present. During depositions, and in trial, good lawyers choose words carefully and ask questions calculated to advance their cause. A fine line separates ethical, probing questions from those that are tricky, and a similar line divides answers that are merely unhelpful from perjury.

Deponent
The person being questioned.

Production of Documents and Things. Each side may ask the other side to produce relevant documents for inspection and copying; to produce physical objects, such as part of a car alleged to be defective; and for permission to enter on land to make an inspection, for example, at the scene of an accident.

Physical and Mental Examination. A party may ask the court to order an examination of the other party, if his physical or mental condition is relevant, for example, in a case of medical malpractice.

Janet Booker begins her discovery with interrogatories. Her goal is to learn Coastal's basic position and factual evidence and then follow up with more detailed questioning during depositions. Her interrogatories ask for every fact Coastal relied on in denying the claim. She asks for the names of all witnesses, the identity of all documents, including electronic records, the description of all things or objects that they considered. She requests the names of all corporate officers who played any role in the decision and of any expert witnesses Coastal plans to call. Interrogatory No. 18 demands extensive information on all *other* claims in the past three years that Coastal has denied based on alleged suicide. Janet is looking for evidence that would support a class action.

Beth remarks on how thorough the interrogatories are. "This will tell us what their case is." Janet frowns and looks less optimistic: she's done this before.

Coastal has 30 days to answer Janet's interrogatories. Before it responds, Coastal mails to Janet a notice of deposition, stating its intention to depose Beth Smiles. Beth and Janet will go to the office of Coastal's lawyer, and Beth will answer questions under oath. But at the same time Coastal sends this notice, it sends *25 other notices of deposition*. The company will depose Karen Caruso as soon as Beth's deposition is over. Coastal also plans to depose all seven employees of Enviro-Vision; three neighbors who lived near Tony and Karen's beach house; two policemen who participated in the search; the doctor and two nurses involved in the case; Tony's physician; Jerry Johnson, Tony's tennis partner; Craig Bergson, a college roommate; a couple who had dinner with Tony and Karen a week before his death; and several other people.

Beth is appalled. Janet explains that some of these people might have relevant information. But there may be another reason that Coastal is doing this: the company wants to make this litigation hurt. Janet will have to attend every one of these depositions. Costs will skyrocket.

Motion for a protective order
A request that the court limit discovery.

Janet files a **motion for a protective order**. This is a request that the court limit Coastal's discovery by decreasing the number of depositions. Janet also calls Rich Stewart and suggests that they discuss what depositions are really necessary. Rich insists that all of the depositions are important. This is a $2 million case and Coastal is entitled to protect itself. As both lawyers know, **the parties are entitled to discover anything that could reasonably lead to valid evidence**.

But there may be another reason that Coastal is doing this: the company wants to make this litigation hurt.

Before Beth's deposition date arrives, Rich sends Coastal's answers to Enviro-Vision's interrogatories. The answers contain no useful information whatsoever. For example, Interrogatory No. 10 asked, "If you claim that Anthony Caruso committed suicide, describe every fact upon which you rely in reaching that conclusion." Coastal's answer simply says, "His state of mind, his poor business affairs, and the circumstances of his death all indicate suicide."

Janet calls Rich and complains that the interrogatory answers are a bad joke. Rich disagrees, saying that it is the best information they have so early in the case. After they debate it for 20 minutes, Rich offers to settle the case for $100,000. Janet refuses and makes no counteroffer.

Janet files a **motion to compel answers to interrogatories**, in other words, a formal request that the court order Coastal to supply more complete answers. Janet submits a **memorandum** with the motion, which is a supporting argument. Although it is only a few pages long, the memorandum takes several hours of online research and writing to prepare—more costs. Janet also informs Rich Stewart that Beth will not appear for the deposition, since Coastal's interrogatory answers are inadequate.

Rich now files *his* motion to compel, asking the court to order Beth Smiles to appear for her deposition. The court hears all of the motions together. Janet argues that Coastal's interrogatory answers are hopelessly uninformative and defeat the whole purpose of discovery. She claims that Coastal's large number of depositions creates a huge and unfair expense for a small firm.

Rich claims that the interrogatory answers are the best that Coastal can do thus far and that Coastal will supplement the answers when more information becomes available. He argues against Interrogatory No. 18, the one in which Janet asked for the names of other policyholders whom Coastal considered suicides. He claims that Janet is engaging in a fishing expedition that would violate the privacy of Coastal's insurance customers and provide no information relevant to this case. He demands that Janet make Beth available for a deposition.

These discovery rulings are critical because they will color the entire lawsuit. A trial judge has to make many discovery decisions before a case reaches trial. At times, the judge must weigh the need of one party to see documents against the other side's need for privacy. One device a judge can use in reaching a discovery ruling is an **in camera inspection**, meaning that the judge views the requested documents alone, with no lawyers present, and decides whether the other side is entitled to view them.

E-Discovery. The biggest change in litigation in the last decade is the explosive rise of electronic discovery. Companies send hundreds, or thousands, or millions of e-mails—every day. Many have attachments, sometimes hundreds of pages long. In addition, businesses large and small have vast amounts of data stored electronically. All of this information is potentially subject to discovery.

It is enormously time-consuming and expensive for companies to locate all of the relevant material, separate it from irrelevant or confidential matter, and furnish it. A firm may be obligated to furnish *millions* of e-mails to the opposing party. In one recent case, a defendant had to pay 31 lawyers full time, for six months, just to wade through the e-ocean of documents and figure out which had to be supplied and how to produce it. Not surprisingly, this data eruption has created a new industry: high-tech companies that assist law firms in finding, sorting, and delivering electronic data.

Who is to say what must be supplied? What if an e-mail string contains individual e-mails that are clearly privileged (meaning a party need not divulge them), but others that are not privileged? May a company refuse to furnish the entire string? Many will try. However, some courts have ruled that companies seeking to protect e-mail strings must create a log describing every individual e-mail and allow the court to determine which are privileged.[5]

When the cost of furnishing the data becomes burdensome, who should pay, the party seeking the information or the one supplying it? In a recent $4 million corporate lawsuit, the defendant turned over 3,000 e-mails and 211,000 other documents. But the trial judge noted that many of the e-mail attachments—sometimes 12 to an e-mail—had gone missing, and required the company to produce them. The defendant protested that finding the attachments would cost an additional $206,000. The judge ordered the company to do it, and bear the full cost.

Both sides in litigation sometimes use gamesmanship during discovery. Thus, if an individual sues a large corporation, for example, the company may deliberately make discovery so expensive that the plaintiff cannot afford the legal fees. And if a plaintiff has a poor case, he might intentionally try to make the discovery process more expensive for the defendant than his settlement offer. Even if a defendant expects to win at trial, an offer to settle a case for $50,000 can look like a bargain if discovery alone will cost $100,000. Some defendants refuse, but others are more pragmatic.

The following case illustrates another common discovery problem: refusal by one side to appear for deposition. Did the defendant cynically believe that long delay would win the day, given that the plaintiff was 78 years old? What can a court do in such a case?

STINTON V. ROBIN'S WOOD, INC.

45 A.D. 3d 203, 842 NYS2d 477
New York App. Div., 2007

Facts: Ethel Flanzraich, 78 years old, slipped and fell on the steps of property owned by Robin's Wood. She broke her left leg and left arm. Flanzraich sued, claiming that Robin's Wood caused her fall because its employee, Anthony Monforte, had negligently painted the stairs. In its answer to the complaint, Robin's Wood denied all of the significant allegations.

During a preliminary conference with the trial judge, the parties agreed to hold depositions of both parties on August 4. Flanzraich appeared for deposition but Robin's Wood did not furnish its employee, Monforte, nor did it offer any other company representative. The court then ordered the deposition of the defendant to take place the following April 2. Again, Robin's Wood produced neither Monforte nor anyone else. On July 16, the court ordered the defendant to produce its representative within 30 days. Once more, no one showed up for deposition.

[5] *Universal Service Fund Telephone Billing Practices Litigation*, 232 F.R.D. 669 (D. Kan. 2005).

On August 18—over *one year* after the original deposition date—Flanzraich moved to strike the defendant's answer, meaning that the plaintiff would win by default. The company argued that it had made diligent efforts to locate Monforte and force him to appear. However, all of the letters sent to Monforte were addressed care of Robin's Wood. Finally, the company stated that it no longer employed Monforte.

The trial judge granted the motion to strike the answer. That meant that Robin's Wood was liable for Flanraich's fall. The only remaining issue was damages. The court determined that Robin's Wood owed $22,631 for medical expenses, $150,000 for past pain and suffering, and $300,000 for future pain and suffering. One day later, Flanraich died, of other causes. Robin's Wood appealed.

Issue: ***Did the trial court abuse its discretion by striking the defendant's answer?***

Excerpts from Judge McCarthy's Decision: We find no merit to the defendant's claim that the [trial court] improvidently exercised its discretion in striking its answer. An action should be determined on the merits whenever possible. However, a court, in its discretion, may invoke the drastic remedy of striking an answer if it determines that the defendant's failure to comply with discovery demands is willful and contumacious.

The willful and contumacious character of [defendant's] conduct may be inferred from the defendant's noncompliance with [three] court orders directing such a deposition. Although the defendant may not have been able to produce Monforte after he left its employ, the defendant failed to explain why it produced neither another representative for the deposition nor timely disclosed to the decedent that it no longer employed Monforte. Either of these actions would have afforded the decedent the opportunity to subpoena Monforte for a nonparty deposition, had she so desired. For instance, by producing its representative for a deposition, the decedent would have had the ability to explore the whereabouts of Monforte and, in all likelihood, would have obtained information regarding how to contact him since the record indicates that the defendant had such information. This is especially important here where the decedent was elderly at the time of the accident and delays in discovery could only serve to prejudice her and unjustly benefit the defendant. Moreover, the defendant failed to explain why it did not produce Monforte for a deposition during the time he was under its employ.

Affirmed.

In the Enviro-Vision case, the judge rules that Coastal must furnish more complete answers to the interrogatories, especially as to why the company denied the claim. However, he rules against Interrogatory No. 18, the one concerning other claims Coastal has denied. This simple ruling kills Janet's hope of making a class action of the case. He orders Beth to appear for the deposition. As to future depositions, Coastal may take any 10 but then may take additional depositions only by demonstrating to the court that the deponents have useful information.

Rich proceeds to take Beth's deposition. It takes two full days. He asks about Enviro-Vision's past and present. He learns that Tony appeared to have won their biggest contract ever from Rapid City, Oregon, but that he then lost it when he had a fight with Rapid City's mayor. He inquires into Tony's mood, learns that he was depressed, and probes in every direction he can to find evidence of suicidal motivation. Janet and Rich argue frequently over questions and whether Beth should have to answer them. At times, Janet is persuaded and permits Beth to answer; other times, she instructs Beth not to answer. For example, toward the end of the second day, Rich asks Beth whether she and Tony had been sexually involved. Janet instructs Beth not to answer. This fight necessitates another trip into court to determine whether Beth must answer. The judge rules that Beth must discuss Tony's romantic life only if Coastal has some evidence that he was involved with someone outside his marriage. The company lacks any such evidence.

Now limited to 10 depositions, Rich selects his nine other deponents carefully. For example, he decides to depose only one of the two nurses; he chooses to question Jerry Johnson, the tennis partner, but not Craig Bergson, the former roommate; and so forth. When we look at the many legal issues this case raises, his choices seem minor. In fact, unbeknownst to Rich or anyone else, his choices may determine the outcome of the case.

As we will see later, Craig Bergson has evidence that is possibly crucial to the lawsuit. If Rich decides not to depose him, neither side will ever learn the evidence and the jury will never hear it. A jury can decide a case only based on the evidence presented to it. *Facts are elusive—and often controlling.*

In each deposition, Rich carefully probes with his questions, sometimes trying to learn what he actually does not know, sometimes trying to pin down the witness to a specific version of facts so that Rich knows how the witness will testify at trial. Neighbors at the beach testify that Tony seemed tense; one testifies about seeing Tony, unhappy, on the beach with his dog. Another testifies he had never before seen Blue tied up on the beach. Karen Caruso admits that Tony had been somewhat tense and unhappy the last couple of months. She reluctantly discusses their marriage, admitting there were problems.

Other Discovery. Rich sends Requests to Produce Documents, seeking medical records about Tony. Once again, the parties fight over which records are relevant, but Rich gets most of what he wants. Janet does less discovery than Rich because most of the witnesses she will call are friendly witnesses. She can interview them privately without giving any information to Coastal. With the help of Beth and Karen, Janet builds her case just as carefully as Rich, choosing the witnesses who will bolster the view that Tony was in good spirits and died accidentally.

She deposes all the officers of Coastal who participated in the decision to deny insurance coverage. She is particularly aggressive in pinning them down as to the limited information they had when they denied Beth's claim.

Summary Judgment

When discovery is completed, both sides may consider seeking summary judgment. **Summary judgment** is a ruling by the court that no trial is necessary because some essential facts are not in dispute. The purpose of a trial is to determine the facts of the case, that is, to decide who did what to whom, why, when, and with what consequences. If there are no relevant facts in dispute, then there is no need for a trial.

Summary judgment
A ruling by the court that no trial is necessary because some essential facts are not in dispute.

In the following case, the defendant won summary judgment, meaning that the case never went to trial. And yet, this was only the beginning of trouble for that defendant, Bill Clinton.

JONES V. CLINTON

990 F. Supp. 657, 1998 U.S. Dist. LEXIS 3902
United States District Court for the Eastern District of Arkansas, 1998

Facts: In 1991, Bill Clinton was governor of Arkansas. Paula Jones worked for a state agency, the Arkansas Industrial Development Commission (AIDC). When Clinton became president, Jones sued him, claiming that he had sexually harassed her. She alleged that, in May 1991, the governor arranged for her to meet him in a hotel room in Little Rock, Arkansas. When they were alone, he put his hand on her leg and slid it toward her pelvis. She escaped from his grasp, exclaimed, "What are you doing?" and said she was "not that kind of girl." She was upset and confused, and sat on a sofa near the door. She claimed that Clinton approached her, "lowered his trousers and underwear, exposed his penis and told her to kiss it." Jones was horrified, jumped up and said she had to leave. Clinton responded by saying, "Well, I don't want to make you do anything you don't want to do," and pulled his pants up. He added that if she got in trouble for leaving work, Jones should "have Dave call me immediately and I'll take care of it." He also said, "You are smart. Let's keep this between ourselves." Jones remained at AIDC until February 1993, when she moved to California because of her husband's job transfer.

President Clinton denied all of the allegations. He also filed for summary judgment, claiming that Jones had not alleged facts that justified a trial. Jones opposed the motion for summary judgment.

Issue: ***Was Clinton entitled to summary judgment or was Jones entitled to a trial?***

Excerpts from Judge Wright's Decision: [To establish this type of a sexual harassment case, a plaintiff must show that her refusal to submit to unwelcome sexual advances resulted in a tangible job detriment, meaning that she suffered a specific loss. Jones claims that she was denied promotions, given a job with fewer responsibilities, isolated physically, required to sit at a workstation with no work to do, and singled out as the only female employee not to be given flowers on Secretary's Day.]

There is no record of plaintiff ever applying for another job within AIDC, however, and the record shows that not only was plaintiff never downgraded, her position was reclassified upward from a Grade 9 classification to a Grade 11 classification, thereby increasing her annual salary. Indeed, it is undisputed that plaintiff received every merit increase and cost-of-living allowance for which she was eligible during her nearly two-year tenure with the AIDC and consistently received satisfactory job evaluations.

Although plaintiff states that her job title upon returning from maternity leave was no longer that of purchasing assistant, her job duties prior to taking maternity leave and her job duties upon returning to work both involved data input. That being so, plaintiff cannot establish a tangible job detriment. A transfer that does not involve a demotion in form or substance and involves only minor changes in working conditions, with no reduction in pay or benefits, will not constitute an adverse employment action, otherwise every trivial personnel action that an irritable employee did not like would form the basis of a discrimination suit.

Finally, the Court rejects plaintiff's claim that she was subjected to hostile treatment having tangible effects when she was isolated physically, made to sit in a location from which she was constantly watched, made to sit at her workstation with no work to do, and singled out as the only female employee not to be given flowers on Secretary's Day. Plaintiff may well have perceived hostility and animus on the part of her supervisors, but these perceptions are merely conclusory in nature and do not, without more, constitute a tangible job detriment. Although it is not clear why plaintiff failed to receive flowers on Secretary's Day in 1992, such an omission does not give rise to a federal cause of action.

In sum, the Court finds that a showing of a tangible job detriment or adverse employment action is an essential element of plaintiff's sexual harassment claim and that plaintiff has not demonstrated any tangible job detriment or adverse employment action for her refusal to submit to the Governor's alleged advances. The President is therefore entitled to summary judgment [on this claim].

In other words, the court acknowledged that there were factual disputes, but concluded that even if Jones proved each of her allegations, she would *still* lose the case, because her allegations fell short of a legitimate case of sexual harassment. Jones appealed the case. Later the same year, as the appeal was pending and the House of Representatives was considering whether to impeach President Clinton, the parties settled the dispute. Clinton, without acknowledging any of the allegations, agreed to pay Jones $850,000 to drop the suit.

Janet and Rich each consider moving for summary judgment, but both correctly decide that they would lose. There is one major fact in dispute: Did Tony Caruso commit suicide? Only a jury may decide that issue. As long as there is *some evidence* supporting each side of a key factual dispute, the court may not grant summary judgment.

EXAM strategy

Question: You are a judge. Mel has sued Kevin, claiming that while Kevin was drunk, he negligently drove his car down Mel's street, and destroyed rare trees on a lot that Mel owns, next to his house. Mel's complaint stated that three witnesses at a bar saw Kevin take at least eight drinks less than an hour before the damage was done. In Kevin's answer, he denied causing the damage and denied being in the bar that night.

Kevin's lawyer has moved for summary judgment. He proves that three weeks before the alleged accident, Mel sold the lot to Tatiana.

Mel's lawyer opposes summary judgment. He produces a security camera tape proving that Kevin was in the bar, drinking beer, 34 minutes before the damage was done. He produces a signed statement from Sandy, a landscape gardener who lives across the street from the scene. Sandy states that she heard a crash, hurried to the windows, and saw

Kevin's car weaving away from the damaged trees. She is a landscape gardener and estimates the tree damage at $30,000 to $40,000. How should you rule on the motion?

Strategy: Do not be fooled by red herrings about Kevin's drinking or the value of the trees. Stick to the question: Should you grant summary judgment? Trials are necessary to resolve disputes about essential factual issues. Summary judgment is appropriate when there are no essential facts in dispute. Is there an essential fact not in dispute? Find it. Apply the rule. Being a judge is easy!

Result: It makes no difference whether Kevin was drunk or sober, whether he caused the harm or was at home in bed. Because Mel does not own the property, he cannot recover for the damage to it. He cannot win. You should grant Kevin's summary judgment motion.

Final Preparation

Well over 90 percent of all lawsuits are settled before trial. But the parties in the Enviro-Vision dispute are unable to compromise, so each side gears up for trial. The attorneys make lists of all witnesses they will call. They then prepare each witness very carefully, rehearsing the questions they will ask. It is considered ethical and proper to rehearse the questions, provided the answers are honest and come from the witness. It is unethical and illegal for a lawyer to tell a witness what to say. It also makes for a weaker presentation of evidence—witnesses giving scripted answers are often easy to spot. The lawyers also have colleagues cross-examine each witness, so that the witnesses are ready for the questions the other side's lawyer will ask.

This preparation takes hours and hours, for many days. Beth is frustrated that she cannot do the work she needs to for Enviro-Vision because she is spending so much time preparing the case. Other employees have to prepare as well, especially for cross-examination by Rich Stewart, and it is a terrible drain on the small firm. More than a year after Janet filed her complaint, they are ready to begin trial.

Trial

Adversary System

Our system of justice assumes that the best way to bring out the truth is for the two contesting sides to present the strongest case possible to a neutral factfinder. Each side presents its witnesses and then the opponent has a chance to cross-examine. The adversary system presumes that by putting a witness on the stand and letting both lawyers question her, the truth will emerge.

The judge runs the trial. Each lawyer sits at a large table near the front. Beth, looking tense and unhappy, sits with Janet. Rich Stewart sits with a Coastal executive. In the back of the courtroom are benches for the public. On one bench sits Craig Bergson. He will watch the entire proceeding with intense interest and a strange feeling of unease. He is convinced he knows what really happened.

Janet has demanded a jury trial for Beth's case, and Judge Rowland announces that they will now impanel the jury.

Right to Jury Trial

Not all cases are tried to a jury. As a general rule, both plaintiff and defendant have a right to demand a jury trial when the lawsuit is one for money damages. For example, in a typical contract lawsuit, such as Beth's insurance claim, both plaintiff and defendant have a jury trial right whether they are in state or federal court. Even in such a case, though, the parties may *waive* the jury right, meaning they agree to try the case to a judge. Also, if the plaintiff is seeking an equitable remedy such as an injunction, there is no jury right for either party.

Voir Dire

Voir dire
The process of selecting a jury.

The process of selecting a jury is called **voir dire**, which means "to speak the truth."[6] The court's goal is to select an impartial jury; the lawyers will each try to get a jury as favorable to their side as possible. A court sends letters to potential jurors who live in its county. Those who do not report for jury duty face significant consequences.

Challenges for cause
A claim that a juror has demonstrated probable bias.

Peremptory challenges
The right to excuse a juror for virtually any reason.

When voir dire begins, potential jurors are questioned individually, sometimes by the judge and sometimes by the two lawyers, as each side tries to ferret out potential bias. Each lawyer may make any number of **challenges for cause**, claiming that a juror has demonstrated probable bias. For example, if a prospective juror in the Enviro-Vision case works for an insurance company, the judge will excuse her on the assumption that she would be biased in favor of Coastal. If the judge perceives no bias, the lawyer may still make a limited number of **peremptory challenges**, entitling him to excuse that juror for virtually any reason, which need not be stated in court. For example, if Rich Stewart believes that a juror seems hostile to him personally, he will use a peremptory challenge to excuse that juror, even if the judge sensed no animosity. The process continues until 14 jurors are seated. Twelve will comprise the jury; the other two are alternates who hear the case and remain available in the event one of the impaneled jurors becomes ill or otherwise cannot continue.

Although jury selection for a case can sometimes take many days, in the Enviro-Vision case, the first day of the hearing ends with the jury selected. In the hallway outside the court, Rich offers Janet $200,000 to settle. Janet reports the offer to Beth and they agree to reject it. Craig Bergson drives home, emotionally confused. Only three weeks before his death, Tony had accidentally met his old roommate and they had had several drinks. Craig believes that what Tony told him answers the riddle of this case.

PEREDA V. PARAJON

957 So.2d 1194
Florida Court of Appeals, 2007

Facts: Maria Parajon sued Diana Pereda for injuring her in a car accident. During voir dire, Parajon's lawyer asked the panel of prospective jurors these questions: "Is there anybody sitting on this panel now that has ever been under the care of a physician for personal injuries, whether you had a lawsuit or not? In other words, you may not have had any sort of lawsuit, but you slipped and fell—you had any accidents?"

Several of the prospective jurors raised their hands, allowing the lawyers to question more deeply into possible bias. However, Lisa Berg, a prospective juror who happened to be a lawyer, did not respond. Berg and others were seated as jurors, and ultimately awarded Parajon $450,000 for medical damages and pain and suffering.

After the trial, questioned in court by the judge, Berg admitted that three years earlier she had been injured in a

---

[6]Students of French note that *voir* means "to see" and assume that *voir dire* should translate as "to see, to speak." However, the legal term is centuries old and derives not from modern French but from Old French, in which *voir* meant "truth."

car accident, hired a lawyer to sue, and settled out of court for $4,000. Asked about the settlement, Berg replied, "I think everyone always wants more money."

Parajon moved for a new trial but the judge denied the motion. Parajon appealed.

Issue: ***Is Parajon entitled to a new trial based on Berg's failure to disclose her own personal injury lawsuit?***

Excerpts from Judge Rothenberg's Decision: To determine whether a juror's nondisclosure warrants a new trial, the complaining party must show that: (1) the information is relevant and material to jury service in the case; (2) the juror concealed the information during questioning; and (3) the failure to disclose the information was not attributable to the complaining party's lack of diligence.

Both Parajon's and Pereda's respective counsels may indeed have been influenced to challenge Berg peremptorily had the facts of her personal injury litigation history been known. Berg's personal injury claim was not remote in time. Berg settled out of court at the urging of her parents in order to put the matter behind her. Her involvement in this matter may have affected her point of view in [this case]. Her nondisclosure, which precluded counsel's ability to question Berg about the experience and to fairly evaluate her as a prospective juror, was material.

It is clear from the record that Berg concealed her personal injury litigation history. She is a lawyer and an officer of the court. It is, therefore, difficult to imagine that she did not think the questions posed by Parajon's counsel applied to her.

The record evidence demonstrates that other prospective jurors, none of whom were lawyers, clearly understood what type of information Parajon's counsel was asking them to disclose. We find that Parajon's counsel made a diligent inquiry.

Reversed and remanded for a new trial.

Opening Statements

The next day, each attorney makes an opening statement to the jury, summarizing the proof he or she expects to offer, with the plaintiff going first. Janet focuses on Tony's successful life, his business and strong marriage, and the tragedy of his accidental death.[7]

Rich works hard to establish a friendly rapport with the jury. If members of the jury like him, they will tend to pay more attention to his presentation of evidence. He expresses regret about the death. Nonetheless, suicide is a clear exclusion from the policy. If insurance companies are forced to pay claims never bargained for, everyone's insurance rates will go up.

civil case = preponderance of the evidence
criminal case = beyond a reasonable doubt

Burden of Proof

In civil cases, the plaintiff has the burden of proof. That means that the plaintiff must convince the jury that its version of the case is correct; the defendant is not obligated to disprove the allegations.

The plaintiff's burden in a civil lawsuit is to prove its case by a **preponderance of the evidence**. It must convince the jury that its version of the facts is at least *slightly more likely* than the defendant's version. Some courts describe this as a "51–49" persuasion, that is, that plaintiff's proof must "just tip" credibility in its favor. By contrast, in a criminal case, the prosecution must demonstrate **beyond a reasonable doubt** that the defendant is guilty. The burden of proof in a criminal case is much tougher because the likely consequences are, too. See Exhibit 3.3.

Preponderance of the evidence
The plaintiff's burden in a civil lawsuit.

Beyond a reasonable doubt
The government's burden in a criminal prosecution.

[7]Janet Booker has dropped her claim for triple damages against Coastal. To have any hope of such a verdict, she would have to show that Coastal had no legitimate reason at all for denying the claim. Discovery has convinced her that Coastal will demonstrate some rational reasons for what it did.

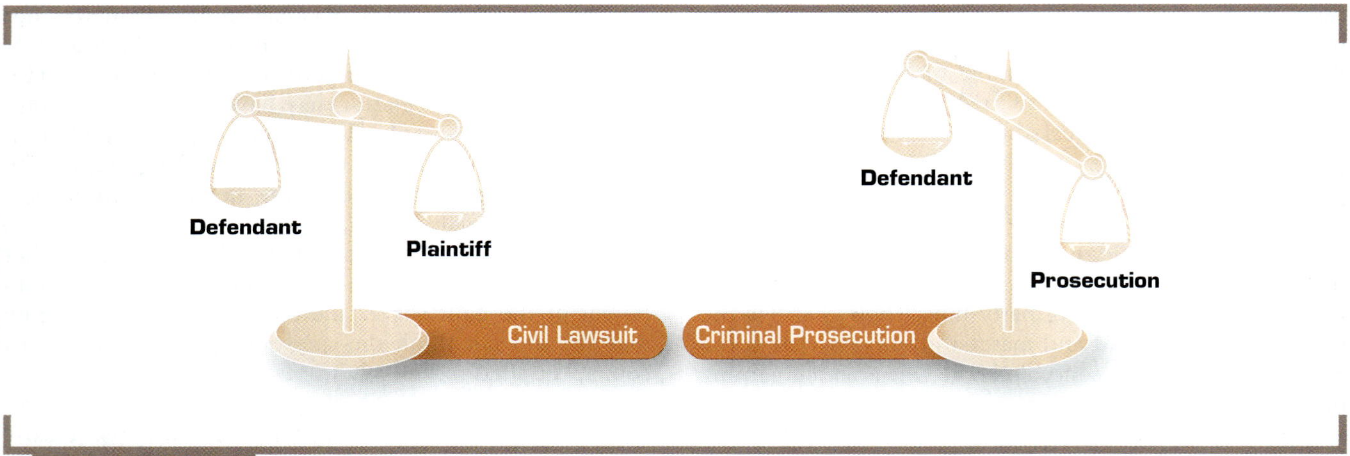

EXHIBIT 3.3 *Burden of Proof.* In a civil lawsuit, a plaintiff wins with a mere preponderance of the evidence. But the prosecution must persuade a jury beyond a reasonable doubt in order to win a criminal conviction.

Plaintiff's Case

Because the plaintiff has the burden of proof, Janet puts in her case first. She wants to prove two things. First, that Tony died. That is easy because the death certificate clearly demonstrates it and Coastal does not seriously contest it. Second, in order to win double indemnity damages, she must show that the death was accidental. She will do this with the testimony of the witnesses she calls, one after the other. Her first witness is Beth. When a lawyer asks questions of her own witness, it is **direct examination**. Janet brings out all the evidence she wants the jury to hear: that the business was basically sound, though temporarily troubled, that Tony was a hard worker, why the company took out life insurance policies, and so forth.

Direct examination
When a lawyer asks questions of her own witness.

Cross-examine
To ask questions of an opposing witness.

Then Rich has a chance to **cross-examine** Beth, which means to ask questions of an opposing witness. He will try to create doubt in the jury's mind. He asks Beth only questions for which he is certain of the answers, based on discovery. Rich gets Beth to admit that the firm was not doing well the year of Tony's death; that Tony had lost the best client the firm ever had; that Beth had reduced salaries; and that Tony had been depressed about business.

Rules of Evidence

The lawyers are not free simply to ask any question they want. The **law of evidence** determines what questions a lawyer may ask and how the questions are to be phrased, what answers a witness may give, and what documents may be introduced. The goal is to get the best evidence possible before the jurors so they can decide what really happened. In general, witnesses may only testify about things they saw or heard.

These rules are complex, and a thorough look at them is beyond the scope of this chapter. However, they can be just as important in resolving a dispute as the underlying substantive law. Suppose that a plaintiff's case depends upon the jury hearing about a certain conversation, but the rules of evidence prevent the lawyer from asking about it. That conversation might just as well never have occurred.

Janet calls an expert witness, a marine geologist, who testifies about the tides and currents in the area where Tony's body was found. The expert testifies that even experienced swimmers can be overwhelmed by a sudden shift in currents. Rich objects strenuously that this is irrelevant, because there is no testimony that there *was* such a current at the time of Tony's death. The judge permits the testimony.

Karen Caruso testifies that Tony was in "reasonably good" spirits the day of his death, and that he often took Blue for walks along the beach. Karen testifies that Blue was part Newfoundland. Rich objects that testimony about Blue's pedigree is irrelevant, but Janet insists it will show why Blue was tied up. The judge allows the testimony. Karen says that whenever Blue saw them swim, he would instinctively go into the water and pull them to shore. Does that explain why Blue was tied up? Only the jury can answer.

Cross-examination is grim for Karen. Rich slowly but methodically questions her about Tony's state of mind and brings out the problems with the company, his depression, and tension within the marriage. Janet's other witnesses testify essentially as they did during their depositions.

Is the breed relevant?

Motion for Directed Verdict

At the close of the plaintiff's case, Rich moves for a directed verdict, that is, a ruling that the plaintiff has entirely failed to prove some aspect of her case. Rich is seeking to win without even putting in his own case. He argues that it was Beth's burden to prove that Tony died accidentally and that she has entirely failed to do that.

A directed verdict is permissible only if the evidence so clearly favors the defendant that reasonable minds could not disagree on it. If reasonable minds could disagree, the motion must be denied. Here, Judge Rowland rules that the plaintiff has put in enough evidence of accidental death that a reasonable person could find in Beth's favor. The motion is denied.

Directed verdict
A ruling that the plaintiff has entirely failed to prove some aspect of her case.

There is no downside for Rich to ask for a directed verdict. The trial continues as if he had never made such a motion.

Defendant's Case

Rich now puts in his case, exactly as Janet did, except that he happens to have fewer witnesses. He calls the examining doctor, who admits that Tony could have committed suicide by swimming out too far. On cross-examination, Janet gets the doctor to acknowledge that he has no idea whether Tony intentionally drowned. Rich also questions several neighbors as to how depressed Tony had seemed and how unusual it was that Blue was tied up. Some of the witnesses Rich deposed, such as the tennis partner Jerry Johnson, have nothing that will help Coastal's case, so he does not call them.

Craig Bergson, sitting in the back of the courtroom, thinks how different the trial would have been had he been called as a witness. When he and Tony had the fateful drink, Tony had been distraught: business was terrible, he was involved in an extramarital affair that he could not end, and he saw no way out of his problems. He had no one to talk to and had been hugely relieved to speak with Craig. Several times Tony had said, "I just can't go on like this. I don't want to, anymore." Craig thought Tony seemed suicidal and urged him to see a therapist Craig knew and trusted. Tony had said that it was good advice, but Craig is unsure whether Tony sought any help.

This evidence would have affected the case. Had Rich Stewart known of the conversation, he would have deposed Craig and the therapist. Coastal's case would have been far stronger, perhaps overwhelming. But Craig's evidence will never be heard. Facts are critical. Rich's decision to depose other witnesses and omit Craig may influence the verdict more than any rule of law.

Closing Arguments

Both lawyers sum up their case to the jury, explaining how they hope the jury will interpret what they have heard. Janet summarizes the plaintiff's version of the facts, claiming that Blue was tied up so that Tony could swim without worrying about him. Rich claims that business and personal pressures had overwhelmed Tony. He tied up his dog, neatly folded his clothes, and took his own life.

Jury Instructions

Judge Rowland instructs the jury as to its duty. He tells them that they are to evaluate the case based only on the evidence they heard at trial, relying on their own experience and common sense.

He explains the law and the burden of proof, telling the jury that it is Beth's obligation to prove that Tony died. If Beth has proven that Tony died, she is entitled to $1 million; if she has proven that his death was accidental, she is entitled to $2 million. However, if Coastal has proven suicide, Beth receives nothing. Finally, he states that if they are unable to decide between accidental death and suicide, there is a legal presumption that it was accidental. Rich asks Judge Rowland to rephrase the "legal presumption" part but the judge declines.

Verdict

The jury deliberates informally, with all jurors entitled to voice their opinion. Some deliberations take two hours; some take two weeks. Many states require a unanimous verdict; others require only, for example, a 10–2 vote in civil cases.

This case presents a close call. No one saw Tony die. Yet even though they cannot know with certainty, the jury's decision will probably be the final word on whether he took his own life. After a day and a half of deliberating, the jury notifies the judge that it has reached a verdict. Rich Stewart quickly makes a new offer: $350,000. (The two sides have the right to settle a case until the moment when the last appeal is decided.) Beth hesitates but turns it down.

The judge summons the lawyers to court, and Beth goes as well. The judge asks the foreman if the jury has reached a decision. He states that it has: the jury finds that Tony Caruso drowned accidentally, and awards Beth Smiles $2 million.

Motions after the Verdict

Judgment *non obstante veredicto*

A judgment notwithstanding the jury's verdict.

Rich immediately moves for a **judgment *non obstante veredicto*** (JNOV), meaning a judgment notwithstanding the jury's verdict. He is asking the judge to overturn the jury's verdict. Rich argues that the jury's decision went against all of the evidence. He also claims that the judge's instructions were wrong and misled the jury.

Judge Rowland denies the JNOV. Rich immediately moves for a new trial, making the same claim, and the judge denies the motion. Beth is elated that the case is finally over—until Janet says she expects an appeal. Craig Bergson, leaving the courtroom, wonders if he did the right thing. He felt sympathy for Beth and none for Coastal. Yet now he is neither happy nor proud.

APPEALS

Two days later, Rich files an appeal to the court of appeals. The same day, he phones Janet and increases his settlement offer to $425,000. Beth is tempted but wants Janet's advice. Janet says the risks of an appeal are that the court will order a new trial, and they would start all over. But to accept this offer is to forfeit over $1.5 million. Beth is unsure what to do. The firm desperately needs cash now, and appeals may take years. Janet suggests they wait until oral argument, another eight months.

Rich files a brief arguing that there were two basic errors at the trial: first, that the jury's verdict is clearly contrary to the evidence; and second, that the judge gave the wrong instructions to the jury. Janet files a reply brief, opposing Rich on both issues. In her brief, Janet cites many cases that she claims are **precedent**: earlier decisions by the state appellate courts on similar or identical issues.

Precedent
Earlier decisions by the state appellate courts on similar issues.

Eight months later, the lawyers representing Coastal and Enviro-Vision appear in the court of appeals to argue their case. Rich, the appellant, goes first. The judges frequently interrupt his argument with questions. They show little sympathy for his claim that the verdict was against the facts. They seem more sympathetic with his second point, that the instructions were wrong.

When Janet argues, all of their questions concern the judge's instructions. It appears they believe the instructions were in error. The judges take the case under advisement, meaning they will decide some time in the future—maybe in two weeks, maybe in five months.

Appeals Court Options

The court of appeals can **affirm** the trial court, allowing the decision to stand. The court may **modify** the decision, for example, by affirming that the plaintiff wins but decreasing the size of the award. (That is unlikely here; Beth is entitled to $2 million or nothing.) The court might **reverse and remand**, nullifying the lower court's decision and returning the case to the lower court for a new trial. Or it could simply **reverse**, turning the loser (Coastal) into the winner, with no new trial.

Affirm
To allow the decision to stand.

Modify
To affirm the outcome but with changes.

Reverse and remand
To nullify the lower decision and return the case for reconsideration or retrial.

Reverse
To turn the loser into the winner.

What will it do here? On the factual issue it will probably rule in Beth's favor. There *was* evidence from which a jury could conclude that Tony died accidentally. It is true that there was also considerable evidence to support Coastal's position, but that is probably not enough to overturn the verdict. If reasonable people could disagree on what the evidence proves, an appellate court generally refuses to change the jury's factual findings. The court of appeals is likely to rule that a reasonable jury *could* have found accidental death, even if the appellate judges personally suspect that Tony may have killed himself.

The judge's instructions raise a more difficult problem. Some states would require a more complex statement about "presumptions."[8]

What does a court of appeals do if it decides the trial court's instructions were wrong? If it believes the error rendered the trial and verdict unfair, it will remand the case, that is, send it back to the lower court for a new trial. However, the court may conclude that the mistake was **harmless error**. A trial judge cannot do a perfect job, and not every error is fatal. The court may decide the verdict was fair in spite of the mistake.

Harmless error
A mistake by the trial judge that was too minor to affect the outcome.

Janet and Beth talk. Beth is very anxious and wants to settle. She does not want to wait four or five months, only to learn that they must start all over. Janet urges that they wait a few weeks to hear from Rich: they don't want to seem too eager.

A week later, Rich telephones and offers $500,000. Janet turns it down, but says she will ask Beth if she wants to make a counter-offer. She and Beth talk. They agree that they will settle for $1 million. Janet then calls Rich and offers to settle for $1.7 million. Rich and Janet

[8]Judge Rowland probably should have said, "The law presumes that death is accidental, not suicide. So if there were no evidence either way, the plaintiff would win because we presume accident. But if there is competing evidence, the presumption becomes irrelevant. If you think that Coastal Insurance has introduced some evidence of suicide, then forget the legal presumption. You must then decide what happened based on what you have seen and heard in court, and on any inferences you choose to draw." Note that the judge's instructions were different, though similar.

debate the merits of the case. Rich later calls back and offers $750,000, saying he doubts that he can go any higher. Janet counters with $1.4 million, saying she doubts she can go any lower. They argue, both predicting that they will win on appeal.

Rich calls, offers $900,000 and says, "That's it. No more." Janet argues for $1.2 million, expecting to nudge Rich up to $1 million. He doesn't nudge, instead saying, "Take it or leave it." Janet and Beth talk it over. Janet telephones Rich and accepts $900,000 to settle the case.

If they had waited for the court of appeals decision, would Beth have won? It is impossible to know. It is certain, though, that whoever lost would have appealed. Months would have passed waiting to learn if the state supreme court would accept the case. If that court had agreed to hear the appeal, Beth would have endured another year of waiting, brief writing, oral argument, and tense hoping. The high court has all of the options discussed: to affirm, modify, reverse and remand, or simply reverse.

Alternative Dispute Resolution

As we have seen in the previous section, trials can be trying. Lawsuits can cause prolonged periods of stress, significant legal bills, and general unpleasantness. Many people and companies prefer to settle cases out of court. Alternative dispute resolution (ADR) provides several semi-formal methods of resolving conflicts. We will look at different types of ADR and analyze their strengths and weaknesses.

Negotiation

In most cases, the parties negotiate, whether personally or through lawyers. Fortunately, the great majority of disputes are resolved this way. Negotiation often begins as soon as a dispute arises and may last a few days or several years.

Mediation

Mediation is the fastest growing method of dispute resolution in the United States. Here, a neutral person, called a *mediator*, attempts to guide the two disputing parties toward a voluntary settlement. (In some cases, there may be two or more mediators, but we will use the singular.) Generally, the two disputants voluntarily enter mediation, although some judges order the parties to try this form of ADR before allowing a case to go to trial.

A mediator does not render a decision in the dispute, but uses a variety of skills to move the parties toward agreement. Often a mediator will shuttle between the antagonists, hearing their arguments, sorting out the serious issues from the less important, prompting the parties and lawyers alike to consider new perspectives, and looking for areas of agreement. Mediators must earn the trust of both parties, listen closely, try to diffuse anger and fear, and build the will to settle. Good mediators do not need a law degree, but they must have a sense of humor and low blood pressure.

Mediation has several major advantages. Because the parties maintain control of the process, the two antagonists can speak freely. They need not fear conceding too much, because no settlement takes effect until both parties sign. All discussions are confidential, further encouraging candid talk. This is particularly helpful in cases involving proprietary information that might be revealed during a trial.

Of all forms of dispute resolution, mediation probably offers the strongest "win–win" potential. Since the goal is voluntary settlement, neither party needs to fear that it will end up the loser. This is in sharp contrast to litigation, where one party is very likely to lose.

Removing the fear of defeat often encourages thinking and talking that are more open and realistic than negotiations held in the midst of a lawsuit. Studies show that over 75 percent of mediated cases do reach a voluntary settlement. Such an agreement is particularly valuable to parties that wish to preserve a long-term relationship. Consider two companies that have done business successfully for 10 years but now are in the midst of a million-dollar trade dispute. A lawsuit could last three or more years and destroy any chance of future trade. However, if the parties mediate the disagreement, they might reach an amicable settlement within a month or two and could quickly resume their mutually profitable business.

This form of ADR works for disputes both big and small. Two college roommates who cannot get along may find that a three-hour mediation session restores tranquility in the apartment. On a larger scale, consider the work of former U.S. Senator George Mitchell, who mediated the Anglo-Irish peace agreement, setting Northern Ireland on the path to peace for the first time in three centuries. Like most good mediators, Mitchell was remarkably patient. In an early session, Mitchell permitted the head of one militant party to speak without interruption—for seven straight hours. The diatribe yielded no quick results, but Mitchell believed that after Northern Ireland's tortured history, any nonviolent discussions represented progress.

Arbitration

In this form of ADR, the parties agree to bring in a neutral third party, but with a major difference: the arbitrator has the power to impose an award. The arbitrator allows each side equal time to present its case and, after deliberation, issues a binding decision, generally without giving reasons. Unlike mediation, arbitration ensures that there will be a final result, although the parties lose control of the outcome.

Judge Judy and similar TV court shows are examples of arbitration. Before the shows are taped, people involved in a real dispute sign a contract in which they give up the right to go to court over the incident and agree to be bound by the judge's decision.

Parties in arbitration give up many additional rights that litigants retain, including discovery and class action. In arbitration, as already discussed as applied to trials, *discovery* allows the two sides in a lawsuit to obtain documentary and other evidence from the opponent before the dispute is decided. Arbitration permits both sides to keep secret many files that would have to be divulged in a court case, potentially depriving the opposing side of valuable evidence. A party may have a stronger case than it realizes, and the absence of discovery may permanently deny it that knowledge. As discussed earlier in this chapter, a *class action* is a suit in which one injured party represents a large group of people who have suffered similar harm. Arbitration eliminates this possibility, since injured employees face the employer one at a time. Finally, the fact that an arbitrator may not provide a written, public decision bars other plaintiffs, and society generally, from learning what happened.

Traditionally, parties sign arbitration agreements *after* some incident took place. A car accident would happen first, and the drivers would agree to arbitration second. But today, many parties agree *in advance* to arbitrate any disputes that may arise in the future. For example, a new employee may sign an agreement requiring arbitration of any future disputes with his employer; a customer opening an account with a stockbroker or bank—or health plan—may sign a similar form, often without realizing it. The good news is fewer lawsuits; the bad news is you might be the person kept out of court.

Assume that you live in Miami. Using the Internet, you order a $1,000 ThinkLite laptop computer, which arrives in a carton loaded with six fat instructional manuals and many small leaflets. You read some of the documents and ignore others. For four weeks, you struggle to make your computer work, to no avail. Finally, you call ThinkLite and demand a refund, but the company refuses. You file suit in your local court, at which time the company points out that buried among the hundreds of pages it mailed you was a *mandatory arbitration form*. This document prohibits you from filing suit against the company and states that if you have any complaint with the company, you must fly to Chicago, pay a $2,000 arbitrator's fee, plead your case before an arbitrator selected by the Laptop Trade Association of America, and, should you lose, pay ThinkLite's attorneys' fees, which could be several thousand dollars. Is that mandatory arbitration provision valid? It is too early to say with finality, but thus far, the courts that have faced such clauses have enforced them.[9]

Chapter Conclusion

No one will ever know for sure whether Tony Caruso took his own life. Craig Bergson's evidence might have tipped the scales in favor of Coastal. But even that is uncertain, since the jury could have found him unpersuasive. After two years, the case ends with a settlement and uncertainty—both typical lawsuit results. The missing witness is less common but not extraordinary. The vaguely unsatisfying feeling about it all is only too common and indicates why most parties settle out of court.

EXAM REVIEW

1. **COURT SYSTEMS** There are many *systems* of courts, one federal and one in each state. A federal court will hear a case only if it involves a federal question or diversity jurisdiction. (pp. 43–49)

2. **TRIAL AND APPELLATE COURTS** Trial courts determine facts and apply the law to the facts; appeals courts generally accept the facts found by the trial court and review the trial record for errors of law. (pp. 49–51)

EXAM Strategy

Question: Jade sued Kim, claiming that Kim promised to hire her as an in-store model for $1,000 per week for 8 weeks. Kim denied making the promise, and the jury was persuaded: Kim won. Jade has appealed, and now offers Steve as a witness. Steve will testify to the Appeals Court that he saw Kim hire Jade as a model, exactly as Jade claimed. Will Jade win on appeal?

Strategy: Before you answer, make sure you know the difference between trial and appellate courts. What is the difference? Apply that distinction here. (See the "Result" at the end of this section.)

[9]See, e.g., *Hill v. Gateway* 2000, 105 F.3d 1147, 1997 U.S. App. LEXIS 1877 (7th Cir. 1997), upholding a similar clause.

3. **PLEADINGS** A complaint and an answer are the two most important pleadings, that is, documents that start a lawsuit. (pp. 51–54)

4. **DISCOVERY** Discovery is the critical pre-trial opportunity for both parties to learn the strengths and weaknesses of the opponent's case. Important forms of discovery include interrogatories, depositions, production of documents and objects, physical and mental examinations, and requests for admission. (pp. 54–59)

5. **MOTIONS** A motion is a formal request to the court. (pp. 54, 66)

6. **SUMMARY JUDGMENT** Summary judgment is a ruling by the court that no trial is necessary because there are no essential facts in dispute. (pp. 59–61)

7. **JURY TRIALS** Generally, both plaintiff and defendant may demand a jury in any lawsuit for money damages. (pp. 61–66)

8. **VOIR DIRE** Voir dire is the process of selecting jurors in order to obtain an impartial panel. (p. 62)

Question: You are a lawyer, representing the plaintiff in a case of alleged employment discrimination. The court is selecting a jury. Based on questions you have asked, you believe that juror number 3 is biased against your client. You explain this to the judge, but she disagrees. Is there anything you can do?

Strategy: The question focuses on your rights during voir dire. If you believe that a juror will not be fair, you may make two different types of challenge. What are they? (See the "Result" at the end of this section.)

9. **BURDEN OF PROOF** The plaintiff's burden of proof in a civil lawsuit is preponderance of the evidence, meaning that its version of the facts must be at least slightly more persuasive than the defendant's. In a criminal prosecution, the government must offer proof beyond a reasonable doubt in order to win a conviction. (pp. 63–64)

10. **RULES OF EVIDENCE** The rules of evidence determine what questions may be asked during trial, what testimony may be given, and what documents may be introduced. (pp. 65–65)

11. **VERDICTS** The verdict is the jury's decision in a case. The losing party may ask the trial judge to overturn the verdict, seeking a JNOV or a new trial. Judges seldom grant either. (pp. 65–66)

12. **APPEALS** An appeals court has many options. The court may affirm, upholding the lower court's decision; modify, changing the verdict but leaving the same party victorious; reverse, transforming the loser into the winner; and/or remand, sending the case back to the lower court. (pp. 47–50, 66–68)

13. **ADR** Alternative dispute resolution is any formal or informal process to settle disputes without a trial. Mediation, arbitration, and other forms of ADR are growing in popularity. (pp. 68–70)

2. Result: Trial courts use witnesses to help resolve fact disputes. Appellate courts review the record to see if there have been errors of law. Appellate courts never hear witnesses, and they will not hear Steve. Jade will lose her appeal.

8. Result: You have already made a *challenge for cause*, claiming bias, but the judge has rejected your challenge. If you have not used up all of your *peremptory challenges*, you may use one to excuse this juror, without giving any reason.

Multiple-Choice Questions

1. The burden of proof in a civil trial is to prove a case ____________________. The burden of proof rests with the ____________________.

(a) beyond a reasonable doubt; plaintiff

(b) by a preponderance of the evidence; plaintiff

(c) beyond a reasonable doubt; defendant

(d) by a preponderance of the evidence; defendant

2. Alice is suing Betty. After the discovery process, Alice believes that no relevant facts are in dispute, and that there is no need for a trial. She should move for…

(a) a judgment on the pleadings

(b) a directed verdict

(c) a summary judgment

(d) a JNOV

3. Glen lives in Illinois. He applies for a job with an Missouri company, and he is told, amazingly, that the job is open only to white applicants. He will now sue the Missouri company under the Civil Rights Act, a federal statute. Can Glen sue in federal court?

(a) Yes, absolutely.

(b) Yes, but only if he seeks damages of at least $75,000. Otherwise, he must sue in a state court.

(c) Yes, but only if the Missouri company agrees. Otherwise, he must sue in a state court.

(d) No, absolutely not. He must sue in a state court.

4. A default judgment can be entered if which of the following is true?

(a) A plaintiff presents her evidence at trial and clearly fails to meet her burden of proof.

(b) A defendant loses a lawsuit and does not pay a judgment within 180 days.

(c) A defendant fails to file an answer to a plaintiff's complaint on time.

(d) A citizen fails to obey an order to appear for jury duty.

5. Barry and Carl are next-door neighbors. Barry's dog digs under Carl's fence and does $500 worth of damage to Carl's garden. Barry refuses to pay for the damage, claiming that Carl's cats "have been digging up my yard for years."

The two argue repeatedly, and the relationship turns frosty. Of the following choices, which has no outside decision maker and is most likely to allow the neighbors to peacefully coexist after working out the dispute?

(a) Trial
(b) Arbitration
(c) Mediation

Essay Questions

1. You plan to open a store in Chicago, specializing in rugs imported from Turkey. You will work with a native Turk who will purchase and ship the rugs to your store. You are wise enough to insist on a contract establishing the rights and obligations of both parties and would prefer an ADR clause. But you do not want a clause that will alienate your overseas partner. What kind of ADR clause should you include, and why?

2. Which court(s) have jurisdiction over each of these lawsuits—state or federal? Explain your reasoning for each answer.

- Pat wants to sue his next-door neighbor, Dorothy, claiming that Dorothy promised to sell him the house next door.
- Paula, who lives in New York City, wants to sue Dizzy Movie Theatres, whose principal place of business is Dallas. She claims that while she was in Texas on holiday, she was injured by their negligent maintenance of a stairway. She claims damages of $30,000.
- Phil lives in Tennessee. He wants to sue Dick, who lives in Ohio. Phil claims that Dick agreed to sell him 3,000 acres of farmland in Ohio, worth over $2 million.
- Pete, incarcerated in a federal prison in Kansas, wants to sue the United States government. He claims that his treatment by prison authorities violates three federal statutes.

3. British discovery practice differs from that in the United States. Most discovery in Britain concerns documents. The lawyers for the two sides, called *solicitors*, must deliver to the opposing side a list of all relevant documents in their possession. Each side may then request to look at and copy those it wishes. Depositions are rare. What advantages and disadvantages are there to the British practice?

4. Trial practice also is dramatically different in Britain. The parties' solicitors do not go into court. Courtroom work is done by different lawyers, called barristers. The barristers have very limited rights to interview witnesses before trial. They know the substance of what each witness intends to say but do not rehearse questions and answers, as in the United States. Which approach do you consider more effective? More ethical? What is the purpose of a trial? Of pre-trial preparation?

5. Claus Scherer worked for Rockwell International and was paid over $300,000 per year. Rockwell fired Scherer for alleged sexual harassment of several workers, including his secretary, Terry Pendy. Scherer sued in United States District Court, alleging that Rockwell's real motive in firing him was his high salary.

Rockwell moved for summary judgment, offering deposition transcripts of various employees. Pendy's deposition detailed instances of harassment, including comments about her body, instances of unwelcome touching, and discussions of extramarital affairs. Another deposition, from a Rockwell employee who investigated the allegations, included complaints by other employees as to Scherer's harassment. In his own deposition, which he offered to oppose summary judgment, Scherer testified that he could not recall the incidents alleged by Pendy and others. He denied generally that he had sexually harassed anyone. The district court granted summary judgment for Rockwell. Was its ruling correct?

Discussion Questions

1. In the Tony Caruso case described throughout this chapter, the defendant offers to settle the case at several stages. Knowing what you do now about litigation, would you have accepted any of the offers? If so, which one(s)? If not, why not?

2. The burden of proof in civil cases is fairly low. A plaintiff wins a lawsuit if he is 51 percent convincing, and then he collects 100 percent of his damages. Is this result reasonable? Should a plaintiff in a civil case be required to prove his case beyond a reasonable doubt? Or, if a plaintiff is only 51 percent convincing, should he get only 51 percent of his damages?

3. Large numbers of employees have signed mandatory arbitration agreements in employment contracts. Courts usually uphold these clauses. Imagine that you signed a contract with an arbitration agreement, that the company later mistreated you, and that you could not sue in court. Would you be upset? Or would you be relieved to go through the faster and cheaper process of arbitration?

4. Imagine a state law that allows for residents to sue "spammers"—those who send uninvited commercial messages through e-mail—for $30. One particularly prolific spammer sends messages to hundreds of thousands of people.

   John Smith, a lawyer, signs up 100,000 people to participate in a class-action lawsuit. According to the agreements with his many clients, Smith will keep one-third of any winnings. In the end, Smith wins a $3 million verdict and pockets $1 million. Each individual plaintiff receives a check for $20.

   Is this lawsuit a reasonable use of the court's resources? Why or why not?

5. Higher courts are reluctant to review a lower court's *factual* findings. Should this be so? Would appeals be fairer if appellate courts reviewed *everything*?

CHAPTER 4

© r.nagy/Shutterstock.com

Common Law, Statutory Law, and Administrative Law

Harry Homicide captures Gary and hauls him to the Old Abandoned Mill. Inside the mill, Harry sets a plank of wood atop a conveyor belt and ties Gary securely to the board.

> "Just hit the big red STOP button on the wall next to you, and I'll untie myself."
> The hiker looks at the button, then back at Gary.
> "I really need to go," he says.
> "WHAT?!"
> "If I don't get home soon, I'm going to miss *Oprah*."

"And now, Gary ... my arch-enemy ... I will have my REVENGE," Harry shouts. With a flourish, he presses a large green button marked START. The conveyor belt starts to move. A very large circular blade at the end of the belt begins to turn and cut into the plank. "Bwah hah hah hah!" Harry laughs in triumph.

Gary moves slowly toward the blade. Very, very slowly. Harry Homicide taps his foot. He sighs, frowns, and checks his watch. "Well," he says, "I think it is safe to assume that it's all over for you, Gary. You should never have crossed me. And so, farewell!" Harry makes a dramatic exit.

Gary works at his bonds frantically. He begins to weep. But then—a hiker appears in the doorway! "Hey! Help! Untie me!" Gary shouts. He can't believe his good fortune.

The hiker mumbles something. "What's that?" Gary shouts. "I can't hear you. Help me—hurry!"

The hiker speaks up. "I said I'm not any good untying knots. Never have been."

Gary's mouth drops open. "Fine, that's fine," he says. "Just hit the big red STOP button on the wall next to you, and I'll untie myself."

The hiker looks at the button, then back at Gary. "I really need to go," he says.

"WHAT?!"

"If I don't get home soon, I'm going to miss *Oprah*."

"You can't be serious!"

"I am serious. I find her empathy and common sense refreshing."

"Oh, boy," Gary mutters to himself. Then, louder, "That's fine, just fine. Just punch the button and you can be on your way in two seconds. Please!"

The hiker takes one last look at the STOP button. "I have to go," he says. Without another word, he leaves.

In his last moments, Gary cannot decide whether he is more irritated with the hiker or Harry Homicide.

Common Law

Gary and the hiker present a classic legal puzzle: what, if anything, must a bystander do when he sees someone in danger? We will examine this issue to see how the common law works.

Common law
Judge-made law.

The **common law** is judge-made law. It is the sum total of all the cases decided by appellate courts. The common law of Pennsylvania consists of all cases decided by appellate courts in that state. The Illinois common law is made up of all of the cases decided by Illinois appellate courts. Two hundred years ago, almost all of the law was common law. Today, common law still predominates in tort, contract, and agency law, and it is very important in property, employment, and some other areas.

Stare Decisis

Stare decisis
"Let the decision stand," that is, the ruling from a previous case.

Precedent
An earlier case that decided the issue.

Nothing perks up a course like Latin. ***Stare decisis*** means "let the decision stand." It is the essence of the common law. Once a court has decided a particular issue, it will generally apply the same rule in similar cases in the future . Suppose the highest court of Arizona must decide whether a contract signed by a 16-year-old can be enforced against him. The court will look to see if there is **precedent**, that is, whether the high court of Arizona has already decided a similar case. The Arizona court looks and finds several earlier cases, all holding that such contracts may not be enforced against a minor. The court will probably apply that precedent and refuse to enforce the contract in this case. Courts do not always follow precedent, but they generally do: *stare decisis.*

A desire for predictability created the doctrine of *stare decisis.* The value of predictability is apparent: people must know what the law is. If contract law changed daily, an entrepreneur who leased factory space and then started buying machinery would be uncertain if the factory would actually be available when she was ready to move in. Will the landlord slip out of the lease? Will the machinery be ready on time? The law must be knowable. Yet there must also be flexibility in the law, some means to respond to new problems and a changing social climate. Sometimes, we are better off if we are not encumbered by ironclad rules established before electricity was discovered. These two ideas are in conflict: the more flexibility we permit, the less predictability we enjoy. We will watch the conflict play out in the bystander cases.

Bystander Cases

This country inherited from England a simple rule about a **bystander's obligations: you have no duty to assist someone in peril unless you created the danger.** In *Union Pacific Railway Co. v. Cappier*,[1] through no fault of the railroad, a train struck a man. Railroad employees saw the incident happen but did nothing to assist him. By the time help arrived, the victim had died. The court held that the railroad had no duty to help the injured man:

> With the humane side of the question courts are not concerned. It is the omission or negligent discharge of legal duties only which come within the sphere of judicial cognizance. For withholding relief from the suffering, for failure to respond to the calls of worthy charity, or for faltering in the bestowment of brotherly love on the unfortunate, penalties are found not in the laws of men but in [the laws of God].

As harsh as this judgment might seem, it was an accurate statement of the law at that time in both England and the United States: bystanders need do nothing. Contemporary writers found the rule inhumane and cruel, and even judges criticized it. But—*stare decisis*—they followed it. With a rule this old and well established, no court was willing to scuttle it. What courts did do was seek openings for small changes.

Eighteen years after the Kansas case of *Cappier*, a court in nearby Iowa found the basis for one exception. Ed Carey was a farm laborer, working for Frank Davis. While in the fields, Carey fainted from sunstroke and remained unconscious. Davis simply hauled him to a nearby wagon and left him in the sun for an additional four hours, causing serious permanent injury. The court's response:

> It is unquestionably the well-settled rule that the master is under no legal duty to care for a sick or injured servant for whose illness or injury he is not at fault. Though not unjust in principle, this rule, if carried unflinchingly and without exception to its logical extreme, is sometimes productive of shocking results. To avoid this criticism [we hold that where] a servant suffers serious injury, or is suddenly stricken down in a manner indicating the immediate and emergent need of aid to save him from death or serious harm, the master, if present is in duty bound to take such reasonable measures as may be practicable to relieve him, even though such master be not chargeable with fault in bringing about the emergency.[2]

And this is how the common law often changes: bit by tiny bit. In Iowa, a bystander could now be liable *if* he was the employer and *if* the worker was suddenly stricken and *if* it was an emergency and *if* the employer was present. That is a small change but an important one.

For the next 50 years, changes in bystander law came very slowly. Consider *Osterlind v. Hill*, a case from 1928.[3] Osterlind rented a canoe from Hill's boatyard, paddled into the lake, and promptly fell into the water. For *30 minutes*, he clung to the side of the canoe and shouted for help. Hill heard the cries but did nothing; Osterlind drowned. Was Hill liable? No, said the court: a bystander has no liability. Not until half a century later did the same court reverse its position and begin to require assistance in extreme cases. Fifty years is a long time for the unfortunate Osterlind to hold on.[4]

In the 1970s, changes came more quickly.

---

[1] 66 Kan. 649, 72 P. 281 (1903).
[2] *Carey v. Davis*, 190 Iowa 720, 180 N.W. 889 (1921).
[3] 263 Mass. 73, 160 N.E. 301 (1928).
[4] *Pridgen v. Boston Housing Authority*, 364 Mass. 696, 308 N.E.2d 467 (Mass. 1974).

Tarasoff v. Regents of the University of California

17 Cal. 3d 425, 551 P.2d 334, 131 Cal. Rptr. 14
Supreme Court of California, 1976

Facts: On October 27, 1969, Prosenjit Poddar killed Tatiana Tarasoff. Tatiana's parents claimed that two months earlier, Poddar had confided his intention to kill Tatiana to Dr. Lawrence Moore, a psychologist employed by the University of California at Berkeley. They sued the university, claiming that Dr. Moore should have warned Tatiana and/or should have arranged for Poddar's confinement.

Issue: ***Did Dr. Moore have a duty to Tatiana Tarasoff, and did he breach that duty?***

Excerpts from Justice Tobriner's Decision: Although under the common law, as a general rule, one person owed no duty to control the conduct of another, nor to warn those endangered by such conduct, the courts have carved out an exception to this rule in cases in which the defendant stands in some special relationship to either the person whose conduct needs to be controlled or in a relationship to the foreseeable victim of that conduct. Applying this exception to the present case, we note that a relationship of defendant therapists to either Tatiana or Poddar will suffice to establish a duty of care.

We recognize the difficulty that a therapist encounters in attempting to forecast whether a patient presents a serious danger of violence. Obviously we do not require that the therapist, in making that determination, render a perfect performance; the therapist need only exercise that reasonable degree of skill, knowledge, and care ordinarily possessed and exercised by members of [the field] under similar circumstances.

In the instant case, however, the pleadings do not raise any question as to failure of defendant therapists to predict that Poddar presented a serious danger of violence. On the contrary, the present complaints allege that defendant therapists did in fact predict that Poddar would kill, but were negligent in failing to warn.

In our view, once a therapist does in fact determine, or under applicable professional standards reasonably should have determined, that a patient poses a serious danger of violence to others, he bears a duty to exercise reasonable care to protect the foreseeable victim of that danger.

[The Tarasoffs have stated a legitimate claim against Dr. Moore.]

The *Tarasoff* exception applies when there is some special relationship, such as therapist–patient. What if there is no such relationship? Remember the *Soldano v. O'Daniels* case from Chapter 1, in which the bartender refused to call the police.

As in the earlier cases we have seen, this lawsuit presented an emergency. But the exception created in *Carey v. Davis* applied only if the bystander was an employer, and that in *Tarasoff* only for a doctor. In *Soldano*, the bystander was neither. Should the law require him to act, that is, should it carve a new exception? Here is what the California court decided:

> Many citizens simply "don't want to get involved." No rule should be adopted [requiring] a citizen to open up his or her house to a stranger so that the latter may use the telephone to call for emergency assistance. As Mrs. Alexander in Anthony Burgess' *A Clockwork Orange* learned to her horror, such an action may be fraught with danger. It does not follow, however, that use of a telephone in a public portion of a business should be refused for a legitimate emergency call.
>
> We conclude that the bartender owed a duty to [Soldano] to permit the patron from Happy Jack's to place a call to the police or to place the call himself. It bears emphasizing that the duty in this case does not require that one must go to the aid of another. That is not the issue here. The employee was not the good samaritan intent on aiding another. The patron was.

And so, courts have made several subtle changes to the common law rule. Let's apply them to the opening scenario. If Gary's family sues the hiker, will they be successful? Probably not.

The hiker did not employ Gary, nor did the two men have any special relationship. The hiker did not stand in the way of someone else trying to call the police. He may be morally culpable for refusing to press a button and save a life, but he will not be legally liable unless an entirely new change to the common law occurs.

The bystander rule, that hardy oak, is alive and well. Various initials have been carved into its bark—the exceptions we have seen and a variety of others—but the trunk is strong and the leaves green. Perhaps someday the proliferating exceptions will topple it, but the process of the common law is slow and that day is nowhere in sight.

EXAM Strategy

Question: When Rachel is walking her dog, Bozo, she watches a skydiver float to earth. He lands in an enormous tree, suspended 45 feet above ground. "Help!" the man shouts. Rachel hurries to the tree and sees the skydiver bleeding profusely. She takes out her cell phone to call 911 for help, but just then Bozo runs away. Rachel darts after the dog, afraid that he will jump in a nearby pond and emerge smelling of mud. She forgets about the skydiver and takes Bozo home. Three hours later, the skydiver expires.

The victim's family sues Rachel. She defends by saying she feared that Bozo would have an allergic reaction to mud, and that in any case she could not have climbed 45 feet up a tree to save the man. The family argues that the dog is not allergic to mud, that even if he is, a pet's inconvenience pales compared to human life, and that Rachel could have phoned for emergency help without climbing an inch. Please rule.

Strategy: The family's arguments might seem compelling, but are they relevant? Rachel is a bystander, someone who perceives another in danger. What is the rule concerning a bystander's obligation to act? Apply the rule to the facts of this case.

Result: A bystander has no duty to assist someone in peril unless she created the danger. Rachel did not create the skydiver's predicament. She had no obligation to do anything. Rachel wins.

STATUTORY LAW

More law is created by statute than by the courts. Statutes affect each of us every day, in our business, professional, and personal lives. When the system works correctly, this is the one part of the law over which "we the people" have control. We elect the legislators who pass state statutes; we vote for the senators and representatives who create federal statutes.

Every other November, voters in all 50 states cast ballots for members of Congress. The winners of congressional elections convene in Washington, D.C. and create statutes. In this section, we look at how Congress does its work creating statutes.[5] Using the Civil Rights Act as a backdrop, we will follow a bill as it makes its way through Congress and beyond.

[5]State legislatures operate similarly in creating state laws.

Bill
A proposed statute.

Veto
The power of the president to reject bills passed by Congress.

Bills

Congress is organized into two houses, the House of Representatives and the Senate. Either house may originate a proposed statute, which is called a **bill**. To become law, the bill must be voted on and approved by both houses. Once both houses pass it, they will send it to the president. If the president signs the bill, it becomes law and is then a statute. If the president opposes the bill, he will **veto** it, in which case it is not law.[6]

If you visit either house of Congress, you will probably find half a dozen legislators on the floor, with one person talking and no one listening. This is because most of the work is done in committees. Both houses are organized into dozens of committees, each with special functions. The House currently has about 25 committees (further divided into about 150 subcommittees) and the Senate has approximately 20 committees (with about 86 subcommittees). For example, the armed services committee of each house oversees the huge defense budget and the workings of the armed forces. Labor committees handle legislation concerning organized labor and working conditions. Banking committees develop expertise on financial institutions. Judiciary committees review nominees to the federal courts. There are dozens of other committees, some very powerful, because they control vast amounts of money, and some relatively weak. Few of us ever think about the House Agricultural Subcommittee on Specialty Crops. But if we owned a family peanut farm, we would pay close attention to the subcommittee's agenda, because those members of Congress would pay close attention to us.

When a bill is proposed in either house, it is referred to the committee that specializes in that subject. Why are bills proposed in the first place? For any of several reasons:

- ***New Issue, New Worry.*** If society begins to focus on a new issue, Congress may respond with legislation. We consider below, for example, the congressional response in the 1960s to employment discrimination.
- ***Unpopular Judicial Ruling.*** If Congress disagrees with a judicial interpretation of a statute, the legislators may pass a new statute to modify or "undo" the court decision. For example, if the Supreme Court misinterprets a statute about musical copyrights, Congress may pass a new law correcting the Court's error. However, the legislators have no such power to modify a court decision based on the Constitution. When the Supreme Court ruled that lawyers had a right *under the First Amendment* to advertise their services, Congress lacked the power to change the decision.
- ***Criminal Law.*** Statutory law, unlike common law, is prospective. Legislators are hoping to control the future. And that is why almost all criminal law is statutory. A court cannot retroactively announce that it *has been* a crime for a retailer to accept kickbacks from a wholesaler. Everyone must know the rules in advance because the consequences—prison, a felony record—are so harsh.

Discrimination: Congress and the Courts

The civil rights movement of the 1950s and 1960s convinced most citizens that African Americans suffered significant and unacceptable discrimination in jobs, housing, voting, schools, and other basic areas of life. Demonstrations and boycotts, marches and counter-marches, church bombings and killings persuaded the nation that the problem was vast and urgent.

In 1963 President Kennedy proposed legislation to guarantee equal rights in these areas. The bill went to the House Judiciary Committee, which heard testimony for

[6] Congress may, however, attempt to override the veto. See the discussion following.

weeks. Witnesses testified that blacks were often unable to vote because of their race, that landlords and home sellers adamantly refused to sell or rent to African Americans, that education was grossly unequal, and that blacks were routinely denied good jobs in many industries. Eventually, the Judiciary Committee approved the bill and sent it to the full House.

The bill was dozens of pages long and divided into "titles," with each title covering a major issue. Title VII concerned employment. We will consider the progress of Title VII in Congress and in the courts. Here is one section of Title VII, as reported to the House floor:[7]

© AP Photo/Bill Hudson

A civil rights demonstrator being arrested by the police.

> Sec. 703(a). It shall be an unlawful employment practice for an employer—
>
> (1) to fail or refuse to hire or to discharge any individual, or otherwise to discriminate against any individual with respect to his compensation, terms, conditions, or privileges of employment, because of such individual's race, color, religion, or national origin; or
>
> (2) to limit, segregate, or classify his employees in any way which would deprive or tend to deprive any individual of employment opportunities or otherwise adversely affect his status as an employee, because of such individual's race, color, religion, or national origin.

Debate

The proposed bill was intensely controversial and sparked argument throughout Congress. Here are some excerpts from one day's debate on the House floor, on February 8, 1964:[8]

> MR. WAGGONNER. I speak to you in all sincerity and ask for the right to discriminate if I so choose because I think it is my right. I think it is my right to choose my social companions. I think it is my right if I am a businessman to run it as I please, to do with my own as I will. I think that is a right the Constitution gives to every man. I want the continued right to discriminate and I want the other man to have the right to continue to discriminate against me, because I am discriminated against every day. I do not feel inferior about it.
>
> I ask you to forget about politics, forget about everything except the integrity of the individual, leaving to the people of this country the right to live their lives in the manner they choose to live. Do not destroy this democracy for a Socialist government. A vote for this bill is no less.
>
> MR. CONTE. If the serious cleavage which pitted brother against brother and citizen against citizen during the tragedy of the Civil War is ever to be justified, it can be justified in this House and then in the other body with the passage of this legislation which can and must reaffirm the rights to all individuals which are inherent in our Constitution.
>
> The distinguished poet Mark Van Doren has said that "equality is absolute or no, nothing between can stand," and nothing should now stand between us and the passage of strong and effective civil rights legislation. It is to this that we are united in a strong bipartisan coalition today, and when the laws of the land proclaim that the 88th Congress acted effectively, judiciously, and wisely, we can take pride in our accomplishments as free men.

---

[7]The section number in the House bill was actually 704(a); we use 703 here because that is the number of the section when the bill became law and the number to which the Supreme Court refers in later litigation.
[8]The order of speakers is rearranged, and the remarks are edited.

Other debate was less rhetorical and aimed more at getting information. The following exchange anticipates a 30-year controversy on quotas:

> MR. JOHANSEN. I have asked for this time to raise a question and I would ask particularly for the attention of the gentleman from New York [MR. GOODELL] because of a remark he made—and I am not quarreling with it. I understood him to say there is no plan for balanced employment or for quotas in this legislation .... I am raising a question as to whether in the effort to eliminate discrimination—and incidentally that is an undefined term in the bill—we may get to a situation in which employers and conceivably union leaders, will insist on legislation providing for a quota system as a matter of self-protection.
>
> Now let us suppose this hypothetical situation exists with 100 jobs to be filled. Let us say 150 persons apply and suppose 75 of them are Negro and 75 of them are white. Supposing the employer ... hires 75 white men. [Does anyone] have a right to claim they have been discriminated against on the basis of color?
>
> MR. GOODELL. It is the intention of the legislation that if applicants are equal in all other respects there will be no restriction. One may choose from among equals. So long as there is no distinction on the basis of race, creed, or color it will not violate the act.

The debate on racial issues carried on. Later in the day, Congressman Smith of Virginia offered an amendment that could scarcely have been smaller—or more important:

> Amendment offered by MR. SMITH of Virginia: On page 68, line 23, after the word "religion," insert the word "sex."

In other words, Smith was asking that discrimination on the basis of sex also be outlawed, along with the existing grounds of race, color, national origin, and religion. Congressman Smith's proposal produced the following comments:

> MR. CELLER. You know, the French have a phrase for it when they speak of women and men. They say "vive la difference." I think the French are right. Imagine the upheaval that would result from adoption of blanket language requiring total equality. Would male citizens be justified in insisting that women share with them the burdens of compulsory military service? What would become of traditional family relationships? What about alimony? What would become of the crimes of rape and statutory rape? I think the amendment seems illogical, ill timed, ill placed, and improper.
>
> MRS. ST. GEORGE. Mr. Chairman, I was somewhat amazed when I came on the floor this afternoon to hear the very distinguished chairman of the Committee on the Judiciary [MR. CELLER] make the remark that he considered the amendment at this point illogical. I can think of nothing more logical than this amendment at this point.
>
> There are still many States where women cannot serve on juries. There are still many States where women do not have equal educational opportunities. In most States and, in fact, I figure it would be safe to say, in all States—women do not get equal pay for equal work. That is a very well known fact. And to say that this is illogical. What is illogical about it? All you are doing is simply correcting something that goes back, frankly to the Dark Ages.

The debate continued. Some supported the "sex" amendment because they were determined to end sexual bias. But politics are complex. Some *opponents* of civil rights supported the amendment because they believed that it would make the legislation less popular and cause Congress to defeat the entire Civil Rights bill.

That strategy did not work. The amendment passed, and sex was added as a protected trait. And, after more debate and several votes, the entire bill passed the House. It went to the Senate, where it followed a similar route from Judiciary Committee to full Senate. Much of the Senate debate was similar to what we have seen. But some senators raised a new issue, concerning §703(2), which prohibited *segregating or classifying* employees based on any of the protected categories (race, color, national origin, religion, or sex). Senator Tower was concerned that §703(2) meant that an employee in a protected category could never be given any sort of job test. So the Senate amended §703 to include a new subsection:

> Sec. 703(h). Notwithstanding any other provision of this title, it shall not be an unlawful employment practice for an employer ... to give and to act upon the results of any professionally developed ability test provided that such test ... is not designed, intended or used to discriminate because of race, color, religion, sex or national origin.

With that amendment, and many others, the bill passed the Senate.

Conference Committee

Civil rights legislation had now passed both houses, but the bills were no longer the same due to the many amendments. This is true with most legislation. The next step is for the two houses to send representatives to a House–Senate Conference Committee. This committee examines all of the differences between the two bills and tries to reach a compromise. With the Civil Rights bill, Senator Tower's amendment was left in; other Senate amendments were taken out. When the Conference Committee had settled every difference between the two versions, the new, modified bill was sent back to each house for a new vote.

The House of Representatives and the Senate again angrily debated the compromise language reported from the Conference Committee. Finally, after years of violent public demonstrations and months of debate, each house passed the same bill. President Johnson promptly signed it. The Civil Rights Act of 1964 was law. See Exhibit 4.1.

But the passing of a statute is not always the end of the story. Sometimes courts must interpret congressional language and intent.

Statutory Interpretation

Title VII of the Civil Rights Act obviously prohibited an employer from saying to a job applicant, "We don't hire minorities." In some parts of the country, that had been common practice; after the Civil Rights Act passed, it became rare. Employers who routinely hired whites only, or promoted only whites, found themselves losing lawsuits. A new group of cases arose, those in which some job standard was set that appeared to be racially neutral, yet had a discriminatory effect. In North Carolina, the Duke Power Co. required that applicants for higher paying, promotional positions meet two requirements: they must have a high school diploma, and they must pass a standardized written test. There was no evidence that either requirement related to successful job performance. Blacks met the requirements in lower percentages than whites, and consequently whites obtained a disproportionate share of the good jobs.

Title VII did not precisely address this kind of case. It clearly outlawed overt discrimination. Was Duke Power's policy overt discrimination, or was it protected by Senator Tower's amendment, §703(h)? The case went all the way to the Supreme Court, where the Court had to interpret the new law.

Courts are often called upon to interpret a statute, that is, to explain precisely what the language means and how it applies in a given case. There are three primary steps in a court's statutory interpretation:

- ***Plain Meaning Rule.*** When a statute's words have ordinary, everyday significance, the court will simply apply those words. Section 703(a)(1) of the Civil Rights Act prohibits firing someone because of her religion. Could an employer who had fired a Catholic because of her religion argue that Catholicism is not really a religion, but more of a social group? No. The word "religion" has a plain meaning and courts apply its commonsense definition.

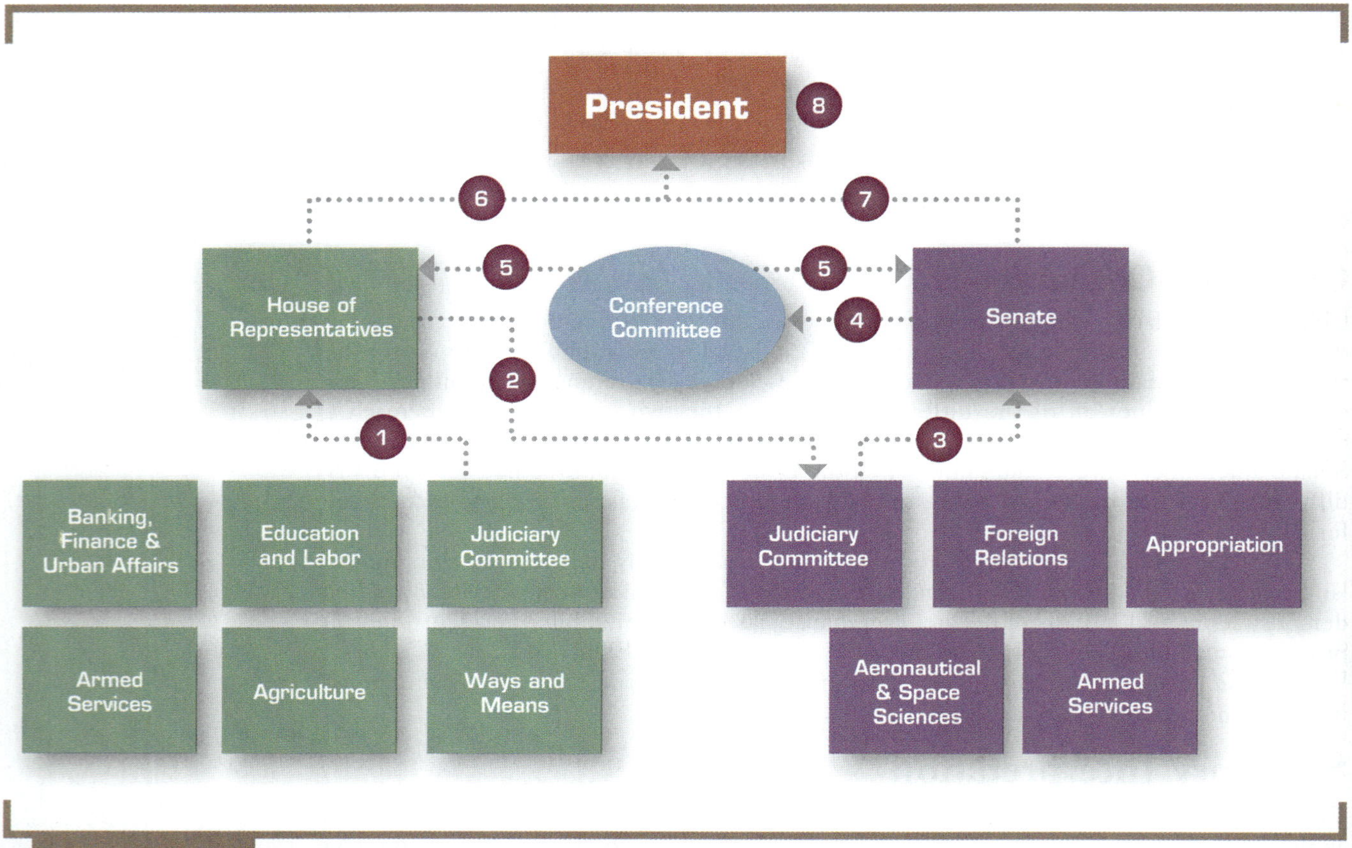

EXHIBIT 4.1 The two houses of Congress are organized into dozens of committees, a few of which are shown here. The path of the 1964 Civil Rights Act (somewhat simplified) was as follows: (1) The House Judiciary Committee approved the bill and sent it to the full House; (2) the full House passed the bill and sent it to the Senate, where it was assigned to the Senate Judiciary Committee; (3) the Senate Judiciary Committee passed an amended version of the bill and sent it to the full Senate; (4) the full Senate passed the bill with additional amendments. Since the Senate version was now different from the bill the House passed, the bill went to a Conference Committee. The Conference Committee (5) reached a compromise and sent the new version of the bill back to both houses. Each house passed the compromise bill (6 and 7) and sent it to the president, who signed it into law (8).

- ***Legislative History and Intent.*** If the language is unclear, the court must look deeper. Section 703(a)(2) prohibits classifying employees in ways that are discriminatory. Does that section prevent an employer from requiring high school diplomas, as Duke Power did? The explicit language of the statute does not answer the question. The court will look at the law's history to determine the intent of the legislature. The court will examine committee hearings, reports, and the floor debates that we have seen.
- ***Public Policy.*** If the legislative history is unclear, courts will rely on general public policies, such as reducing crime, creating equal opportunity, and so forth. They may include in this examination some of their own prior decisions. Courts assume that the legislature is aware of prior judicial decisions, and if the legislature did not change those decisions, the statute will be interpreted to incorporate them.

Here is how the Supreme Court interpreted the 1964 Civil Rights Act.

Landmark Case

Griggs v. Duke Power Co.

401 U.S. 424, 91 S. Ct. 849, 1971 U.S. LEXIS 134
United States Supreme Court, 1971

Facts: See the discussion of the Duke Power Company's job requirements in the "Conference Committee" section above.

Issue: ***Did Title VII of the 1964 Civil Rights Act require that employment tests be job-related?***

Excerpts from Chief Justice Burger's Decision: The objective of Congress in the enactment of Title VII is plain from the language of the statute. It was to achieve equality of employment opportunities and remove barriers that have operated in the past to favor an identifiable group of white employees over other employees. Under the Act, practices, procedures, or tests neutral on their face, and even neutral in terms of intent, cannot be maintained if they operate to "freeze" the status quo of prior discriminatory employment practices.

The Act proscribes not only overt discrimination but also practices that are fair in form, but discriminatory in operation. The touchstone is business necessity. If an employment practice which operates to exclude Negroes cannot be shown to be related to job performance, the practice is prohibited.

On the record before us, neither the high school completion requirement nor the general intelligence test is shown to bear a demonstrable relationship to successful performance of the jobs for which it was used.

Senator Tower offered an amendment which was adopted verbatim and is now the testing provision of section 703(h). Speaking for the supporters of Title VII, Senator Humphrey endorsed the amendment, stating: "Senators on both sides of the aisle who were deeply interested in Title VII have examined the text of this amendment and have found it to be in accord with the intent and purpose of that title." The amendment was then adopted. From the sum of the legislative history relevant in this case, the conclusion is inescapable that the ... requirement that employment tests be job related comports with congressional intent.

And so the highest Court ruled that if a job requirement had a discriminatory impact, the employer could use that requirement only if it was related to job performance. Many more cases arose. For almost two decades courts held that, once workers showed that a job requirement had a discriminatory effect, the employer had the burden to prove that the requirement was necessary for the business. The requirement had to be essential to achieve an important goal. If there was any way to achieve that goal without discriminatory impact, the employer had to use it.

Changing Times

But things changed. In 1989, a more conservative Supreme Court decided *Wards Cove Packing Co. v. Atonio.*[9] The plaintiffs were nonwhite workers in salmon canneries in Alaska. The canneries had two types of jobs, skilled and unskilled. Nonwhites (Filipinos and native Alaskans) invariably worked as low-paid, unskilled workers, canning the fish. The higher paid, skilled positions were filled almost entirely with white workers, who were hired during the off-season in Washington and Oregon.

There was no overt discrimination. But plaintiffs claimed that various practices led to the racial imbalances. The practices included failing to promote from within the company, hiring through separate channels (cannery jobs were done through a union hall, skilled positions were

[9]490 U.S. 642, 109 S. Ct. 2115, 1989 U.S. LEXIS 2794 (1989).

filled out of state), nepotism, and an English language requirement. Once again the case reached the Supreme Court, where Justice White wrote the Court's opinion.

If the plaintiffs succeeded in showing that the job requirements led to racial imbalance, said the Court, the employer now only had to demonstrate that the requirement or practice "serves, in a significant way, the legitimate employment goals of the employer .... [T]here is no requirement that the challenged practice be 'essential' or 'indispensable' to the employer's business." In other words, the Court removed the "business necessity" requirement of *Griggs* and replaced it with "legitimate employment goals."

Voters' Role

The response to *Wards Cove* was quick. Liberals decried it; conservatives hailed it. Everyone agreed that it was a major change that would make it substantially harder for plaintiffs to bring successful discrimination cases. Democrats introduced bills to reverse the interpretation of *Wards Cove*. President George H.W. Bush strongly opposed any new bill. He said it would lead to "quotas," that is, that employers would feel obligated to hire a certain percentage of workers from all racial categories to protect themselves from suits. This was the issue that Congressman Johansen had raised in the original House debate in 1964.

Both houses passed bills restoring the "business necessity" holding of *Griggs*. Again there were differences, and a Conference Committee resolved them. After acrimonious debate, both houses passed the compromise bill in October 1990. Was it therefore law? No. President Bush immediately vetoed the bill. He said it would compel employers to adopt quotas.

Congressional Override

When the president vetoes a bill, Congress has one last chance to make it law: an override. If both houses repass the bill, each by a two-thirds margin, it becomes law over the president's veto. Congress attempted to pass the 1990 Civil Rights bill over the Bush veto, but it fell short in the Senate by one vote.

Civil rights advocates tried again, in January 1991, introducing a new bill to reverse the *Wards Cove* rule. Again both houses debated and bargained. The new bill stated that, once an employee proves that a particular employment practice causes a discriminatory impact, the employer must "demonstrate that the challenged practice is job related for the position in question and consistent with business necessity."

Now the two sides fought over the exact meanings of two terms: "job related" and "business necessity." Each side offered definitions, but they could not reach agreement. It appeared that the entire bill would founder over those terms. So Congress did what it often does when faced with a problem of definition: it dropped the issue. Liberals and conservatives agreed not to define the troublesome terms. They would leave that task to courts to perform through statutory interpretation.

With the definitions left out, the new bill passed both houses. In November 1991, President Bush signed the bill into law. The president stated that the new bill had been improved and no longer threatened to create racial quotas. His opponents charged he had reversed course for political reasons, anticipating the 1992 presidential election.

And so, the Congress restored the "business necessity" interpretation to its own 1964 Civil Rights Act. No one would say, however, that it had been a simple process.

EXAM Strategy

Question: Kelly Hackworth took a leave of absence from her job at Progressive Insurance to care for her ailing mother. When she offered to return, Progressive refused to give her the same job or one like it. She sued based on the Family Medical Leave Act, a federal statute that requires firms to give workers returning from family leave their original job or an equivalent one. However, the statute excludes from its coverage workers whose company employs "fewer than 50 people within 75 miles" of the worker's jobsite. Between Ms. Hackworth's job site in Norman, Oklahoma, and the company's Oklahoma City workplace (less than 75 miles away), Progressive employed 47 people. At its Lawton, Oklahoma facility, Progressive employed three more people – but Lawton was 75.6 miles (wouldn't you know it) away from Norman. Progressive argued that the job was not covered by the statute. Hackworth claimed that this distance should be considered "within 75 miles," thereby rendering her eligible for FMLA leave. Even if it were not, she urged, it would be absurd to disqualify her from important rights based on a disparity of six-tenths of a mile. Please rule.

Strategy: The question asks you to interpret a statute. How do courts do that? There are three steps: the plain meaning rule; legislative history; and public policy. Apply those steps to these facts.

Result: In this real case, the court ruled that the plain meaning of "within 75 miles" was *75 miles or less*. Lawton was not 75 miles or less from Norman. The statute did not apply and Ms. Hackworth lost.[10]

Administrative Law

Before beginning this section, please return your seat to its upright position. Stow the tray firmly in the seatback in front of you. Turn off any laptops, cell phones, or other electronic devices. Sound familiar? Administrative agencies affect each of us every day in hundreds of ways. They have become the fourth branch of government. Supporters believe that they provide unique expertise in complex areas; detractors regard them as unelected government run amok.

Before beginning this section, please return your seat to its upright position. Stow the tray firmly in the seatback in front of you.

Many administrative agencies are familiar. The Federal Aviation Administration, which requires all airlines to ensure that your seats are upright before takeoff and landing, is an administrative agency. The Internal Revenue Service expects to hear from us every April 15. The Environmental Protection Agency regulates the water quality of the river in your town. The Federal Trade Commission oversees the commercials that shout at you from your television set.

Other agencies are less familiar. You may never have heard of the Bureau of Land Management, but if you go into the oil and gas industry, you will learn that this powerful agency has more control over your land than you do. If you develop real estate in Palos Hills, Illinois, you will tremble every time the Appearance Commission of the City of Palos Hills speaks, since you cannot construct a new building without its approval. If your software corporation wants to hire an Argentine expert on databases, you will get to know the complex workings of Immigration and Customs Enforcement: no one lawfully enters this country without its nod of approval.

[10]*Hackworth v. Progressive Casualty Ins. Co.*, 468 F.3d 722, 10th Cir. 2006 (10th Cir. 2006).

Background

By the 1880s, trains crisscrossed America. But this technological miracle became an economic headache. Congress worried that the railroads' economic muscle enabled a few powerful corporations to reap unfair profits. The railroad industry needed closer regulation. Who would do it? Courts decide individual cases, they do not regulate industries. Congress itself passes statutes, but it has no personnel to oversee the day-to-day working of a huge industry. For example, Congress lacks the expertise to establish rates for freight passing from Kansas City to Chicago, and it has no personnel to enforce rates once they are set.

A new entity was needed. Congress passed the Interstate Commerce Act, creating the Interstate Commerce Commission (ICC), the first administrative agency. The ICC began regulating freight and passenger transportation over the growing rail system and continued to do so for over 100 years. Congress gave the ICC power to regulate rates and investigate harmful practices, to hold hearings, issue orders, and punish railroads that did not comply.

The ICC was able to hire and develop a staff that was expert in the issues that Congress wanted controlled. The agency had enough flexibility to deal with the problems in a variety of ways: by regulating, investigating, and punishing. And that is what has made administrative agencies an attractive solution for Congress: one entity, focusing on one industry, can combine expertise and flexibility. However, the ICC also developed great power, which voters could not reach, and thereby started the great and lasting conflict over the role of agencies.

During the Great Depression of the 1930s, the Roosevelt administration and Congress created dozens of new agencies. Many were based on social demands, such as the need of the elderly population for a secure income. Political and social conditions dominated again in the 1960s, as Congress created agencies, such as the Equal Employment Opportunity Commission, to combat discrimination.

Then during the 1980s the Reagan administration made an effort to decrease the number and strength of the agencies. For several years some agencies declined in influence, though others did not. Today, there is still controversy about how much power agencies should have.

Classification of Agencies

Agencies exist at the federal, state, and local level. We will focus on federal agencies because they have national impact and great power. Most of the principles discussed apply to state and local agencies as well. Virtually any business or profession you choose to work in will be regulated by at least one administrative agency, and it may be regulated by several.

Executive-Independent

Some federal agencies are part of the executive branch while others are independent agencies. This is a major distinction. The president has much greater control of executive agencies for the simple reason that he can fire the agency head at any time. An executive agency will seldom diverge far from the president's preferred policies. Some familiar executive agencies are the Internal Revenue Service (part of the Treasury Department); the Federal Bureau of Investigation (Department of Justice); the Food and Drug Administration (Department of Health and Human Services); and the Nuclear Regulatory Commission (Department of Energy).

The president has no such removal power over independent agencies. The Federal Communications Commission (FCC) is an independent agency. For many corporations involved in broadcasting, the FCC has more day-to-day influence on their business than

Congress, the courts, and the president combined. Other powerful independent agencies are the Federal Trade Commission, the Securities and Exchange Commission, the National Labor Relations Board, and the Environmental Protection Agency.

Enabling Legislation

Congress creates a federal agency by passing **enabling legislation**. The Interstate Commerce Act was the enabling legislation that established the ICC. Typically, the enabling legislation describes the problems that Congress believes need regulation, establishes an agency to do it, and defines the agency's powers.

Critics argue that Congress is delegating to another body powers that only the legislature or courts are supposed to exercise. This puts administrative agencies above the voters. But legal attacks on administrative agencies have consistently failed for several decades. Courts acknowledge that agencies have become an integral part of a complex economy, and so long as there are some limits on an agency's discretion, courts will generally uphold its powers

Power of Agencies

Administrative agencies use three kinds of power to do the work assigned to them: they make rules, they investigate, and they adjudicate.

Rulemaking

One of the most important functions of an administrative agency is to make rules. In doing this, the agency attempts, prospectively, to establish fair and uniform behavior for all businesses in the affected area. **To create a new rule is to promulgate it**. Agencies promulgate two types of rules: legislative and interpretive.

Types of Rules: Legislative and Interpretive

Legislative rules are the most important agency rules, and they are much like statutes. Here, an agency creates law by requiring businesses or private citizens to act in a certain way. Suppose you operate a website for young shoppers, aged 10 to 18. Like most online merchants, you consider yourself free to collect as much data as possible about consumers. Wrong. The Federal Trade Commission, a federal agency, has promulgated detailed rules governing any site directed to young children. Before obtaining private data from these immature consumers, you must let them know exactly who you are, how to contact site operators, precisely what you are seeking, and how it will be used. You must also obtain verifiable parental consent before collecting, using, or disclosing any personal information. Failure to follow the rules can result in a substantial civil penalty. This modest legislative rule, in short, will be more important to your business than most statutes passed by Congress.

Interpretive rules do not change the law. They are the agency's interpretation of what the law already requires. But they can still affect all of us. For example, in 1977 Congress amended the Clean Air Act in an attempt to reduce pollution from factories. The act required the Environmental Protection Agency (EPA) to impose emission standards on "stationary sources" of pollution. But what did "stationary source" mean? It was the EPA's job to define that term. Obscure work, to be sure, yet the results could be seen and even smelled, because the EPA's definition would determine the quality of air entering our lungs every time we breathe. Environmentalists wanted the term defined to include every smokestack in a factory so that the EPA could regulate each one. The EPA, however, developed the "bubble concept," ruling that "stationary source" meant an entire factory, but not the individual smokestacks. As a result, polluters could shift emission among smokestacks in a single factory to avoid EPA regulation. Environmentalists howled that this gutted the purpose of the statute, but to no avail. The agency had spoken, merely by interpreting a statute.[11]

© Photodisc/Getty Images

An agency's interpretation of an environmental statue may be obscure, but the consequences affect us all.

How Rules Are Made

Corporations fight many a court battle over whether an agency has the right to issue a particular rule and whether it was promulgated properly. The critical issue is this: how much participation is the public entitled to before an agency issues a rule? There are two basic methods of rulemaking.[12]

Informal Rulemaking. On many issues, agencies may use a simple "notice and comment" method of rulemaking. The agency must publish a proposed rule in advance and permit the public a comment period. During this period, the public may submit any objections and arguments, with supporting data. The agency will make its decision and publish the final rule.

For example, the Department of Transportation may use the informal rulemaking procedure to require safety features for all new automobiles. The agency must listen to objections from interested parties, notably car manufacturers, and it must give a written response to the objections. The agency is required to have rational reasons for the final choices it makes. However, it is not obligated to satisfy all parties or do their bidding.

Formal Rulemaking. In the enabling legislation, Congress may require that an agency hold a hearing before promulgating rules. Congress does this to make the agency more accountable to the public. After the agency publishes its proposed rule, it must hold a public hearing. Opponents of the rule, typically affected businesses, may cross-examine the agency experts about the need for the rule and may testify against it. When the agency makes its final decision about the rule, it must prepare a formal, written response to everything that occurred at the hearing.

When used responsibly, these hearings give the public access to the agency and can help formulate sound policy. When used irresponsibly, hearings can be manipulated to stymie needed regulation. The most famous example concerns peanut butter. The Food and Drug Administration (FDA) began investigating peanut butter content in 1958. It found, for example, that Jif peanut butter, made by Procter & Gamble, had only 75 percent peanuts and 20 percent of a Crisco-type base. P&G fought the investigation, and any changes, for years. Finally, in 1965, the FDA proposed a minimum of 90 percent peanuts in peanut butter; P&G wanted 87 percent. The FDA wanted no more than 3 percent hydrogenated vegetable oil; P&G wanted no limit.

The hearings dragged on for months. One day, the P&G lawyer objected to the hearing going forward because he needed to vote that day. Another time, when an FDA official testified that consumer letters indicated the public wanted to know what was really in peanut butter, the P&G attorney demanded that the official bring in and identify the

[11]An agency's interpretation can be challenged in court, and this one was.

[12]Certain rules may be made with no public participation at all. For example, an agency's internal business affairs and procedures can be regulated without public comment, as can its general policy statements. None of these directly affect the public, and the public has no right to participate.

letters—all 20,000 of them. Finally, in 1968, a decade after beginning its investigation, the FDA promulgated final rules requiring 90 percent peanuts but eliminating the 3 percent cap on vegetable oil.[13]

Investigation

Agencies do an wide variety of work, but they all need broad factual knowledge of the field they govern. Some companies cooperate with an agency, furnishing information and even voluntarily accepting agency recommendations. For example, the U.S. Consumer Product Safety Commission investigates hundreds of consumer products every year and frequently urges companies to recall goods that the agency considers defective. Many firms comply.

Other companies, however, jealously guard information, often because corporate officers believe that disclosure would lead to adverse rules. To force disclosure, agencies use *subpoenas* and *searches.*

Subpoenas

A **subpoena** is an order to appear at a particular time and place to provide evidence. A **subpoena *duces tecum*** requires the person to appear and bring specified documents. Businesses and other organizations intensely dislike subpoenas and resent government agents plowing through records and questioning employees. What are the limits on an agency's investigation? The information sought:

Subpoena
An order to appear at a particular place and time. A subpoena *duces tecum* requires the person to produce certain documents or things.

- Must be *relevant* to a lawful agency investigation. The FCC is clearly empowered to investigate the safety of broadcasting towers, and any documents about tower construction are obviously relevant. Documents about employee racial statistics might indicate discrimination, but the FCC lacks jurisdiction on that issue and thus may not demand such documents.
- Must not be *unreasonably burdensome.* A court will compare the agency's need for the information with the intrusion on the corporation.
- Must not be *privileged.* The Fifth Amendment privilege against self-incrimination means that a corporate officer accused of criminal securities violations may not be compelled to testify about his behavior.

Search and Seizure. At times an agency will want to conduct a surprise **search** of an enterprise and **seize** any evidence of wrongdoing. May an agency do that? Yes, although there are limitations. When a particular industry is *comprehensively regulated,* courts will assume that companies know they are subject to periodic, unannounced inspections. In those industries, an administrative agency may conduct a search without a warrant and seize evidence of violations. For example, the mining industry is minutely regulated, with strict rules covering equipment, mining depths, and air quality. Mining executives understand that they are closely watched. Accordingly, the Bureau of Mines may make unannounced, warrantless searches to ensure safety.[14]

The following case established many of the principles just described.

[13]For an excellent account of this high-fat hearing, see Mark J. Green, *The Other Government* (New York: W. W. Norton & Co., 1978), pp. 136–150.
[14]*Donovan v. Dewey*, 452 U.S. 594, 101 S. Ct. 2534, 1980 U.S. LEXIS 58 (1981).

Landmark Case

UNITED STATES v. BISWELL

406 U.S. 311
Supreme Court Of The United States (1972)

Facts: Biswell operated a pawnshop and had a license to sell "sporting weapons." Treasury agents demanded to inspect Biswell's locked storeroom. The officials claimed that the Gun Control Act of 1968 gave them the right to search without a warrant.

That law says, in part, "the Secretary [of the Treasury] may enter during business hours the premises of any firearms dealer for the purpose of inspecting or examining (1) any records or documents required to be kept by such dealer, and (2) any firearms or ammunition kept or stored by such dealer."

Biswell voluntarily opened the storeroom, and the agent found two sawed-off rifles inside. The guns did not remotely meet the definition of "sporting weapons," and Biswell was convicted on firearms charges.

The appellate court found that because the search violated the Fourth Amendment, the rifles could not be admitted as evidence. It reversed the conviction, and the government appealed to the Supreme Court.

Issue: ***Did the agent's warrantless search violate the Constitution?***

Excerpts from Justice White's Decision: When the officers asked to inspect respondent's locked storeroom, they were merely asserting their statutory right, and respondent was on notice as to their identity and the legal basis for their action. Respondent's submission to lawful authority and his decision to step aside and permit the inspection rather than face a criminal prosecution is analogous to a householder's acquiescence in a search pursuant to a warrant when the alternative is a possible criminal prosecution for refusing entry or a forcible entry. In neither case does the lawfulness of the search depend on consent; in both, there is lawful authority independent of the will of the householder who might, other things being equal, prefer no search at all.

In the context of a regulatory inspection system of business premises that is carefully limited in time, place, and scope, the legality of the search depends not on consent but on the authority of a valid statute.

Federal regulation of the interstate traffic in firearms is undeniably of central importance to federal efforts to prevent violent crime. Large interests are at stake, and inspection is a crucial part of the regulatory scheme.

Here, if inspection is to be effective and serve as a credible deterrent, unannounced, even frequent, inspections are essential. In this context, the prerequisite of a warrant could easily frustrate inspection; and if the necessary flexibility as to time, scope, and frequency is to be preserved, the protections afforded by a warrant would be negligible.

It is also plain that inspections for compliance with the Gun Control Act pose only limited threats to the dealer's justifiable expectations of privacy. When a dealer chooses to engage in this pervasively regulated business and to accept a federal license, he does so with the knowledge that his business records, firearms, and ammunition will be subject to effective inspection. Each licensee is annually furnished with a revised compilation of ordinances that describe his obligations. The dealer is not left to wonder about the purposes of the inspector or the limits of his task.

We have little difficulty in concluding that where, as here, regulatory inspections further urgent federal interest, and the possibilities of abuse and the threat to privacy are not of impressive dimensions, the inspection may proceed without a warrant where specifically authorized by statute. The seizure of respondent's sawed-off rifles was not unreasonable under the *Fourth Amendment*, the judgment of the Court of Appeals is reversed, and the case is remanded to that court.

Adjudication

To **adjudicate** a case is to hold a hearing about an issue and then decide it. Agencies adjudicate countless cases. The FCC adjudicates which applicant for a new television license is best qualified. The Occupational Safety and Health Administration (OSHA) holds adversarial hearings to determine whether a manufacturing plant is dangerous.

Adjudicate
To hold a formal hearing about an issue and then decide it.

Most adjudications begin with a hearing before an **administrative law judge** (ALJ). There is no jury. An ALJ is an employee of the agency but is expected to be impartial in her rulings. All parties are represented by counsel. The rules of evidence are informal, and an ALJ may receive any testimony or documents that will help resolve the dispute.

Administrative law judge
An agency employee who acts as an impartial decision maker.

After all evidence is taken, the ALJ makes a decision. The losing party has a right to appeal to an appellate board within the agency. The appellate board may ignore the ALJ's decision. If it does not, an unhappy party may appeal to federal court.

Limits on Agency Power

There are four primary methods of reining in these powerful creatures: statutory, political, judicial, and informational.

Statutory Control

As discussed, the enabling legislation of an agency provides some limits. It may require that the agency use formal rulemaking or investigate only certain issues. The Administrative Procedure Act imposes additional controls by requiring basic fairness in areas not regulated by the enabling legislation.

Political Control

The president's influence is greatest with executive agencies. Congress, though, "controls the purse." No agency, executive or independent, can spend money it does not have. An agency that angers Congress risks having a particular program defunded or its entire budget cut. Further, Congress may decide to defund an agency as a cost-cutting measure. In its effort to balance the budget, Congress abolished the Interstate Commerce Commission, transferring its functions to the Transportation Department.

Congress has additional control because it must approve presidential nominees to head agencies. Before approving a nominee, Congress will attempt to determine her intentions. And, finally, Congress may amend an agency's enabling legislation, limiting its power.

Judicial Review

An individual or corporation directly harmed by an administrative rule, investigation, or adjudication may generally have that action reviewed in federal court.[15] The party seeking review, for example, a corporation, must have suffered direct harm; the courts will not listen

[15]In two narrow groups of cases, a court may not review an agency action. In a few cases, courts hold that a decision is "committed to agency discretion," a formal way of saying that courts will keep hands off. This happens only with politically sensitive issues, such as international air routes. In some cases, the enabling legislation makes it absolutely clear that Congress wanted no court to review certain decisions. Courts will honor that.

to theoretical complaints about an agency action.[16] And that party must first have taken all possible appeals within the agency itself.[17]

Standard on Review

Suppose OSHA promulgates a new rule limiting the noise level within steel mills. Certain mill operators are furious because they will have to retool their mills in order to comply. After exhausting their administrative appeals, they file suit seeking to force OSHA to withdraw the new rule. How does a court decide the case? Or, in legal terms, what standard does a court use in reviewing the case? Does it simply substitute its own opinion for that of the agency? No, it does not. The standard a court uses must take into account:

Facts. Courts generally defer to an agency's fact finding. If OSHA finds that human hearing starts to suffer when decibels reach a particular level, a court will probably accept that as final. The agency is presumed to have expertise on such subjects. As long as there is *substantial evidence* to support the fact decision, it will be respected.

Law. Courts often—but not always—defer to an agency's interpretation of the law. This is due in part to the enormous range of subjects that administrative agencies monitor. Consider the following example. "Chicken catchers" work in large poultry operations, entering coops, manually capturing broilers, loading them into cages, and driving them to a processing plant where they … well, never mind. On one farm, the catchers wanted to organize a union, but the company objected, pointing out that *agricultural* workers had no right to do so. Were chicken catchers agricultural workers? The National Labor Relations Board, an administrative agency, declared that chicken catchers were in fact *ordinary* workers, entitled to organize. The Supreme Court ruled that courts were obligated to give deference to the agency's decision about chicken catchers. If the agency's interpretation was *reasonable* it was binding, even if the court itself might not have made the same analysis. The workers were permitted to form a union—though the chickens were not.

The following case contains vulgar language, so *please do not read it.*

Fox Television Stations, Inc. v. Federal Communications Commission

613 F.3d 317
Second Circuit Court of Appeals, 2010

Facts: "People have been telling me I'm on the way out every year, right? So f*** 'em," said Cher, on a televised Billboard Music Awards ceremony. A year later, on the same program, Nicole Richie asked, "Have you ever tried to get cow s*** out of a Prada purse? It's not so f****** simple." The FCC, which regulates the broadcast industry, received complaints about this and other profanity on the airwaves.

---

[16]The law describes this requirement by saying that a party must have standing to bring a case. A college student who has a theoretical belief that the EPA should not interfere with the timber industry has no standing to challenge an EPA rule that prohibits logging in a national forest. A lumber company that was ready to log that area has suffered a direct economic injury: it has standing to sue.

[17]This is the doctrine of exhaustion of remedies. A lumber company may not go into court the day after the EPA publishes a proposed ban on logging. It must first exhaust its administrative remedies by participating in the administrative hearing and then pursuing appeals within the agency before venturing into court.

The FCC declared that these words were *invariably* indecent, explicit, and shocking. Their utterance violated the Commission's decency standards, and the Commission had the right to fine the networks for broadcasting them. The networks protested, arguing that the utterances were fleeting and isolated. They claimed that the Commission had traditionally permitted such sporadic usage, that this new ruling was an arbitrary change of policy, and that it violated the networks' First Amendment free speech rights. The Commission disagreed, declaring that it had the right to prohibit even the *occasional* use of the words. The networks appealed to federal court.

Issue: ***Did the FCC abuse its discretion and violate the First Amendment by prohibiting even the occasional use of profanity?***

Excerpts from Judge Pooler's Decision: In 2001, in an attempt to provide guidance to the broadcast industry regarding enforcement policies, the FCC issued a statement in which it explained that an indecency finding involved the following two determinations: (1) whether the material describe[s] or depict[s] sexual or excretory organs or activities; and (2) whether the broadcast is patently offensive as measured by contemporary community standards for the broadcast medium. The Industry Guidance reiterated that fleeting and isolated expletives were not actionably indecent.

In 2004, however, the FCC's policy on indecency changed. During the 2003 Golden Globe Awards, U2 band member Bono exclaimed, upon receiving an award, "this is really, really, f****** brilliant." In response to complaints filed after the incident, the FCC declared, for the first time, that a single, nonliteral use of an expletive (a so-called "fleeting expletive") could be actionably indecent.

A law or regulation is impermissibly vague if it does not "give the person of ordinary intelligence a reasonable opportunity to know what is prohibited." The First Amendment places a special burden on the government to ensure that restrictions on speech are not impermissibly vague.

The Networks argue that the FCC's indecency test is unconstitutionally vague because it provides no clear guidelines as to what is covered and thus forces broadcasters to steer far wider of the unlawful zone, rather than risk massive fines. The FCC argues that the indecency policy in its Industry Guidance, together with its subsequent decisions, give the broadcasters sufficient notice as to what will be considered indecent.

We agree with the Networks that the indecency policy is impermissibly vague. As we stated in a previous opinion:

> Although the Commission has declared that all variants of "f***" and "s***" are presumptively indecent and profane, repeated use of those words in "Saving Private Ryan," for example, was neither indecent nor profane. And while multiple occurrences of expletives in "Saving Private Ryan" was not gratuitous, a single occurrence in the Golden Globe Awards was shocking and gratuitous.

There is little rhyme or reason to these decisions and broadcasters are left to guess.

The FCC's application of its policy to live broadcasts creates an even more profound chilling effect. In the case of the 2003 Billboard Music Awards broadcasts, Fox had an audio delay system in place to bleep fleeting expletives. It also pre-cleared the scripts of the presenters. Ritchie, however, departed from her script and used three expletives in rapid sequence. While the person employed to monitor and bleep expletives was bleeping the first, the following two slipped through. Even elaborate precautions will not protect a broadcaster against such occurrences. In fact, the only way that Fox can be sure that it won't be sanctioned by the FCC is by refusing to air the broadcast live. The absence of reliable guidance in the FCC's standards chills a vast amount of protected speech.

For the foregoing reasons, we strike down the FCC's indecency policy.

Informational Control and the Public

We started this section describing the pervasiveness of administrative agencies. We should end it by noting one way in which all of us have some direct control over these ubiquitous authorities: information.

> A popular government, without popular information, or the means of acquiring it, is but a Prologue to a Farce or a Tragedy—or perhaps both. Knowledge will forever govern ignorance, and a people who mean to be their own Governors must arm themselves with the power which knowledge gives.
>
> *James Madison, President, 1809–17*

Two federal statutes arm us with the power of knowledge.

Freedom of Information Act

Congress passed the landmark Freedom of Information Act (known as "FOIA") in 1966. It is designed to give all of us, citizens, businesses, and organizations alike, access to the information that federal agencies are using. The idea is to avoid government by secrecy.

Any citizen or executive may make a "FOIA request" to any federal government agency. It is simply a written request that the agency furnish whatever information it has on the subject specified. Two types of data are available under FOIA. Anyone is entitled to information about how the agency operates, how it spends its money, and what statistics and other information it has collected on a given subject. People routinely obtain records about agency policies, environmental hazards, consumer product safety, taxes and spending, purchasing decisions, and agency forays into foreign affairs. A corporation that believes that OSHA is making more inspections of its textile mills than it makes of the competition could demand all relevant information, including OSHA's documents on the mill itself, comparative statistics on different inspections, OSHA's policies on choosing inspection sites, and so forth.

Second, all citizens are entitled to any records the government has *about them*. You are entitled to information that the Internal Revenue Service, or the Federal Bureau of Investigation, has collected about you.

FOIA does not apply to Congress, the federal courts, or the executive staff at the White House. Note also that, since FOIA applies to federal government agencies, you may not use it to obtain information from state or local governments or private businesses.

Exemptions. An agency officially has 10 days to respond to the request. In reality, most agencies are unable to meet the deadline but are obligated to make good faith efforts. FOIA exempts altogether nine categories from disclosure. The most important exemptions permit an agency to keep confidential information that relates to national security, criminal investigations, internal agency matters such as personnel or policy discussions, trade secrets or financial institutions, or an individual's private life.

Privacy Act

This 1974 statute prohibits federal agencies from giving information about an individual to other agencies or organizations without written consent. There are exceptions, but overall this act has reduced the government's exchange of information about us "behind our back."

EXAM Strategy

Question: Builder wants to develop 1,000 acres in rural Montana, land that is home to the Kite Owl. The EPA rules that the Kite Owl is an endangered species, and prohibits development of the property. The developer appeals to court. The EPA based its decision on five statistical studies, and the opinions of three out of seven experts. The court looks at the same evidence and acknowledges that the EPA decision is carefully reasoned and fair. However, the judges believe that the other four experts were right: the owl is *not* endangered. Should the court permit development?

Strategy: What is the legal standard for deciding whether a court should affirm or reverse an agency decision? As long as there is *substantial evidence* to support the factual conclusions, and a *reasonable basis* for the legal conclusion, the court should not impose its judgment. Agencies are presumed to have special expertise in their areas. As the *Fox Television* case tells us, an agency ruling should generally be affirmed unless it is arbitrary and capricious. Apply that standard here.

Result: The EPA made a careful, reasoned decision. The court may disagree, but it should not impose its views. The court must affirm the agency's ruling and prohibit development.

Chapter Conclusion

"Why can't they just fix the law?" They can, and sometimes they do—but it is a difficult and complex task. "They" includes a great many people and forces, from common law courts to members of Congress to campaign donors to administrative agencies. The courts have made the bystander rule slightly more humane, but it has been a long and bumpy road. Congress managed to restore the legal interpretation of its own 1964 Civil Rights Act, but it took months of debate and compromising. The FDA squeezed more peanuts into a jar of Jif, but it took nearly a decade to get the lid on.

A study of law is certain to create some frustrations. This chapter cannot prevent them all. However, an understanding of how law is made is the first step toward controlling that law.

Exam Review

1. **COMMON LAW** The common law evolves in awkward fits and starts because courts attempt to achieve two contradictory purposes: predictability and flexibility. (pp. 77–79)

2. **STARE DECISIS** *Stare decisis* means "let the decision stand," and indicates that once a court has decided a particular issue, it will generally apply the same rule in future cases. (p. 77)

3. **BYSTANDER RULE** The common law bystander rule holds that, generally, no one has a duty to assist someone in peril unless the bystander himself created the danger. Courts have carved some exceptions during the last 100 years, but the basic rule still stands. (pp. 77–79)

4. **LEGISLATION** Bills originate in congressional committees and go from there to the full House of Representatives or Senate. If both houses pass the bill, the legislation normally must go to a Conference Committee to resolve differences between the two versions. The compromise version then goes from the Conference Committee back to both houses, and if passed by both, to the president. If the president signs the bill, it becomes a statute; if he vetoes it, Congress can pass it over his veto with a two-thirds majority in each house. (pp. 80–83)

5. **STATUTORY INTERPRETATION** Courts interpret a statute by using the plain meaning rule; then, if necessary, legislative history and intent; and finally, if necessary, public policy. (p. 83)

EXAM Strategy

Question: Whitfield, who was black, worked for Ohio Edison. Edison fired him, but then later offered to rehire him. Another employee argued that Edison's original termination of Whitfield had been race discrimination. Edison rescinded its offer to rehire Whitfield. Whitfield sued Edison, claiming that the company was retaliating for the other employee's opposition to discrimination. Edison pointed out that Title VII of the 1964 Civil Rights Act did not explicitly apply in such cases. Among other things, Title VII prohibits an employer from retaliating against *an employee* who has opposed illegal discrimination. But it does not say anything about retaliation based on *another employee's* opposition to discrimination. Edison argued that the statute did not protect Whitfield.

Strategy: What three steps does a court use to interpret a statute? First, the plain meaning rule. Does that rule help us here? The statute neither allows nor prohibits Edison's conduct. The law does not mention this situation, and the plain meaning rule is of no help. Second step: Legislative history and intent. What did Congress intend with Title VII generally? With the provision that bars retaliation against a protesting employee? Resolving those issues should give you the answer to this question. (See the "Result" at the end of this section.)

6. **ADMINISTRATIVE AGENCIES** Congress creates federal administrative agencies with enabling legislation. The Administrative Procedure Act controls how agencies do their work. (pp. 87–89)

7. **RULEMAKING** Agencies may promulgate legislative rules, which generally have the effect of statutes, or interpretive rules, which merely interpret existing statutes. (pp. 89–91)

8. **INVESTIGATION** Agencies have broad investigatory powers and may use subpoenas and, in some cases, warrantless searches to obtain information. (pp. 91–93)

EXAM Strategy

Question: When Hiller Systems, Inc., was performing a safety inspection on board the M/V *Cape Diamond*, an ocean-going vessel, an accident killed two men. The Occupational Safety and Health Administration (OSHA), a federal agency, attempted to investigate, but Hiller refused to permit any of its employees to speak to OSHA investigators. What could OSHA do to pursue the investigation? What limits would there have been on OSHA's actions?

Strategy: Agencies make rules, investigate, and adjudicate. Which is involved here? Investigation. During an investigation, what power has an agency to force a company to produce data? What are the limits on that power? (See the "Result" at the end of this section.)

9. **ADJUDICATION** Agencies adjudicate cases, meaning that they hold hearings and decide issues. Adjudication generally begins with a hearing before an administrative law judge and may involve an appeal to the full agency or ultimately to federal court. (p. 93)

10. AGENCY LIMITATIONS The four most important limitations on the power of federal agencies are statutory control in the enabling legislation and the APA; political control by Congress and the president; judicial review; and the informational control created by the FOIA and the Privacy Act. (pp. 93–95)

5. Result: Congress passed Title VII as a bold, aggressive move to end race discrimination in employment. Further, by specifically prohibiting retaliation against an employee, Congress indicated it was aware that companies might punish those who spoke in favor of the very goals of Title VII. Protecting an employee from anti-discrimination statements made by a *co-worker* is a very slight step beyond that, and appears consistent with the goals of Title VII and the anti-retaliation provision. Whitfield should win, and in the real case, he did.[18]

9. Result: OSHA can issue a subpoena *duces tecum*, demanding that those on board the ship, and their supervisors, appear for questioning, and bring with them all relevant documents. OSHA may ask for anything that is (1) relevant to the investigation, (2) not unduly burdensome, and (3) not privileged. Conversations between one of the ship inspectors and his supervisor is clearly relevant; a discussion between the supervisor and the company's lawyer is privileged.

Multiple-Choice Questions

1. A bill is vetoed by ____________.

(a) the Speaker of the House
(b) a majority of the voting members of the Senate
(c) the president
(d) the Supreme Court

2. If a bill is vetoed, it may still become law if it is approved by ____________.

(a) two-thirds of the Supreme Court
(b) two-thirds of registered voters
(c) two-thirds of the Congress
(d) the president
(e) an independent government agency

3. Which of the following presidents was most influential in the passing of the Civil Rights Act?

(a) Franklin D. Roosevelt
(b) Ronald Reagan
(c) Abraham Lincoln
(d) John F. Kennedy
(e) George W. Bush

---

[18] *EEOC v. Ohio Edison*, 7 F.3d 541 (6th Cir. 1993).

4. Under FOIA, any citizen may demand information about ____________.
   (a) how an agency operates
   (b) how an agency spends its money
   (c) files that an agency has collected on the citizen herself
   (d) all of the above

5. If information requested under FOIA is not exempt, an agency has ____________ to comply with the request.
   (a) 10 days
   (b) 30 days
   (c) 3 months
   (d) 6 months

Essay Questions

1. Until recently, every state had a statute outlawing the burning of American flags. But in *Texas v. Johnson*,[19] the Supreme Court declared such statutes unconstitutional, saying that flag burning is symbolic speech protected by the First Amendment. Does Congress have the power to overrule the Court's decision?

2. In 1988, terrorists bombed Pan Am Flight 103 over Lockerbie, Scotland, killing all passengers on board. Congress sought to remedy security shortcomings by passing the Aviation Security Improvement Act of 1990, which, among other things, ordered the Federal Aviation Authority (FAA) to prescribe minimum training requirements and staffing levels for airport security. The FAA promulgated rules according to the informal rulemaking process. However, the FAA refused to disclose certain rules concerning training at specific airports. A public interest group called Public Citizen, Inc., along with family members of those who had died at Lockerbie, wanted to know the details of airport security. What steps should they take to obtain the information? Are they entitled to obtain it?

3. The Aviation Security Improvement Act (ASIA) states that the FAA can refuse to divulge information about airport security. The FAA interprets this to mean that it can withhold data in spite of the FOIA. Public Citizen and the Lockerbie family members interpret FOIA as being the controlling statute, requiring disclosure. Is the FAA interpretation binding?

4. An off-duty, out-of-uniform police officer and his son purchased some food from a 7-Eleven store and were still in the parking lot when a carload of teenagers became rowdy. The officer went to speak to them, and the teenagers assaulted him. The officer shouted to his son to get the 7-Eleven clerk to call for help. The son entered the store, told the clerk that a police officer needed help, and instructed the clerk to call the police. He returned 30 seconds later and repeated the request, urging the clerk to say it was a Code 13. The son claimed that the clerk laughed at him and refused to do it. The policeman sued the store. **Argument for the Store:** We sympathize with the policeman and his family, but the store has no liability.

[19] 491 U.S. 397, 109 S. Ct. 2533, 1989 U.S. LEXIS 3115 (1989).

A bystander is not obligated to come to the aid of anyone in distress unless the bystander created the peril, and obviously the store did not do so. The policeman should sue those who attacked him. **Argument for the Police Officer:** We agree that in general a bystander has no obligation to come to the aid of one in distress. However, when a business that is open to the public receives an urgent request to call the police, the business should either make the call or permit someone else to do it

5. Federal antitrust statutes are complex, but the basic goal is straightforward: to prevent a major industry from being so dominated by a small group of corporations that they destroy competition and injure consumers. Does Major League Baseball violate the antitrust laws? Many observers say that it does. A small group of owners not only dominate the industry, but actually *own* it, controlling the entry of new owners into the game. This issue went to the United States Supreme Court in 1922. Justice Holmes ruled, perhaps surprisingly, that baseball is exempt from the antitrust laws, holding that baseball is not "trade or commerce." Suppose that members of Congress dislike this ruling and the current condition of baseball. What can they do?

Discussion Questions

1. Courts generally follow precedent, but in the *Tarasoff* and *Soldano* cases discussed earlier in this chapter, they did not. Consider the opening scenario at the Old Abandoned Mill. *Should* the hiker bear any *legal* responsibility for Gary's untimely end; or should a court follow precedent and hold the lazy hiker blameless?

2. Revisit the *Fox Television Stations* case. Do you agree with the opinion? What would a sensible broadcast obscenity policy contain? When (if ever) should a network face fines for airing bad language?

3. In 2010, President Barack Obama signed a major health care reform bill into law. Seventeen state attorneys general filed a lawsuit challenging the constitutionality of the new statute. A key argument in the case will revolve around "interstate commerce." The states will argue that a provision in the law that requires Americans to purchase health insurance or face fines should be struck down because the Constitution allows for the *regulation* of commerce but does not allow the federal government to require people to *participate in* commerce; that is, to buy something.

   Does this argument seem sensible to you? Should the government be able to require those who can afford to purchase health insurance to purchase it?

4. FOIA applies to government agencies, but it exempts Congress. Should top lawmakers be obligated to comply with FOIA requests, or would that create more problems than it would solve?

5. Suppose you were on a state supreme court and faced with a restaurant-choking case. Should you require restaurant employees to know and employ the Heimlich maneuver to assist a choking victim? If they do a bad job, they could cause additional injury. Should you permit them to do nothing at all? Is there a compromise position? What social policies are most important?

CHAPTER 5

CONSTITUTIONAL LAW

© r.nagy/Shutterstock.com

The consultant started his presentation to the energy company's board of directors. "So I don't have to tell you that if the Smith-Jones bill ever passes Congress, it will be an utter disaster for your company. The House has already passed it. The president wants it. The only thing that kept it from becoming law this summer is that the Senate was too chicken to bring it up for a vote in an election year.

"Here's the bottom line: to be comfortable, you need three candidates who see things your way to beat current senators who support the bill."

The next slide showed a large map of the United States with three states highlighted in red. "These are your best bets. Attempting wins here would cost $60 million total—not so much for a billion-dollar-a-year operation like yours.

"In state #3, we go negative. Really negative."

"The money would go to saturation advertising from Labor Day to Election Day. I want to buy TV ads during local news programs all day, and during most prime time shows. I want the viewers to see your ads at least a dozen times before they go to the polls.

"In state #1, the challenger—your candidate—is a squeaky-clean state representative, but no one knows much about her outside her own district. She carries herself well, has a nice family. People will like her if they see her. Your money makes sure people will see her.

"In state #2, your guy hasn't really done much. But his grandfather was a hero at Normandy, and his dad was a coal miner. Great-grandparents were immigrants who came through New York with nothing in their pockets—I can see the ad with the Statue of Liberty already. A lot of voters will appreciate his family's story. This strategy will work if we have the funds to tell the story often enough.

"In state #3, we go negative. Really negative. Our opponent has been in the Senate a long time, and he's taken maybe 100,000 photos. We have three of them showing him with world leaders who have become unpopular of late. We're going to use them to tell a story about the senator putting foreign interests above American jobs and national security. People are angry—they think America is losing its place in the world. Our polling shows that this kind of campaign will be highly effective.

"You need to get into this election. All of your stakeholders benefit if the Smith-Jones bill dies—your workers stay on the job, your shareholders make more money, and your customers pay lower prices. Corporations are nothing more or less than the people who work for them, and they have the right to express their political opinions. These ads would simply give your workers the chance to exercise their right to free speech."

The CFO interrupted, "Look, we're all against the Smith-Jones bill. But is this plan *legal*?"

Government Power

One in a Million

The Constitution of the United States is the greatest legal document ever written. No other written constitution has lasted so long, governed so many, or withstood such challenge. This amazing work was drafted in 1787, when two weeks were needed to make the horseback ride from Boston to Philadelphia, a pair of young cities in a weak and disorganized nation. Yet today, when that trip requires less than two hours by jet, the same Constitution successfully governs the most powerful country on earth. This longevity is a tribute to the wisdom and idealism of the Founding Fathers.The Constitution is not perfect, but overall, it has worked astonishingly well and has become the model for many constitutions around the world.

The Constitution sits above everything else in our legal system. No law can conflict with it. The chapter opener raises a constitutional issue: does Congress have the right to prohibit corporations from spending money to affect elections, or are these actions protected as free speech under the First Amendment? We will explore this later in the chapter when we discuss the *Citizens United* case.

The Constitution is short and relatively easy to read. This brevity is potent. The Founding Fathers, or **Framers**, wanted it to last for centuries, and they understood that would happen only if the document permitted interpretation and "fleshing out" by later generations. The Constitution's versatility is striking. In this chapter, the first part provides an overview of the Constitution, discussing how it came to be and how it is organized. The second part describes the power given to the three branches of government. The third part explains the individual rights the Constitution guarantees to citizens.

Overview

Thirteen American colonies declared independence from Great Britain in 1776, and gained it in 1783. The new status was exhilarating. Ours was the first nation in modern history founded on the idea that the people could govern themselves, democratically. The idea was daring, brilliant, and fraught with difficulties. The states were governing themselves under the Articles of Confederation, but these articles gave the central government no real power. The government could not tax any state or its citizens and had no way to raise money. The national government also lacked the power to regulate commerce between the states or between foreign nations and any state. This was disastrous. States began to impose taxes on goods entering from other states. The young "nation" was a collection of poor relations, threatening to squabble themselves to death.

In 1787, the states sent a group of 55 delegates to Philadelphia. Rather than amend the old articles, the Framers set out to draft a new document and to create a government that had never existed before. It was hard going. What structure should the government have? How much power? Representatives like Alexander Hamilton, a *federalist,* urged a strong central government. The new government must be able to tax and spend, regulate commerce, control the borders, and do all things that national governments routinely do. But Patrick Henry and other *antifederalists* feared a powerful central government. They had fought a bitter war precisely to get rid of autocratic rulers; they had seen the evil that a distant government could inflict. The antifederalists insisted that the states retain maximum authority, keeping political control closer to home.

The debate continues to this day, and periodically it plays a key role in elections. The "tea party" movement, for example, is a modern group of antifederalists with a growing political influence.

Another critical question was how much power the *people* should have. Many of the delegates had little love for the common people and feared that extending this idea of democracy too far would lead to mob rule. Antifederalists again disagreed. The British had been thrown out, they insisted, to guarantee individual liberty and a chance to participate in the government. Power corrupted. It must be dispersed amongst the people to avoid its abuse.

How to settle these basic differences? By compromise, of course. **The Constitution is a series of compromises about power.** We will see many provisions granting power to one branch of the government while at the same time restraining the authority given.

Separation of Powers

The Framers did not want to place too much power in any single place. One method of limiting power was to create a national government divided into three branches, each independent and equal. Each branch would act as a check on the power of the other two. Article I of the Constitution created a Congress, which was to have legislative, or lawmaking, power. Article II created the office of president, defining the scope of executive, or enforcement, power. Article III established judicial, or interpretive, power by creating the Supreme Court and permitting additional federal courts.

Consider how the three separate powers balance one another: Congress was given the power to pass statutes, a major grant of power. But the president was permitted to veto, or block, proposed statutes, a nearly equal grant. Congress, in turn, had the right to override the veto, ensuring that the president would not become a dictator. The president was allowed to appoint federal judges and members of his cabinet, but only with a consenting vote from the Senate.

Individual Rights

The original Constitution was silent about the rights of citizens. This alarmed many who feared that the new federal government would have unlimited power over their lives. So in 1791 the first 10 amendments, known as the **Bill of Rights,** were added to the Constitution, guaranteeing many liberties directly to individual citizens.

In the next two sections, we look in more detail at the two sides of the great series of compromises: power granted and rights protected.

POWER GRANTED

Congressional Power

To recap two key ideas from Chapter 1:

1. Voters in all 50 states elect representatives who go to Washington, D.C., to serve in Congress.
2. The Congress is comprised of the House of Representatives and the Senate. The House has 435 voting members, and states with large populations send more representatives. The Senate has 100 members—two from each state.

Congress wields tremendous power. Its members create statutes that influence our jobs, money, health care, military, communications, and virtually everything else. But can Congress create *any* kind of law that it wishes? No.

Article I, section 8 is a critically important part of the Constitution. It lists the 18 types of statutes that Congress is allowed to pass, such as imposing taxes, declaring war, and coining money. Thus, only the national government may create currency. The state of Texas cannot print $20 bills with George W. Bush's profile.

States like Texas *are* supposed to create all other kinds of laws for themselves because the Tenth Amendment says, "All powers not delegated to the United States by the Constitution ... are reserved to the States."

The **Commerce Clause** is the specific item in Article I, Section 8, most important to your future as a businessperson. It calls upon Congress "to regulate commerce ... among the several States," and its impact is described in the next section.

Commerce Clause
The part of Article I, Section 8, that gives Congress the power to regulate commerce with foreign nations and among states.

Interstate Commerce

With the Commerce Clause, the Framers sought to accomplish several things in response to the commercial chaos that existed under the Articles of Confederation. They wanted the federal government to speak with one voice when regulating commercial relations with foreign governments.[1] The Framers also wanted to give Congress the power to bring coordination and fairness to trade among the states, and to stop the states from imposing the taxes and regulations that were wrecking the nation's domestic trade.

Virtually all of the numerous statutes that affect businesses are passed under the Commerce Clause. But what does it mean to regulate interstate commerce? Are all business transactions "interstate commerce," or are there exceptions? In the end, the courts must interpret what the Constitution means.

Substantial Effect Rule

An important test of the Commerce Clause came in the Depression years of the 1930s, in *Wickard v. Filburn*.[2] The price of wheat and other grains had fluctuated wildly, severely harming farmers and the national food market. Congress sought to stabilize prices by limiting the bushels per acre that a farmer could grow. Filburn grew more wheat than federal law allowed and was fined. In defense, he claimed that Congress had no right to regulate him because none of his wheat went into *interstate* commerce. He sold some locally and used the rest on his own farm as food for livestock and as seed. The Commerce Clause, Filburn claimed, gave Congress no authority to limit what he could do.

---

[1]*Michelin Tire Corp. v. Wages, Tax Commissioner*, 423 U.S. 276, 96 S. Ct. 535, 1976 U.S. LEXIS 120 (1976).

[2]317 U.S. 111, 63 S. Ct. 82, 1942 U.S. LEXIS 1046 (1942).

The Supreme Court disagreed and held that **Congress may regulate any activity that has a substantial economic effect on interstate commerce.** Filburn's wheat *affected* interstate commerce because the more he grew for use on his own farm, the less he would need to buy in the open market of interstate commerce. In the end, "interstate commerce" does not require that things travel from one state to another.

In *United States v. Lopez,*[3] however, the Supreme Court ruled that Congress *had* exceeded its power under the Commerce Clause. Congress had passed a criminal statute called the "Gun-Free School Zones Act," which forbade any individual from possessing a firearm in a school zone. The goal of the statute was obvious: to keep schools safe. Lopez was convicted of violating the act and appealed his conviction all the way to the high Court, claiming that Congress had no power to pass such a law. The government argued that the Commerce Clause gave it the power to pass the law, but the Supreme Court was unpersuaded.

> The possession of a gun in a local school zone is in no sense an economic activity that might, through repetition elsewhere, substantially affect any sort of interstate commerce. [Lopez] was a local student at a local school; there is no indication that he had recently moved in interstate commerce, and there is no requirement that his possession of the firearm have any concrete tie to interstate commerce. To uphold the Government's contentions here, we would have to pile inference upon inference in a manner that would bid fair to convert congressional authority under the Commerce Clause to a general police power of the sort retained by the States. [The statute was unconstitutional and void.]
>
> Congress's power is great—but still limited.

Current Application: The Affordable Healthcare Act. In 2010, Congress passed the Affordable Healthcare Act and President Barack Obama signed it into law. The wide-ranging legislation may result in as many as 30 million uninsured Americans gaining health care coverage. Almost immediately after it passed, many states sued and argued that the law violated the Constitution by exceeding Congress's power to regulate interstate commerce.

The challenge centers on a provision (which the press refers to as the "individual mandate") in the Act that requires many people to purchase health insurance or face fines. The states argue that requiring people to buy something is fundamentally different from regulating people who *voluntarily* decided to participate in commerce.

At this writing, the lower courts are divided on whether the healthcare statute is constitutional. The Supreme Court will surely have the final word. In the end, the fate of this law hinges upon how the justices define "commerce."

State Legislative Power

The "dormant" or "negative" aspect of the Commerce Clause governs state efforts to regulate interstate commerce. **The dormant aspect holds that a state statute which discriminates against interstate commerce is almost always unconstitutional.** Here is an example, but please do not read it if you plan to drive later today. Michigan and New York permitted in-state wineries to sell directly to consumers. They both denied this privilege to out-of-state producers, who were forced to sell to wholesalers, who offered the wine to retailers, who sold to consumers. This created an impossible barrier for many small vineyards, which did not produce enough wine to attract wholesalers. Even if they did, the multiple resales drove their prices prohibitively high.

Local residents and out-of-state wineries sued, claiming that the state regulations violated the dormant Commerce Clause. The Supreme Court ruled that these statutes obviously discriminated against out-of-state vineyards; the schemes were illegal unless Michigan and

[3] 514 U.S. 549, 115 S. Ct. 1624, 1995 U.S. LEXIS 3039 (1995).

New York could demonstrate an important goal that could not be met any other way. The states' alleged motive was to prevent minors from purchasing wine over the Internet. However, Michigan and New York offered no evidence that such purchases were really a problem. The Court said that minors seldom drink wine, and when they do, they seek instant gratification, not a package in the mail. States that allowed direct shipment to consumers reported no increase in purchases by minors. This discrimination against interstate commerce, like most, was unconstitutional.[4]

Devil's Advocate Underage drinking is a serious problem. The Court should allow states wide leeway in their efforts to limit the harm. Even if the regulations are imperfect, they may help reduce the damage.

Supremacy Clause

What happens when both the federal and state governments pass regulations that are permissible, but conflicting? For example, Congress passed the federal Occupational Safety and Health Act (OSHA) establishing many job safety standards, including those for training workers who handle hazardous waste. Congress had the power to do so under the Commerce Clause. Later, Illinois passed its own hazardous waste statutes, seeking to protect both the general public and workers. The state statute did not violate the Commerce Clause because it imposed no restriction on interstate commerce.

Each statute specified worker training and employer licensing. But the requirements differed. Which statute did Illinois corporations have to obey? Article VI of the Constitution contains the answer. **The Supremacy Clause** states that the Constitution, and federal statutes and treaties, shall be the supreme law of the land.

The Supremacy Clause
Makes the Constitution, and federal statutes and treaties, the supreme law of the land.

- If there is a conflict between federal and state statutes, the federal law **preempts** the field, meaning it controls the issue. The state law is void.
- Even in cases where there is no conflict, if Congress demonstrates that it intends to exercise exclusive control over an issue, federal law preempts.

Thus state law controls only when there is no conflicting federal law *and* Congress has not intended to dominate the issue. In the Illinois case, the Supreme Court concluded that Congress intended to regulate the issue exclusively. Federal law therefore preempted the field, and local employers were obligated to obey only the federal regulations.

EXAM Strategy

Question: Dairy farming was more expensive in Massachusetts than in other states. To help its farmers, Massachusetts taxed all milk sales, regardless of where the milk was produced. The revenues went into a fund that was then distributed to in-state dairy farmers. Discuss.

[4]*Granholm v. Heald*, 544 U.S. 460, 1255 S.Ct. 1885 (2005).

Strategy: By giving a subsidy to local farmers, the state is treating them differently than out-of-state dairies. This raises Commerce Clause issues. The dormant aspect applies. What does it state? Apply that standard to theses facts.

Result: The dormant aspect holds that a state statute which discriminates against interstate commerce is almost always invalid. Massachusetts was subsidizing its farmers at the expense of those from other states. The tax violates the Commerce Clause and is void.

Executive Power

Article II of the Constitution defines executive power. The president's most basic job function is to enforce the nation's laws. Three of his key powers concern appointment, legislation, and foreign policy.

Appointment

Administrative agencies play a powerful role in business regulation, and the president nominates the heads of most of them. These choices dramatically influence what issues the agencies choose to pursue and how aggressively they do it. For example, a president who seeks to expand the scope of regulations on air quality may appoint a forceful environmentalist to run the Environmental Protection Agency (EPA), whereas a president who dislikes federal regulations will choose a more passive agency head.[5]

Legislation

The president and his advisers propose bills to Congress. During the last 50 years, a vast number of newly proposed bills have come from the executive branch. Some argue that *too many* proposals come from the president and that Congress has become overly passive. When a president proposes controversial legislation on a major issue, such as Social Security reform, the bill can dominate the news—and Congress—for months or even years. The president, of course, also has the power to veto bills.[6]

Foreign Policy

The president conducts the nation's foreign affairs, coordinating international efforts, negotiating treaties, and so forth. The president is also the commander in chief of the armed forces, meaning that he heads the military. But Article II does not give him the right to declare war—only the Senate may do that. A continuing tension between the president and Congress has resulted from the president's use of troops overseas *without* a formal declaration of war.

Judicial Power

Article III of the Constitution creates the Supreme Court and permits Congress to establish lower courts within the federal court system.[7] Federal courts have two key functions: adjudication and judicial review.

---

[5]For a discussion of administrative agency power, see Chapter 4, on administrative law.

[6]For a discussion of the president's veto power and Congress's power to override a veto, see Chapter 4, on statutory law.

[7]For a discussion of the federal court system, see Chapter 3, on dispute resolution.

Adjudicating Cases

The federal court system hears criminal and civil cases. Generally, prosecutions of federal crimes begin in United States District Court. That same court has limited jurisdiction to hear civil lawsuits, a subject discussed in Chapter 3, on dispute resolution.

Judicial Review

One of the greatest "constitutional" powers appears nowhere in the Constitution. In 1803, the Supreme Court decided *Marbury v. Madison*.[8] Congress had passed a relatively minor statute that gave certain powers to the Supreme Court, and Marbury wanted the Court to use those powers. The Court refused. In an opinion written by Chief Justice John Marshall, the Court held that the statute violated the Constitution because Article III of the Constitution did not grant the Court those powers. The details of the case were insignificant, but the ruling was profound: because the statute violated the Constitution, said the Court, it was void. **Judicial review refers to the power of federal courts to declare a statute or governmental action unconstitutional and void.**

Chief Justice John Marshall

This formidable grab of power has produced two centuries of controversy. The Court was declaring that it alone had the right to evaluate acts of the other two branches of government—the Congress and the executive—and to decide which were valid and which void. The Constitution nowhere grants this power. Undaunted, Marshall declared that "[I]t is emphatically the province and duty of the judicial department to say what the law is." In later cases, the Supreme Court expanded on the idea, holding that it could also nullify state statutes, rulings by state courts, and actions by federal and state officials. In this chapter we have already encountered an example of judicial review in the *Lopez* case, where the justices declared that Congress lacked the power to pass local gun regulations.

Is judicial review good for the nation? Those who oppose it argue that federal court judges are all appointed, not elected, and that we should not permit judges to nullify a statute passed by elected officials because that diminishes the people's role in their government. Those who favor judicial review insist that there must be one cohesive interpretation of the Constitution and the judicial branch is the logical one to provide it. The following example of judicial review shows how immediate and emotional the issue can be. This is a criminal prosecution for a brutal crime. Cases like this force us to examine two

KENNEDY V. LOUISIANA

128 S.Ct. 2641
United States Supreme Court, 2008

Facts: Patrick Kennedy raped his eight-year-old stepdaughter. Her injuries were the most severe that the forensic expert had ever seen. Kennedy was convicted of aggravated rape because the victim was under 12 years of age.

The jury voted to sentence Kennedy to death, which was permitted by the Louisiana statute. The state supreme court affirmed the death sentence, and Kennedy appealed to the United States Supreme Court. He argued

[8] 5 U.S. 137, 1 Cranch 137 (1803).

that the Louisiana statute was unconstitutional. The Eighth Amendment prohibits cruel and unusual punishment, which includes penalties that are out of proportion to the crime. Kennedy claimed that capital punishment was out of proportion to rape and violated the Eighth Amendment.

Issues: ***Did the Louisiana statute violate the Constitution by permitting the death penalty in a case of child rape? Is it proper for the Supreme Court to decide this issue?***

Excerpts from Justice Kennedy's Decision: The constitutional prohibition against excessive or cruel and unusual punishments mandates that the State's power to punish be exercised within the limits of civilized standards. Evolving standards of decency that mark the progress of a maturing society counsel us to be most hesitant before interpreting the Eighth Amendment to allow the extension of the death penalty, a hesitation that has special force where no life was taken in the commission of the crime.

Consistent with evolving standards of decency and the teachings of our precedents we conclude that, in determining whether the death penalty is excessive, there is a distinction between intentional first-degree murder on the one hand and nonhomicide crimes against individual persons, even including child rape, on the other. The latter crimes may be devastating in their harm, as here, but in terms of moral depravity and of the injury to the person and to the public, they cannot be compared to murder in their severity and irrevocability.

Louisiana reintroduced the death penalty for rape of a child in 1995. Five States have since followed Louisiana's lead: Georgia, Montana, Oklahoma, South Carolina, and Texas. By contrast, 44 States have not made child rape a capital offense. As for federal law, Congress in the Federal Death Penalty Act of 1994 expanded the number of federal crimes for which the death penalty is a permissible sentence, including certain nonhomicide offenses; but it did not do the same for child rape or abuse. [The court concludes that there is a national consensus against imposing the death penalty for rape, and strikes down the Louisiana statute.]

Justice Alito, dissenting: If anything can be inferred from state legislative developments, the message is very different from the one that the Court perceives. In just the past few years, five States have enacted targeted capital child-rape laws. Such a development would not be out of step with changes in our society's thinking. During that time, reported instances of child abuse have increased dramatically; and there are many indications of growing alarm about the sexual abuse of children.

questions about judicial review. What is the proper punishment for such a horrible crime? Just as important, *who should make that decision*—appointed judges, or elected legislators?

Judicial Activism/Judicial Restraint. The power of judicial review is potentially dictatorial. The Supreme Court nullifies statutes passed by Congress (*Marbury v. Madison, United States v. Lopez*) and executive actions. May it strike down any law it dislikes? In theory, no—the Court should nullify only laws that violate the Constitution. But in practice, yes—the Constitution means whatever the majority of the current justices says that it means, since it is the Court that tells us which laws are violative.

Judicial activism
A court's willingness to decide issues on constitutional grounds.

Judicial restraint
A court's attitude that it should leave law making to legislators.

Judicial activism refers to a court's willingness, or even eagerness, to become involved in major issues and to decide cases on constitutional grounds. Activists are sometimes willing to "stretch" laws beyond their most obvious meaning. **Judicial restraint** is the opposite, an attitude that courts should leave lawmaking to legislators and nullify a law only when it unquestionably violates the Constitution. Some justices believe that the Founding Fathers never intended the judicial branch to take a prominent role in sculpting the nation's laws and its social vision.

From the 1950s through the 1970s, the Supreme Court took an activist role, deciding many major social issues on constitutional grounds. The landmark 1954 decision in *Brown v. Board of Education* ordered an end to racial segregation in public schools, not only changing the nation's educational systems but altering forever its expectations about race.[9] The Court also struck down many state laws that denied minorities the right to vote. Beginning with *Miranda v. Arizona*, the Court began a sweeping reappraisal of the police power of the state and the rights of criminal suspects during searches, interrogations, trials, and appeals.[10] And in *Roe v. Wade*, the

[9]347 U.S. 483, 74 S. Ct. 686, 1954 U.S. LEXIS 2094 (1954).
[10]384 U.S. 436, 86 S. Ct. 1602, 1966 U.S. LEXIS 2817 (1966).

Supreme Court established certain rights to abortion, most of which remain after nearly 40 years of continuous litigation.[11]

Beginning in the late 1970s, and lasting to the present, the Court has pulled back from its social activism. Exhibit 5.1 illustrates the balance among Congress, the president, and the Court.

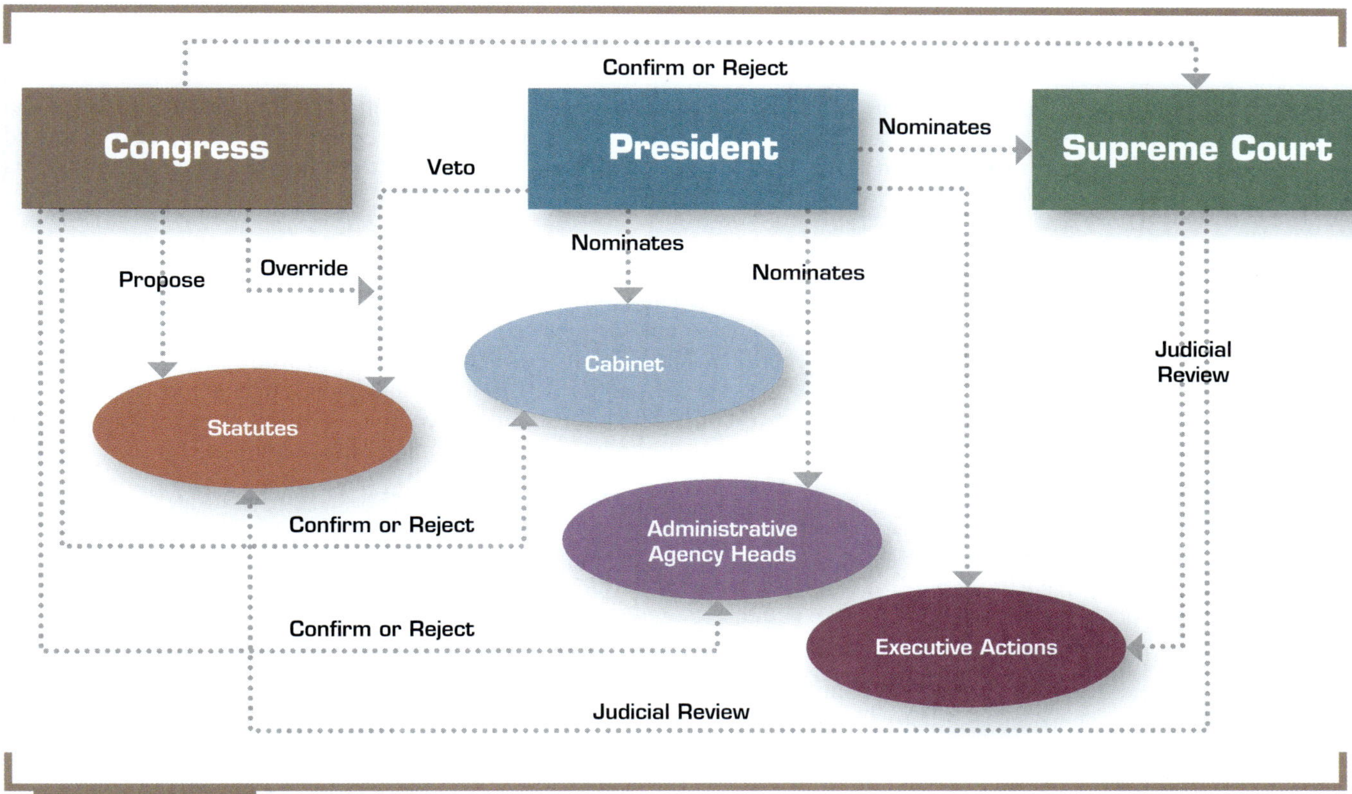

EXHIBIT 5.1 The Constitution established a federal government of checks and balances. Congress may propose statutes; the president may veto them; and Congress may override the veto. The president nominates cabinet officers, administrative heads, and Supreme Court justices, but the Senate must confirm his nominees. Finally, the Supreme Court (and lower federal courts) exercise judicial review over statutes and executive actions. Unlike the other checks and balances, judicial review is not provided for in the Constitution, but is a creation of the Court itself in *Marbury v. Madison*.

PROTECTED RIGHTS

The amendments to the Constitution protect the people of this nation from the power of state and federal government. The First Amendment guarantees rights of free speech, free press, and religion; the Fourth Amendment protects against illegal searches; the Fifth Amendment ensures due process; the Sixth Amendment demands fair treatment for defendants in criminal prosecutions; and the Fourteenth Amendment guarantees equal protection of the law. We consider the First, Fifth, and Fourteenth Amendments in this chapter and the Fourth, Fifth, and Sixth Amendments in Chapter 8, on crime.

---

[11] 410 U.S. 113, 93 S. Ct. 705, 1973 U.S. LEXIS 159 (1973).

The "people" who are protected include citizens and, for most purposes, corporations. Corporations are considered persons and receive most of the same protections. The great majority of these rights also extend to citizens of other countries who are in the United States.

Constitutional rights generally protect only against governmental acts. The Constitution generally does not protect us from the conduct of private parties, such as corporations or other citizens.

Incorporation

A series of Supreme Court cases has extended virtually all of the important constitutional protections to *all levels* of national, state, and local government. This process is called **incorporation** because rights explicitly guaranteed at one level are incorporated into rights that apply at other levels.

First Amendment: Free Speech

The First Amendment states that "Congress shall make no law ... abridging the freedom of speech...." In general, we expect our government to let people speak and hear whatever they choose. The Founding Fathers believed democracy would work only if the members of the electorate were free to talk, argue, listen, and exchange viewpoints in any way they wanted. The people could only cast informed ballots if they were informed. "Speech" also includes symbolic conduct, as the following case flamingly illustrates.

Texas v. Johnson

491 U.S. 397, 109 S. Ct. 2533, 1989 U.S. LEXIS 3115
United States Supreme Court, 1989

Facts: Outside the Republican National Convention in Dallas, Gregory Johnson participated in a protest against policies of the Reagan administration. Participants gave speeches and handed out leaflets. Johnson burned an American flag. He was arrested and convicted under a Texas statute that prohibited desecrating the flag, but the Texas Court of Criminal Appeals reversed on the grounds that the conviction violated the First Amendment. Texas appealed to the United States Supreme Court.

Issue: ***Does the First Amendment protect flag burning?***

Excerpts from Justice Brennan's Decision: The First Amendment literally forbids the abridgment only of "speech," but we have long recognized that its protection does not end at the spoken or written word. While we have rejected the view that an apparently limitless variety of conduct can be labeled "speech," we have acknowledged that conduct may be sufficiently imbued with elements of communication to fall within the scope of the First and Fourteenth Amendments.

In deciding whether particular conduct possesses sufficient communicative elements to bring the First Amendment into play, we have asked whether an intent to convey a particularized message was present, and [whether] the likelihood was great that the message would be understood by those who viewed it. Hence, we have recognized the expressive nature of students' wearing of black armbands to protest American military involvement in Vietnam; of a sit-in by blacks in a "whites only" area to protest segregation; of the wearing of American military uniforms in a dramatic presentation criticizing American involvement in Vietnam; and of picketing about a wide variety of causes.

[The Court concluded that burning the flag was in fact symbolic speech.]

It remains to consider whether the State's interest in reserving the flag as a symbol of nationhood and national unity justifies Johnson's conviction. Johnson was prosecuted because he knew that his politically charged expression would cause "serious offense."

If there is a bedrock principle underlying the First Amendment, it is that the Government may not prohibit the expression of an idea simply because society finds the idea itself offensive or disagreeable. Nothing in our precedents suggests that a State may foster its own view of the flag by prohibiting expressive conduct relating to it.

Could the Government, on this theory, prohibit the burning of state flags? Of copies of the Presidential seal? Of the Constitution? In evaluating these choices under the First Amendment, how would we decide which symbols were sufficiently special to warrant this unique status? To do so, we would be forced to consult our own political preferences, and impose them on the citizenry, in the very way that the First Amendment forbids us to do.

The way to preserve the flag's special role is not to punish those who feel differently about these matters. It is to persuade them that they are wrong. We can imagine no more appropriate response to burning a flag than waving one's own, no better way to counter a flagburner's message than by saluting the flag that burns, no surer means of preserving the dignity even of the flag that burned than by—as one witness here did—according its remains a respectful burial. We do not consecrate the flag by punishing its desecration, for in doing so we dilute the freedom that this cherished emblem represents.

The judgment of the Texas Court of Criminal Appeals is therefore *affirmed*.

Political Speech

Because the Framers were primarily concerned with enabling democracy to function, political speech has been given an especially high degree of protection. Such speech may not be barred even when it is offensive or outrageous. A speaker, for example, could accuse a U.S. senator of being insane and could use crude, violent language to describe him. The speech is still protected. **Political speech is protected unless it is intended and likely to create imminent lawless action.**[12] For example, suppose the speaker said, "The senator is inside that restaurant. Let's get some matches and burn the place down." Speech of this sort is not protected. The speaker could be arrested for attempted arson or attempted murder.

© Gordon Galbraith/Shutterstock

Protected speech?

One of the most important recent developments in constutitional law concerns the ability of *organizations* to engage in political speech. In the case that follows, a sharply divided Supreme Court weighed in on the issue raised in this chapter's opening scenario.

Citizens United v. Federal Election Commission

130 S. Ct. 876
Supreme Court of the United States, 2010

Facts: Citizens United, a nonprofit organization, produced a documentary on presidential candidate Hillary Clinton. The group wanted to run television ads promoting *Hillary: The Movie*. The Bipartisan Campaign Reform Act of 2002 banned "electioneering communication" by corporations and unions for the 30 days before a presidential primary. Citizens United challenged the Act, arguing that it violated the First Amendment.

Issue: ***Did the Bipartisan Campaign Reform Act violate the First Amendment?***

Excerpts from Justice Kennedy's Decision: The First Amendment provides that "Congress shall make no law … abridging the freedom of speech." The law before us makes it a felony for all corporations—including nonprofit advocacy corporations—either to expressly advocate the election

[12]*Brandenburg v. Ohio*, 395 U.S. 444, 89 S. Ct. 1827, 1969 U.S. LEXIS 1367 (1969).

or defeat of candidates or to broadcast electioneering communications within 30 days of a primary election and 60 days of a general election. These prohibitions are classic examples of censorship.

As a restriction on the amount of money a person or group can spend on political communication during a campaign, that statute necessarily reduces the quantity of expression by restricting the number of issues discussed, the depth of their exploration, and the size of the audience reached.

Speech is an essential mechanism of democracy, for it is the means to hold officials accountable to the people. The right of citizens to inquire, to hear, to speak, and to use information to reach consensus is a precondition to enlightened self-government and a necessary means to protect it. For these reasons, political speech must prevail against laws that would suppress it, whether by design or inadvertence.

The Government may not deprive the public of the right and privilege to determine for itself what speech and speakers are worthy of consideration. The First Amendment protects speech and speaker, and the ideas that flow from each.

The Court has recognized that First Amendment protection extends to corporations. This protection has been extended by explicit holdings to the context of political speech. Corporations and other associations, like individuals, contribute to the discussion, debate, and the dissemination of information and ideas that the First Amendment seeks to foster. The Court has thus rejected the argument that political speech of corporations or other associations should be treated differently under the First Amendment simply because such associations are not "natural persons."

The Government falls back on the argument that corporate political speech can be banned in order to prevent corruption or its appearance. We must give weight to attempts by Congress to seek to dispel either the appearance or the reality of these influences. The remedies enacted by law, however, must comply with the First Amendment; and, it is our law and our tradition that more speech, not less, is the governing rule. An outright ban on corporate political speech during the critical preelection period is not a permissible remedy.

Modern-day movies, television comedies, or skits on YouTube might portray public officials or public policies in unflattering ways. Yet if a covered transmission during the blackout period creates the background for candidate endorsement or opposition, a felony occurs solely because a corporation has made the purchase in order to engage in political speech. Speech would be suppressed in the realm where its necessity is most evident: in the public dialogue preceding a real election. Governments are often hostile to speech, but under our law and our tradition it seems stranger than fiction for our Government to make this political speech a crime. Yet this is the statute's purpose and design.

Some members of the public might consider Hillary to be insightful and instructive; some might find it to be neither high art nor a fair discussion on how to set the Nation's course; still others simply might suspend judgment on these points but decide to think more about issues and candidates. Those choices and assessments, however, are not for the Government to make.

The judgment of the District Court is reversed.

It is so ordered.

Time, Place, and Manner

Even when speech is protected, the government may regulate the *time, place,* and *manner* of such speech. A town may require a group to apply for a permit before using a public park for a political demonstration. The town may insist that the demonstration take place during daylight hours and that there be adequate police supervision and sanitation provided. However, the town may not prohibit such demonstrations outright.

Many public universities have designated "free speech zones" located in high-traffic areas of campus which are not immediately adjacent to a large number of classrooms. The zones allow for debates to proceed and reach many students, but they minimize the chances that noisy demonstrations will interfere with lectures.

Morality and Obscenity

The regulation of morality and obscenity presents additional problems. Obscenity has never received constitutional protection. The Supreme Court has consistently held that it does not play a valued role in our society and has refused to give protection to obscene works. That is well and good, but it merely forces the question: what is obscene?

In *Miller v. California*,[13] the Court created a three-part test to determine if a creative work is obscene. The basic guidelines for the factfinder are:

- Whether the average person, applying contemporary community standards, would find that the work, taken as a whole, appeals to the prurient interest;
- Whether the work depicts or describes, in a patently offensive way, sexual conduct specifically defined by the applicable state law; and
- Whether the work, taken as a whole, lacks serious literary, artistic, political, or scientific value.

If the trial court finds that the answer to all three of those questions is "yes," it may judge the material obscene; the state may then prohibit the work. If the state fails to prove any one of the three criteria, though, the work is not obscene.[14] A United States District Court ruled that "As Nasty As They Wanna Be," recorded by 2 Live Crew, was obscene. The appeals court, however, reversed, finding that the state had failed to prove lack of artistic merit.[15]

Commercial Speech

This refers to speech that has a dominant theme to propose a commercial transaction. For example, most advertisements on television and in the newspapers are commercial speech. This sort of speech is protected by the First Amendment, but the government is permitted to regulate it more closely than other forms of speech. Commercial speech that is false or misleading may be outlawed altogether. **The government may regulate other commercial speech, provided that the rules are reasonable, and directed to a legitimate goal.** The following case demonstrates the very different treatment given to this type of speech.

Commercial speech
Communication, such as advertisements, that has the dominant theme of proposing a business transaction.

Salib v. City of Mesa

133 P.3d 756, 212 Ariz. 446
Arizona Court of Appeals, 2006.

Facts: Edward Salib owned a Winchell's Donut House in Mesa, Arizona. To attract customers, he displayed large signs in his store window. The city ordered him to remove the signs, because they violated its Sign Code, which prohibited covering more than 30% of a store's windows with signs. Salib sued, claiming that the Sign Code violated his First Amendment free speech rights. The trial court gave summary judgment for Mesa, and the store owner appealed.

Issue: ***Did Mesa's Sign Code violate the First Amendment?***

Excerpts from Judge Irvine's Decision: Under [a Supreme Court case called] *Central Hudson*, commercial speech that concerns unlawful activity or is misleading is not protected by the First Amendment. Commercial speech that falls into neither of these categories may be regulated if the government satisfies a three-prong test. First, the government must assert a substantial interest in support of the regulation. Mesa argues, and Salib concedes, that the governmental regulation of aesthetics constitutes a substantial interest, so the first prong of *Central Hudson* is not at issue.

Under the second prong of *Central Hudson*, the government must demonstrate that the challenged regulation advances its interest in a direct and material way. Salib argues that this prong has not been met because no

[13] 413 U.S. 15, 93 S. Ct. 2607, 1973 U.S. LEXIS 149 (1973).
[14] *Penthouse Intern Ltd. v. McAuliffe*, 610 F.2d 1353 (5th Cir. 1980).
[15] *Luke Records, Inc. v. Navarro*, 960 F.2d 134, 1992 U.S. App. LEXIS 9592 (11th Cir. 1992).

studies were conducted to determine what aesthetic or safety problems existed and how the Sign Code could solve such problems.

Mesa responds that the Sign Code was enacted because of legitimate concerns among business owners that many businesses in the area had 100% coverage of their storefront windows and that this total coverage was unattractive and detracted from the aesthetics of the city. The First Amendment does not require a formal study before a regulation may be enacted. The record shows that the city council received considerable input on the subject of window coverage and aesthetics before enacting the Sign Code. Although its final adoption of the Sign Code may have rested on anecdote, history, consensus or simple common sense, rather than a formal study or survey addressed specifically to the window coverage provision, the constitution requires no greater proof.

Salib argues the restriction is not narrow enough and therefore violates the third prong of *Central Hudson*. It is clear from the First Amendment cases that narrowly tailored or narrowly drawn does not mean that the least restrictive means must be used. Rather, a "reasonable fit" between the intent and purpose of the regulation and the means chosen to accomplish those goals is required. The regulation does not have to be perfect, but its scope must be in proportion to the interest served.

Mesa argues that 30% is a reasonable compromise between 100% coverage and a total ban of signage. Further, Mesa argues, the Sign Code is narrow because it only addresses signs that are inside the pane, and the Code allows alternative methods of communication, including signs hanging outside of the window sill area. Additionally, Mesa conducted comparisons with other communities and found that the 30% restriction on window coverage was comparable to other cities' restrictions.

We are not in a position to determine what percentage of window coverage is optimal. Rather, we only decide if the 30% figure that was adopted by the Sign Code is a reasonable fit to further the goal of improving aesthetics. We conclude that it is. Reasonable minds can differ as to whether Mesa's interest would best be served by a 15%, 25%, 30% or 40% limitation on window coverage, but under the facts of this case we cannot conclude that these differences of degree are of a constitutional dimension. The exact balance between the size of the signs and the aesthetic benefits attained is ultimately a subjective decision best left to the city council.

We conclude the Sign Code directly advances a substantial governmental interest and is narrowly tailored to directly advance the goal of improved aesthetics. We therefore affirm the trial court's granting of Mesa's Motion for Summary Judgment.

EXAM Strategy

Question: Maria owns a lot next to a freeway that passes through Tidyville. She has rented a billboard to Huge Mart, a nearby retailer, and a second billboard to Green, a political party. However, Tidyville prohibits off-premises signs (those not on the advertiser's property) that are visible from the freeway. Tidyville's rule is designed to make the city more attractive, to increase property values, and to eliminate distractions that may cause freeway accidents. Huge Mart and Green sue, claiming that Tidyville's law violates their First Amendment rights.

A. Huge Mart is likely to win; Green is likely to lose.

B. Green is likely to win; Huge Mart is likely to lose.

C. Huge Mart and Green are both likely to win.

D. Huge Mart and Green are both likely to lose.

Strategy: What is the difference between the two cases? Huge Mart wants the billboard for commercial speech, Green wants it for a political message. What are the legal standards for commercial and political free speech? Apply those standards.

Result: The government may regulate commercial speech, provided that the rules are reasonable and directed to a legitimate goal. Political speech is given much stronger protection, and can be prohibited only if it is intended and likely to create imminent lawless action. The regulation outlawing *advertising* will be upheld, but Tidyville will not be allowed to block political messages.

Fifth Amendment: Due Process and the Takings Clause

You are a senior at a major state university. You feel great about a difficult exam you took in Professor Watson's class. The Dean's Office sends for you, and you enter curiously, wondering if your exam was so good that the dean is awarding you a prize. Not quite. The exam proctor has accused you of cheating. Based on the accusation, Watson has flunked you. You protest that you are innocent and demand to know what the accusation is. The dean says that you will learn the details at a hearing, if you wish to have one. She reminds you that if you lose the hearing, you will be expelled from the university. Four years of work and your entire career are suddenly on the line.

Four years of work and your entire career are suddenly on the line.

The hearing is run by Professor Holmes, who will make the final decision. Holmes is a junior faculty member in Watson's department. (Next year, Watson will decide Holmes's tenure application.) At the hearing, the proctor accuses you of copying from a student sitting in front of you. Both Watson and Holmes have already compared the two papers and concluded that they are strongly similar. Holmes tells you that you must convince him the charge is wrong. You examine the papers, acknowledge that there are similarities, but plead as best you can that you never copied. Holmes doesn't buy it. The university expels you, placing on your transcript a notation of cheating.

Have you received fair treatment? To answer that, we must look to the Fifth Amendment, which provides several vital protections. We will consider two related provisions, the Due Process Clause and the Takings Clause. Together, they state: "No person shall be . . . deprived of life, liberty, or property without due process of law; nor shall private property be taken for public use, without just compensation." These clauses prevent the government from arbitrarily taking the most valuable possessions of a citizen or corporation. The government has the right to take a person's liberty or property. But there are three important limitations:

- ***Procedural Due Process.*** Before depriving anyone of liberty or property, the government must go through certain steps, or procedures, to ensure that the result is fair.
- ***The Takings Clause.*** When the government takes property for public use, such as to build a new highway, it has to pay a fair price.
- ***Substantive Due Process.*** Some rights are so fundamental that the government may not take them from us at all. The substance of any law or government action may be challenged on fundamental fairness grounds.

Takings Clause
A clause in the Fifth Amendment which ensures that when any governmental unit takes private property for public use, it must compensate the owner.

Procedural Due Process

The government deprives citizens or corporations of their property in a variety of ways. The Internal Revenue Service may fine a corporation for late payment of taxes. The Customs Service may seize goods at the border. As to liberty, the government may take it by confining someone in a mental institution or by taking a child out of the home because of

Procedural due process
The doctrine which ensures that before the government takes liberty or property, the affected person has a fair chance to oppose the action.

parental neglect. The purpose of **procedural due process** is to ensure that before the government takes liberty or property, the affected person has a fair chance to oppose the action.

There are two steps in analyzing a procedural due process case:

- Is the government attempting to take liberty or property?
- If so, how much process is due? (If the government is *not* attempting to take liberty or property, there is no due process issue.)

Is the Government Attempting to Take Liberty or Property? Liberty interests are generally easy to spot: confining someone in a mental institution and taking a child from her home are both deprivations of liberty. A property interest may be obvious. Suppose that, during a civil lawsuit, the court **attaches** a defendant's house, meaning it bars the defendant from selling the property at least until the case is decided. This way, if the plaintiff wins, the defendant will have assets to pay the judgment. The court has clearly deprived the defendant of an important interest in his house, and the defendant is entitled to due process. However, a property interest may be subtler than that. A woman holding a job with a government agency has a "property interest" in that job, because her employer has agreed not to fire her without cause, and she can rely on it for income. If the government does fire her, it is taking away that property interest, and she is entitled to due process. A student attending any public school has a property interest in her education. If a public university suspends a student as described above, it is taking her property, and she, too, should receive due process.

How Much Process Is Due? Assuming that a liberty or property interest is affected, a court must decide how much process is due. Does the person get a formal trial, or an informal hearing, or merely a chance to reply in writing to the charges against her? If she gets a hearing, must it be held before the government deprives her of her property, or is it enough that she can be heard shortly thereafter? **What sort of hearing the government must offer depends upon how important the property or liberty interest is and on whether the government has a competing need for efficiency.** The more important the interest, the more formal the procedures must be.

Neutral Factfinder. Regardless of how formal the hearing, one requirement is constant: the factfinder must be neutral. Whether it is a superior court judge deciding a multimillion dollar contract suit or an employment supervisor deciding the fate of a government employee, the factfinder must have no personal interest in the outcome. In *Ward v. Monroeville*,[16] the plaintiff was a motorist who had been stopped for traffic offenses in a small town. He protested his innocence and received a judicial hearing. But the "judge" at the hearing was the town mayor. Traffic fines were a significant part of the town's budget. The motorist argued that the town was depriving him of procedural due process because the mayor had a financial interest in the outcome of the case. The United States Supreme Court agreed and reversed his conviction.

Attachment of Property. As described earlier, a plaintiff in a civil lawsuit often seeks to *attach* the defendant's property. This protects the plaintiff, but it may also harm the defendant if, for example, he is about to close a profitable real estate deal. Attachments used to be routine. In *Connecticut v. Doehr*, the Supreme Court required more caution.[17] Based on *Doehr*, when a plaintiff seeks to attach at the beginning of the trial, a court must look at the plaintiff's likelihood of winning. Generally, the court must grant the defendant a hearing

---

[16]409 U.S. 57, 93 S. Ct. 80, 1972 U.S. LEXIS 11 (1972).

[17]501 U.S. 1, 111 S. Ct. 2105, 1991 U.S. LEXIS 3317 (1991).

before attaching the property. The defendant, represented by a lawyer, may offer evidence as to how attachment would harm him and why it should be denied.

Government Employment. A government employee must receive due process before being fired. Generally, this means some kind of hearing, but not necessarily a formal court hearing. The employee is entitled to know the charges against him, to hear the employer's evidence, and to have an opportunity to tell his side of the story. He is not entitled to have a lawyer present. The hearing "officer" need only be a neutral employee. Further, in an emergency, where the employee is a danger to the public or the organization, the government may suspend with pay, before holding a hearing. It then must provide a hearing before the decision becomes final.

Academic Suspension. There is still a property interest here, but it is the least important of those discussed. When a public school concludes that a student has failed to meet its normal academic standards, such as by failing too many courses, it may dismiss him without a hearing. Due process is served if the student receives notice of the reason and has some opportunity to respond, such as by writing a letter contradicting the school's claims.

In cases of disciplinary suspension or expulsion, courts generally require schools to provide a higher level of due process. In the hypothetical at the beginning of this section, the university has failed to provide adequate due process.[18] The school has accused the student of a serious infraction. The school must promptly provide details of the charge and cannot wait until the hearing to do so. The student should see the two papers and have a chance to rebut the charge. Moreover, Professor Holmes has demonstrated bias. He appears to have made up his mind in advance. He has placed the burden on the student to disprove the charges. And he probably feels obligated to support Watson's original conclusion, since Watson will be deciding his tenure case next year.

The Takings Clause

Florence Dolan ran a plumbing store in Tigard, Oregon. She and her husband wanted to enlarge it on land they already owned. But the city government said that they could expand only if they dedicated some of their own land for use as a public bicycle path and for other public use. Does the city have the right to make them do that? For an answer we must look to a different part of the Fifth Amendment.

The Takings Clause prohibits a state from taking private property for public use without just compensation. A town wishing to build a new football field may boot you out of your house. But the town must compensate you. The government takes your land through the power of **eminent domain**. Officials must notify you of their intentions and give you an opportunity to oppose the project and to challenge the amount the town offers to pay. But when the hearings are done, the town may write you a check and level your house, whether you like it or not.

Eminent domain
The power of the government to take private property for public use.

More controversial issues arise when a local government does not physically take the property but passes regulations that restrict its use. Tigard is a city of 30,000 in Oregon. The city developed a comprehensive land use plan for its downtown area in order to preserve green space, to encourage transportation other than autos, and to reduce its flooding problems. Under the plan, when a property owner sought permission to build in the downtown section, the city could require some of her land to be used for public purposes. This has become a standard method of land use planning throughout the nation. States have used it to preserve coastline, urban green belts, and many environmental features.

When Florence Dolan applied for permission to expand, the city required that she dedicate a 15-foot strip of her property to the city as a bicycle pathway and that she

[18]See, e.g., *University of Texas Medical School at Houston v. Than*, 901 S.W.2d 926, 1995 Tex. LEXIS 105 (Tex. 1995).

preserve, as greenway, a portion of her land within a floodplain. She sued, and though she lost in the Oregon courts, she won in the United States Supreme Court. The Court held that Tigard City's method of routinely forcing all owners to dedicate land to public use violated the Takings Clause. The city was taking the land, even though title never changed hands.[19]

The Court did not outlaw all such requirements. What it required was that, **before a government may require an owner to dedicate land to a public use, it must show that this owner's proposed building requires this dedication of land.** In other words, it is not enough for Tigard to have a general plan, such as a bicycle pathway, and to make all owners participate in it. Tigard must show that it needs *Dolan's* land *specifically for a bike path and greenway*. This will be much harder for local governments to demonstrate than merely showing a city-wide plan. A related issue arose in the following controversial case. A city used eminent domain to take property on behalf of *private developers*. Was this a valid public use?

The Kelo decision was controversial, and in response some states passed statutes prohibiting eminent domain for private development.

Kelo v. City of New London, Connecticut

545 U.S. 469, 125 S.Ct. 2655
United States Supreme Court, 2005

Facts: New London, Connecticut, was declining economically. The city's unemployment rate was double that of the state generally, and the population at its lowest point in 75 years. In response, state and local officials targeted a section of the city, called Fort Trumbull, for revitalization. Located on the Thames River, Fort Trumbull comprised 115 privately owned properties and 32 additional acres of an abandoned naval facility. The development plan included one section for a waterfront conference hotel and stores; a second one for 80 private residences; and one for research facilities.

The state bought most of the properties from willing sellers. However, nine owners of 15 properties refused to sell, and filed suit. The owners claimed that the city was trying to take land for *private* use, not public, in violation of the Takings Clause. The case reached the United States Supreme Court.

Issue: ***Did the city's plan violate the Takings Clause?***

Excerpts from Justice Stevens' Decision: It has long been accepted that the sovereign may not take the property of *A* for the sole purpose of transferring it to another private party *B*, even though *A* is paid just compensation. On the other hand, it is equally clear that a State may transfer property from one private party to another if future "use by the public" is the purpose of the taking; the condemnation of land for a railroad with common-carrier duties is a familiar example.

This is not a case in which the City is planning to open the condemned land—at least not in its entirety—to use by the general public. Nor will the private lessees of the land in any sense be required to operate like common carriers, making their services available to all comers. But this Court long ago rejected any literal requirement that condemned property be put into use for the general public, [embracing] the broader and more natural interpretation of public use as "public purpose." Thus, in a case upholding a mining company's use of an aerial bucket line to transport ore over property it did not own, Justice Holmes' opinion for the Court stressed "the inadequacy of use by the general public as a universal test."

The City has carefully formulated an economic development plan that it believes will provide appreciable benefits to the community, including—but by no means limited to—new jobs and increased tax revenue. As with other exercises in urban planning and development, the City is endeavoring to coordinate a variety of commercial, residential, and recreational uses of land, with the hope that they will form a whole greater than the sum of its parts. Because that plan unquestionably serves a public purpose, the takings challenged here satisfy the public use requirement of the Fifth Amendment.

---

[19] *Dolan v. City of Tigard*, 512 U.S. 374, 114 S. Ct. 2309, 1994 U.S. LEXIS 4826 (1994).

To avoid this result, petitioners urge us to adopt a new bright-line rule that economic development does not qualify as a public use. [However, promoting] economic development is a traditional and long accepted function of government. There is, moreover, no principled way of distinguishing economic development from the other public purposes that we have recognized. In our cases upholding takings that facilitated agriculture and mining, for example, we emphasized the importance of those industries to the welfare of the States in question. Clearly, there is no basis for exempting economic development from our traditionally broad understanding of public purpose.

The judgment of the Supreme Court of Connecticut is affirmed.

Justice O'Connor, dissenting: The Court today significantly expands the meaning of public use. It holds that the sovereign may take private property currently put to ordinary private use, and give it over for new, ordinary private use, so long as the new use is predicted to generate some secondary benefit for the public—such as increased tax revenue, more jobs, maybe even esthetic pleasure. But nearly any lawful use of real private property can be said to generate some incidental benefit to the public. Thus, if predicted (or even guaranteed) positive side-effects are enough to render transfer from one private party to another constitutional, then the words "for public use" do not realistically exclude *any* takings, and thus do not exert any constraint on the eminent domain power.

Any property may now be taken for the benefit of another private party, but the fallout from this decision will not be random. The beneficiaries are likely to be those citizens with disproportionate influence and power in the political process, including large corporations and development firms. As for the victims, the government now has license to transfer property from those with fewer resources to those with more.

Substantive Due Process

This doctrine is part of the Due Process Clause, but it is entirely different from procedural due process and from government taking. During the first third of the twentieth century, the Supreme Court frequently nullified state and federal laws, asserting that they interfered with basic rights. For example, in a famous 1905 case, *Lochner v. New York*,[20] the Supreme Court invalidated a New York statute that had limited the number of hours that bakers could work in a week. New York had passed the law to protect employee health. But the Court declared that private parties had a basic constitutional right to contract. In this case, the statute interfered with the rights of the employer and the baker to make any bargain they wished. Over the next three decades, the Court struck down dozens of state and federal laws that were aimed at working conditions, union rights, and social welfare generally. This was called **substantive due process**[21] because the Court was looking at the underlying rights being affected, such as the right to contract, not at any procedures.

Substantive due process
A form of due process that holds that certain rights are so fundamental that the government may not eliminate them.

Critics complained that the Court was interfering with the desires of the voting public by nullifying laws that the justices personally disliked (judicial activism). During the Great Depression, however, things changed. Beginning in 1934, the Court completely reversed itself and began to uphold the types of laws it earlier had struck down.

The Supreme Court made an important substantive due process ruling in the case of *BMW v. Gore*[22]. A BMW dealership sold Gore a car that had sustained water damage. Instead of telling him of the damage, they simply repainted the car and sold it as new.

In Chapter 6, we will examine two different types of cash awards that juries may make in tort cases. For now, let's call them "ordinary" and "punitive" damages. When plaintiffs win tort cases, juries may always award ordinary damages to offset real, measureable losses. In addition, juries are sometimes allowed to add to an award to further punish a defendant for bad behavior.

[20] 198 U.S. 45, 25 S. Ct. 539, 1905 U.S. LEXIS 1153 (1905).

[21] Be the first on your block to pronounce this word correctly. The accent goes on the first syllable: *sub*stantive.

[22] 517 U.S. 559 (1996).

In the BMW case, the jury awarded Gore $4,000 in ordinary damages as the difference in value between a flawless new car and a water-damaged car. The jury then awarded a delighted Gore $4 *million* in punitive damages. In the end, the Supreme Court decided that the punitive award was so disproportionate to the harm actually caused that it violated substantive due process rights.

Fourteenth Amendment: Equal Protection Clause

Shannon Faulkner wanted to attend The Citadel, a state-supported military college in South Carolina. She was a fine student who met every admission requirement that The Citadel set except one: she was not a man. The Citadel argued that its long and distinguished history demanded that it remain all male. Faulkner responded that she was a citizen of the state and ought to receive the benefits that others got, including the right to a military education. Could the school exclude her on the basis of gender?

Equal Protection Clause
A clause in the Fourteenth Amendment that generally requires the government to treat people equally.

The Fourteenth Amendment provides that "No State shall ... deny to any person within its jurisdiction the equal protection of the laws." This is the **Equal Protection Clause**, and it means that, generally speaking, **governments must treat people equally**. Unfair classifications among people or corporations will not be permitted. A notorious example of unfair classification would be race discrimination: permitting only white children to attend a public school violates the Equal Protection Clause.

Yet clearly, governments do make classifications every day. People with high incomes pay a higher tax rate than those with low incomes; some corporations are permitted to deal in securities, while others are not. To determine which classifications are constitutionally permissible, we need to know what is being classified. There are three major groups of classifications. The outcome of a case can generally be predicted by knowing which group it is in.

- ***Minimal Scrutiny: Economic and Social Relations.*** Government actions that classify people or corporations on these bases are almost always upheld.
- ***Intermediate Scrutiny: Gender.*** Government classifications are sometimes upheld.
- ***Strict Scrutiny: Race, Ethnicity, and Fundamental Rights.*** Classifications based on any of these are almost never upheld.

Minimal Scrutiny: Economic and Social Regulation

Just as with the Due Process Clause, laws that regulate economic or social issues are presumed valid. They will be upheld if they are *rationally related to a legitimate goal.* This means a statute may classify corporations and/or people and the classifications will be upheld if they make any sense at all. The New York City Transit Authority excluded all methadone users from any employment. The United States District Court concluded that this violated the Equal Protection Clause by unfairly excluding all those who were on methadone. The court noted that even those who tested free of any illegal drugs and were seeking non-safety-sensitive jobs, such as clerks, were turned away. That, said the district court, was irrational.

Not so, said the United States Supreme Court. The Court admitted that the policy might not be the wisest. It would probably make more sense to test individually for illegal drugs rather than automatically exclude methadone users. But, said the Court, it was not up to the justices to choose the best policy. They were only to decide if the policy was rational. Excluding methadone users related rationally to the safety of public transport and therefore did not violate the Equal Protection Clause.[23]

Intermediate Scrutiny: Gender

Classifications based on sex must meet a tougher test than those resulting from economic or social regulation. Such laws must *substantially relate to important government objectives.* Courts have increasingly nullified government sex classifications as societal concern with gender equality has grown.

---

[23] *New York City Transit Authority v. Beazer*, 440 U.S. 568, 99 S. Ct. 1355, 1979 U.S. LEXIS 77 (1979).

At about the same time Shannon Faulkner began her campaign to enter The Citadel, another woman sought admission to the Virginia Military Institute, an all-male state school. The Supreme Court held that Virginia had violated the Equal Protection Clause by excluding women from VMI. The Court ruled that gender-based government discrimination requires an "exceedingly persuasive justification," and that Virginia had failed that standard of proof. The Citadel promptly opened its doors to women as well.[24]

Strict Scrutiny: Race, Ethnicity, and Fundamental Rights

Any government action that intentionally discriminates against racial or ethnic minorities, or interferes with a fundamental right, is presumed invalid. In such cases, courts will look at the statute or policy with *strict scrutiny;* that is, courts will examine it very closely to determine whether there is compelling justification for it. The law will be upheld only if it is *necessary to promote a compelling state interest.* Very few meet that test.

- ***Racial and Ethnic Minorities.*** Any government action that intentionally discriminates on the basis of race, or ethnicity is presumed invalid. For example, in *Palmore v. Sidoti,*[25] the state had refused to give child custody to a mother because her new spouse was racially different from the child. The practice was declared unconstitutional. The state had made a racial classification, it was presumed invalid, and the government had no *compelling need* to make such a ruling.
- ***Fundamental Rights.*** A government action interfering with a fundamental right also receives strict scrutiny and will likely be declared void. For example, New York State gave an employment preference to any veteran who had been a state resident when he entered the military. Newcomers who were veterans were less likely to get jobs, and therefore this statute interfered with the right to travel, a fundamental right. The Supreme Court declared the law invalid.[26]

Fundamental rights
Rights so basic that any governmental interference with them is suspect and likely to be unconstitutional.

EXAM Strategy

Question: Megan is a freshman at her local public high school; her older sister Jenna attends a nearby private high school. Both girls are angry because their schools prohibit them from joining their respective wrestling teams, where only boys are allowed. The two girls sue based on the U.S. Constitution. Discuss the relevant law and predict the outcomes.

Strategy: One girl goes to private and one to public school. Why does that matter? Now ask what provision of the Constitution is involved, and what legal standard it establishes.

Result: The Constitution offers protection from the *government.* A private high school is not part of the government, and Jenna has no constitutional case. Megan's suit is based on the Equal Protection Clause. This is gender discrimination, meaning that Megan's school must convince the court that keeping girls off the team *substantially relates to an important government objective.* The school will probably argue that wrestling with stronger boys will be dangerous for girls. However, courts are increasingly suspicious of any gender discrimination and are unlikely to find the school's argument persuasive.

---

[24] *United States v. Virginia,* 518 U.S. 515, 116 S. Ct. 2264, 1996 U.S. LEXIS 4259 (1996).
[25] 466 U.S. 429, 104 S. Ct. 1879, 1984 U.S. LEXIS 69 (1984).
[26] *Attorney General of New York v. Soto-Lopez,* 476 U.S. 898, 106 S. Ct. 2317, 1986 U.S. LEXIS 59 (1986).

Chapter Conclusion

The legal battle over power never stops. The obligation of a state to provide equal educational opportunity for both genders relates to whether Tigard, Oregon, may demand some of Ms. Dolan's store lot for public use. Both issues are governed by one amazing document. That same Constitution determines what tax preferences are permissible, and even whether a state may require you to wear clothing. As social mores change in step with broad cultural developments, as the membership of the Supreme Court changes, the balance of power between federal government, state government, and citizens will continue to evolve. There are no easy answers to these constitutional questions because there has never been a democracy so large, so diverse, or so powerful.

Exam Review

1. **CONSTITUTION** The Constitution is a series of compromises about power. (pp. 103–105)

2. **ARTICLES I, II AND III** Article I of the Constitution creates the Congress and grants all legislative power to it. Article II establishes the office of president and defines executive powers. Article III creates the Supreme Court and permits lower federal courts; the article also outlines the powers of the federal judiciary. (pp. 105–111)

3. **COMMERCE CLAUSE** Under the Commerce Clause, Congress may regulate any activity that has a substantial effect on interstate commerce. (pp. 105–107)

4. **INTERSTATE COMMERCE** A state may not regulate commerce in any way that will interfere with interstate commerce. (p. 105)

EXAM Strategy

Question: Maine exempted many charitable institutions from real estate taxes but denied this benefit to a charity that primarily benefited out-of-state residents. Camp Newfound was a Christian Science organization, and 95 percent of its summer campers came from other states. Camp Newfound sued Maine. Discuss.

Strategy: The state was treating organizations differently depending on what states their campers come from. This raised *Commerce Clause* issues. Did the positive aspect or dormant aspect of that clause apply? The dormant aspect applied. What does it state? Apply that standard to theses facts. (See the "Result" at the end of this section.)

5. **SUPREMACY CLAUSE** Under the Supremacy Clause, if there is a conflict between federal and state statutes, the federal law preempts the field. Even without a conflict, federal law preempts if Congress intended to exercise exclusive control. (p. 107)

6. **PRESIDENTIAL POWERS** The president's key powers include making agency appointments, proposing legislation, conducting foreign policy, and acting as commander in chief of the armed forces. (p. 108)

7. **FEDERAL COURTS** The federal courts adjudicate cases and also exercise judicial review, which is the right to declare a statute or governmental action unconstitutional and void. (pp. 108–111)

8. **FREEDOM OF SPEECH** Freedom of speech includes symbolic acts. Political speech by both people and organizations is protected unless it is intended and likely to create imminent lawless action. (pp. 112–117)

9. **REGULATION OF SPEECH** The government may regulate the time, place, and manner of speech. (p. 114)

10. **COMMERCIAL SPEECH** Commercial speech that is false or misleading may be outlawed; otherwise, regulations on this speech must be reasonable and directed to a legitimate goal. (pp. 115–117)

Question: A federal statute prohibits the broadcasting of lottery advertisements, except by stations that broadcast in states permitting lotteries. The purpose of the statute is to support efforts of states that outlaw lotteries. Truth Broadcasting operates a radio station in State A (a nonlottery state) but broadcasts primarily in State B (a lottery state). Truth wants to advertise State A's lottery but is barred by the statute. Does the federal statute violate Truth's constitutional rights?

Strategy: This case involves a particular kind of speech. What kind? What is the rule about that kind of speech? (See the "Result" at the end of this section.)

11. **PROCEDURAL DUE PROCESS** Procedural due process is required whenever the government attempts to take liberty or property. The amount of process that is due depends upon the importance of the liberty or property threatened. (pp. 117–119)

Question: Fox's Fine Furs claims that Ermine owes $68,000 for a mink coat on which she has stopped making payments. Fox files a complaint and also asks the court clerk to *garnish* Ermine's wages. A garnishment is a court order to an employer to withhold an employee's wages, or a portion of them, and pay the money into court so that there will be money for the plaintiff, if it wins. What constitutional issue does Fox's request for garnishment raise?

Strategy: Ermine is in danger of losing part of her income, which is property. The Due Process Clause prohibits the government (the court) from taking life, liberty or property without due process. What process is Ermine entitled to? (See the "Result" at the end of this section.)

12. **TAKINGS CLAUSE** The Takings Clause prohibits a state from taking private property for public use without just compensation. (pp. 119–121)

13. **SUBSTANTIVE DUE PROCESS** A substantive due process analysis presumes that any economic or social regulation is valid, and presumes invalid any law that infringes upon a fundamental right. (pp. 121–122)

14. **EQUAL PROTECTION CLAUSE** The Equal Protection Clause generally requires the government to treat people equally. Courts apply strict scrutiny in any equal protection case involving race, ethnicity, or fundamental rights; intermediate scrutiny to any case involving gender; and minimal scrutiny to an economic or social regulation. (pp. 122–123)

4. Result: The dormant aspect holds that a state statute which discriminates against interstate commerce is almost always invalid. Maine was subsidizing charities that served in-state residents, and penalizing those that attracted campers from elsewhere. The tax rules violated the Commerce Clause and was void.[27]

10. Result: An advertisement is *commercial* speech. The government may regulate this speech as long as the rules are reasonable and directed to a legitimate goal.
The goal of supporting nonlottery states is reasonable, and there is no violation of Truth's free speech rights.[28]

11. Result: Ermine is entitled to notice of Fox's claim and to a hearing *before* the court garnishes her wages.[29]

Multiple-Choice Questions

1. Greenville College, a public community college, has a policy of admitting only male students. If the policy is challenged under the Fourteenth Amendment, ______________ scrutiny will be applied.
   (a) strict
   (b) intermediate
   (c) rational
   (d) none of the above

2. You begin work at Everhappy Corp. at the beginning of November. On your second day at work, you wear a political button on your overcoat, supporting your choice for governor in the upcoming election. Your boss glances at it and says, "Get that stupid thing out of this office or you're history, chump." Your boss ______________ violated your First Amendment rights. After work, you put the button back on and start walking home. You pass a police officer who blocks your path and says, "Take off that stupid button or you're going to jail, chump." The officer ______________ violated your First Amendment rights.

[27] *Camps Newfound/Owatonna, Inc. v. Town of Harrison, Maine,* 520 U.S. 564, 117 S.Ct. 1590 (1997).
[28] *United States v. Edge Broadcasting,* 509 U.S. 418, 113 S.Ct. 2696 (1993).
[29] *Sniadach v. Family Finance Corp.,* 395 U.S. 337 (1969).

(a) has; has
(b) has; has not
(c) has not; has
(d) has not; has not

3. Which of the following statements accurately describes statutes that Congress and the president may create?
(a) Statutes must be related to a power listed in Article I, section 8 of the Constitution.
(b) Statutes must not infringe on the liberties in the Bill of Rights.
(c) Both A and B
(d) None of the above

4. Which of the following is true of the origin of judicial review?
(a) It was created by Article II of the Constitution.
(b) It was created by Article III of the Constitution.
(c) It was created in the *Marbury v. Madison* case.
(d) It was created by the Fifth Amendment.
(e) It was created by the Fourteenth Amendment.

5. Consider *Kelo v. City of New London*, in which a city with a revitalization plan squared off against property owners who did not wish to sell their property. The key constitutional provision was the Takings Clause in the ______________ Amendment. The Supreme Court decided the city ______________ use eminent domain and take the property from the landowners.
(a) Fifth; could
(b) Fifth; could not
(c) Fourteenth; could
(d) Fourteenth; could not

Essay Questions

1. **YOU BE THE JUDGE WRITING PROBLEM** Scott Fane was a CPA licensed to practice in New Jersey and Florida. He built his New Jersey practice by making unsolicited phone calls to executives. When he moved to Florida, the Board of Accountancy there prohibited him (and all CPAs) from personally soliciting new business. Fane sued. Does the First Amendment force Florida to forgo foreclosing Fane's phoning? **Argument for Fane:** The Florida regulation violates the First Amendment, which protects commercial speech. Fane was not saying anything false or misleading, but was just trying to secure business. This is an unreasonable regulation, designed to keep newcomers out of the marketplace and maintain steady business and high prices for established CPAs. **Argument for the Florida Board of Accountancy:** Commercial speech deserves—and gets—a lower level of protection than other speech. This regulation is a reasonable method of ensuring that the level of CPA work in our state remains high. CPAs who personally solicit clients are obviously in need of business. They are more likely to bend legal and ethical rules to obtain clients and keep them happy, and will lower the standards throughout the state.

2. President George H.W. Bush insisted that he had the power to send American troops into combat in the Middle East, without congressional assent. Yet before authorizing force in Operation Desert Storm, he secured congressional authorization. President Bill Clinton stated that he was prepared to invade Haiti without a congressional vote. Yet he bargained hard to avoid an invasion, and ultimately American troops entered without the use of force. Why the seeming doubletalk by both presidents?

3. In the landmark 1965 case of *Griswold v. Connecticut*, the Supreme Court examined a Connecticut statute that made it a crime for any person to use contraception. The majority declared the law an unconstitutional violation of the right of privacy. Justice Black dissented, saying, "I do not to any extent whatever base my view that this Connecticut law is constitutional on a belief that the law is wise or that its policy is a good one. [It] is every bit as offensive to me as it is to the majority. [There is no criticism by the majority of this law] to which I cannot subscribe—except their conclusion that the evil qualities they see in the law make it unconstitutional." What legal doctrines are involved here? Why did Justice Black distinguish between his personal views on the statute and the power of the Court to overturn it?

4. Gilleo opposed American participation in the war in the Persian Gulf. She displayed a large sign on her front lawn that read, "Say No to War in the Persian Gulf, Call Congress Now." The city of Ladue prohibited signs on front lawns and Gilleo sued. The city claimed that it was regulating "time, place, and manner." Explain that statement, and decide who should win.

5. David Lucas paid $975,000 for two residential lots on the Isle of Palms near Charleston, South Carolina. He intended to build houses on them. Two years later, the South Carolina legislature passed a statute that prohibited building seaward of a certain line, and Lucas's property fell in the prohibited zone. Lucas claimed that his land was now useless and that South Carolina owed him its value. Explain his claim. Should he win?

Discussion Questions

1. Return to the opening scenario and the *Citizens United* case. Is political advertising purchased by corporations appropriate? Do you agree with the five members of the Supreme Court who voted to allow it, or with the four who dissented and would have drawn distinctions between free speech by individuals and organizations? Why?

2. **Ethics** Is political advertising by a nonprofit political organization like Citizens United any more or less appropriate than advertising by for-profit corporations like the one described in the opening scenario? If you were a board member in the opening scenario, which (if any) of the three ads would you vote to authorize?

3. Consider the "tea party" movement. Do you believe that the federal government should be able to create whatever laws it deems to be in the country's best interests, or do you believe that individual states, like Florida and California, should have more control over the laws within their own borders?

4. This chapter is filled with examples of statutes that have been struck down by the courts. A Texas law banning flag burning was rejected by the Supreme Court, as was a Louisiana death penalty statute. The Affordable Healthcare Act has been voided by two lower court judges, and the Supreme Court may or may not agree with the action.

   Do you like the fact that courts can void laws that they determine to be in violation of the Constitution? Or is it wrong for appointed judges to overrule "the will of the majority," as expressed by elected members of Congress and state legislatures?

5. Gender discrimination currently receives "intermediate" Fourteenth Amendment scrutiny. Is this right? Should gender receive "strict" scrutiny as does race? Why or why not?

CHAPTER 6

INTENTIONAL TORTS AND BUSINESS TORTS

© r.nagy/Shutterstock.com

In a small Louisiana town, Don Mashburn ran a restaurant called Maison de Mashburn. The *New Orleans States-Item* newspaper reviewed his eatery, and here is what the article said:

> "'Tain't Creole, 'tain't Cajun, 'tain't French, 'tain't country American, 'tain't good. I don't know how much real talent in cooking is hidden under the mélange of hideous sauces which make this food and the menu a travesty of pretentious amateurism, but I find it all quite depressing. Put a yellow flour sauce on top of the duck, flame it for drama, and serve it with some horrible multiflavored rice in hollowed-out fruit and what have you got? A well-cooked duck with an ugly sauce that tastes too sweet and thick and makes you want to scrape off the glop to eat the plain duck. [The stuffed eggplant was prepared by emptying] a shaker full (more or less) of paprika on top of it. [One sauce created] trout à la green plague [while another should have been called] yellow death on duck."

'Tain't Creole, 'tain't Cajun, 'tain't French, 'tain't country American, 'tain't good.

Mashburn sued, claiming that the newspaper had committed libel, damaging his reputation and hurting his business.[1] Trout à la green plague will be the first course on our menu of tort law. Mashburn learned, as you will, why filing such a lawsuit is easier than winning it.

[1]*Mashburn v. Collin*, 355 So.2d 879 (La. 1977).

tort = a wrong

The odd word "tort" is borrowed from the French, meaning "wrong." And that is what it means in law: a wrong. More precisely, a **tort** is a violation of a duty imposed by the civil law. When a person breaks one of those duties and injures another, it is a tort. The injury could be to a person or her property. Libel, which the restaurant owner in the opening scenario alleged, is one example of a tort. A surgeon who removes the wrong kidney from a patient commits a different kind of tort, called negligence. A business executive who deliberately steals a client away from a competitor, interfering with a valid contract, commits a tort called interference with a contract. A con artist who tricks you out of your money with a phony offer to sell you a boat commits fraud, yet another tort.

Tort
A violation of a duty imposed by the civil law.

Because tort law is so broad, it takes a while—and two chapters—to understand its boundaries. To start with, we must distinguish torts from two other areas of law: criminal law and contract law.

It is a *crime* to steal a car, to embezzle money from a bank, to sell cocaine. As discussed in Chapter 1, society considers such behavior so threatening that the government itself will prosecute the wrongdoer, whether or not the car owner or bank president wants the case to go forward. A district attorney, who is paid by the government, will bring the case to court, seeking to send the defendant to prison, fine him, or both. If there is a fine, the money goes to the state, not to the victim.

In a tort case, it is up to the injured party to seek compensation. She must hire her own lawyer, who will file a lawsuit. Her lawyer must convince the court that the defendant breached some legal duty and ought to pay money damages to the plaintiff. The plaintiff has no power to send the defendant to jail. Bear in mind that a defendant's action might be both a crime and a tort. A man who punches you in the face for no reason commits the tort of battery. You may file a civil suit against him and will collect money damages if you can prove your case. He has also committed a crime, and the state may prosecute, seeking to imprison and fine him.

Differences between Contract, Tort, and Criminal Law

Type of Obligation	Contract	Tort	Criminal Law
How the obligation is created	The parties agree on a contract, which creates duties for both.	The civil law imposes duties of conduct on all persons.	The criminal law prohibits certain conduct.
How the obligation is enforced	Suit by plaintiff.	Suit by plaintiff.	Prosecution by government.
Possible result	Money damages for plaintiff.	Money damages for plaintiff.	Punishment for defendant, including prison and/or fine.
Example	Raul contracts to sell Deirdre 5,000 pairs of sneakers at $50 per pair, but fails to deliver them. Deirdre buys the sneakers elsewhere for $60 per pair and receives $50,000, her extra expense.	A newspaper falsely accuses a private citizen of being an alcoholic. The plaintiff sues and wins money damages to compensate for her injured reputation.	Leo steals Kelly's car. The government prosecutes Leo for grand theft, and the judge sentences him to two years in prison. Kelly gets nothing.

A tort is also different from a contract dispute. A contract case is based on an agreement two people have already made. For example, Deirdre claims that Raul promised to sell her 10,000 pairs of sneakers at a good price but has failed to deliver them. She files a contract lawsuit. In a tort case, there is usually no "deal" between the parties. Don Mashburn had never met the restaurant critic who attacked his restaurant and obviously had never made any kind of contract. The plaintiff in a tort case claims that the law itself creates a duty that the defendant has breached.

Intentional torts
Harm caused by a deliberate action.

Tort law is divided into categories. In this chapter, we consider **intentional torts**, that is, harm caused by a deliberate action. The newspaper columnist who wrongly accuses someone of being a drunk has committed the intentional tort of libel. In the next chapter, we examine negligence and strict liability, which involve injuries and losses caused by neglect and oversight rather than by deliberate conduct.

A final introductory point: when we speak of intentional torts, we do not necessarily mean that the defendant intended to harm the plaintiff. If the defendant does something deliberately and it ends up injuring somebody, she is probably liable even if she meant no harm. For example, intentionally throwing a snowball at a friend is a deliberate act. If the snowball permanently damages his eye, the *harm* is unintended, but the defendant is liable for the intentional tort of battery because the *act* was intentional.

We look first at the most common intentional torts and then at the most important intentional torts that are related to business.

Intentional Torts

Defamation

written = libel
oral = slander

The First Amendment guarantees the right to free speech, a vital freedom that enables us to protect other rights. But that freedom is not absolute.

The law of defamation concerns false statements that harm someone's reputation. Defamatory statements can be written or spoken. Written defamation is called **libel**. Suppose a newspaper accuses a local retail store of programming its cash registers to overcharge customers when the store has never done so. That is libel. Oral defamation is **slander**. If Professor Wisdom, in class, refers to Sally Student as a drug dealer when she has never sold drugs, he has slandered her.

There are four elements to a defamation case. An element is something that a plaintiff must prove to win a lawsuit. The plaintiff in any kind of lawsuit must prove *all* of the elements to prevail. The elements in a defamation case are

- **Defamatory statement.** This is a statement likely to harm another person's reputation. Professor Wisdom's accusation will clearly harm Sally's reputation.
- **Falseness.** The statement must be false. If Sally Student actually sold marijuana to a classmate, then Professor Wisdom has a defense to slander.
- **Communicated.** The statement must be communicated to at least one person *other than the plaintiff.* If Wisdom speaks privately to Sally and accuses her of dealing drugs, there is no slander.
- **Injury.** In many slander cases, the plaintiff generally must show some injury. Sally's injury would be lower reputation in the school, embarrassment, and humiliation. But in slander cases that involve false statements about sexual behavior, crimes, contagious diseases, and professional abilities, the law is willing to assume injury without requiring the plaintiff to prove it. Lies in these four categories amount to **slander per se**.

Libel cases are treated like cases of slander per se, and courts award damages without proof of injury.[2]

Opinion

Thus far, what we have seen is uncontroversial. If a television commentator refers to Frank Landlord as a "vicious slumlord who rents uninhabitable units," and Frank actually maintains his buildings perfectly, Frank will be compensated for the harm. But what if the television commentator states a harsh *opinion* about Frank? Remember that the plaintiff must demonstrate a "false" statement. Opinions generally cannot be proven true or false, and so they do not usually amount to defamation.

Suppose that the television commentator says, "Frank Landlord certainly does less than many rich people do for our community." Is that defamation? Probably not. Who are the "rich people"? How much do they do? How do we define "does less"? These vague assertions indicate the statement is one of opinion. Even if Frank works hard feeding homeless families, he will probably lose a defamation case.

A related defense involves cases where a supposed statement of fact clearly should not be taken literally. Mr. Mashburn, who opened the chapter suing over his restaurant review, lost his case. The court held that a reasonable reader would have understood the statements to be opinion only. "A shaker full of paprika" and "yellow death on duck" were not to be taken literally but were merely the author's expression of his personal dislike.

Public Personalities

The rules of the game change for those who play in the open. Government officials and other types of public figures such as actors and athletes receive less protection from defamation. In the landmark case *New York Times Co. v. Sullivan,*[3] the Supreme Court ruled that the free exchange of information is vital in a democracy and is protected by the First Amendment to the Constitution.

The rule from the *New York Times* case is that a public official or public figure can win a defamation case only by proving **actual malice** by the defendant. Actual malice means that the defendant knew the statement was false or acted with reckless disregard of the truth. If the plaintiff merely shows that the defendant newspaper printed incorrect statements, even

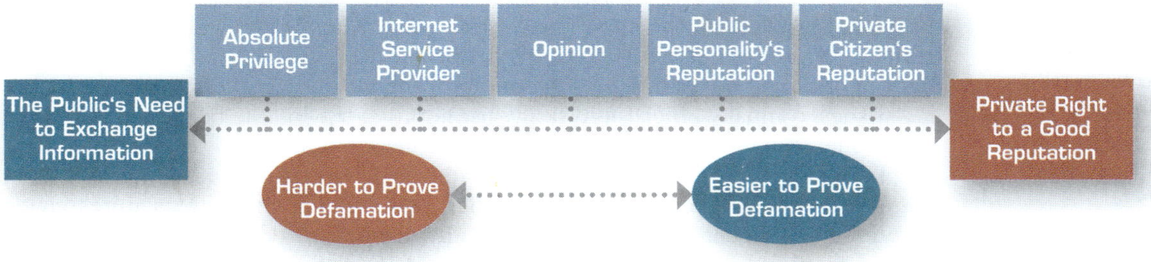

EXHIBIT 6.1 Defamation cases show a tension between the public's need for information and a citizen's right to protect his reputation.

---

[2]When defamation by radio and television became possible, the courts chose to consider it libel, analogizing it to newspapers because of the vast audience. This means that in broadcasting cases, a plaintiff generally does not have to prove damages.

[3]376 U.S. 254, 84 S.Ct. 710, 1964 U.S. LEXIS 1655 (1964).

very damaging ones, that will not suffice to win the suit. In the *New York Times* case, the police chief of Birmingham, Alabama, claimed that the *Times* falsely accused him of racial violence in his job. He lost because he could not prove that the *Times* had acted with actual malice. If he had shown that the *Times* knew the accusation was false, he would have won.

Online Defamation

Kenneth Zeran awoke one day to learn he had become notorious. An unidentified person had posted a message on an AOL bulletin board advertising "Naughty Oklahoma T-Shirts." The shirts featured deeply offensive slogans relating to the 1995 bombing of a federal building in Oklahoma City, in which hundreds of innocent people died. Those interested in purchasing such a t-shirt were instructed to call "Ken" at Zeran's home telephone number. In fact, Zeran had nothing to do with the posting or the t-shirts. He was quickly inundated with phone messages from furious callers, some of whom made death threats.

Zeran could not conveniently change his number because he ran his business from his home. A radio talk show host in Oklahoma City angrily urged its listeners to call Zeran, which they did. Before long, Zeran was receiving an abusive call every two minutes. He sued AOL for defamation—and lost.

The court held that AOL was immune from a defamation suit based on a third-party posting, based on the Communications Decency Act (CDA). Section 230 of the CDA creates this immunity for any Internet service provider, the court declared, adding:

> It would be impossible for service providers to screen each of their millions of postings for possible problems. Faced with potential liability for each message republished by their services, interactive computer service providers might choose to severely restrict the number and type of messages posted. Congress considered the weight of the speech interests implicated and chose to immunize service providers to avoid any such restrictive effect.[4]

Privilege

Absolute privilege
A witness testifying in a court or legislature may never be sued for defamation.

Defendants receive additional protection from defamation cases when it is important for them to speak freely. **Absolute privilege** exists in courtrooms and legislative hearings. Anyone speaking there, such as a witness in court, can say anything at all and never be sued for defamation. (Deliberately false testimony would be *perjury*, but still not *slander*.)

False Imprisonment

False imprisonment
Is the intentional restraint of another person without reasonable cause and without consent.

False imprisonment is the intentional restraint of another person without reasonable cause and without consent. Suppose that a bank teller becomes seriously ill and wants to go to the doctor, but the bank will not permit her to leave until she makes a final tally of her accounts. Against her wishes, company officials physically bar her from leaving the bank. That is false imprisonment. The restraint was unreasonable because her accounts could have been verified later.[5]

False imprisonment cases most commonly arise in retail stores, which sometimes detain employees or customers for suspected theft. Most states now have statutes governing the detention of suspected shoplifters. **Generally, a store may detain a customer or worker for alleged shoplifting provided there is a reasonable basis for the suspicion and the detention is done reasonably**. To detain a customer in the manager's office for 20 minutes and question him about where he got an item is lawful. To chain that customer to a display counter for three hours and humiliate him in front of other customers is unreasonable and constitutes false imprisonment.

---

[4] *Zeran v. America Online, Inc.*, 129 F.3d 327, 1997 U.S. App. LEXIS 31791 (4th Cir. 1997).
[5] *Kanner v. First National Bank of South Miami*, 287 So.2d 715, 1974 Fla. App. LEXIS 8989 (Fla. Dist. Ct. App. 1974).

Intentional Infliction of Emotional Distress

What should happen when a defendant's conduct hurts a plaintiff emotionally but not physically? Historically, not much did happen. Courts once refused to allow recovery, assuming that if they awarded damages for mere emotional injury, they would be inviting a floodgate of dubious claims. But gradually judges reexamined their thinking and reversed this tendency. Today, most courts allow a plaintiff to recover for emotional injury that a defendant intentionally caused. As we see in the next chapter, some courts will also permit recovery when a defendant's negligent conduct caused the emotional injury.

The **intentional infliction of emotional distress** results from extreme and outrageous conduct that causes serious emotional harm. A credit officer was struggling vainly to locate Sheehan, who owed money on his car. The officer phoned Sheehan's mother, falsely identified herself as a hospital employee, and said she needed to find Sheehan because his children had been in a serious auto accident. The mother provided Sheehan's whereabouts, which enabled the company to seize his car. But Sheehan spent seven hours frantically trying to locate his supposedly injured children, who in fact were fine. The credit company was liable for the intentional infliction of emotional distress.[6]

Intentional infliction of emotional distress
An intentional tort in which the harm results from extreme and outrageous conduct that causes serious emotional harm.

By contrast, a muffler shop, trying to collect a debt from a customer, made six phone calls over three months, using abusive language. The customer testified that this caused her to be upset, to cry, and to have difficulty sleeping. The court ruled that the muffler shop's conduct was neither extreme nor outrageous.[7]

The following case arose in a setting that guarantees controversy—an abortion clinic.

Jane Doe and Nancy Roe v. Lynn Mills

212 Mich. App. 73, 536 N.W.2d 824, 1995 Mich. App. LEXIS 313
Michigan Court of Appeals, 1995

Facts: Late one night, an anti-abortion protestor named Robert Thomas climbed into a dumpster located behind the Women's Advisory Center, an abortion clinic. He found documents indicating that the plaintiffs were soon to have abortions at the clinic. Thomas gave the information to Lynn Mills. The next day, Mills and Sister Lois Mitoraj created signs, using the women's names, indicating that they were about to undergo abortions, and urging them not to "kill their babies."

Doe and Roe (not their real names) sued, claiming intentional infliction of emotional distress (as well as breach of privacy, discussed later in this chapter). The trial court dismissed the lawsuit, ruling that the defendants' conduct was not extreme and outrageous. The plaintiffs appealed.

Issue: ***Have the plaintiffs made a valid claim of intentional infliction of emotional distress?***

Excerpts from the Court's *Per Curiam* Decision: Liability for the intentional infliction of emotional distress has been found only where the conduct complained of has been so outrageous in character, and so extreme in degree, as to go beyond all possible bounds of decency, and to be regarded as atrocious and utterly intolerable in a civilized community. Liability does not extend to mere insults, indignities, threats, annoyances, petty oppressions, or other trivialities. It has been said that the case is generally one in which the recitation of the facts to an average member of the community would arouse his resentment against the actor, and lead him to exclaim, "Outrageous!"

The conduct in this case involved defendants identifying plaintiffs by name and publicizing the fact of their abortions by displaying such information on large signs that were held up for public view. In ruling that defendants'

[6] *Ford Motor Credit Co. v. Sheehan*, 373 So.2d 956, 1979 Fla. App. LEXIS 15416 (Fla. Dist. Ct. App. 1979).
[7] *Midas Muffler Shop v. Ellison*, 133 Ariz. 194, 650 P.2d 496, 1982 Ariz. App. LEXIS 488 (Ariz. Ct. App. 1982).

conduct was not sufficiently extreme and outrageous so as to permit recovery, the trial court was influenced in part by its conclusion that the information disclosed did not concern a private matter, inasmuch as it was obtained from a document that had been discarded into the trash. [But the plaintiffs themselves never placed their names on the discarded papers, and even if they had, such an act would not have indicated consent to such publicity.] The trial court also observed that defendants have a constitutional right to "protest peaceably against abortion." However, the objectionable aspect of defendants' conduct does not relate to their views on abortion or their right to express those views, but, rather, to the fact that defendants gave unreasonable or unnecessary publicity to purely private matters involving plaintiffs. Finally, the trial court observed that there is no statute prohibiting the kind of activity engaged in by defendants. It is not necessary, however, that a defendant's conduct constitute a statutory violation in order for it to be found extreme and outrageous.

We are of the opinion that the trial court erred in granting the defendants' motion for summary disposition of plaintiffs' claim of intentional infliction of emotional distress. Defendants' conduct involved more than mere insults, indignities, threats, annoyances, or petty oppressions. We believe this is the type of case that might cause an average member of the community, upon learning of defendants' conduct, to exclaim, "Outrageous!" Because reasonable men may differ with regard to whether defendants' conduct may be considered sufficiently outrageous and extreme so as to subject them to liability for intentional infliction of emotional distress, this matter should be determined by the trier of fact.

[Summary judgment for the defendants is reversed, and the case is remanded for trial.]

Battery and Assault

Battery
An intentional touching of another person in a way that is harmful or offensive.

Assault and battery are related, but not identical. **Battery** is an intentional touching of another person in a way that is harmful or offensive.

If an irate parent throws a chair at a referee during his daughter's basketball game, breaking the man's jaw, he has committed battery. But a parent who cheerfully slaps the winning coach on the back has not committed battery because a reasonable coach would not be offended.

As mentioned earlier, there need be no intention to hurt the plaintiff. If the defendant intended to do the physical act, and a reasonable plaintiff would be offended by it, battery has occurred. An executive who gives an unwanted sexual caress to a secretary also commits this tort, even if he assumed that any normal female would be ecstatic over his attentions. (This is also sexual harassment, discussed in Chapter 29, on employment law.)

Assault
An act that makes a person reasonably fear an imminent battery.

Assault occurs when a defendant does some act that makes a plaintiff *fear* an imminent battery. This tort is based on apprehension—it does not matter whether a battery ever occurs. Suppose Ms. Wilson shouts "Think fast!" at her husband and hurls a toaster at him. He turns and sees it flying at him. His fear of being struck is enough to win a case of assault, even if the toaster misses. If the toaster happens to strike him, Ms. Wilson has also committed battery.

Recall the shoplifting problem. Assume that a store guard pulls an unloaded pistol on Sandra Shopper, suspecting her of theft. Sandra faints and strikes her head on a counter. When sued for assault, the store defends by claiming the guard never touched her and the gun was unloaded. Obviously, the store did not have the benefit of this law course. A reasonable shopper would have feared imminent battery, and the store is liable for assault.

EXAM Strategy

Question: Mark is furious because his girlfriend, Denise, just told him she is leaving him. He never saw it coming. On the sidewalk, he picks up a rock and hurls it at Denise's head. She *does* see it coming, and she ducks. The rock misses Denise but hits Terrance (who never saw it coming) in the back of his head. Denise and Terrance both sue Mark for assault and for battery. Outcomes?

Strategy: Separate the two plaintiffs. What injury did Denise suffer? She saw a rock flying at her and thought she would be struck. Now recall the elements of the two torts. Battery is an intentional touching that is offensive. Assault is an act that makes another person *fear* an imminent battery.

Result: Was Denise touched? No. Did she fear an imminent battery? Yes. Denise wins a suit for assault but loses one for battery. Now Terrance: Was he touched? Yes. Did he fear an imminent battery? No. Terrance wins a suit for battery but loses one for assault.

Trespass, Conversion, and Fraud

Trespass

Trespass is intentionally entering land that belongs to someone else or remaining on the land after being asked to leave. It is also trespass if you have some object, let's say a car, on someone else's property and refuse to remove it. "Intentionally" means that you deliberately walk onto the land. If you walk through a meadow, believing it to be a public park, and it belongs to a private owner, you have trespassed.

Trespass
Intentionally entering land that belongs to someone else or remaining on the land after being asked to leave.

Conversion

Conversion is taking or using someone's personal property without consent. Personal property is any possession other than land or structures permanently attached to land, such as houses. Priceless jewels, ratty sneakers, and sailboats are all personal property. If Stormy sails away in Jib's sailboat and keeps it all summer, that is conversion. Stormy owes Jib the full value of the boat. This, of course, is similar to the crime of theft. The tort of conversion enables a plaintiff to pursue the case herself, without awaiting a criminal prosecution, and to obtain compensation.

© GSPhotography /Shutterstock.com

When does a trespasser intentionally enter onto another's property?

Fraud

Fraud is injuring another person by deliberate deception. Later in this chapter, a plaintiff claims that for many years a cigarette manufacturer fraudulently suggested its product was safe, knowing its assurances were deadly lies. Fraud is a tort, but it typically occurs during the negotiation or performance of a contract, and it is discussed in detail in Unit 2, on contracts.

Conversion
Taking or using someone's personal property without consent.

Fraud
Injuring another person by deliberate deception.

EXAM Strategy

Question: Raymond, a billionaire businessman widely known in the state, is running for the U.S. Senate. A newspaper reports that Raymond received $150,000 from an organization with "proven links to terrorist groups." The story came from a woman working in Raymond's own campaign, and two other witnesses, all three of whom had proven reliable in the past. Raymond, leading in the polls by 18%, plummets in popularity and loses the election. Raymond sues the paper. Outcome?

Strategy: First, determine the injury that Raymond has suffered. His reputation has been damaged. Second, ask what tort protects reputation. Defamation. Third, apply the elements to these facts.

Result: The newspaper's story, very likely to harm reputation, was widely communicated and did injure Raymond. But we don't know whether the article was true or false. Do we need to know? Usually we do, because a defendant is only liable for false statements. However, notice that a public personality must also prove *actual malice.* Was Raymond a public figure? Yes, he was a prominent billionaire and Senate candidate. There was no actual malice. The paper acted in good faith, using three credible sources. Raymond loses his lawsuit.

DAMAGES

Compensatory Damages

Mitchel Bien, who is deaf and mute, enters the George Grubbs Nissan dealership, where folks sell cars aggressively. Very aggressively. Maturelli, a salesman, and Bien communicate by writing messages back and forth. Maturelli takes Bien's own car keys, and the two then test drive a 300ZX. Bien says he does not want the car, but Maturelli escorts him back inside and fills out a sales sheet. Bien repeatedly asks for his keys, but Maturelli only laughs, pressuring him to buy the new car. Minutes pass. Hours pass. Bien becomes frantic, writing a dozen notes, begging to leave, threatening to call the police. Maturelli mocks Bien and his physical disabilities. Finally, after four hours, the customer escapes.

Bien becomes frantic, writing a dozen notes, begging to leave, threatening to call the police.

Bien sues for the intentional infliction of emotional distress. Two former salesmen from Grubbs testify they have witnessed customers cry, yell, and curse as a result of the aggressive tactics. Doctors state that the incident has traumatized Bien, dramatically reducing his confidence and self-esteem and preventing his return to work even three years later.

The jury awards Bien damages. But how does a jury calculate the money? For that matter, why should a jury even try? Money can never erase pain or undo a permanent injury. The answer is simple: money, however inexact, is often the only thing a court has to give.

A successful plaintiff generally receives **compensatory damages**, meaning an amount of money that the court believes will restore him to the position he was in before the defendant's conduct caused injury. Here is how damages are calculated.

Compensatory damages
Money intended to restore a plaintiff to the position he was in before the injury.

Single recovery principle
Requires a court to settle the matter once and for all, by awarding a lump sum for past and future expenses.

First, a plaintiff receives money for medical expenses that he has proven by producing bills from doctors, hospitals, physical therapists, and psychotherapists. Bien receives all the money he has paid. If a doctor testifies that he needs future treatment, Bien will offer evidence of how much that will cost. The **single recovery principle** requires a court to settle the matter once and for all, by awarding a lump sum for past *and future* expenses, if there will be any. A plaintiff may not return in a year and say, "Oh, by the way, there are some new bills."

Second, the defendants are liable for lost wages. The court takes the number of days or months that Bien missed work and multiplies that times his salary. If Bien is currently unable to work, a doctor estimates how many more months he will miss work, and the court adds that to his damages.

Third, a plaintiff is paid for pain and suffering. Bien testifies about how traumatic the four hours were and how the experience has affected his life. He may state that he now fears shopping, suffers nightmares, and seldom socializes. To bolster the case, a plaintiff uses expert testimony, such as the psychiatrists who testified for Bien. Awards for pain and suffering vary enormously, from a few dollars to many millions, depending on the injury and depending on the jury. In some lawsuits, physical and psychological pain are momentary and insignificant; in other cases, the pain is the biggest part of the verdict. In this case, the jury awarded Bien $573,815, calculated as in the following table.[8]

Past medical	$ 70.00
Future medical	6,000.00
Past rehabilitation	3,205.00
Past lost earning capacity	112,910.00
Future lost earning capacity	34,650.00
Past physical symptoms and discomfort	50,000.00
Future physical symptoms and discomfort	50,000.00
Past emotional injury and mental anguish	101,980.00
Future emotional injury and mental anguish	200,000.00
Past loss of society and reduced ability to socially interact with family, former fiancée, and friends, and hearing (i.e., nondeaf) people in general	10,000.00
Future loss of society and reduced ability to socially interact with family, former fiancee, and friends, and hearing people	5,000.00
TOTAL	**$573,815.00**

[8]The compensatory damages are described in *George Grubbs Enterprises v. Bien*, 881 S.W.2d 843, 1994 Tex. App. LEXIS 1870 (Tex. Ct. App. 1994). In addition to the compensatory damages described, the jury awarded $5 million in punitive damages. The Texas Supreme Court reversed the award of punitive damages, but not the compensatory. *Id.*, 900 S.W.2d 337, 1995 Tex. LEXIS 91 (Tex. 1995). The high court did not dispute the appropriateness of punitive damages, but reversed because the trial court failed to instruct the jury properly as to how it should determine the assets actually under the defendants' control, an issue essential to punitive damages but not compensatory.

Awards for future harm (such as future pain and suffering) involve the court making its best estimate of the plaintiff's hardship in the years to come. This is not an exact science. If the judgment is reasonable, it will rarely be overturned. Ethel Flanzraich, aged 78, fell on stairs that had been badly maintained. In addition to her medical expense, the court awarded her $150,000 for future pain and suffering. The day after the court gave its award, Ms. Flanzraich died of other causes. Did that mean her family must forfeit that money? No. The award was reasonable when made and had to be paid.[9]

Punitive Damages

Punitive damages
Damages that are intended to punish the defendant for conduct that is extreme and outrageous.

Here we look at a different kind of award, one that is more controversial and potentially more powerful: punitive damages. The purpose is not to compensate the plaintiff for harm, because compensatory damages will have done that. **Punitive damages** are intended to punish the defendant for conduct that is extreme and outrageous. Courts award these damages in relatively few cases. The idea behind punitive damages is that certain behavior is so unacceptable that society must make an example of it. A large award of money should deter the defendant from repeating the mistake and others from ever making it. Some believe punitive damages represent the law at its most avaricious, while others attribute to them great social benefit.

Although a jury has wide discretion in awarding punitive damages, the Supreme Court has ruled that a verdict must be reasonable. Ira Gore purchased a new BMW automobile from an Alabama dealer and then discovered that the car had been repainted. He sued. At trial, BMW acknowledged a nationwide policy of not informing customers of predelivery repairs when the cost was less than 3% of the retail price. The company had sold about 1,000 repainted cars nationwide. The jury concluded that BMW had engaged in gross, malicious fraud and awarded Gore $4,000 in compensatory damages and $4 million in punitive damages. The Alabama Supreme Court reduced the award to $2 million, but the United States Supreme Court ruled that even that amount was grossly excessive. The Court held that in awarding punitive damages, a court must consider three "guideposts":

- The reprehensibility of the defendant's conduct;
- The ratio between the harm suffered and the award; and
- The difference between the punitive award and any civil penalties used in similar cases.

The Court concluded that BMW had shown no evil intent and that Gore's harm had been purely economic (as opposed to physical). Further, the Court found the ratio of 500 to 1, between punitive and compensatory damages, to be excessive, although it offered no definitive rule about a proper ratio. On remand, the Alabama Supreme Court reduced the punitive damages award to $50,000.[10]

The U.S. Supreme Court gave additional guidance on punitive damages in the following landmark case.

---

[9]We looked at discovery issues from this case in Chapter 3. *Stinton v. Robin's Wood,* 45 A.D.3d 203, 842 N.Y.S.2d 477 (N.Y.App.Div., 2007).

[10]*BMW of North America, Inc. v. Gore,* 517 U.S. 559, 116 S.Ct. 1589, 1996 U.S. LEXIS 3390 (1996).

Landmark Case

State Farm v. Campbell

538 U.S. 408
Supreme Court of the United States (2003)

Facts: While attempting to pass several cars on a two-lane road, Campbell drove into oncoming traffic. An innocent driver swerved to avoid Campbell and died in a collision with a third driver. The family of the deceased driver and the surviving third driver both sued Campbell.

As Campbell's insurer, State Farm represented him in the lawsuit. It turned down an offer to settle the case for $50,000, the limit of Campbell's policy. The company had nothing to gain by settling because even if Campbell lost big at trial, State Farm's liability was capped at $50,000.

A jury returned a judgment against Campbell for $185,000. He was responsible for the $135,000 that exceeded his policy limit. He argued with State Farm, claiming that it should have settled the case. Eventually, State Farm paid the entire $185,000, but Campbell still sued the company, alleging fraud and intentional infliction of emotional distress.

His lawyers presented evidence that State Farm had deliberately acted in its own best interests rather than his. The jury was convinced, and in the end, Campbell won an award of $1 million in compensatory damages and $145 million in punitive damages. State Farm appealed.

Issue: ***What is the limit on punitive damages?***

Excerpts from Justice Kennedy's Opinion: We address whether an award of $145 million in punitive damages, where full compensatory damages are $1 million, is excessive and in violation of the Due Process Clause. The Utah Supreme Court relied upon testimony indicating that State Farm's actions, because of their clandestine nature, will be punished at most in 1 out of every 50,000 cases as a matter of statistical probability, and concluded that the ratio between punitive and compensatory damages was not unwarranted.

Compensatory damages are intended to redress the concrete loss that the plaintiff has suffered by reason of the defendant's wrongful conduct. By contrast, punitive damages serve a broader function; they are aimed at deterrence and retribution.

The Due Process Clause prohibits the imposition of grossly excessive or arbitrary punishments. The reason is that elementary notions of fairness dictate that a person receive fair notice not only of the conduct that will subject him to punishment, but also of the severity of the penalty that a State may impose. To the extent an award is grossly excessive, it furthers no legitimate purpose and constitutes an arbitrary deprivation of property. A defendant should be punished for the conduct that harmed the plaintiff, not for being an unsavory.

We decline to impose a bright-line ratio which a punitive damages award cannot exceed. Our jurisprudence and the principles it has now established demonstrate, however, that, in practice, few awards exceeding a single-digit ratio between punitive and compensatory damages, to a significant degree, will satisfy due process. Single-digit multipliers are more likely to comport with due process, while still achieving the State's goals of deterrence and retribution, than awards with ratios in the range of 145 to 1.

Nonetheless, because there are no rigid benchmarks that a punitive damages award may not surpass, ratios greater than those we have previously upheld may comport with due process where a particularly egregious act has resulted in only a small amount of economic damages. The precise award in any case must be based upon the facts and circumstances of the defendant's conduct and the harm to the plaintiff.

In sum, courts must ensure that the measure of punishment is both reasonable and proportionate to the amount of harm to the plaintiff and to the general damages recovered. In the context of this case, we have no doubt that there is a presumption against an award that has a 145-to-1 ratio. The compensatory award in this case was substantial; the Campbells were awarded $ 1 million for a year and a half of emotional distress. This was complete compensation. The harm arose from a transaction in the economic realm, not from some physical assault or trauma; there were no physical injuries; and State Farm paid the excess verdict before the complaint was filed, so the Campbells suffered only minor economic injuries.

The judgment of the Utah Supreme Court is reversed, and the case is remanded for proceedings not inconsistent with this opinion.

Dramatic cases may *still* lead to very large awards.

And so, the Supreme Court seeks to limit, but not completely prohibit, enormous punitive damages. A California Court of Appeals decided the following case two years after *State Farm v. Campbell.* How should it implement the Supreme Court's guidelines? You be the judge.

You be the Judge

Boeken v. Philip Morris, Incorporated

127 Cal. App.4th 1640, 26 CalRptr.3d 638
California Court of Appeals, 2005

Facts: In the mid-1950s, Richard Boeken began smoking Marlboro cigarettes at the age of 10. Countless advertisements, targeted at boys aged 10 to 18, convinced him and his friends that the "Marlboro man" was powerful, healthy, and manly. Eventually Richard changed to "Marlboro Lite" cigarettes but continued smoking into the 1990s, when he was diagnosed with lung cancer. He filed suit against Philip Morris, the cigarette manufacturer, for fraud and other torts. He died of cancer before the case was concluded.

Evidence at trial demonstrated that by the mid-1950s, scientists uniformly accepted that cigarette smoking caused lung cancer. However, at about the same time, Philip Morris and other tobacco companies began a decades-long campaign to convince the public that there was substantial doubt about any link between smoking and illness. The plaintiffs also demonstrated that tobacco was physically addictive, and that Philip Morris added ingredients such as urea to its cigarettes to increase their addictive power. Boeken testified that in the late 1960s he saw the Surgeon General warnings about the risk of smoking but trusted the cigarette company's statements that smoking was safe. By the 1970s he tried many times, and many cures, to stop smoking but always failed. He finally quit just before surgery to remove part of his lung but resumed after the operation.

The jury found Philip Morris liable for fraudulently concealing that cigarettes were addictive and carcinogenic. It awarded Boeken $5.5 million in compensatory damages, and also assessed punitive damages—of $3 *billion.* The trial judge reduced the punitive award to $100 million. Philip Morris appealed.

You Be the Judge: ***Was the punitive damage award too high, too low, or just right?***

Argument for Philip Morris: The court should substantially reduce the $100 million punitive award because it constitutes an "arbitrary deprivation of property." The Supreme Court has indicated that punitive awards should not exceed compensatory damages by more than a factor of nine. The jury awarded Mr. Boeken $5.5 million in compensatory damages, which means that punitive damages should absolutely not exceed $49.5 million. We argue that they should be even lower.

Cigarettes are a legal product, and our packages have displayed the Surgeon General's health warnings for decades. Mr. Boeken's death is tragic, but his cancer was not necessarily caused by Marlboro cigarettes. And even if cigarettes did contribute to his failing health, Mr. Boeken chose to smoke throughout his life, even after major surgery on one of his lungs.

Argument for Boeken: The Supreme Court says that "few" cases may exceed the 9-to-1 ratio, but that "the precise award in any case must be based upon the facts and circumstances of the defendant's conduct and the harm to the plaintiff." Phillip Morris created ads that targeted children, challenged clear scientific data that its products caused cancer, and added substances to its cigarettes to make them more addictive. Does it get worse than that?

As for harm to the plaintiff, he died a terrible death from cancer. Philip Morris cigarettes kill 200,000 American customers each year. The defendant's conduct could not be more reprehensible. Philip Morris's weekly profit is roughly $100 million. At a minimum, the court should keep the punitive award at that figure. But we ask that the court reinstate the jury's original $3 billion award.

Tort Reform and The Exxon Valdez

Some people believe that jury awards are excessive and need statutory reform, while others argue that the evidence demonstrates excessive awards are rare and modest in size. About one-half of the states have passed limits. The laws vary, but many distinguish between **economic damage** and **non-economic damages**. In such a state, a jury is permitted to award any amount for economic damages, meaning lost wages, medical expenses, and other measureable losses. However, noneconomic damages—pain and suffering and other losses that are difficult to measure—are capped at some level, such as $500,000. In some states, punitive awards have similar caps. These restrictions can drastically lower the total verdict.

In the famous *Exxon Valdez* case, the Supreme Court placed a severe limit on a certain type of punitive award. It is unclear how influential the decision will be because the case arises in the isolated area of maritime law, which governs ships at sea. Nonetheless, the justices wrote at length about punitive awards, and the decision may reverberate in future holdings. This is what happened.

Captain Joseph Hazelwood's negligence caused the *Exxon Valdez* to run aground off the coast of Alaska. The ship dumped 11 million gallons of oil into the sea, damaging 3,000 square miles of vulnerable ecosystem. The oil spill forced fishermen into bankruptcy, disrupted entire communities, and killed hundreds of thousands of birds and marine animals. A decade later, many of the damaged species had not recovered. The jury decided that Exxon had been reckless by allowing Hazelwood to pilot the ship when the company knew he was an alcoholic. The jury awarded compensatory damages to the plaintiffs, and punitive damages of $5 *billion*. Exxon appealed.

Almost two decades after the accident, the Supreme Court ruled. The justices discussed punitive damages in general, noting that much of the criticism of punitive awards appeared overstated. The court declared there had been no major increase in how frequently juries gave punitive damages. In the unusual cases where jurors made such awards, the sums were modest. The problem, declared the justices, was the unpredictability of punitive damages.

The court ruled that *in maritime cases*, the ratio should be no higher than 1:1. The court approved the jury's compensatory award of $507 million, and then reduced the punitive award from $5 billion to $507 million. Supporters of the court's decision stated that it would allow businesses to make plans based on predictable outcomes. Opponents said that the justices ignored the jury's finding of reckless behavior and calamitous environmental harm.[11]

EXAM Strategy

Question: Patrick owns a fast food restaurant which is repeatedly painted with graffiti. He is convinced that 15-year-old John, a frequent customer, is the culprit. The next time John comes to the restaurant, Patrick locks the men's room door while John is inside. Patrick calls the police, but because of a misunderstanding, the police are very slow to arrive. John shouts and cries for help, banging on the door, but Patrick does not release him for two hours. John sues. He claims that he has suffered great psychological harm because of the incident; his psychiatrist asserts that John may have unpredictable suffering in the future. John sues for assault, battery, and false imprisonment. Will he win? May John return to court in the future to seek further damages?

[11] *Exxon Shipping Co. v. Baker*, 128 S.Ct. 2605 (2008).

Strategy: The question focuses on two issues: First, the distinction between several intentional torts; second, damages. Analyze one issue at a time. As to the intentional torts, what injury has John suffered? He was locked in the men's room and suffered psychological harm. Recall the elements of the three possible torts. Battery concerns an offensive touching. A defendant commits assault by causing an imminent fear of battery. False imprisonment: a store may detain someone if it does so reasonably.

As to damages, review the *single recovery principle.*

© Sean Gladwell/Shutterstock

Is it reasonable for the owner of this property to detain the suspected vandal?

Result: Locking John up for two hours, based on an unproven suspicion, was clearly unreasonable. Patrick has committed false imprisonment. The single recovery principle forces John to recover now for all past and future harm. He may not return to court later and seek additional damages.

Business Torts

In this section, we look at several intentional torts that occur almost exclusively in a commercial setting: interference with a contract, interference with a prospective advantage, the rights to privacy and publicity, and Lanham Act violations. Note that several business torts are discussed elsewhere in the book:

- Patents, copyrights, and trademarks are discussed in Chapter 42, on intellectual property.
- False advertising, discussed in part under the Lanham Act section (later in this chapter), is considered more broadly in Chapter 39, on consumer law.
- Consumer issues are also covered in Chapter 39. The material in the present chapter focuses not on consumer claims but on disputes between businesses.

Tortious Interference with Business Relations

Competition is the essence of business. Successful corporations compete aggressively, and the law permits and expects them to. But there are times when healthy competition becomes illegal interference. This is called tortious interference with business relations. It can take one of two closely related forms—interference with a contract or interference with a prospective advantage.

Tortious Interference with a Contract

Tortious interference with a contract exists if the plaintiff can establish the following four elements:

- There was a contract between the plaintiff and a third party;
- The defendant knew of the contract;
- The defendant improperly *induced* the third party to breach the contract or made performance of the contract impossible; and
- There was injury to the plaintiff.

Tortious interference with a contract
An intentional tort in which the defendant improperly induced a third party to breach a contract with the plaintiff.

Because businesses routinely compete for customers, employees, and market share, it is not always easy to identify tortious interference. There is nothing wrong with two companies bidding against each other to buy a parcel of land, and nothing wrong with one corporation doing everything possible to convince the seller to ignore all competitors. But once a company has signed a contract to buy the land, it is improper to induce the seller to break the deal. The most commonly disputed issues in these cases concern elements one and three: was there a contract between the plaintiff and another party? Did the defendant improperly induce a party to breach it? Defendants will try to show that the plaintiff had no contract.

A defendant may also rely on the defense of **justification**, that is, a claim that special circumstances made its conduct fair. To establish justification, a defendant must show that:

- It was acting to protect an existing economic interest, such as its own contract with the third party;
- It was acting in the public interest, for example, by reporting to a government agency that a corporation was overbilling for government services; or
- The existing contract could be terminated at will by either party, meaning that although the plaintiff had a contract, the plaintiff had no long-term assurances because the other side could end it at any time.

Texaco v. Pennzoil

The jury returned an enormous verdict in a famous case of contract interference. *Texaco, Inc. v. Pennzoil Co.* illustrates the two key issues: did a contract exist, and was the defendant's behavior improper? Pennzoil made an unsolicited bid to buy 20 percent of Getty Oil at $100 per share. This offer was too low to satisfy the Getty board of directors, but it got the parties talking. The price increased to $110 per share, and the two sides began to put together pieces of a complicated deal: Gordon Getty would control four-sevenths of the Getty Oil stock, and Pennzoil would control three-sevenths. The J. Paul Getty Museum, which owned 11.8 percent of Getty stock, agreed to sell its shares provided it was paid immediately. Talks continued, the price moved up to $112.50 a share, and finally

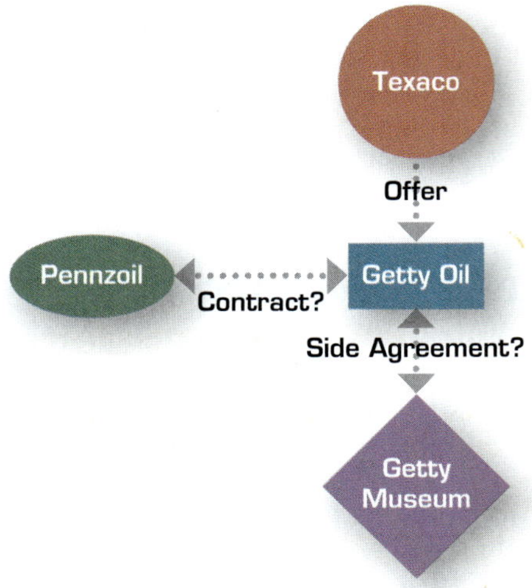

EXHIBIT 6.2 The $10 *billion* question. Texaco offered to pay $125 per share for Getty stock. The key issue was this: when Texaco made the offer, did a contract exist between Pennzoil and Getty? If, as the jury decided, there was a binding agreement, then Texaco committed tortious interference with a contract. If, however, Getty Corp. had a side agreement with the Getty Museum (one of its owners), then arguably there could be no contract between Getty and Pennzoil, and Texaco would have committed no tort at all.

the Getty board voted to approve the deal. A press release announced an agreement in principle between Pennzoil and Getty.

Before the lawyers for both sides could complete the paperwork for the deal, Texaco appeared and offered Getty stockholders $125 per share for the entire company and later upped that offer to $128. Getty turned its attention to Texaco, leaving Pennzoil the jilted lover. This lover, though, decided to sue. In Texas state court, Pennzoil claimed that Texaco had maliciously interfered with a Pennzoil–Getty contract, costing Pennzoil vast amounts of money.

Texaco argued that it had acted in good faith, asserting that there was no binding contract between the other two. But the jury bought Pennzoil's argument, and they bought it big: $7.53 billion in actual damages, plus $3 billion more in punitive damages. Texaco did not happen to have $10 billion it could spare, and the verdict threatened to destroy the oil company. Texaco appealed, but Texas appeals courts require a bond, in this case a $10 billion bond, meaning that the money must be paid into court while the appeal goes forward. Texaco filed for bankruptcy.

At the state supreme court, Texaco based its argument on an obscure rule of the Securities and Exchange Commission (SEC), Rule 10B-13. This rule prevents the parties in a takeover negotiation from arranging a "side deal" while an offer is pending. Texaco's argument thus became: Pennzoil's original $100 per share offer was still pending when the two sides came up with their $112.50 per share, "three-sevenths/four-sevenths" deal. That deal involved a side arrangement with the Getty Museum, which would get its money faster than any other shareholders would. Because it would get about $1 billion, early receipt was a major financial advantage. The deal violated Rule 10B-13 and was therefore invalid. There was no contract, and Texaco could not legally have interfered.

A $10 billion case would be decided on the classic "interference" issue of whether a contract existed. Then the SEC entered the case, filing a brief that appeared strongly to support Texaco's interpretation of the law. Pennzoil could sense that the tide was turning, and the companies settled: Texaco agreed to pay Pennzoil $3 billion as settlement for having wrongfully interfered with Pennzoil's agreement to buy Getty.

Tortious Interference with a Prospective Advantage (no need of contract)

Tortious interference with a prospective advantage
Malicious interference with a developing economic relationship.

Interference with a prospective advantage is an awkward name for a tort that is simply a variation on interference with a contract. The difference is that, for this tort, there need be no contract; the plaintiff is claiming outside interference with an expected economic relationship. Obviously, the plaintiff must show more than just the hope of a profit. **A plaintiff who has a definite and reasonable expectation of obtaining an economic advantage may sue a corporation that maliciously interferes and prevents the relationship from developing.**

The defense of justification, discussed above, applies here as well. A typical example of justification is that the defendant is simply competing for the same business that the plaintiff seeks. There is nothing wrong with that.

To demonstrate interference with a prospective advantage, most courts require a plaintiff to show that the defendant's conduct was independently unlawful. Suppose Pink manufactures valves used in heart surgery. Pink is about to sign a deal for Rabbit to distribute the products. Zebra then says to Pink, "I want that deal. If you sign with Rabbit, I'll spread false rumors that the valves are unreliable." Pink gives in and signs a contract with Zebra. Zebra has committed interference with a prospective advantage because slander is independently illegal.[12]

The ice cream fight that follows demonstrates why plaintiffs often file but seldom win these cases.

CARVEL V. NOONAN

3 N.Y.3d 182, 785 N.Y.S.2d 359, 818 N.E.2d 1100
New York Court of Appeals, 2004

Facts: For decades, Carvel sold its ice cream only through franchised stores. However, a decline in revenues caused the company to begin selling its product in supermarkets. That effort expanded quickly, but many of the franchised stores (franchisees) went out of business. Franchisees filed suit, claiming tortious interference with a prospective advantage. In particular, the plaintiffs argued that Carvel undersold them in supermarkets and issued coupons only redeemable there. The case reached New York's highest court.

Issue: ***Had Carvel committed tortious interference with a prospective advantage?***

Excerpts from Justice Smith's Decision: The franchisees' tort claim is that Carvel unlawfully interfered with the relationships between the franchisees and their customers. The franchisees do not claim that the customers had binding contracts that Carvel induced them to breach; they allege only that, by implementing its supermarket program, Carvel induced the customers not to buy Carvel products from the franchisees. The juries have found that Carvel did so induce customers, and the question for us is whether that inducement was tortious interference under New York law.

We have recognized that inducing breach of a binding agreement and interfering with a nonbinding "economic relation" can both be torts, but that the elements of the two torts are not the same. Where there has been no breach of an existing contract, but only interference with prospective contract rights, however, plaintiff must show

---

[12]For a more detailed explanation, see *Wal-Mart Stores, Inc. v. Sturges*, 52 S.W.3d 711, 2001 Tex. LEXIS 18 (Tex. 2001).

more culpable conduct on the part of the defendant. The implication is that, as a general rule, the defendant's conduct must amount to a crime or an independent tort.

The franchisees claim that Carvel did use wrongful "economic pressure" but that argument is ill-founded for two independent reasons. First, it is ill-founded because the economic pressure that must be shown is not, as the franchisees assume, pressure on the franchisees, but on the franchisees' customers. Conduct constituting tortious interference with business relations is, by definition, conduct directed not at the plaintiff itself, but at the party with which the plaintiff has or seeks to have a relationship.

Here, all Carvel did to the franchisees' customers was to make Carvel goods available in supermarkets at attractive prices; this was not "pressure" on these third parties but legitimate "persuasion," and thus tortious interference with economic relations was not established.

The franchisees' argument is also ill-founded because the Carvel activities they complain of do not amount to the sort of extreme and unfair "economic pressure" that might be "wrongful." The crux of the franchisees' complaint is that Carvel distributed its products through competitive channels, to an extent and in a way that was inconsistent with the franchisor-franchisee relationship. But the relationship between franchisors and franchisees is a complex one; while cooperative, it does not preclude all competition; and the extent to which competition is allowed should be determined by the contracts between the parties, not by courts or juries seeking after the fact to devise a code of conduct.

Apart from attacking the supermarket program in general as excessively and destructively competitive, the franchisees also attack the coupon-redemption element of that program as excessive "economic pressure." The essence of the coupon program was to give customers who used coupons a better price when they shopped in supermarkets. The mere institution of a coupon program was not "economic pressure" rising to the level of "wrongful" or "culpable" conduct.

[Carvel's conduct was not tortious interference with a prospective advantage.]

Privacy and Publicity

We live in a world of dazzling technology, and it is easier than ever—and more profitable—to spy on someone. Does the law protect us? What power do we have to limit the intrusion of others into our lives and to prohibit them from commercially exploiting information about us?

Intrusion

Intrusion
A tort in which a reasonable person would find the invasion of her private life offensive.

Intrusion into someone's private life is a tort if a reasonable person would find it offensive. Peeping through someone's windows or wiretapping his telephone are obvious examples of intrusion. In a famous case involving a "paparazzo" photographer and Jacqueline Kennedy Onassis, the court found that the photographer had invaded her privacy by making a career out of photographing her. He had bribed doormen to gain access to hotels and restaurants she visited, had jumped out of bushes to photograph her young children, and had driven power boats dangerously close to her. The court ordered him to stop.[13] Nine years later the paparazzo was found in contempt of court for again taking photographs too close to Ms. Onassis. He agreed to stop once and for all—in exchange for a suspended contempt sentence.

Commercial Exploitation

The right to commercial exploitation prohibits the use of someone's likeness or voice for commercial purposes without permission. This business tort is the flip side of privacy and covers the right to make money from publicity. For example, it would be illegal to run a

[13] *Galella v. Onassis*, 487 F.2d 986, 1973 U.S. App. LEXIS 7901 (2d Cir. 1973).

magazine ad showing Keira Knightley holding a can of soda without her permission. The ad would imply that she endorses the product. Someone's identity is her own, and it cannot be used for commercial gain unless she permits it.

Ford Motor Co. hired a singer to imitate Bette Midler's version of a popular song. The imitation was so good that most listeners were fooled into believing that Ms. Midler was endorsing the product. That, ruled a court, violated her right to commercial exploitation.[14]

The Lanham Act

The Lanham Act provides broad protection against false statements intended to hurt another business. In order to win a case, a plaintiff must prove three things:

- That the defendants made false or misleading fact statements about the plaintiff's business. This could be a false comparative ad, showing the plaintiff's product to be worse than it is, or it could be a misleading ad, which, though literally accurate, is misleading about the defendant's own product.
- That the defendants used the statements in commercial advertising or promotion. In order to protect First Amendment rights of free speech, particularly political and social commentary, this act covers only commercial speech. A radio ad for beer could violate the Lanham Act; but a radio ad urging that smoking be abolished in public places is not a commercial statement and cannot violate the act.
- That statements created the likelihood of harm to the plaintiff.[15]

"Knock It Off brand food supplement will help you lose weight and gain muscle faster than any competing supplement," shrieks the television commercial, offering an independent study as proof. However, a competitor sues, and demonstrates that during the study, users of Knock It Off received free health club memberships and low-fat gourmet meals, distorting the results. Knock It Off has violated the Lanham Act. The court will order the company to knock it off and stop showing the commercial, and also to pay damages to the injured competitor.

Chapter Conclusion

This chapter has been a potpourri of misdeeds, a bubbling cauldron of conduct best avoided. Although tortious acts and their consequences are diverse, two generalities apply. First, the boundaries of intentional torts are imprecise, the outcome of a particular case depending to a considerable extent upon the factfinder who analyzes it. Second, the thoughtful executive and the careful citizen, aware of the shifting standards and potentially vast liability, will strive to ensure that his or her conduct never provides that factfinder an opportunity to give judgment.

[14] 18 U.S.C. § 2701.

[15] 18 U.S.C. § 2511.

Exam Review

1. **TORT** A tort is a violation of a duty imposed by the civil law. (pp. 131–132)

EXAM Strategy

Question: Keith is driving while intoxicated. He swerves into the wrong lane and causes an accident, seriously injuring Caroline. Which statement is true?

a. Caroline could sue Keith, who might be found guilty in her suit.

b. Caroline and the state could start separate criminal cases against Keith.

c. Caroline could sue Keith, and the state could prosecute Keith for drunk driving.

d. The state could sue Keith but only with Caroline's consent.

e. The state could prosecute Keith and sue him at the same time, for drunk driving.

Strategy: What party prosecutes a criminal case? The government does, not the injured party. What is the result in a criminal case? Guilt or innocence. What about a tort lawsuit? The injured party brings a tort suit. The defendant may be found liable but never guilty. (See the "Result" at the end of this section.)

2. **DEFAMATION** Defamation involves a defamatory statement that is false, uttered to a third person, and causes an injury. Opinion and privilege are valid defenses. (pp. 132–134)

EXAM Strategy

Question: Benzaquin had a radio talk show. On the program, he complained about an incident in which state trooper Fleming had stopped his car, apparently for lack of a proper license plate and safety sticker. Benzaquin explained that the license plate had been stolen and the sticker fallen onto the dashboard, but Fleming refused to let him drive away. Benzaquin and two young grandsons had to find other transportation. On the show, Benzaquin angrily recounted the incident, then described Fleming and troopers generally: "we're not paying them to be dictators and Nazis"; "this man is an absolute barbarian, a lunkhead, a meathead." Fleming sued Benzaquin for defamation. Comment.

Strategy: Review the elements of defamation. Can these statements be proven true or false? If not, what is the result? Look at the defenses. Does one apply? (See the "Result" at the end of this section.)

3. **MALICE** Public personalities can win a defamation suit only by proving actual malice. (pp. 133–134)

4. **FALSE IMPRISONMENT** False imprisonment is the intentional restraint of another person without reasonable cause and without consent. (p. 134)

5. **EMOTIONAL DISTRESS** The intentional infliction of emotional distress involves extreme and outrageous conduct that causes serious emotional harm. (pp. 135–136)

6. **BATTERY** Battery is an intentional touching of another person in a way that is unwanted or offensive. Assault involves an act that makes the plaintiff fear an imminent battery. (p. 136)

Question: Caudle worked at Betts Lincoln-Mercury dealer. During an office party, many of the employees, including president Betts, were playing with an electric auto condenser, which gave a slight shock when touched. Some employees played catch with it. Betts shocked Caudle on the back of his neck, and chased him around. The shock later caused Caudle to suffer headaches, pass out, feel numbness, and eventually to require nerve surgery. He sued Betts for battery. Betts defended by saying that it was all horseplay and that he had intended no harm. Please rule.

Strategy: Betts argues he intended no harm. Is intent to harm an element? (See the "Result" at the end of this section.)

7. **DAMAGES** Compensatory damages are the normal remedy in a tort case. In unusual cases, the court may award punitive damages, not to compensate the plaintiff but to punish the defendant. (pp. 138–144)

8. **TORTIOUS INTERFERENCE** Tortious interference with business relations involves the defendant harming an existing contract or a prospective relationship that has a definite expectation of success. (pp. 145–148)

9. **PRIVACY AND PUBLICITY** The related torts of privacy and publicity involve unreasonable intrusion into someone's private life and unfair commercial exploitation by using someone's name, likeness, or voice without permission. (p. 148)

10. **LANHAM ACT** The Lanham Act prohibits false statements in commercial advertising or promotion. (p. 149)

1. Result: (a) is wrong because a defendant cannot be found guilty in a civil suit. (b) is wrong because a private party has no power to prosecute a criminal case. (c) is correct. (d) is wrong because the state will prosecute Keith, not sue him. (e) is wrong for the same reason.

2. Result: The court ruled in favor of Benzaquin because a reasonable person would understand the words to be opinion and ridicule. They are not statements of fact because most of them could not be proven true or false. A statement like "dictators and Nazis" is not taken literally by anyone.[16]

[16] *Fleming v. Benzaquin*, 390 Mass. 175, 454 N.E.2d 95 (1983).

> **6. Result:** The court held that it was irrelevant that Betts had shown no malice toward Caudle nor intended to hurt him. Betts *intended the physical contact* with Caudle, and even though he could not foresee everything that would happen, he is liable for all consequences of his intended physical action.[17]

Multiple-Choice Questions

1. Jane writes an article for a newspaper reporting that Ann was arrested for stealing a car. The story is entirely false. Ann is not a public figure. Which of the following torts has Jane committed?

(a) Ordinary slander
(b) Slander per se
(c) Libel
(d) None of the above

2. Refer back to Question 1. If Ann decides to sue, she ________________ have to show evidence that she suffered an injury. If she ultimately wins her case. a jury ________________ have the option to award punitive damages.

(a) will; will
(b) will; will not
(c) will not; will
(d) will not; will not

3. Sam sneaks up on Tom, hits him with a baseball bat, and knocks him unconscious. Tom never saw Sam coming. He wakes up with a horrible headache. Which of the following torts has Sam committed?

(a) Assault
(b) Battery
(c) Both A and B
(d) None of the above

4. Imagine a case in which a jury awards compensatory damages of $1 million. If this is not a maritime case, a jury would rarely be allowed to award more than ___________________ in punitive damages.

(a) $1 million
(b) $3 million
(c) $9 million
(d) $10 million
(e) $25 million

---

[17] *Caudle v. Betts*, 512 So.2d 389 (La.1987).

5. Al runs a red light and hits Carol's car. She later sues, claiming the following losses:

$10,000—car repairs

$10,000—medical expenses

$10,000—lost wages (she could not work for two months after the accident)

$10,000—pain and suffering

If the jury believes all of Carol's evidence and she wins her case, how much will she receive in *compensatory* damages?

(a) $40,000
(b) $30,000
(c) $20,000
(d) $10,000
(e) $0

Essay Questions

1. You are a vice president in charge of personnel at a large manufacturing company. In-house detectives inform you that Gates, an employee, was seen stealing valuable computer equipment. Gates denies the theft, but you believe the detectives and fire him. The detectives suggest that you post notices around the company, informing all employees what happened to Gates and why, because it will discourage others from stealing. While you are considering that, a phone call from another company's personnel officer asks for a recommendation for Gates. Should you post the notices? What should you say to the other officer?

2. Caldwell was shopping in a K-Mart store, carrying a large purse. A security guard observed her looking at various small items such as stain, hinges, and antenna wire. On occasion, she bent down out of sight of the guard. The guard thought he saw Caldwell put something in her purse. Caldwell removed her glasses from her purse and returned them a few times. After she left, the guard approached her in the parking lot and said that he believed she had store merchandise in her pocketbook, but he could not say what he thought was put there. Caldwell opened the purse, and the guard testified that he saw no K-Mart merchandise in it. The guard then told Caldwell to return to the store with him. They walked around the store for approximately 15 minutes, while the guard said six or seven times that he saw her put something in her purse. Caldwell left the store after another store employee indicated she could go. Caldwell sued. What kind of suit did she file, and what should the outcome be?

3. Tata Consultancy of Bombay, India, is an international computer consulting firm. It spends considerable time and effort recruiting the best personnel from India's leading technical schools. Tata employees sign an initial three-year employment commitment, often work overseas, and agree to work for a specified additional time when they return to India. Desai worked for Tata, but then he quit and formed a competing company, which he called Syntel. His new company contacted Tata employees by phone, offering higher salaries, bonuses, and assistance in obtaining permanent resident visas in the United States if they would come work for Syntel. At least 16 former Tata employees left their jobs without completing their contractual obligations and went to work for Syntel. Tata sued. What did it claim, and what should be the result?

4. Pacific Express began operating as an airline in 1982. It had routes connecting western cities with Los Angeles and San Francisco, and by the summer of 1983, it was beginning to show a profit. In 1983, United Airlines tried to enter into a cooperative arrangement with Pacific in which United would provide Pacific with passengers for some routes so that United could concentrate on its longer routes. Negotiations failed. Later that year, United expanded its routes to include cities that only Pacific had served. United also increased its service to cities in which the two airlines were already competing. By early 1984, Pacific Express was unable to compete and sought protection under bankruptcy laws. It also sued United, claiming interference with a prospective advantage. United moved for summary judgment. Comment.

5. **YOU BE THE JUDGE WRITING PROBLEM** Johnny Carson was for many years the star of a well-known television show, *The Tonight Show*. For about 20 years, he was introduced nightly on the show with the phrase, "Here's Johnny!" A large segment of the television watching public associated the phrase with Carson. A Michigan corporation was in the business of renting and selling portable toilets. The company chose the name "Here's Johnny Portable Toilets," and coupled the company name with the marketing phrase, "The World's Foremost Commodian." Carson sued, claiming that the company's name and slogan violated his right to commercial exploitation.

   Argument for Carson: The toilet company is deliberately taking advantage of Johnny Carson's good name. He worked hard for decades to build a brilliant career and earn a reputation as a creative, funny, likable performer. No company has the right to use his name, his picture, or anything else closely identified with him, such as the phrase "Here's Johnny." The pun is personally offensive and commercially unfair.

   Argument for Here's Johnny Portable Toilets: Johnny Carson doesn't own his first name. It is available for anyone to use for any purpose. Further, the popular term "john," meaning toilet, has been around much longer than Carson or even television. We are entitled to make any use of it we want. Our corporate name is amusing to customers who have never heard of Carson, and we are entitled to profit from our brand recognition.

Discussion Questions

1. The Supreme Court limits punitive damages in most cases to nine times the compensatory damages awarded in the same case. Is this a sensible guideline? If not, should it be higher or lower?

2. You have most likely heard of the *Liebeck v. McDonalds* case. Liebeck spilled hot McDonald's coffee in her lap and suffered third-degree burns. At trial, evidence showed that her cup of coffee was brewed at 190 degrees, and that, more typically, a restaurant's "hot coffee" is in the range of 140 to 160 degrees.

A jury awarded Liebeck $160,000 in compensatory damages and $2.7 million in punitive damages. The judge reduced the punitive award to $480,000, or three times the compensatory award.

Comment on the case and whether the result was reasonable.

3. Celebrities often have problems with tabloids and the paparazzi. It is difficult for public figures to win libel lawsuits because they must show actual malice. Intrusion lawsuits are also tricky, and flocks of photographers often stalk celebrities at all hours.

Is this right? Should the law change to offer more privacy to famous people? Or is a loss of privacy just the price of success?

4. With a national debt in the trillions, people are desensitized to "mere" billions. Stop for a moment and consider $1 billion. If you had that sum, invested it conservatively, and got a 5 percent return, you could spend roughly $1 million *a week* for the rest of your life *without reducing your principal.*

This chapter described three lawsuits with jackpot punitive damage awards. The jury award was $10 billion in *Texaco v. Pennzoil,* $5 billion in the *Exxon Valdez* case, and $3 billion in *Boeken v. Philip Morris.* Is there any point at which the raw number of dollars awarded is just too large? Was the original jury award excessive in any of these cases? If so, which one(s)?

5. Many retailers have policies that instruct employees *not* to attempt to stop shoplifters. Some store owners fear false imprisonment lawsuits and possible injuries to workers more than losses related to stolen merchandise.

Are these "don't be a hero" policies reasonable? Would you put one in place if you owned a retail store?

CHAPTER 7

NEGLIGENCE AND STRICT LIABILITY

© r.nagy/Shutterstock.com

If you give a party, should *you* be responsible for any damage caused by intoxicated guests?

Submitted for your consideration: a timeline.

3:25 p.m.—Jake, an 18-year-old freshman, sits in his Calculus I class, bored to tears. He receives a text: "Beta Zeta rush party TONIGHT!!!" He perks up.

9:15 p.m.—Jake drives with his roommate over to the Beta Zeta rush party.

9:32 p.m.—Jake and his roommate arrive at the Beta Zeta house. No one checks for ID.

9:36 p.m.—Jake gets a beer from a keg and drinks it.

9:37 p.m.—Jake pours himself another beer and heads outside.

9:58 p.m.—After listening to the band for awhile, Jake returns to the keg and gets a third beer.

10:24 p.m.—Jake faces off with his roommate. He chugs a beer slightly faster than the roommate, and his skills are praised by the Beta Zetas.

10:48 p.m.—Jake bongs a beer.

10:51 p.m.—Jake bongs another beer.

12:26 p.m.—Jake poses slightly off-balance, and his roommate takes an iPhone photo.

12:27 a.m.—Jake's roommate sends the picture to everyone on his contact list.

12:28 a.m.—Jake receives the first of many texts making fun of him.

12:35 a.m.—Jake finds his roommate, shoves him, and threatens to kick his ***.

12:38 a.m.—Jake tells his roommate, "I love you man," and heads off to find another beer.

1:14 a.m.—Jake drinks a seventh and final beer.

1:48 a.m.—Jake and his roommate leave the Beta Zeta house. Jake drives his car.

1:49 a.m.—Jake's roommate suggests getting some tacos.

1:54 a.m.—Jake tries to park his car at Taco Bell, but he misses the brake pedal. He drives his car through a large plate glass window and does $50,000 damage to the restaurant.

Who should pay for this damage? Jake is clearly at fault, but should the Beta Zetas share legal responsibility for the property damage? The question leads to other, similar issues: should a restaurant that serves alcohol to a minor be liable for harm that the youth might cause? Should the restaurant be responsible for serving an intoxicated adult who causes damage? If you give a party, should *you* be responsible for any damage caused by intoxicated guests?

These are all practical questions—worth considering before you entertain—and moral ones as well. They are also typical issues of negligence law. In this contentious area, courts continually face one question: *when someone is injured, how far should responsibility extend?*

NEGLIGENCE

We might call negligence the "unintentional" tort because it concerns harm that arises by accident. Should a court impose liability? The fraternity members who gave the party were not trying to damage the Taco Bell, but the damage occurred all the same. Is it in society's interest to hold the fraternity responsible?

Things go wrong all the time, and people are hurt in large ways and small. Society needs a means of analyzing negligence cases consistently and fairly. We cannot have each court that hears such a lawsuit extend or limit liability based on an emotional response to the facts. One of America's greatest judges, Benjamin Cardozo, offered an analysis more than 80 years ago. In a case called *Palsgraf v. Long Island Railroad*, he made a decision that still influences negligence thinking today.

Landmark Case

PALSGRAF V. LONG ISLAND RAILROAD

248 N.Y. 339; 162 N.E. 99
Court of Appeals of New York, 1928

Facts: Helen Palsgraf was waiting on a railroad platform. As a train began to leave the station, a man carrying a package ran to catch it. He jumped aboard but looked unsteady, so a guard on the car reached out to help him as another guard, on the platform, pushed from behind. The man dropped the package, which struck the tracks and exploded—since it was packed with fireworks. The shock knocked over some heavy scales at the far end of the platform, and one of them struck Palsgraf, who was injured as a result. She sued the railroad.

Issue: ***Was the railroad liable for Palsgraf's injuries?***

Excerpts from Judge Cardozo's Decision: The conduct of the defendant's guard was not a wrong in its relation to the plaintiff, standing far away. Relatively to her it was not negligence at all. Nothing in the situation gave notice that the falling package had in it the potency of peril to persons thus removed. Negligence is not actionable unless it involves the invasion of a legally protected interest, the violation of a right. Negligence is the absence of care, according to the circumstances.

If no hazard was apparent to the eye of ordinary vigilance, an act innocent and harmless, at least to outward seeming, with reference to her, did not take to itself the quality of a tort because it happened to be a wrong with reference to some one else. "In every instance, before negligence can be predicated of a given act, back of the act must be sought and found a duty to the individual complaining.

What the plaintiff must show is "a wrong" to herself and not merely a wrong to someone else. We are told that one who drives at reckless speed through a crowded city street is guilty of a negligent act because the eye of vigilance perceives the risk of damage. The risk reasonably to be perceived defines the duty to be obeyed.

Here, by concession, there was nothing in the situation to suggest to the most cautious mind that the parcel wrapped in newspaper would spread wreckage through the station.

The law of causation, remote or proximate, is thus foreign to the case before us. If there is no tort to be redressed, there is no occasion to consider what damage might be recovered if there were a finding of a tort. The consequences to be followed must first be rooted in a wrong.

Judge Cardozo ruled that the guard's conduct might have been a wrong as to the passenger, but not as to Ms. Palsgraf, standing far away. Her negligence case failed. "Proof of negligence in the air, so to speak, will not do," declared the judge. Courts are still guided by Judge Cardozo's ruling.

To win a negligence case, a plaintiff must prove five elements. Much of the remainder of the chapter will examine them in detail. They are:

- ***Duty of Due Care.*** The defendant had a legal responsibility *to the plaintiff.* This is the point from the *Palsgraf* case.
- ***Breach.*** The defendant breached her duty of care or failed to meet her legal obligations.
- ***Factual Cause.*** The defendant's conduct actually caused the injury.
- ***Proximate Cause.*** It was *foreseeable* that conduct like the defendant's might cause *this type of harm.*
- ***Damages.*** The plaintiff has actually been hurt or has actually suffered a measureable loss.

To win a case, a plaintiff must prove all the elements listed above. If a defendant eliminates only one item on the list, there is no liability.

Duty of Due Care

Each of us has a duty to behave as a reasonable person would under the circumstances. If you are driving a car, you have a duty to all the other people near you to drive like a reasonable person. If you drive while drunk, or send text messages while behind the wheel, then you fail to live up to your duty of care.

But how *far* does your duty extend? Most courts accept Cardozo's viewpoint in the *Palsgraf* case. Judges draw an imaginary line around the defendant and say that she owes a duty to the people within the circle, but not to those outside it. The test is generally "foreseeability." If the defendant could have foreseen injury to a particular person, she has a duty to him. Suppose that one of your friends posts a YouTube video of you texting behind the wheel and her father is so upset from watching it that he falls down the stairs. You would not be liable for the father's downfall because it was not foreseeable that he would be harmed by your texting.

Let us apply these principles to a case that, like the opening scenario, involves a fraternity party.

HERNANDEZ V. ARIZONA BOARD OF REGENTS

177 Ariz. 244, 866 P.2d 1330, 1994 Ariz. LEXIS 6
Arizona Supreme Court, 1994

Facts: At the University of Arizona, the Epsilon Epsilon chapter of Delta Tau Delta fraternity gave a welcoming party for new members. The fraternity's officers knew that the majority of its members were under the legal drinking age, but they permitted everyone to consume alcohol. John Rayner, who was under 21 years of age, left the party. He drove negligently and caused a collision with an auto driven by Ruben Hernandez. At the time of the accident, Rayner's blood alcohol level was .15, exceeding the legal limit. The crash left Hernandez blind and paralyzed.

Hernandez sued Rayner, who settled the case based on the amount of his insurance coverage. The victim also sued the fraternity, its officers and national organization, all fraternity members who contributed money to buy alcohol, the university, and others. The trial court granted summary judgment for all defendants and the court of appeals affirmed. Hernandez appealed to the Arizona Supreme Court.

Issue: ***Did the fraternity and the other defendants have a duty of due care to Hernandez?***

Excerpts from Justice Feldman's Decision: Before 1983, this court arguably recognized the common-law rule of non-liability for tavern owners and, presumably, for social hosts. Traditional authority held that when "an able-bodied man" caused harm because of his intoxication, the act from which liability arose was the consuming not the furnishing of alcohol.

However, the common law also provides that:

> One who supplies [a thing] for the use of another whom the supplier knows or has reason to know to be likely because of his youth, inexperience, or otherwise to use it in a manner involving unreasonable risk of physical harm to himself and others is subject to liability for physical harm resulting to them.

We perceive little difference in principle between liability for giving a car to an intoxicated youth and liability for giving drinks to a youth with a car. A growing number of cases have recognized that one of the very hazards that makes it negligent to furnish liquor to a minor is the foreseeable prospect that the [youthful] patron will become drunk and injure himself or others. Accordingly, modern authority has increasingly recognized that one who furnishes liquor to a minor breaches a common-law duty owed to innocent third parties who may be injured.

Furnishing alcohol to underaged drinkers violates numerous statutes. The conduct in question violates well-established common-law principles that recognize a duty to avoid furnishing dangerous items to those known to have diminished capacity to use them safely. We join the majority of other states and conclude that as to Plaintiffs and the public in general, Defendants had a duty of care to avoid furnishing alcohol to underage consumers.

Arizona courts, therefore, will entertain an action for damages against [one] who negligently furnishes alcohol to those under the legal drinking age when that act is a cause of injury to a third person. [Reversed and remanded.]

Ethics As the Arizona court notes, its decision agrees with the majority of courts that have considered the issue. In most (but not all) states, anyone serving alcohol to a minor is liable for injuries that result to a third party. The case raises other important issues.

- Should a social host who serves alcohol to an *adult* be liable for resulting harm? New Jersey has answered "Yes" to this question. In the Garden State, if a social host pours drinks for a friend, aware that he is becoming drunk, and the friend injures a third party, the host is fully liable. The majority of states to consider this issue have reached the opposite conclusion, holding that a social host is not liable for harm caused by an adult drinker. Are the majority of states correct to distinguish between adult and underage guests, holding a social host liable only for serving minors? Or is New Jersey correct to scrap this distinction?
- Many states now have some type of **dram act**, making liquor stores, bars, and restaurants liable for serving drinks to intoxicated customers who later cause harm. Dram shop laws force a financial dilemma on such firms. The more a tavern or café encourages its customers to drink, the greater its revenue—but also the larger its risk of a liability lawsuit. Do dram shop laws work? Yes, answer the authors of one economic study. In states with such statutes, bars monitor underage drinking more aggressively, refuse drinks earlier to an intoxicated customer, check the references of their own employees more carefully, and prohibit their workers from drinking on the job. Dram shop laws may be a promising way to reduce drunk driving accidents.[1] But are these laws reasonable? Is holding a bar responsible more reasonable than holding liable a person hosting a party at his house?
- There are many signs that society is fed up with drunk drivers. Some states have considered reducing blood alcohol limits for drunk driving to .05, which would place a typical person "over the limit" after two drinks. Are such proposals reasonable?

Dram act
A law that makes businesses liable for serving drinks to intoxicated customers who later cause harm.

In several circumstances, people have special duties to others. Three of them are outlined below.

Special Duty: Landowners

The common law applies special rules to a landowner for injuries occurring on her property. In most states, the owner's duty depends on the type of person injured.

Trespasser
A person on another's property without consent.

Lowest Liability: Trespassing Adults. A **trespasser** is anyone on the property without consent. A landowner is liable to a trespasser only for intentionally injuring him or for some other gross misconduct. The landowner has no liability to a trespasser for mere negligence. Jake is not liable if a vagrant wanders onto his land and is burned by defective electrical wires.

Mid-level Liability: Trespassing Children. The law makes exceptions when the trespassers are **children**. If there is some manmade thing on the land *that may be reasonably expected to attract children*, the landowner is probably liable for any harm. Daphne lives next door to a day-care center and builds a treehouse on her property. Unless she has fenced off the dangerous area, she is probably liable if a small child wanders onto her property and injures himself when he falls from the rope ladder to the treehouse.

---

[1]Sloan, Liang, Stout, and Whetten-Goldstein, "Liability, Risk Perceptions, and Precautions at Bars," *Journal of Law and Economics*, 2000, vol. 43, p. 473.

Higher Liability: Licensee. A **licensee** is anyone on the land for her own purposes but with the owner's permission. A social guest is a typical licensee. A licensee is entitled to a warning of hidden dangers that the owner knows about. If Juliet invites Romeo for a late supper on the balcony and fails to mention that the wooden railing is rotted, she is liable when her hero plunges to the courtyard.

But Juliet is liable only for injuries caused by *hidden* dangers—she has no duty to warn guests of obvious dangers. She need not say, "Romeo, oh Romeo, don't place thy hand in the toaster, Romeo."

Can the owner of this trampoline be liable?

Highest Liability: Invitee. An **invitee** is someone who has a right to be on the property because it is a public place or a business open to the public. The owner has a duty of reasonable care to an invitee. Perry is an invitee when he goes to the town beach. If riptides have existed for years and the town fails to post a warning, it is liable if Perry drowns. Perry is also an invitee when he goes to Dana's coffee shop. Dana is liable if she ignores spilled coffee that causes Perry to slip.

Licensee
A person on another's land for her own purposes but with the owner's permission.

Invitee
A person who has a right to enter another's property because it is a public place or a business open to the public.

With social guests, you must have *actual knowledge* of some specific hidden danger to be liable. Not so with invitees. You are liable even if you had *no idea* that something on your property posed a hidden danger. Therefore, if you own a business, you must conduct inspections of your property on a regular basis to make sure that nothing is becoming dangerous.

The courts of some states have modified these distinctions, and a few have eliminated them altogether. California, for example, requires "reasonable care" as to all people on the owner's property, regardless of how or why they got there. But most states still use the classifications outlined above.

Special Duty: Professionals

A person at work has a heightened duty of care. While on the job, she must act as a reasonable person *in her profession*. A taxi driver must drive as a reasonable taxi driver would. A heart surgeon must perform bypass surgery with the care of a trained specialist in that field.

Two medical cases illustrate the reasonable person standard. A doctor prescribes a powerful drug without asking his patient about other medicines she is currently taking. The patient suffers a serious drug reaction from the combined medications. The physician is liable for the harm. A reasonable doctor *always* checks current medicines before prescribing new ones.

On the other hand, assume that a patient dies on the operating table in an emergency room. The physician followed normal medical procedures at every step of the procedure and acted with reasonable speed. In fact, the man had a fatal stroke. The surgeon is not liable. A doctor must do a reasonable professional job, but she cannot guarantee a happy outcome.

Special Duty: Hiring and Retention

Employers also have special responsibilities.

In a recent one-year period, more than 1,000 homicides and 2 million attacks occurred in the workplace. Companies must beware because they can be liable for hiring or retaining violent employees. A mailroom clerk with a previous rape and robbery conviction followed a secretary home after work and killed her. Even though the murder took place off the company premises, the court held that the defendant would be liable if it knew or should have known of the mail clerk's criminal history.[2] In other cases, companies have been found liable for failing to check an applicant's driving record, contact personal references, or search criminal records.

Courts have also found companies negligent for *retaining* dangerous workers. If an employee threatens a coworker, the organization is not free to ignore the menacing conduct. If the employee acts on his threats, the company may be liable.[3]

What can an employer do to diminish the likelihood of workplace violence? Many things

- Install adequate lighting in parking lots and common areas, hire security guards if necessary, and use closed-circuit television and identification cards. The judicial trend is toward greater liability. Two decades ago, the victim of a parking lot assault could rarely recover from the store; today, such lawsuits are common and frequently successful. The financial liability can be enormous.

- Ensure that the company uses thorough pre-hire screening, contacts all former employers, and checks all references and criminal records. Nursing homes have been among the most delinquent at this, too often hiring applicants with a violent past who have later attacked elderly residents.

- Respond quickly to dangerous behavior. In many cases of workplace violence, the perpetrator had demonstrated repeated bizarre, threatening, or obsessive behavior on the job, but his supervisors had not taken it seriously. Offer counseling where appropriate and fire employees when necessary.

Breach of Duty

The second element of a plaintiff's negligence case is **breach of duty**. If a legal duty of care exists, then a plaintiff must show that the defendant did not meet it. Did the defendant act as a reasonable person, or as a reasonable professional? Did he warn social guests of hidden dangers he knew to exist in her apartment?

Normally, a plaintiff proves this part of a negligence case by convincing a jury that they would not have behaved as the defendant did—indeed, that no reasonable person would.

Negligence Per Se

In certain areas of life, courts are not free to decide what a "reasonable" person would have done because the state legislature has made the decision for them. **When a legislature sets a minimum standard of care for a particular activity, in order to protect a certain group of people, and a violation of the statute injures a member of that group, the defendant has committed negligence per se.** A plaintiff who can show negligence per se need not prove breach of duty.

In Minnesota, the state legislature became alarmed about children sniffing glue, which they could easily purchase in stores. The legislature passed a statute prohibiting the sale to a minor of any glue containing toluene or benzene. About one month later, 14-year-old Steven Zerby purchased Weldwood Contact Cement from the Coast-to-Coast Store in his hometown. The glue contained toluene. Steven inhaled the glue and died from injury to his central nervous system.

The store clerk had not realized that the glue was dangerous. Irrelevant: he was negligent per se because he violated the statute. Perhaps a reasonable person would have made the same error. Irrelevant. The legislature had passed the statute to protect children,

---

[2]*Gaines v. Monsanto*, 655 S.W.2d 568, 1983 Mo. App. LEXIS 3439 (Mo. Ct. App. 1983).

[3]*Yunker v. Honeywell*, 496 N.W.2d 419, 1993 Minn. App. LEXIS 230 (Minn. Ct. App. 1993).

the sale of the glue violated the law, and a child was injured. The store was automatically liable.

Causation

We have seen that a plaintiff must show that the defendant owed him a duty of care and that the defendant breached the duty. To win, the plaintiff must also show that the defendant's breach of duty *caused* the plaintiff's harm. Courts look at two separate causation issues: Was the defendant's behavior the *factual cause* of the harm? Was it the *proximate cause?*

Factual Cause

If the defendant's breach led to the ultimate harm, it is the factual cause. Suppose that Dom's Brake Shop tells a customer his brakes are now working fine, even though Dom knows that is false. The customer drives out of the shop, cannot stop at a red light, and hits a bicyclist crossing the intersection. Dom is liable to to the cyclist. Dom's unreasonable behavior was the factual cause of the harm. Think of it as a row of dominoes. The first domino (Dom's behavior) knocked over the next one (failing brakes), which toppled the last one (the cyclist's injury).

Suppose, alternatively, that just as the customer is exiting the repair shop, the cyclist hits a pothole and tumbles off her cycle. Dom has breached his duty to his customer, but he is not liable to the cyclist—she would have been hurt anyway. This is a row of dominoes that veers off to the side, leaving the last domino (the cyclist's injury) untouched. No factual causation.

Proximate Cause

For the defendant to be liable, the *type of harm* must have been reasonably *foreseeable*. In the first example just discussed, Dom could easily foresee that bad brakes would cause an automobile accident. He need not have foreseen *exactly* what happened. He did not know there would be a cyclist nearby. What he could foresee was this *general type* of harm involving defective brakes. Because the accident that occurred was of the type he could foresee, he is liable.

By contrast, assume the collision of car and bicycle produces a loud crash. Two blocks away, a pet pig, asleep on the window ledge of a twelfth-story apartment, is startled by the noise, awakens with a start, and plunges to the sidewalk, killing a veterinarian who was making a house call. If the vet's family sues Dom, should it win? Dom's negligence was the factual cause: it led to the collision, which startled the pig, which flattened the vet. Most courts would rule, though, that Dom is not liable. The type of harm is too bizarre. Dom could not reasonably foresee such an extraordinary chain of events, and it would be unfair to make him pay for it. See Exhibit 7.1. Another way of stating that Dom is not liable to the vet's family is by calling the falling pig a *superseding cause.* When one of the "dominoes" in the row is entirely unforeseeable, courts will call that event a superseding cause, letting the defendant off the hook.

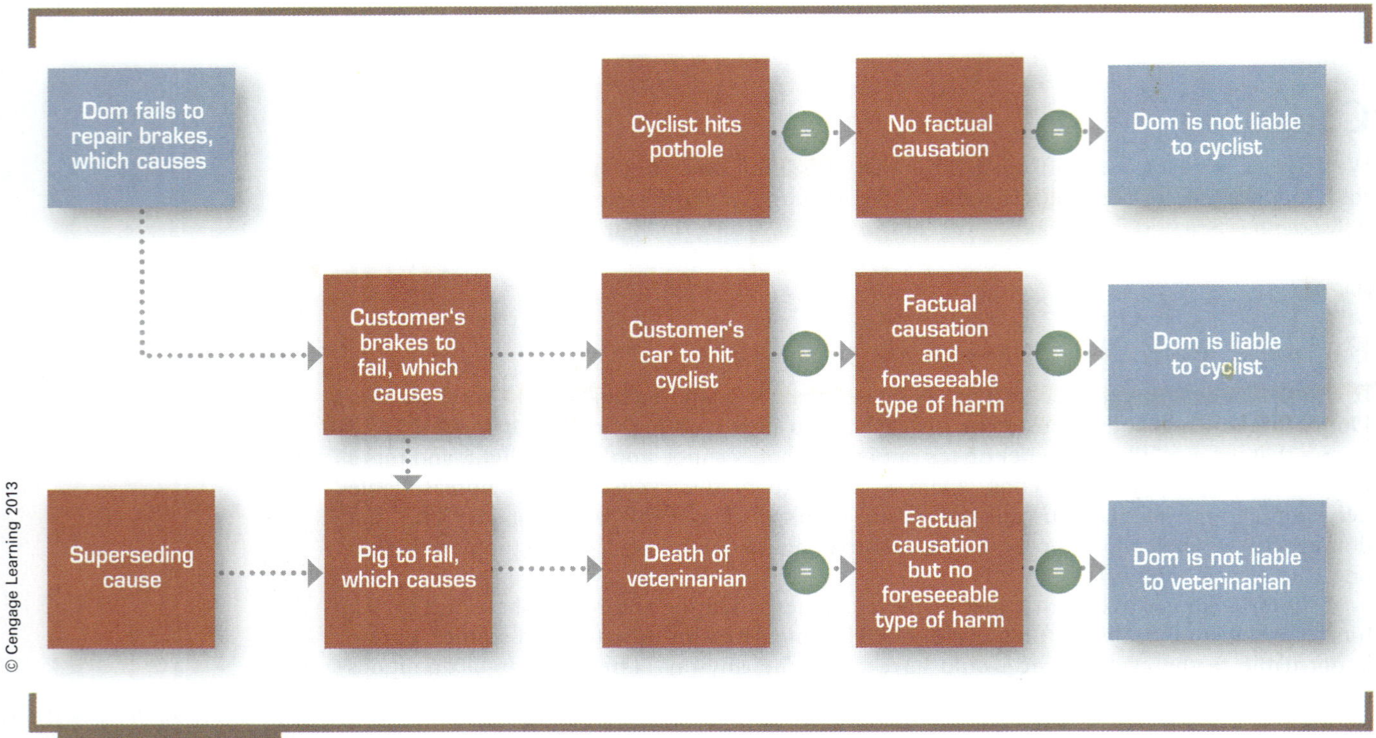

EXHIBIT 7.1

EXAM Strategy

Question: Jenny asked a neighbor, Tom, to water her flowers while she was on vacation. For three days, Tom did this without incident, but on the fourth day, when he touched the outside faucet, he received a violent electric shock that shot him through the air, melted his sneakers and glasses, set his clothes on fire, and seriously burned him. Tom sued, claiming that Jenny had caused his injuries by negligently repairing a second-floor toilet. Water from the steady leak had flooded through the walls, soaking wires and eventually causing the faucet to become electrified. You are Jenny's lawyer. Use one (and only one) element of negligence law to move for summary judgment.

Strategy: The four elements of negligence we have examined thus far are: duty to this plaintiff, breach, factual cause, and proximate cause. Which element seems to be most helpful to Jenny's defense? Why?

Result: Jenny is entitled to summary judgment because this was not a foreseeable type of injury. Even if she did a bad job of fixing the toilet, she could not reasonably have anticipated that her poor workmanship could cause *electrical* injuries to anyone.[4]

[4]Based on *Hebert v. Enos*, 60 Mass. App. Ct. 817, 806 N.E.2d 452 (Mass. Ct. App. 2004).

Res Ipsa Loquitur

Normally, a plaintiff must prove factual cause and foreseeable type of harm in order to establish negligence. But in a few cases, a court may be willing to *infer* that the defendant caused the harm under the doctrine of **res ipsa loquitur** ("the thing speaks for itself"). Suppose a pedestrian is walking along a sidewalk when an air conditioning unit falls on his head from a third-story window. The defendant, who owns the third-story apartment, denies any wrongdoing, and it may be difficult or impossible for the plaintiff to prove why the air conditioner fell. In such cases, many courts will apply *res ipsa loquitur* and declare that **the facts imply that the defendant's negligence caused the accident.** If a court uses this doctrine, then the defendant must come forward with evidence establishing that it did *not* cause the harm.

Res ipsa loquitur
The facts *imply* that the defendant's negligence caused the accident.

Because res ipsa loquitur dramatically shifts the burden of proof from plaintiff to defendant, it applies only when (1) the defendant had exclusive control of the thing that caused the harm, (2) the harm normally would not have occurred without negligence, and (3) the plaintiff had no role in causing the harm. In the air conditioner example, most states would apply the doctrine and force the defendant to prove she did nothing wrong.

The following case illustrates several of the elements of negligence that we have examined so far.

You be the Judge

Griffith v. Valley of Sun Recovery, Inc.

126 Ariz. 227, 613 P.2d 1283
Arizona Court of Appeals, 1980

Facts: Don Gorney was a "repo man"—someone authorized to find and take cars whose owners are behind on payments. A repossessor is allowed to drive away in such a car, provided he can do it peacefully. Gorney worked for Valley of Sun Recovery. He sought a car belonging to Linda Marsalek and Bob Williams. Gorney knew that there had been other, failed efforts to repossess the Marsalek car, including a violent confrontation involving attack dogs. He thought he could do better.

Gorney went to the car at 4:00 in the morning. He unscrewed the bulb in an overhead street lamp. He unlocked the car, setting off its alarm, and quickly hid. The alarm aroused the neighborhood. Williams and a neighbor, Griffith, investigated and concluded it was an attempted theft. They called the police. Gorney watched all of this from his hiding place. When everyone had gone, Gorney entered the car, again setting off the alarm and arousing the neighborhood. Williams and Griffith again emerged, as did another neighbor, dressed in his underwear and carrying a shotgun. They all believed they had caught a thief. Williams shouted for the gun and the neighbor passed it to him, but it went off accidentally and severely injured Griffith.

Griffith sued Valley of Sun. The trial court granted summary judgment for Valley of Sun, and Griffith appealed.

You Be the Judge:

- ***Did Valley of Sun have a duty to Griffith?***
- ***If so, did the company breach its duty?***
- ***If so, was the breach the factual cause of the injury?***
- ***If so, was this type of injury foreseeable?***

Argument for Griffith: Your honors, Mr. Griffith should be allowed to make his case to a jury and let it decide whether Valley of Sun's repossession led to his injury. Mr. Griffith has demonstrated every element of negligence. Valley of Sun had a duty to everyone in the area when it attempted to repossess a car. It could easily have foreseen injury. Car repossessions always involve antagonism between the car owner and the repo company.

Obviously, Gorney breached his duty. He was caught up in some fantasy, dreaming that he was Harrison Ford in an adventure film. He knew from previous repossession attempts that trouble was certain. But rather than minimizing the danger, he exacerbated it. He unscrewed a lightbulb, guaranteeing poor visibility and confusion. He set off the car alarm twice, making the whole neighborhood jittery.

Factual causation is indisputable. Had it not been for his preposterous game playing, no neighbors would have been outside, no guns present—and no accidental shooting. And this type of harm is easily foreseeable. We should have a chance to take our case to a jury.

Argument for Valley of Sun Recovery: Your honors, there are three good reasons to end this case today: no duty, no breach, no causation.

It is preposterous to suggest that Valley of Sun has a legal duty to an entire neighborhood. Car owners who are behind on their payments live in all parts of all communities. Is a repossession company to become an insurer of the entire city?

Yes, some danger is involved because delinquent owners are irresponsible and sometimes dangerous. Should we therefore allow them to keep their cars? Of course not. We must act, and that is what Valley of Sun does.

They do it safely, your honors. Even if there had been a duty, there was no breach. Mr. Gorney attempted to repossess when it was least likely anyone would see him. What should Mr. Gorney have done, asked for permission to take the car? *That* is a recipe for violence. If the owner were reasonable, there would be no repossession in the first place.

Factual causation? Valley of Sun did not create this situation. The car owners did. They bought the car and failed to pay for it. Even if there were factual causation, Valley of Sun is not liable because there is a superseding cause: the negligent use of a firearm by one of Mr. Griffith's neighbors. No jury should hear this case, your honors, because there is no case.

Damages

Finally, a plaintiff must prove that he has been injured, or that he has had some kind of measureable losses. In some cases, injury is obvious. For example, Ruben Hernandez suffered grievous harm when struck by the drunk driver. But in other cases, injury is unclear. **The plaintiff must persuade the court that he has suffered harm that is genuine, not speculative.**

Some cases raise tough questions. Among the most vexing are suits involving *future* harm. Exposure to toxins or trauma may lead to serious medical problems down the road—or it may not. A woman's knee is damaged in an auto accident, causing severe pain for two years. She is clearly entitled to compensation for her suffering. After two years, all pain may cease for a decade—or forever. Yet there is also a chance that in 15 or 20 years, the trauma will lead to painful arthritis. A court must decide today the full extent of present *and future* damages; the single recovery principle, discussed in Chapter 6, prevents a plaintiff from returning to court years later and demanding compensation for newly arisen ailments. The challenge to our courts is to weigh the possibilities and percentages of future suffering and decide whether to compensate a plaintiff for something that might never happen.

The following case examines a different issue: May a plaintiff recover damages because of the emotional injury suffered when a relative is harmed *if she does not see the accident that led to the harm*?

RA V. SUPERIOR COURT

154 Cal. App. 4th 142, 64 Ca. Rptr. 3d 539
California Court of Appeals, 2007

Facts: Michelle Ra and her husband, Phil Ra, were shopping in an Armani Exchange in Old Town, Pasadena. Michelle was looking at merchandise in the women's section while Phil examined men's sweaters about 10 or 15 feet away. Michelle was not facing her husband when she heard a loud bang. A large, overhead store sign had fallen, striking Phil and seriously injuring him. Michelle turned, saw her husband bent over in pain, and hurried to him.

The Ras sued Armani for negligence in permitting the sign to fall, and also for the emotional distress suffered by Michelle. This case concerns only Michelle's claim. The trial court granted summary judgment to the store, declaring that Michelle had not made out a valid claim of bystander recovery because she had not seen the accident occur. She appealed.

Issue: ***May a bystander recover for emotional distress caused by an accident that she did not see?***

Excerpts from Judge Perluss's Decision: [In a pretrial deposition, Michelle was asked:] At that moment you heard the sound, did you know your husband had been involved in any kind of accident; this is before you looked anywhere else?" Ra testified, "I was not sure if he was involved, but I knew the sound came from the direction—the part of the store he was in." [Later, she added that] "although I had some doubt, I believed more likely than not when I heard the loud bang in the Armani store that my husband was involved in an accident. I believed this because when I heard the loud bang, I knew the sound came from where I knew my husband was located. I then immediately turned to look at my husband."

[The state Supreme Court has held that] to recover for negligent infliction of emotional distress as a bystander the plaintiff must prove she (1) is closely related to the injury victim; (2) is present at the scene of the injury-producing event at the time it occurs and is then aware that it is causing injury to the victim; and (3) as a result suffers serious emotional distress—a reaction beyond that which would be anticipated in a disinterested witness and which is not an abnormal response to the circumstances. The [Supreme Court] expressly disapproved suggestions that a negligent actor is liable to all those "who may have suffered emotional distress on viewing or learning about the injurious consequences of his conduct," rather than on viewing the injury-producing event itself.

Although a plaintiff may establish presence at the scene through non-visual sensory perception, "someone who hears an accident but does not then know it is causing injury to a relative does not have a viable bystander claim for emotional distress, even if the missing knowledge is acquired moments later."

In restricting bystander claims to "closely related percipient witnesses," the Supreme Court explained [that it] is the traumatic effect of the perception of the infliction of injury on a closely related person that is actionable, not the observation of the consequences. Absent a reasonable certainty her husband was being injured by whatever caused the loud bang she heard, what Ra experienced at that time was simply fear. Although the emotional distress caused by that fear was no doubt real and substantial (as was the distress resulting from the subsequently acquired knowledge her husband had in fact been injured by the falling sign), it is not compensable in a bystander claim.

In sum, Ra's fear for her husband's safety at the time she heard the loud bang emanating from the part of the store where she knew he was shopping and her belief the possibility of his injury was more likely than not are insufficient as a matter of law to establish contemporaneous awareness of her husband's injuries at the time of the injury-producing accident.

[Affirmed.]

DEFENSES

Contributory and Comparative Negligence

Sixteen-year-old Michelle Wightman was out driving at night, with her friend Karrie Wieber in the passenger seat. They came to a railroad crossing, where the mechanical arm had descended and warning bells were sounding. They had been sounding for a long time. A Conrail train had suffered mechanical problems and was stopped 200 feet from the crossing, where it had stalled for roughly an hour. Michelle and Karrie saw several cars ahead of them go around the barrier and cross the tracks. Michelle had to decide whether she would do the same.

> **... the mechanical arm had descended and warning bells were sounding. They had been sounding for a long time.**

Long before Michelle made her decision, the train's engineer had seen the heavy Saturday night traffic crossing the tracks and realized the danger. The conductor and brakeman also understood the peril, but rather than posting a flagman, who could have stopped traffic when a train approached, they walked to the far end of their train to repair the mechanical problem. A police officer had come upon the scene, told his dispatcher to notify the train's parent company Conrail of the danger, and left.

Michelle decided to cross the tracks. She slowly followed the cars ahead of her. Seconds later, both girls were dead. A freight train traveling at 60 miles per hour struck the car broadside, killing both girls instantly.

Michelle's mother sued Conrail for negligence. The company claimed that it was Michelle's foolish risk that led to her death. Who wins when both parties are partly responsible? It depends on whether the state uses a legal theory called contributory negligence. **Under contributory negligence, if the plaintiff is even slightly negligent, she recovers nothing.** If Michelle's death occurred in a contributory negligence state, and the jury considered her even minimally responsible, her estate would receive no money.

Critics attacked this rule as unreasonable. A plaintiff who was 1 percent negligent could not recover from a defendant who was 99 percent responsible. So most states threw out the contributory negligence rule, replacing it with comparative negligence. **In a comparative negligence state, a plaintiff may generally recover even if she is partially responsible.** The jury will be asked to assess the relative negligence of the two parties.

Michelle died in Ohio, which is a comparative negligence state. The jury concluded that reasonable compensatory damages were $1 million. It also concluded that Conrail was 60 percent responsible for the tragedy and Michelle 40 percent. See Exhibit 7.2. The girl's mother received $600,000 in compensatory damages.

Today, most but not all states have adopted some form of comparative negligence. Critics claim that this principle rewards a careless plaintiff. If Michelle had obeyed the law,

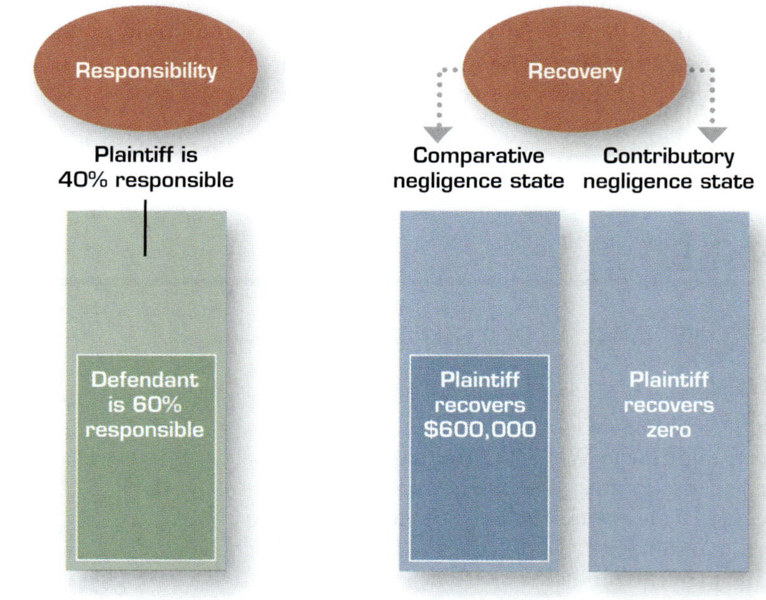

EXHIBIT 7.2 Defendant's negligence injures plaintiff, who suffers $1 million in damages.

she would still be alive. In response to this complaint, many comparative negligence states do *not* permit a plaintiff to recover anything if he was more than 50 percent responsible for his own injury.

In the Conrail case, the jury decided that the rail company was extraordinarily negligent. Expert witnesses testified that similar tragedies occurred every year around the nation and the company knew it. Conrail could easily have prevented the loss of life by posting a flagman on the road. The jury awarded the estate $25 million in punitive damages. The trial judge reduced the verdict by 40 percent to $15 million. The state supreme court affirmed the award.[5]

Assumption of the Risk

Good Guys, a restaurant, holds an ice-fishing contest on a frozen lake to raise money for accident victims. Margie grabs a can full of worms and strolls to the middle of the lake to try her luck, but slips on the ice and suffers a concussion. If she sues Good Guys, how will she fare? She will fall a second time. Wherever there is an obvious hazard, a special rule applies. **Assumption of the risk: a person who voluntarily enters a situation that has an obvious danger cannot complain if she is injured.** Ice is slippery and we all know it. If you venture onto a frozen lake, any falls are your own tough luck.

Do NFL players assume the risk of all on-field injuries?

© REUTERS/Matt Sullivan

However, the doctrine does not apply if someone is injured in a way that is not an inherent part of the dangerous activity. NFL players assume substantial risks each time they take the field, but some injuries fall outside the rule. In a game between the Jets and the Dolphins, Jets assistant coach Sal Alosi, standing on the sideline, tripped Dolphins player Nolan Carroll during a punt return. The trip was not a "normal" part of a football game, and the "assumption of the risk" doctrine would not prevent Carroll from recovering damages.

The following case involves a lake, jet skis—and a great tragedy.

Truong v. Nguyen

67 Cal. Rptr.3d 675, 156 Cal.App.4th 865
California Court of Appeals, 2007

Facts: On a warm California day, there were about 30 personal watercraft (jet skis) operating on Coyote Lake. The weather was fair and visibility good. Anthony Nguyen and Rachael Truong went for a ride on Anthony's Polaris watercraft. Cu Van Nguyen and Chuong Nguyen (neither of whom were related to Anthony) were both riding a Yamaha Waverunner. Both jet skis permitted a driver and passenger, each seated. The two watercraft collided near the middle of the lake. Rachael was killed, and the others all injured.

[5]*Wightman v. Consolidated Rail Corporation*, 86 Ohio St. 3d 431, 715 N.E.2d 546, 1999 Ohio LEXIS 2924 (Ohio 1999).

Rachael's parents sued Anthony, Cu Van, and Chuong, alleging that negligent operation of their watercraft caused their daughter's death. The defendants moved for summary judgment, claiming that assumption of the risk applies to jet skiing. The parents appealed, arguing that jet skiing was not a sport and Rachael never assumed any risk.

Issue: ***Does assumption of the risk apply to jet skiing?***

Excerpts from Judge McAdams's Decision: In a sports context, [assumption of the risk] bars liability because the plaintiff is said to have assumed the particular risks inherent in a sport by choosing to participate. Thus, a court need not ask what risks a particular plaintiff subjectively knew of and chose to encounter, but instead must evaluate the fundamental nature of the sport and the defendant's role in or relationship to that sport.

In baseball, a batter is not supposed to carelessly throw the bat after getting a hit and starting to run to first base. However, assumption of risk recognizes that vigorous bat deployment is an integral part of the sport and a risk players assume when they choose to participate. A batter does not have a duty to another player to avoid carelessly throwing the bat after getting a hit.

Even when a participant's conduct violates a rule of the game and may subject the violator to internal sanctions prescribed by the sport itself, imposition of legal liability for such conduct might well alter fundamentally the nature of the sport by deterring participants from vigorously engaging in activity. Coparticipants' limited duty of care is to refrain from intentionally injuring one another or engaging in conduct that is so reckless as to be totally outside the range of the ordinary activity involved in the sport.

It appears that an activity falls within the meaning of 'sport' if the activity is done for enjoyment or thrill, requires physical exertion as well as elements of skill, and involves a challenge containing a potential risk of injury.

As a matter of common knowledge, jet skiing is an active sport involving physical skill and challenges that pose a significant risk of injury, particularly when it is done—as it often is—together with other jet skiers in order to add to the exhilaration of the sport by racing, jumping the wakes of the other jet skis or nearby boats, or in other respects making the sporting activity more challenging and entertaining. In response to the plaintiff's complaint that the trial court erroneously assumed that the litigants were contestants in some sort of consensual competition event and/or spectator sport, [we conclude] that the doctrine applies equally to competitive and noncompetitive but active sports.

Plaintiffs urge [that] Rachael was merely a passenger on the Polaris and was not actively involved in the sport. The record supports the conclusion that riding as a passenger on a personal watercraft [is participating in a sport], because it is done for enjoyment or thrill, requires physical exertion as well as elements of skill, and involves a challenge containing a potential risk of injury. The vessel is open to the elements, with no hull or cabin. It is designed for high performance, speed, and quick turning maneuvers. The thrill of riding the vessel is shared by both the operator and the passenger. Obstacles in the environment such as spraying water, wakes to be crossed, and other watercraft are part of the thrill of the sport, both for the operator and the passenger.

The summary judgment is affirmed.

Strict Liability

Strict liability
A branch of tort law that imposes a much higher level of liability when harm results from ultrahazardous acts or defective products.

Some activities are so naturally dangerous that the law places an especially high burden on anyone who engages in them. A corporation that produces toxic waste can foresee dire consequences from its business that a stationery store cannot. This higher burden is **strict liability**. There are two main areas of business that incur strict liability: *ultrahazardous activity* and *defective products*. Defective products are discussed in Chapter 22, on product liability.

Ultrahazardous Activity

Ultrahazardous activities include using harmful chemicals, operating explosives, keeping wild animals, bringing dangerous substances onto property, and a few similar activities where the danger to the general public is especially great. **A defendant engaging in an ultrahazardous activity is almost always liable for any harm that results.** Plaintiffs do not have to prove duty or breach or foreseeable harm. Recall the deliberately bizarre case we posed earlier of the pig falling from a window ledge and killing a veterinarian. Dom, the mechanic whose negligence caused the car crash, could not be liable for the veterinarian's death because the plunging pig was a superseding cause.

But now imagine that the pig is jolted off the window ledge by a company engaged in an ultrahazardous activity. Sam's Blasting Co. sets off a perfectly lawful blast to clear ground for a new building down the street. When the pig is startled and falls, the blasting company is liable. Even if Sam took extraordinary care, it will do him no good at trial. The "reasonable person" rule is irrelevant in a strict liability case.

Because "strict liability" translates into "defendant is liable," parties in tort cases often fight over whether the defendant was engaged in an ultrahazardous activity. If the court rules that the activity was ultrahazardous, the plaintiff is assured of winning. If the court rules that it was not ultrahazardous, the plaintiff must prove all elements of negligence.

The line is often hazy. A lawful fireworks display does not incur strict liability, but crop dusting does. Cutting timber is generally not abnormally dangerous, but hauling logs might be. The enormous diversity of business activities in our nation ensures continual disputes over this important principle.

New Jersey Department of Environmental Protection v. Alden Leeds, Inc.

153 N.J. 272, 708 A.2d 1161, 1998 N.J. LEXIS 212
Supreme Court of New Jersey, 1998

Facts: The Alden Leeds Company packages, stores, and ships swimming pool chemicals. The firm does most of its work at its facility in Kearns, New Jersey. At any given time, about 21 different hazardous chemicals are present.

The day before Easter, a fire of unknown origin broke out in "Building One" of the company's site, releasing chlorine gas and other potentially dangerous by-products into the air. There were no guards or other personnel on duty. The fire caused $9 million in damage to company property. Because of the potentially dangerous gas, the Department of Environmental Protection (DEP) closed the New Jersey Turnpike along with half a dozen other major highways, halted all commuter rail and train service in the area, and urged residents to stay indoors with windows closed. An unspecified number of residents went to local hospitals with respiratory problems.

Based on New Jersey's Air Pollution Control Act (APCA), the DEP imposed a civil fine on Alden Leeds for releasing the toxic chemicals. The appellate court reversed, finding that there was no evidence the company had caused the fire or the harm, and the case reached the state's high court.

Issue: ***Did the company cause the harm?***

Excerpts from Justice Coleman's Decision: In 1962, this Court adopted the proposition that "an ultrahazardous activity which introduces an unusual danger into the community should pay its own way in the event it actually causes damage to others." In 1983, the Court expressly recognized "that the law of liability has evolved so that a landowner is strictly liable to others for harm caused by toxic wastes that are stored on his property and flow onto the property of others." The Court explained "that those who use, or permit others to use, land for the conduct of abnormally dangerous activities are strictly liable for resultant damages." The same rationale applies to pollution that is released into the air from chemicals stored at a chemical facility.

An actor who chooses to store dangerous chemicals should be responsible for the release of those chemicals into the air. That Alden Leeds lawfully and properly stored chemicals does not alter that conclusion. The risks attendant to the storage of dangerous substances counsel in favor of precautions to prevent their release. Alden Leeds took no such precautions. On the day of the fire, there was no one stationed at the plant to alert the authorities as soon as a fire or other unforeseen calamity erupted. Nor was there any other early warning system in place. A burglar or smoke alarm sounded, but there was no response to that alarm. The law imposes a duty upon those who store hazardous substances to ensure that the substances on their property do not escape in a manner harmful to the public. Alden Leeds failed to meet that burden.

Although Alden Leeds was not found responsible for the fire, the company's facility caused a release of air pollutants. The required nexus is satisfied by the knowing storage of hazardous chemicals. Regardless of what started the fire, it was the knowing storage of chemicals by Alden

Leeds that caused the release of air contaminants once the fire reached the chemicals.

[Affirmed that the APCA is a strict liability statute and that there must be a causal nexus between the defendant and the harm. Reversed that the storing of hazardous chemicals by Alden Leeds does not satisfy that nexus. The DEP does *not* have to prove that the chemical operator started the fire.]

EXAM Strategy

Facts: Ahmed plans to transport a 25-foot boa constrictor from one zoo to another. The snake is locked in a special cage in Ahmed's truck, approved by the American Zoo Society. Experts check the cage to be sure it is locked and entirely secure. Then Ahmed himself checks the cage. During the transport, his engine begins to fail. He pulls into the breakdown lane and sets up four flares, warning motorists of the stalled vehicle. Katy drives off the road and slams into Ahmed's truck. She is badly injured. Somehow the snake escapes and eats a champion show dog, worth $35,000. Katy and the dog's owner both sue Ahmed. What will be the result in each case?

Strategy: Ahmed's behavior seems reasonable throughout this incident. However, the two suits against him are governed by different rules: negligence in one case, strict liability in the other. Apply each rule to the correct case.

Result: The dog was killed by a dangerous snake. Transporting wild animals is an ultrahazardous activity, and Ahmed is strictly liable. His reasonable behavior will not save him. However, when he parked his truck in the breakdown lane, he did a reasonable job. Katy cannot prove that he breached his duty to her, and she loses.

Chapter Conclusion

Tort issues necessarily remain in flux, based on changing social values and concerns. There is no final word on what is an ultrahazardous activity, or how thoroughly an employer must conduct background checks, or whether a social host can be liable for the destruction caused by a guest. What is clear is that a working knowledge of these issues and pitfalls can help everyone—business executive and ordinary citizen alike.

Exam Review

1. **ELEMENTS** The five elements of negligence are duty of due care, breach, factual causation, proximate causation, and damage. (p. 158)

2. **DUTY** If the defendant could foresee that misconduct would injure a particular person, he probably has a duty to her. Special duties exist for people on the job, landowners, and employers. (pp. 158–162)

Question: A supervisor reprimanded an employee for eating in a restaurant when he should have been at work. Later, the employee showed up at the supervisor's office and shot him. Although the employee previously had been violent, management withheld this information from supervisory personnel. Is the company liable for the supervisor's injury?

Strategy: An employer must do a *reasonable* job of hiring and retaining employees. (See the "Result" at the end of this section.)

3. **BREACH OF DUTY** A defendant breaches his duty of due care by failing to meet his duty of care. (p. 162) breach = failing to meet duty of care

4. **NEGLIGENCE PER SE** If a legislature sets a minimum standard of care for a particular activity in order to protect a certain group of people, and a violation of the statute injures a member of that group, the defendant has committed negligence per se. (pp. 162–163)

5. **FACTUAL CAUSE** If one event directly led to the ultimate harm, it is the factual cause. (p. 163)

6. **PROXIMATE CAUSE** For the defendant to be liable, the type of harm must have been reasonably foreseeable. (p. 163)

7. **DAMAGE** The plaintiff must persuade the court that he has suffered a harm that is genuine, not speculative. Damages for emotional distress, without a physical injury, are awarded only in select cases. (pp. 163–164)

8. **CONTRIBUTORY AND COMPARATIVE NEGLIGENCE** In a contributory negligence state, a plaintiff who is even slightly responsible for his own injury recovers nothing; in a comparative negligence state, the jury may apportion liability between plaintiff and defendant. (pp. 167–169)

Question: There is a collision between cars driven by Candy and Zeke. The evidence is that Candy is about 25 percent responsible, for failing to stop quickly enough, and Zeke about 75 percent responsible, for making a dangerous turn. Candy is most likely to win:

(a) A lawsuit for battery

(b) A lawsuit for negligence in a comparative negligence state

(c) A lawsuit for negligence in a contributory negligence state

(d) A lawsuit for strict liability

(e) A lawsuit for assault

Strategy: Battery and assault are intentional torts, irrelevant in a typical car accident. Are such collisions strict liability cases? No; therefore, the answer must be either (b) or (c). Apply the distinction between comparative and contributory negligence to the evidence here. (See the "Result" at the end of this section.)

9. STRICT LIABILITY A defendant is strictly liable for harm caused by an ultrahazardous activity or a defective product. Ultrahazardous activities include using harmful chemicals, blasting, and keeping wild animals. Strict liability means that if the defendant's conduct led to the harm, the defendant is liable, even if she exercises extraordinary care. (pp. 170–172)

EXAM Strategy

Question: Marko owned a cat and allowed it to roam freely outside. In the three years he had owned the pet, the animal had never bitten anyone. The cat entered Romi's garage. When Romi attempted to move it outside, the cat bit her. Romi underwent four surgeries, was fitted with a plastic finger joint, and spent more than $39,000 in medical bills. She sued Marko, claiming both strict liability and ordinary negligence. Assume that state law allows a domestic cat to roam freely. Evaluate both of Romi's claims.

Strategy: Negligence requires proof that the defendant breached a duty to the plaintiff by behaving unreasonably, and that the resulting harm was foreseeable. Was it? When would harm by a domestic cat be foreseeable? A defendant can be strictly liable for keeping a wild animal. Apply that rule as well. (See the "Result" at the end of this section.)

2. Result: This employer *may* have been liable for negligently hiring a previously violent employee, and it *certainly* did an unreasonable job in retaining him without advising his supervisor of the earlier violence. The assault was easily foreseeable, and the employer is liable.[6]

8. Result. In a contributory negligence state, a plaintiff even 1 percent responsible for the harm loses. Candy was 25 percent responsible. She can win *only* in a comparative negligence state.

9. Result: If Marko's cat had bitten or attacked people in the past, this harm was foreseeable and Marko is liable. If the cat had never done so, and state law allows domestic animals to roam, Romi probably loses her suit for negligence. Her strict liability case definitely fails: a housecat is not a wild animal.

Multiple-Choice Questions

1. Two cars, driven by Fred and Barney, collide. At trial, the jury determines that the accident was 90 percent Fred's fault and 10 percent Barney's fault. Barney's losses total $100,000. If he lives in a state that uses contributory negligence, Barney will recover ________________.

---

[6]Based on *Smith v. National R.R. Passenger Corp.*, 856 F.2d 467 (2d Cir. 1988).

(a) $0
(b) $10,000
(c) $50,000
(d) $90,000
(e) $100,000

2. Assume the same facts as in Question 1, except now Barney lives in a state that follows comparative negligence. Now Barney will recover ____________________.

(a) $0
(b) $10,000
(c) $50,000
(d) $90,000
(e) $100,000

3. Zack lives in a state that prohibits factory laborers from working more than 12 hours in any 24-hour period. The state legislature passed the law to cut down on accidents caused by fatigued workers.

Ignoring the law, Zack makes his factory employees put in 14-hour days. Eventually, a worker at the end of a long shift makes a mistake and severely injures a coworker. The injured worker sues Zack.

Which of the following terms will be most relevant to the case?

(a) *Res ipsa loquitur*
(b) Assumption of the risk
(c) Negligence per se
(d) Strict liability

4. Randy works for a vending machine company. One morning, he fills up an empty vending machine that is on the third floor of an office building. Later that day, Mark buys a can of PepsiCo from that machine. He takes the full can to a nearby balcony and drops it three floors onto Carl, a coworker who recently started dating Mark's ex-girlfriend. Carl falls unconscious. Which of the following can be considered a factual cause of Carl's injuries?

(a) Randy
(b) Mark
(c) Both Randy and Mark
(d) None of the above

5. For this question, assume the same facts as in Question 4. Now determine which of the following can be considered a proximate cause of Carl's injuries?

(a) Randy
(b) Mark
(c) Both Randy and Mark
(d) None of the above

Essay Questions

1. At approximately 7:50 p.m, bells at the train station rang and red lights flashed, signaling an express train's approach. David Harris walked onto the tracks, ignoring a yellow line painted on the platform instructing people to stand back. Two men shouted to Harris, warning him to get off the tracks. The train's engineer saw him too late to stop the train, which was traveling at approximately 55 mph. The train struck and killed Harris as it passed through the station. Harris's widow sued the railroad, arguing that the railroad's negligence caused her husband's death. Evaluate her argument.

2. Ryder leased a truck to Florida Food Service; Powers, an employee, drove it to make deliveries. He noticed that the strap used to close the rear door was frayed, and he asked Ryder to fix it. Ryder failed to do so in spite of numerous requests. The strap broke, and Powers replaced it with a nylon rope. Later, when Powers was attempting to close the rear door, the nylon rope broke and he fell, sustaining severe injuries to his neck and back. He sued Ryder. The trial court found that Powers's attachment of the replacement rope was a superseding cause, relieving Ryder of any liability, and granted summary judgment for Ryder. Powers appealed. How should the appellate court rule?

3. A new truck, manufactured by General Motors Corp. (GMC), stalled in rush hour traffic on a busy interstate highway because of a defective alternator, which caused a complete failure of the truck's electrical system. The driver stood nearby and waved traffic around his stalled truck. A panel truck approached the GMC truck, and immediately behind the panel truck, Davis was driving a Volkswagen fastback. Because of the panel truck, Davis was unable to see the stalled GMC truck. The panel truck swerved out of the way of the GMC truck, and Davis drove straight into it. The accident killed him. Davis's widow sued GMC. GMC moved for summary judgment, alleging (1) no duty to Davis, (2) no factual causation, and (3) no foreseeable harm. Comment.

4. ***YOU BE THE JUDGE* WRITING PROBLEM** When Thomas and Susan Tamplin were shopping at Star Lumber with their six-year-old daughter Ann Marie, a 150-pound roll of vinyl flooring fell on the girl, seriously injuring her head and pituitary gland. Ann was clearly entitled to recover for the physical harm, such as her fractured skull. The plaintiffs also sought recovery for potential future harm. Their medical expert was prepared to testify that although Ann would probably develop normally, he could not rule out the slight possibility that her pituitary injury might prevent her from sexually maturing. Is Ann entitled to damages for future harm? **Argument for Ann:** This was a major trauma, and it is impossible to know the full extent of the future harm. Sexual maturation is a fundamental part of life; if there is a possibility that Ann will not develop normally, she is entitled to present her case to a jury and receive damages. **Argument for Star Lumber:** A plaintiff may not recover for speculative harm. The "slight possibility" that Ann could fail to develop is not enough for her to take her case to the jury.

5. Irving was a lawyer who prepared income tax returns for Maroevich. Irving agreed to draft a will for Maroevich, leaving all of the property to Maroevich's sister, Biakanja. When Maroevich died, the probate court refused to accept the will because Irving had failed to have the signatures properly witnessed. As a result, Biakanja inherited only

one-eighth of the estate. She sued Irving, who defended by saying that he had no duty of due care to Biakanja because all his dealings were with Maroevich and none were with her. Do you agree?

Discussion Questions

1. Imagine an undefeated high school football team on which the average lineman weighs 300 pounds. Also, imagine an 0–10 team on which the average lineman weighs 170 pounds. The undefeated team sets out to hit as hard as they can on every play and to run up the score as much as possible. Before the game is over, 11 players from the lesser team have been carried off the field with significant injuries. All injuries were the result of "clean hits"—none of the plays resulted in a penalty. Even late in the game, when the score is 70–0, the undefeated team continues to deliver devastating hits that are far beyond what would be required to tackle and block. The assumption of the risk doctrine exempts the undefeated team from liability. Is this reasonable?

2. Should the law hold landowners to different standards of care for trespassers, social guests, and invitees? Or do the few states that say, "Just always be reasonable," have a better rule?

3. Are strict liability rules fair? Someone has to dispose of chemicals. Someone has to use dynamite if road projects are to be completed. Is it fair to say to those companies, "You are responsible for all harm caused by your activities, even if you are as careful as you can possibly be?"

4. Steve is making copies. Lonnie, his coworker, politely asks, "When will you be done with the copier?" Steve punches Lonnie in the face. Later, Lonnie learns that Steve's last two employers fired him for punching coworkers. He also finds out that his company did not do a background check of any kind on Steve before hiring him. Would it be fair to hold Lonnie's company liable for the attack, or should Lonnie's only action be against Steve?

5. People who serve alcohol to others take a risk. In some circumstances, they can be held legally responsible for the actions of the people they serve. Is this fair? Should an intoxicated person be the only one liable if harm results? If not, in what specific circumstances is it fair to stretch liablility to other people?

CHAPTER 8

CRIME

© r.nagy/Shutterstock.com

Crime can take us by surprise. Stacey tucks her nine-year-old daughter, Beth, into bed. Promising her husband, Mark, that she will be home by 11:00 PM, she jumps into her car and heads back to Be Patient, Inc. She plugs her iPhone into the player of her $85,000 sedan and tries to relax by listening to music. Be Patient is a health care organization that owns five geriatric hospitals. Most of its patients use Medicare, and Stacey supervises all billing to their largest client, the federal government.

She parks in a well-lighted spot on the street and walks to her building, failing to notice two men, collars turned up, watching from a parked truck. Once in her office, she goes straight to her computer and works on billing issues. Tonight's work goes more quickly than she expected, thanks to new software she helped develop. At 10:30 she emerges from the building with a quick step and a light heart, walks to her car—and finds it missing.

A major crime has occurred during the 90 minutes Stacey was at her desk, but she will never report it to the police. It is a crime that costs Americans countless dollars each year, yet Stacey will not even mention it to friends or family. Stacey is the criminal.

A major crime has occurred during the 90 minutes Stacey was at her desk, but she will never report it to the police.

When we think of crime, we imagine the drug dealers and bank robbers endlessly portrayed on television. We do not picture corporate executives sitting at polished desks. "Street crimes" are indeed serious threats to our security and happiness. They deservedly receive the attention of the public and the law. But when measured only in dollars, street crime takes second place to white-collar crime, which costs society *tens of billions* of dollars annually.

The hypothetical about Stacey is based on many real cases and is used to illustrate that crime does not always dress the way we expect. Her car was never stolen; it was simply towed. Two parking bureau employees, watching from their truck, saw Stacey park illegally and did their job. It is Stacey who committed a crime—Medicare fraud. Every month, she has billed the government about $10 million for work that her company has not performed. Stacey's scheme was quick and profitable—and a distressingly common crime.

Crime, whether violent or white-collar, is detrimental to all society. It imposes a huge cost on everyone. Just the *fear* of crime is expensive—homeowners buy alarm systems and businesses hire security guards. But the anger and fear that crime engenders sometimes tempt us to forget that not all accused people are guilty. Everyone suspected of a crime should have the protections that you yourself would want in that situation. As the English jurist William Blackstone said, "Better that ten guilty persons escape than that one innocent suffer."

Thus, criminal law is a balancing act—between making society safe and protecting us all from false accusations and unfair punishment.

This chapter has four parts:

- The differences between a civil and criminal case;
- **Criminal procedure**—the *process* by which criminals are accused, tried, and sentenced;
- Crimes that *harm* businesses;
- Crimes committed *by* businesses.

Criminal procedure
The process by which criminals are accused, tried, and sentenced.

The Differences between a Civil and Criminal Case

Most of this book focuses on civil law, so we begin with a discussion of the differences between a civil and criminal case.

Civil law involves the rights and liabilities that exist between private parties. As we have seen, if one person claims that another has caused her a civil injury, she must file a lawsuit and convince a court of her damages.

Criminal law is different. Conduct is criminal when society outlaws it. When a state legislature or Congress concludes that certain behavior threatens public safety and welfare, it passes a statute forbidding that behavior; in other words, declaring it criminal. Medicare fraud, which Stacey committed, is a crime because Congress has outlawed it. Money laundering is a crime because Congress concluded that it was a fundamental part of the drug trade and prohibited it.

Criminal law
Prohibits and punishes conduct that threatens public safety and welfare.

Prosecution

Suppose the police arrest Roger and accuse him of breaking into a store and stealing 50 computers. The owner of the store is the one harmed, and he has the right to sue the thief in civil court to recover money damages. But **only the government can prosecute a crime and punish Roger by sending him to prison.** The government may also impose a fine on Roger, but it keeps the fine and does not share it with the victim. (However, the court will sometimes order **restitution**, meaning that the defendant must reimburse the victim for

Restitution
A court order that a guilty defendant reimburse the victim for the harm suffered.

harm suffered.) The local prosecutor has total discretion in deciding whether to bring Roger to trial on criminal charges.

Burden of Proof

In a civil case, the plaintiff must prove her case only by a preponderance of the evidence.[1] But because the penalties for conviction in a criminal case are so serious, the government must prove its case **beyond a reasonable doubt**. Also, the stigma of a criminal conviction would stay with Roger forever, making it more difficult to obtain work and housing. Therefore, in all criminal cases, if the jury has any significant doubt at all that Roger stole the computers, it *must* acquit him.

Beyond a reasonable doubt
The very high burden of proof in a criminal trial, demanding much more certainty than required in a civil trial.

Right to a Jury

The facts of a case are decided by a judge or jury. A criminal defendant has a right to a trial by jury for any charge that could result in a sentence of six months or longer. The defendant may demand a jury trial or may waive that right, in which case the judge will be the factfinder.

Felony/Misdemeanor

A **felony** is a serious crime, for which a defendant can be sentenced to one year or more in prison. Murder, robbery, rape, drug dealing, money laundering, wire fraud, and embezzlement are felonies. A **misdemeanor** is a less serious crime, often punishable by a year or less in a county jail. Public drunkenness, driving without a license, and simple possession of a single marijuana cigarette are considered misdemeanors in most states.

Felony
A serious crime, for which a defendant can be sentenced to one year or more in prison.

Misdemeanor
A less serious crime, often punishable by less than a year in a county jail.

Criminal Procedure

The title of a criminal case is usually the government versus someone: *The United States of America v. Simpson* or *The State of Texas v. Simpson*, for example. This name illustrates a daunting thought—if you are Simpson, the vast power of the government is against you. Because of the government's great power and the severe penalties it can impose, criminal procedure is designed to protect the accused and ensure that the trial is fair. Moreover, a criminal defendant is often engaged in an uphill climb from the beginning because people often assume that anyone accused of a crime must be guilty. Many of the protections for those accused of a crime are found in the first 10 amendments to the United States Constitution, known as the Bill of Rights.

Conduct Outlawed

Crimes are created by statute. The prosecution must demonstrate to the court that the defendant's conduct is indeed outlawed by a statute. Returning to Roger, the alleged computer thief, the state charges that he stole computer equipment from a store, a crime clearly defined by statute as larceny.

The Fifth and Fourteenth Amendments to the Constitution require that the language of criminal statutes be clear and definite enough that (1) ordinary people can understand what conduct is prohibited and (2) the police are discouraged from arbitrary and discriminatory enforcement. Thus, for example, the Supreme Court ruled that a statute that prohibited loitering was unconstitutionally vague because it did not clarify exactly what behavior was prohibited and it tended to be enforced arbitrarily.[2]

---

[1]See the earlier discussion in Chapter 3, on dispute resolution.
[2]*Kolender v. Lawson*, 461 U.S. 352 (S. Ct., 1983).

State of Mind

Voluntary Act

A defendant is not guilty of a crime if she was forced to commit it. In other words, she is not guilty if she acted under duress. However, the defendant bears the burden of proving by a preponderance of the evidence that she did act under duress. In 1974, a terrorist group kidnapped heiress Patricia Hearst from her apartment near the University of California at Berkeley. After being tortured for two months, she participated in a bank robbery with the group. Despite opportunities to escape, she stayed with the criminals until her capture by the police a year later. The State of California put on her on trial for bank robbery. One question for the jury was whether she had voluntarily participated in the crime. This was an issue on which many people had strong opinions. Ultimately Hearst was convicted, sent to prison, and then later pardoned.

Guilty
A judge or jury's finding that a defendant has committed a crime.

© Bettmann/CORBIS

Patty Hearst, before she was kidnapped.

Entrapment

When the government induces the defendant to break the law, the prosecution must prove beyond a reasonable doubt that the defendant was predisposed to commit the crime. The goal is to separate the cases where the defendant was innocent before the government tempted him from those where the defendant was only too eager to break the law.

Kalchinian and Sherman met in the waiting room of a doctor's office where they were both being treated for drug addiction. After several more meetings, Kalchinian told Sherman that the treatment was not working for him and he was desperate to buy drugs. Could Sherman help him? Sherman repeatedly refused, but ultimately agreed to help end Kalchinian's suffering by providing him with drugs. Little did Sherman know that Kalchinian was a police informant. Sherman sold drugs to Kalchinian a number of times. Kalchinian rewarded this act of friendship by getting Sherman hooked again and then turning him in to the police. A jury convicted Sherman of drug dealing, but the Supreme Court overturned the conviction on the grounds that Sherman had been entrapped.[3] The court felt there was no evidence that Sherman was predisposed to commit the crime.

Gathering Evidence: The Fourth Amendment

If the police suspect that a crime has been committed, they will need to obtain evidence. **The Fourth Amendment to the Constitution prohibits the government from making illegal searches and seizures of individuals, corporations, partnerships, and other organizations.** The goal of the Fourth Amendment is to protect the individual from the powerful state.

Warrant

As a general rule, the police must obtain a warrant before conducting a search. A warrant is written permission from a neutral official, such as a judge or magistrate, to conduct a search.[4] **The warrant must specify with reasonable certainty the place to be searched and the items to be seized.** Thus, if the police say they have reason to believe that they will find bloody clothes in the suspect's car in his garage, they cannot also look through his house and confiscate file folders.

[3] *Sherman v. United States*, 356 U.S. 369 (S. Ct., 1958).
[4] A magistrate is a judge who tries minor criminal cases or undertakes primarily administrative responsibilities.

If the police search without a warrant, they have violated the Fourth Amendment. **But even a search conducted with a warrant violates the Fourth Amendment if:**

- There was no probable cause to issue the warrant;
- The warrant does not specify the place to be searched and the things sought; or
- The search extends beyond what is specified in the warrant.

Probable Cause

Probable cause
It is likely that evidence of crime will be found in the place to be searched.

The magistrate will issue a warrant only if there is probable cause. **Probable cause** means that based on all the information presented, **it is likely that evidence of a crime will be found in the place to be searched.** Often, the police base their applications for a warrant on data provided by an informant. The magistrate will want evidence to support the informant's reliability. If it turns out that this informant has been wrong the last three times he gave evidence to the police, the magistrate will probably refuse the request for a warrant.

Searches Without a Warrant

There are seven circumstances under which police may **search without a warrant**:

- **Plain View.** Police may search if they see a machine gun, for example, sticking out from under the front seat of a parked car.
- **Stop and Frisk.** None of us wants to live in a world in which police can randomly stop and frisk us on the street anytime they feel like it. The police do have the right to stop and frisk, but *only if* they have a clear and specific reason to suspect that criminal activity may be afoot and that the person may be armed and dangerous.[5]
- **Emergencies.** If, for example, the police believe that evidence is about to be destroyed, they can search.
- **Automobiles.** If police have lawfully stopped a car and observe evidence of other crimes in the car, such as burglary tools, they may search.
- **Lawful Arrest.** Police may always search a suspect they have arrested. The point of this exception is to protect the officers and preserve evidence.
- **Consent.** Anyone lawfully living in a house can allow the police in to search without a warrant. If your roommate gives the police permission to search your house, that search is legal.
- **No Expectation of Privacy.** The police have a right to search any area in which the defendant does not have a reasonable expectation of privacy. For example, Rolando Crowder was staying at his friend Bobo's apartment. Hearing the police in the hallway, he ran down to the basement. The police found Crowder in the basement with drugs nearby. Crowder argued that the police should have obtained a warrant, but the court ruled that Crowder had no expectation of privacy in Bobo's basement.[6]

Apart from these seven exceptions, a warrant is required.

Exclusionary Rule

Under the exclusionary rule, evidence obtained illegally may not be used at trial. The Supreme Court created the exclusionary rule to ensure that police conduct legal searches. The theory is simple: if police know in advance that illegally obtained evidence cannot be

---

[5] *Terry v. Ohio*, 392 U.S. 1 (S. Ct., 1968).

[6] *Ohio v. Crowder*, 2010 Ohio 3766; 2010 Ohio App. LEXIS 3210 (2010).

used in court, they will not be tempted to make improper searches. Is the exclusionary rule a good idea?

Opponents of the rule argue that a guilty person may go free because one police officer bungled. They are outraged by cases like *Coolidge v. New Hampshire.*[7] Pamela Mason, a 14-year-old babysitter, was brutally murdered. Citizens of New Hampshire were furious, and the state's attorney general personally led the investigation. Police found strong evidence that Edward Coolidge had done it. They took the evidence to the attorney general, who personally issued a search warrant. A search of Coolidge's car uncovered incriminating evidence, and he was found guilty of murder and sentenced to life in prison. But the United States Supreme Court reversed the conviction. The warrant had not been issued by a neutral magistrate. A law officer may not lead an investigation and simultaneously decide what searches are permissible.

After the Supreme Court reversed Coolidge's conviction, New Hampshire scheduled a new trial, attempting to convict him with evidence lawfully obtained. Before the trial began, Coolidge pleaded guilty to second degree murder. He was sentenced and remained in prison until his release years later.

In fact, very few people do go free because of the exclusionary rule. One study showed that evidence is actually excluded in only 1.3 percent of all prosecutions; and in about one-half of *those* cases, the court convicted the defendant on other evidence. Only in 0.7 percent of all prosecutions did the defendant go free after the evidence was suppressed.[8]

There are two exceptions to the exclusionary rule:

- **Inevitable Discovery.** The inevitable discovery exception permits the use of evidence that would inevitably have been discovered even without the illegal search. If an informant was about to tell the police about Coolidge's car, then the evidence found there would have been admissible, so long as the court believed the testimony was true.
- **Good Faith Exception.** Suppose the police use a search warrant believing it to be proper, but it later proves to have been defective. Is the search therefore illegal? No, so long as the police reasonably believed the warrant was valid, the search is legal.[9]

Should the exclusionary rule apply in the following case? You be the judge.

---

[7]403 U.S. 443, 91 S. Ct. 2022, 1971 U.S. LEXIS 25 (S. Ct., 1971).
[8]See the discussion in *United States v. Leon* (Justice Brennan, dissenting), 468 U.S. 897, 1985 U.S. LEXIS 153 (S. Ct., 1984).
[9]Ibid.

You be the Judge

Ohio v. Smith

2009 Ohio 6426; 920 N.E.2d 949; 2009 Ohio Lexis 3496
Supreme Court of Ohio, 2009

Facts: Wendy Northern was hospitalized for a drug overdose. When police questioned her in the hospital, she identified her drug dealer as Antwaun Smith. She then called him to arrange for the purchase of crack cocaine at her house that evening. When Smith arrived at her house, the police arrested him, searched him, and confiscated his cell phone. When the police looked at the phone some time later, they discovered call records and phone numbers confirming that this phone had been used to speak with Northern.

The police had neither a warrant nor Smith's consent to search the phone. Smith filed a motion requesting that the evidence from his cell phone be excluded because it had been obtained without a warrant. After the judge denied this motion, Smith was found guilty and sentenced to 12 years in prison. The appeals court upheld his conviction. He appealed to the Ohio Supreme Court.

You Be the Judge: ***Was the search of Smith's cell phone legal? Should the evidence found on the phone be excluded?***

Argument for the Police: The police have the right to search anyone they arrest. During a perfectly legal search, they discovered Smith's cell phone. Prior courts have ruled that defendants have a low expectation of privacy in address books and that police can search them without a warrant. A cell phone is an electronic address book. Therefore, the search of Smith and the subsequent search of the contents of the phone were both legal. The evidence was properly admitted in court.

Argument for Smith: Police have the right to search someone they have arrested so that they can protect themselves and prevent evidence from being destroyed. A search of the cell phone's contents was not necessary to ensure officer safety, and there was no evidence that the call records and phone numbers were in danger of being destroyed. Once the police had the phone, they had plenty of time to ensure that the data were preserved. In addition, they might have been able to obtain Smith's phone records from his service provider.

The police were entitled to search Smith and discover his cell phone. But they did not have the right to search the phone without a warrant. Modern cell phones are much more similar to a laptop than to an old-fashioned address book—they have the ability to transmit large amounts of personal data in various forms. Courts have ruled that defendants have a high expectation of privacy in laptop computers and that the police must obtain a warrant before searching one. It would be a terrible precedent to declare that the police could search cell phones without a warrant.

The Patriot Act

In response to the devastating attacks of September 11, 2001, Congress passed a sweeping antiterrorist law known as the Patriot Act. The statute was designed to give law enforcement officials greater power to investigate and prevent potential terrorist assaults. The bill raced through Congress nearly unopposed. Proponents hailed it as a vital weapon for use against continuing lethal threats. Opponents argued that the hastily passed law would not provide serious benefits but did threaten the liberties of the very people it purported to shield.

In an early legal test, a federal judge permitted the government to use secret evidence in its effort to freeze the assets of Global Relief Foundation, a religious organization suspected of terrorist activity. The group, which claimed to be purely humanitarian, asserted that it could hardly defend itself against unseen evidence. Finding "acute national security concerns," the judge allowed the government to introduce the evidence in private, without the foundation ever seeing it.[10]

The law also permitted the FBI to issue a **national security letter** (NSL) to communications firms such as Internet service providers (ISPs) and telephone companies. An NSL typically demanded that the recipient furnish to the government its customer records, *without ever divulging* to anyone what it had done. NSLs could be used to obtain access to subscriber billing records, phone, financial, credit, and other information—even records of books taken from libraries. However, an appeals court ruled that a secret NSL could be issued only if the government first demonstrated to a court's satisfaction that disclosure of the NSL would risk serious harm.[11]

---

[10] *Global Relief Found., Inc. v. O'Neill*, 315 F.3d 748, 2002 U.S. App. LEXIS 27172 (7th Cir., 2002).

[11] *Doe v. Mukasey*, 549 F.3d 861; 2008 U.S. App. LEXIS 25193, (2d Cir., 2008).

EXAM Strategy

Question: Police bang down the door of Mary Beth's apartment, enter without her permission, and search the apartment. They had no warrant. When the officers discover that she is smoking marijuana, they arrest her. What motion will the defense lawyer make before trial? Please rule on the defendant's motion. Are there any facts that would make you change your ruling?

Strategy: The defendant's motion is based on the police conduct. What was wrong with that conduct, and what are the consequences?

Result: The defense lawyer will argue that the police violated the Fourth Amendment because they lacked a warrant for the search. He will ask that the court suppress the drug evidence. Ordinarily, the court would grant that motion unless there was other evidence—for example, the police smelled marijuana from the hallway and Mary Beth would have smoked it all if the police had taken the time to obtain a warrant.

The Case Begins

The trial is now ready to begin. But, the government may not be able to use all the evidence it has gathered.

The Fifth Amendment

The Fifth Amendment to the Constitution protects criminal defendants—both the innocent and the guilty—in several ways.

Due Process **Due process** requires fundamental fairness at all stages of the case. The basic elements of due process are discussed in Chapter 5, on constitutional law. In the context of criminal law, due process sets additional limits. The requirement that the prosecution disclose evidence favorable to the defendant is a due process rule. Similarly, if a witness says that a tall white male robbed the liquor store, it would violate due process for the police to place the male suspect in a lineup with four short women.

Due process
Requires fundamental fairness at all stages of the case.

Self-Incrimination The Fifth Amendment bars the government from forcing any person to provide evidence against himself. In other words, the police may not use mental or physical coercion to force a confession or any other information out of someone. Society does not want a government that engages in torture. Such abuse might occasionally catch a criminal, but it would grievously injure innocent people and make all citizens fearful of the government that is supposed to represent them. Also, coerced confessions are inherently unreliable. The defendant may confess simply to end the torture. (The protection against self-incrimination applies only to people; corporations and other organizations are not protected and may be required to provide incriminating information.)

Exclusionary Rule (Again) If the police do force a confession, the exclusionary rule prohibits the prosecution from using it or any information they obtain as a result of what the defendant has said. (This secondary information is referred to as "the fruit of the poisonous tree.") For example, when the police illegally arrest Alice, she tells them that she has bought drugs from Beau. The police go to Beau's house, where they find drugs. He tells them that Caitlyn is his dealer and, indeed, the police find drugs in Caitlyn's bedroom. None of this evidence—neither the confessions nor the drugs—is admissible in court because it all stemmed from Alice's illegal arrest.

The rationale is the same as for Fourth Amendment searches: suppressing the evidence means that police will not attempt to get it illegally. But remember that the confession is void only if it results from custodial questioning. Suppose a policeman, investigating a bank robbery, asks a pedestrian if he noticed anything peculiar. The pedestrian says, "You mean after I robbed the bank?" Result? There was no custodial questioning, and the confession *may* be used against him.

Miranda Rights The police cannot legally force a suspect to provide evidence against himself. But sometimes, under forceful interrogation, he might forget his constitutional rights. In the following landmark case, the Supreme Court established the requirement that police remind suspects of their rights—with the very same warning that we have all heard so many times on television shows.

Landmark Case

Miranda v. Arizona

384 U.S. 436; 1966 U.S. Lexis 2817
Supreme Court of the United States, 1966

Facts: Ernesto Miranda was a mentally ill, indigent citizen of Mexico. The Phoenix police arrested him at his home and brought him to a police station, where a rape victim identified him as her assailant. Two police officers took him to an interrogation room but did not tell him that he had a right to have a lawyer present during the questioning. Two hours later, the officers emerged with a written confession signed by Miranda. At the top of the statement was a typed paragraph stating that the confession was made voluntarily "with full knowledge of my legal rights, understanding any statement I make may be used against me."

At Miranda's trial, the judge admitted this written confession into evidence over the objection of defense counsel. The officers testified that Miranda had also made an oral confession during the interrogation. The jury found Miranda guilty of kidnapping and rape. He was sentenced to 20 to 30 years imprisonment. On appeal, the Supreme Court of Arizona affirmed the conviction. In reaching its decision, the court relied heavily on the fact that Miranda did not specifically request a lawyer. The Supreme Court of the United States granted *certiorari.*

Issues: ***Was Miranda's confession admissible at trial? Should his conviction be upheld?***

Excerpts from Chief Justice Warren's Decision: Our holding briefly stated is this: the prosecution may not use statements, whether exculpatory or inculpatory, stemming from custodial interrogation of the defendant unless it demonstrates the use of procedural safeguards effective to secure the privilege against self-incrimination. By custodial interrogation, we mean questioning initiated by law enforcement officers after a person has been taken into custody or otherwise deprived of his freedom of action in any significant way. As for the procedural safeguards to be employed, the following measures are required. Prior to any questioning, the person must be warned that he has a right to remain silent, that any statement he does make may be used as evidence against him, and that he has a right to the presence of an attorney, either retained or appointed.

The defendant may waive these rights, provided the waiver is made voluntarily, knowingly, and intelligently. If, however, he indicates in any manner and at any stage of the process that he wishes to consult with an attorney before speaking, there can be no questioning. Likewise, if the individual is alone and indicates in any manner that he does not wish to be interrogated, the police may not question him. The mere fact that he may have answered some questions or volunteered some statements on his own does not deprive him of the right to refrain from answering any further inquiries until he has consulted with an attorney and thereafter consents to be questioned.

In a series of cases decided by this Court, the police resorted to physical brutality—beating, hanging, whipping—and to sustained and protracted questioning incommunicado in order to extort confessions. Only recently in Kings County, New York, the police brutally beat, kicked, and placed lighted cigarette butts on the back of a potential witness under interrogation for the purpose of securing a statement incriminating a third party.

Unless a proper limitation upon custodial interrogation is achieved, there can be no assurance that practices of this nature will be eradicated in the foreseeable future. Not only does the use of the third degree involve a flagrant violation of law by the officers of the law, but it involves also the dangers of false confessions, and it tends to make police and prosecutors less zealous in the search for objective evidence. As [an official] remarked: "If you use your fists, you are not so likely to use your wits."

[C]oercion can be mental as well as physical, and the blood of the accused is not the only hallmark of an unconstitutional inquisition. In a serious case, the interrogation may continue for days, with the required intervals for food and sleep, but with no respite from the atmosphere of domination. It is possible in this way to induce the subject to talk without resorting to duress or coercion.

Even without employing brutality, the very fact of custodial interrogation exacts a heavy toll on individual liberty and trades on the weakness of individuals. In [this case before the Court], the defendant was thrust into an unfamiliar atmosphere and run through menacing police interrogation procedures. It is obvious that such an interrogation environment is created for no purpose other than to subjugate the individual to the will of his examiner. This atmosphere carries its own badge of intimidation. To be sure, this is not physical intimidation, but it is equally destructive of human dignity. The current practice of incommunicado interrogation is at odds with one of our Nation's most cherished principles—that the individual may not be compelled to incriminate himself.

All these policies point to one overriding thought: the constitutional foundation underlying the privilege is the respect a government—state or federal—must accord to the dignity and integrity of its citizens. To maintain a fair state-individual balance, to respect the inviolability of the human personality, our accusatory system of criminal justice demands that the government seeking to punish an individual produce the evidence against him by its own independent labors, rather than by the cruel, simple expedient of compelling it from his own mouth.

From the testimony of the officers and by the admission of [the defendant], it is clear that Miranda was not in any way apprised of his right to consult with an attorney and to have one present during the interrogation, nor was his right not to be compelled to incriminate himself effectively protected in any other manner. Without these warnings, the statements were inadmissible. The mere fact that he signed a statement which contained a typed-in clause stating that he had "full knowledge" of his "legal rights" does not approach the knowing and intelligent waiver required to relinquish constitutional rights.

Right to a Lawyer

As *Miranda* made clear, a criminal defendant has the right to a lawyer before being interrogated by the police. The Sixth Amendment guarantees the **right to a lawyer** at all important stages of the criminal process. Because of this right, the government must **appoint a lawyer** to represent, free of charge, any defendant who cannot afford one.

After Arrest

Indictment

Grand jury
A group of ordinary citizens that decides whether there is probable cause the defendant committed the crime with which she is charged.

Once the police provide the local prosecutor with evidence, he presents this evidence to a **grand jury** and asks its members to indict the defendant. The grand jury is a group of ordinary citizens, like a trial jury, but the grand jury holds hearings for several weeks at a time, on many different cases. It is the grand jury's job to determine whether there is probable cause that this defendant committed the crime with which she is charged. At the hearing in front of the grand jury, only the prosecutor presents evidence, not the defense attorney because it is better for the defendant to save her evidence for the trial jury. After all, the defense attorney may want to see what evidence the prosecution has before deciding how to present the case.

Indictment
The government's formal charge that the defendant has committed a crime and must stand trial.

If the grand jury determines that there is probably cause, an **indictment** is issued. An indictment is the government's formal charge that the defendant has committed a crime and must stand trial.

Arraignment

At an arraignment, a clerk reads the formal charges of the indictment. The judge asks whether the defendant has a lawyer. If she does not, the judge urges her to get one quickly. If a defendant cannot afford a lawyer, the court will appoint one to represent her free of charge. The judge now asks the lawyer how the defendant pleads to the charges. At this stage, most defendants plead not guilty.

Discovery

During the months before trial, both prosecution and defense will prepare the most effective case possible. There is less formal discovery than in civil trials. The prosecution is obligated to hand over any evidence favorable to the defense that the defense attorney requests. The defense has a more limited obligation to inform the prosecution of its evidence. In most states, for example, if the defense will be based on an alibi, counsel must reveal the alibi to the government before trial.

Plea Bargaining

Plea bargain
An agreement in which the defendant pleads guilty to a reduced charge, and the prosecution recommends to the judge a relatively lenient sentence.

Sometime before trial, the two attorneys will meet to try to negotiate a plea bargain. A **plea bargain** is an agreement between prosecution and defense that the defendant will plead guilty to a reduced charge, and the prosecution will recommend to the judge a relatively lenient sentence. In the federal court system, about 75 percent of all prosecutions end in a plea bargain. In state court systems, the number is often higher. A judge need not accept the bargain but usually does.

For example, astronaut Lisa Nowak drove across country dressed in a wig and trench-coat to attack fellow astronaut Colleen Shipman, whom she viewed as a romantic rival. After Nowak's arrest, police found in her car a BB gun, a knife, and surgical tubing, which was thought to be evidence of her violent intent. Nowak was charged with attempted murder and attempted kidnapping, but much of the evidence was thrown out of court under the exclusionary rule because of police misconduct. Nowak ultimately pleaded guilty to battery and burglary of a car. At that point, she had served two days in jail. She did not receive further jail time, but she was required to complete 50 hours of community service and to attend anger-management classes.

Trial and Appeal

When there is no plea bargain, the case must go to trial. The mechanics of a criminal trial are similar to those for a civil trial, described in Chapter 3, on dispute resolution. It is the prosecution's job to convince the jury beyond a reasonable doubt that the defendant committed every element of the crime charged. The defense counsel will do everything possible to win an acquittal. In federal courts, prosecutors obtain a conviction in about 80 percent of cases; in state courts, the percentage is slightly lower. Convicted defendants have a right to appeal, and again, the appellate process is similar to that described in Chapter 3.

Double Jeopardy

Double jeopardy
A criminal defendant may be prosecuted only once for a particular criminal offense.

The prohibition against **double jeopardy** means that a defendant may be prosecuted only once for a particular criminal offense. The purpose is to prevent the government from destroying the lives of innocent citizens with repetitive prosecutions. Imagine that Rod and Lucy are accused of murdering a taxi driver. Rod is tried first and wins an acquittal. At Lucy's trial, Rod testifies that he is, indeed, the murderer. The jury acquits Lucy. The Double Jeopardy Clause prohibits the state from retrying Rod again for the same offense, even though he has now confessed to it.

Punishment

The Eighth Amendment prohibits cruel and unusual punishment. The most dramatic issue litigated under this clause is the death penalty. The Supreme Court has ruled that capital punishment is not inherently unconstitutional. Most state statutes divide a capital case into two parts, so that the jury first considers only guilt or innocence, and then, if the defendant is found guilty, deliberates on the death penalty. As part of that final decision, the jury must consider aggravating and mitigating circumstances that may make the ultimate penalty more or less appropriate.[12]

As you might expect from the term "cruel and unusual," courts are generally unsympathetic to such claims unless the punishment is truly outrageous. For example, Mickle pleaded guilty to rape. The judge sentenced him to prison for five years and also ordered that he undergo a vasectomy. The appeals court ruled that this sentence was cruel and unusual. Although the operation in itself is not cruel (indeed, many men voluntarily undergo it), when imposed as punishment, it is degrading and in that sense cruel. It is also an unusual punishment.[13]

In the following case, the Supreme Court was not moved to overturn a harsh punishment.

Ewing v. California

538 U.S. 11, 123 S. Ct. 1179, 155 L. Ed. 2d 108
United States Supreme Court, 2003

Facts: California passed a "three strikes" law, dramatically increasing sentences for repeat offenders. A defendant with two or more serious convictions, who was convicted of a third felony, had to receive a sentence of life imprisonment. Such a sentence required the defendant to serve a minimum of 25 years, and in some cases much more.

Gary Ewing, on parole from a nine-year prison term, stole three golf clubs worth $399 each, and was prosecuted. Because he had prior convictions, the crime, normally a misdemeanor, was treated as a felony. Ewing was convicted and sentenced to 25 years to life. He appealed, claiming that the sentence violated the Eighth Amendment.

Issue: ***Did Ewing's sentence violate the Eighth Amendment?***

Excerpts from Justice O'Connor's Decision: When the California Legislature enacted the three strikes law, it made a judgment that protecting the public safety requires incapacitating criminals who have already been convicted of at least one serious or violent crime. Nothing in the Eighth Amendment prohibits California from making that choice. To the contrary, our cases establish that States have a valid interest in deterring and segregating habitual criminals.

California's justification is no pretext. Recidivism is a serious public safety concern in California and throughout the Nation. According to a recent report, approximately 67 percent of former inmates released from state prisons were charged with at least one "serious" new crime within

[12] *Gregg v. Georgia*, 428 U.S. 153, 96 S. Ct. 2909, 1976 U.S. LEXIS 82 (S. Ct., 1976).
[13] *Mickle v. Henrichs*, 262 F. 687 (1918).

three years of their release. In particular, released property offenders like Ewing had higher recidivism rates than those released after committing violent, drug, or public-order offenses.

To be sure, California's three strikes law has sparked controversy. Critics have doubted the law's wisdom, cost-efficiency, and effectiveness in reaching its goals. This criticism is appropriately directed at the legislature, which has primary responsibility for making the difficult policy choices that underlie any criminal sentencing scheme. We do not sit as a "superlegislature" to second-guess these policy choices.

Ewing's sentence is justified by the State's public-safety interest in incapacitating and deterring recidivist felons, and amply supported by his own long, serious criminal record. Ewing has been convicted of numerous misdemeanor and felony offenses, served nine separate terms of incarceration, and committed most of his crimes while on probation or parole. His prior "strikes" were serious felonies, including robbery and three residential burglaries. To be sure, Ewing's sentence is a long one. But it reflects a rational legislative judgment, entitled to deference, that offenders who have committed serious or violent felonies and who continue to commit felonies must be incapacitated. The State of California was entitled to place upon Ewing the onus of one who is simply unable to bring his conduct within the social norms prescribed by the criminal law of the State.

We hold that Ewing's sentence of 25 years to life in prison, imposed for the offense of felony grand theft under the three strikes law, is not grossly disproportionate and therefore does not violate the Eighth Amendment's prohibition on cruel and unusual punishments.

Devil's Advocate Are we really going to send Ewing to prison for a minimum of 25 years—for *shoplifting?* It is true that Ewing is a recidivist, and undoubtedly a state is entitled to punish chronic troublemakers more harshly than first-time offenders. However, this still seems excessive. In California, a first-time offense of "arson causing *great bodily injury*" incurs a maximum nine-year sentence. A first-time offender convicted of voluntary manslaughter receives a sentence of no more than 11 years. Only a first-time murderer receives a penalty equal to Ewing's—25 years to life. It is unfair to Ewing to equate his property crimes with a homicide, and foolish for society to spend this much money locking him up.

The Eighth Amendment also outlaws excessive fines. Forfeiture is the most controversial topic under this clause. **Forfeiture** is a *civil* law proceeding that is permitted by many different *criminal* statutes. Once a court has convicted a defendant under certain criminal statutes—such as a controlled substance law—the government may seek forfeiture of property associated with the criminal act. *How much* property can the government take? To determine if forfeiture is fair, courts generally look at three factors: whether the property was used in committing the crime, whether it was purchased with proceeds from illegal acts, and whether the punishment is disproportionate to the defendant's wrongdoing. Neal Brunk pleaded guilty to selling 2.5 ounces of marijuana, and the government promptly sought forfeiture of his house on 90 acres, worth about $99,000. The court found that forfeiture was legitimate because Brunk had used drug money to buy the land and then sold narcotics from the property.[14] By contrast, Hosep Bajakajian attempted to leave the United States without reporting $375,000 cash to customs officials as the law requires. The government demanded forfeiture of the full sum, but the Supreme Court ruled that seizure of the entire amount was grossly disproportionate to the minor crime of failing to report cash movement.[15]

[14] *U.S. v. Brunk*, 2001 U.S. App. LEXIS 7566 (4th Cir., 2001).

[15] *U.S. v. Bajakajian*, 524 U.S. 321, 118 S. Ct. 2028, 1998 U.S. LEXIS 4172 (S. Ct., 1998).

CRIMES THAT HARM BUSINESS

Businesses must deal with four major crimes: larceny, fraud, arson, and embezzlement.

Larceny

It is holiday season at the mall, the period of greatest profits—and the most crime. At the Foot Forum, a teenager limps in wearing ragged sneakers and sneaks out wearing Super Sneakers, valued at $145. Down the aisle at a home furnishing store, a man is so taken by a $375 power saw that he takes it. Sweethearts swipe sweaters, pensioners pocket produce. All are committing larceny.

Economists estimate that *12 cents out of every dollar* spent in retail stores covers the cost of shoplifting.

Larceny is the trespassory taking of personal property with the intent to steal it. "Trespassory taking" means that someone else originally has the property. The Super Sneakers are personal property (not real estate), they were in the possession of the Foot Forum, and the teenager deliberately left without paying, intending never to return the goods. That is larceny. By contrast, suppose Fast Eddie leaves Bloomingdale's in New York, descends to the subway system, and jumps over a turnstile without paying. Larceny? No. He has "taken" a service—the train ride—but not personal property.

Each year, about $10 billion in merchandise is stolen from retail stores in the United States. Economists estimate that *12 cents out of every dollar* spent in retail stores covers the cost of shoplifting. Some criminal experts believe that drug addicts commit over half of all shoplifting to support their habits. Stores have added electronic surveillance, security patrols, and magnetic antitheft devices, but the problem will not disappear.

Fraud

Robert Dorsey owned Bob's Chrysler in Highland, Illinois. When he bought cars, the First National Bank of Highland paid Chrysler, and Dorsey—supposedly—repaid the bank as he sold the autos. Dorsey, though, began to suffer financial problems, and the bank suspected he was selling cars without repaying his loans. A state investigator notified Dorsey that he planned to review all dealership records. One week later, a fire engulfed the dealership. An arson investigator discovered that an electric iron, connected to a timer, had been placed on a pile of financial papers doused with accelerant.

The saddest part of this true story is that it is only too common. Some experts suggest that 1 percent of corporate revenues are wasted on fraud alone. Dorsey was convicted and imprisoned for committing two crimes that cost business billions of dollars annually—fraud (for failing to repay the loans) and arson (for burning down the dealership).[16]

Fraud
Deception for the purpose of obtaining money or property.

Fraud refers to various crimes, all of which have a common element: **the deception of another person for the purpose of obtaining money or property from him**. Robert Dorsey's precise violation was bank fraud, a federal crime.[17] It is bank fraud to use deceit to obtain money, assets, securities, or other property under the control of any financial institution.

---

[16] *United States v. Dorsey*, 27 F.3d 285, 1994 U.S. App. LEXIS 15010 (7th Cir., 1994).

[17] 18 U.S.C. §1344.

Wire Fraud and Mail Fraud

Wire and mail fraud are additional federal crimes, involving the use of interstate mail, telegram, telephone, radio, or television to obtain property by deceit.[18] For example, if Marsha makes an interstate phone call to sell land that she does not own, that is wire fraud.

Theft of Honest Services

Under traditional standards, a culprit could only be convicted of fraud if he had deceived the victim to get something of value from *her*. But what if a CEO manipulates the financial results of his company and otherwise misleads investors to keep the stock price high? He has not committed fraud under this traditional definition because he did not personally obtain money from the investors—they bought their stock either from other shareholders or from the company.

To find a way to punish these wrongdoers, prosecutors looked to a statute that prohibits the **theft of honest services.**[19] Originally, this law was used to prosecute public officials who took bribes or kickbacks. But then prosecutors began to apply it to employees in the private sector as well. Prosecutors took the view that an employee violated this law if she did not fully perform the job for which she was paid. Thus, the CEO could be charged for not having done his job properly. But under this standard, the scope of the statute became enormous. In theory, an employee who called in sick so that he could watch his son's play has violated this statute. The scope of the statute permitted enormous discretion on the part of prosecutors.

The Supreme Court recently stepped in to limit its scope. As the following case reveals, **the theft of honest services statute prohibits public and private employees from taking bribes or kickbacks**.

Skilling v. United States

130 S. Ct. 2896, 2010 U.S. LEXIS 5259
Supreme Court of the United States, 2010

Facts: The Enron Corporation was founded as an energy company in Houston, Texas, Five years later, it hired Jeffrey Skilling, a young Harvard Business School graduate, to run one of its subsidiaries. He was promoted to president and chief operating officer 11 years later. At that time, only six companies in the United States had higher revenues than Enron. Six months after Skilling's promotion, he resigned. Four months after that, Enron filed for bankruptcy protection.

The company's stock, which had been trading at $90 per share, became virtually worthless. A government investigation uncovered an elaborate conspiracy to prop up Enron's stock prices by overstating the company's financial well-being. The government prosecuted dozens of Enron employees who participated in the scheme. Skilling's indictment charged that he had violated the honest services statute. He was convicted and sentenced to 292 months imprisonment, 3 years supervised release, and $45 million in restitution. Skilling appealed, arguing that he had not violated the honest services statute because it only applied to bribery and kickback schemes. The Fifth Circuit affirmed his conviction. The Supreme Court granted *certiorari*.

Issue: ***Did Skilling violate the honest services statute?***

Excerpts from Justice Ginsburg's Opinion: Unlike fraud, in which the victim's loss of money or property supplied the defendant's gain, with one the mirror image of the other, the honest-services theory targeted corruption that lacked similar symmetry. While the offender profited, the betrayed party suffered no deprivation of money or

---

[18] 18 U.S.C. §§1341–1346.
[19] 18 U.S.C. § 1346.

property; instead, a third party, who had not been deceived, provided the enrichment. For example, if a city mayor (the offender) accepted a bribe from a third party in exchange for awarding that party a city contract, yet the contract terms were the same as any that could have been negotiated at arm's length, the city (the betrayed party) would suffer no tangible loss. Even if the scheme occasioned a money or property *gain* for the betrayed party, courts reasoned, actionable harm lay in the denial of that party's right to the offender's "honest services." Over time, an increasing number of courts recognized that a recreant employee—public or private—could be prosecuted under this statute if he breached his allegiance to his employer by accepting bribes or kickbacks in the course of his employment.

Skilling asserts that [the honest services statute] is unconstitutionally vague. To satisfy due process, a penal statute must define the criminal offense [1] with sufficient definiteness that ordinary people can understand what conduct is prohibited and [2] in a manner that does not encourage arbitrary and discriminatory enforcement. According to Skilling, [the honest services statute] meets neither of the two due process essentials. First, the phrase "the right of honest services," he contends, does not adequately define what behavior it bars. Second, he alleges, [the honest services statute's] standardless sweep allows policemen, prosecutors, and juries to pursue their personal predilections, thereby facilitating opportunistic and arbitrary prosecutions.

In the main, prosecutions under this statute involved fraudulent schemes to deprive another of honest services through bribes or kickbacks supplied by a third party who had not been deceived. Confined to these paramount applications, [the honest services statute] presents no vagueness problem. Reading the statute to proscribe a wider range of offensive conduct, we acknowledge, would raise the due process concerns underlying the vagueness doctrine. To preserve the statute without transgressing constitutional limitations, we now hold that [the honest services statute] criminalizes only the bribe-and-kickback core.

The Government did not, at any time, allege that Skilling solicited or accepted side payments from a third party in exchange for making these misrepresentations. It is therefore clear that Skilling did not commit honest-services fraud.

Skilling had been found guilty of three crimes: honest services fraud, wire fraud, and securities fraud. Although the Supreme Court ruled that Skilling had not violated the honest services statute, they remanded the case to the appeals court to determine if the other two convictions were independent enough to stand on their own without the honest services element. If not, he would have to be retried. The appeals court did uphold Skilling's two other convictions.

Insurance Fraud

Insurance fraud is another common crime. A Ford suddenly swerves in front of a Toyota, causing it to brake hard. A Mercedes, unable to stop, slams into the Toyota, as the Ford races away. Regrettable accident? No: a "swoop and squat" fraud scheme. The Ford and Toyota drivers were working together, hoping to cause an accident with someone else. The "injured" Toyota driver now goes to a third member of the fraud team—a dishonest doctor—who diagnoses serious back and neck injuries and predicts long-term pain and disability. The driver files a claim against the Mercedes's driver, whose insurer may be forced to pay tens or even hundreds of thousands of dollars for an accident that was no accident. Insurance companies investigate countless cases like this each year, trying to distinguish the honest victim from the criminal.

EXAM Strategy

Question: Eric mails glossy brochures to 25,000 people, offering to sell them a one-month time-share in a stylish apartment in Las Vegas. The brochure depicts an imposing building, an opulent apartment, and spectacular pools. To reserve a space, customers need only send in a $2,000 deposit. Three hundred people respond, sending in the money. In fact, there is no such building. Eric, planning to flee with the cash, is arrested and prosecuted. His sentence could be as long as 20 years. (1) With what crime is he charged? (2) Is this a felony or misdemeanor prosecution? (3) Does Eric have a right to a jury trial? (4) What is the government's burden of proof?

Strategy: (1) Eric is deceiving people, and that should tell you the *type* of crime. (2, 3) The potential 20-year sentence determines whether Eric's crime is a misdemeanor or felony, and whether or not he is entitled to a jury trial. (4) We know that the government has the burden of proof in criminal prosecutions—but *how much* evidence must it offer?

Result: Eric has committed fraud. A felony is one in which the sentence could be a year or more. The potential penalty here is 20 years, so the crime is a felony. Eric has a right to a jury, as does any defendant whose sentence could be six months or longer. The prosecution must prove its case beyond a reasonable doubt, a much higher burden than that in a civil case.

© Patricia Marks/Shutterstock

Tragic accident…or felony?

Arson

Robert Dorsey, the Chrysler dealer, committed a second serious crime. **Arson** is the malicious use of fire or explosives to damage or destroy any real estate or personal property. It is both a federal and a state crime. Dorsey used arson to conceal his bank fraud. Most arsonists hope to collect on insurance policies. Every year thousands of buildings burn, particularly in economically depressed neighborhoods, as owners try to make a quick kill or extricate themselves from financial difficulties. Everyone who purchases insurance ends up paying higher premiums because of this immorality.

Embezzlement

This crime also involves illegally obtaining property, but with one big difference: the culprit begins with legal possession. **Embezzlement** is the fraudulent conversion of property already in the defendant's possession.

This is a story without romance: for 15 years, Kristy Watts worked part-time as a bookkeeper for romance writer Danielle Steele, handling payroll and accounting. During that time, Watts stole $768,000 despite earning a salary of $200,000 a year. Watts said that she had been motivated by envy and jealousy. She was sentenced to three years in prison and agreed to pay her former boss almost $1 million.

Arson
The malicious use of fire or explosives to damage or destroy real estate or personal property.

Embezzlement
The fraudulent conversion of property already in the defendant's possession.

Crimes Committed by Business

A corporation can be found guilty of a crime based on the conduct of any of its **agents**, who include anyone undertaking work on behalf of the corporation. An agent can be a corporate officer, an accountant hired to audit a statement, a sales clerk, or almost any other person performing a job at the company's request.

If an agent commits a criminal act within the scope of his employment and with the intent to benefit the corporation, the company is liable.[20] This means that the agent himself must first be guilty. If the agent is guilty, the corporation is, too.

[20]*New York Central & Hudson River R.R. Co. v. United States*, 212 U.S. 481, 29 S. Ct. 304, 1909 U.S. LEXIS 1832 (S. Ct., 1909). Note that what counts is the intention to benefit, not actual benefit. A corporation will not escape liability by showing that the scheme failed.

Critics believe that the criminal law has gone too far. It is unfair, they argue, to impose *criminal* liability on a corporation, and thus penalize the shareholders, unless high-ranking officers were directly involved in the illegal conduct. The following case concerns a corporation's responsibility for a death caused by its employee.

Commonwealth v. Angelo Todesca Corp.

446 Mass. 128, 842 N.E. 2d 930
Supreme Judicial Court of Massachusetts, 2006

Facts: Brian Gauthier, an experienced truck driver, worked for Todesca, a paving company. After about a year driving a particular 10-wheel tri-axle dump truck, Gauthier noticed that the back-up alarm had stopped working. When he reported this, the company mechanic realized that the old alarm needed replacement. The mechanic had none in stock, so the company instructed Gauthier to drive the truck without the alarm.

About a month later, Gauthier and other Todesca drivers were delivering asphalt to the work site on a highway at the entrance to a shopping mall. A police officer directed the construction vehicles and the routine mall traffic. A different driver asked the officer to "watch our backs" as the trucks backed through the intersection. All of the other trucks were equipped with back-up alarms. When it was Gauthier's turn to back up, he struck the police officer, killing him.

The state charged the Todesca corporation with motor vehicle homicide, and the jury found the company guilty. The trial judge imposed a fine—of $2,500. The court of appeals reversed the conviction, and the prosecution appealed to the state's highest court.

Issue: ***Could the company be found guilty of motor vehicle homicide?***

Excerpts from Justice Spina's Decision: Before criminal liability may be imposed on a corporate defendant, the Commonwealth must prove that the individual for whose conduct it seeks to charge the corporation criminally was placed in a position by the corporation where he had enough responsibility to act for the corporation, and that he was acting in behalf of the corporation [when] he committed a criminal act.

The defendant maintains that a corporation never can be criminally liable for motor vehicle homicide because the language of a criminal statute must be construed strictly, and a "corporation" cannot "operate" a vehicle. We agree with the Commonwealth. Because a corporation is not a living person, it can act only through its agents. By the defendant's reasoning, a corporation never could be liable for any crime. A "corporation" can no more serve alcohol to minors, or bribe government officials, or falsify data on loan applications, than operate a vehicle negligently: only human agents, acting for the corporation, are capable of these actions. Nevertheless, we consistently have held that a corporation may be criminally liable for such acts when performed by corporate employees, acting within the scope of their employment and on behalf of the corporation.

It was undisputed that Gauthier's truck was not equipped with a functioning back-up alarm at the time of the collision, and that he knew the alarm was missing. Although a back-up alarm was not required by statute, the defendant had a written safety policy mandating that all its trucks be equipped with such alarms. An employee's violation of his employer's rules, intended to protect the safety of third persons, is evidence of the employee's negligence, for which the employer may be held liable.

Other drivers at the work site had functioning back-up alarms, and although they spoke moments before the collision, Gauthier never informed the victim that his truck did not have an alarm. The jury could have inferred that the victim, a veteran police officer, was aware that the defendant's custom was to equip its trucks with back-up alarms, and that the victim expected to hear a back-up alarm when a driver operated a truck in reverse.

The jury also could have inferred that an alarm on Gauthier's truck would have sounded practically in the victim's ear, alerting him to the truck's movement in time to get out of its way. The back-up alarm makes a distinctive beeping sound, intended to warn people behind the vehicle that it is operating in reverse, and the victim did not realize Gauthier's truck was backing up because he did not hear that sound.

Affirmed.

Selected Crimes Committed by Business

Workplace Crimes

The workplace can be dangerous. Working on an assembly line exposes factory employees to fast-moving machinery. For a roofer, the first slip may be the last. The invisible radiation in a nuclear power plant can be deadlier than a bullet. The most important statute regulating the workplace is the federal **Occupational Safety and Health Act of 1970 (OSHA)**,[21] which sets safety standards for many industries.[22] May a state government go beyond standards set by OSHA and use the criminal law to punish dangerous conditions? In *People v. O'Neill*,[23] the courts of Illinois answered that question with a potent "yes," permitting a *murder prosecution* against corporate executives themselves.

Film Recovery Systems was an Illinois corporation in business to extract silver from used X-ray film and then resell it. Steven O'Neill was president of Film Recovery, Charles Kirschbaum was its plant manager, and Daniel Rodriguez the foreman. To extract the silver, workers at Film Recovery soaked the X-ray film in large, open, bubbling vats that contained sodium cyanide.

A worker named Stefan Golab became faint. He left the production area and walked to the lunchroom, where workers found him trembling and foaming at the mouth. He lost consciousness. Rushed to a hospital, he was pronounced dead on arrival. The Cook County medical examiner determined that Golab died from acute cyanide poisoning caused by inhalation of cyanide fumes in the plant.

Illinois indicted Film Recovery and several of its managers for murder. The indictment charged that O'Neill and Kirschbaum committed murder by failing to disclose to Golab that he was working with cyanide and other potentially lethal substances and by failing to provide him with appropriate and necessary safety equipment.

The case was tried to a judge without a jury. Workers testified that O'Neill, Kirschbaum, and other managers never told them they were using cyanide or that the fumes they inhaled could be harmful; that management made no effort to ventilate the factory; that Film Recovery gave the workers no goggles or protective clothing; that the chemicals they worked with burned their skin; that breathing was difficult in the plant because of strong, foul orders; and that workers suffered frequent dizziness, nausea, and vomiting.

The trial judge found O'Neill, Kirschbaum, and others guilty of murder. Illinois defines murder as performing an act that the defendant *knows will create a strong probability of death* in the victim, and the judge found they had done that. He found Film Recovery guilty of involuntary manslaughter. Involuntary manslaughter is *recklessly* performing an act that causes death. He sentenced O'Neill, Kirschbaum, and Rodriguez to 25 years in prison.

The defendants appealed, contending that the verdicts were inconsistent. They argued, and the Illinois Court of Appeals agreed, that the judge had made contradictory findings. Murder required the specific intent of *knowing there was a strong probability of death*, whereas the manslaughter conviction required *reckless* conduct. The appeals court reversed the convictions and remanded for a new trial.

Moments before the new trial was to start, O'Neill, Kirschbaum, and Rodriguez all pleaded guilty to involuntary manslaughter. They received sentences of three years, two years, and four months, respectively.

---

[21] 29 U.S.C. §§651 et seq. (1982).

[22] See Chapter 29 on employment law.

[23] 194 Ill. App. 3d 79, 550 N.E.2d 1090, 1990 Ill. App. LEXIS 65 (Ill. App. Ct. 1990).

Hiring Illegal Workers

Employers are required to verify their workers' eligibility for employment in the United States. It is illegal to knowingly employ unauthorized workers. Within three days of hiring a worker, the employer must complete an I-9 form, which lists the items that can be used as documentation of eligibility. The government has the right to arrest illegal employees, and it can also bring charges against the business that hired them.

RICO

The **Racketeer Influenced and Corrupt Organizations Act** (RICO) is one of the most powerful and controversial statutes ever written.[24] Congress passed the law primarily to prevent gangsters from taking money they earned illegally and investing it in legitimate businesses. But RICO has expanded far beyond the original intentions of Congress and is now used more often against ordinary businesses than against organized criminals. Some regard this wide application as a tremendous advance in law enforcement, but others view it as an oppressive weapon used to club ethical companies into settlements they should never have to make.

Racketeer Influenced and Corrupt Organizations Act (RICO)
A powerful Federal statute, originally aimed at organized crime, now used in many criminal prosecutions and civil lawsuits.

What is a violation of this law? **RICO prohibits using two or more racketeering acts to accomplish any of these goals: (1) investing in or acquiring legitimate businesses with criminal money; (2) maintaining or acquiring businesses through criminal activity; or (3) operating businesses through criminal activity.**

What does that mean in English? It is a two-step process to prove that a person or an organization has violated RICO.

- The prosecutor must show that the defendant committed two or more **racketeering acts**, which are any of a long list of specified crimes: embezzlement, arson, mail fraud, wire fraud, and so forth. Thus, if a gangster ordered a building torched in January and then burned a second building in October, that would be two racketeering acts. If a stockbroker told two customers that Bronx Gold Mines was a promising stock, when she knew that it was worthless, that would be two racketeering acts.

Racketeering acts
Any of a long list of specified crimes, such as embezzlement, arson, mail fraud, wire fraud, and so forth.

- The prosecutor must then show that the defendant used these racketeering acts to accomplish one of the three *purposes* listed above. If the gangster committed two arsons and then used the insurance payments to buy a dry cleaning business, that would violate RICO. If the stockbroker gave fraudulent advice and used the commissions to buy advertising for her firm, that would violate RICO.

The government may prosecute both individuals and organizations for violating RICO. For example, the government prosecuted financier Michael Milken for manipulating stock prices. It also threatened to prosecute his employer, Drexel Burnham Lambert. If the government proves its case, the defendant can be hit with large fines and a prison sentence of up to 20 years. RICO also permits the government to seek forfeiture of the defendant's property. A court may order a convicted defendant to hand over any property or money used in the criminal acts or derived from them. Courts often freeze a defendant's assets once charges are brought to ensure that he will not hide the assets. If all his assets are frozen, he will have a hard time paying his defense lawyer, so a freeze often encourages a defendant to plea bargain on a lesser charge. Both Milken and Drexel entered into plea agreements with the government, rather than face a freeze on their assets, or in Milken's case, a long prison sentence.

[24] 18 U.S.C. §§1961–1968.

In addition to criminal penalties, RICO also creates civil law liabilities. The government, organizations, and individuals all have the right to file civil lawsuits, seeking damages and, if necessary, injunctions. For example, a physician sued State Farm Insurance, alleging that the company had hired doctors to produce false medical reports that the company used to cut off claims by injured policy holders. As a result of these fake reports, the company refused to pay the plaintiff for legitimate services he performed on the policy holders. RICO is powerful (and for defendants, frightening) in part because a civil plaintiff can recover **treble damages**, that is, a judgment for three times the harm actually suffered, as well as attorney's fees.

Money Laundering

Money laundering
Using the proceeds of criminal acts either to promote crime or conceal the source of the money.

Money laundering consists of taking the proceeds of certain criminal acts and either (1) using the money to promote crime, or (2) attempting to conceal the source of the money.[25]

Money laundering is an important part of major criminal enterprises. Successful criminals earn enormous sums, which they must filter back into the flow of commerce so that their crimes go undetected. Laundering is an essential part of the corrosive traffic in drugs. Profits, all in cash, may mount so swiftly that dealers struggle to use the money without attracting the government's attention. For example, Colombian drug cartels set up a sophisticated system in which they shipped money to countries such as Dubai that do not keep records on cash transactions. This money was then transferred to the U.S. disguised as offshore loans. Prosecution by the U.S. government led to the demise of some of the banks involved.

But drug money is not the only or even major component of so-called flight capital. Criminals also try to hide the vast sums they earn from arms dealing and tax evasion. Some of this money is used to support terrorist organizations.

EXAM Strategy

Question: Explain the difference between embezzlement and money laundering. Give an example of each.

Strategy: Both crimes involve money illegally obtained, but they are very different. As to embezzlement, how did the criminal obtain the funds? In a laundering case, to what use is the criminal trying to put the cash?

Result: Embezzlement refers to fraudulently taking money that is already in the defendant's possession. For example, if a financial advisor, *lawfully entrusted* with his client's funds for investing, uses some of the cash to buy himself a luxurious yacht, he has embezzled the client's money. Money laundering consists of taking *illegally obtained* money and either using the funds to promote additional crimes or attempting to *conceal* the source of the cash. Thus, an arms dealer might launder money so that he can use it to finance a terrorist organization.

[25] 18 U.S.C. §§1956 et seq.

Other Crimes

Additional crimes that affect business appear elsewhere in the text. An increasing number of federal and state statutes are designed to punish those who harm the environment. (See Chapter 40, on environmental law.) Antitrust violations, in which a corporation fixes prices, can lead to criminal prosecutions. (See Chapter 38, on antitrust law.) Finally, securities fraud is a crime and can lead to severe prison sentences. (See Chapter 36, on securities regulation.)

Punishing a Corporation

Fines

The most common punishment for a corporation is a fine, as demonstrated in the Todesca case. This makes sense in that the purpose of a business is to earn a profit, and a fine, theoretically, hurts. But most fines are modest by the present standards of corporate wealth. In the Todesca prosecution, does a $2,500 fine force corporate leaders to be more cautious, or does it teach them that cutting corners makes economic sense, because the penalties will be a tolerable cost of doing business?

Sometimes the fines are stiffer. British Petroleum was found guilty of two serious environmental violations. In Alaska, the company's failure to inspect and clean pipelines caused 200,000 gallons of crude oil to spill onto the tundra. In Texas, the company's failure to follow standard procedures for ensuring safe refineries caused a catastrophic explosion that killed 15 people and injured 170 more. The total fine for both criminal violations was $62 million.[26] Is that enough to change BP's practices? Evidently not. In the spring of 2010, a BP well called Deepwater Horizon exploded, killing 11 workers and releasing into the Gulf of Mexico the largest marine oil spill ever. The Deepwater rig had violated many safety requirements.

Compliance Programs

The **Federal Sentencing Guidelines** are the detailed rules that judges must follow when sentencing defendants convicted of crimes in federal court. The guidelines instruct judges to determine whether, at the time of the crime, the corporation had in place a serious **compliance program**, that is, a plan to prevent and detect criminal conduct at all levels of the company. A company that can point to a detailed, functioning compliance program may benefit from a dramatic reduction in the fine or other punishment meted out. Indeed, a tough compliance program may even convince federal investigators to curtail an investigation and to limit any prosecution to those directly involved, rather than attempting to get a conviction against high-ranking officers or the company itself.

Federal Sentencing Guidelines
The detailed rules that judges must follow when sentencing defendants convicted of crimes in federal court.

Compliance program
A plan to prevent and detect criminal conduct at all levels of the company.

For a compliance plan to be deemed effective:

- The program must be reasonably capable of reducing the prospect of criminal conduct.
- Specific, high-level officers must be responsible for overseeing the program.
- The company must not place in charge any officers it knows or should have known, from past experience, are likely to engage in illegal conduct.
- The company must effectively communicate the program to all employees and agents.
- The company must ensure compliance by monitoring employees in a position to cheat and by promptly disciplining any who break the law.

[26] Source: **http://epa.gov/**.

Chapter Conclusion

Crime has an enormous impact on business. Companies are victims of crimes, and sometimes they also commit criminal actions. Successful business leaders are ever-vigilant to protect their company from those who wish to harm it, whether from the inside or the outside.

EXAM REVIEW

1. **BURDEN OF PROOF** In all prosecutions, the government must prove its case beyond a reasonable doubt. (p. 180)

EXAM Strategy

Question: Arnie owns a two-family house in a poor section of the city. A fire breaks out, destroying the building and causing $150,000 damage to an adjacent store. The state charges Arnie with arson. Simultaneously, Vickie, the store owner, sues Arnie for the damage to her property. Both cases are tried to juries, and the two juries hear identical evidence of Arnie's actions. But the criminal jury acquits Arnie, while the civil jury awards Vickie $150,000. How did that happen?

Strategy: The opposite outcomes are probably due to the different burdens of proof in a civil and criminal case. Make sure you know that distinction. (See the "Result" at the end of this section.)

2. **RIGHT TO A JURY.** A criminal defendant has a right to a trial by jury for any charge that could result in a sentence of six months or longer. (p. 180)

3. **DURESS** A defendant is not guilty of a crime if she committed it under duress. However, the defendant bears the burden of proving by a preponderance of the evidence that she acted under duress. (p. 181)

4. **ENTRAPMENT.** When the government induces the defendant to break the law, the prosecution must prove beyond a reasonable doubt that the defendant was predisposed to commit the crime. (p. 181)

5. **FOURTH AMENDMENT.** The Fourth Amendment to the Constitution prohibits the government from making illegal searches and seizures of individuals, corporations, partnerships, and other organizations. (pp. 181–185)

6. **WARRANT.** As a general rule, the police must obtain a warrant before conducting a search but there are seven circumstances under which the police may search without a warrant. (pp. 181–182)

7. **THE EXCLUSIONARY RULE.** Under the exclusionary rule, a prosecutor may not use evidence obtained illegally. (pp. 182–183)

8. **FIFTH AMENDMENT** The Fifth Amendment requires due process in all criminal procedures and prohibits double jeopardy and self-incrimination. (pp. 185–187)

9. **SIXTH AMENDMENT** The Sixth Amendment guarantees criminal defendants the right to a lawyer. (p. 187)

10. **EIGHTH AMENDMENT** The Eighth Amendment prohibits excessive fines and cruel and unusual punishments. (pp. 189–190)

11. **LARCENY** Larceny is the trespassory taking of personal property with the intent to steal. (p. 191)

12. **FRAUD** Fraud refers to a variety of crimes, all of which involve the deception of another person for the purpose of obtaining money or property. (pp. 191–193)

Question: Chuck is a DJ on a radio station. A music company offers to pay him every time he plays one of its songs. Soon enough, Chuck is earning $10,000 a week in these extra payments, and his listeners love the music. In Chuck's view, this is a win-win situation. Is Chuck right?

Strategy: This is not traditional fraud because Chuck is not getting money from the people he is cheating—his listeners. Indeed, they are happy. Is there another type of fraud that applies in this situation? (See the "Result" at the end of this section.)

13. **ARSON** Arson is the malicious use of fire or explosives to damage or destroy real estate or personal property. (p. 193)

14. **EMBEZZLEMENT** Embezzlement is the fraudulent conversion of property already in the defendant's possession. (p. 193)

15. **CORPORATE LIABILITY** If a company's agent commits a criminal act within the scope of her employment and with the intent to benefit the corporation, the company is liable. (pp. 196–197)

16. **RICO** RICO prohibits using two or more racketeering acts to invest in legitimate business or carry on certain other criminal acts. RICO permits civil lawsuits as well as criminal prosecutions. (pp. 197–198)

Question: Cheryl is a bank teller. She figures out a way to steal $99.99 per day in cash without getting caught. She takes the money daily for eight months and invests it in a catering business she is starting with Floyd, another teller. When Floyd learns what she is doing, he tries it, but is caught in his first attempt. He and Cheryl are both prosecuted.

(a) Both are guilty only of larceny.

(b) Both are guilty of larceny and violating RICO.

(c) Both are guilty of embezzlement; Cheryl is also guilty of violating RICO.

(d) Both are guilty of embezzlement and violating RICO.

Strategy: You need to know the difference between larceny and embezzlement. What is it? Once you have that figured out, focus on RICO. The government must prove two things: First, that the defendant committed crimes more than once—how many times? Second, that the defendant used the criminal proceeds for a specific purpose—what? (See the "Result" at the end of this section.)

17. MONEY LAUNDERING Money laundering consists of taking profits from a criminal act and either using them to promote crime or attempting to conceal their source. (p. 198)

1. Result: The plaintiff offered enough proof to convince a jury by a preponderance of the evidence that Arnie had damaged her store. However that same evidence, offered in a criminal prosecution, was not enough to persuade the jury beyond a reasonable doubt that Arnie had lit the fire.

12. Result: Chuck has committed a theft of honest services because he has taken a bribe.

16. Result: Cheryl and Floyd both committed embezzlement, which refers to fraudulently taking money that was properly in their possession. Floyd did it once, but a RICO conviction requires two or more racketeering acts—Floyd has not violated RICO. Cheryl embezzled dozens of times and invested the money in a legitimate business. She is guilty of embezzlement and RICO; the correct answer is C.

Multiple-Choice Questions

1. In a criminal case, which statement is true?

(a) The prosecution must prove the government's case by a preponderance of the evidence.

(b) The criminal defendant is entitled to a lawyer even if she cannot afford to pay for it herself.

(c) The police are never allowed to question the accused without a lawyer present.

(d) All federal crimes are felonies.

2. The police are not required to obtain a warrant before conducting a search if:

(a) a reliable informant has told them they will find evidence of a crime in a particular location.

(b) they have a warrant for part of a property and another section of the property is in plain view.

(c) they see someone on the street who could possibly have committed a criminal act.

(d) someone living on the property has consented to the search.

3. Under the exclusionary rule, which statement is true?
   (a) Evidence must be excluded from trial if the search warrant is defective, even if the police believed at the time of the search that it was valid.
   (b) The prosecution cannot use any evidence the police found at the site of the illegal search, but it can use any evidence the police discover elsewhere as a result of the illegal search.
   (c) Any statements a defendant makes after arrest are inadmissible if the police do not read him his Miranda rights.
   (d) If a conviction is overturned because of the exclusionary rule, the prosecution is not allowed to retry the defendant.

4. Benry asks his girlfriend, Alina, to drive his car to the repair shop. She drives his car all right—to Las Vegas, where she hits the slots. Alina has committed
   (a) fraud.
   (b) embezzlement.
   (c) larceny.
   (d) a RICO violation.

5. Which of the following elements is required for a RICO conviction?
   (a) Investment in a legitimate business.
   (b) Two or more criminal acts.
   (c) Maintaining or acquiring businesses through criminal activity.
   (d) Operating a business through criminal activity.

ESSAY QUESTIONS

1. **YOU BE THE JUDGE WRITING PROBLEM** An undercover drug informant learned from a mutual friend that Philip Friedman "knew where to get marijuana." The informant asked Friedman three times to get him some marijuana, and Friedman agreed after the third request. Shortly thereafter, Friedman sold the informant a small amount of the drug. The informant later offered to sell Friedman three pounds of marijuana. They negotiated the price and then made the sale. Friedman was tried for trafficking in drugs. He argued entrapment. Was Friedman entrapped? **Argument for Friedman**: The undercover agent had to ask three times before Friedman sold him a small amount of drugs. A real drug dealer, predisposed to commit the crime, leaps at an opportunity to sell. If the government spends time and money luring innocent people into the commission of crimes, all of us are the losers. **Argument for the Government**: Government officials suspected Friedman of being a sophisticated drug dealer, and they were right. When he had a chance to buy three pounds, a quantity only a dealer would purchase, he not only did so, but he bargained with skill, showing a working knowledge of the business. Friedman was not entrapped—he was caught.

2. Conley owned video poker machines. Although they are outlawed in Pennsylvania, he placed them in bars and clubs. He used profits from the machines to buy more machines. Is he guilty of money laundering?

3. Karin made illegal firearm purchases at a gun show. At her trial, she alleged that she had committed this crime because her boyfriend had threatened to harm her and her two daughters if she did not. Her lawyer asked the judge to instruct the jury that the prosecution had an obligation to prove beyond a reasonable doubt that Karin had acted freely. Instead, the judge told the jury that Karin had the burden of proving duress by a preponderance of the evidence. Who is correct?

4. An informant bought drugs from Dorian. The police obtained a search warrant to search Dorian's house. But before they acted on the warrant, they sent the informant back to try again. This time, Dorian said he did not have any drugs. The police then acted on the warrant and searched his house. Did the police have probable cause?

5. Shawn was caught stealing letters from mailboxes. After pleading guilty, he was sentenced to two months in prison and three years supervised release. One of the supervised release conditions required him to stand outside a post office for eight hours wearing a signboard stating, "I stole mail. This is my punishment." He appealed this requirement on the grounds that it constituted cruel and unusual punishment. Do you agree?

Discussion Questions

1. Under British law, a police officer must now say the following to a suspect placed under arrest: "You do not have to say anything. But if you do not mention now something which you later use in your defense, the court may decide that your failure to mention it now strengthens the case against you. A record will be made of anything you say and it may be given in evidence if you are brought to trial." What is the goal of this British law? What does a police officer in the United States have to say, and what difference does it make at the time of an arrest? Which approach is better?

2. **ETHICS** You are a prosecutor who think it is possible that Naonka, in her role as CEO of a brokerage firm, has stolen money from her customers, many of whom are not well off. If you charge her and her company with RICO violations, you know that she is likely to plea bargain because otherwise her assets and those of the company may be frozen by the court. As part of the plea bargain, you might be able to get her to disclose evidence about other people who might have taken part in this criminal activity. But you do not have any hard evidence at this point. Would such an indictment be ethical? Do the ends justify the means? Is it worth it to harm Naonka for the chance of protecting thousands of innocent investors?

3. Van is brought to the police station for questioning about a shooting at a mall. The police read him his Miranda rights. For the rest of the three-hour interrogation, he remains silent except for a few one-word responses. Has he waived his right to remain silent? Can those few words be used against him in court?

4. Police arrested Bennie on a warrant issued in a neighboring county. When they searched him, the police found drugs and a gun. Only later did the police discover that when they had used the warrant, it was not valid because it had been recalled months earlier. The notice of recall had not been entered into the database. Should the evidence of drugs and a gun be suppressed under the exclusionary rule?

5. Andy was arrested for driving under the influence of alcohol (DUI). He had already been convicted of another driving offense. The court in the *first* offense was notified of this later DUI charge and took that information into consideration when determining Andy's sentence. Did the state violate Andy's protection against double jeopardy when it subsequently tried and convicted him for the DUI offense?

CHAPTER 9

INTERNATIONAL LAW

© r.nagy/Shutterstock.com

The month after Anfernee graduates from business school, he opens a clothing store. Sales are brisk, but Anfernee is making little profit because his American-made clothes are expensive. Then an Asian company offers to sell him identical merchandise for 45 percent less than the American suppliers charge. Anfernee is elated, but quickly begins to wonder: Why is the new price so low? The sales representative expects Anfernee to sell no clothes except his. Is that legal? He also requests a $50,000 cash "commission" to smooth the export process in his country. That sounds suspicious, too. The questions multiply. Will the contract be written in English or a foreign language? Must Anfernee pay in dollars or some other currency? The foreign company wants a letter of credit. What does that mean? What law will govern the agreement? If the clothes are defective, how will disputes be resolved—and where?

The world is now one vast economy, and deals can cross borders quickly.

Transnational business grows with breathtaking speed. The United States now exports more than $1 trillion worth of goods and services. Leading exports include industrial machinery, computers, aircraft, agricultural products, electronic equipment, and chemicals. Anfernee should put this lesson under his cap: the world is now one vast economy, and deals can cross borders quickly.

TRADE REGULATION: THE BIG PICTURE

Nations regulate international trade in many ways. In this section we look at export and import controls that affect trade out of and into the United States. **Exporting** is shipping goods or services out of a country. The United States, with its huge farms, is the world's largest exporter of agricultural products. **Importing** is shipping goods and services into a country. The United States suffers trade deficits every year because the value of its imports exceeds that of its exports, as the following table demonstrates.

Exporting
Shipping goods or services out of a country.

Importing
Shipping goods or services into a country.

Rank	Country	Exports (in billions of U.S. dollars)	Imports (in billions of U.S. dollars)
	Total, All Countries	1,278	1,912
1	Canada	249	277
2	China	92	365
3	Mexico	163	230

Export Controls

You and a friend open an electronics business, intending to purchase goods in this country for sale abroad. A representative of Interlex stops in to see you. Interlex is a Latin American electronics company, and the firm wants you to help it acquire a certain kind of infrared dome which helps helicopters identify nearby aircraft. You find a Pennsylvania company that manufactures the domes, and you realize that you can buy and sell them to Interlex for a handsome profit. Any reason not to? As a matter of fact, there is.

All nations limit what may be exported. In the United States, several statutes do this. The **Export Administration Act of 1985**[1] is one. This statute balances the need for free trade, which is essential in a capitalist society, with important requirements of national security. The statute permits the federal government to restrict exports if they endanger national security, harm foreign policy goals, or drain scarce materials.

The Secretary of Commerce makes a **Controlled Commodities List** of those items that meet any of these criteria. No one may export any commodity on the list without a license.

A second major limitation comes from the **Arms Export Control Act.**[2] This statute permits the President to create a second list of controlled goods, all related to military weaponry. Again, no person may export any listed item without a license.

The AECA will prohibit you from exporting the infrared domes. They are used in the guidance system of one of the most sophisticated weapons in the American defense arsenal. Foreign governments have attempted to obtain the equipment through official channels, but the federal government has placed the domes on the list of restricted military items. When a U.S. citizen did send such goods overseas, he was convicted and imprisoned.[3]

---

[1] 50 U.S.C. §2402 (1994).
[2] 22 U.S.C. §2778 (1994).
[3] *United States v. Tsai*, 954 F.2d 155, 1992 U.S. App. LEXIS 601 (3d Cir. 1992).

Import Controls

Tariffs

Tariff
A tax imposed on goods when they enter a country.

Tariffs are the most widespread method of limiting what may be imported into a nation. **A tariff is a tax imposed on goods when they enter a country.** Tariffs are also called *duties*. Nations use tariffs primarily to protect their domestic industries. Because the company importing the goods must pay this duty, the importer's costs increase, making the merchandise more expensive for consumers. This renders domestic products more attractive. High tariffs unquestionably help local industry, but they may harm local buyers. Consumers often benefit from zero tariffs because the unfettered competition drives down prices.

Tariffs change frequently and vary widely from one country to another. For manufactured goods, the United States imposes an average tariff of less than 4 percent, about the same as that in the European Union. However, some major trading partners around the world set tariffs of 10 to 30 percent for identical items, with those duties generally being highest in developing countries. Foodstuffs show even greater diversity. For agricultural products, average tariffs are about 25 percent in North America, but over 100 percent in South Asia. As we will see later in the chapter, regional trade treaties have changed the tariff landscape. The majority of all U.S. products entering Mexico are duty free. Almost all trade between Canada and the United States is done with zero tariffs, which is partly why the two nations do more bilateral commerce than any others in the world.

Classification. The U.S. Customs Service[4] imposes tariffs at the point of entry into the United States. A customs official inspects the merchandise as it arrives and classifies it, in other words, decides precisely what the goods are. This decision is critical because tariffs can vary greatly depending on the classification. Disputes at this stage typically involve an importer claiming that the Customs Service has imposed the wrong classification. Companies will often go to great lengths to convince a court to lower tariffs on their products.

In the following case, Isotoner claimed that a tariff violated the Constitution.

Did the company make a sensible argument? You be the judge.

[4]The Customs Service is part of the United States Customs and Border Protection, which is itself a division of the Department of Homeland Security.

You be the Judge

Totes-Isotoner Co. v. United States

594 F.3d 1346
United States Court of Appeals for the Federal Circuit, 2010

Facts: Isotoner imports gloves for sale in the United States. The U.S. imposes a higher tariff on "men's" leather gloves than it does on gloves manufactured "for other persons." Isotoner argued that this difference violated the Constitution's Equal Protection Clause and amounted to illegal gender discrimination. The lower court dismissed the complaint, and Isotoner appealed.

Issue: ***Do differing tariff rates for men's and women's gloves amount to illegal gender discrimination?***

Argument for Isotoner: Because the Constitution requires equal protection under the law, the government must treat people the same. In this instance, the government treats men worse than women—with the result that men will have to pay more for gloves. This

Is it acceptable for the government to set differing tariff rates on men's and women's gloves?

is unacceptable. Surely this court would not allow a special tax on yarmulkes, or higher tariffs linked to race. Distinctions that disfavor an entire group of people cannot stand.

Argument for the United States: To be in violation of the Equal Protection Clause, the government must intend to discriminate. That is not the case here. Tariff rates are set for a variety of reasons. Men's and women's gloves may be made by different companies, in different countries, with different impacts on American industry. Surely the government has the discretion to set different tariff rates for gloves or any other kind of imported goods.

Valuation. After classifying the imported goods, customs officials impose the appropriate duty ***ad valorem***, meaning "according to the value of the goods." In other words, the service must determine the value of the merchandise before it can tax a percentage of that value. This step can be equally contentious, since goods will have different prices at each stage of manufacturing and delivery. The question is supposed to be settled by the **transaction value** of the goods, meaning the price actually paid for the merchandise when sold for export to the United States (plus shipping and other minor costs). But there is often room for debate, so importers use customs agents to help negotiate the most favorable valuation.

Ad valorem
Customs officials impose duties "according to the value of the goods."

Duties for Dumping and Subsidizing

Dumping means selling merchandise at one price in the domestic market and at a cheaper, unfair price in an international market. Suppose a Singapore company, CelMaker, makes cellular telephones for $20 per unit and sells them in the United States for $12 each, vastly undercutting domestic American competitors. CelMaker may be willing to suffer short-term losses in order to bankrupt competitors. Once it has gained control of that market, it will raise its prices, more than compensating for its initial losses. And CelMaker may get help from its home government. Suppose the Singapore government prohibits foreign cellular phones from entering Singapore. CelMaker may sell its phones for $75 at home, earning such high profits that it can afford the temporary losses in America.

In the United States, the Commerce Department investigates suspected dumping. If the department concludes that the foreign company is selling items at **less than fair value**, and that this harms an American industry, it will impose a **dumping duty** that is sufficiently high to put the foreign goods back on fair footing with domestic products.

Dumping
Selling merchandise at one price in the domestic market and at a cheaper, unfair price in an international market.

Subsidized goods are also unfair. Suppose the Singapore government permits CelMaker to pay no taxes for 10 years. This enormous benefit will enable the company to produce cheap phones and undersell competitors. Again, the United States imposes a tariff on subsidized goods, called **countervailing duties**. If CelMaker sells phones for $15 that would cost an unsubsidized competitor $21 to make, it will pay a $6 countervailing duty on every phone entering the United States.

Treaties

Recall from Chapter 1 that the President makes treaties with foreign nations. To take effect, treaties must then be approved by at least two-thirds of the United States Senate. This section will examine three significant trade agreements.

General Agreement on Tariffs and Trade (GATT)

What is GATT? The greatest boon to American commerce in a century—or perhaps it is the worst assault on the American economy in 200 years. It depends on whom you ask. Let's start where everyone agrees.

GATT
The General Agreement on Tariffs and Trade.

GATT is the General Agreement on Tariffs and Trade. This massive international treaty has been negotiated on and off since the 1940s as nations have sought to eliminate trade barriers and bolster commerce. GATT has already had a considerable effect. In 1947, the worldwide average tariff on industrial goods was about 40 percent. Now it is about 4 percent. The world's economies have exploded over the past six decades. Leading supporters of GATT suggest that its lower tariffs vastly increase world trade. The United States is one of the biggest beneficiaries because for decades, this country has imposed lower duties than most other nations. A typical American family's annual income has increased due to the more vigorous domestic economy, and at the same time, many goods are less expensive because they enter with low duties.

But opponents claim that the United States now competes against nations with unlimited pools of exploited labor. These countries dominate labor-intensive industries such as textiles, clothing, and manufacturing, and are steadily taking jobs from millions of American workers. Because domestic job losses come in low-end employment, those put out of work are precisely those least able to find a new job.

World Trade Organization (WTO)
Organization created by GATT to stimulate international commerce and resolve trade disputes.

GATT created the **World Trade Organization** (WTO) to stimulate international commerce and resolve trade disputes. The WTO is empowered to hear arguments from any signatory nation about tariff violations or nontariff barriers. This international "court" may order compliance from any nation violating GATT and may penalize countries by imposing trade sanctions.

Here is how the WTO decides a trade dispute. Suppose that the United States believes that Brazil is unfairly restricting trade. The United States uses the WTO offices to request a consultation with Brazil's trade representative. In the majority of cases, these discussions lead to a satisfactory settlement. If the consultation does not resolve the problem, the United States asks the WTO's Dispute Settlement Body (DSB) to form a panel, which consists of three nations uninvolved in the dispute. After the panel hears testimony and arguments from both countries, it releases its report. The DSB generally approves the report, unless either nation appeals. If there is an appeal, the WTO Appellate Body hears the dispute and generally makes the final decision, subject to approval by the entire WTO. No single nation has the power to block final decisions. If a country refuses to comply with the WTO's ruling, affected nations may retaliate by imposing punitive tariffs. The following case forced the WTO to weigh the merits of two important, competing goals: environmental protection and trade growth.

United States—Import Prohibition of Certain Shrimp and Shrimp Products

AB-1998-4
WTO Appellate Body, 1998

Facts: Sea turtles are migratory animals that live throughout the world. The United States recognizes the animals as an endangered species. Studies showed that the greatest threat to the turtles, around the world, came from shrimp fishermen inadvertently catching the animals in their nets. The federal government responded by requiring any importers to certify that shrimp had been caught using Turtle Excluder Devices (TEDs), which keep the animals out of the nets.

India, Pakistan, Malaysia, and Thailand filed complaints with the WTO, claiming that the United States had no right to impose its environmental concerns on world trade. The United States argued that Article XX of the WTO Agreement permitted trade restrictions based on environmental concerns. Article XX states in part:

> Nothing in this Agreement shall be construed to prevent the adoption or enforcement by any Member of measures:
> (b) necessary to protect human, animal or plant life or health;
> (g) relating to the conservation of exhaustible natural resources if such measures are made effective in conjunction with restrictions on domestic production or consumption;

The Dispute Settlement Body declared that the United States had no right to impose its policies on shrimp importers, and the United States appealed.

Issue: ***Did Article XX permit the United States to impose environmental restrictions on shrimp importers?***

Excerpts from the Appellate Body's Report: The [shrimp policy] requires other WTO Members to adopt a regulatory program that is not merely comparable, but rather essentially the same, as that applied to the United States shrimp trawl vessels. The effect is to establish a rigid and unbending standard by which United States officials determine whether or not countries will be certified, thus granting or refusing other countries the right to export shrimp to the United States.

The United States requires the use of approved TEDs at all times by domestic, commercial shrimp trawl vessels. It may be quite acceptable for a government to adopt a single standard applicable to all its citizens throughout that country. However, it is not acceptable, in international trade relations, for one WTO Member to use an economic embargo to require other Members to adopt essentially the same comprehensive regulatory program, without taking into consideration different conditions which may occur in the territories of those other Members.

The United States [failed] to engage other Members exporting shrimp to the United States, in serious, across-the-board negotiations with the objective of concluding bilateral or multilateral agreements for the protection and conservation of sea turtles.

We have not decided that the protection and preservation of the environment is of no significance to the Members of the WTO. Clearly, it is. We have not decided that the sovereign nations that are Members of the WTO cannot adopt effective measures to protect endangered species, such as sea turtles. Clearly, they can and should.

What we have decided in this appeal is simply this: although the measure of the United States in dispute in this appeal serves an environmental objective that is recognized as legitimate, this measure has been applied by the United States in a manner which constitutes arbitrary and unjustifiable discrimination between Members of the WTO.

Environmental groups attacked the ruling, declaring that the WTO paid lip service to the environment but ensured further killing of an important endangered species. Trade supporters applauded it. In addition to the trade versus environment tension, there is a second conflict: rich versus poor. Critics of the shrimp regulations claim that it is unseemly for a wealthy nation to punish subsistence fishermen because of environmental concerns. Their opponents argue that we all share this planet, and long term growth for each of us depends upon living in harmony with limited resources and fragile ecosystems. Which of the competing goals is more important to you?

Ethics **Child labor** is a wrenching issue. The practice exists to some degree in all countries and is common throughout the developing world. The International Labor Organization estimates that more than 250 million children under the age of 14 work full or part time. As the world generally becomes more prosperous, this ugly problem has actually increased. Children in developing countries typically work in agriculture and domestic work, but many toil in mines and factories.

The rug industry illustrates the international nature of this tragedy. In the 1970s, the Shah of Iran banned child labor in rug factories, but many manufacturers simply packed up and moved to southern Asia. Today, tens of millions of children, some as young as four, toil in rug workrooms, seven days a week, 12 hours a day.Child labor raises compelling moral questions—and economic ones as well. In 1997, Congress passed a statute prohibiting the import of goods created by forced or indentured child labor. The first suit under the new law targeted the carpet factories of southern Asia and sought an outright ban on most rugs from that area. Is this statute humane legislation or cultural imperialism dressed as a nontariff barrier? Should the voters of this country or the WTO decide the issue? In answering such difficult questions, we must bear in mind that child labor is truly universal. The United Farm Workers union estimates that 800,000 underage children help their migrant parents harvest U.S. crops.

Our response to such a troubling moral issue need not take the form of a statute or lawsuit. Duke University is one of the most popular names in sports apparel, and the school sells millions worth of T-shirts, sweatshirts, jackets, caps, and other sportswear bearing its logo. In response to the troubling issue of child labor, Duke adopted a code of conduct that prohibits its manufacturers from using forced or child labor and requires all of the firms to pay a minimum wage, permit union organizing, and maintain a safe workplace. The university plans to monitor the companies producing its apparel and terminate the contract for any firm that violates its rules.

Is this right? Who should decide?

Regional Agreements: NAFTA and The European Union

In 1993, the United States, Canada, and Mexico signed the **North American Free Trade Agreement** (NAFTA). The principal goal was to eliminate almost all trade barriers between the three nations. Like GATT, this treaty has been controversial. Unquestionably, trade between the three nations has increased enormously. Mexico now exports more goods to the United States than do Germany, Britain, and Korea combined. Opponents of the treaty argue that NAFTA costs the United States jobs and lowers the living standards of American workers by forcing them to compete with low-paid labor. For example, Swingline Staplers closed a factory in Queens, New York, after 75 years of operation and moved to Mexico. Instead of paying its American workers $11.58 per hour, Swingline decided to pay Mexican workers 50 cents an hour to do the same job.

Proponents contend that although some jobs are lost, many others are gained, especially in fields with a bright future, such as high technology. They claim that as new jobs invigorate the Mexican economy, consumers there will be able to afford American goods for the first time, providing an enormous new market.

EXAM Strategy

Question: California producers of sea salt protest to the American government that they cannot compete with the same product imported from China. How do the California producers want the United States government to respond? May the U.S. government legally oblige?

Strategy: Domestic producers who cannot compete with foreign competition typically ask their government to impose higher tariffs on the imported goods. However, the whole point of GATT, and the WTO, is to avoid trade wars. There are two instances in which the U.S. government is free to levy increased duties on the Chinese goods. What are they?

Result: When a company *dumps* goods, it sells them overseas at an artificially low price, generally to destroy competition and gain a foothold. That is illegal, and the domestic (U.S.) government may impose dumping duties to protect local producers. Subsidized goods—those supported by the foreign company's government—are also illegal. If the United States government can demonstrate illegal subsidies, it will impose countervailing duties designed to give all producers an equal chance.

Twenty-seven countries belong to the **European Union (EU),** including Great Britain, Germany, France, Italy, and Spain, as well as Latvia and Slovakia.

The EU is one of the world's most powerful associations, with a population of nearly half a billion people. Its sophisticated legal system sets EU-wide standards for tariffs, dumping, subsidies, antitrust, transportation, and many other issues. The first goals of the EU were to eliminate trade barriers between member nations, establish common tariffs with respect to external countries, permit the free movement of citizens across its borders, and coordinate its agricultural and fishing policies for the collective good. The EU has largely achieved these goals. Most, but not all, of the EU countries have adopted a common currency, the euro. During the next decade the union will focus on further economic integration and effective coordination of foreign policy.

The EU (European Union Countries)

INTERNATIONAL SALES AGREEMENTS

Overseas markets offer tremendous growth potential. Foreign customers have an astonishing desire for some kinds of American goods and services.

Cowboy boots are hot in France. Imagine that you own and operate Big Heel, Inc., a small Texas company that makes superb boots. You realize that France could be a bonanza. What should you consider as you proceed? Several things.

The Sales Contract

Le Pied D'Or, a new, fast-growing French chain of shoe stores, is interested in buying 10,000 pairs of your boots at about $300 per pair. You are wise enough to know that you must have a written contract—$3 million is a lot of money for Big Heel.

What Law Governs?

Potentially, three conflicting laws could govern your boot contract: Texas law, French law, and an international treaty. Each is different, and it is therefore essential to negotiate which law will control.

Texas lawyers are familiar with the Texas law and will generally prefer that it govern. French law is obviously different, and French lawyers and business executives are naturally partial to it. How to compromise? Perhaps by using a neutral law.

The **United Nations Convention on Contracts for the International Sale of Goods (CISG)** is the result of 50 years of work by various international groups, all seeking to create a uniform, international law on this important subject. The United States and most of its principal trading partners have adopted this important treaty.

Signatory
A nation that signs a treaty.

The CISG applies automatically to any contract for the sale of goods between two parties from different countries if each operates in a country that is a signatory. (Goods are moveable objects like boots.) France and the United States have both signed. Thus, the CISG automatically applies to the Big Heel–Pied D'Or deal unless the parties *specifically opt out.* If the parties want to be governed by other law, their contract must state very clearly that they exclude the CISG and elect, for example, French law.

Choice of Forum

The parties must decide not only what law governs, but where disagreements will be resolved. This can be a significant part of a contract, because the French and American legal systems are dramatically different. In a French civil lawsuit, generally neither side is entitled to depose the other or to obtain interrogatories or even documents. This is in sharp contrast to the American system, where such discovery methods dominate litigation. American lawyers, accustomed to discovery to prepare a case and advance settlement talks, are sometimes frankly unnerved by the French system. Similarly, French lawyers are dismayed at the idea of spending two years taking depositions, exchanging paper, and arguing motions, all at great expense. At trial, the contrasts grow. In a French civil trial, there is generally no right to a jury. The rules of evidence are more flexible (and unpredictable), neither side employs its own expert witnesses, and the parties themselves never appear as witnesses.

Choice of Language and Currency

The parties must select a language for the contract and a currency for payment. Language counts because legal terms seldom translate literally. Currency is vital because the exchange rate may alter between the signing and payment. Suppose the Argentine peso falls 30 percent against the dollar in one week. An Argentine company that contracted on Monday to pay $1 million for U.S. aircraft engines will suddenly have to pay 30 percent more in pesos to meet its contractual obligations. To avoid such calamities, companies engaged in international commerce often purchase from currency dealers a guarantee to obtain the needed currency at a future date for a guaranteed price. Assuming that Big Heel insists on being paid in U.S. dollars, Pied D'Or could obtain a quote from a currency dealer as to the present cost of obtaining $3 million at the time the boots are to be delivered. Pied D'Or might pay a 5 percent premium for this guarantee, but it will have insured itself against disastrous currency swings.

Choices Made. The parties agree that the contract price will be paid in U.S. dollars. Pied D'Or is unfamiliar with U.S. law and absolutely refuses to make a deal unless either French law or the CISG governs. Your lawyer, Susan Fisher, recommends accepting the CISG, provided that the contract is written in English and that any disputes will be resolved in Texas courts. Pied D'Or balks at this, but Fisher presses hard, and ultimately those are the terms agreed upon. Fisher is delighted with the arrangement, pointing out that the CISG provisions can all be taken into account as the contract is written, and that by using Texas courts to settle any dispute, Big Heel has an advantage in terms of familiarity and location.

Letter of Credit

Because Pied D'Or is new and fast growing, you are not sure it will be able to foot the bill. Pied D'Or provides a letter of reference from its bank, La Banque Bouffon, but this is a small bank and it is unfamiliar to you. You need greater assurance of payment, and your lawyer recommends that payment be made by **letter of credit**. Here is how the letter will work.

Letter of credit
A commercial device used to guarantee payment in international trade.

Big Heel demands that the contract include a provision requiring payment by confirmed, irrevocable letter of credit. Le Pied D'Or agrees. The French company now contacts its bank, La Banque Bouffon, and instructs Bouffon to issue a letter of credit to Big Heel. The letter of credit is a promise *by the bank itself* to pay Big Heel if Big Heel presents certain documents. Banque Bouffon, of course, expects to be repaid by Pied D'Or. The bank is in a good position to assess Pied D'Or's creditworthiness since it is local and can do any investigating it wants before issuing the credit. It may also insist that Pied D'Or give Bouffon a mortgage on property, or that Pied D'Or deposit money in a separate Bouffon account. Pied D'Or is the **account party** on the letter of credit, and Big Heel is the **beneficiary**.

But at Big Heel, you are still not entirely satisfied. You feel that a bank is unlikely to default on its promises, but still, you don't know anything about Bouffon. That is why you have required a *confirmed* letter of credit. Bouffon will forward its letter of credit to Big Heel's own bank, Wells Fargo. Wells Fargo examines the letter and then *confirms* the letter. This is *Wells Fargo's own legal guarantee* that it will pay Big Heel. Wells Fargo will do this only if it knows, through international banking contacts, that Bouffon is a sound and trustworthy bank. The risk has now been spread to two banks, and at Big Heel, you are finally confident of payment.

You get busy, make excellent boots, and pack them. When they are ready, you truck them to Galveston, where they are taken alongside a ship, *Le Fond de la Mer*. Your agent presents the goods to the ship's officials, along with customs documents that describe the goods. *Le Fond de la Mer*'s officer in turn issues your agent a **negotiable bill of lading**. This document describes *exactly* the goods received—their quantity, color, quality, and anything else important.

You now take the negotiable bill of lading to Wells Fargo. You also present to Wells Fargo a **draft**, which is simply a formal order to Wells Fargo to pay, based on the letter of credit. Wells Fargo will look closely at the bill of lading, which must specify *precisely* the goods described in the letter of credit. Why so cautious? Because the bank is dealing only in paper. It never sees the boots. Wells Fargo is exchanging $3 million of its own money based on instructions in the letter of credit. The bank should pay only if the bill of lading indicates that *Le Fond de la Mer* received exactly what is described in the letter of credit. Wells Fargo will decide whether the bill of lading is *conforming* or *nonconforming*. If the terms of both documents are identical, the bill of lading is conforming and Wells Fargo must pay. If the terms vary, the bill of lading is nonconforming and Wells Fargo will deny payment. Thus, if the bill of lading indicated 9,000 pairs of boots and 1,000 pairs of sneakers, it is nonconforming and Big Heel would get no money.

Wells Fargo concludes that the documents are conforming, so it issues a check to Big Heel for $3 million. In return, you endorse the bill of lading and other documents over to Wells Fargo, which endorses the same documents and sends them to Banque Bouffon. Bouffon makes the same minute inspection and then writes a check to Wells Fargo. Bouffon then demands payment from Le Pied D'Or. Pied D'Or pays its bank, receiving in exchange the bill of lading and customs documents. Note that payment in all stages is now complete, though the boots are still rolling on the high seas. Finally, when the boots arrive in Le Havre, Pied D'Or trucks roll up to the wharf and, using the bill of lading and customs documents, collect the boots. See Exhibit 9.1.

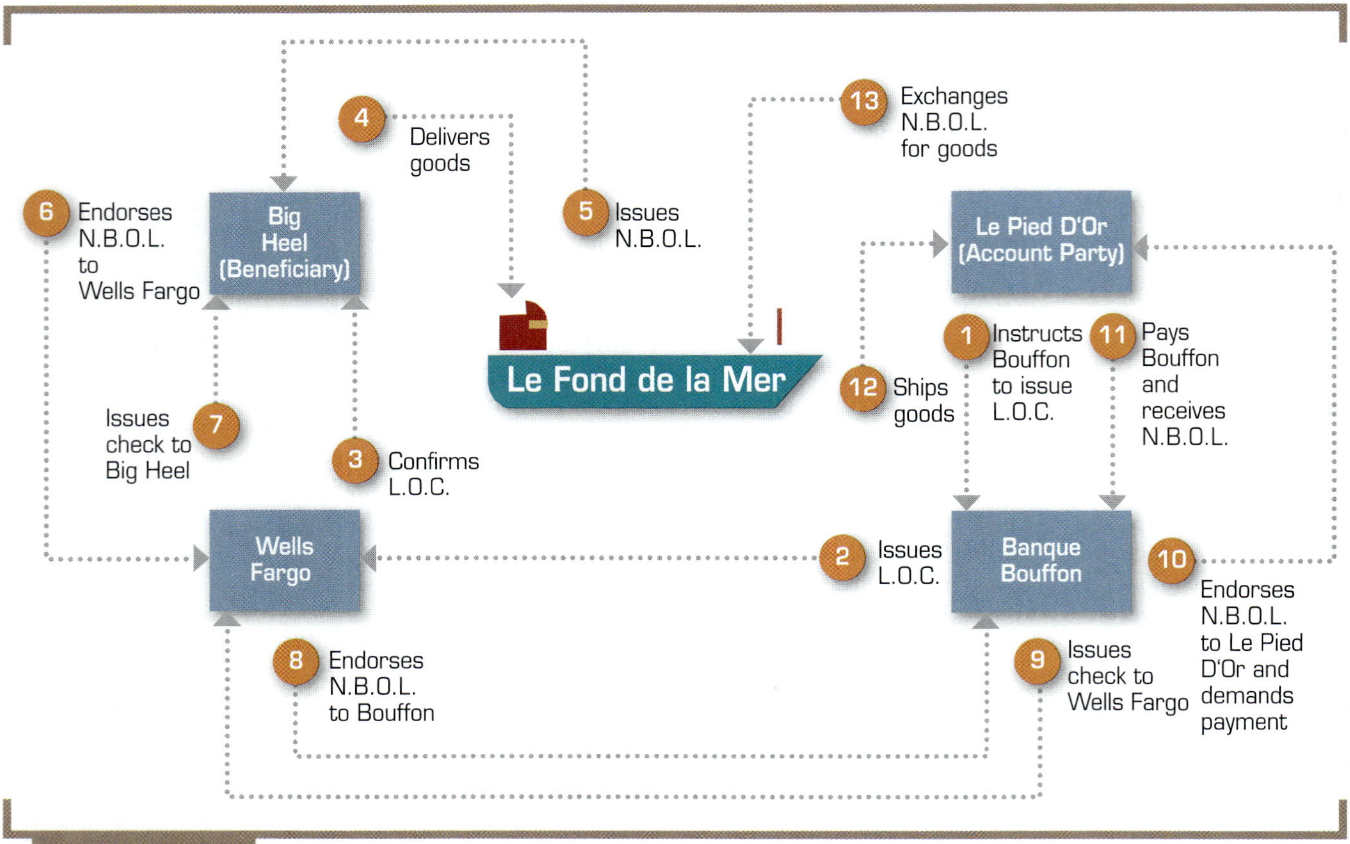

EXHIBIT 9.1

Good news: They fit! Not all customers walk away in such comfort, as the following case indicates.

Centrifugal Casting Machine Co., Inc. v. American Bank & Trust Co.

966 F.2d 1348, 1992 U.S. App. LEXIS 13089
Tenth Circuit Court of Appeals, 1992

Facts: Centrifugal Casting Machine Co. (CCM) entered into a contract with the State Machinery Trading Co. (SMTC), an agency of the Iraqi government. CCM agreed to manufacture cast iron pipe plant equipment for a total price of $27 million. The contract specified payment of the full amount by confirmed irrevocable letter of credit. The Central Bank of Iraq then issued the letter, on behalf of SMTC (the "account party") to be paid to CCM (the "beneficiary"). The Banca Nazionale del Lavorov (BNL) confirmed the letter.

Following Iraq's invasion of Kuwait on August 2, 1990, President George H.W. Bush issued two executive orders blocking the transfer of property in the United States in which Iraq held any interest. In other words, no one could use, buy, or sell any Iraqi property or cash. When CCM attempted to draw upon the letter of credit, the United States government intervened. The government claimed that like all Iraqi money in the United States, this money was frozen by the executive order. The United States District Court rejected the government's claim, and the government appealed.

Issue: ***Is CCM entitled to be paid pursuant to the letter of credit?***

Excerpts from Judge Sentelle's Decision: The United States contends on appeal that the freeze of Iraq's assets furthers national policy to punish Iraq by preventing it from obtaining economic benefits from transactions with American citizens, and by preserving such assets both for use as a bargaining chip in resolving this country's differences with Iraq and as a source of compensation for claims Americans may have against Iraq. We agree that these policy considerations are compelling and that we are therefore required to construe Iraqi property interests broadly. However, we are not persuaded these policies would be furthered by [creating] a property interest on behalf of Iraq that would not otherwise be cognizable under governing legal principles.

Two interrelated features of the letter of credit provide it with its unique value in the marketplace and are of critical importance in our consideration of the United States' claim here. First, the simple result [of a letter of credit] is that the issuer [i.e., the bank] substitutes its credit, preferred by the beneficiary, for that of the account party. Second, the issuer's obligation to pay on a letter of credit is completely independent from the underlying commercial transaction between the beneficiary and the account party. Significantly, the issuer must honor a proper demand even though the beneficiary has breached the underlying contract; even though the insolvency of the account party renders reimbursement impossible; and notwithstanding supervening illegality, impossibility, war or insurrection. This principle of independence is universally viewed as essential to the proper functioning of a letter of credit and to its particular value, i.e., its certainty of payment.

This assurance of payment gives letters of credit a central role in commercial dealings, and gives them a particular value in international transactions, in which sophisticated investors knowingly undertake such risks as political upheaval or contractual breach in return for the benefits to be reaped from international trade. Law affecting such an essential instrument of the economy must be shaped with sensitivity to its special characteristics. Accordingly, courts have concluded that the whole purpose of a letter of credit would be defeated by examining the merits of the underlying contract dispute to determine whether the letter should be paid.

Because of the nature of a letter of credit, we conclude that Iraq does not have a property interest in the money CCM received under the letter. The United States contends in essence that Iraq has a property interest in this money because it was allegedly a contract payment made by Iraq, which Iraq should recover because CCM breached the contract. In so arguing, the United States makes a breach of contract claim on behalf of Iraq that Iraq has never made, creates a remedy for the contracting parties in derogation of the remedy they themselves provided and, most importantly, disregards the controlling legal principles with respect to letters of credit.

Affirmed.

EXAM Strategy

Question: In an international contract for the sale of goods, Seller is to be paid by a confirmed irrevocable letter of credit. Buyer claims that the goods are defective and threatens to sue. If the parties are going to end up in court anyway, why bother with a letter of credit?

Strategy: A confirmed letter of credit is unique because the seller is assured of payment as soon as it presents a proper bill of lading to the appropriate local bank—regardless of the quality of the goods. Seller would much rather defend this lawsuit against Buyer than sue for its money in foreign courts.

Result: There *may* be a lawsuit, but Seller is not worried. It is Buyer who must sue, probably in Seller's home country. Buyer now risks substantial time and cash for an uncertain outcome. When the parties discuss a settlement, as surely they will, Seller is holding a big advantage—the cash.

Many countries impose a much higher tax on repatriated profits than on normal income in order to keep the money in domestic commerce.

International Trade Issues

Assume that Ambux is an American communications corporation that decides to invest in a growing overseas market. The president of Ambux is particularly interested in building telephone systems in the former republics of the Soviet Union, reasoning that these economies offer great opportunity for growth. She hires a consultant to advise her on the most important issues concerning possible investment in Uzbekistan and other former Soviet republics. The consultant presents several related issues:

- Repatriation of profits
- Expropriation
- Sovereign immunity
- Act of State doctrine
- The Foreign Corrupt Practices Act (FCPA)
- Extraterritoriality

Repatriation of Profits

Repatriation of profits occurs when an investing company pulls its earnings out of a foreign country and takes them back home. If Ambux builds a telephone system in Uzbekistan, it will plan to make money and then repatriate the profit to its headquarters in the United States. But Ambux must not assume an automatic right to do so. Many countries impose a much higher tax on repatriated profits than on normal income in order to keep the money in domestic commerce. Others bar repatriation altogether. Developing countries in particular want the money to "stay home." Thus, before Ambux invests anywhere, it must ensure that it can repatriate profits or live with any limitations the foreign country might impose.

Fortunately, investing in Uzbekistan is relatively secure. Uzbekistan and the United States have signed a trade treaty guaranteeing unlimited repatriation for American investors. This treaty should suffice. But Ambux might still feel cautious. Uzbekistan is a relatively new nation, and the mechanisms for actually getting the money out of Uzbekistan banks may be slow or faulty. The solution is to get a written agreement from the Minister of Commerce explicitly permitting Ambux to repatriate all profits and providing a clear mechanism to do it through the local banks.

Expropriation

Nationalize
Action in which a government assumes ownership of property.

Many nations, both developed and developing, **nationalize** property, meaning that they declare the national government to be the new owner. For example, during the 1940s and 1950s, Great Britain nationalized its coal, steel, and other heavy industries. The state assumed ownership and paid compensation to the previous owners. In the United States, nationalization is rare, but local governments often take land by eminent domain, to be used for roads or other public works. As we have seen, the United States Constitution requires that the owners be fairly compensated.

When a government takes property owned by *foreign* investors, it is called **expropriation**. The U.S. government historically has acknowledged that the expropriation of American interests is legal, provided the host government pays the owners *promptly and fully, in dollars.* But if compensation is inadequate or long delayed, or made in a local currency that is hard to exchange, the taking is a **confiscation.**

The courts of almost all nations agree that confiscation is illegal. But it can be difficult or impossible to prevent because courts of a host country may be partial to their own government.

Sovereign Immunity

Sovereign immunity holds that the courts of one nation lack the jurisdiction (power) to hear suits against foreign governments. Most nations respect this principle. In the United States, the **Foreign Sovereign Immunities Act** (FSIA) states that American courts generally cannot entertain suits against foreign governments. This is a difficult hurdle for a company to overcome when seeking compensation for foreign expropriation, but there are three possible exceptions.

Foreign Sovereign Immunities Act (FSIA)
A statute which states that American courts generally cannot entertain suits against foreign governments.

Waiver. A lawsuit is permitted against a foreign country that waives its immunity, that is, voluntarily gives up this protection. Suppose the Czech government wishes to buy fighter planes from an American manufacturer. The manufacturer might insist on a waiver in the sales contract, and the Czech Republic might be willing to grant one to get the weapons it desires. If the planes land safely but the checks bounce, the manufacturer may sue.

Commercial Activity. A plaintiff in the United States can sue a foreign country engaged in commercial, but not political, activity. Suppose the government of Iceland hires an American ecology-consulting firm to help its fishermen replenish depleted fishing grounds. Since fishing is a for-profit activity, the contract is commercial, and if Iceland refuses to pay, the company may sue in American courts.

Violation of International Law. A plaintiff in this country may sue a foreign government that has confiscated property in violation of international law, provided that the property either ends up in the United States or is involved in commercial activity that affects someone in the United States. Suppose a foreign government confiscates a visiting American ship, with no claim of right, and begins to use it for shipping goods for profit. Later, the ship carries some American produce. The taking was illegal, and it now affects American commerce. The original owner may sue.

Investment Insurance

Companies eager to do business abroad but anxious about expropriation should consider publicly funded insurance. In 1971, Congress established the **Overseas Private Investment Corporation (OPIC)** to insure U.S. investors against overseas losses due to political violence and expropriation. OPIC insurance is available to investors at relatively low rates for investment in almost any country.

Should Ambux investigate OPIC insurance before investing in Uzbekistan? Absolutely. While the Uzbekistan government has the best of intentions with respect to foreign investment, the nation is young and the government has no track record. A government can change course quickly. Why take unnecessary risks?

Foreign Corrupt Practices Act

The Foreign Corrupt Practices Act (FCPA)[5] makes it illegal for an American businessperson to give "anything of value" to any foreign official in order to influence an official decision. It is sad but true that in many countries, bribery is routine and widely accepted. When Congress investigated foreign bribes to see how common they were, more than 450 U.S. companies

[5] 15 U.S.C. §§78 et seq.

admitted paying hundreds of millions of dollars in bribes to foreign officials. Legislators concluded that such massive payments distorted competition among American companies for foreign contracts, interfered with the free market system, and undermined confidence everywhere in our way of doing business. In response, Congress passed the FCPA.

American executives have long complained that the FCPA puts their companies at a competitive disadvantage. Of the more than 200 nations in the world, very few aggressively prevent their nationals from bribing foreign officials. (In some countries, a bribe paid to a foreign official may even be treated as a tax deduction!) Others argue that the United States should not try to affect the way other countries do business by creating laws that apply outside its own borders.

The FCPA has two principal requirements:

- ***Bribes.*** The statute makes it illegal for U.S. companies and citizens to bribe foreign officials to influence a governmental decision. The statute prohibits giving anything of value and also bars using third parties as a conduit for such payments. Interestingly, the bribe need not be actually paid. A *promise* to pay bribes violates the Act. Also, the bribe need not be successful. If an American company makes an unauthorized payment but never gains any benefit, the company has still violated the law.

- ***Recordkeeping.*** All publicly traded companies—whether they engage in international trade or not—must keep detailed records that prevent hiding or disguising bribes. These records must be available for inspection by U.S. officials.

Not all payments violate the FCPA. A **grease or facilitating payment is legal.** Grease payments are common in many foreign countries to obtain a permit, process governmental papers, or obtain utility service. For example, the cost of a permit to occupy an office building might be $100, but the government clerk suggests that you will receive the permit faster (within this lifetime) if you pay $150, one-third of which he will pocket. Such small payments are legal. You cannot bribe the high-level decision makers who award contracts in the first place. But, once a contract has been secured, you may often bribe lower-level government workers to encourage them to speed things along.

Further, a payment **does not violate the FCPA if it was legal under the written laws of the country in which it was made.** Since few countries establish written codes *permitting* officials to receive bribes, this defense is unlikely to help many Americans who hand out gifts.

Punishments can be severe. A company may face large fines and the loss of profits earned as a result of illegal bribes. In 2011, Johnson & Johnson agreed to pay $77 million to settle an FCPA action. In addition to financial penalties, individuals who violate the FCPA can face up to five years in prison.

The following case is a classic example of bribery. Not much loyalty within Owl Securities. Why is that? What does it teach us?

United States v. King

354 F.3d 859
Eighth Circuit Court of Appeals, 2004

Facts: Owl Securities and Investments, Ltd., hoped to develop a large port in Limon, Costa Rica. The project included docks, housing, recreational facilities, an airport, and more. Richard King was one of Owl's largest investors, and Stephen Kingsley its CEO. The government charged King with attempting to bribe Costa Rican officials to obtain land and other concessions needed for their project. At trial, several of Owl's officers, including Kingsley, Richard Halford, and Albert Reitz, testified against King. A jury convicted King of violating the FCPA. He received a 30-month sentence and a fine of $60,000. He appealed.

Issue: ***Was there sufficient evidence that King had violated the FCPA?***

Excerpts from Judge Beam's Decision: Viewing the evidence in the light most favorable to the verdict, there was ample evidence in the record to support the jury's convictions. The tape recordings, alone, support the jury's verdict. There was sufficient evidence to prove King's knowledge of the proposed payment long before Kingsley became an informant for the government.

For example, the following exchanges are just a small sample of what the jury heard:

> Kingsley: Well you've always known about the closing cost fees and that.
> King: I've known what?
> Kingsley: You've known about the closing costs.
> King: The one million dollars?
> Kingsley: Yeah.
> King: I've known about that for five years, yeah, . . .
> [A later tape recording:]
> Kingsley: Yeah, what, um, what Pablo had said, was why just pay, pay off the current politicians. Pay off the future ones.
> King: That's right. Because we're gonna have to work with them anyway.
> Kingsley: And so what he was saying was double, you know, give them more money. Buy the opposition. If you buy the current party and the opposition, then it doesn't matter who's in because there's only two parties.
> King: The thing that really worries me is that, uh, if the Justice Department gets a hold of. Finds out how many people we've been paying off down there. Uh, or even if they don't. Are we gonna have to spend the rest of our lives paying off these petty politicians to keep them out of our hair? I can just see us, every, every day some politician on our doorstep down there wanting a hand out for this or that . . . . Think we could pay the top people enough, that the rest of the people won't bother us any. That's what I'm hoping this million and a half dollars does. I'm hoping it pays enough top people . . .
> [A later recording:]
> Kingsley: Now Pablo's continued to talk to the politicians. They know about the toll, closing costs call it what you will.
> King: Does everybody agree to what we talked about recently?
> Kingsley: Yeah, a million into escrow for the toll.
> King: And then we get the property and then we do the (unintelligible)?
> Kingsley: Um hum. Yeah now let me I'll, I'll, I'll come on to that because I'll explain how we work through that. Uh, essentially once the politicians see the money in escrow, they'll move. That's what it comes down to [clears throat]. Pablo's gonna send a list, an e-mail with a list of politicians already paid off and the ones he's gonna pay off.
> King: Isn't that awfully dangerous?
> Kingsley: No, e-mail's probably the most secure form of communication.
> King: From what I read it's not, number one and number two, there's got to be a better way.

We affirm the judgment of the district court.

Ethics What's wrong with bribery, anyway? Many businesspeople think it is relatively harmless—just a cost of doing business, like New York City's high taxes or Germany's high labor costs. Corruption is not a victimless crime. Poor people in poor countries are the losers when officials are on the take; corruption means that good projects are squeezed out by bad ones. And corruption can reduce a country's entire administration to a state of decay. Honest officials give up. Bribes grow ever bigger and more ubiquitous. The trough becomes less well stocked; the snouts plunge deeper. Worldwide about $400 billion is lost each year to corruption in government procurement. The anticorruption czar in Mexico estimated that bribes reduce Mexico's gross domestic product annually by 9.5 percent. This sum is twice the country's education budget.[6]

[6] "Who Will Listen to Mr. Clean?" *The Economist*, August 2, 1997, p. 52.

EXAM Strategy

Question: Splash is a California corporation that develops resorts. Lawrence, a Splash executive, is hoping to land a $700 million contract with a developing country in Southeast Asia. He seeks your advice. "I own a beach house in Australia, worth about $2 million. If I give it to a certain government official in the Asian country, I know that will close the resort deal. If I don't, someone else will, and my company loses out. Do you think that's wrong? Should I do it?" Please advise him.

Strategy: Lawrence has phrased his question in terms of ethics, but there is more involved. What law governs his proposed conduct? Is Lawrence legally safe, given that the land is foreign and the contract will be signed overseas?

Result: If Lawrence gives anything of value (such as a house) to secure a government contract, he has violated the FCPA. It makes no difference where the property is located or the deal signed. He could go to jail, and his company could be harshly penalized. Ethically, his gift would exacerbate corruption in a developing nation and mean that the agreement was determined by a bribe, not the merits of Splash. Other companies might do a superior job employing local workers, constructing an enduring resort, and protecting the environment, all for less money.

Extraterritoriality

The United States has many statutes designed to protect employees, such as those that prohibit discrimination on race, religion, gender, and so forth. Do these laws apply overseas? This is an issue of **extraterritoriality—the power of one nation to impose its laws in other countries.**[7] Many American companies do business through international **subsidiaries**—foreign companies that they control. The subsidiary may be incorporated in a nation that denies workers the protection they would receive in the United States. What should happen when an employee of a foreign subsidiary argues that his rights under an American statute have been violated? You make the call.

[7]Extraterritoriality can also refer to exemption from local laws. For example, ambassadors are generally exempt from the law of the nation in which they serve.

You be the Judge

Carnero v. Boston Scientific Corporation

433 F.3d 1
First Circuit Court of Appeals, 2006

Facts: Boston Scientific (BSC) was an American company that manufactured medical equipment. The company had its headquarters in Massachusetts but did business around the world through foreign subsidiaries. One of the company's subsidiaries was Boston Scientific Argentina (BSA), and it was there that Ruben Carnero began working. His employment contract stated he would work at BSA's headquarters in Buenos Aires and be paid in pesos. Argentine law was to govern the contract. Four years later, Carnero took an assignment to work as country manager for a different BSC subsidiary, Boston Scientific Do Brasil (BSB). Carnero frequently traveled to Massachusetts to meet with company executives, but he did most of his work in South America.

About a year later, BSB fired Carnero, and BSA soon did the same. Carnero claimed that the companies terminated him in retaliation for his reporting to BSC executives that the Argentine and Brazilian subsidiaries inflated sales figures and engaged in other accounting fraud. Carnero filed suit in Massachusetts, alleging that his firing violated an American statute, the Sarbanes-Oxley Act of 2002 (SOX).

Congress passed that law in response to the massive fraud cases involving Enron, Arthur Andersen, and others. The law was passed primarily to protect investors, but included a "whistleblower" provision. That section was designed to guard employees who informed superiors or investigating officials of fraud within the company. The law allows injured employees reinstatement and back pay.

BSC argued that SOX did not apply overseas and the District Court agreed, dismissing the case. Carnero appealed.

Issue: ***Does SOX protect a whistleblower employed overseas by a subsidiary of an American company?***

Argument for Carnero: Congress passed SOX because the American people were appalled by the massive fraud in major corporations, and the resulting harm to employees, investors, the community, and the economy. The whistleblower protection is designed to encourage honest employees to come forward and report wrongdoing—an act that no employee wants to do, and one which has historically led to termination. Mr. Carnero knew his report would be poorly received, but believed he had an ethical obligation to protect his company. For that effort, he was fired, and now Boston Scientific attempts to avoid liability using the technicality of corporate hierarchy.

Yes, Mr. Carnero was employed by BSB and BSA. But both of those companies are owned and operated by Boston Scientific. It is the larger company, with headquarters in the United States, which calls the shots. That is why executives in Massachusetts frequently asked Mr. Carnero to report to them—and why he brought them his unhappy news.

A whistleblower deserves gratitude and a pay raise. Mr. Carnero may well have saved his employer from massive losses and public disgrace. Would Boston Scientific like to wind up as Enron did—the company in bankruptcy court, its executives in prison? If Boston Scientific is too petty to acknowledge Mr. Carnero's contribution, the company should at least honor the purpose and intent of SOX by protecting his job.

Argument for Boston Scientific: First, we do not know whether there have been any accounting irregularities or not. Second, the fact that Mr. Carnero is employed by companies incorporated in Argentina and Brazil is more than a technicality. He is asking an American court to go into two foreign countries—sovereign nations with good ties to the United States—and investigate accounting and employment practices of companies incorporated and operating there. The very idea is offensive. No nation can afford to treat its allies and trading partners with such contempt.

If the United States can impose its whistleblowing law in foreign countries, may those nations impose their rules and values here? Suppose that a country forbids women to do certain work. May companies in those nations direct American subsidiaries to reject all female job applicants? Neither the citizens nor courts of this country would tolerate such interference for a moment.

Mr. Carnero's idea is also impractical. How would an American court determine why he was fired? Must the trial judge here subpoena Brazilian witnesses and demand documentary evidence from that country?

Finally, the SOX law does not apply overseas because Congress never said it did. The legislators—well aware that American corporations operate subsidiaries abroad—made no mention of those companies when they passed this statute.

Chapter Conclusion

Overseas investment, like sales abroad, offers potentially great rewards but significant pitfalls. A working knowledge of international law is essential to any entrepreneur or executive seriously considering foreign commerce. Issues such as choice of law, repatriation of profits, and expropriation can mean the difference between profit and loss. As the WTO lowers barriers, international trade will only increase, and your awareness of these principles will grow still more valuable.

Exam Review

1. **EXPORT RESTRICTIONS** Several statutes restrict exports from the United States that would harm national security, foreign policy, or certain other goals. (p. 207)

2. **TARIFFS** A tariff is a tax imposed on goods entering a country. The Customs Service classifies goods when they enter the United States and imposes appropriate tariffs. (pp. 208–209)

EXAM Strategy

Question: Sports Graphics, Inc. imports "Chill" brand coolers from Taiwan. Chill coolers have an outer shell of vinyl, with handles and pockets, and an inner layer of insulation. In a recent lawsuit, the issue was whether "Chill" coolers were "luggage" or "articles used for preparing, serving, or storing food or beverages," as Sports Graphics claimed. Who was the other party to the dispute, why did the two sides care about this, and what arguments did they make?

Strategy: The Customs Service (the other party) classifies goods and then imposes an appropriate *ad valorem* tax. What is at stake, of course, is money. (See the "Result" at the end of this section.)

3. **DUMPED AND SUBSIDIZED IMPORTS** Most countries, including the United States, impose duties for goods that have been dumped (sold at an unfairly low price in the international market) and for subsidized goods (those benefiting from government financial assistance in the country of origin). (p. 210)

4. **GATT** The General Agreement on Tariffs and Trade (GATT) is lowering the average duties worldwide. Proponents see it as a boon to trade; opponents see it as a threat to workers. (pp. 210–212)

5. **WTO** GATT created the WTO, which resolves disputes between signatories to the treaty. (pp. 210–212)

EXAM Strategy

Question: In a recent WTO case, several nations claimed that American laws concerning shrimp fishing were unfair and illegal. The case demonstrated a conflict between two important values. What were the values? In your view, which is more important? Who won and why?

Strategy: Make sure you understand the *Shrimp Products* case in the text. (See the "Result" at the end of this section.)

6. **CISG** A sales agreement between an American company and a foreign company may be governed by American law, by the law of the foreign country, or by the CISG. (p. 214)

7. **LETTERS OF CREDIT** A confirmed, irrevocable letter of credit is an important means of facilitating international sales contracts, because the seller is assured of payment by a local bank so long as it delivers the specified goods. (pp. 215–216)

Question: Flyby Knight (FK) contracts to sell 12 helicopters to Air Nigeria for $8 million each. Payment is to be made by letter of credit, issued by the Bank of Nigeria, confirmed by Citibank in New York, and due when the confirming bank receives a bill of lading indicating all helicopters are on board ship, ready for sailing to Nigeria. FK loads the aircraft on board ship, and the next day delivers the bill of lading to Citibank. The same day, Air Nigeria informs FK that its inspectors onboard ship have discovered serious flaws in the rotator blades and the fuel lines. Air Nigeria states it will neither accept nor pay for the helicopters. Is FK entitled to its $96 million?

a. FK is entitled to no money.

b. FK is entitled to no money *provided* Air Nigeria can prove the helicopters are defective.

c. Air Nigeria is obligated to pay FK the full price.

d. Bank of Nigeria is obligated to pay FK the full price.

e. Citibank is obligated to pay FK the full price.

Strategy: Payment is to be made by confirmed letter of credit. Ask yourself what that means. In such a case, the confirming bank is obligated to pay the seller when the bank receives a bill of lading indicating that conforming goods have been delivered. What about the fact that the goods seem defective? That is irrelevant. It is precisely to avoid long-distance arguments over such problems that sellers insist on these letters. (See the "Result" at the end of this section.)

8. **REPATRIATION** A foreign government may restrict repatriation of profits. (p. 218)

9. **EXPROPRIATION** Expropriation refers to a government taking property owned by foreign investors. U.S. courts regard this as lawful, provided the country pays the American owner promptly and fully in dollars. (pp. 218–219)

10. **SOVEREIGN IMMUNITY** Sovereign immunity means that, in general, American courts lack jurisdiction to hear suits against foreign governments unless the foreign nation has waived immunity, is engaging in commercial activity, or has violated international law. (p. 219)

11. **FOREIGN CORRUPT PRACTICES ACT (FCPA)** The FCPA makes it illegal for an American businessperson to bribe foreign officials. (pp. 219–221)

12. **EXTRATERRITORIALITY** The principle that refers to the power of one nation to impose its laws in other countries. (pp. 222–223)

2. Result: Customs evidently claimed the goods were luggage, with a higher tariff than food storage articles. Customs argued that the handles and portability made the articles luggage. But Sports Graphics prevailed, convincing the court that the primary purpose of the containers was the storage of food. The lawsuit reduced the company's tariff from 20 percent to 3.4 percent.

5. Result: Small nations sued, claiming that American regulations made it difficult or impossible for them to fish, devastating their economic growth. The United States argued that vital environmental concerns mandated such rules. The WTO found in favor of the small nations, ruling that before the United States imposed its environmental standards on other countries, it must engage in multinational negotiations, seeking an acceptable compromise. Environmentalists argued that the decision was short-sighted, and contributed to the destruction of an endangered species. Supporters of the decision responded that long-term environmental concerns sound patronizing and hollow to people with empty stomachs.

7. Result: When Citibank receives the bill of lading, indicating delivery of the helicopters, it is obligated to pay. The correct answer is (E).

Multiple-Choice Questions

1. A letter of credit is issued by a ________________.

(a) buyer
(b) seller
(c) shipping company
(d) bank

2. Tariffs are a tax on ________________. Treaties like NAFTA seek to ________________ tariffs.

(a) imports; increase
(b) imports; decrease
(c) exports; increase
(d) exports; decrease

3. The President negotiates a defense agreement with a foreign government. To take effect, the agreement must be ratified by which of the following?

(a) Two-thirds of the House of Representatives
(b) Two-thirds of the Senate
(c) The Supreme Court
(d) A and B
(e) A, B, and C

4. Lynn owns a small printing company in Nevada. She makes a contract with a company in France to print custom children's books and ship them to France. The contract does not say anything about which body of law will be used to resolve any disputes that arise. If there is a conflict, which body of law will actually be applied to the case?

(a) Nevada law

(b) French law

(c) The CISG

(d) None of the above

5. Countervailing duties are imposed when ______________.

(a) dumping occurs

(b) goods are unreasonably subsidized

(c) Both A and B

(d) None of the above

Essay Questions

1. Arnold Mandel exported certain high-technology electronic equipment. Later, he was in court arguing that the equipment he shipped should not have been on the Department of Commerce's Commodity Control List. What items may be on that list, and why does Mandel care?

2. ***YOU BE THE JUDGE* WRITING PROBLEM** Continental Illinois National Bank issued an irrevocable letter of credit on behalf of Bill's Coal Co. for $805,000, with the Allied Fidelity Insurance Co. as beneficiary. Bill's Coal Co. then went bankrupt. Allied then presented to Continental documents that were complete and conformed to the letter of credit. Continental refused to pay. Since Bill's Coal was bankrupt, there was no way Continental would collect once it had paid on the letter. Allied filed suit. Who should win? **Argument for Allied Fidelity:** An irrevocable letter of credit serves one purpose: to assure the seller that it will be paid if it performs the contract. Allied has met its obligation. The company furnished documents demonstrating compliance with the agreement. Continental *must* pay. Continental's duty to pay is an independent obligation, unrelated to the status of Bill's Coal. The bank issued this letter knowing the rules of the game and expecting to make a profit. It is time for Continental to honor its word. **Argument for Continental Bank:** In this transaction, the bank was merely a middleman, helping to facilitate payment of a contract. Allied has fulfilled its obligations under the contract, and we understand the company's desire to be paid. Regrettably, Bill's Coal is bankrupt. No one is going to be paid on this deal. Allied should have researched Bill's financial status more thoroughly before entering into the agreement. While we sympathize with Allied's dilemma, it has only itself to blame and cannot expect the bank to act as some sort of insurance company for a deal gone awry.

3. Jean-François, a French wine exporter, sues Bobby Joe, a Texas importer, claiming that Bobby Joe owes him $2 million for wine. Jean-François takes the witness stand to describe how the contract was created. Where is the trial taking place?

4. The Kyrgyz Republic is one of the new nations that broke away from the old Soviet Union. In September 1994, the government of Kyrgyzstan made two independent announcements: (1) it was abolishing all taxes on repatriation; and (2) the government was resigning and would shortly be replaced. Explain the significance of these announcements for an American company considering a major investment in Kyrgyzstan.

5. The Instituto de Auxilios y Viviendas is a government agency of the Dominican Republic. Dr. Marion Fernandez, the general administrator of the Instituto and Secretary of the Republic, sought a loan for the Instituto. She requested that Charles Meadows, an American citizen, secure the Instituto a bank loan of $12 million. If he obtained a loan on favorable terms, he would receive a fee of $240,000. Meadows secured a loan on satisfactory terms, which the Instituto accepted. He then sought his fee, but the Instituto and the Dominican government refused to pay. He sued the government in United States District Court. The Dominican government claimed immunity. Comment.

Discussion Questions

1. The United States consistently imports much more than it exports. The annual gap is consistently several hundred billion dollars. Does this concern you? If so, what should be done about it? If not, why not?

2. Does the FCPA seem sensible? Is fighting corruption the right thing to do, or does the statute place American companies at an unacceptable competitive disadvantage?

3. Generally speaking, should the United States pass laws that seek to control behavior outside its borders? Or, when in Rome, should our companies and subsidiaries be allowed to do as the Romans do?

4. Do you favor free trade agreements like NAFTA? Do you believe that free trade benefits everyone in the long run, or are you more concerned that American jobs may be lost?

5. Imagine that you read an article that reports the maker of your favorite brand of clothing uses child labor in its overseas factories. Being realistic, would you avoid buying that kind of clothing in the future? Why or why not?

UNIT 2

Contracts

CHAPTER 10

Introduction to Contracts

Austin Electronics had a terrible year. John, the store's owner, decided to get out of the electronics business. Before closing his doors, he hung a sign reading "Everything Must Go!" and held a going-out-of-business sale.

Customer #1—Fran

"Nice TV," Fran commented. "Price says $400. I'll give you $250 for it."

"Sorry, but I need at least $400," John replied.

"Hmm. Nope, that's just too much."

"OK, OK, I'll let it go for $250."

"Well…no. No, I've changed my mind. No deal."

Customer #2—Ricky

"How much for that iPod, mister?" said Ricky, a 10-year-old boy.

"Twenty bucks, kid," John said.

"Wow! I'll take it! Keep it for me while I ride home to get my money."

"Sure thing, kid."

"Well, how's about you sell them to me for $50 or I'll beat your face in for you."

Customer #3—Carla

"That's a good-looking home theater projector," Carla said. "I don't see a price tag. How much?"

"Well," John replied, "how much are you offering?"

"Hmm … I could give you $700 for it."

John was pleasantly surprised. "You've got yourself a deal." The two shook hands.

"I'll be back with my checkbook later today," Carla said.

Customer #4—Dave

As the sun set and the shadows lengthened, John waited patiently for his last customer to finish looking around. Truth be told, the guy looked kind of creepy.

"I'll give you $50 for these speakers," Dave said in a raspy voice.

"Sorry, man, but I can't let them go for less than $100," John replied.

"Well," Dave said, leaning closer, "how's about you sell them to me for $50 or I'll beat your face in for you."

"O … kay," John said, startled. "$50 it is, then."

Dave smiled. He slid a fifty-dollar bill across the counter, picked up the speakers, and left without a word.

John has made four agreements, but are they contracts? Can he require Fran to buy the TV for $250? If Ricky and Carla never return to buy the iPod and the projector, can John take them to court and force them to follow through on the deals? Can John undo his transaction with the disreputable Dave?

Throughout this unit on contracts, we will consider issues like these. It is vital for a businessperson to understand the difference between an ordinary promise and a legally enforceable contract.

Most contracts work out precisely as intended because the parties fulfill their obligations. Most—but not all. In this unit, we will study contracts that have gone wrong. We look at these errant deals so that you can learn how to avoid problems.

Contracts

Elements of a Contract

A contract is merely a legally enforceable agreement. People regularly make promises, but only some of them are enforceable. For a contract to be enforceable, seven key characteristics *must* be present. We will study this "checklist" at length in the next several chapters.

- Offer. All contracts begin when a person or a company proposes a deal. It might involve buying something, selling something, doing a job, or anything else. But only proposals made in certain ways amount to a legally recognized offer.
- Acceptance. Once a party receives an offer, he must respond to it in a certain way. We will examine the requirements of both offers and acceptances in the next chapter.
- Consideration. There has to be bargaining that leads to an *exchange* between the parties. Contracts cannot be a one-way street; both sides must receive some measureable benefit.
- Legality. The contract must be for a lawful purpose. Courts will not enforce agreements to sell cocaine, for example.
- Capacity. The parties must be adults of sound mind.
- Consent. Certain kinds of trickery and force can prevent the formation of a contract.
- Writing. While verbal agreements often amount to contracts, some types of contracts must be in writing to be enforceable.

Contracts Checklist

- ☐ Offer
- ☐ Acceptance
- ☐ Consideration
- ☐ Legality
- ☐ Capacity
- ☐ Consent
- ☐ Writing

Other Important Issues

Once we have examined the essential parts of contracts, the unit will turn to other important issues:

- Third-Party Interests. If Jerome and Tara have a contract, and if the deal falls apart, can Kevin sue to enforce the agreement? It depends.
- Performance and Discharge. If a party fully accomplishes what the contract requires, his duties are discharged. But what if his obligations are performed poorly, or not at all?
- Remedies. A court will award money or other relief to a party injured by a breach of contract.

Let's apply these principles to the opening scenario.

Fran is not obligated to buy the TV for $250 because John did not accept her offer. Ricky does not have to buy the iPod because he is under 18. If he changes his mind, there is nothing John can do about it. Nor is Carla required to buy the projector. Agreements concerning a sale of goods valued at more than $500 must be in writing. John can successfully sue Dave. He accepted Dave's offer to buy the speakers for $50, but he did so under duress. Agreements made under threats of violence are not enforceable contracts.

All Shapes and Sizes

Some contracts—like those in the opener—are small. But contracts can also be large. Lockheed Martin and Boeing spent years of work and millions of dollars competing for a U.S. Defense Department aircraft contract. Why the fierce effort? The deal was potentially good for 25 years and *$200 billion*. Lockheed won. The company earned the right to build the next generation of fighter jets—3,000 planes, with different varieties of the aircraft to be used by each of the American defense services and some allied forces as well.

Many contracts involve public issues. The Lockheed agreement concerns government agencies deciding how to spend taxpayer money for national defense. Other contracts concern intensely private matters. Mary Beth Whitehead signed a contract with William and Elizabeth Stern, of New Jersey. For a fee of $10,000, Whitehead agreed to act as a surrogate mother, and then deliver the baby to the Sterns for adoption after she carried it to term. But when little Melissa was born, Whitehead changed her mind and fled to Florida with the baby. The Sterns sued for breach of contract. Surrogacy contracts now lead to hundreds of births per year. Are the contracts immoral? Should they be illegal? Are there limits to what one person may pay another to do? The New Jersey Supreme Court, the first to rule on the issue, declared the contract illegal and void. The court nonetheless awarded Melissa to the Sterns, saying that it was in the child's best interest to live with them. Inevitably, legislators disagree about this emotional issue. Some states have passed statutes permitting surrogacy, while others prohibit it.

At times, we even enter contracts without knowing it. Suppose you try to book a flight using your frequent-flyer miles, but the airline tells you the terms of the frequent-flyer program have changed and you must earn more mileage. According to the Supreme Court, you may well have an enforceable agreement based on the terms the airline quoted when you earned the miles.[1]

Contracts Defined

Contract
A legally enforceable agreement.

We have seen that a **contract** is a promise that the law will enforce. As we look more closely at the elements of contract law, we will encounter some intricate issues. This is partly because we live in a complex society, which conducts its business in a wide variety of ways. Remember, though, that we are usually interested in answering three basic questions, all relating to promises:

[1] *American Airlines, Inc. v. Wolens*, 513 U.S. 219, 115 S. Ct. 817, 1995 U.S. LEXIS 690 (1995).

- Is it certain that the defendant promised to do something?
- If she did promise, is it fair to make her honor her word?
- If she did not promise, are there unusual reasons to hold her liable anyway?

Development of Contract Law

Courts have not always assumed that promises are legally significant. In the twelfth and thirteenth centuries, promises were not binding unless a person made them *in writing and affixed a seal* to the document. This was seldom done, and therefore most promises were unenforceable.

The common law changed very slowly, but by the fifteenth century, courts began to allow some suits based on a broken promise. There were still major limitations. Suppose a merchant hired a carpenter to build a new shop, and the carpenter failed to start the job on time. Now courts would permit the suit, but only if the merchant had paid some money to the carpenter. If the merchant made a 10 percent down payment, the contract would be enforceable. But if the merchant merely *promised* to pay when the building was done, and the carpenter never began work, the merchant could recover nothing.

In 1602, English courts began to enforce mutual *promises;* that is, deals in which neither party gave anything to the other but both promised to do something in the future. Thus, if a farmer promised to deliver a certain quantity of wheat to a merchant and the merchant agreed on the price, both parties were now bound by their promise, even though there had been no down payment. This was a huge step forward in the development of contract law, but many issues remained. Consider the following employment case from 1792, which raises issues of public policy that still challenge courts today.

Davis v. Mason

Court of King's Bench
Michaelmas Term, 33d George III, p. 118 (1792)

Facts: Mason was a surgeon/apothecary in the English town of Thetford. Davis wished to apprentice himself to Mason. The two agreed that Davis would work for Mason and learn his profession. They further agreed that if Davis left Mason's practice, he would not set up a competing establishment within 10 miles of Thetford at any time within 14 years. Davis promised to pay £200 if he violated the agreement not to compete.

Davis began working for Mason in July 1789. In August 1791, Mason dismissed Davis, claiming misconduct, though Davis denied it. Davis then established his own practice within 10 miles of Thetford. Mason sued for the £200.

Davis admitted promising to pay the money. But he claimed that the agreement should be declared illegal and unenforceable. He argued that 14 years was unreasonably long to restrict him from the town of Thetford, and that 10 miles was too great a distance. (In those days, 10 miles might take the better part of a day to travel.) He added an additional policy argument, saying that it was harmful to the public health to restrict a doctor from practicing his profession: if the people needed his service, they should have it. Finally, he said that his "consideration" was too great for this deal. In other words, it was unfair that he should pay £200 because he did not receive anything of that value from Mason.

Issue: ***Was the contract too unreasonable to enforce?***

Excerpts from Lord Kenyon's Decision: Here, the plaintiff being established in business as a surgeon at Thetford, the defendant wished to act as his assistant with a view of deriving a degree of credit from that situation; on which the former stipulated that the defendant should not come to live there under his auspices and steal away his patients: this seems to be a fair consideration. Then it was objected that the limits within which the defendant engaged not to practise are unreasonable: but I do not see that they are necessarily unreasonable, nor do I know how to draw the line. Neither are the public likely to be injured by an agreement of this kind, since every other person is at liberty to practise as a surgeon in this town.

Judgment for the Plaintiff.

Noncompetition agreement
A contract in which one party agrees not to compete with another.

The contract between Davis and Mason is called a **noncompetition agreement**. Today they are more common than ever, and frequently litigated. The policy issues that Davis raised have never gone away. You may well be asked to sign a noncompetition agreement sometime in your professional life. We look at the issue in detail in Chapter 12, on consideration. That outcome was typical of contract cases for the next 100 years. Courts took a *laissez-faire* approach, declaring that parties had *freedom to contract* and would have to live with the consequences. Lord Kenyon saw Davis and Mason as equals, entering a bargain that made basic sense, and he had no intention of rewriting it. After 500 years of evolution, courts had come to regard promises as almost sacred. The law had gone from ignoring most promises to enforcing nearly all.

By the early twentieth century, bargaining power in business deals had changed dramatically. Farms and small businesses were yielding place to huge corporations in a trend that accelerated throughout the century. In the twenty-first century, multinational corporations span many continents, wielding larger budgets and more power than many of the nations in which they do business. When such a corporation contracts with a small company or an individual consumer, the latter may have little or no leverage. Courts increasingly looked at the basic fairness of contracts. Noncompetition agreements are no longer automatically enforced. Courts may alter them or ignore them entirely because the parties have such unequal power and because the public may have an interest in letting the employee go on to compete. Davis's argument—that the public is entitled to as many doctors as it needs—is frequently more successful in court today than it was in the days of Lord Kenyon.

Legislatures and the courts limit the effect of promises in other ways. Suppose you purchase a lawn mower with an attached tag, warning you that the manufacturer is not responsible in the event of any malfunction or injury. You are required to sign a form acknowledging that the manufacturer has no liability of any kind. That agreement is clear enough—but a court will not enforce it. The law holds that the manufacturer *has* warranted the product to be good for normal purposes, regardless of any language included in the sales agreement. If the blade flies off and injures a child, the manufacturer is liable. This is socially responsible, even though it interferes with a private agreement.

The law has not come full circle back to the early days of the common law. Courts still enforce the great majority of contracts. But the possibility that a court will ignore an agreement means that any contract is a little less certain than it would have been a century ago.

Types of Contracts

Before undertaking a study of contracts, you need to familiarize yourself with some important vocabulary. This section will present five sets of terms.

Bilateral and Unilateral Contracts

only one of 2

Bilateral contract
A promise made in exchange for another promise.

In a **bilateral contract**, both parties make a promise. A producer says to Gloria, "I'll pay you $2 million to star in my new romantic comedy, which we are shooting three months from now in Santa Fe." Gloria says, "It's a deal." That is a bilateral contract. Each party has made a promise to do something. The producer is now bound to pay Gloria $2 million, and Gloria is obligated to show up on time and act in the movie. The vast majority of contracts are bilateral contracts. They can be for services, such as this acting contract; they can be for the sale of goods, such as 1,000 tons of steel, or for almost any other purpose. When the bargain is a promise for a promise, it is a bilateral agreement.

In a unilateral contract, one party makes a promise that the other party can accept only by *actually doing* something. These contracts are less common. Suppose the movie producer tacks a sign to a community bulletin board. It has a picture of a dog with a phone number, and it reads, "I'll pay $100 to anyone who returns my lost dog." If Leo sees the sign, finds the producer, and merely promises to find the dog, he has not created a contract. Because of the terms on the sign, Leo must actually find and return the dog to stake a claim to the $100.

Executory and Executed Contracts

A contract is **executory** when it has been made, but one or more parties has not yet fulfilled its obligations. Recall Gloria, who agrees to act in the producer's film beginning in three months. The moment Gloria and the producer strike their bargain, they have an executory bilateral express contract.

A contract is **executed** when all parties have fulfilled their obligations. When Gloria finishes acting in the movie and the producer pays her final fee, their contract will be fully executed.

Executory contract
An agreement in which one or more parties has not yet fulfilled its obligations.

Executed contract
An agreement in which all parties have fulfilled their obligations.

EXAM Strategy

Question: Abby has long coveted Nicola's designer handbag because she saw one of them in a movie. Finally, Nicola offers to sell her friend the bag for $350 in cash. "I don't have the money right now," Abby replies, "but I'll have it a week from Friday. Is it a deal?" Nicola agrees to sell the bag. Use two terms to describe the contract.

Strategy: In a bilateral contract, both parties make a promise, but in a unilateral agreement, only one side does so. An executory contract is one with unfulfilled obligations, while an executed agreement is one with nothing left to be done.

Result: Nicola promised to sell the bag for $350 cash, and Abby agreed to pay. Because both parties made a promise, this a bilateral agreement. The deal is not yet completed, meaning that they have an executory contract.

Valid, Unenforceable, Voidable, and Void Agreements

A **valid contract** is one that satisfies all of the law's requirements. It has no problems in any of the seven areas listed at the beginning of this chapter, and a court will enforce it. The contract between Gloria and the producer is a valid contract, and if the producer fails to pay Gloria, she will win a lawsuit to collect the unpaid fee.

An **unenforceable agreement** occurs when the parties intend to form a valid bargain, but a court declares that some rule of law prevents enforcing it. Suppose Gloria and the producer orally agree that she will star in his movie, which he will start filming in 18 months. The law, as we will see in Chapter 15, requires that this contract be in writing because it cannot be completed within one year. If the producer signs up another actress two months later, Gloria has no claim against him.

A **voidable contract** occurs when the law permits one party to terminate the agreement. This happens, for example, when the other party has committed fraud, or when an agreement has been signed under duress. In the opening scenario, Dave threatened John when he would not sell the speakers for $50. The agreement is voidable at John's option. If John later decides that the $50 is acceptable, he may keep it. But if he decides that he wants to cancel the agreement and sue for the return of his speakers, he can do that as well.

A **void agreement** is one that neither party can enforce, usually because the purpose of the deal is illegal or because one of the parties had no legal authority to make a contract.

The following case illustrates the difference between voidable and void agreements.

Voidable contract
An agreement that may be terminated by one of the parties.

Void agreement
A contract that neither party can enforce, because the bargain is illegal or one of the parties had no legal authority to make it.

MR. W FIREWORKS, INC. v. OZUNA

2009 Tex. App. LEXIS 8237
Court of Appeals of Texas, Fourth District, San Antonio, 2009

Facts: Mr. W sells fireworks. Under Texas law, retailers may sell fireworks to the public only during the two weeks immediately before the Fourth of July and during two weeks immediately before New Year's Day. And so, fireworks sellers like Mr. W tend to lease property.

Mr. W leased a portion of Ozuna's land. The lease contract contained two key terms:

> "In the event the sale of fireworks on the aforementioned property is or shall become unlawful during the period of this lease and the term granted, this lease shall become void.
>
> "Lessor(s) agree not to sell or lease any part of said property, including any adjoining, adjacent, or contiguous property, to any person(s) or corporation for the purpose of selling fireworks in competition to the Lessee during the term of this lease, *and for a period of ten years after lease is terminated*." (Emphasis added.)

A longstanding San Antonio city ordinance bans the sale of fireworks inside city limits, and also within 5,000 feet of city limits. Like all growing cities, San Antonio sometimes annexes new land, and its city limits change. One annexation caused the Ozuna property to fall within 5,000 feet of the new city limits, and it became illegal to sell fireworks from the property. Mr. W stopped selling fireworks and paying rent on Ozuna's land.

Two years later, San Antonio's border shifted again. This time, the city *disannexed* some property and *shrank*. The new city limits placed Ozuna's property just beyond the 5,000-foot no-fireworks zone. Ozuna then leased a part of his land to Alamo Fireworks, a competitor of Mr. W.

Mr. W sued for breach of contract, arguing that Ozuna had no right to lease to a competitor for a period of 10 years. The trial court granted Ozuna's motion for summary judgment. Mr. W appealed.

Issue: ***Did Ozuna breach his contract with Mr. W by leasing his land to a competitor?***

Excerpts from Judge Angelini's Decision: The property owners [argue] that when the city ordinance made the sale of fireworks illegal on the subject properties, the leases became void, resulting in the property owners and Mr. W no longer having an enforceable agreement. Mr. W's argues that the provision restricting the property owners from leasing to competitors survived the agreement. This is inconsistent with the meaning of "voidable" contracts. For example, when a minor enters into a contract, that contract is not void, but is voidable at the election of the minor. This means that the minor may set aside the entire contract at his option, but he *is not entitled to enforce portions that are favorable to him and at the same time disaffirm other provisions that he finds burdensome.* He is not permitted to retain the benefits of a contract while repudiating its obligations.

Could Ozuna declare independence from contractual obligations?

Here, while Mr. W is arguing that the illegalization of the sale of fireworks made the contract "voidable," it is still seeking to enforce the provision of the contract prohibiting the property owners from leasing to competitors. We decline to adopt such an interpretation.

Further, contracts requiring an illegal act are void. We therefore hold that the illegalization of the sale of the fireworks on the respective properties did not trigger the provision in the leases prohibiting the property owners from leasing to competitors of Mr. W.

We affirm the judgment of the trial court.

Express and Implied Contracts only 1 of 2

Express contract
An agreement with all the important terms explicitly stated.

In an **express contract**, the two parties explicitly state all the important terms of their agreement. The vast majority of contracts are express contracts. The contract between the producer and Gloria is an express contract because the parties explicitly state what Gloria will do, where and when she will do it, and how much she will be paid. Some express contracts are oral, as that one was, and some are written. They might be bilateral express contracts, as Gloria's was, or unilateral express contracts, as Leo's was. Obviously, it is wise to make express contracts, and to put them in writing. We emphasize, however, that many oral contracts are fully enforceable.

In an implied contract, the words and conduct of the parties indicate that they intended an agreement. Suppose every Friday, for two months, the producer asks Lance to mow his lawn, and loyal Lance does so each weekend. Then, for three more weekends, Lance simply shows up without the producer asking, and the producer continues to pay for the work done. But on the 12th weekend, when Lance rings the doorbell to collect, the producer suddenly says, "I never asked you to mow it. Scram." The producer is correct that there was no express contract because the parties had not spoken for several weeks. But a court will probably rule that the conduct of the parties has *implied* a contract. Not only did Lance mow the lawn every weekend, but the producer even paid on three weekends when they had not spoken. It was reasonable for Lance to assume that he had a weekly deal to mow and be paid.

Today, the hottest disputes about implied contracts continue to arise in the employment setting. Many corporate employees have at-will relationships with their companies. This means that the employees are free to quit at any time and the company has the right to fire them, for virtually any reason. But often a company provides its workers with personnel manuals that lay out certain rights. Does a handbook create a contract guaranteeing those rights? What is your opinion?

ı be the **Judge**

DEMASSE V. ITT CORPORATION

194 Ariz. 500, 984 P.2d 1138
Supreme Court of Arizona, 1999

Roger DeMasse and five were employees-at-will at Corporation, where they working at various times :n 1960 and 1979. Each id an hourly wage.

'T issued an employee ɔok, which it revised four ɔver two decades.

ıe first four editions of the handbook stated that each job classification, any layoffs would be made :rse order of seniority. The fifth handbook made ıportant changes. First, the document stated that ıg contained herein shall be construed as a guaran- continued employment. ITT does not guarantee ıed employment to employees and retains the right ıinate or lay off employees."

:cond, the handbook stated that "ITT reserves the amend, modify, or cancel this handbook, as well as all of the various policies [or rules] outlined in it." ears later, ITT notified its hourly employees that layoff guidelines for hourly employees would be based not on seniority, but on ability and performance. About 10 days later, the six employees were laid off, though less-senior employees kept their jobs. The six employees sued.

You Be The Judge: ***Did ITT have the right to unilaterally change the layoff policy?***

Argument for the workers: It is true that all of the plaintiffs were originally employees-at-will, subject to termination at the company's whim. However, things changed when the company issued the first handbook. ITT chose to include a promise that layoffs would be based on seniority. Long-term workers and new employees all understood the promise and relied on it. The company put it there to attract and retain good workers. The policy worked. Responsible employees understood that the longer they remained at ITT, the safer their job was. Company and employees worked together for many years with a common understanding, and that is a textbook definition of an implied contract.

Once a contract is formed, whether express or implied, it is binding on both sides. That is the whole point of a contract. If one side could simply change the terms of an agreement on its own, what value would any contract have? The company's legal argument is a perfect symbol of its arrogance: It believes that because these workers are mere hourly workers, they have no rights, even under contract law. The company is mistaken. Implied contracts are binding, and ITT should not make promises it does not intend to keep.

Argument for ITT: Once an at-will employee, always one. ITT had the right to fire any of its employees at any time—just as the workers had the right to quit whenever they wished. That never changed, and in case any workers forgot it, the company reiterated the point in its most recent handbook. If the plaintiffs thought layoffs would happen in any particular order, that is their error, not ours.

All workers were bound by the terms of whichever handbook was then in place. For many years, the company had made a seniority-layoff promise. Had we fired a senior worker during that period, he or she would have had a legitimate complaint—and that is why we did not do it. Instead, we gave everyone four years' notice that things would change. Any workers unhappy with the new policies should have left to find more congenial work.

Why should an employee be allowed to say, "I prefer to rely on the old, outdated handbooks, not the new one"? The plaintiffs' position would mean that no company is ever free to change its general work policies and rules. Since when does an at-will employee have the right to dictate company policy? That would be disastrous for the whole economy—but fortunately it is not the law.

Promissory Estoppel and Quasi-Contracts

Now we turn away from "true" contracts and consider two unusual circumstances. Sometimes, courts will enforce agreements even if they fail to meet the usual requirement of a contract. We emphasize that these remedies are uncommon exceptions to the general rules. Most of the agreements that courts enforce are the express contracts that we have already studied. Nonetheless, the next two remedies are still pivotal in some lawsuits. In each case, a sympathetic plaintiff can demonstrate an injury but *there is no contract.* The plaintiff cannot claim that the defendant breached a contract, because none ever existed. The plaintiff must hope for more "creative" relief.

The two remedies can be confusingly similar. The best way to distinguish them is this:

- In promissory estoppel cases, the defendant made a promise that the plaintiff relied on.
- In quasi-contract cases, the defendant received a *benefit* from the plaintiff.

Promissory Estoppel

A fierce fire swept through Dana and Derek Andreason's house in Utah, seriously damaging it. The good news was that agents for Aetna Casualty promptly visited the Andreasons and helped them through the crisis. The agents reassured the couple that all of the damage was covered by their insurance, instructed them on which things to throw out and replace, and helped them choose materials for repairing other items. The bad news was that the agents were wrong: the Andreasons' policy had expired six weeks before the fire. When Derek Andreason presented a bill for $41,957 worth of meticulously itemized work that he had done under the agents' supervision, Aetna refused to pay.

Promissory estoppel
A *possible* remedy for an injured plaintiff in a case with no valid contract, where the plaintiff can show a promise, reasonable reliance, and injustice.

The Andreasons sued—but not for breach of contract. There *was* no contract—they allowed their policy to expire. They sued Aetna under the legal theory of promissory estoppel: even when there is no contract, a plaintiff may use **promissory estoppel** to enforce the defendant's promise if he can show that:

- The defendant made a promise knowing that the plaintiff would likely rely on it;
- The plaintiff did rely on the promise; and
- The only way to avoid injustice is to enforce the promise.

Aetna made a promise to the Andreasons—namely, its assurance that all of the damage was covered by insurance. The company knew that the Andreasons would rely on that promise, which they did by ripping up a floor that might have been salvaged, throwing out some furniture, and buying materials to repair the house. Is enforcing the promise the only way to avoid injustice? Yes, ruled the Utah Court of Appeals.[2] The Andreasons' conduct was reasonable and based entirely on what the Aetna agents told them. Under promissory estoppel, the Andreasons received virtually the same amount they would have obtained had the insurance contract been valid.

Is enforcing the promise the only way to avoid injustice?

There was plenty of romance in the following case. Was there an enforceable promise?

NORTON V. HOYT

278 F. Supp. 2d 214
United States District Court for the District of Rhode Island, 2003

Facts: Gail Norton sued Russell Hoyt, and this is what she alleged. The two met when Norton, who was single, worked as an elementary school teacher. Hoyt told her he was also single, and they began an affair. She later learned that he was married, but he assured her he was getting a divorce, and they continued their relationship.

Six years later, Hoyt, who was rich, convinced Norton to quit her job so that they could travel together. The couple lived lavishly, spending time in Newport, Rhode Island, where Hoyt was part of the yachting crowd, in London, the Bahamas, and other agreeable places. Hoyt rented Norton an apartment, bought her cars, and repeated his promises to divorce his wife and marry his lover. He never did either.

After 23 years, Hoyt ended the relationship. Norton became ill, and saw various doctors for anxiety, depression, headaches, stomach maladies, and weight loss. During one joint therapy session, Hoyt told Norton and the psychiatrist that he would continue to support her with $80,000 a year. But he did not.

Norton sued, claiming promissory estoppel. Hoyt moved for summary judgment. In ruling on the motion, the court assumed that Norton's allegations were true.

Issue: ***Was Norton entitled to support, based on promissory estoppel?***

Excerpts from Judge Lageux's Decision: Even viewed most favorably to the Plaintiff, the record fails to reveal a clear, unconditional, and unambiguous promise. Plaintiff's vacillations have not helped her cause. First, she claimed that Hoyt promised to divorce his wife, marry her, and provide lifetime support to her. Then she changed her mind and the promise became one to provide lifetime support to her regardless of whether Hoyt divorced his wife or not. Finally at the hearing on this motion, counsel argued that Hoyt had simply promised to take care of Norton for life. However, there can be many interpretations of the phrase "take care of for life." It could refer to care in a social, emotional, or financial context. As other courts have recognized, this is certainly not a clear and unambiguous promise.

Even assuming, *arguendo*, that there was a clear and unambiguous promise, Norton's reliance upon that promise was unreasonable. Though the couple had discussions about their life together and even discussed potential wedding plans, Plaintiff knew that Hoyt was married, and that he spent time at the marital domicile with his wife and children. Norton and Hoyt never openly associated as husband and wife, their friends and family knew that they were not married, and they did not exclusively cohabitate. Furthermore, Norton knew that Hoyt had lied in the past,

---

[2]*Andreason v. Aetna Casualty & Surety Co.*, 848 P.2d 171, 1993 Utah App. LEXIS 26 (Utah App. 1993).

was in an adulterous relationship, and apparently had made little effort to fulfill the terms of the promise. Reliance upon an unclear and ambiguous promise made by an apparently unreliable man was imprudent.

In any event, whatever form her reliance took, it is insufficient to overcome the other fatal flaws in her claim. Any promise for support that Hoyt made prior to the breakup is ambiguous at best, and, considering the source, was not a reasonable basis upon which to ground reliance. Sometime between year one and year 23 of the affair, it should have become clear to Norton that her reliance on Hoyt's promise to divorce his wife and marry her was misplaced.

[The defendant's motion for summary judgment is granted.]

Devil's Advocate Why should one person be able to make repeated promises over two decades and escape all responsibility? Even if Hoyt's precise words varied, each of his promises involved long-term emotional and financial security for Norton. Norton was naïve, but Hoyt was dishonest. The law should be a tool for teaching people like him a lesson.

Why have we chosen to illustrate an important point of law—promissory estoppel—with a case that fails? Because that is the typical outcome. Plaintiffs allege promissory estoppel very frequently, but seldom succeed. They do occasionally win, as the Andreasons demonstrated earlier, but courts are skeptical of these claims. The lesson is clear: Before you rely on a promise, negotiate a binding contract.

© Photodisc/Getty Images

Quasi-contract may require compensation even when no contract exists.

Quasi-Contract

Don Easterwood leased over 5,000 acres of farmland in Jackson County, Texas, from PIC Realty for one year. The next year, he obtained a second one-year lease. During each year, Easterwood farmed the land, harvested the crops, and prepared the land for the following year's planting. Toward the end of the second lease, after Easterwood had harvested his crop, he and PIC began discussing the terms of another lease. While they negotiated, Easterwood prepared the land for the following year, cutting and plowing the soil. But the negotiations for a new lease failed, and Easterwood moved off the land. He sued PIC Realty for the value of his work preparing the soil.

Easterwood had neither an express nor an implied contract for the value of his work. How could he make any legal claim? By relying on the legal theory of a quasi-contract: Even when there is no contract, a court may use **quasi-contract** to compensate a plaintiff who can show that:

- The plaintiff gave some benefit to the defendant;
- The plaintiff reasonably expected to be paid for the benefit and the defendant knew this; and
- The defendant would be unjustly enriched if he did not pay.

Quasi-contract

A *possible* remedy for an injured plaintiff in a case with no valid contract, where the plaintiff can show benefit to the defendant, reasonable expectation of payment, and unjust enrichment.

If a court finds all of these elements present, it will generally award the value of the goods or services that the plaintiff has conferred. The damages awarded are called ***quantum meruit***, meaning that the plaintiff gets "as much as he deserves." The court is awarding money that it believes the plaintiff *morally ought to have*, even though there was no valid contract entitling her to it. This again is judicial activism, with the courts inventing a "quasi" contract where no true contract exists. The purpose is justice, the term is contradictory.

Don Easterwood testified that in Jackson County, it was quite common for a tenant farmer to prepare the soil for the following year but then be unable to farm the land. In those cases, he claimed, the landowner compensated the farmer for the work done. Other witnesses agreed that this was the local custom. The court ruled that indeed there was no contract, but that all elements of quasi-contract had been satisfied. Easterwood gave a benefit to PIC because the land was ready for planting. Jackson County custom caused Easterwood to assume he would be paid, and PIC Realty knew it. Finally, said the court, it would be unjust to let PIC benefit without paying anything. The court ordered PIC to pay the fair market value of Easterwood's labors.

Quantum meruit
"As much as he deserves"—the damages awarded in a quasi-contract case.

FOUR THEORIES OF RECOVERY

Theory	Did the Defendant Make a Promise?	Is There a Contract?	Description
Express Contract	Yes	Yes	The parties intend to contract and agree on explicit terms.
Implied Contract	Not explicitly	Yes	The parties do not formally agree, but their words and conduct indicate an intention to create a contract.
Promissory Estoppel	Yes	No	There is no contract, but the defendant makes a promise that she can foresee will induce reliance; the plaintiff relies on it; and it would be unjust not to enforce the promise.
Quasi-Contract	No	No	There is no intention to contract, but the plaintiff gives some benefit to the defendant, who knows that the plaintiff expects compensation; it would be unjust not to award the plaintiff damages.

EXAM Strategy

Question: The table above lists the different theories a plaintiff may use to recover damages in a contract dispute. In the following examples, which one will each plaintiff use in trying to win the case?

1. Company pays all employees 10 percent commission on new business they develop. Company compensates each employee when the new customer pays its first bill. After Leandro obtains three new clients, Company fires him. When

the new customers pay their bill, Company refuses to pay Leandro a commission because he is no longer an employee. Leandro sues.

2. Burt agrees in writing to sell Red 100 lobsters for $15 each, payable by credit card, in exactly 30 days. When the lobsters fail to arrive, Red sues.
3. Company handbook, given to all new hires, states that no employee will be fired without a hearing and an appeal. Company fires Delores without a hearing or appeal. She sues.

Strategy: In (1), the Company never promised to pay a commission to nonemployees, so there is no contract. However, the Company *benefited* from Leandro's work. In (2), the parties have *clearly stated all terms* to a simple sales agreement. In (3), the Company and Delores never negotiated termination, but *the handbook suggests* that all employees have certain rights.

Result: (1) is a case of quasi-contract because the company benefited and should reasonably expect to pay. (2) is an express contract because all terms are clearly stated. (3) is an implied contract, similar to the *DeMasse* case, based on the handbook.

Sources of Contract Law

Common Law

We have seen the evolution of contract law from the twelfth century to the present. Express and implied contracts, promissory estoppel, and quasi-contract were all crafted, over centuries, by courts deciding one contract lawsuit at a time. Many contract lawsuits continue to be decided using common-law principles developed by courts.

Uniform Commercial Code

Business methods changed quickly during the first half of the last century. Transportation speeded up. Corporations routinely conducted business across state borders and around the world. These developments presented a problem. Common-law principles, whether related to contracts, torts, or anything else, sometimes vary from one state to another. New York and California courts often reach similar conclusions when presented with similar cases, but they are under no obligation to do so. Business leaders became frustrated that, to do business across the country, their companies had to deal with many different sets of common-law rules.

Executives, lawyers, and judges wanted a body of law for business transactions that reflected modern commercial methods and provided uniformity throughout the United States. It would be much easier, they thought, if some parts of contract law were the same in every state. That desire gave birth to the Uniform Commercial Code (UCC), created in 1952. The drafters intended the UCC to facilitate the easy formation and enforcement of contracts in a fast-paced world. The Code governs many aspects of commerce, including the sale and leasing of goods, negotiable instruments, bank deposits, letters of credit, investment securities, secured transactions, and other commercial matters. Every state has adopted at least part of the UCC to govern commercial transactions within that state. For our purposes in studying contracts, the most important part of the Code is Article 2, which governs the sale of goods. **"Goods" means anything movable, except for money, securities, and certain legal rights.** Goods include pencils, commercial aircraft, books, and Christmas trees. Goods do not include land or a house because neither is movable, nor do they include a stock certificate. A contract for the sale of 10,000 sneakers is governed by the UCC; a contract for the sale of a condominium in Marina del Rey is governed by the California common law.

When analyzing any contract problem as a student or businessperson, you must note whether the agreement concerns the sale of goods. For many issues, the common law and the UCC are reasonably similar. But sometimes, the law is quite different under the two sets of rules.

And so, the UCC governs contracts for a sale of goods, while common-law principles govern contracts for sales of services and everything else. Most of the time, it will be clear whether the UCC or the common law applies. But what if a contract involves both goods and services? When you get your oil changed, you are paying in part for the new oil and oil filter (goods) and in part for the labor required to do the job (services). In a mixed contract, Article 2 governs only if the *primary purpose* was the sale of goods. In the following case, the court had to decide the primary purpose.

Fallsview Glatt Kosher Caterers, Inc. v. Rosenfeld

2005 WL 53623
Civil Court, City of New York, 2005

Facts: During the Jewish holidays, Fallsview Glatt Kosher Caterers organized programs at Kutcher's Country Club, where it provided all accommodations, food, and entertainment.

Fallsview sued Willie Rosenfeld, alleging that he had requested accommodations for 15 members of his family, agreeing to pay $24,050, and then failed to appear or pay.

Rosenfeld moved to dismiss, claiming that even if there had been an agreement, it was never put in writing. Under UCC §2-201, any contract for the sale of goods worth $500 or more can be enforced only if it is in writing and signed. Fallsview argued that the agreement was not for the sale of goods, but for services. The company claimed that because the contract was not governed by the UCC, it should be enforced even with no writing.

Issue: ***Was the agreement one for the sale of goods, requiring a writing, or for services, enforceable with no writing?***

Excerpts from Judge Battaglia's Decision: Mr. Rosenfeld contends that the "predominant purpose" and "main objective" of the agreement alleged by Fallsview was the "service of Kosher food," while the hotel accommodations and entertainment were merely "incidental or collateral" services.

Defendant's contention that the "predominant purpose" of the alleged agreement is the sale of food is said to be compelled by the very nature of the Passover holiday. [He argues that] "the essential religious obligation during this eight-day period and the principal reason why people attend events similar to the Program sponsored by plaintiff is in order to facilitate their fulfillment of the requirement to eat only food which is prepared in strict accordance with the mandate of Jewish law for Passover, i.e., food which is 'Kosher for Passover.' It is the desire to obtain these 'goods' and not the urge for 'entertainment' or 'accommodations' that motivates customers to subscribe to such 'Programs.' "

[Fallsview submitted] ten sheets, designated "Kutcher's Country Club Daily Activities" for Sunday, April 4, through Tuesday, April 13, 2004. The activities possible include tennis, racquetball, swimming, Swedish massage, "make over face lift show," "trivia time," aerobics, bingo, ice skating, dancing, "showtime," "power walk," arts and crafts, day camp, ping-pong, Yiddish theater, board games, horse racing, horseback riding, wine tasting, and indoor baci and that is only through Wednesday. These activities are provided, together with accommodations and food, for an "all inclusive" price that is apparently determined by the size and location of the room(s) and the numbers and ages of the persons in each party.

A review of the characteristics of the "program," which is the subject matter of the alleged agreement, leads the Court to conclude that the "essence" of the family and communal "experience" is defined primarily by "services" and not by "goods."

The intended scope of UCC section 2-201 is also indicated by its provision that "[a] writing is not insufficient because it omits or incorrectly states a term agreed upon but the contract is not enforceable under this paragraph beyond the quantity of goods shown in the writing." For the Code, quantity is even more important than price. A contract of the type involved here would rarely, if ever, specify the "quantity" of the "goods" to be provided. Nor would, for example, a contract for a week's stay at a weight-loss spa, or a zen-vegetarian retreat, or a cruise of the islands.

Plaintiff argues that "Defendant's proposition that a hotel reservation is a sale of goods would render all reservations made via telephone or the Internet unenforceable and would leave hotels in a precarious economic position." That may or may not be true, but the argument does highlight the importance of ensuring that a Statute of Frauds structured and outfitted by the Legislature for a particular transactional context not be casually applied to a very different commercial segment and model. The structure and terms of section 2-201 tell us that it was not intended to cover the agreement alleged in this Complaint.

Defendant's motion to dismiss is denied.

EXAM Strategy

Question: Leila agrees to pay Kendrick $35,000 to repair windmills. Confident of this cash, Kendrick contracts to buy Derrick's used Porsche for $33,000. Then Leila informs Kendrick she does not need his help and will not pay him. Kendrick tells Derrick that he no longer wants the Porsche. Derrick sues Kendrick, and Kendrick files suit against Leila. What law or laws govern these lawsuits?

Strategy: Always be conscious of whether a contract is for services or the sale of goods. Different laws govern. To make that distinction, you must understand the term "goods." If you are clear about that, the question is answered easily.

Result: *Goods* means anything movable, and a Porsche is movable—one might say "super-movable." The UCC will control Derrick's suit. Repairing windmills is primarily a service. Kendrick's lawsuit is governed by the common law of contracts.

Chapter Conclusion

Contracts govern countless areas of our lives, from intimate family issues to multibillion-dollar corporate deals. Understanding contract principles is essential for a successful business or professional career and is invaluable in private life. This knowledge is especially important because courts no longer rubber-stamp any agreement that two parties have made. If we know the issues that courts scrutinize, the agreement we draft is likelier to be enforced. We thus achieve greater control over our affairs—the very purpose of a contract.

EXAM REVIEW

1. **CONTRACTS: DEFINITION AND ELEMENTS** A contract is a legally enforceable promise. Analyzing whether a contract exists involves inquiring into these issues: offer, acceptance, consideration, capacity, legal purpose, consent, and sometimes, whether the deal is in writing. (pp. 232–233)

2. DEVELOPMENT The development of contract law stretches into the distant past. Before the fifteenth century, courts rarely enforced promises at all. By the 1600s, courts enforced many mutual promises, and by 1900, most promises containing the seven elements of a contract were strictly enforced. (pp. 233–235)

3. UNILATERAL AND BILATERAL CONTRACTS In bilateral contracts, the parties exchange promises. In a unilateral contract, only one party makes a promise, and the other must take some action—his return promise is insufficient to form a contract. (p. 235)

4. EXECUTORY AND EXECUTED CONTRACTS In an executory contract, one or both of the parties have not yet have not done everything that they promised to do. In an executed contract, all parties have fully performed. (pp. 235–236)

5. ENFORCEABILITY

- Valid contracts are fully enforceable.
- An unenforceable agreement is one with a legal defect.
- A voidable contract occurs when one party has an option to cancel the agreement.
- A void agreement means that the law will ignore the deal regardless of what the parties want. (pp. 236–237)

Question: Yasmine is negotiating to buy Stewart's house. She asks him what condition the roof is in.

"Excellent," he replies. "It is only 2 years old, and should last 25 more." In fact, Stewart knows that the roof is 26 years old and has had a series of leaks. The parties sign a sales contract for $600,000. A week before Yasmine is to pay for the house and take possession, she discovers the leaks and learns that the mandatory new roof will cost $35,000. At the same time, she learns that the house has increased in value by $60,000 since she signed the agreement. What options does Yasmine have?

Strategy: You know intuitively that Stewart's conduct is as shabby as his roof. What is the legal term for his deception? Fraud. Does fraud make an agreement void or voidable? Does it matter? (See the "Result" at the end of this section.)

6. EXPRESS AND IMPLIED CONTRACTS If the parties formally agreed and stated explicit terms, there is probably an express contract. If the parties did not formally agree but their conduct, words, or past dealings indicate they intended a binding agreement, there may be an implied contract. (pp. 237–238)

7. OTHER REMEDIES If there is no contract, are there other reasons to give the plaintiff damages?

- A claim of promissory estoppel requires that the defendant made a promise knowing that the plaintiff would likely *rely*, and the plaintiff did so. It would be wrong to deny recovery.

- A claim of quasi-contract requires that the defendant received a benefit, knowing that the plaintiff would expect compensation, and it would be unjust not to grant it. (pp. 239–242)

EXAM Strategy

Question: The Hoffmans owned and operated a successful small bakery and grocery store. They spoke with Lukowitz, an agent of Red Owl Stores, who told them that for $18,000, Red Owl would build a store and fully stock it for them. The Hoffmans sold their bakery and grocery store and purchased a lot on which Red Owl was to build the store. Lukowitz then told Hoffman that the price had gone up to $26,000. The Hoffmans borrowed the extra money from relatives, but then Lukowitz informed them that the cost would be $34,000. Negotiations broke off, and the Hoffmans sued. The court determined that there was no contract because too many details had not been worked out—the size of the store, its design, and the cost of constructing it. Can the Hoffmans recover any money?

Strategy: Because there is no contract, the Hoffmans must rely on either promissory estoppel or quasi-contract. Promissory estoppel focuses on the defendant's promise and the plaintiff's reliance. Those suing in quasi-contract must show that the defendant received a benefit for which it should reasonably expect to pay. Does either fit here? (See the "Result" at the end of this section.)

8. **SOURCES OF CONTRACT LAW** If a contract is for the sale of goods, the UCC is the relevant body of law. For anything else, the common law governs. If a contract involves both goods and services, a court will determine the agreement's primary purpose. (pp. 243–244)

EXAM Strategy

Question: Honeywell, Inc., and Minolta Camera Co. had a contract providing that Honeywell would give to Minolta various technical information on the design of a specialized camera lens. Minolta would have the right to use the information in its cameras, provided that Minolta also used certain Honeywell parts in its cameras. Honeywell delivered to Minolta numerous technical documents, computer software, and test equipment, and Honeywell engineers met with Minolta engineers at least 20 times to discuss the equipment. Several years later, Honeywell sued, claiming that Minolta had taken the design information but failed to use Honeywell parts in its cameras. Minolta moved to dismiss, claiming that the UCC required lawsuits concerning the sale of goods to be filed within four years of the breach and that this lawsuit was too late. Honeywell answered that the UCC did not apply, and that therefore, Minnesota's six-year statute of limitations governed. Who is right?

Strategy: Like many contracts, this one involves both goods, which are governed by the UCC, and services, controlled by the common law. We decide which of those two laws governs by using the predominant purpose test. Was this contract primarily about selling goods or about providing services? (See the "Result" at the end of this section.)

5. Result: Indeed, it does matter. Stewart's fraud makes the contract voidable by Yasmine. She has the right to terminate the agreement and pay nothing. However, she may go through with the contract if she prefers. The choice is hers—but not Stewart's.

7. Result: Red Owl received no benefit from the Hoffmans' sale of their store or purchase of the lot. However, Red Owl did make a promise and expected the Hoffmans to rely on it, which they did. The Hoffmans won their claim of promissory estoppel.

8. Result: The primary purpose of this agreement was not the sale of goods, but rather the exchange of technical data, ideas, designs, and so forth. The common law governs the contract, and Honeywell's suit may go forward.

Multiple-Choice Questions

1. A sitcom actor, exhausted after his 10-hour workweek, agrees to buy a briefcase full of cocaine from Lewis for $12,000. Lewis and the actor have a ____________ contract.

(a) valid

(b) unenforceable

(c) voidable

(d) void

2. Carol says, "Pam, you're my best friend in the world. I just inherited a million bucks, and I want you to have some of it. Come with me to the bank tomorrow, and I'll give you $10,000." "Sweet!" Pam replies. Later that day, Carol has a change of heart. She is allowed to do so. Examine the list of the elements of a contract, and cite the correct reason.

(a) The agreement was not put into writing.

(b) The agreement lacks a legal purpose.

(c) Pam did not give consideration.

(d) Pam does not have the capacity to make a contract.

3. On the first day of the baseball season, Dean orders a new Cardinals hat from Amazon. At the moment he submits his order, Dean and Amazon have an ____________ contract. Two days later, Amazon delivers the hat to Dean's house. At this point, Dean and Amazon have an ____________ contract.

(a) executory; executory

(b) executory; executed

(c) executed; executory

(d) executed; executed

4. Linda goes to an electronics store and buys a high-definition TV. Lauren hires a company to clean her swimming pool once a week. The ____________ governs Linda's contract with the store, and the ____________ governs Lauren's contract with the cleaning company.

(a) common law; common law

(b) common law; UCC

(c) UCC; common law

(d) UCC; UCC

5. Consider the following scenarios:

I. Madison says to a group of students, "I'll pay $35 to the first one of you who shows up at my house and mows my lawn."

II. Lea posts a flyer around town that reads, "Reward: $500 for information about the person who keyed my truck last Saturday night in the Wag-a-Bag parking lot. Call Lea at 555-5309."

Which of these proposes a *unilateral* contract?

(a) I only

(b) II only

(c) Both I and II

(d) None of the above

Essay Questions

1. Pennsylvania contracted with Envirotest Systems, Inc., an Arizona company, to build 86 automobile emissions inspection stations in 25 counties and operate them for seven years. This contract is worth hundreds of millions of dollars to Envirotest. But Pennsylvania legislators suddenly opposed the entire system, claiming that it would lead to long delays and high expenses for motorists. These lawmakers urged that Pennsylvania simply stop construction of the new system. Was Pennsylvania allowed to get out of the contract because its legislators concluded the whole system is unwise?

2. Central Maine Power Co. made a promotional offer in which it promised to pay a substantial sum to any homeowner or builder who constructed new housing heated with electricity. Motel Services, Inc., which was building a small housing project for the city of Waterville, Maine, decided to install electrical heat in the units in order to qualify for the offer. It built the units and requested payment for the full amount of the promotional offer. Is Central Maine obligated to pay? Why or why not?

3. Interactive Data Corp. hired Daniel Foley as an assistant product manager at a starting salary of $18,500. Over the next six years, Interactive steadily promoted Foley until he became Los Angeles branch manager at a salary of $56,116. Interactive's officers repeatedly told Foley that he would have his job as long as his performance was adequate. In addition, Interactive distributed an employee handbook that specified "termination guidelines," including a mandatory seven-step pre-termination procedure. Two years later, Foley learned that his recently hired supervisor, Robert Kuhne, was under investigation by the FBI for embezzlement at his previous job. Foley reported this to Interactive officers. Shortly thereafter, Interactive fired Foley. He sued, claiming that Interactive could fire him only for good cause, after the seven-step procedure. What kind of a claim is he making? Should he succeed?

4. ***ETHICS*** You want to lease your automobile to a friend for the summer but do not want to pay a lawyer to draw up the lease. Joanna, a neighbor, is in law school. She is not licensed to practice law. She offers to draft a lease for you for $100, and you unwisely accept. Later, you refuse to pay her fee, and she sues to collect. Who will win the lawsuit, and why? Apart from the law, was it morally right for the law student to try to help you by drafting the lease? Was she acting helpfully, or foolishly, or fraudulently? Is it just for you to agree to her fee and then refuse to pay it? What is society's interest in this dispute? Should a court be more concerned with the ethical issue raised by the conduct of the two parties or with the social consequences of this agreement?

5. ***YOU BE THE JUDGE* WRITING PROBLEM** John Stevens owned a dilapidated apartment that he rented to James and Cora Chesney for a low rent. The Chesneys began to remodel and rehabilitate the unit. Over a four-year period, they installed two new bathrooms, carpeted the floors, installed new septic and heating systems, and rewired, replumbed, and painted. Stevens periodically stopped by and saw the work in progress. The Chesneys transformed the unit into a respectable apartment. Three years after their work was done, Stevens served the Chesneys with an eviction notice. The Chesneys counterclaimed, seeking the value of the work they had done. Are they entitled to it? **Argument for Stevens:** Mr. Stevens is willing to pay the Chesneys exactly the amount he agreed to pay: nothing. The parties never contracted for the Chesneys to fix up the apartment. In fact, they never even discussed such an agreement. The Chesneys are making the absurd argument that anyone who chooses to perform certain work, without ever discussing it with another party, can finish the job and then charge it to the other person. If the Chesneys expected to get paid, obviously they should have said so. If the court were to allow this claim, it would be inviting other tenants to make improvements and then bill the landlord. The law has never been so foolish. **Argument for the Chesneys:** The law of quasi-contract was crafted for cases exactly like this. The Chesneys have given an enormous benefit to Stevens by transforming the apartment and enabling him to rent it at greater profit for many years to come. Stevens saw the work being done and understood that the Chesneys expected some compensation for these major renovations. If Stevens never intended to pay the fair value of the work, he should have stopped the couple from doing the work or notified them that there would be no compensation. It would be unjust to allow the landlord to seize the value of the work, evict the tenants who did it, and pay nothing.

Discussion Questions

1. Have you ever made an agreement that mattered to you, only to have the other person refuse to follow through on the deal? Looking at the list of elements in the chapter, did your agreement amount to a contract? If not, which element did it lack?

2. Consider promissory estoppel and quasi-contracts. Do you like the fact that these doctrines exist? Should courts have "wiggle room" to enforce deals that fail to meet

formal contract requirements? Or, should the rule be "If it's not an actual contract, too bad. No deal."

3. Is it sensible to have two different sets of contract rules—one for sales of goods and another for everything else? Would it be better to have a single set of rules for all contracts?

4. In the case *Davis v. Mason*, a court considered an early non-compete agreement. Did the court in that case reach a proper conclusion? What should courts say in similar cases in modern times?

5. Return to the opening scenario. Fran, Ricky, Carla, and Dave each made an agreement with John. None is valid under contract law. For the sake of fairness, *should* any of them be legally enforceable? If so, which?

CHAPTER 11

The Agreement: Offers and Acceptances

I should talk with my agent. I'd need something in writing about the nude scene ...

Interior. A glitzy café, New York. Evening. Bob, a famous director, and Katrina, a glamorous actress, sit at a table, near a wall of glass looking onto a New York sidewalk that is filled with life and motion. Bob sips a margarita while carefully eyeing Katrina. Katrina stares at her wine glass.

Bob *(smiling confidently)*: *Body Work* is going to be huge—for the right actress. I know a film that's gonna gross a hundred million when I'm holding one. I'm holding one.

Katrina *(perking up at the mention of money)*: It is quirky. It's fun. And she's very strong, very real.

Bob: She's you. That's why we're sitting here. We start shooting in seven months.

Katrina *(edging away from the table)*: I have a few questions. That nude scene.

Bob: The one on the toboggan run?

Katrina: *That* one was O.K. But the one in the poultry factory—very explicit. I don't work nude.

Bob: It's not really nude. Think of all those feathers fluttering around.

Katrina: It's nude.

Bob: We'll work it out. This is a romantic comedy, not tawdry exploitation. Katrina, we're talking $2.5 million. A little accommodation, please. We'll give you $600,000 up front, and the rest deferred, the usual percentages.

Katrina: Bob, my fee is $3 million. As you know. That hasn't changed.

Katrina picks up her drink, doesn't sip it, places it on the coaster, using both hands to center it perfectly. He waits, as she stares silently at her glass.

Bob: We're shooting in Santa Fe, the weather will be perfect. You have a suite at the Excelsior, plus a trailer on location.

KATRINA: I should talk with my agent. I'd need something in writing about the nude scene, the fee, percentages—all the business stuff. I never sign without talking to her.

Bob shrugs and sits back.

KATRINA *(made anxious by the silence)*: I love the character, I really do.

BOB: You and several others love her. *(That jolts her.)* Agents can wait. I have to put this together fast. We can get you the details you want in writing. *Body Work* is going to be bigger than *Sex in the City*.

That one hooks her. She looks at Bob. He nods reassuringly. Bob sticks out his hand, smiling. Katrina hesitates, lets go of her drink, and SHAKES HANDS, looking unsure. Bob signals for the check.

Do Bob and Katrina have a deal? *They* seem to think so. But is her fee $2.5 million or $3 million? What if Katrina demands that all nude scenes be taken out, and Bob refuses? Must she still act in the film? Or suppose her agent convinces her that *Body Work* is no good even with changes. Has Katrina committed herself? What if Bob auditions another actress the next day, likes her, and signs her? Does he owe Katrina her fee? Or suppose Bob learns that the funding has fallen apart and there will be no film. Is Katrina entitled to her money?

Bob and Katrina have acted out a classic problem in *agreement,* one of the basic issues in contract law. Their lack of clarity means that disputes are likely and lawsuits possible. Similar bargaining goes on every day around the country and around the world, and the problems created are too frequently resolved in court. Some negotiating is done in person; more is done over the phone, by fax, by email—or all of them combined. This chapter highlights the most common sources of misunderstanding and litigation so that you can avoid making contracts you never intended—or deals that you cannot enforce.

There almost certainly is no contract between Bob and Katrina. Bob's offer was unclear. Even if it was valid, Katrina counteroffered. When they shook hands, it is impossible to know what terms each had in mind.

Contracts Checklist

- ☑ Offer
- ☑ Acceptance
- ☐ Consideration
- ☐ Legality
- ☐ Capacity
- ☐ Consent
- ☐ Writing

MEETING OF THE MINDS

Remember from the last chapter that contracts have seven key characteristics. Agreements that have a problem in any of the areas do not amount to valid contracts. In this chapter, we examine the first two items on the checklist.

Offer
An act or statement that proposes definite terms and permits the other party to create a contract by accepting those terms.

Parties form a contract only if they have a meeting of the minds. For this to happen, one side must make an **offer** and the other must make an **acceptance**. An offer proposes definite terms, and an acceptance unconditionally agrees to them.

Throughout the chapter, keep in mind that courts make *objective* assessments when evaluating offers and acceptances. A court will not try to get inside Katrina's head and decide what she was thinking as she shook hands. It will look at the handshake *objectively,* deciding how a reasonable person would interpret her words and conduct. Katrina may honestly have meant to conclude a deal for $3 million with no nude scenes, while Bob might in good faith have believed he was committing himself to $2.5 million and absolute control of the script. Neither belief will control the outcome.

OFFER

Bargaining begins with an offer. The person who makes an offer is the **offeror**. The person to whom he makes that offer is the **offeree**. The terms are annoying but inescapable because, like handcuffs, all courts use them.

Offeror
The person who makes an offer.

Offeree
The person to whom an offer is made.

Two questions determine whether a statement is an offer:

- Do the offeror's words and actions indicate an *intention* to make a bargain?
- Are the terms of the offer reasonably definite?

Zachary says to Sharon, "Come work in my English language center as a teacher. I'll pay you $800 per week for a 35-hour week, for six months starting Monday." This is a valid offer. Zachary's words seem to indicate that he intends to make a bargain and his offer is definite. If Sharon accepts, the parties have a contract that either one can enforce.

In the section below, we present several categories of statements that are generally *not* valid offers.

Statements that Usually do not Amount to Offers

(generally not valid offers)

Invitations to Bargain

An invitation to bargain is not an offer. Suppose Martha telephones Joe and leaves a message on his answering machine, asking if Joe would consider selling his vacation condo on Lake Michigan. Joe faxes a signed letter to Martha saying, "There is no way I could sell the condo for less than $150,000." Martha promptly sends Joe a cashier's check for that amount. Does she own the condo? No. Joe's fax was not an offer. It is merely an invitation to negotiate. Joe is indicating that he might well be happy to receive an offer from Martha, but he is not promising to sell the condo for $150,000 or for any amount.

Price Quotes

A price quote is generally not an offer. If Imperial Textile sends a list of fabric prices for the new year to its regular customers, the list is not an offer. Once again, the law regards it merely as a solicitation of offers. Suppose Ralph orders 1,000 yards of fabric, quoted in the list at $40 per yard. *Ralph* is making the offer, and Imperial may decline to sell at $40, or at any price, for that matter.

This can be an expensive point to learn. Leviton Manufacturing makes electrical fixtures and switches. Litton Microwave manufactures ovens. Leviton sent a price list to Litton, stating what it would charge for specially modified switches for use in Litton's microwaves. The price letter included a statement greatly limiting Leviton's liability in the event of any problem with the switches. Litton purchased thousands of the switches and used them in manufacturing its microwaves. But consumers reported fires due to defects in the switches. Leviton claimed that under the contract it had no liability. But the court held that the price letter was not an offer. It was a request to receive an offer. Thus the contract ultimately formed did not include Leviton's liability exclusion. Litton won over $4 million.[1] See Exhibit 11.1

Letters of Intent

In complex business negotiations, the parties may spend months bargaining over dozens of interrelated issues. Because each party wants to protect itself during the discussions, ensuring that the other side is serious without binding itself to premature commitments,

[1]*Litton Microwave Cooking Products v. Leviton Manufacturing Co., Inc.*, 15 F.3d 790, 1994 U.S. App. LEXIS 1876 (8th Cir. 1994).

EXHIBIT 11.1 The Litton case demonstrates why it is important to distinguish a valid offer from a mere price quote. Leviton's price list (including a limited warranty) was *not* an offer. When Litton ordered goods (with no limit to the warranty), it was making an offer, which Leviton accepted by delivering the goods. The resulting contract did not contain the limited warranty that Leviton wanted, costing that company a $4 million judgment.

Letter of intent
A letter that summarizes negotiating progress.

it may be tempting during the negotiations to draft a **letter of intent**. The letter *might* help distinguish a serious party from one with a casual interest, summarize the progress made thus far, and assist the parties in securing necessary financing. Usually, letters of intent do not create any legal obligation. They merely state what the parties are considering, not what they have actually agreed to. But note that is possible for a letter of intent to bind the parties if its language indicates that the parties *intended* to be bound.

Advertisements

Mary Mesaros received a notice from the United States Bureau of the Mint, announcing a new $5 gold coin to commemorate the Statue of Liberty. The notice contained an order form stating:

> VERY IMPORTANT—PLEASE READ: YES, Please accept my order for the U.S. Liberty Coins I have indicated. I understand that all sales are final and not subject to refund. Verification of my order will be made by the Department of the Treasury, U.S. Mint. If my order is received by December 31, I will be entitled to purchase the coins at the Pre-Issue Discount price shown.

Mesaros ordered almost $2,000 worth of the coins. But the Mint was inundated with so many requests for the coin that the supply was soon exhausted. Mesaros and thousands of others never got their coins. This was particularly disappointing because the market value of the coins doubled shortly after their issue. Mesaros sued on behalf of the entire class of disappointed purchasers. Like most who sue based on an advertisement, she lost.[2] **An advertisement is generally not an offer.** An advertisement is merely a request for offers. The consumer makes the offer, whether by mail, as above, or by arriving at a merchant's store ready to buy. The seller is free to reject the offer.

Advertisers should be careful, however, not to be too specific in their ads. Some ads do count as offers, as the following case illustrates.

[2] *Mesaros v. United States*, 845 F.2d 1576, 1988 U.S. App. LEXIS 6055 (Fed. Cir. 1988).

Landmark Case

Carlill v. Carbolic Smoke Ball Company

1 QB 256
Court of Appeal, 1892

Facts: In the early 1890s, English citizens greatly feared the Russian flu. The Carbolic Smoke Ball Company ran a newspaper ad that contained two key passages:

> "£100 reward will be paid by the Carbolic Smoke Ball Company to any person who contracts the influenza after having used the ball three times daily for two weeks according to the printed directions supplied with each ball.
>
> "£1000 is deposited with the Alliance Bank, shewing our sincerity in the matter."

The product was a ball that contained carbolic acid. Users would inhale vapors from the ball through a long tube.

Carlill purchased a smoke ball and used it as directed for two months. She then caught the flu. She sued, arguing that because her response to the ad had created a contract with the company, she was entitled to £100.

The trial court agreed, awarding Carlill the money. The company appealed.

Issues: ***Did the advertisement amount to an offer? If so, was the offer accepted?***

Excerpts from Lord Justice Lindley's Decision: The first observation I will make is that we are dealing with an express promise to pay £100 in certain events. Read the advertisement how you will, and twist it about as you will, here is a distinct promise expressed in language which is perfectly unmistakable.

We must first consider whether this was intended to be a promise at all. The deposit is called by the advertiser as proof of his sincerity in the matter—that is, the sincerity of his promise to pay this £100 in the event which he has specified. I say there is the promise, as plain as words can make it.

Then it is contended that it is not binding. In the first place, the performance of the conditions is the acceptance of the offer. Unquestionably, as a general proposition, when an offer is made, it is necessary that the acceptance should be notified. But is that so in cases of this kind? I think that in a case of this kind that the person who makes the [offer] shews by his language and from the nature of the transaction that he does not expect and does not require notice of the acceptance apart from notice of the performance.

We, therefore, find here all the elements which are necessary to form a binding contract enforceable in point of law.

It appears to me, therefore, that the defendants must perform their promise, and, if they have been so unwary as to expose themselves to a great many actions, so much the worse for them. Appeal dismissed.

Carlill lived 50 years more, dying at the age of 96—of the flu.

This case serves as a cautionary tale. Running a "normal" ad which describes a product, its features, and its price does not amount to an offer. But, if a company proposes to take an action—like pay $100 to customers who take certain, specific actions—then it may find itself contractually obligated to follow through on its promises. The acceptance of the offer makes a unilateral contract.

Note also that, regardless of whether an ad counts as an offer, consumers have protection from those shopkeepers who are intent upon deceit. Almost every state has some form of **consumer protection statute,** which outlaws false advertising. For example, an automobile dealer who advertises a remarkably low price but then has only one automobile at that price has probably violated a consumer protection statute because the ad was published in bad faith, to trick consumers into coming to the dealership. In the *Mesaros* case, the United States Mint did not violate any consumer protection statute because it acted in good faith and simply ran out of coins.

© AP Photo/Seth Wenig

You have the high bid—but you may not have the property.

Auctions

It is the property you have always dreamed of owning—and it is up for auction! You arrive bright and early, stand in front, bid early, bid often, bid higher, bid highest of all—it's yours! For five seconds. Then, to your horror, the auctioneer announces that none of the bids were juicy enough and he is withdrawing the property. Robbery! Surely he cannot do that? But he can. Auctions are exciting and useful, but you must understand the rules.

Every day, auctions are used to sell exquisite works of art, real estate, and many other things. **Placing an item up for auction is *not* an offer—it is merely a request for an offer.** The *bids* are the offers. If and when the hammer falls, the auctioneer has accepted the offer.

The important thing to know about a particular auction is whether it is conducted with or without reserve. Most auctions are *with reserve*, meaning that the items for sale have a minimum price. The law assumes that an auction is with reserve unless the auctioneer clearly states otherwise. The auctioneer will not sell anything for less than its reserve (minimum price). So when the bidding for your property failed to reach the reserve, the auctioneer was free to withdraw it.

The rules are different in an auction *without reserve*. Here, there is no minimum. Once the first bid is received, the auctioneer *must* sell the merchandise to the highest bidder.

EXAM Strategy

Question: Ahn and Chet are both unhappy. (1) Ahn, an interior designer, is working on a hotel project. In the annual catalog of a furniture wholesaler, she sees that sofa beds cost $3,000. Based on the catalog, she sends an order for 100 sofa beds to the wholesaler. The wholesaler notifies Ahn that the price has gone up to $4,000. (2) At an estate auction, held without reserve, Chet is high bidder on a rare violin. The seller considers Chet's bid too low and refuses to sell. Both Ahn and Chet sue, but only one will win. Which plaintiff will win, and why?

Strategy: (1) A contract requires an offer and an acceptance. When the furniture wholesaler sent out its catalog, did it make an offer that Ahn could accept? (2) Chet was high bidder. At some auctions, the high bidder is merely making an offer, but at others, he wins the item. Which kind of auction was this?

Result: (1) A price quote is generally not an offer. Ahn's order for 100 sofas was the offer, and the company was free to reject it. Ahn loses. (2) Most auctions are with reserve, meaning that the high bidder is merely making an offer. However, this one was without reserve. Chet gets the violin.

Problems with Definiteness

It is not enough that the offeror indicates that she intends to enter into an agreement. **The terms of the offer must also be definite.** If they are vague, then even if the offeree agrees to the deal, a court does not have enough information to enforce it and there is no contract.

You want a friend to work in your store for the holiday season. This is a definite offer: "I offer you a job as a sales clerk in the store from November 1 through December 29, 40 hours per week at $10 per hour." But suppose, by contrast, you say: "I offer you a job as a sales clerk in the store during the holiday season. We will work out a fair wage once we see how busy things get." Your friend replies, "That's fine with me." This offer is indefinite, and there is no contract. What is a fair wage? $15 per hour? Or $20 per hour? What is the "holiday season"? How will the determinations be made? There is no binding agreement.

The following case, which concerns a famous television show, presents a problem with definiteness.

BAER V. CHASE

392 F.3d 609
Third Circuit Court of Appeals, 2004

Facts: David Chase was a television writer-producer with many credits, including a detective series called *The Rockford Files*. He became interested in a new program, set in New Jersey, about a "mob boss in therapy," a concept he eventually developed into *The Sopranos*. Robert Baer was a prosecutor in New Jersey who wanted to write for television. He submitted a *Rockford Files* script to Chase, who agreed to meet with Baer.

When they met, Baer pitched a different idea, concerning "a film or television series about the New Jersey Mafia." He did not realize Chase was already working on such an idea. Later that year, Chase visited New Jersey. Baer arranged meetings for Chase with local detectives and prosecutors, who provided the producer with information, material, and personal stories about their experiences with organized crime. Detective Thomas Koczur drove Chase and Baer to various New Jersey locations and introduced Chase to Tony Spirito. Spirito shared stories about loan sharking, power struggles between family members connected with the mob, and two colorful individuals known as Big Pussy and Little Pussy, both of whom later became characters on the show.

Back in Los Angeles, Chase wrote and sent to Baer a draft of the first *Sopranos* teleplay. Baer called Chase and commented on the script. The two spoke at least four times that year, and Baer sent Chase a letter about the script.

When *The Sopranos* became a hit television show, Baer sued Chase. He alleged that on three separate occasions Chase had agreed that if the program succeeded, Chase would "take care of" Baer, and would "remunerate Baer in a manner commensurate to the true value of his services." This happened twice on the phone, Baer claimed, and once during Chase's visit to New Jersey. The understanding was that if the show failed, Chase would owe nothing. Chase never paid Baer anything.

The district court dismissed the case, holding that the alleged promises were too vague to be enforced. Baer appealed.

Issue: ***Was Chase's promise definite enough to be enforced?***

Excerpts from Judge Greenberg's Decision: A contract arises from offer and acceptance, and must be sufficiently definite so that the performance to be rendered by each party can be ascertained with reasonable certainty. Therefore parties create an enforceable contract when they agree on its essential terms and manifest an intent that the terms bind them. If parties to an agreement do not agree on one or more essential terms of the purported agreement courts generally hold it to be unenforceable.

New Jersey law deems the price term, that is, the amount of compensation, an essential term of any contract.

An agreement lacking definiteness of price, however, is not unenforceable if the parties specify a practicable method by which they can determine the amount. However, in the absence of an agreement as to the manner or method of determining compensation the purported agreement is invalid. Additionally, the duration of the contract is deemed an essential term and therefore any agreement must be sufficiently definitive to allow a court to determine the agreed upon length of the contractual relationship.

Baer premises his argument on his view that New Jersey should disregard the well-established requirement of definiteness in its contract law when the subject-matter of the contract is an "idea submission." [However,] New Jersey precedent does not support Baer's attempt to carve out an exception to traditional principles of contract law for submission-of-idea cases. The New Jersey courts have not provided even the slightest indication that they intend to depart from their well-established requirement that enforceability of a contract requires definiteness with respect to the essential terms of that contract.

Nothing in the record indicates that the parties agreed on how, how much, where, or for what period Chase would compensate Baer. The parties did not discuss who would determine the "true value" of Baer's services, when the "true value" would be calculated, or what variables would go into such a calculation. There was no discussion or agreement as to the meaning of "success" of *The Sopranos*. There was no discussion how "profits" were to be defined. There was no contemplation of dates of commencement or termination of the contract. And again, nothing in Baer's or Chase's conduct, or the surrounding circumstances of the relationship, shed light on, or answers, any of these questions.

Affirmed.

Ethics Was it fair for Chase to use Baer's services without compensation? Did Baer really *expect* to get paid, or was he simply hoping that his work would land him a job?

EXAM Strategy

Question: Niels owned three adjoining parcels of land in Arizona ranging from 60 to 120 acres. Hannah wanted to buy one. The two had dinner in Chicago and then sketched this agreement: "Binding Contract: Niels agrees to sell one of his three Arizona lots to Hannah. Within 14 days, the parties will meet on the land, decide which lot Hannah is buying, and settle on a price. If they cannot agree on a price, they will decide a fair method of doing so. Both parties agree to be bound by this contract." Each signed. When they meet in Arizona, Niels refuses to sell any land, and Hannah sues. What will happen?

Strategy: Do not be fooled by wording such as "Binding Contract." Focus on the legal issues: Was there a meeting of the minds? Niels and Hannah *thought* they had a contract—but courts make an objective assessment, not subjective. Did Niels make an offer? Were the terms definite?

Result: Both parties believed they had a binding deal, and both parties were wrong. There are two primary issues—which lot is being sold and how much will it cost—and neither is specified. How are they to select a lot? What is a "fair method" of determining price? Other issues are not touched upon: When will the deal close, how will payment be made, what happens if Hannah cannot finance the purchase? The terms are too vague. The parties never reached a meeting of the minds, and Hannah will lose her suit.

The UCC and Open Terms

In the last chapter, we introduced the Uniform Commercial Code (UCC). Article 2 of the UCC governs contracts when the primary purpose is a sale of goods. Remember that goods are moveable, tangible objects. Usually, UCC provisions are not significantly different from common-law rules. But on occasion, the UCC modifies the common-law rule in some major way. In such cases, we will present a separate description of the key UCC provision. The UCC as a whole is covered in Unit 3. Depending on the class time available, some instructors prefer to discuss the UCC separately, while others like to include it in the general discussion of contracts. This book is designed to work with either approach.

We have just seen that, under the common law, the terms of an offer must be definite. But under the UCC, many indefinite contracts are allowed to stand. Throughout this unit, we witness how the Uniform Commercial Code makes the law of sales more flexible. There are several areas of contract law where imperfect negotiations may still create a binding agreement under the Code, even though the same negotiations under the common law would have yielded no contract. "Open terms" is one such area.

Yuma County Corp. produced natural gas. Yuma wanted a long-term contract to sell its gas so that it could be certain of recouping the expenses of exploration and drilling. Northwest Central Pipeline, which operated an interstate pipeline, also wanted a deal for 10 or more years so it could make its own distribution contracts, knowing it would have a steady supply of natural gas in a competitive market. But neither Yuma nor Northwest wanted to make a long-term *price* commitment, because over a period of years the price of natural gas could double—or crash. Each party wanted a binding agreement without a definitive price. If their negotiations had been governed by the common law, they would have run smack into the requirement of definiteness—no price, no contract. But because this was a sale of goods, it was governed by the UCC.

Under UCC §2-204(3), even though one or more terms are left open, a contract does not fail for indefiniteness if the parties have intended to make a contract and there is a reasonably certain basis for giving an appropriate remedy. Thus, a contract for the sale of goods may be enforced when a key term is missing. Business executives may have many reasons to leave open a delivery date, a price, or some other term. But note that the parties must still have *intended* to create a contract. The UCC will not create a contract where the parties never intended one.

In some cases, the contract will state how the missing term is to be determined. Yuma County and Northwest drafted a contract with alternative methods of determining the price. In the event that the price of natural gas was regulated by the Federal Energy Regulatory Commission (FERC), the price would be the highest allowed by the FERC. If the FERC deregulated the price (as it ultimately did), the contract price would be the average of the two highest prices paid by different gas producers in a specified geographic area.

Gap Filler Provisions

Even if a UCC contract lacks a specific method for determining missing terms, the Code itself contains **gap-filler provisions**, which are rules for *supplying* missing terms. Some of the most important gap-filler provisions of the Code follow.

Gap-filler provisions
UCC rules for supplying missing terms.

Open Price. In general, if the parties do not settle on a price, the Code establishes that the goods will be sold for a reasonable price. This will usually be the market value or a price established by a neutral expert or agency. (UCC §2-305.)

Output and Requirements Provisions. An **output contract** obligates the seller to sell all of his output to the buyer, who agrees to accept it. For example, a cotton grower might agree to sell all of his next crop to a textile firm. A **requirements contract** obligates a buyer to obtain all of his needed goods from the seller. A vineyard might agree to buy all of its wine bottles from one supplier. Output and requirements contracts are by definition

Output contract
Obligates the seller to sell all of his output to the buyer, who agrees to accept it.

Requirements contract
Obligates a buyer to obtain all of his needed goods from the seller.

incomplete, since the exact quantity of the goods is unspecified. The Code requires that in carrying out such contracts, both parties act in good faith. Neither party may suddenly demand a quantity of goods (or offer a quantity of goods) that is disproportionate to their past dealings or their reasonable estimates. (UCC §2-306.)

Termination of Offers

Once an offer has been made, it faces only two possible fates—it can be terminated or accepted. If an offer is terminated, it can never be accepted. If it is accepted, and if there are no problems with any of the five remaining elements on the Contracts Checklist, then a valid contract is created. Offers can be terminated in four ways: revocation, rejection, expiration, and by operation of law.

Termination by Revocation

An offer is **revoked** when the offeror "takes it back" before the offeree accepts. In general, the offeror may revoke the offer any time before it has been accepted. Imagine that I call you and say, "I'm going out of town this weekend. I'll sell you my ticket to this weekend's football game for $75." You tell me that you'll think it over and call me back. An hour later, my plans change. I call you a second time and say, "Sorry, but the deal's off—I'm going to the game after all." I have revoked my offer, and you can no longer accept it.

In the next case, this rule was worth $100,000 to one of the parties.

Nadel v. Tom Cat Bakery

2009 N.Y. Misc. Lexis 5105
Supreme Court of New York, New York County, 2009

Facts: A Tom Cat Bakery delivery van struck Elizabeth Nadel as she crossed a street. Having suffered significant injuries, Nadel filed suit. Before the trial began, the attorney representing the bakery's owner offered a $100,000 settlement, which Nadel refused.

While the jury was deliberating, the bakery's lawyer again offered Nadel the $100,000 settlement. She decided to think about it during lunch. Later that day, the jury sent a note to the judge. The bakery owner told her lawyer that if the note indicated the jury had reached a verdict, that he should revoke the settlement offer.

Back in the courtroom, the bakery's lawyer said, "My understanding is that there's a note.... I was given an instruction that if the note is a verdict, my client wants to take the verdict."

Nadel's lawyer then said, "My client will take the settlement. My client will take the settlement."

The trial court judge allowed the forewoman to read the verdict, which awarded Nadel—nothing. She appealed, claiming that a $100,000 settlement had been reached.

Issue: ***Did Nadel's lawyer accept the settlement offer in time?***

Excerpts from Judge Figueroa's Decision: Plaintiff's motion to enforce "the settlement" has generated considerable debate between the parties. Plaintiff asserts that the defendant is bound to a settlement. Plaintiff's problem is that there was no "agreement" to speak of. To be sure, there was an offer from defendant. During the above-quoted colloquy, clearly there were also words of acceptance from plaintiff. But when the words, "my client will take the settlement" were uttered, it was too late for them to be effective. By that time, defense counsel had made it clear that if the jury had already come to a verdict, the offer was off the table. That condition could not be ignored, as the verdict that would mean all bets were off had already been reached. For the foregoing reasons, plaintiff's motion is denied.

Making Contracts Temporarily Irrevocable

Some offers cannot be revoked, at least for a time. Often, people and businesses need time to evaluate offers. If a car dealer offers you a green sedan for $25,000, you may want to shop around for a few days to try to find a better price. In the meantime, you may want to make sure that the green sedan is still available if you decide to return. Can you legally prevent the car dealer from selling the car to anyone else while you ponder the offer? In some circumstances, yes.

Option Contract (All types of contracts). With an option contract, an interested purchaser *buys* the right to have the offer held open. **The offeror may not revoke an offer during the option period.** Suppose you pay the car dealer $250 to hold open its offer until February 2. Later that day, the dealership notifies you that it is selling to someone else. Result? You can enforce *your* contract. The car dealer had no power to revoke because you purchased an option.

Firm Offers (UCC contracts only). Once again, the UCC has changed the law on the sale of goods. If a promise made in writing is signed by a *merchant,* and if it agrees to hold open an offer for a stated period, then an offer may not be revoked. The open period may not exceed three months. So, if the car dealer gives you a piece of paper that reads, "The offer on the green sedan is open at $25,000 until Friday at noon," he cannot revoke the offer before Friday at noon, even though you have not paid him anything. (UCC §2-205.)

Termination by Rejection

If an offeree clearly indicates that he does not want to take the offer, then he has **rejected** it. **If an offeree rejects an offer, the rejection immediately terminates the offer.** Suppose a major accounting firm telephones you and offers a job, starting at $80,000. You respond, "Nah. I'm gonna work on my surfing for a year or two." The next day, you come to your senses and write the firm, accepting its offer. No contract. Your rejection terminated the offer and ended your power to accept it.

Counteroffer. A party makes a **counteroffer** when it responds to an offer with a new and different proposal. Frederick faxes Kim, offering to sell a 50 percent interest in the Fab Hotel in New York for only $135 million. Kim faxes back and says, "That's too much, but I'll pay $115 million." Moments later, Kim's business partner convinces her that Frederick's offer was a bargain, and she faxes an acceptance of his $135 million offer. Does Kim have a binding deal? No. **A counteroffer is a rejection.** When Kim offered $115 million, she rejected Frederick's offer. Her original fax created a new offer, for $115 million, which Frederick never accepted. The parties have no contract at any price.

Termination by Expiration

An offeror may set a time limit. Quentin calls you and offers you a job in his next motion picture. He tells you, "I've got to know by tomorrow night." If you call him in three days to accept, you are out of the picture. **When an offer specifies a time limit for acceptance, that period is binding.**

If the offer specifies no time limit, the offeree has a *reasonable* period in which to accept. A reasonable period varies, depending upon the type of offer, previous dealings between the parties, and any normal trade usage or customary practices in a particular industry.

Termination by Operation of Law

In some circumstances, the law itself terminates an offer. **If an offeror dies or becomes mentally incapacitated, the offer terminates automatically and immediately.** Arnie offers you a job as an assistant in his hot-air balloon business. Before you can even accept, Arnie tumbles out of a balloon at 3,000 feet. The offer terminates along with Arnie.

Destruction of the subject matter terminates the offer. A car dealer offers to sell you a rare 1938 Bugatti for $7,500,000 if you bring cash the next day. You arrive, suitcase stuffed with cash, just in time to see Arnie drop 3,000 feet through the air and crush the Bugatti. The dealer's offer is terminated.

ACCEPTANCE

As we have seen, when there is a valid offer outstanding, it remains effective until it is terminated or accepted. An offeree accepts by saying or doing something that a reasonable person would understand to mean that he definitely wants to take the offer. Assume that Ellie offers to sell Gene her old iPod for $50. If Gene says, "I accept your offer," then he has indeed accepted, but there is no need to be so formal. He can accept the offer by saying, "It's a deal," or, "I'll take it," or any number of things. He need not even speak. If he hands her a $50 bill, he also accepts the offer.

It is worth noting that **the offeree must say or do *something* to accept.** Marge telephones Vick and leaves a message on his answering machine: "I'll pay $75 for your business law textbook from last semester. I'm desperate to get a copy, so I will assume you agree unless I hear from you by 6:00 tonight." Marge hears nothing by the deadline and assumes she has a deal. She is mistaken. Vick neither said nor did anything to indicate that he accepted.

Mirror Image Rule

If only he had known! A splendid university, an excellent position as department chair—gone. And all because of the mirror image rule.

Ohio State University wrote to Philip Foster offering him an appointment as a professor and chair of the art history department. His position was to begin July 1, and he had until June 2 to accept the job. On June 2, Foster telephoned the dean and left a message accepting the position, *effective July 15.* Later, Foster thought better of it and wrote the university, accepting the school's starting date of July 1. Too late! Professor Foster never did occupy that chair at Ohio State. The court held that since his acceptance varied the starting date, it was a counteroffer. And a counteroffer, as we know, is a rejection.[3]

Was it sensible to deny the professor a job over a mere 14-day difference? Sensible or not, that is the law.

Was it sensible to deny the professor a job over a mere 14-day difference? Sensible or not, that is the law. The common-law **mirror image rule** requires that acceptance be on *precisely* the same terms as the offer. If the acceptance contains terms that add or contradict the offer, even in minor ways, courts generally consider it a counteroffer. The rule worked reasonably well in the 19th century, when parties would write an original contract and exchange it, penciling in any changes. But now that businesses use standardized forms to purchase most goods and services, the rule creates enormous difficulties. Sellers use forms they have prepared, with all conditions stated to their advantage, and buyers employ their own forms, with terms they prefer. The forms are exchanged in the mail or electronically, with neither side clearly agreeing to the other party's terms.

Mirror image rule
Requires that acceptance be on precisely the same terms as the offer.

The problem is known as the "battle of forms." Once again, the UCC has entered the fray, attempting to provide flexibility and common sense for those contracts involving the

[3]*Foster v. Ohio State University*, 41 Ohio App. 3d 86, 534 N.E.2d 1220, 1987 Ohio App. LEXIS 10761 (Ohio Ct. App. 1987).

sale of goods. But for contracts governed by the common law, such as Professor Foster's, the mirror image rule is still the law.

UCC and the Battle of Forms

UCC §2-207 dramatically modifies the mirror image rule for the sale of goods. Under this provision, an acceptance that adds additional or different terms often will create a contract.

Additional or Different Terms

One basic principle of the common law of contracts remains unchanged: the key to creation of a contract is a valid offer that the offeree *intends* to accept. If there is no intent to accept, there is no contract. The big change brought about by UCC §2-207 is this: **an offeree who accepts may include in the acceptance terms that are additional to or different from those in the offer.** Thus, even with additional or different terms, the acceptance may well create a contract.

Example A. Wholesaler writes to Manufacturer, offering to buy "10,000 wheelbarrows at $50 per unit. Payable on delivery, 30 days from today's date." Manufacturer writes back, "We accept your offer of 10,000 wheelbarrows at $50 per unit, payable on delivery. *Interest at normal trade rates for unpaid balances.*" Manufacturer clearly intends to form a contract. The company has added a new term, but there is still a valid contract.

However, if the offeree states that her acceptance is *conditioned on the offeror's assent* to the new terms, there is no contract.

Example B. Same offer as above. Manufacturer adds the interest rate clause and states, "Our acceptance is conditional upon your agreement to this interest rate." Manufacturer has made a counteroffer. There is no contract, yet. If Wholesaler accepts the counteroffer, there is a contract; if Wholesaler does not accept it, there is no contract.

Additional terms are those that bring up *new* issues, such as interest rates, not contained in the original offer. Additional terms in the acceptance are considered proposals to add to the contract. Assuming that both parties are merchants, the additional terms ***will generally become part of the contract.*** Thus, in Example A, the interest rate will become a part of the binding deal. If Wholesaler is late in paying, it must pay whatever interest rate is current.

In three circumstances, the additional terms in the acceptance *do not* become part of the contract:

- If the original offer *insisted on its own terms.* In other words, if Wholesaler wrote, "I offer to buy them on the following terms and *no other terms*," then the Manufacturer is not free to make additions.
- If the additional terms *materially alter* the original offer. Suppose Manufacturer wrote back, "We accept your offer for 10,000 wheelbarrows. Delivery will be made within 180 days, unless we notify you of late delivery." Manufacturer has changed the time from 30 days to 180 days, with a possible extension beyond that. That is a material alteration, and it will not become part of the contract. By contrast, Manufacturer's new language concerning "interest at normal trade rates" was not a material alteration, and therefore that interest rate becomes part of the contract.
- If the offeror receives the additional terms and *promptly objects* to them.

Different terms are those that contradict terms in the offer. For example, if the seller's form clearly states that no warranty is included, and the buyer's form says the seller warrants all goods for three years, the acceptance contains different terms. An acceptance may contain different terms and still create a contract. But in these cases, courts have struggled to decide what the terms of the contract are. **The majority of states hold that different**

(contradictory) terms cancel each other out. Neither term is included in the contract. Instead, the neutral terms from the Code itself are "read into" the contract. These are the gap-filler terms discussed above. If, for example, the forms had contradictory warranty clauses (as they almost always do), the different terms would cancel each other out, and the warranty clauses from the UCC would be substituted.[4]

EXAM Strategy

Question: Elaine faxes an offer to Raoul. Raoul writes, "I accept. Please note, I will charge 2 percent interest per month for any unpaid money." He signs the document and faxes it back to Elaine. Do the two have a binding contract?

Strategy: Slow down, this is trickier than it seems. Raoul has added a term to Elaine's offer. We must take two steps to decide whether there is a contract. In a contract for services, acceptance must mirror the offer, but not so in an agreement for the sale of goods.

Result: If this is an agreement for services, there is no contract. However, if this agreement is for goods, the additional term *may* become part of an enforceable contract.

Question: Assume that Elaine's offer concerns goods. Is there an agreement?

Strategy: Under UCC §2-207, an additional term will become part of a binding agreement for goods except in three instances. What are the three exceptions?

Result: Raoul's extra term will be incorporated in a binding contract unless (1) Elaine's offer made clear she would accept no other terms; (2) Raoul's interest rate is a material alteration of the offer (almost never the case for interest rates); or (3) Elaine promptly rejects the interest rate.

Clickwraps And Shrinkwraps

You want to purchase Attila brand software and download it to your computer. You type in your credit card number and other information, agreeing to pay $99. Attila also requires that you "read and agree to" all of the company's terms. You click "I agree," without having read one word of the terms. Three frustrating weeks later, tired of trying to operate defective Attilaware, you demand a refund and threaten to sue. The company replies that you are barred from suing because the terms you agreed to included an arbitration clause. To resolve any disputes, you must travel to Attila's hometown, halfway across the nation, use an arbitrator that the company chooses, pay one-half the arbitrator's fee, and also pay Attila's legal bills if you should lose. The agreement makes it financially impossible for you to get your money back. Is that contract enforceable?

You have entered into a "clickwrap" agreement. Similar agreements, called "shrinkwraps," are packaged inside many electronic products. A shrinkwrap notice might require that before inserting a purchased CD into your computer, you must read and agree to all terms in the brochure. Clickwraps and shrinkwraps often include arbitration clauses. They

[4]Not all states follow this rule, however. Some courts have held that when the acceptance contains terms that contradict those in the offer, the language in the offer should be final. A few courts have ruled that the terms in the acceptance should control.

frequently limit the seller's liability if anything goes wrong, saying that the manufacturer's maximum responsibility is to refund the purchase price (even if the software destroys your hard drive).

Many courts that have analyzed these issues have ruled that clickwrap and shrinkwrap agreements are indeed binding, even against consumers. The courts have emphasized that sellers are entitled to offer a product on any terms they wish, and that shrinkwrap and clickwrap are the most efficient methods of including complicated terms in a small space. Think before you click![5]

However, some courts have *refused* to enforce such contracts against a consumer, stating that the buyer never understood or agreed to the shrinkwrapped terms. The court in the following case works hard to balance the competing interests, and in the process demonstrates that this new area of law is very much in flux.

SPECHT V. NETSCAPE COMMUNICATIONS CORPORATION

306 F.3d 17
Second Circuit Court of Appeals, 2002

Facts: A group of plaintiffs sued Netscape, claiming that two of the company's products illegally captured private information about files that they downloaded from the Internet. The plaintiffs alleged that this was electronic eavesdropping, in violation of two federal statutes.

From Netscape's Web page, the plaintiffs had downloaded SmartDownload, a software plug-in that enabled them to download the company's Communicator software. The Web page advertised the benefits of SmartDownload, and near the bottom of the screen was a tinted button labeled "Download." The plaintiffs clicked to download. If, instead of downloading, they had scrolled further down, they would have seen an invitation to "review and agree to the terms of the Netscape SmartDownload software license agreement." By clicking the appropriate button, they would have been sent to a series of linked pages, and finally arrived at a license agreement. Among the terms was an agreement to arbitrate any dispute. In other words, a consumer downloading SmartDownload was in theory giving up the right to file suit if anything went wrong, and agreeing to settle the dispute by arbitration. However, the plaintiffs never reviewed the license terms.

In the district court, Netscape moved to dismiss the case and compel arbitration. Netscape claimed that the plaintiffs had forfeited any right to sue based on the license agreement. The district court denied the company's motion, ruling that the plaintiffs had not agreed to the terms of the license. Netscape appealed.

Issue: ***Had the plaintiffs agreed to arbitrate their claims?***

Excerpts from Judge Sotomayor's Decision: Defendants argue that plaintiffs must be held to a standard of reasonable prudence and that, because notice of the existence of SmartDownload license terms was on the next scrollable screen, plaintiffs were on "inquiry notice" of those terms. We disagree with the proposition that a reasonably prudent offeree in plaintiffs' position would necessarily have known or learned of the existence of the SmartDownload license agreement prior to acting, so that plaintiffs may be held to have assented to that agreement with constructive notice of its terms.

Receipt of a physical document containing contract terms or notice thereof is frequently deemed, in the world of paper transactions, a sufficient circumstance to place the offeree on inquiry notice of those terms. These principles apply equally to the emergent world of online product delivery, pop-up screens, hyperlinked pages, clickwrap licensing, scrollable documents, and urgent admonitions

[5] *ProCD, Inc. v. Zeidenberg*, 86 F.3d 1447 (7th Cir. 1996), is the leading case to enforce shrinkwrap agreements (and, by extension, clickwraps). *Klocek v. Gateway*, 104 F. Supp. 1332 (D. Kan. 2000), is one of the few cases to reject such contracts. *Klocek*, however, was dismissed for failure to reach the federal court $75,000 jurisdictional level.

to "Download Now!" What plaintiffs saw when they were being invited by defendants to download this fast, free plug-in called SmartDownload was a screen containing praise for the product and, at the very bottom of the screen, a "Download" button. Defendants argue that a fair and prudent person using ordinary care would have been on inquiry notice of SmartDownload's license terms.

We are not persuaded that a reasonably prudent offeree in these circumstances would have known of the existence of license terms. Plaintiffs were responding to an offer that did not carry an immediately visible notice of the existence of license terms or require unambiguous manifestation of assent to those terms. Thus, plaintiffs' apparent manifestation of consent was to terms contained in a document whose contractual nature was not obvious. Moreover, the fact that, given the position of the scroll bar on their computer screens, plaintiffs may have been aware that an unexplored portion of the Netscape Web page remained below the download button does not mean that they reasonably should have concluded that this portion contained a notice of license terms.

We conclude that in circumstances such as these, where consumers are urged to download free software at the immediate click of a button, a reference to the existence of license terms on a submerged screen is not sufficient to place consumers on inquiry or constructive notice of those terms. There is no reason to assume that viewers will scroll down to subsequent screens simply because screens are there.

For the foregoing reasons, we affirm the district court's denial of defendants' motion to compel arbitration and to stay court proceedings.

The plaintiffs in *Specht* won because they knew nothing about the arbitration clause and were unlikely to discover it on the company's website. Notice what happens when a user *does* know about terms posted online. Register.com was a registrar of Internet domain names, meaning that it issued domain names to people and companies establishing a new website. The company was legally obligated to make available to the public, for free, the names and contact information of its customers. Register was also in the business of assisting owners, for a fee, to develop their websites.

Verio, Inc. competed in the site development business. Verio's automated software program (robot) would search Register.com daily, seeking information about new sites. *After* Verio obtained contact information, a notice would appear on the Register site, stating:

> By submitting a query, you agree that under no circumstances will you use this data to support the transmission of mass unsolicited, commercial advertising or solicitation via email.

In fact, though, Verio used the contact information for exactly that purpose, sending mass emailings to owners of new websites, soliciting their development business. Register sued. Verio defended by stating it was not bound by the notice because the notice did not appear until after it had obtained the information. Verio argued that when it sent the queries, it was unaware of any restrictions on use of the data. The court was unpersuaded, and explained its reasoning with a simple but telling metaphor:

> The situation might be compared to one in which plaintiff P maintains a roadside fruit stand displaying bins of apples. A visitor, defendant D, takes an apple and bites into it. As D turns to leave, D sees a sign, visible only as one turns to exit, which says "Apples—50 cents apiece." D does not pay for the apple. D believes he has no obligation to pay because he had no notice when he bit into the apple that 50 cents was expected in return. D's view is that he never agreed to pay for the apple. Thereafter, each day, several times a day, D revisits the stand, takes an apple, and eats it. D never leaves money.
>
> P sues D in contract for the price of the apples taken. D defends on the ground that on no occasion did he see P's price notice until after he had bitten into the apples. D may well prevail as to the first apple taken. D had no reason to understand upon taking it that P was demanding the payment. In our view, however, D cannot continue on a daily basis to take apples for free, knowing full well that P is offering them only in exchange for 50 cents in compensation, merely because the sign demanding payment is so placed that on each occasion D does not see it until he has bitten into the apple.

Register.com won its case. Verio was prohibited from using the contact information for mass emailings because it had actual knowledge of the restrictions placed on its use.[6]

Communication of Acceptance

The offeree must communicate his acceptance for it to be effective. The questions that typically arise concern the method, the manner, and the time of acceptance.

Method and Manner of Acceptance

The term "method" refers to whether acceptance is done in person or by mail, telephone, email, or fax. The term "manner" refers to whether the offeree accepts by promising, by making a down payment, by performing, and so forth. **If an offer demands acceptance in a particular method or manner, the offeree must follow those requirements.** An offer might specify that it be accepted in writing, or in person, or before midnight on June 23. An offeror can set any requirements she wishes. Omri might say to Oliver, "I'll sell you my bike for $200. You must accept my offer by standing on a chair in the lunchroom tomorrow and reciting a poem about a cow." Oliver can only accept the offer in the exact manner specified if he wants to form a contract.

If the offer does not specify a type of acceptance, the offeree may accept in any reasonable manner and method. An offer generally may be accepted by performance or by a promise, unless it specifies a particular method. The same freedom applies to the method. If Masako faxes Eric an offer to sell 1,000 acres in Montana for $800,000, Eric may accept by mail or fax. Both are routinely used in real estate transactions, and either is reasonable.

© Stocklite/Shutterstock.com

If the offer does not specify a type of acceptance, the offeree may accept in any reasonable manner and medium.

Time of Acceptance: The Mailbox Rule

An acceptance is generally effective upon dispatch, meaning the moment it is out of the offeree's control. Terminations, on the other hand, are effective when received. When Masako faxes her offer to sell land to Eric, and he mails his acceptance, the contract is binding the moment he puts the letter into the mail. In most cases, this **mailbox rule** is just a detail. But it becomes important when the offeror revokes her offer at about the same time the offeree accepts. Who wins? Suppose Masako's offer has one twist:

Mailbox rule
Acceptance is generally effective upon dispatch. Terminations are effective when received.

- On Monday morning, Masako faxes her offer to Eric.
- On Monday afternoon, Eric writes, "I accept" on the fax, and Masako mails a revocation of her offer.
- On Tuesday morning, Eric mails his acceptance.
- On Thursday morning, Masako's revocation arrives at Eric's office.
- On Friday morning, Eric's acceptance arrives at Masako's office.

[6] *Register.Com v. Verio, Inc.*, 353 F.3d 393 (2d Cir. 2004).

Outcome? Eric has an enforceable contract. Masako's offer was effective when it reached Eric. His acceptance was effective on Tuesday morning, when he mailed it. Nothing that happens later can "undo" the contract.

Soldau v. Organon, Inc.

860 F.2d 355, 1988 U.S. App. LEXIS 14757
United States Court of Appeals for the Ninth Circuit, 1988

Facts: Organon fired John Soldau. Then the company sent to him a letter offering to pay him double the normal severance pay, provided Soldau would sign a full release, that is, a document giving up any and all claims he might have against Organon. The release was included with the letter. Soldau signed it, dated it, and took it to the nearest post office, where he deposited it in the mailbox. When he returned home, Soldau discovered in the mail a check from Organon for the double severance pay. He hustled back to the post office, where he persuaded a postal clerk to open the mailbox and retrieve the release he had posted. He then cashed Organon's check and finally filed a suit against the company, alleging that his firing was age discrimination.

The federal district court gave summary judgment for Organon, ruling that Soldau's acceptance of the proposed release was effective when he mailed it, creating a contract. He appealed.

Issue: ***Did Soldau create a contract by mailing the release?***

Excerpts from the *Per Curiam* Decision: The district court was clearly correct under California law. Soldau does not argue to the contrary. Instead, he contends that the formation and validity of the release are governed by federal law, and would not have been effective unless and until it had been received by Organon. We need not decide which body of law controls. Under federal as well as California law, Soldau's acceptance was effective when it was mailed.

The so-called mailbox or effective when mailed rule was adopted and followed as federal common law by the Supreme Court [at the beginning of the 20th century]. We could not change the rule, and there is no reason to believe the Supreme Court would be inclined to do so. It is almost universally accepted in the common law world. It is enshrined in the Restatement (Second) of Contracts and endorsed by the major contract treatises.

Commentators are also virtually unanimous in [supporting the "effective upon dispatch" rule,] pointing to the long history of the rule; its importance in creating certainty for contracting parties; its essential soundness, on balance, as a means of allocating the risk during the period between the making of the offer and the communication of the acceptance or rejection to the offeror; and the inadequacy of the rationale offered by the Court of Claims for the change.

Since Soldau's contractual obligation to release Organon in return for Organon's obligation to make the enhanced severance payment arose when Soldau deposited his acceptance in the post office mailbox, his subsequent withdrawal of the acceptance was ineffectual.

Affirmed.

Chapter Conclusion

The law of offer and acceptance can be complex. Yet for all its faults, the law is not the principal source of dispute between parties unhappy with negotiations. Most litigation concerning offer and acceptance comes from *lack of clarity* on the part of the people negotiating. The many examples discussed are all understandable given the speed and fluidity of the real world of business. But the executive who insists on clarity is likelier in the long run to spend more time doing business and less time in court.

EXAM REVIEW

1. **MEETING OF THE MINDS** The parties can form a contract only if they have a meeting of the minds, which requires that they understand each other and show that they intend to reach an agreement. (p. 252)

Question: Norv owned a Ford dealership and wanted to expand by obtaining a BMW outlet. He spoke with Jackson and other BMW executives on several occasions. Norv now claims that those discussions resulted in an oral contract that requires BMW to grant him a franchise, but the company disagrees. Norv's strongest evidence of a contract is the fact that Jackson gave him forms on which to order BMWs. Jackson answered that it was his standard practice to give such forms to prospective dealers, so that if the franchise were approved, car orders could be processed quickly. Norv states that he was "shocked" when BMW refused to go through with the deal. Is there a contract?

Strategy: A court makes an *objective* assessment of what the parties did and said to determine whether they had a meeting of the minds and intended to form a contract. Norv's "shock" is irrelevant. Do the order forms indicate a meeting of the minds? Was there additional evidence that the parties had reached an agreement? (See the "Result" at the end of this section.)

2. **OFFER** An offer is an act or statement that proposes definite terms and permits the other party to create a contract by accepting those terms. (p. 253)

3. **OTHER STATEMENTS** Invitations to bargain, price quotes, letters of intent, and advertisements are generally not offers. However, an ad in which a company proposes to take a specific action when a customer takes a specific action can amount to an offer. And letters of intent that indicate the parties intended to be bound can also count as offers. (pp. 253–255)

Question: **"Huge** selection of Guernsey sweaters," reads a newspaper ad from Stuffed Shirt, a clothing retailer. "Regularly $135, today only $65." Waldo arrives at Stuffed Shirt at 4:00 that afternoon, but the shop clerk says there are no more sweaters. He shows Waldo a newly arrived Shetland sweater that sells for $145. Waldo sues, claiming breach of contract and violation of a consumer protection statute. Who will prevail?

(a) Waldo will win the breach of contract suit and the consumer protection suit.

(b) Waldo will lose the breach of contract suit but might win the consumer protection suit.

(c) Waldo will lose the consumer protection suit but should win the breach of contract suit.

(d) Waldo will win the consumer protection suit only if he wins the contract case.

(e) Waldo will lose both the breach of contract suit and the consumer protection suit.

Strategy: Waldo assumes that he is accepting the store's offer. But did Stuffed Shirt make an offer? If not, there cannot be a contract. Does the consumer protection statute help him? (See the "Result" at the end of this section.)

4. **DEFINITENESS** The terms of the offer must be definite, although under the UCC the parties may create a contract that has open terms. (pp. 257–258)

5. **TERMINATION** An offer may be terminated by revocation, rejection, expiration, or operation of law. (pp. 260–262)

EXAM Strategy

Question: Rick is selling his Espresso Coffee Maker. He sends Tamara an email, offering to sell the machine for $350. Tamara promptly emails back, offering to buy the item for $300. She hears nothing from Rick, so an hour later Tamara stops by his apartment, where she learns that he just sold the machine to his roommate for $250. She sues Rick. Outcome?

(a) Tamara will win because her offer was higher than the roommate's.

(b) Tamara will win because Rick never responded to her offer.

(c) Tamara will win because both parties made clear offers, in writing.

(d) Tamara will lose because she rejected Rick's offer.

(e) Tamara will lose because her offer was not definite.

Strategy: A valid contract requires a definite offer and acceptance. Rick made a valid offer. When Tamara said she would buy the machine for a lower amount, was that acceptance? If not, what was it? (See the "Result" at the end of this section.)

6. **MIRROR IMAGE RULE AND UCC §2-207** The common-law mirror image rule requires acceptance on precisely the same terms as the offer. Under the UCC, an offeree may often create a contract even when the acceptance includes terms that are additional to or different from those in the offer. (pp. 262–264)

7. **CLICKWRAPS** Clickwrap and shrinkwrap agreements are generally enforceable. (pp. 264–267)

8. **MANNER OF ACCEPTANCE** If an offer demands acceptance in a particular method or manner, the offeree must follow those requirements. If the offer does not specify a type of acceptance, the offeree may accept in any reasonable manner and medium. (p. 267)

9. MAILBOX RULE An acceptance is generally effective upon dispatch, meaning from the moment it is out of the offeree's control. Terminations usually are not effective until received. (pp. 267–268)

1. Result: The order forms are neither an offer nor an acceptance. Norv has offered no evidence that the parties agreed on price, date of performance, or any other key terms. There is no contract. Norv allowed eagerness and optimism to replace common sense.[7]

3. Result: An advertisement is usually not an offer, but merely a solicitation of one. It is Waldo who is making the offer, which the store may reject. Waldo loses his contract case, but he may win under the consumer protection statute. The correct answer is B. If Stuffed Shirt proclaimed "Huge selection" when there were only five sweaters, the store was deliberately misleading consumers, and Waldo wins. However, if there was indeed a large selection, and Waldo arrived too late, he is out of luck.

5. Result: Tamara made a counteroffer of $300. A counteroffer is a rejection. Tamara rejected Rick's offer and simultaneously offered to buy the coffee maker at a lower price. Rick was under no obligation to sell to Tamara at any price. He will win Tamara's suit.

Multiple-Choice Questions

1. Rebecca, in Honolulu, faxes a job offer to Spike, in Pittsburgh, saying, "We can pay you $55,000 per year, starting June 1." Spike faxes a reply, saying, "Thank you! I accept your generous offer, though I will also need $3,000 in relocation money. See you June 1. Can't wait!" On June 1, Spike arrives, to find that his position is filled by Gus. He sues Rebecca.

(a) Spike wins $55,000.
(b) Spike wins $58,000.
(c) Spike wins $3,000.
(d) Spike wins restitution.
(e) Spike wins nothing.

2. Arturo hires Kate to work in his new sporting goods store. "Look," he explains, "I can only pay you $9.00 an hour. But if business is good a year from now, and you're still here, I'm sure I can pay you a healthy bonus." Four months later, Arturo terminates Kate. She sues.

(a) Kate will win her job back, plus the year's pay and the bonus.
(b) Kate will win the year's pay and the bonus.
(c) Kate will win only the bonus.
(d) Kate will win only her job back.
(e) Kate will win nothing.

[7]Based on *Arnold Pontiac-GMC, Inc. v. General Motors Co.*, 786 F.2d 564 (3d Cir. 1986).

3. Manny offers to sell Gina his TV for $100 on January 1. On January 2, Gina writes out a letter of acceptance. On January 3, Gina drops the letter in a mailbox. On January 4, a postal worker gets the letter out of the mailbox and takes it to the post office. On January 5, the letter arrives in Manny's mailbox. When (if ever) was a contract formed?

(a) January 2
(b) January 3
(c) January 4
(d) January 5
(e) None of the above—a contract has not been formed.

4. Frank, an accountant, says to Missy, "I'll sell you my laptop for $100." Missy asks, "Will you give me until tomorrow to make up my mind?" "Sure," Frank replies. Which of the following is true?

(a) Frank cannot revoke his offer, no matter what.
(b) Frank cannot revoke his offer, but only if Missy pays him to keep the offer open until tomorrow.
(c) Frank can revoke his offer no matter what, because he is not a merchant.
(d) Frank can revoke his offer no matter what, because he did not promise Missy anything in writing.

5. Which of the following amounts to an offer?

(a) Ed says to Carmen, "I offer to sell you my pen for $1."
(b) Ed says to Carmen, "I'll sell you my pen for $1."
(c) Ed writes, "I'll sell you my pen for $1," and gives the note to Carmen.
(d) All of the above.
(e) A and C only.

Essay Questions

1. The town of Sanford, Maine, decided to auction off a lot it owned. The town advertised that it would accept bids through the mail, up to a specified date. Arthur and Arline Chevalier mailed in a bid that turned out to be the highest. When the town refused to sell them the lot, they sued. Result?

2. The Tufte family leased a 260-acre farm from the Travelers Insurance Co. Toward the end of the lease, Travelers mailed the Tuftes an option to renew the lease. The option arrived at the Tuftes' house on March 30, and gave them until April 14 to accept. On April 13, the Tuftes signed and mailed their acceptance, which Travelers received on April 19. Travelers claimed there was no lease and attempted to evict the Tuftes from the farm. May they stay?

3. Consolidated Edison Co. of New York (Con Ed) sought bids from General Electric Co. (GE) and others to supply it with two huge transformers. Con Ed required that the bids be held open for 90 days. GE submitted a written bid and included a clause holding the bid open for 90 days. During that period, Con Ed accepted GE's bid, but GE refused to honor it. Is there a contract?

4. The Dukes leased land from Lillian Whatley. Toward the end of their lease, they sent Ms. Whatley a new contract, renewing the lease for three years and giving themselves the option to buy the land at any time during the lease for $50,000. Ms. Whatley crossed out the clause giving them an option to buy. She added a sentence at the bottom, saying, "Should I, Lillian Whatley, decide to sell at end [sic] of three years, I will give the Dukes the first chance to buy." Then she signed the lease, which the Dukes accepted in the changed form. They continued to pay the rent until Ms. Whatley sold the land to another couple for $35,000. The Dukes sued. Are the Dukes entitled to the land at $50,000? At $35,000?

5. ***YOU BE THE JUDGE WRITING PROBLEM*** Academy Chicago Publishers (Academy) approached the widow of author John Cheever about printing some of his unpublished stories. She signed a contract, which stated:

The Author will deliver to the Publisher on a mutually agreeable date one copy of the manuscript of the Work as finally arranged by the editor and satisfactory to the Publisher in form and content.... Within a reasonable time and a mutually agreeable date after delivery of the final revised manuscript, the Publisher will publish the Work at its own expense, in such style and manner and at such price as it deems best, and will keep the Work in print as long as it deems it expedient.

Within a year, Academy had located and delivered to Mrs. Cheever more than 60 unpublished stories. But she refused to go ahead with the project. Academy sued for the right to publish the book. The trial court ruled that the agreement was valid; the appeals court affirmed; and the case went to the Illinois Supreme Court. Was Academy's offer valid, and was the contract enforceable? **Argument for Mrs. Cheever:** The agreement is too vague to be enforceable. None of the essential terms are specified: the number of stories, their length, who selects them, the date of publication, the size or cost of the book, or anything else. There is no contract. **Argument for Academy:** Mrs. Cheever wanted to publish this book and agreed in writing to help Academy do so. Both parties understood the essential nature of the book and were willing to permit some flexibility, to ensure a good edition. She has no right to back out now.

Discussion Questions

1. Advertisements usually do not amount to offers. Is this fair? Should businesses have legal obligations to sell items at an advertised price?

2. Most auctions are held "with reserve." If you place the highest bid at such an auction, and if your bid is below the reserve, then you do not get the item. Is this fair? Should the law award you the item at the price you bid?

3. Someone offers to sell you a concert ticket for $50, and you reply, "I'll give you $40," The seller refuses to sell at the lower price, and you say, "OK, OK, I'll pay you $50." Clearly, no contract has been formed, because you made a counteroffer. If the seller has changed her mind and no longer wants to sell for

$50, she doesn't have to. But is this fair? If it is all part of the same conversation, should you be able to accept the $50 offer and get the ticket?

4. If you click an "I agree" box, odds are that its terms are binding on you, even if the box contains dozens or even hundreds of lines of dense text. Is this fair? Should the law change to limit the enforceability of clickwraps?

5. Courts stick to objective (reasonable person) standards when evaluating offers and acceptances. Juries are not asked to "get inside someone's head," they are instructed to determine what a reasonable person would think of offerors' and offereees' statements. Is this practice reasonable? Would it be better if the law directly considered whether people *wanted* to make contracts?

CHAPTER 12

© picsbyst/Shutterstock.com

CONSIDERATION

Have you ever rented a movie that you did not want every one of your friends to know about? Cathryn Harris did. Imagine her shock when she rented a movie online from Blockbuster, only to find out that this news was automatically transmitted to her Facebook page and then broadcast to all her "friends." Just think how bad that could be.

Harris sued Blockbuster for this violation of her privacy, only to find out she had clicked away her right to sue. To rent the movie, she had had to click that little box saying she agreed to all the terms and conditions. And one of those terms and conditions was an agreement to arbitrate, not litigate. Can Blockbuster get away with this?

To rent the movie, she had to click that little box saying she agreed to all the terms and conditions.

It turns out that this movie has a happy ending. The court ruled that the contract between Harris and Blockbuster was unenforceable because there was no *consideration*.

Consideration is our next step on the road to understanding contracts. In the last chapter, we learned what it takes to create an agreement. But an agreement is not necessarily a legally enforceable contract.

This is the first of four chapters that will examine problems that can prevent an agreement from becoming a contract. A lack of consideration is one of them. Without it, a promise is "just a promise" and nothing more.

WHAT IS CONSIDERATION?

Contracts Checklist

- ☐ Offer
- ☐ Acceptance
- ☑ Consideration
- ☐ Legality
- ☐ Capacity
- ☐ Consent
- ☐ Writing

The central idea of consideration is simple: contracts must be a two-way street. If one side gets all the benefit and the other side gets nothing, then an agreement lacks consideration and is not an enforceable contract.

There are three rules of consideration:

1. Both parties must get something of *measureable value* from the contract. That thing can be money, boots, an agreement not to sue, or anything else that has real value.
2. A *promise* to give something of value counts as consideration. A *promise* to mow someone's lawn next week is the equivalent of actually *doing* the yardwork when evaluating whether consideration exists.
3. The two parties must have *bargained for* whatever was exchanged and struck a deal: "If you do this, I'll do that." If you just decide to deliver a cake to your neighbor's house without her knowing, that may be something of value, but since you two did not bargain for it, there is no contract and she does not owe you the price of the cake.

Let's take an example: Sally's Shoe Store and Baker Boots agree that she will pay $20,000 for 100 pairs of boots. They both get something of value—Sally gets the boots, Baker gets the money. A contract is formed when the promises are made because a promise to give something of value counts. The two have bargained for this deal, so there is valid consideration.

Now for an example where there is no consideration. Marvin works at Sally's. At 9 a.m., he is in a good mood and promises to buy his coworker a Starbucks during the lunch hour. The delighted coworker agrees. Later that morning, the coworker is rude to Marvin, who then changes his mind about buying the coffee. He is free to do so. His promise created a one-way street: the coworker stood to receive all the benefit of the agreement, while Marvin got nothing. Because Marvin received no value, there is no contract.

What Is Value?

As we have seen, an essential part of consideration is that both parties must get something of value. That item of value can be either an "act" or a "forbearance."

Act

Act
Any action that a party was not legally required to take in the first place.

A party commits an **act** when she does something she was not legally required to do in the first place. She might do a job, deliver an item, or pay money, for example. An act does not count if the party was simply complying with the law or fulfilling her obligations under an existing contract. Thus, for example, suppose that your professor tells the university that she will not post final grades unless she is paid an extra $5,000. Even if the university agrees to this outrageous demand, that agreement is not a valid contract because the professor is already under an obligation to post final grades.

Forbearance

Forbearance
Refraining from doing something that one has a legal right to do.

A **forbearance** is, in essence, the opposite of an act. A plaintiff forbears if he agrees *not* to do something he had a legal right to do. An entrepreneur might promise a competitor not to open a competing business, or an elderly driver (with a valid driver's license) might promise concerned family members that he will not drive at night.

Let's apply these ideas to the most famous of all consideration lawsuits. Our story begins in 1869, when a well-meaning uncle makes a promise to his nephew. Ever since *Hamer v. Sidway* appeared, generations of American law students have dutifully inhaled the facts and sworn by its wisdom; now you, too, may drink it in.

Landmark Case

Hamer v. Sidway

124 N.Y. 538, 27 N.E. 256, 1891 N.Y. LEXIS 1396
New York Court of Appeals, 1891

Facts: This is a story with two Stories. William Story wanted his nephew to grow up healthy and prosperous. In 1869, he promised the 15-year-old boy (who was also named William Story) $5,000 if the lad would refrain from drinking liquor, using tobacco, swearing, and playing cards or billiards for money until his twenty-first birthday. (In that wild era—can you believe it?—the nephew had a legal right to do all those things.) The nephew agreed and, what is more, he kept his word. When he reached his twenty-first birthday, the nephew notified his uncle that he had honored the agreement. The uncle congratulated the young man and promised to give him the money, but said he would wait a few more years before handing over the cash, until the nephew was mature enough to handle such a large sum. The uncle died in 1887 without having paid, and his estate refused to honor the promise. Because the nephew had transferred his rights in the money, it was a man named Hamer who eventually sought to collect from the uncle's estate. The estate argued that since the nephew had given no consideration for the uncle's promise, there was no enforceable contract. The trial court found for the plaintiff, and the uncle's estate appealed.

Issue: ***Did the nephew give consideration for the uncle's promise?***

Excerpts from Justice Parker's Decision: The defendant contends that the contract was without consideration to support it, and therefore invalid. He asserts that the promisee, by refraining from the use of liquor and tobacco, was not harmed, but benefited; that that which he did was best for him to do, independently of his uncle's promise, and insists that it follows that, unless the promisor was benefited, the contract was without consideration, a contention which, if well founded, would seem to leave open for controversy in many cases whether that which the promisee did or omitted to do was in fact of such benefit to him as to leave no consideration to support the enforcement of the promisor's agreement. Such a rule could not be tolerated, and is without foundation in the law. Courts will not ask whether the thing which forms the consideration does in fact benefit the promisee or a third party, or is of any substantial value to anyone. It is enough that something is promised, done, forborne, or suffered by the party to whom the promise is made as consideration for the promise made to him.

Now applying this rule to the facts before us, the promisee used tobacco, occasionally drank liquor, and he had a legal right to do so. That right he abandoned for a period of years upon the strength of the promise of the testator [that is, the uncle] that for such forbearance he would give him $5,000. We need not speculate on the effort which may have been required to give up the use of those stimulants. It is sufficient that he restricted his lawful freedom of action within certain prescribed limits upon the faith of his uncle's agreement, and now, having fully performed the conditions imposed, it is of no moment whether such performance actually proved a benefit to the promisor, and the court will not inquire into it.

The issue of value in a contract is an important one, so let's look at another case. In the movies, when a character wants to get serious about keeping a promise—*really* serious—he sometimes signs an agreement in blood. As it turns out, this kind of thing actually happens in real life. In the following case, did the promise of forbearance have value? Did a contract signed in blood count? You be the judge.

You be the Judge

KIM V. SON

2009 Cal. App. LEXIS 2011
Court of Appeal of California, 2009

Facts: Stephen Son was a part owner and operator of two corporations. Because the businesses were corporations, Son was not personally liable for the debts of either one.

Jinsoo Kim invested a total of about $170,000 in the companies. Eventually, both of them failed, and Kim lost his investment. Son felt guilty over Kim's losses.

Later, Son and Kim met in a sushi restaurant and drank heroic quantities of alcohol. At one point, Son pricked his finger with a safety pin and wrote the following in his own blood: "Sir, please forgive me. Because of my deeds, you have suffered financially. I will repay you to the best of my ability." In return, Kim agreed not to sue him for the money owed.

Son later refused to honor the bloody document and pay Kim the money. Kim filed suit to enforce their contract.

The judge determined that the promise did not create a contract because there had been no consideration.

You Be The Judge: ***Was there consideration?***

Argument for Kim: As a part of the deal made at the sushi restaurant, Kim agreed not to sue Son. What could be more of a forbearance than that? Kim had a right to sue at any time, and he gave the right up. Even if Kim was unlikely to win, Son would still prefer not to be sued.

Besides, the fact that Son signed the agreement in blood indicates how seriously he took the obligation to repay his loyal investor. At a minimum, Son eased his guilty conscience by making the agreement, and surely that is worth something.

Argument for Son: Who among you has not at one point or another become intoxicated, experienced emotions more powerful than usual, and regretted them the next morning? Whether calling an ex-girlfriend and professing endless love or writing out an agreement in your own blood, it is all the same.

A promise not to file a meritless lawsuit has no value at all. It did not matter to Son whether or not Kim filed suit because Kim could not possibly win. If this promise counts as value, then the concept of consideration is meaningless because anyone can promise not to sue anytime. Son had no obligation to pay Kim. And the bloody napkin does not change that fact because it was made without consideration of any kind. It is an ordinary promise, not a contract that creates any legal obligation.

Adequacy of Consideration

Gold can make people crazy. At the turn of the 20th century, John Tuppela joined the gold rush to Alaska. He bought a mine and worked it hard, a disciplined man in an unforgiving enterprise. Sadly, his prospecting proved futile and mental problems overwhelmed him. In 1914, a court declared him insane and locked him in an institution in Portland, Oregon. Four years later, Tuppela emerged and learned to his ecstasy that gold had been discovered in his mine, now valued at over half a million dollars. Then the bad news hit: a court-appointed guardian had sold the mine for pennies while Tuppela was institutionalized. Destitute and forlorn, Tuppela turned to his lifelong friend, Embola, saying, "If you will give me $50 so I can go to Alaska and get my property back, I will pay you $10,000 when I win my property." Embola accepted the offer, advancing the $50.

After a long and bitter fight, Tuppela won back his mine, though a guardian would still supervise his assets. Tuppela asked the guardian to pay the full $10,000 to Embola, but the guardian refused. Embola sued, and the issue was whether his $50 was *adequate consideration* to support Tuppela's promise of $10,000. A happy ending: Embola won and recovered his money.

Courts seldom inquire into the *adequacy* of consideration. Although the difference between Embola's $50 and Tuppela's $10,000 was huge, it was not for a court to decide whether the parties had made an intelligent bargain. Embola undertook a risk, and his $50 was valid consideration. The question of adequacy is for the parties as they bargain, not for the courts.

Law professors often call this the "peppercorn rule," a reference to a Civil War–era case in which a judge mused, "What is a valuable consideration? A peppercorn."[1] Even the tiniest benefit to a plaintiff counts, so long as it has a measureable value.

REUTERS/Mario Anzuoni

How does the peppercorn rule apply in this situation?

EXAM Strategy

Question: 50 Cent has been rapping all day, and he is very thirsty. He pulls his Ferrari into the parking lot of a convenience store. The store turns out to be closed, but luckily for him, a PepsiCo machine sits outside. While walking over to it, he realizes that he has left his wallet at home. Frustrated, he whistles to a 10-year-old kid who is walking by. "Hey kid!" he shouts. "I need to borrow fifty cents!" "I know you are!" the kid replies. Fiddy tries again. "No, no, I need to *borrow* fifty cents!" The kid walks over. "Well, I'm not going to just give you my last fifty cents. But maybe you can sell me something." 50 Cent cannot believe it, but he really is very thirsty. He takes off a Rolex, which is his least expensive bling. "How about this?" "Deal," the kid says, handing over two quarters. Is the kid entitled to keep the watch?

Strategy: Even in extreme cases, courts rarely take an interest in *how much* consideration is given, or whether everyone got a "good deal." Even though the Rolex is worth thousands of times more than the quarters, the quarters still count under the peppercorn rule.

Result: After this transaction, 50 Cent may have second thoughts, but they will be too late. The kid committed an act by handing over his money—he was under no legal obligation to do so. And 50 Cent received something of small but measureable value. So there is consideration to support this deal, and 50 Cent would not get his watch back.

[1] *Hobbs v. Duff*, 23 Cal. 596 (1863).

Illusory Promises

Annabel calls Jim and says, "I'll sell you my bicycle for 325 bucks. Interested?" Jim says, "I'll look at it tonight in the bike rack. If I like what I see, I'll pay you in the morning." At sunrise, Jim shows up with the $325, but Annabel refuses to sell. Can Jim enforce their deal? No. He said he would buy the bicycle *if he liked it*, keeping for himself the power to get out of the agreement for any reason at all. He is not *committing* himself to do anything, and the law considers his promise illusory—that is, not really a promise at all. **An illusory promise is not consideration.** Because he has given no consideration, there is no contract, and *neither party* can enforce the deal.

Let's revisit the Blockbuster case from the opening scenario. Blockbuster's clickwrap box read, in part:

> "Blockbuster may at any time, and at its sole discretion, modify these Terms and Conditions of Use, including without limitation the Privacy Policy, with or without notice. Such modifications will be effective immediately upon posting."

Because Blockbuster had the ability to change the rules at any time for any reason, the court determined that the contract was illusory and that Harris was not bound by Blockbuster's arbitration clause.[2]

APPLICATIONS OF CONSIDERATION

We will spend the remainder of the chapter looking at specific situations in which consideration plays a central role.

The UCC: Consideration in Requirements and Output Contracts

In a requirements contract, the buyer agrees to purchase 100 percent of her goods from one seller. The seller agrees to sell the buyer whatever quantity she reasonably needs. The quantity is not stated in the contract, though it may be estimated based on previous years or best calculations. The common law regarded requirements contracts as void because the buyer held all the power. She could purchase a vast quantity or none at all. She was making no commitment, and hence was giving no consideration. Common-law courts refused to enforce requirements contracts, as well as their counterpart, output contracts.

In an output contract, the seller guarantees to sell 100 percent of its output to one buyer, and the buyer agrees to accept the entire quantity. For example, a timber company might agree to sell all of its wood products to a lumber wholesaler. The common law frowned on this because now it was the seller who was making no real commitment.

The problem with the common-law rule was that many merchants valued these contracts. Consider the utility of requirements contracts. From the buyer's viewpoint, a requirements contract provides flexibility. The buyer can adjust purchases based on consumer demands. The agreement also guarantees her a source of goods in a competitive market. For a seller, the requirements agreement will ensure him at least this one outlet and will prevent competitors from selling to this buyer. The contract should enable the seller to spend less on marketing and may enable him to predict sales more accurately. Output contracts have similar value.

[2]*Harris v. Blockbuster Inc.*, 622 F. Supp. 2d 396 (N.D. Tex. 2009).

The UCC responded in a forthright fashion: **Section 2-306 expressly allows output and requirements contracts in the sale of goods.**[3] However, the Code places one limitation on how much the buyer may demand (or the seller may offer):

> A term which measures the quantity by the output of the seller or the requirements of the buyer means such actual output or requirements as may occur *in good faith,* ...

The "good faith" phrase is critical. In requirements contracts, courts have ruled that it is the "good faith" that a buyer brings to the deal that represents her consideration.[4] In other words, by agreeing to act in good faith, she actually is limiting her options. Because she is obligating herself, the deal becomes binding. Beware that this is not just wordplay. A buyer *must make its requirement demands in good faith,* based on the expectations the parties had when they signed the deal.

Suppose that you operate a T-shirt business. You and a wholesaler agree on a two-year requirements contract with a fixed price of $3 per T-shirt and an estimate of 150 T-shirts per week. If business is slow the first two months, you are permitted to purchase only 25 T-shirts per week if that is all you are selling. Should sales suddenly boom and you need 200 per week, you may also require that many. Both of those demands are made in good faith. But suppose the price of cotton skyrockets and the wholesale cost of T-shirts everywhere suddenly doubles. You have a two-year guaranteed price of $3 per T-shirt. Could you demand 2,000 T-shirts per week, knowing that you will be able to resell the shirts to other retailers for a big profit? No. That is not acting in good faith based on the original expectations of the parties. The wholesaler is free to ignore your exorbitant demand. The legal requirement has come full circle: your good faith is valid consideration and makes the deal enforceable—but it is binding on you, too.

EXAM Strategy

Question: Will bought simple wood furniture and custom-painted it for sale to interior designers. He entered into a written agreement to buy all the furniture he needed, for two years, from Wood Knot, Inc. Wood Knot agreed to supply Will with all the furniture he requested. During the second year, Will's business grew, and he requested 28 percent more furniture than in the first year. Wood Knot would not deliver unless Will would pay a higher price per unit, which Will would not. Will sued. What kind of a contract was this? Will Will win? Why or why not?

Strategy: Because this agreement did not specify the quantity of goods being sold, we know that it was either a requirements contract or an output contract. Review the difference between the two. Which was this agreement? These contracts are now legal, with one major limitation. What is that limitation? Apply it here.

Result: This was a requirements contract because Will agreed to purchase all his furniture from Wood Knot. Under the UCC, requirements contracts are enforceable, provided the buyer makes his demands in good faith. Will's increased order was a result of his booming business. Indeed, he entered into this agreement to protect his ability to grow his company. He made the request in good faith, the contract is enforceable, and yes—Will will win.

---

[3]UCC §2-306(2) permits a related type of contract, the exclusive dealing agreement. Here, either a buyer or a seller of goods agrees to deal exclusively with the other party. The results are similar to an output or requirements agreement. Once again, one party is receiving a guarantee in exchange for a promise that the common law would have considered illusory. Under the Code, such a deal is enforceable.

[4]*Famous Brands, Inc. v. David Sherman Corp.*, 814 F.2d 517, 1987 U.S. App. LEXIS 3634 (8th Cir. 1987).

Of course, exceptions are the spice of law …

Preexisting Duty

As we have seen, **a promise to do something that a party is already obligated to do is not consideration.** Of course, exceptions are the spice of law, and the preexisting duty rule provides us with a rackful. Courts have created these exceptions because a rigid application of the rule might interfere with legitimate business goals.

Exception: Additional Work

When a party agrees to do something above and beyond what he is obligated to do, his promise is generally valid consideration. Cecil has promised to build a fabulous swimming pool/cabana for Nathalie for $250,000. When the work is half complete, he offers to build the cabana out of seashells rather than pine wood. If Nathalie agrees to a new price of $300,000 for the pool complex, she is obligated to pay because Cecil's extra work is valid consideration for her promise.

Exception: Modification

If both parties agree that a modification is necessary, the surest way to accomplish that is to rescind the original contract and draft a new one. **To rescind means to cancel.** Thus, if neither party has completed its obligations, the agreement to rescind will terminate each party's rights and obligations under the old contract. This should be done in writing. Then the parties sign the new agreement. Courts will *generally* enforce a rescission and modification provided both parties voluntarily entered into it, in good faith. If one side, determined to earn greater profits, unfairly coerces the other into the changes, the modification is invalid.

Once again, the UCC has changed the common law, making it easier for merchants to modify agreements for the sale of goods. UCC §2-209 provides:

- An agreement modifying a contract within this Article needs no consideration to be binding.
- A signed agreement which excludes modification or rescission except by a signed writing cannot be otherwise modified or rescinded.

Here is how these two provisions work together. Mike's Magic Mania (MMM) agrees to deliver 500 rabbits and 500 top hats to State University for the school's Sleight of Hand 101 course. The goods, including 100 cages and 1,000 pounds of rabbit food, are to arrive no later than September 1, in time for the new semester, with payment on delivery. By September 20, no rabbits have appeared, in or out of hats. The university buys similar products from another supply house at a 25 percent steeper price and sues MMM for the difference. Mike claims that in early September, the dean had orally agreed to permit delivery in October. The dean is on sabbatical in Tahiti and cannot be reached for comment. Is the alleged modification valid?

Under the common law, the modification would have been void because MMM gave no consideration for the extended delivery date. However, this is a sale of goods, and under UCC §2-209, an oral modification may be valid even without consideration. Unfortunately for Mike, though, the original agreement included a clause forbidding oral modification. Any changes had to be in writing, signed by both parties. Mike never obtained such a document. Even if the dean did make the oral agreement, the university wins.

The following case arose in a setting that is traumatic and lamentably common: a homeowner could not make his mortgage payments. Foreclosure loomed. Did the parties agree to save the home?

You be the Judge

Citizens Trust Bank v. White

274 Ga.App.508, 618 S.E.2d 9
Georgia Court of Appeals, 2005

Facts: Herbert White owned a house in Atlanta. He refinanced his home through Citizens Trust Bank, but fell behind on his loan payments. He owed about $43,000. The Bank notified White that it intended to foreclose. After some delays, the Bank sent White a formal notice that it would sell his house at a foreclosure sale on the courthouse steps, on May 7. The finance agreement provided that if the Bank foreclosed, White owed the full amount.

On that date, White arrived and offered the Bank $35,000 to stop the foreclosure. The Bank's collection manager, D.J. Hughlett, accepted the money and drafted a letter, which he and White signed:

> Citizens Trust Bank agrees to postpone the foreclosure [based on] a payment of $33,000.00 in certified funds and a possible $2,000.00 from the account of Cora White Cummings on the above-referenced property. Our Attorney, William A. Broughman, will forward to you a written agreement, for your signature, to consummate this transaction. The payoff balance as of 11:05 AM is $7,986.43. If his sister pays the $2,000.00, the balance will be $5,986.43.

White did pay the extra $2,000. Hughlett decided that the signed letter was a forbearance agreement with White, so he did not bother to send an additional document. Hughlett believed that White would pay the balance within 30 days, but White never did so. The Bank sent a new foreclosure notice and did in fact sell the house.

White sued the Bank, claiming that it had breached its agreement not to foreclose. The jury agreed, awarding White $250,000 in compensatory damages. The Bank appealed, arguing that White gave no consideration for the agreement because he was already obligated to pay the full balance.

You Be The Judge: ***Was the signed letter an enforceable contract?***

Argument for the Bank: Mr. White fell behind on his mortgage payments. As soon as the Bank notified him that it was foreclosing, his full debt became due. When he offered to pay a percentage of that debt, he was fulfilling a preexisting duty. He was *legally obligated* to pay the $35,000 that he "offered," along with the full balance due. A promise to do what a party is required to do is never consideration. Without consideration, there is no contract.

The jury made an emotional decision based on sympathy for the debtor. That leads to bad policy and bad law. The policy is poor because if everyone were allowed to default without suffering a loss, no bank would lend money and most citizens could never buy a house. The law is even worse because the case should not have gone to a jury. The trial judge should have dismissed the suit based on the preexisting duty rule.

Argument for Mr. White: There were two parties to this agreement, and both believed they had a binding agreement. The Bank's officer agreed to postpone foreclosure. He also promised to forward a formal document confirming the understanding but did not do so. And why did he send no other document? Because he believed the Bank had already agreed to halt any foreclosure effort. He was right.

Mr. White paid 80 percent of the balance due. It is wrong for the Bank to take the money and then break its promise. Furthermore, it is absurd to foreclose based on such a modest debt. The legal argument about consideration is nonsense. Mr. White's consideration was a check for $35,000.

The jury award indicates a group of average citizens who were angry about what the Bank did. The verdict should be affirmed.

EXAM Strategy

Question: Star Struck, a Hollywood talent agency, employs Puneet as one of its young agents and Max as a part-time delivery boy. Puneet's contract is for one year. She earns $5,000 per month, payable on the last day of each month. After she has worked at the firm for four months, a Star Struck executive says to her, "We are having cash flow problems. We cannot pay you this month, and will probably fall about two months behind. However, if you will agree to do Max's job for the next few months, we can pay you on time." Puneet cheerfully agrees to the deal. However, after a few weeks of the extra labor, Puneet confesses that she is overwhelmed and can no longer do Max's job. Star Struck fires her. Puneet sues. Was there a binding agreement for Puneet to do Max's work?

Strategy: Star Struck made an offer to Puneet and she accepted it. But a contract needs more than offer and acceptance. Both parties must give consideration. Had they done more than they were required to do under their preexisting duty?

Result: A promise to do what a party is already obligated to do is not consideration. Star Struck was required to pay Puneet every month, so its "offer" included no consideration. Without consideration, there can be no agreement. Puneet was not obligated to do Max's job, and she will win this lawsuit.

Exception: Unforeseen Circumstances

Hugo has a deal to repair major highways. Hugo hires Hal's Hauling to cart soil and debris. Hal's trucks begin work, but after crossing the work site several times, they sink to their axles in sinister, sucking slime. Hal demands an additional 35 percent payment from Hugo to complete the job, pointing out that the surface was dry and cracked and that neither Hal nor Hugo was aware of the subsurface water. Hal howls that he must use different trucks with different tires and work more slowly to permit the soil to dry. Hugo hems and haws and finally agrees. But when the hauling is finished, Hugo refuses to pay the extra money. Is Hugo liable?

Yes. When unforeseen circumstances cause a party to make a promise regarding an unfinished project, that promise is generally valid consideration. Even though Hal is only promising to finish what he was already obligated to do, his promise is valid consideration because neither party knew of the subsoil mud. Hal was facing a situation quite different from what the parties anticipated. It is almost as though he were undertaking a new project. Hal has given consideration, and Hugo is bound by his promise to pay extra money.

Settlement of Debts

You claim that your friend Felicity owes you $90,000, but she refuses to pay. Finally, when you are desperate, Felicity offers you a cashier's check for $60,000—provided you accept it as full settlement. To get your hands on some money, you agree and cash the check. The next day, you sue Felicity for $30,000. Who wins? It will depend principally upon one major issue: was Felicity's debt liquidated or unliquidated?

Liquidated Debt

A **liquidated debt** is one in which there is no dispute about the amount owed. A loan is a typical example. If a bank lends you $10,000, and the note obligates you to repay that amount on June 1 of the following year, you clearly owe that sum. The debt is liquidated.

Liquidated debt
A debt in which there is no dispute about the amount owed.

In cases of liquidated debt, if the creditor agrees to take less than the full amount as full payment, her agreement is not binding. The debtor has given no consideration to support the creditor's promise to accept a reduced payment, and therefore the creditor is not bound by her word. The reasoning is simply that the debtor is already obligated to pay the full amount, so no bargaining could reasonably cause the creditor to accept less. If Felicity's debt to you is liquidated, your agreement to accept $60,000 is not binding, and you will successfully sue for the balance.

Exception: Different Performance

There is one important exception to this rule. If the debtor offers a *different performance* to settle the liquidated debt, and the creditor agrees to take it as full settlement, the agreement is binding. Suppose that Felicity, instead of paying $60,000, offers you five acres in Alaska, and you accept. When you accept the deed to the land, you have given up your entire claim, regardless of the land's precise value.

Unliquidated Debt: Accord and Satisfaction

A debt is **unliquidated** for either of two reasons: (1) the parties dispute whether any money is owed, or (2) the parties agree that some money is owed but dispute how much. When a debt is unliquidated for either reason, the parties may enter into a binding agreement to settle for less than what the creditor demands.

Unliquidated debt
A debt that is disputed because the parties disagree over its existence or amount.

Such a compromise will be enforced if:

- The debt is unliquidated;
- The parties agree that the creditor will accept as full payment a sum less than she has claimed; and
- The debtor pays the amount agreed upon.

This agreement is called an **accord and satisfaction**. The accord is the agreement to settle for less than the creditor claims. The satisfaction is the actual payment of that compromised sum. An accord and satisfaction is valid consideration to support the creditor's agreement to drop all claims. Each party is giving up something: the creditor gives up her full claim, and the debtor gives up his assertion that he owed little or nothing.

Accord and satisfaction
A completed agreement to settle a debt for less than the sum claimed.

Accord and Satisfaction by Check

Most accord and satisfaction agreements involve payment by check. UCC §3-311 governs these agreements, using the same common-law rules described above.[5] The Code specifies that when the debtor writes "full settlement" on the check, a creditor who cashes the check generally has entered into an accord and satisfaction. If Felicity's debt is unliquidated, and she gives you a check with "full payment of all debts" written on the face in bold letters, the moment you deposit the check, you lose any claim to more money. What happens if the debtor makes such a notation but the creditor changes it? A massage therapist learned the answer and felt sore for days.

[5]A check is legally an instrument, which is why this section comes from Article 3 of the Code. For a full discussion of instruments, see Chapters 23–36.

Henches v. Taylor

138 Wash. App. 1026, 2007 WL 1241525
Washington Court of Appeals, 2007

Facts: Jim Henches, a licensed massage therapist, treated Benjamin Taylor after he was injured in a car accident. When all treatments were finished, Henches billed Taylor for more than $7,000. Taylor's insurance company claimed the bill was exorbitant and paid only $2,625, for 24 massage treatments.

Henches continued to send bills to Taylor, not only for the balance due but for additional time spent consulting with Taylor's other health care providers, preparing to testify in Taylor's personal injury lawsuit, and attempting to collect his debts. In response to a bill for $11,945.86, Taylor's lawyer, James Harris, sent Henches a letter, stating:

> I have reviewed your billing statements and am having a difficult time understanding a number of charges you included. By my calculations, the amount owed to you is approximately $5,243.45. I have enclosed a check for that amount as payment in full to settle Mr. Taylor's account with you.

The letter was accompanied by a check with "final payment" written on the notation line. Henches filed suit, seeking the full balance. Then he wrote "attorney/fee" on the check, over the word "final," and deposited the check.

The trial court gave summary judgment to Taylor, ruling that deposit of the check constituted accord and satisfaction. Henches appealed.

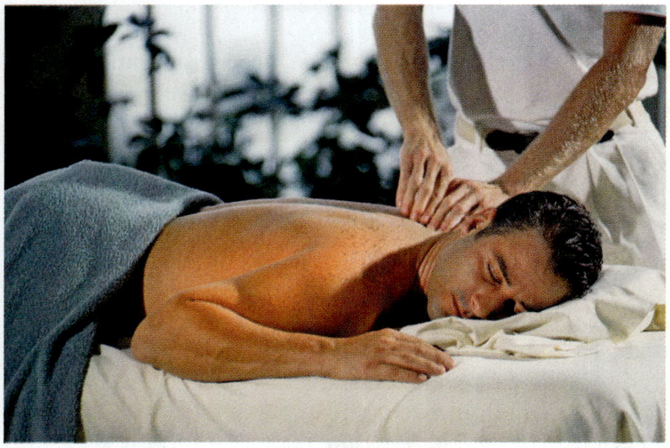

The massage feels great, but how much is it really worth?

Issue: ***Was there an accord and satisfaction, discharging the debt?***

Excerpts from Judge Ellington's Decision: A debt is discharged by accord and satisfaction when the debtor and creditor agree to settle a claim by some performance other than that which is claimed due, and the creditor accepts the substituted performance as full satisfaction of the claim. Accord and satisfaction requires a bona fide dispute, an agreement to settle the dispute for a certain sum, and performance of the agreement.

Taylor easily satisfied the first element of accord and satisfaction. The parties' contracts did not establish a liquidated amount for the services provided, and the letter that accompanied Taylor's check to Henches demonstrates a good faith dispute over the amount owed.

As with any contract, an accord and satisfaction cannot be formed without a meeting of the minds. But the required intent is shown when payment is offered in full satisfaction and is accompanied by conduct from which the creditor cannot fail to understand that payment is tendered on condition its acceptance constitutes satisfaction.

Given the undisputed facts here, Henches could not fail to understand that the check was offered on condition of full settlement. Henches' alteration of the "final payment" language is further demonstration that he read and understood the notation. Taylor tendered a check in final payment and Henches deposited the check, thereby accepting that payment.

A creditor can accept payment and avoid formation of an accord only where both parties understand before payment is accepted that the payment will not settle the claim. Henches contends his alteration of the check prevents accord and satisfaction. But a creditor cannot prevent formation of an accord by making a unilateral change to a draft tendered in full payment, even if the creditor endorses the check with the words accepted as partial payment and not as payment in full and not as an accord and satisfaction of the known full amount legally due and owing.

Where the amount due is in dispute, and the debtor sends cash or check for less than the amount claimed, clearly expressing his intention that it is sent as a settlement in full, and not on account or in part payment, the retention and use of the money or the cashing of the check is almost always held to be an acceptance of the offer operating as full satisfaction, even though the creditor may assert or send word to the debtor that the sum is received only in part payment.

Henches' alteration of the check was a unilateral act not communicated to Taylor. Accord and satisfaction discharged Taylor's debts to Henches. We affirm the trial court's summary judgment dismissal of Henches' suit.

UCC Exceptions

The Code creates two exceptions for accord and satisfaction cases involving checks. The first exception concerns "organizations," which typically are businesses. The general rule of §3-311 is potentially calamitous to them because a company that receives thousands of checks every day is unlikely to inspect all notations. A consumer who owes $12,000 on a credit card might write "full settlement" on a $200 check, potentially extinguishing the entire debt through accord and satisfaction. Under the exception, if an organization notifies a debtor that any offers to settle for less than the debt claimed must be made to a particular official, and the check is sent to anyone else in the organization, depositing the check generally does *not* create an accord and satisfaction. Thus a clerk who deposits 900 checks daily for payment of MasterCard debts will not have inadvertently entered into dozens of accord and satisfaction agreements.

The second exception allows a way out to most creditors who have inadvertently created an accord and satisfaction. If, within 90 days of cashing a "full payment" check, the creditor offers repayment of the same amount to the debtor, there is no accord and satisfaction. Homer claims that Virgil owes him $7 million but foolishly cashes Virgil's check for $3 million, without understanding that "paid in full" means just what it says. Homer has created an accord and satisfaction. But if he promptly sends Virgil a check for $3 million, he has undone the agreement and may sue for the full amount.

Consideration: Trends

Employment Agreements

In a noncompete agreement, an employee promises not to work for a competitor for some time after leaving the company. It used to be that these covenants were rare and reserved for top officers, but they have now become commonplace throughout many organizations. We will talk about them more in the next chapter, but often these covenants raise an issue of consideration: what consideration does the employee receive for signing a covenant not to compete? After all, the company is already under an obligation to pay the employee for working. What additional value does the employee receive in return for signing the agreement?

Although this area of law is developing and is a bit murky, the following case reflects the current majority view. Sometimes consideration issues can drive you nuts.

Snider Bolt & Screw v. Quality Screw & Nut

2009 U.S. Dist. LEXIS 50797
United States District Court for the Western District of Kentucky, 2009

Facts: James Scott signed a covenant not to compete when he went to work for Snider Bolt & Screw. The agreement prohibited him from taking a job with a competitor for one year after leaving Snider. Three years later, Scott quit his job at Snider and immediately went to work for Quality Screw & Nut (QSN).

Snider obtained a temporary restraining order that banned Scott from working at his new job. QSN argued that the covenant not to compete was void for lack of consideration. It asked the court to lift the temporary restraining order.

Issue: ***Did the covenant not to compete lack consideration?***

Excerpt from Judge Heyburn's Decision: Snider says that when Scott signed his covenant not to compete, he did so based upon an implied promise that Snider would continue his employment. Indeed, Snider did maintain Scott's employment until Scott himself left his job. Kentucky courts have found quite specifically that "where an employer has fulfilled an implied promise to continue the employee's employment, that promise is sufficient consideration

[to] support enforcement of the employee's promise not to compete." The Kentucky Supreme Court subsequently held that even continued at-will employment would be sufficient consideration. Here, Scott worked for another three years and left on his own accord to join QSN. These circumstances fit within the rule and the Court finds that the Covenant is supported by adequate consideration.

Consequently, the Court has no basis for sustaining QSN's motion.

Promissory Estoppel and "Moral Consideration"

Judges have a tool by which they can enforce agreements even if there is no consideration. Under the doctrine of promissory estoppel, a judge has the discretion to "ignore" the fact that consideration does not exist if a promise causes foreseeable reliance by a plaintiff and a great injustice would be done if the promise were broken. Some courts will use the phrase "moral consideration" to describe this basic idea.

For example, consider a pledge to charity. If Dave promises to give money to charity and then fails to make the donation, there is no consideration because he has received nothing in return. If the charity sues to enforce the promise, it cannot show that it has committed an act or forbearance.[6]

Nevertheless, some courts will force donors to make good on their donations anyway. Especially in the case of large donations, courts will often cite the "grave injustices" that can follow from this kind of promise breaking. "If you don't give the 'Coats for Kids' program the $100,000 you've pledged, then thousands of children will go without a coat this winter," a judge might say. Also, it may be that the charity has relied on the pledge to open another storefront or undertake a new program. Courts are likely to enforce the pledge in these circumstances.

It is unwise to make charitable pledges, especially large pledges, if you might change your mind.

EXAM Strategy

Question: In an Alabama case, Webb saved McGowin's life by preventing a giant block of wood from falling on his head.[7] Webb was permanently disabled in the accident and was never able to work again. Later, McGowin promised to give Webb money every two weeks for the rest of his life. McGowin made the payments for awhile but then stopped. Webb sued.

Strategy: No consideration exists here. McGowin made the promise to pay the money *after* Webb's heroic act. Webb did not give McGowin anything of value *in return for* the promise to pay money. But what about promissory estoppel?

[6] An exception to this, of course, would be if the charity agreed to give Dave something at the time he made the pledge. As a "fix" for consideration problems, many charities send donors something of trivial value when pledges are made—maybe a water bottle or a tote bag. Under the peppercorn rule, even something of small value counts as a legal act, and it converts a mere promise of a donation into an enforceable contract.

[7] *Webb v. McGowin*, 168 So. 196 (Ala.1935).

Result: In the case, the court found that "moral consideration" was present, and that Webb was entitled to the payments to prevent substantial injustice.

It is important to note that applications of promissory estoppel and similar doctrines are rare. Ordinarily, if there is no consideration, then there is no contract. However, in extreme cases, it is possible for a court to enforce a deal even without consideration. But this is not something you can count on.

Chapter Conclusion

This ancient doctrine of consideration is simple to state but subtle to apply. The parties must bargain and enter into an exchange of promises or actions. If they do not, there is no consideration and the courts are unlikely to enforce any promise made. A variety of exceptions modify the law, but a party wishing to render its future more predictable—the purpose of a contract—will rely on a solid bargain and exchange.

Exam Review

1. **CONSIDERATION** There are three rules of consideration:
   - Both parties must get something of *measureable value* from the contract.
   - A *promise* to give something of value counts as consideration.
   - The two parties must have *bargained for* whatever was exchanged. (pp. 276–278)

2. **ACT OR FORBEARANCE** The item of value can be either an act or a forbearance. (pp. 276–277)

Question: An aunt saw her eight-year-old nephew enter the room, remarked what a nice boy he was, and said, "I would like to take care of him now." She promptly wrote a note, promising to pay the boy $3,000 upon her death. Her estate refused to pay. Is it obligated to do so?

Strategy: A contract is enforceable only if the parties have given consideration. The consideration might be an act or a forbearance. Did the nephew give consideration? (See the "Result" at the end of this section.)

3. **ADEQUACY** The courts will seldom inquire into the adequacy of consideration. This is the "peppercorn rule." (pp. 278–279)

4. **ILLUSORY PROMISES** An illusory promise is not consideration. (pp. 278–280)

EXAM Strategy

Question: Eagle ran convenience stores. He entered into an agreement with Commercial Movie in which Commercial would provide Eagle with DVDs for rental. Eagle would pay Commercial 50 percent of the rental revenues. If Eagle stopped using Commercial's service, Eagle could not use a competitor's services for 18 months. The agreement also provided: "Commercial shall not be liable for compensation or damages of any kind, whether on account of the loss by Eagle of profits, sales or expenditures, or on account of any other event or cause whatsoever." Eagle complied with the agreement for two years but then began using a competitor's service, and Commercial sued. Eagle claimed that the agreement was unenforceable for lack of consideration. Please rule.

Strategy: In this case, both parties seem to have given consideration. But there is a flaw in the "promise" that Commercial made. Commercial can never be liable to Eagle—no matter what happens. (See the "Result" at the end of this section.)

5. **REQUIREMENT AND OUTPUT CONTRACTS** Under sales law, requirement and output contracts are valid. Although one side controls the quantity, its agreement to make demands *in good faith* is consideration. (pp. 280–283)

6. **PREEXISTING DUTY** Under the doctrine of preexisting duty, a promise to do something that the party is already legally obligated to perform is generally not consideration. (p. 282)

7. **LIQUIDATED DEBT** A liquidated debt is one in which there is no dispute about the amount owed. For a liquidated debt, a creditor's promise to accept less than the full amount is not binding. (pp. 285–287)

8. **UNLIQUIDATED DEBT** For an unliquidated debt, if the parties agree that the creditor will accept less than the full amount claimed and the debtor performs, there is an accord and satisfaction and the creditor may not claim any balance. (pp. 285–287)

9. **"FULL PAYMENT" NOTATIONS** In most states, payment by a check that has a "full payment" notation will create an accord and satisfaction unless the creditor is an organization that has notified the debtor that full payment offers must go to a certain officer. (pp. 285–287)

EXAM Strategy

Question: When White's wife died, he filed a claim with Boston Mutual for $10,000 death benefits under her insurance policy. The insurer rejected the claim, saying that his wife had misrepresented her medical condition in the application form. The company sent White a check for $478.75, which it said represented "a full refund of all applicable premiums paid" for the coverage. White deposited the check. Had the parties reached an accord and satisfaction?

Strategy: The UCC permits parties to enter into an accord and satisfaction by check. The debtor must make clear that the check is offered in full payment of a disputed debt. Debtors generally do that by writing "Final Settlement," "Accepted as Full Payment of All Debts," or some similar notation on the check. Had the insurance company complied with that requirement? (See the "Result" at the end of this section.)

10. PROMISSORY ESTOPPEL Sometimes, to prevent injustice, courts will enforce agreements even if no consideration is present. These deals are still not formal contracts, but the courts will enforce a promise nonetheless. (pp. 288–289)

Question: Phil Philanthropist called PBS during a fund drive and pledged to donate $100,000. PBS then planned and began to produce a Fourth of July *Sesame Street* special, counting on the large donation to fund it. Later, Phil changed his mind and said he had decided not to donate the money after all. PBS sued because without the money, it would not be able to complete the show. Will PBS win the lawsuit?

Strategy: Analyze the promise to donate the $100,000. Does it contain consideration? If not, is there any other legal possibility? (See the "Result" at the end of this section.)

2. Result: The nephew gave no consideration. He did not promise to do anything. He committed no act or forbearance. Without consideration, there is no enforceable contract. The estate wins.

4. Result: Commercial's promise was illusory. The company was free to walk away from the deal at any time. Commercial could never be held liable. Commercial gave no consideration, and there was no binding contract for either party to enforce.

9. Result: The insurer merely stated that its check was a refund of premiums. Nowhere did the company indicate that the check was full payment of its disputed obligation. The company should have made it clear that it would not pay any benefits and that this payment was all that it would offer. There was no accord and satisfaction.

10. Result: There is no "regular" consideration here because Phil received no measureable benefit and PBS did not act or forbear. But PBS can likely make a strong case that a great injustice will be done if the money is not paid. A judge might well decide to apply the doctrine of promissory estoppel and require Phil to make the donation.

Multiple-Choice Questions

1. For consideration to exist, there must be:
   (a) A bargained-for exchange
   (b) A manifestation of mutual assent
   (c) Genuineness of assent
   (d) Substantially equal economic benefits to both parties

2. Which of the following requires consideration in order to be binding on the parties?
   (a) Modification of a contract involving the sale of real estate
   (b) Modification of a sale of goods contract under the UCC
   (c) Both A and B
   (d) None of the above

3. Ted's wallet is as empty as his bank account, and he needs $3,500 immmediately. Fortunately, he has three gold coins that he inherited from his grandfather. Each is worth $2,500, but it is Sunday, and the local rare coins store is closed. When approached, Ted's neighbor Andrea agrees to buy the first coin for $2,300. Another neighbor, Cami, agrees to buy the second for $1,100. A final neighbor, Lorne, offers "all the money I have on me"—$100—for the last coin. Desperate, Ted agrees to the proposal. Which of the deals is supported by consideration?
   (a) Ted's agreement with Andrea only
   (b) Ted's agreements with Andrea and Cami only
   (c) All three of the agreements
   (d) None of the agreements

4. In a(n) ____________ contract, the seller guarantees to sell 100 percent of its output to one buyer, and the buyer agrees to accept the entire quantity. This kind of arrangement ____________ acceptable under the UCC.
   (a) output; is
   (b) output; is not
   (c) requirements; is
   (d) requirements; is not

5. Noncompete agreements are common features of employment contracts. Currently, courts ____________ enforce these clauses.
   (a) always
   (b) usually
   (c) rarely
   (d) never

Essay Questions

1. American Bakeries had a fleet of over 3,000 delivery trucks. Because of the increasing cost of gasoline, the company was interested in converting the trucks to propane fuel. It signed a requirements contract with Empire Gas, in which Empire would convert "approximately 3,000" trucks to propane fuel, as American Bakeries requested, and would then sell all the required propane fuel to run the trucks. But American Bakeries changed its mind and never requested a single conversion. Empire sued for lost profits. Who won?

2. CeCe Hylton and Edward Meztista, partners in a small advertising firm, agreed to terminate the business and split assets evenly. Meztista gave Hylton a two-page document showing assets, liabilities, and a bottom line of $35,235.67, with half due to each partner. Hylton questioned the accounting and asked to see the books. Meztista did not permit Hylton to see any records and refused to answer her phone calls. Instead, he gave her a check in the amount of $17,617.83, on which he wrote "Final payment/payment in full." Hylton cashed the check, but she wrote on it, "Under protest—cashing this check does not constitute my acceptance of this amount as payment in full." Hylton then filed suit, demanding additional monies. Meztista claimed that the parties had made an accord and satisfaction. What is the best argument for each party? Who should win?

3. ***ETHICS*** Melnick built a house for Gintzler, but the foundation was defective. Gintzler agreed to accept the foundation if Melnick guaranteed to make future repairs caused by the defects. Melnick agreed but later refused to make any repairs. Melnick argued that his promise to make future repairs was unsupported by consideration. Who will win the suit? Is either party acting unethically? Which one, and why?

4. Sami walks into a restaurant. She is given a menu, which indicates that lobster is $30. Sami orders the lobster. It arrives, and Sami thinks it is very tasty. When the bill arrives, Sami tries to execute a clever ploy she learned about in her business law class. She writes a check to the restaurant for $20 and writes "full settlement" across the top. The waiter accepts the check without looking at it, and the restaurant manager later deposits it in the restaurant's bank account. Is this a liquidated or an unliquidated debt? Is Sami off the hook for the last $10?

5. In the bleachers…

"You're a prince, George!" Mike exclaimed. "Who else would give me a ticket to the big game?"

"No one, Mike, no one."

"Let me offer my thanks. I'll buy you a beer!"

"Ah," George said. "A large beer would hit the spot right now."

"Small. Let me buy you a small beer."

"Ah, well, good enough."

Mike stood and took his wallet from his pocket. He was distressed to find a very small number of bills inside. "There's bad news, George!" he said.

"What's that?"

"I can't buy you the beer, George."

George considered that for a moment. "I'll tell you what, Mike," he said. "If you march to the concession stand right this minute and get me my beer, I won't punch you in the face."

"It's a deal!" Mike said.

Discuss the consideration issues raised by this exchange.

6. Jack Tallas came to the United States from Greece in 1914. He lived in Salt Lake City for nearly 70 years, achieving great success in insurance and real estate. During the last 14 years of his life, his friend Peter Dementas helped him with numerous personal and business chores. Two months before his death, Tallas dictated a memorandum to Dementas, in Greek, stating:

> PETER K. DEMENTAS is my best friend I have in this country, and since he came to the United States, he treats me like a father and I think of him as my own son. He takes me in his car grocery shopping. He drives me to the doctor and also takes me every week to Bingham to pick up my mail, collect the rents, and manage my properties. For all the services Peter has given me all these years, I owe to him the amount of $50,000 (Fifty Thousand Dollars). I will shortly change my will to include him as my heir.

Tallas signed the memorandum, but he did not in fact alter his will to include Dementas. The estate refused to pay, and Dementas sued. Was there consideration? Please rule.

Discussion Questions

Apply the following material to the next three questions.

Some view consideration as a technicality that allows people to make promises and then back out of them. Perhaps all promises should be enforced. In Japan, for example, promises to give gifts are enforceable without consideration.[8]

In the United States, if I promise to give you a gift merely because I feel like being nice, I can freely change my mind as far as contract law is concerned. A court will not make me follow through because there is no consideration.

In Japan, I would be obligated to buy the gift if all other elements of a contract were present—an offer, an acceptance, and so forth.

Some argue that consideration in U.S. law is a doctrine left over from centuries long past, that it lacks any reasonable modern purpose, and that it should be abolished.

1. Do you agree with this statement: "A person should always keep his or her word."

2. When it comes to giving gifts, which is better—the Japanese or American rule?

3. Are there any specific types of agreements (perhaps high-value, long-term, extremely time-consuming ones) that should definitely require consideration?

4. In the gold rush example, Embola gave Tuppela $50 in exchange for a promise of $10,000 later. Under the peppercorn rule, the deal was a contract. Is the peppercorn rule sensible? Should courts require a more *even* exchange of value?

5. In the last two chapters, we have examined clickwrap boxes. Sometimes courts refuse to enforce clickwrap terms because of problems with acceptance or consideration, but usually the terms are enforced. Is there a way to make clickwraps fair to both sides? Would it be better to ban clickwrap boxes altogether?

[8]See Japan's Civil Code, Article 549.

CHAPTER 13

© picsbyst/Shutterstock.com

LEGALITY

Soheil Sadri, a California resident, did some serious gambling at Caesar's Tahoe casino in Nevada. And lost. To keep gambling, he wrote checks to Caesar's and then signed two memoranda pledging to repay all money advanced. After two days, with his losses totaling more than $22,000, he went home. Back in California, Sadri stopped payment on the checks and refused to pay any of the money he owed Caesar's. The casino sued. In defense, Sadri claimed that California law considered his agreements illegal and unenforceable. He was unquestionably correct about one thing: a contract that is illegal is void and unenforceable.

A contract that is illegal is void and unenforceable.

Contracts that Violate a Statute

In this chapter, we examine a variety of contracts that may be void, or unenforceable. Illegal agreements fall into two groups: those that violate a statute, and those that violate public policy.

Wagers

Gambling is big business. Almost all states now permit some form of wagering, from casinos to racetracks to lotteries, and they eagerly collect the billions of dollars in revenue generated. Supporters urge that casinos create jobs and steady income, boost state coffers, and take business away from organized crime. Critics argue that naive citizens inevitably lose money they can ill afford to forfeit, and that addicted gamblers destroy their families and weaken the fabric of communities. With citizens and states divided over the ethics of gambling, it is inevitable that we have conflicts such as the dispute between Sadri and Caesar's. The basic rule, however, is clear: **a gambling contract is illegal unless it is a type of wagering *specifically authorized* by state statute.**

In California, as in many states, gambling on credit is not allowed. In other words, it is illegal to lend money to help someone wager. But in Nevada, gambling on credit is legal, and debt memoranda such as Sadri's are enforceable contracts. Caesar's sued Sadri in California (where he lived). The result? The court admitted that California's attitude toward gambling had changed, and that bingo, poker clubs, and lotteries were common. Nonetheless, the court denied that the new tolerance extended to wagering on credit:

> There is a special reason for treating gambling on credit differently from gambling itself. Having lost his or her cash, the pathological gambler will continue to play on credit, if extended, in an attempt to win back the losses. This is why enforcement of gambling debts has always been against public policy in California and should remain so, regardless of shifting public attitudes about gambling itself. If Californians want to play, so be it. But the law should not invite them to play themselves into debt. The judiciary cannot protect pathological gamblers from themselves, but we can refuse to participate in their financial ruin.[1]

© Elena Ray/Shutterstock

The gambling is legal—but what about a gambling contract?

Caesar's lost and Sadri kept his money. However, do not become too excited at the prospect of risk-free wagering. Casinos responded to cases like *Sadri* by changing their practices. Most now extend credit only to a gambler who agrees that disputes about repayment will be settled in *Nevada* courts. Because such contracts are legal in that state, the casino is able to obtain a judgment against a defaulting debtor and—yes—enforce that judgment in the gambler's home state.

Despite these more restrictive casino practices, Sadri's dispute is a useful starting place from which to examine contract legality because it illustrates two important themes.

First, morality is a significant part of contract legality. In refusing to enforce an obligation that Sadri undeniably had made, the California court relied on the human and social consequences of gambling and on the ethics of judicial enforcement of gambling debts. Second, "void" really means just that: a court will not

[1]*Metropolitan Creditors Service of Sacramento v. Sadri*, 15 Cal. App. 4th 1821, 1993 Cal. App. LEXIS 559, 19 Cal. Rptr. 2d 646 (Cal. Ct. App. 1993).

intercede to assist either party to an illegal agreement, even if its refusal leaves one party shortchanged.

Insurance

Another market in which "wagering" unexpectedly pops up is that of insurance. You may certainly insure your own life for any sum you choose. But may you insure someone else's life? **Anyone taking out a policy on the life of another must have an insurable interest in that person.** The most common insurable interest is family connection, such as spouses or parents. Other valid interests include creditor-debtor status (the creditor wants payment if the debtor dies) and business association (an executive in the company is so valuable that the firm will need compensation if something happens to him). If there is no insurable interest, there is generally no contract.

EXAM Strategy

Question: Jimenez sold Breton a used motorcycle for $5,500, payable in weekly installments. Jimenez then purchased an insurance policy on Breton's life, worth $320,000 if Breton died in an accident. Breton promptly died in a collision with an automobile. The insurance company offered only $5,500, representing the balance due on the motorcycle. Jimenez sued, demanding $320,000. Make an argument that the insurance company should win.

Strategy: The issue is whether Jimenez had an insurable interest in Breton's life. If he had no interest, he cannot collect on an insurance policy. If he had an interest, what was it? For how much money?

Result: Jimenez's had an interest in Breton's life to insure payment of the motorcycle debt—$5,500. Beyond that, this policy represented a wager by Jimenez that Breton was going to die. Contracts for such wagers are unenforceable. Jimenez is entitled only to $5,500.[2]

Licensing Statutes

You sue your next-door neighbor in small claims court, charging that he keeps a kangaroo in his backyard and that the beast has disrupted your family barbecues by leaping over the fence, demanding salad, and even kicking your cousin in the ear. Your friend Foster, a graduate student from Melbourne, offers to help you prepare the case, and you agree to pay him 10 percent of anything you recover. Foster proves surprisingly adept at organizing documents and arguments. You win $1,200, and Foster demands $120. Must you pay? The answer is determined by the law of licensing.

States require licenses for anyone who practices a profession, such as law or medicine, works as a contractor or plumber, and for many other kinds of work. These licenses are required in order to protect the public. States demand that an electrician be licensed because the work is potentially dangerous to a homeowner: the person doing the work must know an amp from a watt. **When a licensing requirement is designed to protect the public, any contract made by an unlicensed worker is unenforceable.** Your friend Foster is

[2] *Jimenez v. Protective Life Insurance Co.*, 8 Cal. App. 4th 528 (Cal. App. 1992).

unlicensed to practice law. Even though Foster did a fine job with your small claims case, he cannot enforce his contract for $120.

States use other licenses simply to raise money. For example, most states require a license to open certain kinds of retail stores. This requirement does not protect the public because the state will not investigate the store owner the way it will examine a prospective lawyer or electrician. The state is simply raising money. **When a licensing requirement is designed merely to raise revenue, a contract made by an unlicensed person is generally enforceable.** Thus, if you open a stationery store and forget to pay the state's licensing fee, you can still enforce a contract to buy 10,000 envelopes from a wholesaler at a bargain price.

Many cases, such as the following one, involve contractors seeking to recover money for work they did without a license.

Authentic Home Improvements v. Mayo

2006 WL 2687533
District of Columbia Superior Court, 2006

Facts: Authentic Home Improvements (Authentic) performed work on Diane Mayo's home, but she sued for return of the money she had paid. In court, Authentic's owner acknowledged that he had no contractor's license when it began the work, but he expected to obtain it soon. The court ordered Authentic to refund Mayo the entire sum she had paid, and the company agreed. Later, however, Authentic returned to court, stating that things had changed. The license had in fact been issued soon after work began. Authentic argued that it should not be obligated to return Mayo's money and was in fact entitled to its full fee for the work accomplished.

Issue: ***Did the new license entitle Authentic to its home improvement fee?***

Excerpts from Judge Goodbread's Decision: This is not a matter of a trial judge doggedly cleaving to his original ruling—one that he frankly wishes he could modify under these circumstances. To use the words of Proteus, "My duty pricks me on to utter that which else no worldly good should draw from me." Shakespeare, "The Two Gentlemen of Verona." Not that it makes any difference to anyone, but the undersigned, a carpenter's son dwelling at this end of the Judicial Food Chain, disagrees with the harsh general rule in these cases and [believes that exceptions to the licensing requirement should be made in deserving cases]. Nevertheless, the undersigned is bound by the repeated rulings of the Court of Appeals.

As early as 1974, our Court of Appeals noted the high incidence of complaints emanating from the home improvement industry, noting that, even then, it was estimated that fraudulent practices in the industry cost consumers from 500 million to 1 billion dollars annually (this would amount to over $4.3 billion in today's dollars). A simple search of the Internet for the term "home improvement fraud" brings up over two million sites.

Not only is it immaterial that the parties may be in equal fault in the home improvement contract matter, but it has also been held that the unlicensed contractor may not recover even in instances wherein the homeowner *already knew* at all times relevant that the contractor was not licensed and impliedly or expressly "waived" that requirement in return for the work being done promptly. Moreover—turning the purpose of the rule inside out—even where it was the contractor who was the "victim" and the home owner herself who knew in advance that the contract would be invalid and unenforceable, yet still benefitted unfairly from the contractor's good work, the homeowner was allowed to prevail, despite what might be termed "malice aforethought."

The unique defense of a "retroactive" license presented in this case does not vitiate the rule. [Authentic's owner argues that he] had every reasonable *expectation* of receiving a license and that, in fact, he *did* receive the license within a reasonable time of beginning work. Yet the requirement to have *already* had issued, and in hand, a license or permit to conduct or perform the act at issue is not a difficult concept to grasp and one need go no further than the common driver's permit or license tags to understand it. No one could legally drive a vehicle in *anticipation* of the license and the plates that had already been approved, on the premise that they would eventually arrive in the mail in due course, and that it would be all right to drive until they do.

The Court's original ruling in this case must stand.

Usury

It pays to understand usury.

Henry Paper and Anthony Pugliese were real estate developers. They bought property in Florida, intending to erect an office building. Walter Gross, another developer, agreed to lend them $200,000 at 15 percent interest. Gross knew the partners were desperate for the money, so at the loan closing, he demanded 15 percent equity (ownership) in the partnership, in addition to the interest. Paper and Pugliese had no choice but to sign the agreement. The two partners never repaid the loan, and when Gross sued, the court ruled that they need never pay a cent.

Usury laws prohibit charging excess interest on loans. Some states, such as New York, set very strict limits. Others, like Utah, allow for virtually any rate. A lender who charges a usurious rate of interest may forfeit the illegal interest, all interest, or, in some states, the entire loan.

Florida law requires a lender who exceeds 25 percent interest to forfeit the entire debt. Where was the usury in Gross's case? Just here: when Gross insisted on a 15 percent share of the partnership, he was simply extracting additional interest and disguising it as partnership equity. The Paper-Pugliese partnership had equity assets of $600,000. A 15 percent equity, plus interest payments of 15 percent over 18 months, was the equivalent of a per annum interest rate of 45 percent. Gross probably thought he had made a deal that was too good to be true. And in the state of Florida, it was. He lost the entire debt.[3]

Credit Card Debt

Many consumers are desperate to obtain credit cards on any terms. When First Premier Bank launched a credit card with a 79.9 percent rate of interest, 700,000 people applied for it within the next two years.

How can such a rate exist?

Even if a state's usury statute applies to credit cards, savvy lenders can often avoid limits on interest rates. The Supreme Court has ruled that when national banks issue a credit card, they can use the rate of their own state or of that of the consumer, whichever is higher. Also, many card issuers require borrowers to sign contracts that say the laws of a lender-friendly state will be applied to all future disputes. New York customers might agree to live by Utah laws, for example.

Most courts continue to enforce these contracts that impose high out-of-state rates. But since the financial meltdown of 2008, some courts have started to express distaste for this practice. In the following case, a New York court addressed the issue.

American Express Travel Related Services Company, Inc. v. Assih

893 N.Y.S.2d 438
Civil Court of the City of New York, Richmond County, 2009

Facts: American Express Travel Related Services (American Express) alleged that New York resident Titus Assih missed a credit card payment. His interest rate ballooned from 12.24 percent to 21 percent, and eventually to 27.99 percent. Assih made small payments for a time, but soon he stopped paying altogether.

American Express sued Assih. The company sought to enforce this provision of its agreement: "This Agreement

[3] *Jersey Palm-Gross, Inc. v. Paper*, 639 So.2d 664, 1994 Fla. App. LEXIS 6597 (Fla. Ct. App. 1994).

is governed by Utah law and applicable federal law." The agreement's only connection to Utah was that American Express assigned its interest to a one-branch bank in Utah.

Assih argued that New York law, which sets strict limits on maximum rates of credit card interest, should apply instead.

Issues: *Should New York or Utah law apply? Did the increased rates violate usury statutes?*

Excerpts from Judge Straniere's Opinion: Having dealt with thousands of consumer credit cases over the years, the court is sometimes caused to wonder if the regulations governing this industry originated in the Wonderful Land of Oz. For example, the scene where Dorothy and friends approach the gates of the Emerald City and ring the bell seeking entrance seems to present a number of the issues arising in debt collection litigation.

> Guardian: Well, that's more like it! Now state your business!
> Dorothy and Friends: We want to see the Wizard!
> Guardian: The Wizard? But nobody can see the Great Oz! Nobody's ever seen the Great Oz! Even I've never seen him!
> Dorothy: Well, then how do you know there is one?

Like the Land of Oz, run by a Wizard who no one has ever seen, the Land of Credit Cards permits consumers to be bound by agreements they never sign, agreements they may have never received, subject to change without notice and the laws of a state other than those existing where they reside.

The Utah usury statute provides: The parties to a lawful contract may agree upon any rate of interest for the loan that is the subject of their contract.

Is it any wonder that credit card issuers, such as plaintiff, make their agreements subject to Utah law? An interest rate is not usurious so long as the parties "agree upon any rate of interest." If Nathan Detroit had known he could make loans charging 100% interest a day by reducing them to writing, signed and subject to Utah law, he would not have had to seek a living running the "oldest, established, permanent floating crap game in New York." Incredibly courts are expected to enforce these agreements against unsophisticated, unrepresented consumers who reside in states such as New York which do not have similar statutes and who have no idea that their agreement is subject to Utah law.

Is New York required to apply the Utah usury statute to credit card interest charges which far exceed the legal rate in New York? New York follows the "substantial relationship" approach that provides:

> The law of the state chosen by the parties to govern their contractual rights and duties will be applied.... unless the chosen state has no substantial relationship to the parties.

The corporate plaintiff is incorporated in New York and its principal place of business is in New York. Defendant resides in New York. Most of the transactions charged to the credit card took place in New York. Payments on the credit card are mailed to a New York address. Utah has no substantial relationship to the parties.

Taking all of the above into account, it is clear that New York has the most significant contacts to the parties and New York law will apply to the Agreement.

The legal rate of interest in New York in general obligations [is] sixteen per cent. New York still retains a criminal usury statute for interest rates which exceed twenty-five per cent. Except for the initial interest rate charged on defendant's account by plaintiff of 12.24%, all other interest charges assessed by plaintiff violated the New York civil usury statutes. The last billings on this account in fact exceeded the criminal usury rate of 25% when they reached 27.99%.

Under New York law, all usurious contracts are void and the lender forfeits both principal and interest.

The Wizard in the "Wizard of Oz" warned Dorothy and friends, "Do not arouse the wrath of the great and powerful Oz." I am sure the court will likewise be arousing the wrath of the plaintiff.

Plaintiff's cause of action is dismissed.

Contracts that Violate Public Policy

In the preceding section, we saw that courts refuse to enforce contracts that violate a *statute*. However, a judge may declare a contract illegal even if it does not violate a statute. In this section, we examine cases in which a *public policy* prohibits certain contracts. In other words, we focus primarily on common law rules.

Restraint of Trade: Noncompete Agreements

Free trade is the basis of the U.S. economy, and any bargain that restricts it is suspect. Most restraint of free trade is barred by antitrust law. But it is the common law that still regulates one restriction on trade: agreements to refrain from competition. Some of these agreements are legal, and some are void.

Recall that a noncompete agreement is a contract in which one party agrees not to compete with another in a stated type of business. For example, an anchorwoman for an NBC news affiliate in Miami might agree that she will not anchor any other Miami station's news for one year after she leaves her present employer. Noncompetes are often valid, but the common law places some restrictions on them.

To be valid, an agreement not to compete must be ancillary to a legitimate bargain. "Ancillary" means that the noncompetition agreement must be part of a larger agreement. Suppose Cliff sells his gasoline station to Mina, and the two agree that Cliff will not open a competing gas station within 5 miles anytime during the next two years. Cliff's agreement not to compete is ancillary to the sale of his service station. His noncompetition promise is enforceable. But suppose that Cliff and Mina already had the only two gas stations within 35 miles. They agree between themselves not to hire each other's workers. Their agreement might be profitable to them because each could now keep wages artificially low. But their deal is ancillary to no legitimate bargain, and it is therefore void. Mina is free to hire Cliff's mechanic despite her agreement with Cliff.

The two most common settings for legitimate noncompetition agreements are the sale of a business and an employment relationship.

Sale of a Business

Kory has operated a real estate office, Hearth Attack, in a small city for 35 years, building an excellent reputation and many ties with the community. She offers to sell you the business and its goodwill for $300,000. But you need assurance that Kory will not take your money and promptly open a competing office across the street. With her reputation and connections, she would ruin your chances of success. You insist on a noncompete clause in the sale contract. In this clause, Kory promises that for one year, she will not open a new real estate office or go to work for a competing company within a 10-mile radius of Hearth Attack. Suppose, six months after selling you the business, Kory goes to work for a competing real estate agency two blocks away. You seek an injunction to prevent her from working. Who wins?

When a noncompete agreement is ancillary to the sale of a business, it is enforceable if reasonable in time, geographic area, and scope of activity. In other words, a court will not enforce a noncompete agreement that lasts an unreasonably long time, covers an unfairly large area, or prohibits the seller of the business from doing a type of work that she never had done before. Measured by this test, Kory is almost certainly bound by her agreement. One year is a reasonable time to allow you to get your new business started. A 10-mile radius is probably about the area that Hearth Attack covers, and realty is obviously a fair business from which to prohibit Kory. A court will probably grant the injunction, barring Kory from her new job.

With her reputation and connections, she would ruin your chances of success.

If, on the other hand, the noncompetition agreement had prevented Kory from working anywhere within 200 miles of Hearth Attack, and she started working 50 miles away, a court would refuse to enforce the contract. That geographic restriction would be unreasonable since Kory never previously did business 50 miles away, and Hearth Attack is unlikely to be affected if she works there now. An overly broad restriction would make for bad public policy, and it would lack a legal purpose.

Employment

When you sign an employment contract, the document may well contain a noncompete clause. Employers have legitimate worries that employees might go to a competitor and take with them trade secrets or other proprietary information. Some employers, though, attempt to place harsh restrictions on their employees, perhaps demanding a blanket agreement that the employee will never go to work for a competitor. Once again, courts look at the reasonableness of restrictions placed on an employee's future work. Because the agreement now involves the very livelihood of the worker, a court scrutinizes the agreement more closely.

A noncompete clause in an employment contract is generally enforceable only if it is essential to the employer, fair to the employee, and harmless to the general public. Judges usually enforce these agreements to protect trade secrets and confidential information. They may protect customer lists that have been expensive to produce. Courts rarely restrain an employee simply because he wants to work for a competitor, and they disfavor agreements that last too long or apply in a very wide area. The following chart summarizes the factors that courts look at in all types of noncompetition agreements.

THE LEGALITY OF NONCOMPETITION CLAUSES (NONCOMPETES)

Type of Noncompetition Agreement	When Enforceable	
Not ancillary to a sale of business or employment	Never	
Ancillary to a sale of business	If reasonable in time, geography, and scope of activity	
Ancillary to employment	Contract is *more* likely to be enforced when it involves: • Trade secrets or confidential information: these are almost always protected • Customer lists developed over extended period of time and carefully protected • Limited time and geographical scope • Terms essential to protect the employer's business	Contract is *less* likely to be enforced when it involves: • Employee who already had the skills when he arrived, or merely developed general skills on the job • Customer lists that can be derived from public sources • Excessive time or geographical scope • Terms that are unduly harsh on the employee or contrary to public interest

Suppose that Gina, an engineer, goes to work for Fission Chips, a silicon chip manufacturer that specializes in defense work. She signs a noncompete agreement promising never to work for a competitor. Over a period of three years, Gina learns some of Fission's proprietary methods of etching information onto the chips. She acquires a great deal of new expertise about chips generally. And she periodically deals with Fission Chip's customers, all of whom are well-known software and hardware manufacturers. Gina accepts an offer from WriteSmall, a competitor. Fission Chips races to court, seeking an injunction that would prevent Gina from (1) working for WriteSmall; (2) working for any other competitor; (3) revealing any of Fission's trade secrets; (4) using any of the general expertise she acquired at Fission Chips; and (5) contacting any of Fission's customers.

This injunction threatens Gina's career. If she cannot work for a competitor, or use her general engineering skills, what *will* she do? And for exactly that reason, no court will grant such a broad order. The court will allow Gina to work for competitors, including WriteSmall. It will order her not to use or reveal any trade secrets belonging to Fission. She will, however, be permitted to use the general expertise she has acquired, and she may contact former customers since anyone could get their names from the yellow pages.

Was the noncompete in the following case styled fairly, or was the employee clipped?

King v. Head Start Family Hair Salons, Inc.

886 So.2d 769
Supreme Court of Alabama, 2004

Facts: Kathy King was a single mother supporting a college-age daughter. For 25 years, she had worked as a hair stylist. For the most recent 16 years, she had worked at Head Start, which provided haircuts, coloring, and styling for men and women. King was primarily a stylist, though she had also managed one of the Head Start facilities.

King quit Head Start and began working as manager of a Sport Clips shop, located in the same mall as the store she just left. Sport Clips offered only haircuts and primarily served men and boys. Head Start filed suit, claiming that King was violating the noncompetition agreement that she had signed. The agreement prohibited King from working at a competing business within a two-mile radius of any Head Start facility for 12 months after leaving the company. The trial court issued an injunction enforcing the noncompete. King appealed.

Issue: ***Was the noncompetition agreement valid?***

Excerpts from Justice Lyons's Decision: King's most persuasive argument is that the geographic restriction contained in the noncompetition agreement imposes an undue hardship on her. King has been in the hair-care industry for 25 years, and it is the only industry in which she is skilled and the only industry in which she can find employment. Head Start has 30 locations throughout the Jefferson County and Shelby County area, making it virtually impossible for her to find employment in the hair-care industry at a facility that does not violate the terms of the noncompetition agreement. According to King, the geographic restriction constitutes a blanket prohibition on practicing her trade.

It cannot reasonably be argued that King, at the age of 40 and having spent more than half of her life as a hair stylist, can learn a new job skill that would allow her to be gainfully employed and meet her needs and the needs of her daughter. Under the circumstances presented here, enforcement of the noncompetition agreement works an undue hardship upon King. The noncompetition agreement cannot so burden King that it would result in her impoverishment.

Head Start is nevertheless entitled to some of the protection it sought in the noncompetition agreement. Head Start has a valid concern that King would be able to attract many of her former Head Start customers if she is allowed to provide hair-care services unencumbered by any limitations. To prevent an undue burden on King and to afford some protection to Head Start, the trial court should enforce a more reasonable geographic restriction—such as one prohibiting King from providing hair-care services within a two-mile radius of the location of the Head Start facility at which she was formerly employed or imposing some other limitation that does not unreasonably interfere with King's right to gainful employment while, at the same time, protecting Head Start's interest in preventing King from unreasonably competing with it during the one-year period following her resignation.

Reversed and remanded.

EXAM Strategy

Question: Caf-Fiend is an expanding chain of coffeehouses. The company offers to buy Bessie's Coffee Shop, in St. Louis, on these terms: Bessie will manage the store, as Caf-Fiend's employee, for one year after the sale. For four years after the sale, Bessie will not open a competing restaurant anywhere within 12 miles. For the same four years, she will not work anywhere in the United States for a competing coffee retailer. Are the last two terms enforceable against Bessie?

Strategy: This contract includes two noncompete clauses. In the first, Bessie agrees not to open a competing business. Courts generally enforce such clauses if they are reasonable in time, geography, and scope of activity. Is this clause reasonable? The second clause involves employment. Courts take a dimmer view of these agreements. Is this clause essential to protect the company's business? Is it unduly harsh for Bessie?

Result: The first restriction is reasonable. Caf-Fiend is entitled to prevent Bessie from opening her own coffeehouse around the corner and drawing her old customers. The second clause is unfair to Bessie. If she wants to move from St. Louis to San Diego and work as a store manager, she is prohibited. It is impossible to see how such employment would harm Caf-Fiend—but it certainly takes away Bessie's career options. The first restriction is valid, the second one unenforceable.

Exculpatory Clauses

You decide to capitalize on your expert ability as a skier and open a ski school in Colorado, "Pike's Pique." But you realize that skiing sometimes causes injuries, so you require anyone signing up for lessons to sign this form:

> I agree to hold Pike's Pique and its employees entirely harmless in the event that I am injured in any way or for any reason or cause, including but not limited to any acts, whether negligent or otherwise, of Pike's Pique or any employee or agent thereof.

The day your school opens, Sara Beth, an instructor, deliberately pushes Toby over a cliff because Toby criticized her clothes. Eddie, a beginning student, "blows out" his knee attempting an advanced racing turn. And Maureen, another student, reaches the bottom of a steep run and slams into a snowmobile that Sara Beth parked there. Maureen, Eddie, and Toby's families all sue Pike's Pique. You defend based on the form you had them sign. Does it save the day?

Exculpatory clause
A contract provision that attempts to release one party from liability in the event the other is injured.

The form on which you are relying is an **exculpatory clause**, that is, one that attempts to release you from liability in the event of injury to another party. Exculpatory clauses are common. Ski schools use them, and so do parking lots, landlords, warehouses, sports franchises, and day-care centers. All manner of businesses hope to avoid large tort judgments by requiring their customers to give up any right to recover. Is such a clause valid? Sometimes. Courts frequently—but do not always—ignore exculpatory clauses, finding that one party was forcing the other party to give up legal rights that no one should be forced to surrender.

An exculpatory clause is generally unenforceable when it attempts to exclude an intentional tort or gross negligence. When Sara Beth pushes Toby over a cliff, that is the intentional tort of battery. A court will not enforce the exculpatory clause. Sara Beth is clearly liable.[4] As to the snowmobile at the bottom of the run, if a court determines that was gross negligence

[4]Note that Pike's Pique is probably not liable under agency law principles that preclude an employer's liability for an employee's intentional tort.

(carelessness far greater than ordinary negligence), then the exculpatory clause will again be ignored. If, however, it was ordinary negligence, then we must continue the analysis.

An exculpatory clause is usually unenforceable when the affected activity is in the public interest, such as medical care, public transportation, or some essential service. Suppose Eddie goes to a doctor for surgery on his damaged knee, and the doctor requires him to sign an exculpatory clause. The doctor negligently performs the surgery, accidentally leaving his cuff links in Eddie's left knee. The exculpatory clause will not protect the doctor. Medical care is an essential service, and the public cannot give up its right to demand reasonable work.

© Photodisc/Getty Images

Exculpatory clauses are important to the operators of businesses that involve some risk, such as ski resorts.

But what about Eddie's suit against Pike's Pique? Eddie claims that he should never have been allowed to attempt an advanced maneuver. His suit is for ordinary negligence, and the exculpatory clause probably *does* bar him from recovery. Skiing is a recreational activity. No one is obligated to do it, and there is no strong public interest in ensuring that we have access to ski slopes.

An exculpatory clause is generally unenforceable when the parties have greatly unequal bargaining power. When Maureen flies to Colorado, suppose that the airline requires her to sign a form contract with an exculpatory clause. Because the airline almost certainly has much greater bargaining power, it can afford to offer a "take it or leave it" contract. The bargaining power is so unequal, though, that the clause is probably unenforceable. Does Pike's Pique have a similar advantage? Probably not. Ski schools are not essential and are much smaller enterprises. A dissatisfied customer might refuse to sign such an agreement and take her business elsewhere. A court probably will not see the parties as *grossly* unequal.

An exculpatory clause is generally unenforceable unless the clause is clearly written and readily visible. If Pike's Pique gave all ski students an eight-page contract, and the exculpatory clause was at the bottom of page seven in small print, the average customer would never notice it. The clause would be void.

In the following case, the court focused on the public policy concerns of exculpatory clauses used in a very common setting. Should the exculpatory clause stop the tenant from suing the landlord? You be the judge.

You be the Judge

Ransburg v. Richards

770 N.E.2d 393
Indiana Court of Appeals, 2002

Facts: Barbara Richards leased an apartment at Twin Lakes, a complex owned by Lenna Ransburg. The written lease declared that:

- Twin Lakes would "gratuitously" maintain the common areas.
- Richards's use of the facilities would be "at her own risk."
- Twin Lakes was not responsible for any harm to the tenant or her guests, anywhere on the property (including the parking lot), even if the damage was caused by Twin Lakes' negligence.

It snowed. As Richards walked across the parking lot to her car, she slipped and fell on snow-covered ice. Richards sued Ransburg, who moved for summary judgment based on the exculpatory clause. The trial court denied Ransburg's motion, and she appealed.

You Be the Judge: ***Was the exculpatory clause valid?***

Argument for Tenant: An exculpatory clause in a contract for an essential service violates public policy. When an ill person seeks medical care, his doctor cannot require him to sign an exculpatory clause. In the same way, a person has to live somewhere. Her landlord cannot force her to sign a waiver.

Landlords tend to be wealthy and powerful. There is generally no equality of bargaining power between them. The tenants are not freely agreeing to the exculpatory language.

Moreover, if a landlord fails to maintain property, not just the tenant is at risk. Visitors, the mail carrier, and the general public could all walk through the Twin Lakes parking lot. The public's interest is served when landlords maintain their properties. They must be held liable when they negligently fail to maintain common areas and injuries result.

Argument for Landlord: Ms. Richards does indeed have to live somewhere, but she does not have to live on the plaintiff's property. Surely there are many dozens of properties nearby. If Richards had been dissatisfied with any part of the proposed lease—excessive rent, strict rules, or an exculpatory clause—she was free to take her business to another landlord.

Landlords may generally be wealthier than their tenants, but that fact alone does not mean that a landlord is so powerful that leases are offered on a "take it or leave it" basis. Here, the landlord stated the exculpatory clause plainly. This is a clear contract between adults, and it should stand in its entirety.

Bailment Cases

Bailment
Giving possession and control of personal property to another person.

Bailor
One who creates a bailment by delivering goods to another.

Bailee
A person who rightfully possesses goods belonging to another.

Exculpatory clauses are very common in bailment cases. **Bailment** means giving possession and control of personal property to another person. The person giving up possession is the **bailor**, and the one accepting possession is the **bailee**. When you leave your laptop computer with a dealer to be repaired, you create a bailment. The same is true when you check your coat at a restaurant or lend your Matisse to a museum. Bailees often try to limit their liability for damage to property by using an exculpatory clause.

Judges are slightly more apt to enforce an exculpatory clause in a bailment case because any harm is to *property* and not persons. But courts will still look at many of the same criteria we have just examined to decide whether a bailment contract is enforceable. In particular, when the bailee is engaged in an important public service, a court is once again likely to ignore the exculpatory clause. The following contrasting cases illustrate this.

In *Weiss v. Freeman*,[5] Weiss stored personal goods in Freeman's self-storage facility. Freeman's contract included an exculpatory clause relieving it of any and all liability. Weiss's goods were damaged by mildew, and she sued. The court held the exculpatory clause valid. The court considered self-storage to be a significant business, but not as vital as medical care or housing. It pointed out that a storage facility would not know what each customer stored and therefore could not anticipate the harm that might occur. Freedom of contract should prevail, the clause was enforceable, and Weiss got no money.

But in *Gardner v. Downtown Porsche Audi*,[6] Gardner left his Porsche 911 at Downtown for repairs. He signed an exculpatory clause saying that Downtown was "Not Responsible for Loss or Damage to Cars or Articles Left in Cars in Case of Fire, Theft, or Any Other Cause Beyond Our Control." Due to Downtown's negligence, Gardner's Porsche was stolen. The court held the exculpatory clause void. It ruled that contemporary society is utterly dependent upon automobile transportation and Downtown was therefore in a business of great

---

[5]1994 Tenn. App. LEXIS 393 (Tenn. Ct. App. 1993).

[6]180 Cal. App. 3d 713, 225 Cal. Rptr. 757, 1986 Cal. App. LEXIS 1542 (Cal. Ct. App. 1986).

public importance. No repair shop should be able to contract away liability, and Gardner won. (This case also illustrates that using 17 uppercase letters in one sentence does not guarantee legal victory.)

EXAM Strategy

Facts: Shauna flew a World War II fighter aircraft as a member of an exhibition flight team. While the team was performing in a delta formation, another plane collided with Shauna's aircraft, causing her to crash-land and leaving her permanently disabled. Shauna sued the other pilot and the team. The defendants moved to dismiss based on an exculpatory clause that Shauna had signed. The clause was one paragraph long, and it stated that Shauna knew team flying was inherently dangerous and could result in injury or death. She agreed not to hold the team or any members liable in case of an accident. Shauna argued that the clause should not be enforced against her if she could prove the other pilot was negligent. Please rule.

Strategy: The issue is whether the exculpatory clause is valid. Courts are likely to declare such clauses void if they concern vital activities like medical care, exclude an intentional tort or gross negligence, or if the parties had unequal bargaining power.

Result: This is a clear, short clause, between parties with equal bargaining power, and does not exclude an intentional tort or gross negligence. The activity is unimportant to the public welfare. The clause is valid. Even if the other pilot was negligent, Shauna will lose, meaning the court should dismiss her lawsuit.

Unconscionable Contracts

Gail Waters was young, naive, and insecure. A serious injury when she was 12 years old left her with an annuity, that is, a guaranteed annual payment for many years. When Gail was 21, she became involved with Thomas Beauchemin, an ex-convict, who introduced her to drugs. Beauchemin suggested that Gail sell her annuity to some friends of his, and she agreed. Beauchemin arranged for a lawyer to draw up a contract, and Gail signed it. She received $50,000 for her annuity, which at that time had a cash value of $189,000 and was worth, over its remaining 25 years, $694,000. Gail later decided this was not a wise bargain. Was the contract enforceable? That depends on the law of unconscionability.

An unconscionable contract is one that a court refuses to enforce because of fundamental unfairness. Even if a contract does not violate any specific statute or public policy, it may still be void if it "shocks the conscience" of the court.

Historically, a contract was considered unconscionable if it was "such as no man in his senses and not under delusion would make on the one hand, and as no honest and fair man would accept on the other."[7] The two factors that most often led a court to find unconscionability were (1) **oppression**, meaning that one party used its superior power to force a

Oppression
One party uses its superior power to force a contract on the weaker party.

[7] *Hume v. United States*, 132 U.S. 406, 411, 10 S.Ct. 134, 1889 U.S. LEXIS 1888 (1889), quoting *Earl of Chesterfield v. Janssen*, 38 Eng. Rep. 82, 100 (Ch. 1750).

contract on the weaker party, and (2) **surprise**, meaning that the weaker party did not fully understand the consequences of its agreement.

These cases have always been controversial because it is not easy to define oppression and unfair surprise. Further, anytime a court rejects a contract as unconscionable, it diminishes freedom of contract. If one party can escape a deal based on something as hard to define as unconscionability, then no one can rely as confidently on any agreement. As an English jurist said in 1824, "public policy is a very unruly horse, and when once you get astride it, you never know where it will carry you."[8]

Gail Waters won her case. The Massachusetts high court ruled:

> Beauchemin introduced the plaintiff to drugs, exhausted her credit card accounts to the sum of $6,000, unduly influenced her, suggested that the plaintiff sell her annuity contract, initiated the contract negotiations, was the agent of the defendants, and benefited from the contract between the plaintiff and the defendants. The defendants were represented by legal counsel; the plaintiff was not. The cash value of the annuity policy at the time the contract was executed was approximately four times greater than the price to be paid by the defendants. For payment of not more than $50,000 the defendants were to receive an asset that could be immediately exchanged for $189,000, or they could elect to hold it for its guaranteed term and receive $694,000.
>
> The defendants assumed no risk and the plaintiff gained no advantage. We are satisfied that the disparity of interests in this contract is so gross that the court cannot resist the inference that it was improperly obtained and is unconscionable.[9]

Adhesion Contracts

Adhesion contracts
Standard form contracts prepared by one party and presented to the other on a "take it or leave it" basis.

A related issue concerns **adhesion contracts**, which are standard form contracts prepared by one party and given to the other on a "take it or leave it" basis. We have all encountered them many times when purchasing goods or services. When a form contract is vigorously negotiated between equally powerful corporations, the resulting bargain is generally enforced. However, when the contract is simply presented to a consumer who has no ability to bargain, it is an adhesion contract and subject to an unconscionability challenge.

Worldwide Insurance v. Klopp

603 A.2d 788, 1992 Del. LEXIS 13
Supreme Court of Delaware, 1992

Facts: Ruth Klopp had auto insurance with Worldwide. She was injured in a serious accident that left her with permanent neck and back injuries. The other driver was uninsured, so Klopp filed a claim with Worldwide under her "uninsured motorist" coverage. Her policy required arbitration of such a claim, and the arbitrators awarded Klopp $90,000. But the policy also stated that if the arbitrators awarded more than the statutory minimum amount of insurance ($15,000), either side could appeal the award and request a full trial. Worldwide appealed and demanded a trial.

In the trial court, Klopp claimed that the appeal provision was unconscionable and void. The trial court agreed and entered judgment for the full $90,000. Worldwide appealed.

Issue: ***Is the provision that requires arbitration and then permits appeal by either party void as unconscionable?***

---

[8] *Richardson v. Mellish*, 2 Bing. 229, 103 Eng. Rep. 294, 303 (1824).
[9] *Waters v. Min Ltd.*, 412 Mass. 64, 587 N.E.2d 231, 1992 Mass. LEXIS 66 (1992).

Excerpts from Justice Walsh's Decision: The parties' views of the arbitration provision are polar opposites. Worldwide contends that the provision is a clear and unambiguous contractual undertaking granting both the insured and the insurer the right to appeal any award in excess of financial responsibility limits. Klopp argues that this provision is unconscionable and void as against public policy because it affords an advantage to one of the parties under a contract of adhesion.

The public policy of this State favors the resolution of disputes through arbitration. An insurance policy which provides for arbitration as its primary mechanism for dispute resolution is thus enforceable against the wishes of either contractual party. [But] our approval of the arbitration concept does not extend to any feature of a contract of adhesion, which, in whole or in part, is unconscionable.

Under the present policy language, both parties are bound by a low award which an insurance company is unlikely to appeal. While high awards may be appealed by either party, common experience suggests that it is unlikely that an insured would appeal such an award. It is the insurer who, generally, would be dissatisfied with a high award. The policy provision thus presents an "escape hatch" to the insurer for avoidance of high arbitration awards, whether or not the award was fair and reasonable. However, the insured, who would tend to be dissatisfied with a low award, is barred from appealing such an award, i.e., an award under [$15,000].

In our view, the policy provision at issue here promotes litigation, circumvents the arbitration process, and provides an arbitration escape device in favor of an insurance company. So viewed, the provision is contrary to the public policy of this State. Accordingly, we hold that a provision in an insurance policy which allows either party to demand a trial de novo, if the amount of an arbitrators' award exceeds a stated minimum amount but denies review for lesser awards, is void as against public policy and unenforceable. The Chancery Court was correct in striking this unconscionable clause.

The judgment of the Court of Chancery is *affirmed.*

The UCC: Unconscionability and Sales Law

With the creation of the Uniform Commercial Code (UCC), the law of unconscionability got a boost. The Code explicitly adopts unconscionability as a reason to reject a contract.[10] Although the Code directly applies only to the sale of goods, its unconscionability section has proven to be influential in other cases as well, and courts today are more receptive than they were 100 years ago to a contract defense of fundamental unfairness.

The drafters of the UCC reinforced the principle of unconscionability by including it in §2-302:

> If the court as a matter of law finds the contract or any clause of the contract to have been unconscionable at the time it was made the court may refuse to enforce the contract, or it may enforce the remainder of the contract without the unconscionable clause, or it may so limit the application of any unconscionable clause as to avoid any unconscionable result.

In Code cases, the issue of unconscionability often arises when a company attempts to limit the normal contract law remedies. Yet the Code itself allows such limitations, provided they are reasonable.

Section 2-719 provides in part:

> [A contract] may provide for remedies in addition to or in substitution for those provided [by the Code itself] *and may limit or alter the measure of damages recoverable*... as by limiting the buyer's remedies to return of the goods and repayment of the price...

In other words, the Code includes two potentially competing sections: §2-719 permits a seller to insist that the buyer's only remedy for defective goods is return of the purchase

[10]UCC §2-302.

price, but §2-302 says that *any unconscionable* provision is unenforceable. In lawsuits concerning defective goods, the seller often argues that the buyer's only remedies are those stated in the agreement, and the buyer responds that the contract limitation is unconscionable.

Electronic Data Systems (EDS) agreed to create complex software for Chubb Life America at a cost of $21 million. Chubb agreed to make staggered payments over many months as the work proceeded. The contract included a limitation on remedies, stating that if EDS became liable to Chubb, its maximum liability would be equal to two monthly payments.

EDS's work was woefully late and unusable, forcing Chubb to obtain its software elsewhere. Chubb sued, claiming $40 million in damages based on the money paid to EDS and additional funds spent purchasing alternative goods. EDS argued that the contract limited its liability to two monthly payments, a fraction of Chubb's damage. Chubb, of course, responded that the limitation was unconscionable.

The court noted that both parties were large, sophisticated corporations. As they negotiated the agreement, the companies both used experienced attorneys and independent consultants. This was no contract of adhesion presented to a meek consumer, but an allocation of risk resulting from hard bargaining. The court declared that the clause was valid, and EDS owed no more than two monthly payments.[11]

Chapter Conclusion

It is not enough to bargain effectively and obtain a contract that gives you exactly what you want. You must also be sure that the contract is legal. What appears to be an insurance contract might legally be an invalid wager. Unintentionally forgetting to obtain a state license to perform a certain job could mean you will never be paid for it. Bargaining a contract with a noncompete or exculpatory clause that is too one-sided may lead a court to ignore it. Legality is multifaceted, sometimes subtle, and always important.

Exam Review

Illegal contracts are void and unenforceable. Illegality most often arises in these settings:

1. **WAGERING** A purely speculative contract—whether for gambling or insurance—is likely to be unenforceable. (pp. 296–297)

2. **LICENSING** When the licensing statute is designed to protect the public, a contract by an unlicensed plaintiff is generally unenforceable. When such a statute is designed merely to raise revenue, a contract by an unlicensed plaintiff is generally enforceable. (pp. 297–298)

[11] *Colonial Life Insurance Co. v. Electronic Data Systems Corp.*, 817 F. Supp. 235, 1993 U.S. Dist. LEXIS 4123 (D.N.H. 1993).

Question: James Wagner agreed to build a house for Nancy Graham. Wagner was not licensed as a contractor, and Graham knew it. When the house was finished, Graham refused to pay the final $23,000, and Wagner sued. Who will prevail?

Strategy: A licensing statute designed to protect the public is strictly enforced, but that is not true for one intended only to raise revenue. What was the purpose of this statute? (See the "Result" at the end of this section.)

3. USURY Excessive interest is generally unenforceable and may be fatal to the entire debt. Credit card debt is often exempt from usury laws. (pp. 299–300)

Question: McElroy owned 104 acres worth about $230,000. He got into financial difficulties and approached Grisham, asking to borrow $100,000. Grisham refused, but ultimately the two reached this agreement: McElroy would sell Grisham his property for $80,000, and the contract would include a clause allowing McElroy to repurchase the land within two years for $120,000. McElroy later claimed the contract was void. Is he right?

Strategy: Loans involving usury do not always include a clearly visible interest rate. You may have to do some simple math to see the interest being charged. McElroy wanted to borrow $100,000, but instead sold his property, with the right to repurchase. If he did repurchase, how much interest would he have effectively paid? (See the "Result" at the end of this section.)

4. NONCOMPETE A noncompete clause in the sale of a business must be limited to a reasonable time, geographic area, and scope of activity. In an employment contract, such a clause is considered reasonable—and enforceable—only to protect trade secrets, confidential information, and customer lists. (pp. 301–304)

Question: The purchaser of a business insisted on putting this clause in the sales contract: The seller would not compete, for five years, "anywhere in the United States, the continent of North America, or anywhere else on earth." What danger does that contract represent *to the purchaser?*

Strategy: This is a noncompete clause based on the sale of a business. Such clauses are valid if reasonable. Is this clause reasonable? If it is unreasonable, what might a court do? (See the "Result" at the end of this section.)

5. EXCULPATORY CLAUSES These clauses are generally void if the activity involved is in the public interest, the parties are greatly unequal in bargaining power, or the clause is unclear. In other cases, they are generally enforced. (pp. 304–307)

6. **UNCONSCIONABILITY** Oppression and surprise may create an unconscionable bargain. An adhesion contract is especially suspect when it is imposed by a corporation on a consumer or small company. Under the UCC, a limitation of liability is less likely to be unconscionable when both parties are sophisticated corporations. (pp. 307–310)

2. Result: This statute was designed to protect the public. Wagner was unlicensed and cannot enforce the contract. Graham wins.

3. Result: By selling at $80,000 and repurchasing at $120,000, McElroy would be paying $40,000 in interest on an $80,000 loan. The 50 percent rate is usurious. The court prohibited Graham from collecting the interest.

4. Result: "Anywhere else on earth"? This is almost certainly unreasonable. It is hard to imagine a purchaser who would legitimately need such wide-ranging protection. In some states, a court might rewrite the clause, limiting the effect to the seller's state, or some reasonable area. However, in other states, a court finding a clause unreasonable will declare it void in its entirety—enabling the seller to open a competing business next door.

Multiple-Choice Questions

1. At a fraternity party, George mentions that he is going to learn to hang-glide during spring break. Vicki, a casual friend, overhears him, and the next day she purchases a $100,000 life insurance policy on George's life. George has a happy week of hang-gliding. But on the way home, he is bitten by a parrot and dies of a rare tropical illness. Vicki files a claim for $100,000. The insurance company refuses to pay.
   (a) Vicki will win $100,000, but only if she mentioned animal bites to the insurance agent.
   (b) Vicki will win $100,000 regardless of whether she mentioned animal bites to the insurance agent.
   (c) Vicki will win $50,000.
   (d) Vicki will win nothing.

2. Now assume that Vicky has loaned George $50,000. George again mentions that he is going to learn to hang-glide during spring break, so Vicki purchases the $100,000 life insurance policy on George's life. If George dies and the insurance company refuses to pay…
   (a) Vicki will win $100,000, but only if she mentioned animal bites to the insurance agent.
   (b) Vicki will win $100,000 regardless of whether she mentioned animal bites to the insurance agent.
   (c) Vicki will win $50,000.
   (d) Vicki will win nothing.

3. KwikFix, a Fortune 500 company, contracts with Allied Rocket, another huge company, to provide the software for Allied's new Jupiter Probe rocket for

$14 million. The software is negligently designed, and when the rocket blasts off from Cape Kennedy, it travels only as far as Fort Lauderdale before crashing to Earth. Allied Rocket sues for $200 million and proves that as a result of the disaster, it lost a huge government contract, worth at least that much, which KwikFix was aware of. KwikFix responds that its contract with Allied included a clause limiting its liability to the value of the contract. Is the contract clause valid?

(a) The clause is unenforceable because it is unconscionable.

(b) The clause is unenforceable because it is exculpatory.

(c) The clause is enforceable because both parties are sophisticated corporations.

(d) The clause is enforceable because $200 million is an unconscionable claim.

4. Ricki goes to a baseball game. The back of her ticket clearly reads: "Fan agrees to hold team blameless for all injuries—pay attention to the game at all times for your own safety!" In the first inning, a foul ball hits Ricki in the elbow. She ____________ sue the team over the foul ball. Ricki spends the next several innings riding the opposing team's first baseman. The *nicest* thing she says to him is, "You suck, Franklin!" In the eighth inning, Franklin has had enough. He grabs the ballboy's chair and throws it into the stands, injuring Ricki's other elbow. Ricki ____________ sue the team over the thrown chair.

(a) can; can

(b) can; cannot

(c) cannot; can

(d) cannot; cannot

5. Jim, about to start a pickup soccer game, asks Desiree if she will hold his wallet while he plays. Desiree, a law student, says, "Sure, if you'll sign this exculpatory clause holding me blameless for negligence." Jim is very surprised, but he signs the paper that Desiree holds out for him. A bailment ____________ been created. If Desiree is careless and loses the wallet, she ____________ be liable to Jim.

(a) has; will

(b) has; will not

(c) has not; will

(d) has not; will not

Essay Questions

1. For 20 years, Art's Flower Shop relied almost exclusively on advertising in the yellow pages to bring business to its shop in a small West Virginia town. One year, the yellow pages printer accidentally did not print Art's ad, and Art's suffered an enormous drop in business. Art's sued for negligence and won a judgment of $50,000 from the jury, but the printing company appealed, claiming that under an exculpatory clause in the contract, the company could not be liable to Art's for more than the cost of the ad, about $910. Art's claimed that the exculpatory clause was unconscionable. Please rule.

2. Brockwell left his boat to be repaired at Lake Gaston Sales. The boat contained electronic equipment and other personal items. Brockwell signed a form stating that Lake Gaston had no responsibility for any loss to any property in or on the boat. Brockwell's electronic equipment was stolen and other personal items were damaged, and he sued. Is the exculpatory clause enforceable?

3. Guyan Machinery, a West Virginia manufacturing corporation, hired Albert Voorhees as a salesman and required him to sign a contract stating that if he left Guyan, he would not work for a competing corporation anywhere within 250 miles of West Virginia for a two-year period. Later, Voorhees left Guyan and began working at Polydeck Corp., another West Virginia manufacturer. The only product Polydeck made was urethane screens, which comprised half of 1 percent of Guyan's business. Is Guyan entitled to enforce its noncompete clause?

4. 810 Associates owned a 42-story skyscraper in midtown Manhattan. The building had a central station fire alarm system, which was monitored by Holmes Protection. A fire broke out and Holmes received the signal. But Holmes's inexperienced dispatcher misunderstood the signal and failed to summon the fire department for about nine minutes, permitting tremendous damage. 810 sued Holmes, which defended based on an exculpatory clause that relieved Holmes of any liability caused in any way. Holmes's dispatcher was negligent. Does it matter *how* negligent he was?

5. ***YOU BE THE JUDGE* WRITING PROBLEM** Oasis Waterpark, located in Palm Springs, California, sought out Hydrotech Systems, Inc., a New York corporation, to design and construct a surfing pool. Hydrotech replied that it could design the pool and sell all the necessary equipment to Oasis, but it could not build the pool because it was not licensed in California. Oasis insisted that Hydrotech do the construction work because Hydrotech had unique expertise in these pools. Oasis promised to arrange for a licensed California contractor to "work with" Hydrotech on the construction; Oasis also assured Hydrotech that it would pay the full contract price of $850,000, regardless of any licensing issues. Hydrotech designed and installed the pool as ordered. But Oasis failed to make the final payment of $110,000. Hydrotech sued. Can Hydrotech sue for either breach of contract or fraud (trickery)? **Argument for Oasis:** The licensing law protects the public from incompetence and dishonesty. The legislature made the section strict: no license, no payment. If the court were to start picking and choosing which unlicensed contractors could win a suit, it would be inviting incompetent workers to endanger the public and then come into court and try their luck. That is precisely the danger the legislature seeks to avoid. **Argument for Hydrotech:** This is not the kind of case the legislature was worried about. Hydrotech has never solicited work in California. Hydrotech went out of its way to avoid doing any contracting work, informing Oasis that it was unlicensed in the state. Oasis insisted on bringing Hydrotech into the state to do work. If Oasis has its way, word will go out that any owner can get free work done by hiring an *unlicensed* builder. Make any promises you want, get the work done to your satisfaction, and then stiff the contractor—you'll never have to pay.

Discussion Questions

1. ***ETHICS:*** Richard and Michelle Kommit traveled to New Jersey to have fun in the casinos. While in Atlantic City, they used their MasterCard to withdraw cash from an ATM conveniently located in the "pit"—the gambling area of a casino. They ran up debts of $5,500 on the credit card and did not pay. The Connecticut National Bank sued for the money. Law aside, who has the moral high ground? Is it acceptable for the *casino* to offer ATM services in the gambling pit? If a *credit card* company allows customers to withdraw cash in a casino, is it encouraging them to lose money? Do *the Kommits* have any ethical right to use the ATM, attempt to win money by gambling, and then seek to avoid liability?

2. The Justice Department recently shut down three of the most popular online poker websites (Poker Stars, Absolute Poker, and Full Tilt Poker). State agencies take countless actions each year to stop illegal gaming operations. Do you believe that gambling by adults *should* be regulated? If so, which types? Rate the following types of gambling from most acceptable to least acceptable:

– online poker	– state lotteries	– horse racing
– casino gambling	– bets on pro sports	– bets on college sports

3. Van hires Terri to add an electrical outlet to his living room for his new HDTV. Terri does an excellent job, and the new outlet works perfectly. She presents Van with a bill for $200. But Terri is not a licensed electrician. Her state sets licensing standards in the profession to protect the public. And so, Van can refuse to pay Terri's bill. Is this reasonable? *Should* he be able to avoid payment?

4. Should noncompete agreements in employment contracts be illegal altogether? Is there equality of bargaining power between the company and the employee? Should non-competes be limited to top officers of a company? Would you be upset if a prospective employer asked *you* to agree to a one year covenant not to compete?

5. Revisit the Gail Waters example on page **[307]**. Imagine now that Beauchemin was not her boyfriend, and that he had not introduced her to the drugs to which she became addicted. If all other facts in the case remain the same, would the purchase of the annuity for $50,000 still be unconscionable, in your opinion?

CHAPTER 14

VOIDABLE CONTRACTS: CAPACITY AND CONSENT

Katie, age 17, visits her local electronics store to buy a new laptop. At the register, she pays $400 in cash for the machine. No one is with her, and the cashier does not ask her to show her ID.

Out in the parking lot, Katie's cell phone rings. As she fumbles for it, she loses her grip on the new laptop. It falls to the pavement—crack!—bounces once, and comes to rest a few feet away from her.

Just then, an H2 Hummer rounds the corner. It runs over Katie's new laptop. "Ugg …" she says, feeling nauseous. The SUV stops, and the reverse lights come on. It backs slowly over the laptop again. The driver, oblivious, rolls down his window and asks Katie, "Say, is there a gas station around here?"

Just then, an H2 Hummer rounds the corner. It runs over Katie's new laptop.

"Ah … that way," a shocked Katie says, pointing to a sign in the distance. "But you just …"

"Oh, I see it! Thanks a million!" The driver puts the Hummer in gear and drives over the laptop a third time. The small jolt loosens the one lug nut securing the spare tire to the back of the SUV. The heavy spare falls directly on top of what remains of Katie's new laptop.

Scooping up wires, bits of plastic, and pieces of metal, she goes back inside the store. Dumping the pieces on the customer service desk, she says, "I've changed my mind about this computer."

The clerk looks at the collection of laptop parts, shakes his head, and points to a sign behind him. "Look, I can't take merchandise back if it's damaged. And this laptop is, ah, damaged."

"Too bad," Katie says. " I want my money back. Now."

Is Katie entitled to a full refund? In most states, *yes*.

This chapter examines **voidable contracts**. When a contract is voidable, one party has the option either to enforce or terminate the agreement. Two specific issues are presented.

Capacity concerns the legal ability of a party to enter a contract in the first place. Someone may lack capacity because of his young age or mental infirmity. **Consent** refers to whether a contracting party truly understood what she was getting into and whether she made the agreement voluntarily. Consent issues arise in cases of fraud, mistake, duress, and undue influence.

CAPACITY

Capacity is the legal ability to enter into a contract. An adult of sound mind has capacity. Generally, any deal she enters into will be enforced if all elements on the Contracts Checklist—agreement, consideration, and so forth—are present. But two groups of people usually lack legal capacity: minors and those with a mental impairment.

Contracts Checklist

- ☐ Offer
- ☐ Acceptance
- ☐ Consideration
- ☐ Legality
- ☑ Capacity
- ☐ Consent
- ☐ Writing

Minors

In contract law, a minor is someone under the age of 18. Because a minor lacks legal capacity, she normally can create only a voidable contract. **A voidable contract may be canceled by the party who lacks capacity.** Notice that *only the party lacking capacity* may cancel the agreement. So a minor who enters into a contract generally may choose between enforcing the agreement or negating it. The other party—an adult, or perhaps a store—has no such right. Voidable contracts are very different from those that are void, which we examined in Chapter 13, on legality. A *void* contract is illegal from the beginning and may not be enforced by either party. A *voidable* contract is legal but permits one party to escape, if she so wishes.

Disaffirmance

A minor who wishes to escape from a contract generally may **disaffirm** it; that is, he may notify the other party that he refuses to be bound by the agreement. There are several ways a minor may disaffirm a contract. He may simply tell the other party, orally or in writing, that he will not honor the deal. Or he may disaffirm a contract by refusing to perform his obligations under it. A minor may go further—he can undo a contract that has already been completed by filing a suit to **rescind** the contract; that is, to have a court formally cancel it.

Disaffirm
To give notice of refusal to be bound by an agreement.

Rescind
To cancel a contract.

Kevin Green was 16 when he signed a contract with Star Chevrolet to buy a used Camaro. Because he was a minor, the deal was voidable. When the Camaro blew a gasket and Kevin informed Star Chevrolet that he wanted his money back, he was disaffirming the contract. He happened to do it because the car suddenly seemed a poor buy, but he could have disaffirmed for any reason at all, such as deciding that he no longer liked Camaros. When Kevin disaffirmed, he was entitled to his money back.

Restitution

A minor who disaffirms a contract must return the consideration he has received, to the extent he is able. Restoring the other party to its original position is called **restitution**. The consideration that Kevin Green received in the contract was, of course, the Camaro.

Restitution
Restoring an injured party to its original position.

What happens if the minor is not able to return the consideration because he no longer has it or it has been destroyed? Most states hold that the minor is *still* entitled to his money back. A minority of states follow the **status quo rule**, which provides that, if a minor cannot return the consideration, the adult or store is only required to return its *profit margin* to the minor.

In the opening scenario, Katie attempted to return a destroyed laptop for the full purchase price of $400. Assume that the store paid a computer manufacturer $350 for the laptop and then marked it up $50.

In most states, Katie would be entitled to the full $400 purchase price, even though the laptop is now worthless. The sign at the customer service desk would have no effect, and the store would have to absorb the loss. But, if Katie lives in a state with the status quo rule, then the store will have to refund only $50 to Katie. It is permitted to keep the other $350 so that it breaks even on the transaction, or is "returned to the status quo."

Ethics The rule permitting a minor to disaffirm a contract is designed to discourage adults from making deals with innocent children and it is centuries old. Is this rule still workable in our modern consumer society? There are entire industries devoted to (and dependent upon) minors. Think of children's films, music, sneakers, and toys. Does this rule imperil retailers? Is it *right* to give a 17-year-old high school senior so much power to cancel agreements? In the opening scenario, is it reasonable for Katie to seek a full refund, or is she taking advantage of the system?

Timing of Disaffirmance/Ratification

A minor may disaffirm a contract anytime before she reaches age 18. She also may disaffirm within a reasonable time *after* turning 18. Suppose that 17-year-old Betsy signs a contract to buy a $3,000 stereo. The following week, she picks up the system and pays for it in full. Four months later, she turns 18, and two months after that, she disaffirms the contract. Her disaffirmance is effective. In most states, she gets 100 percent of her money back. In some cases, minors have been entitled to disaffirm a contract several *years* after turning 18. But the minor's right to disaffirm ends if she ratifies the contract. **Ratification** is made by any words or action indicating an intention to be bound by the contract. Suppose Betsy, age 17, buys her stereo on credit, promising to pay $150 per month. She has made only four payments by the time she turns 18, but after reaching her majority, she continues to pay every month for six more months. Then she attempts to disaffirm. Too late. Her actions—payment of the monthly bill for six months as an adult—ratified the contract she entered into as a minor. She is now fully obligated to pay the entire $3,000, on the agreed-upon schedule.

Ratification
Words or actions indicating an intention to be bound by a contract.

Exception: Necessaries

A necessary is something essential to the minor's life and welfare. **On a contract for necessaries, a minor must pay for the value of the benefit received.** In other words, the minor may still disaffirm the contract and return whatever is unused. But he is liable to pay for whatever benefit he obtained from the goods while he had them. Food, clothing, housing, and medical care are necessaries. Thus a 16-year-old who buys and eats a 99-cent cheeseburger cannot later seek his 99 cents from the fast food restaurant.

Exception: Misrepresentation of Age

The rules change somewhat if a minor lies about his age. Sixteen-year-old Dan is delighted to learn from his friend Betsy that a minor can buy a fancy stereo system, use it for a year or so, and then get his money back. Dan drops into SoundBlast and asks to buy a $4,000 surround-sound system. The store clerk says that the store no longer sells expensive systems to underage customers. Dan produces a fake driver's license indicating that he is 18, and the clerk sells him the system. A year later, Dan drives up to SoundBlast and unloads the system, now in shambles. He asks for his $4,000 back. Is he still permitted to disaffirm?

States have been troubled by this problem, and there is no clear rule. A few states will still permit Dan to disaffirm the contract entirely. The theory is that a minor must be saved from his own poor judgment, including his foolish lie. Many states, though, will prohibit Dan from disaffirming the contract. They take the reasonable position that the law was intended to protect childhood innocence, not calculated deceit.

Mentally Impaired Persons

You are a trial court judge. Don wants you to rule that his father, Cedric, is mentally incompetent and, on behalf of Cedric, to terminate a contract he signed. Here is the evidence:

Cedric is a 75-year-old millionaire who keeps $300,000 stuffed in pillow cases in the attic. He lives in a filthy house with a parrot whom he calls the Bishop, an iguana named Orlando, and a tortoise known as Mrs. Sedgely. All of the pets have small beds in Cedric's grungy bedroom, and each one eats at the dining table with its master. Cedric pays college students $50 an hour to read poetry to the animals, but he forbids the reading of sonnets, which he regards as "the devil's handiwork."

Don has been worried about Cedric's bizarre behavior for several years and has urged his father to enter a nursing home. Last week, when Don stopped in to visit, Cedric became angry at him, accusing his son of disrespecting the Bishop and Mrs. Sedgely, who were enjoying a 15th-century Castilian poem that Jane, a college student, was reading. Don then blurted out that Cedric was no longer able to take care of himself. Cedric snapped back, "I'll show you how capable I am." On the back of a 40-year-old menu, he scratched out a contract promising to give Jane "$100,000 today and $200,000 one year from today if she agrees to feed, house, and care for the Bishop, Orlando, and Mrs. Sedgely for the rest of their long lives." Jane *quickly* signed the agreement. Don urges that the court, on Cedric's behalf, declare the contract void. How will you rule? Courts often struggle when deciding cases of mental competence.

A person suffers from a mental impairment if, by reason of mental illness or defect, he is unable to understand the nature and consequences of the transaction.[1] The mental impairment can be due to some mental illness, such as schizophrenia, or to mental retardation, brain injury, senility, or any other cause that renders the person unable to understand the nature and consequences of the contract.

A party suffering a mental impairment usually creates only a voidable contract. The impaired person has the right to disaffirm the contract just as a minor does. But again, the contract is voidable, not void. The mentally impaired party generally has the right to full performance if she wishes.

The law creates an exception: if a person has been adjudicated insane, then all of his future agreements are void. "Adjudicated insane" means that a judge has made a formal finding that a person is mentally incompetent and has assigned the person a guardian.

How will a court evaluate Cedric's mental status? Of course, if there had already been a judicial determination that he was insane, any contract he signed would be void. Since no judge has issued such a ruling about Cedric, the court will listen to doctors or therapists who have evaluated him and to anyone else who can testify about Cedric's recent conduct. The court may also choose to look at the contract itself, to see if it is so lopsided that no competent person would agree to it.

---

[1]Restatement (Second) of Contracts §15.

How will Don fare in seeking to preserve Cedric's wealth? Poorly. Unless Don has more evidence than we have heard thus far, he is destined to eat canned tuna while Jane and the Bishop dine on caviar. Cedric is decidedly eccentric, and perhaps unwise. But those characteristics do not prove mental impairment. Neither does leaving a fortune to a poetry reader. If Don could produce evidence from a psychiatrist that Cedric, for example, was generally delusional or could not distinguish a parrot from a religious leader, that would persuade a court of mental impairment. But on the evidence presented thus far, Mrs. Sedgely and friends will be living well.[2]

Intoxication

Similar rules apply in cases of drug or alcohol intoxication. When one party is so intoxicated that he cannot understand the nature and consequences of the transaction, the contract is voidable.

We wish to stress that courts are *highly* skeptical of intoxication arguments. If you go out drinking and make a foolish agreement, you are probably stuck with it. Even if you are too drunk to drive, you are probably not nearly too drunk to make a contract. If your blood alcohol level is, say, .08, your coordination and judgment are poor. Driving in such a condition is dangerous. But you probably have a fairly clear awareness of what is going on around you.

Upon the question of his intoxication, he was corroborated abundantly.

To back out of a contract on the grounds of intoxication, you must be able to provide evidence that you did not understand the "nature of the agreement," or the basic deal that you made.

The following landmark case is a rare exception, and the defendant was able to escape the deal. The defendant had lots of witnesses who testified that he had no idea what he was doing.

[2]For a similar case, see *Harwell v. Garrett*, 239 Ark. 551, 393 S.W.2d 256, 1965 Ark. LEXIS 1033 (1965).

Landmark Case

Babcock v. Engel

58 Mont. 597; 194 P. 137
Supreme Court of Montana, 1920

Facts: While Charles Engel's wife was out of town, he sat home alone, drinking mightily. During this period, he made an agreement with G. M. Babcock to trade a 320-acre farm and $2,000 worth of personal property for a hotel. Engel's property was worth approximately twice the value of the hotel. Engel later refused to honor the deal on the grounds that he had been intoxicated when he made the agreement. Babcock sued, but the jury sided with Engel and dismissed the complaint. Babcock appealed.

Issue: ***Was Engel so intoxicated that his agreement with Babcock became voidable?***

Excerpts from Justice Holloway's Decision: If, as a matter of fact, Engel was so far under the influence of intoxicating liquor when he signed the contract that he was incapable of giving his assent, it would be voidable at the election of Engel when he became sober.

[T]he jury answered that on November 22, Engel was "so under the influence of intoxicating liquors as to deprive him of his powers of reasoning and render him unable to comprehend the consequences of his act in executing said agreement."

Engel himself testified to the effect that, availing himself of his wife's absence from home, he had been indulging greatly to excess and had been drunk on November 21; that he drank heavily of whisky which he had at his home on the morning of November 22; that immediately upon his arrival in the town, he had four or five drinks of whisky and blackberry before he entered upon the negotiations with Babcock.

Four other witnesses, each apparently disinterested, testified that at the time in question, Engel was intoxicated, could not comprehend the nature of his acts, in other words, that he was not qualified to transact business. The jury determined upon the credibility of the witnesses.

Intoxication is not made a defense by the Codes, and there was a time in the history of our jurisprudence when courts refused to lend their aid to relieve one from the consequences of his own voluntary intemperance, but the doctrine has long since been abandoned. The courts do not now concern themselves so much with the question of intoxication as with the question of contractual capacity, and if in fact either party is not mentally capable of giving his free consent to the terms disclosed by the writing, it is altogether immaterial by what cause his incapacity was produced. The courts have simply recognized the fact that intoxication, among other things, may render a person incapable of making a binding contract.

The test approved by the great majority of the decisions is the same which is applied in other forms of mental derangement, namely, that the deed or contract will be voidable if the person, at the time of its execution, was so far under the influence of intoxicants as to be unable to understand the nature and consequences of his act, and unable to bring to bear upon the business in hand any degree of intelligent choice and purpose.

Affirmed.

Restitution

A mentally infirm party who seeks to void a contract must make restitution. If a party succeeds with a claim of mental impairment, the court will normally void the contract but will require the impaired party to give back whatever she got. Suppose Danielle buys a Rolls-Royce and promises in writing to pay $4,000 per month for five years. Three weeks later, she seeks to void the contract on the grounds of mental impairment. She must return the Rolls. If the car has depreciated, Danielle normally will have to pay for the decrease in value. What happens if restitution is impossible? Generally, courts require a mentally infirm person to make full restitution if the contract is to be rescinded. If restitution is impossible, the court will not rescind the agreement unless the infirm party can show bad faith by the other. This is because, unlike minority, which is generally easy to establish, mental competence may not be so apparent to the other person negotiating.

Reality of Consent

Smiley offers to sell you his house for $300,000, and you agree in writing to buy it. After you move in, you discover that the house is sinking into the earth at the rate of six inches per week. In twelve months, your only access to the house may be through the chimney. You sue, seeking to rescind. You argue that when you signed the contract, you did not truly consent because you lacked essential information. In this section we look at four claims that parties make in an effort to rescind a contract based on lack of valid consent: (1) fraud, (2) mistake, (3) duress, and (4) undue influence.

Contracts Checklist

- ☐ Offer
- ☐ Acceptance
- ☐ Consideration
- ☐ Legality
- ☐ Capacity
- ☑ Consent
- ☐ Writing

Fraud

Fraud begins when a party to a contract says something that is factually wrong. "This house has no termites," says a homeowner to a prospective buyer. If the house is swarming with the nasty pests, the statement is a misrepresentation. But does it amount to fraud? An injured person must show the following:

1. The defendant knew that his statement was false, or that he made the statement recklessly and without knowledge of whether it was false.
2. The false statement was material.
3. The injured party justifiably relied on the statement.

Element One: Intentional or Reckless Misrepresentation of Fact

The injured party must show a false statement of fact. Notice that this does not mean the statement was a necessarily a "lie." If a homeowner says that the famous architect Stanford White designed her house, but Bozo Loco actually did the work, it is a false statement.

Now, if the owner knows that Loco designed the house, she has committed the first element of fraud. And, if she has no idea who designed the house, her assertion that it was "Stanford White" also meets the first element.

But the owner might have a good reason for the error. Perhaps a local history book identifies the house as a Stanford White. If she makes the statement with a reasonable belief that she is telling the truth, she has made an innocent misrepresentation (discussed in the next section) and not fraud.

Opinions and "puffery" do not amount to fraud. An opinion is not a statement of fact. A seller says, "I think land values around here will be going up 20 or 30 percent for the foreseeable future." That statement is pretty enticing to a buyer, but it is not a false statement of fact. The maker is clearly stating her own opinion, and the buyer who relies on it does so at his peril. A close relative of opinion is something called "puffery."

Get ready for one of the most astonishing experiences you've ever had! This section on puffery is going to be the finest section of any textbook you have ever read! You're going to find the issue intriguing, the writing dazzling, and the legal summary unforgettable!

"But what happens," you might wonder, "if this section fails to astonish? What if I find the issue dull, the writing mediocre, and the legal summary incomprehensible? Can I sue for fraud?" No. The promises we made were mere puffery. A statement is puffery when a reasonable person would realize that it is a sales pitch, representing the exaggerated opinion of the seller. Puffery is not a statement of fact. Because puffery is not factual, it is never a basis for rescission.

Consumers filed a class action against Intel Corporation, claiming fraud. They asserted that Intel advertised its "Pentium 4" computer chip as the "best" in the market when in fact it was no faster than the Pentium III chip. The Illinois Supreme Court dismissed the claims, asserting that no reasonable consumer would make a purchase relying solely on the name "Pentium 4." Even if the consumers could show that Intel plotted to persuade the market that the Pentium 4 was the finest processor, they are demonstrating nothing but puffery.

[Saying that the Pentium 4 is "better" or "best"] could mean that the Pentium 4 is cheaper, smaller, more reliable, of higher quality, better for resale, more durable, creates less heat, uses less electricity, is more compatible with some versions of software, or is simply the latest in a temporal line of processors. Because the term "better" as a mere suggestion in the name "Pentium 4" is not capable of precise measuring, it is mere puffery and therefore not actionable. That is true even if Intel specifically set out to show the market that the Pentium 4 was the best processor to date.[3]

[3]*Barbara's Sales, Inc. v. Intel Corp.*, 879 N.E.2d 910 (Ill. 2007).

Courts have found many similar phrases to be puffery, including "high-quality," "expert workmanship," and "you're in good hands with us."

Element Two: Materiality

The injured party must demonstrate that the statement was material, or important. A minor misstatement does not meet this second element of fraud. Was the misstatement likely to influence the decision of the misled party significantly? If so, it was material.

Imagine a farmer selling a piece of his land. He measures the acres himself, and calculates a total of 200. If the actual acreage is 199, he has almost certainly not made a *material* misstatement. But if the actual acreage is 150, he has.

Element Three: Justifiable Reliance

The injured party also must show that she actually did rely on the false statement and that her reliance was reasonable. Suppose the seller of a gas station lies through his teeth about the structural soundness of the building. The buyer believes what he hears but does not much care because he plans to demolish the building and construct a day-care center. There was a material misstatement but no reliance, and the buyer may not rescind.

The reliance must be justifiable—that is, reasonable. If the seller of wilderness land tells Lewis that the area is untouched by pollution, but Lewis can see a large lake on the property covered with six inches of oily red scum, Lewis is not justified in relying on the seller's statements. If he goes forward with the purchase, he may not rescind.

No Duty to Investigate In the previous example, Lewis must act reasonably and keep his eyes open if he walks around the "wilderness" property. But he has no duty to undertake an investigation of what he is told. In other words, if the seller states that the countryside is pure and the lake looks crystal clear, Lewis is not obligated to take water samples and have them tested by a laboratory. A party to a contract has no obligation to investigate the other party's factual statements.

Plaintiff's Remedies for Fraud

In the case of fraud, the injured party generally has a choice of rescinding the contract or suing for damages or, in some cases, doing both. The contract is voidable, which meant that injured party is not *forced* to rescind the deal but may if he wants. Fraud *permits* the injured party to cancel. Alternatively, the injured party can sue for damages—the difference between what the contract promised and what it delivered.

Nancy learns that the building she bought has a terrible heating system. A new one will cost $12,000. If the seller told her the system was "like new," Nancy may rescind the deal. But it may be economically harmful for her to do so. She might have sold her old house, hired a mover, taken a new job, and so forth. What are her other remedies? She could move into the new house and sue for the difference between what she got and what was promised, which is $12,000, the cost of replacing the heating system.

In some states, a party injured by fraud may both rescind *and* sue for damages. In these states, Nancy could rescind her contract, get her deposit back, and then sue the seller for any damages she has suffered. Her damages might be, for example, a lost opportunity to buy another house or wasted moving expenses.

In fact, this last option—rescinding and still suing for damages—is available in all states when a contract is for the sale of goods. **UCC §2-721 permits a party to rescind a contract and then sue for damages when fraud is committed.**

Innocent Misrepresentation

If all elements of fraud are present except the misrepresentation of fact was not made intentionally or recklessly, then **innocent misrepresentation** has occurred. So, if a person misstates a material fact and induces reliance, but he had good reason to believe that his statement was true, then he has not committed fraud. Most states allow recission of a contract, but not damages, in such a case.

Special Problem: Silence

We know that a party negotiating a contract may not misrepresent a material fact. The house seller may not say that "the roof is in great shape" when she sleeps under an umbrella to avoid rain. But what about silence? Suppose the seller knows the roof is in dreadful condition but the buyer never asks. Does the seller have an affirmative obligation to disclose what she knows?

This is perhaps the hottest topic today in the law of misrepresentation. In 1817, the United States Supreme Court laid down the general rule that a party had no duty to disclose, even when he knew that the other person was negotiating under a mistake.[4] In other words, the Court was reinforcing the old rule of *caveat emptor*, "let the buyer beware." But social attitudes about fairness have changed. Today, a seller who knows something that the buyer does not know is often required to divulge it.

Nondisclosure of a fact amounts to misrepresentation in these four cases: (1) where disclosure is necessary to *correct a previous assertion;* (2) where disclosure would correct a *basic mistaken assumption* that the other party is relying on; (3) where disclosure would correct the other party's *mistaken understanding about a writing;* or (4) where there is *a relationship of trust* between the two parties.[5]

To Correct a Previous Assertion. During the course of negotiations, one party's perception of the facts may change. When an earlier statement later appears inaccurate, the change generally must be reported.

W. R. Grace & Co. wanted to buy a natural-gas field in Mississippi. An engineer's report indicated the presence of large gas reserves. On the basis of the engineering report, the Continental Illinois National Bank committed to a $75 million nonrecourse production loan. A "nonrecourse loan" meant that Continental would be repaid only with revenues from the gas field. After Continental committed, but before it had closed on the loan, Grace had an exploratory well drilled and struck it rich—with water. The land would never produce any gas. Without informing Continental of the news, Grace closed the $75 million loan. When Grace failed to repay, Continental sued and won. A party who learns new information indicating that a previous statement is inaccurate must disclose the bad news.[6]

She also knew that a reasonable buyer might avoid a haunted house, fearing grisly events ...

To Correct a Basic Mistaken Assumption. When one party knows that the other is negotiating with a mistaken assumption about an important fact, the party who knows of the error must correct it. Jeffrey Stambovsky agreed to buy Helen Ackley's house in Nyack, New York, for $650,000. Stambovsky signed a contract and made a $32,500 down payment.

---

[4] *Laidlaw v. Organ*, 15 U.S. 178, 1817 U.S. LEXIS 396 (1817).

[5] Restatement (Second) of Contracts §161.

[6] *FDIC v. W.R. Grace & Co.*, 877 F.2d 614, 1989 U.S. App. LEXIS 8905 (7th Cir. 1989).

Before completing the deal, he learned that in several newspaper articles, Ackley had publicized the house as being haunted. Ackley had also permitted the house to be featured in a walking tour of the neighborhood as "a riverfront Victorian (*with ghost*)." Stambovsky refused to go through with the deal and sued to rescind. He won. The court ruled that Ackley sold the house knowing Stambovsky was ignorant of the alleged ghosts. She also knew that a reasonable buyer might avoid a haunted house, fearing grisly events—or diminished resale value. Stambovsky could not have discovered the apparitions himself, and Ackley's failure to warn permitted him to rescind the deal.[7]

© Galina Barskaya/Shutterstock

What if the defect is…a ghost?

A seller generally must report any latent defect he knows about that the buyer should not be expected to discover himself. As social awareness of the environment increases, a buyer potentially worries about more and more problems. We now know that underground toxic waste, carelessly dumped in earlier decades, can be dangerous or even lethal. Accordingly, any property seller who realizes that there is toxic waste underground, or any other hidden hazard, must reveal that fact.

To Correct a Mistaken Understanding about a Writing. Suppose the potential buyer of a vacation property has a town map showing that the land he wants to buy has a legal right of way to a beautiful lake. If the seller of the land knows that the town map is out of date and that there is no such right of way, she must disclose her information.

A Relationship of Trust. Maria is planning to sell her restaurant to her brother Ricardo. Maria has a greater duty to reveal problems in the business because Ricardo assumes she will be honest. **When one party naturally expects openness and honesty, based on a close relationship, the other party must act accordingly.** If the building's owner has told Maria he will not renew her lease, she must pass that information on to Ricardo.

What happens if an owner, rather than disclosing hidden defects, sells the property "as is"? The following case provides insight.

Hess v. Chase Manhattan Bank, USA, N.A.

220 S.W.3d 758
Missouri Supreme Court, 2007

Facts: Billy Stevens owned a paint company. On several occasions, he ordered employees to load a trailer with 55-gallon paint drums and pallets of old paint cans and then dump them on property he owned. This illegal dumping saved Stevens the cost of proper disposal. Later, employees notified the Environmental Protection Agency (EPA) of what Stevens had done, and the EPA began an investigation. (Stevens later served time for environmental crimes.)

Stevens defaulted on his mortgage to the land. While Chase Manhattan Bank was in the process of foreclosing, it learned that the EPA was investigating the property for contamination. Chase foreclosed and put the property up for sale "as is." Several buyers expressed interest. The bank did not inform any of them of the ongoing EPA investigation. Dennis Hess bought the property for $52,000.

---

[7] *Stambovsky v. Ackley*, 169 A.D.2d 254, 572 N.Y.S.2d 672, 1991 N.Y. App. Div. LEXIS 9873 (N.Y. App. Div. 1991).

After Hess bought the land, he discovered the illegal waste and sued Chase for failing to disclose the EPA's investigation. The jury awarded Hess $52,000 and Chase appealed.

Issue: ***Did Chase have a duty to disclose to Hess the ongoing investigation?***

Excerpts from Judge Stith's Decision: The buyer has a right to rely on the seller to disclose where the undisclosed material information would not be discoverable through ordinary diligence. Chase learned that the EPA was investigating the property before Chase completed its foreclosure of the mortgage. Even with superior knowledge, a duty to disclose will be imposed only if the material facts would not be discovered through the exercise of ordinary diligence. Chase asserts that a reasonable inspection of the property by Hess would have disclosed the presence of the paint cans near the old barn foundation. Chase's argument misapprehends the factual basis of Hess's fraudulent non-disclosure claim. It is the *EPA investigation* into hazardous waste dumping on the property that is the material fact that Hess asserts Chase had a duty to disclose, not the presence (or absence) of paint cans.

Hess presented evidence that two potential buyers who did discover the paint cans each still made an offer to purchase the property. Both testified that the presence of paint cans did not give them notice that the EPA was investigating and that, had they known of its investigation, they would not have made offers for the property. From this evidence, the jury could have found that even had Hess further inspected the property and discovered the paint cans, this would not have put him on notice that the EPA had an ongoing investigation into hazardous waste dumping on the property.

Chase asserts that in spite of the evidence of its knowledge and Hess's inability to discover the EPA investigation, a duty to disclose should not be imposed because the contract specified that Chase was making "no representations, guaranties, or warranties, either written or implied, regarding the property" and that "the property is being sold in AS-IS condition with no express or implied representations or warranties by the seller or its agents." It claims that through these provisions, it bargained for the right to remain silent and no duty to speak ever arose.

What Chase misapprehends is that Hess alleges *fraud in the inducement* to contract, not fraud in the terms of the contract. Missouri law holds that a party may not, by disclaimer or otherwise, contractually exclude liability for fraud in inducing that contract. Each of the individuals who made an offer to purchase this property did so without knowledge that it was under EPA investigation. They all testified that, had they known, they would not have made an offer to purchase this property and would not, therefore, have "bargained for" Chase's silence. Chase's duty to speak arose from its superior knowledge prior to the execution of this contract. The presence of a clause disclaiming warranties in a contract does not negate a pre-contractual duty to speak.

Affirmed.

EXAM Strategy

Question: Mako is selling his country house for $400,000. Guppy, an interested buyer, asks whether there is sufficient water from the property's well. Mako replies, "Are you kidding? Watch this." He turns on the tap, and the water flows bountifully. Mako then shows Guppy the well, which is full. Guppy buys the property, but two weeks later, the well runs dry. In fact, Mako knew the water supply was inadequate, and he had the well filled by a tanker truck while the property was being sold. A hydrologist tells Guppy it will cost $100,000 to dig a better well, with no guarantee of success. Guppy sues Mako. What remedy should Guppy seek? Who will win?

Strategy: Is this a case of innocent misrepresentation or fraud? Fraud. Therefore, Guppy may seek two remedies: damages or rescission. Make sure that you understand the difference. To win, Guppy must show he relied on a fact that was both false and material.

Result: When Mako responded to Guppy's question by demonstrating the apparent abundance of water, he made a false statement. This was fraud (not innocent misrepresentation), because Mako knew the well was inadequate. That was a material fact. Guppy reasonably relied on the demonstration. Guppy will win. He can elect to rescind the contract (return the property to Mako and get his money back) or choose damages (the cost of digging a proper well). Given the uncertain nature of well digging, he would be wise to rescind.

Mistake

Contract law principles come from many sources, and in the area of "legal mistake," a cow significantly influenced the law. The cow was named Rose. She was a gentle animal that lived in Michigan in 1886. Rose's owner, Hiram Walker & Sons, bought her for $850. After a few years, the company concluded that Rose could have no calves. As a barren cow, she was worth much less than $850, so Walker contracted to sell her to T. C. Sherwood for a mere $80. But when Sherwood came to collect Rose, the parties realized that (surprise!) she was pregnant. Walker refused to part with the happy mother, and Sherwood sued. Walker defended, claiming that both parties had made a *mistake* and that the contract was voidable.

A mistake can take many forms. It may be a basic error about an essential characteristic of the thing being sold, as in Rose's case. It could be an erroneous prediction about future prices, such as an expectation that oil prices will rise. It might be a mechanical error, such as a builder offering to build a new home for $300 when he clearly meant to bid $300,000. Some mistakes lead to voidable contracts, others create enforceable deals. The first distinction is between bilateral and unilateral mistakes.

Bilateral Mistake

Bilateral mistake
Occurs when both parties negotiate based on the same factual error.

A **bilateral mistake** occurs when both parties negotiate based on the same factual error. Sherwood and Walker both thought Rose was barren, both negotiated accordingly, and both were wrong. The Michigan Supreme Court gave judgment for Walker, the seller, permitting him to rescind the contract because the parties were *both* wrong about the essence of what they were bargaining for.

If the parties contract based on an important factual error, the contract is voidable by the injured party. Sherwood and Walker were both wrong about Rose's reproductive ability, and the error was basic enough to cause a tenfold difference in price. Walker, the injured party, was entitled to rescind the contract. Note that the error must be *factual.* Suppose Walker sold Rose thinking that the price of beef was going to drop, when in fact the price rose 60 percent in five months. That would be simply a *prediction* that proved wrong, and Walker would have no right to rescind.

Conscious Uncertainty. No rescission is permitted where one of the parties knows he is taking on a risk; that is, he realizes there is uncertainty about the quality of the thing being exchanged. Rufus offers 10 acres of mountainous land to Priscilla. "I can't promise you anything about this land," he says, "but they've found gold on every adjoining parcel." Priscilla, eager for gold, buys the land, digs long and hard, and discovers—mud. She may not rescind the contract. She understood the risk she was assuming, and there was no mutual mistake.

Unilateral Mistake

Unilateral mistake
Occurs when only one party enters a contract under a mistaken assumption.

Sometimes only one party enters a contract under a mistaken assumption, a situation called **unilateral mistake**. In these cases, it is more difficult for the injured party to rescind a contract. This makes sense since in a bilateral error, neither side really knew what it was getting into, and rescission seems a natural remedy. But with unilateral mistakes, one side may simply have made a better bargain than the other. As we have seen throughout this unit on contracts, courts are unwilling to undo an agreement merely because someone made a foolish deal. Nonetheless, if her proof is strong, the injured party in a case of unilateral mistakes still may sometimes rescind a contract.

To rescind for unilateral mistake, a party must demonstrate that she entered the contract because of a basic factual error and that *either* (1) enforcing the contract would be *unconscionable* or (2) the nonmistaken party *knew* of the error.[8]

A town obtains five bids for construction of a new municipal swimming pool. Four are between $100,000 and $111,000. Fred's bid is for $82,000. His offer includes a figure of $2,000 for excavation work, while the others have allotted about $20,000 for that work. Fred has inadvertently dropped a zero, resulting in a bid that is $18,000 too low. Town officials accept Fred's offer. When he sues to rescind, Fred wins. Town officials knew that the work could not be done that cheaply, and it would be unfair to hold Fred to a mathematical error that the other side perceived.[9]

In contrast, suppose that Rebecca sues Pierce, whose bad driving caused an accident, and Amy, who owned the car that Pierce was driving. While the case is pending, Amy's insurance company, Risknaught, pays Rebecca a $70,000 settlement. Later, the state supreme court rules that Pierce was an unauthorized driver, and an owner's insurer is never liable in such a case. Risknaught seeks to rescind its settlement, claiming unilateral mistake as to its liability. The company loses. Risknaught was aware that an appellate ruling might establish new precedent. The insurer settled based on a decision calculated to minimize its risk.[10]

In the following case an automobile dealer made a mistake—how often does *this* happen?—in the customer's favor.

Donovan v. RRL Corporation

26 Cal.4th 261, 27 P.3d 702, 109 Ca. Rptr.2d 807
Supreme Court of California, 2001

Facts: Brian Donovan was in the market for a used car. As he scanned the Costa Mesa *Daily Pilot*, he came upon a "Pre-Owned Coup-A-Rama Sale!" at Lexus of Westminster. Of the 16 cars listed in the ad (with vehicle identification numbers), one was a sapphire-blue Jaguar XJ6 Vanden Plas, priced at $25,995.

Brian drove to a Jaguar dealership to do some comparison shopping. Jaguars of the same year and mileage cost about $8,000 to $10,000 more than the auto at the Lexus agency. The next day, Brian and his wife hurried over to the Coup-A-Rama event, spotted the Jaguar (which had the correct VIN) and asked a salesperson if they might test-drive it. Pleased with the ride, Brian said to the salesman, "O.K. We will take it at your price, $26,000." This figure startled the sales representative, who glanced at the newspaper ad Brian showed him, and responded, "That's a mistake."

As indeed it was. The Lexus agency had paid $35,000 for the Jaguar and intended to sell it for about $37,000. Brian was adamant. "No, I want to buy it at your advertised price, and I will write you a check right now." The sales manager was called in, and he refused to sell the car for less than $37,000.

It turned out that the *Daily Pilot*'s typographical and proofreading errors had caused the mistake, although the Lexus dealership had failed to review the proof sheet, which would have revealed the error before the ad went to press.

Brian sued. The trial court found that unilateral mistake prevented enforcement of the contract. The appel-

[8]Restatement (Second) of Contracts §153.

[9]See examples provided in Restatement (Second) of Contracts §153.

[10]See, e.g., *AID Hawai'i Ins. Co. v. Bateman*, 82 Haw. 453, 923 P.2d 395 (Haw. 1996).

late court reversed, and Donovan appealed to the state's highest court.

The state supreme court first ruled that there *was* in fact a contract between the parties. (Generally, a newspaper advertisement is merely a solicitation for an offer, but a California statute generally holds *automobile dealers* to the terms of their offers.) The court then went on to examine the mistake.

Issue: ***Did the Lexus dealer's mistake entitle it to rescind the contract?***

Excerpts from Justice George's Decision: A significant error in the price term of a contract constitutes a mistake regarding a basic assumption upon which the contract is made, and such a mistake ordinarily has a material effect adverse to the mistaken party. The defendant must show that the resulting imbalance in the agreed exchange is so severe that it would be unfair to require the defendant to perform.

Measured against this standard, defendant's mistake in the contract for the sale of the Jaguar automobile constitutes a material mistake regarding a basic assumption upon which it made the contract. Enforcing the contract with the mistaken price of $25,995 would require defendant to sell the vehicle to plaintiff for $12,000 less than the intended advertised price of $37,995—an error amounting to 32 percent of the price defendant intended. The exchange of performances would be substantially less desirable for defendant and more desirable for plaintiff.

The mere fact that a mistaken party could have avoided the mistake by the exercise of reasonable care does not preclude avoidance on the ground of mistake. Indeed, since a party can often avoid a mistake by the exercise of such care, the availability of relief would be severely circumscribed if he were to be barred by his negligence. Nevertheless, in *extreme cases,* the mistaken party's fault is a proper ground for denying him relief for a mistake that he otherwise could have avoided.

If we were to accept plaintiff's position that that the dealer always must be held to the strict terms of a contract arising from an advertisement, we would be holding that the dealer intended to assume the risk of all typographical errors in advertisements, no matter how serious the error and regardless of the circumstances in which the error was made. For example, if an automobile dealer proofread an advertisement but, through carelessness, failed to detect a typographical error listing a $75,000 automobile for sale at $75, the defense of mistake would be unavailable to the dealer.

No evidence presented at trial suggested that defendant knew of the mistake before plaintiff attempted to purchase the automobile, that defendant intended to mislead customers, or that it had adopted a practice of deliberate indifference regarding errors in advertisements. The uncontradicted evidence established that the *Daily Pilot* made the proofreading error resulting in defendant's mistake.

We conclude that the municipal court correctly entered judgment in defendant's favor.

EXAM Strategy

Question: Joe buys an Otterhound named Barky, from Purity Dog Shop. He pays $2,500 for the puppy. The high cost is a result of the certificate Purity gives him, indicating that the puppy's parents were both AKC champions (elite dogs). Two months later, Joe sells the hound to Emily for $2,800. Joe and Emily both believe that Barky is descended from champions. Then a state investigation reveals that Purity has been cheating and its certificates are fakes. Barky is just a regular dog, worth about $100. Emily sues Joe. Who wins?

Strategy: Both parties are mistaken about the kind of dog Joe is selling, so this is an instance of bilateral mistake. What is the rule in such cases?

Result: If the two sides agree based on an important factual error, the contract is voidable by the injured party. A mutt is entirely different from a dog that might become a champion. The parties erred about the essence of their deal. Joe's good faith does not save him, and Emily is entitled to rescind.

Duress

Duress
An improper threat made to force another party to enter into a contract.

True consent is also lacking when one party agrees to a contract under **duress**. If kindly Uncle Hugo signs over the deed to the ranch because Niece Nelly is holding a gun to his head, Hugo has not consented in any real sense, and he will have the right to rescind the contract. **If one party makes an improper threat that causes the victim to enter into a contract, and the victim had no reasonable alternative, the contract is voidable.**[11]

On a Sunday morning, Bancroft Hall drove to pick up his daughter Sandra, who had slept at a friend's house. The Halls are black and the neighborhood was white. A suspicious neighbor called the police, who arrived, aggressively prevented the Halls from getting into their own car, and arrested the father. The Halls had not violated any law or done anything wrong whatsoever. Later an officer told Hall that he could leave immediately if he signed a full release (stating that he had no claims of any kind against the police), but that if he refused to sign it, he would be detained for a bail hearing. Hall signed the release but later filed suit. The police defended based on the release.

The court held that the release was voidable because Hall had signed it under duress. The threat to detain Hall for a bail hearing was clearly improper because he had committed no crime. He also had no reasonable alternative to signing. A jury awarded the Halls over half a million dollars.[12]

Can "improper threats" take other forms? Does *economic* intimidation count? Many plaintiffs have posed that question over the last half century, and courts have grudgingly yielded.

Today, in most states, economic duress *can* also be used to void a contract. But economic duress sounds perilously close to hard bargaining—in other words, business. The free market system is expected to produce tough competition. A smart, aggressive executive may bargain fiercely. How do we distinguish economic duress from legal, successful business tactics? Courts have created no single rule to answer the question, but they do focus on certain issues.

In analyzing a claim of economic duress, courts look at these factors:

- Acts that have no legitimate business purpose
- Greatly unequal bargaining power
- An unnaturally large gain for one party
- Financial distress to one party

Is the following case one of duress or hard bargaining?

How do we distinguish hard bargaining from economic duress?

[11]Restatement (Second) of Contracts §175(1).

[12]*Halls v. Ochs*, 817 F.2d 920, U. S. App. LEXIS 5822 (1st Cir. 1987).

You be the Judge

In Re RLS Legal Solutions, L.L.C.

2005 WL 171381
Texas Court of Appeals, 2005

Facts: Amy Maida sued her employer, RLS Legal Solutions, for various claims relating to her job. RLS asked that the case be dismissed because Maida had signed an arbitration agreement. Maida had in fact signed the contract while already working at RLS. However, she responded that the agreement should not be enforced because she had signed it under economic duress. At trial, she was asked whether she had found the agreement acceptable:

> I did not. The arbitration clause was going to allow me not to be able to be in a position that I needed to be in now, and that is, to have someone represent me to help me where I feel like the company did me wrong.
>
> After I refused to agree to this arbitration clause, I was told that my payroll checks would not be direct deposited into my account until I signed the agreement and that I would not be paid until I signed the agreement. I had received my paychecks by direct deposit for three years. [RLS did in fact stop the direct deposit payment of Maida's salary.]
>
> I needed my paycheck to meet my financial responsibilities since I am a single family income household provider. I had no way to pay my mortgage, vehicle note, car and homeowner's insurance as well as any household bills.

Maida testified that after signing and returning the agreement, she received a manual check. Maida said that when she asked why she had not been paid by direct deposit as usual, she was told her paycheck would be held until she signed the agreement.

RLS argued that Maida had eventually received every paycheck to which she was entitled, had suffered no losses, and was free to leave RLS at any time if she found her employment terms unacceptable.

The trial court refused to dismiss the case or order arbitration, and RLS appealed.

You Be the Judge: ***Did Maida sign the arbitration under economic duress?***

Argument for RLS: Your honors, it is hard to take seriously a claim of economic duress when the plaintiff has not lost one cent and was never forced to sign anything. RLS runs a business, not a community center. To stay competitive, we constantly revise our commercial practices, and this was one such change. We did not ask for a bizarre or inappropriate change: arbitration is a widely favored method of settling disputes, quicker and cheaper *for all parties*. Maida signed. Yes, we stopped direct deposit of her check, but in the end, we paid her all she was due. We were not obligated to pay her in any particular fashion, or even to continue her employment. If she wanted to stay with us, she had to play by our rules.

Argument for Maida: The company could offer an arbitration contract to all workers. But that is distinct from forcing such agreements down employee throats, which is what they did here. RLS knows that its workers depend on prompt payment of payroll checks to avoid falling quickly into debt. The company offered Maida the arbitration agreement, she rejected it, and they responded by stopping direct deposit of her check. Knowing that she was the sole provider for her family, the firm intended to subject her to intolerable economic pressure. It worked. However, the court should have no part of this coercion. The two sides had hugely differing bargaining power, and RLS attempted to use financial distress to obtain what it could not by persuasion.

Undue Influence

She was single and pregnant. A shy young woman in a large city with no family nearby, she needed help and support. She went to the Methodist Mission Home of Texas where she found room and board, support—and a lot of counseling. Her discussions with a minister and a private counselor stressed one point: that she should give up her baby for adoption. She signed the adoption papers, but days later, she decided she wanted the baby after all. Was there any ground to rescind? She claimed *undue influence*, in other words, that the Mission Home so dominated her thinking that she never truly consented. Where one party has used undue influence, the contract is voidable at the option of the injured party. There are two elements to the plaintiff's case. **To prove undue influence, the injured party must demonstrate:**

- A relationship between the two parties either of trust or of domination, and
- Improper persuasion by the stronger party.[13]

In the Methodist Mission case, the court held that the plaintiff had been young and extremely vulnerable during the days following the birth of her child. The mission's counselor, to whom she turned for support, had spent day after day forcefully insisting that the young woman had no moral or legal right to keep her child. This amounted to undue influence. The court voided the adoption agreement.[14] In the following case, the age difference is reversed.

Sepulveda v. Aviles

762 N.Y.S.2d 358, 308 A.D.2d 1
New York Supreme Court, Appellate Division, 2003

Facts: Agnes Seals owned and lived in a 10-unit apartment building on East 119th Street in New York City. When she was 80 years old, a fire damaged much of the building's interior, leaving Seals physically and mentally unable to care for the property. Shortly after the fire, she met David Aviles, a 35-year-old neighbor. Aviles convinced Seals to sell him the building, promising to care for her for the rest of her life. She sold him the building for $50,000, taking a down payment of $10,000, with the rest to be paid over time. At the closing, Seals was represented by an attorney, Martin Freedman, whom she had never met before, and who had been referred to her by Aviles's lawyer (with whom he shared office space).

Three years later, Seals died. Her will left her entire estate to Elba and Victor Sepulveda, but the building had been Seals's principal asset. The Sepulvedas sued Aviles, asking the court to set aside the sale of the building, claiming that Aviles had used undue influence to trick Seals into a sale that was not in her interest. The jury found that Aviles had not used undue influence, and the Sepulvedas appealed.

Issue: ***Did Aviles use undue influence to obtain the apartment building?***

Excerpts from Judge Gonzalez's Decision: The jury's verdict here was completely at odds with any fair interpretation of the evidence. The trial testimony established that at the time of the transfer, Seals was an 80-year-old woman in declining health who had recently suffered a traumatic crisis resulting from [the fire], requiring her to vacate the premises for two months. The testimony of social worker Blair established that only 16 months after the conveyance, Seals was totally homebound and dependent on others, especially Aviles, to do her banking and shopping and to provide her with transportation to medical appointments. She also was suffering from significant memory impairment by that time. This evidence of Seals's mental condition was corroborated by the medical testimony of Dr. Forster, who provided his expert opinion that Seals was suffering from severe Alzheimer's dementia [at the time of the sale]. In our view, the evidence of Seals's severe mental impairment far outweighed the self-serving, lay opinions of Aviles and Freedman that Seals appeared coherent and lucid at the closing.

Seals's dependence on Aviles was further confirmed by the testimony of two disinterested witnesses, Blair and Sister Lachapelle, who testified that Aviles told Seals shortly before the sale that if she transferred the building to him, he would take care of her for the rest of her life. In addition, that Seals was represented at the closing by an attorney she had never met before and who was referred by the buyer, Mr. Aviles, is a circumstance noted in many prior cases as raising a serious question of improper influence.

---

[13]Restatement (Second) of Contracts §177.

[14]*Methodist Mission Home of Texas v. N A B*, 451 S.W.2d 539, 1970 Tex. App. LEXIS 2055 (Tex. Civ. App. 1970).

Additional clear and convincing evidence adduced by plaintiffs reveal a series of transactions permeated by undue influence. Aviles's unfettered use of Seals's funds and credit cards, which Aviles admitted at trial, provides convincing evidence that he was exploiting Seals's impaired condition for his own financial gain. Finally, his brazen conduct in writing out mortgage checks to Seals, having her endorse them, and then depositing them back into his own account raises the strongest inference that the mortgage agreement was a sham, and his intent was to obtain Seals's building through improper means. In light of the trial evidence, we find that the jury's verdict that Aviles did not obtain Seals's property by undue influence could not have been reached on any fair interpretation of the evidence.

[Reversed and remanded for new trial.]

Chapter Conclusion

An agreement between two parties may not be enough to make a contract enforceable. A minor or a mentally impaired person may generally disaffirm contracts. Even if both parties are adults of sound mind, courts will insist that consent be genuine. Misrepresentation, mistake, duress, and undue influence all indicate that at least one party did not truly consent. As the law evolves, it imposes an increasingly greater burden of *good faith negotiating* on the party in the stronger position.

Exam Review

1. **VOIDABLE CONTRACT** Capacity and consent are different contract issues that can lead to the same result: a voidable contract. A voidable agreement is one that can be canceled by a party who lacks legal capacity or who did not give true consent. (p. 317)

2. **MINORS** A minor (someone under the age of 18) generally may disaffirm any contract while she is still a minor or within a reasonable time after reaching age18. (pp. 317–319)

Question: John Marshall and Kirsten Fletcher decided to live together. They leased an apartment, each agreeing to pay one-half of the rent. When he signed the lease, Marshall was 17. Shortly after signing the lease, Marshall turned 18, and two weeks later, he moved into the apartment. He paid his half of the rent for two months and then moved out because he and Fletcher were not getting along. Fletcher sued Marshall for one-half of the monthly rent for the remainder of the lease. Who wins?

Strategy: Marshall was clearly a minor when he signed the lease, and he could have rescinded the agreement at that time. However, after he turned 18, he moved in and began to pay rent. What effect did that have on his contract obligation? (See the "Result" at the end of this section.)

3. **MENTAL IMPAIRMENT** A mentally impaired person may generally disaffirm a contract. In such a case, though, he generally must make restitution. (pp. 319–320)

4. **INTOXICATION** A person who is so intoxicated that he fails to understand the nature of an agreement may disaffirm a contract. (pp. 320–321)

5. **FRAUD** Fraud is grounds for rescinding a contract. The injured party must prove all of the following:

   a. A false statement of fact made intentionally or recklessly

   b. Materiality

   c. Justifiable reliance (pp. 322–324)

6. **INNOCENT MISREPRESENTATION** Innocent misrepresentation also allows an injured party to rescind a contract, but it does not allow a plaintiff to sue for damages. It has the same elements as fraud, but it does not require intent or recklessness. (p. 324)

EXAM Strategy

Question: Ron buys 1,000 "Smudgy Dolls" for his toy store. Karen, the seller, tells him the dolls are in perfect condition, even though she knows their heads are defectively attached. Ron sells all of the products, but then he has to face 1,000 angry customers with headless dolls. Ron sues Karen seeking recission. What is the likely outcome?

a. This is fraud, and Ron will be able to rescind.

b. This is an innocent misrepresentation, and Ron will be able to rescind.

c. This is fraud, but Ron will not be able to rescind.

d. This is an innocent misrepresentation, but Ron will not be able to rescind.

e. This is neither fraud nor an innocent misrepresentation.

Strategy: Karen knew her statement was false, so this is a case of fraud if all elements can be met. Ron must prove a false statement of fact, materiality, and reliance. Can he do so? (See the "Result" at the end of this section.)

7. **SILENCE** Silence amounts to misrepresentation only in four instances:

- Where disclosure is necessary to *correct a previous assertion*
- Where disclosure would correct a *basic mistaken assumption* on which the other party is relying
- Where disclosure would correct the other party's *mistaken understanding about a writing;* or
- Where there is a *relationship of trust* between the two parties. (pp. 324–327)

8. **MISTAKE** In a case of bilateral mistake, either party may rescind the contract. In a case of unilateral mistake, the injured party may rescind only upon a showing that enforcement would be unconscionable or that the other party knew of her mistake. (pp. 327–330)

9. **DURESS** If one party makes an improper threat that causes the victim to enter into a contract, and the victim had no reasonable alternative, the contract is voidable. (pp. 330–332)

Question: Andreini's nerve problem diminished the use of his hands. Dr. Beck operated, but the problem grew worse. A nurse told the patient that Beck might have committed a serious error that exacerbated the problem. Andreini returned for a second operation, which Beck assured him would correct the problem. But after Andreini had been placed in a surgical gown, shaved, and prepared for surgery, the doctor insisted that he sign a release relieving Beck of liability for the first operation. Andreini did not want to sign it, but Beck refused to operate until he did. Later, Andreini sued Beck for malpractice. A trial court dismissed Andreini's suit based on the release. You are on the appeals court. Will you affirm the dismissal or reverse?

Strategy: Adreini is claiming physical duress. Did Beck act *improperly* in demanding a release? Did Adreini have a *realistic alternative?* (See the "Result" at the end of this section.)

10. **UNDUE INFLUENCE** Once again the injured party may rescind a contract, but only upon a showing of a special relationship and improper persuasion. (pp. 332–333)

2. Result: A minor can disaffirm a contract. However, if he turns 18 and then ratifies the agreement, he is fully liable. When he paid the rent, Marshall ratified the contract, and thus he is fully liable.

5. Result: Karen made a false statement of fact, knowing it was wrong. It was material, and Ron reasonably relied on her. Karen has committed fraud. Ron is entitled to rescind the agreement. The correct answer is "a."

8. Result: The Utah Supreme Court reversed the trial court, so you probably should as well. Beck forced Adreini to sign under duress. The threat to withhold surgery was improper, and Adreini had no reasonable alternative.

MULTIPLE-CHOICE QUESTIONS

1. Kerry finds a big green ring in the street. She shows it to Leroy, who says, "Wow. That could be valuable." Neither Kerry nor Leroy knows what the ring is made of or whether it is valuable. Kerry sells the ring to Leroy for $100, saying, "Don't come

griping if it turns out to be worth two dollars." Leroy takes the ring to a jeweler who tells him it is an unusually perfect emerald, worth at least $75,000. Kerry sues to rescind.

(a) Kerry will win based on fraud.

(b) Kerry will win based on mutual mistake.

(c) Kerry will win based on unilateral mistake.

(d) Kerry will lose.

2. Veronica has a beer and then makes a contract. She continues drinking, and her blood alcohol level eventually rises to .09, which is just above her state's threshold for drunk driving. She makes a second contract while in this condition. Veronica's first contract is ________________, and her second contract is ________________.

(a) valid; valid

(b) valid; voidable

(c) voidable; voidable

(d) voidable; void

3. Jerry is so mentally ill that he is unable to understand the nature and consequences of his transactions, but he has not been adjudicated insane. Penny has been adjudicated insane, and a court has appointed a guardian to handle her affairs. Jerry's contracts are ____________, and Penny's contracts are ____________.

(a) valid; valid

(b) valid; voidable

(c) valid; void

(d) voidable; voidable

(e) voidable; void

4. Angela makes a material misstatement of fact to Lance, which he relies on when he signs Angela's contract. Fraud exists if Angela made the misstatement ...

(a) intentionally

(b) recklessly

(c) carelessly

(d) A and B only

(e) A, B, and C

5. Scarborough's Department Store opens for business on a busy shopping day just before Christmas. A hurried clerk places a sign in the middle of a table piled high with red cashmere sweaters. The sign reads, "SALE—100% Cashmere—$0.99 Each." The sign, of course, was supposed to read "$99 each."

This is a __________ mistake, and customers ____________ be able to demand that Scarborough's sell the sweaters for 99 cents.

(a) unilateral; will

(b) unilateral; will not

(c) bilateral; will

(d) bilateral; will not

Essay Questions

1. Raymond Barrows owned a 17-acre parcel of undeveloped land in Seaford, Delaware. For most of his life, Mr. Barrows had been an astute and successful businessman, but by the time he was 85 years old, he had been diagnosed as "very senile and confused 90 percent of the time." Glenn Bowen offered to buy the land. Barrows had no idea of its value, so Bowen had it appraised by a friend, who said it was worth $50,000. Bowen drew up a contract, which Barrows signed. In the contract, Barrows agreed to sell the land for $45,000, of which Bowen would pay $100 at the time of closing; the remaining $44,900 was due whenever Bowen developed the land and sold it. There was no time limit on Bowen's right to develop the land nor any interest due on the second payment. Comment.

2. On television and in magazines, Maurine and Mamie Mason saw numerous advertisements for Chrysler Fifth Avenue automobiles. The ads described the car as "luxurious," "quality-engineered," and "reliable." When they went to inspect the car, the salesman told them the warranty was "the best ... comparable to Cadillacs and Lincolns." After the Masons bought a Fifth Avenue, they began to have many problems with it. Even after numerous repairs, the car was unsatisfactory and required more work. The Masons sued, seeking to rescind the contract based on the ads and the dealer's statement. Will they win?

3. The McAllisters had several serious problems with their house, including leaks in the ceiling, a buckling wall, and dampness throughout. They repaired the buckling wall by installing I-beams to support it. They never resolved the leaks and the dampness. When they decided to sell the house, they said nothing to prospective buyers about the problems. They stated that the I-beam had been added for reinforcement. The Silvas bought the house for $60,000. Soon afterwards, they began to have problems with leaks, mildew, and dampness. Are the Silvas entitled to any money damages? Why or why not?

4. Roy Newburn borrowed money and bought a $49,000 truck from Treadwell Ford. A few months later, the truck developed transmission problems. Newburn learned that the truck had 170,000 more miles on it than the odometer indicated. The company admitted the mileage error and promised to install a new transmission for free. Treadwell did install the new transmission, but when Newburn came to pick up the truck, Treadwell demanded that he sign a general release absolving the dealership of any claims based on the inaccurate mileage. Treadwell refused to turn over the truck until Newburn finally signed. The truck broke down again, and delays cost Newburn so much income that he fell behind on his loan payments and lost the truck. He sued Treadwell, which defended based on the release. Is the release valid?

5. Morell bought a security guard business from Conley, including the property on which the business was located. Neither party knew that underground storage tanks were leaking and contaminating the property. After the sale, Morell discovered the tanks and sought to rescind the contract. Should he be allowed to do so?

Discussion Questions

1. Sixteen-year-old Travis Mitchell brought his Pontiac GTO into M&M Precision Body and Paint for body work and a paint job. M&M did the work and charged $1,900, which Travis paid. When Travis later complained about the quality of the work, M&M did some touching up, but Travis was still dissatisfied. He demanded his $1,900 back, but M&M refused to refund it because all of the work was "in" the car and Travis could not return it to the shop. The state of Nebraska, where this occurred, follows the majority rule on this issue. Does Travis get his money? Is this a *fair* result?

2. Contract law gives minors substantial legal protection. But does a modern high school student *need* so much protection? Older teens may have been naive in the 1700s, but today, they are quite savvy. Should the law change so that only younger children—perhaps those aged 14 and under—have the ability to undo agreements? Or is the law reasonable the way it currently exists?

3. In the old Michigan case featuring Rose the Cow, the court refused to enforce the agreement. Was this a fair result? Should bilateral mistakes create voidable contracts, or should Walker have been required to sell the cow for $80?

4. Susan drops by Dean's garage sale. She buys a painting for $10. Both she and Dean think that the painting is a copy of a Matisse. Later, Susan is delighted to discover that the painting is actually a Matisse and is worth $50,000,000. Dean hears the news, and wants the painting back. Will he get it? Why or why not?

5. Do you have sympathy for intoxicated people who make agreements? Should the law ever let them back out of deals when they sober up? After all, no one forced them to get drunk. Should the law be more lenient, or is is it reasonable as it currently exists?

© picsbyst/Shutterstock.com

WRITTEN CONTRACTS

Oliver and Perry were college roommates, two sophomores with contrasting personalities. They were sitting in the cafeteria with some friends, Oliver chatting away, Perry slumped on a plastic bench. Oliver suggested that they buy a lottery ticket, as the prize for that week's drawing was $13 million. Perry muttered, "Nah. You never win if you buy just one ticket." Oliver bubbled up, "O.K., we'll buy a ticket every week. We'll keep buying them from now until we graduate. Come on, it'll be fun. This month, I'll buy the tickets. Next month, you will, and so on." Other students urged Perry to do it and, finally, he agreed.

The two friends carefully reviewed their deal. Each party was providing consideration—namely, the responsibility for purchasing tickets during his month. The amount of each purchase was clearly defined at one dollar. They would start that week and continue until graduation day, two and a half years down the road. Finally, they would share equally any money won. As three witnesses looked on, they shook hands on the bargain. That month, Oliver bought a ticket every week, randomly choosing numbers, and won nothing. The next month, Perry bought a ticket with equally random numbers—and won $52 million. Perry moved out of their dorm room into a suite at the Ritz and refused to give Oliver one red cent. Oliver sued, seeking $26 million, and the return of an Eric Clapton compact disc. If the former friends had understood the Statute of Frauds, they would never have gotten into this mess.[1]

Perry moved out of their dorm room into a suite at the Ritz and refused to give Oliver one red cent.

[1]Based loosely on *Lydon v. Beauregard* (Middlesex Sup. Ct., Mass., Dec. 22, 1989), reported in Paul Langher, "Couple Lose Suit to Share $2.8M Prize," *Boston Globe*, December 23, 1989, p. 21.

The rule we examine in this chapter is not exactly news. Originally passed by the British Parliament in 1677, the Statute of Frauds has changed little over the centuries. The purpose was to prevent lying (fraud) in civil lawsuits. Jury trials of that era invited perjury. Neither the plaintiff nor the defendant was permitted to testify, meaning that the jury never heard from the people who really knew what had happened. Instead, the court heard testimony from people who claimed to have witnessed the contract being created. Knowing that he would never be subjected to aggressive cross-examination, a plaintiff might easily allege that a fake contract was real, and then bribe witnesses to support his case. A powerful earl, seeking to acquire 300 acres of valuable land owned by a neighboring commoner, might claim that the neighbor had orally promised to sell his land. Although the claim was utterly false, the earl would win if he could bribe enough "reputable" witnesses to persuade the jury.

To provide juries with more reliable evidence that a contract did or did not exist, Parliament passed the Statute of Frauds. It required that in several types of cases, a contract would be enforced only if it were in writing. Contracts involving interests in land were first on the list.

In the days before the Revolutionary War, when Pennsylvania was still a British possession, the colony's supreme court heard the following case, which centered on the Statute of Frauds. Notice the case citation. This is very nearly the first case reported in United States history. Back then, rulings were expressed quite differently (and everything was capitalized), but you will be able to see Judge Coleman's point.

Landmark Case

The Lessee of Richardson v. Campbell

1 U.S. 10
Supreme Court of Pennsylvania, 1764

Facts: A tenant had rented land from Richardson. However, Campbell claimed the property was really his. Unless the tenant could prove that Richardson owned the land, he would have no right to stay there.

Richardson's tenant offered a deed (which was then called a *patent*) to support his claim; Campbell provided receipts as evidence that he had bought the property.

To prove that the receipts were for the disputed property, Campbell wanted to introduce statements from an important person—Thomas Penn, whose father, William, had founded the Pennsylvania colony. Obviously, the tenant did not want that evidence admitted in court.

Issue: ***Was oral evidence about the ownership of land admissible in court?***

Excerpts from Justice Coleman's Decision: PLAINTIFF supported his Title by a Patent. The Defendant produced Receipts several Years prior to Plaintiff's Patent; but the Plaintiff contend[ed] that the Receipts were only for Money paid on an adjacent Tract; the Defendant produced a Witness to prove a parol Declaration of Mr. Thomas Penn that the Land in dispute was sold to Defendant.

This piece of Evidence was opposed by the Plaintiff, and refused BY THE COURT.

Almost all states of this country have passed their own version of the Statute of Frauds. It is important to remember, as we examine the rules and exceptions, that Parliament and the state legislatures all had a commendable, straightforward purpose in passing their respective statutes of fraud: *to provide a court with the best possible evidence of whether the parties intended to make a contract.* Ironically, the British government has repealed the writing requirement for most contracts. Parliament concluded that the old statute, far from preventing wrongdoing, was *helping* people commit fraud. A wily negotiator could orally agree to terms and then, if the deal turned unprofitable, walk away from the contract, knowing it was unenforceable without written evidence.

Thus far, no state in this country has entirely repealed its Statute of Frauds. Instead, courts have carved exceptions into the original statute to prevent unfairness. Some scholars have urged state legislatures to go further and repeal the law altogether. Other commentators defend the Statute of Frauds as a valuable tool for justice. They argue that, among other benefits, the requirement of a writing cautions people to be careful before making—or relying on—a promise. For now, the Statute of Frauds is a vital part of law. Sadly, Oliver from the opening scenario will learn this the hard way.

The Statute of Frauds: A plaintiff may not enforce any of the following agreements unless the agreement, or some memorandum of it, is in writing and signed by the defendant.

The agreements that must be in writing are those:

- For any interest in **land**
- That **cannot be performed within one year**
- To pay the **debt of another**
- Made by an **executor of an estate**
- Made **in consideration of marriage**; and
- For the sale of goods worth $500 or more.

In other words, when two parties make an agreement covered by any one of these six topics, it must be in writing to be enforceable. Oliver and Perry made a definite agreement to purchase lottery tickets during alternate months and share the proceeds of any winning ticket. But their agreement was to last two and a half years. As the second item on the list indicates, a contract must be in writing if it cannot be performed within one year. The good news is that Oliver gets back his Eric Clapton CD. The bad news is he gets none of the lottery money. Even though three witnesses saw the deal made, it is unlikely to be enforced in any state. Perry will walk away with all $52 million.

Note that although the Oliver-Perry agreement is unenforceable, it is not void. Suppose that Perry does the right thing, agreeing to share the winnings with Oliver. Over the next 20 years, as he receives the winnings, Perry gives one-half to his friend. But then, having squandered his own fortune, Perry demands the money back from Oliver, claiming that the original contract violated the Statute of Frauds. Perry loses. **Once a contract is fully executed, it makes no difference that it was unwritten.** The Statute of Frauds prevents the enforcement of an executory contract; that is, one in which the parties have not fulfilled their obligations. But the contract is not *illegal.* Once both parties have fully performed, neither party may demand rescission. The Statute of Frauds allows a party to cancel future obligations but not undo past actions.

Ethics The *law* permits Perry to keep all of the lottery money. But does Perry have a *moral* right to deny Oliver his half-share? Is the Statute of Frauds serving a useful purpose here? Remember that Parliament passed the original Statute of Frauds believing that a written document would be more reliable than the testimony of alleged witnesses. If we permitted Oliver to enforce the oral contract, based on his testimony and that of the witnesses, would we simply be inviting other plaintiffs to invent lottery "contracts" that had never been made?

Common Law Statute of Frauds: Contracts That Must Be in Writing

Agreements for an Interest in Land

A contract for the sale of any interest in land must be in writing to be enforceable. Notice the phrase "interest in land." This means *any legal right* regarding land. A house on a lot is an interest in land. A mortgage, an easement, and a leased apartment are all interests in land. As a general rule, leases must therefore be in writing, although most states have created an exception for short-term leases. A short-term lease is often one for a year or less, although the length varies from state to state.

© oksana.perkins/Shutterstock

"Any interest in land" may sound obscure, but those who understand it are better off than those who do not.

Kary Presten and Ken Sailer were roommates in a rental apartment in New Jersey that had a view of the Manhattan skyline. The lease was in Sailer's name, but the two split all expenses. Then the building became a "cooperative," meaning that each tenant would have the option of buying the apartment.[2] Sailer learned he could buy his unit for only $55,800 if he promptly paid a $1,000 fee to maintain his rights. He mentioned to Presten that he planned to buy the unit, and Presten asked if he could become half-owner. Sailer agreed and borrowed the $1,000 from Presten to pay his initial fee. But as the time for closing on the purchase came nearer, Sailer realized that he could sell the apartment for a substantial profit. He placed an ad in a paper and promptly received a firm offer for $125,000. Sailer then told Presten that their deal was off, and that he, Sailer, would be buying the unit alone. He did exactly that, and Presten filed suit. Regrettably, the outcome of Presten's suit was only too easy to predict.

A cooperative apartment is an interest in land, said the court. This agreement could be enforced only if put in writing and signed by Sailer. The parties had put nothing in writing, and therefore Presten was out of luck. He was entitled to his $1,000 back, but nothing more. The apartment belonged to Sailer, who could live in it or sell it for a large, quick profit.[3]

Suppose that you are interested in buying five expensive acres in a fast-growing rural area. There is no water on the property, and the only way to bring public water to it is through land owned by the neighbor, Joanne, who agrees to sell you an easement through her property. An *easement* is a legal right that an owner gives to another person to make some use of the owner's land. In other words, Joanne will permit you to dig a 200-foot trench through her land and lay a water pipe there in exchange for $15,000. May you now safely purchase the five acres? Not until Joanne has signed the written easement. You might ignore this "technicality," since Joanne seems friendly and honest. But

[2]Technically, the residents of a "co-op" do not own their apartments. They own a share of the corporation that owns the building. Along with their ownership shares, residents have a right to lease their unit for a modest fee.

[3]*Presten v. Sailer*, 225 N.J. Super. 178, 542 A.2d 7, 1988 N.J. Super. LEXIS 151 (N.J. Super. Ct. App. Div. 1988).

you could then spend $300,000 buying your property only to learn that Joanne has changed her mind. She might refuse to go through with the deal unless you pay $150,000 for the easement. Without her permission to lay the pipe, your new land is worthless. Avoid such nightmares: get it in writing.

Exception: Full Performance by the Seller

If the seller completely performs her side of a contract for an interest in land, a court is likely to enforce the agreement even if it was oral. Adam orally agrees to sell his condominium to Maggie for $150,000. Adam delivers the deed to Maggie and expects his money a week later, but Maggie fails to pay. Most courts will allow Adam to enforce the oral contract and collect the full purchase price from Maggie.

Exception: Part Performance by the Buyer

The buyer of land may be able to enforce an oral contract if she paid part of the purchase price *and either* entered upon the land *or* made improvements to it. Suppose that Eloise sues Grover to enforce an alleged oral contract to sell a lot in Happydale. She claims they struck a bargain in January. Grover defends based on the Statute of Frauds, saying that even if the two did reach an oral agreement, it is unenforceable. Eloise proves that she paid 10 percent of the purchase price, that she began excavating on the lot in February to build a house, and that Grover knew of the work. Eloise has established part performance and will be allowed to enforce her contract.

This exception makes sense if we recall the purpose of the Statute of Frauds: to provide the best possible evidence of the parties' intentions. The fact that Grover permitted Eloise to enter upon the land and begin building on it is compelling evidence that the two parties had reached an agreement. But be aware that most claims of part performance fail. Merely paying a deposit on a house is not part performance. A plaintiff seeking to rely on part performance must show partial payment *and* either entrance onto the land *or* physical improvements to it.

Exception: Promissory Estoppel

The other exception to the writing requirement is our old friend promissory estoppel. **If a promisor makes an oral promise that should reasonably cause the promisee to rely on it, and the promisee does rely, the promisee may be able to enforce the promise,** despite the Statute of Frauds, if that is the only way to avoid injustice. This exception potentially applies to any contract that must be written, such as those for land, those that cannot be performed within one year, and so forth.

Maureen Sullivan and James Rooney lived together for seven years, although they never married. They decided to buy a house. The two agreed that they would be equal owners, but Rooney told Sullivan that in order to obtain Veterans Administration financing, he would have to be the sole owner on the deed. They each contributed to the purchase and maintenance of the house, and Rooney repeatedly told Sullivan that he would change the deed to joint ownership. He never did. When the couple split up, Sullivan sued, seeking a 50 percent interest in the house. She won. The agreement was for an interest in land and should have been in writing, said the court. But Rooney had clearly promised Sullivan that she would be a half-owner, and she had relied by contributing to the purchase and maintenance. The Statute of Frauds was passed to *prevent* fraud, not to enable one person to mislead another and benefit at her expense.[4]

---

[4]*Sullivan v. Rooney*, 404 Mass. 160, 533 N.E.2d 1372, 1989 Mass. LEXIS 49 (1989).

EXAM Strategy

Question: Aditi and Danielle, MBA students, need an apartment for next September. They find a lovely two-bedroom unit that the owner is rehabbing. The students can see that the owner is honest, his workmanship excellent. The owner agrees to rent them the apartment beginning September 1, for $1,200 per month for one year. "Come back at the end of August. By then, my work will be done and I'll have the papers to sign." Aditi asks, "Should we sign something now, to be sure?" The landlord laughs and replies, "I trust you. You don't trust me?" They both trust him, and they shake hands on the deal. When the students return in August, the landlord has rented it to Danielle's former boyfriend for $1,400 per month. Aditi and Danielle sue. Who wins?

Strategy: Under the statute of frauds, a contract for the sale of any interest in land must be in writing to be enforceable. What does "any interest" mean? Does the Statute of Frauds apply to this case?

Result: An "interest" means any legal right. A lease is an interest in land, meaning that the students cannot enforce this agreement unless it is in writing, signed by the owner—and it is not. The students need to look for a new apartment.

Agreements That Cannot Be Performed within One Year

Contracts that cannot be performed within one year are unenforceable unless they are in writing. This one-year period begins on the date the parties make the agreement. The critical word here is "cannot." If a contract *could possibly* be completed within one year, it need not be in writing. Betty gets a job at Burger Brain, throwing fries in oil. Her boss tells her she can have Fridays off for as long as she works there. That oral contract is enforceable whether Betty stays one week or twenty years. "As long as she works there" *could* last for less than one year. Betty might quit the job after six months. Therefore, it does not need to be in writing.[5]

If an agreement will *necessarily* take longer than one year to finish, it must be in writing to be enforceable. If Betty is hired for a term of three years as manager of Burger Brain, the agreement is unenforceable unless put in writing. She cannot perform three years of work in one year.

Or, if you hire a band to play at your wedding 15 months from today, the agreement must be in writing. The gig may take only a single day, but that day will definitely not fall in the next 12 months.

The following case starts with a notorious diet pill and ends with a paralegal suing her boss. Which argument carries greater weight?

---

[5]This is the majority rule. In most states, for example, if a company hires an employee "for life," the contract need not be in writing because the employee could die within one year. "Contracts of uncertain duration are simply excluded [from the Statute of Frauds]; the provision covers only those contracts whose performance cannot possibly be completed within a year." Restatement (Second) of Contracts §130, Comment a, at 328 (1981). See, e.g., *Mackay v. Four Rivers Packing Co.*, 2008 WL 427789 (Id. 2008). However, a few states disagree. The Illinois Supreme Court ruled that a contract for lifetime employment is enforceable only if written. *McInerney v. Charter Golf, Inc.*, 176 Ill. 2d 482, 680 N.E.2d 1347, 1997 Ill. LEXIS 56 (Ill. 1997).

You be the Judge

Sawyer v. Mills
2007 WL 1113038
Kentucky Court of Appeals, 2007

Facts: Barbara Sawyer, a paralegal, worked for attorney Melbourne Mills, assisting him in a class action lawsuit against the makers of a popular diet drug called Fen-Phen. Mills promised Sawyer a large bonus "when the ship comes in," but he never specified how much he would pay her. Mills successfully settled the Fen-Phen case for millions of dollars, and he later met with Sawyer and her husband to discuss her bonus. The Sawyers secretly recorded the conversation.

The Sawyers asked Mills for a $1 million bonus, to be paid as a lump sum. Mills refused. However, the parties kept talking and Mills eventually agreed to pay Sawyer $1 million, plus $65,000 for a luxury automobile. Payments were to be made in monthly installments of $10,000, for 10 years. Mills also agreed to sign a document confirming his promise. Sawyer's lawyer drafted the writing, but Mills never signed it. He did pay nine monthly installments, along with an extra payment of $100,000.

At trial, jurors heard the tape recording, which confirmed the oral agreement. The jury concluded that the parties had reached a binding agreement and awarded Sawyer $900,000. However, the court granted a judgment notwithstanding the verdict for Mills. He ruled that the agreement was barred by the Statute of Frauds. Sawyer appealed.

You Be the Judge: ***Does the Statute of Frauds prevent enforcement of Mills's promise?***

Argument for Sawyer: The Statute of Frauds exists to make sure that a plaintiff does not come into court and allege an oral promise that never existed. The fear of fraudulent claims is legitimate, but obviously it does not apply in this case. We *know* that Mills agreed to pay a million dollars because we can *hear* him make the promise. We know the exact terms of the agreement, and we know it was a reasonable arrangement based on years of work and a massive settlement. We even hear Mills agree to sign a document confirming his promise.

The Statute of Frauds was designed to prevent fraud—not encourage it. Mills's tiresome, technical arguments did not fool the jurors. After hearing—literally—the evidence, the jury knew there had been a deal and awarded Sawyer her fair share. Let's stop playing legal games, start doing justice, and restore the verdict.

Argument for Mills: This is a simple case. The plaintiffs allege an oral contract for 10 years' worth of installment payments. In other words, *if* there was an agreement, it was for 10 years' duration. Sawyer's own lawyer drafted a contract—never signed—for compensation lasting a full decade. Under the Statute of Frauds, an agreement that cannot be performed within one year is unenforceable unless written and signed. End of case.

If our legislature wanted to encourage secret tape recordings and deception, it could have included an exception to the Statute of Frauds, giving tricky plaintiffs a reward for bad-faith negotiating. However, the legislators wisely have made no such exception. The alleged oral contract is worthless.

Promise to Pay the Debt of Another

When one person agrees to pay the debt of another as a favor to that debtor, it is called a collateral promise, and it must be in writing to be enforceable. D. R. Kemp was a young entrepreneur who wanted to build housing in Tuscaloosa, Alabama. He needed $25,000 to complete a project he was working on, so he went to his old college professor, Jim Hanks, for help. The professor said he would see what he could do about getting Kemp a loan. Professor Hanks spoke with his good friend Travis Chandler, telling him that Kemp was highly responsible and would be certain to repay any money loaned. Chandler trusted Professor Hanks but wanted to be sure of his money. Professor Hanks assured Chandler that if for any reason Kemp did not repay the loan, he, Hanks, would pay Chandler in full.

With that assurance, Chandler wrote out a check for $25,000, payable to Kemp, never having met the young man.

Kemp, of course, never repaid the loan. (Thank goodness he did not; this textbook has no use for people who do what they are supposed to.) Kemp exhausted the cash trying to sustain his business, which failed anyway, so he had nothing to give his creditor. Chandler approached Professor Hanks, who refused to pay, and Chandler sued. The outcome was easy to predict. Professor Hanks had agreed to repay Kemp's debt *as a favor to Kemp*, making it a collateral promise. Chandler had nothing in writing, and that is exactly what he got from his lawsuit—nothing.

Exception: The Leading Object Rule

There is one major exception to the collateral promise rule. When the promisor guarantees to pay the debt of another and *the leading object of the promise is some benefit to the promisor himself*, then the contract will be enforceable even if unwritten. In other words, if the promisor makes the guarantee not as a favor to the debtor, but primarily out of *self-interest*, the Statute of Frauds does not apply.

Robert Perry was a hog farmer in Ohio. He owed $26,000 to Sunrise Cooperative, a supplier of feed. Because Perry was in debt, Sunrise stopped giving him feed on credit and began selling him feed on a cash-only basis. Perry also owed money to Farm Credit Services, a loan agency. Perry promised Farm Credit he would repay his loans as soon as his hogs were big enough to sell. But Perry couldn't raise hogs without feed, which he lacked the money to purchase. Farm Credit was determined to bring home the bacon, so it asked Sunrise Cooperative to give Perry the feed on credit. Farm Credit orally promised to pay any debt that Perry did not take care of. When Perry defaulted on his payments to Sunrise, the feed supplier sued Farm Credit based on its oral guarantee. Farm Credit claimed the promise was unenforceable, based on the Statute of Frauds. But the court found in favor of Sunrise. The *leading object* of Farm Credit's promise to Sunrise was self-interest, and the oral promise was fully enforceable.[6]

Promise Made by an Executor of an Estate

This rule is merely a special application of the previous one, concerning the debt of another person. An executor is the person who is in charge of an estate after someone dies. The executor's job is to pay debts of the deceased, obtain money owed to him, and disburse the assets according to the will. In most cases, the executor will use only the estate's assets to pay those debts. The Statute of Frauds comes into play when an executor promises to pay an estate's debts with her own funds. An executor's promise to use her own funds to pay a debt of the deceased must be in writing to be enforceable.

Suppose Esmeralda dies penniless, owing Tina $35,000. Esmeralda's daughter, Sapphire, is the executor of her estate. Tina comes to Sapphire and demands her $35,000. Sapphire responds, "There is no money in mamma's estate, but don't worry, I'll make it up to you with my own money." Sapphire's oral promise is unenforceable. Tina should get it in writing while Sapphire is feeling generous.

Promise Made in Consideration of Marriage

Barney is a multimillionaire with the integrity of a gangster and the charm of a tax collector. He proposes to Li-Tsing, who promptly rejects him. Barney then pleads that if Li-Tsing will be his bride, he will give her an island he owns off the coast of California. Li-Tsing begins to see his good qualities and accepts. After they are married, Barney refuses to

---

[6] *Sunrise Cooperative v. Robert Perry*, 1992 Ohio App. LEXIS 3913 (Ohio Ct. App. 1992).

deliver the deed. Li-Tsing will get nothing from a court either, because **a promise made in consideration of marriage must be in writing to be enforceable**.

The Common Law Statute of Frauds: What the Writing Must Contain

Each of the types of contract described above must be in writing in order to be enforceable. What must the writing contain? It may be a carefully typed contract, using precise legal terminology, or an informal memo scrawled on the back of a paper napkin at a business lunch. The writing may consist of more than one document, written at different times, with each document making a piece of the puzzle. But there are some general requirements: the writing

- **Must be signed by the defendant, and**
- **Must state with reasonable certainty the name of each party, the subject matter of the agreement, and all of the essential terms and promises.**[7]

Signature

A state's Statute of Frauds typically requires that the writing be "signed by the party to be charged therewith"; that is, the party who is resisting enforcement of the contract. Throughout this chapter, we refer to that person as the defendant because when these cases go to court, it is the defendant who is disputing the existence of a contract.

Judges define "signature" very broadly. Using a pen to write one's name certainly counts, but it is not required. A secretary who stamps an executive's signature on a letter fulfills this requirement. In fact, any mark or logo placed on a document to indicate acceptance, even an "X," will generally satisfy the Statute of Frauds. And electronic commerce, as we discuss below, creates new methods of signing.

Reasonable Certainty

Suppose Garfield and Hayes are having lunch, discussing the sale of Garfield's vacation condominium. They agree on a price and want to make some notation of the agreement even before their lawyers work out a detailed purchase and sales agreement. A perfectly adequate memorandum might say, "Garfield agrees to sell Hayes his condominium at 234 Baron Boulevard, Apartment 18, for $350,000 cash, payable on June 18, 2015, and Hayes promises to pay the sum on that day." They should make two copies of their agreement and sign both. Notice that although Garfield's memo is short, it is *certain* and *complete*. This is critical because problems of vagueness and incompleteness often doom informal memoranda.

Vagueness

Ella Hayden owned valuable commercial property on a highway called Route 9. She wrote a series of letters to her stepson Mark, promising that several of the children, including Mark, would share the property. One letter said: "We four shall fairly divide on the Route 9 property. [sic]" Other letters said: "When the Route 9 Plaza is sold, you can take a long vacation," and

---

[7]Restatement (Second) of Contracts §131.

"The property will be sold. You and Dennis shall receive the same amount." Ella Hayden died without leaving Mark anything. He sued, but got nothing. The court ruled:

> The above passages written by Ms. Hayden do not recite the essential elements of the alleged contract with reasonable certainty. The writings do not state unequivocally or with sufficient particularity the subject matter to which the writings relate, nor do they provide the terms and conditions of alleged promises made which constitute a contract. The alleged oral contract between Ms. Hayden and Mr. Hayden cannot be identified from the passages from Ms. Hayden's letters quoted above when applied to existing facts. In sum, Mr. Hayden's cause of action seeking an interest in the Route 9 property is foreclosed by the Statute of Frauds.[8]

Incompleteness

During Ronald McCoy's second interview with Spelman Memorial Hospital, the board of directors orally offered him a three-year job as assistant hospital administrator. McCoy accepted. Spelman's CEO, Gene Meyer, sent a letter confirming the offer, which said:

> To reconfirm the offer, it is as follows: 1. We will pay for your moving expenses. 2. I would like you to pursue your Master's Degree at an area program. We will pay 100 percent tuition reimbursement. 3. Effective September 26, you will be eligible for all benefits. 4. A starting salary of $48,000 annually with reviews and eligibility for increases at 6 months, 12 months, and annually thereafter. 5. We will pay for the expenses of 3 trips, if necessary, in order for you to find housing. 6. Vacation will be for 3 weeks a year after one year; however, we do allow for this to be taken earlier. [Signed] Gene Meyer.

Spelman Hospital fired McCoy less than a year after he started work, and McCoy sued. The hospital's letter seems clear, and it is signed by an authorized official. The problem is, it is incomplete. Can you spot the fatal omission? The court did.

McCoy wanted to hold the hospital's board to its spoken promise that he would have a job for a term of three years. To be enforceable, a contract for a term of over one year must be in writing under the Statute of Frauds.

To satisfy the Statute of Frauds, an employment contract—[or] its memorandum or note—must contain *all* essential terms, including *duration of the employment relationship*. Without a statement of duration, an employment-at-will arrangement is created, which is terminable at any time by either party with no liability for breach of contract. McCoy's argument that the letter constituted a memorandum of an oral contract fails because the letter does not state an essential element: duration. The letter did not state that Spelman was granting McCoy employment for any term—only that his salary would be reviewed at 6 months, 12 months, and "annually thereafter."[9]

The lawsuits in this section demonstrate the continuing force of the Statute of Frauds. If the promisor had truly wanted to make a binding commitment, he or she could have written the appropriate contract or memorandum in a matter of minutes. Great formality and expense are unnecessary. But the written document *must be clear and complete,* or it will fail.

EXAM Strategy

Question: Major Retailer and Owner negotiated a lease of a strip mall, the tenancy to begin August 1. Retailer's lawyer then drafted a lease accurately reflecting all terms agreed to, including the parties, exact premises, condition of the store, dates of the

[8] *Hayden v. Hayden*, Mass. Lawyers Weekly No. 12-299-93 (Middlesex Sup. Ct. 1994).

[9] *McCoy v. Spelman Memorial Hospital*, 845 S.W.2d 727, 1993 Mo. App. LEXIS 105 (Mo. Ct. App. 1993).

lease, and monthly rent of $18,000. Retailer signed the lease and delivered it to Owner on July 1. On July 20, Owner leased the same space to a different tenant for $23,000 per month. Retailer sued, claiming that the parties had a binding deal, and the Owner had breached his agreement in order to obtain higher rent. Who will win?

Strategy: To comply with the Statute of Frauds, a writing must state all essential terms. This lease appears to do that. However, the writing must contain one other thing. What is it?

Result: The writing must be *signed* by the party claiming that there is no contract; that is, by the defendant. Owner never signed the lease. This lease does not comply with the Statute of Frauds, and the Retailer will lose his case.

Electronic Contracts and Signatures

E-commerce has grown at a dazzling rate—each year, U.S. enterprises buy and sell tens of billions of dollars worth of goods and services over the Internet. What happens to the writing requirement, though, when there is no paper? The present Statute of Frauds requires some sort of "signature" to ensure that the defendant committed to the deal. Today, an "electronic signature" could mean a name typed (or automatically included) at the bottom of an e-mail message, a retinal or vocal scan, or a name signed by electronic pen on a writing tablet, among others.

E-signatures are valid in all 50 states. Almost all states have adopted the Uniform Electronic Transactions Act[10]. UETA declares that *electronic* contracts and signatures are as enforceable as those on paper. In other words, the normal rules of contract law apply, and neither party can avoid such a deal merely because it originated in cyberspace. A federal statute, the **Electronic Signatures in Global and National Commerce Act (E-SIGN),** also declares that contracts cannot be denied enforcement simply because they are in electronic form, or signed electronically. It applies in states that have not adopted UETA.

Note that, in many states, certain documents still require a traditional (non-electronic) signature. Wills, adoptions, court orders, and notice of foreclosure are common exceptions. If in doubt, get a hard copy, signed in ink.

THE UCC'S STATUTE OF FRAUDS

We have reached another section dedicated to the Uniform Commercial Code. Remember that UCC rules govern only contracts involving a sale of goods. Because some merchants make dozens or even hundreds of oral contracts every year, the drafters of the UCC wanted to make the writing requirement less onerous for the sale of goods.

The UCC requires a writing for the sale of goods worth $500 or more. The Code's requirements are easier to meet than those of the common law. **UCC §2-201,** the Statute of Frauds section, has three important elements:

1. The basic rule
2. The merchants' exception
3. Special circumstances

[10]The states that have not adopted the Uniform Electronic Transactions Act, at the time of this writing, are Illinois, New York, and Washington.

> The key difference between the common-law rule and the UCC rule is that the Code does *not* require *all* of the terms of the agreement to be in writing.

UCC §2-201(1)—The Basic Rule

A contract for the sale of goods worth $500 or more is not enforceable unless there is some writing, signed by the defendant, indicating that the parties reached an agreement. The key difference between the common-law rule and the UCC rule is that the Code does *not* require *all* of the terms of the agreement to be in writing. The Code looks for something simpler: *an indication that the parties reached an agreement.* Only two things are required: the signature of the defendant and the quantity of goods being sold. Suppose a short memorandum between textile dealers indicates that Seller will sell to Buyer "grade AA 100 percent cotton, white athletic socks." If the writing does not state the price, the parties can testify at court about what the market price was at the time of the deal. If the writing says nothing about the delivery date, the court will assume a reasonable delivery date, say, 60 days. But how many socks were to be delivered? 100 pairs or 100,000? The court will have no objective evidence, and so, the quantity must be written.

Writing	Result
"Confirming phone conversation today, I will send you 1,000 reams of paper for laser printing, usual quality & price. [Signed,] Seller."	This memorandum satisfies UCC §2-201 (1), and the contract may be enforced against the seller. The buyer may testify as to the "usual" quality and price between the two parties, and both sides may rely on normal trade usage.
"Confirming phone conversation today, I will send you best quality paper for laser printing, $3.25 per ream, delivery date next Thursday. [Signed,] Seller."	This memorandum is not enforceable because it states no quantity.

UCC §2-201(2)—The Merchants' Exception

When both parties are "merchants," that is, businesspeople who routinely deal in the goods being sold, the Code will accept an even more informal writing. **Within a reasonable time of making an oral contract, if a merchant sends a written confirmation to another, and if the confirmation is definite enough to bind the *sender herself,* then the merchant who receives the confirmation will *also* be bound by it unless he objects in writing within 10 days.** This exception dramatically changes the rules from the common law, but it applies only between two merchants. The drafters of the Code assumed that experienced merchants are able to take care of themselves in fast-moving negotiations. The critical difference is this: a writing may create a binding contract *even when it is not signed by the defendant.*

Madge manufactures "beanies," that is, silly caps with plastic propellers on top. Rachel, a retailer, telephones her, and they discuss the price of the beanies, shipping time, and other details. Madge then faxes Rachel a memo: "This confirms your order for 2,500 beanies at $12.25 per beanie. Colors: blue, green, black, orange, red. Delivery date: 10 days. [Signed] Madge." Rachel receives the fax, reads it while negotiating with another manufacturer, and throws it in the wastebasket. Rachel buys her beanies elsewhere, and Madge sues. Rachel defends, claiming there is no written contract because she, Rachel, never signed anything. Madge wins under UCC §2-201(2). Both parties were merchants because they routinely dealt in these goods. Madge signed and sent a confirming memo that could have been used to hold her, Madge, to the deal. When Rachel read it, she was not free to disregard it. Obviously, the intelligent business practice would have been to promptly fax a reply saying, "I disagree. We do not have any deal for beanies." Since Rachel failed to respond within 10 days, Madge has an enforceable contract.

For a confirming memo to count, a merchant must send it within a *reasonable* time. But how long is that? A few days certainly qualifies. Could 13 months be quick enough?

Seton Co. v. Lear Corp.

198 Fed. Appx. 496, 2006 WL 2860774
Sixth Circuit Court of Appeals, 2006

Facts: General Motors hired Lear Corporation to supply all of the leather seats for its trucks and SUVs. In October 1998, Lear reached an agreement with Seton Company to provide Lear with the actual cut-to-pattern leather, which Lear would then assemble. Seton agreed to give Lear certain rebates based on the size of the orders. Despite the great value of this contract, the parties initially put nothing in writing. (Note to students: Later in life, if you negotiate a multimillion dollar deal and fail to put it in writing, your grade in this course will be *retroactively lowered!*)

Both parties performed the contract satisfactorily for about a year. Then they agreed to a slight modification in the rebates. All was still well. In the fall of 1999, Lear asked Seton to send a written summary of the agreement, including the modified rebates. In November 1999, Seton sent a one-page memorandum to Lear, summarizing the agreement. It stated: "Lear is to award Seton the entire [truck and SUV program] cut-to-pattern business for the life of the program." The letter ended with a request that Lear "kindly return with acknowledgment signature," but Lear did not do so.

For two more years, the parties worked together amicably. Then Seton became anxious that Lear was planning to take its business elsewhere. In January 2002, Seton sent a letter requesting that Lear affirm its commitment to deal exclusively with Seton for the life of the GMC program. Lear responded that there had never been any such agreement. Seton filed suit.

At trial, Lear claimed that no contract had ever been signed. Seton replied that its memo summarizing the agreement created a valid contract under the "merchant exception" rule. The jury agreed with Seton and awarded the company $34 million. Lear appealed.

Issue: ***Did Seton's memorandum create a contract under the merchant exception?***

Excerpts from the Court's Per Curiam Decision: The attention of the jurors was focused upon two inquiries: first, whether Seton actually produced a "writing in confirmation of the contract"; and second, whether any such writing was sent to Lear "within a reasonable time." The defendant argues that the November 23, 1999, letter from Seton to Lear was not a confirmation of a contract but, rather, an offer to contract. To bolster that argument, Lear now emphasizes language in the letter stating, "We hope that the above meets with your understanding of this agreement." The jury, however, obviously gave more credence to the opening sentence of the letter directing Lear to "please find below the agreement reached by Messrs. M. Duross, Director of Purchasing for Lear Corporation and N. Showich, Vice President of Sales and Marketing for Seton Company."

Similarly, a closer look at the language of the entire November 23 letter reveals the falsity of the defendant's claim that the fact that the correspondence asked for an acknowledgment signature necessarily means that the letter was merely an offer that has not yet been accepted by Lear. As explained by the district judge, "Seton's November 23, 1999 letter did not *require* Lear to take an additional step in order to indicate its acceptance of the letter's terms. Therefore, the Court does not conclude as a matter of law that the letter merely was an offer."

The defendant also contests the timeliness of the letter. Although recognizing that the concept of a "reasonable time" for sending a written confirmation of the agreement depends on the nature, purpose, and circumstances of such action, Lear argues that the 13-month period between the making of the alleged contract and the letter is far too lengthy a period to be considered "reasonable." Again, the jury came to a contrary conclusion, possibly because the parties had engaged in congenial business relations with each other without incident for a lengthy period of time after negotiation of the 1998 agreement. Furthermore, a short time prior to issuance of the letter, Lear and Seton modified the terms of their agreement to extend the rebates that the plaintiff paid to the defendant. Even Lear does not argue that the period of time between that subsequent modification and the November 23 letter should be considered unreasonably long as a matter of law.

Affirmed.

UCC §2-201(3)—Special Circumstances

An oral contract *may* be enforceable, even without a written memorandum, if:

- **The seller is specially manufacturing the goods for the buyer, *or***
- **The defendant admits in court proceedings that there was a contract, *or***
- **The goods have been delivered or they have been paid for.**

Specially Manufactured Goods

If a seller, specially manufacturing goods for the buyer, begins work on them before the buyer cancels, and the goods cannot be sold elsewhere, the oral contract is binding. Bernice manufactures solar heating systems. She phones Jason and orders 75 special electrical converter units designed for her heating system, at $150 per unit. Jason begins manufacturing the units, but then Bernice phones again and says she no longer needs them. Bernice is bound by the contract. The goods are being manufactured for her and cannot be sold elsewhere. Jason had already begun work when she attempted to cancel. If the case goes to court, Jason will win.

The UCC gives merchants special leeway—and important responsibilities.

Admissions in Court

When the defendant admits in court proceedings that the parties made an oral contract, the agreement is binding. Rex sues Sophie, alleging that she orally agreed to sell him five boa constrictors that have been trained to stand in a line and pass a full wine glass from one snake to the next. Sophie defends the lawsuit, but during a deposition, she says, "OK, we agreed verbally, but nothing was ever put in writing, and I knew I didn't have to go through with it. When I went home, the snakes made me feel really guilty, and I decided not to sell." Sophie's admission under oath dooms her defense.

Goods Delivered or Paid For

If the seller has delivered the goods, or the buyer has paid for them, the contract may be enforced even with nothing in writing. Malik orally agrees to sell 500 plastic chairs to a university for use in its cafeteria. Malik delivers 300 of the chairs, but then the university notifies him that it will not honor the deal. Malik is entitled to payment for the 300 chairs, though not for the other 200. Conversely, if the university had sent a check for one-half of the chairs, it would be entitled to 250 chairs.

EXAM Strategy

Question: Beasley is a commercial honey farmer. He orally agrees to sell 500,000 pounds of honey to Grizzly at $1 per pound. Grizzly immediately faxes Beasley a signed confirmation, summarizing the deal. Beasley receives the fax but ignores it, and he never responds to Grizzly. Five days later, Beasley sells his honey to Brown for $1.15 per pound. Grizzly sues Beasley for breach of contract. Beasley claims that he signed nothing and was free to sell his honey anywhere he wanted. Who will win?

Strategy: Honey is a moveable thing, meaning that this contract is governed by the UCC. Under the Code, contracts for the sale of goods worth $500 or more must be in writing. However, the merchant exception changes things when both parties are merchants. Beasley and Grizzly are both merchants. Apply the merchant exception.

Result: Beasley breached the contract. Within a reasonable time after making the agreement, Grizzly sent a memo to Beasley confirming it. Beasley had 10 days either to object in writing or be held to the agreement. Beasley will lose this lawsuit because he ignored the faxed confirmation.

PAROL EVIDENCE

Tyrone agrees to buy Martha's house for $800,000. The contract obligates Tyrone to make a 10 percent down payment immediately and pay the remaining $720,000 in 45 days. As the two parties sign the deal, Tyrone discusses his need for financing. Unfortunately, at the end of 45 days, he has been unable to get a mortgage for the full amount. He claims that the parties orally agreed that he would get his deposit back if he could not obtain financing. But the written agreement says no such thing, and Martha disputes the claim. Who will win? Probably Martha, because of the parol evidence rule.

Parol evidence refers to anything (apart from the written contract itself) that was said, done, or written *before* the parties signed the agreement or *as they signed it.* Martha's conversation with Tyrone about financing the house was parol evidence because it occurred as they were signing the contract. Another important term is **integrated contract**, which means a writing that the parties intend as the final, complete expression of their agreement. Now for the rule.

Integrated contract
A writing that the parties intend as the final, complete expression of their agreement.

The parol evidence rule: When two parties make an integrated contract, neither one may use parol evidence to contradict, vary, or add to its terms. Negotiations may last for hours, weeks, or even months. Almost no contract includes everything that the parties said. When parties consider their agreement integrated, any statements they made before or while signing are irrelevant. If a court determines that Martha and Tyrone intended their agreement to be integrated, it will prohibit testimony about Martha's oral promises. One way to avoid parol evidence disputes is to include an *integration clause.* That is a statement clearly proclaiming that this writing is the "full and final expression" of the parties' agreement, and that anything said before signing or while signing is irrelevant. In the following case, learned people learned about parol evidence the hard way.

Mayo v. North Carolina State University

2005 WL 350567
North Carolina Court of Appeals, 2005

Facts: Dr. Robert Mayo was a tenured faculty member of the engineering department at North Carolina State University (NCSU), and director of the school's nuclear engineering program. In July, he informed his department chair, Dr. Paul Turinsky, that he was leaving NCSU effective September 1. Turinsky accepted the resignation.

In October, after Mayo had departed, Phyllis Jennette, the university's payroll coordinator, informed him that he had been overpaid. She explained that for employees who worked 9 months but were paid over 12 months, the salary checks for July and August were in fact prepayments for the period beginning that September. Because Mayo had not worked after September 1, the checks for July and August were overpayment. When he refused to refund the money, NCSU sought to claim it in legal proceedings. The first step was a hearing before an administrative agency.

At the hearing, Turinsky and Brian Simet, the university's payroll director, explained that the "prepayment" rule was a basic part of every employee's contract. However, both acknowledged that the prepayment rule was not included in any of the documents that formed Mayo's contract, including his appointment letter, annual salary letter, and policies adopted by the university's trustees. The university officials used other evidence, outside the written documents, to establish the prepayment policy.

Based on the additional evidence, the agency ruled that NCSU was entitled to its money. However, Mayo appealed to court, and the trial judge declared that he owed nothing, ruling that the university was not permitted to rely on parol evidence to establish its policy. NCSU appealed.

Issue: ***May NCSU rely on parol evidence to establish its prepayment rule?***

Excerpts from Judge Bryant's Decision: Here, the language of the employment agreement is clear and unambiguous—petitioner is to be paid in twelve monthly installments for his service as a nine-month, academic year, tenured faculty member.

The terms relied upon by NCSU were not expressly included in the employment agreement. Dr. Turinsky testified that petitioner's written employment agreement is comprised of terms found in petitioner's appointment letter, annual salary letter, and written policies adopted and amended by the UNC Board of Governors and the NCSU Board of Trustees. However, none of these documents forming the employment agreement set forth the compensation policies upon which NCSU bases its claim. Simet, Director of NCSU's Payroll Department, admitted at the agency hearing that the policies were "not stated anywhere specifically." Further, Dr. Turinsky testified he did not know of the existence of the terms until September, after petitioner left his employment with NCSU. NCSU, however, attempts to offer parol evidence to explain that payments made in July and August were prepayments for the following academic year.

The parol evidence rule prohibits the admission of parol evidence to vary, add to, or contradict a written instrument intended to be the final integration of the transaction. The rule is otherwise where it is shown that the writing is not a full integration of the terms of the contract, or when a contract is ambiguous, parol evidence is admissible to show and make certain the intention behind the contract.

Here Dr. Turinsky testified that petitioner's employment agreement consisted only of petitioner's appointment letter, his annual salary letter, and the policies adopted and amended by the UNC Board of Governors and by the NCSU Board of Trustees. It therefore appears the parties intended the above documents to be the final integration of the employment agreement. Additionally, we have already noted the language contained in the documents are unambiguous; thus, parol evidence may not be introduced to explain the terms of the agreement.

We hold petitioner does not owe a debt to NCSU as result of an alleged overpayment of salary.

[Affirmed.]

Exception: An Incomplete or Ambiguous Contract

If a court determines that a written contract is incomplete or ambiguous, it will permit parol evidence. Suppose that an employment contract states that the company will provide "full health coverage for Robert Watson and his family," but does not define *family*. Three years later, Watson divorces and remarries, acquiring three stepchildren, and a year later, his second wife has a baby. Watson now has two children by his first marriage and four by the second. The company refuses to insure Watson's first wife or his stepchildren. A court will probably find a key clause in his health care contract—"coverage for ... *his family*"—is ambiguous. A judge cannot determine exactly what the clause means from the contract itself, so the parties will be permitted to introduce parol evidence to prove whether or not the company must insure Watson's extended family.[11]

Fraud, Misrepresentation, or Duress

A court will permit parol evidence of fraud, misrepresentation, or duress. To encourage Annette to buy his house, Will assures her that no floodwaters from the nearby river have ever come within two miles of the house. Annette signs a contract that is silent about flooding and includes an integration clause stating that neither party is relying on any oral statements made during negotiations. When Annette moves in, she discovers that the foundation is collapsing due to earlier flooding and that Will knew of the flooding and the damage. Despite the integration clause, a court will probably allow Annette to testify about Will's misrepresentations.[12]

Chapter Conclusion

Some contracts must be in writing to be enforceable, and the writing must be clear and unambiguous. Drafting the contract need not be arduous. The disputes illustrated in this chapter could all have been prevented with a few carefully crafted sentences. It is worth the time and effort to write them.

Exam Review

1. **THE STATUTE OF FRAUDS** Several types of contract are enforceable only if written:
   - **LAND** The sale of any interest in land (pp. 342–344)
   - **ONE YEAR** An agreement that *cannot* be performed within one year (pp. 344–345)

CPA Question: Able hired Carr to restore Able's antique car for $800. The terms of their oral agreement provided that Carr had 18 months to complete the work. Actually, the work could be completed within one year. The agreement is:

(a) Unenforceable because it covers services with a value in excess of $500

(b) Unenforceable because it covers a time period in excess of one year

[11]See, e.g., *Eure v. Norfolk Shipbuilding & Drydock Corp., Inc.*, 561 S.E.2d 663 (Va. 2002).

[12]*Lindberg v. Roseth*, 137 Idaho 222, 46 P.3d 518 (Idaho 2002).

(c) Enforceable because personal service contracts are exempt from the Statute of Frauds

(d) Enforceable because the work could be completed within one year

Strategy: This is a subtle question. Notice that the contract is for a sum greater than $500. But that is a red herring. Why? The contract also might take 18 months to perform. But it *could* be finished in less than a year. (See the "Result" at the end of this section.)

- **DEBT OF ANOTHER** A promise to pay the debt of another, including promises made by executors to pay an estate's debts. (pp. 345–346)

EXAM Strategy

Question: Donald Waide had a contracting business. He bought most of his supplies from Paul Bingham's supply center. Waide fell behind on his bills, and Bingham told Waide that he would extend no more credit to him. That same day, Donald's father, Elmer Waide, came to Bingham's store, and said to Bingham that he would "stand good" for any sales to Donald made on credit. Based on Elmer's statement, Bingham again gave Donald credit, and Donald ran up $10,000 in goods before Bingham sued Donald and Elmer. What defense did Elmer make, and what was the outcome?

Strategy: This was an oral agreement, so the issue is whether the promise had to be in writing to be enforceable. Review the list of six contracts that must be in writing. Is this agreement there? (See the "Result" at the end of this section.)

- **EXECUTORS** A promise made by an executor of an estate (p. 346)
- **MARRIAGE** A promise made in consideration of marriage; and (pp. 346–347)
- **GOODS** The sale of goods worth $500 or more (p. 350)

EXAM Strategy

Question: James River-Norwalk, Inc., was a paper and textile company that needed a constant supply of wood. James River orally contracted with Gary Futch to supply wood for the company, and Futch did so for several years. The deal was worth many thousands of dollars, but nothing was put in writing. Futch actually purchased the wood for his own account and then resold it to James River. After a few years, James River refused to do more business with Futch. Did the parties have a binding contract?

Strategy: If this is a contract for services, it is enforceable without anything in writing. However, if it is one for the sale of goods, it must be in writing. Clearly what James River wanted was the wood, and it did not care where Futch found it. (See the "Result" at the end of this section.)

2. **CONTENTS** The writing must be signed by the defendant and must state the name of all parties, the subject matter of the agreement, and all essential terms and promises. Electronic signatures usually are valid. (pp. 347–349)

3. **UNIFORM COMMERCIAL CODE (UCC)** A contract or memorandum for the sale of goods may be less complete than those required by the common law.

   - The basic UCC rule requires only a memorandum signed by the defendant, indicating that the parties reached an agreement and specifying the quantity of goods.
   - Between merchants, even less is required. If one merchant sends written confirmation of a contract, the merchant who receives the document must object within 10 days or be bound by the writing.
   - In the following special circumstances, no writing may be required: the goods are specially manufactured, one party admits in litigation that there was a contract, or one party pays for part of the goods or delivers some of the goods. (pp. 349–353)

4. **PAROL EVIDENCE** When an integrated contract exists, neither party may generally use parol evidence to contradict, vary, or add to its terms. Parol evidence refers to anything (apart from the written contract itself) that was said, done, or written before the parties signed the agreement or as they signed it. (pp. 353–355)

1. "One Year" Result: (d) A contract for the sale of goods worth $500 or more must be in writing—but this is a contract for *services*, not the sale of goods, so the $800 price is irrelevant. The contract *can* be completed within one year, and thus it falls outside the Statute of Frauds. This is an enforceable agreement.

1. "Debt of Another" Result: Elmer made a promise to pay the debt of another. He did so as a favor to his son. This is a collateral promise. Elmer never signed any such promise, and the agreement cannot be enforced against him.

1. "Goods" Result: James River was buying wood, and this is a contract for the sale of goods. With nothing in writing, signed by James River, Futch has no enforceable agreement.

MULTIPLE-CHOICE QUESTIONS

1. **CPA QUESTION** Two individuals signed a contract that was intended to be their entire agreement. The parol evidence rule will prevent the admission of evidence offered to:
   (a) Explain the meaning of an ambiguity in the written contract
   (b) Establish that fraud had been committed in the formation of the contract
   (c) Prove the existence of a contemporaneous oral agreement modifying the contract
   (d) Prove the existence of a subsequent oral agreement modifying the contract

2. Raul wants to plant a garden, and he agrees to buy a small piece of land for $300. Later, he agrees to buy a table for $300. Neither agreement is put in writing. The

agreement to buy the land ____________ enforceable, and the agreement to buy the table ____________ enforceable.

(a) is; is

(b) is; is not

(c) is not; is

(d) is not; is not

3. The common-law Statute of Frauds requires that to be "in writing," an agreement must be signed by ...

(a) the plaintiff

(b) the defendant

(c) both A and B

(d) none of the above

4. Mandy verbally tells a motorcycle dealer that she will make her son's motorcycle payments if he falls behind on them. Will Mandy be legally required to live up to this agreement?

(a) Yes, absolutely

(b) Yes, if her son is under 18

(c) Yes, if Mandy will be the primary driver of the motorcycle

(d) Yes, if the motorcycle is worth less than $500

(e) No, absolutely not

5. In December 2012, Eric hires a band to play at a huge graduation party he is planning to hold in May, 2014. The deal is never put into writing. In January 2014, if he wanted to cancel the job, Eric ____________ be able to do so. If he does not cancel, and if the band shows up and plays at the party in May 2014, Eric ____________ have to pay them.

(a) will; will

(b) will; will not

(c) will not; will

(d) will not; will not

Essay Questions

1. Richard Griffin and three other men owned a grain company called Bearhouse, Inc., which needed to borrow money. First National Bank was willing to loan $490,000, but it insisted that the four men sign personal guaranties on the loan, committing themselves to repaying up to 25 percent of the loan each if Bearhouse defaulted. Bearhouse went bankrupt. The bank was able to collect some of its money from Bearhouse's assets, but it sued Griffin for the balance. At trial, Griffin wanted to testify that before he signed his guaranty, a bank officer assured him that he would only owe 25 percent of *whatever balance was unpaid,* not 25 percent of the total loan. How will the court decide whether Griffin is entitled to testify about the conversation?

2. When Deana Byers married Steven Byers, she was pregnant with another man's child. Shortly after the marriage, Deana gave birth. The marriage lasted only two months, and the couple separated. In divorce proceedings, Deana sought child support. She claimed that Steven had orally promised to support the child if Deana would marry him. Steven claims he never made the promise. Comment on the outcome.

3. Lonnie Hippen moved to Long Island, Kansas, to work in an insurance company owned by Griffiths. After he moved there, Griffiths offered to sell Hippen a house he owned, and Hippen agreed in writing to buy it. He did buy the house and moved in, but two years later, Hippen left the insurance company. He then claimed that at the time of the sale, Griffiths had orally promised to buy back his house at the selling price if Hippen should happen to leave the company. Griffiths defended based on the Statute of Frauds. Hippen argued that the Statute of Frauds did not apply because the repurchase of the house was essentially part of his employment with Griffiths. Comment.

4. Landlord owned a clothing store and agreed in writing to lease the store's basement to another retailer. The written lease, which both parties signed, (1) described the premises exactly, (2) identified the parties, and (3) stated the monthly rent clearly. But an appeals court held that the lease did not satisfy the Statute of Frauds. Why not?

5. **YOU BE THE JUDGE WRITING PROBLEM** Harrison Epperly operated United Brake Systems in Indianapolis, Indiana, and wanted to open a similar store in Nashville. He offered Kenneth Jarrett a job as manager, promising six months' severance pay if the store was not profitable in six months, and 49 percent ownership if he managed the new store for 10 years. Jarrett agreed, but the two men never put the deal in writing. Under Jarrett's management, the Nashville branch grew dramatically. After four years of renting space, the company purchased the land and buildings it used. Epperly periodically acknowledged his promise to make Jarrett 49 percent owner of the Nashville branch, and from time to time, he mentioned the arrangement to other workers. But after 10 years, Epperly sold United Brake, which had grown to 23 branches, to another company for $11 million. Jarrett sued Epperly for 49 percent of the Nashville branch. The trial court awarded Jarrett $812,000. Epperly appealed. Is Jarrett's contract with Epperly barred by the Statute of Frauds? **Argument for Epperly:** This alleged contract is unenforceable for two reasons. First, the agreement includes real estate; namely, the valuable land and buildings the company uses. A contract for the sale of any interest in land is unenforceable unless written. Second, the contract could not have been performed within 1 year. If there was a deal, then by Jarrett's own words, the parties intended it to last 10 years. And 10 years' work cannot be performed in 1 year. **Argument for Jarrett:** The agreement had nothing to do with land. Jarrett and Epperly agreed that Mr. Jarrett would obtain a 49 percent ownership of the *Nashville branch*. At the time they made that agreement, the Nashville branch had no real estate. There is no rule saying that a valid contract becomes invalid because a corporation acquires some land. The "not in one year" argument also misses the point. The primary obligation was to open the branch and manage it for six months. If it was not profitable, Mr. Jarrett would immediately receive six months' severance pay, and the contract would be fully performed by both parties in less than a year. Finally, Epperly made a binding commitment, and Mr. Jarrett relied. Promissory estoppel prohibits Mr. Epperly from using deceit to profit.

Discussion Questions

1. **ETHICS** Jacob Deutsch owned commercial property. He orally agreed to rent it for six years to Budget Rent-A-Car. Budget took possession, began paying monthly rent, and, over a period of several months, expended about $6,000 in upgrading the property. Deutsch was aware of the repairs. After a year, Deutsch attempted to evict Budget. Budget claimed it had a six-year oral lease, but Deutsch claimed that such a lease was worthless. Please rule. Is it ethical for Deutsch to use the Statute of Frauds in attempting to defeat the lease? Assume that, as landlord, you had orally agreed to rent premises to a tenant, but then for business reasons, you preferred not to carry out the deal. Would you evict a tenant if you thought the Statute of Frauds would enable you to do so? How should you analyze the problem? What values are most important to you?

2. Mast Industries and Bazak International were two textile firms. Mast orally offered to sell certain textiles to Bazak for $103,000. Mast promised to send documents confirming the agreement, but it never did. Finally, Bazak sent a memorandum to Mast confirming the agreement, describing the goods, and specifying their quantity and the price. Bazak's officer signed the memo. Mast received the memo but never agreed to it in writing. When Mast failed to deliver the goods, Bazak sued. Who will win? Why?

3. Is the Statute of Frauds reasonable, or does it unacceptably allow people to escape their obligations on a mere technicality?

4. Does the coverage of the Statute of Frauds make sense as it currently stands? Would it be better to expand the law and require that all contracts be in writing? Or should the law be done away with altogether?

5. Compare the common-law Statute of Frauds to the UCC version. What are the specific differences? Which is more reasonable? Why?

CHAPTER 16

© picsbyst/Shutterstock.com

THIRD PARTIES

Morty is 80, and a back injury makes it impossible for him to keep up with his yardwork. The weeds in his front yard are knee-high by the Fourth of July, when his son John comes to visit for a week.

Surprised at the condition of the lawn, John gets the old mower out of the garage and mows it himself. Later in the visit, John calls a local landscaping company. He agrees to pay $500 for the company to send workers to mow Morty's lawn every two weeks for the rest of the year.

The company bills John's credit card, but it never sends anyone to cut the grass. As the summer wears on, John and Morty make several angry phone calls to the landscaper, without result. The owner of the company seems not to care, and it may take a lawsuit to motivate him to refund John's money so that he can hire someone else to do the job.

But if John is too busy to take legal action, can *Morty* do so?

If John is too busy to take legal action, can *Morty* do so?

The last four chapters examined the Contracts Checklist, so you now know all the elements that must be present for a valid contract to exist. In this chapter and the next two, we turn our attention to other contracts issues.

Third Party Beneficiary

The two parties who make a contract always intend to gain some benefit for themselves. Often, though, their bargain will also benefit *someone else.* **A third party beneficiary is someone who was not a party to the contract but stands to benefit from it.** Many contracts create third party beneficiaries. In the opening scenario, Morty is a third party beneficiary of John's agreement with the landscaping company. As another example, suppose a major league baseball team contracts to purchase from Seller 20 acres of an abandoned industrial site to be used for a new stadium. The owner of a pizza parlor on the edge of Seller's land might benefit enormously, since 40,000 hungry fans in the neighborhood for 81 home games every season could turn her once-marginal operation into a gold mine of cheese and pepperoni.

But what if the contract falls apart? What if the team backs out of the deal to buy the land? Seller can certainly sue because it is a party to the contract. But what about the pizza parlor owner? Can she sue to enforce the deal and recover lost profits for unsold sausage and green pepper?

The outcome in cases like these depends upon the intentions of the two contracting parties. If they *intended* to benefit the third party, she will probably be permitted to enforce their contract. If they did not intend to benefit her, she probably has no power to enforce the agreement.

Intended Beneficiaries

Intended beneficiary
Someone who may enforce a contract made between two other parties.

Promisor
Makes the promise that a third party seeks to enforce.

Promisee
The contract party *to whom* a promise is made.

A person is an **intended beneficiary** and may enforce a contract if the parties intended her to benefit and if either (a) enforcing the promise will satisfy a *duty* of the promisee to the beneficiary, or (b) the promisee intended to make a *gift* to the beneficiary. (The **promisor** is the one who makes the promise that the third party beneficiary is seeking to enforce. The **promisee** is the other party to the contract.)

In other words, a third party beneficiary must show two things in order to enforce a contract that two other people created. First, she must show that the two contracting parties were aware of her situation and knew that she would receive something of value from their deal. Second, she must show that the promisee wanted to benefit her for one of two reasons: either to satisfy some duty owed or to make her a gift.

If the promisee is fulfilling some duty, the third party beneficiary is called a **creditor beneficiary**. Most often, the duty that a promisee will be fulfilling is a debt already owed to the beneficiary. If the promisee is making a gift, the third party is a **donee beneficiary.**[1] So long as the third party is either a creditor or a donee beneficiary, she may enforce the contract. If she is only an incidental beneficiary, she may not.

We will apply this rule to the dispute over Morty's lawn. Like most contracts, the deal between John and the landscaping company had two promises: the company's promise to mow the lawn every two weeks and John's agreement to pay $500. The one that interests us is the promise to mow the lawn. The company is the promisor and John is the promisee.

Did the two parties intend to benefit Morty? Yes, they did. John wanted his father's property maintained. Did John owe Morty a legal duty? No. Did John intend to make a gift to Morty? Yes. So, Morty is an intended, donee beneficiary, and he can sue the landscaping company to enforce the contract himself.

[1] "Donee" comes from the word "donate".

By contrast, the pizza parlor owner will surely lose. A stadium is a multimillion-dollar investment, and it is most unlikely that the baseball team and the seller of the land were even aware of the owner's existence, let alone that they intended to benefit her. She probably cannot prove either the first element or the second element, and certainly not both.

In the following case, a dazzling diamond loses its luster. Who is entitled to sue?

SCHAUER V. MANDARIN GEMS OF CALIFORNIA, INC.

2005 WL 5730
Court of Appeal of California, 2005

Facts: Sarah Schauer and her fiance, Darin Erstad, went shopping for an engagement ring at Mandarin Gems, where they were captivated by a 3-carat diamond with a high clarity rating. Erstad bought the ring for $43,121. Later, Mandarin supplied Erstad with a written appraisal valuing the ring at $45,500. A certified gemologist signed the appraisal.

Diamonds may last forever, but this marriage was short-lived. The divorce decree gave each party the right to keep whatever personal property they currently held, meaning that Schauer could keep the ring. She had the ring appraised by the Gem Trade Laboratory, which gave it a poor clarity rating and a value of only $20,000.

Schauer sued Mandarin for misrepresentation and breach of contract, but the jeweler defended by saying that it had never made a contract with her. The trial court dismissed Schauer's suit, and she appealed.

Issue: ***Does Schauer have any right to sue for breach of contract as a third party beneficiary?***

Excerpts from Judge Ikola's Decision: Plaintiff has standing in her own right to sue for breach of contract as a third party beneficiary. [D]efendant entered into a written contract with Plaintiff's fiance to purchase the subject engagement ring for the sole and stated purpose of giving it to Plaintiff.

A contract, made expressly for the benefit of a third person, may be enforced by him or her at any time before the parties rescind it. Because third party beneficiary status is a matter of contract interpretation, a person seeking to enforce a contract as a third party beneficiary must plead a contract which was made expressly for his or her benefit and one in which it clearly appears that he or she was a beneficiary.

An intent to make the obligation inure to the benefit of the third party must have been clearly manifested by the contracting parties. Although this means persons only incidentally or remotely benefited by the contract are not entitled to enforce it, it does not mean both of the contracting parties must intend to benefit the third party: Rather, it means the promisor—in this case, defendant jeweler—must have understood that the promisee (Erstad) had such intent. No specific manifestation by the promisor of an intent to benefit the third person is required.

We conclude the pleading here meets the test of demonstrating plaintiff's standing as a third party beneficiary to enforce the contract between Erstad and defendant. Erstad allegedly bought the ring for the sole and *stated* purpose of giving the ring to plaintiff. Under the alleged facts, the jeweler *must* have understood Erstad's intent to enter the sales contract for plaintiff's benefit. Thus, plaintiff has adequately pleaded her status as a third party beneficiary, and she is entitled to proceed with her contract claim against defendant.

EXAM Strategy

Question: Mr. Inspector examines houses and gives its reports to potential buyers. Mr. Inspector contracts with Greenlawn, a real estate agent, to furnish reports on houses that Greenlawn is selling. The agreement allows the agent to give the reports to potential buyers. Greenlawn gives Molly one of Mr. Inspector's reports and, relying upon it, she buys a house. Although the report states that the house is structurally sound, it turns out that chronic roof leaks have caused water to seep into the walls. Molly sues Mr. Inspector. The inspector requests summary judgment, claiming that he had no contract with Molly.

Strategy: Mr. Inspector is right in saying he had no agreement with Molly. To prevail, Molly must demonstrate she is a third party beneficiary of the contract between the other two. A third party beneficiary may enforce a contract if the parties intended to benefit her and either (a) enforcing the promise will satisfy a duty of the promisee to the beneficiary or (b) the promisee intended to make a gift to the beneficiary.

Result: Greenlawn used the inspection summaries as sales tools. When Greenlawn assured a potential buyer that she could rely upon a report, the real estate agent took on a duty to deliver reliable information. Mr. Inspector understood that. The two parties intended to benefit Greenlawn's buyers. Molly may sue Mr. Inspector for breach of his contract with the agent. Mr. Inspector's motion for summary judgment is denied.

Incidental Beneficiaries

Incidental beneficiary
Someone who might have benefited from a contract between two others but has no right to enforce that agreement.

A person who fails to qualify as a donee beneficiary or a creditor beneficiary is merely an **incidental beneficiary** and may not enforce the contract. The pizza parlor owner is an incidental beneficiary.

In an effort to persuade courts, many plaintiffs make creative arguments that they are intended beneficiaries with enforcement rights. Is every taxpayer an intended beneficiary of a government contract? Do labor unions have rights if a contract refers to them in general terms? Or are these plaintiffs incidental beneficiaries? The following case answers these questions.

Unite Here Local 30 v. California Department of Parks and Recreation

2011 Cal. App. LEXIS 510
Court of Appeal of California, 2011

Facts: The California Department of Parks and Recreation (DPR) and Delaware North Companies (DNC) entered into a contract giving DNC the right to operate a concession stand at a state park in San Diego for 10 years. Four years into the contract, DNC assigned its rights to operate the stand to another company.

DNC fired many of its employees, and the new operator did not rehire them. Some of these workers were members of the union Unite Here Local 30. Local 30 sued to block the assignment. It was joined in the suit by Bridgette Browning, who lived in the area and seemed to care who provided her hot dogs.

The trial court rejected the plaintiff's claims, and the plaintiffs appealed.

Issue: ***Were the plaintiffs incidental or donee beneficiaries?***

Excerpts from Judge Hull's Decision: Paragraph 37(a) of the contract limits assignments and reads: "No assignment shall be made unless first consented to in writing by State." Before State considers such assignment, the proposed assignment must comply with applicable law. DPR reviewed the evidence submitted by Delaware North and determined that the proposed assignment met the requirements under paragraph 37(a).

Plaintiffs contend a third party who is within the class of those for whose benefit a contract is made have standing to sue for breach of that contract. They further argue, Local 30 and the employees it represents are clearly intended beneficiaries of the original contract.

The test for determining whether a contract was made for the benefit of a third person is whether an intent to benefit a third person appears from the terms of the contract. Under the intent test, it is not enough that the third party would incidentally have benefited from performance. On the other hand, the third person need not be named or identified individually. A third party may enforce a contract where he shows that he is a member of a class of persons for whose benefit it was made.

Plaintiffs contend Bridgette Browning has a right to sue as a taxpayer of California. They point out that paragraph 37 procedures are intended to eliminate favoritism, fraud, corruption, and misuse of public funds. Thus, plaintiffs argue, can be said to have the intent to benefit the general public and the taxpayer. Of course, any contract entered into by the state would presumably be for the benefit of the state's residents and taxpayers, just as a contract entered into by a corporation would presumably be for the benefit of the corporation's shareholders. However, the fact that members of the public derive a benefit from the contract does not make them intended beneficiaries. A person is a donee beneficiary only if the promisee's contractual intent is to make a gift to him. Browning is no more than an incidental beneficiary who benefits merely because the state as a whole benefits.

Likewise, Local 30 is no more than an incidental beneficiary. Plaintiffs argue that because the Concession Contract contains a neutrality agreement regarding union organizing, Local 30 and the employees it represents are clearly intended beneficiaries of the original contract. The neutrality agreement states, in part, "Concessionaire shall not use the Premises to hold a meeting if the purpose is to promote or deter union organizing." This provision hardly reveals an intent to confer a benefit on Local 30, or any union for that matter. At best, it shows an intent not to provide either a benefit or a detriment to union organizing.

We conclude the trial court correctly determined plaintiffs are not third party beneficiaries and therefore lack standing to sue on that basis.

The judgment is affirmed.

Assignment and Delegation

After a contract is made, one or both parties may wish to substitute someone else for themselves. Six months before Maria's lease expires, an out-of-town company offers her a new job at a substantial increase in pay. After taking the job, she wants to sublease her apartment to her friend Sarah.

A contracting party may transfer his rights under the contract, which is called an **assignment** of rights. Or a party may transfer her obligations under the contract, which is a **delegation** of duties. Frequently, a party will make an assignment and delegation simultaneously, transferring both rights (such as the right to inhabit an apartment) and duties (like the obligation to pay monthly rent) to a third party.

Assignment
Transferring contract *rights*.

Delegation
Transferring contract *duties*.

Assignment

Lydia needs 500 bottles of champagne. Bruno agrees to sell them to her for $10,000, payable 30 days after delivery. He transports the wine to her.

Bruno owes Doug $8,000 from a previous deal. He says to Doug, "I don't have your money, but I'll give you my claim to Lydia's $10,000." Doug agrees. Bruno then *assigns* to Doug his rights to Lydia's money, and in exchange Doug gives up his claim against Bruno for $8,000. Bruno is the **assignor, the one making an assignment**, and Doug is the **assignee, the one receiving an assignment**.

Why would Bruno offer $10,000 when he owed Doug only $8,000? Because all he has is a *claim* to Lydia's money. Cash in hand is often more valuable. Doug, however, is willing to assume some risk for a potential $2,000 gain.

Obligor
The party obligated to do something.

Bruno notifies Lydia of the assignment. Lydia, who owes the money, is called the **obligor;** that is, the one obligated to do something. At the end of 30 days, Doug arrives at

Lydia's doorstep, asks for his money, and gets it, since Lydia is obligated to him. Bruno has no claim to any payment. See Exhibit 16.1.

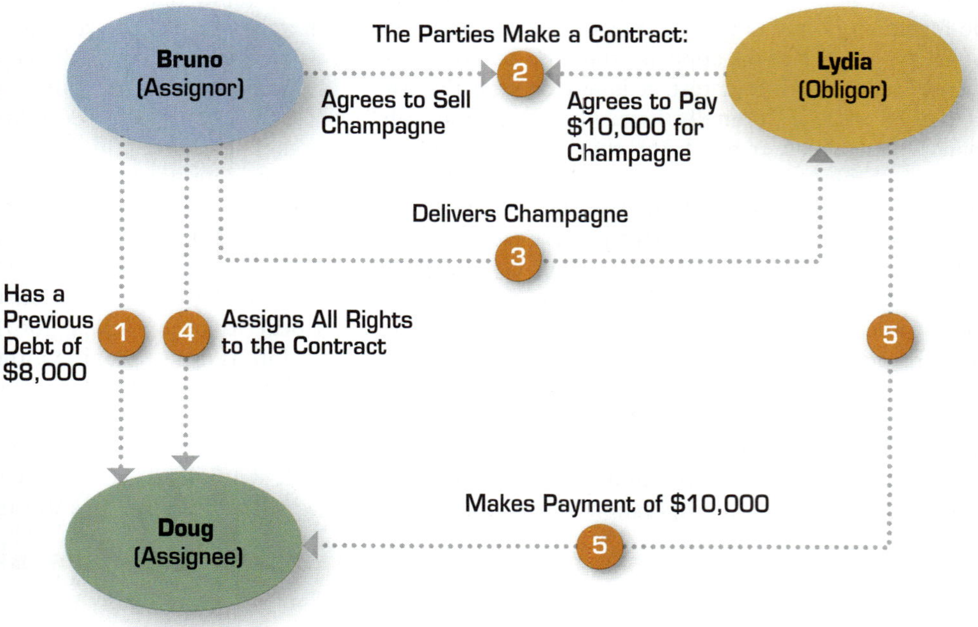

EXHIBIT 16.1

EXAM Strategy

Question: Hasannah, an art dealer, signs a contract with Jason. Hasannah will deliver a David Hockney painting to Jason's house. Jason may keep it for 30 days and then either return it or pay Hasannah $2 million. Hasannah delivers the painting. Hasannah finds a better building to house her gallery and agrees to buy it from Shannon. She and Shannon sign a contract allowing Shannon to receive Jason's payment if he keeps the picture. Hasannah then notifies Jason to pay Shannon the $2 million. Identify the obligor, the assignor, and the assignee.

Strategy: The obligor is the one obligated to do something. The assignor makes an assignment and the assignee receives it.

Result: Jason is obligated either to return the picture or pay $2 million for it. He is the obligor. Hasannah is entitled to the money, but she assigns her right to Shannon. Hasannah is the assignor and Shannon the assignee.

What Rights Are Assignable?

Most contract rights are assignable, but not all. Disputes sometimes arise between the two contracting parties about whether one of the parties could legally assign her rights to a third party. Any **contractual right may be assigned unless assignment**

(a) would substantially change the obligor's rights or duties under the contract;

(b) is forbidden by law or public policy; or

(c) is validly precluded by the contract itself.[2]

Substantial Change. An assignment is prohibited if it would substantially change the obligor's situation. For example, Bruno is permitted to assign to Doug his rights to payment from Lydia because it makes no difference to Lydia whether she writes a check to one person or another. But suppose that, before delivery, Lydia had wanted to assign her rights to the shipment of 500 bottles of champagne to a business in another country. In this example, Bruno would be the obligor, and his duties would substantially change. Shipping heavy items over long distances adds substantial costs, so Lydia would not be able to make the assignment.

Assignment is also prohibited when the obligor is agreeing to perform **personal services**. The close working relationship in such agreements makes it unfair to expect the obligor to work with a stranger. Warner, a feature film director, hires Mayer to be his assistant on a film to be shot over the next 10 weeks. Warner may not assign his right to Mayer's work to another director.

Public Policy. Some assignments are prohibited by public policy. For example, someone who has suffered a personal injury may not assign her claim to a third person. Vladimir is playing the piano on his roof deck when the instrument rolls over the balustrade and drops 35 stories before smashing Wanda's foot. Wanda has a valid tort claim against Vladimir, but she may not assign the claim to anyone else. As a matter of public policy, all states have decided that the sale of personal injury claims could create an unseemly and unethical marketplace.

Contract Prohibition. Finally, one of the contracting parties may try to prohibit assignment in the agreement itself. For example, most landlords include in the written lease a clause prohibiting the tenant from assigning the tenancy without the landlord's written permission.

Subleasing disputes between landlord and tenant are common. How much leeway does a landlord have in rejecting a proposed assignment? The following case provides the answer.

Tenet Healthsystem Surgical, L.L.C. v. Jefferson Parish Hospital Service District No. 1

426 F.3d 738
Fifth Circuit Court of Appeals, 2005

Facts: MSC, Inc. owned the Marrero Shopping Center, and leased space to Tenet Healthsystem for use in outpatient surgery and general medical practice. The lease allowed Tenet to assign the lease with MSC's consent, and stated that consent would not be unreasonably withheld.

Two years later, MSC sold the shopping center to West Jefferson Medical Center, which owned an adjacent hospital and wanted the space for expansion. A few months after that, Tenet requested permission from West Jefferson to assign its lease to Pelican Medical, which intended to use the space for an occupational medical

[2]Restatement (Second) of Contracts §317(2). And note that UCC §2-210 is, for our purposes, nearly identical.

clinic. West Jefferson denied permission, stating that Pelican would be performing work not permitted under the original lease, and also because Pelican would compete with West Jefferson.

Tenet sued, claiming that West Jefferson was unreasonably withholding permission to assign. The trial court granted summary judgment for West Jefferson. Tenet appealed.

Issue: ***Did West Jefferson unreasonably withhold permission to assign the lease?***

Excerpts from Judge Davis's Decision: West Jefferson asserts that Pelican's contemplated uses of the facility exceed those permitted under the lease [and also argues] that its refusal was reasonable because the proposed use of the facility poses more competition to its adjacent hospital.

Tenet used the facility for an outpatient surgery center. Pelican planned to use the facility for an occupational medical clinic. The services offered by an occupational medicine practice are quite comprehensive, from physical examinations and drug screening to low acuity emergencies. The clinic can treat patients with depression, lacerations, broken bones [and] pneumonia, and provides related lab and x-ray services. Nothing in this description takes the proposed practice outside the limits of a "general medical and physician's offices, including related uses," a permitted use under the lease.

West Jefferson also opposes the lease assignment from Tenet to Pelican on the basis that Pelican's broadened scope of operations would include new areas of competition with its hospital. When determining the reasonableness of a landlord's refusal to consent to an assignment of a lease, the standard is that of a reasonable prudent man.

In determining whether a landlord's refusal to consent was reasonable in a commercial context, only factors that relate to the landlord's interest in preserving the leased property or in having the terms of prime lease performed should be considered. Among factors a landlord can consider are the financial responsibility of the proposed subtenant, the legality and suitability of proposed use and nature of the occupancy. A landlord's personal taste or convenience is not properly considered. Rather the landlord's objection must relate to ownership and operation of leased property, not lessor's general economic interest. Under this standard, West Jefferson's refusal to consent to the assignment of the Tenet lease because Pelican would be a new competitor relates not to the ownership and operation of the leased property, but to West Jefferson's general economic interest.

West Jefferson's reason for denying consent to the assignment to Pelican based on increased competition is wholly personal to West Jefferson and does not relate in any way to an objective evaluation of Pelican as a tenant. Further, allowing West Jefferson to deny consent on a basis personal to it, a successor owner who took subject to the existing lease, would expand West Jefferson's rights under the lease to the detriment of the lessee in a manner not bargained for in the lease itself. Accordingly, we conclude that West Jefferson's refusal of consent to the assignment of the lease on the basis of increased competition was unreasonable.

Reversed and remanded.

How Rights Are Assigned

Writing. In general, an assignment may be written or oral, and no particular formalities are required. However, when someone wants to assign rights governed by the statute of frauds, she must do it in writing. Suppose City contracts with Seller to buy Seller's land and then brings in Investor to complete the project. If City wants to assign to Investor its rights to the land, it must do so in writing.

Consideration. An assignment can be valid with or without consideration, but the lack of consideration may have consequences. Two examples should clarify this. Recall Bruno, who sells champagne to Lydia and then assigns to Doug his right to payment. In that case, there *is* consideration for the assignment. Bruno assigns his rights only because Doug cancels the old debt, and his agreement to do that is valid consideration. **An assignment for consideration is irrevocable.** Once the two men agree, Bruno may not telephone Doug and say, "I've changed my mind, I want Lydia to pay me after all." Lydia's $10,000 now belongs to Doug.

Gratuitous assignment
One made as a gift, for no consideration.

But suppose that Bruno assigns his contract rights to his sister Brunhilde as a birthday present. This is a **gratuitous assignment;** that is, one made as a gift, for no consideration. **A**

gratuitous assignment is generally revocable if it is oral and generally irrevocable if it is written. If Bruno verbally assigns his rights to Brunhilde, but then changes his mind, telephones Lydia, and says, "I want you to pay me after all," that revocation is effective and Brunhilde gets nothing. But if Bruno puts his assignment in writing and Brunhilde receives it, Bruno has given up his right to receive Lydia's payment.

© Joel Blit/Shutterstock

If you assign your rights under a contract, inform the obligor immediately.

Notice to Obligor. The assignment is valid from the moment it is made, regardless of whether the assignor notifies the obligor. But an assignor with common sense will immediately inform the obligor of the assignment. Suppose Maude has a contract with Nelson, who is obligated to deliver 700 live frogs to her shop. If Maude (assignor) assigns her rights to Obie (assignee), Maude should notify Nelson (obligor) the same day. If she fails to inform Nelson, he may deliver the frogs to Maude. Nelson will have no further obligations under the contract, and Maude will owe Obie 700 frogs.

Rights of the Parties after Assignment

Once the assignment is made and the obligor notified, the assignee may enforce her contractual rights against the obligor. If Lydia fails to pay Doug for the champagne she gets from Bruno, Doug may sue to enforce the agreement. The law will treat Doug as though he had entered into the contract with Lydia.

But if a lawsuit arises, the reverse is also true. **The obligor may generally raise all defenses against the assignee that she could have raised against the assignor.** Suppose Lydia opens the first bottle of champagne—silently. "Where's the pop?" she wonders. There is no pop because all 500 bottles have gone flat. Bruno has failed to perform his part of the contract, and Lydia may use Bruno's nonperformance as a defense against Doug. If the champagne was indeed worthless, Lydia owes Doug nothing.

Assignor's Warranty. The law implies certain warranties, or assurances, on the part of the assignor. Unless the parties expressly agree to exclude them, the assignor warrants that (1) the rights he is assigning actually do exist, and (2) there are no defenses to the rights other than those that would be obvious, like nonperformance. But the assignor *does not* warrant that the obligor is solvent. Bruno is impliedly warranting to Doug that Lydia has no defenses to the contract, but he is not guaranteeing Doug that she has the money to pay, or that she will pay.

Special Issue: The Uniform Commercial Code and Assignments of Security Interests

The provisions of the Uniform Commercial Code regarding assignments in contracts for the sale of goods are very similar to common-law rules.[3] However, Article 9 of the Code has special rules about the assignment of **security interests**, which are the legal rights in personal

Security interests
Rights in personal property that assure payment or the performace of some obligation.

[3]UCC §2-210.

property that assure payment. When an automobile dealer sells you a new car on credit, the dealer will keep a security interest in your car. If you do not make your monthly payments, the dealer retains a right to repossess the vehicle. That authority is called a *security interest.* (See Chapter 24 for a full discussion.)

Companies that sell goods often prefer to assign their security interests to some other firm, such as a bank or finance company. The bank is the assignee. Just as we saw with the common law, the assignee of a security interest generally has all of the rights that the assignor had. And the obligor (the buyer) may also raise all of the defenses against the assignee that she could have raised against the assignor.

Under UCC §9-404, the obligor on a sales contract may generally assert any defenses against the assignee that arise from the contract, and any other defenses that arose before notice of assignment. The Code's reference to any defenses that arise from the contract means that if the assignor breached his part of the deal, the obligor may raise that as a defense. Suppose a dealer sells you a new Porsche on credit, retaining a security interest. He assigns the security interest to the bank. The car is great for the first few weeks, but then the roof slides onto the street and both doors fall off. You refuse to make any more monthly payments. When the bank sues you, you may raise the automobile's defects as a defense, just as you could have raised them against the dealer itself. Where the Code talks about other defenses that arose before notice of assignment, it refers, for example, to fraud. Suppose the dealer knew that before you bought the Porsche, it had been smashed up and rebuilt. If the dealer told you it was brand new, that was fraud, and you could raise the defense against the bank.

A contract may prohibit an obligor from raising certain defenses against an assignee. Sometimes a seller of goods will require the buyer to sign a contract that permits the seller to assign *and* prohibits the buyer from raising defenses against the assignee that he could have raised against the seller. University wants to buy a computer system on credit from Leland for $85,000. Leland agrees to the deal but insists that the contract permit him to assign his rights to anyone he chooses. He also wants this clause: "University agrees that it will not raise against an assignee any defenses that it may have had against Leland." This clause is sometimes called a *waiver clause* because the obligor is waiving (giving up) rights. Courts may also refer to it as an *exclusion clause* since the parties are excluding potential defenses. Leland wants a waiver clause because it makes his contract more valuable. As soon as University signs the agreement, Leland can take his contract to Krushem Collections, a finance company. Krushem might offer Leland $70,000 cash for the contract. Leland can argue, "You have to pay $85,000 for this. You are guaranteed payment by University since they cannot raise any defenses against you, even if the computer system collapses in the first half-hour." Leland gets cash and need not worry about collecting payments. Krushem receives the full value of the contract, with interest, spread out over several years.

Under UCC §9-403, an agreement by a buyer (or lessee) that he will not assert against an assignee any claim or defense that he may have against the seller (or lessor) is generally enforceable by the assignee if he took the assignment in good faith, for value, without notice of the potential defenses. In other words, Leland's waiver clause with University is enforceable. If Leland assigns the contract to Krushem Collections and the system proves worthless, Krushem is still entitled to its monthly payments from University. The school must seek its damages against Leland—a far more arduous step than simply withholding payment.

These waiver clauses are generally *not* valid in consumer contracts. If Leland sold a computer system to a consumer (an individual purchasing it for her personal use), the waiver would generally be unenforceable.

In the following case, one side pushes the waiver rule to its extreme. Can an assignee recover for money advanced . . . when the money was never advanced? You be the judge.

You be the Judge

Wells Fargo Bank Minnesota v. BrooksAmerica Mortgage Corporation

419 F.3d 107
Second Circuit Court of Appeals, 2005

Facts: Michael Brooks desperately needed financing for his company, BrooksAmerica, so he agreed to a sale-leaseback agreement with Terminal Marketing Company. Terminal would pay BrooksAmerica $250,000, and in exchange it would obtain title to BrooksAmerica's computers and office equipment. BrooksAmerica would then lease the equipment for three years, for $353,000. The equipment would never leave BrooksAmerica's offices.

The contract included a "hell or high water clause" stating that BrooksAmerica's obligation to pay was "absolute and unconditional." Another clause permitted Terminal to assign its rights without notice to BrooksAmerica and stated that the assignee took its rights "free from all defenses, setoffs, or counterclaims."

Brooks also signed a "Delivery and Acceptance Certificate" stating that BrooksAmerica had received the $250,000 (even though no money had yet changed hands) and reaffirming BrooksAmerica's absolute obligation to pay an assignee, despite any defenses BrooksAmerica might have.

Terminal assigned its rights to Wells Fargo, which had taken about 2,000 other equipment leases from Terminal. Terminal never paid any portion of the promised $250,000. Brooks refused to make the required payments (about $10,000 per month) and Wells Fargo sued. Brooks acknowledged that Wells Fargo paid Terminal for the assignment.

Both parties moved for summary judgment. The trial court ruled in favor of Wells Fargo, and Brooks appealed.

You Be the Judge: ***Is Wells Fargo entitled to its monthly lease payments despite the fact that BrooksAmerica never received financing?***

Argument for BrooksAmerica: We acknowledge the general validity of UCC §9-403. However, in this case, Wells Fargo makes an absurd argument. Neither Terminal nor any assignee has a right to enforce a financing contract when Terminal failed to deliver the financing. There is no valid contract to enforce here because Terminal never paid the $250,000 owed to BrooksAmerica. "Good faith" required Wells Fargo to make sure that Terminal had performed. A simple inquiry would have informed Wells Fargo that Terminal was entitled to no money. This entire transaction is a sham, and §9-403 was never drafted to encourage financial swindles.

The trial court *penalized* BrooksAmerica for acting in good faith. Mr. Brooks signed the Delivery Certificate assuming that any reasonable company would promptly deliver the money it had promised. Unfortunately, Terminal does not operate at the same ethical level—a fact that Wells Fargo should know from its earlier assignments.

Argument for Wells Fargo: Under UCC §9-403, an assignee such as Wells Fargo may enforce a waiver of defenses clause if the assignment was taken in good faith, for value, and free of knowledge of any claims or defenses. Wells Fargo meets that test.

The "simple inquiry" argument has two flaws. First, §9-403 does not require one. The UCC requires good faith, not an investigation. Second, Wells Fargo *did* investigate by checking the contract and the Delivery Certificate. We have done more than required. We have taken thousands of equipment leases as assignees. In this case, we examined the contract and the Delivery Certificate, and assumed that BrooksAmerica had received its money. If Terminal had not paid, why did Mr. Brooks sign a certificate stating he had received his cash? We are entitled to payment. Any dispute between BrooksAmerica and Terminal is for those parties to resolve.

Delegation of Duties

Garret has always dreamed of racing stock cars. He borrows $250,000 from his sister, Maybelle, in order to buy a car and begin racing. He signs a promissory note, which is a document guaranteeing that he will repay Maybelle the full amount, plus interest, on a monthly basis over 10 years. Regrettably, during his first race, Garret discovers that he has a

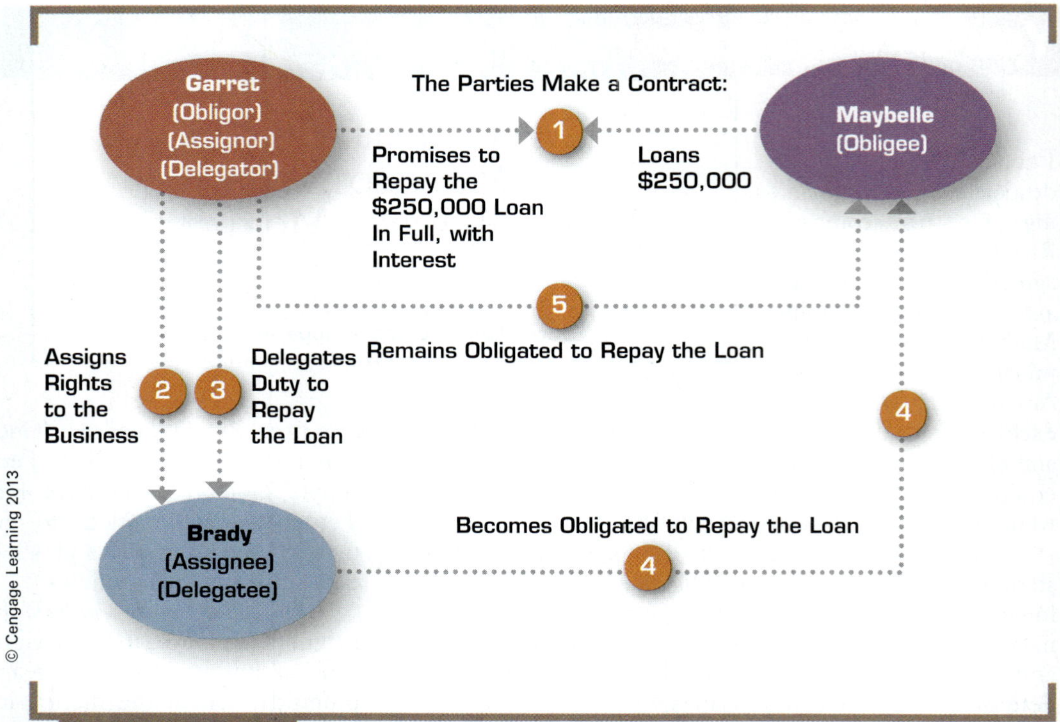

EXHIBIT 16.2

speed phobia and quits the business. Garret transfers the car and all of his equipment to Brady, who agrees in writing to pay all money owed to Maybelle. Brady sends a check for a few months, but then the payments stop. Maybelle sues Garret, who defends based on the transfer to Brady. Will his defense work?

Garret has assigned his rights in the car and business to Brady, and that is entirely legal. But more important, he has *delegated his duties* to Brady. Garret was the **delegator** and Brady was the **delegatee**. In other words, the promissory note he signed was a contract, and the agreement imposed certain *duties* on Garret, primarily the obligation to pay Maybelle $250,000 plus interest. Garret had a right to delegate his duties to Brady, but delegating those duties did not relieve Garret of *his own* obligation to perform them. When Maybelle sues, she will win. Garret, like many debtors, would have preferred to wash his hands of his debt, but the law is not so obliging.

Most duties are delegable. But delegation does not by itself relieve the delegator of his own liability to perform the contract.

Garret's delegation to Brady was typical in that it included an assignment at the same time. If he had merely transferred ownership, that would have been only an assignment. If he had convinced Brady to pay off the loan without getting the car, that would have been merely a delegation. He did both at once. See Exhibit 16.2.

What Duties Are Delegable?

The rules concerning what duties may be delegated mirror those about the assignment of rights. And once again, the common law agrees with the UCC. An obligor may delegate his duties unless:

1. delegation would violate public policy, or
2. the original contract prohibits delegation, or
3. the obligee has a substantial interest in personal performance by the obligor.[4]

© Photodisc/Getty Images

© Dhannte/Shutterstock

One may delegate and one may not.

Public Policy. Delegation may violate public policy, such as in a public works contract. If City hires Builder to construct a subway system, state law may prohibit Builder from delegating his duties to Beginner. The theory is that a public agency should not have to work with parties that it never agreed to hire.

Contract Prohibition. It is very common for a contract to prohibit delegation. We saw in the "Assignment" section that courts may refuse to enforce a clause that limits one party's ability to assign its contract rights. That does not hold true with delegation. The parties may forbid almost any delegation, and the courts will enforce the agreement. Hammer, a contractor, is building a house and hires Spot as his painter, including in his contract a clause prohibiting delegation. Just before the house is ready for painting, Spot gets a better job elsewhere and wants to delegate his duties to Brush. Hammer may refuse the delegation, even if Brush is equally qualified.

Substantial Interest in Personal Performance. Suppose Hammer had omitted the "nondelegation" clause from his contract with Spot. Could Hammer still refuse the delegation on the grounds that he has a substantial interest in having Spot do the work? No. Most duties are delegable, so long as they do not violate public policy or a clause in a contract. There is nothing so special about painting a house that one particular painter is required to do it. But some kinds of work do require personal performance, and obligors may not delegate these tasks. The services of lawyers, doctors, dentists, artists, and performers are considered too personal to be delegated. There is no single test that will perfectly define this group, but generally when the work will test the *character, skill, discretion, and good faith of the obligor,* she may *not* delegate her job.

EXAM STRATEGY

Question: Parker is a well-known actress. She agrees to act in Will's play for four weeks, for $30,000 per week. A week before rehearsals are to begin, Parker notifies Will that she cannot appear because a film producer has offered her over $1 million to start shooting immediately. She has arranged for Claire, another well-known actress,

[4]Restatement (Second) of Contracts §318. And see UCC §2-210, establishing similar limits.

to appear in her place. Will objects. Parker claims, correctly, that their agreement does not prohibit her from making this substitution. Is Parker allowed to do this?

Strategy: Parker is attempting to delegate her duties. Under the Restatement, delegation is allowed unless (1) it would violate public policy, (2) it is prohibited by the contract, or (3) the obligee has a substantial interest in the obligor's personal performance.

Result: This is hardly a matter of public concern, and the contract does not speak to the issue. However, acting is a very personal kind of work. The actor must be right for the part, interact smoothly with other cast members, work well with the director, and help draw the audience. Will is entitled to have Parker perform the work, and she may not delegate her role.

Improper Delegation and Repudiation. Sometimes parties delegate duties they should not. Suppose Spot, having agreed not to delegate his painting job, is so tempted by the higher offer from another contractor that he delegates the work anyway. Hammer informs Spot he will not allow Brush on the job site. If Spot still refuses to work, he has **repudiated** the agreement; in other words, he has formally notified the other side that he will not perform his side of the contract. Hammer will probably sue him. On the other hand, if Hammer allows Brush up the ladder and Brush completes the job, Hammer has no claim against anybody.

Novation

Novation
A three-way agreement in which the obligor transfers all rights and duties to a third party.

As we have seen, a delegator does not automatically get rid of his duties merely by delegating them. But there is one way a delegator *can* do so. A **novation** is a three-way agreement in which the obligor transfers all rights and duties to a third party. The obligee agrees to look only to that third party for performance.

Recall Garret, the forlorn race car driver. When he wanted to get out of his obligations to Maybelle, he should have proposed a novation. Were one created, he would assign all rights and delegate all duties to Brady, and Maybelle would agree that *only Brady* was obligated by the promissory note, releasing Garret from his responsibility to repay. Why would Maybelle do this? She might conclude that Brady was a better bet than Garret and that this was the best way to get her money. Maybelle would prefer to have both people liable. But Garret might refuse to bring Brady into the deal until Maybelle permits a novation. In the example given, Garret failed to obtain a novation, and hence he and Brady were *both* liable on the promissory note.

Since a novation has the critical effect of releasing the obligor from liability, you will not be surprised to learn that two parties to a contract sometimes fight over whether some event was a simple delegation of duties or a novation. Here is one such contest.

ROSENBERG V. SON, INC.

491 N.W.2d 71, 1992 N.D. LEXIS 202
Supreme Court of North Dakota, 1992

Facts: The Rosenbergs owned a Dairy Queen in Grand Forks, North Dakota. They agreed in writing to sell the Dairy Queen to Mary Pratt. The contract required her to pay $10,000 down and $52,000 over 15 years, at 10 percent interest. Two years later, Pratt assigned her rights and delegated her duties under the sales contract to Son, Inc. The agreement between Pratt and Son contained a "Consent to Assignment" clause, which the Rosenbergs signed. Pratt then moved to Arizona and had nothing further to do with the Dairy Queen. The Rosenbergs never received full payment for the Dairy Queen. They sued Mary Pratt.

The trial court gave summary judgment for Pratt, finding that she was no longer obligated on the original contract. The Rosenbergs appealed.

Issue: ***Did Pratt obtain a novation relieving her of her duties under the original sales contract?***

Excerpts from Chief Justice Erickstad's Decision: It is a well-established principle in the law of contracts that a contracting party cannot escape its liability on the contract by merely assigning its duties and rights under the contract to a third party.

It is evident from the express language of the assignment agreement between Pratt and Son, Inc., that only an assignment was intended, not a novation. The agreement made no mention of discharging Pratt from any further liability on the contract.

Furthermore, the agreement was between Pratt and Son, Inc.; they were the parties signing the agreement, not the Rosenbergs. An agreement between Pratt and Son, Inc., cannot unilaterally affect the Rosenbergs' rights under the contract. As mentioned earlier, the Rosenbergs did sign a consent to the assignment at the bottom of the agreement. However, by merely consenting to the assignment, the Rosenbergs did not consent to a discharge of the principal obligor—Pratt. Nothing in the language of the consent clause supports such an allegation. A creditor is free to consent to an assignment without releasing the original obligor.

We *reverse* the summary judgment and *remand* for further proceedings.

It appears that Mary Pratt, moving to Arizona, honestly thought she was not only out of the ice cream business but relieved of any debt to the Rosenbergs. This lawsuit undoubtedly came as a cold shock. What should she have done to avoid the dispute?

Chapter Conclusion

A moment's caution! It is important to remember that the parties to a contract may not have the right to substitute someone else into the contract. The parties to a contract always have legal rights themselves, but when outsiders enter the picture, subtle differences in key areas determine whether additional rights exist.

Exam Review

1. **THIRD PARTY BENEFICIARY** A third party beneficiary is an intended beneficiary and may enforce a contract if the parties intended her to benefit from the agreement and if either (1) enforcing the promise will satisfy a debt of the promisee to the beneficiary, or (2) the promisee intended to make a gift to the beneficiary. The intended beneficiary described in (1) is a *creditor beneficiary*, while (2) describes a *donee beneficiary*. Any beneficiary who meets neither description is an *incidental beneficiary* and has no right to enforce the contract. (pp. 362–365)

2. **ASSIGNMENT AND DELEGATION** An assignment transfers the assignor's contract rights to the assignee. A delegation transfers the delegator's duties to the delegatee. (pp. 365–366)

3. **RIGHTS ASSIGNABLE** A party generally may assign contract rights unless doing so would substantially change the obligor's rights or duties, is forbidden by law, or is validly precluded by the contract. (pp. 367–369)

EXAM Strategy

Question: Angelo Zavarella and Yvette Rodrigues were injured in an automobile accident allegedly caused by a vehicle belonging to Truck Equipment of Boston. Travelers Insurance Co. paid insurance benefits to Zavarella and Rodrigues, who then assigned to Travelers their claims against Truck Equipment. Travelers sued Truck Equipment, which moved to dismiss. What is Truck Equipment's claim that the case should be dismissed, and how would you rule?

Strategy: Travelers is claiming to be the assignee of the plaintiffs' claims. Any contractual right may be assigned except in the three instances listed above. Does one of those prohibitions apply? (See the "Result" at the end of this section.)

4. **ENFORCEMENT** Once the assignment is made and the obligor notified, the assignee may enforce her contractual rights against the obligor. The obligor, in turn, may generally raise all defenses against the assignee that she could have raised against the assignor. (p. 369)

5. **THE UCC AND SECURITY INTERESTS:** Article 9 of the UCC governs security interests, which are the legal rights to personal property that assure payment of a debt. Under Article 9, obligors may assert defenses against assignees that arise from contracts, and agreements not to enforce such defenses are generally valid. (pp. 369–371)

6. **DUTIES DELEGABLE** Duties are delegable unless delegation would violate public policy, the contract prohibits delegation, or the obligee has a substantial interest in personal performance by the obligor. (pp. 371–375)

EXAM Strategy

Question: Pizza of Gaithersburg, Maryland, owned five pizza shops. Pizza arranged with Virginia Coffee Service to install soft drink machines in each of its stores and maintain them. The contract made no mention of the rights of either party to delegate. Virginia Coffee delegated its duties to the Macke Co., leading to litigation between Pizza and Macke. Pizza claimed that Virginia Coffee was barred from delegating because Pizza had a close working relationship with the president of Virginia Coffee, who personally kept the machines in working order. Was the delegation legal?

Strategy: Any contractual duty may be delegated except in the three instances listed above. Does one of those prohibitions apply? (See the "Result" at the end of this section.)

7. **DISCHARGE** Unless the obligee agrees otherwise, delegation does not discharge the delegator's duty to perform. (pp. 371–372)

8. **NOVATION** A *novation* is a three-way agreement in which the obligor delegates all duties to the delegatee and the obligee agrees to hold only the delegatee responsible. (pp. 374–375)

Question: Mardy, a general contractor, is building a house. He contracts with Plumbco to do all plumbing work for $120,000. Before Plumbco begins the work, it notifies Mardy in writing that Leo will be doing the work instead. Mardy does not respond. When Leo fails to perform, Mardy sues Plumbco. Plumbco is

(a) Liable

(b) Liable only if Plumbco agreed to remain responsible for the job

(c) Not liable because Mardy failed to repudiate the delegation

(d) Not liable because Plumbco validly delegated its duties

(e) Not liable because the parties entered into a novation

Strategy: Delegation does not by itself relieve the delegator of his own liability to perform the contract. In a novation, the obligee agrees to look only to the third party for performance. Was this a delegation or a novation? (See the "Result" at the end of this section.)

3. Result: Truck Equipment's winning argument was one sentence long: Claims for personal injury may not be assigned. Such assignments would transform accident claims into commercial commodities and encourage assignees to exaggerate the gravity of the harm.

6. Result: There is no public policy issue involved. The contract is silent as to delegation. And Pizza's only legitimate interest was in seeing that installation and maintenance were adequate. There is no reason to believe that Virginia Coffee would perform the work better than others. The duty was delegable, and Virginia Coffee wins.

8. Result: When Plumbco announced that Leo would do the work, Mardy did not respond. Mardy certainly did not agree to look exclusively to Leo for performance. There has not been a novation, and Plumbco remains liable on the contract. The correct answer is (a).

Multiple-Choice Questions

1. **CPA QUESTION** Yost contracted with Egan for Yost to buy certain real property. If the contract is otherwise silent, Yost's rights under the contract are:

   (a) Assignable only with Egan's consent

   (b) Nonassignable because they are personal to Yost

   (c) Nonassignable as a matter of law

   (d) Generally assignable

2. **CPA QUESTION** One of the criteria for a valid assignment of a sales contract to a third party is that the assignment must:
   (a) Not materially increase the other party's risk or duty
   (b) Not be revocable by the assignor
   (c) Be supported by adequate consideration from the assignee
   (d) Be in writing and signed by the assignor

3. Amanda agrees to pay Jennifer $300 for a pair of tickets to see Jerry Seinfeld. "Seinfeld is my boyfriend Octavio's favorite comedian, and the tickets will be a great birthday present for him," she tells Jennifer. Amanda pays up and tells a delighted Octavio about the tickets, but Jennifer never delivers them. Octavio is a(n) ____________ beneficiary of the agreement, and as such, he ____________ have a right to enforce the contract himself.
   (a) donee; does
   (b) donee; does not
   (c) incidental; does
   (d) incidental; does not

4. A novation completely releases an ____________ from any further liability. To be effective, it ____________ require the agreement of both the obligor and obligee.
   (a) obligor; does
   (b) obligor; does not
   (c) obligee; does
   (d) obligee; does not

5. Will misses three straight payments on his SUV, and his bank repossesses it. The right to repossess ____________ a security interest. Security interests are governed by Article ____________ of the Uniform Commercial Code.
   (a) is; 2
   (b) is; 9
   (c) is not; 2
   (d) is not; 9

Essay Questions

1. Intercontinental Metals Corp. (IMC) contracted with the accounting firm of Cherry, Bekaert, & Holland to perform an audit. Cherry issued its opinion about IMC, giving all copies of its report directly to the company. IMC later permitted Dun & Bradstreet to examine the statements, and Raritan River Steel Co. saw a report published by Dun & Bradstreet. Relying on the audit, Raritan sold IMC $2.2 million worth of steel on credit, but IMC promptly went bankrupt. Raritan sued Cherry, claiming that IMC was not as sound as Cherry had reported and that the accounting firm had breached its contract with IMC. Comment on Raritan's suit.

2. Woodson Walker and Associates leased computer equipment from Park Ryan Leasing. The lease said nothing about assignment. Park Ryan then assigned the lease to TCB as security for a loan. Park Ryan defaulted on its loan, and Walker failed to make several payments on the lease. TCB sued Walker for the lease payments. Was the assignment valid, given the fact that the original lease made no mention of it? If the assignment was valid, may Walker raise defenses against TCB that it could have raised against Park Ryan?

3. C. Gaston Whiddon owned Gaston's LP Gas Co., Inc. Curtis Dufour purchased the company. Since Whiddon had personally operated the company for many years, Dufour was worried about competition from him and insisted on a noncompetition clause in the sales contract. The clause stated that Whiddon would not "compete with Gaston's LP Gas Co. anywhere south of Interstate Highway 20 for nine years." Three years later, the Herring Gas Co. offered to buy all of Dufour's gas business, assuming that Whiddon would not be a competitor for six more years. Dufour sold all of the assets to Herring, keeping the actual corporation "Gaston's LP Gas Co." for himself. What mistake in drafting have Dufour and Herring made?

4. **YOU BE THE JUDGE WRITING PROBLEM** David Ricupero suspected his wife Polly of having an affair, so he taped her phone conversations and, based on what he heard, sued for divorce. David's lawyer, William Wuliger, had the recorded conversations transcribed for use at trial. The parties settled the divorce out of court and signed an agreement that included this clause:

> Except as herein otherwise provided, each party hereto completely and forever releases the other and his attorneys from any and all rights each has or may have ... to any property, privileges, or benefits accruing to either by virtue of their marriage, or conferred by the Statutory or Common Law of Ohio or the United States of America.

After the divorce was final, Polly sued William Wuliger for invasion of privacy and violation of federal wiretapping law. Wuliger moved to dismiss the case based on the clause quoted. Polly argued that Wuliger was not a party to the divorce settlement and had no right to enforce it. May Wuliger enforce the waiver clause from the Ricuperos' divorce settlement? **Argument for Wuliger:** The contract language demonstrates that the parties intended to release one another and their attorneys from any claims. That makes Wuliger an intended third party beneficiary, and he is entitled to enforce the agreement. If Polly did not want to release Wuliger from such claims, she was free not to sign the agreement. **Argument for Polly Ricupero:** A divorce agreement settles the affairs between the couple. That is all it is ever intended to do, and the parties here never intended to benefit a lawyer. Wuliger is only an incidental beneficiary and cannot use this contract to paper over his violation of federal wiretapping law.

5. Judith and John Brooks hired Wayne Hayes to build a house. The contract required Hayes to "provide all necessary labor and materials and perform all work of every nature whatsoever to be done in the erection of the residence." Hayes hired subcontractors to do all of the work. One of Hayes's employees checked on the work site daily, but neither Hayes nor any of his employees actively supervised the building. The Brookses were aware of this working arrangement and consented to it. The mason negligently installed the fireplace, ultimately leading to a serious fire. The Brookses sued Hayes for breach of contract. Hayes contended that when the Brookses approved of his hiring of subcontractors to do all work, that created a novation relieving him of any liability. Discuss.

Discussion Questions

1. A century and a half ago, an English judge stated: "All painters do not paint portraits like Sir Joshua Reynolds, nor landscapes like Claude Lorraine, nor do all writers write dramas like Shakespeare or fiction like Dickens. Rare genius and extraordinary skill are not transferable." What legal doctrine is the judge describing? What is the ethical basis of this rule?

2. Nationwide Discount Furniture hired Rampart Security to install an alarm in its warehouse. A fire would set off an alarm in Rampart's office, and the security company was then supposed to notify Nationwide immediately. A fire did break out, but Rampart allegedly failed to notify Nationwide, causing the fire to spread next door and damage a building owned by Gasket Materials Corp. Gasket sued Rampart for breach of contract, and Rampart moved for summary judgment. Comment.

3. If a person promises to give you a gift, there is usually no consideration. The person can change his mind and decide not to give you the present, and there is nothing you can do about it. But if a person makes a contract with *someone else* and intends that you will receive a gift under the agreement, you are a donee beneficiary and you *do* have rights to enforce the deal. Are these rules unacceptably inconsistent? If so, which rule should change?

4. Imagine that you hire your trusted friend, Fran, to paint your house, and that you do not include a nondelegation clause in the agreement. Fran delegates the job to Sam, who is a stranger to you. The delegation is legal, but should it be? Is it reasonable that you must accept the substitute painter?

5. In our society, a person can buy and sell almost anything. But as this chapter describes, you cannot sell personal injury claims. Should you be able to? Imagine that you are injured in a car wreck. You are told that you might win $100,000 in a lawsuit eventually, but that you might not receive payment for years, and you might also lose the case and recover nothing. If someone is willing to pay you $20,000 cash-on-the-barrelhead today for the rights to your claim, is it fair that public policy concerns prohibit you from taking the money?

CHAPTER 17

PERFORMANCE AND DISCHARGE

© picsbyst/Shutterstock.com

Polly was elated. It was the grand opening of her new restaurant, Polly's Folly, and everything was bubbling. The wait staff hustled, and Caesar, the chef, churned out succulent dishes. Polly had signed a contract promising him $1,500 per week for one year, "provided Polly is personally satisfied with his cooking." Polly was determined that her restaurant would be glorious. Her three-year lease would cost $6,000 per month, and she had signed an advertising deal with Billboard Bonanza for the same period. Polly had also promised Eddie, a publicity agent, a substantial monthly fee, to begin as soon as the restaurant was 80 percent booked for one month. Tonight, with candles flickering at packed tables, Polly beamed.

Polly disliked a veal dish and gagged on one of Caesar's soups. She fired her chef.

After a week, Polly's smiles were a bit forced. Some of Caesar's new dishes had been failures, including a grilled swordfish that was hard to pierce and shrimp jambalaya that was too spicy. The restaurant was only 60 percent full, and the publicity agent yelled at Caesar for costing him money. Later that month, Polly disliked a veal dish and gagged on one of Caesar's soups. She fired her chef.

Then troubles gushed forth—literally. A water main burst in front of Polly's restaurant, flooding the street. The city embarked on a two-month repair job that ultimately took four times that long. The street was closed to traffic, and no one could park within blocks of Polly's restaurant. Patronage dropped steadily as hungry customers refused to deal with the bad parking and construction noise. After several months, behind on the rent and in debt to everyone, Polly closed her doors for good.

Shortly, the court doors swung open, offering a full menu of litigation. Polly's landlord sued for three years' rent, and Billboard Bonanza demanded its money for the same period. Caesar claimed his year's pay. Eddie, the agent, insisted on some money for his hard work. Polly defended vigorously, seeking to be *discharged* from her various contracts.

Discharge
A party is discharged when she has no more duties under the contract.

If a party is **discharged,** she is "finished," and has no more duties under a contract. In each lawsuit, Polly asked a court to declare that her obligations were terminated and that she owed no money.

Most contracts are discharged by full performance. In other words, the parties generally do what they promise. Suppose, before the restaurant opened, Walter had promised to deliver 100 sets of cutlery to Polly and she had promised to pay $20 per set. Walter delivered the goods on time, and Polly paid $2000 on delivery. The parties got what they expected, and that contract was fully discharged.

Rescind
To terminate a contract by mutual agreement.

Sometimes the parties discharge a contract by agreement. For example, the parties may agree to **rescind** their contract, meaning that they terminate it by mutual agreement.[1] If Polly's landlord believed he could get more rent from a new tenant, he might agree to rescind her lease. But he was dubious about the rental market and refused to rescind.

At times, a court may discharge a party who has not performed. When things have gone amiss, a judge must interpret the contract and issues of public policy to determine who in fairness should suffer the loss. In the lawsuits brought by the landlord and Billboard Bonanza, Polly argued a defense called "commercial impracticability," claiming that she should not be forced to rent space that was useless to her or buy advertising for a restaurant that had closed. From Polly's point of view, the claim was understandable. But we can also respect the arguments made by the landlord and the advertiser, that they did not cause the burst water main. Claims of commercial impracticability are difficult to win, and Polly lost against both of these opponents. Though she was making no money at all from the restaurant, the court found her liable in full for the lease and the advertising contract.[2]

Polly's argument against Caesar raised another issue of discharge. Caesar claimed that his cooking was good professional work and that all chefs have occasional disasters, especially in a new restaurant. But Polly responded that they had a "personal satisfaction" contract. Under such contracts, "good" work may not suffice if it fails to please the promisee. Polly won this argument, and Caesar recovered nothing.

As to Eddie's suit, Polly raised a defense called "condition precedent," meaning that some event had to occur before she was obligated to pay. Polly claimed that she owed Eddie money only if and when the restaurant was 80 percent full for a month, and that had never happened. The court agreed and discharged Polly on Eddie's claim.

We will analyze each of these issues, and begin with a look at conditions.

CONDITIONS

Condition
An event that must occur before a party becomes obligated under a contract.

Parties often put conditions in a contract. A **condition** is an event that must occur before a party becomes obligated under a contract. "I'll agree to do something, but only if something else happens first." Polly agreed to pay Eddie, the agent, a percentage of her profits, but with an important condition: 80 percent of the tables had to be booked for a month. Unless and until those tables were occupied, Polly owed Eddie nothing. That never happened, or, in contract language, the *condition failed*, and so Polly was discharged.

Conditions can take many forms. Alex would like to buy Kevin's empty lot and build a movie theater on it, but the city's zoning law will not permit that kind of business in that

[1]The parties could also decide that one party's duties will be performed by someone else, a modification called a **novation**. Alternatively, they could create an **accord and satisfaction**, in which they agree that one party will substitute a new kind of performance in place of his contract obligations. See Chapter 16, on third parties, and Chapter 12, on consideration.

[2]Based on *Luminous Neon v. Parscale*, 17 Kan. App. 2d 241, 836 P.2d 1201, 1992 Kan. App. LEXIS 572 (Kan. Ct. App. 1992).

location. Alex signs a contract to buy Kevin's empty lot in 120 days, *provided that* within 100 days, the city re-zones the area to permit a movie theater. If the city fails to re-zone the area by day 100, Alex is discharged and need not complete the deal.

Another example: Friendly Insurance issues a policy covering Vivian's house, promising to pay for any loss due to fire, but only if Vivian furnishes proof of her losses within 60 days of the damage. If the house burns down, Friendly becomes liable to pay. But if Vivian arrives with her proof 70 days after the fire, she collects nothing. Friendly, though it briefly had a duty to pay, was discharged when Vivian failed to furnish the necessary information on time.

How Conditions Are Created

Express Conditions

The parties may expressly state a condition. Alex's contract with Kevin expressly discharged all obligations if the city failed to re-zone within the stated period. Notice that **no special language is necessary to create the condition**. Phrases such as "provided that" frequently indicate a condition, but neither those nor any other specific words are essential. So long as the contract's language indicates that the parties *intended* to create a condition, a court will enforce it.

Because informal language can create a condition, the parties may dispute whether they intended one or not. Sand Creek Country Club, in Indiana, was eager to expand its clubhouse facilities and awarded the design work to CSO Architects. The club wanted the work done quickly but had not secured financing. The architects sent a letter confirming their agreement:

> It was our intent to allow Mr. Dan Moriarty of our office to start work on your project as early as possible in order to allow you to meet the goals that you have set for next fall. Also, it was the intent of CSO to begin work on your project and delay any billings to you until your financing is in place. As I explained to you earlier, we will continue on this course until we reach a point where we can no longer continue without receiving some payment.

The club gave CSO the go-ahead to begin design work, and the architects did their work and billed Sand Creek for $33,000. But the club, unable to obtain financing, refused to pay. Sand Creek claimed that CSO's letter created a *condition* in their agreement; namely, that the club would have to pay only if and when it obtained financing. The court was unpersuaded and ruled that the parties had never intended to create an express condition. The architects were merely delaying their billing as a convenience to the club. It would be absurd, said the court, to assume that CSO intended to perform $33,000 worth of work for free.[3]

Professional sports contracts are often full of conditions. Assume that the San Francisco Giants want to sign Tony Fleet to play center field. The club considers him a fine defensive player but a dubious offensive performer. The many conditional clauses in his contract reflect hard bargaining over an athlete who may or may not become a star. The Giants guarantee Fleet only $500,000, a very modest salary by Major League Baseball standards. If the speedy outfielder appears in at least 120 games, his pay increases to $1 million. Winning a Gold Glove award is worth an extra $200,000 to him. The Giants insist on a team option to re-sign Fleet for the following season at a salary of $800,000, but if the center-fielder plays in fewer than 100 games, the team loses that right, leaving Fleet free to negotiate for higher pay with other teams.

---

[3] *Sand Creek Country Club, Ltd. v. CSO Architects, Inc.*, 582 N.E.2d 872, 1991 Ind. App. LEXIS 2151 (Ind. Ct. App. 1991).

Implied Conditions

At other times, the parties say nothing about a condition, but it is clear from their agreement that they have implied one. Charlotte orally rents an apartment to Hakan for one year and promises to fix any problems in the unit. It is an implied condition that Hakan will promptly notify Charlotte of anything needing repair. Although the parties have not said anything about notice, it is only common sense that Hakan must inform his landlord of defects since she will have no other way to learn of them.

Types of Conditions

Courts divide conditional clauses into three categories: (1) condition precedent, (2) condition subsequent, and (3) concurrent conditions.[4] But what they have in common is more important than any of their differences. The key to all conditional clauses is this: **if the condition does not occur, one party will probably be discharged without having to perform his obligations under a contract.**

Condition Precedent

In this kind of condition, an event must occur *before* a duty arises. Polly's contract with Eddie concerned a condition precedent. Polly had no obligation to pay Eddie anything *unless and until* the restaurant was 80 percent full for a month. Since that never happened, she was discharged. If the parties agreed to a condition precedent, the *plaintiff* has the burden to prove that the condition happened and that the defendant was obligated to perform.

In the following case, the plaintiff claimed that it had met a condition precedent and was entitled to a payment. Not surprisingly, the defendant had a different point of view.

American Electronic Components, Inc. v. Agere Systems, Inc.

2009 U.S. App. LEXIS 12763
Third Circuit Court of Appeals, 2009

Facts: American Electronic Components, Inc. (AECI), agreed to a three-year contract under which it would sell Agere Systems's equipment. The contract said in part, "AECI shall receive a percentage of the sale price for each item of Equipment sold."

Agere announced that it planned to close a subsidiary in Madrid. AECI found potential buyers for the Madrid equipment, but Agere ultimately sold it to a different buyer.

AECI sued, arguing that it should be paid a commission because of its effort in trying to sell the equipment. It also argued that when Agere sold the equipment, it had interfered with AECI's ability to fulfill the contract's condition precedent.

The trial court dismissed the complaint, and AECI appealed.

Issues: ***Was a* completed sale *a condition precedent in this agreement? Was Agere liable for interfering with AECI's sales efforts?***

Excerpts from Judge Smith's Decision: As the District Court determined, the contract clearly sets forth when AECI is owed a commission: when AECI consummated a sale of equipment.

AECI argues that summary judgment is not appropriate because the parties dispute whether AECI expended substantial effort to find a buyer for the equipment. AECI

[4]The Restatement (Second) of Contracts has officially abandoned the terms *condition precedent* and *condition subsequent*. See Restatement §§224 et seq. But courts routinely use the terms, so it is difficult to avoid the old distinctions.

claims that it acted as Agere's broker and is thus owed a commission for merely finding a buyer for the Madrid equipment. This argument is unavailing, as the contract specifically limits AECI's entitlement to a commission to situations where it actually sold the designated equipment. Thus, whether AECI expended resources to—and did in fact—find a buyer for the Madrid equipment, are not material to whether AECI is owed a commission.

Finally, there is not sufficient evidence for a reasonable jury to conclude that Agere should be required to pay AECI a commission because Agere improperly prevented AECI from fulfilling the contract's condition precedent—consummating the sale. AECI correctly asserts that a party may not escape contractual liability by relying on the failure of a condition precedent where the party wrongfully prevented the performance of that condition. The record does not support this conclusion here. The facts that AECI located potential buyers for the Madrid equipment and that Agere eventually sold the equipment do not lead to the inference that Agere engaged in some sort of subterfuge to prevent AECI from earning a commission. Further, the non-exclusive contract allows Agere to sell its own equipment.

For the reasons stated above, we affirm.

Condition Subsequent

This type of condition must occur *after* a particular duty arises. If the condition does not occur, the duty is discharged. Vivian's policy with Friendly Insurance contains a condition subsequent. As soon as the fire broke out, Friendly became obligated to pay for the damage. But if Vivian failed to produce her proof of loss on time, Friendly's obligation ended – it was discharged. Note that, with a condition subsequent, it is the *defendant* who must prove that the condition occurred, relieving him of any obligation.

CONDITION PRECEDENT AND CONDITION SUBSEQUENT COMPARED

	Condition Created	**Does Condition Occur?**	**Duty Is Determined**	**Result**
Condition Precedent	"Fee to be paid when restaurant is filled to 80% capacity for one month."	Condition DOES occur: restaurant is packed.	Duty arises: Polly owes Eddie his fee.	Polly pays the fee.
		Condition DOES NOT occur: restaurant is empty.	Duty never arises: Polly is discharged.	Polly pays nothing.
	Condition Created	**Duty Is Determined**	**Does Condition Occur?**	**Result**
Condition Subsequent	"Vivian must give proof of loss within 60 days."	Fire damages property, and Friendly Insurance becomes obligated to pay Vivian.	Condition DOES occur: Vivian proves her losses within 60 days.	Friendly pays Vivian for her losses.
			Condition DOES NOT occur: Vivian fails to prove her losses within 60 days.	Friendly is discharged and owes nothing

Concurrent Conditions

Here, both parties have a duty to perform *simultaneously*. Renee agrees to sell her condominium to Tim on July 5. Renee agrees to furnish a valid deed and clear title to the property on that date, and Tim promises to present a cashier's check for $200,000. The parties have agreed to concurrent conditions. Each performance is the condition for the other's performance. If Renee arrives at the Registry of Deeds and can say only, "Don't worry. I'm totally sure I own this property," Tim need not present his check; similarly, if Tim arrives with only an "IOU" scribbled on the back of a candy wrapper, Renee has no duty to hand over a valid deed.

EXAM Strategy

Question: Roberto wants to buy Naomi's house for $350,000 and is willing to make a 20 percent down payment, which satisfies Naomi. However, he needs a $280,000 mortgage in order to complete the purchase, and he is not certain he can obtain one. Naomi is worried that Roberto might change his mind about buying the house and then use alleged financing problems to skip out of the deal. How can the two parties protect themselves?

Strategy: Both parties should use conditional clauses in the sales agreement. Naomi must force Roberto to do his best to obtain a mortgage. How? Roberto's clause should protect him if he cannot obtain a sufficient mortgage. How?

Result: Naomi should demand the 20 percent down payment. Further, her conditional clause should state that Roberto forfeits the down payment unless he demonstrates that, within two weeks, he has applied in good faith for a mortgage to at least three banks. Roberto should insist that if he promptly and fully applies to three banks but fails to obtain a mortgage, his down payment is refunded.

Public Policy

At times, a court will refuse to enforce an express condition on the grounds that it is unfair and harmful to the general public. In other words, a court might agree that the parties created a conditional clause but conclude that permitting its enforcement would hurt society. Did the insurance contract in the following case harm society? You be the judge.

You be the Judge

Anderson v. Country Life Insurance Co.

180 Ariz. 625, 886 P.2d 1381, 1994 Ariz. App. LEXIS 240
Arizona Court of Appeals, 1994

Facts: On November 26, a Country Life Insurance agent went to the house of Donald and Anna Mae Anderson. He persuaded the Andersons to buy a life insurance policy and accepted a check for $1,600. He gave the Andersons a "conditional receipt for medical policy," dated that day. The form stated that the Andersons would have a valid life insurance policy with Country Life, effective November 26, but only when all conditions were met. The most important of these conditions was that the Country Life home office accepts the Andersons as medical risks. The Andersons were pleased with the new policy and glad that it was effective that same day.

It was not. Donald Anderson died of a heart attack a few weeks later. Country Life declined the Andersons as medical risks and refused to issue a policy. Anna Mae Anderson sued. Country Life pointed out that medical approval was a condition precedent. In other words, the company argued that the policy would be effective as of November 26, but only if it later decided to make the policy effective. Based on this argument, the trial court gave summary judgment for Country Life. Ms. Anderson appealed, claiming that the conditional clause was a violation of public policy.

You Be the Judge: ***Did the conditional clause violate public policy?***

Argument for Ms. Anderson: Your honors, this policy is a scam. This so-called "conditional receipt for medical policy" is designed to trick customers and then steal their money. The company leads people to believe they are covered as of the day they write the check. But they aren't covered until *much later,* when the insurer gets around to deciding the applicant's medical status.

The company gets the customer's money right away and gives nothing in exchange. If the company, after taking its time, decides the applicant is not medically fit, it returns the money, having used it for weeks or even months to earn interest. If, on the other hand, the insurance company decides the applicant is a good bet, it then issues the policy effective for weeks or months *in the past, when coverage is of no use.* No one can die retroactively, your honors. The company is being paid for a period during which it had no risk.This is a fraud and a disgrace, and the company should pay the benefits it owes.

Argument for Country Life: Your honors, is Country Life supposed to issue life insurance policies without doing a medical check? That is the road to bankruptcy and would mean that no one could obtain this valuable coverage. Of course we do a medical inquiry, as quickly as possible. It's in our interest to get the policy decided one way or the other.

The policy clearly stated that coverage was effective *only when approved by the home office,* after all inquiries were made. The Andersons knew that as well as the agent. If they were covered immediately, why would the company do a medical check? Country Life resents suggestions that this policy is a scam, when in reality it is Ms. Anderson who is trying to profit from a tragedy that the company had nothing to do with.

The facts of this case are unusual. Obviously, most insureds do not die between application and acceptance. It would be disastrous for society to rewrite every insurance policy in this state based on one very sad fact pattern. The contract was clear and it should be enforced as written.

PERFORMANCE

Caitlin has an architect draw up plans for a monumental new house, and Daniel agrees to build it by September 1. Caitlin promises to pay $900,000 on that date. The house is ready on time, but Caitlin has some complaints. The living room was supposed to be 18 feet high, but it is only 17 feet; the pool was to be azure, yet it is aquamarine; the maid's room was not supposed to be wired for cable television, but it is. Caitlin refuses to pay anything for the house. Is she justified? Of course not, it would be absurd to give her a magnificent house for free when it has only tiny defects. But in this easy answer lurks a danger. Technically, Daniel did breach the contract, and yet the law allows him to recover the full contract price, or virtually all of it. Once that principle is established, how far will a court stretch it? Suppose the living room is only 14 feet high, or 12 feet, or 5 feet? What if the foundation has a small crack? A vast and dangerous split? What if Daniel finishes the house a month late? Six months late? Three years late? At some point, a court will conclude that Daniel has so thoroughly botched the job that he deserves little or no money. But where, exactly, is that point? This is a question that businesses—and judges—face often.

The more complex a contract, the more certain that at least one party will perform imperfectly. Nearly every house ever built has at least some small defects. A delivery of a thousand bushels of apples is sure to include a few rotten ones. A custom-designed computer system for a huge airline is likely to have some glitches. The cases raise several related doctrines, all concerning *how well* a party performed its contractual obligations.

Strict Performance and Substantial Performance

Strict Performance

When Daniel built Caitlin's house with three minor defects, she refused to pay, arguing that he had not *strictly performed* his obligations. Her assertion was correct, yet she lost anyway. Courts dislike strict performance because it enables one party to benefit without paying and sends the other one home empty-handed. A party is generally not required to render

Strict performance
Requires one party to perform its obligations precisely, with no deviation from the contract terms.

strict performance unless the contract expressly demands it *and* such a demand is reasonable. Caitlin's contract never suggested that Daniel would forfeit all payment if there were minor problems. Even if Caitlin had insisted on such a clause, few courts would have enforced it because the requirement would be unreasonable for a project as complicated as the construction of a $900,000 home.

There are some cases where strict performance does make sense. Marshall agrees to deliver 500 sweaters to Leo's store, and Leo promises to pay $20,000 cash on delivery. If Leo has only $19,000 cash and a promissory note for $1,000, he has failed to perform, and Marshall need not give him the sweaters. Leo's payment represents 95 percent of what he promised, but there is a big difference between getting the last $1,000 in cash and receiving a promissory note for that amount.

Substantial Performance

Substantial performance
Occurs when one party fulfills enough of its contract obligations to warrant payment.

Daniel, the house builder, won his case against Caitlin because he fulfilled *most* of his obligations, even though he did an imperfect job. Courts often rely on the substantial performance doctrine, especially in cases involving services as opposed to those concerning the sale of goods or land. In a contract for services, a party that **substantially performs** its obligations will generally receive the full contract price, minus the value of any defects. Daniel receives $900,000, the contract price, minus the value of a ceiling that is 1 foot too low, a pool the wrong color, and so forth. It will be for the trial court to decide how much those defects are worth. If the court decides the low ceiling is a $10,000 defect, the pool color is worth $5,000, and the cable television wiring error is worth $500, then Daniel receives $884,500.

© Wally Stemberger/Shutterstock
Substantial performance is vital, unless you enjoy working for free.

On the other hand, a **party that fails to perform substantially receives nothing on the contract itself and will recover only the value of the work, if any.** If the foundation cracks in Caitlin's house and the walls collapse, Daniel will not receive his $900,000. In such a case, he collects only the market value of the work he has done, which, since the house is a pile of rubble, is probably zero.

When is performance substantial? There is no perfect test, but courts look at these issues:

- How much benefit has the promisee received?
- If it is a construction contract, can the owner use the thing for its intended purpose?
- Can the promisee be compensated with money damages for any defects?
- Did the promisor act in good faith?

EXAM Strategy

Question: Jade owns a straight track used for drag racing. She hires Trevor to resurface it, for $180,000, paying $90,000 down. When the project is completed, Jade refuses to pay the balance and sues Trevor for her down payment. He counterclaims for the $90,000 still due. At trial, Trevor proves that all of the required materials were applied by trained workers in an expert fashion, the dimensions were perfect, and his profit margin very modest. The head of the national drag racing association testifies that his group considers the strip unsafe. He noticed puddles in both asphalt lanes, found the concrete starting pads unsafe, and believed the racing surface needed to be ground off and reapplied. His organization refuses to sanction races at the track until repairs are made. Who wins the suit?

Strategy: When one party has performed imperfectly, we have an issue of substantial performance. To decide whether Trevor is entitled to his money, we apply four factors: (1) How much benefit did Jade receive? (2) Can she use the racing strip for its intended purpose? (3) Can Jade be compensated for defects? (4) Did Trevor act in good faith?

Result: Jade has received no benefit whatsoever. She cannot use her drag strip for racing. Compensation will not help Jade—she needs a new strip. Trevor's work must be ripped up and replaced. Trevor may have acted in good faith, but he failed to deliver what Jade bargained for. Jade wins all of the money she paid. (As we will see in the next chapter, she may also win additional sums for her lost profits.)

Personal Satisfaction Contracts

Sujata, president of a public relations firm, hires Ben to design a huge multimedia project for her company, involving computer software, music, and live actors, all designed to sell frozen bologna sandwiches to supermarkets. His contract guarantees him two years' employment, provided all of his work "is acceptable in the sole judgment of Sujata." Ben's immediate supervisor is delighted with his work and his colleagues are impressed, but Sujata is not. Three months later, she fires him, claiming that his work is "uninspired." Does she have the right to do that?

This is a **personal satisfaction contract**, in which the promisee makes a personal, subjective evaluation of the promisor's performance. Employment contracts may require personal satisfaction of the employer; agreements for the sale of goods may demand that the buyer be personally satisfied with the product; and deals involving a credit analysis of one party may insist that his finances be satisfactory to the other party. In resolving disputes like Ben and Sujata's, judges must decide: when is it *fair* for the promisee to claim that she is not satisfied? May she make that decision for any reason at all, even on a whim?

Personal satisfaction contracts
Permit the promisee to make a subjective evaluations of the promisor's performance.

A court applies a subjective standard only if assessing the work involves personal feelings, taste, or judgment and the contract explicitly demanded personal satisfaction. A "subjective standard" means that the promisee's personal views will greatly influence her judgment, even if her decision is foolish and unfair. Artistic or creative work, or highly specialized tasks designed for a particular employer, may involve subtle issues of quality and personal preference. Ben's work combines several media and revolves around his judgment. Accordingly, the law applies a subjective standard to Sujata's decision. Since she concludes that his work is uninspired, she may legally fire him, even if her decision is irrational.

Either the system works or it does not.

Note that the promisee, Sujata, has to show two things: that assessing Ben's work involves her personal judgment *and* that their contract explicitly demands personal satisfaction. If the contract were vague on this point, Sujata would lose. Had the agreement merely said, "Ben will at all times make his best efforts," Sujata could not fire him.

In all other cases, a court applies an *objective* standard to the promisee's decision. In other words, the objective standard will be used if assessing the work does not involve personal judgment *or* if the contract failed to explicitly demand personal satisfaction. An objective standard means that the promisee's judgment of the work must be reasonable. Suppose Sujata hires Leila to install an alarm system for her company, and the contract requires that Sujata be "personally satisfied." Leila's system passes all tests, but Sujata claims, "It just doesn't make me feel secure. I know that someday it's going to break down." May Sujata refuse to pay? No. Even though the contract used the phrase "personally satisfied," a mechanical alarm system does not involve personal judgment and taste. Either the system works or it does not. A reasonable person would find that Leila's system is just fine and therefore, under the objective standard, Sujata must pay. The law strongly favors the objective standard because the subjective standard gives unlimited power to the promisee.

Good Faith

The parties to a contract must carry out their obligations in good faith. The difficulty, of course, is applying this general rule to the wide variety of problems that may arise when people or companies do business. How far must one side go to meet its good faith burden? Marvin Shuster was a physician in Florida. Three patients sued him for alleged malpractice. Shuster denied any wrongdoing and asked his insurer to defend the claims. But the insurance company settled all three claims without defending and with a minimum of investigation. Shuster paid nothing out of his own pocket, but he sued the insurance company, claiming that it acted in bad faith. The doctor argued that the company's failure to defend him caused emotional suffering and meant that it would be impossible for him to obtain new malpractice insurance. The Florida Supreme Court found that the insurer acted in good faith. The contract clearly gave all control of malpractice cases to the company. It could settle or defend as it saw fit. Here, the company considered it more economical to settle quickly, and Shuster should have known, from the contract language, that the insurer might choose to do so.[5]

How far must one side go to meet its good faith burden?

In the following case, one party to a contract played its cards very close to its chest. Too close?

Brunswick Hills Racquet Club Inc. v. Route 18 Shopping Center Associates

182 N.J. 210, 864 A.2d 387
Supreme Court of New Jersey, 2005

Facts: Brunswick Hills Racquet Club (Brunswick) owned a tennis club on property that it leased from Route 18 Shopping Center Associates (Route 18). The lease ran for 25 years, and Brunswick had spent about $1 million in capital improvements. The lease expired, and Brunswick had the option of either buying the property

[5] *Shuster v. South Broward Hospital Dist. Physicians' Prof. Liability Ins. Trust*, 591 So. 2d 174, 1992 Fla. LEXIS 20 (Fla. 1992).

or purchasing a 99-year lease, both on very favorable terms. To exercise its option, Brunswick had to notify Route 18 no later than September 30 and had to pay the option price of $150,000. If Brunswick failed to exercise its options, the existing lease automatically renewed as of September 30, for 25 more years, but at more than triple the current rent.

Brunswick's lawyer wrote to Rosen Associates, the company that managed Route 18, nineteen months before the option deadline, stating that Brunswick intended to exercise the option for a 99-year lease. He requested that the lease be sent well in advance so that he could review it. He did not make the required payment of $150,000. Rosen replied that it had forwarded Spector's letter to its attorney, who would be in touch. In April, Spector again wrote, asking for a reply from Rosen or its lawyer.

Over the next six months, the lawyer continually asked for a copy of the lease or further information, but neither Route 18's lawyer nor anyone else provided any data. Eventually, the September deadline passed.

Route 18's lawyer notified Brunswick that it could not exercise its option to lease because it had failed to pay the $150,000 by September 30.

Brunswick sued, claiming that Route 18 had breached its duty of good faith and fair dealing. The trial court found that Route 18 had no duty to notify Brunswick of impending deadlines, and it gave summary judgment for Route 18. The appellate court affirmed, and Brunswick appealed to the state supreme court.

Issue: ***Did Route 18 breach its duty of good faith and fair dealing?***

Excerpts from Justice Albin's Decision: Courts generally should not tinker with a finely drawn and precise contract entered into by experienced business people that regulates their financial affairs. [However,] every party to a contract is bound by a duty of good faith and fair dealing in both the performance and enforcement of the contract. Good faith is a concept that defies precise definition. Good faith conduct is conduct that does not violate community standards of decency, fairness, or reasonableness. The covenant of good faith and fair dealing calls for parties to a contract to refrain from doing anything which will have the effect of destroying or injuring the right of the other party to receive the benefits of the contract.

Our review of the undisputed facts of this case leads us to the inescapable conclusion that defendant breached the covenant of good faith and fair dealing. Nineteen months in advance of the option deadline, plaintiff notified defendant in writing of its intent to exercise the option to purchase the 99-year lease. Plaintiff mistakenly believed that the purchase price was not due until the time of closing.

During a 19-month period, defendant, through its agents, engaged in a pattern of evasion, sidestepping every request by plaintiff to discuss the option and ignoring plaintiff's repeated written and verbal entreaties to move forward on closing the 99-year lease despite the impending option deadline and obvious potential harm to plaintiff.

Defendant never requested the purchase price of the lease. Indeed, as defendant's attorney candidly admitted at oral argument, defendant did not want the purchase price because the successful exercise of the option was not in defendant's economic interest.

Ordinarily, we are content to let experienced commercial parties fend for themselves and do not seek to introduce intolerable uncertainty into a carefully structured contractual relationship by balancing equities. But there are ethical norms that apply even to the harsh and sometimes cutthroat world of commercial transactions. We do not expect a landlord or even an attorney to act as his brother's keeper in a commercial transaction. We do expect, however, that they will act in good faith and deal fairly with an opposing party. Plaintiff's repeated letters and telephone calls to defendant concerning the exercise of the option and the closing of the 99-year lease obliged defendant to respond, and to respond truthfully.

[Plaintiff is entitled to exercise the 99-year lease.]

EXAM Strategy

Question: Sun operates an upscale sandwich shop in New Jersey, in a storefront that she leases from Ricky for $18,000 per month. The lease, which expires soon, allows Sun to renew for five years at $22,000 per month. Ricky knows, but Sun does not, that in a year, Prada will open a store on the same block. The dramatic increase in pedestrian traffic will render Sun's space more valuable. Ricky says nothing about Prada, Sun declines to renew, and Ricky leases the space for $40,000 a month. Sun sues Ricky, claiming he breached his duty of good faith and fair dealing. Based on the *Brunswick Hills* case, how would the New Jersey Supreme Court rule?

Strategy: In the *Brunswick Hills* case, the court, on the one hand, criticized the defendant for cynically evading the plaintiff's efforts to renew. However, the court also said, "We do not expect a landlord or even an attorney to act as his brother's keeper in a commercial transaction." Using those opposing themes as guidelines, examine the court's decision and predict the ruling in Sun's suit.

Result: *Brunswick Hills* begins: "Courts generally should not tinker with a finely drawn and precise contract entered into by experienced business people." Sun's lease imposes no responsibility on Ricky to report on neighborhood changes or forecast profitability. Further, Sun made no requests to Ricky about the area's future. Sun is asking Ricky to be "her brother's keeper," and neither this court nor any other will do that. She loses.

Time of the Essence Clauses

> Go, sir, gallop, and don't forget that the world was made in six days. You can ask me for anything you like, except time.
>
> *Napoleon, to an aide, 1803*

Generals are not the only ones who place a premium on time. Ask Gene LaSalle. The Seabreeze Restaurant agreed to sell him all of its assets. The parties signed a contract stating the price and closing date. Seabreeze insisted on a clause saying, "Seabreeze considers that time is of the essence in consummating the proposed transaction." Such clauses are common in real estate transactions and in any other agreement where a delay would cause serious damage to one party. LaSalle was unable to close on the date specified and asked for an extension. Seabreeze refused and sold its assets elsewhere. A Florida court affirmed that Seabreeze acted legally.

Time of the essence clauses
Generally make contract dates strictly enforceable.

A **time of the essence clause** will generally make contract deadlines strictly enforceable. Seabreeze regarded a timely sale as important, and LaSalle agreed to the provision. There was nothing unreasonable about the clause, and LaSalle suffered the consequences of his delay.[6]

Suppose the contract had named a closing date but included no time of the essence clause. If LaSalle offered to close three days late, could Seabreeze sell elsewhere? No. **Merely including a date for performance does not make time of the essence.** Courts dislike time of the essence arguments because even a short delay may mean that one party forfeits everything it expected to gain from the bargain. If the parties do not *clearly* state that prompt performance is essential, then both are entitled to reasonable delays.

Breach

When one party breaches a contract, the other party is discharged. The discharged party has no obligation to perform and may sue for damages. Edwin promises that on July 1, he will deliver 20 tuxedos, tailored to fit male chimpanzees, to Bubba's circus for $300 per suit.

---

[6] *Seabreeze Restaurant, Inc. v. Paumgardhen*, 639 So.2d 69, 1994 Fla. App. LEXIS 4546 (Fla. Dist. Ct. App. 1994).

After weeks of delay, Edwin concedes he hasn't a cummerbund to his name. Bubba is discharged and owes nothing. In addition, he may sue Edwin for damages.

Material Breach

As we know, parties frequently perform their contract duties imperfectly, which is why courts accept substantial performance rather than strict performance, particularly in contracts involving services. In a more general sense, **courts will discharge a contract only if a party committed a *material* breach.** A material breach is one that substantially harms the innocent party and for which it would be hard to compensate without discharging the contract. Suppose Edwin fails to show up with the tuxedos on June 1 but calls to say they will arrive under the big top the next day. He has breached the agreement. Is his breach material? No. This is a trivial breach, and Bubba is not discharged. When the tuxedos arrive, he must pay.

The following case raises the issue in the context of a major college sports program.

O'Brien v. Ohio State University

2007 WL 2729077
Ohio Court of Appeals, 2007

Facts: The Ohio State University (OSU), experiencing a drought in its men's basketball program, brought in Coach Jim O'Brien to turn things around. The plan was successful. In only his second year, he guided the team to its best record ever. The team advanced to the Final Four, and O'Brien was named national coach of the year. OSU's athletic director promptly offered the coach a new, multiyear contract worth about $800,000 per year.

Section 5.1 of the contract included termination provisions. The university could fire O'Brien *for cause* if (a) there was a material breach of the contract by the coach or (b) O'Brien's conduct subjected the school to NCAA sanctions. OSU could also terminate O'Brien *without cause,* but in that case, it had to pay him the full salary owed.

O'Brien began recruiting a talented 21-year-old Serbian player named Alex Radojevic. While getting to know the young man, O'Brien discovered two things. First, it appeared that Radojevic had been paid to play briefly for a Yugoslavian team, meaning that he was ineligible to play college basketball. Second, it was clear that Radojevic's family had suffered terribly during the strife in his homeland.

O'Brien concluded that Radojevic would never play for OSU or any major college. He also decided to loan Radojevic's mother some money. Any such loan would violate an NCAA rule if done to recruit a player, but O'Brien believed the loan was legal since Radojevic could not play in the NCAA anyway. Several years later, the university learned of the loan and realized that O'Brien had never reported it. Hoping to avoid trouble with the NCAA, OSU imposed sanctions on itself. The university also fired the coach, claiming he had lied, destroyed the possibility of postseason play, and harmed the school's reputation.

O'Brien sued, claiming he had not materially breached the contract. The trial court awarded the coach $2.5 million, and the university appealed.

Issue: ***Did O'Brien materially breach the contract?***

Excerpts from Judge Tyack's Decision: OSU argued that it was substantially injured by the self-imposed sanctions, which included a ban from post-season and NCAA tournament play [during the current season], and relinquishing two basketball scholarships from the [next] recruiting class. Contrary to OSU's argument, however, the trial court found these sanctions to be insubstantial. [Athletic Director] Geiger announced the one-year post-season ban in December, and it appears from the timing of that announcement that Geiger made the decision based on the fact that the team was unlikely to be invited to a post-season tournament in the first place.

The second alleged harm was harm to OSU's reputation. The trial court found that any reputational harm was similarly exaggerated, at least as it specifically related to the Radojevic matter. Radojevic never enrolled at OSU, and never played a single second for OSU's basketball team.

NCAA violations happen all the time. It's the nature of the beast. Also relevant to the issue of OSU's allegedly damaged reputation is the fact that almost immediately after firing O'Brien, OSU was able to lure one of the nation's top coaching prospects, [Thad Matta], to assume O'Brien's former position. Shortly thereafter, Matta successfully recruited possibly the best recruiting class ever. Based on this evidence, the trial court could reasonably find the Radojevic loan did not cause serious harm to OSU.

OSU argues that O'Brien acted in bad faith by covering up his misconduct for several years. In the words of OSU's counsel at oral argument: *"If lying to your employer for four years is not a material breach, it's hard to imagine what would be!"* Although the premise for counsel's argument is sound, it is unsound in application because it assumes facts not in evidence. Counsel for OSU assumes for the purposes of the argument that O'Brien systematically either denied allegations about the Radojevic loan, or took affirmative steps to conceal it from OSU. The evidence does not support such a conclusion. After Radojevic was drafted by the NBA, there is not a single inference that can be drawn from the record to suggest that O'Brien even thought about the loan. In O'Brien's own mind, he did not believe he had done anything wrong; thus, he would not have had a motive to conceal what he had done.

[There was no material breach.]

Affirmed.

Anticipatory Breach

Sally will receive her bachelor's degree in May and already has a job lined up for September. She has signed a two-year contract to work as window display designer for Surebet Department Store. The morning of graduation, she reads in the paper that Surebet is going out of business that very day. Surebet has told Sally nothing about her status. Sally need not wait until September to learn her fate. Surebet has committed an **anticipatory breach by making it unmistakably clear that it will not honor the contract**. Sometimes a promisor will actually inform the promisee that it will not perform its duties. At other times, as here, the promisor takes some step that makes the breach evident. Sally is discharged and may immediately seek other work. She is also entitled to file suit for breach of contract. The court will treat Surebet's anticipatory breach just as though the store had actually refused to perform on September 1.

Statute of Limitations

Statute of limitations
A statutory time limit within which an injured party must file suit.

A party injured by a breach of contract should act promptly. A **statute of limitations** begins to run at the time of injury and will limit the time within which the injured party may file suit. These laws set time limits for filing lawsuits. Statutes of limitation vary from state to state and from issue to issue within a state. Failure to file suit within the time limits discharges the party who breached the contract. Always consult a lawyer promptly in the case of a legal injury.

IMPOSSIBILITY

"Your honor, my client wanted to honor the contract. He just couldn't. *Honest.*" This plea often echoes around courtrooms as one party seeks discharge without fulfilling his contract obligations. Does the argument work? It depends. If performing a contract was truly impossible, a court will discharge the agreement. But if honoring the deal merely imposed a financial burden, the law will generally enforce the contract.

True Impossibility

These cases are easy—and rare. **True impossibility means that something has happened making it literally impossible to do what the promisor said he would do.** Francoise owns a vineyard that produces Beaujolais Nouveau wine. She agrees to ship 1,000 cases of her wine to Tyrone, a New York importer, as soon as this year's vintage is ready. Tyrone will pay $50 per case. But a fungus wipes out her entire vineyard. Francoise is discharged. It is theoretically impossible for Francoise to deliver wine from her vineyard, and she owes Tyrone nothing.

Meanwhile, though, Tyrone has a contract with Jackson, a retailer, to sell 1,000 cases of Beaujolais Nouveau wine at $70 per case. Tyrone has no wine from Francoise, and the only other Beaujolais Nouveau available will cost him $85 per case. Instead of earning $20 per case, Tyrone will lose $15. Does this discharge Tyrone's contract with Jackson? No. It is possible for him to perform—it's just more expensive. He must fulfill his agreement.

True impossibility is generally limited to these three causes:

- ***Destruction of the Subject Matter,*** as happened with Francoise's vineyard.
- ***Death of the Promisor in a Personal Services Contract.*** When the promisor agrees personally to render a service that cannot be transferred to someone else, her death discharges the contract. Producer hires Josephine to write the lyrics for a new Broadway musical, but Josephine dies after writing only two words: "Act One." The contract was personal to Josephine and is now discharged. Neither Josephine's estate nor Producer has any obligation to the other. But notice that most contracts are not for personal services. Suppose that Tyrone, the wine importer, dies. His contract to sell wine to Jackson is not discharged because anyone can deliver the required wine. Tyrone's estate remains liable on the deal with Jackson.
- ***Illegality.*** Chet, a Silicon Valley entrepreneur, wants to capitalize on his computer expertise. He contracts with Construction Co. to build a factory in Iran that will manufacture computers for sale in that country. Construction Co. fails to build the factory on time, and Chet sues. Construction Co. defends by pointing out that the President of the United States has issued an executive order barring trade between the United States and Iran. Construction Co. wins; the executive order discharged the contract.

Commercial Impracticability and Frustration of Purpose

It is rare for contract performance to be truly impossible but very common for it to become a financial burden to one party. Suppose Bradshaw Steel in Pittsburgh agrees to deliver 1,000 tons of steel beams to Rice Construction in Saudi Arabia at a given price, but a week later, the cost of raw ore increases 30 percent. A contract once lucrative to the manufacturer is suddenly a major liability. Does that change discharge Bradshaw? Absolutely not. Rice signed the deal *precisely to protect itself against price increases.* As we have seen, the primary purpose of contracts is to enable the parties to control their future.

Yet there may be times when a change in circumstances is so extreme that it would be unfair to enforce a deal. What if a strike made it impossible for Bradshaw to ship the steel to Saudi Arabia, and the only way to deliver would be by air, at *five times* the sea cost? Must Bradshaw fulfill its deal? What if a new war meant that any ships or planes delivering the goods might be fired upon? Other changes could make the contract undesirable for *Rice.* Suppose the builder wanted steel for a major public building in Riyadh, but the Saudi government decided not to go forward with the construction. The steel would then be worthless to Rice. Must the company still accept it?

None of these hypotheticals involves true impossibility. It is physically possible for Bradshaw to deliver the goods and for Rice to receive. But in some cases, it may be so dangerous, costly, or pointless to enforce a bargain that a court will discharge it instead.

Courts use the related doctrines of commercial impracticability and frustration of purpose to decide when a change in circumstances should permit one side to escape its duties.

Commercial impracticability means some event has occurred that neither party anticipated and *fulfilling the contract would now be extraordinarily difficult and unfair to one party.* If a shipping strike forces Bradshaw to ship by air, the company will argue that neither side expected the strike and that Bradshaw should not suffer a fivefold increase in shipping costs. Bradshaw will probably win the argument.

Frustration of purpose means some event has occurred that neither party anticipated and *the contract now has no value for one party.* If Rice's building project is canceled, Rice will argue that the steel now is useless to the company. Frustration cases are hard to predict. Some states would agree with Rice, but others would hold that it was Rice's obligation to protect itself with a government guarantee that the project would be completed. Courts consider the following factors in deciding impracticability and frustration claims:

- *Mere financial difficulties will never suffice to discharge a contract.* Barbara and Michael Luber divorced, and Michael agreed to pay alimony. He stopped making payments and claimed that it was impracticable for him to do so because he had hit hard times and simply did not have the money. The court dismissed his argument, noting that commercial impracticability requires some objective event that neither party anticipated, not merely the financial deterioration of one party.[7]

- *The event must have been truly unexpected.* Wayne Carpenter bought land from the state of Alaska, intending to farm it and agreeing to make monthly payments. The sales contract stated that Alaska did not guarantee the land for agriculture or any other purpose. Carpenter struggled to farm the land but failed; as soon as the ground thawed, the water table rose too high for crops. Carpenter abandoned the land and stopped making payments. Alaska sued and won. The high court rejected Carpenter's claim of impracticability since the "event"—bad soil—was not unexpected. Alaska had warned that the land might prove unworkable, and Carpenter had no claim for commercial impracticability.[8]

- *If the promisor must use a different means to accomplish her task, at a greatly increased cost, she probably does have a valid claim of impracticability.* If a shipping strike forces Bradshaw to use a different means of delivery—say, air—and this multiplies its costs several times, the company is probably discharged. But a mere increase in the cost of raw materials, such as a 30 percent rise in the price of ore, will almost never discharge the promisor.

- *A* force majeure *clause is significant but not necessarily dispositive.* To protect themselves from unexpected events, companies sometimes include a *force majeure* clause, allowing cancellation of the agreement in case of extraordinary and unexpected events. A typical clause might permit the seller of goods to delay or cancel delivery in the event of "acts of God, fire, labor disputes, accidents, or transportation difficulties." A court will always consider a *force majeure* clause, but it may not enforce it if one party is trying to escape from routine financial problems.

---

[7] *Luber v. Luber*, 418 Pa. Super. 542, 614 A.2d 771, 1992 Pa. Super. LEXIS 3338 (Pa. Super. Ct. 1992).
[8] *State v. Carpenter*, 869 P.2d 1181, 1994 Alaska LEXIS 23 (Alaska 1994).

Chapter Conclusion

Negotiate carefully. A casually written letter may imply a condition precedent that the author never intended. The term *personal satisfaction* should be defined so that both parties know whether one party may fire the other on a whim. Never assume that mere inconvenience or financial loss will discharge contractual duties.

Exam Review

1. **CONDITION** A condition is an event that must occur before a party becomes obligated. It may be stated expressly or implied, and no formal language is necessary to create one. (pp. 382–387)

Question: Stephen Krogness, a real estate broker, agreed to act as an agent for Best Buy Co., which wanted to sell several of its stores. The contract provided that Best Buy would pay Krogness a commission of 2 percent for "a sale to any prospect submitted directly to Best Buy by Krogness." Krogness introduced Corporate Realty Capital (CRC) to Best Buy, and the parties negotiated but could not reach agreement. CRC then introduced Best Buy to BB Properties (BB). Best Buy sold several properties to BB for $46 million. CRC acted as the broker. Krogness sought a commission of $528,000. Is he entitled to it?

Strategy: This contract contains a conditional clause. What is it? What must occur before Best Buy is obligated to pay Krogness? Did that event happen? (See the "Result" at the end of this section.)

2. **SUBSTANTIAL PERFORMANCE** Strict performance, which requires one party to fulfill its duties perfectly, is unusual. In construction and service contracts, substantial performance is generally sufficient to entitle the promisor to the contract price, minus the cost of defects in the work. (pp. 388–389)

3. **PERSONAL SATISFACTION** Personal satisfaction contracts are interpreted under an objective standard, requiring reasonable ground for dissatisfaction, unless the work involves personal judgment *and* the parties intended a subjective standard. (pp. 389–390)

4. **GOOD FAITH** Good faith performance is required in all contracts. (pp. 390–392)

5. **TIME OF THE ESSENCE** Time of the essence clauses result in strict enforcement of contract deadlines. (p. 392)

EXAM Strategy

Question: Colony Park Associates signed a contract to buy 44 acres of residential land from John Gall. The contract stated that closing would take place exactly one year later. The delay was to enable Colony Park to obtain building permits to develop condominiums. Colony Park worked diligently to obtain all permits, but delays in sewer permits forced Colony Park to notify Gall it could not close on the agreed date. Colony Park suggested a date exactly one month later. Gall refused the new date and declined to sell. Colony Park sued. Gall argued that since the parties specified a date, time was of the essence and Colony Park's failure to buy on time discharged Gall. Please rule.

Strategy: A time of the essence clause generally makes a contract date strictly enforceable. Was there one in this agreement? (See the "Result" at the end of this section.)

6. **MATERIAL BREACH** A material breach is the only kind that will discharge a contract; a trivial breach will not. (pp. 393–394)

7. **IMPOSSIBILITY** True impossibility means that some event has made it impossible to perform an agreement. It is typically caused by destruction of the subject matter, the death of an essential promisor, or intervening illegality. (pp. 394–396)

EXAM Strategy

Question: Omega Concrete had a gravel pit and factory. Access was difficult, so Omega contracted with Union Pacific Railroad (UP) for the right to use a private road that crossed UP property and tracks. The contract stated that use of the road was solely for Omega employees and that Omega would be responsible for closing a gate that UP planned to build where the private road joined a public highway. In fact, UP never constructed the gate; Omega had no authority to construct the gate. Mathew Rogers, an Omega employee, was killed by a train while using the private road. Rogers's family sued Omega, claiming that Omega failed to keep the gate closed as the contract required. Is Omega liable?

Strategy: True impossibility means that the promisor cannot do what he promised to do. Is this such a case? (See the "Result" at the end of this section.)

8. **COMMERCIAL IMPRACTICABILITY** Commercial impracticability means that some unexpected event has made it extraordinarily difficult and unfair for one party to perform its obligations. (pp. 395–396)

9. **FRUSTRATION OF PURPOSE** Frustration of purpose may occur when an unexpected event renders a contract completely useless to one party. (pp. 395–396)

1. Result: The conditional clause requires Best Buy to pay a commission for "a sale to any prospect submitted directly to Best Buy by Krogness." Krogness did not in fact introduce BB Properties to Best Buy. The condition has not occurred, and Best Buy is under no obligation to pay.

5. Result: Merely including a date for performance does not make time of the essence. A party that considers a date critical must make that clear. This contract did not indicate that the closing date was vital to either party, so a short delay was reasonable. Gail was ordered to convey the land to Colony Park.

7. Result: There was no gate, and Omega had no right to build one. This is a case of true impossibility. Omega was not liable.

Multiple-Choice Questions

1. ***CPA QUESTION*** Nagel and Fields entered into a contract in which Nagel was obligated to deliver certain goods by September 10. On September 3, Nagel told Fields that he had no intention of delivering the goods. Prior to September 10, Fields may successfully sue Nagel under the doctrine of:

(a) Promissory estoppel

(b) Accord and satisfaction

(c) Anticipatory breach

(d) Substantial performance

2. Most contracts are discharged by ...

(a) Agreement of the parties

(b) Full performance

(c) Failure of conditions

(d) Commercial impracticability

(e) A material breach

3. If a contract contains a condition precedent, the ____________ has the burden of proving that the condition actually happened. If a condition subsequent exists, the ____________ has the burden of showing that the condition occurred.

(a) plaintiff; plaintiff

(b) plaintiff; defendant

(c) defendant; plaintiff

(d) defendant; defendant

4. Big Co., a construction company, builds a grocery store. The contract calls for a final price of $5 million. Big Co. incurred $4.5 million in costs and stands to make a profit of $500,000. On a final inspection, the grocery store owner is upset. His blueprints called for 24 skylights, but the finished building has only 12. Installing the additional skylights would cost $100,000. Big Co. made no other errors. How much must the grocery store owner pay Big Co.?

(a) $5,000,000

(b) $4,900,000

(c) $4,500,000

(d) $0

5. Lenny makes K2, a synthetic form of marijuana, in his basement. He signs an agreement with the Super Smoke Shop to deliver 1,000 cans of K2 for $10,000. After the contract is signed, but before the delivery, Super Smoke Shop's state legislature makes the sale of K2 illegal. Lenny's contract will be discharged because of ___________.

   (a) true impossibility
   (b) commercial impracticability
   (c) frustration of purpose
   (d) None of the above

Essay Questions

1. **ETHICS** Commercial Union Insurance Co. (CU) insured Redux, Ltd. The contract made CU liable for fire damage but stated that the insurer would not pay for harm caused by criminal acts of any Redux employees. Fire destroyed Redux's property. CU claimed that the "criminal acts" clause was a condition precedent, but Redux asserted it was a condition subsequent. What difference does it make, and who is legally right? Does the insurance company's position raise any ethical issues? Who drafted the contract? How clear were its terms?

2. Stephen Muka owned U.S. Robotics. He hired his brother Chris to work in the company. His letter promised Chris $1 million worth of Robotics stock at the end of one year, "provided you work reasonably hard & smart at things in the next year." (We should all have such brothers.) Chris arrived at Robotics and worked the full year, but toward the end of the year, Stephen died. His estate refused to give Chris the stock, claiming their agreement was a personal satisfaction contract and only Stephen could decide whether Chris had earned the reward. Comment.

3. Ken Ward was an Illinois farmer who worked land owned by his father-in-law, Frank Ruda. To finance his operation, he frequently borrowed money from Watseka First National Bank, paying back the loans with farming profits. But Ward fell deeper and deeper into debt, and Watseka became concerned. When Ward sought additional loans, Watseka insisted that Ruda become a guarantor on all of the outstanding debt, and the father-in-law agreed. The new loans had an acceleration clause, permitting the bank to demand payment of the entire debt if it believed itself "insecure"; that is, at risk of a default. Unfortunately, just as Ward's debts reached more than $120,000, Illinois suffered a severe drought, and Ward's crops failed. Watseka asked Ruda to sell some of the land he owned to pay back part of the indebtedness. Ruda reluctantly agreed but never did so. Meanwhile, Ward decreased his payments to the bank because of the terrible crop. Watseka then "accelerated" the loan, demanding that Ruda pay off the entire debt. Ruda defended by claiming that Watseka's acceleration at such a difficult time was bad faith. Who should win?

4. Loehmann's clothing stores, a nationwide chain with headquarters in New York, was the anchor tenant in the Lincoln View Plaza Shopping Center in Phoenix, Arizona, with a 20-year lease from the landlord, Foundation Development, beginning in 1978. Loehmann's was obligated to pay rent the first of every month and to pay common-area charges four times a year. The lease stated that if Loehmann's failed

to pay on time, Foundation could send a notice of default, and that if the store failed to pay all money due within 10 days, Foundation could evict. On February 23, 1987, Foundation sent to Loehmann's the common-area charges for the quarter ending January 31, 1987. The balance due was $3,500. Loehmann's believed the bill was in error and sent an inquiry on March 18, 1987. On April 10, 1987, Foundation insisted on payment of the full amount within 10 days. Foundation sent the letter to the Loehmann's store in Phoenix. On April 13, 1987, the Loehmann's store received the bill and, since it was not responsible for payments, forwarded it to the New York office. Because the company had moved offices in New York, a Loehmann's officer did not see the bill until April 20. Loehmann's issued a check for the full amount on April 24 and mailed it the following day. On April 28, Foundation sued to evict; on April 29, the company received Loehmann's check. Please rule.

5. **YOU BE THE JUDGE WRITING PROBLEM** Kuhn Farm Machinery, a European company, signed an agreement with Scottsdale Plaza Resort, of Arizona, to use the resort for its North American dealers' convention during March 1991. Kuhn agreed to rent 190 guest rooms and spend several thousand dollars on food and beverages. Kuhn invited its top 200 independent dealers from the United States and Canada and about 25 of its own employees from the United States, Europe, and Australia, although it never mentioned those plans to Scottsdale.

   On August 2, 1990, Iraq invaded Kuwait, and on January 16, 1991, the United States and allied forces were at war with Iraq. Saddam Hussein and other Iraqi leaders threatened terrorist acts against the United States and its allies. Kuhn became concerned about the safety of those traveling to Arizona, especially its European employees. By mid-February, 11 of the top 50 dealers with expense-paid trips had either canceled their plans to attend or failed to sign up. Kuhn postponed the convention. The resort sued. The trial court discharged the contract under the doctrines of commercial impracticability and frustration of purpose. The resort appealed. Did commercial impracticability or frustration of purpose discharge the contract? **Argument for Scottsdale Plaza Resort:** The resort had no way of knowing that Kuhn anticipated bringing executives from Europe, and even less reason to expect that if anything interfered with their travel, the entire convention would become pointless. Most of the dealers could have attended the convention, and the resort stood ready to serve them. **Argument for Kuhn:** The parties never anticipated the threat of terrorism. Kuhn wanted this convention so that its European executives, among others, could meet top North American dealers. That is now impossible. No company would risk employee lives for a meeting. As a result, the contract has no value at all to Kuhn, and its obligations should be discharged by law.

Discussion Questions

1. Evans built a house for Sandra Dyer, but the house had some problems. The garage ceiling was too low. Load-bearing beams in the "great room" cracked and appeared to be steadily weakening. The patio did not drain properly. Pipes froze. Evans wanted the money promised for the job, but Dyer refused to pay. Comment.

2. Krug International, an Ohio corporation, had a contract with Iraqi Airways to build aeromedical equipment for training pilots. Krug then contracted for Power Engineering, an Iowa corporation, to build the specialized gearbox to be used in

the training equipment for $150,000. Power did not know that Krug planned to resell the gearbox to Iraqi Airways. When Power had almost completed the gearbox, the Gulf War broke out and the United Nations declared an embargo on all shipments to Iraq. Krug notified Power that it no longer wanted the gearbox. Power sued. Please rule.

3. The death of a promisor in a *personal services* contract discharges an agreement. But if a promisor dies, other kinds of contracts live on. Is this sensible? Would it be better to discharge all kinds of agreements if one of the parties passes away?

4. Is commercial impracticability (such as the shipping strike described earlier in the chapter) a good reason for discharge? What about frustration of purpose (such as the cancellation of the construction project in Saudi Arabia)? Is one more justified than the other? Are parties who back out of contracts on these grounds acting reasonably?

5. Franklin J. Moneypenny hires Angela to paint his portrait. She is to be paid $50,000 if the painting is acceptable "in Franklin's sole judgment." At the big unveiling, 99 of 100 attendees think that Angela has done a masterful job. Franklin disagrees. He thinks the painting makes him look like a toad. (He does in fact look like a toad, but he does not like to contemplate this fact.) Franklin refuses to pay, and, because he signed a personal satisfaction contract, Angela gets nothing. Is this fair? Should the law allow personal satisfaction contracts?

CHAPTER 18

REMEDIES

© picsbyst/Shutterstock.com

Ben is the general manager of an NFL football team. Driving home in his truck, he is in a sour humor. Spencer, the team's best running back, under contract to play for one more year at $2.5 million, has announced he is leaving the team to act in a new sitcom. Ben wonders whether he can stop Spencer from leaving the team. Even if it is possible, would it be worthwhile to make a disgruntled, out-of-condition athlete carry (and fumble) the ball? If Spencer leaves, it will cost at least $5 million to hire a runner with equal speed and power.

The G.M.'s phone rings. Louise, a dealer in rare autos, has bad news.

"I hate to tell you, Ben, but the deal just fell through."

"What are you talking about? We both signed! That's a binding contract!" A seller in Florida had agreed in writing to sell Ben a 1955 Ferrari for $900,000.

"*I* know it's true, and *you* know it," Louise murmurs soothingly. "But the seller has decided he just can't part with it."

Ben slams his cell phone down, turns into his driveway—and notices that the back door is open. Did he leave it that way? No. The burglar did. Ben has lost about $100,000 worth of jewelry, clothing, and sports memorabilia. Why didn't the alarm sound? When he demands an explanation from Alarmist, his home security provider, the quality assurance representative assures Ben that he will receive the full compensation due under his contract—$600. Later that night, Ben will have a long talk with his lawyer about breached contracts and remedies.

Ben slams his cell phone down, turns into his driveway—and notices that the back door is open. Did he leave it that way? No. The burglar did.

Breaching a Contract

Someone breaches a contract when he fails to perform a duty without a valid excuse. Spencer is legally committed to play for the team for one more year and is clearly breaching his contract when he informs the team that in the future, he will be playing for laughs. But what can the team do about the runner's breach? In other words, what is the team's *remedy?* **A remedy is the method a court uses to compensate an injured party.**

Injunction
A court order that requires someone to do something or refrain from doing something.

Should a court stop Spencer from performing in his new sitcom? Force him to carry the ball instead? An order forcing someone to refrain from doing something is an **injunction.** Courts frequently grant injunctions to an employer, blocking an employee from *leaving* to work elsewhere. However, courts almost never use an order to force an employee to *complete* a contract with his employer because that would force two antagonistic parties to work together. In other words, Ben can probably stop Spencer from working in television, but no court will order the running back to suit up and play.

Expectation damages
The money required to put one party in the position she would have been in had the other side performed the contract.

Courts also award **expectation damages**, meaning the money required to put one party in the position he would have been in had the other side performed the contract. If Spencer's team is forced to hire another running back for double the money they expected to pay Spencer, the team will probably recover the difference between the two players' salaries.

Specific performance
Forces both parties to complete the deal.

The Ferrari seller has breached his deal with Ben. What is Ben's remedy? He does not want money damages; he wants that lovely red car. In cases of property that is rare or difficult to replace, courts often award **specific performance**, forcing both parties to complete the deal. Ben should get his car.

Liquidated damages clause
A provision in the contract that declares in advance what one party will receive if the other side breaches.

Finally, the alarm company is trying to *insist* upon a remedy—a very limited one, which will leave Ben largely uncompensated for the burglary. Alarmist is relying on a **liquidated damages clause,** meaning a provision in the contract that declares in advance what one party will receive if the other side breaches. Courts sometimes enforce these clauses. But as we will see later, Alarmist's liquidated clause may be too harsh, and thus unenforceable.

How to best help an injured party, without unfairly harming the other person, is the focus of remedies. The questions and issues created by Ben's Bad Day are typical remedy problems. Courts have struggled with remedies for centuries, but we will master the subject in one chapter.

Ethics Though a court may have several alternative remedies available, it is important to note that most have one thing in common: the focus is on compensating the injured party rather than punishing the party in breach. A court must decide whether to prevent Spencer from leaving the gridiron for the television studio, but it will not consider fining or jailing him.

Some critics argue that someone who willfully breaches a contract should pay a penalty. The Ferrari seller knows he is obligated to part with his car but tries to keep it anyway. Spencer blithely ignores his obligations to the team. Should a remedy reflect morality? In this chapter, we will see very few instances in which a court *punishes* unethical conduct. Is this right? Should contract law exact a price for bad behavior?

Identifying the "Interest" to Be Protected

Interest
A legal right in something.

The first step that a court takes in choosing a remedy is to decide what interest it is trying to protect. An **interest** is a legal right in something. Someone can have an interest in property, for example, by owning it, or renting it to a tenant, or lending money so someone else may buy it. He can have an interest in a *contract* if the agreement gives him some benefit. There are four principal contract interests that a court may seek to protect:

- ***Expectation interest.*** This refers to what the injured party reasonably thought she would get from the contract. The goal is to put her in the position she would have been in if both parties had fully performed their obligations.
- ***Reliance interest.*** The injured party may be unable to demonstrate expectation damages, perhaps because it is unclear he would have profited. But he may still prove that he *spent money* in reliance on the agreement and that in fairness, he should receive compensation.
- ***Restitution interest.*** The injured party may be unable to show an expectation interest or reliance. But perhaps she has conferred a benefit *on the other party*. Here, the objective is to restore to the injured party the benefit she has provided.
- ***Equitable interest.*** In some cases, money damages will not suffice to help the injured party. Something more is needed, such as an order to transfer property to the injured party (specific performance) or an order forcing one party to stop doing something (an injunction).

In this chapter, we look at all four interests.

Expectation Interest

This is the most common remedy that the law provides for a party injured by a breach of contract. **The expectation interest is designed to put the injured party in the position she would have been in had both sides fully performed their obligations.** A court tries to give the injured party the money she would have made from the contract. If accurately calculated, this should take into account all the gains she reasonably expected and all the expenses and losses she would have incurred. The injured party should not end up better off than she would have been under the agreement, nor should she suffer a loss.

If you ever go to law school, you will almost certainly encounter the following case during your first week of classes. It has been used to introduce the concept of damages in contract lawsuits for generations. Enjoy the famous "case of the hairy hand."

Landmark Case

Hawkins v. McGee

84 N.H. 114, 146 A. 641
Supreme Court of New Hampshire, 1929

Facts: Hawkins suffered a severe electrical burn on the palm of his right hand. After years of living with disfiguring scars, he went to visit Dr. McGee, who was well known for his early attempts at skin-grafting surgery. The doctor told Hawkins "I will guarantee to make the hand a hundred percent perfect." Hawkins hired him to perform the operation.

McGee cut a patch of healthy skin from Hawkins's chest and grafted it over the scar tissue on Hawkins' palm. Unfortunately, the chest hair on the skin graft was very thick, and it continued to grow after the surgery. The operation resulted in a hairy palm for Hawkins. Feeling rather ... embarrassed ... Hawkins sued Dr. McGee.

The trial court judge instructed the jury to calculate damages in this way: "If you find the plaintiff entitled to anything, he is entitled to recover for what pain and suffering he has been made to endure and what injury he has sustained over and above the injury that he had before."

The jury awarded Hawkins $3,000, but the court reduced the award to $500. Dissatisfied, Hawkins appealed.

Issue: ***How should Hawkins' damages be calculated?***

Excerpts from Justice Branch's Decision: The jury was permitted to consider two elements of damage, (1) pain and suffering due to the operation, and (2) positive ill effects of the operation upon the plaintiff's hand. [T]he foregoing instruction was erroneous.

By damages as that term is used in the law of contracts, is intended compensation to put the plaintiff in as good a position as he would have been in had the defendant kept his contract. The measure of recovery is what the defendant should have given the plaintiff, not what the plaintiff has given the defendant or otherwise expended.

We conclude that the true measure of the plaintiff's damage in the present case is the difference between the value to him of a perfect hand and the value of his hand in its present condition, including any incidental consequences fairly within the contemplation of the parties when they made their contract.

The extent of the plaintiff's suffering does not measure this difference in value. The pain necessarily incident to a serious surgical operation was a part of the contribution which the plaintiff was willing to make to his joint undertaking with the defendant to produce a good hand. It furnished no test of the difference between the value of the hand which the defendant promised and the one which resulted from the operation.

[Remanded for a] new trial.

Now let's consider a more modern example.

William Colby was a former director of the CIA. He wanted to write a book about his 15 years in Vietnam. He paid James McCarger $5,000 for help in writing an early draft and promised McCarger another $5,000 if the book was published. Then he hired Alexander Burnham to cowrite the book. Colby's agent secured a contract with Contemporary Books, which included a $100,000 advance. But Burnham was hopelessly late with the manuscript and Colby missed his publication date. Colby fired Burnham and finished the book without him. Contemporary published *Lost Victory* several years late, and the book flopped, earning no significant revenue. Because the book was so late, Contemporary paid Colby a total of only $17,000. Colby sued Burnham for his lost expectation interest. The court awarded him $23,000, calculated as follows:

	$100,000	advance, the only money Colby was promised
	– 10,000	agent's fee
	= 90,000	Fee for the two authors, combined
divided by 2	= 45,000	Colby's fee (the other half went to the coauthor)
	– 5,000	owed to McCarger under the earlier agreement
	= 40,000	Colby's expectation interest
	– 17,000	Fee Colby eventually received from Contemporary
	= 23,000	Colby's expectation damages; that is, the additional amount he would have received had Burnham finished on time

The *Colby* case[1] presented a relatively easy calculation of damages. Other contracts are complex. Courts typically divide the expectation damages into three parts: (1) direct (or "compensatory") damages, which represent harm that flowed directly from the contract's breach; (2) consequential (or "special") damages, which represent harm caused by the injured party's unique situation; and (3) incidental damages, which are minor costs such as

[1]*Colby v. Burnham,* 31 Conn. App. 707, 627 A.2d 457, 1993 Conn. App LEXIS 299 (Conn. App. Ct. 1993).

storing or returning defective goods, advertising for alternative goods, and so forth. The first two, direct and consequential, are the important ones.

Note that punitive damages are absent from our list. The golden rule in contracts cases is to give successful plaintiffs "the benefit of the bargain" and not to punish defendants. Punitive damages are occasionally awarded in lawsuits that involve both a contract *and* either an intentional tort (such as fraud) or a breach of fiduciary duty, but they are not available in "simple" cases involving only a breach of contract.

Direct Damages

Direct damages are those that flow directly from the contract. They are the most common monetary award for the expectation interest. These are the damages that inevitably result from the breach. Suppose Ace Productions hires Reina to star in its new movie, *Inside Straight.* Ace promises Reina $3 million, providing she shows up June 1 and works until the film is finished. But in late May, Joker Entertainment offers Reina $6 million to star in its new feature, and on June 1, Reina informs Ace that she will not appear. Reina has breached her contract, and Ace should recover direct damages.

Direct damages
Are those that flow directly from the contract.

What are the damages that flow directly from the contract? Ace has to replace Reina. If Ace hires Kayla as its star and pays her a fee of $4 million, Ace is entitled to the difference between what it expected to pay ($3 million) and what the breach forced it to pay ($4 million), or $1 million in direct damages.

Consequential Damages

In addition to direct damages, the injured party may seek consequential damages or, as they are also known, "special damages." **Consequential damages** reimburse for harm that results from the *particular* circumstances of the plaintiff. These damages are only available if they are a *foreseeable consequence* of the breach. Suppose, for example, Raould breaches two contracts—he is late picking both Sharon and Paul up for a taxi ride. His breach is the same for both parties, but the consequences are very different. Sharon misses her flight to San Francisco and incurs a substantial fee to rebook the flight. Paul is simply late for the barber, who manages to fit him in anyway. Thus, Raould's damages would be different for these two contracts. The rule concerning this remedy comes from a famous 1854 case, *Hadley v. Baxendale.* This is another case that all American law students read. Now it is your turn.

Consequential damages
Are those resulting from the unique circumstances of *this injured party.*

Landmark Case

Hadley v. Baxendale

9 Ex. 341, 156 Eng. Rep. 145
Court of Exchequer, 1854

Facts: The Hadleys operated a flour mill in Gloucester. The crankshaft broke, causing the mill to grind to a halt. The Hadleys employed Baxendale to cart the damaged part to a foundry in Greenwich, where a new one could be manufactured. Baxendale promised to make the delivery in one day, but he was late transporting the shaft, and as a result, the Hadleys' mill was shut for five extra days. They sued, and the jury awarded damages based in part on their lost profits. Baxendale appealed.

Issue: ***Should the defendant be liable for profits lost because of his delay in delivering the shaft?***

Excerpts from Judge Alderson's Decision: Where two parties have made a contract which one of them has broken, the damages which the other party ought to receive in respect of such breach of contract should be such as may fairly and reasonably be considered either arising naturally, i.e. according to the usual course of things, from such breach of contract itself, or such as may reasonably be supposed to have been in the contemplation of both parties, at the time they made the contract, as the probable result of the breach of it. Now, if the special circumstances under which the contract was actually made were communicated by the plaintiffs to the defendants, and thus known to both parties, the damages resulting from the breach of such a contract, which they would reasonably contemplate, would be the amount of injury which would ordinarily follow from a breach of contract under these special circumstances so known and communicated. But, on the other hand, if these special circumstances were wholly unknown to the party breaking the contract, he, at the most, could only be supposed to have had in his contemplation the amount of injury which would arise generally, and in the great multitude of cases not affected by any special circumstances, from such a breach of contract.

Now, in the present case, if we are to apply the principles above laid down, we find that the only circumstances here communicated by the plaintiffs to the defendants at the time the contract was made, were that the article to be carried was the broken shaft of a mill, and that the plaintiffs were the millers of that mill. But how do these circumstances shew reasonably that the profits of the mill must be stopped by an unreasonable delay in the delivery of the broken shaft by the carrier to the third person? Suppose the plaintiffs had another shaft in their possession put up or putting up at the time, and that they only wished to send back the broken shaft to the engineer who made it; it is clear that this would be quite consistent with the above circumstances, and yet the unreasonable delay in the delivery would have no effect upon the intermediate profits of the mill. It follows, therefore, that the loss of profits here cannot reasonably be considered such a consequence of the breach of contract as could have been fairly and reasonably contemplated by both the parties when they made this contract.

[The court ordered a new trial, in which the jury would *not* be allowed to consider the plaintiffs' lost profits.]

The rule from *Hadley v. Baxendale* has been unchanged ever since: **The injured party may recover consequential damages only if the *breaching party* should have *foreseen* them when the two sides formed the contract.**

Let us return briefly to *Inside Straight.* Suppose that, long before shooting began, Ace had sold the film's soundtrack rights to Spinem Sound for $2 million. Spinem believed it would make a profit only if Reina appeared in the film, so it demanded the right to discharge the agreement if Reina dropped out. When Reina quit, Spinem terminated the contract. Now, when Ace sues Reina, it will also seek $2 million in consequential damages for the lost music revenue.

The $2 million is not a direct damage. The contract between Reina and Act has nothing directly to do with selling soundtrack rights. But the loss is nonetheless a consequence of Reina bailing out on the project. And so, if Reina knew about Ace's contract with Spinem when she signed to do the film, the loss would be foreseeable to her, and she would be liable for $2 million. If she never realized she was an essential part of the music contract, and if a jury determines that she had no reason to expect the $2 million loss, she owes nothing for the lost soundtrack profits.

Injured plaintiffs often try to recover lost profits. Courts will generally award these damages if (1) the lost profits were foreseeable and (2) plaintiff provides enough information so that the fact finder can reasonably estimate a fair amount. The calculation need not be done with mathematical precision. In the following case, the plaintiffs lost not only profits—but their entire business. Can they recover for harm that is so extensive? You decide.

You be the Judge

BI-ECONOMY MARKET, INC. v. HARLEYSVILLE INS. CO. OF NEW YORK

2008 WL 423451
New York Court of Appeals, 2008

Facts: Bi-Economy Market was a family-owned meat market in Rochester, New York. The company was insured by Harleysville Insurance. The "Deluxe Business Owner's" policy provided replacement cost for damage to buildings and inventory. Coverage also included "business interruption insurance" for one year, meaning the loss of pretax profit plus normal operating expenses, including payroll.

The company suffered a disastrous fire, which destroyed its building and all inventory. Bi-Economy immediately filed a claim with Harleysville, but the insurer responded slowly. Harleysville eventually offered a settlement of $163,000. A year later, an arbitrator awarded the Market $407,000. During that year, Harleysville paid for seven months of lost income but declined to pay more. The company never recovered or reopened.

Bi-Economy sued, claiming that Harleysville's slow, inadequate payments destroyed the company. The company also sought consequential damages for the permanent destruction of its business. Harleysville claimed that it was only responsible for damages specified in the contract: the building, inventory, and lost income. The trial court granted summary judgment for Harleysville. The appellate court affirmed, claiming that when they entered into the contract, the parties did not contemplate damages for termination of the business. Bi-Economy appealed to the state's highest court.

You Be the Judge: ***Is Bi-Economy entitled to consequential damages for the destruction of its business?***

Argument for Bi-Economy: Bi-Economy is a small, family business. We paid for business interruption insurance for an obvious reason: in the event of a disaster, we lacked the resources to keep going while buildings were constructed and inventory purchased. We knew that in such a calamity, we would need prompt reimbursement—compensation covering the immediate damage and our ongoing lost income. Why else would we pay the premiums?

At the time we entered into the contract, Harleysville could easily foresee that if it responded slowly, with insufficient payments, we could not survive. They knew that is what we wanted to avoid—and it is just what happened. The insurer's bad faith offer of a low figure, and its payment of only seven months' lost income, ruined a fine family business. When the insurance company agreed to business interruption coverage, it was declaring that it would act fast and fairly to sustain a small firm in crisis. The insurer should now pay for the full harm it has wrought.

Argument for Harleysville: We contracted to insure the Market for three losses: its building, inventory, and lost income. After the fire, we performed a reasonable, careful evaluation and made an offer we considered fair. An arbitrator later awarded Bi-Market additional money, which we paid. However it is absurd to suggest that in addition to that, we are liable for an open-ended commitment for permanent destruction of the business.

Consequential damages are appropriate in cases where a plaintiff suffers a loss that was not covered in the contract. In this case, though, the parties bargained over exactly what Harleysville would pay in the event of a major fire. If the insurer has underpaid for lost income, let the court award a fair sum. However, the parties never contemplated an additional, enormous payment for cessation of the business. There is almost no limit as to what that obligation could be. If Bi-Market was concerned that a fire might put the company permanently out of business, it should have said so at the time of negotiating for insurance. The premium would have been dramatically higher.

Neither Bi-Market nor Harleysville ever imagined such an open-ended insurance obligation, and the insurer should not pay an extra cent.

Incidental Damages

Incidental damages are the relatively minor costs that the injured party suffers when *responding to* the breach. When Reina, the actress, breaches the film contract, the producers may have to leave the set and fly back to Los Angeles to hire a new actress. The travel cost is an incidental damage. In another setting, suppose Maud, a manufacturer, has produced 5,000 pairs of

Incidental damages
Relatively minor costs that the injured party suffers when responding to the breach.

running shoes for Foot The Bill, a retail chain, but Foot The Bill breaches the agreement and refuses to accept the goods. Maud will have to store the shoes and advertise for alternate buyers. The storage and advertising costs are incidental expenses, and Maud will recover them.

The UCC and Damages

Under the Uniform Commercial Code (UCC), remedies for breach of contract in the sale of goods are similar to the general rules discussed throughout this chapter. UCC §§2-703 through 2-715 govern the remedies available to buyers and sellers.[2]

Seller's Remedies

If a buyer breaches a sale of goods contract, the seller generally has at least two remedies. She may resell the goods elsewhere. If she acts in good faith, she will be awarded **the difference between the original contract price and the price she was able to obtain in the open market**. Assume that Maud, the manufacturer, had a contract to sell her shoes to Foot The Bill for $55 per pair and Foot The Bill's breach forces her to sell them on the open market, where she gets only $48 per pair. Maud will win $7 per pair times 5,000 pairs, or $35,000, from Foot The Bill.

Alternatively, the buyer may choose not to resell and settle for the difference between the contract price and the market value of the goods. Maud, in other words, may choose to keep the shoes. If she can prove that their market value is $48 per pair, for example, by showing what other retailers would have paid her for them, she will still get her $7 each, representing the difference between what the contract promised her and what the market would support. In either case, the money represents direct damages. Maud is also entitled to incidental damages, such as the storage and advertising expenses described above. But there is one significant difference under the UCC: **most courts hold that the seller of goods is *not* entitled to consequential damages**. Suppose Maud hired two extra workers to inspect, pack, and ship the shoes for Foot The Bill. Those are consequential damages, but Maud will not recover them because she is the seller and the contract is for the sale of goods.

Buyer's Remedies

Cover
To make a good faith purchase of goods similar to those in the contract.

The buyer's remedies in sale of goods contracts (which are, as always, governed by the Uniform Commercial Code) are similar to those we have already considered. She typically has two options. First, the buyer can "cover" by purchasing substitute goods. To **cover** means to make a good faith purchase of goods similar to those in the contract. The buyer may then obtain **the difference between the original contract price and her cover price**. Alternatively, if the buyer chooses not to cover, she is entitled to the difference between the original contract price and the market value of the goods.

Suppose Mary has contracted to buy 1,000 six-foot Christmas trees at $25 per tree from Elmo. The market suddenly rises, and not feeling the spirit of the season, Elmo breaches his deal and sells the trees elsewhere. If Mary makes a good faith effort to cover but is forced to pay $40 per tree, she may recover the difference from Elmo, meaning $15 per tree times 1,000 trees, or $15,000. Similarly, if she chooses not to cover but can prove that $40 is now the market value of the trees, she is entitled to her $15 per tree.

Under the UCC, **the buyer *is* entitled to consequential damages, provided that the seller could reasonably have foreseen them**. If Mary tells Elmo, when they sign their deal, that she has a dozen contracts to resell the trees for an average price of $50 per tree, she may recover $25 per tree, representing the difference between her contract price with Elmo and the value of the tree *to her*, based on her other contracts.[3] If she failed to inform Elmo of the

[2]We discuss these remedies in greater detail in Unit 3, on commercial transactions.

[3]As we discuss in the section on mitigation later in the chapter, Mary will get only her consequential damages if she attempts to cover.

other contracts, she would not receive any money based on them. The buyer is also entitled to whatever incidental damages may have accrued.

EXAM Strategy

Question: Chloe is a fashion designer. Her recent collection of silk-velvet evening gowns was gobbled up by high-end retailers, who now clamor for more. Chloe needs 300 yards of the same fabric by August 15. Mill House, which has supplied fabric to Chloe for many years, agrees to sell her 300 yards at $100 per yard, delivered on August 15. The market value of the fabric is $125, but Mill House gives Chloe a break because she is a major customer.

Chloe contracts with Barney's and Neiman Marcus to sell a total of 50 dresses, at an *additional* profit to Chloe of $800 per dress. On August 15, Mill House delivers defective fabric. Chloe cannot make her dresses in time, and the retailers cancel their orders. Chloe sues Mill House and wins—but what are her damages?

Strategy: To determine damages, first ask whether the contract is governed by the common law or the UCC. This agreement concerns goods, so the Code applies. The UCC permits a buyer to recover damages for the difference between the contract price and the market value of the goods. The Code also allows consequential damages if the seller could have foreseen them. Apply those standards.

For a fashion designer, defective fabric is a calamity. But how do we calculate the damages?

Result: Because Chloe's contract enabled her to save $25 per yard for 300 yards, she is entitled to $7,500. Chloe has also lost profits of $40,000. Mill House could easily have foreseen those losses because the supplier knew that Chloe was a designer who fabricated and sold dresses. Chloe is entitled to $47,500.

We turn now to cases where the injured party cannot prove expectation damages.

Reliance Interest

To win expectation damages, the injured party must prove the breach of contract caused damages that can be *quantified with reasonable certainty*. This rule sometimes presents plaintiffs with a problem.

George plans to manufacture and sell silk scarves during the holiday season. In the summer, he contracts with Cecily, the owner of a shopping mall, to rent a high-visibility stall for $100 per day. George then buys hundreds of yards of costly silk and gets to work cutting and sewing. But in September, Cecily refuses to honor the contract. George sues and proves Cecily breached a valid contract. But what is his remedy?

George cannot establish an expectation interest in his scarf business. He *hoped* to sell each scarf for a $40 gross profit. He *planned* on making $2,000 per day. But how much would he *actually* have earned? Enough to retire on? Enough to buy a salami sandwich for lunch? He has no way of proving his profits, and a court cannot give him his expectation interest.

Reliance interest
Puts the injured party in the position he would have been in had the parties never entered into a contract.

Instead, George will ask for *reliance damages*. The **reliance interest** is designed to put an injured party in the position he would have been in had the parties never entered into a contract. This remedy focuses on the time and money the injured party spent performing his part of the agreement.

George should be able to recover reliance damages from Cecily. Assuming he is unable to sell the scarves to a retail store, which is probable since retailers will have made purchases long ago, George should be able to recover the cost of the silk fabric he bought and perhaps something for the hours of labor he spent cutting and sewing. But reliance damages can be difficult to win because *they are harder to quantify*. Courts prefer to compute damages using the numbers provided in a contract. If a contract states a price of $25 per Christmas tree and one party breaches, the arithmetic is easy. Judges can become uncomfortable when asked to base damages on vague calculations. How much was George's time worth in making the scarves? How good was his work? How likely were the scarves to sell? If George has a track record in the industry, he will be able to show a market price for his services. Without such a record, his reliance claim becomes a tough battle.

Promissory Estoppel

We have seen in earlier chapters that a plaintiff may sometimes recover damages based on promissory estoppel even when there is no valid contract. The plaintiff must show that the defendant made a promise knowing that the plaintiff would likely rely on it, that the plaintiff did rely, and that the only way to avoid injustice is to enforce the promise. **In promissory estoppel cases, a court will generally award *reliance damages*.** It would be unfair to give expectation damages for the full benefit of the bargain when, legally speaking, there has been no bargain.

In the following case, the victorious plaintiff demonstrates how unreliable reliance damages are and how winning can be hard to distinguish from losing.

Toscano v. Greene Music

124 Ca. App. 4th 685, 21 Ca. Rptr. 3d 732
Court of Appeal of California, 2004

Facts: Joseph Toscano was the general manager of Fields Pianos (Fields) in Santa Ana, California. He was unhappy with his job and decided to seek other employment. Toscano contacted Michael Greene, who owned similar stores. In July, Greene offered Toscano a sales management job starting September 1. Relying on that offer, Toscano resigned from Fields on August 1. However, in mid-August, Greene withdrew his employment offer. Toscano later found lower-paying jobs in other cities.

Toscano sued Greene for breach of contract and promissory estoppel. Greene argued that Toscano was not entitled to any expectation damages because his employment with Greene would have been at will, meaning he could lose the job at any time. Greene also urged that because Toscano was an at-will employee at Fields, he could recover at most one month's lost wage.

The trial court ruled that Toscano was entitled to reliance damages for all lost wages at Fields, starting from the day he resigned, going forward until his anticipated retirement in 2017. Toscano's expert accountant calculated his past losses (until the time of trial) at $119,061, and his future lost earnings at $417,772. The trial court awarded Toscano $536,833, and Greene appealed.

Issue: ***Was Toscano entitled to reliance damages?***

Excerpts from Judge O'Rourke's Decision: Given the equitable underpinnings of the promissory estoppel doctrine, we hold that a plaintiff such as Toscano, who relinquished his job in reliance on an unfulfilled promise of employment, may on an appropriate showing recover the lost wages he would have expected to earn from his former employer but for the defendant's promise. Such a damage measure is in keeping with the equitable nature of promissory estoppel. The object of equity is to do right and justice.

Our holding necessarily rejects the notion that the at-will nature of Toscano's former employment with Fields (undisputed by the parties here) is a strict impediment to recovery of future wages that Toscano would have earned at Fields had he not relied on Greene's promise.

[However,] we conclude that even drawing all inferences in Toscano's favor, the evidence was too speculative to lend support to the trial court's award of Toscano's lost future earnings from September 1 to his retirement.

Roberta Spoon, Toscano's damages expert, testified that in calculating Toscano's lost wages for the remainder of his career, "[a]ll I have done is arithmetic. I have simply analyzed the numbers." She testified she was not aware that Toscano's employment with Fields called for any specific tenure. Indeed, Spoon admitted Toscano could have quit or been fired from that job from the time he resigned to the present. She simply assumed Toscano would have continued employment with Fields or another employer at a comparable salary, observing that he had never in the past changed employers for anything other than a pay increase.

Spoon's testimony does not establish Toscano had a definite expectation of continued employment with Fields for any particular period of time. It is evident her supposition was based only on Toscano's history of remaining with his employers until offered new employment. However, *Toscano's* intentions or practices are not relevant to whether he could expect to remain with Fields until his retirement. Evidence of Toscano's intentions does not establish with any reasonable certainty that Fields, an at-will employer who had the right to terminate Toscano at any time for any reason, had some different understanding of the terms of Toscano's employment, or that it would have continued to employ him until the end of his career. Neither party presented testimony from Jerry Goldman, Toscano's boss at Fields. An expert's opinion must not be based upon speculative or conjectural data.

The award of future earnings calculated from [the day he quit] to the date of Toscano's retirement in 2017 is vacated and the matter remanded for a new trial on the issue of damages only. The judgment is otherwise affirmed.

Notice that the court never even mentions that Toscano acted in good faith, relying on Greene's promise, while the latter offered no excuse for suddenly withdrawing his offer. Is it fair to permit Greene to escape all liability? This court, like most, simply will not award significant damages where there is no contract permitting a clear calculation of losses.

The judges, though, have not entirely closed the door on Toscano. What is the purpose of the remand? What might Toscano demonstrate on remand? What practical difficulties will he encounter?

Restitution Interest

Lillian and Harold Toews signed a contract to sell 1,500 acres of Idaho farmland to Elmer Funk. (No, not him—the Bugs Bunny character you are thinking of is Elmer Fudd.) He was to take possession immediately, but he would not receive the deed until he finished paying for the property, in 10 years. This arrangement enabled him to enroll in a government

He did move onto the land and did receive $76,000 from the government for a year's worth of inactivity. (Nice work if you can get it.)

program that would pay him "set-asides" for *not* farming. Funk kept most aspects of his agreement. He did move onto the land and did receive $76,000 from the government for a year's worth of inactivity. (Nice work if you can get it.) The only part of the bargain Funk did not keep was his promise to pay. Lillian and Harold sued. Funk had clearly breached the deal. But what remedy?

The couple still owned the land, so they did not need it reconveyed. Funk had no money to pay for the farm, so they would never get their expectation interest. And they had expended almost no money based on the deal, so they had no reliance interest. What they had done, though, was to *confer a benefit* on Funk. They had enabled him to obtain $76,000 in government money. Harold and Lillian wanted a return of the benefit they had conferred on Funk, a remedy called *restitution*. The **restitution interest** is designed to return to the injured party a benefit that he has conferred on the other party, which it would be unjust to leave with that person. The couple argued that they had bestowed a $76,000 benefit on Funk and that it made absolutely no sense for him to keep it. The Idaho Court of Appeals agreed. It ruled that the couple had a restitutionary interest in the government set-aside money and ordered Funk to pay them the money.[4]

Restitution interest
Is designed to return to the injured party a benefit he has conferred on the other party.

Restitution is awarded in two types of cases. First, the law allows restitution when the parties have reached a contract and one of them breaches, as Funk did. In such cases, a court may choose restitution because no other remedy is available or because no other remedy would be as fair. Second, courts may award restitution in cases of quasi-contract, which we examined in Chapter 10. In quasi-contract cases, the parties never made a contract, but one side did benefit the other. We consider each kind of restitution interest in turn.

Restitution in Cases of a Voidable Contract

Restitution is a common remedy in contracts involving fraud, misrepresentation, mistake, and duress. In these cases, restitution often goes hand in hand with **rescission**, which means to "undo" a contract and put the parties where they were before they made the agreement. Courtney sells her favorite sculpture to Adam for $95,000, both parties believing the work to be a valuable original by Barbara Hepworth. Two months later, Adam learns that the sculpture is a mere copy, worth very little. A court will permit Adam to rescind the contract on the ground of mutual mistake. At the same time, Adam is entitled to restitution of the purchase price. Courtney gets the worthless carving, and Adam receives his money back.

Rescission
To "undo" a contract and put the parties where they were before they made the agreement.

The following case involved fraud in the sale of a valuable property.

Putnam Construction & Realty Co. v. Byrd

632 So. 2d 961, 1992 Ala. LEXIS 1289
Supreme Court of Alabama, 1992

Facts: Putnam Construction & Realty Co. owned the University Square Business Center (USBC), an office complex with several major tenants. William Byrd and his partners (the "buyers") entered into a contract to buy USBC. They financed the purchase with a $16.2 million loan from Northwestern Mutual Life. Northwestern's loan was secured with a mortgage on the USBC, meaning that if the borrowers failed to repay the loan,

[4] *Toews v. Funk*, 129 Idaho 316, 924 P.2d 217, 1994 Idaho App. LEXIS 75 (Idaho Ct. App. 1994).

Northwestern would own the property. Shortly after the sale closed, Byrd learned that several of the major tenants were leaving. The buyers sued Putnam, seeking rescission of the contract and restitution of their money. The trial court found that Putnam (the "sellers") had committed fraud. It rescinded the sales contract, returning the property to the sellers. It ordered the sellers to assume full liability for the mortgage. The trial court did not, however, order restitution of the buyers' expenses, such as the closing costs. The sellers appealed—which proved to be a big mistake.

Issue: ***Were the buyers entitled to rescission and/or restitution?***

Excerpts from Justice Steagall's Decision: With the departure of its major tenants, the USBC does not have the profit potential the buyers bargained for and is, in fact, a liability to them. While the buyers could receive money damages to approximate the value of the lost leases, such an award would be speculative at best and would not abrogate the fact that the buyers now have a property that operates at an increasing loss. The equitable remedy of rescission, while difficult to execute, would more completely provide the buyers with the compensation they seek. The jury was, therefore, correct in determining that rescission is the proper remedy to be applied in this case.

We agree with the trial court that a reconveyance of USBC to the sellers, subject to the mortgage, "constitutes the most equitable result which can be achieved." Accordingly, we affirm those portions of the court's order relating to the reconveyance of USBC subject to the mortgage. We must also recognize, however, that the buyers incurred other substantial out-of-pocket costs to finance a transaction that was born out of the sellers' fraud. After carefully considering the evidence in this case, we conclude that repayment of the following costs is necessary to more equitably restore the buyers to the position they occupied before the sale: $483,006.75 in closing costs on the purchase of USBC; $121,000 in interest payments they paid to the sellers on the $1.5 million note; and the $500,000 in nonrefundable fees the buyers paid to Northwestern to obtain the loan. We remand this case for the trial court to enter a judgment ordering repayment of these costs.

Ethics Imagine that you are the officer from Putnam in charge of negotiating the sale of USBC to the buyers. You learn that several major tenants are soon to depart and realize that if the buyers learn this, they will lower their offer or reject the deal altogether. Your boss insists you tell the buyers that all tenants will be staying. What will you do? What Life Principles will you apply?

Restitution in Cases of a Quasi-Contract

George Anderson owned a valuable 1936 Plymouth. He took it to Ronald Schwegel's repair shop, and the two orally agreed that Schwegel would restore the car for $6,000. Unfortunately, they never agreed on the meaning of the word *restore*. Anderson thought the term meant complete restoration, including body work and engine repairs, whereas Schwegel intended body work but no engine repairs. After doing some of the work, Schwegel told Anderson that the car needed substantial engine work, and he asked for Anderson's permission to allow an engine shop to do it. Anderson agreed, believing the cost was included in the original estimate. When the car was finished and running smoothly, Schwegel demanded $9,800. Anderson refused to pay more than the $6,000 agreed price, and Schwegel sued.

The court held that there was no valid contract between the parties. A contract requires a meeting of the minds. Here, said the court, there was no meeting of the minds on what *restore* included, and hence Schwegel could not recover either his expectation or his reliance interest since both require an enforceable agreement. Schwegel then argued that a quasi-contract existed. In other words, he claimed that even if there had been no valid agreement, he had performed a service for Anderson and that it would be unjust for Anderson to keep it without paying. **A court may award restitution, even in the absence of a contract, where one party has conferred a benefit on another and it would be unjust for the other party to retain**

the benefit. The court ruled that Schwegel was entitled to the full $3,800 above and beyond the agreed price because that was the fair market value of the additional work. Anderson had asked for the repairs and now had an auto that was substantially improved. It would be unjust, ruled the court, to permit him to keep that benefit for free.[5]

Other Remedies

In contract lawsuits, plaintiffs are occasionally awarded the remedies of specific performance, injunction, and reformation.

Specific Performance

Leona Claussen owned Iowa farmland. She sold some of it to her sister-in-law, Evelyn Claussen, and, along with the land, granted Evelyn an option to buy additional property at $800 per acre. Evelyn could exercise her option anytime during Leona's lifetime or within six months of Leona's death. When Leona died, Evelyn informed the estate's executor that she was exercising her option. But other relatives wanted the property, and the executor refused to sell. Evelyn sued and asked for *specific performance.* She did not want an award of damages; she wanted *the land itself.* The remedy of specific performance forces the two parties to perform their contract.

A court will award specific performance, ordering the parties to perform the contract, only in cases involving the sale of land or some other asset that is considered "unique." Courts use this remedy when money damages would be inadequate to compensate an injured party. If the subject is unique and irreplaceable, money damages will not put the injured party in the same position she would have been in had the agreement been kept. So a court will order the seller to convey the rare object and the buyer to pay for it.

Historically, every parcel of land has been regarded as unique, and therefore specific performance is always available in real estate contracts. Family heirlooms and works of art are also often considered unique. Evelyn Claussen won specific performance. The Iowa Supreme Court ordered Leona's estate to convey the land to Evelyn for $800 per acre.[6] Generally speaking, either the seller or the buyer may be granted specific performance. One limitation in land sales is that a buyer may obtain specific performance only if she was ready, willing, and able to purchase the property on time. If Evelyn had lacked the money to buy Leona's property for $800 per acre within the six-month time limit, the court would have declined to order the sale.

EXAM Strategy

Question: The Monroes, a retired couple who live in Illinois, want to move to Arizona to escape the northern winter. In May, the Monroes contract in writing to sell their house to the Temples for $450,000. Closing is to take place June 30. The Temples pay a deposit of $90,000. However, in early June, the Monroes travel through Arizona and discover it is too hot for them. They promptly notify the Temples they are no longer willing to sell, and return the $90,000, with interest. The Temples sue, seeking the house. In response, the Monroes offer evidence that

---

[5] *Anderson v. Schwegel,* 118 Idaho 362, 796 P.2d 1035, 1990 Idaho App. LEXIS 150 (Idaho Ct. App. 1990).

[6] *In re Estate of Claussen*, 482 N.W.2d 381, 1992 Iowa Sup. LEXIS 52 (Iowa 1992).

the value of the house has dropped from about $450,000 to about $400,000. They claim that the Temples have suffered no loss. Who will win?

Strategy: Most contract lawsuits are for money damages, but not this one. The Temples want the house. Because they want the house itself, and not money damages, the drop in value is irrelevant. What legal remedy are the Temples seeking? They are suing for specific performance. When will a court grant specific performance? Should it do so here?

Result: In cases involving the sale of land or some other unique asset, a court will grant specific performance, ordering the parties to perform the agreement,. All houses are regarded as unique. The court will force the Monroes to sell their house, provided the Temples have sufficient money to pay for it.

Other unique items, for which a court will order specific performance, include such things as secret formulas, patents, and shares in a closely held corporation. Money damages would be inadequate for all these things since the injured party, even if she got the cash, could not go out and buy a substitute item. By contrast, a contract for a new Cadillac Escalade is not enforceable by specific performance. If the seller breaches, the buyer is entitled to the difference between the contract price and the market value of the car. The buyer can take his money elsewhere and purchase a virtually identical SUV.

Injunction

In the opening scenario, the NFL team's general manager considered whether to seek an injunction against his running back who wanted to leave the team and act in a TV show. An **injunction** is a court order that requires someone to refrain from doing something.

In the increasingly litigious world of professional sports, injunctions are commonplace. In the following basketball case, the trial court issued a **preliminary injunction;** that is, an order issued early in a lawsuit prohibiting a party from doing something *during the course of the lawsuit.* The court attempts to protect the interests of the plaintiff immediately. If, after trial, it appears that the plaintiff has been injured and is entitled to an injunction, the trial court will make its order a **permanent injunction**. If it appears that the preliminary injunction should never have been issued, the court will terminate the order.

Milicic v. Basketball Marketing Company, Inc.

2004 Pa.A Super. 333, 857 A.2d 689
Superior Court of Pennsylvania, 2004

Facts: The Basketball Marketing Company (BMC) markets, distributes, and sells basketball apparel and related products. BMC signed a long-term endorsement contract with a 16-year-old Serbian player, Darko Milicic, who was virtually unknown in the United States. Two years later, Milicic became the second pick in the National Basketball Association draft, making him an immensely marketable young man.

Four days after his 18th birthday, Milicic made a buyout offer to BMC, seeking release from his contract so that he could arrange a more lucrative one elsewhere. BMC refused to release him. A week later, Milicic notified BMC in writing that he was disaffirming the contract, and he returned all money and goods he had received from the company. BMC again refused to release Milicic.

Believing that Milicic was negotiating an endorsement deal with either Reebok or Adidas, BMC sent both companies letters informing them it had an enforceable endorsement deal with Milicic that was valid for several more years. Because of BMC's letter, Adidas ceased negotiating with Milicic just short of signing a contract. Milicic sued BMC, seeking a preliminary injunction that would prohibit BMC from sending such letters to competitors. The trial court granted the preliminary injunction, and BMC appealed.

Issue: ***Is Milicic entitled to a preliminary injunction?***

Excerpts from Judge McCaffery's Decision:[7] BMC argues that the trial court erred by concluding that Milicic had proven the four essential prerequisites necessary for injunctive relief. However, Milicic did meet these four requirements.

1. Milicic had a strong likelihood of success on the merits.

   Pennsylvania law recognizes, except as to necessities, the contract of a minor is voidable if the minor disaffirms it at any reasonable time after the minor attains majority. Just 11 days after his 18th birthday, Milicic sent BMC a letter withdrawing from the agreement. This letter was sent within a reasonable time after Milicic's reaching the age of majority and stated his unequivocal revocation and voidance of the agreement. There exists more than a reasonable probability that Milicic will succeed in [nullifying the contract with BMC].

2. Injunctive relief was necessary to prevent immediate and irreparable harm that could not be adequately compensated by the awarding of monetary damages.

   Top N.B.A. draft picks generally solicit, negotiate, and secure endorsement contracts within a short time after the draft to take advantage of the publicity, excitement, and attendant marketability associated with the promotion. BMC blocked Milicic's efforts to enter into such an endorsement agreement. After being contacted by BMC, advanced negotiations between Milicic and Adidas were suspended. These business opportunity and market advantage losses may aptly be characterized as irreparable injury for purposes of equitable relief.

3. Greater injury would have occurred from denying the injunction than from granting the injunction.

   BMC's refusal to acknowledge Milicic's ability to disaffirm the contract is at odds with public policy. Because infants are not competent to contract, the ability to disaffirm protects them from their own immaturity and lack of discretion. It is established practice in Pennsylvania to petition the court to appoint a guardian for the child, to protect the interests of both parties. It confounds the Court that BMC, a corporation of great magnitude, whose business may be said to be based in contract law, failed to have a guardian appointed for Milicic.
   Harm to the public is an additional consideration. The public policy consideration underlying the rule which allows a child to disaffirm a contract within a reasonable time after reaching the age of majority is that minors should not be bound by mistakes resulting from their immaturity or the overbearance of unscrupulous adults.

4. The preliminary injunction restored the parties to the status quo that existed prior to the wrongful conduct:

   Enjoining BMC from further interfering with Milicic's ability to contract will place the parties where they were prior to BMC's wrongful conduct. As all four of the essential prerequisites have been satisfied in this case, the Court properly granted injunctive relief. Order affirmed.

Was Darko Milicic entitled to a preliminary injunction against BMC?

[7]Because we are unwilling to assume, as the court apparently does, that this decision will be read only by robots, the authors have substituted *BMC* for *appellant* and *Milicic* for *appellee*.

Reformation

The final remedy, and perhaps the least common, is **reformation**, a process in which a court will partially rewrite a contract. Courts seldom do this because the whole point of a contract is to enable the parties to control their own futures. But a court may reform a contract if it believes a written agreement includes a simple mistake. Suppose that Roger orally agrees to sell 35 acres to Hannah for $600,000. The parties then draw up a written agreement, accidentally describing the land as including 50 additional acres that neither party considered part of the deal. Roger refuses to sell. Hannah sues for specific performance but asks the court to *reform* the written contract to reflect the true agreement. Most but not all courts would reform the agreement and enforce it.

Reformation
A process in which a court will partially rewrite a contract.

A court may also reform a contract to save it. If Natasha sells her advertising business to Joseph and agrees not to open a competing agency in the same city anytime in the next 10 years, a court may decide that it is unfair to force her to wait a decade. It could reform the agreement and permit Natasha to compete, say, 3 years after the sale. But some courts are reluctant to reform contracts and would throw out the entire noncompetition agreement rather than reform it. Parties should never settle for a contract that is sloppy or overbroad, assuming that a court will later reform errors. They may find themselves stuck with a bargain they dislike, or with no contract at all.

SPECIAL ISSUES

Finally, we consider some special issues of damages, beginning with a party's obligation to minimize its losses.

Mitigation of Damages

A party injured by a breach of contract may not recover for damages that he could have avoided with reasonable efforts. In other words, when one party perceives that the other has breached or will breach the contract, the injured party must try to prevent unnecessary loss. A party is expected to **mitigate** his damages; that is, to keep damages as low as he reasonably can.

Mitigate
To keep damages as low as reasonable.

Malcolm agrees to rent space in his mall to Zena, for a major department store. As part of the lease, Malcolm agrees to redesign the interior to meet her specifications. After Malcolm has spent $20,000 in architect and design fees, Zena informs Malcolm that she is renting other space and will not occupy his mall. Malcolm nonetheless continues the renovation work, spending an additional $50,000 on materials and labor. Malcolm will recover the lost rental payments and the $20,000 expended in reliance on the deal. He will *not* recover the extra $50,000. He should have stopped work when he learned of Zena's breach.

Nominal Damages

Nominal damages are a token sum, such as one dollar, given to a plaintiff who demonstrates that the defendant breached the contract but cannot prove serious injury. A school board unfairly fires Gemma, a teacher. If she obtains a teaching job at a better school for identical pay the very next day, she probably can show no damages at all. Nonetheless, the school wrongfully terminated her, and a court may award nominal damages. Nominal damages provide plaintiff with a "moral victory."

Nominal damages
A token sum, such as one dollar, given to a plaintiff who demonstrates a breach but no serious injury.

Liquidated Damages

It can be difficult or even impossible to prove how much damage the injured party has suffered. So lawyers and executives negotiating a deal may include in the contract a **liquidated damages** clause, a provision stating in advance how much a party must pay if it

Liquidated damages
A clause stating in advance how much a party must pay if it breaches.

breaches. Assume that Laurie has hired Bruce to build a five-unit apartment building for $800,000. Bruce promises to complete construction by May 15. Laurie insists on a liquidated damages clause providing that if Bruce finishes late, Laurie's final price is reduced by $3,000 for each week of delay. Bruce finishes the apartment building June 30, and Laurie reduces her payment by $18,000. Is that fair? The answer depends on two factors: **A court will generally enforce a liquidated damages clause if (1) at the time of creating the contract, it was very difficult to estimate actual damages, and (2) the liquidated amount is reasonable.** In any other case, the liquidated damage will be considered a mere penalty and will prove unenforceable.

We will apply the two factors to Laurie's case. When the parties made their agreement, would it have been difficult to estimate actual damages caused by delay? Yes. Laurie could not prove that all five units would have been occupied or how much rent the tenants would have agreed to pay. Was the $3,000 per week reasonable? Probably. To finance an $800,000 building, Laurie will have to pay at least $6,000 interest per month. She must also pay taxes on the land and may have other expenses. Laurie does not have to prove that every penny of the liquidated damages clause is justified, but only that the figure is reasonable. A court will probably enforce her liquidated damages clause.

On the other hand, suppose Laurie's clause demanded $3,000 per day. There is no basis for such a figure, and a court will declare it a penalty clause and refuse to enforce it. Laurie will be back to square one, forced to prove in court any damages she claims to have suffered from Bruce's delay.

In the chapter's opening scenario, the alarm company tries to invoke a liquidated damages clause that would leave Ben largely uncompensated. Depending on what the parties knew when they made the agreement, a court may well find the clause too harsh and permit Ben to sue for his actual losses.

EXAM Strategy

Question: In March, James was accepted into the September ninth-grade class at the Brookstone Academy, a highly competitive private school. To reserve his spot, James's father, Rex, sent in a deposit of $2,000 and agreed in writing to pay the balance due, $19,000. If James withdrew in writing from the school by August 1, Rex owed nothing more to Brookstone. However, once that date passed, Rex was obliged to pay the full $19,000, whether or not James attended. On August 5, Rex hand-delivered to Brookstone a letter stating that James would not attend. Brookstone demanded the full tuition and, when Rex refused to pay, sued for $19,000. Analyze the case.

Strategy: When one party seeks contract damages that are specified in the agreement, it is relying on a liquidated damages clause. A court will generally enforce a liquidated damages clause provided the plaintiff can prove two things. What are those two things? Can this plaintiff meet that standard?

Result: Brookstone must prove that at the time of creating the contract it was difficult to estimate actual damages and that the liquidated amount is reasonable. Rex will probably argue that the liquidated amount is unreasonable, contending that a competitive school can quickly fill a vacancy with another eager applicant. Brookstone will counter that budgeting, which begins in January, is difficult and imprecise. Tuition money goes toward staff salaries, maintenance, utilities, and many other expenses. If the school cannot not rely in January on a certain income, the calculation becomes impossible. Rex had four months to make up his mind, and by August 1, the school was firmly committed to its class size and budget. In a similar case, the court awarded the full tuition to the school, concluding that the sum was a reasonable estimate of the damages.

Chapter Conclusion

The powers of a court are broad and flexible and may suffice to give an injured party what it deserves. But problems of proof and the uncertainty of remedies demonstrate that the best solution is a carefully drafted contract and socially responsible behavior.

Exam Review

1. **BREACH** Someone breaches a contract when he fails to perform a duty without a valid excuse. (pp. 404–405)

2. **REMEDY** A remedy is the method a court uses to compensate an injured party. (p. 405)

3. **INTERESTS** An interest is a legal right in something, such as a contract. The first step that a court takes in choosing a remedy is to decide what interest it is protecting. (pp. 404–405)

4. **EXPECTATION** The expectation interest puts the injured party in the position she would have been in had both sides fully performed. It has three components:

   (a) Direct damages, which flow directly from the contract.
   (b) Consequential damages, which result from the unique circumstances of the particular injured party. The injured party may recover consequential damages only if the breaching party should have foreseen them.
   (c) Incidental damages, which are the minor costs an injured party incurs responding to a breach. (pp. 405–411)

Question: Mr. and Ms. Beard contracted for Builder to construct a house on property he owned and sell it to the Beards for $785,000. The house was to be completed by a certain date, and Builder knew that the Beards were selling their own home in reliance on the completion date. Builder was late with construction, forcing the Beards to spend $32,000 in rent. Ultimately, Builder never finished the house, and the Beards moved elsewhere. They sued. At trial, expert testimony indicated the market value of the house as promised would have been $885,000. How much money are the Beards entitled to, and why?

Strategy: Normally, in cases of property, an injured plaintiff may use specific performance to obtain the land or house. However, there *is* no house, so there will be no specific performance. The Beards will seek their expectation interest. Under the contract, what did they reasonably expect? They anticipated a finished house, on a particular date, worth $885,000. They did not expect to pay rent while waiting. Calculate their losses. (See the "Result" at the end of this section.)

5. **RELIANCE** The reliance interest puts the injured party in the position he would have been in had the parties never entered into a contract. It focuses on the time and money that the injured party spent performing his part of the agreement. If there was no valid contract, a court might still award reliance damages under a theory of promissory estoppel. (pp. 412–413)

EXAM Strategy

Question: Bingo is emerging as a rock star. His last five concerts have all sold out. Lucia signs a deal with Bingo to perform two concerts in one evening in Big City for a fee of $50,000 for both shows. Lucia then rents the Auditorium for that evening, guaranteeing to pay $50,000. Bingo promptly breaks the deal before any tickets are sold. Lucia sues, pointing out that the Auditorium seats 3,000 and she anticipated selling all tickets for an average of $40 each, for a total gross of $120,000. How much will Lucia recover, if anything?

Strategy: The parties created a valid contract, and Lucia relied on it. She claims two losses: the payment to rent the hall and her lost profits. A court may award reliance damages if the plaintiff can quantify them, provided the damages are not speculative. Can Lucia quantify either of those losses? Both of them? Were they speculative? (See the "Result" at the end of this section.)

6. **RESTITUTION** The restitution interest returns to the injured party a benefit that she has conferred on the other party which would be unjust to leave with that person. Restitution can be awarded in the case of a contract created, for example, by fraud, or in a case of quasi-contract, where the parties never created a binding agreement. (pp. 413–416)

7. **SPECIFIC PERFORMANCE** Specific performance, ordered only in cases of land or a unique asset, requires both parties to perform the contract. (pp. 416–417)

8. **INJUNCTION** An injunction is a court order that requires someone to do something or refrain from doing something. (pp. 417–418)

9. **REFORMATION** Reformation is the process by which a court will—occasionally—rewrite a contract to ensure that it accurately reflects the parties' agreement and/or to maintain the contract's viability. (p. 419)

10. **MITIGATION** The duty to mitigate means that a party injured by a breach of contract may not recover for damages that he could have avoided with reasonable efforts. (p. 419)

Question: Ambrose hires Bierce for $25,000 to supervise the production of Ambrose's crop, but then breaks the contract by firing Bierce at the beginning of the season. A nearby grower offers Bierce $23,000 for the same growing season, but Bierce refuses to take such a pay cut. He stays home and sues Ambrose. How much money, if any, will Bierce recover from Ambrose, and why?

Strategy: Ambrose has certainly breached the contract. The injured party normally receives the difference between his expectation interest and what he actually received. Bierce expected $25,000 and received nothing. However, Bierce made no effort to minimize his losses. How much would Bierce have lost had he mitigated? (See the "Result" at the end of this section.)

11. **NOMINAL DAMAGES** Nominal damages are a token sum, such as one dollar, given to an injured plaintiff who cannot prove damages. (p. 419)

12. **LIQUIDATED DAMAGES** A liquidated damages clause will be enforced if and only if, at the time of creating the contract, it was very difficult to estimate actual damages and the liquidated amount is reasonable. (pp. 419–420)

4. Result: The Beards' direct damages represent the difference between the market value of the house and the contract price. They expected a house worth $100,000 more than their contract price, and they are entitled to that sum. They also suffered consequential damages. The Builder knew they needed the house as of the contract date, and he could foresee that his breach would force them to pay rent. He is liable for a total of $132,000.
5. Result: Lucia can easily demonstrate that Bingo's breach cost her $50,000—the cost of the hall. However, it is uncertain how many tickets she would have sold. Unless Lucia has a strong track record selling tickets to concerts featuring Bingo, a court is likely to conclude that her anticipated profits were speculative. She will probably receive nothing for that claim.
10. Result: Even if he had mitigated, Bierce would have lost $2,000. He is entitled to that sum. However, he cannot recover the remaining $23,000. After Ambrose breached, Bierce had identical work available to him, but he failed to take it. His failure to mitigate is fatal.

Multiple-Choice Questions

1. ***CPA QUESTION*** Master Mfg., Inc. contracted with Accur Computer Repair Corp. to maintain Master's computer system. Master's manufacturing process depends on its computer system operating properly at all times. A liquidated damages clause in the contract provided that Accur would pay $1,000 to Master for each day that Accur was

late responding to a service request. On January 12, Accur was notified that Master's computer system had failed. Accur did not respond to Master's service request until January 15. If Master sues Accur under the liquidated damage provision of the contract, Master will:

(a) Win, unless the liquidated damages provision is determined to be a penalty

(b) Win, because under all circumstances liquidated damage provisions are enforceable

(c) Lose, because Accur's breach was not material

(d) Lose, because liquidated damage provisions violate public policy

2. **CPA QUESTION** Kaye contracted to sell Hodges a building for $310,000. The contract required Hodges to pay the entire amount at closing. Kaye refused to close the sale of the building. Hodges sued Kaye. To what relief is Hodges entitled?

(a) Punitive damages and direct damages

(b) Specific performance and direct damages

(c) Consequential damages or punitive damages

(d) Direct damages or specific performance

3. A manufacturer delivers a new tractor to Farmer Ted on the first day of the harvest season. But, the tractor will not start. It takes two weeks for the right parts to be delivered and installed. The repair bill comes to $1,000. During the two weeks, some acres of Farmer Ted's crops die. He argues in court that his lost profit on those acres is $60,000. If a jury awards $1,000 for tractor repairs, it will be in the form of ____________ damages. If it awards $60,000 for the lost crops, it will be in the form of ____________ damages.

(a) direct; direct

(b) direct; consequential

(c) consequential; direct

(d) consequential; consequential

(e) direct; incidental

4. Julie signs a contract to buy Nick's 2002 Mustang GT for $5,000. Later, Nick changes his mind and refuses to sell his car. Julie soon buys a similar 2002 Mustang GT for $5,500. She then sues Nick and wins $500. The $500 represents her ____________.

(a) expectation interest

(b) reliance interest

(c) restitution interest

(d) None of the above

5. Under the Uniform Commercial Code, a seller ____________ generally entitled to recover consequential damages, and a buyer ____________ generally entitled to recover consequential damages.

(a) is; is

(b) is; is not

(c) is not; is

(d) is not; is not

Essay Questions

1. Lewis signed a contract for the rights to all timber located on Nine-Mile Mine. He agreed to pay $70 per thousand board feet ($70/mbf). As he began work, Nine-Mile became convinced that Lewis lacked sufficient equipment to do the job well and forbade him to enter the land. Lewis sued. Nine-Mile moved for summary judgment. The mine offered proof that the market value of the timber was exactly $70/mbf, and Lewis had no evidence to contradict Nine-Mile. The evidence about market value proved decisive. Why? Please rule on the summary judgment motion.

2. Twin Creeks Entertainment signed a deal with U.S. JVC Corp. in which JVC would buy 60,000 feature-film videocassettes from Twin Creeks over a three-year period. JVC intended to distribute the cassettes nationwide. Relying on its deal with JVC, Twin Creeks signed an agreement with Paramount Pictures, agreeing to purchase a minimum of $600,000 worth of Paramount cassettes over a two-year period. JVC breached its deal with Twin Creeks and refused to accept the cassettes it had agreed upon. Twin Creeks sued and claimed, among other damages, the money it owed to Paramount. JVC moved to dismiss the claim based on the Paramount contract, on the ground that Twin Creeks, the seller of goods, was not entitled to such damages. What kind of damages is Twin Creeks seeking? Please rule on the motion to dismiss.

3. Racicky was in the process of buying 320 acres of ranchland. While that sale was being negotiated, Racicky signed a contract to sell the land to Simon. Simon paid $144,000, the full price of the land. But Racicky went bankrupt before he could complete the *purchase* of the land, let alone its sale. Which of these remedies should Simon seek: expectation, restitution, specific performance, or reformation?

4. Parkinson was injured in an auto accident by a driver who had no insurance. Parkinson filed a claim with her insurer, Liberty Mutual, for $2,000 under her "uninsured motorist" coverage. Liberty Mutual told her that if she sought that money, her premiums would go "sky high," so Parkinson dropped the claim. Later, after she had spoken with an attorney, Parkinson sued. What additional claim was her attorney likely to make?

5. **YOU BE THE JUDGE WRITING PROBLEM** John and Susan Verba sold a Vermont lakeshore lot to Shane and Deborah Rancourt for $115,000. The Rancourts intended to build a house on the property, but after preparing the land for construction, they learned that a wetland protection law prevented building near the lake. They sued, seeking rescission of the contract. The trial court concluded that the parties had reached their agreement under a "mutual, but innocent, misunderstanding." The trial judge gave the Verbas a choice: they could rescind the contract and refund the purchase price, or they could give the Rancourts $55,000, the difference between the sales price and the actual market value of the land. The Rancourts appealed. Were the Rancourts entitled to rescission of the contract? **Argument for the Rancourts:** When the parties have made a mutual mistake about an important factual issue, either party is entitled to rescind the contract. The land is of no use to us and we want our money back. **Argument for the Verbas:** Both sides were acting in good faith and both sides made an honest mistake. We are willing to acknowledge that the land is worth somewhat less than we all thought, and we are willing to refund $55,000. The buyers shouldn't complain—they are getting the property at about half the original price, and the error was as much their fault as ours.

Discussion Questions

1. **ETHICS** The National Football League owns the copyright to the broadcasts of its games. It licenses local television stations to telecast certain games and maintains a "blackout rule," which prohibits stations from broadcasting home games that are not sold out 72 hours before the game starts. Certain home games of the Cleveland Browns team were not sold out, and the NFL blocked local broadcast. But several bars in the Cleveland area were able to pick up the game's signal by using special antennas. The NFL wanted the bars to stop showing the games. What did it do? Was it unethical of the bars to broadcast the games that they were able to pick up? Apart from the NFL's legal rights, do you think it had the moral right to stop the bars from broadcasting the games?

2. Consequential damages can be many times higher than direct damages. Consider the "Farmer Ted" scenario raised in multiple-choice question 3, which is based on a real case.[8] Is it fair for consequential damages to be 60 times higher than direct damages? The Supreme Court is skeptical that *punitive* damages should be more than 9 times compensatory damages in a tort case. Should a similar "soft limit" apply to consequential damages in contract cases?

3. Is reformation ever a reasonable remedy? Should courts be in the business of rewriting contracts, or should they stick to determining whether agreements are enforceable?

4. If someone breaks a contract, the other party can generally sue and win some form of damages. But for centuries, the law has considered land to be unique. And so, a lawsuit that involves a broken agreement for a sale of land will usually result in an order of specific performance. Is this ancient rule still reasonable? If someone backs out of an agreement to sell an acre of land, should he be ordered to turn over the land itself? Why not just require him to pay an appropriate number of dollars in damages?

5. Is it reasonable to require the mitigation of damages? If a person is wronged because the other side breached a contract, should she have any obligations at all? For example, suppose that a tenant breaches a lease by leaving early. Should the landlord have an obligation to try to find another tenant before the end of the lease?

---

[8] *Prutch v. Ford*, 574 P.2d 102 (Colo. 1977).

CHAPTER 19

© picsbyst/Shutterstock.com

Practical Contracts

Two true stories:

One

Holly (on the phone to her client Judd): Harry's lawyer just emailed me a letter that Harry says he got from you last year. I'm reading from the letter now: "Each year that you meet your revenue goals, you'll get a 1 percent equity interest." Is it possible you sent that letter?

Judd: I don't remember the exact wording, but probably something like that.

Holly: You told me, absolutely, positively, you had never promised Harry any stock. That he was making the whole thing up.

Judd: He was threatening to leave unless I gave him some equity, so I said what he wanted to hear. But that letter didn't *mean* anything. This is a family business, and no one but my children will ever get stock.

I don't know what the *contract* says—that's just the legal stuff.

Two

Grace (on the phone with her lawyer): Providential has raised its price to $12 a pound. I can't afford to pay that! We had a deal that the price would never go higher than 10 bucks. I've talked to Buddy over there, but he is refusing to back down. We need to do something!

Lawyer: Let me look at the contract.

Grace (her voice rising): I don't know what the *contract* says—that's just the legal stuff. Our *business* deal was no more than $10 a pound!

You have been studying the *theory* of contract law. This chapter is different—its purpose is to demonstrate how that theory operates in *practice*. We will look at the structure and content of a standard agreement and answer questions such as: do you need a written agreement? What do all these legal terms mean? Are any important provisions missing? By the end of the chapter, you will have a road map for understanding a written contract.[1] (Note that we do not repeat here what you have learned in prior chapters about the *substantive* law of contracts.) This chapter has another goal, too: we will look at the relationship between lawyers and their clients and their different roles in creating a contract.

Businesspeople, not surprisingly, tend to focus more on business than on the technicalities of contract law. However, *ignoring* the role of a written agreement can lead to serious trouble. Both of the clients in the opening scenario ended up being bound by a contract they did not want.

To illustrate our discussion of specific contract provisions, we will use a real contract between an actor and a producer to make a movie. For reasons of confidentiality, however, we have changed the names.

Before we begin our discussion of written contracts, let's ask: **do you need a written agreement at all?** Some years ago, this author was with a group of lawyers, all of whom had done a major home renovation and *none of whom* had signed a contract with their builder. All of the projects had turned out well. The lawyers had not prepared a written contract because they trusted their builders. They all had good recommendations from prior clients. Also, a building project by its very nature requires regular negotiations because it is impossible to predict all the potential changes: How much would it cost to move that door? How much do we save if we use Caesarstone instead of granite?

These cases worked out well without a written contract, but there are times when you should *definitely* sign an agreement:

1. The Statute of Frauds requires it.
2. The deal is crucial to your life or the life of your business.
3. The terms are complex.
4. You do not have an ongoing relationship of trust with the other party.

Once you decide you need a written contract, then what?

THE LAWYER

The American Bar Association commissioned a study to find out what people think of lawyers. Survey participants responded with these words: greedy, corrupt, manipulative, snakes, and sharks.[2] Businesspeople refer to their lawyers with terms like *business prevention department*. They are reluctant to ask an attorney to draft a contract for fear of the time and expense that lawyers can inject into the process. And they worry that the lawyers will interfere in the business deal itself, at best causing unnecessary hindrance, at worst killing the deal. Part of the problem is that lawyers and clients have different views of the future.

---

[1]For further reading on practical contracts, see Scott Burnham, *Drafting and Analyzing Contracts,* Lexis/Nexis, 2003; Charles M. Fox, *Working with Contracts,* Practical Law Institute, 2008; George W. Kuney, *The Elements of Contract Drafting,* Thomson/West, 2006.

[2]Robert Clifford, *Opening Statement: Now More than Ever,* Litigation, 28 Litigation 1, Spring 2002.

Lawyers and Clients

Businesspeople are optimists—they believe that they have negotiated a great deal and everything is going to go well—sales will boom, the company will prosper. **Lawyers have a different perspective—their primary goal is to protect their clients by avoiding litigation, now and in the future.** For this reason, lawyers are trained to be pessimists—they try to foresee and protect against everything that can possibly go wrong. Businesspeople sometimes view this lawyering as a waste of time and a potential deal-killer. What if the two parties cannot agree about what to do in the event of a very unlikely circumstance? The deal might just collapse.

To take one example of this lawyerly perspective, a couple happily married nigh on 40 years went to see a lawyer about changes in their will. The husband wanted to transfer some assets to his wife. The lawyer advised against it—after all, the couple might divorce. They became angry and indignant because *they would never divorce.* And they may very well be right. However, just that week, the lawyer had seen another couple who did divorce after 41 years of marriage. He thought it better to be on the safe side and consider the possibility that such events might happen.

Lawyers also prefer to negotiate touchy subjects at the beginning of a relationship, when everyone is on friendly terms and eager to make a deal, rather than waiting until trouble strikes. In the long run, nothing harms a relationship more than unpleasant surprises. For example, the Artist in the movie contract we will refer to throughout this chapter did not know in advance what conditions on the set would be, how grueling the shooting schedule, or how many friends and family would visit him. So his lawyer negotiated a deal in which the Producer agreed to provide a driver, a "first-class star trailer (which shall be a double pop-out)," a luxury hotel suite, and an adjacent room for visitors. In the end, because the role called for the Artist to live in the wilderness, he ultimately slept in a tent on the set to experience his part more fully, so he did not need the double pop-out trailer or the luxury suite. He also dispensed with the driver. But, under different circumstances, he might have wanted those luxuries, and his lawyer's goal was to protect his interests. It is a lot easier to forgo an expense than to add one to a movie budget.

Another advantage of using lawyers to conduct these negotiations is that they can serve as the bad guys. Instead of the client raising tough issues, the lawyers do. Many a client has said, "but my lawyer insists ..." If the lawyer takes the blame, the client is able to maintain a better relationship with the other party. And hiring a lawyer communicates to the other parties that you are taking the deal seriously, and they will not be able to pull a fast one on you.

Of course, this lawyerly protection comes at a cost—legal fees, time spent bargaining, the hours used to read complex provisions, and the potential for good will to erode during negotiations.

Do you need a lawyer? The answer largely depends on the complexity of the deal. Most people do not hire a lawyer to review an apartment lease—the language is standard, and the prospective tenant has little power to change the terms of the deal. On the other hand, you should not undertake a significant acquisition or purchase agreement on your own.

Hiring a Lawyer

If you do hire a lawyer, be aware of certain warning signs. Although the lawyer's goal is to protect you, a good attorney should be a dealmaker, not a deal-breaker. She should help you do what you want and, therefore, should never (or, at least, hardly ever) say, "You cannot do this." Instead, she should say, "Here are the risks to this approach" or "Here is another way to achieve your goal."

Moreover, your lawyer's goal should not be to annihilate the other side. In the end, the contract will be more beneficial to everyone if the parties' relationship is harmonious. Trying to exact every last ounce of flesh, using whatever power you have to an abusive extreme, is not a sound long-term strategy. In the end, the best deals are those in which all the parties' incentives are aligned. Success for one means success for all—or at least, success for one party does not *prohibit* a positive outcome for the other side. If either side in the movie contract behaved unreasonably, word would quickly spread in the insular Hollywood world, damaging the troublemaker's ability to make other deals.

Now either you have a lawyer or you do not. The next step is to think about developing the contract.

The Contract

In this section, we discuss how a contract is prepared and what provisions it should include.

Who Drafts It?

Once businesspeople have agreed to the terms of the deal, it is time to prepare a draft of the contract. Generally, both sides would prefer to *control the pen* (that is, to prepare the first draft of the contract) because the drafter has the right to choose a structure and wording that best represents his interests. Typically, the party with the most bargaining power prepares the drafts. In the movie contract, Producer's lawyer prepared the first draft. The contract then went to Artist's lawyer, who added the provisions that mattered to the client.

How to Read a Contract

Reading a contract is not like cracking open a novel. Instead, it should be a focused, multi-step process:

- **Pre-reading.** Before you begin reading the first draft of a contract, spend some time thinking about the provisions that are important to you. If you skip this step, you may find that as you read, your attention is so focused on the specific language of the contract that you lose sight of the larger picture.
- **The first read.** Read through once, just to get the basic idea of the contract—its structure and major provisions.
- **What-ifs.** This is the time to think about various outcomes, good and bad. Under the terms of the contract, what happens if all goes according to your plan? Also consider worst-case scenarios. In both situations, does the contract produce the result that you want? What happens if sales are higher than you expect, or if the product causes unexpected harm?
- **The second read.** Now read the contract to make sure that it handles the what-ifs in a manner that is satisfactory to you. Think about the relationship between various provisions—does it make sense?

Following this approach will help you avoid mistakes.

Mistakes

This author once worked with a lawyer who made a mistake in a contract. "No problem," he said. "I can win that one in court." Not a helpful attitude, given that one purpose of a contract is to *avoid* litigation. In this section, we look at the most common types of mistakes and how to avoid them.

Vagueness

Businesspeople sometimes *deliberately* choose vagueness. They do not want the terms of the contract to be clear. It may be that they are not sure what they can get from the other side, or in some cases, even what they really want. So they try to form a contract that leaves their options open. However, as the following case illustrates: **Vagueness is your enemy.**

Quake Construction v. American Airlines

141 Ill. 2d 281, 565 N.E.2d 990, 1990 Ill. LEXIS 151
Supreme Court of Illinois, 1990

Facts: Jones Brothers Construction was the general contractor on a job to expand American Airlines' facilities at O'Hare International Airport. Jones Brothers invited Quake Construction to bid on the employee facilities and automotive maintenance shop ("the project"). After Quake bid, Jones Brothers orally informed Quake that it was awarding Quake the project and would forward a contract soon. Jones Brothers wanted the license numbers of the subcontractors that Quake would be using, but Quake could not furnish those numbers until it had assured its subcontractors that they had the job. Quake did not want to give that assurance until *it* was certain of its own work. So Jones Brothers sent a letter of intent that stated, among other things:

> We have elected to award the contract for the subject project to your firm as we discussed on April 15. A contract agreement outlining the detailed terms and conditions is being prepared and will be available for your signature shortly.
>
> Your scope of work includes the complete installation of expanded lunchroom, restaurant, and locker facilities for American Airlines employees, as well as an expansion of American Airlines' existing Automotive Maintenance Shop. A sixty (60) calendar day period shall be allowed for the construction of the locker room, lunchroom, and restaurant area beginning the week of April 22. The entire project shall be completed by August 15.
>
> Subject to negotiated modifications for exterior hollow metal doors and interior ceramic floor tile material as discussed, this notice of award authorizes the work set forth in the [attached] documents at a lump sum price of $1,060,568.00. Jones Brothers Construction Corporation reserves the right to cancel this letter of intent if the parties cannot agree on a fully executed subcontract agreement.

The parties never signed a more detailed written contract, and ultimately Jones Brothers hired another company. Quake sued, seeking to recover the money it spent in preparation and its loss of anticipated profit.

Issue: ***Was the letter of intent a valid contract?***

Excerpts from Justice Calvo's Decision: [A]lthough letters of intent may be enforceable, such letters are not necessarily enforceable unless the parties intend them to be.

In determining whether the parties intended to reduce their agreement to writing, the following factors may be considered: whether the type of agreement involved is one usually put into writing, whether the agreement contains many or few details, whether the agreement involves a large or small amount of money, whether the agreement requires a formal writing for the full expression of the covenants, and whether the negotiations indicated that a formal written document was contemplated at the completion of the negotiations.

[We conclude that] the letter was ambiguous. The letter of intent included detailed terms of the parties' agreement. The letter stated that Jones awarded the contract for the project to Quake. The letter stated further, "this notice of award authorizes the work." Moreover the letter indicated that the work was to commence approximately 4 to 11 days after the letter was written. This short period of time reveals the parties intent to be bound by the letter so that work could begin on schedule. We also agree that the cancellation clause exhibited the parties' intent to be bound by the letter because no need would exist to provide for the cancellation of the letter unless the letter had some binding effect. The cancellation clause also implies the parties' intention to be bound by the letter, at least until they entered into the formal contract. These factors evinced the parties' intent to be bound by the letter.

On the other hand, the letter referred several times to the execution of a formal contract by the parties, thus indicating the parties' intent not to be bound by the letter. The cancellation clause could be interpreted to mean that the parties did not intend to be bound until they entered into a formal agreement.

Thus, we hold that the letter of intent in the case at bar is ambiguous regarding the parties' intent to be bound by it. Therefore, on remand, the circuit court shall allow the parties to present parol evidence regarding their intent. The trier of fact must then determine, based on the parties' intent, whether the letter of intent is a binding contract.

So after years of litigation, Jones Brothers and Quake had to go *back* to court to try to prove whether they intended the letter to be binding. The problem is that both sides permitted vagueness to enter their negotiations. Sometimes parties adopt vagueness as a *strategy*. One party may be trying to get a commitment from the other side without obligating itself. A party may feel *almost* ready to commit and yet still have reservations. It wants the *other* party to make a commitment so that planning can go forward. This is understandable but dangerous.

If you were negotiating for Jones Brothers and wanted to clarify negotiations without committing your company, how could you do it? State in the letter that it is *not a contract*, and that *neither side is bound by it*. State that it is a memorandum summarizing negotiations thus far, but that neither party will be bound until a full written contract is signed.

But what if Quake cannot get a commitment from its subcontractors until they are certain that it has the job? Quake should take the initiative and present Jones Brothers with its own letter of intent, stating that the parties *do* have a binding agreement for $1 million worth of work. Insist that Jones Brothers sign it. Jones Brothers would then be forced to decide whether it is willing to make a binding commitment. If Jones Brothers is not willing to commit, let it openly say so. At least both parties will know where they stand.

The movie contract provides another example of deliberate vagueness. In these contracts, nudity is always a contentious issue. Producers believe that nudity sells movie tickets; actors are afraid that it may tarnish their reputation. In the first draft of our contract, Artist's lawyer specified:

> Artist may not be photographed and shall not be required to render any services nude below the waist or in simulated sex scenes without Artist's prior written consent.

(This clause also applied to any double depicting Artist.) However, the script called for a scene in which Artist was swimming nude and the director wanted the option of showing him below the waist from the back. Ultimately, the nudity clause read as follows:

> Producer has informed Artist that Artist's role in the Picture might require Artist to appear and be photographed (a) nude, which nudity may include only above-the-waist nudity and rear below-the-waist nudity, but shall exclude frontal below-the-waist nudity; and (b) in simulated sex scenes. Artist acknowledges and agrees that Artist has accepted such employment in the Picture with full knowledge of Artist's required participation in nude scenes and/or in simulated sex scenes and Artist's execution of the Agreement constitutes written consent by Artist to appear in the nude scenes and simulated sex scenes and to perform therein as reasonably required by Producer. A copy of the scenes from the screenplay requiring Artist's nudity and/or simulated sex are attached hereto. Artist shall have a right of meaningful prior consultation with the director of the Picture regarding the manner of photography of any scenes in which Artist appears nude or engaged in simulated sex acts.
>
> Artist may wear pants or other covering that does not interfere with the shooting of the nude scenes or simulated sex scenes. Artist's buttocks and/or genitalia shall not be shown, depicted, or otherwise visible without Artist's prior written consent. Artist shall have the absolute right to change his mind and not perform in any nude scene or simulated sex scene, notwithstanding that Artist had prior thereto agreed to perform in such scene.

What does this provision mean? Has Artist agreed to perform in nude scenes or not? He has acknowledged that the script calls for nude scenes and he has agreed, in principle, that he will appear in them. However, he did not want to agree categorically, before shooting had even started and he had experience working with this director. Actor has a number of options—he can refuse to shoot nude scenes altogether, or he can shoot them and then, after viewing them, decide not to allow them in the movie. With a clause such as this one, the director shot different versions of the scene—some with nudity and some without—so that if Artist rejected the nude scene, the director still had options.

The true test of whether a vague clause belongs in a contract is this: would you sign the contract if you knew that the other side's interpretation would prevail in litigation? In this example, each side was staking out its position, and deferring a final negotiation until there was an actual disagreement about a nude scene. If you would be happy enough with the other side's position in the end, the vague clause simply defers a fight that you can afford to lose. But if the point is really important to you, it may be wiser to resolve the issue before you sign the contract by writing the clause in a way that clearly reflects your desired outcome.

EXAM Strategy

Question: The nudity provision in the movie contract is vague. Rewrite it so that it accurately expresses the agreement between the parties.

Strategy: This is easy! Just say what the parties intended the deal to be.

Result: "The script for the Picture includes scenes showing Artist (a) with frontal nudity from the waist up and with rear below-the-waist nudity (but no frontal below-the-waist nudity); and (b) in simulated sex scenes. However, no scenes shall be shot in which Artist's buttocks and/or genitalia are shown, depicted, or otherwise visible without Artist's prior written consent. Artist shall have the absolute right not to perform in any nude scene or simulated sex scene. If shot, no nude or sex scenes may appear in the Picture without Artist's prior written consent."

Ambiguity

Vagueness occurs when the parties do not want the contract to be clear. Ambiguity is different—it means that the provision is *accidentally* unclear. It occurs in contracts when the parties think only about what *they* want a provision to mean, without considering the literal meaning or the other side's perspective. When reading a contract, try to imagine all the different ways a clause can be interpreted. Because you think it means one thing does not mean that the other side will share your view. For example, suppose that an employment contract says, "Employee agrees not to work for a competitor for a period of three years from employment." Does that mean three years from the date of hiring or the date of termination? Unclear, so who knows?

To take another example, the dictionary defines vandalism as *deliberately mischievous or malicious destruction or damage of property*. Arson is *the malicious burning of a house or property*. Seems clear enough—but does arson count as vandalism? In the following case, no one thought about this question until a house burned down.

Cipriano v. Patrons Mutual Insurance Company of Connecticut

2005 Conn. Super. LEXIS 3577
Superior Court of Connecticut, 2005

Facts: Juacikino Cipriano purchased an insurance policy on his house from Patrons Mutual Insurance Company. The policy stated that the company would not pay for any damage to the residence caused by vandalism or burglary if the residence was vacant for more than 30 days in a row just before the loss. Furthermore, the company would not pay for damage to personal property caused by fire, lightning, or vandalism.

After Cipriano's house had been vacant for more than 30 days, an arsonist burned it down. Patrons denied his claim on the grounds that arson is vandalism, which his policy did not cover. Cipriano filed suit against Patrons. The insurance company filed a motion for summary judgment.

Issues: ***Does arson count as vandalism? Must Patrons pay Cipriano's claim?***

Excerpts from Judge Devine's Decision: [T]here are no genuine issues of fact that the fire was the result of arson and that the dwelling house was vacant for more than 30 days prior to the fire. The defendant contends that the term "vandalism" includes the act of arson. The plaintiff argues that, in reviewing the insurance policy as a whole, an insured may not be able to discern what "vandalism" means, as that term is used in the separate sections of the insurance policy.

Under our law, the terms of an insurance policy are to be construed according to the general rules of contract construction. It is a basic principle of insurance law that policy language will be construed as laymen would understand it and not according to the interpretation of sophisticated underwriters, and that ambiguities in contract documents are resolved against the party responsible for its drafting; the policyholder's expectations should be protected, as long as they are objectively reasonable from the layman's point of view. However, a court will not torture words to import ambiguity where the ordinary meaning leaves no room for ambiguity, and words do not become ambiguous simply because lawyers or laymen contend for different meanings.

In the present case, the defendant has drafted an insurance policy where "vandalism" and "fire" are undefined terms. Reading the insurance policy as whole, the terms "vandalism" and "fire" are found to be included as separate perils covered under the personal property coverage. In the exclusionary provision for the coverage of the residence, "vandalism" is listed as an excluded loss. "Fire" is not mentioned.

Because the terms "vandalism" and "fire" are undefined, and are listed as two distinct perils, it is ambiguous as to which peril, "vandalism" or "fire," covers arson. Therefore, "vandalism" is susceptible of two reasonable interpretations. As such, the insurance policy must be construed against the party responsible for its drafting.

The defendant's motion for summary judgment is hereby denied.

This case illustrates an important rule of contract drafting: **Any ambiguity is interpreted against the drafter of the contract**. (The *Cipriano* policy is a good example of how incomprehensible insurance policies can be. This complexity tends to erode judicial sympathy for the perpetrator.) Although both sides need to be careful in reading a contract—litigation benefits no one—the side that prepares the documents bears a special burden. This rule is meant to

1. Protect laypeople from the dangers of form contracts that they have little power to change. Even if the insured in this case had read the contract carefully, it is unlikely that an insurance company would change its form contract for him.
2. Protect people who are unlikely to be represented by a lawyer. Most people do not hire a lawyer to read insurance contracts (or any form contract). And without an experienced lawyer, it is highly unlikely that an insured would ask, "So is arson included in the vandalism clause?"
3. Encourage those who prepare contracts to do so carefully.

Typos

The bane of a lawyer's existence! This author worked on a securities offering in which the sales document almost went out with part of the company's name spelled *Pertoleum* instead of *Petroleum*. (And legend has it that a United Airlines securities offering once featured "Untied Airlines.") Although clients tend not to have a sense of humor about such errors, at least there would be no adverse legal result. That is not always the case with typos.

A group of condominium buyers ended up in litigation over a tiny typo in their purchase agreements: an "8" instead of a "9." What difference could that possibly make? A lot, it turns out. Extell Development Corporation built the Rushmore, a luxury condominium complex in Manhattan. When Extell began selling the units, it agreed to refund any buyer's down payment if the first closing did not occur by September 1, 2009. (The goal was to protect buyers who might not have any place to live if the building was not finished on time.) In the end, the first closing occurred in February 2009. No problem, right? No problem except that, by accident, the purchase contract said September 1, *2008* rather than *2009*. In the meantime, the Manhattan real estate market tumbled, and many purchasers of Rushmore condominiums wanted to back out. After litigation all the way to the Federal Court of Appeals, Extell was required to refund the deposits.

What is the law of typos? First of all, the law has a fancier word than *typo*—it is **scrivener's error.** A scrivener is a clerk who copies documents. **In the case of a scrivener's error, a court will reform a contract if there is clear and convincing evidence that the mistake does not reflect the true intent of the parties.** In the Rushmore case, an arbitrator refused to reform the contract, ruling that there was no clear and convincing evidence that the parties intended something other than the contract term as written.

In the following case, even more money was at stake. What would you do if you were the judge?

Daisy Beatty

Because of a tiny typo, purchasers of condominiums in this building were able to back out of their deals.

Scrivener's error A typo.

You be the Judge

Heritage Technologies v. Phibro-Tech

2008 U.S. Dist. LEXIS 329
United States District Court for the Southern District of Indiana, 2008

Facts: Heritage wanted to buy a substance called tribasic copper chloride (TBCC) from Phibro but, because of uncertainty in the industry, the two companies could not agree on a price for future years. It turned out, though, that the price of TBCC tended to rise and fall with that of copper sulfate, so Heritage proposed that the amount it paid for TBCC would increase an additional $15 per ton for each $0.01 increase in the cost of copper sulfate over $0.38 per pound.

Two top officers of Heritage and Phibro met in the Delta Crown Room at LaGuardia Airport to negotiate the purchase contract. At the end of their meeting, the Phibro officer hand wrote a document stating the terms of their deal and agreeing to the Heritage pricing proposal.

Negotiations between the two companies continued, leading to some changes and additions to their Crown Room agreement. In a draft prepared by Phibro, the $.01 number was changed to $0.1—that is, from 1 cent to 10 cents. In other words, in the original draft, Heritage agreed to a first increase if copper sulfate went above 39 cents per pound, an additional price rise at 40 cents, and so on. But in the Phibro draft, Heritage's first increase would not occur until the price of copper sulfate went to 48 cents a pound, with a second rise at 58 cents. In short, the Phibro draft was much more favorable to Heritage than the Heritage proposal had been.

At some point during the negotiations, the lawyer for Heritage asked his client if the $0.1 figure was accurate. The Heritage officer said that the increase in this amount was meant to be payment for other provisions that favored Phibro. There is no evidence that this statement was true. The contract went through eight drafts and numerous changes, but after the Crown Room meeting, the two sides never again discussed the $0.1 figure.

After the execution of the agreement, Heritage discovered a different mistake. When Heritage brought the error to Phibro's attention, Phibro agreed to make the change even though it was to Phibro's disadvantage to do so.

All was peaceful until the price of copper sulfate went to \$0.478 per pound. Phibro believed that because the price was above \$0.38 per pound, it was entitled to an increased payment. Heritage responded that the increase would not occur until the price went above \$0.48. Phibro then looked at the agreement and noticed the \$0.1 term for the first time. Phibro contacted Heritage to say that the \$0.1 term was a typo and not what the two parties had originally agreed in the Delta Crown Room. Heritage refused to amend the agreement and Phibro filed suit.

You Be the Judge: ***Should the court enforce the contract as written or as the parties agreed in their Crown Room meeting? Which number is correct—\$0.10 or \$0.01?***

Argument for Phibro: In the Delta Crown Room, the two negotiators agreed to a \$15 per ton increase in the price of TBCC for each 1-cent increase in copper sulfate price. Then by mistake, the contract said 10 cents. The two parties never negotiated the 10-cent provision, and there is no evidence that they had agreed to it. The court should revise this contract to be consistent with the parties' agreement, which was 1 cent.

Also, the 10-cent figure makes no economic sense. The point of the provision was that the price of TBCC would go up at the same rate as copper sulfate, and 1 cent for each ton is a much more accurate reflection of the relationship between these two commodities than 10 cents per ton.

Argument for Heritage: The Delta Crown Room agreement was nothing more than a draft. The contract went through eight rounds of changes. The change in price was in return for other provisions that benefited Phibro.

The parties conducted negotiations by sending drafts back and forth rather than by talking on the phone. Both parties were represented by a team of lawyers, the agreement went through eight drafts, and this pricing term was never altered despite several other changes and additions. There is no clear and convincing evidence that both parties were mistaken about what the document actually said. Ultimately, the parties agreed to 10 cents, and that is what the court should enforce.

Ethics When Heritage found a different mistake in the contract, Phibro agreed to correct it, even though the correction was unfavorable to Phibro. But when a mistake occurred in Heritage's favor, it refused to honor the intended terms of the agreement. Is Heritage behaving ethically? Does Heritage have an obligation to treat Phibro as well as Phibro behaved towards Heritage? Is it right to take advantage of other people's mistakes? What Life Principle would you apply in this situation?

Preventing Mistakes

Here are ways to prevent mistakes in a contract.

> As a general rule, your lawyer is less likely to make mistakes than you are.

Let your lawyer draft the contract. As a general rule, your lawyer is less likely to make mistakes than you are. Of all the players in the *Heritage* case, only one person noticed the error—Heritage's lawyer.

Resist overlawyering. Yes, your lawyer should draft the contract, but that does not mean she should have free rein, no matter what. This author once worked with a real estate attorney who had developed his own standard mortgage contract, of which he was immensely proud. Whenever he saw a provision in another contract that was missing from his own, he immediately added it. His standard form contract soon topped 100 pages. That contract was painful to read and did no service to his clients.

Read the important terms carefully. Before signing a contract, check *carefully* and *thoughtfully* the names of the parties, the dates, dollar amounts, and interest rates. If all these elements are correct, you are unlikely to go too far wrong. And, of course, having read this chapter, *you* will never mistake $0.10 for $0.01.

Finally, when your lawyer presents you with a written contract, you should follow these rules:

1. Complain if your lawyer gives you a contract with provisions that are irrelevant to your situation.
2. If you do not know what a provision means, ask. If you still do not know (or if your lawyer does not know), ask her to take it out. Lawyers rarely draft from scratch; they tend to use other contracts as templates. Just because a provision was in another agreement does not mean that it is appropriate for you.
3. Remember that a contract is also a reference document. During the course of your relationship with the other party, you may need to refer to the contract regularly. That will be difficult if you do not understand portions of it, or if the contract is so disorganized you cannot find a provision when you need it.

Which brings us to our next topic—the structure of a contract. Once you understand the standard outline of a contract, it will be much easier for you to find your way through the thicket of provisions.

The Structure of a Contract

Traditional contracts tended to use archaic words—*whereas* and *heretofore* were common. Modern contracts are more straightforward, without as many linguistic flourishes. Our movie contract takes the modern approach.

Title

Contracts have a title, which generally is in capital letters, underlined, and centered at the top of the page. The title should be as descriptive as possible—a generic title such as AGREEMENT does not distinguish one contract from another. Much better to entitle it EMPLOYMENT AGREEMENT or CONFIDENTIALITY AGREEMENT. The title of our movie contract is MEMORANDUM OF AGREEMENT (not a particularly useful name), but in the upper right-hand corner, there is space for the date of the contract and the subject. Let's say the subject is Dawn Rising/Clay Parker. It would have been even better if the title of the movie had been: Agreement between Clay Parker and Winterfield Productions for Dawn Rising.

Introductory Paragraph

The introductory paragraph includes the date, the names of the parties, and the nature of the contract. The names of the parties and the movie are defined terms, e.g., Clay Parker ("Artist"). By defining the names, the actual names do not have to be repeated throughout the agreement. In this way, a standard form contract can be used in different deals without worrying about whether the names of the parties are correct throughout the document.

The introductory paragraph should also include specific language indicating that the parties entered into an agreement. In our contract, the opening paragraph states:

> This shall confirm the agreement ("Agreement") between WINTERFIELD PRODUCTIONS ("Producer') and CLAY PARKER ("Artist") regarding the acting services of Artist in connection with the theatrical motion picture tentatively entitled "DAWN RISING" (the "Picture")[3], as follows:

This introductory paragraph is not numbered.

[3]These are not the parties' real names but are offered to illustrate the concepts.

It is here that traditional contracts included their "Whereas" provisions. Thus, for example, a traditional movie contract might say the following:

> WHEREAS, Producer desires to retain the services of Artist for the purpose of making a theatrical motion picture; and
>
> WHEREAS, Artist desires to work for Producer on the terms and subject to the conditions set forth herein;
>
> NOW, THEREFORE, in consideration of the mutual covenants contained herein, and for other good and valuable consideration, the receipt and adequacy of which are hereby acknowledged, the parties agree as follows:

None of these flourishes are necessary, but some people prefer them.

Definitions

Most contracts have some definitions. As we have seen in the movie contract, *Artist, Producer*, and *Movie* were defined in the introductory paragraph. Sometimes, definitions are included in a separate section. Alternatively, they can appear throughout the contract. The movie contract does not have a definitions section, but many terms, such as *fixed compensation* and *teaser*, are defined within it.

Covenants

Covenant
A promise in a contract.

Now we get to the heart of the contract: What are the parties agreeing to do? Failure to perform these obligations constitutes a breach of the contract and damages will result. **Covenant** is a legal term that means a promise in a contract.

At this stage, the relationship between lawyer and client is particularly important. They will obtain the best result if they work well together. And to achieve a successful outcome, both need to contribute. Clients should figure out what they need for the agreement to be successful. It is at this point that they have the most control over the deal, and they should exercise it. *It is a mistake to assume that everything will work itself out.* Instead, clients need to protect themselves now as best they can. Lawyers can help in this process because they have worked on other similar deals and they know what can go wrong. Listen to them—they are on your side.

Imagine you are an actor about to sign a contract to make a movie. What provisions would you want? Begin by asking what your goals are for the project. Certainly, to make a movie that gets good reviews and good box office. So you will ask for as much control over the process and product as you can get—selection of the director and co-stars, for instance. Maybe influence on the editing process. But you also want to make sure that the movie does not hurt your career. What provisions would you need to achieve that goal? And shooting a movie can be grueling work, so you want to ensure that your physical and emotional needs are met, particularly when you are on location away from home. Try to think of all the different events that could happen and how they would affect you. The contract should make provisions for these occurrences.

Now take the other side and imagine what you would want if you were the producer. The producer's goal is to make money—which means creating a quality movie while spending as little as possible and maintaining control over the process and final product. As you can see, some of the goals conflict—both Artist and Producer want control over the final product. Who will win that battle?

Here are the terms of the movie contract.

The Artist negotiated:

1. A fixed fee of $1,800,000, to be paid in equal installments at the end of each week of filming.
2. Extra payment if the filming takes longer than 10 weeks.
3. 7.5 percent of the gross receipts of the movie.

4. A royalty on any product merchandising, the rate to be negotiated in good faith.
5. Approval over (but approval shall not be unreasonably withheld):
    a. the director, costars, hairdresser, makeup person, costume designer, stand-ins, and the look of his role (although he lists one director and costar whom he has preapproved)
    b. any changes in the script that materially affect his role
    c. all product placements, but he preapproves the placement of Snickers candy bars
    d. locations where the filming takes place
    e. all videos, photos, and interviews of him
    f. the translation of the script for French subtitles (he is fluent in French)
6. Approval (at his sole discretion) over the release of any blooper videos.
7. His name to be listed first in the movie credits, on a separate card (i.e., alone on the screen).
8. That the producer not give any photographs from the set to a tabloid (such as, the *National Enquirer* or the *Star*).
9. At least 12 hours off duty from the end of each day of filming to the start of the next day.
10. That he fly first class to any locations outside of Los Angeles.
11. That the producer pay for 10 first-class airline tickets for his friends to visit him on location.
12. A luxury hotel suite for himself and a room for his friends.
13. A driver and four-wheel-drive SUV to transport him to the set.
14. The right to keep some wardrobe items.

The Producer negotiated:

1. All intellectual property rights to the movie.
2. The right not to make the movie, although he would still have to pay Artist the fixed fee.
3. Control over the final cut of the movie.
4. That the Artist will show up on a certain date and work in good faith for
    a. 2 weeks in pre-production (wardrobe and rehearsals)
    b. 10 weeks shooting the movie
    c. 2 free weeks after the shooting ends, in case the director wants to reshoot some scenes. The Artist must in good faith make himself available whenever the director needs him.
5. The right to fire Artist if his appearance or voice materially changes before or during the filming of the movie.
6. That the Artist help promote the movie on dates subject to Artist's approval, which shall not be unreasonably withheld.

Breach

So now we have the covenants in the movie contract. What happens if one of the parties breaches a covenant? Throughout the life of a contract, there could be many small breaches. Say, Artist shows up one day late for filming or he gains five pounds. Maybe Producer deposits Artist's paycheck a few days late. Perhaps a pop-out trailer is not available. Although these events may technically be violations, a court would not impose sanctions

Material breach
A violation of a contract that defeats an essential purpose of the agreement.

over such minor issues. To constitute a violation of the contract, the breach must be material. A **material breach** is important enough to defeat an essential purpose of the contract. Although a court would probably not consider one missed day to be a material breach, if Artist repeatedly failed to show up, that would be material.

Given that the goal of a contract is to avoid litigation, it is can be useful to define what a breach is. The movie contract uses this definition:

> Artist fails or refuses to perform in accordance with Producer's instructions or is otherwise in material breach or material default hereof," and "Artist's use of drugs [other than prescribed by a medical doctor]."

The contract goes on, however, to give Artist one free pass:

> It being agreed that with regard to one instance of default only, Artist shall have 24 hours after receipt of notice during principal photography, or 48 hours at all other times, to cure any alleged breach or default hereof.

Sometimes, you will recall, contracts state the consequences of a breach, such as the amount of damages. A damages clause can specify a certain amount, a limitation on the total, or other variations. In other words, the contract could say, "If Artist breaches, Producer is entitled to $1 million in damages." (You remember from prior chapters that these are called *liquidated damages.*) Alternatively, a damage clause could say, "Damages will not exceed $1 million." But the vast majority of contracts have neither liquidated damages nor damage caps.

Sole discretion
A party to a contract has the absolute right to make a decision on that issue.

Reasonable
Ordinary or usual under the circumstances.

Good faith
An honest effort to meet both the spirit and letter of a contract.

Good faith. Note that many of the covenants in the movie contract provide that the right must be exercised *reasonably* or that a decision must be made in *good faith* (except for the right to approve blooper videos, over which Artist has *sole discretion.*) A party with **sole discretion** has the absolute right to make any decision on that issue. Sole discretion clauses are not entered into lightly. **Reasonable** means ordinary or usual under the circumstances. **Good faith** means an honest effort to meet both the spirit and letter of the contract. These are the technical definitions. What do *material, reasonably,* and *in good faith* mean in practice?

In the following case, a famous athlete felt that the other party had committed a material breach of their contract, behaved unreasonably, and acted in bad faith. Do you agree?

LeMond Cycling, Inc. v. PTI Holding, Inc.

2005 U.S. Dist. LEXIS 742
United States District Court for the District of Minnesota, 2005

Facts: Before Lance Armstrong, Greg LeMond won the Tour de France, cycling's most prestigious race. *Sports Illustrated* named him one of the 40 most influential people in sports during the prior 40 years. He formed LeMond Cycling, Inc. (LCI) to handle his business dealings. Protective Technologies International, Inc. (PTI) sold cycling accessories under brand names like Barbie, Playskool, and Tonka to retailers such as Target, Wal-Mart, K-Mart, and Toys R Us.

LeMond and PTI signed a contract (the Deal Memo) providing that PTI would use LeMond's name to sell bicycle accessories. In return, PTI would pay LCI $500,000 a year plus a 6 percent royalty on annual sales exceeding $8.33 million. The Deal Memo required PTI to

- Use commercially reasonable efforts to produce and market LeMond bicycle accessories
- Keep LCI apprised of PTI's efforts, including information about marketing and media plans

PTI tried to sell LeMond products to Target, Wal-Mart, and Toys R Us. Only Target was interested, and then only in a minor way. It agreed to allocate just 6 feet of shelf space to LeMond products. It also rejected PTI's proposal to install a video kiosk that featured LeMond. PTI did not tell LCI about this deal.

LeMond accessories sold poorly at Target. PTI itself did not do any promotional activities or advertising for the products beyond the initial video for the kiosk, which

Thierry Prat/Sygma/Corbis

Greg LeMond was one of the greatest cyclists ever. Why didn't his products sell?

Target rejected. PTI argued that it was Target's role to advertise the products.

Because of poor sales, Target reduced the amount of shelf space for LeMond items to just 4 feet. Ultimately, Target discontinued these products altogether. In neither instance did PTI inform LCI. PTI did try to sell LeMond accessories to Wal-Mart, Toys R Us, and other stores, but there were no takers.

Shortly thereafter, PTI began to sell Schwinn bicycle accessories to the retailers that had rejected LeMond products. PTI earned over $30 million from Schwinn sales. The company then abandoned all efforts to sell LeMond items.

LCI filed suit against PTI for breach of contract. In response, PTI filed a motion for summary judgment, seeking to have the suit dismissed.

Issue: ***Did PTI breach its contract with LCI?***

Excerpts from Judge Magnuson's Decision: To prevail on a breach of contract claim, LCI must prove that PTI breached a material term of the contract. A material breach goes to the root or essence of the contract and is so fundamental to the contract that the failure to perform that obligation defeats an essential purpose of the contract. Even when express conditions of the contract are violated, the breach is not necessarily material.

LCI contends that PTI's alleged failure to provide LCI with annual marketing and media plans was material. LCI submits that these documents serve a critical purpose in licensing agreements because they allow the licensor to monitor sales and corresponding royalty payments.

The Court disagrees. The fact that PTI failed to give reports or other documents to LeMond does not frustrate the essential purpose of the contract. Furthermore, there is no causal connection between PTI's failure to provide LCI with these reports and LCI's lost profit. Therefore, these terms of the Deal Memo, by themselves, are not material as a matter of law.

However, whether or not PTI used commercially reasonable efforts to produce [and] market the Product Line is a material term of the contract, as it is the primary purpose of the contract itself. Thus, the issue is whether PTI breached this duty.

The Deal Memo fails to define commercially reasonable. LCI is convinced that commercially reasonable requires an examination of customary practices within the licensing industry. LCI's broad argument that only industry standards are relevant to the commercial reasonableness determination is unpersuasive. Although an objective component is instructive as to whether or not PTI acted with commercial reasonableness, there must be a subjective evaluation as well. No business would agree to perform to its detriment, and therefore whether or not PTI performed with commercial reasonableness also depends on the financial resources, business expertise, and practices of PTI.

The Complaint also alleges that PTI breached its implied covenant of good faith and fair dealing with LCI. Good faith requires a party to act honestly. Bad faith exists when a party's refusal to fulfill its obligations is based on an ulterior motive. LCI submits that PTI abandoned LCI and its obligations under the Deal Memo when it engaged in its relationship with Schwinn. Indeed, LCI has submitted evidence that PTI narrowly focused on its Schwinn obligations despite its continuing obligation to LCI under the Deal Memo. There is a dispute of fact as to whether PTI exercised good faith in its performance under the terms of the Deal Memo. Thus, PTI's Motion on this point is denied.

IT IS HEREBY ORDERED that:

Defendants' Motion for Summary Judgment is GRANTED in part and DENIED in part as set forth in this Order.

In drafting covenants, there are two issues to keep in mind.

Reciprocal Promises and Conditions. Suppose that a contract provides that:

1. Actor shall take part in the principal photography of Movie for 10 weeks, commencing on March 1.
2. Producer shall pay Artist $180,000 per week.

Reciprocal promises
Promises that are each enforceable independently.

Conditional promises
Promises that a party agrees to perform only if the other side has first done what it promised.

In this case, even if Artist does not show up for shooting, Producer is still required to pay him. These provisions are **reciprocal promises, which means that they are each enforceable independently.** Producer must make payment and then sue Artist, hoping to recover damages in court.

The better approach is for the covenants to be **conditional**—a party agrees to perform them only if the other side has first done what it promised. For example, in the real movie contract, Producer promises to pay Artist "On the condition that Artist fully performs all of Artist's services and obligations and agreements hereunder and is not in material breach or otherwise in material default hereof." And Artist has the right to attend any premieres of the movie and invite three friends, "On the condition that Artist fully performs all services and material obligations hereunder."

In short, if you do not expect to perform under the contract until the other side has met its obligations, be sure to say so.

Language of the covenants. To clarify *who* exactly is doing what, covenants in a contract should use the active, not passive voice. In other words, a contract should say "Producer shall pay Artist $1.8 million," not "Artist shall be paid $1.8 million."

For important issues where disputes are likely to arise, the language should be precise, detailed, and complete. The movie contract uses 453 words to define the Artist's services just for shooting the movie, not including promotional efforts once the film is released. These acting services include, "dubbing, retakes, reshoots, and added scenes."

Representations and Warranties

Representations and warranties
Statements of fact about the past or present.

Covenants are the promises the parties make about what they will do in the future. Representations and warranties are statements of fact about the past or present; they are true when the contract is signed (or at some other specific, designated time).[4] These representations and warranties are important—without them, the other party might not have agreed to the contract. For example, in the movie contract, Artist warrants that he is a member of the Screen Actors Guild. This provision is important because, if it were not true, Producer would either have to obtain a waiver or pay a substantial penalty.

In a contract between two companies, each side will generally represent and warrant facts such as: they legally exist, they have the authority to enter into the contract, their financial statements are accurate, they have revealed all material litigation, and they own all relevant assets. In a contract for the sale of goods, the contract will include warranties about the condition of the goods being sold.

EXAM Strategy

Question: Producer does not want Artist to pilot an airplane during the term of the contract. Would that provision be a warranty and representation or a covenant? How would you phrase it?

Strategy: Warranties and representations are about events in the past or present. A covenant is a promise for the future. If, for example, Producer wanted to know that Artist had never used drugs in the past, that provision would be a warranty and representation.

[4]Although, technically, there is a slight difference between a representation and a warranty, many lawyers confuse the two terms, and the distinction is not important. We will treat them as synonyms, as many lawyers do.

Result: A promise not to pilot an airplane is a covenant. The contract could say, "Until Artist completes all services required hereunder, he shall not pilot an airplane."

Boilerplate

These standard previsions are typically placed in a section entitled *Miscellaneous*. Many people think that *boilerplate* is a synonym for *boring and irrelevant*, but it is worth remembering that the term comes from the iron or steel that protects the hull of a ship—something that shipbuilders ignore to the passengers' peril. A contract without boilerplate is valid and enforceable—so it can be tempting to skip these provisions, but they do play an important protective role. In essence, boilerplate creates a private law that governs disputes between the parties. Courts can also play this role and, indeed, in the absence of boilerplate they will. But remember that an important goal of a contract is to avoid court involvement.

Here are some standard, and important, boilerplate provisions.

Choice of Law and Forum. **Choice of law** provisions determine which state's laws will be used to interpret the contract. **Choice of forum** determines the state in which any litigation would take place. (One state's courts can apply another state's laws.) Lawyers often view these two provisions as the most important boilerplate. Individual states might have dramatically different laws. Even the so-called uniform statutes, such as the Uniform Commercial Code, can vary widely from state to state. Variations are even more pronounced in other areas of the law, in particular in the common law, which is created by state courts. As for forum, it is a lot more convenient and cheaper to litigate a case in one's home courts.

Choice of law provisions
Determine which state's laws will be used to interpret the contract.

Choice of forum provisions
Determine the state in which any litigation would take place.

When resolving a dispute, the choice of law and forum can strongly influence the outcome. For this reason, sometimes parties are reluctant to negotiate the provision and instead decide not to designate a forum and just take their chances. Or they may choose a neutral, equally inconvenient forum like Delaware. Without a choice of forum clause, the parties may well end up litigating where to litigate, or they may find themselves even worse off—with parallel cases filed by each in his preferred forum.

The movie contract states: "This Agreement shall be deemed to have been made in the State of California and shall be construed and enforced in accordance with the law of the State of California." The contract did not, but might have, also specified the forum—that any litigation would be tried in California.

Modification. Contracts should contain a provision governing modification. The movie contract states: "This Agreement may not be amended or modified except by an instrument in writing signed by the party to be charged with such amendment or modification."

"Charged with such amendment" means the party who is adversely affected by the change. For example, if Producer agrees to pay Artist more, then Producer must sign the amendment. Without this provision, a conversation over beers between Producer and Artist about a change in pay might turn out to be an enforceable amendment.

The original version of the movie contract said that Artist would be photographed nude only above the waist. He ultimately agreed to rear-below-the-waist photography. That amendment (which the parties called a **rider**—another term for amendment or addition) took the form of a letter from Artist agreeing to the change. Producer then signed the letter, acknowledging receipt and acceptance. The amendment would have been valid even without Producer's signature because Artist was "charged with such Amendment."

Rider
An amendment or addition to a contract.

If a contract has a provision requiring that amendments be in writing, there are three ways to amend it:

1. Signing an amendment (or rider).
2. Crossing out by hand the wrong language and replacing it with the correct terms. It is good practice for both parties to initial each change. This method is typically used before the document is signed—say, at the closing if the parties notice a mistake.
3. Rewriting the entire contract to include the changed provisions. In this case, the contract is typically renamed: The Amended and Restated Agreement. This method is most appropriate if there are many complex alterations.

Note that amending a contract may raise issues of consideration, a topic discussed in Chapter 12.

Assignment of rights
A transfer of benefits under a contract to another person.

Delegation of duties
A transfer of obligations in a contract.

Assignment of Rights and Delegation of Duties. An **assignment of rights** is a transfer of your benefits under a contract to another person, while **delegation of duties** is a transfer of your obligations. In the movie contract, Producer has the right to *assign* the contract, but he must stay secondarily liable to it. In other words, someone else can take over the contract for him, but if that person fails to live up to his obligations, Producer is liable. Artist might be unhappy if another production company takes over the movie, but he is still required under the contract to perform his acting services. At least he knows that Producer is liable for his paycheck.

Delegation means that someone else performs the duties under the contract. It certainly matters to Producer which actor shows up to do the shooting. Artist cannot say, "I'm too busy—here's my cousin Jack." So the movie contract provides:

> It is expressly understood and agreed that the services to be rendered by Artist hereunder are of the essence of this Agreement and that such services shall not be delegated to any other person or entity, nor shall Artist assign the right to receive compensation hereunder.

In essence, Producer not only cares who shows up for shooting, he also wants to make sure that no one else cashes the checks. He wants to deal only with Artist. And he worries that if Artist assigns the right to receive payment, he will feel less motivated to do his job well.

Arbitration. Some contracts prohibit the parties from suing in court and require that disputes be settled by an arbitrator. The parties to a contract do not have to arbitrate a dispute unless the contract specifically requires it. Arbitration has its advantages—flexibility and savings in time and money—but it also has disadvantages. For example, most contracts between consumers and brokerage houses require arbitration. Consumer advocates argue that the arbitrators in these disputes are biased in favor of the brokerage houses—who engage in many arbitrations—over consumers who are likely to be one-time customers. And many believe that employees receive a less favorable result when they arbitrate, rather than litigate, disputes with their employer. Also, if a court makes a mistake in applying the law, an appellate court can correct the error. But if an arbitrator makes a mistake, there is generally no appeal. The movie contract does not include an arbitration provision.

Attorney's fees. As a general rule, parties to a contract must pay their own legal fees, no matter who is in the wrong. But contracts may override this general rule and provide that the losing party in a dispute must pay the attorney's fees for both sides. Such a provision tends to discourage the poorer party from litigating with a rich opponent for fear of having to pay two sets of attorney's fees. The movie contract provides:

> Artist hereby agrees to indemnify Producer from and against any and all losses, costs (including, without limitation, reasonable attorneys' fees), liabilities, damages, and claims of any nature arising from or in connection with any breach by Artist of any agreement, representation, or warranty made by Artist under this Agreement.

There is no equivalent provision for breaches by Producer. What does that omission tell you about the relative bargaining power of the two parties?

Integration. During contract negotiations, the parties may discuss many ideas that are not ultimately included in the final version. The point of an integration clause is to prevent either side from later claiming that the two parties had agreed to additional provisions. The movie contract states:

> This Agreement, along with the exhibits attached hereto, shall constitute a binding contract between the parties hereto and shall supersede any and all prior negotiations and communications, whether written or oral, with respect hereto.

Without this clause, even a detailed written contract can be amended by an undocumented conversation—a dangerous situation since the existence and terms of the amendment will depend on what a court *thinks* was said and intended, which may or may not be what actually happened.

EXAM Strategy

Question: Daniel and Annie signed a contract providing that Annie would sell craft beers to Daniel's grocery stores at a price of $20 per case. During negotiations, Daniel and Annie agreed that the price would go up to $22 per case once he had bought 1,000 cases. This provision never made it into the contract. After the contract had been signed, Daniel agreed to a price of $23 per case once volume exceeded 1,000 cases. The contract had an integration provision but no modification clause. What price must Daniel pay for cases in excess of 1,000?

Strategy: If a contract has an integration provision, then side agreements made during negotiations are unenforceable unless included in the written contract. Without a modification provision, oral agreements made after the contract was signed may be enforceable.

Result: A court would not enforce the side agreement that required Daniel to pay $22 a case. It is possible that a court would enforce the $23 agreement—which leaves Daniel with a choice of paying $23 a case or the cost of having his lawyer defend a lawsuit.

Severability. If, for whatever reason, some part of the contract turns out to be unenforceable, a severability provision asks the court simply to delete the offending clause and enforce the rest of the contract. For example, courts will not enforce *unreasonable* non-compete clauses. (California courts will not enforce *any* non-competes, unless made in connection with the sale of a business.) In one case, a consultant signed an employment contract that prohibited him from engaging in his occupation "anyplace in the world." The court struck down this non-compete provision but ruled that the rest of the contract (which contained trade secret clauses) was valid.

The movie contract states:

> In the event that there is any conflict between any provision of this Agreement and any statute, law, or regulation, the latter shall prevail; provided, however, that in such event, the provision of this Agreement so affected shall be curtailed and limited only to the minimum extent necessary

> to permit compliance with the minimum requirement, and no other provision of this Agreement shall be affected thereby and all other provisions of this Agreement shall continue in full force and effect.

Force majeure event
A disruptive, unexpected occurrence for which neither party is to blame that prevents one or both parties from complying with a contract.

Force Majeure. A **force majeure event** is a disruptive, unexpected occurrence for which neither party is to blame that prevents one or both parties from complying with the contract. Force majeure events typically include war, terrorist attack, fire, flood, or general acts of God. If, for example, a major terrorist event were to halt air travel, Artist might not be able to appear on set as scheduled. The movie contract defines force majeure events thus:

> fire, war, governmental action or proceeding, third-party breach of contract, injunction, or other material interference with the production or distribution of motion pictures by Producer, or any other unexpected or disruptive event sufficient to excuse performance of this Agreement as a matter of law or other similar causes beyond Producer's control or by reason of the death, illness, or incapacity of the producer, director, or a member of the principal cast or other production personnel.

Notices. After a contract is signed, there may be times when the parties want to send each other official notices—of a breach, an objection, or an approval, for example. In this section, the parties list the addresses where these notices may be sent. For Producer, it is company headquarters. For Artist, there are three addresses: his agent, his manager, and his lawyer. The notice provision also typically specifies when the notice is effective: when sent, when it would normally be expected to arrive, or when it actually does arrive.

Closing. To indicate that the parties have agreed to the terms of the contract, they must sign it. A simple signature is sufficient, but contracts often contain flourishes. The movie contract, for example, states:

> IN WITNESS WHEREOF, the parties hereto have executed this Agreement as of the date first written above.

With clauses like this, it is important to make sure that there is an (accurate) date on the first page. If not otherwise provided in the "Notices" section, it is a good idea to include the parties' addresses. The movie contract also listed Artist's social security number.

When a party to the contract is a corporation, the signature lines should read like this:

Winterfield Productions, Inc.
By:____________
Name:
Title:

If an individual signs her own name without indicating that she is doing so in her role as an employee of Winterfield Productions, Inc., she would be personally liable.

In the end, both parties signed the contract and the movie was made. According to Rotten Tomatoes, the online movie site, professional reviewers rated it 7.9 out of 10.

Chapter Conclusion

You will undoubtedly sign many contracts in your life. Their length and complexity can be daunting. (In the movie contract, one of the paragraphs is 1,000 words.) The goal of this chapter is to help you understand the structure and meaning of the most important provisions so that you can read and analyze contracts more effectively.

Exam Review

1. **AMBIGUITY** Any ambiguity in a contract is interpreted against the party that drafted the agreement. (pp. 433–434)

2. **SCRIVENER'S ERROR** A scrivener's error is a typographical mistake. In the case of a scrivener's error, a court will reform a contract if there is clear and convincing evidence that the mistake does not reflect the true intent of the parties. (p. 435)

Question: Martha intended to transfer a piece of land to Paul. By mistake, she signed a contract transferring two parcels of land. Each piece was accurately described in the contract. Will the court reform this contract and transfer one piece of land back to her?

Strategy: Begin by asking if this was a scrivener's error. Then consider whether the court will correct the mistake.

3. **BEFORE SIGNING A CONTRACT** Before signing a contract, check carefully and thoughtfully the names of the parties, the dates, dollar amounts, and interest rates. (p. 437)

4. **MATERIAL BREACH** A material breach is important enough to defeat an essential purpose of the contract. (pp. 439–442)

Question: Laurie's contract to sell her tortilla chip business to Hudson contained a provision that she must continue to work at the business for five years. One year later, she quit. Hudson refused to pay her the amounts still owing under the contract. Laurie alleged that he is liable for the full amount because her breach was not material. Is Laurie correct?

Strategy: What was the essential purpose of the contract? Was Laurie's breach important enough to defeat it?

5. **SOLE DISCRETION** A party with sole discretion has the absolute right to make any decision on that issue. (p. 440)

Question: A tenant rented space from a landlord for a seafood restaurant. Under the terms of the lease, the tenant could assign the lease only if the landlord gave her consent, which she had the right to withhold "for any reason whatsoever, at her sole discretion." The tenant grew too ill to run the restaurant and asked permission to assign the lease. The landlord refused. In court, the tenant argued that the landlord could not unreasonably withhold her consent. Is the tenant correct?

Strategy: A sole discretion clause grants the absolute right to make a decision. Are there any exceptions?

6. **REASONABLE** Reasonable means ordinary or usual under the circumstances. (p. 440)

7. **GOOD FAITH** Good faith means an honest effort to meet both the spirit and letter of the contract. (p. 440)

8. **STRUCTURE OF A CONTRACT** The structure of a contract looks like this:

   a. Title
   b. Introductory Paragraph
   c. Definitions
   d. Covenants
   e. Conditions
   f. Representations and Warranties
      i. Covenants are the promises the parties make about what they will do in the future.
      ii. Representations and warranties are statements of fact about the present or past—they are true when the contract is signed (or at some other specific, designated time).
   g. Remedies
   h. Boilerplate
      i. Choice of Law and Forum
      ii. Modification
      iii. Assignment of Rights and Delegation of Duties
      iv. Arbitration
      v. Attorney's Fees
      vi. Integration
      vii. Severability
      viii. Force Majeure
      ix. Notices
      x. Closing (pp. 437–446)

2. Result: The court ruled that it was not a scrivener's error because it was not a typo or clerical error. Therefore, the court did not reform the contract and the land was not transferred back to Martha.

4. Result: The purpose of the contract was for Hudson to build up the business and make a profit. Laurie's departure interfered with that goal. The court ruled that the breach was material and Hudson did not have to pay the sums still owing under the contract.

5. Result: The court ruled for the landlord. She had the absolute right to make any decision as long as the decision was not illegal. The moral: Sole discretion clauses are serious business. Do not enter into one lightly.

Multiple-Choice Questions

1. In the *Quake* case, the appellate court ruled
(a) the letter of intent was a valid contract.
(b) letters of intent are *never* a valid contract.
(c) a letter of intent can be a valid contract, but this one was not.
(d) the trial court had to determine if the letter of intent was a valid contract.

2. In the *Cipriano* case, what happened?
(a) The jury decided in favor of Cipriano because arson is vandalism.
(b) The jury decided against Cipriano because arson is not vandalism.
(c) The judge dismissed the motion for summary judgment because the contract was ambiguous.
(d) The judge granted the motion for summary judgment because the contract was not ambiguous.

3. In the case of a scrivener's error, what happens?
(a) A court will not reform the contract. The parties must live with the document they signed.
(b) A court will reform the contract if there is clear and convincing evidence that the clause in question does not reflect the true intent of the parties.
(c) A court will reform the contract if a preponderance of the evidence indicates that that the clause in question does not reflect the true intent of the parties.
(d) A court will invalidate the contract in its entirety.

4. In the *LeMond* case, the court ruled:
(a) PTI's failure to supply marketing and media plans was a material breach of the contract because without those plans, LCI could not monitor sales.
(b) PTI's failure to supply marketing and media plans was a material breach of the contract because PTI had agreed to supply the plans.
(c) the requirement that PTI use commercially reasonable means to promote the product line was not enforceable because the term was ambiguous.
(d) PTI's failure to supply marketing and media plans was not a material breach of the contract.

5. A contract states (1) that Buzz Co. legally exists and (2) will provide 2,000 pounds of wild salmon each week. Which of the following statements is true?
(a) Clause 1 is a covenant and Clause 2 is a representation.
(b) Clause 1 is a representation and Clause 2 is a covenant.
(c) Both clauses are representations.
(d) Both clauses are covenants.

Essay Questions

1. List three types of contracts that should definitely be in writing, and one that probably does not need to be.

2. Make a list of provisions that you would expect in an employment contract.

3. List three provisions in a contract that would be material, and three that would not be.

4. Slimline and Distributor signed a contract which provided that Distributor would use reasonable efforts to promote and sell Slimline's diet drink. Slimline was already being sold in Warehouse Club. After the contract was signed, Distributor stopped conducting in-store demos of Slimline. It did not repackage the product as Slimline and Warehouse requested. Sales of Slimline continued to increase during the term of the contract. Slimline sued Distributor, alleging a violation of the agreement. Who should win?

5. **YOU BE THE JUDGE WRITING PROBLEM** Chip bought an insurance policy on his house from Insurance Co. The policy covered damage from fire but explicitly excluded coverage for harm caused "by or through an earthquake." When an earthquake struck, Chip's house suffered no fire damage, but the earthquake caused a building some blocks away to catch on fire. That fire ultimately spread to Chip's house, burning it down. Is Insurance Co. liable to Chip? **Argument for Insurance Co.:** The policy could not have been clearer or more explicit. If there had been no earthquake, Chip's house would still be standing. The policy does not cover his loss. **Argument for Chip:** His house was not damaged by an earthquake; it burned down. The policy covered fire damage. If a contract is ambiguous, it must be interpreted against the drafter of the contract.

Discussion Questions

1. In the movie contract, which side was the more successful negotiator? Can you think of any terms that either party left out? Are any of the provisions unreasonable?

2. What are the advantages and disadvantages of hiring a lawyer to draft or review a contract?

3. What are the penalties if Artist breaches the movie contract? Why are the penalties so light?

4. **ETHICS** In the *Heritage* case, the two companies had agreed to a price change of \$0.01. When Heritage's lawyer pointed out to his client the change to \$0.10, the Heritage officer did not tell Phibro. The change was subtle in appearance but important in its financial impact. Was Heritage's behavior ethical? When the opposing side makes a mistake in a contract, do you have an ethical obligation to tell them? What Life Principles would you apply in this situation?

5. Blair Co.'s top officers approached an investment bank to find a buyer for the company. The bank sent an engagement letter to Blair with the following language:

   > If, within 24 months after the termination of this agreement, Blair is bought by anyone with whom Bank has had substantial discussions about such a sale, Blair must pay Bank its full fee.

   Is there any problem with the drafting of this provision? What could be done to clarify the language?

UNIT 3

Commercial Transactions

CHAPTER 20

INTRODUCTION TO SALES

© Stas Volik/Shutterstock.com

He Sued, She Sued. Harold and Maude made a great couple because both were compulsive entrepreneurs. One evening they sat on their penthouse roofdeck, overlooking the twinkling Chicago skyline. Harold sipped a decaf coffee while negotiating, over the phone, with a real estate developer in San Antonio. Maude puffed a cigar as she bargained on a different line with a toy manufacturer in Cleveland. They hung up at the same time. "I did it!" shrieked Maude, "I made an incredible deal for the robots—five bucks each!" "No, *I* did it!" trumpeted Harold, "I sold the 50 acres in Texas for $300,000 more than it's worth." They dashed indoors.

Confirming our deal—100,000 Psychopath Robots—you deliver Chicago—end of summer.

Maude quickly scrawled a handwritten memo, which said, "Confirming our deal—100,000 Psychopath Robots—you deliver Chicago—end of summer." She didn't mention a price, or an exact delivery date, or when payment would be made. She signed her memo and faxed it to the toy manufacturer. Harold took more time. He typed a thorough contract, describing precisely the land he was selling, the $2.3 million price, how and when each payment would be made and the deed conveyed. He signed the contract and faxed it, along with a plot plan showing the surveyed land. Then the happy couple grabbed a bottle of champagne, returned to the deck—and placed a side bet on whose contract would prove more profitable. The loser would have to cook and serve dinner for six months.

Neither Harold nor Maude ever heard again from the other parties. The toy manufacturer sold the Psychopath Robots to another retailer at a higher price. Maude was forced to buy comparable toys elsewhere for $9 each. She sued. And the Texas property buyer changed his mind, deciding to develop a Club Med in Greenland and refusing to pay Harold for his land. He sued. Only one of the two plaintiffs succeeded. Which one?

The adventures of Harold and Maude illustrate the Uniform Commercial Code (UCC) in action. The Code is the single most important source of law for people engaged in commerce and controls the vast majority of contracts made every day in every state. The Code is ancient in origin, contemporary in usage, admirable in purpose, and flawed in application. "Yeah, yeah, that's fascinating," snaps Harold, "but who wins the bet?" Relax, Harold, we'll tell you in a minute.

Development of Commercial Law

In England in the 1500s, it was far more important to hold land than it was to have money. Large landowners—barons, earls, and dukes—stood in excellent positions. They had access to the king or queen, they were exempt from many kinds of arrest, and, if they did get into trouble, they generally were tried before other members of the nobility in special courts. It is not surprising that law was then centered squarely upon *real property*, which mainly consists of land and permanent structures. But society changes, and so do businesses. When this happens, the law may fall behind the times.

In the 1500s, merchants in England began to have problems using existing law to resolve commercial disputes. There were many laws about land, but few for contracts. English judges were only beginning to acknowledge that an exchange of mere promises, with no money or property changing hands, might lead to an enforceable agreement. But merchants dealt in the sale of goods, not real estate. Their livelihood depended upon promises, on the rapid movement of their wares, and on their ability to enforce bargains. Dissatisfied with the few remedies that courts offered, businessmen throughout England and the Continent began to treat their own customs as law and to settle disputes in trade organizations rather than civil courts. The body of rules they relied on became known as the *lex mercatoria*, or **law merchant**. The law merchant was thus a "custom made" law, created by the merchants who used it. The new doctrine focused on promises, the sale and exchange of goods, and payment.

In the middle of the 20th century, contract law again required a reinvention. Two problems had become apparent in the United States.

1. Old contract law principles often did not reflect modern business practices.
2. Laws had become different from one state to another.

On many legal topics, contract law included, the national government has had little to say and has allowed the states to act individually. Texas decides what kinds of agreements count as contracts in Texas, and next door in Oklahoma, the rules may be very different. On many issues, states reached essentially similar conclusions, so contract law developed in the same direction. But sometimes, the states disagreed, and contract law took on the aspect of a patchwork quilt.

The UCC was created as an attempt to solve these two problems. It was a proposal written by legal scholars and not a law drafted by members of Congress or state legislatures. The scholars at the American Law Institute and the National Conference of Commissioners on Uniform State Laws had great ideas, but they had no legal authority to make anyone do anything.

Over time, lawmakers in all 50 states were persuaded to adopt many parts of the Uniform Commerical Code. They responded to these persuasive arguments:

1. Businesses will benefit if most commercial transactions are governed by the modern and efficient contract law principles that are outlined in the UCC.
2. Businesses everywhere will be able to operate more efficiently, and transactions will be more convenient, if the law surrounding most of their transactions is the same in all 50 states.

This chapter will focus on Article 2 of the UCC, which applies to the sale of goods. A **good** is a moveable physical object except for money and securities (like stock certificates). A house is not a good, but the *stuff* in the house—the car in the garage, the televisions, the furniture, and almost everything else—is. Article 2 applies to contracts that sell goods, as well as to contracts that sell a mix of goods and services if the *predominant purpose* of the deal is to sell goods.

It is worth noting that the UCC is not a total replacement for older principles in contract law. Contract lawsuits not involving goods are still resolved using the older common law rules. The table below outlines the UCC and the types of contracts that it does govern.

The entire Code is available online at **http://www.law.cornell.edu/ucc/ucc.table.html.**

Article 1:	
General Provisions	The purpose of the code, general guidance in applying it, and definitions.
Article 2:	
Sale of Goods	The sale of *goods,* such as a new car, 20,000 pairs of gloves, or 101 Dalmatians. This is one of the two most important articles in the UCC.
Article 2A:	
Leases	A temporary exchange of goods for money, such as renting a car.
Article 3:	
Negotiable Instruments	The use of checks, promissory notes, and other negotiable instruments.
Article 4:	
Bank Deposits and Collections	The rights and obligations of banks and their customers.
Article 4A:	
Funds Transfers	An instruction, given by a bank customer, to credit a sum of money to another's account.
Article 5:	
Letters of Credit	The use of credit, extended by two or more banks, to facilitate a contract between two parties who do not know each other and require guarantees by banks they trust.
Article 6:	
Bulk Transfers	The sale of a major part of a company's inventory or equipment. This article has been repealed in all but a few states.
Article 7:	
Warehouse Receipts, Bills of Lading, and Other Documents of Title	Documents proving ownership of goods that are being transported or stored. This article is being revised as we go to press.

Article 8:	
Investment Securities	Rights and liabilities concerning shares of stock or other ownership of an enterprise.
Article 9:	
Secured Transactions	A sale of goods in which the seller keeps a financial stake in the goods he has sold, such as a car dealer who may repossess the car if the buyer fails to make payments. This is one of the two most important articles in the Code.

Harold and Maude, Revisited

Harold and Maude each negotiated what they believed was an enforceable agreement, and both filed suit: Harold for the sale of his land, Maude for the purchase of toy robots. Only one prevailed. The difference in outcome demonstrates one of the changes that the UCC has wrought in the law of commercial contracts and illustrates why everyone in business needs a working knowledge of the Code. As we revisit the happy couple, Harold is clearing the dinner dishes. Maude sits back in her chair, lights a cigar, and compliments her husband on the apple tart. Harold, scowling and spilling coffee, wonders what went wrong.

Harold's contract was for the sale of land and governed by the common law of contracts. The common law statute of frauds requires any agreement for the sale of land to be in writing and *signed by the defendant,* in this case the buyer in Texas. Harold signed it, but the buyer never did, so Harold's meticulously detailed document was worth less than a five-cent cigar.

Maude's quickly scribbled memorandum concerning psychotic robot toys was for the sale of goods and was governed by Article 2 of the UCC. The Code requires less detail and formality in a writing. Because Maude and the seller were both merchants, the document she scribbled could be enforced *even against the defendant,* who had never signed anything. The fact that Maude left out the price and other significant terms was not fatal to a contract under the UCC, although under the common law such omissions would have made the bargain unenforceable. We will look in greater detail at these UCC changes. For now it is enough to see that the Code has carved major changes into the common law of contracts, alterations that Harold is beginning to appreciate.

This Unit and This Chapter

This unit covers three principal subjects, all relating to commercial transactions that the Code governs. The first chapters concern the sale of goods and focus primarily on Article 2. In the present chapter we emphasize how Code provisions work together to change the common law. In the following chapters we examine title to goods (Chapter 21), then warranties and product liability (Chapter 22), and, finally, performance and remedies (Chapter 23).

Future chapters (Chapters 25–26) survey the law of negotiable instruments. Checks are the most common kind of negotiable instrument, but we will see that there are many other varieties and that each creates different rights and obligations. We include in the unit a chapter devoted to secured transactions (Chapter 24), that is, a sale of goods in which the seller keeps a financial stake in the goods he has sold, and later in the text a chapter that analyzes bankruptcy law (Chapter 37).

The remainder of this chapter examines contract formation under Article 2 of the UCC. When an agreement is struck, the first fundamental question of contract law is this: has an enforceable contract been formed? As you read the chapter, keep the following ideas in mind:

1. *The UCC is pro-business.* The whole point of the UCC is to make business transactions more reliable, convenient, and predictable.
2. *Tie goes to the contract.* In baseball, a tie goes to the runner. Under the UCC, the preference is to declare an agreement to be a contract if no clear reason exists to declare it invalid.

UCC Basics

Code's Purpose

The Uniform Commercial Code proclaims its purposes clearly:

UCC §1-102(2): Underlying purposes and policies of this Act are

(a) to simplify, clarify and modernize the law governing commercial transactions;

(b) to permit the continued expansion of commercial practices through custom, usage and agreement of the parties;

(c) to make uniform the law among the various jurisdictions.

This is not mere boilerplate. To "modernize," in (a), requires a focus on the needs of contemporary businesspeople, not on rules developed when judges rode horseback. Suppose a court must decide whether a writing is detailed enough to satisfy the Code's statute of frauds. The judge may rely on §1-102 to decide that because modern commerce is so fast, even the skimpiest of writings is good enough to demonstrate that the parties had reached a bargain. In doing so, the judge would deliberately be turning away from legal history to accommodate business practices in an electronic age.

Section 1-102 also states that "[t]his Act shall be liberally construed and applied to promote its underlying purposes," meaning that when in doubt, courts should focus on the goals described. The Code emphasizes *getting the right results* rather than following rigid rules of contract law.

Scope of Article 2

Because the UCC changes the common law, it is essential to know whether the Code applies in a given case. Negotiations may lead to an enforceable agreement when the UCC applies, even though the same bargaining would create no contract under the common law.

Goods
Are things that are moveable, other than money and investment securities.

UCC §2-102: Article 2 applies to the sale of goods.[1] **Goods** are things that are moveable, other than money and investment securities. Hats are goods, and so are railroad cars, lumber, books, and bottles of wine. Land is not a good, nor is a house. So an agreement for the delivery of 10,000 board feet of white pine is a contract for the sale of goods, and Article 2 governs it. But the article does not apply to a contract for the sale of an office building. A skyscraper is not moveable (although an entire city *may* be[2]).

---

[1]Officially, Article 2 tells us that it applies to *transactions* in goods, which is a slightly broader category than sale of goods. But most sections of Article 2, and most court decisions, focus exclusively on sales, and so shall we.

[2]"If you are lucky enough to have lived in Paris as a young man, then wherever you go for the rest of your life, it stays with you, for Paris is a moveable feast." Ernest Hemingway, 1950.

Article 2 regulates **sales**, which means that one party transfers title to the other in exchange for money. If you sell your motorcycle to a friend, that is a sale of goods. If you lend the bike to your friend for the weekend, that is not a sale and Article 2 does not apply. Article 2 also does not apply to the leasing of goods, for example, when you rent a car. A sale involves a permanent change in ownership whereas a lease concerns a temporary change in possession.

Mixed Contracts

To determine whether the UCC governs, we need to know what kind of an agreement the parties made. Was it one for the sale of goods (UCC) or one for services (common law)? In fact the agreement combined both goods and services and was therefore a *mixed contract.* **In a mixed contract involving sales and services, the UCC will govern if the *predominant purpose* is the sale of goods, but the common law will control if the predominant purpose is providing services.**

For example, assume that you take your car to a mechanic for repairs and that there are problems with the work. If a lawsuit ensues, a court will have to determine whether the predominant purpose of the contract was the parts (goods) which were replaced or the labor (service) involved in the work.

Merchants

UCC §2-104: A **merchant** is someone who routinely deals in the particular goods involved, *or* who appears to have special knowledge or skill in those goods, *or* who uses agents with special knowledge or skill in those goods. A used car dealer is a "merchant" when it comes to selling autos, because he routinely deals in them. A man selling his own car to someone who responded to his classified ad is not acting a merchant.

Merchant
Generally, someone who routinely deals in the particular goods involved.

The UCC frequently holds a merchant to a higher standard of conduct than a non-merchant. For example, a merchant may be held to an oral contract if she received written confirmation of it, even though the merchant herself never signed the confirmation. That same confirmation memo, arriving at the house of a non-merchant, would *not* create a binding deal. We will see many instances of this dual level of responsibility, one for a merchant and the other for a non-merchant.

© Brand X/Corbis

The UCC gives merchants greater freedom to contract—and greater responsibility.

Good Faith and Unconscionability

The UCC imposes a duty of good faith in the performance of all contracts. For *non-merchants,* good faith means honesty in fact. For a *merchant,* good faith means honesty in fact *plus* the exercise of reasonable commercial standards of fair dealing.[3] Thus, when parties perform a contract, or in certain cases when they negotiate, neither side may lie or mislead. Further, a party who is a merchant must act as fairly as the business community routinely expects.

The UCC employs a second principle to encourage fair play and just results: the doctrine of unconscionability. UCC §2-302: A contract may be **unconscionable** if it is shockingly one-sided and fundamentally unfair. If a court concludes that some part of a contract is

Unconscionable
A contract that is shockingly one-sided and fundamentally unfair.

[3]UCC §§1-201(19), 1-203, and 2-103.

unconscionable, it will refuse to enforce that provision. Courts seldom find a contract unconscionable if the two parties are businesses, but they are quicker to apply the doctrine when one party is a consumer.

The doctrine of good faith focuses on a party's behavior as it performs an agreement: was it attempting to carry out its obligations in a reasonable manner and do what both sides expected when they made the deal? Unconscionability looks primarily at the contract itself. Are any terms so grossly unfair that a court should reform or ignore them?

CONTRACT FORMATION

The common law expected the parties to form a contract in a fairly predictable and traditional way: the offeror made a clear offer that included all important terms, and the offeree agreed to all terms. Nothing was left open. The drafters of the UCC recognized that businesspeople frequently do not think or work that way and that the law should reflect business reality.

Formation Basics: Section 2-204

UCC §2-204 provides three important rules that enable parties to make a contract quickly and informally:

1. ***Any Manner That Shows Agreement.*** The parties may make a contract in any manner sufficient to show that they reached an agreement. They may show the agreement with words, writings, or even their conduct. Lisa negotiates with Ed to buy 300 barbecue grills. The parties agree on a price, but other business prevents them from finishing the deal. Then six months later, Lisa writes, "Remember our deal for 300 grills? I still want to do it if you do." Ed doesn't respond, but a week later, a truck shows up at Lisa's store with the 300 grills and Lisa accepts them. The combination of their original discussion, Lisa's subsequent letter, Ed's delivery, and her acceptance all adds up to show that they reached an agreement. The court will enforce their deal, and Lisa must pay the agreed-upon price.
2. ***Moment of Making Is Not Critical.*** The UCC will enforce a deal even though it is difficult, in common law terms, to say exactly when it was formed. Was Lisa's deal formed when they orally agreed? When he delivered? She accepted? The Code's answer: it does not matter. The contract is enforceable.
3. ***One or More Terms May Be Left Open.*** The common law insisted that the parties clearly agree on all important terms. If they did not, there was no meeting of minds and no enforceable deal. The Code changes that. **Under the UCC, a court may enforce a bargain even though one or more terms were left open.** Lisa's letter never said when she required delivery of the barbecues or when she would pay. Under the UCC, the omission is not fatal. As long as there is some certain basis for giving damages to the injured party, the court will do just that. Suppose Lisa refused to pay, claiming that the agreement included no date for her payment. A court would rule that the parties assumed she would pay within a commercially reasonable time, such as 30 days.

In the following case, we can almost see the roller coasters, smell the cotton candy—and hear the carnival owners arguing. Because the cases in this chapter involve more than one Code section, we will outline the relevant provisions at the outset.

CODE PROVISIONS DISCUSSED IN THIS CASE

Issue	Relevant Code Section
1. What law governs?	UCC §2-102: Article 2 applies to the sale of goods.
2. Did the parties form a contract?	UCC §2-204: The parties may make a contract in any manner sufficient to show agreement.

JANNUSCH V. NAFFZIGER

2008 WL 540877
Illinois Court of Appeals, 2008

Facts: Gene and Martha Jannusch owned a food concession business. They believed they had an agreement to sell it to Lindsey and Louann Naffziger. When the Naffzigers backed out, the Jannuschs sued. The trial court ruled that there had been no meeting of the minds and hence no contract. The Jannuschs appealed. Because the court's decision refers to its exposition of the facts, we will allow a judge to explain what happened.

Issues: ***Does the common law govern or the UCC? Did the parties form a contract?***

Excerpts from Justice Cook's Decision: Plaintiffs operated a business, Festival Foods, which served concessions at festivals and events throughout Illinois and Indiana. The assets included a truck and servicing trailer and equipment such as refrigerators, roasters, chairs and tables, and lighting equipment.

Defendants were interested in purchasing the concession business, met several times with plaintiffs, and observed the business in operation. Gene testified that plaintiffs entered into an oral agreement to sell Festival Foods to defendants for $150,000. Defendants would receive the truck and trailer, all necessary equipment, and the opportunity to work at event locations secured by plaintiffs. Defendants paid $10,000 immediately, with the balance to be paid when defendants received their loan money from the bank. Defendants took possession of Festival Foods the next day and operated Festival Foods for the remainder of the season.

Louann acknowledged testifying during a deposition that an oral agreement to purchase Festival Foods for $150,000 existed but later testified she could not recall specifically making an oral agreement on any particular date. Lindsey testified she and Louann met with plaintiffs and paid the $10,000 for the right to continue to purchase the business because plaintiffs had another interested buyer. According to Lindsey, Gene suggested the parties sign something and she replied that defendants were "in no position to sign anything" because they had not received any loan money from the bank and did not have an attorney. Lindsey admitted taking possession of Festival Foods, receiving the income from the business, purchasing inventory, replacing equipment, paying taxes on the business and paying employees.

Defendants operated six events. Gene attended the first two festivals with defendants, who paid him $10 an hour. Two days after the business season ended, defendants returned Festival Foods to the storage facility where it had been stored by Gene. Lindsey testified one of the reasons defendants returned Festival Foods was because the income from the events they operated was lower than expected.

[Application of the UCC]

Defendants argue the UCC should not apply because this case involves the sale of a business rather than just the sale of goods. The "predominant purpose" test is used to determine whether a contract for both the sale of goods and the rendition of services falls within the scope of article 2 of the UCC. Certainly significant tangible assets were involved in this case. The evidence presented in this case was sufficient to support the conclusion that the proposed agreement was predominantly one for the sale of goods.

[Formation of Contract]

Defendants argue that nothing was said in the contract about allocating a price for good will, a covenant not to compete, allocating a price for the equipment, how to release liens, what would happen if there was no loan approval, and other issues. Defendants argue these are essential terms for the sale of a business.

A contract may be enforced even though some contract terms may be missing or left to be agreed upon, but if the essential terms are so uncertain that there is no basis for deciding whether the agreement has been kept or broken, there is no contract.

The essential terms were agreed upon in this case. The purchase price was $150,000, and the items to be transferred were specified. No essential terms remained to be agreed upon; the only action remaining was the performance of the contract. Defendants took possession of the items to be transferred and used them as their own.

Louann admitted there was an agreement to purchase Festival Foods for $150,000 but could not recall specifically making an oral agreement on any particular date. An agreement sufficient to constitute a contract for sale may be found even though the moment of its making is undetermined. Returning the goods at the end of the season was not a rejection of plaintiffs' offer to sell, it was a breach of contract.

We conclude there was an agreement to sell Festival Foods for the price of $150,000 and that defendants breached that agreement. Reversed and remanded.

Based on the UCC, the Jannuschs won a case they would have lost under the common law. Next we look at changes the Code has made in the centuries-old requirement of a writing.

Statute of Frauds

UCC §2-201 requires a writing for any sale of goods worth $500 or more. However, under the UCC, the writing need not summarize the agreement completely, and it need not even be entirely accurate. Once again, the Code is modifying the common law rule, permitting parties to enforce deals with less formality. In some cases, the court grants an exception and enforces an agreement with no writing at all. Here are the rules.

Contracts for Goods Worth $500 or More

Section 2-201 demands a writing for any contract of goods over this limit, meaning that virtually every significant sale of goods has some writing requirement. Remember that a contract for goods costing less than $500 is still covered by the UCC, but it may be oral.

Writing Sufficient to Indicate a Contract

The Code only requires a writing *sufficient to indicate* that the parties made a contract. In other words, the writing need not *be* a contract. A simple memo is enough, or a letter or informal note, mentioning that the two sides reached an agreement, is enough. **In general, the writing must be signed by the defendant,** that is, whichever party is claiming there was no deal. Dick signs and sends to Shirley a letter saying, "This is to acknowledge your agreement to buy all 650 books in my rare book collection for $188,000." Shirley signs nothing. A day later, Louis offers Dick $250,000. Is Dick free to sell? No. He signed the memo, it indicates a contract, and Shirley can enforce it against him.

Now reverse the problem. Suppose that after Shirley receives Dick's letter, she decides against rare books in favor of original scripts from the *South Park* television show. Dick sues. Shirley wins because *she* signed nothing.

Incorrect or Omitted Terms

If the writing demonstrates the two sides reached an agreement, it satisfies §2-201 even if it omits important terms or states them incorrectly. Suppose Dick writes "$1888,000," indicating almost $2 million, when he meant to write "$188,000." The letter still shows that the parties made a deal, and the court will enforce it, relying on oral testimony to determine the correct price.

Enforceable Only to the Quantity Stated

Since the writing only has to indicate that the parties agreed, it need not state every term of their deal. But one term is essential: quantity. **The Code will enforce the contract only up to the quantity of goods stated in the writing.** This is logical, since a court can surmise other terms, such as price, based on market conditions. Buyer agrees to purchase pencils from Seller. The market value of the pencils is easy to determine, but a court would have no way of knowing whether Buyer meant to purchase 1,000 pencils or 100,000; the quantity must be stated.

Exceptions

In the following three sets of circumstances, the UCC statute of frauds is "turned off".

Merchant Exception. This is a major change from the common law. **When two merchants make an oral contract, and one sends a confirming memo to the other within a reasonable time, and the memo is sufficiently definite that it could be enforced against the sender herself, then the memo is also valid against the merchant who receives it, unless he objects within 10 days.** Laura, a tire wholesaler, signs and sends a memo to Scott, a retailer, saying, "Confm yr order today—500 tires cat #886—cat price." Scott realizes he can get the tires cheaper elsewhere and ignores the memo. Big mistake. Both parties are merchants, and Laura's memo is sufficient to bind her. So it also satisfies the statute of frauds *against Scott*, unless he objects within 10 days.

Specialty Goods Exception. If a buyer orders goods that are to be specially manufactured for the buyer and are not suitable for sale to others in the ordinary course of the seller's business, then a verbal agreement is enforceable even if it exceeds $500.

Judicial Admission Exception. If a defendant admits in his pleading, testimony, or otherwise in court that a contract for sale was made, then the contract he admitted to is enforceable against him.

The following case examines all three of these exceptions in the context of an agreement to buy carpet and tile. When the Supreme Court of Virginia issued its ruling, one company was floored.

CODE PROVISIONS DISCUSSED IN THIS CASE

Issue	Relevant Code Section
1. Is there a confirmatory memo?	UCC 2-201(2)
2. Has the buyer ordered specialty goods?	UCC 2-201(3)(a)
3. Did the buyer admit in its testimony that an agreement existed?	UCC 2-201(3)(b)

Delta Star, Inc. v. Michael's Carpet World

276 Va. 524
Supreme Court of Virginia, 2008

Facts: Ivan Tepper, the CEO of Delta Star, met with the sales manager at Michael's, a flooring company. In a verbal agreement, he hired Michael's to install carpet in the entryway of his office suite, and tile in his personal office and the office of Nash, his assistant.

Michael's faxed Delta Star a purchase order which read, "Carpet for entrance to lobby, $832.22." Michael's installed the carpet and Delta Star paid the $832.22. But, Delta Star sought to cancel part of the remaining work installing tile, and Michael's sued.

At trial, Delta Star argued that, because the tiling was priced at more than $500, the UCC statute of frauds made the agreement unenforceable. The trial court disagreed, holding that the tile was specially manufactured, because Michael's had never ordered that type of tile for a customer before. The lower court also determined that Delta Star had admitted the existence of the contract in its testimony, and that the purchase order amounted to a writing in any event. Michael's was awarded $2,565 in damages, and Delta Star appealed.

Issue: ***Was the contract enforceable?***

Excerpts from Judge Stephenson's Decision: We first consider the trial court's finding that the flooring materials were specially manufactured goods or products for [Delta Star] and not readily suitable for sale [to] others in the ordinary course of [Michael's] business. The flooring materials chosen by Delta Star were selected from samples displayed, were not altered in any way to suit only Delta Star, and were suitable for sale to others in Michael's ordinary course of business. Therefore, the flooring materials were not "specifically manufactured" for Delta Star.

We next consider the trial court's finding that there exists a confirmatory writing establishing an enforceable contract. We do not agree that such a writing exists. At trial, Michael's contended that its invoice for the purchase and installation of flooring in Delta Star's entryway constituted confirmatory writings. [It] cannot serve as confirmation of a contract for the purchase and installation of flooring in Tepper's office. The invoice confirms only the parties' agreement with regard to the entryway flooring.

Finally, we consider the trial court's ruling that Delta Star admitted in its testimony the existence of a contract for the purchase and installation of flooring in Tepper's office. At trial, Michael's contended that Nash's testimony regarding her attempt to cancel that portion of the alleged contract dealing with Tepper's office constituted an admission that a contract existed because "you can't cancel something unless you're admitting that you got a contract and you want to cancel it." Delta Star contends that Nash did not admit that there existed a contract for the purchase and installation of flooring in Tepper's office.

We agree with Delta Star. A review of Nash's trial testimony reveals that she stated that Delta Star "didn't want to act on the estimate" [and] that Delta Star "hadn't agreed to ... order [the flooring for Tepper's office] yet." Therefore, Nash did not admit the existence of a contract for the purchase and installation of flooring in Tepper's office.

For the foregoing reasons, we hold that the trial court erred in overruling Delta Star's Statute of Frauds defense and in finding that an enforceable contract existed between Michael's and Delta Star for the purchase and installation of flooring in Tepper's office.

Reversed.

Added Terms: Section 2-207

Under the common law's mirror image rule, when one party makes an offer, the offeree must accept those exact terms. If the offeree adds or alters any terms, the acceptance is ineffective and the offeree's response becomes a counteroffer. In one of its most significant modifications of contract law, the UCC changes that result. **Under §2-207, an acceptance that adds or alters terms will often create a contract.** The Code has made this change in response to *battles of the form*. Every day, corporations buy and sell millions of dollars of goods using pre-printed forms. The vast majority of all contracts involve such documents. Typically, the buyer places an order using a pre-printed form, and the seller acknowledges with its own pre-printed acceptance form. Because each form contains language favorable to the party sending it, the two documents rarely agree. The Code's drafters concluded that the law must cope with real practices.

We discuss §2-207 in detail in Chapter 11 and summarize it here only to emphasize how it works with other UCC provisions. The section is confusing, and a diagram helps. **For a schematic look at UCC §2-207, see the illustration on page 463.**

Intention

The parties must still *intend* to create a contract. Section 2-207 is full of exceptions, but there is no change in this basic requirement of contract law. If the differing forms indicate that the parties never reached agreement, there is no contract.

Additional or Different Terms

An offeree may include a new term in his acceptance and still create a binding deal. Suppose Breeder writes to Pet Shop, offering to sell 100 guinea pigs at $2 each. Pet Shop faxes a memo saying, "We agree to buy 100 g.p. We get credit for any unhealthy pig." Pet Shop has added a new term, concerning unhealthy pigs, but the parties *have* created a binding contract because the writings show they intended an agreement. Now the court must decide what the terms of the contract are, since there is some discrepancy. The first step is to decide whether the new language is an *additional term* or a *different term*.

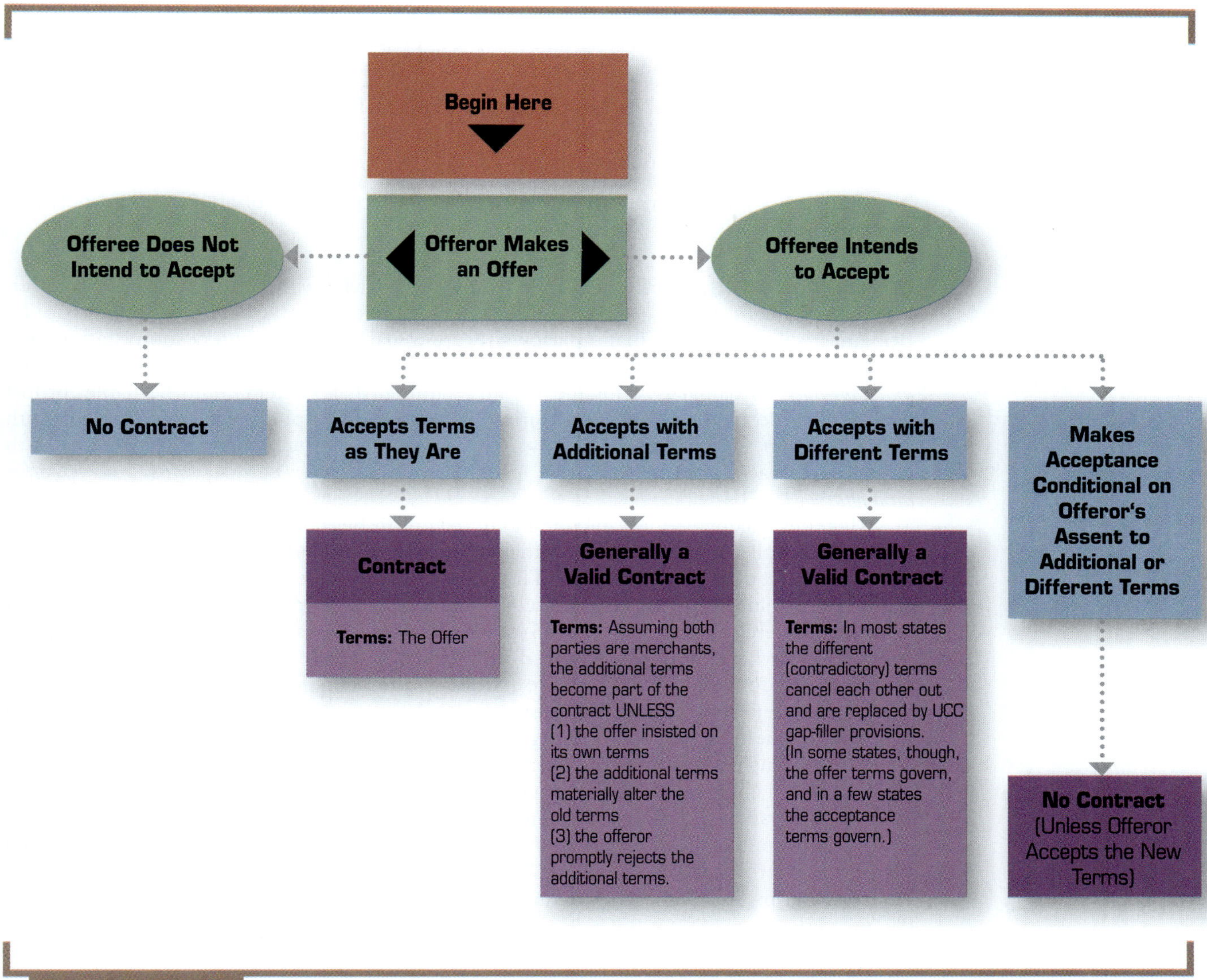

EXHIBIT 20.1 UCC §2-207.

Additional Terms. **Additional terms** are those that raise issues not covered in the offer. The "unhealthy pig" issue is an additional term because the offer said nothing about it. **When both parties are *merchants*, additional terms generally become part of the bargain.** Pet Shop's insistence on credit for sick guinea pigs is binding on Breeder. In three circumstances, however, additional terms *do not* bind the parties:

Additional terms
Terms that raise issues not covered in the offer.

- If the original offer *insisted on its own terms*. If Breeder offered the pets for sale "on these and no other terms," Pet Shop's additional language would not become part of their deal.
- If the additional terms *materially alter* the offer. Pet Shop's new language about credit for unhealthy animals is fairly uncontroversial. But suppose Pet Shop wrote back, "Breeder is liable for any illness of any animal in Pet Shop within 90 days of shipment

of guinea pigs." Breeder would potentially have to pay for a $500 iguana with pneumonia or a $6,000 parrot with gout. This is a material alteration of the bargain and is not part of the contract.

- If the offeror *promptly objects* to the new terms. If Breeder received Pet Shop's fax and immediately called up to say "No credit for unhealthy pigs," then Pet Shop's additional term is not part of their deal.

In all other circumstances, additional terms do become part of an agreement between merchants.

Different Terms. Different terms are terms that *contradict* those in the offer. Suppose Brilliant Corp. orders 1,500 cellular phones from Makem Co., for use by Brilliant's sales force. Brilliant places the order using a pre-printed form stating that the product is fully warranted for normal use and that seller is liable for compensatory *and consequential* damages. This means, for example, that Makem could be liable for lost profits if a salesman's phone fails during a lucrative sales pitch. Makem responds with its own memo stating that in the event of defective phones, Makem is liable only to repair or replace, and *is not liable for consequential damages, lost profits, or any other damages*.

Makem's acceptance has included a *different* term because its language contradicts the offer. Almost all courts would agree that the parties intended to reach an agreement and therefore the contract is enforceable. The question is, what are its terms? Is the full warranty of the offer included, or the very limited warranty of the acceptance? The majority of states hold that **different terms cancel each other out**. Neither party's language goes into the contract. But what then *are* the terms of the deal?

If the evidence indicates that the parties had orally agreed on the issue disputed in the forms, then the courts will ignore the contradictory writings and enforce the oral contract. **If there is no clear oral agreement, the Code supplies its own terms, called gap-fillers,** which cover prices, delivery dates and places, warranties, and other subjects. In the cellular phone case, the contradicting warranty provisions cancel each other out. The parties had not orally agreed on a warranty, so a court would enforce the Code's gap-filler warranty, which does permit recovery of compensatory and consequential damages. Therefore, Makem *would* be liable for lost profits. We outline most of the gap-filler terms in Chapter 11. Warranty provisions are analyzed in greater detail in Chapter 22.

In the following case, the Rhode Island Supreme Court seeks the fairest method of sorting out conflicting terms.

CODE PROVISIONS DISCUSSED IN THIS CASE

Issue	Relevant Code Section
1. Which are the terms of this agreement?	UCC §2-207: *Additional* terms generally but not always become part of the bargain. *Different* terms generally cancel each other out.
2. What is the Code's provision concerning delivery?	UCC §2-309: The time for shipment or delivery if not agreed upon is a reasonable time.
3. What is a "reasonable" delivery time?	UCC §1-204: A "reasonable" time depends on the nature, purpose, and circumstances of the action.

Superior Boiler Works, Inc. v. R. J. Sanders, Inc.

1998 R.I. LEXIS 153
Supreme Court of Rhode Island, 1998

Facts: R. J. Sanders, Inc., had a contract with the federal government to install the heating system at a federal prison camp. The company negotiated with Superior Boiler Works to purchase three large commercial units. On March 27, Superior sent a proposal to Sanders, offering to sell three boilers for a total of $156,000 and estimating time of delivery at four weeks. The parties exchanged further documents and held various discussions. Finally, on July 20, Sanders sent a "purchase order" for three boilers, agreeing to pay $145,827 and stating "Date required: 4 Weeks," that is, August 20. On August 6, Superior sent a "sales order," agreeing to sell the three boilers at that price, but providing a shipping date of October 1. This later delivery date forced Sanders to rent temporary boilers at a cost of $45,315. On October 1, Superior shipped the boilers, which arrived on October 5. Sanders sent a check in the amount of $100,000, claiming that Superior had delivered the boilers late and deducting the cost of its rental equipment. Superior sued for the additional $45,000 and moved for summary judgment, which the trial court granted. Sanders appealed, claiming that the contract had required Superior to deliver the boilers within four weeks.

Issue: ***Did Superior's October delivery breach the contract?***

Excerpts from Justice Flanders's Decision: Sanders' amended purchase order of July 20 and Superior's August 6 response agree exactly on the specifications and on the price of the boilers. The fact that these two documents disagree on one important term—the time for delivery—does not prevent the formation of a contract under the UCC because it is apparent from their subsequent conduct that both parties intended to be bound contractually. What becomes of the parties' conflicting positions on the shipment period (Sanders' specified four-week delivery versus Superior's stated October 1 shipping date) is a question that must be considered in light of section 2-207(2).

[The court mentioned that other states had responded in various ways to "different" terms, that is, those that conflict. Judge Flanders declared that Rhode Island would side with the majority and adopt the "knock-out" rule, meaning that conflicting terms knock each other out, leaving a hole in the contract that is filled by one of the Code's gap-filler provisions.] Here, the void relating to delivery time would be filled by Section 2-309, which reads, "The time for shipment or delivery ... if ... not agreed upon shall be a reasonable time."

Because of the UCC's gap-filling provisions, we recognize that this approach might result in the enforcement of a contract term that neither party agreed to and, in fact, in regard to which each party expressed an entirely different preference. We note in response to this concern that the offeror and the offeree both have the power to protect any term they deem critical by expressly making acceptance conditional on assent to that term. And as merchants, both parties should have been well aware that their dealings were subject to the UCC and to its various gap-filling provisions. In this case, because the two variant shipping-date terms cancel each other out, the amended purchase order and the August 6 sales order formed a contract that required the three boilers to be delivered within a reasonable period after August 6.

In the usual case the question of what constitutes a reasonable time under the UCC is one for the finder of fact to determine from the nature, the purpose, and the circumstances surrounding the transaction, including the parties' course of dealing, usages of trade in the pertinent industry, or the parties' course of performance. See [UCC §1-204(2). In this case, however, the only available evidence indicated that Superior's performance was reasonable, by industry standards.]

For the foregoing reasons the appeal is denied, and the Superior Court's judgment is affirmed.

EXAM Strategy

Question: Martin, a diamond wholesaler, writes Serge, a jewelry retailer, offering to sell 75 specified diamonds for $2 million. Martin's offer sheet specifies the price, quantity, date of delivery and other key terms. The sheet also states, "Offer is made on these terms and no other." Serge sends Martin his own purchase order, naming the diamonds, price and so forth, but adding a clause requiring any disputes to be settled by a diamond-industry arbitrator. In the diamond industry, arbitration by such a person is standard. Martin does not object to the arbitration clause. Martin delivers the gems but Serge refuses to pay the full price, claiming that many of the stones are of inferior quality. Martin sues for the balance due, but Serge insists that any dispute must be settled by arbitration. May Martin litigate, or must he arbitrate the case?

Strategy: Under the common law, there might not be a contract between these parties, because Serge added a new term. However, this agreement concerns the sale of goods, meaning that the UCC governs. Under UCC §2-207, when both parties are merchants (as they are here), additional terms become part of the contract except in three instances. Review those three instances, and apply them here.

Result: Additional terms become part of the agreement unless the original offeror insisted on its own terms, the new term materially alters the offer, or the offeror promptly rejects the new term. Martin's offer insisted on its own terms and Serge's arbitration clause does not become part of the agreement. Martin may litigate his dispute.

Open Terms: §§2-305 and 2-306

Open Prices

Under §2-305, the parties may conclude a contract even though they have not settled the price. Again, this is a change from the common law, which required certainty of such an important contract term. Under the Code, if the parties have not stated one, **the price is a reasonable price at the time of delivery.** A court will use market value and other comparable sales to determine what a reasonable price would have been. If the contract permits the buyer or seller to *determine* the price during contract performance, §2-305 requires that she do so in good faith, as the following case demonstrates.

CODE PROVISIONS DISCUSSED IN THIS CASE

Issue	Relevant Code Sections
1. May the parties form a binding agreement without specifying the price?	UCC §2-305(1): The parties may conclude a contract even though they have not settled the price.
2. May a contract permit one party to settle the price?	UCC §2-305(2): "A price to be fixed by the seller or by the buyer" requires that it be fixed in good faith.
3. What does *good faith* mean?	UCC §§1-201(19), 1-203 and 2-103: For *non-merchants*, good faith means honesty in fact. For a *merchant*, good faith means honesty in fact *plus* the exercise of reasonable commercial standards of fair dealing.

Mathis v. Exxon Corporation

302 F.3d 448
Fifth Circuit Court of Appeals, 2002

Facts: Exxon marketed gasoline to retailers in three ways. *Franchisees* (who owned local gas stations) were required to purchase a minimum number of gallons per month. Exxon set the price each month, known as the dealer tank wagon price (DTW). *Jobbers* (distributors who could resell to dealers) paid the "rack price," which was generally lower than the DTW. *Company-operated retail stores* (CORS) paid nothing, because Exxon owned them.

A group of 54 Texas franchisees sued, claiming that Exxon set their gasoline prices artificially high. The plaintiffs alleged that Exxon wanted to drive them out of business and replace their franchises with more profitable CORS. The evidence indicated that the franchisees' DTW was consistently higher than the rack price paid by jobbers. Many plaintiffs testified that their franchises had become unprofitable. One study showed that 62 percent of franchisees in Corpus Christi, Texas, were selling gas below the price they paid for it. Plaintiffs' expert testified that 75 percent of their competitors could buy gasoline at a lower price.

The plaintiffs argued that this evidence demonstrated that Exxon set the prices in bad faith. The jury agreed, awarding the plaintiffs $5.7 million, plus $2.3 million in attorney's fees. Exxon appealed.

Issue: ***Did Exxon set the prices in bad faith?***

Excerpts from Judge Smith's Decision: [UCC §2-305(2) rejects the idea that the seller may fix any price he wants.] The price must be fixed in good faith. Good faith includes observance of reasonable commercial standards of fair dealing in the trade if the party is a merchant. In the normal case a "posted price" or a future seller's or buyer's "given price," "price in effect," "market price," or the like satisfies the good faith requirement.

The franchisees here are alleging a breach of good faith grounded not in Exxon's failure to price in accord with an established schedule, but in its failure to set the price in good faith. Suits recognizing such a cause of action are rare, and with good reason: We would be ill-advised to consider a case to be outside the norm based only on an allegation of improper motive by the party setting the price.

Plaintiffs produced enough evidence to escape [the] "normal case" limitation. They showed, for example, that Exxon planned to replace a number of its franchises with CORS, that the DTW price was higher than the sum of the rack price and transportation, that Exxon prevented the franchisees from purchasing gas from jobbers, and that a number of franchisees were unprofitable or noncompetitive.

For example, one Exxon document stated that the company's "Marketing Strategy is to reduce Dealer stores (est. 30%)." Another document set forth Exxon's plans to reduce dealer stations in Houston from 95 to 45, and to increase CORS from 83 to 150. James Carter, the regional director of the Exxon/Mobil Fuels Marketing Company, testified that Exxon made more of a profit from a CORS than from an independent lessee store. These plans and observations were validated by the fact that the number of dealer stations steadily declined.

Further indication of plans to shift from dealer-lessees to CORS is shown by Exxon's dissatisfaction with outlets featuring service bays. Exxon documents showed that service bays—generally associated with lessee-dealer locations—were becoming less profitable, while stations with convenience stores—generally associated with CORS—were the wave of the future.

Exxon's bad faith, in this regard, is shown by the record. Facing the competition of self-service stations that were either selling food and other goods or had bare pumps with no overhead costs incurred in servicing vehicles, Exxon decided years ago that retail marketing through franchise dealers was becoming economically unsound. Although Exxon decided to move to CORS in Houston and jobbers in Corpus Christi, this decision was not communicated to its franchisees. Because of profit from their other sales, CORS could, and did, sell gas for less than the franchise dealers paid to Exxon for their gas. And the jobbers delivered Exxon gas to their dealers for less than Exxon franchisees were required to pay for their delivered gas, but Exxon prohibited its franchisees from buying at this lower price from the jobbers.

Accordingly, the jury's finding that Exxon breached its duty of good faith in setting the DTW price it charged the plaintiffs is not without foundation in the law or the evidence. As we have recounted, plaintiffs offered ample evidence tending to prove their version of price-setting.

[Affirmed.]

EXAM Strategy

Facts: Coffee Retailer sends a form to Cupper, ordering 100 cartons of specified coffee cups to be delivered the first of each month for six months. The order form says nothing about price. For three months, Cupper delivers on time and sends an invoice, which Retailer pays. On the fourth month, Cupper's invoice is 8 percent higher than before. Retailer refuses to pay the increase and informs Cupper that it will accept no more deliveries. Cupper sues. Retailer claims there was no enforceable contract. Cupper says there was a bargain and that it has the right to determine the price. Who is right?

Strategy: Retailer's offer included no price. Under the common law, the absence of such an essential term would mean there was no contract. However, these are goods, and under the UCC the parties can make an enforceable deal without specifying the price. This is a valid contract. The companies may, if they choose, permit one party to determine the price. Did they do so here? If so, is Cupper's conduct reasonable? If the parties did not allow one side to set the price, how would a court do so?

Result: This contract neither stated a price nor allowed one party to determine it. That means that the price is a reasonable one at the time of delivery. A court will use market value, and any comparable sales, to determine the price.

Output and Requirements Contracts

Under §2-306, an output contract obligates the seller to sell all of his output to the buyer, who agrees to accept it. Suppose Joel has a small plant in which he manufactures large plants; that is, handcrafted artificial flowers and trees, made of silk and other expensive materials. Joel isn't sure how many he can produce in a year, but wants a guaranteed market. He makes an output contract with Yolanda, in which he promises to sell the entire output of his plant, and she agrees to buy it all.

A requirements contract is the reverse, obligating a buyer to purchase all his needed goods from the seller. Joel might sign a requirements contract with Worm Express, agreeing to buy from Worm all the silk he needs. Both output and requirements contracts are valid under the Code, although they create certain problems. By definition, the exact quantity of goods is not specified. But then how much may one party demand? Is there any upper or lower limit?

The UCC requires that the parties in an output or requirements contract make their demands in good faith. For example, in a requirements contract, a buyer may not suddenly increase her demand far beyond what the parties expected merely because there has been a market change. Suppose the price of silk skyrockets. Joel's requirements contract obligates Worm Express to sell him all the silk he needs. Could Joel demand 10 times the silk he had anticipated, knowing he could resell it at a big profit to other manufacturers? No. That would be bad faith. Come on, Joel, play by the rules.

May the buyer *reduce* his demand far below what the parties anticipated? Yes, as long as he makes the reduction in good faith.

The following case involves several issues, including a claim that an output contract existed. Some contracts are meticulously written by veteran lawyers who use deliberate and precise legal terms in every part of the agreement. Of course, agreements are not always done so carefully. See what sense you can make of the "Weaner Pig Purchase Agreement."

CODE PROVISIONS DISCUSSED IN THIS CASE

Issue	Relevant Code Section
Which law governs this agreement?	UCC 2-102
Is there a writing sufficient to indicate a contract?	UCC 2-201
Was an output contract formed?	UCC 2-306

You be the Judge

Lohman v. Wagner

862 A.2d 1042
Court of Special Appeals of Maryland, 2004

Facts: Legal research can take you in odd directions. Today, for example, we learn that a "weaner pig" is a very young pig that has just been weaned from its mother. You must raise and sell a lot of them to make a living. Farmers who raise pigs to full size need to sell fewer animals to get by.

Farmer Charles Lohman talked extensively with John Wagner about raising weaner pigs for a new "pork network" that Wagner, the owner of Swine Services, was thinking of putting together. Lohman eventually decided to join Wagner and convert his pig farm to one that specialized in raising weaner pigs. He needed to borrow money to remodel his farm, and he needed to convince his bankers that, if they loaned him the necessary money, he would be in a reasonable position to repay them.

He told Wagner that he "would need something to show his banker." Wagner faxed over a document with several blanks entitled "Weaner Pig Purchase Agreement." It said, in part, "PRODUCER agrees to supply _ weaner pigs weekly." When he received the fax, Lohman wrote "300" in the blank. After showing the fax to his banker, Lohman was able to secure his loan. He never sent Wagner a copy of the document with the blank filled in.

For awhile, everyone was happy. Lohman shipped weaner pigs to Wagner and was paid $28 each for them. But eventually, problems arose. The price Wagner offered for weaner pigs dropped to $18, and Wagner never assembled the promised pork network, which Lohman argued would have helped to boost prices. Lohman sued Wagner for breach of contract.

The trial court found that the agreement did not meet the UCC's requirement that a quantity term be included, that it was unenforceable, and that Lohman was entitled to nothing. Lohman appealed.

You Be the Judge: ***Does Lohman have an enforceable agreement with Wagner?***

Argument for Lohman: Your honor, I'm not a ham, and I won't "boar" you with a long story. Our arguments, briefly stated, are these.

First, the UCC's statute of frauds, and its requirement that a quantity term be included, should not apply. This agreement is essentially one for services, and not for goods. My client furnishes housing for weaner pigs, labors to raise them, and ships them to the defendant. His services are the largest part of this contract.

Even if this contract is deemed to be a sale of goods, there is a quantity term included in the Weaner Pig Purchase Agreement—300. The number was entered by my client as a good-faith estimate of the number of animals he could produce.

In any event, UCC 2-306 does not require a quantity term in this case. This agreement was an output contract. Lohman sold every weaner pig he produced to Wagner, and Wagner accepted and paid for them. Output contracts, by definition, do not include specific quantity terms; they merely obligate a seller to sell all of his output to the buyer.

This case amounts to nothing more or less than a greedy man trying to reap what he did not sow and to use legal technicalities to hog all the profits for himself.

Argument for Wagner: My counterpart has managed to make several nifty pig-related references in his argument, but nevertheless, no contract exists. The

UCC does apply to this agreement, because pigs are clearly goods. Most products require some labor to assemble and bring to market. Someone "labored" to make my shoes, my necktie, and my pen. But all are goods.

In a UCC contract, a quantity must be written by the defendants, but here the "300" was written by the plaintiff. It was never communicated to my client. He never agreed to it, or even had a chance to review it. The same holds true for the claim that this is an output contract. My client never agreed to buy all the pigs that Lohman produced.

My opponent is grasping at straws. Which pigs eat. I think. Get it? Oh, forget it ...

Modification

Another way in which the UCC is pro-contract and pro-business is in its treatment of contract modifications. If two sides have a contract and seek to make changes, are the changes enforceable?

Example 1. Being the best at almost anything pays well, and soccer is no exception. Cristiano Ronaldo's contract with Real Madrid runs through 2015 and averages a whopping $22 million per season. Assume that this year, he leads Real to the fabled treble—a La Liga championship, a victory in the Copa del Rey, and a win in the Champions League. Afterward, the club offers him a raise to $28 million per season through 2015, and Ronaldo accepts. If Spanish law is the same as American law, does the team have a legal obligation to pay the extra millions? No.

This is a services contract, and not a sale of goods. Therefore, common law principles would apply, and they require new consideration for contract modifications to stand. Since Ronaldo did not agree to play any additional seasons or give any other new value to the team, no consideration exists.

We hate to leave out fans of Spain's other big club, so for the next example, we will pay our 65 euros for a ticket on the AVE train and settle in for a three-hour, 500-kilometer trip eastward to Barcelona.

Example 2. FC Barcelona is planning "Lionel Messi Bobblehead Day," and the team orders 10,000 units for the occasion. Unfortunately, the boat carrying the shipment from China is boarded by Somali pirates, who are, it turns out, Barca supporters. The entire shipment is stolen, and the headlines read, "*Trade Hobbled! Pirates Gobble Bobbles!*"

The manufacturer calls the team and asks for a three-week extension on the original delivery deadline. The team is very understanding, agrees to the delay, and reschedules the promotion for a later game. Is this modification which extends the delivery deadline now a valid part of the contract? Yes.

In §2-209, the UCC does away with the consideration requirement for changes to contracts, so long as both sides agree to the modification. In this example, no consideration exists to support the extended deadline because the manufacturer gets all the benefit, and the team gets nothing. But, that does not create a problem in enforcing the new deal.

Parties make a contract attempting to control their futures. But one party's certainty can be undercut by the ease with which the other party may obtain a modification. Section 2-209 acknowledges this tension by enabling the parties to limit changes. The UCC allows the parties to modify some contracts orally, but **they may agree to prohibit oral modifications and insist that all modifications be in writing and signed. Between merchants, such a clause is valid. But if either party is *not* a merchant, such a clause is valid only if the non-merchant *separately* signs it.**

Once again the Code gives greater protection to non-merchants than to merchants. Two merchants may agree, as part of their bargain, that any future modifications will be valid only if written and signed. But this limitation on modifications is not valid against a non-merchant unless she separately signs the limiting clause itself. Suppose a furniture retailer orders 200 beds from a manufacturer. The retailer's order form requires any modifications to be in writing. The manufacturer initials the retailer's form at the bottom. The parties have a valid agreement and no oral modifications will be enforced. But suppose the retailer sells a bed to a customer. The sales form also bars oral modifications. That prohibition is void unless the customer separately signs it.

EXAM Strategy

Question: Dale turns 18. For his birthday, he gets $500 cash and his grandmother's ancient station wagon. And yes, it is the kind with wood paneling on the side. Dale can't do much about how the car looks, but he decides that he can at least make it sound awesome. So, he immediately takes the car to Big Mike's Custom Stereo.

At Big Mike's, Dale makes a verbal agreement to buy an amplifier and two Rockford Fosgate speakers and to have them installed at a cost of $499. The amp and speakers come to $420, and the installation charge is $79. He decides to have them installed while he waits.

After an hour, a clerk finds him and says, "Hey, man, we're out of stock on those speakers. But I can get you some Alpines right now—same size, same price, just as loud." Dale is eager to drive out with a new system, and agrees to the speaker substitution. Moments later, Dale finds the clerk and says, "Wait, I'm not sure about all of this. I don't think I want to buy any of it after all." Can Dale get his money back, or is he stuck with his purchases?

Strategy: Under UCC principles, a contract is considered to be for the sale of goods if the value of the items far exceeds the cost of the labor (installation), and the contract's predominant purpose is a sale of goods. The UCC statute of Frauds does not apply to a transaction under $500. A contract can be modified without consideration.

Result: The UCC governs this contract because the speakers are much more expensive than the labor. The contract does not have to be in writing because it is for less than $500. The agreement to use Alpine speakers rather than Rockford Fosgates is enforceable, even without consideration for the change. Dale will have to live with the deal, including the Alpine speakers.[4]

[4]Bonus point from chapter 14 material: Since this is Dale's 18th birthday, if he were even one day younger, he could back out of this deal on the grounds that he is a minor and has formed a voidable agreement.

The following table concludes this chapter with an illustration of the Code's impact on the common law.

SELECTED CODE PROVISIONS THAT CHANGE THE COMMON LAW

Issue	Common Law Rule	UCC Sec.	UCC Rule	Example
Contract formation	Offer must be followed by acceptance that shows meeting of the minds on all important terms.	§2-204 and §2-305	Contract can be made in any manner sufficient to show agreement; moment of making not critical; one or more terms, including the price, may be left open.	Tilly writes Meg, "I need a new van for my delivery company." Meg delivers a van and Tilly starts to use it. Under the common law, there is no contract, because no price was ever mentioned; under the UCC, the writing plus the conduct show an intention to contract (2-204). The price is a *reasonable* one (2-305).
Writing requirement	All essential terms must be in writing.	§2-201	Any writing is sufficient if it indicates a contract; terms may be omitted or misstated; "merchant" exception can create a contract enforceable against a party who receives the writing and does nothing within 10 days.	Douglas, a car dealer, signs and sends to Michael, another dealer, a memo saying, "Confirming our deal for your blue Rolls." Michael reads it but ignores it; 10 days later Douglas has satisfied the statute of frauds under the UCC's merchant exception.
Added terms in acceptance	An acceptance that adds or changes any term is a counteroffer.	§2-207	Additional or different terms are not necessarily counteroffers; their presence does not prevent a contract from being formed, and in some cases the new terms will become a part of the bargain.	Roberts sends a pre-printed form to Julia, offering to buy 25 computers and stating a price; Julia responds with her own pre-printed form, accepting the offer but adding a term that balances unpaid after 30 days incur a finance charge. The additional term is not a counteroffer; there is a valid contract; and the finance charge is part of the bargain.
Modification	A modification is valid only if supported by new consideration.	§2-209	A modification needs no consideration to be binding.	Martin, a computer manufacturer, agrees to sell Steve, a retailer, 500 computers at a specified price, including delivery. The next day Martin learns that his delivery costs have gone up 20%; he calls Steve, who faxes a note agreeing to pay 15% extra. Under the common law, the modification would be void; under the Code, it is enforceable.

Chapter Conclusion

The Uniform Commercial Code (UCC) enables parties to create a contract quickly. While this can be helpful in a fast-paced business world, it also places responsibility on executives. Informal conversations may cause at least one party to conclude that it has a binding agreement—and the law may agree.

Exam Review

1. **UNIFORM COMMERCIAL CODE** The Code is designed to modernize commercial law and make it uniform throughout the country. (pp. 453–455)

2. **SALE OF GOODS** Article 2 applies to the sale of goods, which are movable things other than money and investment securities. (pp. 456–457)

Question: While shopping at his local mall, Fred buys an iPad for $499, a barbecue grill for $509, and then pays $25 to have his watchband cleaned. Which of Fred's transactions are governed by Article 2 of the UCC?

Strategy: To answer this question, you must identify the transactions that amount to a sale of goods. Land and buildings are not goods. Neither are money and securities, but other moveable physical objects are. Also, be sure not to confuse the question "Does Article 2 apply?" with the question "Does this agreement need to be in writing?" (See the "Result" at the end of this section)

3. **LEASING** Article 2A governs the leasing of goods. (p. 454)

4. **MIXED CONTRACTS** In a mixed contract involving goods and services, the UCC applies if the predominant purpose is the sale of goods. (p. 457)

5. **MERCHANTS** A merchant is someone who routinely deals in the particular goods involved, or who appears to have special knowledge or skill in those goods, or who uses agents with special knowledge or skill. The UCC frequently holds a merchant to a higher standard of conduct than a non-merchant. (p. 457)

6. **GOOD FAITH** The UCC imposes a duty of good faith in the performance of all contracts. (pp. 457–458)

7. **UNCONSCIONABILITY** A contract is unconscionable if it is shockingly one-sided and fundamentally unfair. A court is much likelier to use unconscionability to protect a consumer than a corporation. (pp. 457–458)

EXAM Strategy

Question: Jim Dan, Inc. owned a golf course that had trouble with crabgrass. Jim Dan bought 20 bags of Scotts Pro Turf Goosegrass/Crabgrass Control for $835 and applied it to the greens. The Pro Turf caused over $36,000 in damage to the greens. Jim Dan sued Scotts. Scotts defended by claiming that it sold the Pro Turf with a clearly written, easy-to-read disclaimer that stated that in the event of damage, the buyer's only remedy would be a refund of the purchase price. Jim Dan, Inc. argued that the clause was unconscionable. Please rule.

Strategy: There are two steps to deciding an issue of unconscionability. First, does the contract involve a consumer, or is this an agreement between two businesses? Second, is the agreement shockingly one-sided? (See the "Result" at the end of this section.)

8. **FORMATION** UCC §2-204 permits the parties to form a contract in any manner that shows agreement. (pp. 458–460)

9. **WRITING** For the sale of goods worth $500 or more, UCC §2-201 requires some writing that indicates an agreement. Terms may be omitted or misstated, but the contract will be enforced only to the extent of the quantity stated. (p. 460)

EXAM Strategy

Question: To satisfy the UCC statute of frauds regarding the sale of goods, which of the following must generally be in writing?

a. Designation of the parties as buyer and seller

b. Delivery terms

c. Quantity of the goods

d. Warranties to be made

Strategy: Okay, this may be overkill. But the question illustrates two basic points of UCC law: first, the Code allows a great deal of flexibility in the formation of contracts. Second, there is one term for which no flexibility is allowed. Make sure you know which it is. (See the "Result" at the end of this section.)

10. **MERCHANT'S EXCEPTION** When two merchants make an oral contract, and one sends a confirming memo to the other within a reasonable time, and the memo is sufficiently definite that it could be enforced against the sender herself, then the merchant who receives it will also be bound unless he objects within 10 days. (pp. 461–462)

11. **ADDITIONAL TERMS** UCC §2-207 governs an acceptance that does not "mirror" the offer. *Additional terms* usually, but not always, become part of the contract. *Different terms* contradict a term in the offer. When that happens, most courts reject both parties' proposals and rely on gap-filler terms. (pp. 462–464)

Question: Cookie Co. offered to sell Distrib Markets 20,000 pounds of cookies at $1.00 per pound, subject to certain specified terms for delivery. Distrib replied in writing as follows: "We accept your offer for 20,000 pounds of cookies at $1.00 per pound, weighing scale to have valid city certificate." Under the UCC:

a. A contract was formed between the parties.

b. A contract will be formed only if Cookie agrees to the weighing scale requirement.

c. No contract was formed because Distrib included the weighing scale requirement in its reply.

d. No contract was formed because Distrib's reply was a counteroffer.

Strategy: Distrib's reply included a new term. That means it is governed by UCC §2-207. Is the new term an additional term or a different term? An additional term goes beyond what the offeror stated. Additional terms become a part of the contract except in three specified instances. A different term contradicts one made by the offeror. Different terms generally cancel each other out. (See the "Result" at the end of this section.)

12. PRICE Under UCC §2-305 a contract is enforceable even if the price is not stated. In such cases the price must be reasonable. (pp. 466–468)

13. MODIFICATION UCC §2-209 permits contracts to be modified even if there is no consideration. The parties may prohibit oral modifications, but such a clause is ineffective against a non-merchant unless she signed it. (pp. 470–471)

2. Result: The purchases of the iPad and the barbecue grill are covered by Article 2 of the UCC. Both agreements involve goods. $500 is a figure that is relevant to whether the statute of frauds applies to the agreements, but it is not material to the threshold question of whether Article 2 applies in the first place. All sales of goods, from pencils to Ferarris, fall under Article 2.

The watch cleaning is a service, and not a sale of goods. It is not governed by Article 2.

7. Result: This is a bargain between two businesses, and courts rarely find clauses in such agreements unconscionable. The assumption is that sophisticated businesspeople understand what they are getting into and are able to protect themselves. If Jim Dan could run a golf course, the company was sophisticated enough to understand the simple disclaimer in this contract. Scotts wins.

9. Result: (D). The contract will be enforced only to the extend of the quantity stated.

11. Result: The "valid city certificate" phrase raises a new issue; it does not contradict anything in Cookie's offer. That means it is an additional term, and becomes part of the deal unless Cookie insisted on its own terms, the additional term materially alters the offer, or Cookie promptly rejects it. Cookie did not insist on its terms, this is a minor addition, and Cookie never rejected it. The new term is part of a valid contract and the answer is "a."

Multiple-Choice Questions

1. For a contract governed by the UCC sales article, which one of the following statements is correct?

(a) Merchants and non-merchants are treated alike.

(b) The contract may involve the sale of any type of personal property.

(c) The obligations of the parties to the contract must be performed in good faith.

(d) The contract must involve the sale of goods for a price of $500 or more.

2. Which of the following transactions is *not* governed by Article 2 of the UCC?

(a) Purchasing an automobile for $35,000

(b) Leasing an automobile worth $35,000

(c) Purchasing a stereo worth $501

(d) Purchasing a stereo worth $499

3. Fred assembles computers in his garage and sells them. He makes an agreement with Alpha Company under which Alpha will deliver 100 keyboards. The agreement does not specify when payment is due. Which of the following is true?

(a) Fred has no obligation to pay, because there was no "meeting of the minds" and no contract was formed

(b) Fred must pay within 10 days of making the agreement.

(c) Fred must pay within 10 days of accepting the keyboards.

(d) Fred must pay within a commercially reasonable time.

4. Under the UCC statute of frauds, a contract must be signed by the __________ to count as being "in writing." Also, the __________ of the goods must be written.

(a) plaintiff; price

(b) plaintiff; quantity

(c) defendant; price

(d) defendant; quantity

5. Assume that a contract is modified. New consideration must be present for the modification to be binding if the deal is governed by which of the following?

(a) The common law

(b) The UCC

(c) Both A and B

(d) Neither A nor B

Essay Questions

1. The Massachusetts Bay Transit Authority (MBTA) awarded the Perini Corp. a large contract to rehabilitate a section of railroad tracks. The work involved undercutting the existing track, removing the ballast and foundation, rebuilding the track, and disposing of the old material. Perini solicited an offer from Atlantic Track &

Turnout Co. for Atlantic to buy whatever salvageable material Perini removed. Perini estimated the quantity of salvageable material that would be available. Atlantic offered to purchase "all available" material over the course of Perini's deal with the MBTA, and Perini accepted. But three months into the project, the MBTA ran short of money and told Perini to stop the undercutting part of the project. That was the work that made Perini its profit, so Perini requested that the MBTA terminate the agreement, which the agency did. By that point Perini had delivered to Atlantic only about 15 percent of the salvageable material that it had estimated. Atlantic sued. What kind of contract do the parties have? Who should win and why?

2. Hasbro used to manufacture a toy called "Wonder World Aquarium." The toy included a powder that, when mixed with water, formed a gel that filled a plastic aquarium. Children could then place plastic fish in the aquarium and create underwater scenes. Cloud Corporation supplied the powder to Hasbro. The toy sold poorly, and Hasbro's need for the powder diminished.

The two companies discussed changing the powder's formula. Cloud believed the conversation amounted to an indication that Hasbro would continue to buy powder, so it produced large quantities. Although it did not receive an order from Hasbro, Cloud sent an order acknowledgment for 9.5 million packets to Hasbro. Hasbro made no objection to it.

Did the order acknowledgment creat an enforceable agreement? What specific facts determine your answer?

3. Nina owns a used car lot. She signs and sends a fax to Seth, a used car wholesaler who has a huge lot of cars in the same city. The fax says, "Confirming our agrmt—I pick any 15 cars fr yr lot—30% below blue book." Seth reads the fax, laughs, and throws it away. Two weeks later, Nina arrives and demands to purchase 15 of Seth's cars. Is he obligated to sell?

4. The Brugger Corp. owned a farm, operated by Jason Weimer, who acted as the company's business agent. Tri-Circle, Inc. was a farm equipment company. On behalf of Brugger, Weimer offered to buy from Tri-Circle certain equipment for use on the farm. Tri-Circle accepted the offer, using a pre-printed form. The form included a finance charge for late payment. Weimer's offer had said nothing about finance charges, but he made no objection to the new term. Tri-Circle supplied the farm equipment but later alleged that Brugger had refused to pay for $12,000 worth of the supplies. Tri-Circle sued. In deciding whether Tri-Circle was entitled to finance charges, the court first inquired whether Brugger, Weimer, and Tri-Circle were merchants. Why did it look into that issue? *Were* they merchants?

5. ***YOU BE THE JUDGE* WRITING PROBLEM** Brewster manufactured plastic bottles. Dial made personal care products at many plants around the country, including one in Salem, Virginia. The companies agreed that Dial would purchase from Brewster all of the plastic bottles it needed for its Salem factory. Dial estimated its requirements for one year at 7,850,000 bottles, but added a clause stating that "quantities are estimated only and do not bind Dial to purchase any minimum quantity." A few months later, Dial concluded that its Salem plant was unprofitable. The company closed the factory and notified Brewster that it would buy no bottles at all. Brewster sued. Did Dial have the right to reduce its orders to zero? **Argument for Brewster:** The parties had a clear contract for a massive number of bottles. Dial knew that this contract was extremely important to Brewster. Although Dial had some right to adjust its orders, it had no right to reduce them to zero. **Argument for Dial:** The issue is whether Dial acted in good faith. It did. The company had a legitimate reason for closing the factory—it was losing money—and with no factory it certainly did not need any bottles.

Discussion Questions

Apply the following facts to the next two questions.

The publication of the original UCC in 1952 sparked an expansion of the statute of frauds in the United States to cover sales of goods of $500 or more. At about the same time (in 1954), the British Parliament repealed its longstanding statute of frauds as applied to sales of goods. Some have argued that we should scrap UCC §2-201 on the grounds that it encourages misdealing as much as it prevents fraud. Consider the following two hypotheticals:

(In the United States) Johnny is looking at a used Chevy Tahoe. He knows that the $7,000 price is a good one, but he wants to go online and see if he can find an even better deal. In the 20 minutes he has been with the car's current owner, the owner has received three phone calls about the car. Johnny wants to make sure that no one else buys the car while he is thinking the deal over, so he makes a verbal agreement to buy the car and shakes the seller's hand. He knows that because of the statute of frauds and the fact that nothing is in writing, he does not yet have any enforceable obligation to buy the car.

(In the United Kingdom) Nigel sells used Peugeots in Liverpool. When he senses interest from customers, he aggressively badgers them until they verbally commit to buy. If the customers later get cold feet and try to back out of the deal, he holds them to the verbal contracts. Because there is no longer a UCC-style statute of frauds in Britain, the buyers are stuck.

1. Rate the degree to which you believe Johnny and Nigel acted wrongfully. Did one behave more wrongfully than the other? If so, which one, and why?

2. Do you think that the UCC statute of frauds as it currently exists is more likely to prevent fraud, or is it more likely to encourage misunderstandings and deception? Why? Overall, is it sensible to require that purchases of big-ticket items be in writing before they are final?

3. The Uniform Commercial Code was written by a group of scholars and adopted by elected state legislators. But many contracts that do not involve a sale of goods are still governed by old common-law principles that have been created by judges over a period of centuries. Who makes for better lawmakers—judges or legislators? Do you prefer the way in which common-law principles or UCC rules were created?

4. Under UCC §2-207, "added terms" in an acceptance can become part of a contract between merchants. Does this seem reasonable to you? Are businesses likely to take advantage of it?

5. This chapter revisits the idea of unconscionability. Courts will sometimes refuse to enforce deals that are, as UCC §2-302 states it, "shocking and fundamentally unfair".

Consider the following two cases. In each, an electronics store sells an HDTV with a fair market value of $600 for $1500.

(a) Sale #1 is made to Ann. She has a terrible credit score, and is willing to pay $1500 because the store offers to finance the TV, and she has no other available credit.

(b) Sale #2 is made to Franklin J. Moneypenny, a very wealthy investment banker, on Christmas Eve. He knows the price is much too high, but he is in a big hurry to finish his last minute shopping.

In both cases, the consumers paid 2.5 times the fair value of the TV. In your opinion, is either transaction unconscionable? If so, why? If not, why not?

CHAPTER 21

Ownership and Risk

© Stas Volik/Shutterstock.com

He drove his truck fast along the rough country road, hurrying through the shadows of the Cascade Mountains, passing close to the Rogue River. The door panel, freshly painted, read "Ernest Jenkins, Cattle Buyer." Spinning the wheel hard left, he drove through an impressive gate and under a wooden sign which read "Double Q Ranch." He knew the ranch by reputation and quickly saw that it was prosperous—a good place for a man like him to do business.

He introduced himself to Kate Vandermeer, the Double Q's business manager, and expressed an interest in buying 300 head of cattle. Vandermeer and the man mounted horses and rode out to inspect the herd. Vandermeer noticed that his boots were brand new and that he rode awkwardly.

Vandermeer noticed that his boots were brand new and that he rode awkwardly.

He was satisfied with the cattle, so the two bargained, sitting on horseback and looking into the sunset. Vandermeer started at $310,000 and was surprised at how quickly they reached an agreement, at $285,000, a price she considered excellent. They agreed that Vandermeer would deliver the cattle by truck, in one week, in a nearby town. He would pay with a cashier's check and take possession of the cattle and all ownership documents, such as brand inspection certificates and veterinarian's certificates. Back at the ranch, Vandermeer offered him a drink, but he said he had to hurry to another appointment.

The next week, right on schedule, he arrived on Thursday and presented his cashier's check for the full amount. When they had transferred the livestock, Vandermeer suggested they talk over some future business, but he was again in a rush. They shook hands and parted, the man heading due east, fast.

The Double Q's bank sent the cashier's check for collection but learned early the following week that it was forged. Vandermeer called the State Police, who traced the man's movements to the state line. Three weeks later and 1,600 miles east, the FBI located the cattle, with the prominent "QQ" brand, in stockyards in Omaha. Ned Munson had purchased the cattle from the man for $225,000, which he considered a bargain. He had paid with a cashier's check. Ernest Jenkins, of course, had disappeared—literally. The truck's freshly painted door now read, "Ted J. Pringle, Grain Merchant," and it was parked a long, long way from Omaha.

Legal Interest

Who owns the cows? The Double Q wanted its cattle back or $285,000. If Munson was foolish enough to pay money to a thief, that wasn't the ranch's problem. But Ned Munson claimed the cows were his. He had paid a fair price to a man who appeared to own them. If Vandermeer was so foolish as to give up the cattle to a con artist, let the ranch suffer the consequences. The Double Q sued. Both parties to this lawsuit are unhappy, but fortunately for us, they have illustrated the theme for our chapter: When two parties claim a conflicting legal interest in particular goods, *who wins?* Who obtains the law's protection? These are disputes over *conflicting interests in goods.*

An interest is a legal right in something. More than one party can have an interest in particular goods. Suppose you lease a new car from a dealer, agreeing to pay $400 per month for three years. Several parties will have legal interests in the car. The dealer still *owns* the car—interest number one. At the end of three years, the dealer gets it back. For three years, you have the *use* of the car—interest number two. You may use the car for all normal purposes, and you are obligated to make monthly payments. Your payments go to a finance agency, which has made an arrangement with the dealer to obtain the right to your $400 monthly payment. The finance agency has a *security interest* in the car—interest number three. If you fail to pay on time, the finance company has the right to repossess your car. If you take the car to a garage for maintenance, the garage has *temporary possession* of the car—interest number four. The garage has the right to keep the car locked up overnight, to work on it, and to test-drive it. Sometimes legal interests clash, and it is those conflicts we look at here.

Often the parties will claim ownership, each arguing that his interest is stronger than the other's. But in this chapter, we also consider cases where each party argues that the *other* one owns the goods. Suppose a seller manufactures products for a buyer, but while the goods are being shipped, they are destroyed in a fire. The seller may argue that it no longer owned the goods, and the fire is the buyer's misfortune. But the buyer will claim it had not yet acquired the items.

In other cases, a *third party* will be involved. You pay $30,000 cash to buy a new car and expect to pick it up in three days. But the day before you arrive, the dealer's bank seizes all of the cars on the lot, claiming the dealer has defaulted on loans. Now the fight over legal interest is between you and the bank, with the dealer a relatively passive observer.

In the cattle case, three parties had a legal interest in the goods. The Double Q ranch originally had valid **title** to the cattle, meaning the normal rights of ownership. Ernest Jenkins, the con artist, acquired a lesser interest. His contract with Double Q was fraudulent because Jenkins intended to cheat the ranch. Nonetheless, he did have an agreement. He obtained **voidable title**, meaning limited rights in the goods, inferior to those of the owner.[1] Finally, Ned Munson makes a claim to the cattle based on his payment and his possession of the cows and all documents.

Voidable title
Limited rights in goods, inferior to those of the owner.

The court will use various sections of the Uniform Commercial Code (UCC) to determine who keeps the cows and who ultimately bears the loss. Ned Munson should

[1]We discuss voidability in detail in Chapter 14, on capacity and consent.

win the cattle. He was acting in good faith and a commercially reasonable manner when he bought the cows from a man who appeared to be a lawful cattle buyer. The Double Q must bear the loss. If, however, the Double Q can convince a court that Munson acted irresponsibly because he had specific grounds for suspecting Jenkins, the court might order Munson to pay for the cattle.[2]

Ethics As we look at this issue and others like it, ask yourself whether the UCC rules and the court decisions accomplish two sensible goals: (1) to be fair to innocent parties and (2) to encourage reasonable business practices. Both Munson and the Double Q were innocent parties. Jenkins was the bad guy. Why let Munson keep the livestock? Because he probably did all that a reasonable businessperson should do in buying cattle. He paid a fair (though low) price to a man who had all the normal ownership documents. The law *could* place a greater burden on Munson and require, for example, that he investigate Jenkins's background. The law *could* force Munson to thoroughly check the history of the cattle and find out how Jenkins acquired them. But such rules would hogtie the cattle industry. Most sales are legitimate; cattle ranchers and buyers must be able to buy and sell quickly, responding to market conditions and opportunities for profit.

Notice that in this case and most others, the UCC focuses on basic fairness and sensible business practices. Munson wins because he acted reasonably and in good faith, not simply because he happens to hold certain certificates to the animals. The Code's authors have labored to get away from legal formalities and give results that make sense.

Identification, Title, and Insurable Interest

Historically, courts settled disputes about legal interest by looking at one thing: title. But the drafters of the UCC concluded that "title" was too abstract an answer for the assorted practical questions that arose. It sometimes could be hard to prove exactly who did have title, and it made no sense to settle a wide variety of business problems with one legal idea. Today, title is only one of several issues that a court will use to resolve conflicting interests in goods. *Identification* and *insurable interest* have become more important, and title has diminished in significance. We can begin to understand all three doctrines if we examine how title passes from seller to buyer.

Existence and Identification

Title in goods can pass from one person to another only if the goods exist and have been identified to the contract.

Existence

Goods must exist before title can pass.[3] Although most goods do exist when people buy and sell them, some have not yet come into being, such as crops to be grown later or goods that have not yet been manufactured. A farmer may contract to sell corn even before it is planted, but title to the corn cannot pass until it actually exists.

---

[2]For a cattle case that raises these and other issues, see *Rudiger Charolais Ranches v. Van De Graaf Ranches*, 994 F.2d 670, 1993 U.S. App. LEXIS 12412 (9th Cir. 1993).
[3]UCC §2-105(2).

Identification

Goods must be identified to the contract before title can pass.[4] This means that the parties must have designated the specific goods being sold. Often, identification is obvious. If Dealer agrees to sell to Buyer a 60-foot yacht with identification number AKX472, the parties have identified the goods. But suppose Paintco agrees to sell Brushworks 1,000 gallons of white base paint at a specified price. Paintco has 25,000 gallons in its warehouse. Title cannot pass until Paintco identifies the specific gallons that will go to Brushworks.

The parties may agree in their contract how and when they will identify the goods.[5] They are free to identify them to the contract in any way they want. Paintco and Brushworks might agree, for example, that within one week of signing the sales agreement, Paintco will mark appropriate gallons. If the gallons are stored 50 to a crate, then Paintco will have a worker stick a "Brushworks" label on 20 crates. Once the label is on, the goods are identified to the contract.

If the parties do not specify any particular method, identification will occur according to these rules:

- Identification occurs when the parties enter into a contract if the agreement describes specific goods that already exist. If the Dealer agrees to sell a yacht and the parties include the ID number in their contract, the goods are identified (even though the parties never use the term "identify").
- For unborn animals, identification generally takes place when they are conceived; for crops, identification normally happens when they are planted.
- For other goods, identification occurs when the seller marks, ships, or in some other way indicates the *exact* goods that are going to the buyer.[6]

EXAM *Strategy*

Question: Arielle, an artist, has 25 hand-painted room screens in her studio. She contracts to sell five of them to Retailer for $5,000 each. The contract allows Arielle to choose which five she will sell. Arielle moves five screens from her studio to a warehouse, but a week later, a fire destroys the building and its contents. Two insurance companies dispute whether title to the screens has passed to Retailer. The warehouse insurer claims the goods were identified and title passed; Retailer's insurer says the goods were not identified and title never passed. The contract says nothing about identification. Have the goods been identified?

Strategy: Title cannot pass until the goods have been identified to the contract. Identification can occur in three ways: the parties describe specific goods that already exist; animals are conceived or crops planted; or the seller marks, ships, or otherwise indicates which are going to the buyer. Did any of those things happen?

---

[4]UCC §2-401(1).
[5]UCC §2-501(1).
[6]UCC §2-501.

Result: The parties never described the goods. The goods are neither animals nor crops. However, when Arielle moved five of the screens to the warehouse, she "indicated which goods were going to the buyer." The goods were identified.

Passing of Title

Once goods exist and are identified to the contract, ownership can pass from one person to another. **Title may pass in any manner on which the parties agree (UCC §2-401).** Once again, the Code allows the parties to control their affairs with commonsense decisions. The parties can agree, for example, that title passes when the goods leave the manufacturer's factory, or when they reach the shipper who will transport them, or at any other time and place. If the parties do not agree on passing title, §2-401 decides. There are three possibilities:

- *When the goods are being moved,* title passes to the buyer when the seller completes whatever transportation it is obligated to do. Suppose the Seller is in Milwaukee and the Buyer is in Honolulu. The contract requires the Seller to deliver the goods to a ship in San Francisco. Title passes when the Seller completes its last *contractually required* step. In this example, that happens when the goods reach the ship in San Francisco.
- *When the goods are* not *being moved and a contract calls for delivery of ownership documents,* title passes when the seller delivers these documents to the buyer. Suppose Seller, located in Louisville, has manufactured 5,000 baseball bats, which are stored in a warehouse in San Diego. Under the terms of their contract, Buyer will take possession of the bats at the warehouse. When Seller gives Buyer ownership documents, title passes.
- *When the goods are* not *being moved and the contract does* not *call for delivery of ownership documents,* title passes when the parties form the contract. For example, if the Buyer owns the warehouse where the bats are stored, Buyer needs no documents to take possession; title passes when the parties reach agreement.

Where the goods were identified will determine whether sales tax is due.

The following case raises issues of identification and title.

CODE PROVISIONS DISCUSSED IN THIS CASE

Issue	Relevant Code Section
1. In which state were goods identified to the contracts?	UCC §2-501(1): The parties may agree in their contract how and when they will identify the goods; otherwise, they are identified as specified in §2-501 (a),(b) or (c).
2. In which state did title pass?	UCC §2-402: Title may pass in any manner on which the parties agree; otherwise, it passes as specified in §2-401.

Circuit City Stores, Inc. v. Commissioner of Revenue

439 Mass. 629, 790 N.E.2d 636
Supreme Judicial Court of Massachusetts, 2003

Facts: Circuit City, which sold electronic goods, permitted customers to pay for goods at one store but pick them up at another. Because Massachusetts imposed a 5 percent sales tax on all goods sold in the state, but neighboring New Hampshire had no sales tax, many Massachusetts customers chose to save the 5 percent by collecting their goods at a New Hampshire store.

For these "alternative location" sales, the customer receipt indicated where the item had been bought and where it would be picked up. The receipt also said, "reserved," meaning simply that in the collection store, one less item was available to other customers. Until the merchandise was picked up, the customer could demand a refund or request to collect the item in the store where she had paid for it.

The Massachusetts Commissioner of Revenue demanded sales tax on the "alternative location" sales, claiming that it was a sale in Massachusetts because that is where title passed. Circuit City claimed that it owed no sales tax because (1) the goods were not identified to the contract until a customer picked them up in New Hampshire, and (2) title passed in New Hampshire. The case reached the highest court in Massachusetts.

Issue: ***Where were the goods identified to the contract? Where did title to the goods pass?***

Excerpts from Justice Greaney's Decision: We discern no explicit agreement between the parties concerning passage of title. Circuit City claims that testimony at the hearing with respect to its handling of alternative location sales (i.e., that Circuit City does not book the sale, credit the sale, or consider the sale to have occurred until the product is physically released to the customer) indicates an understanding between the parties that the transaction that takes place in Massachusetts constitutes, not a concluded sale, but only an order for merchandise. We disagree. The events transpiring at the cash register in Massachusetts reflect a significant degree of understanding between Circuit City and its customers that a sale, and not a mere deposit on an order, has occurred. The customer sales receipt, although not a document of title, contains a description of the item or items purchased, as well as the time and date of the sale. The record suggests that, in an ordinary case, any period of warranty relevant to the purchase begins as of this date. The purchase price reflected on the receipt represents full consideration paid for the merchandise. From the vantage point of the customer, the sales receipt represents proof of his or her right to the purchased merchandise. The fact the sale is credited to the Massachusetts store, and the commission accorded the sales associate in Massachusetts, in our view, is indicative of an intent on Circuit City's part that more than an order for merchandise takes place in Massachusetts.

As under the UCC, the inquiry centers, not on physical transfer of the goods, but on whether goods are placed within the actual or constructive possession of another. Here, Circuit City performed its obligations with respect to delivery when the sale was entered as an alternative location sale into Circuit City's system and the purchased merchandise was "reserved" for the customer at the designated location. It was the customer from that point on who assumed responsibility for acquiring physical receipt of the purchased merchandise.

It is clear that, under the UCC, no title can pass under a contract for sale "prior to their identification to the contract." G.L. c. 106, §2-401(1). This was also true in common law. We reject, however, Circuit City's argument that "identification to the contract" cannot be made in alternative location sales prior to the time that the merchandise is physically removed from inventory and the serial number is scanned in the New Hampshire store. The reserve notation marked on the customer sales receipt for the purchased merchandise sufficiently reflects its status of being set aside, or identified, to that particular transaction. The Circuit City district manager described the reserving system as moving merchandise to a "phantom" location to await customer pick-up, and, indeed, the situation presented to the customer is just as though the merchandise actually is set aside and waiting for the customer at the pick-up counter. Because customers do not choose items in a store such as Circuit City by a particular serial number, but only by make and model, identification by serial number is unnecessary to the sale.

Affirmed.

Insurable Interest

Closely related to identification and title is the idea of insurable interest. Anyone buying or selling expensive goods should make certain that the goods are insured. There are some limits, though, on who may insure goods, and when. As we saw in Chapter 13, a party may insure something such as property or a a human life only when she has a legitimate interest in it. If the person buying the policy lacks a real interest in the thing insured, the law regards the policy as a gambling agreement and considers it void.

When does someone have an insurable interest in goods? The UCC gives one answer for buyers and one for sellers. **A buyer obtains an insurable interest when the goods are identified to the contract (UCC §2-501).** Suppose that in January, Grain Broker contracts with Farmer to buy his entire wheat crop. Neither party mentions "identification." In January, the crop is not identified and Broker has no insurable interest. In May, after weeks of breaking the soil, Farmer plants his wheat crop. Once he has planted it, the goods are identified. The Broker now has an insurable interest and purchases insurance. In July, a drought destroys the crop, and the Broker never gets one grain of wheat. The Broker need not worry: his insurance policy will cover his losses.

The seller's insurable interest is different. **The seller retains an insurable interest in goods as long as she has either title to the goods or a security interest in them (UCC §2-501).** "Security interest" refers to cases in which the buyer still owes money for the goods and the seller can repossess the goods if payment is not made. Suppose Flyola Manufacturing sells a small aircraft to WingIt, a dealer, for $300,000. WingIt pays $30,000 cash and agrees to pay interest on the balance until it sells the plane. Flyola has an insurable interest even while the aircraft is in WingIt's showroom and may purchase insurance anytime until WingIt pays off the last dime.

And so, a seller and buyer can have an insurable interest in the same goods simultaneously. Suppose the heavy-metal band Flulike Symptoms hires Inkem Corp., in Minneapolis, to make 25,000 T-shirts with the band's logo, for sale at rock concerts. The parties agree that the T-shirts are identified as soon as the logo is printed, and that title will pass when Inkem delivers the T-shirts to the office of the Symptoms' manager in Kansas City. Inkem obviously has an insurable interest while the company is making the T-shirts and continues to have an interest until it delivers the T-shirts in Kansas City. But the Flulike Symptoms' insurable interest arises the moment their logo is stamped on each shirt, so the Symptoms could insure the goods while they are still stored in Inkem's factory. Why would the Symptoms spend hard-earned cash to insure goods they do not have? They may be uncertain that Inkem has obtained proper insurance.

In the following case, a car accident leads several insurance companies to dispute who owned the damaged auto. Each company wants to claim that the car belonged to—someone *else*.

CODE PROVISIONS DISCUSSED IN THIS CASE

Issue	Relevant Code Section
1. Which party had title to the car?	UCC §2-401: Title to goods may pass in any manner on which the parties agree.
2. Did the seller have an insurable interest in the car?	UCC §2-501: The seller retains an insurable interest in the goods as long as it holds title to or a security interest in them.

Valley Forge Insurance Co. v. Great American Insurance Co.

1995 Ohio App. LEXIS 3939
Ohio Court of Appeals, 1995

Facts: On a Friday afternoon, Karl and Linda Kennedy went to John Nolan Ford to buy a new Mustang. The parties signed all necessary documents, including a New Vehicle Buyer's Order, an Agreement to Provide Insurance, and credit applications. The Kennedys made a down payment, but they could not arrange financing before the dealership closed. John Nolan Ford determined that the Kennedys were creditworthy and allowed them to take the car home for the weekend. That evening, Karl Kennedy permitted his brother-in-law, Cella, to take the car for a drive, along with a passenger named Campbell. Cella wrecked the car, injuring his passenger. Campbell sued, and the question was which insurance company was liable: John Nolan Ford's insurer (Milwaukee Mutual), Cella's insurer (Valley Forge), or Kennedy's insurer (Great American). The trial court ruled that title had never passed to Kennedy and found Milwaukee Mutual liable. The insurance company appealed.

Issue: ***Had title passed to Kennedy at the time of the accident?***

Excerpts from the *Per Curiam* Decision: Milwaukee argues that the risk of loss and insurable interest had passed because the car had been delivered. Further, Milwaukee states that the Kennedys explicitly agreed to provide insurance. Great American counters that the parties had "otherwise explicitly agreed" in the New Vehicle Buyer's Order that any interest in the car would not pass until "either the full purchase price is paid in cash or a satisfactory deferred payment agreement is executed by the parties[.]" No financing had been arranged at the time of the accident.

Two terms of the New Vehicle Buyer's Order apply to the situation at bar. Under the "Agreement" provision, the contract states that "it is expressly agreed that the purchaser acquires no right, title or interest in or to the property which he agrees to purchase hereunder until such property is delivered to him and either the full purchase price is paid in cash or a satisfactory deferred payment agreement is executed by the parties hereto[.]"

Milwaukee also argues that the Kennedys explicitly agreed to provide insurance by signing the "Agreement to Provide Insurance." While the agreement does state that the Kennedys agreed to provide insurance, it is not clear when the Kennedys were to obtain the insurance. In fact, because the agreement refers to an "instalment [sic] contract," it is possible that the Kennedys were to provide insurance once a financing agreement was reached. In light of the fact that the agreement is ambiguous, we construe the contract strictly against the drafter and hold that any agreement to provide insurance was to take effect after financing was obtained.

We hold that because the parties had otherwise agreed that interest in the car, including insurable interest, would not pass until the financing was complete, John Nolan Ford still had the risk of loss and the insurable interest when the accident occurred. [Affirmed.]

Imperfect Title

Bona Fide Purchaser

Some people are sleazy, and sales law must accommodate that reality. In the chapter opener we saw a scam artist purchase cattle from a respectable ranch and sell them to an honest dealer. The bad guy skipped town, leaving a dispute between two innocent parties. Either the original owner (the ranch) or the buyer (the cattle dealer) must bear the loss. Who loses?

THE QUESTION: WHO MUST SUFFER THE LOSS?

Owner ⟶	**Bad Guy** ⟶	**Buyer**
(has valid title)	(obtains goods from Owner and sells)	(buys goods from Bad Guy)

Let's consider a new example, from the beginning. First, we need to know what kind of title Bad Guy obtains: is it void or voidable? The key is this: did Bad Guy *take* the item against the will of the owner, or did he fraudulently *trick* the owner into voluntarily handing the item to him?

Abe steals Marvin's BMW in the middle of the night and promptly sells it to Elaine for $35,000 cash. Two weeks later, the police locate the car. When Abe stole it, he obtained void title, which is no title at all. When Bad Guy sells the goods to Buyer, she also gets *no title at all.* Elaine must return the car to Marvin and suffer the $35,000 loss for Abe's theft. This policy makes sense because Marvin has done nothing wrong. If the law permitted Elaine to get valid title, it would encourage theft.

If Bad Guy *attempts to purchase* the goods from Owner using fraud or deception, he obtains **voidable** title, meaning limited rights in the goods, inferior to those of the owner. The owner should be able to recover the goods from Bad Guy (if he can be found), but not from anyone else who ends up with them. Suppose Connie agrees to buy Mark's Jeep. She gives him a check for $20,000 and he signs the vehicle over to her. Connie knows her check will bounce; she has used fraud to obtain the car. As a result, Connie obtains only voidable title. If Mark learns of the deception before Connie sells the car to someone else, he will get his Jeep back.

Unfortunately, Connie is slippery, not stupid. She quickly sells the Jeep to Seth for cash. By the time Connie's check bounces, she is long gone, and Seth has the car. Who keeps the Jeep? Seth wins the car if he is a bona fide purchaser. **A person with voidable title has power to transfer valid title for value to a good faith purchaser, generally called a *bona fide purchaser* or *BFP*.**[7]

Seth can prove that he is a bona fide purchaser by showing two things:

- That he gave value for the goods, *and*
- That he acted in good faith.

It is generally easy for purchasers to show that they gave value. The buyer could give cash or a check or could agree to extinguish a debt; that is, to forgive some money that Bad Guy owed. The real issue becomes whether the buyer acted in good faith. If Seth paid a reasonable purchase price and Connie showed him convincing identification and signed over to him all purchase documents, Seth acted in good faith. He keeps the Jeep and Mark loses.

On the other hand, suppose Seth knows the brand-new Jeep is worth more than $28,000. Connie seems in a frantic hurry to sell the car. She cannot produce the car's registration but promises to send it within three days. Connie's conduct, together with the $8,000 discount, would make a reasonable person suspicious. Seth is not acting in good faith and therefore is not a bona fide purchaser. Mark receives the car back, and Seth pays dearly for his automotive lust.

In the following case, German soldiers confiscated property during World War II. What kind of title did they obtain? Could ownership of looted art be passed on to someone else?

---

[7]UCC §2-403(1).

Bakalar v. Vavra

619 F.3d 136
Second Circuit Court of Appeals, 2010

Facts: Franz Grunbaum was a Jewish man who lived in Vienna before World War II. In 1938, the Nazis imprisoned him in the Dachau concentration camp, where he died three years later. The Nazis also confiscated his property, which included a valuable drawing.

This drawing changed hands several times until it was eventually sold to David Bakalar in 1963. Years later, Franz Grumbaum's heirs, Milos Vavra and Leon Fischer, argued that they were the true owners of the picture. At this point, it was was worth an estimated $675,000. The trial court disagreed, finding that Bakalar was the drawing's owner. Vavra and Fischer appealed.

Issue: ***Did Bakalar own the painting?***

Excerpts from Judge Korman's Decision: [I]n New York, a thief cannot pass good title. This means that, under New York law, absent other considerations, an artwork stolen during World War II still belongs to the original owner, even if there have been subsequent buyers and even if each of those buyers was completely unaware that she was buying stolen goods. The manner in which the rule is applied reflects an overarching concern that New York not become a marketplace for stolen goods. New York case law has long protected the right of the owner whose property has been stolen to recover that property, even if it is in the possession of a good-faith purchaser for value.

Until demand is made, the statute of limitations does not begin to run.

Consequently, if the Drawing was stolen or otherwise unlawfully taken from Grunbaum, that circumstance would affect the validity of Bakalar's title. Indeed, if Vavra and Fischer have made a showing that they have a claim to the Drawing, New York law places the burden on Bakalar, the current possessor, to prove that the Drawing was not stolen.

Accordingly, we vacate the judgment of the district court and remand the case.

EXAM *Strategy*

Question: In this chapter's introduction, a con artist uses a forged check to buy cattle. The issue raised is who must bear the loss—the original owner or the buyer. As presented, Vandermeer (the original owner) would lose the case. Add facts to the story such that Vandermeer *wins* the case.

Strategy: If the con artist had *stolen* the cattle, he could convey no title, and Vandermeer would win. However, the bad guy in fact used a forged check, so he obtained *voidable* title. A buyer is a BFP, and receives good title from such a seller, if the buyer gives value and acts in good faith. We know that Munson gave value. Focus on the issue of good faith.

Result: Facts such as these would disqualify Munson as a BFP: "Munson knew that the market value of the cattle was about $275,000. The 'merchant' wanted to sell him the cows instantly and was willing to give an enormous discount, down to $225,000. In a liquid market, with plenty of buyers, there was no legitimate business reason for such a discount." Under those facts, Munson should have been suspicious, and is not a BFP.

Entrustment

Your old Steinway grand piano needs a complete rebuilding. You hire Fred Showpan, Inc., a company that repairs and sells instruments. Showpan hauls your piano away and promises to return it in perfect shape. Two months later, you are horrified to spot Showpan's showroom boarded up and pasted with bankruptcy notices. Worse still, you learn that Fred sold your beloved instrument to a customer, Frankie List. When you track down List, he claims he paid $18,000 for the piano and likes it just fine. Is he entitled to keep it?

Quite likely he is. Section 2-403(1), the BFP provision we just discussed, would not apply because Showpan did not *purchase* the piano from you. But §2-403(2) does apply. This is the "entrustment" section, and it covers cases in which the owner of goods voluntarily *leaves* them with a merchant, who then sells the goods without permission. According to **UCC §2-403(2), any entrusting to a merchant who deals in goods of that kind gives him power to transfer all rights of the entruster to a buyer in the ordinary course of business (BIOC).** There are several important ideas in this section:

Buyer in the ordinary course of business (BIOC) One who acts in good faith, without knowing that the sale violates the owner's rights.

Entrusting means delivering goods to a merchant or permitting the merchant to retain them.[8] In the piano example, you clearly entrusted goods to a merchant. If you buy a used car from Fast Eddie's and then leave it there for a week while you obtain insurance, you have entrusted it to Eddie.

Deals in Goods of That Kind

The purpose of the section is to protect innocent buyers who enter a store, see the goods they expect to find, and purchase something, having no idea that the storekeeper is illegally selling the property of others. Shoppers should not have to demand proof of title to everything in the store. Further, if someone has to bear the risk, let it be the person who has entrusted her goods; she is in the best position to investigate the merchant's integrity. But this protection does not extend to a buyer who arrives at a vacuum cleaner store and buys an $80,000 mobile home parked in the lot.

In the Ordinary Course of Business

A **buyer in the ordinary course of business (BIOC)** is one who acts in good faith, without knowing that the sale violates the owner's rights. If Frank List buys your piano assuming that Showpan owns it, he has acted in good faith. If Frank was your neighbor, recognized your instrument, and bought it anyway, he is not buying in the ordinary course of business and must hand over the piano.

Of course, a merchant who violates the owner's rights is liable to that owner. If Showpan were still in business when you discovered your loss, you could sue and recover the value of the piano. The problems arise when the merchant is bankrupt or otherwise unable to reimburse the owner.

EXAM *Strategy*

Question: Pamela went to University Used Auto and asked if the company had a Lincoln Navigator. University had no such SUV, but a sales representative told Pamela that he would find her one. The representative contacted Royal auto dealership, which sold new and used cars. Royal agreed to supply University with a car, on the understanding that an interested buyer would pay *Royal*, which in turn would give a finder's fee to University. The companies had worked this way in the past. Royal delivered a Navigator as requested. But when the used car company sold

[8]For a discussion of who is and who is not a merchant, see Chapter 20.

the vehicle to Pamela, the company instructed her to pay University directly, which she did. Royal sued Pamela, seeking the car, and the court had to determine whether there had been an entrustment. Royal argued that it never entrusted the Navigator to University because the parties agreed to require payment to Royal.

Strategy: Entrustment means delivering goods to a merchant who routinely deals in such articles.

Result: Royal delivered a used car to a used car dealer. That is entrustment. It is true that both dealers understood that Pamela was to pay Royal—but she did not know that. Entrustment protects good faith buyers, and Pamela wins.

Entrustment protects good faith buyers—but was there entrustment?

In the following case, we definitely have an entrustment. Do we have a BIOC?

Lindholm v. Brant

283 Conn. 65, 925 A.2d 1048
Supreme Court of Connecticut, 2007

Facts: Kerstin Lindholm and her husband, Magnus, were art collectors. For over 30 years, an art dealer named Anders Malmberg sold paintings for the couple and bought others for them, including an Andy Warhol picture called *Red Elvis*. In 1989, Malmberg arranged for Kerstin Lindholm to loan Red Elvis to the Museum of Modern Art in New York, as part of a major exhibition on Warhol. The exhibit also included paintings owned by Peter Brant. Brant saw *Red Elvis* at the show, was interested in the painting, and learned that Kerstin was the owner, represented by Malmberg.

A decade later, another dealer, Stellan Holm, told Brant that Malmberg had purchased *Red Elvis* and might sell it. In fact, the Lindholms still owned the picture.

Brant orally agreed to pay Malmberg $2.9 million for *Red Elvis*. With nothing put in writing, he made a $900,000 deposit. Then Brant learned that the Lindholms were involved in a bitter divorce. Concerned that Magnus Lindholm might make claims to the picture, he hired a lawyer to investigate. The lawyer reported finding no liens or art-loss claims but told Brant that this did not prove that Malmberg owned the painting.

Brant asked Malmberg for documents proving that Kerstin had sold him the picture, but Malmberg refused, pointing out that confidentiality was the norm in the art world. Eventually, after Malmberg arranged loans of *Red Elvis* to the Guggenheim Museum and yet another exhibition, in Denmark, Brant paid the remaining $2 million and received the picture. Meanwhile Kerstin, assuming she owned *Red Elvis*, arranged to sell to a Japanese buyer for $4.6 million, only to learn that Brant now claimed to own it.

Kerstin sued. The trial court ruled that Brant was a BIOC, entitled to keep the painting. Kerstin appealed, and the case reached Connecticut's highest court.

Issue: ***Was Brant a BIOC?***

Excerpts from Justice Sullivan's Decision: As we have indicated, the defendant presented expert testimony that the vast majority of art transactions, in which the buyer has no reason for concern about the seller's ability to convey good title, are "completed on a handshake and an exchange of an invoice." It is not customary for sophisticated buyers and sellers to obtain a signed invoice from the original seller to the dealer prior to a transaction, nor is it an ordinary or customary practice to request the underlying invoice or corroborating information as to a dealer's authority to convey title.

We are compelled to conclude, however, that the sale from Malmberg to the defendant was unlike the vast majority of art transactions. Because of his concern that Magnus Lindholm might make a claim to *Red Elvis*, the defendant took the extraordinary step of hiring counsel to conduct an investigation and to negotiate a formal contract of sale on his behalf. In addition, during the course of the investigation, the defendant's counsel conducted both a lien search and an Art Loss Register search that revealed no competing claims to *Red Elvis*. Although the defendant was cautioned that the searches provided only minimal assurance that Malmberg had good title to the painting, such searches typically are not conducted during the course of a normal art transaction and, therefore, provided the defendant with at least some assurance that Lindholm had no claims to the painting.

Both Malmberg and Holm had reputations as honest, reliable, and trustworthy art dealers. The defendant had little reason to doubt Malmberg's claim that he was the owner of *Red Elvis*, and any doubts that he did have reasonably were allayed by relying on Holm's assurances that Malmberg had bought the painting from the plaintiff because she needed money due to her divorce. The defendant established that it is customary to rely on the assurances of respected art dealers when conducting a transaction, and the defendant had no reason to depart from this practice.

The defendant's concerns were further allayed when Malmberg delivered *Red Elvis* to a bonded warehouse in Denmark, the delivery location the parties had agreed to in the contract of sale. At the time of the sale, the painting was on loan to the Guggenheim, whose policy it was to release a painting on loan only to the true owner, or to someone the true owner had authorized to take possession.

The judgment is affirmed.

CREDITOR'S RIGHTS

In the "Entrustment" section of this chapter, we considered the rights of the *owner* of goods and how her interests might conflict with those of a merchant and a buyer. A related issue concerns a *creditor;* that is, someone with a financial stake in the goods that the merchant is selling. Suppose a merchant borrows money from a finance company to buy fish tanks with built-in televisions to entertain bored guppies. The finance company is now the merchant's creditor. The merchant agrees that when she sells any of the TV tanks, she will pay a percentage of the proceeds to the finance company. But if she sells tanks to a buyer without giving one cent to her creditor, does the buyer get to keep the fish tanks? To determine an answer, we need to know whether the sale was made in the ordinary course of business.

> **Yoyo grabs the money and sails into the horizon, leaving the bank in his wake.**

Ordinary Sales

Article 9 of the UCC controls the rights of secured parties. We look closely at it in Chapter 24. Briefly stated, **UCC §9-320 generally permits a buyer in the ordinary course of business to take goods free and clear of a security interest.** Suppose the Nickel & Dime Bank loans Yoyo's Yachts $100,000 to purchase two yachts wholesale. The yachts arrive at Yoyo's and remain in the showroom, but Nickel & Dime retains a security interest in both. If Yoyo fails to repay its loan, the bank is entitled to repossess the yachts. Further, Yoyo is obligated to notify the bank immediately of a sale and hold the money until the bank gets its share. Unaware of Nickel & Dime's security interest, Liz pays $80,000 for one of the yachts. Yoyo grabs the money and sails into the horizon, leaving the bank in his wake. May Nickel & Dime take Liz's new yacht? No, because Liz was a buyer in the ordinary course, she takes the yacht free of any security interest.

Naturally, there are exceptions, and you will *not* want to miss the full story in Chapter 24, on secured transactions. But for present purposes, the ordinary customer who purchases goods from a store will keep them regardless of any problems the store has with its creditors. The policy behind the law is obvious: to enable consumers to buy and merchants to sell. If you had to trace the chain of title before you bought a pair of sneakers at Discount City, commerce would grind to a halt and many of us would be barefoot. Section 9-320 keeps things flowing along.

Returnable Goods

Sometimes the seller will allow the buyer to return goods even when he has no complaints about their quality. This, too, can create a problem for creditors. A bank may extend a loan to a business based on the inventory. The bank is willing to lend money because it can seize the goods if the merchant fails to pay on time. But what if the merchant *does not own* some of the goods because he intends to return them to the original owner? If the merchant fails to pay his loan, who gets the goods—the creditor (bank) or the owner of the goods? The UCC considers two types of contract that permit a buyer to return goods.

Sale on Approval

If a buyer takes goods intending to use them herself but has the right to return the goods to the seller, it is a **"sale on approval."** Max manufactures bar code readers, the machines that scan bar codes at checkout lines. He wants to sell half a dozen to Pinky's store, but Pinky isn't sure the machines are worth the price. To encourage Pinky, Max allows her to take the machines and try them out. At the end of 60 days, she may return them or pay full price. There really is no *sale* until Pinky has formally accepted the goods.

Sale on approval
Occurs when a buyer takes goods intending to use them herself but has the right to return them.

Under UCC §2-326(2), in a sale on approval, the goods *are not* subject to the buyer's creditors until the buyer accepts them. Suppose Pinky has borrowed $200,000 from the bank and has given a security interest "in all goods in the store now or in the future." The bar code machines are "goods in the store," and if Pinky fails to pay her loans, the bank will try to seize the equipment. But this is a sale on approval, and the bank has no right to Max's machines.

A finance company will often extend credit based on a merchant's inventory. A creditor considering such a loan must determine what goods, if any, are "sale on approval" since those goods give the creditor no security.

Sale or Return

If a buyer takes goods intending to *resell* them but has the right to return the goods to the seller, it is a **"sale or return."** This is generally the same as a *consignment.* Yvonne runs a used car lot. Trent offers to sell Yvonne his extremely used car for $1,000, but it is in such poor shape Yvonne doubts there's a teenager in the county dumb enough to buy it. "My sister's boyfriend is real dumb," Trent suggests hopefully. Yvonne offers instead to place the car on

Sale or return
Occurs when a buyer takes goods intending to *resell* them but has the right to return them to the seller.

her lot and try to sell it. She will pay Trent nothing upfront for the car and will keep 20 percent of the price if she can sell it.

Under **UCC §2-326, in a sale or return, the goods are subject to the claims of the buyer's creditors**. Suppose Yvonne fails to pay back some loans. Her creditors will instantly round up Trent's car, and he will never get a dime.[9]

Risk of Loss

Many of the issues we have looked at thus far involve someone doing something wrong, often a scoundrel selling goods that he never owned. Now we turn to cases where there may be no wrongdoer.

Accidents hurt businesses. When goods are damaged, the law may again need to decide whether it is the seller or buyer who must suffer the loss. In the cases we have seen thus far, the parties were arguing, "It's mine!"—"Like heck it is, it's *mine!*" In risk of loss cases, the parties are generally shouting, "It was yours!"—"No way, dude, it was *yours!*"

Athena, a seafood wholesaler, is gearing up for the Super Bowl, which will bring 150,000 hungry visitors to her city for a week of eating and gabbing. Athena orders 25,000 lobsters from Poseidon's Fishfoods, 500 miles distant, and simultaneously contracts with a dozen local restaurants to resell them. Poseidon loads the lobsters, still kicking, into refrigerated railcars owned by Demeter Trucking. But halfway to the city, the train collides with a prison van. None of the convicts escape, but the lobsters do, hurtling into swamps from which they are never recaptured. Athena loses all of her profits and sues. As luck would have it, Demeter Trucking had foolishly let its insurance lapse. Poseidon claims the goods were out of its hands. Who loses?

The common law answered this problem by looking at which party had title to the goods at the time of loss. But the Uniform Commercial Code again rejects the old concept, striving once more for a practical solution. The UCC permits the parties to agree on who bears the risk of loss. **UCC §2-509(4) states that the parties may allocate the risk of loss any way they wish.**

Often the parties will do just that, avoiding arguments and litigation in the event of an accident. As part of her agreement with Poseidon, Athena should have included a one-sentence clause, such as "Seller bears all risk of loss until the lobsters are delivered to Athena's warehouse." So long as the parties make their risk allocation clear, the Code will enforce their terms.

Shipping Terms

The parties can quickly and easily allocate the risk of loss by using common shipping terms that the Code defines. FOB means free on board; FAS indicates free alongside a ship; and CIF stands for cost, insurance, and freight. By combining these designations with other terms, the parties can specify risk in a few words:

- ***FOB place of shipment.*** The seller is obligated to put the goods into the possession of the carrier at the place named. The seller bears the expense and risk until they are in the carrier's possession. From that moment onward, the buyer bears the risk.
- ***FOB place of destination.*** The seller must deliver the goods at the place named and bears the expense *and risk* of shipping.

[9]**Article 2 Alert.** Section 2-326 previously permitted a consignor to protect her goods from a creditor by taking any of three specified steps. Those three protective steps *have been deleted* (the changes are not mere proposals), so that this section conforms to Article 9 revisions. Anyone considering consignment should be aware of the risk of losing goods to a creditor, and should take appropriate steps to protect them pursuant to Article 9.

- ***FAS a named vessel.*** The seller at his expense *and risk* must deliver the goods alongside the named vessel and obtain proper receipts.
- ***CIF.*** The price includes in a lump sum: the cost of the goods and the insurance and freight to the named destination.
- ***C & F.*** The price includes in a lump sum: the cost of the goods and freight, but *not* insurance.

Thus, if Athena had put a clause in her contract saying, "FOB Athena's warehouse," Poseidon would have had the risk of any loss up to the time the lobsters were unloaded in Athena's possession. Poseidon would then have known that it must insure the lobsters during transit.

When the Parties Fail to Allocate the Risk

If the parties fail to specify when the risk passes from seller to buyer, the Code provides the answer. When neither party breached the contract, §2-509 determines the risk; when a party has breached the contract, §2-510 governs. The full analysis of risk is somewhat intricate, so we first supply you with a short version: **when neither party has breached the contract, the risk of loss generally passes from seller to buyer when the seller has transported the goods as far as he is obligated to. When a party has breached, the risk of loss generally lies with that party.**

And now, for the courageous student, the full version of how the UCC allocates the risk of loss when the parties failed to specify it.

When Neither Party Breaches

In the example of Athena and Poseidon, both parties did what they were supposed to do, so there was no breach of contract. To settle these cases, we need to know whether the contract obligated the seller to ship the goods or whether the goods were handled in some other way. There are three possibilities: (1) the contract required the seller to ship the goods, or (2) the contract involved a bailment, or (3) other cases.

If the Seller Must Ship the Goods. Most contracts require the seller to arrange shipment of the goods. In a *shipment contract*, the seller must deliver the goods *to a carrier*, which will then transport the goods to the buyer. The carrier might be a trucking company, railroad, airline, or ship, and is generally located near the seller's place of business. **In a shipment contract, the risk passes to the buyer when the seller delivers the goods to the carrier.** Suppose Old Wood, in North Carolina, agrees to sell $100,000 worth of furniture to Pioneer Company, in Anchorage. The contract requires Old Wood to deliver the goods to Great Northern Railroad lines in Chicago. From North Carolina to Chicago, Old Wood bears the risk of loss. If the furniture is damaged, stolen, or destroyed, Old Wood is out of luck. But once the furniture is on board the train in Chicago, the risk of loss passes to Pioneer. If the train derails in Montana and every desk and chair is smashed to kindling, Pioneer must nevertheless pay the full $100,000 to Old Wood.

In a *destination contract*, the seller is responsible for delivering the goods *to the buyer*, and risk passes to the buyer when the goods reach the destination. If the contract required Old Wood to deliver the furniture to Pioneer's warehouse in Anchorage, then Old Wood bears the loss for the entire trip. If the train travels 3,000 miles and then plunges off a bridge in Alaska, 45 feet from its destination, Old Wood picks up the tab.

If There Is a Bailment. Freezem Corp. produces 500 room air conditioners and stores them in Every-Ware's Warehouse. This is a **bailment, meaning that one person or company is legally holding goods for the benefit of another**. Freezem is the **bailor**, the one who owns the goods, and Every-Ware is the **bailee**, the one with temporary possession. Suppose Freezem agrees to sell 300 of its air conditioners to KeepKool Appliances. KeepKool does

Bailor
The one who owns goods legally held by another.

Bailee
The one with temporary possession of another's goods.

not need the machines in its store for six months, so it plans to keep them at Every-Ware's until then. But two weeks after Freezem and KeepKool make their deal, Every-Ware burns to the ground. Who bears the loss of the 300 air conditioners? **If the contract requires a bailee to hold the goods for the buyer, the risk passes when the buyer obtains documents entitling her to possession, or when the bailee acknowledges her right to the goods.** If fire broke out in Every-Ware's before KeepKool received any documents enabling it to take the air conditioners away, then the loss would fall on Freezem.

Other Cases. The great majority of contracts involve either shipment by the seller or a bailment. In the remaining cases, if the seller is a *merchant*, risk passes to the buyer on receipt. This means that a merchant is only off the hook if the buyer actually accepts the goods. If the seller is *not a merchant*, risk passes when the seller tenders the goods, meaning that she makes them available to the buyer. The Code is giving more protection to buyers when they deal with a merchant.

When One Party Breaches

Still there? Really? Excellent. You are indeed a dedicated student. We strive to make all legal topics interesting, but every once in awhile, we find ourselves ... largely powerless. Ah, well, so it goes.

We now look at how the Code allocates risk when one of the parties *does* breach. Again there are three possibilities: (1) seller breaches and buyer rejects; (2) seller breaches, buyer accepts, but then revokes; or (3) buyer breaches.

Seller Breaches and Buyer Rejects. PlayStore, a sporting goods store, orders 75 canoes from Floataway. PlayStore specifies that the canoes must be 12 feet long, lightweight metal, dark green. Floataway delivers 75 canoes to Truckit, a trucking company. When Truckit's trucks arrive, PlayStore finds that the canoes are the right material and color, but 18 feet long. PlayStore rejects the craft, and Truckit heads back to Floataway. But one of the trucks is hijacked and the 25 canoes it carries are never recovered. Floataway demands its money for the 25 lost canoes. Who loses?

Nonconforming goods
Merchandise that differs from that specified in the contract.

Floataway had delivered **nonconforming goods;** that is, merchandise which differs from that specified in the contract. A buyer has a right to reject such goods. **When the buyer rejects nonconforming goods, the risk of loss remains with the seller until he cures the defect or the buyer decides to accept the goods.** In our example, Floataway must suffer the loss for the stolen canoes. If PlayStore had decided to accept the canoes, even though they were the wrong size, then the risk would have passed to the sports store.

Seller Breaches, Buyer Accepts, but Then Revokes. PlayStore orders 200 tennis rackets from High Strung. When the rackets arrive, they seem fine, so the store accepts them. But then a salesperson notices that the grips are loose. Every racket has the same problem. PlayStore returns the rackets to High Strung, but they are destroyed when a blimp crashes into the delivery truck. **When a buyer accepts goods but then rightfully revokes acceptance, the risk remains with the seller to the extent that the buyer's insurance will not cover the loss.** If PlayStore's insurance covers the damaged rackets, there is no problem. If PlayStore's insurance does not cover the loss of goods in transit, High Strung must pay.

Buyer Breaches. One last time. PlayStore orders 60 tents from ExploreMore. About the time the tents leave the factory, PlayStore decides to drop its line of camping goods and specialize in team sports. PlayStore notifies ExploreMore that it wants to explore less and will not pay. The tents are destroyed in a collision involving a prison van and a train carrying lobsters. This time, PlayStore is liable. **When a buyer breaches the contract before taking possession, it assumes the risk of loss to the extent that the seller's insurance is deficient.**

Exhibit 21.1 should clarify.

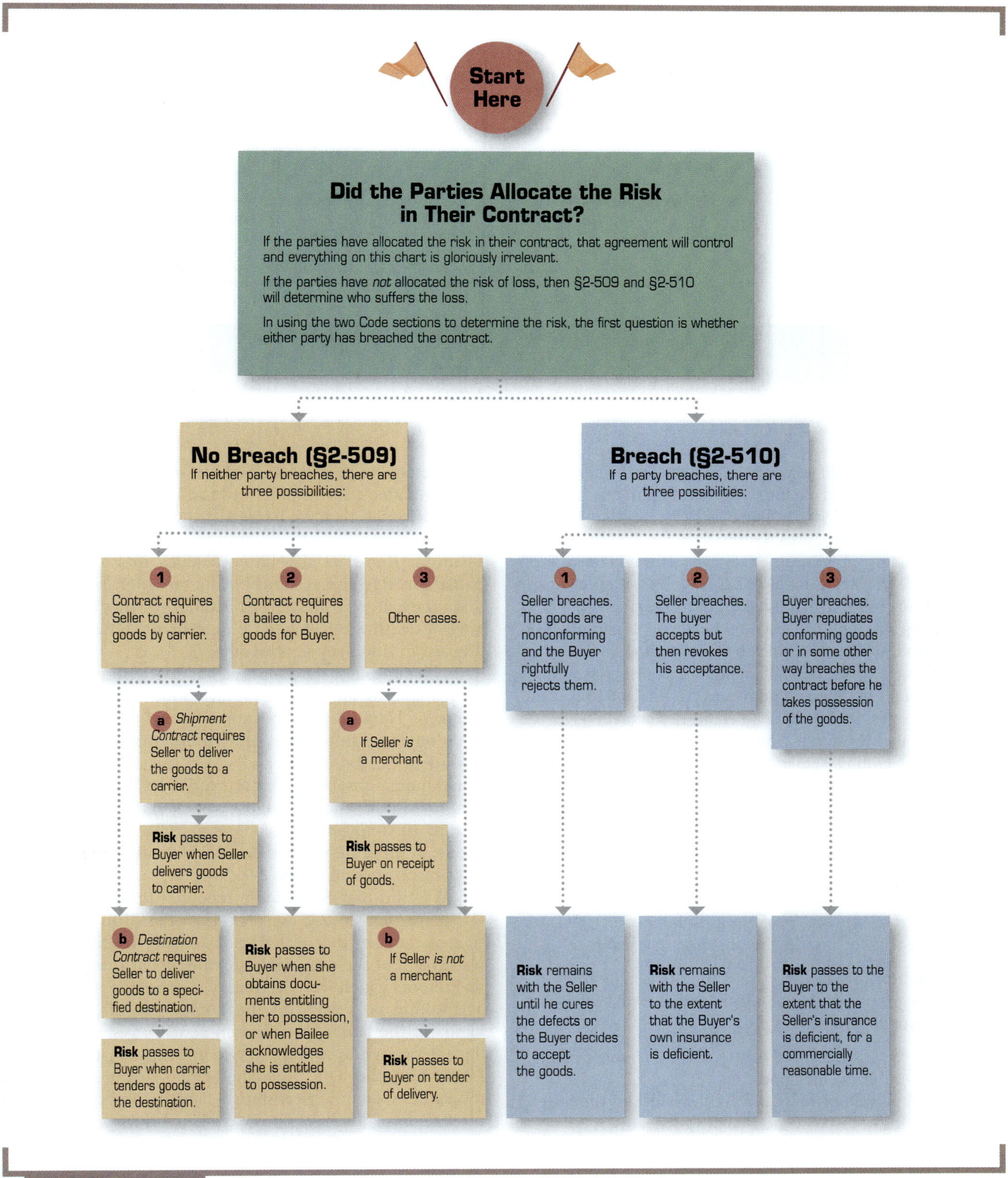
Start Here
Did the Parties Allocate the Risk in Their Contract?
If the parties have allocated the risk in their contract, that agreement will control and everything on this chart is gloriously irrelevant.
If the parties have not allocated the risk of loss, then §2-509 and §2-510 will determine who suffers the loss.
In using the two Code sections to determine the risk, the first question is whether either party has breached the contract.
No Breach (§2-509)
If neither party breaches, there are three possibilities:
Breach (§2-510)
If a party breaches, there are three possibilities:
1 Contract requires Seller to ship goods by carrier.
2 Contract requires a bailee to hold goods for Buyer.
3 Other cases.
1 Seller breaches. The goods are nonconforming and the Buyer rightfully rejects them.
2 Seller breaches. The buyer accepts but then revokes his acceptance.
3 Buyer breaches. Buyer repudiates conforming goods or in some other way breaches the contract before he takes possession of the goods.
a Shipment Contract requires Seller to deliver the goods to a carrier.
Risk passes to Buyer when Seller delivers goods to carrier.
a If Seller is a merchant
Risk passes to Buyer on receipt of goods.
b Destination Contract requires Seller to deliver goods to a specified destination.
Risk passes to Buyer when carrier tenders goods at the destination.
Risk passes to Buyer when she obtains documents entitling her to possession, or when Bailee acknowledges she is entitled to possession.
b If Seller is not a merchant
Risk passes to Buyer on tender of delivery.
Risk remains with the Seller until he cures the defects or the Buyer decides to accept the goods.
Risk remains with the Seller to the extent that the Buyer's own insurance is deficient.
Risk passes to the Buyer to the extent that the Seller's insurance is deficient, for a commercially reasonable time.

EXHIBIT 21.1

In the following case, neither party breached, so §2-509 governs.

CODE PROVISIONS DISCUSSED IN THIS CASE

Issue	Relevant Code Section
1. Did the parties create a bailment?	In a bailment, one person legally holds goods for the benefit of another.
2. Which party bore the risk of the horse's death?	UCC §2-509(2): If the contract requires a bailee to hold the goods for the buyer, the risk passes when the buyer obtains documents entitling her to possession, or when the bailee acknowledges her right to the goods.

Harmon v. Dunn

1997 Tenn. App. LEXIS 217
Tennessee Court of Appeals, 1997

Facts: Bess Harmon owned a two-year-old Tennessee Walking Horse named Phantom Recall. Harmon, who lived in Tennessee, boarded her horse with Steve Dunn at his stables in Florence, Alabama. Dunn cared for Phantom Recall and showed him at equestrian events. Harmon instructed Dunn to sell the horse for $25,000, and Dunn arranged for his friend Scarbrough to buy the colt. On June 30, Dunn delivered Scarbrough's $25,000 check to Harmon, who handed over the horse's certificate of registration and a "transfer of ownership" document. That night at a horse show, Dunn told Scarbrough that he had delivered the check and had the ownership papers in his car. Dunn did not actually give the documents to his friend. Scarbrough knew that Phantom Recall was at Dunn's stable, where Scarbrough had boarded other horses. Sadly, the colt developed colitis and died suddenly, on July 4. Scarbrough stopped payment on his check, and Harmon sued for her money. The trial court found for Harmon, and Scarbrough appealed.

Issue: ***Which party bore the risk of Phantom Recall's death?***

Excerpts from Judge Farmer's Decision: [UCC §2-509 states:] Risk of loss in the absence of breach....

(2) Where the goods are held by a bailee to be delivered without being moved, the risk of loss passes to the buyer:

(a) on his receipt of a negotiable document of title covering the goods, or

(b) on acknowledgment by the bailee of the buyer's right to possession of the goods, or

(c) after his receipt of a non-negotiable document of title or other written direction to deliver...

We conclude that the facts before us clearly establish a bailor-bailee relationship between Harmon and Dunn. It is not disputed that the latter was the agent of the former. Here, it was agreed that Dunn would train and care for Phantom Recall at the Dunn Stables in Florence, Alabama. He was also responsible for transporting the horse to various shows. The record establishes that prior to the horse's death, he had been entered and shown by Dunn himself in three separate events.

Having established Dunn a bailee for purposes of [§2-509(2)] and in the absence of any prior arrangement with Dunn or Harmon that the horse be delivered elsewhere upon purchase from the latter, we find that the risk of loss passed to Scarbrough if and when the applicable provisions under subsection (2) occurred. Subsection (2)(a) and (b) provide that the risk of loss passes to the buyer "on his receipt of a negotiable document of title covering the goods; or on acknowledgment by the bailee of the buyer's right to possession of the goods."

We find that Scarbrough received the ability to control possession of the horse no later than July 1 irrespective of the fact that he did not actually receive physical possession of the ownership documents at that time. The documents which were necessary for transfer of ownership and taking possession of the horse were already in the hands of the bailee. We find an actual physical back and forth exchange between the two unnecessary under these facts where the bailee and the seller's agent are one and the same. Certainly Scarbrough had the ability to control possession of the horse no later than July 1 when he was made aware that Dunn had the transfer papers.

[Affirmed.]

Chapter Conclusion

The Code enables the parties in most commercial transactions to control their own destiny. It reduces the importance of abstract terms like "title" and allows buyer and seller to specify when goods are identified and when risk shifts. Owners and creditors can anticipate problems and protect themselves. But the provisions only work if businesspeople understand the rules and apply them.

Exam Review

1. **INTEREST AND TITLE** An *interest* is a legal right in something. *Title* means the normal rights of ownership. (pp. 481–486)

2. **IDENTIFICATION** Goods must *exist* and be *identified* to the contract before title can pass. The parties may agree in their contract how and when they will identify goods; if they do not specify, the Code stipulates when it happens. The parties may also state when title passes, and once again, if they do not, the Code provides rules. (pp. 482–484)

Question: On September 10, Bell Corp. entered into a contract to purchase 50 lamps from Glow Manufacturing. Bell prepaid 40 percent of the purchase price. Glow became insolvent on September 19 before segregating, in its inventory, the lamps to be delivered to Bell. Bell will not be able to recover the lamps because:

a. Bell is regarded as a merchant.

b. The lamps were not identified to the contract.

c. Glow became insolvent fewer than 10 days after receipt of Bell's prepayment.

d. Bell did not pay the full price at the time of purchase.

Strategy: In analyzing issues about ownership, remember that title can never change hands until the goods have been identified to the contract. Identification can occur in three ways: the parties describe specific goods that already exist; animals are conceived or crops planted; or the seller marks, ships, or otherwise indicates which are going to the buyer. (See the "Result" at the end of this section.)

3. **INSURABLE INTEREST** A buyer obtains an *insurable interest* when the goods are identified to the contract. A seller retains an insurable interest in goods as long as she has either title or a security interest in them. (pp. 486–487)

4. **VOID AND VOIDABLE TITLE** *Void title* is no title at all. *Voidable title* means limited rights in the goods, inferior to those of the owner. A person with voidable title has power to transfer good title to a *bona fide purchaser (BFP);* that is, someone who purchases in good faith, for value. (pp. 487–489)

5. **ENTRUSTING** Any *entrusting* of goods to a merchant who deals in goods of that kind gives him the power to transfer all rights of the entruster to a buyer in the ordinary course of business. (pp. 490–492)

6. **BIOC** A buyer in the ordinary course of business generally takes goods free and clear of any security interest. (p. 490)

EXAM Strategy

Question: Fay Witcher owned a Ford Bronco. Steve Risher operated a used car lot. Witcher delivered his automobile to Risher, asking him to resell it if he could. Witcher specified that he wanted all cash for his car, not cash plus a trade-in. Risher sold the car to Richard Parker for $12,800, but he took a trade-in as part payment. Risher promised to deliver the Bronco's certificate of title to Parker within a few days but never did. He was also obligated to deliver proceeds of the sale to Witcher, and, of course, he failed to do that. Parker claimed that the car was rightfully his. Witcher argued that Parker owned nothing because he never got the title and because Witcher never got his money. Who loses?

Strategy: Any *entrusting* of goods to a merchant who deals in goods of that kind gives him the power to transfer all rights of the entruster to a buyer in the ordinary course of business. A buyer in the ordinary course of business generally takes goods free and clear of any security interest. Did Witcher entrust the auto? Was Parker a BIOC? Why or why not? (See the "Result" at the end of this section.)

7. **SALE ON APPROVAL** In a sale on approval, the goods *are not* subject to the buyer's creditors until the buyer accepts them; in a sale or return, the goods *are* subject to the buyer's creditors. (p. 493)

8. **RISK OF LOSS** In their contract, the parties may allocate the *risk of loss* any way they wish. If they fail to do so, the Code provides several steps to determine who pays for any damage. When neither party has breached, the risk of loss generally passes from seller to buyer when the seller has transported the goods as far as he is obligated to. When a party has breached, the risk of loss generally lies with the party that has breached. (pp. 494–498)

EXAM Strategy

Question: Bradkeyne International, Ltd., an English company, bought a large quantity of batteries from Duracell, Inc. The contract specified delivery "FOB cargo ship, Jacksonville, Florida." Duracell supervised the loading of the batteries onto a ship in Jacksonville in early July, and they arrived in England in August. When loaded onto the ship, the batteries were conforming goods that could be used for normal purposes. But on board the ship, excessive heat damaged them. By the time they reached England, they were worth only a fraction of the original price. Bradkeyne sued Duracell. Who loses?

Strategy: The advantage of standard shipping terms is that they make business predictable and exam questions easy. If you know what "FOB cargo ship, Jacksonville, Florida" means, you know the answer. (See the "Result" at the end of this section.)

2. Result: The contract was silent about which goods were involved; neither animals nor plants were involved; and Glow never segregated the lamps. The lamps were never identified to the contract, and the correct answer is (b).

6. Result: Risher was a merchant dealing in automobiles, meaning that Witcher did entrust the car to him. Parker was a BIOC: he acted in good faith, without knowing that the sale violated the agreement between Witcher and Risher. Parker wins, and he keeps the car.

8. Result: "FOB cargo ship, Jacksonville, Florida" means that the seller bears all risks until the goods are placed in the carrier's possession. From that moment onward, the buyer bears the risk. The batteries were fine when delivered, so Duracell was off the hook once they were on board. Bradkeyne bears the loss.

Multiple-Choice Questions

1. CPA QUESTION On Monday, Wolfe paid Aston Co., a furniture retailer, $500 for a table. On Thursday, Aston notified Wolfe that the table was ready to be picked up. On Saturday, while Aston was still in possession of the table, it was destroyed in a fire. Who bears the loss of the table?

(a) Wolfe, because Wolfe had title to the table at the time of loss
(b) Aston, unless Wolfe is a merchant
(c) Wolfe, unless Aston breached the contract
(d) Aston, because Wolfe had not yet taken possession of the table

2. CPA QUESTION Under UCC Article 9 on secured transactions, which of the following statements is correct concerning the disposition of goods by a secured creditor after a debtor defaults on a loan?

(a) A good faith purchaser of the goods, for value and without knowledge of any defects in the sale, takes free of any security interest.
(b) The debtor may not redeem the goods after the default.
(c) Secured creditors retain the right to redeem the goods after they are sold to a third party.
(d) The goods may be disposed of only at a public sale.

3. CPA QUESTION Quick Corp. agreed to purchase 200 typewriters from Union Suppliers, Inc. Union is a wholesaler of appliances and Quick is an appliance retailer. The contract required Union to ship the typewriters to Quick by common carrier, "FOB Union Suppliers, Inc. Loading Dock." Which of the parties bears the risk of loss during shipment?

(a) Union, because the risk of loss passes only when Quick receives the typewriters
(b) Union, because both parties are merchants
(c) Quick, because title to the typewriters passed to Quick at the time of shipment
(d) Quick, because the risk of loss passes when the typewriters are delivered to the carrier

4. Sheri signs a contract with Farmer Charlie on February 1. Under the deal, she will pay $25,000 for Charlie's entire pumpkin crop on October 1. Charlie plants pumpkin seeds on March 1, and they begin to sprout on April 1. When are the pumpkins identified?

(a) February 1

(b) March 1

(c) April 1

(d) October 1

5. Sam obtains a Patek Philippe watch from Greg by fraud. It has a retail price of $10,000. He sells it to Melissa for $9,000. She believes he owns the watch. Melissa ____________ a bona fide purchaser. Sam disappears. If Greg discovers that she has the watch and demands that it be returned, Melissa ____________ have to give the watch to Greg.

(a) is; will

(b) is; will not

(c) is not; will

(d) is not; will not

Essay Questions

1. Franklin Miller operated Miller Seed Co. in Pea Ridge, Arkansas. He bought, processed, and sold fescue seed, which is used for growing pasture and fodder grass. Farmers brought seed to Miller, who would normally clean, bag, and store it. In some cases, the farmers authorized Miller to sell the seed, in some cases not. Miller mixed together the seed that was for sale with the seed in storage so that a customer could not see any difference between them. Miller defaulted on a $380,000 loan from the First State Bank of Purdy. First State attempted to seize all of the seed in the store. Tony Havelka, a farmer, protested that his 490,000 pounds of seed was merely in storage and not subject to First State's claim. Who is entitled to the seed?

2. **ETHICS** Myrna and James Brown ordered a $35,000 motor home from R.V. Kingdom, Inc. The manufacturer delivered the vehicle to R.V. Kingdom, with title in the dealer's name. The Browns agreed to accept the motor home, but they soon regretted spending the money and asked R.V. Kingdom to resell it. The motor home stayed on R.V. Kingdom's lot for quite a few months, but when the Browns decided to come get it, they learned that R.V. Kingdom had illegally used the vehicle as collateral for a loan and that a bank had repossessed it. The Browns filed a claim with their insurance company, State Farm. The insurer agreed that the vehicle had been stolen and agreed that the Browns' policy covered newly acquired vehicles. But the company refused to pay, claiming that the Browns had not taken title or possession to the goods and therefore had no insurable interest. The Browns sued. Please rule on their case.

Let us also look at the ethics of the case by creating a contrasting hypothetical. Suppose that among the insurance company's thousands of customers was Arvee, a recreational vehicle dealership similar to the one in the real case. Imagine that Arvee had taken in an automobile for resale from a customer named Parker and kept the vehicle on its lot. If Parker's auto were stolen, what argument would the insurance company be making? How would the company define insurable interest in *that* case?

3. John C. Clark, using an alias, rented a Lexus from Alamo Rent-A-Car in San Diego, California. Clark never returned the car to Alamo and obtained a California "quick title" using forged signatures. He then advertised in the *Las Vegas Review Journal* newspaper and sold the car to Terry and Yvonne Mendenhall for $34,000 in cash. The Mendenhalls made improvements to the car, had it insured, smog- and safety-tested, registered, licensed, and titled in the state of Utah. When Alamo reported the car stolen, the Nevada Department of Motor Vehicles seized the auto and returned it to Alamo. The Mendenhalls sued Alamo. The trial court concluded that the Mendenhalls had purchased the car for value and without notice that it was stolen, and so they were bona fide purchasers entitled to the Lexus. Alamo appealed. Please rule.

4. Universal Consolidated Cos. contracted with China Metallurgical Import and Export Corp. (CMIEC) to provide CMIEC with new and used equipment for a cold rolling steel mill. Universal then contracted with Pittsburgh Industrial Furnace Co. (Pifcom) to engineer and build much of the equipment. The contract required Pifcom to deliver the finished equipment to a trucking company, which would then transport it to Universal. Pifcom delivered the goods to the trucking company as scheduled. But before all of the goods reached Universal, CMIEC notified Universal it was canceling the deal. Universal, in turn, notified Pifcom to stop work, but all goods had been delivered to the shipper and ultimately reached Universal. Pifcom claimed that it retained title to the goods, but Universal claimed that title had passed to it. Who is right?

5. **YOU BE THE JUDGE WRITING PROBLEM** Construction Helicopters paid Heli-Dyne Systems $315,000 for three helicopters that were in Argentina. Two were ready to fly, and one was disassembled for routine maintenance. The contract said nothing about risk of loss (the parties could have saved a lot of money by reading this chapter). Heli-Dyne arranged for an Argentine company to oversee their loading on board the freight ship *Lynx*. The two helicopters and 25 crates containing the disassembled craft were properly loaded, but when the ship arrived in Miami, only 7 of the crates appeared. Heli-Dyne refused to supply more parts, and Construction sued. Who bears the loss? **Argument for Construction:** Construction had no control over the goods until they reached Miami. Although we do not know exactly what happened to the crates, we know the one party that had *nothing* to do with the loss: Construction. The company should not pay for damage it never caused. **Argument for Heli-Dyne:** Because the contract failed to specify risk of loss, it is a shipment contract. In such an agreement, risk of loss passes to the buyer when the seller delivers the goods to a carrier. Heli-Dyne delivered the goods and has no further responsibility.

Discussion Questions

1. In the opening scenario with the con artist and the cattle, we learned that the original owner would be left out in the cold under the UCC. Is this a fair result? Would it be better to require Vandermeer and the buyer in Omaha to share the loss?

2. In the *Bakalar* case involving artwork stolen during World War II, do you agree with the court's decision? Should the heirs get a chance to recover the drawing that was stolen from their ancestor? Or should Bakalar, who has owned the drawing for 50 years and knew nothing about its origin, be able to keep ownership?

3. Imagine that your laptop gets a virus, and you take it to a local computer repair shop. The shop sells your computer to Heidi. Under the entrustment rules in the UCC, Heidi is a buyer in the ordinary course of business. And so, even if you find Heidi and demand that she return your laptop, *she gets to keep it*. Is this fair? Does the law give too much protection to purchasers in this situation, and not enough to victims?

4. You are about to move, and you take your furniture to a consignment shop. The shop's creditors seize everything in the store, including your furniture. You demand that the creditors give back your stuff, but under UCC §2-326, *they don't have to*. Is this fair? Should the law change?

5. Greg manufactures and sells T-shirts. As a seller, would he be better off if his contracts indicated "FOB (place of shipment)" or "FOB (place of destination)" ? Explain your answer.

CHAPTER 22

© Stas Volik/Shutterstock.com

WARRANTIES AND PRODUCT LIABILITY

You are sitting in a fast-food restaurant. Your friend Harley, who works for a state senator, is eating with one hand and gesturing with the other.

"I'm mostly working on product liability reform. We think it might actually pass this time," he proclaims, stabbing the air with his free hand. "Some of our constituents want it *right now*."

"What would be different?" you ask.

"Well, for starters, we'd cap lawsuit judgments. It's absurd, these multimillion dollar verdicts, just because something has a *slight defect*."

"But if someone gets hurt," you reply, "shouldn't she get everything she's entitled to?"

Harley waves off your remark. "Ridiculous!" he exclaims. "Most of these 'victims' wouldn't have any problem if they'd just be more careful in the first place." Still feeling agitated, he takes a ferocious bite from his burger—and *CRACK*—he breaks a tooth.

Feeling agitated, he takes a ferocious bite from his burger—and *CRACK*—he breaks a tooth.

"Aaaahhhh! My toof! My TOOF!" Harley howls in pain and throws down the bun, revealing a large piece of bone in the meat. He tips his chair back in disbelief and says loudly, "I'll sue these sons of aaaahhhh …" Just then, his defective chair collapses. Harley falls backwards and slams into the tile floor, knocking himself unconscious. Hours later, when he revives in the hospital, he refuses to speak to you until he puts in a call to his lawyer.

Harley and his lawyer will be chatting about **product liability**, which refers to goods that have caused an injury. The harm may be physical, as it was in Harley's case. Sometimes, it is purely economic, as when a corporation buys a computer so defective it must be replaced, costing the buyer lost time and profits. The injured party's remedies may be derived from several legal ideas, including:

- ***Warranty***, which is an assurance provided in a sales contract;
- ***Negligence***, which refers to unreasonable conduct by the defendant; and
- ***Strict liability***, which allows lawsuits over defective products whether the defendant acted reasonably or not.

We discuss each of these ideas in this chapter. What all product liability cases have in common is that a person or business has been hurt by goods. We focus primarily on cases where the *sale* of goods leads to the injury, but we also examine product liability issues where there has been no sale. We begin with warranties.

Express Warranties

Warranty
A contractual assurance that goods will meet certain standards.

A **warranty** is a contractual assurance that goods will meet certain standards. It is normally a manufacturer or a seller who gives a warranty and a buyer who relies on it. A warranty might be explicit and written: "The manufacturer warrants that the light bulbs in this package will illuminate for 2,000 hours." Or a warranty could be oral: "Don't worry, this machine can harvest any size of wheat crop ever planted in the state." The manufacturer may offer a warranty as a means of attracting buyers: "We provide the finest bumper-to-bumper warranty in the automobile industry." Or *the law itself* may impose a warranty on goods, requiring the manufacturer to meet certain standards whether it intends to or not. Here we consider express warranties.

Express warranty
One that the seller creates with his words or actions.

An **express warranty** is one that the seller creates with his words or actions.[1] Whenever a seller *clearly indicates* to a buyer that the goods being sold will meet certain standards, she has created an express warranty. For example, if the sales clerk for a paint store tells a professional house painter that "this exterior paint will not fade for three years, even in direct sunlight," that is an express warranty and the store is bound by it. Or, if the clerk gives the painter a brochure that makes the same promise, the store is again bound by its express warranty. On the other hand, if the salesperson merely says, "I know you're going to be happy with this product," there is no warranty because the promise is too vague. The Uniform Commercial Code establishes that the seller may create an express warranty in three ways: (1) with an affirmation of fact or a promise; (2) with a description of the goods; or (3) with a sample or model. In addition, the buyer must demonstrate that what the seller said or did was part of the *basis of the bargain*.

Affirmation of Fact or Promise

Any affirmation of fact—or any promise—can create an express warranty.[2] An affirmation of fact is simply a statement about the nature or quality of the goods, such as "this scaffolding is made from the highest grade of steel available at any price" or "this car will accelerate

[1] UCC §2-313.
[2] UCC §2-313(1)(a).

from 0 to 60 in 5.3 seconds." A promise can include phrases such as, "we guarantee you that this air conditioning system will cool your building to 72 degrees, regardless of the outdoor temperature."

A common problem in cases of express warranty is to separate true affirmations of fact from mere sales puffery or seller's opinion, which creates no express warranty. "You meet the nicest people when you ride a Honda motorcycle," is mere puffery. If you purchase a Honda and meet only deadbeats, the manufacturer owes you nothing.

A statement is more likely to be an affirmation of fact if:

- ***It is specific and can be proven true or false.*** Suppose the brochures of a home builder promise to meet "the strictest building codes." Since there is a code on file, the builder's work can be compared to it, and his promise is binding.
- ***It is written.*** An oral promise *can* create an express warranty. But promises in brochures are more likely to be taken seriously. Statements in a *written contract* are the likeliest of all to create a binding warranty.
- ***Defects are not obvious.*** If a used car salesman tells you that a car is rust-free when the driver's door is pockmarked with rust, you should not take the statement seriously—since a court will not, either.
- ***Seller has greater expertise.*** If the seller knows more than the buyer, his statements will be more influential with buyer and court alike. If your architect assures you that the new porch will be warm in winter, the law recognizes that you will naturally rely on her expertise.

Description of Goods

Any description of the goods can create an express warranty.[3] The statement can be oral or written. A description might be a label on a bag of seed, referring to the seed as a particular variety of tomato; it could be a tag on airplane parts, assuring the buyer that the goods have met safety tests. Wherever the words appear, if they describe the goods as having particular characteristics or qualities, the seller has probably created an express warranty.

Sample or Model

Any sample or model can create an express warranty.[4] A sample can be a very effective way of demonstrating the quality of goods to a customer. However, a seller who uses a sample is generally warranting that the merchandise sold will be just as good.

Basis of Bargain

The seller's conduct must have been part of the basis of the bargain. To prove an express warranty, a buyer must demonstrate that the two parties *included the statements or acts in their bargain*. Some courts have interpreted this to mean that the buyer must have *relied* on the seller's statements. There is logic to this position. For example, suppose a sales brochure makes certain assurances about the quality of goods, but the buyer never sees the brochure until she files suit. Should the seller be held to an express warranty? Some courts would rule that the seller is not liable for breach of warranty.

Other courts, however, have ruled that a seller's statement can be part of the basis of the bargain even when the buyer has not clearly relied on it. These courts are declaring that a seller who chooses to make statements about his goods will be held to them *unless the seller*

---

[3] UCC §2-313(1)(b).

[4] UCC §2-313(1)(c).

can convince a court that he should not be liable. This is a policy decision, taken by many courts, to give the buyer the benefit of the doubt since the seller is in the best position to control what he says. The issue arises in the following case.

Rite Aid Corp. v. Levy-Gray

894 A.2d 563, 391 Md. 698
Court of Appeals of Maryland, 2006

Facts: Dr. Ronald Geckler diagnosed Ellen Levy-Gray with Lyme disease and prescribed doxycycline. Geckler told Levy-Gray that while taking the drug, she must stop nursing her son, but he provided her with no other information. Levy-Gray had the prescription filled at a Rite-Aid pharmacy she knew and trusted. With the medication, the pharmacy included its own pamphlet, called "Rite Advice." The cover page said, "Inside is everything you need to know about your prescription. It covers everything in writing from dosage to side effects." The inside of the pamphlet stated, in part:

> IMPORTANT NOTE: THE FOLLOWING INFORMATION IS INTENDED TO SUPPLEMENT, NOT SUBSTITUTE FOR, THE EXPERTISE AND JUDGMENT OF YOUR PHYSICIAN, PHARMACIST, OR OTHER HEALTHCARE PROFESSIONAL.
>
> HOW TO TAKE THIS MEDICATION: Take each dose with a full glass of water (4 oz. or 120 ml) or more. Take with food or milk if stomach upset occurs unless your doctor directs you otherwise.

Doxycycline immediately upset Levy-Gray's stomach, so she began to take the medicine with milk. In order to maintain her breast milk so that she could resume nursing when the treatment ended, Levy-Gray also consumed eight glasses of milk per day, grilled cheese sandwiches, ice cream, and so forth. Because her Lyme disease did not improve, her brother, a doctor in another specialty, recommended that she stop using dairy products. Her symptoms briefly improved, but ultimately she was diagnosed with post-Lyme syndrome, a chronic autoimmune response.

Levy-Gray sued Rite-Aid for breach of an express warranty. She claimed that the instructions to take Doxycycline with milk rendered the drug ineffective and caused her chronic condition. At trial, her expert witness testified that taking dairy products with the drug prevented the drug from being absorbed into the body. Rite-Aid's expert stated any loss of absorption was modest and had no effect on her treatment. The company also claimed that the pamphlet could not have been part of the basis of the bargain because Levy-Gray never saw it until after she bought the medication.

The jury found that Rite-Aid had breached a warranty and awarded Levy-Gray $250,000. Rite-Aid appealed; the intermediate appeals court affirmed, and the state's highest court took the case.

Issue: ***Did Rite-Aid breach an express warranty?***

Excerpts from Justice Battaglia's Decision: Rite Aid contends that the statements about doxycycline contained in the "Rite Advice" pamphlet were not part of the basis of the bargain because Ms. Levy-Gray did not receive them and was not aware of their existence until after the sale was completed. Rite Aid argues that for an affirmation to become "part of the basis of the bargain," the affirmation must be a negotiated term of the agreement, or the consumer must at least have been aware of its existence prior to the consummation of the deal. Based on the circumstances surrounding most purchases in modern commercial dealing, we disagree.

The precise time when words of description or affirmation are made or samples are shown is not material. The sole question is whether the language is fairly to be regarded as part of the contract. Express warranties may be formed prior to the completion of the sale or even after the sale has been consummated. What is paramount is the relationship between the sale of the goods and the affirmations made by the seller. As it is common knowledge that sellers will deliver written warranties after the contract has been made, some courts are recognizing that later statements found in these writings are part of the basis of the bargain.

Rite Aid also relies on the "learned intermediary" doctrine, which applies to the tripartite relationship between the drug manufacturer, the prescribing physician, and the patient, as supporting the proposition that pharmacists cannot be held liable for the breach of express warranty because the patient is presumed to have relied upon the advice rendered by her physician.

The jury further could have inferred from the evidence presented at trial that the language contained in the "Rite Advice" pamphlet encouraged Ms. Levy-Gray to rely on the information contained therein based upon its assertion on the cover that "[i]nside is everything that you need to know about your prescription"; thus, the statement "take with food or milk if upset stomach occurs" had the effect of warranting that for the duration of Ms. Levy-Gray's doxycycline treatment, the doxycycline will not be adversely affected by her consumption of milk. The jury reasonably could have inferred that Ms. Levy-Gray relied on the veracity of Rite Aid's affirmation each time she took the dose of doxycycline with milk.

Affirmed.

Devil's Advocate How can a statement be the basis of the bargain if one party never heard or read it until *after* she purchased the product? Obviously, the pamphlet had no influence on the consumer's decision to form the contract. And even if the unread notice was somehow part of the bargain, it never urged users to consume eight glasses of milk per day while eating grilled cheese sandwiches and ice cream. The right step for any patient, before adopting such an extreme course, is to check with her doctor. Common sense should be part of good legal doctrine.

EXAM Strategy

Question: Melinda, a rock singer, goes to Stereo Shop to buy equipment for her home recording studio. She likes a $5,000 unit on display, and the sales clerk shows her how to record and edit her music. "It's a terrific unit," he says. "Record a song, see if you like it." She records a song in the store, and the audio file she creates is flawless. Impressed, Melinda buys the equipment. However, when the equipment is set up in her home, Melinda's recordings frequently have static in them, forcing her to re-record them. When Stereo Shop is unable to remedy the problem, Melinda sues for breach of warranty. Did Stereo Shop create a warranty? Who is likely to win?

Strategy: Begin by recalling how a seller creates a warranty. One way that this can happen is with an affirmation of fact. These claims are generally strongest if the statement was in writing and specific. A description of the goods may also lead to a warranty, as may use of a sample or model.

Result: The clerk's statement that "It's a terrific unit" is oral and general. Courts will consider it nothing more than puffery. The clerk made no additional description of the goods. However, the clerk used a model, knowing that Melinda would rely on the demonstration, which she did. A seller who takes advantage of a model warrants that the merchandise sold will be just as good. Melinda will win her claim for breach of an express warranty unless Stereo Shop can show that the static is caused by Melinda's improper use of the equipment.

Implied Warranties

Sean decides to plow driveways during the winter. Emily sells him a snowplow and installs it on his truck, but she makes no promises about its performance. When winter arrives, Sean has plenty of business, but he finds that the plow cannot be raised or lowered whenever the temperature falls below 40 degrees. He demands a refund from Emily, but she declines, saying, "I never said that thing would work in the winter. Tough luck." Is she off the hook? No. It is true she made no express warranties. But many sales are covered by implied warranties.

Implied warranties are those created by the Uniform Commercial Code itself, not by any act or statement of the seller. The Code's drafters concluded that goods should generally meet certain standards of quality, regardless of what the seller did or did not say. So the UCC creates both an implied warranty of merchantability and an implied warranty of fitness.

Implied Warranty of Merchantability

This is the most important warranty in the UCC. Buyers, whether individual consumers or billion-dollar corporations, are more likely to rely on this than any other section, and sellers must understand it thoroughly when they market goods. **Unless excluded or modified, a warranty that the goods shall be merchantable is implied in a contract for their sale if the seller is a merchant with respect to goods of that kind. Merchantable** means that the goods are fit for the ordinary purposes for which they are used.[5] This rule contains several important principles:

Merchantable
Means that the goods are fit for the ordinary purposes for which they are used.

- *Unless excluded or modified* means that the seller does have a chance to escape this warranty. We later discuss what steps a seller may take if she wants to sell goods that are *not* merchantable.
- *Merchantability* requires that goods be fit for their normal purposes. To be merchantable, a ladder must be able to rest securely against a building and support someone who is climbing it. The ladder need not be serviceable as a boat ramp.
- *Implied* means that the law itself imposes this liability on the seller even if it is not written down.
- *A merchant with respect to goods of that kind* means that the seller is someone who routinely deals in these goods or holds himself out as having special knowledge about these goods. If it is selling vehicles, a car dealer is acting as a merchant. An accountant who sells his used car by listing it online is not a merchant.

Dacor Corp. manufactured and sold scuba diving equipment. Dacor ordered air hoses from Sierra Precision, specifying the exact size and couplings so that the hose would fit tightly and safely into Dacor's oxygen units. Within about one year, customers returned a dozen Dacor units, complaining that the hose connections had cracked or sheared and were unusable. Dacor recalled 16,000 units and refit them with safe hoses, at a cost of more than $136,000. Dacor sued Sierra, claiming a breach of the implied warranty of merchantability. The Illinois court first ruled that Sierra was a merchant with respect to scuba hoses because it routinely manufactured and sold them. The court then ruled:

> There is no evidence suggesting that these hose assemblies were subjected to anything other than normal use. Since the kind of failure experienced in connection with the returned hose assemblies would be life-threatening if it occurred under water, the hose assemblies were not fit for the purpose for which they were used within the meaning of UCC section 2-314.

The court ordered Sierra to pay the cost of Dacor's recall.[6]

The scuba equipment was not merchantable because a properly made scuba hose should never crack under normal use. But what if the product being sold is food, and the food contains something that is harmful—yet quite normal? Remember the legislative aide in the opening scenario? Let's see how a similar real case turned out.

---

[5]UCC §2-314(1).

[6]*Dacor Corp. v. Sierra Precision*, 1993 U.S. Dist. LEXIS 8009 (N.D. Ill. 1993).

Goodman v. Wenco Foods, Inc.

333 N.C. 1, 423 S.E.2d 444, 1992 N.C. LEXIS 671
Supreme Court of North Carolina, 1992

Facts: Fred Goodman and a friend stopped for lunch at a Wendy's restaurant in Hillsborough, North Carolina. Goodman had eaten about half of his double hamburger when he bit down and felt immediate pain in his lower jaw. He took from his mouth a triangular piece of cow bone, about one-sixteenth to one-quarter inch thick and one-half inch long, along with several pieces of his teeth. Goodman's pain was intense, and his dental repairs took months.

The restaurant purchased all of its meat from Greensboro Meat Supply Company (GMSC). Wendy's required its meat to be chopped and "free from bone or cartilage in excess of 1/8 inch in any dimension." GMSC beef was inspected continuously by state regulators and was certified by the United States Department of Agriculture (USDA). The USDA considered any bone fragment less than three-quarters of an inch long to be "insignificant."

Goodman sued, claiming a breach of the implied warranty of merchantability. The trial court dismissed the claim, ruling that the bone was natural to the food and that the hamburger was therefore fit for its ordinary purpose. The appeals court reversed this, holding that a hamburger could be unfit even if the bone occurred naturally. Wendy's appealed to the state's highest court.

Issue: ***Was the hamburger unfit for its ordinary purpose?***

Excerpts from Justice Exum's Decision: We hold that when a substance in food causes injury to a consumer, it is not a bar to recovery against the seller that the substance was "natural" to the food, provided that the substance's presence should not reasonably have been anticipated by the consumer.

A triangular, one-half-inch, inflexible bone shaving is indubitably "inherent" in or "natural" to a cut of beef, but whether it is so "natural" to hamburger as to put a consumer on his guard—whether it "is to be reasonably expected by the consumer"—is, in most cases, a question for the jury. We are not requiring that the respondent's hamburgers be perfect, only that they be fit for their intended purpose. It is difficult to conceive of how a consumer might guard against the type of injury present here, short of removing the hamburger from its bun, breaking it apart and inspecting its small components.

Wendy's argues that the evidence supported its contention that its hamburger complied with [legal] standards. Wendy's reasons that [regulators permit] some bone fragments in meat and that its hamburgers are therefore merchantable as a matter of law. The court of appeals rejected this argument, noting that compliance "with all state and federal regulations is only some evidence which the jury may consider in determining whether the product was merchantable." We agree.

We thus conclude, as did the court of appeals majority, that a jury could reasonably determine the meat to be of such a nature and the bone in the meat of such a size that a consumer should not reasonably have anticipated the bone's presence. The court of appeals therefore properly reversed the directed verdict for Wendy's on plaintiff's implied warranty of merchantability claim.

Implied Warranty of Fitness for a Particular Purpose

The other warranty that the Uniform Commercial Code imposes on sellers is the implied warranty of fitness for a particular purpose. This cumbersome name is often shortened and referred to as simply the *warranty of fitness*. **Where the seller at the time of contracting *knows* about a particular purpose for which the buyer wants the goods, and knows that the buyer is relying on the seller's skill or judgment, there is (unless excluded or modified) an implied warranty that the goods shall be fit for the purpose.**[7] Here are the key points:

- ***Particular purpose.*** The seller must know about some *special* use that the buyer plans for the goods. For example, if a lumber salesman knows that a builder is purchasing lumber to construct houses in a swamp, the UCC implies a warranty that the lumber will withstand water.

[7]UCC §2-315.

- ***Seller's skill.*** The buyer must be depending upon the seller's skill or judgment in selecting the product, and the seller must know it. Suppose the builder says to the lumber salesman, "I need four-by-eights that I will be using to build a house in the swamp. What do you have that will do the job?" The builder's reliance is obvious, and the warranty is established. By contrast, suppose that an experienced Alaskan sled driver offers to buy your three huskies, telling you she plans to use them to pull sleds. She has the experience and you do not, and if the dogs refuse to pull more than a one-pound can of dog food, you have probably not breached the implied warranty of fitness.
- ***Exclusion or modification.*** Once again, the seller is allowed to modify or exclude any warranty of fitness.

WARRANTIES COMPARED

Express Warranty	Implied Warranty of Merchantability	Implied Warranty of Fitness for a Particular Purpose
The Rule: Seller can create an express warranty with any affirmation or promise, with any description of the goods, or with any sample or model, provided the words or sample is part of the basis of the bargain	*The Rule:* With certain exceptions, the Code implies a warranty that the goods will be fit for their ordinary purpose.	*The Rule:* With some exceptions, the Code implies a warranty that the goods are fit for the buyer's special purpose, provided that the seller knows of that purpose when the contract is made and knows of the buyer's reliance.
Example: Manufacturer sends Retailer a brochure describing its brand of children's bicycle. The brochure states that "these bikes will last for a minimum of eight years of normal use." If the handlebars snap off after six months, Manufacturer has breached its express warranty.	*Example:* Manufacturer sells Retailer 300 "children's bicycles." There is no brochure and no promise made by Manufacturer about the bikes' quality. The UCC implies a warranty that the bikes will be fit for ordinary riding by children. But the cycles might not be strong enough to withstand mountain racing, and there is no warranty to that effect.	*Example:* Retailer orders from Manufacturer "300 mountain bikes, for racing," and Manufacturer agrees. The UCC implies a warranty that the bikes will withstand the added stress of mountain racing.

Two Last Warranties: Title and Infringement

Strapped for cash, Maggie steals her boyfriend's rusty Chevy and sells it to Paul for $2,500. As we saw in Chapter 21, Maggie gets no valid title by her theft, and therefore Paul receives no title either. When the boyfriend finds his car parked at a nightclub, he notifies the police and gets his wheels back. Poor Paul is out of pocket $2,500 and has no car to show for it. That clearly is unjust, and the UCC provides Paul with a remedy: **the seller of goods warrants that her title is valid and that the goods are free of any security interest that the buyer knows nothing about unless the seller has clearly excluded or modified this warranty.**[8] Once again, the Code is imposing a warranty on any seller except those who explicitly exclude or modify it. When Maggie sells the car to Paul, she warrants her valid title to the car and simultaneously breaches that warranty since she obviously has no title. If he can find her, Paul will win a lawsuit against Maggie for $2,500.

The same Code section imposes a warranty against claims of infringement by third parties. **Unless otherwise agreed, a seller who is a merchant warrants that the goods are free of any rightful claim of copyright, patent, or trademark infringement.**[9] Wesley sells to Komputer Corp. a device that automatically blasts purple smoke out of a computer screen anytime a student's paper is really dreadful. Unless Komputer Corp. agrees otherwise, Wesley is automatically giving the buyer a warranty that no one else invented the device or has any copyright, patent, or trademark in it.

[8] UCC §2-312(1).
[9] UCC §2-313(3).

DISCLAIMERS AND DEFENSES

There are several limitations on warranties. A seller may disclaim *warranties*, meaning that he eliminates express or implied warranties covering the goods. Or the seller may limit the buyer's *remedy*, which means that even if there is a breach of warranty, the buyer still may have only a very limited chance to recover against the seller.

Disclaimers

A **disclaimer** is a statement that a particular warranty *does not* apply. The Code permits the seller to disclaim most warranties.

Disclaimer
A statement that a particular warranty does not apply.

Oral Express Warranties

Under the Code, a seller may disclaim an oral express warranty. Suppose Traffic Co. wants to buy a helicopter from HeliCorp for use in reporting commuter traffic. HeliCorp's salesman tells Traffic Co., "Don't worry, you can fly this bird day and night for six months with nothing more than a fuel stop." HeliCorp's contract may disclaim the oral warranty. The contract could say, "HeliCorp's entire warranty is printed below. Any statements made by any agent or salesperson are disclaimed and form no part of this contract." That disclaimer is valid. If the helicopter requires routine servicing between flights, HeliCorp has not breached an oral warranty.

VisionsofAmerica/Joe Sohm/Getty Images

Would you fly in a helicopter protected by an oral express warranty?

Written Express Warranties

This is the one type of warranty that is almost impossible to disclaim. If a seller includes an express warranty in the *sales contract*, any disclaimer is definitely invalid. Suppose HeliCorp sells an industrial helicopter for use in hauling building equipment. The sales contract describes the aircraft as "operable to 14,000 feet." Later, in the contract, a limited warranty disclaims "any other warranties or statements that appear in this document or in any other document." That disclaimer is invalid and does not cancel the assurance that the helicopter can operate to 14,000 feet. The Code will not permit a seller to take contradictory positions in a document. The goal is simply to be fair, and the UCC assumes that it is confusing and unjust for a seller to say one thing to help close a deal and the opposite to limit its losses.[10]

What if the express written statement is in a different document, such as a sales brochure? The disclaimer is void if it would *unfairly surprise* the buyer. Assume, again, that HeliCorp promises a helicopter that requires no routine maintenance for six months, but this time, the promise appears in a sales brochure that Traffic Co. reads and relies on. If HeliCorp attempts to disclaim the written warranty, it will probably fail. Most people take written information seriously, and courts usually find that consumers would be unfairly surprised if a company tried to go back on promises made in a sales brochure.

[10]UCC §2-316(1).

Implied Warranties

A seller may disclaim the implied warranty of merchantability provided he *actually mentions the word* merchantability *and makes the disclaimer conspicuous*. Courts demand to see the specific word *merchantability* in the disclaimer to be sure the buyer realized she was giving up this fundamental protection. If the word is there, and the disclaimer is conspicuous enough that the buyer should have seen it, she has forfeited the warranty. A seller may disclaim the implied warranty of fitness with any language that is clear and conspicuous.

To make life easier, the Uniform Commercial Code permits a seller to disclaim *all* implied warranties by conspicuously stating that the goods are sold "as is" or "with all faults." Notice the tension between this provision and the one just discussed. A seller who wants to disclaim *only* the warranty of merchantability must explicitly mention that term; but a seller wishing to exclude *all* implied warranties may do so with a short expression, such as "sold as is."

Many states, though, prohibit a seller from disclaiming implied warranties in the sale of consumer goods. In these states, if a home furnishings store sells a bunk bed to a consumer, and the top bunk tips out the window on the first night, the seller is liable. Even if the sales contract clearly stated "no warranties of merchantability," the court would reject the clause and find that the seller breached the implied warranty of merchantability.

As the following case illustrates, courts tend to impose high standards on defendants who disclaim warranties.

CCB Ohio, LLC v. Chemque, Inc.

649 F. Supp. 2d 757
United States District Court for the Southern District of Ohio, 2009

Facts: CCB Ohio specializes in upgrading power lines in a way that makes it possible to offer broadband service over an electrical grid. Chemque manufactures Q-gel.

Transformers reduce the 100,000 or more volts flowing through a typical power line to the 120 volts that actually arrive at the outlets in your home. Unfortunately, transformers completely block digital signals, so, to offer broadband over an electrical grid, data must take a "detour" around transformers. Couplers allow for this detour.

CCB and its contractors purchased Q-gel. This substance was supposed to create a waterproof seal that would bind newly installed couplers to power lines. Unfortunately, the gel did not gel, at least not for long. Within 18 months, 40 percent of CCB Ohio's couplers were leaking liquefied Q-gel. Ultimately, 90 percent of the couplers throughout the Cincinnati area leaked and caused millions of dollars in losses.

CCB Ohio sued for breach of warranty. Chemque argued that it had disclaimed all implied warranties. It moved for summary judgment.

Issue: ***Did Chemque disclaim its warranties?***

Excerpts from Judge Spiegel's Decision: Defendant's argument is that [it] disclaimed any warranties, as its specification sheet states "all information is given without warranty or guarantee." Plaintiffs respond that several genuine issues of fact remain as to whether Defendant effectively disclaimed all warranties. Specifically, Plaintiffs argue facts remain as to whether Plaintiffs ever received the specification sheet containing the disclaimer, whether the disclaimer was conspicuous, and whether the disclaimer effectively disclaimed the implied warranty of merchantability and Defendant's express warranties.

The Court finds Plaintiffs' argument well-taken that the record neither establishes they received a disclaimer, nor that the disclaimer Defendant has proffered amounts to a conspicuous disclaimer that a reasonable person ought to have noticed. The Court further concludes that Defendant's purported disclaimer that "all information is given without warranty or guarantee" did not effectively disclaim the implied warranty of merchantability, as the disclaimer does not mention merchantability. Finally, questions of fact exist as to whether Defendant's disclaimer is reasonable vis à vis its express warranties.

As such, the Court rejects Defendant's motion for summary judgment as to Plaintiffs' warranty claims.

EXAM Strategy

Question: Marcos's backyard pool, which measured 35 feet by 18 feet, needed a new filter. A sales brochure stated, "This filter will keep any normal backyard pool, up to 50 feet by 25, clean and healthy all summer for a minimum of 5 years." Marcos signed a sales contract, which included this disclaimer: "The filter will work to normal industry standards. This is the only warranty. No other statements, written or oral, apply. Pools vary widely, and the Seller cannot guarantee any specific level of performance or cleanliness. Buyer agrees to this disclaimer." The filter failed to keep Marcos's pool clean, and he sued for breach of warranty. Who should win?

Strategy: Sellers are often able to disclaim oral warranties, but written warranties are difficult to disclaim. Here, the initial promise and the disclaimer were in different documents. Does that change the outcome? Finally, Marcos was a consumer. Courts treat consumers differently from corporate buyers.

Result: It is difficult or impossible for sellers to disclaim written warranties, even if the promise and disclaimer are in different documents. A disclaimer that would unfairly surprise the buyer is void. Marcos relied on the sales brochure—as the company intended—and the seller will probably lose. Furthermore, most states give extra protection to consumers, knowing that they are less sophisticated buyers. A court is likely to find in favor of Marcos based on the seller's express warranty, as well as the implied warranties of merchantability and fitness.

Remedy Limitations

Simon Aerials, Inc., manufactured boomlifts, the huge cranes used to construct multistoried buildings. Simon agreed to design and build eight unusually large machines for Logan Equipment Corp. Simon delivered the boomlifts late, and they functioned poorly. Logan requested dozens of repairs and modifications, which Simon attempted to accomplish over many months, but the equipment never worked well. Logan gave up and sued for $7.5 million, representing the profits it expected to make from renting the machines and the damage to its reputation. Logan clearly had suffered major losses, and it recovered—nothing. How could that be?

Simon had negotiated a **limitation of remedy** clause, by which the parties may limit or exclude the normal remedies permitted under the Uniform Commercial Code.[11] These important rights are entirely distinct from disclaimers. A disclaimer limits the seller's warranties and thus affects whether the seller has breached her contract in the first place. A remedy limitation, by contrast, states that if a party *does* breach its warranty, the injured party will not get all of the damages the Code normally allows.

In its contract, Simon had agreed to repair or replace any defective boomlifts, but that was all. The agreement said that if a boomlift was defective, and Logan lost business, profits, and reputation, Simon was not liable. The court upheld the remedy limitation. Since Simon had repeatedly attempted to repair and redesign the defective machines, it had done everything it promised to do. Logan got nothing.[12]

[11]UCC §2-719. A few states prohibit remedy limitations, but most permit them.

[12]*Logan Equipment Corp. v. Simon Aerials, Inc.*, 736 F. Supp. 1188, 1990 U.S. Dist. LEXIS 5720 (D. Mass. 1990).

We compare disclaimers and remedy limitations in the table below.

COMPARISON OF DISCLAIMERS AND REMEDY LIMITATIONS

Code Section	Purpose	Setting	Contract Language	Result
Disclaimers: UCC §2-316	Limits warranties, whether express or implied. This section will determine *whether there has been a breach.*	Seller sells Buyer a used "tire shredding machine." UCC §2-314 implies a warranty of merchantability, meaning that the machine will be good for its ordinary purpose, which is shredding tires in a commercial recycling business.	Seller includes in the contract a clause stating that the tire shredder is sold "as is." Under §2-316, this phrase excludes all implied warranties, meaning that the implied warranty of merchantability will NOT apply here.	One tire goes through the machine, the tire emerges completely intact, and the machine falls to pieces. *Result:* Seller has NOT breached the contract, and Buyer gets no damages.
Remedy limitations: UCC §2-719	Limits the remedies available *when one party has breached* the contract.	Seller sells Buyer 10,000 computer circuit boards at $200 each, which Buyer uses in its laptops.	Seller requires a clause limiting Buyer's remedies to "replace or repair." If the boards fail, Seller will replace or repair them for free. But Buyer is permitted NO OTHER REMEDY. Buyer may not seek consequential damages, which would include lost profits and injured reputation.	All of the boards malfunction, and Buyer's customers are angry *at Buyer.* Buyer must take the computers back, losing all of its expected profits and also suffering a serious loss of reputation in the high-tech world. Seller IS in breach of the contract and must repair or replace all circuit boards at its expense. But Seller owes NOTHING for Buyer's lost profits or injured reputation.

Consequential Damages

Simon's contract clause was a typical one. Sellers frequently use a remedy limitation to avoid liability for consequential damages, which can be vast. Recall that a party injured by breach of contract normally gets direct, or *compensatory* damages.[13] In the sale of goods, that means the difference between the value of the goods promised and those actually delivered. A seller can anticipate and probably tolerate such damages since the seller understands exactly how much it costs to repair or replace the goods it has sold. **Consequential damages**, however, are different. They are losses stemming from the particular requirements of the buyer. The buyer might have entered into dozens of contracts in reliance on the goods it expects from the seller. The seller will have no way of knowing how great the consequential damages could be. Logan Equipment claimed that it would have earned profits in the millions, and it was just such a claim that Simon had determined to avoid.

Notice that there is one major restriction on limitation of remedy clauses: **an exclusion of consequential damages is void if it is unconscionable.** The word *unconscionable* means that a remedy restriction is shockingly one-sided and fundamentally unfair.[14] If the buyer is a consumer, a court will be likelier to consider such an exclusion unfair since the typical consumer will not understand the terms and may never even notice them. If the buyer is a

[13]Compensatory, consequential, and incidental damages are discussed in Chapter 18, on remedies.
[14]UCC §2-719.

consumer who suffers a *personal injury*, a court is nearly certain to reject the exclusion. It is unfair for a corporation to market defective goods and escape liability because an unsuspecting consumer failed to understand contract language. Suppose Byron buys a hot-air popcorn popper that comes with a label which attempts to limit remedies. Byron is seriously burned when the popper ignites. Virtually all courts will ignore the label and permit Byron to recover his full damages. However, when the buyer is a corporation, courts assume it had adequate legal advice and an opportunity to reject unacceptable terms. When two companies agree to a remedy limitation, they are allocating the risk of loss as one part of their bargain. A court will seldom substitute its judgment for that of the contracting companies. In the *Logan Equipment* case, both parties were corporations, and sophisticated executives negotiated the boomlift sale. The court found nothing unconscionable in the bargain and enforced the limitation that the parties had agreed to.[15]

Privity

When two parties contract, they are *in privity*. If Lance buys a chainsaw from the local hardware store, he is in privity with the store. But Lance has no privity with Kwiksaw, the manufacturer of the chainsaw. Under traditional contract law, a plaintiff injured by a breach of contract could sue only a defendant with whom he had privity. So, many years ago, if Lance's chainsaw had been seriously defective, he could have sued only the store. Kwiksaw would have defended successfully, claiming "lack of privity." This hurt consumers because the local retailer might have lacked assets to compensate for serious injuries. Today, privity is gradually disappearing as a defense. Various states are approaching the issue in different ways, so there is no one rule. We can, however, highlight the trends.

Personal Injury

Where a product causes a personal injury, most states permit a warranty lawsuit even without privity. If the chain on Lance's power saw flies off and slashes his arm, he has suffered a personal injury. Of course, he may sue the store, with which he has privity. But he will want to sue the manufacturer, which has more money. In the majority of states, he will be able to sue the manufacturer for breach of warranty even though he had no privity with it.[16] (Note that Lance is sure to make other claims against the manufacturer, including *negligence* and *strict liability*, both discussed below.)

---

[15]*Logan Equipment*, 736 F. Supp. at 1195.

[16]The Code offers three alternative versions of its rule concerning privity: UCC §2-318, Alternatives A, B, and C, with each state free to adopt whichever version the legislature prefers. Alternative A, the most restrictive, extends a warranty in the cases of personal injury to the buyer and members of his household. But the comments of this section indicate that this extension to household members does not *preclude* claims brought by non-household members. The drafters have left it up to the states to decide whether additional injured parties could sue. Several states that have adopted this version of the privity rule have permitted warranty claims by injured parties who were not household members. Dahlia buys a weed cutter manufactured by Thorn and sold by Hardware, and she loans it to Rose, who is cut when it malfunctions. Many, but not all, states that have adopted Alternative A would allow Rose to sue Thorn.

Alternative B is more expansive, explicitly permitting a warranty suit by any injured natural person (non-corporation), who could reasonably be affected by the product. In states that have adopted this section, Rose would certainly be permitted to sue Thorn. Alternative C, the most expansive, permits recovery by natural persons and corporations and allows suits for economic loss as well as personal injury. What does all this mean? The privity requirement is disappearing in personal injury cases and diminishing in cases of economic loss.

Economic Loss

If the buyer suffers only economic loss, privity may still be required to bring a suit for breach of warranty. If the buyer is a *business*, the majority of states require privity. Fab-Rik makes fabric for furniture and drapes, which it sells to various wholesalers. Siddown makes sofas. Siddown buys Fab-Rik fabric from a wholesaler and, after installing it on 200 sofas, finds the material defective. Siddown may sue the wholesaler but, in most states, will be unable to sue Fab-Rik for breach of any warranties. There was no privity.

By contrast, when the buyer is a *consumer*, more states will permit a suit against the manufacturer, even without privity. Lance, the consumer, buys his power saw to landscape his property. This time, the saw malfunctions without injuring him, but Lance must buy a replacement saw for considerably more money. Many states—but not all—will permit him to recover his losses from Kwiksaw, the manufacturer, on the theory that Kwiksaw intends its product to reach consumers and is in the best position to control losses.

In the following case, a jailhouse tragedy prompts a product liability suit.

Reed v. City of Chicago

263 F.Supp.2d 1123
United States District Court for the Northern District of Illinois, 2003

Facts: J. C. Reed was arrested and brought to Chicago's Fifth District Police Station. Police were allegedly aware that he was suicidal, having seen him slash his wrists earlier. They removed his clothing and dressed him in a paper isolation gown. Sadly, Reed used the gown to hang himself.

Reed's mother, on his behalf, sued the police (for failing to monitor a suicidal inmate) and also Cypress Medical Products, the manufacturer of the isolation gown. The claim was that the gown should have been made of material that would tear if someone attempted to hang himself with it. Cypress moved to dismiss the suit, claiming that Reed had no privity with the company.

Issue: ***Could Reed maintain a lawsuit against Cypress despite lack of privity?***

Excerpts from Judge Moran's Decision: The single issue we must decide is whether plaintiff, as a non-purchaser, can recover from the manufacturer and designer of the gown for breach of warranty. Historically, Illinois law has required privity. Lack of privity occurs when a user of the product, beside the consumer, is injured. Section 2-318 of the Uniform Commercial Code (UCC), as adopted by the Illinois legislature, contains mandatory exceptions to the general requirement of privity:

> A seller's warranty whether express or implied extends to any natural person who is in the family or household of his buyer or who is a guest in his home if it is reasonable to expect that such person may use, consume or be affected by the goods and who is injured in person by breach of the warranty.

The Illinois Supreme Court has determined that the privity is no longer an absolute requirement for breach of warranty actions. While section 2-318 lists specific exceptions to the privity requirement, Illinois courts have noted that this list is not necessarily exhaustive.

The vast majority of cases examining the limits of section 2-318 in Illinois have dealt with the employment context, expanding the class of potential breach of warranty plaintiffs to employees of the ultimate purchaser. In [a case called *Whitaker*,] plaintiff was injured while using a bandsaw that had been purchased by his employer. The court determined that the employee was essentially a third party beneficiary to the sale in that the employee's safety while using the bandsaw was "either explicitly or implicitly part of the basis of the bargain when the employer purchased the goods."

In cases examining the limits of section 2-318 in other contexts, courts have been reluctant to find additional exceptions to the privity requirement. In [a case called *Hemphill*,] the court refused to allow a breach of warranty claim by a university football player against the manufacturer of his helmet.

While no Illinois courts have expanded the plaintiff class for breach of warranty actions beyond employees, we believe that the law requires us to do so here. The beneficiary of any warranty made by the manufacturer and designer of the gown is necessarily a potentially suicidal detainee like Reed. If protection is not provided to plaintiffs like Reed, any warranty as to the safety of the gown would have little, if any, effect. In designing and manufacturing the gown, defendants contemplated that the users of the gown would be detainees. Moreover, the safety of these detainees was necessarily a part of the bargain, whether explicitly or implicitly, between the seller and buyer. For these reasons, a detainee of the City like Reed must be able to enforce the protections of any warranties made by the manufacturer and designer of the gown.

For the foregoing reasons, defendants' motion to dismiss is denied.

Buyer's Misuse

Misuse by the buyer will generally preclude a warranty claim.[17] Common sense tells us that the seller only warrants its goods if they are properly used. Lord & Taylor warranted that its false eyelashes would function well and cause no harm. But when Ms. Caldwell applied them, they severely irritated one eye. She sued, but the store prevailed. Why? Caldwell applied the eyelashes improperly, getting the glue into one eye. On her other eye, she used the product correctly and suffered no harm. Her misuse proved painful to her eye—and fatal to her lawsuit.[18]

Statute of Limitations and Notice of Breach

It is right that a seller be responsible for the goods it places in the market. On the other hand, a seller should not face potential liability *forever*. A company cannot be a perpetual insurer for goods that it sold decades earlier. And so the UCC imposes two important time limits on a buyer's claim of breach.

The Code prescribes a four-year statute of limitations. This means that the buyer must bring any lawsuit for breach of a warranty no later than four years after the goods were delivered. When the parties contract, they may shorten that period to no less than one year, but they may not extend it. Suppose PlaneJane, an airline, buys 10 new aircraft from Flyem, a manufacturer, taking delivery on June 1, 2012. In the fall of 2015, PlaneJane begins to discover structural weaknesses in the wings, which Flyem repeatedly repairs over the next few months. PlaneJane must decide whether to file a lawsuit. If the airline believes all problems are corrected, fine. But if it has any doubts about the aircraft fitness, PlaneJane must sue promptly. On June 2, 2016, any lawsuit for breach of warranty is barred by the statute of limitations.

The Code puts an additional burden on a buyer asserting a breach of warranty. **The UCC requires that a buyer notify the seller of defects within a reasonable time.**[19] The purpose here is to enable the seller to cure, by repairing or replacing, any problems with the goods. Ideally, a seller that receives notice of a potential breach will fix the problem and there will *be* no lawsuit.

The circumstances will determine what is a "reasonable" amount of time. An inexperienced consumer could reasonably take many months to figure out that a new laptop computer had a serious operating defect. Further, a delay of six or eight months would not harm a large computer manufacturer. On the other hand, a corporate buyer of perishable food products must act very quickly if it wishes to claim the goods are defective.

---

[17]Some courts characterize the misuse as "comparative negligence" or "contributory negligence" or "failure of proximate cause." These tort terms are discussed in Chapter 7, dealing with negligence and strict liability. For our purposes here, though, it is enough to understand that misuse generally precludes a warranty claim.

[18]*Caldwell v. Lord & Taylor, Inc.*, 142 Ga. App. 137, 235 S.E.2d 546 (Ga. Ct. App. 1977).

[19]UCC §2-607.

Negligence

A consumer injured by an exploding cola bottle is unlikely to have bargained for her beverage with the CEO of the cola company.

A buyer of goods may have remedies other than warranty claims. One is negligence, which we discussed in detail in Chapter 7. Here, we focus on how this law applies to the sale of goods. Negligence, as you will recall, is notably different from contract law. In a contract case, the two parties have reached an agreement, and the terms of their bargain will usually determine how to settle any dispute. If the parties agreed that the seller disclaimed all warranties, then the buyer may be out of luck. But in a negligence case, there has been no bargaining between the parties, and they may never have met. A consumer injured by an exploding cola bottle is unlikely to have bargained for her beverage with the CEO of the cola company. Instead, the law *imposes* a standard of conduct on everyone in society, corporation and individual alike. The two key elements of this standard, for present purposes, are *duty* and *breach*. A plaintiff injured by goods she bought must show that the defendant, usually a manufacturer or seller of a product, had a duty to her and breached that duty.[20] A defendant has a duty of due care to anyone who could *foreseeably* be injured by its misconduct. Generally, the duty is to act as a reasonable person would in like circumstances; a defendant who acts unreasonably has breached its duty.

In negligence cases concerning the sale of goods, plaintiffs most often raise one or more of these claims:

- ***Negligent design.*** The buyer claims that the product injured her because the manufacturer designed it poorly. Negligence law requires a manufacturer to design a product free of *unreasonable* risks. The product does not have to be absolutely safe. An automobile that nearly guaranteed a driver's safety could be made, in theory, but it would be prohibitively expensive. Reasonable safety features must be built in, if they can be included at a tolerable cost.
- ***Negligent manufacture.*** The buyer claims that the design was adequate but that failure to inspect or some other careless conduct caused a dangerous product to leave the plant.
- ***Failure to warn.*** A manufacturer is liable for failing to warn the purchaser or users about the dangers of normal use and also foreseeable misuse. However, there is no duty to warn about obvious dangers, a point evidently lost on some manufacturers. A Batman costume came with this statement: "For play only: cape does not enable user to fly."

In the following case, the plaintiffs raise issues of negligent design and failure to warn, concerning a disposable lighter. Did they breach their duty? You decide.

---

[20] A plaintiff in a negligence case must also prove three other elements: factual causation, foreseeable type of harm, and injury. For a discussion of those elements, see Chapter 7. We focus in this chapter on duty and breach because those two elements take on special importance in product liability cases.

You be the Judge

Boumelhem v. Bic Corp.

211 Mich. App. 175, 535 N.W.2d 574, 1995
Mich. App. LEXIS 228
Michigan Court of Appeals, 1995

Facts: Ibrahim Boumelhem, aged four, began playing with a Bic disposable lighter that his parents had purchased. He started a fire that burned his legs and severely burned his six-month-old brother over 85 percent of his body. Ibrahim's father sued Bic, claiming that the lighter was negligently designed because it could have been childproof. He also claimed failure to warn because the lighter did not clearly warn of the danger to children.

The *Boumelhem* court considered evidence and analyses from several other cases against Bic. The court noted that consumers use over 500 million disposable lighters annually in the United States. Each lighter provides 1,000 to 2,000 lights. During one three-year period, children playing with disposable lighters started 8,100 fires annually, causing an average of 180 people to die every year, of whom 140 were children under five. Another 990 people were injured. The average annual cost of deaths, injuries, and property damage from child-play fires was estimated at $310 to $375 million, or 60 to 75 cents per lighter sold. Bic had acknowledged in earlier litigation that it was foreseeable lighters would get into children's hands and injure them. Bic had also agreed that it was feasible to make a more child-resistant lighter.

The trial court relied on a Michigan case. In *Adams v. Perry Furniture Co.*,[21] four minor children had died in a fire started when one of them was playing with a Bic lighter. The *Adams* court had found no negligent design and no failure to warn, and it dismissed all claims. The trial court in the present case followed *Adams* and dismissed Boumelhem's claims. He appealed.

You Be the Judge: ***Did Bic negligently design its disposable lighter? Did Bic negligently fail to warn of the lighter's dangers?***

Argument for Boumelhem: Your honors, the *Adams* court decided the issues wrongly. There is a reason that new plaintiffs are back in this court, the year after *Adams*, raising related issues against Bic: the company is killing hundreds of children every year. In its efforts to maximize corporate profits, it is literally burning these children to death and injuring hundreds more. That's wrong.

Bic has acknowledged that its disposable lighters can and will get into the hands of children. Bic knows full well that its product will injure or kill a certain percentage of these children—very young children. Bic has admitted that it could design a childproof lighter, and it knows perfectly well how to include effective warnings on its lighters. But rather than improve product design and give effective warnings, Bic prefers to do business as usual and litigate liability for injured children.

We ask this court to rule that Bic breached its duty to design and manufacture a lighter that will keep our kids safe, and breached its duty to warn.

Argument for Bic: Your honors, the Bic Corp. is as horrified as anyone over the injuries to these children and the deaths of other kids. But Bic is not responsible. The children's parents are responsible. We sympathize with their grief, but not with their attempt to pass parental responsibility onto the shoulders of a corporation. There are several reasons Bic is not liable in this case.

First, the *Adams* court decided the matter, and that precedent is binding.

Second, Bic has no duty to design a different lighter. The test in design defect cases is whether the risks are unreasonable in light of the foreseeable injuries. Young children can hurt themselves in countless ways, from falls to poisonings to automobile injuries. There is one answer to these dangers, and it is called good parenting. The parents who bought this lighter purchased it because it could start a fire. The moment they purchased it, they assumed the obligation to keep it away from their children. These are useful products, which is why Bic sells hundreds of millions per year. Other consumers should not be forced to pay an outrageously high price for a simple tool, just because some parents fail to do their job.

The failure to warn argument is even weaker. The law imposes no failure to warn when the danger is obvious. Every adult knows that lighters are *potentially* dangerous, if misused, or if passed on to children. No one would be helped by a warning that said, "This lighter starts fires. Don't give it to children."

---

[21] 198 Mich. App. 1, 497 N.W.2d 514, 1993 Mich. App. LEXIS 33 (Mich. Ct. App. 1993).

STRICT LIABILITY

The other tort claim that an injured person can often bring against the manufacturer or seller of a product is strict liability. Like negligence, strict liability is a burden created by the law rather than by the parties. And, as with all torts, strict liability concerns claims of physical harm. But there is a key distinction between negligence and strict liability: in a negligence case, the injured buyer must demonstrate that the seller's conduct was unreasonable. Not so in strict liability.

In strict liability, the injured person need not prove that the defendant's conduct was unreasonable. The injured person must show only that the defendant manufactured or sold a product that was defective and that the defect caused harm. Almost all states permit such lawsuits, and most of them have adopted the following model:

1. One who sells any product in a defective condition unreasonably dangerous to the user or consumer or to his property is subject to liability for physical harm thereby caused to the ultimate user or consumer, or to his property, if
   a. the seller is engaged in the business of selling such a product, and
   b. it is expected to and does reach the user or consumer without substantial change in the condition in which it is sold.
2. The rule stated in Subsection (1) applies although
   a. the seller has exercised all possible care in the preparation and sale of his product, and
   b. the user or consumer has not bought the product from or entered into any contractual relation with the seller.[22]

These are the key terms in subsection (1):

- ***Defective condition unreasonably dangerous to the user.*** The defendant is liable only if the product is defective when it leaves his hands. There must be something wrong with the goods. If they are reasonably safe and the buyer's mishandling of the goods causes the harm, there is no strict liability. If you attempt to open a soda bottle by knocking the cap against a counter, and the glass shatters and cuts you, the manufacturer owes nothing. A carving knife can produce a lethal wound, but everyone knows that, and a sharp knife is not unreasonably dangerous. On the other hand, prescription drugs may harm in ways that neither a layperson nor a doctor would anticipate. The manufacturer *must provide adequate warnings* of any dangers that are not apparent.
- ***In the business of selling.*** The seller is liable only if she normally sells this kind of product. Suppose your roommate makes you a peanut butter sandwich and, while eating it, you cut your mouth on a sliver of glass that was in the jar. The peanut butter manufacturer faces strict liability, as does the grocery store where your roommate bought the goods. But your roommate is not strictly liable because he is not in the food business.

Because prescription drugs may cause harm even when taken correctly, drug manufacturers are required to provide adequate warnings of potential dangers involved in taking their products.

[22] Restatement (Second) of Torts §402A.

- ***Reaches the user without substantial change.*** Obviously, if your roommate put the glass in the peanut butter thinking it was funny, neither the manufacturer nor the store is liable.

And here are the important phrases in subsection (2).

- ***Has exercised all possible care.*** This is the heart of strict liability, which makes it a potent claim for consumers. *It is no defense that the seller used reasonable care.* If the product is dangerously defective and injures the user, the seller is liable even if it took every precaution to design and manufacture the product safely. Suppose the peanut butter jar did in fact contain a glass sliver when it left the factory. The manufacturer proves that it uses extraordinary care in keeping foreign particles out of the jars and thoroughly inspects each container before it is shipped. The evidence is irrelevant. The manufacturer has shown that it was not *negligent* in packaging the food, but reasonable care is irrelevant in strict liability cases.
- ***No contractual relation.*** Remember "privity," from the warranty discussion? Privity only exists between the user and the person from whom she actually bought the goods, but in strict liability cases, *privity is not required.* Suppose the manufacturer that made the peanut butter sold it to a distributor, which sold it to a wholesaler, which sold it to a grocery store, which sold it to your roommate. You may sue the manufacturer, distributor, wholesaler, and store, even though you had no privity with any of them.

Contemporary Trends

If the steering wheel on a brand new car falls off, and the driver is injured, that is a clear case of defective manufacturing, and the company will be strictly liable. Those are the easy cases. But defective design cases have been more contentious. Suppose a vaccine that prevents serious childhood illnesses inevitably causes brain damage in a very small number of children because of the nature of the drug. Is the manufacturer liable? What if a racing sailboat, designed only for speed, is dangerously unstable in the hands of a less-experienced sailor? Is the boat's maker responsible for fatalities? Suppose an automobile made of lightweight metal uses less fuel but exposes its occupants to more serious injuries in an accident. How is a court to decide whether the design was defective? Often, these design cases also involve issues of warnings: did the drug designer diligently detail dangers to doctors? Should a sailboat seller sell speedy sailboats solely to seasoned sailors?

Over the years, most courts have adopted one of two tests for design and warning cases. The first is *consumer expectation.* Here, a court finds the manufacturer liable for defective design if the product is less safe than a reasonable consumer would expect. If a smoke detector has a 3 percent failure rate and the average consumer has no way of anticipating that danger, effective cautions must be included, though the design may be defective anyway.

Many other states use a *risk-utility test.* Here, a court must weigh the benefits for society against the dangers that the product poses. Principal factors in the risk-utility test include:

- The *value* of the product,
- The *gravity*, or seriousness, of the danger,
- The *likelihood* that such danger will occur,
- The mechanical feasibility of a *safer alternative* design, and
- The *adverse consequences* of an alternative design.

Tort Reform

Some people believe that jury awards are excessive and need statutory reform. About two-thirds of the states have passed at least some limits on damages in tort actions. About one-third of states have created new rules for particular kinds of product liability. *Unavoidably unsafe* prescription drugs are an example. Suppose that a plaintiff proves that a prescription medicine caused her grievous, permanent harm, and that 1 percent of all users will suffer similar damage. If the pharmaceutical company can demonstrate that it is impossible to manufacture the drug to eliminate all danger, many states will deny the plaintiff any damages. These states have essentially decided that the benefits of that prescription medicine outweigh its risks. If the medicine is unavoidably unsafe—that is, it cannot be made safer—the company should not be held liable; large verdicts might drive pharmaceutical firms out of a business that has great social value.

Opponents consider tort reform dangerous to society. They argue that the real goal of the so-called reform is to free irresponsible corporations from any potential liability, enabling them to save money while injuring innocent people. They insist that giving the 12 average members of society on a jury a say in product safety benefits everyone.

Time Limits: Statutes of Limitations in Tort Cases

We have seen that for *warranty* cases, the UCC imposes a four-year statute of limitations. By contrast, most states have a different statute of limitations for tort claims. Many states set a three-year limit, though some are shorter and others longer. But the key element is this: in a tort case, the statute of limitations runs *from the time the defect was discovered*.

Many product liability cases involve both warranty and tort claims. Should a court apply the statute of limitations from the Code or from tort law? The analysis begins with the **economic loss doctrine**: when an injury is purely economic and arises from a contract made by two businesses, the injured party may only sue under the UCC. (If the buyer is a consumer, most courts will not apply this doctrine.)

Economic loss doctrine
When an injury is purely economic, and arises from a contract made by two businesses, the injured party may only sue under the UCC.

So, **the four-year statute of limitations will apply in all cases covered by the economic loss doctrine**. Suppose a corporation discovers that a product it purchased six years ago is defective and has caused major losses. The company probably has no remedy. Neibarger purchased an automated milking system for his dairy from Universal Cooperatives. Over the next few years, many of his cows became sick; some died, and others had to be sold for beef. Seven years after he bought the equipment, Neibarger learned that Universal had improperly designed and installed the vacuum system that is an essential part of the machine. He sued, claiming massive damage to his farming operation, but the Michigan Supreme Court applied the economic loss doctrine. Neibarger's loss was commercial, resulting from a contract that two corporations had negotiated. His only possible remedy was under the UCC, but the Code's statute of limitations had expired. In the end, he had no remedy.[23]

A Final Issue: Statutes of Repose

In tort cases, the passage of time provides a seller with two possible defenses. We have seen that the statute of limitations requires that a lawsuit be brought within a specified period, such as three years, beginning when the defect is discovered or should have been discovered. **A statute of repose places an absolute limit on when a lawsuit may be filed,**

[23] *Neibarger v. Universal Cooperatives, Inc.*, 439 Mich. 512, 486 N.W.2d 612, 1992 Mich. LEXIS 1502 (1992).

regardless of when the defect is discovered. Jeffrey Oats was riding in the back seat of a Nissan sports car when it was involved in an accident. Tragically, Oats suffered spinal cord injuries that left him a quadriplegic. Oats sued Nissan, based on defective design, claiming that the rear seat lacked adequate head and leg room and that the car's body panels lacked sufficient strength. He argued that these defects only became apparent in an accident. But the Idaho Supreme Court dismissed his claims because the car was 11 years old at the time of the accident. The Idaho statute of repose prohibits most product liability suits filed more than 10 years after the goods were sold, regardless of when the defects were discoverable.[24]

EXAM Strategy

Question: Stuart lives in a state that sets a three-year statute of limitations on tort claims. His state also has an eight-year statute of repose. Stuart bought a television on June 1, 2010. On July 1, 2017, a manufacturing defect causes the television to malfunction and cause an electrical fire. Stuart waits for a year and then files a lawsuit on July 1, 2018. Will he win, or will his case be dismissed?

Strategy: Since Stuart is a consumer, the court will not apply either the economic loss doctrine or the UCC's four-year statute of limitations. When does the state's three-year statute of limitations begin to run? What effect will the state's statute of repose have on Stuart's case?

Result: The statute of limitations' three-year period starts to run only when Stuart discovers the defect. Since he filed one year from the fire, the statute of limitations does not bar his recovery. But unfortunately, Stuart's lawsuit will fail because of the statute of repose. That eight-year limit begins to expire when Stuart buys the TV, and the lawsuit is not filed for eight years and one month from the time of the sale. Stuart loses.

Other Legislation

Lemon Laws

It is intensely frustrating—and expensive—for consumers when a new car is defective and spends more time in the repair shop than on the road. So, many states have passed lemon laws, which entitle the buyer to receive a refund if the car has defects that substantially impair its value and safety. This right may prove more valuable than a limited warranty, which might only entitle the buyer to repeated attempts at servicing.

Consumer Protection Laws

Virtually all states also have consumer protection laws, which focus on a merchant's bad faith or deceit. Consumers can use these statutes, which are discussed in Chapter 39, to recover for defective goods or inadequate service.

---

[24] *Oats v. Nissan Motor Corp.*, 126 Idaho 162, 879 P.2d 1095, 1994 Ida. LEXIS 116 (1994).

Chapter Conclusion

Both sellers and buyers of goods must understand the basic principles of product liability law. A seller must understand warranty, negligence, and strict liability law and consider all of those principles when designing, manufacturing, marketing, and selling goods. A buyer, on the other hand, should be aware each theory provides a possible basis for compensation and that consumers receive particularly strong protection.

EXAM REVIEW

Products can injure. The harm may be economic or physical. The plaintiff might have a remedy in *warranty*, which is found in the UCC, or one in *tort*, either for negligence or strict liability. The economic loss doctrine states that, when the injured party is a corporation and the harm is purely economic, the only remedies available are the warranty provisions of the Code. If a corporation suffers physical injury, it will probably be able to sue in tort. A consumer who suffers a physical injury can definitely sue in both tort and warranty, and a consumer who suffers an economic injury can generally, but not always, sue in both.

The Code prescribes a four-year statute of limitation for breaches of warranty. In tort cases, the statute of limitations runs from whenever the plaintiff should have discovered the defect. For ease of review, the following chart summarizes the different warranty and tort remedies.

	Contract or Tort	Source of Law	Summary of the Rule	Example	Potential Issue
Express Warranty	Contract	UCC §2-313	May be created by an affirmation of fact, a promise, a description of goods, or a sample, but it must have been the basis of the bargain.	Salesman says, "This helicopter will operate perfectly at 16,000 feet."	Written contract may disclaim any and all *oral* warranties.
Implied Warranty of Merchantability	Contract	UCC §2-314	The Code implies that the goods are fit for their ordinary use.	Buyer purchases a deep freezer. The Code implies a warranty that it will keep food frozen.	Seller may disclaim this warranty only if a conspicuous disclaimer includes the word "merchantability."
Implied Warranty of Fitness	Contract	UCC §2-315	The Code implies that the goods are fit for buyer's special purpose that seller knows about.	Where seller knows (1) buyer wants pine trees to plant in sandy soil, and (2) buyer is relying on seller's judgment, the trees carry an implied warranty that they will grow in that soil.	Seller may disclaim this warranty with conspicuous writing, but note that some states will disregard a disclaimer of *any* implied warranty in a consumer sale.

	Contract or Tort	Source of Law	Summary of the Rule	Example	Potential Issue
Implied Warranty of Title	Contract	UCC §2-312	The Code implies that seller has good title, free of any security interests and claims of patent, copyright, or trademark.	Seller sells a stolen car to buyer, who must later return it to the rightful owner. Seller has breached his warranty of good title and owes buyer her full damages.	Buyer is not protected against any security interests that she knows about.
Negligence	Tort	Common law	Seller is liable if she fails to show level of conduct that a *reasonable person* would use.	Manufacturer sells bathing suit made of miracle fabric; buyer swims in ocean where saltwater makes garment transparent; seller's failure to test the suit in saltwater was unreasonable and leaves seller liable. If seller had thoroughly tested and this was a freak occurrence, there would probably be no negligence.	No duty to warn if the danger is obvious. (In the bathing suit example, the danger is *not* obvious and there was a duty to warn.)
Strict Liability	Tort	State statutes and common law	Seller liable if the product leaves in a dangerously defective condition.	Can of barbecue lighter fluid explodes in the user's hand because the can's metal was defective; manufacturer took every reasonable precaution to test and inspect every can leaving factory; that reasonable care is *irrelevant* and seller is liable.	Injured buyer need not prove negligence but must prove that the product was defective.

Multiple-Choice Questions

1. **CPA QUESTION** Vick bought a used boat from Ocean Marina that disclaimed "any and all warranties." Ocean was unaware the boat had been stolen from Kidd. Vick surrendered it to Kidd when confronted with proof of the theft. Vick sued Ocean. Who prevails?
   (a) Vick, because the implied warranty of title has been breached
   (b) Vick, because a merchant cannot disclaim implied warranties
   (c) Ocean, because of the disclaimer of warranties
   (d) Ocean, because Vick surrendered the boat to Kidd

2. **CPA QUESTION** To establish a cause of action based on strict liability in tort for personal injuries resulting from using a defective product, one of the elements the plaintiff must prove is that the seller (defendant):
   (a) Failed to exercise due care
   (b) Was in privity of contract with the plaintiff
   (c) Defectively designed the product
   (d) Was engaged in the business of selling the product

3. **CPA QUESTION** Which of the following conditions must be met for an implied warranty of fitness for a particular purpose to arise?

   I. The warranty must be in writing.

   II. The seller must know that the buyer was relying on the seller in selecting the goods.

   (a) I only
   (b) II only
   (c) Both I and II
   (d) Neither I nor II

4. **CPA QUESTION** Under the UCC sales article, an action for breach of the implied warranty of merchantability by a party who sustains personal injuries may be successful against the seller of the product only when:
   (a) The seller is a merchant of the product involved.
   (b) An action based on negligence can also be successfully maintained.
   (c) The injured party is in privity of contract with the seller.
   (d) An action based on strict liability in tort can also be successfully maintained.

5. **CPA QUESTION** Which of the following factors is least important in determining whether a manufacturer is strictly liable in tort for a defective product?
   (a) The negligence of the manufacturer
   (b) The contributory negligence of the plaintiff
   (c) Modifications to the product by the wholesaler
   (d) Whether the product caused injuries

Essay Questions

1. Leighton Industries needed steel pipe to build furnaces for a customer. Leighton sent Callier Steel an order for a certain quantity of "A 106 Grade B" steel. Callier confirmed the order and created a contract by sending an invoice to Leighton, stating that it would send "A 106 Grade B" steel, as ordered. Callier delivered the steel, and Leighton built the furnaces, but they leaked badly and required rebuilding. Tests demonstrated that the steel was not in fact "A 106 Grade B," but an inferior steel. Leighton sued. Who wins?

2. **YOU BE THE JUDGE WRITING PROBLEM** United Technologies advertised a used Beechcraft Baron airplane for sale in an aviation journal. Thompson Comerford, an attorney, was interested and spoke with a United agent, who described the plane as "excellently maintained" and said it had been operated "under §135 flight regulations," meaning the plane had been subject to airworthiness inspections every 100 hours. Comerford arrived at a Dallas airport to pick up the plane, where he paid $80,000 for it. He signed a sales agreement stating that the plane was sold "as is" and that there were "no representations or warranties, express or implied, including the condition of the aircraft, its merchantability, or its fitness for any particular

purpose." Comerford attempted to fly the plane home but immediately experienced problems with its brakes, steering, ability to climb, and performance while cruising. (Otherwise, it was fine.) He sued, claiming breach of express and implied warranties. Did United Technologies breach an express or implied warranty? **Argument for Comerford:** United described the airplane as "excellently maintained," knowing that Mr. Comerford would rely on that information. United bragged about §135 servicing when that was obviously a lie. The company should not be allowed to say one thing and put the opposite in writing. **Argument for United Technologies:** Comerford is a lawyer, and we assume he can read. The contract could not have been clearer. The plane was sold as is. There were no warranties. If Comerford disliked the terms, he should have bargained for a different contract—or walked away. He knew he was buying a risky plane, and it is his to keep.

3. Round Tire Co. sells 1,000 tires to Green Rent-a-Car for use on Green's fleet. The same day, it sells one new tire to Betty Blue for use on her car. For both sales, Round uses a sales agreement that includes: "LIMITATION OF REMEDIES. Round agrees to repair or replace any tire which Round determines was defective, within 12 months or 25,000 miles, whichever comes first. Buyer agrees that this is Buyer's SOLE REMEDY; Buyer is not entitled to consequential or incidental damages or any other remedy of any kind." All of Round's tires prove defective. Green is so disgusted, it immediately purchases substitute tires from another manufacturer. Green loses $12,000 in extra tire costs and $75,000 in lost rental payments because many of its cars must be off the road waiting for tires. Betty Blue's new tire blows out as she is driving to church, and Betty suffers broken bones. Green and Blue both sue. Predict the outcomes.

4. Texaco, Inc., and other oil companies sold mineral spirits in bulk to distributors, which then resold to retailers. Mineral spirits are used for cleaning. Texaco allegedly knew that the retailers, such as hardware stores, frequently packaged the mineral spirits (illegally) in used half-gallon milk containers and sold them to consumers, often with no warnings on the packages. Mineral spirits are harmful or fatal if swallowed. David Hunnings, aged 21 months, found a milk container in his home, swallowed the mineral spirits, and died. The Hunnings sued Texaco for negligence. The trial court dismissed the complaint, and the Hunnings appealed. What is the legal standard in a negligence case? Have the plaintiffs made out a valid case of negligence? Remember that at this stage, a court is not deciding who wins, but what standard a plaintiff must meet in order to take its case to a jury. Assume that Texaco knew about the repackaging and the grave risk but continued to sell in bulk because doing so was profitable. (If the plaintiffs cannot prove those facts, they will lose even if they *do* get to a jury.) Would that make you angry? Does that mean such a case should go to a jury? Or would you conclude that the fault still lies with the retailer, the parents, or both?

5. Boboli Co. wanted to promote its "California-style" pizza, which it sold in supermarkets. The company contracted with Highland Group, Inc., to produce 2 million recipe brochures, which would be inserted in the carton when the freshly baked pizza was still very hot. Highland contracted with Comark Merchandising to print the brochures. But when Comark asked for details concerning the pizza, the carton, and so forth, Highland refused to supply the information. Comark printed the first lot of 72,000 brochures, which Highland delivered to Boboli. Unfortunately, the hot bread caused the ink to run, and customers opening the carton often found red or blue splotches on their pizzas. Highland refused to accept additional brochures, and Comark sued for breach of contract. Highland defended by claiming that Comark had breached its warranty of merchantability. Please comment.

Discussion Questions

1. Consider the opening scenario, in which a diner cracked a tooth on a fragment of bone hidden in a hamburger. Would society be better off if lawsuits over such injuries were more difficult to win and yielded smaller damages? Or should the person with the cracked tooth have a good chance to get a large payday in court? Does your answer depend upon whether you are the person with the cracked tooth?

2. A seller can disclaim all implied warranties by stating that goods are sold "as is" (or by using other, more specific language). Is this fair? The UCC's implied warranties seem reasonable—that goods are fit for their normal purposes, for example. Should it be so easy for sellers to escape their obligations?

3. After learning more about implied warranties and disclaimers, would you ever buy an item sold "as is?" Imagine a car salesman who offers you a car for $8,000, but who also says that he can knock the price down to $6,500 if you will buy the car "as is." If you live in a state that does not give consumers special protections, which deal would be more appealing?

4. Assume that two computer manufacturers—Alpha and Beta—deliver identical shipments of malfunctioning laptops. The defective machines each cause customers $10,000 in direct damages and $50,000 in consequential damages. Alpha's contract contained a limitation of damages clause, and it pays only $10,000. Beta's contract had no such clause, and it is on the hook for $60,000. Is this fair?

5. "Lemon laws" usually only cover cars. Are there other products that should be covered by similar laws? If so, which ones?

CHAPTER 23

© Stas Volik/Shutterstock.com

PERFORMANCE AND REMEDIES

Was it a 1930s roadster? A drag racing car from the 1950s? Both. When the Plymouth Prowler first hit the road, with its motorcycle-styled front fenders and low-slung hot rod body, it was nearly impossible to get your hands on one. Dealers were swamped with orders, but they did not know if they would receive a single car from the manufacturer.

Donald Hessler wanted a Prowler—and he was a determined man. Hessler went to Crystal Lake Chrysler-Plymouth, met with its owner, Gary Rosenberg, and signed an agreement to buy a Prowler anytime during the next year for $5,000 over the manufacturer's list price. Three months later, Rosenberg revealed that the list price would be $39,000. However, the car dealer also entered into a contract to sell a Prowler to another customer for $50,000.

Donald Hessler wanted a Prowler—and he was a determined man.

The next time they spoke, Rosenberg told Hessler that Crystal Lake would not be allotted any Prowlers. The eager buyer, though, responded that a Chrysler representative had told him Crystal Lake would receive at least one car. Rosenberg was furious with a customer who had "gone behind his back" to contact Chrysler, and said he would not sell Hessler a car, even if he did receive one.

Hessler telephoned 38 Chrysler dealers, but none would promise him a car. One month later, at a promotional event for the car, he saw a new Prowler—with Crystal Lake's name on it! He located Rosenberg, offered to buy the car on the spot—and was again rebuffed. Frustrated and angry, but still determined, Hessler somehow found a Prowler later the same day from another dealer, and bought it—for $77,706.

Ecstatic with his new car, Hessler drove straight to court, where he sued Crystal Lake. Was Rosenberg within his rights, refusing to sell a car to Hessler? Was the customer entitled to compensation for spending so much more on the coveted auto? These are typical issues of contract performance under the Uniform Commercial Code. We look at the issue in this chapter, along with principles of *remedy*. When Hessler bought a car elsewhere, he was *covering*. Did he act reasonably in spending almost $40,000 above list price? You will have to wait a few pages to find out, but we promise to give you the answer before anyone else gets it.

Obligation on All Parties: Good Faith

Surely it is a good idea to begin this final chapter on sale of goods issues in good faith.

The R. G. Ray Corp. needed T-bolts to use in automobile parts it was manufacturing for the Garrett Co. Ray contracted for Maynard Manufacturing to deliver 57,000 T-bolts and provided Maynard with detailed specifications. The contract stated that Ray would be the "final judge" of whether the T-bolts conformed to its specifications and that Ray had the right to return any or all non-conforming bolts. **Conforming goods satisfy the contract terms. Non-conforming goods do not.**[1]

Unfortunately, Ray rejected the 57,000 bolts and sued, demanding every penny it had paid as well as additional damages for its lost business with Garrett. Ray moved for summary judgment, pointing out that the contract explicitly allowed it to judge the bolts, to reject any it found unsatisfactory, and to cancel the contract. The court acknowledged that the contract did give Ray these one-sided powers, yet it denied summary judgment. There was still an issue of *good faith.*

The UCC requires *good faith* in the performance and enforcement of every contract. Good faith means honesty in fact. Between merchants, it also means the use of reasonable commercial standards of fair dealing.[2] So Ray's right to reject the T-bolts was not absolute. There was some evidence that Ray had lost its contract with Garrett for reasons having nothing to do with Maynard's T-bolts. If that was true, and Ray had rejected the T-bolts simply because it no longer needed them, then Ray acted in bad faith and would be fully liable on the contract. The court ruled that Maynard should have its day in court to prove bad faith.[3]

Seller's Rights and Obligations

The seller's primary obligation is to deliver conforming goods to the buyer.[4] But because a buyer might not be willing or able to accept delivery, the UCC demands only that the seller make a reasonable *attempt* at delivery. **The seller must *tender* the goods, which means to make conforming goods available to the buyer.**[5] Normally, the contract will state where and when the seller is obligated to tender delivery. For example, the parties may agree that Manufacturer is to tender 1,000 printers at a certain warehouse on July 3. If Manufacturer makes the printers available on that date, Buyer is obligated to pick them up then and there and is in breach if it fails to do so.

---

[1]UCC §2-106(2).
[2]UCC §§1-203, 2-103(1)(b).
[3]*R. G. Ray Corp. v. Maynard Manufacturing Co.*, 1993 U.S. Dist. LEXIS 15754 (N.D. Ill. 1993).
[4]UCC §2-301.
[5]UCC §2-503.

Although a seller must always tender delivery, that does not mean a seller always transports the goods. Sometimes the contract will require the buyer to collect the goods. Regardless of where delivery is being made, however, the seller must (1) make the goods available at a reasonable time, (2) keep the goods available for a reasonable period, and (3) deliver to the buyer any documents that it needs to take possession. And as we have said, the seller is expected to deliver *conforming* goods, which brings us to the next rule.

Perfect Tender Rule

Under the perfect tender rule, the buyer may reject the goods if they fail *in any respect* to conform to the contract.[6]

Stanley and Joan Jakowski agreed to buy a new Camaro automobile from Carole Chevrolet. The contract stated that Carole would apply a polymer undercoating. The Jakowskis paid in full for the car, but the next day, they informed Carole that the car lacked the undercoating. Carole acknowledged the defect and promised to apply the undercoating, but before it could do so, a thief stole the car. The Jakowskis demanded their money back, but Carole refused, saying that the risk of loss had passed to the Jakowskis when Carole tendered delivery. The Jakowskis sued, claiming that they had rejected the Camaro as non-conforming. Carole responded that this was absurd: the car was perfect in every respect except for the very minor undercoating, which Carole had promised to fix promptly. Carole Chevrolet lost the case because of the perfect tender rule.

The New Jersey court found that the defect was minor but said that "despite seller's assertion to the contrary, the degree of their nonconformity is irrelevant in assessing the buyer's right to reject them… . [N]o particular quantum of nonconformity is required." The Jakowskis had lawfully rejected non-conforming goods, and Carole Chevrolet was forced to pay them the full value of the missing car.[7]

Restrictions on the Perfect Tender Rule

The UCC includes sections that limit the perfect tender rule's effect. Indeed, courts often apply the limitations more enthusiastically than the rule itself, and so while perfect tender is the law, it must be understood in the context of other provisions. We will look at the most common ways that the law undercuts the perfect tender rule. In doing so, we will see the typically flexible approach that the Code takes to a business transaction.

Usage of Trade, Course of Dealing, and Course of Performance

The Uniform Commercial Code takes the commonsense view that a contract for the sale of goods does not exist in a vacuum. It requires courts to consider three things when they apply the perfect tender rule.

"Usage of trade" means any practice that members of an industry *expect* to be part of their dealings.[8] The perfect tender rule may not permit a buyer to reject goods with minor flaws. For example, the textile industry interprets the phrase "first-quality fabric" to permit a limited number of flaws in most materials. If a seller delivers 1,000 bolts of fabric and 5 of them have minor defects, the seller has *not* violated the perfect tender rule.

The course of dealing between the two parties may also limit the rule. **The term *course of dealing* refers to previous commercial transactions between the *same parties*.**[9] The UCC requires

---

[6]UCC §2-601.

[7]*Jakowski v. Carole Chevrolet, Inc.*, 180 N.J. Super. 122, 433 A.2d 841, 1981 N.J. Super. LEXIS 635 (N.J. Super. Ct. 1981).

[8]UCC §1-205(2).

[9]UCC §1-205(1).

that a current contract be interpreted in the light of any past dealings that have created reasonable expectations. Suppose a buyer orders 20,000 board feet of "highest-grade pine" from a lumber company, just as it has in each of the three previous years. In the earlier deliveries, the buyer accepted the lumber even though 1 or 2 percent was not the highest grade. That course of dealing will probably control the present contract, and the buyer will not be permitted suddenly to reject an entire shipment because 1 percent is a lower grade of pine. Such a tender is not "perfect," but it would be good enough.

The course of performance has the same effect on contract interpretation. **The term *course of performance* refers to the history of dealings between the parties *in a single contract*, and thus assumes that it is the kind of contract demanding an ongoing relationship.**[10] Suppose a newspaper company signs a deal to purchase 5 tons of newsprint from a paper company every week for a year, and the contract also specifies the grade of paper to be delivered. If, during the first three months, the newspaper company routinely accepts paper containing a small number of flaws, that course of performance will control the contract. During the final month, the newspaper may not suddenly reject the type of paper it had earlier accepted.

Parties' Agreement

The parties may also choose to limit the effect of the perfect tender rule *themselves* by drafting a contract that *permits* imperfection in the goods. In some industries, this practice is routine. For example, contracts requiring the seller to design or engineer goods especially for the buyer will generally state a level of performance that the equipment must meet. If the goods meet the level described, the buyer has no right to reject, even if the product has some flaws.

Cure

A basic goal of the UCC is a fully performed contract that leaves both parties satisfied. The seller's right to *cure* helps achieve this goal. **When the buyer rejects non-conforming goods, the seller has the right to cure by delivering conforming goods before the contract deadline.**[11] LightCo is obligated to deliver 10,000 specially manufactured bulbs to Burnout Corp. by September 15. LightCo delivers the bulbs on August 20, and on August 25, Burnout notifies the seller that the bulbs do not meet contract specifications. If LightCo promptly notifies Burnout that it intends to cure and then delivers conforming lightbulbs on September 15, it has fulfilled its contract obligations and Burnout must accept the goods. The seller may even cure *after the contract deadline* if the seller (1) reasonably believed the original goods were acceptable and (2) promptly notified the buyer of his intent to cure within a reasonable time. This gives the seller a second chance to replace defective goods. Suppose Chip Co. delivers 25,000 computer chips to Assembler one day before the contract deadline, and two days later, Assembler notifies Chip that the goods are defective. If Chip had tested the chips thoroughly before they left its factory and reasonably believed they met contract specifications, then Chip may cure by promptly notifying Assembler that it will supply conforming goods within a *reasonable* period. Thus, even if the conforming chips arrive two weeks after the contract deadline, Chip will have cured unless Assembler can show that the delay caused it serious harm.

What if a shipment of goods has several nonconformities and the seller offers to fix *some* of the problems? The following case addresses the issue.

---

[10]UCC §2-208(1).

[11]UCC §2-508.

Zion Temple First Pentecostal Church of Cincinnati, Ohio, Inc. v. Brighter Day Bookstore & Gifts

2004 WL 23150323
Court of Appeals of Ohio, 2004

Facts: Zion Temple First Pentecostal Church ordered new choir robes from Brighter Day Bookstore, a retailer that sold robes manufactured by Murphy Cap & Gown.

When Brighter Day delivered the robes to the Zion Temple, the church members found many faults. They did not like the color or material, which they considered very different from a sample they had reviewed at Brighter Day. The sleeves had been attached facing the wrong way. And on the overlays, the Velcro and tags were visible.

Zion complained to Murphy. The manufacturer offered to repair the sleeves, but Zion declined the offer because of the other problems. Zion returned the robes and, when it failed to get its money back, filed suit.

The trial court gave summary judgment for the defendants, and Zion Temple appealed.

Issue: ***Did Zion Temple afford Murphy a chance to cure?***

Excerpts from Judge Doan's Decision: The record shows that the choir members actually inspected the robes when Brighter Day delivered them and Zion found what it deemed to be nonconformities. This inspection was reasonable and was made within a reasonable time. Thus, Zion never accepted the robes but instead rejected them as not conforming to the contract. Since Zion rejected the goods, Murphy had a right to cure.

Murphy offered to cure any problem with the sleeves. Where the buyer rejects a nonconforming tender which the seller had reasonable ground to believe would be acceptable with or without money allowance, the seller may, if he seasonably notifies the buyer, have a further reasonable time to substitute a conforming tender. Murphy manufactured the sleeves on the robes according to its design specifications. Because of an error in the catalog that Zion had consulted before placing its order, the sleeves as properly manufactured appeared different from the sleeves as depicted in the catalog. Murphy clearly had the right to cure this nonconformity and indicated its intention to do so within a reasonable time.

Zion had other reasons for contending that the robes did not conform to the contract. It claimed that Velcro was visible on the reversible overlays and that the tags on the overlays could be seen when the overlays were reversed. Murphy never indicated its intention to cure these alleged nonconformities. Consequently, the trial court erred in granting Murphy's motion for summary judgment.

We reverse the entry of summary judgment for Murphy and remand this case for trial or further proceedings consistent with this court's opinion.

EXAM Strategy

Question: Xuberant Inc. orders 2000 wristwatches from Timely Co. The watches, with Xuberant's logo on the face, are to be delivered by September 15 so that Xuberant can give them away at its September 25 sales convention. Timely tests the watches and is satisfied they work. But when Xuberant receives them, on September 15, the company rejects them because its name is misspelled. Timely offers to correct the error and deliver the new watches by September 22, but Xuberant refuses and sues. Likely outcome?

Strategy: Timely has delivered nonconforming goods, and Xuberant is entitled to reject them. However, the seller has the right to cure by delivering conforming goods before the contract deadline. Timely is offering to deliver shortly after the deadline. Is it entitled to do so?

Result: If the seller reasonably believed the goods were conforming, it may cure within a reasonable time after the deadline. If the court believes that Timely's spelling error was unreasonable, the company has no right to cure. However, a basic goal of the code is a fully performed contract. A court is likely to declare that the error was excusable and the new delivery date adequate for Xuberant's purpose. Timely will probably win.

Substantial Impairment

Sometimes the Code holds buyers to a higher standard and makes it more difficult to refuse goods. Perfect tender is the usual rule, but in two circumstances, a buyer who claims goods are non-conforming must show that the defects *substantially impair* their value. This standard applies: (1) if the buyer is revoking acceptance of goods or (2) if the buyer is rejecting an installment.

For example, a buyer who initially *accepts* a dozen cement mixers but *later* discovers problems with their engines may revoke his acceptance only by showing that the defects have caused him serious problems. Similarly, if a contract requires a buyer to accept one shipment of diesel fuel each month for two years, the buyer may reject one monthly installment only if the problem with the fuel substantially lowers its value.

Destruction of the Goods

A farmer contracts to sell 250,000 pounds of sunflower seeds to a broker. The contract describes the 125 acres that the farmer will plant to grow the sunflowers. He plants his crop on time, but a drought destroys most of the plants and he is able to deliver only 75,000 pounds. Is the farmer liable for the seeds he could not deliver? No. Is the broker required to accept the smaller crop? No. **If identified goods are *totally* destroyed before risk passes to the buyer, the contract is void. If identified goods are *partially* destroyed, the buyer may choose whether to accept the goods at a reduced price or void the contract.**[12]

© Janos Gehring/Shutterstock.com

If a valuable crop is destroyed, who suffers the loss?

The crop of sunflowers was identified to the contract when the farmer planted it. When a drought destroyed most of the crop, the contract became voidable. The buyer had the right to accept the smaller crop, at a reduced price, or to reject the crop entirely. The farmer is not liable for the shortfall because the destruction was not his fault.[13]

[12]UCC §2-613. Identification of goods is discussed in Chapter 20, on ownership and risk.

[13]Based on *Red River Commodities, Inc. v. Eidsness*, 459 N.W.2d 805, 1990 N.D. LEXIS 159 (N.D. 1990).

Commercial Impracticability

Commercial impracticability means that a supervening event excuses performance of a contract, if the event was *not* within the parties' contemplation when they made the agreement.[14] An event is "supervening" if it interrupts the normal course of business and dominates performance of the contract. But a supervening event will excuse performance only if neither party had thought there was a serious chance it would happen.

Harris RF Systems was an American company that manufactured radio equipment. Svenska, a Swedish corporation, bought Harris radio systems and sold them in many countries, including Iran. One contract required Harris to ship a large quantity of spare radio parts, which Svenska would pay $600,000 for and then resell in Iran. Harris attempted to ship the parts to Svenska, but U.S. Customs seized the goods, and the U.S. Department of Defense notified Harris that it believed the parts would be of military value to Iran.

The Defense Department acknowledged that technically, Harris was licensed to ship the goods, but it made two things clear: first, that it would litigate rather than permit the goods to reach Iran; and second, that if Harris attempted to complete the sale in Iran, the department would place all of Harris's future radio shipments on a Munitions List, making it difficult to ship them anywhere in the world. Svenska, on the other hand, pointed out that it had binding contracts to deliver the radio parts to various customers in Iran. If the parts were not forthcoming, Svenska would hold Harris liable for all of its losses. Harris attempted to reach a satisfactory compromise with all parties but failed and eventually agreed not to ship the parts overseas.

Svenska sued. Harris defended, relying on commercial impracticability. Harris persuaded the court that neither party had foreseen the government's intervention and that both parties realized it would be virtually impossible to export goods the Defense Department was determined to block. The court dismissed Svenska's suit.[15]

Sellers offer many excuses to avoid contracts. In the following case, you decide whether the seller's problem was "within the parties' contemplation" when they made the agreement.

---

[14]UCC §2-615.

[15]*Harriscom Svenska AB v. Harris Corp.*, 1990 U.S. Dist. LEXIS 20006 (W.D.N.Y. 1990).

You be the Judge

United Aluminum Corporation v. Linde, Inc.

2009 U.S. Dist. LEXIS 74259
United States District Court for the District of Connecticut, 2009

Facts: United Aluminum Corporation (UAC) manufactured aluminum coil. For many years, Linde supplied UAC with the nitrogen it needed for its manufacturing processes. The companies signed a long-term contract in 1997, which said, in part:

> Linde agrees that at UAC's sole option, UAC may extend the term of this Agreement for a maximum of five years commencing upon August 31, 2008.

The contract also called for a price of $0.23 per unit of nitrogen.

In 2007, UAC sent Linde a letter which stated, in part, "UAC intends to exercise its option to extend the term for an additional five years from September 1, 2008 to August 31, 2013." Linde replied that the price of nitrogen had risen significantly over the life of the contract and that it would have to increase prices by 38 percent.

UAC sued, seeking the right to continue buying nitrogen from Linde at $0.23 per unit. Linde defended on the grounds of commercial impracticability.

You Be the Judge: ***Should Linde be discharged on the grounds of commercial impracticability?***

Argument for Linde: Your honor, our industry has seen substantial increases in costs since 1997. The price of nitrogen is much higher, but that is just the tip of the iceberg. We must pay our workers more, our property taxes have increased, and, because of the rising price of gasoline, our transportation costs are much higher.

We did not anticipate these increases when we made the original agreement. At that time, costs in our industry had been fairly stable for many years. We have small margins even under ideal circumstances. To continue selling at 1997 prices forces us to operate at a substantial loss. Our request for a 38 percent price increase is reasonable.

It is commercially impracticable for use to ship nitrogen for another five years at the prices quoted in the original contract.

Argument for UAC: The Uniform Commercial Code does not allow for a claim of commercial impracticability every time prices increase. It allows such a claim only in the case of an event that was not in the parties' contemplation when they made an agreement.

In some exceptional circumstances, excusing performance is entirely reasonable. But nothing unusual or unforeseeable has happened here. Nitrogen prices have gone up. But over a decade, the price of nearly everything increases. Gasoline, groceries, cable television—the list goes on. Surely Linde knew that price increases were possible.

We made the original contract because Linde offered us long-term stability on the price of nitrogen. Without that part of the bargain, we would likely have sought another supplier. It is not right to allow Linde to back out of its clear contractual obligations.

The accompanying chart outlines the seller's obligations.

Basic Obligation: The seller's basic obligation is to deliver conforming goods**. The perfect tender rule permits the buyer to reject the goods if they are in any way non-conforming.** But many Code provisions limit the harshness of the perfect tender rule**.**

Limitation on Seller's Obligation	Code Provision	Effect on Seller's Obligations
Good faith	§1-201(19) and §2-103(1)(b)	Prohibits the buyer from using the perfect tender rule as a way out of a contract that has become unprofitable.
Course of dealing, usage of trade, and course of performance	§1-205(1), §1-205(2), and §2-208	If applicable, will limit the buyer's right to reject for relatively routine defects.
The parties' agreement	§2-106	May describe tolerances for imperfections in the goods.
Cure	§2-508	Allows the seller to replace defective goods with conforming goods, if time permits.
Revocation of acceptance	§2-608	A buyer who has accepted goods may later revoke them only if she can show that the defects *substantially impair* its value.
Installment contracts	§2-612	A buyer may reject an installment only if the defects *substantially impair* its value.
Destruction of goods	§2-613	If goods identified to the contract are destroyed, the contract is void.
Commercial impracticability	§2-615	A supervening event excuses performance of a impracticability contract, if the event was not within the parties' contemplation when they made the agreement.

Buyer's Rights and Obligations

The buyer's primary obligation is to accept conforming goods and pay for them.[16] The buyer must also **provide adequate facilities to receive the goods.**[17] For example, if the contract requires the seller to deliver to the buyer's warehouse, and the parties anticipate that delivery will be by rail, then the buyer must have facilities for unloading railcars at its warehouse.

Inspection and Acceptance

The buyer generally has the right to inspect the goods before paying or accepting.[18] If the contract is silent on this issue, the buyer may inspect. Typically, a buyer will insist on this right, but contracts can be created which do *not* give the parties a right to inspect—for example, a contract allowing shipment C.O.D., which means "cash on delivery." In that case, the buyer must pay upon receipt and do her inspecting later.

Along with the right of inspection comes the obligation to do it within a reasonable time and to notify the seller promptly if the buyer intends to reject the goods. **The buyer accepts goods** if (1) after a reasonable opportunity to inspect, she indicates to the seller that the goods are conforming or that she will accept them in spite of non-conformity; or (2) she has had a reasonable opportunity to inspect the goods and has *not rejected them;* or (3) she performs some act indicating that she now owns the goods, such as altering or reselling them.[19]

Partial Acceptance

A buyer has the right to accept some goods while rejecting others if the goods can be divided into *commercial units.* Such a unit is any grouping of goods that the industry normally treats as a whole. For example, one truckload of gravel would be a commercial unit. If the contract called for 100 truckloads of gravel, a buyer could accept 10 that conformed to contract specifications while rejecting 90 that did not.

Revocation

As we mentioned earlier, a buyer has a limited right to revoke acceptance of goods. **A buyer may revoke acceptance but only if the non-conformity *substantially impairs* the value of the goods and only if she had a legitimate reason for the initial acceptance.**[20] This means the perfect tender rule does *not* apply: a buyer in this situation may not revoke because of minor defects. Further, the buyer must show that she had a good reason for accepting the goods originally. Acceptable reasons would include defects that were not visible on inspection or defects that the seller promised but failed to cure.

Rejection

The buyer may reject non-conforming goods by notifying the seller within a reasonable time.[21] Huntsville Hospital purchased electrocardiogram equipment from Mortara Instrument for $155,000. The equipment failed to work properly, and the hospital notified Mortara within a reasonable time that it was rejecting. The hospital asked Mortara to pick up the equipment and refund the full purchase price, but Mortara did neither. When the hospital sued, Mortara claimed that the hospital should have returned the equipment to Mortara and

---

[16]UCC §2-301.
[17]UCC §2-503(1)(b).
[18]UCC §2-513.
[19]UCC §2-606.
[20]UCC §§2-607, 608.
[21]UCC §§2-601, 602.

that its failure left it liable for the full cost. The court of appeals was unpersuaded and gave judgment for the hospital, declaring that the hospital's only obligation was to notify the seller of a rejection and hold the goods for the seller to collect.[22]

The rule is different in the case of an installment contract. An **installment contract** is one that *requires* goods to be delivered in *separate lots*. If Bus Co. contracts for Oil Co. to deliver 5,000 gallons of gasoline every week for one year, that is an installment contract. **A buyer may reject a non-conforming installment but only if it *substantially impairs* the value of that installment and cannot be cured.**[23] The perfect tender rule does not apply. Bus Co. has no right to reject an installment containing 4,900 gallons of gasoline because the minor shortfall does not impair the shipment's substantial value. On the other hand, if Oil Co. delivered gasoline with lead in it, Bus Co. could reject it since Bus Co. would be legally prohibited from using the gas. (Remember, though, that Oil Co., like all sellers, has the right to cure.)

The following case deals with rejection and revocation. Have a peek inside the trailer, but mind the slippery puddles.

LILE v. KIESEL

871 N.E. 2d 995
Indiana Court of Appeals, 2007

Facts: Edward and Kelly Kiesel bought a new pull-behind trailer from James Lile, the owner of Lile's Trailer Sales. That same day, the couple took their new trailer on its first outing. Because this was a camping trip, it rained all night, and in the morning, the Kiesels noticed water inside the trailer near the door. The next time it rained, Edward noticed more water pooling in various parts of the trailer. A week later, Edward brought the trailer in for repairs.

Lile repaired the roof, using new silicone. However, a week later the trailer again leaked, and Kelly reported this to Lile, demanding a full refund. Lile refused a refund but offered to seal any leaks, replace interior walls, and sand and paint the exterior. The Kiesels instead took the trailer to a different auto body shop, where the owner said that extensive interior rust indicated the trailer had leaked longer than the Kiesels owned it. The Kiesels sued. Lile claimed that the Kiesels had accepted the vehicle and unfairly refused repairs. The trial court awarded the Kiesels the full price of the trailer, and Lile appealed.

Issue: ***Were the Kiesels entitled to the trailer's purchase price?***

Excerpts from Judge Riley's Decision:[24] Lile's asserts that the Kiesels accepted the trailer and consequently could not reject the goods. We agree that in purchasing the trailer, using it on more than one occasion, as well as licensing and titling it in their names, the Kiesels accepted the trailer and lost any right to reject the sale of the trailer. However, even though acceptance precludes the rejection of goods, it does not impair a buyer's ability to revoke acceptance and seek a remedy for the nonconformity of goods. Specifically, [UCC § 2-608] provides for the revocation of acceptance of goods in whole or in part, stating:

> The buyer may revoke his acceptance of a lot or commercial unit whose non-conformity substantially impairs its value to him if he has accepted it ... without discovery of such non-conformity if his acceptance was reasonably induced either by the difficulty of discovery before acceptance or by the seller's assurances.

In our view, there is no question that leaking and rust damage substantially impairs the value of a trailer. In addition, leaks due to rain would have been difficult to discover prior to the trailer's purchase. Furthermore, in reporting the

[22] *Huntsville Hospital v. Mortara Instrument,* 57 F.3d 1043, 1995 U.S. App. LEXIS 16925 (11th Cir. 1995).

[23] UCC §2-612.

[24] Once again, the authors of this text have substituted the parties' names for the court's "appellant" and "appellee."

problem to Lile's within less than a week of purchasing the trailer, the Kiesels undoubtedly notified Lile's within a reasonable time after they discovered the leaks. As a result, we conclude the Kiesels met the requisite elements under [§ 2-608] for revocation of acceptance of the trailer.

Lile's also asks this court to hold that the Kiesels did not act in good faith following their acceptance of the trailer when they refused to allow Lile's to make repairs on the trailer. Lile's relies on [§ 2-508] to argue that the Kiesels had to give Lile's an opportunity to cure the trailer's defects. We disagree. First, we note that [§ 2-508] pertains to a buyer's *rejection* of nonconforming goods upon delivery. Lile's has already asked us and we have already concluded that the Kiesels accepted the trailer; consequently, as previously determined, the Kiesels can only *revoke* their acceptance at this point. Additionally, there is no evidence in the record to suggest that the Kiesels did not act in good faith in dealing with Lile's. In fact, although they were not obligated to do so, the record clearly shows that the Kiesels gave Lile's an opportunity to cure the leaks when they brought the trailer into Lile's for replacement of silicone on parts of the trailer's roof.

The trial court properly ordered Lile's to reimburse the Kiesels for the purchase price of the trailer. Affirmed.

Seller's Remedies

When a buyer breaches a contract, the UCC provides the seller with a variety of potential remedies. Exactly which ones are available depends upon who has the goods (buyer or seller) and what steps the seller took after the buyer breached. The seller can always **cancel the contract**. She may also be able to:

- stop delivery of the goods,
- identify goods to the contract,
- resell and recover damages,
- obtain damages for non-acceptance, or
- obtain the contract price.

Stop Delivery

Sometimes a buyer breaches before the seller has delivered the goods (for example, by failing to make a payment due under the contract or perhaps by repudiating the contract). A party **repudiates** when it indicates that it will not perform, which it can do either by its conduct or by failing to answer a written demand for assurances that it intends to perform.

If a buyer breaches, **the seller may refuse to deliver the goods.**[25] If, when the buyer breaches, the seller has already placed the goods in the hands of a carrier (such as UPS), the seller may instruct the carrier not to deliver the goods, provided the shipment is at least a carload or larger.

Identify Goods to the Contract

If the seller has not yet identified goods to the contract when the buyer breaches, he may do so as soon as he learns of the breach.[26] Suppose an electronics manufacturer, with 5,000 Blu-ray players in its warehouse, learns that a retailer refuses to pay for the 800 units it contracted to buy. The manufacturer may now attach a label to 800 units in its warehouse, identifying them

[25]UCC §2-705.

[26]UCC §2-704.

to the contract. This will help it recover damages when it resells the identified goods or uses one of the other remedies described below.

Resale

A seller may resell goods that the buyer has refused to accept, provided she does it reasonably. **If the resale is commercially reasonable, the seller may recover the difference between the resale price and contract price, plus incidental damages, minus expenses saved.**[27] Incidental damages are expenses the seller incurs in holding the goods and reselling them—costs such as storage, shipping, and advertising for resale. The seller must deduct expenses saved by the breach. For example, if the contract required the seller to ship heavy machinery from Detroit to San Diego, and the buyer's breach enables the seller to sell its goods in Detroit, the seller must deduct from its claimed losses the transportation costs that it saved.

A seller who acts in a commercially reasonable manner is entitled to the following damages:

	Contract price (the price Seller expected from the original contract)
–	the resale price (the money Seller got at resale)
+	incidental damages (storage, advertising, etc.)
–	expenses saved
=	Seller's damages

A seller is also permitted to resell goods privately; that is, by simply negotiating a deal with another party. But if the seller does so, she must first give the buyer reasonable notice of the private resale.

EXAM Strategy

Question: Fork manufactures forklift trucks. Fork agrees to sell 10 trucks, for $30,000 each, to McKnife. Fork will store the trucks in a warehouse near McKnife for 3 months, when the buyer will collect them. Storage will cost Fork $2,000 per month. A week after signing the deal, before Fork has moved the trucks to the warehouse, McKnife notifies Fork it cannot pay for the trucks. Fork spends $2,000 advertising the machines and sells them for $25,000 each in a commercially reasonable manner. Fork then sues McKnife. Fork will win—but how much?

Strategy: Apply the formula outlined above.

Result: Fork is entitled to

	The contract price	$300,000
–	the resale price	250,000
+	incidental damages	2,000
–	expenses saved	6,000
=	Fork's damages	46,000

[27]UCC §2-706.

Damages for Non-Acceptance

A seller who does not resell, or who resells unreasonably, may recover the difference between the original contract price and the market value of the goods at the time of delivery.[28] Oilko agrees to sell Refinery 100,000 barrels of oil for $100 per barrel, to be delivered on November 1. Oilko tenders the oil on November 1 but Refinery refuses to accept it. Three months later, on February 20, Oilko resells the oil to another purchaser for $92 per barrel and sues Refinery for $800,000 (the difference between its contract price and what it finally obtained), plus the cost of storage. Will Oilko win? No. Oilko's resale was unreasonable. Because there is a ready market for oil, Oilko should have resold immediately. Because Oilko acted unreasonably, it will not obtain damages under the Code's resale provision. Oilko will be forced to base its damages on market value.

Often this remedy will be less valuable to the seller than resale damages. Suppose that on November 1, the market value of Oilko's oil was $99 per barrel. Oilko's contract with Refinery was actually worth only $1 per barrel to Oilko—the amount by which its contract price exceeded the market value. That is all that Oilko will get in court.[29] A seller with a reasonable chance to resell should be certain to do it.

The following chart compares resale and non-acceptance damages:

Resale Damages §2-706		**Non-Acceptance Damages §2-708**	
Contract price	$10,000,000	Contract price	$10,000,000
Resale price	-9,200,000	Market value of goods	-9,900,000
	$ 800,000		$ 100,000

Action for the Price

The seller may recover the contract price if (1) the buyer has already accepted the goods *or* (2) the seller's goods are conforming and the seller is unable to resell after a reasonable effort.[30] Royal Jones was a company that constructed rendering plants—factories that use sophisticated equipment to extract valuable minerals from otherwise useless material. Royal Jones contracted for First Thermal to construct three rendering tanks, at a cost of $64,350. First Thermal built the tanks to Royal Jones's specifications, but Royal Jones never accepted or paid for them, and First Thermal sued. Royal Jones argued that First Thermal deserved no money because it had not attempted to resell the goods, but the court awarded the full contract price, stating:

> First Thermal proved that any effort at resale would have been unavailing because these were the only rendering tanks First Thermal ever made, the tanks were manufactured according to Royal Jones's specifications, First Thermal had no other customers to which it could resell the tanks, and it was unaware how the tanks could have been marketed for resale.[31]

Resale is normally the safest route for an injured seller to recover the maximum amount, but when it is unrealistic, as in the *First Thermal* case, a lawsuit for the full price is appropriate.

---

[28] UCC §2-708.

[29] Based on *Baii Banking Corp. v. Atlantic Richfield Co.*, 1993 U.S. Dist. LEXIS 14107 (S.D.N.Y. 1993).

[30] UCC §2-709.

[31] *Royal Jones & Associates, Inc. v. First Thermal Systems, Inc.*, 566 So. 2d 853, 1990 Fla. App. LEXIS 6596 (Fla. Ct. App. 1990).

All of the seller's remedies are summarized in the chapter review at the end of the chapter. We now move on to the buyer's remedies.

Buyer's Remedies

The buyer, too, has a variety of potential remedies. If a seller fails to deliver goods, repudiates, or if the buyer rightfully rejects the goods, the buyer is entitled to **cancel the contract**. She may also **recover money paid** to the seller, assuming she has not received the goods. In addition, she may be entitled to:

- incidental and consequential damages,
- specific performance,
- cover,
- damages for non-delivery,
- accept the non-conforming goods and seek damages, or
- liquidated damages.

© Adam Crowley / Photodisc / Jupiterimages

How much should the plaintiff recover per rosebush in consequential damages?

Incidental Damages and Consequential Damages

An injured buyer is generally entitled to incidental *and* consequential damages. Incidental damages for buyers include such costs as advertising for replacements, sending buyers to obtain new goods, and shipping the replacement goods. **Consequential damages**, or losses that are caused by a breach, can be much more extensive and may include lost profits caused by the seller's failure to deliver.

A buyer, however, only gets consequential damages for harm that was *unavoidable*. Suppose Wholesaler has a contract to sell 10,000 rosebushes at $10 per bush to FloraMora. Wholesaler contracts to buy 10,000 rosebushes from Growem at $6 per bush, but Growem fails to deliver. Wholesaler in fact could obtain comparable roses at $8 per bush but fails to do so and loses the chance to sell to FloraMora. Wholesaler sues Growem, seeking the $4-per-bush profit it would have made on the FloraMora deal. The company will receive only $2 per bush, representing the difference between its contract price and the market value of the plants. Wholesaler will be denied the additional $2 per bush.

In the following case, the court decides whether *future* profits may be too speculative to award as consequential damages.

Smith v. Penbridge Associates, Inc.

440 Pa. Super. 410, 655 A.2d 1015, 1995 Pa. Super. LEXIS 574
Superior Court of Pennsylvania, 1995

Facts: Donna and Alan Smith wanted to raise emus, which are flightless Australian birds that look like ostriches. The creatures reproduce rapidly in almost any terrain and are sold for their meat, which is high in protein and low in fat, and for their oil, leather, and feathers. The Smiths paid Tomie Clark, the manager of Penbridge Farms, $4,000 as a down payment for a "proven breeder pair." Since it is impossible to discern an emu's gender by looking, the Smiths asked Clark several times if the two birds were male and female, and he assured them that the pair had successfully produced chicks the previous breeding season.

The Smiths placed the prospective lovebirds in the same pen, but the breeding season passed without a hint of romance. Donna Smith phoned Penbridge Farms, which advised her on a procedure used to determine gender. Donna performed this task and learned that the emus were both gentlemen. The would-be breeders asked for their money back, but Penbridge refused, so the Smiths flew into court. The trial judge awarded the couple $105,215, representing lost profits from their anticipated chicks. Penbridge appealed, arguing that a buyer cannot count her chicks before they have hatched.

Issue: ***Did the trial court err by awarding lost profits?***

Excerpts from Judge Popovich's Decision: [Penbridge claimed that the] evidence was speculative and insufficient to support an award of consequential damages, including damages for lost profits. [Penbridge argued that, since] the breeding of emus is a relatively new business, and there is no reliable data to project the ultimate success in breeding emus, the [Smiths'] claims for loss of chick production are entirely speculative and do not meet the "reasonable certainty" requirement of the law of damages.

The Uniform Commercial Code provides the following circumstances for the recovery of consequential damages resulting from the breach of the seller: any loss resulting from general or particular requirements and needs of which the seller at the time of contracting had reason to know and which could not reasonably be prevented by "cover" or otherwise. [UCC §2-715(2).]

The determination of damages lies with the factfinder, who weighs the evidence and assesses the credibility of the witnesses. Although the court recognized that emu breeding was a relatively new commercial business, it determined that the award of consequential damages could be calculated with a reasonable degree of certainty from the evidence adduced at trial. The court below initially found that the value of a three-month old chick produced from the [previous] season was $5,000. The lower court then concluded that [the Smiths] suffered incidental and consequential damages in the amount of $90,000.00. From our thorough evaluation of the record, we conclude that the evidence was sufficient for the lower court to measure lost profits with a reasonable degree of certainty. The basis for this rule is that the breaching party should not be allowed to shift the loss to the injured party when damages, even if uncertain in amount, were certainly the responsibility of the party in breach.

Order affirmed.

Specific Performance

If the contract goods are rare or unique, the buyer may be allowed *specific performance,* which means a court order requiring the seller to deliver those particular goods.[32] This remedy is most common when the goods are one-of-a-kind. Suppose Gallery agreed to sell to Trisha an original Corot painting for $120,000 but then refused to perform (because another buyer offered more money). Trisha can obtain specific performance because the painting cannot be replaced: the court will order Gallery to deliver the work. By contrast, a car rental company stymied by a dealer's refusal to sell 500 new Ford Mustangs will not obtain specific performance since the rental company can simply buy the same cars from another dealer and sue for the difference.

[32]UCC §2-716.

Cover

If the seller breaches, the buyer may "cover" by reasonably obtaining substitute goods; it may then obtain the difference between the contract price and its cover price, plus incidental and consequential damages, minus expenses saved.[33] Casein, a protein derived from milk, is used to make cheese and to process many other foods. Erie Casein Co. contracted with Anric Corp. to supply several hundred thousand pounds of casein for about $1 per pound. Half was to be delivered in March of the first year and the other half in March of the second year. By May of the first year, Anric had not finished its first delivery because it was having difficulty obtaining the casein, but Erie told Anric to keep trying. Anric delivered some of the casein later the same year, but by March of the second year was forced to admit it could not meet the second delivery. Anric suggested that it might be able to obtain more casein in the autumn of that second year.

Erie waited until August of the second year, but it finally obtained its casein elsewhere at a price of $1.45 per pound. Erie sued Anric for the extra money it had paid, about $66,000. Anric argued that Erie had no right to the difference because Erie had waited until the price of casein was sky-high before obtaining substitute goods.

The court found for Erie. Even though the company might have covered a year earlier, when the price was much lower, it was reasonable for the buyer to wait because Anric indicated it might be able to supply the goods later. Erie had acted in good faith, and when it ultimately covered, it did so at the best price it could find. An injured buyer does not have to do a perfect job of covering, only a reasonable job, and Erie got its full $66,000.[34]

An injured buyer does not have to do a perfect job of covering, only a reasonable job.

Note that an injured buyer may also be awarded consequential damages, which we discuss below. Finally, if covering saves expense, the savings are deducted from any damages.

We hope that you recall Donald Hessler, whom we met in the chapter opener. We last saw him circling the courthouse in his Plymouth Prowler, anxiously awaiting the outcome of his suit against the dealership that promised him the same car for a lot less money. It has been a long wait; you and Donald deserve an answer.

Hessler v. Crystal Lake Chrysler-Plymouth, Inc.

338 Ill.App.3d 1010, 788 N.E.2d 405, 273 Ill.Dec. 96
Appellate Court of Illinois, 2003

Facts: The facts are provided in the chapter opening. The trial court awarded Hessler $29,853, representing the difference between his contract with Crystal Lake and the sum he ultimately spent purchasing a new Prowler. Crystal Lake appealed, arguing that Hessler covered unreasonably.

Issue: ***Did Hessler cover reasonably?***

Excerpts from Judge Callum's Decision: We conclude that the trial court did not err in finding that defendant's foregoing actions reasonably indicated to plaintiff that defendant would not deliver to him a Prowler under the Agreement. As we determined above, defendant contracted to deliver a Prowler to plaintiff as soon as possible. It was not against the manifest weight of the evidence for the trial court to find that defendant [breached] the Agreement

[33] UCC §2-712.

[34] *Erie Casein Co. v. Anric Corp.*, 217 Ill. App. 3d 602, 577 N.E.2d 892, 1991 Ill. App. LEXIS 1429 (Ill. App. Ct. 1991).

when it repeatedly informed plaintiff that it would not deliver to him the first Prowler it received. Such actions made it sufficiently clear to plaintiff that defendant would not perform under the Agreement.

Defendant's final argument is that the trial court erred in calculating the damages award because plaintiff effected an inappropriate cover. Defendant contends that plaintiff did not recontact the 38 dealers he had called in September to inquire if they would sell him a Prowler. Instead, on the same day that Rosenberg refused to sell him a car, plaintiff visited another dealership and purchased a Prowler for about $40,000 over the list price.

Comment 2 to section 2-712 of the UCC provides, in relevant part:

> The test of proper cover is whether at the time and place the buyer acted in good faith and in a reasonable manner, and it is immaterial that hindsight may later prove that the method of cover used was not the cheapest and most effective.

Plaintiff testified that he called Rosenberg on September 22 to inform him that defendant was on a tentative list to receive a Prowler and that Rosenberg responded that he would not sell to plaintiff a car and that plaintiff was not the first person with whom he had contracted. Rosenberg testified that he informed plaintiff on this date that the Prowler was "already committed." The trial court also heard plaintiff's testimony that, following his September 22 conversation with Rosenberg, he had "serious doubts" that defendant would sell to him a Prowler and he contacted about 38 dealerships to inquire about purchasing a vehicle, but was unable to obtain a car.

Following Rosenberg's refusal to sell a car to plaintiff on October 25, plaintiff visited another dealership on that day and purchased a Prowler for about $30,000 over what he would have paid defendant for the same car. The trial court concluded that the price plaintiff ultimately paid for a Prowler was the "best price" he could receive after defendant refused to sell a car to him. We agree. The trial court heard testimony from both parties about the Prowler's limited supply. It also heard plaintiff's testimony about his efforts to obtain a car one month before his purchase date. We conclude that the court's determination that plaintiff effected a proper cover was not against the manifest weight of the evidence.

For the foregoing reasons, the judgment of the circuit court is affirmed.

Devil's Advocate It is fine for a buyer to cover, but Hessler's conduct is absurd. He bought a car for nearly *double* the contract price. A buyer's behavior must be reasonable, and no court should reward conduct that is clearly obsessive. This purchase was not required by business or financial pressures. We have here a man who believes he is entitled to whatever he wants. If Hessler decides he must have a Prowler *at any price,* then in fairness he should be the one to *pay* that price.

Non-Delivery

In some cases, the buyer does not cover, or fails to cover *reasonably,* leaving it with damages for non-delivery. **The measure of damages for non-delivery is the difference between the market price at the time the buyer learns of the breach and the contract price, plus incidental and consequential damages, minus expenses saved.**[35] Suppose that in the case described above, Erie had not covered but simply filed suit against Anric. Instead of its $66,000, Erie would have obtained the difference between its contract price with Anric and the market value on the date of breach. That market price was probably only a few pennies higher than the contract price, and Erie would have obtained less than $10,000.

[35]UCC §2-713.

Acceptance of Non-Conforming Goods

A buyer will sometimes accept non-conforming goods from the seller, either because no alternative is available or because the buyer expects to obtain some compensation for the defects. **Where the buyer has accepted goods but notified the seller that they are non-conforming, he may recover damages for the difference between the goods as promised and as delivered, plus incidental and consequential damages.**[36]

Liquidated Damages

Liquidated damages are those that the parties agree, at the time of contracting, will compensate the injured party. **They are enforceable, but only in an amount that is reasonable in light of the harm, the difficulties of proving actual loss, and the absence of other remedies.**[37] A clause that establishes unreasonably large or unreasonably small liquidated damages is void. Courts only enforce a liquidated damages clause if it would have been difficult to estimate actual damages when the parties reached the agreement.

Cessna Aircraft agreed to build a "Citation V" business jet and sell it to Aero Consulting for $3,995,000. Cessna's contract required Aero to pay an initial deposit of $125,000, a second deposit of $300,000 six months prior to delivery, and the balance upon delivery. The contract also stated that if Aero failed to pay the balance due, Cessna would keep all deposited monies by way of liquidated damages.

How do you avoid a bitter aftertaste?

Aero made both deposits, and Cessna built the plane and tendered it to Aero, but Aero refused to pay the full balance due. Cessna notified Aero that it would keep the $425,000 deposited. When Aero sued, seeking a return of the deposits, the issue was whether this liquidated damage was fair. The court concluded that it was. At the time Cessna entered into the deal, it was difficult to estimate actual damages in the event of Aero's breach. The long period required to build a jet aircraft and the uncertainties about supply and demand in the marketplace meant that neither party could say for sure how much Cessna would lose should Aero breach. Further, the liquidated damage here was about 10 percent of the total cost, not an unreasonably high figure. Cessna kept the money (and the plane).[38]

EXAM Strategy

Question: You have a red wine problem. Your California vineyard has strong sales throughout the United States, and it is time to expand into Europe. To penetrate foreign markets, you offer your product at steep discounts to a Swiss importer. Your intent is that the importer will sell your wine inexpensively to retailers, so that low

[36]UCC §2-714.

[37]UCC §2-718.

[38]*Aero Consulting Corp. v. Cessna Aircraft Co.*, 867 F. Supp. 1480, 1994 U.S. Dist. LEXIS 16668 (D. Kan. 1994).

prices will entice consumers. The danger, though, is that the importer will return the wine to the United States and undersell your own product in an established market, taking advantage of your advertising and infuriating established dealers. Such a resale could occur before your wine ever left the country. What can you do to keep this problem from fermenting?

Strategy: A liquidated damages clause can put teeth into your plan to sell the wine to overseas consumers. You might specify substantial compensation if any of your exported wine finds its way back home. However, an overly aggressive clause will be declared a penalty—and void. How can you avoid such a disaster?

Result: **Liquidated damages are enforceable in an amount that is reasonable in light of the harm and the difficulties of proving actual loss.** Your clause may certainly compensate you for lost goodwill among domestic retailers and for harm to your efforts at establishing the brand in Europe. Make *good faith* estimates of those losses—if the clause gives you too much compensation, a court may void it altogether. Lost profits per case sold in the United States are probably easy to calculate and should *not* be part of the liquidated damages clause.

Chapter Conclusion

The drafters of the UCC intended the law to reflect contemporary commercial practices but also to require a satisfactory level of sensible, ethical behavior. For example, the Code allows numerous exceptions to the perfect tender rule so that a buyer may not pounce on minor defects in goods to avoid a contract that has become financially burdensome. Similarly, a seller forced to resell his goods must do so in a commercially reasonable manner. Good faith and common sense are the hallmarks of contract performance and remedies.

EXAM REVIEW

1. **GOOD FAITH** The Code requires good faith in the performance and enforcement of every contract. (p. 532)

2. **CONFORMING GOODS** Conforming goods are those that satisfy the contract terms; non-conforming goods fail to do so. (pp. 532–533)

3. **TENDER** The seller must tender the goods, which means make conforming goods available to the buyer. The perfect tender rule permits a buyer to reject goods that are non-conforming in any respect, although there are numerous exceptions. (p. 533)

4. **USAGE OF TRADE** Usage of trade, course of dealing, and course of performance may enable a seller to satisfy the perfect tender rule even though there are some defects in the goods. (pp. 533–534)

5. **CURE** When the buyer rejects non-conforming goods, the seller has the right to cure by delivering conforming goods before the contract deadline. (pp. 534–535)

EXAM Strategy

Question: Allied Semi-Conductors International agreed to buy 50,000 computer chips from Pulsar, for a total price of $365,750. Pulsar delivered the chips, which Allied then sold to Apple Computer. But at least 35,000 of the chips proved defective, so Apple returned them to Allied, which sent them back to Pulsar. Pulsar agreed to replace any defective chips, but only after Allied, at its expense, tested each chip and established the defect. Allied rejected this procedure and sued. Who wins?

Strategy: The chips were non-conforming goods, and Allied was entitled to reject them. Pulsar, in turn, had a right to cure the defects; that is, to solve the problem that it created. Did Pulsar offer to cure? (See the "Result" at the end of this section.)

6. **DESTRUCTION OF THE GOODS** If identified goods are destroyed before risk passes to the buyer, the contract is void. (p. 536)

EXAM Strategy

CPA Question Under a contract governed by the UCC sales article, which of the following statements is correct?

a. Unless both the seller and the buyer are merchants, neither party is obligated to perform the contract in good faith.

b. The contract will not be enforceable if it fails to expressly specify a time and a place for delivery of the goods.

c. The seller may be excused from performance if the goods are accidentally destroyed before the risk of loss passes to the buyer.

d. If the price of the goods is less than $500, the goods need not be identified to the contract for title to pass to the buyer.

Strategy: (a) Sounds unlikely. Remind yourself which contracts must be performed in good faith. (b) As we learned in Chapter 19, the Code permits open terms. What are they? (c) Review the rules on destruction of the goods (d) Goods must be identified to the contract before title can pass. Is there an exception for goods under $500? (See the "Result" at the end of this section.)

7. **COMMERCIAL IMPRACTICABILITY** Under commercial impracticability, a supervening event excuses performance if it was not within the parties' contemplation when they made the contract. (pp. 537–538)

8. **INSPECTION** The buyer generally has the right to inspect goods before paying or accepting. If the buyer does not reject goods within a reasonable time after inspecting them, she may be deemed to have accepted them. (pp. 539–541)

CPA Question Smith contracted in writing to sell Peters a used personal computer for $600. The contract did not specifically address the time for payment, place of delivery, or Peters's right to inspect the computer. Which of the following statements is correct?

a. Smith is obligated to deliver the computer to Peters's home.

b. Peters is entitled to inspect the computer before paying for it.

c. Peters may not pay for the computer using a personal check unless Smith agrees.

d. Smith is not entitled to payment until 30 days after Peters receives the computer.

Strategy: This question should be no problem. Three of the four possible answers offer rules that appear *nowhere* in the Code. (a) There is no reference in the Code to "home delivery" of goods. (b) The buyer has the right to inspect goods before paying or accepting, unless the contract specifies otherwise. (c) Nowhere does the UCC prohibit payment by check. (d) You have never read in the Code any presumption of a 30-day delay in payment—so do not imagine one. (See the "Result" at the end of this section.)

9. **REVOCATION** A buyer may revoke his acceptance of non-conforming goods, but only if the defects substantially impair the value of the goods. (p. 539)

10. **REJECTION** A buyer may reject non-conforming goods by notifying the seller within a reasonable time. (pp. 539–540)

The following chart summarizes the contrasting remedies available to the two parties.

Seller's Remedies	Issue	Buyer's Remedies
§2-705: The seller generally may stop delivery, whether it was to be done by the seller herself or a carrier.	Delivery	§2-716: Specific performance: buyer may obtain specific performance only if the goods are unique.
§2-706: Resale: If the resale is made in good faith and a commercially reasonable manner, the seller may recover the difference between the resale price and the contract price, plus incidental costs, minus savings.	When the injured party makes an alternate contract	§2-712: Cover: The buyer may purchase alternate goods and obtain the difference in price, plus incidental and consequential damages, minus expenses saved.
§2-708: Non-acceptance: The measure of damages for non-acceptance is the the time and place of tender and the contract price (plus incidental damages minus expenses saved).	When the goods have not changed hands	§2-713: Non-delivery: If the seller fails to deliver, the buyer's damages are the difference between the market price at the time he learned of the breach and the contract price (plus incidental and consequential damages, minus expenses saved).
§2-709: The seller may sue for the price.	When the buyer has accepted the goods	§2-714: A buyer who has accepted non-conforming goods and notified the seller may recover damages for resulting losses.
§§2-706, 2-708, 2-709, 2-710: The seller is entitled to incidental damages but not consequential damages.	Incidental and consequential damages	§2-715: The buyer is entitled to incidental and consequential damages.

LIQUIDATED DAMAGES
§2-718: Either party may obtain liquidated damages but only in an amount that is reasonable at the time of the contract.

5. Result: Pulsar never offered a true cure. When the seller delivers defective goods and wishes to cure, it must take all steps—at its expense—to fix the problem. Pulsar could cure only by delivering, at its expense and in a timely manner, 50,000 conforming chips. Pulsar failed to cure, and Allied recovers the entire purchase price.

6. Result: Answer (a) is wrong because all contracts must be performed in good faith. Answer (b) is wrong because a contract with open terms is enforceable. Answer (c) is right because it correctly states the rule on destruction of goods. Answer (d) is wrong because title never passes unless the goods were identified to the contract.

8. Result: Answer (b) is correct. Peters is entitled to inspect the computer unless the contract states otherwise, which it did not.

Multiple-Choice Questions

1. **CPA QUESTION** Cara Fabricating Co. and Taso Corp. agreed orally that Taso would custom-manufacture a compressor for Cara at a price of $120,000. After Taso completed the work at a cost of $90,000, Cara notified Taso that the compressor was no longer needed. Taso is holding the compressor and has requested payment from Cara. Taso has been unable to resell the compressor for any price. Taso incurred storage fees of $2,000. If Cara refuses to pay Taso and Taso sues Cara, the most Taso will be entitled to recover is:

(a) $92,000
(b) $105,000
(c) $120,000
(d) $122,000

2. **CPA QUESTION** On February 15, Mazur Corp. contracted to sell 1,000 bushels of wheat to Good Bread, Inc., at $6 per bushel, with delivery to be made on June 23. On June 1, Good advised Mazur that it would not accept or pay for the wheat. On June 2, Mazur sold the wheat to another customer at the market price of $5 per bushel. Mazur had advised Good that it intended to resell the wheat. Which of the following statements is correct?

(a) Mazur can successfully sue Good for the difference between the resale price and the contract price.
(b) Mazur can resell the wheat only after June 23.
(c) Good can retract its anticipatory breach at any time before June 23.
(d) Good can successfully sue Mazur for specific performance.

3. Under the UCC, to tender delivery, a seller must:

(a) Make the goods available at a reasonable time
(b) Keep the goods available for a reasonable period
(c) Deliver to the buyer any documents that it needs to take possession
(d) All of the above
(e) None of the above

4. Blackburn FC (go Rovers!) orders 10,000 soccer jerseys from Alpha Co. to sell in its stadium store. They are to be delivered on July 10. When they arrive early on July 2, Blackburn is disappointed because the collars, which are supposed to be white, are blue. Blackburn notifies Alpha of the error. Alpha says that it wants a chance to "make it right." If Alpha delivers another shipment of 10,000 conforming jerseys on July 10, Blackburn ...
   (a) absolutely must accept the new shipment
   (b) must accept the new shipment if Alpha offers a reasonable discount
   (c) must accept the new shipment if it has suffered no measureable losses
   (d) may accept the new shipment, but has the option to reject it

5. Assume that a year has passed, and Blackburn FC once again orders 10,000 soccer jerseys from Alpha, to be delivered on July 10. This time, nonconforming jerseys are delivered on July 10. Alpha thoroughly inspected the shirts before shipping and had no reason to spot the error. When Blackburn notifies Alpha of the problem, Alpha says that it intends to cure the defect. If Blackburn cannot show that it will suffer any serious harm, does the UCC require Blackburn to give Alpha a chance to cure this time?
   (a) No, because the contract's deadline has passed.
   (b) Yes, it must give Alpha until July 17 to cure.
   (c) Yes, it must give Alpha until July 20 to cure.
   (d) Yes, it must give Alpha a reasonable amount of time to cure.

Discussion Questions

1. Jewell-Rung was a Canadian corporation that imported and sold men's clothing wholesale. Haddad was a New York corporation that manufactured and sold men's clothing under the "Lakeland" label. The companies agreed that Haddad would sell 2,325 Lakeland garments to Jewell-Rung for $250,000. Jewell-Rung began to take orders for the garments from its Canadian customers. Jewell-Rung had orders for about 372 garments when it learned that Haddad planned to allow another company, Olympic, the exclusive Canadian right to manufacture and sell Lakeland garments. Jewell-Rung sued Haddad for its lost profits. Haddad moved for summary judgment, claiming that Jewell-Rung could not recover lost profits because it had not covered. Is Haddad right? If so, why might Jewell-Rung not have covered?

2. Mastercraft Boat manufactured boats and often used instrument panels and electrical systems assembled or manufactured by Ace Industries. Typically, Ace would order electrical instruments and other parts and assemble them to specifications that Mastercraft provided. Mastercraft decided to work with a different assembler, M & G Electronics, so it terminated its relationship with Ace. Mastercraft then requested that Ace deliver all of the remaining instruments and other parts that it had purchased for use in Mastercraft boats. Ace delivered the inventory to Mastercraft, which inspected it and kept some of the items, but returned others to Ace, stating that the shipment had been unauthorized. Later, Mastercraft requested that Ace deliver the remaining parts (which Mastercraft had sent back to Ace) to M & G, which Ace did. Mastercraft then refused to pay for these parts, claiming that they were non-conforming. Is Ace entitled to its money for the parts?

3. Lewis River Golf, Inc., grew and sold sod. It bought seed from defendant, O. M. Scott & Sons, under an express warranty. But the sod grown from the Scott seeds developed weeds, a breach of Scott's warranty. Several of Lewis River's customers sued, unhappy with the weeds in their grass. Lewis River lost most of its customers, cut back its production from 275 acres to 45 acres, and destroyed all remaining sod grown from Scott's seeds. Eventually, Lewis River sold its business at a large loss. A jury awarded Lewis River $1,026,800, largely for lost profits and loss of goodwill. Scott appealed, claiming that a plaintiff may not recover for lost profits and goodwill. Comment.

4. The AM/PM Franchise association was a group of 150 owners of ARCO Mini-Market franchises in Pennsylvania and New York. Each owner had an agreement to operate a gas station and mini-market, obtaining all gasoline, food, and other products from ARCO. The association sued, claiming that ARCO had experimented with its formula for unleaded gasoline, using oxinol, and that the poor-quality gas had caused serious engine problems and a steep drop in customers. The association demanded (1) lost profits for gasoline sales, (2) lost profits for food and other items, and (3) loss of goodwill. The trial court dismissed the case, ruling that the plaintiff's claims were too speculative, and the association appealed. Please rule.

5. **YOU BE THE JUDGE WRITING PROBLEM** Clark Oil agreed to sell Amerada Hess several hundred thousand barrels of oil at $24 each by January 31, with the sulfur content not to exceed 1 percent. On January 26, Clark tendered oil from various ships. Most of the oil met specifications, but a small amount contained excess sulfur. Hess rejected all of the oil. Clark recirculated the oil, meaning that it blended the high-sulfur oil with the rest, and it notified Amerada that it could deliver 100 percent of the oil, as specified, by January 31. Hess did not respond. On January 30, Clark offered to replace the oil with an entirely new shipment, due to arrive February 1. Hess rejected the offer. On February 6, Clark retendered the original oil, all of which met contract terms, and Hess rejected it. Clark sold the oil elsewhere for $17.75 per barrel and filed suit. Is Clark entitled to damages? **Argument for Clark:** A seller is entitled to cure any defects. Clark did so in good faith and offered all of the oil by the contract deadline. Clark went even further, offering an entirely new shipment of oil. Hess acted in bad faith, seeking to obtain cheaper oil. Clark is entitled to the difference between the contract price and its resale price. **Argument for Hess:** Hess was entitled to conforming goods, and Clark failed to deliver. Under the perfect tender rule, that is the end of the discussion. Hess had the right to reject non-conforming goods, and it promptly did so. Hess chose not to deal further with Clark because it had lost confidence in Clark's ability to perform.

Discussion Questions

1. **ETHICS** Laura and Bruce Trethewey hired Basement Waterproofing Nationwide, Inc. (BWNI) to waterproof the walls in their basement for a fee of $2,500. BWNI's contract stated: "BWNI will service any seepage in the areas waterproofed at no additional cost to the customer. All labor and materials will be at the company's expense. Liability for any damage shall be limited to the total price paid for this contract." The material that BWNI used to waterproof the Tretheweys' walls swelled and caused large cracks to open in the walls. Water poured into the basement, and the

Tretheweys ultimately spent $38,000 to repair the damage. They sued, claiming negligence and breach of warranty, but BWNI claimed its liability was limited to $2,500. Please rule. Apart from the legal ruling, comment on ethics. BWNI wanted to protect itself against unlimited damage claims. Is this a legitimate way to do it? Is this how BWNI would wish to be treated itself? If you think BWNI *did* behave ethically, what advice would you have for consumers who hire home improvement companies? If you believe the company did *not* behave ethically, imagine that you are a BWNI executive, charged with drafting a standard contract for customers. How would you protect your company's interests while still acting in a way you consider moral?

2. Consider the UCC's exceptions to the perfect tender rule: usage of trade, course of dealing, and course of performance. Do these all seem reasonable, or are they too lenient on sellers who deliver non-conforming goods?

3. Are the UCC's rules related to cure sensible? If a seller ships goods that are not what you ordered, should you (in many circumstances) be *required* to give them a chance to make it right?

4. The opening scenario presented the true story of a man who paid a great deal of money for a Plymouth Prowler. Do you agree with the court's decision to award him nearly $30,000 in damages? Or do you agree with the Devil's Advocate feature and think that he was overcompensated for foolish spending?

5. Review the section "Damages for Non-Acceptance." In that section's example, Refinery refused Oilko's shipment on November 1, when the oil was worth $99 per barrel. Oilko waited three months to resell the oil, and at that time, it received only $92 per barrel. In such a case, the UCC allows Oilko to receive only $1 per barrel in damages rather than the $8-per-barrel reduction in price it actually received. Is this fair? Would it be more sensible to allow a company like Oilko to receive $8 per barrel in damages?

UNIT 5

Gostock-dot-net/Shutterstock.com

Agency and Employment Law

CHAPTER 28

AGENCY LAW

© Ivan Cholakov Gostock-dot-net/Shutterstock.com

The first time Bella walked into the store, my heart flipped. A lot of hot girls just know you can't keep your eyes off them. But not Bella. She had the shyest, sweetest smile you ever saw. From the beginning, I knew she was out of my league. But it didn't matter. Just to be in the same room with her was awesome. I would have folded shirts forever if I could do it standing next to her. She smelled like flowers, and her skin was beautiful.

Of course, she didn't last long at the store. How could she? All she had to do was walk down the street and good things would happen to her. She got picked to be on one of those reality shows.

Being on TV and all, she had to look good, so a couple of weeks after she left, she texted me: "Need clothes 4 show. Can u help?"

I like to think I wouldn't have murdered someone if Bella had asked me to, but I guess it depends on who the someone was. So I came up with a pretty good idea. I issued merchandise credits made out to fake people, which she used to buy clothes. I also let her use my employee discount. Look, Anthropologie is a big company—it's not like they would miss the clothes or anything. Besides, having Bella wear them on that TV show was great advertising.

I like to think I wouldn't have murdered someone if Bella had asked me to, but I guess it depends on who the someone was.

But you know what those guys at corporate did? Sued me for violating my duty of loyalty! To some big company! Are they kidding?? Like they would ever be loyal to me.

To find out who is in the right here, read the *Otsuka* case later in the chapter. It deals with a similar situation.

Thus far, this book has primarily dealt with issues of individual responsibility: what happens if *you* knock someone down or *you* sign an agreement? Agency law, on the other hand, is concerned with your responsibility for the actions of others. What happens if your agent assaults someone or signs a contract in your name? Agency law presents a significant trade-off: if you do everything yourself, you have control over the result. But the size and scope of your business (and your life) will be severely limited. Once you hire other people, you can accomplish a great deal more, but your risks increase immensely. Your agents may violate your instructions, and still you could be liable for what they have done. Although it might be safer to do everything yourself, that is not a practical decision for most business owners (or most people). The alternative is to hire carefully and to limit the risks as much as possible by understanding the law of agency.

Creating an Agency Relationship

Let us begin with two important definitions:

- **Principal**: A person who has someone else acting for him.
- **Agent:** A person who acts for someone else.

Principal
In an agency relationship, the person for whom an agent is acting.

Agent
In an agency relationship, the person who is acting on behalf of a principal.

Principals have substantial liability for the actions of their agents.[1] Therefore, disputes about whether an agency relationship exists are not mere legal quibbles but important issues with potentially profound financial consequences.

In an agency relationship, someone (the agent) agrees to perform a task for, and under the control of, someone else (the principal). **To create an agency relationship, there must be:**

- A **principal** and
- An **agent**
- Who mutually **consent** that the agent will act on behalf of the principal and
- Be subject to the principal's **control**
- Thereby creating a **fiduciary** relationship.

Consent

To establish consent, the principal must ask the agent to do something, and the agent must agree. In the most straightforward example, you ask a neighbor to walk your dog, and she agrees. Matters were more complicated, however, when Steven James met some friends one evening at a restaurant. During the two hours he was there, he drank four to six beers. (It is probably a bad sign that he cannot remember how many.) From then on, one misfortune piled upon another. After leaving the restaurant at about 7:00 p.m., James sped down a highway and crashed into a car that had stalled on the road, thereby killing the driver. James told the police at the scene that he had not seen the parked car (another bad sign). Evidently, James's lawyer was not as perceptive as the police in recognizing drunkenness. In a misguided attempt to help his client, James's lawyer took him to the local hospital for a blood test. Unfortunately, the test confirmed that James had indeed been drunk at the time of the accident.

[1]The word "principal" is always used when referring to a person. It is not to be confused with the word "principle," which refers to a fundamental idea.

The attorney knew that if this evidence was admitted at trial, his client would soon be receiving free room and board from the Massachusetts Department of Corrections. So at trial, the lawyer argued that the blood test was protected by the client-attorney privilege because the hospital had been his agent and therefore a member of the defense team. The court disagreed, however, holding that the hospital employees were not agents for the lawyer because they had not consented to act in that role.

The court upheld James's conviction of murder in the first degree by reason of extreme atrocity or cruelty.[2]

Control

Principals are liable for the acts of their agents because they exercise control over the agents. If principals direct their agents to commit an act, it seems fair to hold the principal liable when that act causes harm. How would you apply that rule to the following situation?

William Stanford was an employee of the Agency for International Development. While on his way home to Pakistan to spend the holidays with his family, his plane was hijacked and taken to Iran, where he was killed. Stanford had originally purchased a ticket on Northwest Airlines but had traded it for a seat on Kuwait Airways (KA). The airlines had an agreement permitting passengers to exchange tickets from one to the other. Stanford's widow sued Northwest on the theory that KA was Northwest's agent. The court found, however, that no agency relationship existed because Northwest had no control over KA.[3] Northwest did not tell KA how to fly planes or handle terrorists; therefore, it should not be liable when KA made fatal errors. Not only must an agent and principal consent to an agency relationship, but the principal also must have control over the agent.

Fiduciary Relationship

In a **fiduciary relationship**, a trustee acts for the benefit of the beneficiary, always putting the interests of the beneficiary before his own. A fiduciary relationship is a special relationship with high standards. The beneficiary places special confidence in the fiduciary who, in turn, is obligated to act in good faith and candor, putting his own needs second. The purpose of a fiduciary relationship is for one person to benefit another. **Agents have a fiduciary duty to their principals.**

All three elements—consent, control, and a fiduciary duty—are necessary to create an agency relationship. In some relationships, for example, there might be a *fiduciary duty* but no *control.* A trustee of a trust must act for the benefit of the beneficiaries, but the beneficiaries have no right to control the trustee. Therefore, a trustee is not an agent of the beneficiaries. *Consent* is present in every contractual relationship, but that does not necessarily mean that the two parties are agent and principal. If Horace sells his car to Lily, they both expect to benefit under the contract, but neither has a *fiduciary duty* to the other and neither *controls* the other, so there is no agency relationship.

Elements Not Required for an Agency Relationship

Consent, control, and a fiduciary relationship are necessary to establish an agency relationship. The following elements are *not* required:

- *A Written Agreement.* In most cases, an agency agreement does not have to be in writing. An oral understanding is valid, except in one circumstance—the **equal dignities rule**. According to this rule, if an agent is empowered to enter into a contract that must be in writing, then the appointment of the agent must also be written.

Equal dignities rule
If an agent is empowered to enter into a contract that must be in writing, then the appointment of the agent must also be written.

---

[2] *Commonwealth v. James*, 427 Mass. 312, 693 N.E.2nd 148, 1998 Mass. LEXIS 175. (S.J.C. MA, 1998)
[3] *Stanford v. Kuwait Airways Corp.*, 648 F. Supp. 1158, 1986 U.S. Dist. LEXIS 18880 (S.D.N.Y. 1986).

For example, under the statute of frauds, a contract for the sale of land is unenforceable unless in writing, so the agency agreement to sell land must also be in writing.

- *A Formal Agreement.* The principal and agent need not agree formally that they have an agency relationship. They do not even have to think the word "agent." So long as they act like an agent and a principal, the law will treat them as such.
- *Compensation.* An agency relationship need not meet all the standards of contract law. For example, a contract is not valid without consideration, but an agency agreement is valid *even if the agent is not paid.*

Duties of Agents to Principals

Agents owe a fiduciary duty to their principals. There are four elements to this duty.

Duty of Loyalty

An agent has a fiduciary duty to act loyally for the principal's benefit in all matters connected with the agency relationship.[4] The agent has an obligation to put the principal first, to strive to accomplish the principal's goals. As the following case illustrates, this duty applies to all employees, no matter how lowly.

Otsuka v. Polo Ralph Lauren Corporation

2007 U.S. DIST. LEXIS 86523
United States District Court for the Northern District of California, 2007

Facts: Justin Kiser and Germania worked together at a Ralph Lauren Polo store in San Francisco. After she left the job, he let her buy clothing using merchandise credits made out to nonexistent people. He also let her use his employee discount. Not surprisingly, both of these activities were against store policies. Polo sued Kiser, alleging that he had violated his duty of loyalty.

Kiser filed a motion to dismiss on the grounds that he was such a low-level employee that he did not owe a duty of loyalty to Polo.

Issue: ***Do all employees owe a duty of loyalty to their employer?***

Excerpts from Judge Illston's Decision: Kiser moves to dismiss this cause of action, contending that a lower-level employee owes no fiduciary duty to his employer. In response, [Polo] argues that there is a duty of loyalty akin to a fiduciary duty that all employees owe to their employers.

The Court agrees with Kiser that the cases cited by [Polo] address the duty of loyalty with respect to higher-ranking employees than Kiser, who worked as a sales clerk in a retail store. [But t]he Third Restatement provides that all employees are agents, and that "[a]s agents, all employees owe a duty of loyalty to their employers." Restatement (Third) of Agency §1.01. This is true regardless of how ministerial or routinized a work assignment may be.

Accordingly, the Court DENIES Kiser's motion to dismiss the cause of action.

[4]Restatement (Third) of Agency §8.01.

The various components of the duty of loyalty follow.

Outside Benefits

An agent may not receive profits unless the principal knows and approves. Suppose that Hope is an employee of the agency Big Egos and Talents, Inc. (BEAT). She has been representing Will Smith in his latest movie negotiations.[5] Smith often drives her to meetings in his new Maybach. He is so thrilled that she has arranged for him to star in the new movie *Little Men* that he buys her a Maybach. Can Hope keep this generous gift? Only with BEAT's permission. She must tell BEAT about the Maybach; the company may then take the vehicle itself or allow her to keep it.

Confidential Information

The ability to keep secrets is important in any relationship, but especially a fiduciary relationship. Agents can neither disclose nor use for their own benefit any confidential information they acquire during their agency. As the following case shows, this duty continues even after the agency relationship ends.

Abkco Music, Inc. v. Harrisongs Music, Ltd.

722 F.2d 988, 1983 U.S. App. LEXIS 15562
United States Court of Appeals for the Second Circuit, 1983

Facts: Bright Tunes Music Corp. (Bright Tunes) owned the copyright to the song "He's So Fine." The company sued George Harrison, a Beatle, alleging that the Harrison composition "My Sweet Lord" copied "He's So Fine." At the time the suit was filed, Allen B. Klein handled the business affairs of the Beatles.

Klein (representing Harrison) met with the president of Bright Tunes to discuss possible settlement of the copyright lawsuit. Klein suggested that Harrison might be interested in purchasing the copyright to "He's So Fine." Shortly thereafter, Klein's management contract with the Beatles expired. Without telling Harrison, Klein began negotiating with Bright Tunes to purchase the copyright to "He's So Fine" for himself. To advance these negotiations, Klein gave Bright Tunes information about royalty income for "My Sweet Lord"—information that he had gained as Harrison's agent.

The trial judge in the copyright case ultimately found that Harrison had infringed the copyright on "He's So Fine" and assessed damages of $1,599,987. After the trial, Klein purchased the "He's So Fine" copyright from Bright Tunes and with it, the right to recover from Harrison for the breach of copyright.

George Harrison, a few months after writing "My Sweet Lord."

Issue: ***Did Klein violate his fiduciary duty to Harrison by using confidential information after the agency relationship terminated?***

Excerpts from Judge Pierce's Decision: There is no doubt that the relationship between Harrison and [Klein]

[5] Do not be confused by the fact that Hope works as an agent for movie stars. As an employee of BEAT, her duty is to the company. She is an agent of BEAT, and BEAT works for the celebrities.

prior to the termination of the management agreement was that of principal and agent, and that the relationship was fiduciary in nature. [A]n agent has a duty not to use confidential knowledge acquired in his employment in competition with his principal. This duty exists as well after the employment is terminated as during its continuance. On the other hand, use of information based on general business knowledge or gleaned from general business experience is not covered by the rule, and the former agent is permitted to compete with his former principal in reliance on such general publicly available information. The evidence presented herein is not at all convincing that the information imparted to Bright Tunes by Klein was publicly available.

While the initial attempt to purchase [the copyright to "He's So Fine"] was several years removed from the eventual purchase on [Klein]'s own account, we are not of the view that such a fact rendered [Klein] unfettered in the later negotiations. Taking all of these circumstances together, we agree that [Klein's] conduct did not meet the standard required of him as a former fiduciary.

To listen to the two songs involved in this case, google "benedict copyright."

Ethics Klein was angry that the Beatles had failed to renew his management contract. Was it reasonable for him to think that he owed no duty to the principal who had fired him? Why kind of world would it be if everyone acted like Klein? Why would George Harrison prefer to owe money to Bright Tunes rather than to Klein?

Competition with the Principal

Agents are not allowed to compete with their principal in any matter within the scope of the agency business. If Allen Klein had purchased the "He's So Fine" copyright while he was George Harrison's agent, he would have committed an additional sin against the agency relationship. Owning song rights was clearly part of the agency business, so Klein could not make such purchases without Harrison's consent. Once the agency relationship ends, however, so does the rule against competition. Klein was entitled to buy the "He's So Fine" copyright after the agency relationship ended (so long as he did not use confidential information).

Conflict of Interest Between Two Principals

Unless otherwise agreed, an agent may not act for two principals whose interests conflict. Suppose Travis represents both director Steven Spielberg and actor Amy Adams. Spielberg is casting the title role in his new movie, *Nancy Drew: Girl Detective,* a role that Adams covets. Travis cannot represent these two clients when they are negotiating with each other unless they both know about the conflict and agree to ignore it. The following example illustrates the dangers of acting for two principals at once.

EXAM Strategy

Question: The Sisters of Charity was an order of nuns in New Jersey. Faced with growing health care and retirement costs, they decided to sell off a piece of property. The nuns soon found, however, that the world is not always a charitable place. They agreed to sell the land to Linpro for nearly $10 million. But before the deal closed, Linpro signed a contract to resell the property to Sammis for $34 million. So, you say, the sisters made a bad deal. There is no law against that. But it turned out that the nuns' law firm also represented Linpro. Their lawyer at the firm, Peter Berkley, never told the sisters about the deal between Linpro and Sammis. Was that the charitable—or legal—thing to do?

Strategy: Always begin by asking if there is an agency relationship. Was there consent, control, and a fiduciary relationship? *Consent*: Berkley had agreed to work for the nuns. *Control*: they told him what he was to do—sell the land. The purpose of a *fiduciary relationship* is for one person to benefit another. The point of the nuns' relationship with Berkley is for him to help them. Once you know there is an agency relationship, then ask if the agent has violated his duty of loyalty.

Result: You know that an agent is not permitted to act for two principals whose interests conflict. Here, Berkley is working for the nuns, who want the highest possible price for their land, and Linpro, who wants the lowest price. Berkley has violated his duty of loyalty.

Secretly Dealing with the Principal

If a principal hires an agent to arrange a transaction, the agent may not become a party to the transaction without the principal's permission. Matt Damon became an overnight sensation after starring in the movie *Good Will Hunting*. Suppose that he hired Trang to read scripts for him. Unbeknownst to Damon, Trang has written her own script, which she thinks would be ideal for him. She may not sell it to him without revealing that she wrote it herself. Damon may be perfectly happy to buy Trang's script, but he has the right, as her principal, to know that she is the person selling it.

Appropriate Behavior

An agent may not engage in inappropriate behavior that reflects badly on the principal. This rule applies even to *off-duty* conduct. For example, a coed trio of flight attendants went wild at a hotel bar in London. They kissed and caressed each other, showed off their underwear, and poured alcohol down their trousers. The airline fired two of the employees and gave a warning letter to the third.

Other Duties of an Agent

Before Taylor left for a five-week trip to England, he hired Angie to rent his vacation house. Angie never got around to listing his house on the Multiple Listing Service used by all the area brokers, nor did she post it on the Web herself, but when the Fords contacted her looking for rental housing, she did show them Taylor's place. They offered to rent it for $750 per month.

Angie called Taylor in England to tell him. He responded that he would not accept less than $850 a month, which Angie thought the Fords would be willing to pay. He told Angie to call back if there was any problem. The Fords decided that they would go no higher than $800 a month. Although Taylor had told Angie that he could not receive text messages in England, she texted him the Fords' counteroffer. Taylor never received it, so he never responded. When the Fords pressed Angie for an answer, she said she could not get in touch with Taylor. Not until Taylor returned home did he learn that the Fords had rented another house. Did Angie violate any of the duties that agents owe to their principals?

Duty to Obey Instructions

An agent must obey her principal's instructions unless the principal directs her to behave illegally or unethically. Taylor instructed Angie to call him if the Fords rejected the offer. When Angie failed to do so, she violated her duty to obey instructions. If, however, Taylor had asked her to say that the house's basement was dry when in fact it looked like a swamp every spring, Angie would be under no obligation to follow those illegal instructions.

Duty of Care

An agent has a duty to act with reasonable care. In other words, an agent must act as a reasonable person would, under the circumstances. A reasonable person would not have texted Taylor while he was in England.

Under some circumstances, an agent is held to a higher—or lower—standard than usual. **An agent with special skills is held to a higher standard because she is expected to use those skills.** A trained real estate agent should know enough to post all listings on the Web.

But suppose Taylor had asked his neighbor, Jed, to help him sell the house. Jed is not a trained real estate agent, and he is not being paid, which makes him a *gratuitous agent*. A gratuitous agent is held to a lower standard because he is doing his principal a favor and, as the old saying goes, you get what you pay for—up to a point. **Gratuitous agents are liable if they commit *gross* negligence, but not *ordinary* negligence.** If Jed, as a gratuitous agent, texted Taylor an important message because he forgot that Taylor could not receive these messages in England, he would not be liable for that ordinary negligence. But if Taylor had, just that day, sent Jed an email complaining that he could not get any text messages, Jed would be liable for gross negligence and a violation of his duty.

Duty to Provide Information

An agent has a duty to provide the principal with all information in her possession that she has reason to believe the principal wants to know. She also has a duty to provide accurate information. Angie knew that the Fords had counteroffered for $800 a month. She had a duty to pass this information on to Taylor.

EXAM Strategy

Question: Jonah tells his friend Derek that he would like to go parasailing. Derek is very enthusiastic and suggests that they try an outfit called Wind Beneath Your Wings because he has heard good things about them. Derek offers to arrange everything. He makes a reservation, puts the $600 fee on his credit card, and picks Jonah up to drive him to the Wings location. What a friend! But the day does not turn out as Jonah had hoped. While he is soaring up in the air over the Pacific Ocean, his sail springs a leak, he goes plummeting into the sea and breaks both legs. During his recuperation in the hospital, he learns that Wings is unlicensed. He also sees an ad for Wings offering parasailing for only $350. And Derek is listed in the ad as one of the company's owners. Is Derek an agent for Jonah? Has he violated his fiduciary responsibility?

Strategy: There are three issues to consider in answering this question: (1) Was there an agency relationship? This requires consent, control, and a fiduciary relationship. (2) Is anything missing—does it matter if the agent is unpaid or the contract is not in writing? (3) Has the agent fulfilled his duties?

Result: There is an agency relationship: Derek had agreed to help Jonah; it was Jonah who set the goal for the relationship (parasailing); the purpose of this relationship is for one person to benefit another. It does not matter if Derek was not paid or the agreement not written. Derek has violated his duty to exercise due care. He should not have taken Jonah to an unlicensed company. He has also violated his duty to provide information: he should have told Jonah the true cost for the lessons and also revealed that he was a principal of the company. And he violated his duty of loyalty when he worked for two principals whose interests were in conflict.

Principal's Remedies when the Agent Breaches a Duty

A principal has three potential remedies when an agent breaches her duty:

- The principal can recover from the agent any **damages** the breach has caused. Thus, if Taylor can rent his house for only $600 a month instead of the $800 the Fords offered, Angie would be liable for $2,400—$200 a month for one year.
- If an agent breaches the duty of loyalty, he must turn over to the principal any **profits** he has earned as a result of his wrongdoing. Thus, after Klein violated his duty of loyalty to Harrison, he forfeited profits he would have earned from the copyright of "He's So Fine."
- If the agent has violated her duty of loyalty, the principal may **rescind** the transaction. When Trang sold a script to her principal, Matt Damon, without telling him that she was the author, she violated her duty of loyalty. Damon could rescind the contract to buy the script.[6]

Duties of Principals to Agents

In a typical agency relationship, the agent agrees to perform tasks for the principal, and the principal agrees to pay the agent. The range of tasks undertaken by an agent is limited only by the imagination of the principal. Because the agent's job can be so varied, the law needs to define an agent's duties carefully. The role of the principal, on the other hand, is typically less complicated—often little more than paying the agent as required by the agreement. Thus, the law enumerates fewer duties for the principal. Primarily, the principal must reimburse the agent for reasonable expenses and cooperate with the agent in performing agency tasks. The respective duties of agents and principals can be summarized as follows:

Duties of Agents to Principals	Duty of Principals to Agents
Duty of loyalty	Duty to compensate as provided by the agreement
Duty to obey instructions	Duty to reimburse for reasonable expenses
Duty of care	Duty to cooperate
Duty to provide information	

As a general rule, the principal must indemnify (i.e., reimburse) the agent for any expenses she has reasonably incurred. These reimbursable expenses fall into three categories:

- **A principal must indemnify an agent for any expenses or damages reasonably incurred in carrying out his agency responsibilities.** For example, Peace Baptist Church of Birmingham, Alabama, asked its pastor to buy land for a new church. He paid part of the purchase price out of his own pocket, but the church refused to reimburse him. Although the pastor lost in church, he won in court.[7]

[6]A principal can rescind his contract with an agent who has violated her duty, but, as we shall see later in the chapter, the principal might not be able to rescind a contract with a third party when the agent misbehaves.

[7]*Lauderdale v. Peace Baptist Church of Birmingham*, 246 Ala. 178, 19 So. 2d 538, 1944 Ala. LEXIS 508 (S. Ct. AL, 1944).

- **A principal must indemnify an agent for tort claims brought by a third party if the principal authorized the agent's behavior and the agent did not realize he was committing a tort.** Marisa owns all the apartment buildings on Elm Street, except one. She hires Rajiv to manage the units and tells him that, under the terms of the leases, she has the right to ask guests to leave if a party becomes too rowdy. But she forgets to tell Rajiv that she does not own one of the buildings, which happens to house a college sorority. One night, when the sorority is having a rambunctious party, Rajiv hustles over and starts ejecting the noisy guests. The sorority is furious and sues Rajiv for trespass. If the sorority wins its suit against Rajiv, Marisa would have to pay the judgment, plus Rajiv's attorney's fees, because she had told him to quell noisy parties and he did not realize he was trespassing.
- **The principal must indemnify the agent for any liability she incurs from third parties as a result of entering into a contract on the principal's behalf, including attorney's fees and reasonable settlements.** An agent signed a contract to buy cucumbers for Vlasic Food Products Co. to use in making pickles. When the first shipment of cucumbers arrived, Vlasic inspectors found them unsuitable and directed the agent to refuse the shipment. The agent found himself in a pickle when the cucumber farmer sued. The agent notified Vlasic, but the company refused to defend him. He settled the claim himself and, in turn, sued Vlasic. The court ordered Vlasic to reimburse the agent because he had notified them of the suit and had acted reasonably and in good faith.[8]

Duty to Cooperate

Principals have a duty to cooperate with their agent:

- **The principal must furnish the agent with the opportunity to work.** If Lewis agrees to serve as Ida's real estate agent in selling her house, Ida must allow Lewis access to the house. It is unlikely that Lewis will be able to sell the house without taking anyone inside.
- **The principal cannot unreasonably interfere with the agent's ability to accomplish his task.** Ida allows Lewis to show the house, but she refuses to clean it and then makes disparaging comments to prospective purchasers. "I really get tired of living in such a dark, dreary house," she says. "And the neighborhood children are vicious thugs." This behavior would constitute unreasonable interference with an agent.
- **The principal must perform her part of the contract.** Once the agent has successfully completed the task, the principal must pay him, even if the principal has changed her mind and no longer wants the agent to perform. Ida is a 78-year-old widow who has lived alone for many years in a house that she loves. Her asking price is outrageously high. But lo and behold, Lewis finds a couple happy to pay Ida's price. There is only one problem. Ida does not really want to sell. She put her house on the market because she enjoys showing it to all the folks who move to town. She rejects the offer. Now there is a second problem. The contract provided that Lewis would find a willing buyer at the asking price. Because he has done so, Ida must pay his real estate commission even if she does not want to sell her house.

Terminating an Agency Relationship

Either the agent or the principal can terminate the agency relationship at any time. In addition, the relationship terminates automatically if the principal or agent no longer can perform their required duties or a change in circumstances renders the agency relationship pointless.

[8] *Long v. Vlasic Food Products Co.*, 439 F.2d 229, 1971 U.S. App. LEXIS 11455 (4th Cir. 1971).

Termination by Agent or Principal

The two parties—principal and agent—have three choices in terminating their relationship:

- *Term Agreement.* If the principal and agent agree in advance how long their relationship will last, they have a term agreement. For example:
    - *Time.* Alexandra hires Boris to help her add to her collection of guitars previously owned by rock stars. If they agree that the relationship will last two years, they have a term agreement.
    - *Achieving a Purpose.* The principal and agent can agree that the agency relationship will terminate when the principal's goals have been achieved. Alexandra and Boris might agree that their relationship will end when Alexandra has purchased 10 guitars.
    - *Mutual Agreement.* No matter what the principal and agent agree at the start, they can always change their minds later on, so long as the change is mutual. If Boris and Alexandra originally agree to a two-year term, but Boris decides he wants to go back to business school and Alexandra runs out of money after only one year, they can decide together to terminate the agency.
- *Agency at Will.* If they make no agreement in advance about the term of the agreement, either principal or agent can terminate at any time.
- *Wrongful Termination.* An agency relationship is a personal relationship. Hiring an agent is not like buying a book. You might not care which copy of the book you buy, but you do care which agent you hire. If an agency relationship is not working out, the courts will not force the agent and principal to stay together. **Either party always has the *power* to walk out. They may not, however, have the *right*.** If one party's departure from the agency relationship violates the agreement and causes harm to the other party, the wrongful party must pay damages. Nonetheless, he will be permitted to leave. If Boris has agreed to work for Alexandra for two years but he wants to leave after one, he can leave, provided he pays Alexandra the cost of hiring and training a replacement.

  If the agent is a **gratuitous** agent (i.e., is not being paid), he has both the power and the right to quit any time he wants, regardless of the agency agreement. If Boris is doing this job for Alexandra as a favor, he will not owe her damages when he stops work.

Principal or Agent Can No Longer Perform Required Duties

If the principal or the agent is unable to perform the duties required under the agency agreement, the agreement terminates.

- **If either the agent or the principal fails to obtain (or keep) a license necessary to perform duties under the agency agreement, the agreement ends.** Caleb hires Allegra to represent him in a lawsuit. If she is disbarred, their agency agreement terminates because the agent is no longer allowed in court. Alternatively, if Emil hires Bess to work in his gun shop, their agency relationship terminates when he loses his license to sell firearms.
- **The bankruptcy of the agent or the principal terminates an agency relationship only if it affects their ability to perform.** Bankruptcy rarely interferes with an agent's responsibilities. After all, there is generally no reason why an agent cannot continue to act for the principal whether the agent is rich or poor. If Lewis, the real estate agent, becomes bankrupt, he can continue to represent Ida or anyone else who wants to sell a house. The bankruptcy of a principal is different, however, because after filing for

bankruptcy, the principal loses control of his assets. A bankrupt principal may be unable to pay the agent or honor contracts that the agent enters into on his behalf. Therefore, the bankruptcy of a principal is more likely to terminate an agency relationship.

- **An agency relationship terminates upon the death or incapacity of either the principal or the agent.** Agency is a personal relationship, and when the principal dies, the agent cannot act on behalf of a nonexistent person.[9] Of course, a nonexistent person cannot act either, so the relationship also terminates when the agent dies. Incapacity has the same legal effect because either the principal or the agent is at least temporarily unable to act.

- **If the agent violates her duty of loyalty, the agency agreement automatically terminates.** Agents are appointed to represent the principal's interest; if they fail to do so, there is no point to the relationship. Louisa is negotiating a military procurement contract on behalf of her employer, Missiles R Us, Inc. In the midst of these negotiations, she becomes very friendly with Sam, the government negotiator. One night over drinks, she tells Sam what Missiles' real costs are on the project and the lowest bid it could possibly make. By passing on this confidential information, Louisa has violated her duty of loyalty, and her agency relationship terminates.

Change in Circumstances

After the agency agreement is negotiated, circumstances may change. If these changes are significant enough to undermine the purpose of the agreement, the relationship ends automatically. Andrew hires Melissa to sell his country farm for $100,000. Shortly thereafter, the largest oil reserve in North America is discovered nearby. The farm is now worth 10 times Andrew's asking price. Melissa's authority terminates automatically.

Other changes in circumstance that affect an agency agreement are:

- *Change of Law.* If the agent's responsibilities become illegal, the agency agreement terminates. Oscar has hired Marta to ship him succulent avocados from California's Imperial Valley. Before she sends the shipment, Mediterranean fruit flies are discovered, and all fruits and vegetables in California are quarantined. The agency agreement terminates because it is now illegal to ship the California avocados.

- *Loss or Destruction of Subject Matter.* Andrew hired Damian to sell his Palm Beach condominium, but before Damian could even measure the living room, Andrew's creditors attached the condo. Damian is no longer authorized to sell the real estate because Andrew has "lost" the subject matter of his agency agreement with Damian.

Effect of Termination

Once an agency relationship ends, the agent no longer has the authority to act for the principal. If she continues to act, she is liable to the principal for any damages he incurs as a result. The Mediterranean fruit fly quarantine ended Marta's agency. If she sends Oscar the avocados anyway and he is fined for possession of a fruit fly, Marta must pay the fine.

The agent loses her authority to act, but some of the duties of both the principal and agent continue even after the relationship ends:

- *Principal's Duty to Indemnify Agent.* Oscar must reimburse Marta for expenses she incurred before the agency ended. If Marta accumulated mileage on her car during her search for the perfect avocado, Oscar must pay her for gasoline and depreciation. But he owes her nothing for her expenses after the agency relationship ends.

---

[9] Restatement (Third) of Agency §§3.05, 3.06, 3.07, 3.08.

- *Confidential Information.* Remember the "He's So Fine" case earlier in the chapter? George Harrison's agent used confidential information to negotiate on his own behalf the purchase of the "He's So Fine" copyright. An agent is not entitled to use confidential information even after the agency relationship terminates.

LIABILITY

Thus far, this chapter has dealt with the relationship between principals and agents. Although an agent can dramatically increase his principal's ability to accomplish her goals, an agency relationship also dramatically increases the risk of legal liability to third parties. A principal may be liable in tort for any harm the agent causes and also liable in contract for agreements that the agent signs. Indeed, once a principal hires an agent, she may be liable to third parties for his acts, even if he disobeys instructions. Agents may also find themselves liable to third parties.

PRINCIPAL'S LIABILITY FOR CONTRACTS

Many agents are hired for the primary purpose of entering into contracts on behalf of their principals. Salespeople, for example, may do little other than sign on the dotted line. Most of the time, the principal wants to be liable on these contracts. But even if the principal is unhappy (because, say, the agent has disobeyed orders), the principal generally cannot rescind contracts entered into by the agent. After all, if someone is going to be penalized, it should be the principal who hired the disobedient agent, not the innocent third party.

The principal is liable for the acts of an agent if (1) the agent had *authority,* or (2) the principal *ratifies* the acts of the agent.

To say that the principal is "liable for the acts" of the agent means that the principal is as responsible as if he had performed the acts himself. It also means that the principal is liable for statements the agent makes to a third party. Thus, when a lawyer lied on an application for malpractice insurance, the insurance company was allowed to void the policy for the entire law firm. It was as if the firm had lied. In addition, the principal is deemed to know any information that the agent knows or should know.

Authority

A principal is bound by the acts of an agent if the agent has authority. There are three types of authority: express, implied, and apparent. Express and implied authority are categories of actual authority because the agent is truly authorized to act for the principal. In apparent authority, the principal is liable for the agent's actions even though the agent was *not* authorized.

Express Authority

The principal grants **express authority** by words or conduct that, reasonably interpreted, cause the agent to believe the principal desires her to act on the principal's account.[10] In other words, the principal asks the agent to do something and the agent does it. Craig calls his stockbroker, Alice, and asks her to buy 100 shares of Banshee Corp. for his account. She has *express authority* to carry out this transaction.

[10] Restatement (Third) of Agency §2.01.

Implied Authority

Unless otherwise agreed, authority to conduct a transaction includes authority to do acts that are reasonably necessary to accomplish it.[11] The principal does not have to micromanage the agent. David has recently inherited a house from his grandmother. He hires Nell to auction off the house and its contents. She hires an auctioneer, advertises the event, rents a tent, and generally does everything necessary to conduct a successful auction. After withholding her expenses, she sends the tidy balance to David. Totally outraged, he calls her on the phone, "How dare you hire an auctioneer and rent a tent? I never gave you permission! I absolutely *refuse* to pay these expenses!"

© Peter Casolino/Alamy

Did Nell have the authority to hire this auctioneer?

David is wrong. A principal almost never gives an agent absolutely complete instructions. Unless some authority is implied, David would have had to say, "Open the car door, get in, put the key in the ignition, drive to the store, buy stickers, mark an auction number on each sticker ..." and so forth. To solve this problem, the law assumes that the agent has authority to do anything that is reasonably necessary to accomplish her task.

Apparent Authority

A principal can be liable for the acts of an agent who is not, in fact, acting with authority if the *principal's* conduct causes a third party reasonably to believe that the agent is authorized.[12] In the case of *express* and *implied* authority, the principal has authorized the agent to act. Apparent authority is different: the principal has *not* authorized the agent, but has done something to make an innocent third party *believe* the agent is authorized. As a result, the principal is every bit as liable to the third party as if the agent did have authority.

For example, Zbigniew Lambo and Scott Kennedy were brokers at Paulson Investment Co., a stock brokerage firm in Oregon. The two men violated securities laws by selling unregistered stock, which ultimately proved to be worthless. Kennedy and Lambo were liable, but they were unable to repay the money. Either Paulson or its customers would end up bearing the loss. What is the fair result? The law takes the view that the principal is liable, not the third party, because the principal, by word or deed, allowed the third party to believe that the agent was acting on the principal's behalf. The principal could have prevented the third party from losing money.

Although the two brokers did not have *express* or *implied* authority to sell the stock (Paulson had not authorized them to break the law), the company was nonetheless liable on the grounds that the brokers had *apparent* authority. Paulson had sent letters to its customers notifying them when it hired Kennedy. The two brokers made sales presentations at Paulson's offices. The company had never told customers that the two men were not authorized to sell this worthless stock.[13] Thus the agents *appeared* to have authority, even though they did not. Of course, Paulson had the right to recover from Kennedy and Lambo, if it could ever compel them to pay.

Remember that the issue in apparent authority is always what the *principal* has done to make the *third party* believe that the *agent* has authority. Suppose that Kennedy and Lambo never worked for Paulson but, on their own, printed up Paulson stationery. The company would not be liable for the stock the two men sold because it had never done or said anything that would reasonably make a third party believe that the men were its agents.

---

[11] Restatement (Third) of Agency §2.02.

[12] Restatement (Third) of Agency §2.03.

[13] *Badger v. Paulson Investment Co.*, 311 Ore. 14, 803 P.2d 1178, 1991 Ore. LEXIS 7 (S. Ct. OR, 1991).

Ratification

If a person accepts the benefit of an unauthorized transaction or fails to repudiate it, then he is as bound by the act as if he had originally authorized it. He has *ratified* the act.[14] Many of the cases in agency law involve instances in which one person acts *without* authority for another. To avoid liability, the alleged principal shows that he had not authorized the task at issue. But sometimes after the fact, the principal decides that he approves of what the agent has done even though it was not authorized at the time. The law would be perverse if it did not permit the principal, under those circumstances, to agree to the deal the agent has made. The law is not perverse, but it is careful. Even if an agent acts without authority, the principal can decide later to be bound by her actions so long as these requirements are met:

- The "agent" indicates to the third party that she is acting for a principal.
- The "principal" knows all the material facts of the transaction.
- The "principal" accepts the benefit of the whole transaction, not just part.
- The third party does not withdraw from the contract before ratification.

A night clerk at the St. Regis Hotel in Detroit, Michigan, was brutally murdered in the course of a robbery. A few days later, the *Detroit News* reported that the St. Regis management had offered a $1,000 reward for any information leading to the arrest and conviction of the killer. Two days after the article appeared, Robert Jackson turned in the man who was subsequently convicted of the crime. But then it was Jackson's turn to be robbed—the hotel refused to pay the reward on the grounds that the manager who had made the offer had no authority. Jackson still had one weapon left: he convinced the court that the hotel had ratified the offer. One of the hotel's owners admitted he read the *Detroit News*. The court concluded that if someone reads a newspaper, he is sure to read any articles about a business he owns; therefore, the owner must have been aware of the offer. He accepted the benefit of the offer by failing to revoke it publicly by, say, announcing to the press that the reward was invalid. This failure to revoke constituted a ratification, and the hotel was liable.[15]

Subagents

Many of the examples in this chapter involve a single agent acting for a principal. Real life is often more complex. Daniel, the owner of a restaurant, hires Michaela to manage it. She in turn hires chefs, waiters, and dishwashers. Daniel has never even met the restaurant help, yet they are also his agents, albeit a special category called **subagent.** Michaela is called an **intermediary agent**—someone who hires subagents for the principal.

As a general rule, an agent has no authority to delegate her tasks to another unless the principal authorizes her to do so. But when an agent is authorized to hire a subagent, the principal is as liable for the acts of the subagent as he is for the acts of a regular agent. Daniel authorizes Michaela to hire a restaurant staff, so she hires Lydia to serve as produce buyer. When Lydia buys food for the restaurant, Daniel must pay the bill.

Agent's Liability for Contracts

The agent's liability on a contract depends upon how much the third party knows about the principal. Disclosure is the agent's best protection against liability.

[14]Restatement (Third) of Agency §4.01.

[15]*Jackson v. Goodman*, 69 Mich. App. 225, 244 N.W.2d 423, 1976 Mich. App., LEXIS 741 (Mich. Ct. App., 1976).

Fully Disclosed Principal

An agent is not liable for any contracts she makes on behalf of a *fully* disclosed principal. A principal is fully disclosed if the third party knows of his *existence* and his *identity*. Augusta acts as agent for Parker when he buys Tracey's prize-winning show horse. Augusta and Tracey both grew up in posh Grosse Pointe, Michigan, where they attended the same elite schools. Tracey does not know Parker, but she figures any friend of Augusta's must be OK. She figures wrong—Parker is a charming deadbeat. He injures Tracey's horse, fails to pay the full contract price, and promptly disappears. Tracey angrily demands that Augusta make good on Parker's debt. Unfortunately for Tracey, Parker was a fully disclosed principal—Tracey knew of his *existence* and his *identity*. Although Tracey partly relied on Augusta's good character when contracting with Parker, Augusta is not liable because Tracey knew who the principal was and could have (should have) investigated him. Augusta did not promise anything herself, and Tracey's only recourse is against the principal, Parker (wherever he may be).

To avoid liability when signing a contract on behalf of a principal, an agent must clearly state that she is an agent and also must identify the principal. Augusta should sign a contract on behalf of her principal, Parker, as follows: "Augusta, as agent for Parker" or "Parker, by Augusta, Agent."

Unidentified Principal

In the case of an *unidentified* principal, the third party can recover from either the agent or the principal. (An unidentified principal is also sometimes called a "partially disclosed principal.") A principal is unidentified if the third party knew of his *existence* but not his *identity*. Suppose that, when approaching Tracey about the horse, Augusta simply says, "I have a friend who is interested in buying your champion." Any friend of Augusta's is a friend of Tracey's—or so Tracey thinks. Parker is an unidentified principal because Tracey knows only that he exists, not who he is. She cannot investigate his creditworthiness because she does not know his name. Tracey relies solely on what she is able to learn from the agent, Augusta. Both Augusta and Parker are liable to Tracey. (They are jointly and severally liable, which means that Tracey can recover from either or both of them. However, she cannot recover more than the total she is owed: if her damages are $100,000, she can recover that amount from either Augusta or Parker, or partial amounts from both, but in no event more than $100,000.)

Undisclosed Principal

In the case of an *undisclosed* principal, the third party can recover from either the agent or the principal. A principal is undisclosed if the third party did not know of his existence. Suppose that Augusta simply asks to buy the horse herself, without mentioning that she is purchasing it for Parker. In this case, Parker is an undisclosed principal because Tracey does not know that Augusta is acting for someone else. Both Parker and Augusta are jointly and severally liable. As Exhibit 28.1 illustrates, the principal is always liable, but the agent is not unless the principal's identity is a mystery.

In some ways, the concept of an undisclosed principal violates principles of contract law. If Tracey does not even know that Parker exists, how can they have an agreement or a meeting of the minds? Is such an arrangement fair to Tracey? No matter—a contract with an undisclosed principal is binding. The following incident illustrates why.

William Zeckendorf was a man with a plan. For years, he had been eyeing a six-block tract of land along New York's East River. It was a wasteland of slums and slaughterhouses, but he could see its potential. The meat packers had refused to sell to him, however, because they knew they would never be permitted to build slaughterhouses in Manhattan again. Finally, he got the phone call he had been waiting for. The companies were willing to sell—at more than three times the market price of surrounding land. Undeterred, Zeckendorf immediately put down a $1 million deposit. But to make his investment worthwhile, he needed to buy the neighboring property—once the slaughterhouses were gone, the other land would be much more valuable. Zeckendorf was well known as a wealthy developer; he

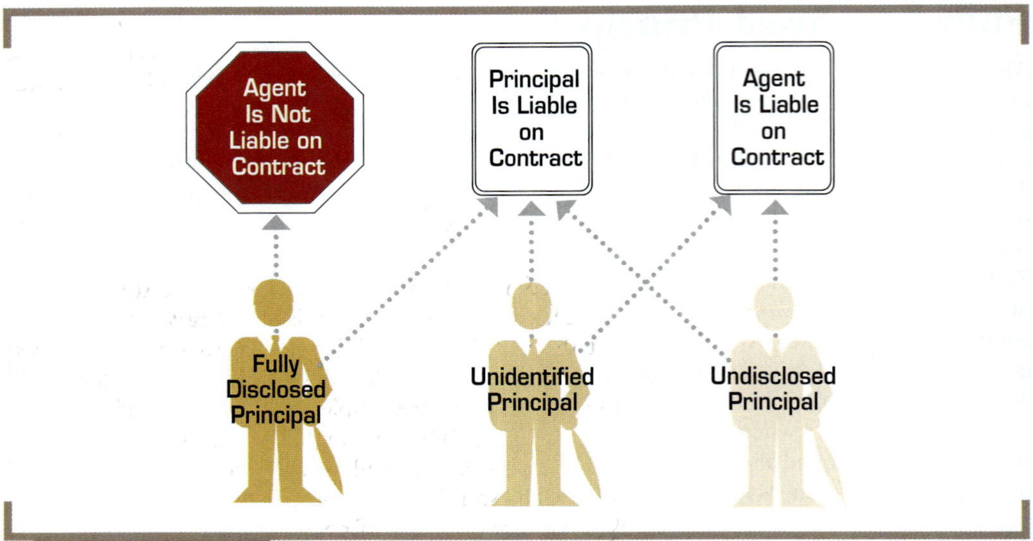

EXHIBIT 28.1

had begun his business career managing the Astor family's real estate holdings. If he personally tried to negotiate the purchase of the surrounding land, word would soon get out that he wanted to put together a large parcel. Prices would skyrocket, and the project would become too costly. So he hired agents to purchase the land for him. To conceal his involvement further, he went to South America for a month. When he returned, his agents had completed 75 different purchases, and he owned 18 acres of land.

Shortly afterwards, the United Nations (UN) began seeking a site for its headquarters. President Truman favored Boston, Philadelphia, or a location in the Midwest. The UN committee suggested Greenwich or Stamford, Connecticut. But John D. Rockefeller settled the question once and for all. He purchased Zeckendorf's land and donated it to the UN (netting Zeckendorf a 25 percent profit). Without the cooperation of agency law, the UN headquarters would not be in New York today.

Without the cooperation of agency law, the UN headquarters would not be in New York today.

Because of concerns about fair play, there are some exceptions to the rule on undisclosed principals. **A third party is not bound to the contract with an undisclosed principal if (1) the contract specifically provides that the third party is not bound to anyone other than the agent, or (2) the agent lies about the principal because she knows the third party would refuse to contract with him.** Suppose that a large university is buying up land in an impoverished area near its campus. An owner of a house there wants to make sure that if he sells to the university, he gets a higher price than if he sells to an individual with more limited resources. A cagey property owner, when approached by one of the university's agents, could ask for a clause in the contract providing that the agent was not representing someone else. If the agent told the truth, the owner could demand a higher price. If the agent lied, then the owner could rescind the contract when the truth emerged.

Unauthorized Agent

Thus far in this section, we have been discussing an agent's liability to a third party for a transaction that was authorized by the principal. Sometimes, however, agents act without the authority of a principal. **If the agent has no authority (express, implied, or apparent), the**

principal is not liable to the third party, and the agent is. Suppose that Augusta agrees to sell Parker's horse to Tracey. Unfortunately, Parker has never met Augusta and has certainly not authorized this transaction. Augusta is hoping that she can persuade him to sell, but Parker refuses. Augusta, but not Parker, is liable to Tracey for breach of contract.

PRINCIPAL'S LIABILITY FOR TORTS

An employer is liable for a tort committed by its employee acting within the scope of employment or acting with authority.[16] This principle of liability is called ***respondeat superior,*** which is a Latin phrase that means "let the master answer." Under the theory of *respondeat superior*, the employer (that is, the principal) is liable for misbehavior by the employee (that is, the agent) whether or not the employer was at fault. Indeed, the employer is liable even if he *forbade* or tried to *prevent* the employee from misbehaving. Thus a company could be liable for the damage a worker causes while driving and talking on her cell phone, even if she is violating company policy at the time. This sounds like a harsh rule. The logic is that because the principal controls the agent, he should be able to *prevent* misbehavior. If he cannot prevent it, at least he can *insure* against the risks. Furthermore, the principal may have deeper pockets than the agent or the injured third party and thus be better able to *afford* the cost of the agent's misbehavior.

To apply the principle of *respondeat superior*, it is important to understand each part of the rule.

Employee

There are two kinds of agents: (1) *employees* and (2) *independent contractors*. **A principal *may be* liable for the torts of an employee but generally is *not* liable for the torts of an independent contractor.** Because of this rule, the distinction between an employee and an independent contractor is important.

Employee or Independent Contractor?

The more control the principal has over an agent, the more likely that the agent will be considered an employee. Therefore, when determining if agents are employees or independent contractors, courts consider whether:

- The principal supervises details of the work.
- The principal supplies the tools and place of work.
- The agents work full time for the principal.
- The agents receive a salary or hourly wages, not a fixed price for the job.
- The work is part of the regular business of the principal.
- The principal and agents believe they have an employer-employee relationship.
- The principal is in business.[17]

Suppose, for example, that Mutt and Jeff work 40 hours a week at Swansong Media preparing food for the company's onsite dining room. They earn a weekly salary. Swansong provides food, utensils, and kitchen. This year, however, Swansong decides to go all out for its holiday party, so it hires FiFi LaBelle to prepare special food. She buys the food, prepares it in her own kitchen, and delivers it to the company in time for the party. She is an independent contractor, while Mutt and Jeff are employees.

[16] Restatement (Third) of Agency §7.07.
[17] Ibid.

Negligent Hiring

Principals prefer agents to be considered independent contractors, not employees, because, as a general rule, principals are not liable for the torts of an independent contractor. There is, however, one exception to this rule: **the principal is liable for the torts of an independent contractor *if* the principal has been negligent in hiring or supervising her.** Remember that, under *respondeat superior*, the principal is liable *without fault* for the torts of employees. The case of independent contractors is different: the principal is liable only if he was *at fault* by being careless in his hiring or supervising.

Exhibit 28.2 illustrates the difference in liability between an employee and an independent contractor.

Scope of Employment

Principals are liable only for torts that an employee commits within the *scope of employment*. If an employee leaves a pool of water on the floor of a store and a customer slips and falls, the employer is liable. But if the same employee leaves water on his own kitchen floor and a friend falls, the employer is not liable because the employee is not acting within the scope of employment. An employee is acting within the scope of employment if the act:

- Is one that employees are generally responsible for
- Takes place during hours that the employee is generally employed
- Is part of the principal's business
- Is similar to the one the principal authorized
- Is one for which the principal supplied the tools; and
- Is not seriously criminal.

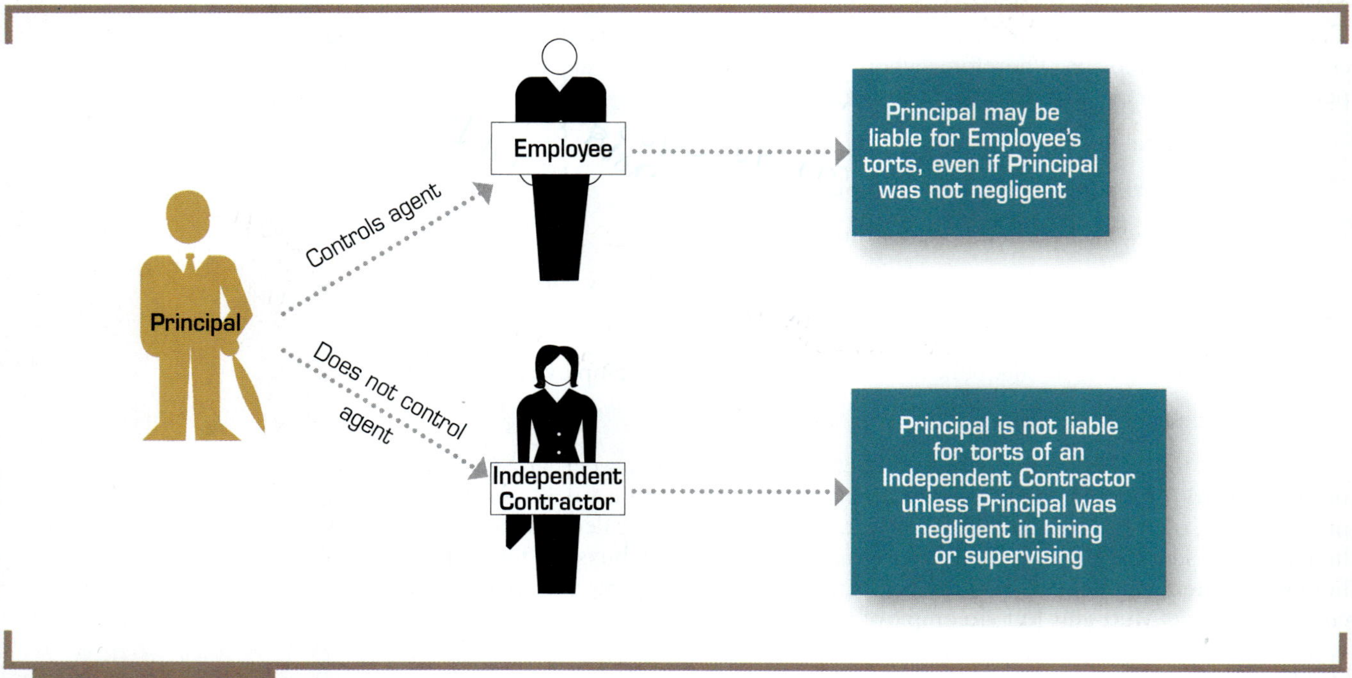

EXHIBIT 28.2

Scope of employment cases raise two major issues: authorization and abandonment.

Authorization

In authorization cases, the agent is clearly working for the principal but commits an act that the principal has not authorized. Although Jane has often told the driver of her delivery van not to speed, Hank ignores her instructions and plows into Bernadette. At the time of the accident, he is working for Jane, delivering flowers for her shop, but his act is not authorized. **An act is within the scope of employment, even if expressly forbidden, if it is of the same general nature as that authorized or if it is incidental to the conduct authorized.** Hank was authorized to drive the van, but not to speed. However, his speeding was of the same general nature as the authorized act, so Jane is liable to Bernadette.

Abandonment

The second major issue in a *scope of employment* case involves abandonment. **The principal is liable for the actions of the employee that occur while the employee is at work, but not for actions that occur after the employee has abandoned the principal's business.** Although the rule sounds straightforward, the difficulty lies in determining whether the employee has in fact abandoned the principal's business. The employer is liable if the employee is simply on a *detour* from company business, but the employer is not liable if the employee is off on a *frolic of his own.* Suppose that Hank, the delivery van driver, speeds during his afternoon commute home. An employee is generally not acting within the scope of his employment when he commutes to and from work, so his principal, Jane, is not liable. Or suppose that, while on the way to a delivery, he stops to view his favorite movie classic, *Dead on Arrival.* Unable to see in the darkened theater, he knocks Anna down, causing grave harm. Jane is not liable because Hank's visit to the movies is outside the scope of his employment. On the other hand, if Hank stops at the Burger Box drive-in window en route to making a delivery, Jane is liable when he crashes into Anna on the way out of the parking lot because this time, he is simply making a detour.

Was the employee in the following case acting within the scope of his employment while driving to work? You be the judge.

You be the Judge

Zankel v. United States of America

2008 U.S. Dist. LEXIS 23655
United States District Court for the Western District of Pennsylvania, 2008

Facts: Staff Sergeant William E. Dreyer was a recruiter for the United States Marine Corps. Driving to work one morning at 6:40 a.m., in a government-owned car, he struck and killed 12-year-old Justin Zankel. The child's parents sued the federal government, claiming that it was liable for Dreyer's actions because he had been acting within the scope of his employment at the time of the accident.

The Marine Corps had provided Dreyer with a car to drive while on government business, but he was not permitted to use this car while commuting to and from home unless he had specific authorization from his boss, Major Michael Sherman. However, Sherman was flexible in giving authorization and even permitted his soldiers simply to leave a message on his voicemail. Indeed, he had denied only about a dozen such requests over a three-year period.

Each month, Dreyer was expected to meet specific quotas for the number of contracts signed and recruits shipped to basic training. However, despite working 16 to 18 hours every day of the week, Dreyer had not met his recruiting quotas for months. Sherman had formally reprimanded him and increased his target for the following month.

On the day before the accident, Dreyer left home at 6:30 a.m., driving his own car. At the office, he switched to a government car and worked until 10:45 p.m. He then discovered that his personal car would not start. He did not want to call Sherman that late, so he drove his government car home without permission. He believed that, had he called, Sherman would have said it was OK.

Dreyer arrived home at midnight. He was under orders to attend an early-morning training session the next day. So he awoke early and left home at 6:35 a.m. At 6:40 a.m., his car hit Justin Zankel.

You Be the Judge: ***Was Dreyer within the scope of employment when he killed Zankel?***

Argument for the Zankels: At the time of the accident, Dreyer was driving a government vehicle. Although he had not requested permission to drive the car, if he had done so, permission certainly would have been granted.

Moreover, even if Dreyer was not authorized to drive the Marine Corps car, the government is still liable because his activity was of the same general nature as that authorized and it was incidental to the conduct authorized. Driving the car was part of Dreyer's work. Indeed, he could not perform his job without it. In addition, Dreyer was on the road early so that he could attend a required training session. He was exhausted from trying to reach impossible goals. The Marine Corps must bear responsibility for this tragic accident.

Argument for United States: The government had a clear policy stating that recruiters were not authorized to drive a government car without first requesting permission. Dreyer had not done so. Therefore, he was not authorized to drive the government car at the time of the accident.

Moreover, it is well established that an employee commuting to and from work is not within the scope of employment. If Dreyer had been driving from one recruiting effort to another, that would be a different story. But in this case, he had not yet started work for the Marine Corps, and therefore the government is not liable.

Intentional Torts

A principal is *not* liable for the *intentional* torts of an employee unless (1) the employee intended to serve some purpose of the employer; or (2) the employer was negligent in hiring or supervising this employee.

During an NBA basketball game, Kobe pushes LeBron into some chairs under the basket to prevent him from scoring a breakaway layup. Kobe's team is liable for his actions because he was motivated, at least in part, by a desire to help his team. But if Kobe hits LeBron in the parking lot after the playoffs are over, Kobe's team is *not* liable because he is no longer motivated by a desire to help the team. His motivation now is personal revenge or frustration.

In the following case, a priest did wrong. Was he serving some purpose of the Church? Was the Church liable for his criminal acts?

Doe v. Liberatore

478 F. Supp. 2d 742; 2007 U.S. Dist. Lexis 19067
United States District Court for the Middle District of Pennsylvania, 2007

Facts: A number of priests wrote to James Timlin, the Bishop of Scranton, warning him that Father Albert Liberatore was engaging in a sexual relationship with one of his male students. Bishop Timlin transferred Liberatore from the school to a parish church.

Fourteen year-old John Doe was a member of Liberatore's parish. Liberatore befriended Doe, taking him on outings and giving him expensive gifts. Doe routinely slept in Liberatore's bed. A number of priests told Bishop Timlin that they feared Liberatore was sexually abusing Doe. One witness reported that she had seen Doe put his hand down Liberatore's pants. Eventually, Doe himself told a priest that he was being sexually abused. The priest instructed Doe to forgive Liberatore and not to tell other people because it would ruin Doe's life and the lives of others.

Only after Liberatore pleaded guilty to multiple counts of sexual abuse did the Church dismiss him from the priesthood. Doe filed suit against the Church and Bishop Timlin, alleging that they were liable for the torts committed by Liberatore. The defendants filed a motion to dismiss.

Issues: ***Was Liberatore acting within the scope of his employment? Was the Church liable for his criminal acts?***

Excerpts from Judge Caputo's Decision: Under Pennsylvania law, an employer is held liable for the negligent acts of his employee which cause injuries to a third party, provided that such acts were committed during the course of and within the scope of the employment.

The conduct of an employee is considered within the scope of employment if: (1) it is of a kind and nature that the employee is employed to perform; (2) it occurs substantially within the authorized time and space limits; (3) it is actuated, at least in part, by a purpose to serve the employer; and (4) if force is intentionally used by the employee against another, the use of force is not unexpected by the employer.

Here, it is clear that Liberatore's sexual molestation of Plaintiff was not within the scope or nature of his employment as a priest. Indeed, the activity of which Plaintiff now complains is wholly inconsistent with the role of one who is received into the Holy Orders as an ordained priest of the Roman Catholic Church. Moreover, the acts of sexual abuse perpetrated by Liberatore were both outrageous and certainly not actuated by any purpose of serving the Diocese, Sacred Heart, or Bishop Timlin. Therefore, the Court will grant summary judgment in favor of the Diocese, Sacred Heart, and Bishop Timlin as to [this issue].

Plaintiff next claims that the Diocese, Sacred Heart, and Bishop Timlin are liable for negligence in their hiring, supervision, and retention of Liberatore as a Diocesan priest. [A]n employer owes a duty to exercise reasonable care in selecting, supervising and controlling employees. The Supreme Court of Pennsylvania has held that, to fasten liability on an employer, it must be shown that the employer knew or, in the exercise of ordinary care, should have known of the necessity for exercising control of his employee.

In the instant case, the Diocese, Sacred Heart, and Bishop Timlin may be liable if they knew or should have known that Liberatore had a propensity for committing sexual abuse and his employment as Pastor at Sacred Heart might create a situation where his propensity would harm a third person, such as Plaintiff. [A] reasonable jury could conclude that the Diocese, Sacred Heart, and Bishop Timlin were negligent or reckless in supervising and retaining Liberatore. However, the Court concludes that a reasonable jury could not find that the Diocese, Sacred Heart, and Bishop Timlin were negligent or reckless in hiring Liberatore because there is no evidence suggesting that Liberatore was or would become a child sex predator when he was hired.

Physical or Non-Physical Harm

In the case of *physical* torts, a principal is liable for the negligent conduct of a employee that occurs within the scope of employment. The rule for *nonphysical* torts (that is, torts that harm only reputation, feelings, or wallet) is different. **Nonphysical torts are treated more like a contract claim, and the principal is liable if the employee acted with express, implied, or apparent authority.**[18] For example, suppose that Dwayne buys a house insurance policy from Andy, who is an agent of the Balls of Fire Insurance Company. Andy throws away Dwayne's policy and pockets his premiums. When Dwayne's house burns down, Balls of Fire is liable because Andy was acting with apparent authority.

EXAM Strategy

Question: Daisy was the founder of an Internet start-up company. Mac was her driver. One day, after he had dropped her at a board meeting, he went to the car wash. There, he told an attractive woman that he worked for a money management firm. She gave him money to invest. On the way out of the car wash, he was so excited that he hit another customer's expensive car. Who is liable for Mac's misdeeds?

Strategy: In determining a principal's liability, begin by figuring out whether the agent has committed a physical or non-physical tort. Remember that the principal is liable for physical torts within the scope of employment, but for nonphysical torts, she is liable only if the employee acted with authority.

Result: In this case, Daisy is liable for the damage to the car because that was a physical tort within the scope of employment. But she is not liable for the investment money because Mac did not have authority (express, implied, or apparent) to take those funds.

Agent's Liability for Torts

The focus of the prior section was on the *principal's* liability for the agent's torts. But it is important to remember that **agents are always liable for their own torts.** Agents who commit torts are personally responsible, whether or not their principal is also liable. Even if the tort was committed to benefit the principal, the agent is still liable. So the sailor who got into a fistfight while rousting a shipmate from bed is liable even though he thought he was acting for the benefit of his principal.

This rule makes obvious sense. If the agent were not liable, he would have little incentive to be careful. Imagine Hank driving his delivery van for Jane. If he were not personally liable for his own torts, he might think, "If I drive fast enough, I can make it through that light even though it just turned red. And if I don't, what the heck, it'll be Jane's problem, not mine." Agents, as a rule, may have fewer assets than their principal, but it is important that their personal assets be at risk in the event of their negligent behavior.

If the agent and principal are *both* liable, which does the injured third party sue? The principal and the agent are *jointly and severally liable,* which means, as we have seen, that the injured third party can sue either one or both, as she chooses. If she recovers from the principal, he can sue the agent.

Chapter Conclusion

When students enroll in a business law course, they fully expect to learn about torts and contracts, corporations and partnerships. They probably do not think much about agency law; many of them have not even heard the term before. Yet it is an area of the law that affects us all because each of us has been and will continue to be both an agent and a principal many times in our lives.

Exam Review

1. **CREATING AN AGENCY RELATIONSHIP** A principal and an agent mutually consent that the agent will act on behalf of the principal and be subject to the principal's control, thereby creating a fiduciary relationship. (pp. 671–672)

2. **ELEMENTS NOT REQUIRED** An agency relationship can exist without either a written agreement, a formal agreement, or compensation. (pp. 672–673)

3. **AN AGENT'S DUTIES TO THE PRINCIPAL** An agent owes these duties to the principal: duty of loyalty, duty to obey instructions, duty of care, and duty to provide information. (pp. 673–677)

4. **THE PRINCIPAL'S REMEDIES IN THE EVENT OF A BREACH** The principal has three potential remedies when the agent breaches her duty: recovery of damages the breach has caused, recovery of any profits earned by the agent from the breach, and rescission of any transaction with the agent. (p. 678)

5. **THE PRINCIPAL'S DUTIES TO THE AGENT** The principal has three duties to the agent: to compensate as provided by the agreement, to reimburse legitimate expenses, and to cooperate with the agent. (pp. 678–679)

6. **POWER AND RIGHT TO TERMINATE** Both the agent and the principal have the power to terminate an agency relationship, but they may not have the right. If the termination violates the agency agreement and causes harm to the other party, the wrongful party must pay damages. (pp. 679–682)

7. **AUTOMATIC TERMINATION** An agency relationship automatically terminates if the principal or agent no longer can perform the required duties or if a change in circumstances renders the agency relationship pointless. (pp. 680–681)

8. **A PRINCIPAL'S LIABILITY FOR CONTRACTS** A principal is liable for the contracts of the agent if the agent has express, implied, or apparent authority. (pp. 682–684)

9. **EXPRESS AUTHORITY** The principal grants express authority by words or conduct that, reasonably interpreted, cause the agent to believe that the principal desires her to act on the principal's account. (p. 682)

10. **IMPLIED AUTHORITY** Implied authority includes authority to do acts that are incidental to a transaction, usually accompany it, or are reasonably necessary to accomplish it. (p. 683)

11. **APPARENT AUTHORITY** Apparent authority means that a principal is liable for the acts of an agent who is not, in fact, acting with authority if the principal's conduct causes a third party reasonably to believe that the agent is authorized. (p. 683)

Question: Dr. James Leonard wrote Dr. Edward Jacobson to offer him the position of chief of audiology at Jefferson Medical College in Philadelphia. In the letter, Leonard stated that this appointment would have to be approved by the promotion and appointment committee. Jacobson believed that the appointment committee acted only as a "rubber stamp," affirming whatever recommendation Leonard made. Jacobson accepted Leonard's offer and proceeded to sell his house and quit his job in Colorado. You can guess what happened next. Two weeks later, Leonard sent Jacobson another letter, rescinding his offer because of opposition from the appointment committee. Did Leonard have apparent authority?

Strategy: In cases of apparent authority, begin by asking what the principal did to make the third party believe that the agent was authorized. What did the Medical College do? (See the "Result" at the end of this section.)

12. AN AGENT'S LIABILITY FOR A CONTRACT An agent is not liable for any contract she makes on behalf of a fully disclosed principal. The principal is liable. In the case of a unidentified or undisclosed principal, both the agent and the principal are liable on the contract. (pp. 684–687)

13. A PRINCIPAL'S LIABILITY FOR TORTS An employer is liable for a tort committed by its employee acting within the scope of employment or acting with authority. (pp. 687–692)

EXAM Strategy

Question: While drunk, the driver of a subway car plows into the back of the car ahead of him, killing a passenger. It was against the rules for the driver to be drunk. Is the subway authority liable for the negligence of its employee?

Strategy: With a tort case, always determine first if the agents are employees or independent contractors. This worker was an employee. Then ask if the employee was acting within the scope of employment. Yes, he was driving a subway car, which is what he was hired to do. Does it matter than he had violated subway rules? No, his violation of the rules does not eliminate his principal's liability. (See the "Result" at the end of this section.)

14. INDEPENDENT CONTRACTOR The principal is liable for the physical torts of an independent contractor only if the principal has been negligent in hiring or supervising him. (p. 687)

15. INTENTIONAL TORTS A principal is not liable for the intentional torts of an employee unless (1) the employee intended to serve some purpose of the employer; or (2) the employer was negligent in hiring or supervising the employee. (pp. 690–691)

EXAM Strategy

Question: What if the subway driver mentioned above had stabbed a passenger?

Strategy: In the case of an intentional tort, the principal is liable only if the agent was intending to serve some purpose of the employer or the employer was negligent in hiring or supervising him. (See the "Result" at the end of this section.)

16. AGENT'S LIABILITY FOR TORTS Agents are always liable for their own torts. (p. 692)

17. NONPHYSICAL TORTS A principal is liable only for the nonphysical torts of an employee who is acting with express, implied or apparent authority. (p. 691)

11. Result: No. Indeed, Leonard had told Jacobson that he did not have authority. If Jacobson chose to believe otherwise, that was his problem.

13. Result: The subway authority is liable.

15. Result: When he stabbed a passenger, the driver was not serving the purpose of the employer, so the subway authority would not be liable. There was no evidence that the subway authority had been negligent in its hiring or supervising of employees.

Multiple-Choice Questions

1. At Business University, semester enrollment begins at midnight on April 1. Jasper asked his roommate, Alonso, to register him for an important required course as a favor. Alonso agreed to do so but then overslept. As a result, Jasper could not enroll in the required course he needed to graduate and had to stay in school for an additional semester. Is Alonso liable to Jasper?

(a) No, because an agency agreement is invalid unless the agent receives payment.
(b) No, because Alonso was not grossly negligent.
(c) No, because the cost of the extra semester is unreasonably high.
(d) Yes, because Alonso disobeyed his instructions.

2. Finn learns that, despite his stellar record, he is being paid less than other salespeople at Barry Co., so he decides to start his own company. During his last month on the Barry payroll, he tells all of his clients about his new business. He also tells them that Barry is a great company, but his fees will be lower. After he opens the doors of his new business, most of his former clients move with him. Is Finn liable to Barry?

(a) No, because he has not been disloyal to Barry—he praised the company.
(b) No, because Barry was underpaying him.
(c) No, because his clients have the right to hire whichever company they choose.
(d) Yes, Finn has violated his duty of loyalty to Barry.

3. Kurt asked his car mechanic, Quinn, for help in buying a used car. Quinn recommends a Ford Focus that she has been taking care of its whole life. Quinn was working for the seller. Which of the following statements is true?

(a) Quinn must pay Kurt the amount of money she received from the Ford's prior owner.
(b) After buying the car, Kurt finds out that it needs $1,000 in repairs. He can recover that amount from Quinn, but only if Quinn knew about the needed repairs before Kurt bought the car.
(c) Kurt cannot recover anything because Quinn had no obligation to reveal her relationship with the car's seller.
(d) Kurt cannot recover anything because he had not paid Quinn for her help.

4. Figgins is the dean of a college. He appointed Sue as acting dean while he was out of the country and posted an announcement on the college website announcing that she was authorized to act in his place. He also told Sue privately that she did not have the right to make admissions decisions. While Figgins was gone, Sue overruled the admissions committee to admit the child of a wealthy alumnus. Does the child have the right to attend this college?
   (a) No, because Sue was not authorized to admit him.
   (b) No, because Figgins did not ratify Sue's decision.
   (c) Yes, because Figgins was a fully disclosed principal.
   (d) Yes, because Sue had apparent authority.

5. ***CPA QUESTION*** A principal will not be liable to a third party for a tort committed by an agent:
   (a) unless the principal instructed the agent to commit the tort.
   (b) unless the tort was committed within the scope of the agency relationship.
   (c) if the agency agreement limits the principal's liability for the agent's tort.
   (d) if the tort is also regarded as a criminal act.

6. ***CPA QUESTION*** Cox engaged Datz as her agent. It was mutually agreed that Datz would not disclose that he was acting as Cox's agent. Instead, he was to deal with prospective customers as if he were a principal acting on his own behalf. This he did and made several contracts for Cox. Assuming Cox, Datz, or the customer seeks to avoid liability on one of the contracts involved, which of the following statements is correct?
   (a) Cox must ratify the Datz contracts to be held liable.
   (b) Datz has no liability once he discloses that Cox was the real principal.
   (c) The third party can avoid liability because he believed he was dealing with Datz as a principal.
   (d) The third party may choose to hold either Datz or Cox liable.

Essay Questions

1. An elementary school custodian hit a child who wrote graffiti on the wall. Is the school district liable for this intentional tort by its employee?

2. What if the custodian hit one of the schoolchildren for calling him a name? Is the school district liable?

3. A soldier was drinking at a training seminar. Although he was told to leave his car at the seminar, he disobeyed orders and drove to a military club. On the way to the club, he was involved in an accident. Is the military liable for the damage he caused?

4. One afternoon while visiting friends, tennis star Vitas Gerulaitis fell asleep in their pool house. A mechanic had improperly installed the swimming pool heater, which leaked carbon monoxide fumes into the house where he slept, killing him.

His mother filed suit against the owners of the estate. On what theory would they be liable?

5. **YOU BE THE JUDGE WRITING PROBLEM** Sarah went to an auction at Christie's to bid on a tapestry for her employer, Fine Arts Gallery. The good news is that she purchased a Dufy tapestry for $77,000. The bad news is that it was not the one her employer had told her to buy. In the excitement of the auction, she forgot her instructions. Fine Art refused to pay, and Christie's filed suit. Is Fine Arts liable for the unauthorized act of its agent? **Argument for Christie's:** Christie's cannot possibly ascertain in each case the exact nature of a bidder's authority. Whether or not Sarah had actual authority, she certainly had apparent authority, and Fine Arts is liable. **Argument for Fine Arts:** Sarah was not authorized to purchase the Dufy tapestry, and therefore Christie's must recover from her, not Fine Arts.

Discussion Questions

1. **ETHICS** Mercedes has just begun work at Photobook.com. What a great place to work! Although the salary is not high, the company has fabulous perks. The dining room provides great food from 7 a.m. to midnight, five days a week. There is also a free laundry and dry-cleaning service. Mercedes's social life has never been better. She invites her friends over for Photobook meals and has their laundry done for free. And because her job requires her to be online all the time, she has plenty of opportunity to stay in touch with her friends by g-chatting, tweeting, and checking Facebook updates. She is, however, shocked that one of her colleagues takes paper home from the office for his children to use at home. Are these employees behaving ethically?

2. Kevin was the manager of a radio station, WABC. A competing station lured him away. In his last month on the job at WABC, he notified two key on-air personalities that if they were to leave the station, he would not hold them to their noncompete agreements. What can WABC do?

3. Jesse worked as a buyer for the Vegetable Co. Rachel offered to sell Jesse 10 tons of tomatoes for the account of Vegetable. Jesse accepted the offer. Later, Jesse discovered that Rachel was an agent for Sylvester Co. Who is liable on this contract?

4. The Pharmaceutical Association holds an annual convention. At the convention, Brittany, who was president of the association, told Luke that Research Corp. had a promising new cancer vaccine. Luke was so excited that he chartered a plane to fly to Research's headquarters. On the way, the plane crashed and Luke was killed. Is the Pharmaceutical Association liable for Luke's death?

5. Betsy has a two-year contract as a producer at Jackson Movie Studios. She produces a remake of the movie *Footloose.* Unfortunately, it bombs, and Jackson is so furious that he fires her on the weekend the movie opens. Does he have the power to do this?

CHAPTER 29

EMPLOYMENT LAW

"On the killing beds you were apt to be covered with blood, and it would freeze solid; if you leaned against a pillar, you would freeze to that, and if you put your hand upon the blade of your knife, you would run a chance of leaving your skin on it. The men would tie up their feet in newspapers and old sacks, and these would be soaked in blood and frozen, and then soaked again, and so on, until by nighttime a man would be walking on great lumps the size of the feet of an elephant. Now and then, when the bosses were not looking, you would see them plunging their feet and ankles into the steaming hot carcass of the steer…. The cruelest thing of all was that nearly all of them—all of those who used knives—were unable to wear gloves, and their arms would be white with frost and their hands would grow numb, and then of course there would be accidents."[1]

… you would see them plunging their feet and ankles into the steaming hot carcass of the steer.

[1]From Upton Sinclair, *The Jungle* (New York: Bantam Books, 1981), p. 80, a 1906 novel about the meat-packing industry.

INTRODUCTION

For most of history, the concept of career planning was unknown. By and large, people were born into their jobs. Whatever their parents had been—landowner, soldier, farmer, servant, merchant, or beggar—they became, too. People not only knew their place, they also understood the rights and obligations inherent in each position. The landowner had the right to receive labor from his tenants, but he also cared for them if they fell ill. Certainly, there were abuses, but at a time when people held religious convictions about their position in life and workers had few expectations that their lives would be better than their parents', the role of law was limited. The primary English law of employment simply established that, in the absence of a contract, an employee was hired for a year at a time. This rule was designed to prevent injustice in a farming society. If an employee worked through harvest time, the landowner could not fire him in the unproductive winter. Conversely, a worker could not stay the winter and then leave for greener pastures in the spring.

In the 18th and 19th centuries, the Industrial Revolution profoundly altered the employment relationship. Many workers left the farms and villages for large factories in the city. Bosses no longer knew their workers personally, so they felt little responsibility toward them. The old laws that had suited an agrarian economy with stable relationships did not fit the new employment conditions. Instead of duties and responsibilities, courts emphasized the freedom to contract. Since employees could quit their factory jobs whenever they wanted, it seemed only fair for employers to have the same freedom to fire a worker. That was indeed the rule adopted by the courts: unless workers had an explicit employment contract, they were employees at will. **An *employee at will* could be fired for a good reason, a bad reason, or no reason at all.** For nearly a century, this was the basic common law rule of employment. A court explained the rule this way:

> Precisely as may the employee cease labor at his whim or pleasure, and, whatever be his reason, good, bad, or indifferent, leave no one a legal right to complain; so, upon the other hand, may the employer discharge, and, whatever be his reason, good, bad, or indifferent, no one has suffered a legal wrong.[2]

However evenhanded this common law rule of employment may have sounded in theory, in practice, it could lead to harsh results. The lives of factory workers were grim. It was not as if they could simply pack up and leave; conditions were no better elsewhere. For the worker, freedom to contract often meant little more than freedom to starve. Courts and legislatures gradually began to recognize that individual workers were generally unable to negotiate fair contracts with powerful employers. Since the beginning of the 20th century, employment law has changed dramatically. Now, the employment relationship is more strictly regulated by statutes and by the common law.

Note well, though: **in the absence of a specific legal exception, the rule in the United States is that an employee at will can be fired for any reason.** But there *are* many exceptions to this rule. They take the form of statutes and common law. Many of the statutes discussed in this chapter were passed by Congress and therefore apply nationally. The common law, however, comes from state courts and only applies locally. We will look at a sampling of cases that illustrates national trends, even though the law may not be the same in every state.

This chapter covers four topics in employment law: (1) employment security, (2) safety and privacy in the workplace, (3) financial protection, and (4) employment discrimination.

---

[2] *Union Labor Hospital Assn. v. Vance Redwood Lumber Co.*, 112 P.886, 888, 1910 Cal. LEXIS 417 (Cal., 1910).

Employment Security

National Labor Relations Act

Without unions to represent employee interests, employers could simply fire any trouble-making workers who complained about conditions in factories or mines. By joining together, workers could bargain with their employers on more equal terms. Naturally, the owners fought against the unions, firing organizers and even hiring goons to beat them up. Distressed by anti-union violence, Congress passed the **National Labor Relations Act** in 1935. Known as the **NLRA** or the **Wagner Act**, this statute:

- Created the National Labor Relations Board to enforce labor laws;
- Prohibits employers from penalizing workers who engage in union activity (for example, joining a preexisting union or forming a new one); and
- Requires employers to "bargain in good faith" with unions.

Family and Medical Leave Act

The Family and Medical Leave Act (FMLA) guarantees both men and women up to 12 weeks of *unpaid* leave each year for childbirth, adoption, or a serious health condition of their own or in their immediate family. A family member is a spouse, child, or parent—but not a sibling or an in-law. An employee who takes a leave must be allowed to return to the same or an equivalent job with the same pay and benefits. The FMLA applies only to companies with at least 50 workers and to employees who have been with the company full time for at least a year. This is about 60 percent of all employees.

Kevin Knussman was the first person to win a lawsuit under the FMLA. While a Maryland state trooper, he requested eight weeks of leave to care for his pregnant wife, who was suffering severe complications. His boss granted only two weeks. After Knussman's daughter was born, his boss again denied leave, saying that "God made women to have babies." Knussman ultimately recovered $40,000.[3]

The Department of Labor has issued regulations to resolve disputes under the FMLA. These regulations provide that:

- Before a worker returns from FMLA leave, an employer may require a "fitness for duty" evaluation to confirm that the worker can perform the essential functions of the job.
- An employer may consider FMLA absences when awarding bonuses.
- Employers are not permitted to seek medical certification directly from the employee's doctor.

Although the FMLA offers important protections, the United States is the only rich country that does not provide mandatory *paid* maternity leave.

Health Insurance

Companies are *not* required to provide their employees with health insurance. However, current legislation specifies that, starting in 2014, employers who have more than 50 full-time employees must pay a penalty if they do not provide basic health insurance. In addition, company insurance policies must cover employees' children up to the age of 26. At this

---

[3]Eyal Press, "Family-Leave Values," *New York Times*, July 29, 2007.

writing, however, some judges have found this statute to be unconstitutional, while others have upheld it. Almost inevitably, the Supreme Court will decide the statute's fate. (For updates, visit bizlawupdate.com.)

Losing your job does not mean that you must also give up your health insurance—at least not right away. Under the Consolidated Omnibus Budget Reconciliation Act (COBRA), **former employees must be allowed to continue their health insurance for 18 months after being terminated from their job.** The catch is that employees must pay for it themselves, up to 102 percent of the cost. (The extra 2 percent covers administrative expenses.) COBRA applies to any company with 20 or more workers.

Common-Law Protections

The employment-at-will doctrine was created by the courts. Because that rule has sometimes led to absurdly unfair results, the courts have now created a major exception to the rule—**wrongful discharge**.

Wrongful discharge
An employer may not fire a worker for a reason that violates basic social rights, duties or responsibilities.

Wrongful Discharge: Violating Public Policy

Olga Monge was a schoolteacher in her native Costa Rica. After moving to New Hampshire, she attended college in the evenings to earn U.S. teaching credentials. At night, she worked at the Beebe Rubber Co. During the day, she cared for her husband and three children. When she applied for a better job at her plant, the foreman offered to promote her if she would be "nice" and go out on a date with him. When she refused, he assigned her to a lower-wage job, took away her overtime, made her clean the washrooms, and generally ridiculed her. Finally, she collapsed at work, and he fired her.[4]

Imagine that you are one of the judges who decided this case. Olga Monge has been treated abominably, but she was an employee at will and, as you well know, could be fired for any reason. But how can you let the foreman get away with this despicable behavior? The New Hampshire Supreme Court decided that even an employee at will has rights:

> We hold that a termination by the employer of a contract of employment at will which is motivated by bad faith or malice or based on retaliation is not in the best interest of the economic system or the public good and constitutes a breach of the employment contract.[5]

The *Monge* case illustrates the concept of wrongful discharge, which prohibits **an employer from firing a worker for a *bad reason.***

How do the courts define a "bad reason"? It is a reason that violates public policy. Unfortunately, this **public policy rule** is easier to name than it is to define because its definition and application vary from state to state. **In essence, the public policy rule prohibits an employer from firing a worker for a reason that violates basic social rights, duties, or responsibilities.** Almost every employee who has ever been fired feels that a horrible injustice has been done. The difficulty, from the courts' perspective, is to distinguish those cases of dismissal that are offensive enough to affront the community at large from those that outrage only the employee. The courts have primarily applied the public policy rule when an employee refuses to violate the law, performs a legal duty, exercises a legal right, or supports basic societal values.

Refusing to Violate the Law. Larry Downs went to Duke Hospital for surgery on his cleft palate. When he came out of the operating room, the doctor instructed a nurse, Marie Sides, to give Downs enough anesthetic to immobilize him. Sides refused because she thought the anesthetic was wrong for this patient. The doctor angrily administered the anesthetic himself. Shortly thereafter, Downs stopped breathing. Before the doctors could

[4]*Monge v. Beebe*, 114 N.H. 130, 316 A.2d 549, 1974 N.H. LEXIS 223 (NH S. Ct., 1974).
[5]*Id.* at 133.

resuscitate him, he suffered permanent brain damage. When Downs's family sued the hospital, Sides was called to testify. A number of Duke doctors told her that she would be "in trouble" if she testified. She did testify, and after three months of harassment, she was fired. When she sued Duke University, the court held:

> It would be obnoxious to the interests of the state and contrary to public policy and sound morality to allow an employer to discharge any employee, whether the employment be for a designated or unspecified duration, on the ground that the employee declined to commit perjury, an act specifically enjoined by statute. To hold otherwise would be without reason and contrary to the spirit of the law.[6]

As a general rule, employees may not be discharged for refusing to break the law. For example, courts have protected employees who refused to participate in an illegal price-fixing scheme, falsify pollution control records required by state law, pollute navigable waters in violation of federal law, or assist a supervisor in stealing from customers.[7]

Performing a Legal Duty. **Courts have consistently held that an employee may not be fired for serving on a jury.** Employers sometimes have difficulty replacing employees who are called up for jury duty and, therefore, prefer that their workers find some excuse for not serving. But jury duty is an important civic obligation that employers are not permitted to undermine.

Exercising a Legal Right. **As a general rule, an employer may not discharge a worker for exercising a legal right if that right supports public policy.** Dorothy Frampton injured her arm while working at the Central Indiana Gas Co. Her employer (and its insurance company) paid her medical expenses and her salary during the four months she was unable to work. When she discovered that she also qualified for benefits under the state's workers' compensation plan, she filed a claim and received payment. One month later, the company fired her without giving a reason. In her suit against the gas company, the court held:

> The [Workers' Compensation] Act creates a duty in the employer to compensate employees for work-related injuries and a right in the employee to receive such compensation. If employers are permitted to penalize employees for filing workmen's compensation claims, a most important public policy will be undermined. Employees will not file claims for justly deserved compensation—opting, instead, to continue their employment without incident. The end result, of course, is that the employer is effectively relieved of his obligation.[8]

Supporting Societal Values. Courts are sometimes willing to protect employees who do the right thing, even if they violate the boss's orders. Kevin Gardner had just parked his armored truck in front of a bank in Spokane, Washington, when he saw a man with a knife chase the manager out of the bank. While running past the truck, the manager looked directly at Gardner and yelled, "Help me, help me." Gardner got out of his truck and locked the door. By then, the suspect had grabbed another woman, put his knife to her throat, and dragged her into the bank. Gardner followed them in, tackled the suspect, and disarmed him. The rescued woman hailed Gardner as a hero, but his employer fired him for violating a "fundamental" company rule that prohibited drivers from leaving their armored

---

[6] *Sides v. Duke University*, 74 N.C. App. 331, 328 S.E.2d 818, 1985 N.C. App. LEXIS 3501 (N.C. Ct. App. 1985).

[7] *Tameny v. Atlantic Richfield Co.*, 27 Cal. 3d 167, 610 P.2d 1330, 1980 Cal. LEXIS 171 (1980); *Trombetta v. Detroit*, T. & I. R., 81 Mich. App. 489, 265 N.W.2d 385, 1978 Mich. App. LEXIS 2153 (Mich. Ct. App. 1978); *Sabine Pilot Service, Inc. v. Hauck*, 28 Tex. Sup. J. 339, 687 S.W.2d 733, 1985 Tex. LEXIS 755 (1985); *Vermillion v. AAA Pro Moving & Storage*, 146 Ariz. 215, 704 P.2d 1360, 1985 Ariz. App. LEXIS 592 (Ariz. Ct. App. 1985).

[8] *Frampton v. Central Indiana Gas Co.*, 260 Ind. 249, 297 N.E.2d 425, 1973 Ind. LEXIS 522 (1973).

trucks unattended. However, the court held for Gardner on the grounds that, although he had no affirmative legal duty to intervene in such a situation, society values and encourages voluntary rescuers when a life is in danger.[9] This issue is, however, one on which the courts are divided. Not all would have made the same decision.

In the following case, two employees objected when their company supplied defective human tissue for transplantation into live patients. Should the court protect them from termination?

KOZLOSKI V. AMERICAN TISSUE SERVICES FOUNDATION

2006 U.S. Dist. LEXIS 95435
United States District Court for the District of Minnesota, 2006

Facts: American Tissue Services Foundation (ATSF) was in the business of supplying human tissue from cadavers for transplantation into live patients. Mike Slack, an employee of ATSF, revealed to his boss that he had falsified a donor medical record and changed the donor's blood type on the form. This falsification was not only dangerous to recipients of the tissue, it violated Food and Drug Administration (FDA) regulations. Slack was fired and the infractions were reported to the FDA, as required by law.

It turned out, however, that Slack was the foster child of the company's chairman. And, in this case, (foster) blood was thicker than water. The chairman not only hired Slack at another company as a quality assurance specialist (believe it or not), but he fired Slack's boss and the two men who had reported the problem to the FDA. The men filed suit against ATSF for wrongful discharge, but the company filed a motion to dismiss on the grounds that the public policy doctrine in Minnesota applied only to employees who had refused to violate the law.

Issue: ***Does the public policy doctrine in Minnesota apply only if the employee has been fired for refusing to violate the law?***

Excerpts from Judge Graham's Decision: Plaintiffs claim their terminations occurred as a direct result of and in retaliation for their reporting to their employer and the FDA concerns about public safety, violations of federal regulations and federal law, and related concerns regarding quality control issues that may directly affect public safety. [T]he Court rejects Defendant's contention that the *only* common law wrongful discharge claim in Minnesota is one based on allegations that termination was in retaliation for refusing to violate the law. Instead the Court concludes the Minnesota Supreme Court has recognized a common law wrongful discharge claim when a discharge is for a reason that *clearly* violates public policy. In other words, it is the clarity of the violation of public policy that defines the existence of the common law claim.

[T]he FDA regulations concerning the safe transfer of tissues from cadavers for use in live patients emphasize the public safety and protection of citizens, and thus encompass *clear* public policy regarding [the] public's safety. Plaintiffs' allegations that they were required by law to report the violations to the FDA for ATSF to remain in compliance also bolsters this determination. [T]he Court concludes Plaintiffs have sufficiently alleged common law claims for wrongful discharge.

Contract Law

Traditionally, many employers (and employees) thought that only a formal, signed document qualified as an employment contract. Increasingly, however, courts have been willing to enforce an employer's more casual promises, whether written or oral. Sometimes courts have also been willing to *imply* contract terms in the absence of an *express* agreement.

Truth in Hiring. **Oral promises made during the hiring process can be enforceable, even if not approved by the company's top executives.** When the Tanana Valley Medical-Surgical Group, Inc., hired James Eales as a physician's assistant, it promised him that so long as he

[9] *Gardner v. Loomis Armored, Inc.*, 913 P.2d 377, 1996 Wash. LEXIS 109 (1996).

did his job, he could stay there until retirement age. Six years later, the company fired him without cause. The Alaska Supreme Court held that the clinic's promise was enforceable.[10]

Employee Handbooks. The employee handbook at Blue Cross & Blue Shield stated that employees could be fired only for just cause and then only after warnings, notice, a hearing, and other procedures. Charles Toussaint was fired summarily five years after he joined the company. Although this decision was ultimately reviewed by the personnel department, company president, and chairman of the board of trustees, Toussaint was not given the benefit of all of the procedures in the handbook. The court held that **an employee handbook creates a contract.**[11]

Covenant of Good Faith and Fair Dealing. A covenant of good faith and fair dealing prohibits one party to a contract from interfering with the other's right to benefit under the contract. All parties are expected to behave in a fair, decent, and reasonable manner. **In almost all states, courts will imply a covenant of good faith and fair dealing in an at-will employment relationship.** These cases, however, have all arisen in situations in which an employer fires a worker to avoid paying promised income or benefits.

When Forrest Fleming went to work for Parametric Technology Corp., the company promised him valuable stock options if he met his sales goals. He would not be able to *exercise* the options (that is, purchase the stock), however, until several years after they were granted, and then only if he was still employed by the company. During his four years with Parametric, Fleming received options to purchase about 18,000 shares for a price as low as 25 cents each. The shares ultimately traded in the market for as much as $50. Although Fleming exercised some options, the company fired him three months before he became eligible to purchase an additional 1,000 shares. The jury awarded him $1.6 million in damages. Although Parametric had not violated the explicit terms of the option agreement, the jury believed it had violated the covenant of good faith and fair dealing by firing Fleming to prevent him from exercising his remaining options.[12]

Tort Law

Workers have successfully sued their employers under the following tort theories.

Defamation. **Employers may be liable for defamation when they give false and unfavorable references about a former employee.** In his job as a bartender at the Capitol Grille restaurant, Christopher Kane often flirted with customers. After he was fired from his job, his ex-boss claimed that Kane had been "fired from every job he ever had for sexual misconduct." In fact, Kane had never been fired before. He recovered $300,000 in damages for this defamation.

Qualified privilege
Employers who give references are liable only for false statements that they know to be false or that are primarily motivated by ill will.

More than half of the states, however, recognize a qualified privilege for employers who give references about former employees. A **qualified privilege** means that employers are liable only for false statements that they know to be false or that are primarily motivated by ill will. After Becky Chambers left her job at American Trans Air, Inc., she discovered that her former boss was telling anyone who called for a reference that Chambers "does not work good with other people," is a "troublemaker," and "would not be a good person to rehire." Chambers was unable, however, to present compelling evidence that her boss had been primarily motivated by ill will. Neither Trans Air nor the boss was held liable for these statements because they were protected by the qualified privilege.[13]

---

[10] *Eales v. Tanana Valley Medical-Surgical Group, Inc.*, 663 P.2d 958, 1983 Alas. LEXIS 430 (Alaska 1983).
[11] *Toussaint v. Blue Cross & Blue Shield*, 408 Mich. 579, 292 N.W.2d 880, 1980 Mich. LEXIS 227 (1980).
[12] *Fleming v. Parametric Tech. Corp.*, 1999 U.S. App. LEXIS 14864.
[13] *Chambers v. American Trans Air, Inc.*, 577 N.E.2d 612, 1991 Ind. App. LEXIS 1413 (Ind. Ct. App. 1991).

Even if the employer wins, a trial is an expensive and time-consuming undertaking. Not surprisingly, companies are leery about offering any references for former employees. The company gains little benefit from giving an honest evaluation and may suffer substantial liability. As a matter of policy, many companies instruct their managers to reveal only a person's salary and dates of employment and not to offer an opinion on job performance.

On the flip side, do employers have any obligation to warn about risky workers? **Generally, courts have held that employers do *not* have a legal obligation to disclose information about former employees.** For example, while Jeffrey St. Clair worked at the St. Joseph Nursing Home, he was disciplined 24 times for actions ranging from extreme violence to drug and alcohol use. When he applied for a job with Maintenance Management Corp., St. Joseph refused to give any information other than St. Clair's dates of employment. After he savagely murdered a security guard at his new job, the guard's family sued, but the court dismissed the case.[14]

In some recent cases, however, courts have held that, when a former worker is potentially dangerous, employers do have an obligation to disclose this information. For example, officials from two junior high schools gave Robert Gadams glowing letters of recommendation without mentioning that he had been fired for inappropriate sexual conduct with students. While an assistant principal at a new school, he molested a 13-year-old. Her parents sued the former employers. The court held that the writer of a letter of recommendation owes to third parties (in this case, the student) "a duty not to misrepresent the facts in describing the qualifications and character of a former employee, if making these misrepresentations would present a substantial, foreseeable risk of physical injury to the third persons."[15] As a result of cases such as this, it makes sense to disclose past violent behavior.

To assist employers who are asked for references, Lehigh economist Robert Thornton has written "The Lexicon of Intentional Ambiguous Recommendations" (LIAR). For a candidate with interpersonal problems, he suggests saying, "I am pleased to say that this person is a former colleague of mine." For a candidate with drug or alcohol problems, there are several possibilities: "She was always high in my opinion," "We remember the hours she spent working with us as happy hours," or "I would say that her real talent is getting wasted at her current job."[16]

Ethics All joking aside, what if someone calls you to check references on a former employee who had a drinking problem? The job is driving a van for junior high school sports teams. What is the manager's ethical obligation in this situation? Many managers say that, in the case of a serious problem such as alcoholism, sexual harassment, or drug use, they will find a way to communicate that an employee is unsuitable. What if the ex-employee says she is reformed? Aren't people entitled to a second chance? Is it right to risk a defamation suit against your company to protect others from harm?

accept & allow

Intentional Infliction of Emotional Distress. **Employers who condone cruel treatment of their workers face liability under the tort of intentional infliction of emotional distress.** For example, when a 57-year-old social-work manager at Yale–New Haven Hospital

[14] *Moore v. St. Joseph Nursing Home, Inc.*, 184 Mich. App. 766, 459 N.W.2d 100, 1990 Mich. App. LEXIS 285 (Mich. Ct. App. 1990).

[15] *Randi W. v. Muroc Joint Unified School District*, 14 Cal. 4th 1066, 929 P.2d 582, 1997 Cal. LEXIS 10 (1997), modified, 14 Cal. 4th 1282c, 97 Cal. Daily Op. Service 1439.

[16] Robert J. Thornton, *Lexicon of Intentionally Ambiguous Recommendations*, Barnes and Noble Books, 2005.

was fired, she was forced to place her personal belongings in a plastic bag and was escorted out the door by security guards in full view of gaping coworkers. A supervisor told her that she would be arrested for trespassing if she returned. A jury awarded her $105,000.

Whistleblowing

No one likes to be accused of wrongdoing even if (or, perhaps, especially if) the accusations are true. **This is exactly what whistleblowers do: they are employees who disclose illegal behavior on the part of their employer.** Not surprisingly, many companies, when faced with such an accusation by an employee, prefer to shoot the messenger. Here is one such story.

Although FMC Corp. sold 9,000 Bradley Fighting Vehicles to the U.S. Army, there had been doubts about the Bradley from the beginning. Its purpose was to ferry soldiers across rivers during a land war in Europe, but whenever a prototype was driven into water, it leaked as badly as any car would have done. When testing supervisor Henry Boisvert refused to sign a report stating that the Bradley functioned well, FMC fired him. A jury ultimately agreed with his version of events and awarded him $171 million.

The law on whistleblowers varies across the country. As a general rule, however, whistleblowers are protected in the following situations:

- *The False Claims Act.* Boisvert recovered under the federal False Claims Act, a statute that permits lawsuits against anyone who defrauds the government. The recovery is shared by the government (who receives 75 percent to 85 percent) and the whistleblower (who gets the rest). The Act prohibits employers from firing workers who file suit under the statute.

- *The Dodd-Frank Wall Street Reform and Consumer Protection Act.* Anyone who provides information to the government about violations of securities or commodities laws is entitled to a payout of from 10 to 30 percent of whatever award the government receives, provided that the award tops $1 million. If a company retaliates against tipsters, they are entitled to reinstatement, double back pay, and attorney's fees. The whistleblowing provision is intended to encourage tips to the government, but companies fear it may also discourage employees from reporting wrongdoing to corporate compliance offices—why report a problem for free when you could get paid a lot of money?

- *Sarbanes-Oxley Act of 2002.* This act protects employees of publicly traded companies who provide evidence of fraud to investigators (whether in or outside the company). A successful plaintiff is entitled to reinstatement, back pay, and attorney's fees.

- *Constitutional protection for government employees.* Employees of federal, state, and local governments have a right to free speech under the United States Constitution. Therefore, the government cannot retaliate against public employees who blow the whistle, so long as the employee is speaking out on a matter of public concern. For example, a New York City social worker complained on TV that the city child welfare agency was not adequately protecting children from horrible abuse. When the city suspended the social worker from her job, she sued. The court ruled that the government has the right to prohibit some employee speech, but if the employee speaks on matters of public concern, the government bears the burden of justifying any retaliation. In this case, the court held for the social worker.[17]

- *Statutory protection for federal employees.* The Civil Service Reform Act and the Whistleblower Protection Act prevent retaliation against federal employees who

[17]*Harman v. City of New York*, 140 F.3d 111, 1998 U.S. App. LEXIS 5567 (2d Cir. 1998).

report wrongdoing. They also permit the award of back pay and attorney's fees to the whistleblower. This statute was used to prevent the National Park Service from disciplining two managers who wrote a report expressing concern over development in Yellowstone National Park.

- *State laws.* The good news is that all 50 states have laws that protect whistleblowers from retaliation by their employers. The bad news is that the scope of this protection varies greatly from state to state. Most courts, however, prohibit the discharge of employees who report illegal activity. For example, a Connecticut court held a company liable when it fired a quality control director who reported to his boss that some products had failed quality tests.[18]

EXAM Strategy

Question: When Shiloh interviewed for a sales job at a medical supply company, the interviewer promised that she could work exclusively selling medical devices and would not have to be involved in the sale of drugs. Once she began work (as an employee at will), Shiloh discovered that the sales force was organized around regions, not products, so she had to sell both devices and drugs. When she complained to her boss over lunch in the employee lunchroom, he said in a loud voice, "You are a big girl now—it's time you learned that you don't always get what you want." That afternoon, she was fired. Does she have a valid claim against the company?

Strategy: We know that Shiloh is an employee at will. We also know that she is not protected by any statute we have studied. What about the *common law*? Shiloh has had two interactions with the company—being hired and being fired. What protections does the common law provide during the hiring process? The employer's promises are enforceable. Here, the company is liable because the interviewer clearly made a promise that the company did not keep. What about the way in which Shiloh was fired? Is it intentional infliction of emotional distress? Was this treatment cruel? Probably not cruel enough to constitute intentional infliction of emotional distress.

Result: The company is liable to Shiloh for making false promises to her during the hiring process, but not for the manner in which she was fired.

SAFETY AND PRIVACY IN THE WORKPLACE

Workplace Safety

In 1970, Congress passed the Occupational Safety and Health Act (OSHA) to ensure safe working conditions. Under OSHA:

- Employers must comply with specific health and safety standards. For example, health care personnel who work with blood are not permitted to eat or drink in areas where the blood is kept and must not put their mouths on any instruments used to store blood. Protective clothing—gloves, gowns, and laboratory coats—must be impermeable to blood.

---

[18] *Smith v. Calgon Carbon Corp.*, 917 F.2d 1338, 1990 U.S. App. LEXIS 19193 (3rd Cir. 1990).

- Employers are under a general obligation to keep their workplace "free from recognized hazards that are causing or are likely to cause death or serious physical harm" to employees.
- Employers must keep records of all workplace injuries and accidents.
- The Occupational Safety and Health Administration (also known as OSHA) may inspect workplaces to ensure that they are safe. OSHA may assess fines for violations and order employers to correct unsafe conditions.

OSHA has done a lot to make the American workplace safer. In 1900, roughly 35,000 workers died at work. A century later, the workforce had grown five times larger, but the number of annual deaths had fallen to about 5,500.

Employee Privacy

Upon opening the country's first moving assembly line in the early 1900s, Henry Ford issued a booklet, "Helpful Hints and Advice to Employees," that warned against drinking, gambling, borrowing money, taking in boarders, and practicing poor hygiene. Ford also created a department of 100 investigators for door-to-door checks on his employees' drinking habits, sexual practices, and housekeeping skills. It may be surprising, but in modern times, employees have been fired or disciplined for such extracurricular activities as playing dangerous sports, dating coworkers, or even having high cholesterol.

The right to hire, fire, and make an honest profit is enshrined in American tradition. But so is the right to privacy. Justice Louis D. Brandeis called it the "right to be let alone—the most comprehensive of rights and the right most valued by civilized men." Employees are entitled under the common law to a **reasonable expectation of privacy**. This protection means that an employer could not, for instance, search an employee's home even if looking for items that the employee might have stolen from the company. What other protection do workers have against intrusive employers?

Off-Duty Conduct

A worker's off-duty conduct may affect her employer. For instance, a smoker may have lower productivity and higher healthcare expenses. The federal government estimates that it costs $3,400 a year to employ a worker who smokes. As a result, some employers refuse to hire smokers or even threaten to fire current workers who smoke. (Nicotine can be detected in a smoker's urine for a week or more.)

These bans on smokers affect a considerable number of people—roughly 20 percent of Americans. As a result, more than half of the states have passed statutes prohibiting job bans on smokers. Indeed, some states have passed laws that protect the right of employees to engage in any *lawful* activity when off duty, including smoking, drinking socially, having high cholesterol, being overweight, or engaging in dangerous hobbies—bungee jumping or rollerblading, for instance. In the absence of such a statute, however, an employer does have the right to fire an employee for off-duty conduct.

Alcohol and Drug Testing

Traditionally, employers primarily tested for illegal drugs, but increasingly, they have been concerned that prescription medications may impair workers as well. For example, in one study, workers who were tested after accidents in the workplace were four times more likely to have opiates in their system than job applicants.

Under federal law, private employers are permitted to test for alcohol and illegal drugs. However, the Equal Employment Opportunity Commission (EEOC), the federal agency charged with enforcing federal employment laws, prohibits testing for prescription drugs unless a worker seems impaired. The EEOC has filed suit against a company that randomly tested for prescription drugs (that were being used legally), but the court has not yet issued an opinion.[19] State laws on drug testing vary widely.

Public safety workers, such as police and firefighters, can be required to report legal drug use that might compromise their ability to perform their jobs. They can be randomly tested for illegal use. Other government employees can be randomly tested only if they show signs of impairment.

↳ disabled

Lie Detector Tests

Under the Employee Polygraph Protection Act of 1988, employers may not require, or even *suggest,* that an employee or job candidate submit to a lie detector test, except (1) as part of an "ongoing investigation" into crimes that have occurred or (2) for jobs in pharmaceutical firms that deal with controlled substances. Before the test is administered, employees are entitled to written notice of their rights.

Electronic Monitoring of the Workplace

Technological advances in communications have raised a host of new privacy issues. Many companies monitor employee use of electronic equipment in the workplace: telephone calls, voicemail, email, and Internet usage. **The Electronic Communications Privacy Act of 1986 (ECPA) permits employers to monitor workers' telephone calls and email messages if (1) the employee consents, (2) the monitoring occurs in the ordinary course of business, or (3) in the case of email, the employer provides the email system.** However, bosses may not disclose any private information revealed by the monitoring.

Sending personal emails through a company server is dangerous. In one case, the court permitted an employer to fire two workers who exchanged (they claimed) joking emails threatening violence to sales managers. The company had an explicit policy stating that emails were confidential and would not be intercepted or used against an employee.[20] On the other hand, a New Jersey court recently held that unless company policy explicitly informs workers otherwise, the company does not have the right to monitor a personal, password-protected, web-based email account.[21]

Unless you enjoy the prospect of engaging in years of litigation to clarify this issue, it is still good advice to consider all email you send through a company server to be public.

Social Media

Social media are the newest challenge facing both employers and workers. On the one hand, employers may find themselves liable for statements that their workers make electronically. For example, Cisco Systems Inc., has settled two lawsuits brought against the company for statements made by a company lawyer on his blog. Not surprisingly, employers have fired workers who posted inappropriate information in cyberspace. But companies may find themselves liable for violations of employee privacy if a boss reads workers' Facebook or MySpace pages. A high school teacher in Georgia sued her school district after she was forced to resign because of vacation photos on Facebook that showed her holding a glass of wine.

Could he be fired for posting this photo on his Facebook page?

[19] *Bates v. Dura Auto Sys*, District Court of Tennessee.
[20] *Smyth v. Pillsbury*, 914 F. Supp. 97, 1996 U.S. Dist. LEXIS 776, (Fed. Dist. Ct., 1996).
[21] *Stengart v. Loving Care Agency, Inc.*, 201 N.J. 300, 2010 N.J. LEXIS 241, (S.Ct. NJ, 2010).

In short, the law is uncertain and varies by state, so employees at will should err on the side of caution and remember that the law does not currently protect their electronic lives from employer prying. They should consider anything they publish on the Internet to be public.

As for companies, it makes sense to establish policies providing that:

1. Employees should never reveal their company's name on a blog or social website such as Facebook.
2. In addition, all employees' personal blogs must contain a disclaimer that "All postings on this blog are my opinion and not those of my employer, who has neither vetted nor approved them." The blogger should not reveal the company's name.
3. Blog comments should never be offensive, impolite, or reflect badly on the employer. Nor should they reveal confidential or proprietary information.
4. Supervisors have the right to read and take action based on any electronic information posted by an employee.

Immigration

Because of discrimination laws, employers should not ask about an applicant's country of origin, but they are permitted to inquire if the person is authorized to work in the United States. If the applicant says, "Yes," the interviewer cannot ask for evidence until the person is hired. At that point, the employer must complete an I-9 form—Employment Eligibility Verification—within three days. This form lists the acceptable documents that can be used for verification. Employees have the right to present whichever documents they want from the list of acceptable items. The employer may not ask for some other document. The I-9 forms must be kept for three years after the worker is hired or one year after termination.

EXAM Strategy

Question: To ensure that its employees did not use illegal drugs in or outside the workplace, Marvel Grocery Store required all employees to take a lie detector test. Moreover, managers began to screen the company email system for drug references. Jagger was fired for refusing to take the polygraph test. Jonathan was dismissed when a search of his email revealed that he had used marijuana during the prior weekend. Has the company acted legally?

Strategy: First: As employees at will, are Jagger and Jonathan protected by a statute? The Employee Polygraph Protection Act permits employers to require a lie detector test as part of ongoing investigation into crimes that have occurred. Here, Marvel has no reason to believe that a crime occurred, so it cannot require a polygraph test.

Second: What about Jonathan's marijuana use? The ECPA permits Marvel to monitor email messages on its own system. But can the company fire Jonathan for illegal off-duty conduct? Some statutes protect employees for *legal* behavior outside the workplace, but no state protects employees for behavior that violates the law.

Result: The company is liable to Jagger for requiring him to take the lie detector test, but not to Jonathan for monitoring his email or firing him for illegal drug use.

FINANCIAL PROTECTION

Congress and the states have enacted laws that provide employees with a measure of financial security. All of the laws in this section were created by statute, not by the courts.

Fair Labor Standards Act: Minimum Wage, Overtime, and Child Labor

Passed in 1938, the Fair Labor Standards Act (FLSA) regulates wages and limits child labor nationally. It provides that hourly workers must be paid a minimum wage of $7.25 per hour, plus time and a half for any hours over 40 in one week. These wage provisions do not apply to salaried workers, such as managerial, administrative, or professional staff. More than half the states set a higher minimum wage, so it is important to check state guidelines as well.

Today, the biggest issue that employers face under the FLSA is: "What counts as work, and how do you keep track of it?" What if a worker answers email during lunch or takes a phone call on the train ride home? Although these activities count as work, how can the employer keep track of it? Carla Bird, an assistant at Oprah Winfrey's production company, submitted timesheets showing 800 hours of overtime in 17 weeks. She said she had worked 12 or 13 hours a day, seven days a week, for four months. The company paid her $32,000 in overtime.[22] If employees work all the time, or even if they are just on call, they are entitled to be paid for those hours.

The FLSA also prohibits "oppressive child labor," which means that children under 14 may work only in agriculture and entertainment. Fourteen- and fifteen-year-olds are permitted to work *limited* hours after school in nonhazardous jobs. Sixteen- and seventeen-year-olds may work *unlimited* hours in nonhazardous jobs.

ages 14-15 = limited hrs
16-17 = unlimited hrs

Workers' Compensation

Workers' compensation statutes ensure that employees receive payment for injuries incurred at work. Before workers' comp, injured employees could recover damages only if they sued their employer. It is the brave (or carefree) worker who is willing to risk a suit against his own boss. Lawsuits poison the atmosphere at work. Moreover, employers frequently won these suits by claiming that (1) the injured worker was contributorily negligent, (2) a fellow employee had caused the accident, or (3) the injured worker had assumed the risk of injury. As a result, seriously injured workers (or their families) often had no recourse against the employer.

Workers' comp statutes provide a fixed, certain recovery to the injured employee, no matter who was at fault for the accident. In return, employees are not permitted to sue their employers for negligence. The amounts allowed (for medical expenses and lost wages) under workers' comp statutes are often less than a worker might recover in court, but the injured employee trades the certainty of some recovery for the higher risk of rolling the dice at trial. Payments are approved by an administrative board that conducts an informal hearing into each claim.

Social Security

The federal social security system began in 1935, during the depths of the Great Depression, to provide a basic safety net for the elderly, ill, and unemployed. **Currently, the social security system pays benefits to workers who are retired, disabled, or temporarily**

[22]Lisa Belkin, "O.T. Isn't as Simple as Telling Time." *The New York Times*, September 20, 2007.

Fox Photos/Hulton Archive/Getty Images

Before Social Security, breadlines were often the only safety net available to the unemployed.

unemployed and to the spouses and children of disabled or deceased workers. It also provides medical insurance to the retired and disabled. The social security program is financed through a tax on wages that is paid by employers, employees, and the self-employed.

Although the social security system has done much to reduce poverty among the elderly, many worry that it cannot survive in its current form. The system was designed to be "pay as you go"; that is, when workers pay taxes, the proceeds do not go into a savings account for their retirement, but instead are used to pay benefits to current retirees. In 1940, there were 40 workers for each retiree; currently, there are 3.3. As a result, the system now pays out more in benefits each year than it receives in tax revenues. By 2025, when the last baby boomers retire, there will be only 2 workers to support each retiree—a prohibitive burden. No wonder baby boomers are often cautioned not to count on social security when making their retirement plans.

The Federal Unemployment Tax Act (FUTA) is the part of the social security system that provides support to the unemployed. FUTA establishes some national standards, but states are free to set their own benefit levels and payment schedules. A worker who quits voluntarily or is fired for just cause is ineligible for benefits. While receiving payments, she must make a good-faith effort to look for other employment.

Pension Benefits

In 1974, Congress passed the Employee Retirement Income Security Act (ERISA) to protect workers covered by private pension plans. Under ERISA, employers are not required to establish pension plans, but if they do, they must follow these federal rules. The law was aimed, in particular, at protecting benefits of retired workers if their companies subsequently go bankrupt. The statute also prohibits risky investments by pension plans. In addition, the statute sets rules on the vesting of benefits. (An employer cannot cancel *vested* benefits; *nonvested* benefits are forfeited when the employee leaves.) Before ERISA, retirement benefits at some companies did not vest until the employee retired—if he quit or was fired before retirement, even after years of service, he lost his pension. Under current law, employee benefits normally must vest within five years of employment.

Employment Discrimination

In the last five decades, Congress has enacted important legislation to prevent discrimination in the workplace.

Equal Pay Act of 1963

Under the Equal Pay Act, an employee may not be paid at a lesser rate than employees of the opposite sex for equal work. "Equal work" means tasks that require equal skill, effort, and responsibility under similar working conditions. If the employee proves that she is not being paid equally, the employer will be found liable unless the pay difference is based on merit, productivity, seniority, or some factor other than sex. A "factor other than sex" includes prior wages, training, profitability, performance in an interview, and value to the company. For example, female agents sued Allstate Insurance Co. because its salary for new agents was based, in part, on prior salary. The women argued that this system was unfair because it perpetuated the historic wage differences between men and women. The court, however, held for Allstate.[23]

Title VII

Before 1964, it was legal to treat men and women, whites and people of color, differently in the workplace. Women, for example, could be paid less than men for the same job and could be fired if they got married or pregnant. Newspapers had different pages for men's and women's job ads and, no matter their education, women were prohibited from applying for the most desirable jobs. They could be secretaries but not writers, lawyers, or bankers. Indeed, in 1952, when Sandra Day O'Connor graduated from Stanford Law School with high honors, law firms only offered her secretarial jobs. She went on to become the first woman justice on the Supreme Court of the United States. This discrimination was a terrible waste of resources—so many talented people who were unable to use their skills. Partly as a result of Title VII, women now make up a majority of the American workforce, although they are still underrepresented at the top of many organizations.

Under Title VII of the Civil Rights Act of 1964, it is illegal for employers to discriminate on the basis of race, color, religion, sex, or national origin. More specifically, Title VII prohibits (1) discrimination in the workplace, (2) sexual harassment, and (3) discrimination because of pregnancy. It also permits employers to develop affirmative action plans.

Proof of Discrimination

Discrimination under Title VII means firing, refusing to hire, failing to promote, or otherwise reducing a person's employment opportunities because of race, color, religion, sex, or national origin. This protection applies to every stage of the employment process, from job ads to postemployment references, and includes placement, wages, benefits, and working conditions.

Plaintiffs in Title VII cases can prove discrimination two different ways: disparate treatment and disparate impact.

Disparate Treatment. To prove a disparate treatment case, the plaintiff must show that she was *treated* differently because of her sex, race, color, religion, or national origin. The required steps in a disparate treatment case are:

Step 1. The plaintiff presents evidence that the defendant has discriminated against her because of a protected trait. This is called a ***prima facie* case.** The plaintiff is not required to prove discrimination; she need only create a *presumption* that discrimination occurred.

Suppose that Louisa applies for a job coaching a boys' high school ice hockey team. She was an All-American hockey star in college. Although Louisa is obviously qualified for the job, Harry, the school principal, rejects her and continues to interview other people. This is not proof of discrimination because Harry may have a perfectly good, nondiscriminatory explanation. However, his behavior *could have been* motivated by discrimination.

Step 2. The defendant must present evidence that its decision was based on *legitimate, nondiscriminatory* reasons. Harry might say, for example, that he wanted someone with prior coaching experience. Although Louisa is clearly a great player, she has never coached before.

---

[23] *Kouba v. Allstate Insurance Co.*, 691 F.2d 873, 1982 U.S. App. LEXIS 24479 (9th Cir. 1982).

Step 3. To win, the plaintiff must now prove that the employer discriminated. She may do so by showing that the reasons offered were simply a *pretext*. Louisa might show that Harry had recently hired a male tennis coach who had no prior coaching experience. Or Harry's assistant might testify that Harry said, "No way I'm going to put a woman on the ice with those guys." If she can present evidence such as this, Louisa wins.

In the following case, was the bartender treated differently because of her sex? You be the judge.

You be the Judge

Jespersen v. Harrah's

444 F.3D 1104, 2006 U.S. APP. LEXIS 9307
United States Court of Appeals for the Ninth Circuit, 2006

Facts: Darlene Jespersen was a bartender at the sports bar in Harrah's Casino in Reno, Nevada. She was an outstanding employee, frequently praised by both her supervisors and customers.

When Jespersen first went to work for Harrah's, female bartenders were encouraged, but not required, to wear makeup. Jespersen tried it for a short period of time, but she did not like it. Moreover, she felt that wearing makeup interfered with her ability to deal with unruly, intoxicated guests because it "took away [her] credibility as an individual and as a person."

After Jespersen had been at Harrah's for almost 20 years, the casino implemented a program that required bartenders to be "well groomed, appealing to the eye." More explicitly, for men:

- Hair must not extend below top of shirt collar. Ponytails are prohibited.
- Hands and fingernails must be clean and nails neatly trimmed at all times.
- No colored polish is permitted.
- Eye and facial makeup is not permitted.
- Shoes will be solid black leather or leather type with rubber (non-skid) soles.

The rules for women were:

- Hair must be teased, curled, or styled. Hair must be worn down at all times, no exceptions.
- Nail polish can be clear, white, pink, or red color only. No exotic nail art or length.
- Shoes will be solid black leather or leather type with rubber (non-skid) soles.
- Makeup (foundation/concealer and/or face powder, as well as blush and mascara) must be worn and applied neatly in complimentary colors, and lip color must be worn at all times.

An expert was brought in to show the employees (both male and female) how to dress. The workers were then photographed and told that they must look like the photographs every day at work.

When Jespersen refused to wear makeup, Harrah's fired her. She sued under Title VII. The district court granted Harrah's motion for summary judgment. Jespersen appealed.

You Be The Judge: ***Did Harrah's requirement that women wear makeup violate Title VII?***

Argument for Jespersen: Jespersen refused to wear makeup to work because the cost—in time, money, and personal dignity—was too high.

Employers are free to adopt different appearance standards for each sex, but these standards may not impose a greater burden on one sex than the other. Men were not required to wear makeup, but women were. That difference meant a savings for men of hundreds of dollars and hours of time. Harrah's did not have the right to fire Jespersen for violating a rule that applies only to women, with no equivalent for men.

Argument for Harrah's: Employers are permitted to impose different appearance rules on women than on men so long as the overall burden on employees is the same. For example, it is not discriminatory to require men to wear their hair short. On balance, Harrah's rules did not impose a heavier burden on women than on men.

Disparate Impact. Disparate impact applies if the employer has a rule that, *on its face*, is not discriminatory, but *in practice* excludes too many people in a protected group. The following landmark case illustrates this principle.

The steps in a disparate impact case are:

Landmark Case

Griggs v. Duke Power Co.

401 U.S. 424, 91 S. Ct. 849, 1971 U.S. LEXIS 134
United States Supreme Court, 1971

Facts: Before Title VII, Duke Power hired black employees only in the Labor department, where the highest pay was less than the lowest earnings in the other departments. After Title VII, the company required all new hires for jobs in the desirable departments to have a high school education or satisfactory scores on two tests that measured intelligence and mechanical ability. Neither test gauged the ability to perform a particular job. The pass rate for whites was much higher than for blacks, and blacks were also less likely than whites to have a high school diploma. The new policy did not apply to the (exclusively white) employees who were already working in the preferred departments. These "unqualified" whites all performed their jobs satisfactorily.

Black employees sued Duke Power, alleging that this hiring policy violated Title VII. The trial court dismissed the case. The Court of Appeals ruled that the policy was not in violation of Title VII because Duke Power did not have a discriminatory purpose. The Supreme Court granted *certiorari*.

Issue: ***Does a policy violate Title VII if it has a discriminatory impact but no discriminatory purpose?***

Excerpts from Chief Justice Burger's Decision: Congress did not intend by Title VII to guarantee a job to every person regardless of qualifications. What is required by Congress is the removal of artificial, arbitrary, and unnecessary barriers to employment when the barriers operate invidiously to discriminate on the basis of racial or other impermissible classification.

The Act proscribes not only overt discrimination but also practices that are fair in form, but discriminatory in operation. The touchstone is business necessity. If an employment practice which operates to exclude Negroes cannot be shown to be related to job performance, the practice is prohibited.

On the record before us, neither the high school completion require-ment nor the general intelligence test is shown to bear a demonstrable relationship to successful performance of the jobs for which it was used. Both were adopted without meaningful study of their relationship to job-performance ability. Rather, the requirements were instituted on the Company's judgment that they generally would improve the overall quality of the work force. The evidence, however, shows that employees who have not completed high school or taken the tests have continued to perform satisfactorily and make progress in departments for which the high school and test criteria are now used.

[G]ood intent or absence of discriminatory intent does not redeem employment procedures or testing mechanisms that operate as "built-in headwinds" for minority groups and are unrelated to measuring job capability. Congress directed the thrust of the Act to the *consequences* of employment practices, not simply the motivation. More than that, Congress has placed on the employer the burden of showing that any given requirement must have a manifest relationship to the employment in question.

History is filled with examples of men and women who rendered highly effective performance without the conventional badges of accomplishment in terms of certificates, diplomas, or degrees. Diplomas and tests are useful servants, but Congress has mandated the commonsense proposition that they are not to become masters of reality.

Nothing in the Act precludes the use of testing or measuring procedures; obviously they are useful. What Congress has commanded is that any tests used must measure the person for the job and not the person in the abstract.

The judgment of the Court of Appeals is reversed.

Step 1. The plaintiff must present a *prima facie* case. The plaintiff is not required to prove discrimination; he need only show a disparate impact—that the employment practice in question excludes a disproportionate number of people in a protected group (women and minorities, for instance). In the *Griggs* case, a far higher percentage of whites than blacks passed the tests required for a job in one of the good departments. The EEOC defines a disparate impact as one in which the pass rate for minorities is less than 80 percent of that for whites.

Step 2. The defendant must offer some evidence that the employment practice was a *job-related business necessity*. Duke Power would have to show that the tests predicted job performance.

Step 3. To win, the plaintiff must now prove either that the employer's reason is a *pretext* or that other, *less discriminatory*, rules would achieve the same results. The plaintiffs in *Griggs* showed that the tests were not a job-related business necessity—after all, whites who had not passed any of these tests performed the jobs well. Duke Power could no longer use them as a hiring screen. If the power company wanted to use tests, it would have to find some that measured an employee's ability to perform particular jobs.

Hiring tests remain controversial. In a recent case, a group of white firefighters sued the city of New Haven, Connecticut, for discarding promotion tests on which they performed better than blacks. Twice as many whites as blacks passed the test. The Supreme Court upheld the use of the examination on the grounds that it was job-related, consistent with business necessity, and there was no strong evidence that an equally valid, less-discriminatory test existed.[24] In short, the mere existence of a disparate impact does not mean that an employment practice violates the law.

Color

Title VII prohibits discrimination based on both race and color. Although many people assume that they are essentially the same, that is not necessarily the case. For example, Dwight Burch alleged that his coworkers at an Applebee's restaurant called him hateful names because of his dark skin color. These colleagues were also African American but were lighter-skinned. Burch sued on the basis of "color discrimination."

Title VII prohibits the type of treatment that Burch allegedly suffered. While denying any wrongdoing, Applebee's settled the case by paying Burch $40,000 and agreeing to conduct antidiscrimination training.

Transgender

David Schroer was in the Army for 25 years, including a stint tracking terrorists. The Library of Congress offered him a job as a specialist in terrorism. (Who knew that libraries needed terrorism specialists?) However, when he revealed that he was in the process of becoming Diane Schroer, the Library of Congress withdrew the offer. As you can guess, he sued under Title VII.

Traditionally, courts took the view that sex under Title VII applied only to how people were born, not what they chose to become. Employers could and did fire workers for changing sex. However, a federal court recently found the Library of Congress in violation of Title VII for withdrawing Schroer's offer.[25] Only time will tell if other federal courts will follow this lead.

---

[24] *Ricci v. DeStefano*, 129 S. Ct. 2658, 2009 U.S. LEXIS 4945 (S. Ct. 2009).

[25] *Schroer v. Billington*, 577 F. Supp. 2d 293, 2008 U.S. Dist. LEXIS 71358, (U.S. Dt. Ct. 2008).

Retaliation

Title VII not only prohibits discrimination, it also penalizes employers who retaliate against workers for *complaining* about discrimination. Retaliation means that the employer has done something so bad it would deter a reasonable worker from complaining about discrimination.[26] For example, when a woman was demoted to a less-desirable job after she complained about sexual harassment by her boss, the company was liable.

Religion

Employers must make *reasonable accommodation* for a worker's religious beliefs unless the request would cause *undue hardship* for the business. What would you do in the following cases if you were the boss:

1. A Christian says he cannot work at Wal-Mart on Sundays—his Sabbath. It also happens to be one of the store's busiest days.
2. A Jewish police officer wants to wear a beard and yarmulke as part of his religious observance. Facial hair and headgear are banned by the force.
3. Muslim workers at a meat-packing plant want to pray at sundown, but break times were specified in the labor contract and sundown changes from day to day. The workers begin to take bathroom breaks at sundown, stopping work on the production line.

Disputes such as these are on the rise and are not easy to handle fairly. In the end, Wal-Mart fired the Christian, but when he sued on the grounds of religious discrimination, the company settled the case. A judge ruled that the police officer could keep his beard because the force allowed other employees with medical conditions to wear facial hair, but the headcovering had to go. The boss at the meat-packing plant fired the Muslim employees who walked off the job.

Defenses to Charges of Discrimination

- protect the defendent of showing discrimination

Under Title VII, the defendant has three possible defenses.

Merit. A defendant is not liable if he shows that the person he favored was the most qualified. Test results, education, or productivity can all be used to demonstrate merit, provided they relate to the job in question. Harry can show that he hired Bruce for the coaching job instead of Louisa because Bruce has a master's degree in physical education and seven years of coaching experience. On the other hand, the fact that Bruce scored higher on the National Latin Exam in the eighth grade is not a good reason to hire him over Louisa.

→ maintain ; continue

Seniority. A legitimate seniority system is legal even if it perpetuates past discrimination. Suppose that Harry has always chosen the most senior assistant coach to take over as head coach when a vacancy occurs. Because the majority of the senior assistant coaches are male, most of the head coaches are, too. Such a system does not violate Title VII.

Bona Fide Occupational Qualification. An employer is permitted to establish discriminatory job requirements if they are *essential* to the position in question. The business must show that it cannot fulfill its primary function unless it discriminates. Such a requirement is called a **bona fide occupational qualification (BFOQ).** Catholic schools may, if they choose, refuse to hire non-Catholic teachers; clothing companies may refuse to hire men to model women's attire. Generally, however, courts are not sympathetic to claims of BFOQ. They have, for example, almost always rejected BFOQ claims that are based on customer preference. Thus, airlines could not refuse to hire male flight attendants even though they

Bona fide occupational qualification (BFOQ)
An employer is permitted to establish discriminatory job requirements if they are essential to the position in question.

[26] *Burlington Northern v. White*, 126 S. Ct. 2405, 2006 U.S. LEXIS 4895, (S. Ct., 2006).

believed that travelers prefer female attendants.[27] The major exception to this customer preference rule is sexual privacy: an employer may refuse to hire women to work in a men's bathroom, and vice versa.

Affirmative Action

Affirmative action is a hot political issue: white males protest that such programs constitute reverse discrimination against them; political candidates campaign on anti–affirmative action platforms.

Affirmative action is not required by Title VII, nor is it prohibited. Affirmative action programs have three different sources:

- *Litigation.* Courts have the power under Title VII to order affirmative action to remedy the effects of past discrimination.
- *Voluntary action.* Employers can voluntarily introduce an affirmative action plan to remedy the effects of past practices or to achieve equitable representation of minorities and women.
- *Government contracts.* In 1965, President Johnson signed Executive Order 11246, which prohibits discrimination by federal contractors. This order had a profound impact on the American workplace because one-third of all workers are employed by companies that do business with the federal government. If an employer found that women or minorities were underrepresented in its workplace, it was required to establish goals and timetables to correct the deficiency.

In 1995, however, the Supreme Court dramatically limited the extent to which the government can *require* contractors to establish affirmative action programs. The Court ruled that these programs are permissible only if they serve a "compelling national interest" and are "narrowly tailored" so that they minimize the harm to white males. The government must be able to show that (1) the programs are needed to overcome specific past discrimination, (2) they have time limits, and (3) nondiscriminatory alternatives are not available.[28] This case led to a sharp decrease in the number of federal contracts awarded to companies owned by women and minorities.

Sexual Harassment

When Professor Anita Hill accused Supreme Court nominee Clarence Thomas of sexually harassing her, people across the country were glued to their televisions, watching the Senate hearings on her charges. Thomas was ultimately confirmed to the Supreme Court, but "sexual harassment" became a household phrase. The number of cases—and the size of the damage awards—skyrocketed.

> Everyone has heard of sexual harassment, but few people know exactly what it is.

Everyone has heard of **sexual harassment**, but few people know exactly what it is. Men fear that a casual comment or glance will be met with career-ruining charges; women claim that men "just don't get it." So what is sexual harassment anyway? **Sexual harassment involves unwelcome sexual advances, requests for sexual favors, and other verbal or physical conduct of a sexual nature.** There are two major categories of sexual harassment: (1) *quid pro quo* and (2) hostile work environment.

---

[27] *Diaz v. Pan American World Airways, Inc.*, 442 F.2d 385, 1971 U.S. App. LEXIS 10920 (5th Cir. 1971).

[28] *Adarand Constructors, Inc. v. Pena*, 515 U.S. 200, 115 S. Ct. 2097, 1995 U.S. LEXIS 4037 (1995).

Quid Pro Quo. From a Latin phrase that means "one thing in return for another," *quid pro quo* harassment occurs if any aspect of a job is made contingent upon sexual activity. In other words, when a banker says to an assistant, "You can be promoted to teller if you sleep with me," that is *quid pro quo* sexual harassment.

Quid pro quo
A Latin phrase that means "one thing in return for another."

understated

Hostile Work Environment. This is a more subtle claim and the one that managers worry about most. **An employee has a valid claim of sexual harassment if sexual talk and innuendo are so pervasive that they interfere with her (or his) ability to work.** Courts have found that offensive jokes, comments about clothes or body parts, and public displays of pornographic pictures can create a hostile environment.

Text messages have become a new frontier in sexual harassment—so-called *textual harassment.* In behavior that can only make you ask, "What were they thinking?" bosses have sent wildly inappropriate text messages to their subordinates—offering promotions for sex or providing evidence of a sexual relationship. News flash: text messages can be recovered, and juries can read. "She said, he said" cases are a lot harder to win than "She said, he texted."

In the following case, the Supreme Court defined the standard for a hostile work environment.

TERESA HARRIS V. FORKLIFT SYSTEMS, INC.

510 U.S. 17, 114 S. CT. 367, 1993 U.S. LEXIS 7155
United States Supreme Court, 1993

Facts: Teresa Harris was a manager at Forklift Systems; Charles Hardy was its president. Hardy frequently made inappropriate sexual comments to Harris and other women at the company. For example, he said to Harris, in the presence of others, "You're a woman, what do you know?" and "We need a man as the rental manager." He called her "a dumb-ass woman" and suggested that the two of them "go to the Holiday Inn to negotiate her raise." He also asked Harris and other female employees to get coins from his front pants pocket. He insisted that Harris and other women pick up objects he had thrown on the ground. When Harris complained to Hardy, he apologized and claimed he was only joking. A month later, while Harris was arranging a deal with one of Forklift's customers, he asked her, in front of other employees, "What did you do, promise the guy some sex Saturday night?"

Harris sued Forklift, claiming that Hardy had created an abusive work environment. The federal trial court ruled against Harris on the grounds that Hardy's comments might offend a reasonable woman, but they were not severe enough to have a serious impact on Harris's psychological well-being. The appeals court confirmed, and the Supreme Court granted *certiorari.*

Issue: ***To be a violation of Title VII, must sexual harassment seriously affect the employee's psychological well-being?***

Excerpts from Justice O'Connor's Decision: Title VII of the Civil Rights Act of 1964 makes it "an unlawful employment practice for an employer to discriminate against any individual with respect to his compensation, terms, conditions, or privileges of employment, because of such individual's race, color, religion, sex, or national origin." [T]his language is not limited to economic or tangible discrimination. The phrase "terms, conditions, or privileges of employment" evinces a congressional intent to strike at the entire spectrum of disparate treatment of men and women in employment, which includes requiring people to work in a discriminatorily hostile or abusive environment. When the workplace is permeated with discriminatory intimidation, ridicule, and insult that is sufficiently severe or pervasive to alter the conditions of the victim's employment and create an abusive working environment, Title VII is violated.

This standard takes a middle path between making actionable any conduct that is merely offensive and requiring the conduct to cause a tangible psychological injury. [M]ere utterance of an epithet which engenders offensive feelings in an employee does not sufficiently affect the conditions of employment to implicate Title VII. Conduct that is not severe or pervasive enough to create an objectively hostile or abusive work environment—an environment that a reasonable person would find hostile or abusive—is beyond Title VII's purview. Likewise, if the victim does not subjectively perceive the environment to be abusive, the conduct has not actually altered the conditions of the victim's employment, and there is no Title VII violation.

But Title VII comes into play before the harassing conduct leads to a nervous breakdown. A discriminatorily abusive work environment, even one that does not seriously affect employees' psychological well-being, can and often will detract from employees' job performance, discourage employees from remaining on the job, or keep them from advancing in their careers. Moreover, even without regard to these tangible effects, the very fact that the discriminatory conduct was so severe or pervasive that it created a work environment abusive to employees because of their race, gender, religion, or national origin offends Title VII's broad rule of workplace equality.

We therefore believe the [trial court] erred in relying on whether the conduct "seriously affected plaintiff's psychological well-being" or led her to "suffer injury." So long as the environment would reasonably be perceived, and is perceived, as hostile or abusive, there is no need for it also to be psychologically injurious.

Employees who commit sexual harassment are liable for their own misdeeds. But is their company also liable? The Supreme Court has held that:

- If the victimized employee has suffered a "tangible employment action" such as firing, demotion, or reassignment, the company is liable to her for sexual harassment by a supervisor.
- If the victimized employee has not suffered a tangible employment action, the company is not liable if it can prove that (1) it used reasonable care to prevent and correct sexually harassing behavior, and (2) the employee unreasonably failed to take advantage of the complaint procedure or other preventive opportunities provided by the company.[29]

In an effort to develop practical guidelines for its employees, Corning Consumer Products Co. asks them to apply four tests in determining whether their behavior constitutes sexual harassment:

- Would you say or do this in front of your spouse or parents?
- What about in front of a colleague of the opposite sex?
- Would you like your behavior reported in your local newspaper?
- Does it need to be said or done at all?

Procedures and Remedies

Before a plaintiff in a Title VII case brings suit, she must first file a complaint with the EEOC. Note, however, that the plaintiff must file within 180 days of the wrongdoing. But if the plaintiff is alleging that she was paid less than she should have been, each paycheck she receives starts the statute of limitations all over again. The EEOC has the right to sue on behalf of the plaintiff. This arrangement is favorable for the plaintiff because the government pays the legal bill. If the EEOC decides *not* to bring the case, or does not make a decision within six months, it issues a **right to sue letter**, and the plaintiff may proceed on her own in court. Many states also have their own version of the EEOC.

Remedies available to the successful plaintiff include hiring, reinstatement, retroactive seniority, back pay, reasonable attorney's fees, and damages of up to $300,000. Two recent trends, however, have reduced employees' chances of taking home substantial damages. Concerned about a rise in discrimination lawsuits, employers now often require new hires to agree in advance to arbitrate, not litigate, any future employment claims. The Supreme

[29] *Burlington Industries, Inc. v. Ellerth*, 524 U.S. 742, 118 S. Ct. 2257, 1998 U.S. LEXIS 4217 (1998); *Faragher v. Boca Raton*, 524 U.S. 775, 118 S. Ct. 2275, 1998 U.S. LEXIS 4216 (1998).

Court has upheld the employers' right to do so.[30] Typically, employees receive worse results in the arbitrator's office than in the courtroom, largely because arbitrators tend to favor repeat customers (such as management) over one-time users (such as employees). But even if a case does go to trial, plaintiffs in job discrimination cases have a much worse track record than other types of plaintiffs—they win less often at trial, and they lose more often on appeal. Discrimination plaintiffs win only about 30 percent of the time, and they eventually lose nearly half of those cases on appeal.

Pregnancy

Lucasfilm Ltd. (owned by filmmaker George Lucas) offered Julie Veronese a job as a manager on his California estate, but then it withdrew the offer when she revealed she was pregnant. Is that a problem? Under the Pregnancy Discrimination Act of 1978, an employer may not fire, refuse to hire, or fail to promote a woman because she is pregnant. An employer must also treat pregnancy as any other temporary disability. If, for example, employees are allowed time off from work for other medical disabilities, women must also be allowed a maternity leave. A jury ordered Lucasfilm to pay Veronese $113,800.

The Pregnancy Discrimination Act also protects a woman's right to terminate a pregnancy. An employer cannot fire a woman for having an abortion.[31]

Parenthood

Suppose that you are in charge of hiring at your company. You receive applications from four people: a mother, a father, a childless woman, and a childless father. All have equivalent qualifications. Which one would you hire? In studies, participants repeatedly rank mothers as less qualified than other employees and fathers as most desirable, even when their credentials are exactly the same.

An employer cannot discriminate because of pregnancy, but what about when the new mother goes back to work? Is parenthood protected by Title VII? Increasingly, courts have held that unequal treatment of mothers is a violation of Title VII. For example, after Dawn Gallina, an associate at the Mintz, Levin law firm, revealed to her boss that she had a young child, he began to treat her differently from her male colleagues and spoke to her "about the commitment differential between men and women." The court ruled that her belief of illegal discrimination was reasonable.[32] The EEOC has issued guidelines indicating that stereotypes are not a legitimate basis for personnel decisions.

Age Discrimination

The Age Discrimination in Employment Act (ADEA) of 1967 prohibits age discrimination against employees or job applicants who are at least 40 years old. An employer may not fire, refuse to hire, fail to promote, or otherwise reduce a person's employment opportunities because he is 40 or older. Under this statute, an employer may not require a worker to retire at any age. (These retirement rules do not apply to police and top-level corporate executives.)

The procedure for an age-bias claim is similar to that under Title VII—plaintiffs must first file a charge with the EEOC. If the EEOC does not take action, they can file suit themselves. However, the standard of proof is tougher in an age discrimination case than in Title VII litigation. Under the ADEA, the plaintiff must show that *but for* his age, the

---

[30] *Circuit City Stores, Inc. v. Adams;* 532 U.S. 105, 2001 U.S. LEXIS 2459 (2001).

[31] *Doe v. C.A.R.S Protection Plus, Inc.*; 527 F.3d 358 (3rd Cir., 2008).

[32] *Gallina v. Mintz, Levin, Cohn, Ferris, Glovsky, and Popeo*; 2005 U.S. App. LEXIS 1710 (4th Cir., 2005).

employer would not have taken the action it did. In other words, to win a case, the plaintiff must show that age was not just one factor, it was the *deciding* factor.[33]

Another issue in age discrimination cases: what happens if a company fires older workers because they are paid more? As a general rule, people in their 60s earn 50 percent more than workers in their early 30s. The older folks are more efficient, but not 50 percent more. What can a company do? Circuit City Stores fired 8 percent of its employees because they could be replaced with people who would work for less. The fired workers were more experienced—and older. This action is legal under the ADEA. Courts have held that an employer is entitled to prefer *lower-paid* workers even if that preference results in the company also choosing *younger* workers. As the court put it in one case, "An action based on price differentials represents the very quintessence of a legitimate business decision."[34] Indeed, economists argue that the U.S. economy's strength is based at least in part on its flexibility—an American employer can hire workers without fear of being stuck with them until retirement.

What protection does the ADEA provide? In passing this statute, Congress was particularly concerned about employers who relied on unfavorable stereotypes rather that job performance. The following case illustrates this issue.

Reid v. Google, Inc.

50 Cal. 4th 512, 2010 Cal. LEXIS 7544
Supreme Court of California, 2010

Facts: Google's vice-president of engineering, Wayne Rosing (aged 55), hired Brian Reid (52) as director of operations and director of engineering. Reid had a Ph.D. in computer science and had been a professor of electrical engineering at Stanford University. At the time, the top executives at Google were CEO Eric Schmidt (47), vice-president of engineering operations Urs Hölzle (38), and founders Sergey Brin (28), and Larry Page (29).

During his two years at Google, Reid's only written performance review stated that he had consistently met expectations. The comments indicated that Reid had an extraordinarily broad range of knowledge, an aptitude and orientation towards operational and IT issues, an excellent attitude, and that he projected confidence when dealing with fast-changing situations, was very intelligent and creative, and was a terrific problem solver. The review also commented that "Adapting to Google culture is the primary task. Right or wrong, Google is simply different: younger contributors, inexperienced first-line managers, and the super-fast pace are just a few examples of the environment."

According to Reid, even as he received a positive review, Hölzle and other employees made derogatory age-related remarks such as his ideas were "obsolete," "ancient," and "too old to matter," that he was "slow," "fuzzy," "sluggish," and "lethargic," an "old man," an "old guy," and an "old fuddy-duddy," and that he did not "display a sense of urgency" and "lacked energy."

Fifteen months after Reid joined Google, cofounder Brin emailed several executives about Google's payroll: "We should avoid the tendency towards bloat here, particularly with highly paid individuals." A month later, Reid's duties were assigned to two men who were 15 and 20 years younger. Google asked Reid to develop two in-house educational programs but did not give him a budget or a staff.

Three months later, Reid was fired. Google says it was because of his poor performance and the termination of the educational programs. Reid alleges he was told it was not related to the educational programs or his performance but rather was based on a lack of "cultural fit."

Reid sued Google for age discrimination. The trial court granted Google's motion for summary judgment on the grounds that Reid did not have enough evidence of discrimination. The Court of Appeal overruled the trial court. The California Supreme Court agreed to hear the case.

Issues: ***Did Reid have enough evidence of age discrimination to warrant a trial? Should the summary judgment motion be granted?***

---

[33] *Gross v. FBL Financial Services, Inc.*, 129 S. Ct. 2343; 2009 U.S. LEXIS 4535 (S. Ct., 2009).
[34] *Marks v. Loral Corp.*, 57 Cal. App. 4th 30, 1997 Cal. App. LEXIS 611 (Cal. Ct. App., 1997).

Excerpts from Justice Chin's Decision expressing the unanimous view of the court: Reid offered discriminatory comments that coworkers and decision makers made and evidence that Google demoted Reid to a nonviable position before terminating him and advanced changing rationales for his termination. Google contends that the Court of Appeal should have applied the stray remarks doctrine, i.e., should have categorized the alleged statements by Hölzle and Rosing as irrelevant stray remarks and disregarded them in reviewing the merits of the summary judgment motion.

[Justice O'Connor of the Supreme Court of the United States has] stated that "'stray remarks'—statements by nondecisionmakers, or statements by decisionmakers unrelated to the decisional process itself"—do not constitute direct evidence of decision makers' illegitimate criterion in reaching their decision." However, Justice O'Connor explained that stray remarks can be probative of discrimination.

Google contends that we should adopt the stray remarks doctrine so that California courts can disregard discriminatory comments by co-workers and nondecisionmakers, or comments unrelated to the employment decision to ensure that unmeritorious cases principally supported by such remarks are disposed of before trial.

[S]trict application of the stray remarks doctrine, as urged by Google, would result in a court's categorical exclusion of evidence even if the evidence was relevant. An age-based remark not made directly in the context of an employment decision or uttered by a non-decision-maker may be relevant, circumstantial evidence of discrimination. In a later decision authored by Justice O'Connor, the United States Supreme Court indicates that even if age-related comments can be considered stray remarks because they were not made in the direct context of the decisional process, a court should not categorically discount the evidence if relevant; it should be left to the factfinder to assess its probative value.

[T]he stray remarks cases merely demonstrate the common-sense proposition that a slur, in and of itself, does not prove actionable discrimination. A stray remark alone may not create a triable issue of age discrimination. But when combined with other evidence, an otherwise stray remark may create an ensemble [that] *is* sufficient to defeat summary judgment.

For the reasons stated above, we affirm the judgment of the Court of Appeal.

Americans with Disabilities Act

The Americans with Disabilities Act (ADA) prohibits employers from discriminating on the basis of disability. As with Title VII, a plaintiff under the ADA must first file a charge with the EEOC. If the EEOC decides not to file suit, the individual may do so himself.

A **disabled person** is someone with a physical or mental impairment that substantially limits a major life activity, or someone who is regarded as having such an impairment. The definition of major life activity includes the following tasks: caring for oneself, performing manual tasks, seeing, hearing, eating, sleeping, walking, standing, lifting, bending, speaking, breathing, learning, reading, concentrating, thinking, communicating, and working. Cell growth and digestive, bowel, bladder, neurological, brain, respiratory, circulatory, endocrine, reproductive, and immune system functions are also considered major life activities. And the definition protects *recovered* drug addicts or alcoholics but does not include the *current* use of drugs, sexual disorders, pyromania, exhibitionism, or compulsive gambling.

Disabled person
Someone with a physical or mental impairment that substantially limits a major life activity, or someone who is regarded as having such an impairment.

Suppose an employee has a disabling illness, but one that can be successfully treated. The employee is still considered to be disabled, even if the illness is well controlled. Thus, someone with diabetes is disabled, even if the illness is managed so well that it does not interfere with major life activities. There is one important exception—someone whose vision is normal when wearing glasses or contact lenses is not disabled for purposes of the ADA.

An employer may not disqualify an employee or job applicant because of disability so long as she can, with *reasonable accommodation*, perform the *essential functions* of the job. An accommodation is not reasonable if it would create *undue hardship* for the employer. In one case, a court held that a welder who could perform 88 percent of a job was doing the essential functions. Reasonable accommodation includes buying necessary equipment, providing readers or interpreters, or permitting a part-time schedule. In determining undue hardship, *relative* cost, not *absolute* cost, is the issue. Even an expensive accommodation—such as hiring a full-time reader—is not considered an undue hardship unless it imposes a significant burden on the overall finances of the company.

An employer may not ask about disabilities before making a job offer. The interviewer may ask only whether an applicant can perform the work. Nor can an employer require applicants to take a medical exam unless the exam is (1) job-related and (2) required of all applicants for similar jobs. However, drug testing is permitted.

After a job offer has been made, an employer may require a medical test, but it must be related to the *essential functions* of the job. For example, an employer could not test the cholesterol of someone applying for an accounting job because high cholesterol is no impediment to good accounting.

An employer may not discriminate against someone because of his *relationship* with a disabled person. For example, an employer cannot refuse to hire an applicant because he has a disabled child or a spouse with cancer.

Under EEOC rules, physical and mental disabilities are to be treated the same. The difficulty is that physical ailments such as diabetes and deafness may be easy to diagnose, but what does a supervisor do when an employee is chronically late, rude, or impulsive? Does this mean that the worker is mentally disabled or just a lazy, irresponsible jerk? Among other accommodations, the EEOC rules indicated that employers should be willing to put up barriers to isolate people who have difficulty concentrating, provide detailed day-to-day feedback to those who need greater structure in performing their jobs, or allow workers on antidepressants to come to work later if they are groggy in the morning.

While lauding the ADA's objectives, many managers have been apprehensive about its impact on the workplace. Most acknowledge, however, that society is better off if every member has the opportunity to work. And as advocates for the disabled point out, we are all, at best, only temporarily able-bodied. Even with the ADA, only 29 percent of the disabled population who are of working age are actually employed, whereas 79 percent of able-bodied persons have jobs.

Genetic Information Nondiscrimination Act

Suppose you want to promote someone to chief financial officer, but you know that her mother and sister both died young of breast cancer. Is it legal to consider that information in making a decision? Not since Congress passed the Genetic Information Nondiscrimination Act (GINA). **Under this statute, employers (with 15 or more workers) may not require genetic testing or discriminate against workers because of their genetic makeup.** Nor may health insurers use such information to decide coverage or premiums. Thus, neither employers nor health insurers may require you to provide your family medical history—who has died of cancer or heart disease, for instance. And if they find this information out from another source (such as a newspaper obituary), they may not use it in making an employment decision.

Every applicant feels slightly apprehensive before a job interview, but now the interviewer may be even more nervous—fearing that every question is a potential land mine of liability. Most interviewers (and students who have read this chapter) would know better than Delta Airlines interviewers who allegedly asked applicants about their sexual preference, birth control methods, and abortion history. The following list provides guidelines for interviewers.

Don't Even Consider Asking	Go Ahead and Ask
Can you perform this function with or without reasonable accommodation?	Would you need reasonable accommodation in this job?
How many days were you sick last year?	How many days were you absent from work last year?
What medications are you currently taking?	Are you currently using drugs illegally?
Where were you born? Are you a United States citizen?	Are you authorized to work in the United States?
How old are you?	What work experience have you had?
How tall are you? How much do you weigh?	Could you carry a 100-pound weight, as required by this job?
When did you graduate from college?	Where did you go to college?
How did you learn this language?	What languages do you speak and write fluently?
Have you ever been arrested?	Have you ever been convicted of a crime that would affect the performance of this job?
Do you plan to have children? How old are your children? What method of birth control do you use?	Can you work weekends? Travel extensively? Would you be willing to relocate?
What is your corrected vision?	Do you have 20/20 corrected vision?
Are you a man or a woman? Are you single or married? What does your spouse do? What will happen if your spouse is transferred? What clubs, societies, or lodges do you belong to?	Talk about the weather instead!

The most common gaffe on the part of interviewers? Asking women about their child-care arrangements. That question assumes the woman is responsible for child-care.

EXAM Strategy

Question: Pippa became pregnant the week she started work as an administrator at Awesome University. Her supervisor was so annoyed at her that he would not consider her for promotion to another job within the university. Under the university's maternity leave policy, Pippa was not entitled to any time off from work because she had not been an employee for at least a year by the time her baby was born. When she quit her job, the university cancelled her health insurance coverage. Has the university violated the law?

Strategy: First: Is Pippa protected by any statutes? The possibilities are: the FMLA, COBRA, and the Pregnancy Discrimination Act.

Second: How do these statutes apply? Under the Pregnancy Discrimination Act, an employer cannot deny a promotion to a woman because she is pregnant. Also, if employees are allowed time off for illness, they must also be allowed time off for pregnancy. Thus, if men who have heart attacks are permitted paid time off from work, women must also be paid while they recuperate from delivery.

Third: The FMLA guarantees at least 12 weeks of unpaid leave each year for childbirth but only for workers who have been employed for at least one year. Therefore, the university's maternity leave policy is legal. Finally, under COBRA, Pippa has the right to continue her health insurance for 18 months (provided she pays for it).

Result: The university has violated two statutes.

Chapter Conclusion

Although managers sometimes feel overwhelmed by the long list of laws that protect workers, the United States guarantees its workers fewer rights than virtually any other industrialized nation. For instance, Japan, Great Britain, France, Germany, and Canada all require employers to show just cause before terminating workers. Although American employers are no longer insulated from minimum standards of fairness, reasonable behavior, and compliance with important policies, they still have great freedom to manage their employees.

Exam Review

1. **TRADITIONAL COMMON LAW RULE** The traditional common law rule of employment provided that an employee at will could be fired for a good reason, a bad reason, or no reason at all. (p. 699)

2. **NLRA** The National Labor Relations Act prohibits employers from penalizing workers for union activity. (p. 700)

3. **FMLA** The Family and Medical Leave Act guarantees workers up to 12 weeks of unpaid leave each year for childbirth, adoption, a serious health condition of their own or in their immediate family. (p. 700)

4. **HEALTH INSURANCE** Starting in 2014, employers who have more than 50 full-time employees must pay a penalty if they do not provide basic health insurance. (pp. 700–701)

5. **COBRA** Under the Consolidated Omnibus Budget Reconciliation Act, former employees must be allowed to continue their health insurance for 18 months after being terminated from their job, but they must pay for it themselves. (p. 701)

6. **WRONGFUL DISCHARGE** An employer who fires a worker for a bad reason is liable under a theory of wrongful discharge. (pp. 701–704)

7. **PUBLIC POLICY** Generally, an employee may not be fired for refusing to violate the law, performing a legal duty, exercising a legal right, or supporting basic societal values. (pp. 701–703)

EXAM Strategy

Question: When Theodore Staats went to his company's "Council of Honor Convention," he was accompanied by a woman who was not his wife, although he told everyone she was. The company fired him. Staats alleged that his termination violated public policy because it infringed upon his freedom of association. He also alleged that he had been fired because he was too successful—his commissions were so high, he outearned even the highest-paid officer of the company. Has Staat's employer violated public policy?

Strategy: Is Staats protected by a statute? No. Is he being asked to break the law? No. Is he trying to perform a legal duty? No. Is he being denied a legal right? (See the "Result" at the end of this section.)

8. **PROMISES MADE DURING THE HIRING PROCESS** Promises made during the hiring process may be enforceable, even if not approved by the company's top executives. (pp. 703–704)

EXAM Strategy

Question: When Phil McConkey interviewed for a job as an insurance agent with Alexander & Alexander, the company did not tell him that it was engaged in secret negotiations to merge with Aon. When the merger went through soon thereafter, Aon fired McConkey. Was Alexander liable for not telling McConkey about the possible merger?

Strategy: Was McConkey protected by a statute? No. Did the company make any promises to him during the hiring process? (See the "Result" at the end of this section.)

9. **HANDBOOKS** An employee handbook may create a contract. (p. 704)

10. **COVENANT OF GOOD FAITH AND FAIR DEALING** In almost all states, courts will imply this covenant in an at-will employment relationship. (p. 704)

11. **IMMIGRATION** After hiring a worker, employers must complete an I-9 form—Employment Eligibility Verification—within three days. This form lists the acceptable documents that can be used for verification. Employees have the right to present whichever documents they want from the lists of acceptable items. (p. 710)

12. **DEFAMATION** Employers may be liable for defamation if they give false and unfavorable references. (pp. 704–705)

13. **WHISTLEBLOWERS** Whistleblowers receive some protection under both federal and state laws. (pp. 706–707)

14. **OSHA** The goal of the Occupational Safety and Health Act is to ensure safe conditions in the workplace. (pp. 707–708)

15. **EMPLOYEE PRIVACY** An employer may not violate a worker's reasonable expectation of privacy. However, unless a state has passed a statute to the contrary, employers may monitor many types of off-duty conduct (even legal activities such as smoking). Most states permit private employers to administer alcohol and drug tests. But employers may not require lie detector tests, except as (1) part of an investigation into a crime or (2) for jobs in pharmaceutical firms that deal with controlled substances. (pp. 708–710)

16. **WORKERS' COMPENSATION** Workers' compensation statutes ensure that employees receive payment for injuries incurred at work. (p. 711)

17. **SOCIAL SECURITY** The social security system pays benefits to workers who are retired, disabled, or temporarily unemployed and to the spouses and children of disabled or deceased workers. (pp. 711–712)

18. **ERISA** The Employee Retirement Income Security Act regulates private pension plans. (p. 713)

19. **EQUAL PAY ACT** Under the Equal Pay Act, an employee may not be paid at a lesser rate than employees of the opposite sex for equal work. (pp. 713–714)

20. **TITLE VII** Title VII of the Civil Rights Act of 1964 prohibits employers from discriminating on the basis of race, color, religion, sex, or national origin. (pp. 713–721)

21. **RETALIATION** Title VII penalizes employers who retaliate against workers for complaining about discrimination. (p. 717)

22. **BFOQ** Under the bona fide occupational qualification standard, an employer is permitted to establish discriminatory job requirements if they are *essential* to the position in question. (pp. 717–718)

23. **PREGNANCY DISCRIMINATION ACT OF 1978** Under the Pregnancy Discrimination Act, an employer may not fire, refuse to hire, or fail to promote a woman because she is pregnant. An employer must also treat pregnancy as any other temporary disability. (p. 721)

24. **ADEA** The Age Discrimination in Employment Act prohibits age discrimination against employees or job applicants who are age 40 or older. (pp. 721–723)

25. **ADA** The Americans with Disabilities Act prohibits employers from discriminating on the basis of disability. (pp. 723–724)

Question: When Thomas Lussier filled out a Postal Service employment application, he did not admit that he had twice pleaded guilty to charges of disorderly conduct. Lussier suffered from Post Traumatic Stress Disorder (PTSD) acquired during military service. Because of this disorder, he sometimes had panic attacks that required him to leave meetings. He was also a recovered alcoholic and drug user. During his stint with the Postal Service, he had some personality conflicts with other employees. Once, another employee hit him. He also had one episode of "erratic emotional behavior and verbal outburst." In the meantime, a postal employee in Ridgewood, New Jersey, killed four colleagues. The postmaster general encouraged all supervisors to identify workers who had dangerous propensities. Lussier's boss discovered that he had lied on his employment application about the disorderly conduct charges and fired him. Is the Postal Service in violation of the law?

Strategy: Was Lussier disabled under the ADA? He had a mental impairment (PTSD) that substantially limited a major life activity. Could Lussier, with reasonable accommodation, perform his job? Yes. Was his firing illegal? (See the "Result" at the end of this section.)

26. GINA Under the Genetic Information Nondiscrimination Act, employers with 15 or more workers may not require genetic testing or discriminate against workers because of their genetic makeup. (pp. 724–725)

7. Result: The court held that freedom of association is an important social right and should be protected. However, being fired for bringing a lover to an employer's convention is not a threat to public policy. Nor is discharge for being too successful.

8. Result: The court held that when Alexander hired him, it was making an implied promise that he would not be fired immediately. The company was liable for not having revealed the merger negotiations.

25. Result: The court held that the Postal Service was in violation of the law because Lussier had been dismissed solely as a result of his disability.

Multiple-Choice Questions

1. Brook moved from Denver to San Francisco to take a job with an advertising agency. His employment contract stated that he was "at will and could be terminated at any time." After 28 months with the company, he was fired without explanation. Which of the following statements is true?
   (a) His contract implied that he could only be fired for cause.
   (b) Because he had a contract, he was not an employee at will.
   (c) He could only be fired for a good reason.
   (d) He could be fired for any reason.
   (e) He could be fired for any reason except a bad reason.

2. ***CPA QUESTION*** An unemployed CPA generally would receive unemployment compensation benefits if the CPA:
   (a) Was fired as a result of the employer's business reversals
   (b) Refused to accept a job as an accountant while receiving extended benefits
   (c) Was fired for embezzling from a client
   (d) Left work voluntarily without good cause

3. During a job interview with Venetia, Jack reveals that he and his wife are expecting twins. Venetia asks him if he is planning to take a leave once the babies are born. When Jack admits that he would like to take a month off work, he can see her face fall. She ultimately decides not to hire him because of the twins. Which of the following statements are true?
   (a) Venetia has violated the FMLA.
   (b) Venetia has violated the Pregnancy Discrimination Act.
   (c) Venetia has violated Title VII.
   (d) All of the above.
   (e) None of the above.

4. Ralph has worked as a model builder at Snowdrop Architects for 30 years. The firm replaces him with Charlotte, who is only 24 and willing to work for 30 percent less than his salary. The firm never offered to let him stay for less pay. When he left, one of the partners told him, "Frankly, it's not a bad thing to have a cute young person working with the clients." Which of the following statements is true?
   (a) Snowdrop is liable because it had an obligation to offer Ralph the lower salary before firing him.
   (b) Snowdrop is liable because it is illegal to replace an older worker with a younger one just to save money.
   (c) Snowdrop is liable because age was a factor in Ralph's firing.
   (d) Snowdrop is liable under Title VII because it replaced an old man with a young woman.
   (e) Snowdrop is not liable because age was not the deciding factor in Ralph's firing.

5. During chemotherapy for bone cancer, a delivery person is exhausted, nauseous, and weak. He has asked permission to come in later, work a shorter day, and limit his lifting to 10 pounds. Delivery people typically carry packages of up to 70 pounds. Does Vulcan, his employer, have the right to fire him?
   (a) Vulcan must create a new position so that the employee can do something else.
   (b) Vulcan must transfer the employee to another position, but only if one is vacant and he is able to perform it.
   (c) Vulcan can fire the man because none of his major life activities has been affected.
   (d) Vulcan can fire the man because he cannot perform the essential functions of his job.
   (e) Vulcan can fire him because he is not disabled—once the chemotherapy treatments end, he will feel fine again.

Essay Questions

1. Reginald Delaney managed a Taco Time restaurant in Portland, Oregon. Some of his customers told Mr. Ledbetter, the district manager, that they would not be eating there so often because there were too many black employees. Ledbetter told Delaney to fire Ms. White, who was black. Delaney did as he was told. Ledbetter's report on the incident said: "My notes show that Delaney told me that White asked him to sleep with her and that when he would not, that she started causing dissension within the crew. She asked him to come over to her house and that he declined." Delaney refused to sign the report because it was untrue, so Ledbetter fired him. What claim might Delaney make against his former employer?

2. Debra Agis worked as a waitress in a Ground Round restaurant. The manager informed the waitresses that "there was some stealing going on." Until he found out who was doing it, he intended to fire all the waitresses in alphabetical order, starting with the letter "A." Dionne then fired Agis. Does she have a valid claim against her employer?

3. The Lillie Rubin boutique in Phoenix would not permit Dick Kovacic to apply for a job as a salesperson. It hired only women to work in sales because fittings and alterations took place in the dressing room or immediately outside. The customers were buying expensive clothes and demanded a male-free dressing area. Has the Lillie Rubin store violated Title VII? What would its defense be?

4. **YOU BE THE JUDGE WRITING PROBLEM** FedEx gave Marcie Dutschmann an employment handbook stating that (1) she was an at-will employee, (2) the handbook did not create any contractual rights, and (3) employees who were fired had the right to a termination hearing. The company fired Dutschmann, claiming that she had falsified delivery records. She said that FedEx was retaliating against her because she had complained of sexual harassment. FedEx refused her request for a termination hearing. Did the employee handbook create an implied contract guaranteeing Dutschmann a hearing? **Argument for FedEx:** The handbook could not have been clearer—it did not create a contract. Dutschmann is an employee at will and is not entitled to a hearing. **Argument for Dutschmann:** FedEx intended that employees would rely on the handbook.The company used promises of a hearing to attract and retain good employees. Dutschmann was entitled to a hearing.

5. After the terrorist attacks of 9/11, the United States tightened its visa requirements. In the process, baseball teams discovered that 300 foreign-born professional players had lied about their age. (A talented 16-year-old is much more valuable than a 23-year-old with the same skills.) In some cases, the players had used birth certificates that belonged to other (younger) people. To prevent this fraud, baseball teams began asking for DNA tests on prospects and their families, to make sure they were not lying about their identity. Is this testing legal? What if a team wanted to test players to see if they were susceptible to certain diseases?

Discussion Questions

1. When Walton Weiner interviewed for a job with McGraw-Hill, Inc., he was assured that the company would not terminate an employee without "just cause." Weiner also signed a contract specifying that his employment would be subject to the provisions of McGraw-Hill's handbook. The handbook said, "[The] company will resort to dismissal for just and sufficient cause only, and only after all practical steps toward rehabilitation or salvage of the employee have been taken and failed. However, if the welfare of the company indicates that dismissal is necessary, then that decision is arrived at and is carried out forthrightly." After eight years, Weiner was fired suddenly for "lack of application." Does Weiner have a valid claim against McGraw-Hill?

2. **ETHICS** Mary Ann Singleton was the librarian at a maximum-security prison located in Tazewell County, Virginia. About four times a week, Gene Shinault, assistant warden for operations, persistently complimented Singleton and stared at her breasts when he spoke to her. On one occasion, he measured the length of her skirt to judge its compliance with the prison's dress code and told her that it looked "real good"; constantly told her how attractive he found her; made references to his physical fitness, considering his advanced age; asked Singleton if he made her nervous (she answered "yes"); and repeatedly remarked to Singleton that if he had a wife as attractive as Singleton, he would not permit her to work in a prison facility around so many inmates. Shinault told Singleton's supervisor in her presence, "Look at her. I bet you have to spank her every day." The supervisor then laughed and said, "No. I probably should, but I don't." Shinault replied, "Well, I know I would." Shinault also had a security camera installed in her office in a way that permitted him to observe her as she worked. Singleton reported this behavior to her supervisor, who simply responded, "Boys will be boys." Did Shinault sexually harass Singleton? Whether or not Shinault violated the law, what *ethical* obligation did Singleton's superviser have to protect her from this type of behavior?

3. Ronald Lockhart, who was deaf, worked for FedEx as a package handler. Although fluent in American Sign Language, he could not read lips. After 9/11, the company held meetings to talk about security issues. Lockhart complained to the EEOC that he could not understand these discussions. FedEx fired him. Has FedEx violated the law?

4. Gregg Young, the CEO of BJY Inc. insisted on calling Mamdouh El-Hakem "Manny" or "Hank." Does this behavior violate the law?

5. Once again, FedEx was in the news when it refused to promote José Rodriguez to a supervisor's position because of his accent and "how he speaks." Is FedEx in violation of the law?

LABOR LAW

A strike! For five weeks, the union workers have been walking picket lines at JMJ, a manufacturer of small electrical engines. An entire town of 70,000 citizens, most of them blue-collar workers, is sharply divided, right down to the McNally's kitchen table. Buddy, age 48, has worked on the assembly lines at JMJ for more than 25 years. Now he's sipping coffee in the house where he grew up. His sister Kristina, age 46, is a vice president for personnel at JMJ. The two have always been close. In high school, Kristina idolized her older brother, the football and track star. Buddy was immensely proud of his kid sister's academic triumphs, boasting to the world that she would "be the first lady president." Today, though, conversation is halting.

An entire town of 70,000 citizens, most of them blue-collar workers, is sharply divided, right down to the McNallys' kitchen table.

"It's time to get back together, Buddy," Kristina murmurs. "The strike is hurting the whole company—and the town."

Not the *whole* town, Kristina," he replies. "Your management pals still have fat incomes and nice houses."

"Oh yeah? You haven't seen our porch lately."

"Go talk to Tony Falcione. He can't pay his rent."

"Talk to the Ericksons," Kristina snaps back. "They don't even work for JMJ. Their sandwich shop is going under because none of you guys stop in for lunch. Come back to work."

"Not with that clause on the table."

That clause is management's proposal for the new union contract—one that Kristina helped draft. The company officers want the right to subcontract work—that is, to send it out for other companies to perform.

"Buddy, we need the flexibility. K-Ball is underselling us by 35 percent. If we can't compete, there won't be *any* jobs or *any* contract!"

"The way to save money is not by sending our jobs overseas, where people will work for 50 bucks a month."

"O.K., fine. Tell me how we *should* save money."

"How you can sit at this table and say these things? In this house? You never would have gone to college if Dad hadn't made union wages."

"If we can't cut costs, we're out of business. *Then* what's your union going to do for you? All we're asking is the right to subcontract some of the smallest components. Everything else gets built here."

"This is just the start. Next it'll be the wiring, then the batteries, then you'll assemble the whole thing over there—and that'll be it for me. You take that clause off the table, we'll be back in 15 minutes."

"You know I can't do that."

Buddy stands up. They stare silently, sadly, at each other, and then Kristina says, in a barely audible voice, "I have to tell you this. My boss is starting to talk about hiring replacement workers."

Buddy walks out.

Some Americans revere unions, believing that organized labor has pulled the working class up from poverty and shielded it from exploitative management. Others loathe organized labor, convinced that unions foment mindless conflicts, decrease productivity, increase costs, and harm corporations and the economy generally. In the next section, we begin at the beginning: why do unions exist?

UNIONS DEVELOP ... AND THE LAW RESPONDS

During the 19th century, as industrialization spread across America, workers found employment conditions increasingly unbearable. Here is an account of mining in the American West:

> View their work! Descending from the surface in the shaft-cages, they enter narrow galleries where the air is scarce respirable. By the dim light of their lanterns a dingy rock surface, braced by rotting props, is visible. The stenches of decaying vegetable matter, hot foul water, and human excretions intensify the effects of the heat. The men throw off their clothes at once. Only a light breech-cloth covers their hips, and thick-soled shoes protect their feet from the scorching rocks and steaming rills of water that trickle over the floor. Except for these coverings they toil naked, with heavy drops of sweat starting from every pore.[1]

Temperatures in the mines were well over 100 degrees. Miners drank more than three gallons of water every day. Some suddenly collapsed, with swollen veins, purple faces, and glazed eyes. Within minutes, they were dead, but even before they died, their places in the mine were taken by other workers desperate for pay.

[1]Eliot Lord, *Comstock Mining and Miners* (Washington: G.P.O., 1883), p. 386, quoted in Richard E. Lingenfelter, *The Hardrock Miners* (Berkeley: University of California Press, 1974), p. 13.

Conditions were also oppressive in the new factories back east. Workers, often women and sometimes children, worked 60 to 70 hours per week and sometimes more, standing at assembly lines in suffocating, dimly lit factories, performing monotonous and dangerous work with heavy machinery. A visitor to a factory in Lowell, Massachusetts, in 1855 was shocked by the degrading conditions and the exhausting hours required of all workers:

> I inquired of the agent of a principal factory whether it was the custom of the manufacturers to do anything for the physical, intellectual, and moral welfare of their work-people. "We never do," he said. "As for myself, I regard my work-people just as I regard my machinery. So long as they can do my work for what I choose to pay them, I keep them, getting out of them all I can. What they do or how they fare outside my walls I don't know, nor do I consider it my business to know. When my machines get old and useless, I reject them and get new, and these people are part of my machinery."[2]

Because of the intolerable conditions and impoverishing wages, workers began to band together into unions. But early in the 19th century, American courts regarded any coordinated effort by workers as a criminal conspiracy. Courts convicted workers merely for the *act of joining together*, even if no strike took place. In 1842, the Massachusetts high court became the first to reject this use of the criminal law. The court ruled that workers could join together for legitimate economic goals; their efforts would become criminal only if the workers used illegal means to achieve them.[3] Other courts came to agree, and so management resorted to the civil law to curtail unions.

In 1890, Congress passed the Sherman Act to outlaw monopolies.[4] But for the next 40 years, courts relied on this statute to issue injunctions, declaring that *strikes* illegally restrained trade. A company could usually obtain an immediate injunction merely by alleging that a strike *might* cause harm. Courts were so quick to issue injunctions that most companies became immune to union efforts. But with the economic collapse of 1929 and the vast suffering of the Great Depression, public sympathy shifted to the workers. Congress responded with the first of several landmark statutes.

Norris-LaGuardia Act
Prohibits federal court injunctions in peaceful labor disputes.

National Labor Relations Act (NLRA)
Ensures the right of workers to form unions and encourages management and unions to bargain collectively.

Pro-Union Statutes

In 1932, Congress passed the **Norris-LaGuardia Act,** which prohibited federal court injunctions in nonviolent labor disputes. No longer could management stop a strike merely by mentioning the word "strike." By taking away the injunction remedy, Congress was declaring that workers should be permitted to organize unions and to use their collective power to achieve legitimate economic ends. The statute led to explosive growth in union membership.

In 1935, Congress passed the Wagner Act, generally known as the **National Labor Relations Act (NLRA).** This is the most important of all labor laws. A fundamental aim of the NLRA is the establishment and maintenance of industrial peace, to preserve the flow of commerce. The NLRA ensures the

© Darren Baker/Shutterstock.com

As industry changes, labor changes with it. Do these changes spell the end of unionization, or are unions merely undergoing a transition as labor catches up with the modern economy?

---

[2]Massachusetts Senate Dock. no. 21, 1868, p. 23, quoted in Norman Ware, *The Industrial Worker* (Chicago: Quadrangle Books, 1964), p. 77.
[3]*Commonwealth v. Hunt*, 45 Mass. 111, 4 Met. 111 (1842).
[4]See Chapter 38, on antitrust law.

right of workers to form unions and encourages management and unions to bargain collectively and productively. For our purposes, Sections 7 and 8 of the NLRA are the most important.

Section 7 guarantees employees the right to organize and join unions, bargain collectively through representatives of their own choosing, and engage in other concerted activities. This is the cornerstone of union power. With the enactment of the NLRA, Congress put an end to any notion that unions were inherently illegal by explicitly recognizing that workers could join together, bargain as a group, and use their collective power to seek better conditions.

Section 8 prohibits employers from engaging in the following unfair labor practices (ULPs):

- Interfering with union organizing efforts,
- Dominating or interfering with any union,
- Discriminating against a union member, or
- Refusing to bargain collectively with a union.

National Labor Relations Board (NLRB)
Administers and interprets the NLRA and adjudicates labor cases.

The NLRA also established the **National Labor Relations Board (NLRB)** to administer and interpret the statute and to adjudicate labor cases. For example, when a union charges that an employer has committed an unfair labor practice—say, by refusing to bargain—the claim goes first to the NLRB.

The NLRB has two primary tasks:

- *Representation.* The Board decides whether a particular union is entitled to represent a group of employees.
- *Unfair labor practices.* The Board adjudicates claims by either the employer or workers that the other side has committed a ULP.

To accomplish these tasks, the NLRB has several divisions. Although the agency is headquartered in Washington, it performs the greatest volume of its work in local offices. Regional offices, each headed by a regional director, are located throughout the country. Each has a General Counsel to investigate ULP claims. If the General Counsel's office believes that a party has committed an unfair labor practice, it prosecutes the case. The Board itself, which sits in Washington, has five members, all appointed by the president. The Board makes final agency decisions about representation and ULP cases.

Throughout the 1930s and 1940s, unions grew in size and power. As strikes became more common, employers complained loudly of union abuse. Unions coerced unwilling workers to join and engaged in *secondary boycotts,* picketing an innocent company to stop it from doing business with an employer the union was fighting. In 1947, Congress responded with the Taft-Hartley Act, also known as the **Labor-Management Relations Act**, designed to curb union abuses. The statute amended §8 of the NLRA to outlaw certain unfair labor practices *by unions.*

Labor-Management Relations Act
Is designed to curb union abuses.

Section 8(b) makes it an unfair labor practice for a union to:

- Interfere with employees who are exercising their labor rights under §7,
- Encourage an employer to discriminate against a particular employee because of a union dispute,
- Refuse to bargain collectively, or
- Engage in an illegal strike or boycott, particularly secondary boycotts.

Finally, in the 1950s, the public became aware that certain labor leaders were corrupt. Some officers stole money from large union treasuries, rigged union elections, and stifled opposition within the organization. In response, in 1959 Congress passed the Landrum-Griffin Act, generally called the **Labor-Management Reporting and Disclosure Act (LMRDA).** The LMRDA requires union leadership to make certain financial disclosures and guarantees free speech and fair elections within a union.

These landmark federal labor laws are outlined below:

Four Key Labor Statutes

Norris-LaGuardia Act (1932)	Prohibits federal court injunctions in peaceful strikes.
National Labor Relations Act (1935)	Guarantees workers' right to organize unions and bargain collectively. Prohibits an employer from interfering with union organizing or discriminating against union members. Requires an employer to bargain collectively.
Labor-Management Relations Act (1947)	Prohibits union abuses such as coercing employees to join. Outlaws secondary boycotts.
Labor-Management Reporting and Disclosure Act (1959)	Requires financial disclosures by union leadership. Guarantees union members free speech and fair elections.

Today, labor abuses are less visible—but as ugly as ever. From New York City to Los Angeles, desperately poor, frightened immigrants cut and sew about half of all the garments this country produces, often working in appalling sweatshops where conditions are little better than in 19th-century factories. Frequently, the employees are undocumented immigrants who speak no English, know nothing of their rights, and fear that any complaints they make will lead to deportation. Owners force the workers to toil 50 to 60 hours a week, with few breaks, in cramped rooms with weak lighting, no ventilation, and inadequate sanitation. Pay is below the minimum wage.

Labor Unions Today

Organized labor is in flux in the United States. In the 1950s, about 1 in 4 workers belonged to a union. Today, only about 1 in 8, or 15 million total U.S. workers, are union members. Employers point to this figure with satisfaction and claim that it shows that unions have failed their memberships. In an increasingly high-tech, service-oriented economy, employers argue, there is no place for organized labor. Union supporters respond that although the country has shed many old factories, workers have not benefited. Throughout the last 20 years, they assert, compensation for executives has soared into the stratosphere while wages for the average worker, in real dollars, have fallen.

Unions continue to attract political attention. In 2011, legislators in Wisconsin voted to strip most collective bargaining rights from schoolteachers and other state government workers. Public employees are five times more likely to be union members than private sector workers, but they are generally not protected by the NLRA. Instead, state labor laws apply, which tend to provide less protection than federal statutes.

Crowds of as many as 100,000 gathered in Madison, Wisconsin, to protest the proposed legislation, but it passed nonetheless. Commentators on the left forecast significant political consequences for the Wisconsin lawmakers, while editorialists on the right predict that many states will soon follow the Wisconsin model.

Although overall membership is down, unions still matter.

Organizing a Union

Exclusivity

It is difficult to organize a union. When a worker starts to talk about collective action, or when an organizer appears from a national union, many employees are suspicious or fearful; some may be hostile. Management will generally be opposed—sometimes fiercely opposed—to any union organizing effort. The fight can become ugly, and all because of one principle: *exclusivity*.

Under §9 of the NLRA, a validly recognized union is the *exclusive* representative of the employees. This means that the union will represent all of the designated employees, regardless of whether a particular worker *wants* to be represented. The company may not bargain directly with any employee in the group, nor with any other organization representing the designated employees.

Collective bargaining unit
The precisely defined group of employees represented by a particular union.

A **collective bargaining unit** is the precisely defined group of employees who will be represented by a particular union. Suppose a hotel workers' union attempts to organize the Excelsior Hotel. The union will seek to represent some of Excelsior's employees, but not all. The union may represent, for example, all maids, busboys, and bellhops. Those employees are in the collective bargaining unit. Many other people who work for the hotel will *not* be in the collective bargaining unit. Managers who run the hotel, reservation agents who work in other cities, launderers who work in separate facilities for a different employer—all of these people are *outside* the collective bargaining unit and will be unaffected by the union's bargaining.

It is the union's *exclusive* right to bargain for the unit that gives the organization its power. But some employees may be unhappy with the way a union exercises this power. Along with a union's exclusive bargaining power goes a duty of fair representation, which requires that a union treat all members fairly, impartially, and in good faith. A union is not entitled to favor some members over others. No union may discriminate against a member based on characteristics such as race or gender.

In the following case, workers believed the union was failing to represent them on a vital issue. Should they be allowed to bargain on their own behalf? You be the judge.

You be the Judge

Emporium Capwell Co. v. Western Additional Community Organization

420 U.S. 50, 95 S. Ct. 977, 1975 U.S. LEXIS 134
United States Supreme Court, 1975

Facts: Emporium Capwell operated a department store in San Francisco. The Department Store Employees Union represented all stock workers. Several black union members complained to the union about racial discrimination in promotions, asserting that highly qualified black workers were routinely passed over in favor of less-qualified whites. The union promised to pursue the issue with management, but the black employees were not satisfied with the union's effort. The unhappy workers demanded to speak with top management of the store and then, without the union's permission, picketed the store and handed out leaflets accusing the company of discrimination. Emporium Capwell fired the picketing employees. The resulting case went all the way to the Supreme Court.

In most labor cases, the union is on one side and management is on the other. In this case, the black employees were on one side, with the union on the other. The union argued that exclusivity prohibited any group of workers from demanding to meet separately with management. It claimed that the disgruntled workers violated the NLRA by insisting on separate bargaining and that it was proper for the company to fire the workers. In other words, the union placed a higher value on exclusivity than on maintaining the jobs of those employees. The black workers, on the other hand, argued that eliminating discrimination was more important than union exclusivity. They insisted that management had no right to fire them and that they were entitled to get their jobs back and to bargain independently.

You Be the Judge: ***Did the picketing employees violate the NLRA by demanding to bargain directly with management?***

Argument for the Union: Your honors, exclusivity is the core of a union's strength. If management is free to talk with employees individually—or if it can be *compelled* to talk with them—the union has no leverage. An astute manager will quickly use worker conflicts as a tool to divide the union and destroy it. By cutting deals with favored employees, management could demonstrate to all workers that affiliation with the union is a losing tactic and that the smart worker bargains for himself—and then does what management tells him to do.

Racial discrimination is a terrible evil. It must be eradicated from the workplace. This union is committed to fighting prejudice. But the union must do it *collectively*. If an exception to the principle of exclusivity can be carved out for one important issue, such as race discrimination, then an exception can be carved out for other important issues, such as gender bias, age discrimination, language differences, retirement pay, health benefits ... and on and on. To allow this group of picketers to pursue a worthy goal with separate bargaining would be to destroy the union—and ensure that *no* valuable goals are obtained.

Argument for the Picketing Workers: Congress granted employees the right to organize *for their mutual benefit,* not to advance the cause of unions. A labor organization is a means to an end, not an end in itself. When a union fails to support its members on a vital issue, employees must be free to fend for themselves. Race discrimination is not a simple bargaining issue; it is a vital matter of human dignity. This union failed to act promptly and vigorously to protect its African American members and end discrimination. It makes no difference *why* the union failed to protect its members. Weak-kneed, docile union leadership can be just as devastating to the cause of racial equality as bad faith. We are not asking that union members be free to pursue every petty complaint directly with management. To equate racial justice with retirement benefits is to ignore the significance of discrimination. We merely ask that, when a union fails to protect its members concerning a profound issue such as this, the injured employees be allowed to speak for themselves.

Organizing: Stages

A union organizing effort generally involves the following pattern.

Campaign

Union organizers talk with employees—or attempt to talk—and interest them in forming a union. The organizers may be employees of the company, who simply chat with fellow workers about unsatisfactory conditions. Or a union may send nonemployees of the company to hand out union leaflets to workers as they arrive and depart from work.

Authorization Cards

Union organizers ask workers to sign authorization cards, which state that the particular worker requests the specified union to act as her sole bargaining representative.

If a union obtains authorization cards from a sizable percentage of workers, it seeks **recognition** as the exclusive representative for the bargaining unit. The union may ask the employer to recognize it as the bargaining representative, but most of the time, employers refuse to recognize the union voluntarily.

Petition

Assuming that the employer does not voluntarily recognize a union, the union generally petitions the NLRB for an election. It must submit to the NLRB regional office authorization cards signed by at least 30 percent of the workers. The regional office verifies whether there are enough valid cards to warrant an election and looks closely at the proposed bargaining unit to make sure that it is appropriate. If the regional director determines that the union has identified an appropriate bargaining unit and has enough valid cards, it orders an election.

Election

The NLRB closely supervises the election to ensure fairness. All members of the proposed bargaining unit vote on whether they want the union to represent them. If more than 50 percent of the workers vote for the union, the NLRB designates that union as the exclusive representative of all members of the bargaining unit. When unions hold representation elections in private corporations, they win about half the time.

Labor organizations claim that management typically uses company time to campaign against the union. Employers respond that labor loses elections because workers fear that a union will hurt them, not help.

The "Card-Check" Debate

Before becoming president, then-U.S. Senator Barack Obama co-introduced a bill called the Employee Free Choice Act. This bill provides that when more than 50 percent of workers sign an authorization card, the NLRB must immediately designate that union as the exclusive representative of all members in the bargaining unit *without an election*.

Supporters argue that, if a majority of workers return authorization cards, an election is unnecessary and only gives companies an opportunity to intimidate workers. Those who dislike the bill argue that workers may feel bullied into signing an authorization card and should always have the right to a final vote by secret ballot.

The bill has generated much debate but has not passed Congress at the time of this writing.

Organizing: Actions

These are some of the issues that most commonly arise during an organizing effort: (1) What may a union do during its organizing campaign? (2) What may the employer do to defeat the campaign? (3) What is an appropriate bargaining unit?

What Workers May Do

The NLRA guarantees employees the right to talk among themselves about forming a union, to hand out literature, and ultimately to join a union.[5] Workers may urge other employees to sign authorization cards and may vigorously push their cause. When employees hand out leaflets, the employer generally may not limit the content. In one case, a union distributed leaflets urging workers to vote against political candidates who opposed minimum-wage laws. The employer objected to the union distributing the information on company property, but the Supreme Court upheld the union's right. Even though the content of the writing was not directly related to the union, the connection was close enough that the NLRA protected the union's activity.[6]

There are, of course, limits to what union organizers may do. The statute permits an employer to restrict organizing discussions if they interfere with discipline or production. A worker on a moving assembly line has no right to walk away from his task to talk with other employees about organizing a union; the employer may insist that the worker stay at his job and leave discussions until lunch or some other break.[7]

---

[5]NLRA §7.

[6]*Eastex, Inc. v. NLRB*, 434 U.S. 1045, 98 S. Ct. 888, 1978 U.S. LEXIS 547 (1978).

[7]*NLRB v. Babcock & Wilcox Co.*, 351 U.S. 105, 76 S. Ct. 679, 1956 U.S. LEXIS 1721 (1956).

What Employers May Do

As mentioned above, an employer may prohibit employees from organizing if the efforts interfere with the company's work. In a retail store, for example, management may prohibit union discussions in the presence of customers because the discussions could harm business.

May the employer speak out against a union organizing drive? Yes. Management is entitled to communicate to the employees why it believes a union will be harmful to the company. But the employer's efforts must be limited to explanation and advocacy. **The employer may vigorously present anti-union views to its employees but may not use either threats or promises of benefits to defeat a union drive.**[8] Notice that the employer is prohibited not only from threatening reprisals, such as firing a worker who favors the union, but also from offering benefits designed to defeat the union. A company that has vigorously rejected employee demands for higher wages may not suddenly grant a 10 percent pay increase in the midst of a union campaign.

It is an unfair labor practice for an employer to interfere with a union organizing effort. Normally, a union claiming such interference will file an unfair labor practice charge. If the Board upholds the union's claim, it will order the employer to stop its interference and permit a fair election. In some cases, though, management's interference is so pervasive and intrusive that the Board may conclude an election would be pointless. **When an employer outrageously interferes with a union organizing campaign, the NLRB may forgo the normal election, certify the union as the exclusive representative, and order the company to bargain.** This *bargaining order* is an extreme measure, and the Board uses it only when an employer has shown extreme anti-union animus.

Here is a case illustrating the tensions and crude language that so often arise during organizing efforts.

Progressive Electric, Inc. v. National Labor Relations Board

453 F.3d 538
District of Columbia Court of Appeals, 2006

Facts: Progressive Electric, Inc. was a non-union electrical contractor. The International Brotherhood of Electrical Workers (IBEW) targeted the company for organizing. Progressive did not go quietly.

Progressive advertised in the local paper that it was accepting applications for electrician/technicians. Without revealing his IBEW membership, David Cousins responded to the ad and was hired. A month later, eight more union members went as a group to Progressive to apply. They carried video and tape recording equipment. Randy Neeman, Progressive's president, realized that they were union members and told them, "You guys, we are not hiring. We are not taking no [sic] applications. We hired a couple of people and filled the spots. So I would love to put you all on and as soon as I get an opening, I will give you guys a call." The union members filled out job applications, and Neeman said he would call when there was an opening. In fact, he immediately threw away the applications.

Don Hildreth, a Progressive foreman, told Cousins and one other employee that Neeman "didn't want any union crap around here." Hildreth continued, "If the unions got into Progressive, Progressive would lose contracts and would go out of business because Progressive couldn't afford the union wages and benefits."

Neeman held a company meeting, where he told the assembled employees: "All right, I've been quiet up 'til now, which is strange for me, I know. But now we're

[8] *NLRB v. Gissel Packing Co.*, 395 U.S. 575, 89 S. Ct. 1918, 1969 U.S. LEXIS 3172 (1969).

gonna talk about this dirty word – *union*." Neeman's presentation was punctuated by phrases such as "Mr. Asshole Union Rep" and "bunch of dummies." At some point in the presentation, Neeman wrote the word "union" on the board, drew a circle around it, and put a slash through it.

Progressive later filled various positions with non-union members, never advertising the jobs nor contacting the IBEW applicants.

The IBEW filed charges with the NLRB, which concluded that Progressive had committed an unfair labor practice by threatening job loss and plant closure if the union organized the company. Progressive appealed.

Issue: ***Did the company commit a ULP?***

Excerpts from Judge Brown's Decision: Under Section 8(a)(3), it is an unfair labor practice for an employer to encourage or discourage membership in any labor organization. An employer violates this provision by refusing to consider or hire job applicants on account of their union affiliation. This protection extends even to applicants that are union "salts," or union members sent in ostensibly to obtain employment but with the objective of inducing union organization.

The Board's finding is reasonable. After Neeman accepted a sheet containing the Union Applicants' information, he lied to them, assuring them he would call them "as soon as [there is] an opening" when in fact he had no such intention. In the ALJ's words, this falsehood had the "effect of luring the applicants into complacency." The Board also pointed to various events over the course of the subsequent year, including multiple Union letters, which Progressive received via fax but refused via certified mail; the decision to use blind advertisements; and the failure to hire the Union Applicants to any of the seven suitable positions that became available. While we doubt any of these actions—including the initial misrepresentation—would be independently sufficient, the Board reasonably found they were collectively "part and parcel of [Progressive's] overall scheme to refuse to consider and hire" the Union Applicants.

The record before us, however, permits a finding that the actions in question were motivated by anti-union animus. The evidence includes [Neeman's] deliberate misrepresentation to the Union Applicants and his admission that he never intended to hire them; his overt hostility at the meeting; and his failure to contact or hire any of the Union Applicants over the time period in question. The contrary evidence—such as Neeman's friendly relationships with union members [and] his hiring of a small number of union members in the past—does not compel a contrary conclusion in this case.

[We will enforce the Board's order.]

EXAM Strategy

Question: We Haul is a trucking company. The Teamsters Union is attempting to organize the drivers. Workers who favor a union have been using the lunchroom to hand out petitions and urge other drivers to sign authorization cards. The company posts a notice in the lunchroom: "No Union Discussions. Many employees do not want unions discussed in the lunchroom. Out of respect for them, we are prohibiting further union efforts in this lunchroom." Comment.

Strategy: The NLRA guarantees employees the right to talk among themselves about forming a union and to hand out literature. Union workers may vigorously push their cause. Management is entitled to communicate to the employees why it believes a union will be harmful to the company, but the employer's efforts must be limited to explanation and advocacy.

Result: We Haul has violated the NLRA. The company has the right to urge employees not to join the union. However, it is not entitled to block the union from its organizing campaign. Even assuming the company is correct that some employees do not want unions discussed, it has no right to prohibit such advocacy.

Appropriate Bargaining Unit

When a union petitions the NLRB for an election, the Board determines whether the proposed bargaining unit is appropriate. **The Board generally certifies a proposed bargaining unit if and only if the employees share a "community of interest."** Employers frequently assert that the bargaining unit is inappropriate. If the Board agrees with the employer and rejects the proposed bargaining unit, it dismisses the union's request for an election. The Board pays particular attention to two kinds of employees: managerial and confidential.

Managerial employees must be excluded from the bargaining unit.[9] An employee is managerial if she is so closely aligned with management that her membership in the bargaining unit would create a conflict of interest between her union membership and her actual work. Courts generally find such a conflict only if *the employee is substantially involved in the employer's labor policy*.

For example, a factory worker who spends one-third of his time performing assembly work but two-thirds of his time supervising a dozen other workers is so closely aligned with management that he could not fairly be part of the bargaining unit. There would be constant tension between his supervisory work and his advocacy on behalf of the union. By contrast, an engineer who analyzes production methods and merely reports her findings to management may not be closely aligned with the employer. Unless the engineer has actual control over personnel decisions, she can probably be included in a bargaining unit of other engineers.[10]

Confidential employees are generally excluded from the bargaining unit.[11] A confidential employee is one who works so closely with executives or other management employees that there would be a conflict of interest if the employee were in the bargaining unit. An executive assistant may be so intimately acquainted with his boss's ideas, plans, and other confidential information that it would be unfair to allow him to join a bargaining unit of other administrative assistants.

Once the Board has excluded managerial and confidential employees, it looks at various criteria to decide whether the remaining employees should logically be grouped in one bargaining unit; that is, whether they share a **community of interest.** The Board looks for:

- Rough equality of pay and benefits and methods of computing both,
- Similar total hours per week and type of work,
- Similar skills and training, and
- Previous bargaining history and the number of authorization cards from any different groups within the unit.

Having applied these criteria to all members of the proposed unit, the Board either certifies the bargaining unit or rejects the unit and dismisses the union's petition. Suppose the employees in a public high school decide to organize. The Board will probably find that an appropriate bargaining unit includes all academic teachers and physical education teachers because they do roughly similar work and are paid similarly. The principal and vice principal will not be included in the unit because their work is supervisory and administrative and they are paid on a separate scale.

---

[9]*NLRB v. Bell Aerospace Co., Div. of Textron, Inc.*, 416 U.S. 267, 94 S. Ct. 1757, 1974 U.S. LEXIS 35 (1974).

[10]See, e.g., *NLRB v. Case Corp.*, 995 F.2d 700, 1993 U.S. App. LEXIS 13246 (7th Cir. 1993).

[11]Ibid.

COLLECTIVE BARGAINING

Collective bargaining agreement (CBA)
A contract between a union and management.

The ultimate goal of bargaining is to create a new contract, which is called a **collective bargaining agreement (CBA).** But problems can arise as union and employer advocate their respective positions. Three of the most common conflicts are (1) whether an issue is a mandatory subject of bargaining, (2) whether the parties are bargaining in good faith, and (3) how to enforce the agreement.

Subjects of Bargaining

The NLRA *permits* the parties to bargain almost any subject they wish, but it only *requires* them to bargain certain issues. **Mandatory subjects include wages, hours, and other terms and conditions of employment.**

Management and unions often disagree as to whether a particular topic is mandatory or not. Typically, unions attempt to expand the number of mandatory subjects while the company argues that many subjects are not mandatory and are none of the union's business. In general, a court is likely to find a given issue mandatory when it *directly relates* to individual workers. Courts generally find these subjects to be mandatory: pay, benefits, order of layoffs and recalls, production quotas, work rules (such as safety practices), retirement benefits, and onsite food service and prices. Courts usually consider these subjects to be nonmandatory: product type and design, advertising, sales, financing, corporate organization, and location of plants.

Today, some of the most heated disputes between management and labor arise from a company's desire to subcontract work and/or to move plants to areas with cheaper costs. **Subcontracting** means that a manufacturer, rather than producing all parts of a product and then assembling them, contracts for other companies, frequently overseas, to make some of the parts. Is a business free to subcontract work? That depends on management's motive. **A company that subcontracts in order to maintain its economic viability is probably *not* required to bargain first; however, bargaining *is* mandatory if the subcontracting is designed to replace union workers with cheaper labor.**

Dorsey Trailers manufactured dump trucks. During a period of heavy sales, Dorsey subcontracted some of its production work to Bankhead Enterprises, which agreed to manufacture two trucks per week and split the profits. The union filed a ULP charge, claiming that subcontracting was a mandatory subject of bargaining, and that Dorsey had no right to make the deal before negotiating with the union.

The court noted that Dorsey was losing business because it could not fill orders fast enough. The dump truck industry was cyclical, and in a period of strong demand, the company had to be able to manufacture its goods quickly. Dorsey had been unable to hire enough welders and other skilled workers to keep up with demand. The court stated that Dorsey could not survive without the subcontracting. Further, the company had not reduced union jobs; it had simply failed to add more union workers—through no fault of its own. Dorsey was free to subcontract without bargaining the issue.[12]

Plant closings, which can result in hundreds or thousands of lost jobs, are also a volatile issue. Although the job losses are potentially greater than those that result from subcontracting, management is not obligated to bargain such a decision. **An employer is not required to bargain over the closing of a plant, only the *effects* of the closing.**[13]

---

[12] *Dorsey Trailers, Inc. Northumberland PA Plant v. NLRB*, 134 F.3d 125, 1998 U.S. App. LEXIS 764 (3rd. Cir. 1998).

[13] *First National Maintenance Corp. v. NLRB*, 452 U.S. 666, 101 S. Ct. 2573, 1981 U.S. LEXIS 117 (1981).

The reasoning behind this rule is basic: the company that opened a plant ought to be able to close it. Further, having concluded that the employer has the right to shut down a facility, courts also allow the employer to do so fairly quickly. Management may need speed and flexibility in effecting such major business changes. In contrast, the union will want to slow down or prevent the closing. The two sides will have few things to discuss, and mandated bargaining will gain little for employees while potentially costing the company time and money. When a plant closing will cost jobs, management must bargain such things as the order of layoffs, but it need not bargain the closing itself.

Employer and Union Security

Both the employer and the union will seek clauses making their positions more secure. Management, above all, wants to be sure that there will be no strikes during the course of the agreement. For its part, the union tries to ensure that its members cannot be turned away from work during the CBA's term, and that all newly hired workers will affiliate with the union. We look at several union security issues.

No Strike/No Lockout. Most agreements include some form of no-strike clause, meaning that the union promises not to strike during the term of the contract. In turn, unions insist on a no-lockout clause, meaning that in the event of a labor dispute, management will not prevent union members from working. **No-strike and no-lockout clauses are both legal.**

Closed Shops. A closed shop means the employer must hire only union members. Though obviously very attractive to a union, effectively giving it veto power over new hires, a closed shop is not possible. **A closed shop is illegal.** Indeed, for a union to bargain for a closed shop violates the NLRA.

Union and Agency Shops. In a union shop, membership in the union becomes compulsory *after* the employee has been hired. Thus management retains an unfettered right to hire whom it pleases, but all new employees who fit into the bargaining unit must affiliate with the union. **A union shop is generally legal.** There are two limitations, however. First, new members need not join the union for 30 days. Second, the new members, after joining the union, can only be required to pay initiation fees and union dues. If the new hire decides he does not want to participate in the union, the union may not compel him to do so, and management may not terminate him (pursuant to a CBA) for his refusal. This is a compromise, designed to protect workers from having to play an active role in a union while ensuring that the union receives normal dues from all employees, whether they participate in union affairs or not. If employees could avoid dues, they would be "free riders," benefiting from the union's bargaining without paying for it.

An **agency shop** is similar to a union shop. Here, the new hire must pay union fees but need not actually join the organization. In both a union shop and an agency shop, the worker may insist on paying only the percentage of dues that is devoted to collective bargaining, contract administration, and grievances. An employee may refuse to pay, for example, the percentage of union dues devoted to organizing other companies.[14]

Some states have passed so-called **right to work** laws, which restrict or even outlaw union shop and agency shop agreements. These statutes typically prohibit a labor organization from demanding that all employees join the union or pay dues.

Hot Cargo Clause. A hot cargo clause would prohibit an employer from doing business with a specified company. A union might like such a clause to put pressure on the *other* company, where the union already has a dispute. But the effort must fail: **hot cargo clauses are illegal.**

---

[14] *Communications Workers of America v. Beck*, 487 U.S. 735, 108 S. Ct. 2641, 1988 U.S. LEXIS 3030 (1988).

Duty to Bargain

Both the union and the employer must bargain in good faith. However, they are *not* obligated to reach an agreement. In the end, this means that the two sides must meet with open minds and make a reasonable effort to reach a contract. Each side must listen to the other's proposals and consider possible compromises.

In the following case, the Supreme Court examined the requirements of bargaining in good faith.

Landmark Case

NLRB v. Truitt Manufacturing Co.

351 U.S. 149
United States Supreme Court, 1956

Facts: A union representing workers at Truitt Manufacturing Company requested a raise of 10 cents per hour for all members. The company offered an additional 2.5 cents per hour and argued that a larger increase would bankrupt the company. The union demanded to examine Truitt's books, and when the company refused, the union complained to the National Labor Relations Board.

The NLRB determined that the company had failed to bargain in good faith and ordered it to allow union representatives to examine its finances. A court of appeals found no unfair labor practice and refused to enforce the Board's order. The Supreme Court granted certiorari.

Issue: ***Did the company refuse to bargain in good faith?***

Excerpts from Justice Black's Decision: We think that in determining whether the obligation of good-faith bargaining has been met, the Board has a right to consider an employer's refusal to give information about its financial status. While Congress did not compel agreement between employers and bargaining representatives, it did require collective bargaining in the hope that agreements would result. [T]he Act admonishes both employers and employees to exert every reasonable effort to make and maintain agreements.

In their effort to reach an agreement here, both the union and the company treated the company's ability to pay increased wages as highly relevant. Claims for increased wages have sometimes been abandoned because of an employer's unsatisfactory business condition; employees have even voted to accept wage decreases because of such conditions.

Good-faith bargaining necessarily requires that claims made by either bargainer should be honest claims. This is true about an asserted inability to pay an increase in wages. If such an argument is important enough to present in the give and take of bargaining, it is important enough to require some sort of proof of its accuracy.

The Board concluded that under the facts and circumstances of this case, the respondent was guilty of an unfair labor practice in failing to bargain in good faith. We see no reason to disturb the findings of the Board.

Reversed.

Sometimes an employer will attempt to make changes without bargaining the issues at all. However, **management may not unilaterally change wages, hours, or terms and conditions of employment without bargaining the issues to impasse**. "Bargaining to impasse" means that both parties must continue to meet and bargain in good faith until it is clear that they cannot reach an agreement. The goal in requiring collective bargaining is to bring the parties together to reach an agreement that brings labor peace. In one case, the union won an election, but before bargaining could begin, management changed the schedule from five 8-hour days to four 10-hour days a week. The company also changed its layoff policy from one of strict seniority to one based on ability and began laying off employees based on alleged poor performance. The court held that each of these acts violated the company's duty to bargain. The employer ultimately might be allowed to make every one of these changes, but first it had to bargain the issues to impasse.[15]

For the same reasons, though the employer may implement new policies after impasse, it may *implement only what it has proposed at the table.* Again, it would defeat the purpose of the NLRA if a company were free to implement a business decision that it had never proposed; the two sides *could not* have discussed plans that were never offered at the table.

EXAM Strategy

Question: The Clerical Workers Union (CWU) represents office workers at General Contracting. International Plumbers Union (IPU) represents plumbers at the same company. Both unions are bargaining new contracts. General Contracting offers the CWU a 2 percent raise, but the union asks for 7 percent. The two sides bargain for five months, but the company never raises its offer. At the same time, General refuses the IPU's demand for an 11 percent raise, stating such a raise would bankrupt the company. General offers the IPU a 3 percent raise. Both unions file ULP charges. What are the outcomes of these cases?

Strategy: What are the two sides obligated to do during bargaining? What are they *not* obligated to do? A company that states it is financially unable to meet a union demand incurs an additional obligation. Make sure you know what that is.

Result: Both sides are obligated to bargain in good faith. However, they are not required to reach agreement. So long as General listened to the CWU demands and responded in good faith, it has done all the NLRA requires. When a company claims financial inability to meet a demand, it must show the union its financial records. If General failed to provide the IPU with such data, it has committed a ULP.

Enforcement

Virtually all collective bargaining agreements provide for their own enforcement, typically through **grievance-arbitration**. Suppose a company transfers an employee from the day shift to the night shift, and the worker believes the contract prohibits such a transfer for any employee with her seniority. The employee complains to the union, which files a grievance, that is, a formal complaint with the company notifying management that the union claims a contract violation. Generally, the CBA establishes some kind of informal hearing, usually conducted by a member of management, at which the employee, represented by the union, may state her case and respond to the company's assertions. The manager has a limited time period—say, seven days—to decide the grievance.

Grievance
A formal complaint alleging a contract violation.

Arbitration
A formal hearing before a neutral party to resolve a contract dispute between a union and a company.

If, after the manager's decision, the employee is still dissatisfied, the union normally has the right to appeal to a more formal hearing, perhaps before a top company executive or committee. If this hearing still fails to satisfy the employee, the union typically may file for arbitration, that is, a formal hearing before a neutral arbitrator. In the arbitration hearing, each side is represented by its lawyer. The arbitrator is required to decide the case based on the CBA. An arbitrator finds either for the employee, and orders the company to take certain corrective action, or for the employer, and dismisses the grievance. A CBA also permits the company to file a grievance. Its complaint normally goes directly to arbitration. In the vast majority of grievances, the arbitrator's decision is final. Courts generally do not examine the

[15] *Adair Standish Corp. v. NLRB*, 912 F.2d 854, 1990 U.S. App. LEXIS 14670 (6th Cir. 1990).

merits of an arbitrator's decision. The idea of all contracts, including CBAs, is to give the parties a chance to control their own destiny. Of course, a rule would hardly be a rule without an exception. A court may refuse to enforce an arbitrator's award that is contrary to public policy. So if an arbitrator's decision encourages either party to violate the law or engage in clearly immoral conduct, a court may nullify the award. The following case demonstrates how reluctant courts are to interfere with an arbitrator's decision.

Brentwood Medical Associates v. United Mine Workers of America

396 F.3d 237
United States Court of Appeals for the Third Circuit, 2005

Facts: Brentwood Medical Associates operated a hospital. The United Mine Workers of America represented one unit of employees, which included Denise Cope, a phlebotomist (someone who draws blood). Exercising her seniority rights, Cope changed jobs to Charge Entry Associate. A year and a half later, BMA announced it was terminating the position. Cope asked to return to her old job. This would have required "bumping" the least-senior phlebotomist out of a job. BMA refused, claiming that bumping was not allowed under the collective bargaining agreement (CBA). Cope filed a grievance, which an arbitrator heard.

The arbitrator ruled in Cope's favor. In his decision, he asked rhetorically why, if the CBA disallowed bumping, did it include the following language:

> ... employees who exercise seniority rights and bump must have the skill to perform all of the work [in the new job].

The problem with the quoted language was that it did not in fact exist anywhere in the CBA. BMA filed suit, asking a federal court to overturn the arbitration decision. The trial court upheld the award and BMA appealed.

Issue: ***Should the arbitration award be affirmed even though the arbitrator relied on language that cannot be found in the CBA?***

Excerpts from Judge Van Antwerpen's Decision: The narrow issue before us is whether the arbitrator's conclusion is supported, in any way, by a rational interpretation of the collective bargaining agreement. We ask merely whether the parties to the collective bargaining agreement got what they bargained for, namely an arbitrator who would first provide an interpretation of the contract that was rationally based on the language of the agreement, and second would produce a rational award. BMA contends that the arbitrator's reference to the language not found in the collective bargaining agreement fatally taints the award, because this reference is essential to the arbitrator's ultimate conclusion and is inseparable from the remainder of the award. As such, our focus must be on whether the arbitrator's discussion can still support the award if we excise the anomalous language.

In additional support for his conclusion, the arbitrator cited several provisions of the agreement. For example, Section 1 defines seniority as "bargaining unit–wide" and not within classification. Section 2 provides that the principle of seniority is a factor in layoffs, recalls, and certain types of promotional opportunities provided the employee is fully qualified. Section 5 specifies that in filling vacancies when the qualifications of two or more applicants are relatively equal, preference will be based on seniority.

After reviewing the totality of the arbitrator's decision, we are confident that his award does not rest solely upon the aberrant language added by the arbitrator. Faced with what he perceived as an incongruity between BMA's position and the bargaining unit–wide seniority rights of employees, the arbitrator attempted to construe together, and then give effect to, all provisions of the agreement. While BMA may take issue with his contractual interpretation, this is not sufficient to justify [overturning] the award.

Full-blown judicial review of the arbitrator's decision would annul the bargain between BMA and UMWA for an arbitrator's construction of their agreement and replace it with a judicial interpretation that was not bargained for. Only where there is manifest disregard for the agreement can we override an arbitrator. Because the remainder of the justification for the award offered by the arbitrator was capable of separation from the aberrant language, his decision reflects an interpretation of the contract that is at least minimally rooted in the collective bargaining agreement, and not his own brand of industrial justice.

For the foregoing reasons, we affirm the decision of the District Court.

Devil's Advocate It is one thing to respect an arbitrator's award and presume it final; it is quite another to rubber-stamp a decision. This arbitrator based his opinion in large part on alleged "CBA language" that in fact came out of thin air. The court blithely suggests that the imaginary language was not of overriding importance—but the *arbitrator* thought so! This is the rare, even bizarre case in which a court should say, "Not good enough. We are taking over."

Concerted Action

Concerted action refers to any tactics union members take in unison to gain some bargaining advantage. It is this power that gives a union strength. **The NLRA guarantees the right of employees to engage in concerted action for mutual aid or protection.**[16] The most common forms of concerted action are strikes and picketing.

Concerted action
Tactics taken by union members to gain bargaining advantage.

Strikes

The NLRA guarantees employees the right to strike, but with some limitations.[17] A union has a guaranteed right to call a strike if the parties are unable to reach a collective bargaining agreement. A union may call a strike to exert economic pressure on management, to protest an unfair labor practice, or to preserve work that the employer is considering sending elsewhere. Note that the right to strike can be waived. Management will generally insist that the CBA include a **no-strike clause**, which prohibits the union from striking while the CBA is in force. A strike is illegal in several other situations as well; here, we mention the most important.

No-strike clause
A clause in a CBA that prohibits the union from striking while the CBA is in force.

Cooling Off Period

Once the union agrees to a CBA, it may not strike to terminate the agreement, or modify it, without giving management 60 days' notice. Suppose a union contract expires July 1. The two sides attempt to bargain a new contract, but progress is slow. The union may strike as an economic weapon, but it must notify management of its intention to do so *and then must wait 60 days*. This cooling off period is designed to give both sides a chance to reassess negotiations and to decide whether some additional compromise would be wiser than enduring a strike.

Statutory Prohibition

Many states have outlawed strikes by public employees. In some states, the prohibition applies to selected employees, such as firefighters or teachers. In other states, all public employees are barred from striking, whether or not they have a contract. The purpose of these statutes is to ensure that unions do not use the public health or welfare as a weapon to secure an unfair bargaining advantage. However, even employees subject to such a rule may find other tactics to press their cause.

[16] NLRA §7.
[17] NLRA §13.

Ethics Jen has worked hard throughout high school, achieving a 3.8 GPA, and now she is ready to apply to some of the best colleges in the country. Her teachers think she is an extraordinary student—yet no one will write her a letter of recommendation.

The teacher's union has been bargaining for a new contract for a year and a half. The teachers seek a 4 percent raise; the school board has offered 1 percent. There will be no strike—state law prohibits that—but the teachers have decided they will "work to rule," meaning that they will do only what their (expired) contract requires: teach classes, issue grades, and so forth.

"This stinks," wails Jen. "I've never asked for extra assistance. I've tried to be helpful in class, and a lot of times, I've tutored other kids. This is the one time in my life I really need my teachers to be there for me, and they're turning their backs."

"My heart goes out to Jen," responds her American history teacher, "but our problem is simple: as long as we quietly ask for decent pay, no one listens. Students and parents notice us only when they suffer inconvenience."

"This is an outrage!" shouts Jen's father. "These so-called teachers have no right to hurt my child over their pay disputes. If they were serious about their profession, they would do everything they could to help the children who are entrusted to them."

"If the parents were serious about education," the history teacher retorts, "or truly concerned about their children's welfare, they would demand that the town pay respectable salaries. They prefer lower taxes so they can spend more on fancy cars."

Who is right? Is the teachers' refusal to perform any "extras" a reasonable tactic?

Violent Strikes

The NLRA prohibits violent strikes. Violence does sometimes occur on the picket line when union members attempt to prevent other workers from entering the job site. Or a union may stage a **sit-down strike**, in which members stop working but remain at their job posts, physically blocking replacement workers from taking their places. Any such action is illegal.

Partial Strikes

A partial strike occurs when employees stop working temporarily, then resume, then stop again, and so forth. This tactic is particularly disruptive because management cannot bring in replacement workers. A union may either walk off the job or stay on it, but it may not alternate.

Replacement Workers

When employees go on strike, management generally wants to replace them to keep the company operating. When replacement workers begin to cross a union picket line, tempers are certain to explode, and entire communities may feel the repercussions. Are replacement workers legal? Yes. **Management has the right to hire replacement workers during a strike.** May the employer offer the replacement workers *permanent* jobs, or must the company give union members their jobs back when the strike is over? It depends on the type of strike.

After an *economic strike,* an employer may not discriminate against a striker, but the employer is *not* obligated to lay off a replacement worker to give a striker his job back. An economic strike is one intended to gain wages or benefits. When a union bargains for a pay raise but fails to get it and walks off the job, that is an economic strike. During such a strike, an employer may hire permanent replacement workers. When the strike is over, the company has no obligation to lay off the replacement workers to make room for the strikers. However, if the company does hire more workers, it may not discriminate against the strikers.

After a *unfair labor practices strike,* a union member is entitled to her job back, even if that means the employer must lay off a replacement worker. Suppose management refuses to bargain in good faith, by claiming poverty without producing records to substantiate its claim. The union strikes. Management's refusal to bargain was an unfair labor practice, and the strike is a ULP strike. When it ends, the striking workers must get their jobs back. The following case raises the pivotal distinction concerning a strike: was this one sparked by a ULP—or by money?

Citizens Publishing and Printing Company v. National Labor Relations Board

263 F.3d 224
United States Court of Appeals for the Third Circuit, 2001

Facts: Citizens Publishing was a family-owned corporation that published the *Ellwood City Ledger* and another local newspaper. Bud Dimeo had been the company's sole photographer for over 35 years. When the needs for daytime photography declined, Citizens began requiring Dimeo to work at night and on weekends as well. Citizens also occasionally employed stringers, meaning freelance photographers who were paid per photo.

Teamsters Local No. 261 was certified as the representative for certain Citizens' employees, including photographers but excluding stringers. While the company and union were negotiating a contract, Dimeo retired, and Citizens assigned most of the night/weekend photography to stringers. The union filed a ULP charge with the NLRB, claiming that Citizens had unilaterally changed the terms and conditions of employment without bargaining, by giving to stringers work previously done by Dimeo, a bargaining unit member.

On July 23, fully 18 months after contract negotiations had started, the union met with employees and informed them that the NLRB intended to issue a complaint based on Citizens' use of stringers. The members voted to strike, and they walked out on July 24. The paper continued to publish, using family members, supervisors, and nonstriking employees. The following February, six months into the strike, Citizens reassured the union that that none of the replacement workers were considered permanent; the strikers could return if they wished.

The parties met to bargain on March 14. The union representative indicated the union was prepared to return to work. Company representatives took a break to caucus; when they returned, they informed the union that all replacements were permanent. In other words, the strikers had lost their jobs. The next day, Citizens informed the replacement workers that they were permanent. The NLRB found that the union's job action was a ULP strike and ordered Citizens to offer the union members their jobs back. Citizens appealed.

Issue: ***Was the job action a ULP strike?***

Excerpts from Judge Fuentes's Decision: An employer violates § 8(a)(5) if, without bargaining to impasse, it effects a unilateral change of an existing term or condition of employment. By unilaterally changing the employees' terms and conditions of employment, an employer minimizes the influence of organized bargaining and emphasizes to the employees that there is no necessity for a collective bargaining agent.

Here, substantial evidence supports the Board's finding that Citizens Publishing's night/weekend work became an integral part of the regular full-time photographer's work, and thus, became bargaining unit work. When Citizens Publishing assigned the night/weekend work to Dimeo, that work became a necessary and integral part of the full-time photographer's position. Additionally, Dimeo did not receive any additional remuneration for his night/weekend work. Thus, at the time of the Union's certification, the status quo included a full-time photographer's position with night/weekend work. Accordingly, substantial evidence supports the determination that Citizens Publishing violated the Act when it unilaterally subcontracted the bargaining unit work during the negotiations over the initial collective-bargaining agreement.

We next address whether the strike was an "unfair labor practice strike," as opposed to a mere economic strike. Unfair labor practice strikers are entitled to immediate reinstatement upon their unconditional offers to return to work; any replacements hired during the strike must be dismissed, if necessary, to effect reinstatement of the strikers.

Here, substantial evidence supports the Board's finding that the strike was an unfair labor practice strike. The Union convened a meeting of bargaining unit members on the day before the strike began. After learning of Citizens Publishing's action, numerous employees indicated their desire to go on strike, and the membership held a strike vote. These facts support the Board's finding that its decision to issue a complaint galvanized the bargaining unit members' belief that an unfair labor practice had been committed and served as the flashpoint for discussion about calling a strike.

Moreover, even if Citizens Publishing's subcontracting of night/weekend work did not constitute an unfair labor practice, its discharge of the striking employees on March 14 converted the strike into an unfair labor practice strike because it prolonged the strike. Citizens Publishing's false declaration that it had permanently replaced the strikers prolonged the strike by thwarting the Union's attempt to make an unconditional offer to return to work that day. Indeed, the Union informed Citizens Publishing at the March 14 bargaining session of its intent to make an unconditional offer to return to work. Before the Union could make its offer, however, Citizens Publishing preemptively notified the Union that it had permanently replaced the strikers, thereby effectively informing the Union that any unconditional offer to return to work would be futile.

We will enforce the Board's order in its entirety.

© AP Photo/Damian Dovarganes

Picketing the employer's workplace in support of a strike is generally lawful.

The workers have bargained with management for weeks, and discussions have turned belligerent.... as 150 employees arrive for work, they are amazed to find the company's gate locked and armed guards standing on the other side.

Picketing

Picketing the employer's workplace in support of a strike is generally lawful. Striking workers are permitted to establish picket lines at the employer's job site and to urge all others—employees, replacement workers, and customers—not to cross the line. But the picketers are not permitted to use physical force to *prevent* anyone from crossing the line. The NLRA does not authorize or protect violence on the picket line. The company may terminate violent picketers and permanently replace them, regardless of the nature of the strike.

Secondary boycotts are generally illegal. A secondary boycott is a picket line established not at the employer's premises, but at the workplace of a *different* company that does business with the union's employer. Such a boycott is designed to put pressure on the union's employer by forcing other companies to stop doing business with it. Suppose Union is on strike against Truck Co. Union is free to picket Truck Co.'s office or terminal. If Truck Co. hires replacement workers, the trucks will be back on the road, making deliveries. Now Union wants to put additional pressure on Truck Co., so it sets up picket lines at a *supermarket* where Truck Co. delivers. Union attempts to persuade customers not to shop at the store and other workers, including delivery drivers, not to enter the premises. If allowed, the picketing might result in the supermarket demanding that Truck Co. compromise with Union. But this is a secondary boycott, so it is illegal. Truck Co. and the supermarket will obtain an injunction prohibiting the secondary boycott. See Exhibit 30.1.

Lockouts

The workers have bargained with management for weeks, and discussions have turned belligerent. It is 6:00 a.m., the start of another day at the factory. But as 150 employees arrive for work, they are amazed to find the company's gate locked and armed guards standing on the other side. What is this? A lockout.

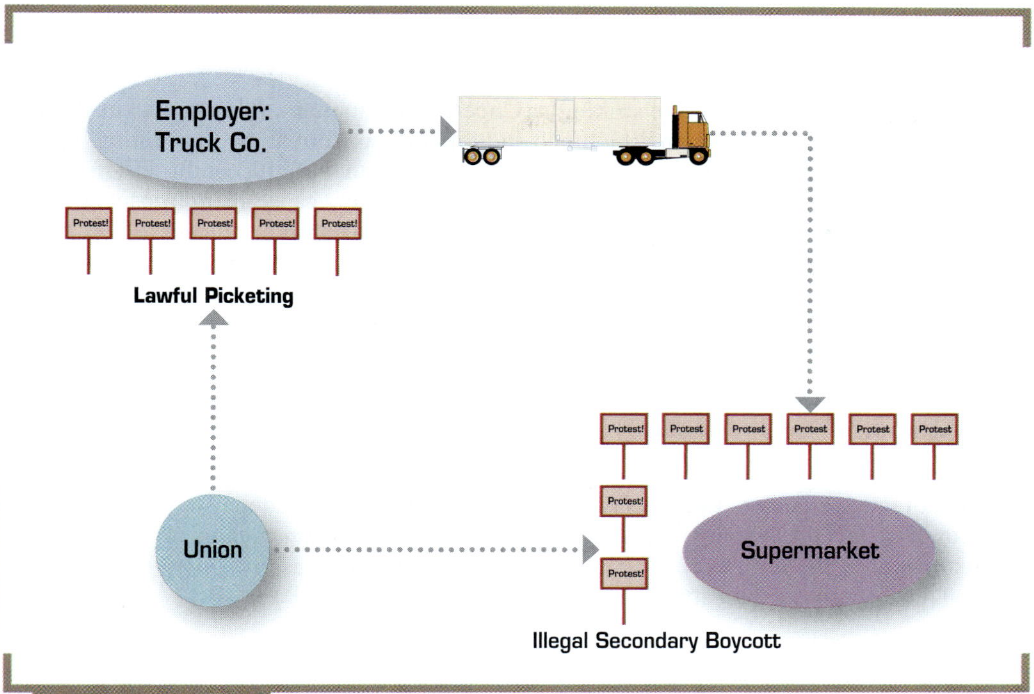

EXHIBIT 30.1 A union striking against Truck Co. may lawfully picket the employer, using peaceful means to urge all others to stay away. But if the union attempts to put indirect pressure on Truck Co. by picketing one of the company's customers, it is engaging in an illegal secondary boycott.

The power of a union comes ultimately from its potential to strike. But management, too, has weapons. In a lockout, management prohibits workers from entering the premises, denying the employees work and a chance to earn a paycheck. Most, but not all, lockouts are legal.

A defensive lockout is almost always legal. It is one way management can respond to union pressure such as a sit-down strike or a **whipsaw strike,** which may occur when a union is simultaneously bargaining with various employers. Suppose a machinists' union is simultaneously bargaining a contract with three engine manufacturers, attempting to obtain an identical contract from all of the companies. To pressure the companies, the union might choose to strike against only *one* of the manufacturers. This is a whipsaw strike, and it can be very effective because the struck company, losing money while the others profit, will push strongly for a compromise. But management of all three companies may respond by locking out the workers from *all* factories, even those where no strike is under way. That is a defensive lockout, and it is legal.

An offensive lockout is legal if the parties have reached a bargaining impasse. Management, bargaining a new CBA with a union, may wish to use a lockout to advance its position. It is allowed to do so *provided the parties have reached an impasse.* If there is no impasse, a lockout will *probably* be illegal. Most courts consider that a lockout before impasse indicates hostility to the union. That kind of general antagonism to a union is illegal because the NLRA guarantees employees the right to organize. In addition, management usually *must notify the union before locking it out.* Again, the purpose of the NLRA is to bring the parties together through bargaining. A lockout is a legitimate method to pressure a union into compromise, but it can have that effect only if the union is warned and given a chance to bargain.

EXAM Strategy

Question: Union workers are striking at Cheesey, a restaurant, forming picket lines in front of the restaurant during the lunch and dinner hours but at no other times. The union members chant slogans denouncing their wages and working conditions, urging diners not to enter. There is no violence, but the picketers cause many prospective customers to stay away, and Cheesey suffers a substantial drop in business. The restaurant files a charge with the NLRB, claiming that the union has committed a ULP by (1) deliberately harming its business and (2) engaging in a secondary boycott. Who will win?

Strategy: Striking workers are allowed to picket. May they *urge* non-union members to stay out of the business? May they *prohibit* others from entering? Secondary boycotts are illegal. Is this one?

Result: Striking workers may urge the public not to cross the picket line. The union may not use violence to keep people out, but this union has not done so. This is not a secondary boycott, which is a picket line established at a *different* company that does business with the employer. The company's loss of business is one possible—and legal—consequence of a strike. The union has not committed a ULP.

Chapter Conclusion

Workers first attempted to organize unions in this country about 200 years ago in response to appalling working conditions. These conditions are generally much better today, and contemporary clashes between union and management are less likely to stem from sweltering temperatures in a mine than from a management decision to subcontract work. But although the flash points have changed, labor law is still dominated by issues of organizing, collective bargaining, and concerted action.

Exam Review

1. **RIGHT TO ORGANIZE** Section 7 of the National Labor Relations Act (NLRA) guarantees employees the right to organize and join unions, bargain collectively, and engage in other concerted activities. (pp. 735–736)

2. **INTERFERENCE WITH ORGANIZING** Section 8(a) of the NLRA makes it an unfair labor practice for an employer to interfere with union organizing, discriminate against a union member, or refuse to bargain collectively. (p. 736)

3. **DISCRIMINATION** Section 8(b) of the NLRA makes it an unfair labor practice for a union to interfere with employees who are exercising their rights under §7, to encourage an employer to discriminate against an employee because of a labor dispute, to refuse to bargain collectively, or to engage in an illegal strike or boycott. (p. 738)

4. **EXCLUSIVITY** Section 9 of the NLRA makes a validly recognized union the *exclusive* representative of the employees. Along with exclusivity comes a duty of fair representation, which requires that a union treat all members fairly, impartially, and in good faith. (pp. 738–739)

Question: Douglas Kuroda worked for the Hertz Corp. He and his supervisor had a heated argument in which Kuroda told his boss, "You may have a master's degree, but you don't know s***." The supervisor instructed Kuroda to punch out for the day, but Kuroda refused to leave until security officers escorted him off the premises. Hertz fired him, and Kuroda filed a grievance. The union represented Kuroda at an arbitration hearing. During the hearing, the union made no objection to certain evidence that the company offered to demonstrate why it fired Kuroda. The arbitrator ruled in favor of the company. Kuroda sued his union. What kind of claim is he making against the union? Is he likely to win his claim?

Strategy: The duty of fair representation requires that a union represent all members fairly, impartially, and in good faith. (See the "Result" at the end of this section.)

5. **EMPLOYER OPPOSITION** During a union organizing campaign, an employer may vigorously present anti-union views to its employees, but it may not use threats or promises of benefits to defeat the union effort. (pp. 741–742)

Question: Power, Inc., which operated a coal mine, suffered financial losses and had to lay off employees. The United Mine Workers of America (UMWA) began an organizing drive. Power's general manager warned miners that if the company was unionized, it would be shut down. An office manager told one of the miners that the company would get rid of union supporters. Shortly before the election was to take place, Power laid off 13 employees, all of whom had signed union cards. A low-seniority employee who had not signed a union card was not laid off. The union claimed that Power had committed ULPs. Comment.

Strategy: Section 7 of the NLRA guarantees employees the right to organize. An employer may vigorously advocate against a union organizing campaign. However, Section 8 (a) makes it a ULP to interfere with union organizing or discriminate against a union member. (See the "Result" at the end of this section.)

6. **CERTIFICATION** The NLRB will certify a proposed bargaining unit only if the employees share a community of interest. (p. 743)

7. **BARGAINING** The employer and the union *must* bargain over wages, hours, and other terms and conditions of employment. They *may* bargain other subjects, but neither side may insist on doing so. (pp. 744–749)

8. GOOD FAITH The union and the employer must bargain in good faith, but they are not obligated to reach an agreement. Management may not unilaterally change wages, hours, or terms and conditions of employment without bargaining to impasse. (p. 746)

EXAM Strategy

Question: Concrete Company was bargaining a CBA with the drivers' union. Negotiations went on for many months. Concrete made its final offer of $9.50 per hour, with step increases of $0.75 per hour in a year, and the same the following two years. The union refused to accept the offer and the two sides reached an impasse. Concrete then implemented its plan, minus the step increases. Was its implementation legal?

Strategy: Management may unilaterally change wages and so forth only if the parties have reached an impasse. At all stages, the two sides must bargain in good faith. The goal of the NLRA is to achieve labor peace through productive negotiations. (See the "Result" at the end of this section.)

9. STRIKES The NLRA guarantees employees the right to strike, with some limitations. (pp. 749–753)

10. ECONOMIC STRIKES After an *economic* strike, an employer is not obligated to lay off replacement workers to give a striker her job back, but it may not discriminate against a striker. After a *ULP* strike, the striking worker must get her job back. (p. 750)

11. PICKETING Picketing the employer's workplace in support of a strike is generally lawful; a secondary boycott is generally illegal. (p. 752)

12. LOCKOUTS An employer may lock out workers, but only after giving them notice. (pp. 752–754)

13. MULTI-EMPLOYER BARGAINING Multi-employer bargaining and implementation do not violate antitrust laws. (p. 753)

4. Result: Kuroda is claiming that the union violated its duty of fair representation. A union violates this duty if its actions are arbitrary or discriminatory. However, courts give unions wide latitude in deciding how to represent members. The union lawyer made a reasonable tactical determination about the evidence. Even if other lawyers might have been more aggressive, this is not evidence of discrimination or bad faith. Kuroda lost.

5. Result: Each of the acts described was a ULP. Threatening layoffs or company closure are classic examples of ULPs. Laying off those who had signed union cards but not those who refused was clear discrimination. The NLRB found the violations so extreme it certified the union and issued an order to bargain.

8. Result: The implementation was illegal. Because the parties had reached an impasse, the company was entitled to implement the last proposal it had made at the bargaining table. But it did not do so. By implementing a reduced plan that it had never proposed, management showed bad faith. To allow the company to implement something that it had never offered would defeat the whole purpose of bargaining.

Multiple-Choice Questions

1. Which of the following statutes prohibits federal court injunctions in nonviolent labor disputes?

(a) The Norris-LaGuardia Act

(b) The National Labor Relations Act

(c) The Labor-Management Relations Act

(d) The Labor-Management Reporting and Disclosure Act

2. Which of the following statutes defines unfair labor practices and ensures workers' right to form a union?

(a) The Norris-LaGuardia Act

(b) The National Labor Relations Act

(c) The Labor-Management Relations Act

(d) The Labor-Management Reporting and Disclosure Act

3. Which of the following type(s) of worker will usually be excluded from a bargaining unit?

(a) Managerial employees

(b) Confidential employees

(c) Both A and B

(d) None of the above

4. When an employer is forced to hire only union members, a ____________ shop exists. This kind of arrangement ____________ legal under the NLRA.

(a) closed; is

(b) closed; is not

(c) union; is

(d) union; is not

5. Alpha Company's workers walk out on strike. The company hires replacement workers so that it can continue to operate its business. When the strike ends, Alpha must rehire the original workers if the strike was over ____________.

(a) wages

(b) an unfair labor practice

(c) Both A and B

(d) None of the above

Essay Questions

1. Triec, Inc., is a small electrical contracting company in Springfield, Ohio, owned by its executives, Yeazell, Jones, and Heaton. Employees contacted the International Brotherhood of Electrical Workers, which began an organizing drive. Six of the

11 employees in the bargaining unit signed authorization cards. The company declined to recognize the union, which petitioned the NLRB to schedule an election. The company then granted several new benefits for all workers, including higher wages, paid vacations, and other measures. When the election was held, only 2 of the 11 bargaining unit members voted for the union. Did the company violate the NLRA?

2. Q-1 Motor Express was an interstate trucking company. When a union attempted to organize Q-1's drivers, it met heavy resistance. A supervisor told one driver that if he knew what was good for him, he would stay away from the union organizer. The company president told another employee that he had the right to fire everybody, close the company, and then rehire new drivers after 72 hours. He made numerous other threats to workers and their families. Based on the extreme nature of the company's opposition, what exceptional remedy did the union seek before the NLRB?

3. Gibson Greetings, Inc., had a plant in Berea, Kentucky, where the workers belonged to the International Brotherhood of Firemen & Oilers. The old CBA expired, and the parties negotiated a new one but were unable to reach an agreement on economic issues. The union struck. At the next bargaining session, the company claimed that the strike violated the *old* CBA, which had a no-strike clause and which stated that the terms of the old CBA would continue in force as long as the parties were bargaining a *new* CBA. The company refused to bargain until the union at least agreed that by bargaining, the company was not giving up its claim of an illegal strike. The two sides returned to bargaining, but meanwhile the company hired replacement workers. Eventually, the striking workers offered to return to work, but Gibson refused to rehire many of them. In court, the union claimed that the company had committed a ULP by (1) insisting the strike was illegal and (2) refusing to bargain until the union acknowledged the company's position. Why is it very important to the union to establish the company's act as a ULP? *Was* it a ULP?

4. Eads Transfer, Inc., was a moving and storage company with a small workforce represented by the General Teamsters, Chauffeurs, and Helpers Union. When the CBA expired, the parties failed to reach agreement on a new one, and the union struck. As negotiations continued, Eads hired temporary replacement workers. After 10 months of the strike, some union workers offered to return to work, but Eads made no response to the offer. Two months later, more workers offered to return to work, but Eads would not accept any of the offers. Eventually, Eads notified all workers that they would not be allowed back to work until a new CBA had been signed. The union filed ULP claims against the company. Please rule.

5. Olivetti Office U.S.A., Inc., was located in Newington, Connecticut, and its workers were represented by the United Automobile, Aerospace, and Agriculture Implement Workers of America. The company's president reported to the union that Olivetti was losing money. He insisted that unless the union renegotiated certain wage increases in the current CBA, Olivetti would subcontract work to cheaper parts of the country to save money. The union requested to bargain over the proposed subcontracting, and Olivetti agreed. But when the sides met, the company would not permit the union to see the financial data that supported its arguments. After several meetings, the company declared an impasse, implemented its subcontracting proposal, and laid off workers in Connecticut. The union claimed this was a ULP. Was it?

Discussion Questions

1. Once a union is recognized, it acts as the exclusive representative for all workers in a bargaining unit, even if some of them do not want the union to represent them. Is this reasonable? Should individual employees be able to "opt out," or would it be unfair for workers to get all the benefit of the union without having to pay dues?

2. Union workers earn an average of $200 per week more than non-union workers. Many people believe that unions are an essential part of creating a broad middle class, while others argue that they create undeserved windfalls for members. Do you have a favorable or unfavorable view of unions?

3. Union membership has fallen steadily in recent decades, in part because many unionized manufacturing jobs have been shipped overseas. Do you believe that unions will make a comeback in new industries? Would you prefer to be a member of a union if you had a choice? Why or why not?

4. Weigh in on the "card check" controversy. Imagine a company with 100 workers. After union organizers talk to the employees, 55 of them sign an authorization card. Should that be enough to establish the union, or should the employees also have to vote in a secret ballot before the union is designated as the employees' representative?

5. Strikes and lockouts frequently make the news, especially when a professional sports league is involved. Pro athletes tend to be highly compensated. Does that fact change your opinions about labor disputes? In the recent NFL lockout, did you side with the players or the owners?

UNIT 6

erstock.com

Business Organizations

CHAPTER 31

STARTING A BUSINESS: LLCS AND OTHER OPTIONS

© Evan Meyer/Shutterstock.com

Poor Jeffrey Horning. If only he had understood business law. Horning owned a thriving construction company which operated as a corporation—Horning Construction Company, Inc. To lighten his crushing workload, he decided to bring in two partners to handle more day-to-day responsibility. It seemed a good idea at the time.

Horning transferred the business to Horning Construction, LLC and then gave one-third ownership each to two trusted employees, Klimowski and Holdsworth. But Horning did not pay enough attention to the legal formalities—the new LLC had no operating agreement.

Jeffrey Horning was stuck in purgatory, with two business partners he loathed and no way out.

Nothing worked out as he had planned. The two men did not take on extra work. Horning's relationship with them went from bad to worse, with the parties bickering over every petty detail and each man trying to sabotage the others. It got to the point that Klimowski sent Horning a letter full of foul language. At his wit's end, Horning proposed that the LLC buy out his share of the business. Klimowski and Holdsworth refused. Really frustrated, Horning asked a court to dissolve the business on the grounds that Klimowski despised him, Holdsworth resented him, and neither of them trusted him. In his view, it was their goal "to make my remaining time with Horning, LLC so unbearable that I will relent and give them for a pittance the remainder of the company for which they have paid nothing to date."

Although the court was sympathetic, it refused to help. Because Horning, LLC did not have an operating agreement that provided for a buyout, it had to depend upon the LLC statute, which only permitted dissolution "whenever it is not reasonably practicable to carry on the business." Unfortunately, Horning, LLC was very successful, grossing over $25 million annually. Jeffrey Horning was stuck in purgatory, with two business partners he loathed and no way out.[1]

Every business, no matter how large, was at one point little more than a gleam in an entrepreneur's eye. The goal of the law is to balance the rights, duties, and liabilities of entrepreneurs, managers, investors, and customers. Time and again in these next chapters, we will see that legal issues can have as profound an impact on the success of a company as any business decision. The law affects virtually every aspect of business. Wise (and successful) entrepreneurs know how to use the law to their advantage. Think of the grief Jeffrey Horning could have saved himself if he had understood the implications of the LLC statute.

To begin, entrepreneurs must select a form of organization. The correct choice can reduce taxes, liability, and conflict while facilitating outside investment. If entrepreneurs do not make a choice for themselves, the law will automatically select a (potentially undesirable) default option.

Sole Proprietorships

Sole proprietorship
An unincorporated business owned by one person.

Sole proprietorships are the most common form of business, so we begin there. A **sole proprietorship** is an unincorporated business owned by one person. For example, Linda runs ExSciTe (which stands for Excellence in Science Teaching), a company that helps teachers prepare hands-on science experiments in the classroom using such basic items as vinegar, lemon juice, and red cabbage.

If an individual runs a business without taking any formal steps to create an organization, she automatically has a sole proprietorship. It is, if you will, the default option. She is not required to hire a lawyer or register with the government. The company is not even required to file a separate tax return—because the business is a *flow-through* tax entity. In other words, Linda must pay *personal* income tax on the profits, but the *business* itself does not pay income taxes. A very few states, and some cities and towns, require sole proprietors to obtain a business license. And states generally require sole proprietors to register their business name if it is different from their own. Linda, for example, would file a "d/b/a" or "doing business as" certificate for ExSciTe.

Sole proprietorships also have some serious disadvantages. First, the owner of the business is responsible for all of the business's debts. If ExSciTe cannot pay its suppliers or if a student is injured by an exploding cabbage, Linda is *personally* liable. She may have to sell her house and car to pay the debt. Second, the owner of a sole proprietorship has limited options for financing her business. Debt is generally her only source of working capital because she has no stock or memberships to sell. If someone else brings in capital and helps with the management of the business, then it is a partnership, not a sole proprietorship. For this reason, sole proprietorships work best for small businesses without large capital needs.

[1] *In the Matter of Jeffrey M. Horning*, 816 N.Y.S.2d 877; 2006 N.Y. Misc. LEXIS 555.

Corporations

Corporations are the dominant form of organization for a simple reason—they have been around for a long time and, as a result, they are numerous and the law that regulates them is well developed.

The concept of a corporation is very old indeed—it began with the Greeks and spread from them through the Romans into English law. At the beginning, however, corporations were viewed with deep suspicion. A British jurist commented that they had "neither bodies to be punished nor souls to be condemned." And what were shareholders doing that they needed limited liability? Why did they have to cower behind a corporate shield? For this reason, shareholders originally had to obtain special permission to form a corporation. In England, corporations could be created only by special charter from the monarch or, later, from Parliament. But with the advent of the Industrial Revolution, large-scale manufacturing enterprises needed huge amounts of capital from investors who were not involved in management and did not want to be personally liable for the debts of an organization that they were not managing. In 1811, New York became the first jurisdiction in the United States to permit routine incorporation.[2]

Despite the initial suspicion with which corporations were viewed, economists now suggest that this form of organization, combined with technological advances such as double-entry bookkeeping and stockmarkets, provided the West with an enormous economic advantage. In particular, corporations permitted the investment of outside capital and were more likely than partnerships to survive the death of their founders. In short, corporations permitted the development of large, enduring businesses.

Corporations in General

As is the case for all forms of organization, corporations have their advantages and disadvantages.

Limited Liability

If a business flops and cannot pay its bills, shareholders lose their investment in the company but not their other assets. Likewise, if an employee is in an accident while driving a company van, the business is liable for any harm to the other driver, but its shareholders are not personally liable. Be aware, however, that limited liability does not protect against all debts. Individuals are always responsible for their *own* acts. Suppose that the careless employee who caused the accident was also a company shareholder. Both he and the company would be liable. If the company did not pay the judgment, the employee would have to, from his personal assets. **A corporation protects managers and investors from personal liability for the debts of the corporation and the actions of others, but not against liability for their *own* negligence (or other torts and crimes).**

Transferability of Interests

Corporations provide flexibility for enterprises small (with one owner) and large (with thousands of shareholders). As we will see, partnership interests are not transferable without the permission of the other partners, whereas corporate stock can be bought and sold easily.

Duration

When a sole proprietor dies, legally so does the business. But corporations have perpetual existence: they can continue without their founders.

---

[2]An Act Relative to Incorporation for Manufacturing Purpose, 1811 N.Y. Laws, ch. 67, §111.

Logistics

Corporations require substantial expense and effort to create and operate. The cost of establishing a corporation includes legal and filing fees, not to mention the cost of the annual filings that states require. Corporations must also hold meetings for both shareholders and directors. Minutes of these meetings must be kept indefinitely in the company minute book.

Taxes

Because corporations are taxable entities, they must pay taxes and file returns. This is a simple sentence that requires a complex explanation. Originally, there were only three ways to do business: as a sole proprietorship, a partnership, or a corporation. The sole proprietor pays taxes on all the business's profits. A partnership is not, as we say, a taxable entity, which means it does not pay taxes itself. All income and losses are passed through to the partners and reported on their personal income tax returns. Corporations, by contrast, are taxable entities and pay income tax on their profits. Shareholders must then pay tax on dividends from the corporation. Thus a dollar is taxed only once before it ends up in a partner's bank account, but twice before it is deposited by a shareholder.

Exhibit 31.1 compares the single taxation of partnerships with the double taxation of corporations. Suppose, as shown in the exhibit, that a corporation and a partnership each receives $10,000 in additional income. The corporation pays tax at a top rate of 35 percent.[3]

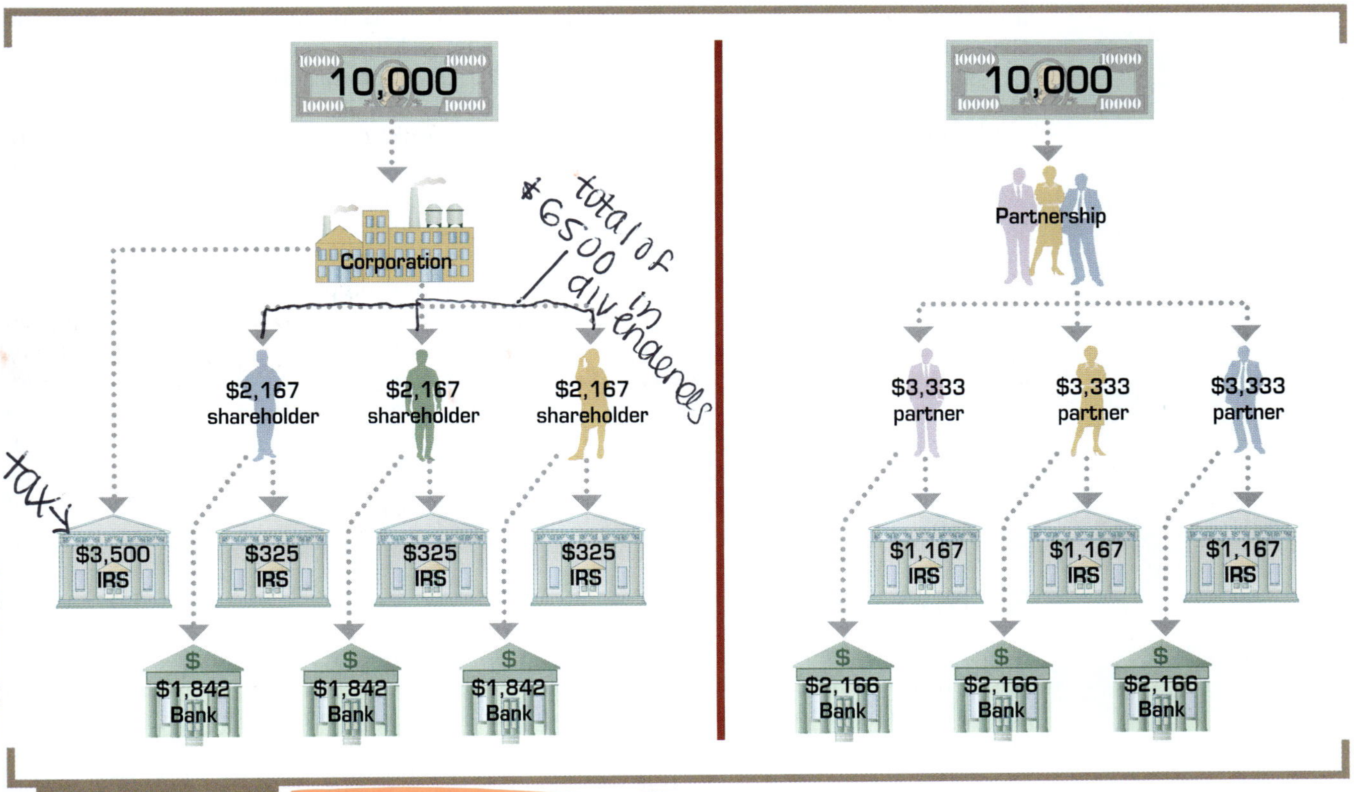

EXHIBIT 31.1 Partners pay lower taxes than shareholders.

---

[3]This is the federal tax rate; most states also levy a corporate tax.

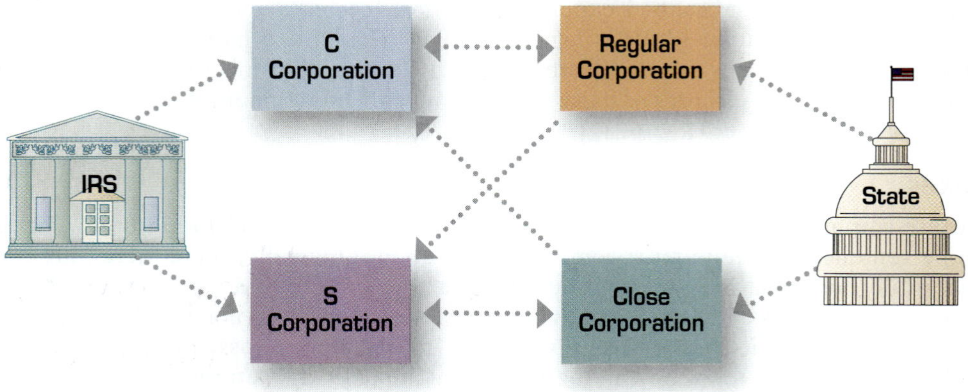

EXHIBIT 31.2 Both a regular and a close corporation can be either a C or an S corporation.

Thus the corporation pays $3,500 of the $10,000 in tax. The corporation pays out the remaining $6,500 as a dividend of $2,167 to each of its three shareholders. Then the shareholders are taxed at the special dividend rate of 15 percent, which means they each pay a tax of $325. They are each left with $1,842. Of the initial $10,000, almost 45 percent ($4,475) has gone to the Internal Revenue Service (IRS).

Compare the corporation to a partnership. The partnership itself pays no taxes, so it can pass on $3,333 to each of its partners. At a 35 percent individual rate, each partner pays an income tax of $1,167. As partners, they pocket $2,166, which is $324 more than they could keep as shareholders. Of the partnership's initial $10,000, 35 percent ($3,501) has gone to the IRS, compared with the corporation's 45 percent.

One further tax issue. Corporations are created and regulated by state law but must pay both federal and state taxes. Federal law gives favorable tax treatment to some small corporations, which it calls "S corporations." Many states also treat small corporations differently but calls them "close corporations." Federal tax law and state corporation statutes are completely independent. Thus, an organization could be a close corporation under state law and not qualify as an S corporation or, conversely, could be an S corporation under federal law but may or may not be a close corporation for state purposes. Exhibit 31.2 illustrates the difference between state corporate law and federal taxation of corporations.

S Corporations

Although entrepreneurs are often optimistic about the likely success of their new enterprise, in truth, the majority of new businesses lose money in their early years. Congress created S corporations (aka "S corps") to encourage entrepreneurship by offering tax breaks. The name "S corporation" comes from the provision of the Internal Revenue Code that created this form of organization.[4] **Shareholders of S corps have both the limited**

[4]26 U.S.C. §1361.

liability of a corporation and the tax status of a partnership. Like a partnership, an S corp is not a taxable entity—all the company's profits and losses pass through to the shareholders, who pay tax at their individual rates. It avoids the double taxation of a regular corporation (called a "C corporation"). If, as is often the case, the startup loses money, investors can deduct these losses against their other income.

S corps do face some major restrictions:

- There can be only one class of stock (although voting rights can vary within the class).
- There can be no more than 100 shareholders.
- Shareholders must be individuals, estates, charities, pension funds, or trusts, not partnerships or corporations.
- Shareholders must be citizens or residents of the United States, not nonresident aliens.
- All shareholders must agree that the company should be an S corporation.

Although *most* states follow the federal lead on S corporations, a small number require these companies to pay state corporate tax.

Close Corporations

Close corporation
A company whose stock is not publicly traded. Also known as a *closely held corporation*.

Originally, the terms ***close corporation*** and ***closely held corporation*** referred simply to a company whose stock was not publicly traded (in other words, a "privately held" company). Most close corporations are small, although some privately held corporations, such as Hallmark Cards, Inc., and Mars, Inc. (maker of Mars candy bars), are huge. Beginning in New York in 1948, some states amended their corporation statutes to make special provisions for entrepreneurs. In some cases, a corporation must affirmatively elect to be treated as a close corporation; in others, any corporation can take advantage of these special provisions. Now when lawyers refer to "close corporations," they usually mean not merely a privately held company, but one that has taken advantage of the close corporation provisions of its state code.

Although the provisions of close corporation statutes vary from state to state, they tend to have certain common themes:

- **Protection of minority shareholders.** As there is no public market for the stock of a close corporation, a minority shareholder who is being mistreated by the majority cannot simply sell his shares and depart. Therefore, close corporation statutes often provide some protection for minority shareholders. For example, the charter of a close corporation could require a unanimous vote of all shareholders to choose officers, set salaries, or pay dividends. It could grant each shareholder veto power over all important corporate decisions.
- **Transfer restrictions.** The shareholders of a close corporation often need to work closely together in the management of the company. Therefore, statutes typically permit the corporation to require that a shareholder first offer shares to the other owners before selling them to an outsider. In that way, the remaining shareholders have some control over who their new co-owners will be.
- **Flexibility.** Close corporations can typically operate without a board of directors, a formal set of bylaws, or annual shareholder meetings.
- **Dispute resolution.** The shareholders are allowed to agree in advance that any one of them can dissolve the corporation if some particular event occurs or, if they choose, for any reason at all. If the shareholders are in a stalemate, the problem

can be solved by dissolving the corporation. Even without such an agreement, a shareholder can ask a court to dissolve a close corporation if the other owners behave "oppressively" or "unfairly."

EXAM Strategy

Question: Consider these two entrepreneurs: Judith formed a corporation to publish a newsletter that will not generate substantial revenues. Drexel operated his construction and remodeling business as a sole proprietorship. Were these forms of organization right for these businesses?

Strategy: Prepare a list of the advantages and disadvantages of each form of organization. Sole proprietorships are best for businesses without substantial capital needs. Corporations can raise capital but are expensive to operate.

Result: Judith would be better off with a sole proprietorship—her revenues will not support the expenses of a corporation. Also, her debts are likely to be small, so she will not need the limited liability of a corporation. And no matter what her form of organization, she would be personally liable for any negligent acts she commits, so a corporation would not provide any additional protection. But for Drexel, a sole proprietorship could be disastrous because his construction company will have substantial expenses and a large number of employees. If an employee causes an injury, Drexel might be personally liable. And if his business fails, the court would liquidate his personal assets. He would be better off with a form of organization that limits his liability, such as a corporation or a limited liability company.

Limited Liability Companies

An LLC offers the limited liability of a corporation and the tax status of a partnership.

Limited liability companies (LLCs) are a relatively new form of organization. Wyoming passed the first LLC statute in 1977, but most states did not follow suit until after 1991. An LLC is an extremely useful form of organization increasingly favored by entrepreneurs. It is not, however, as simple as it perhaps should be. Owing to a complex history that involves painful interaction between IRS regulations and state laws (the details of which we will spare you), the specific provisions of state laws vary greatly. An effort to remedy this confusion—the Uniform Limited Liability Company Act—has not at this point been widely accepted. Indeed, it was so heavily criticized that it was revised, but the revised statute has been adopted by only a handful of states. Thus, we can discuss only general trends in state laws. Before forming an LLC, you should review carefully the laws in your particular state.

Limited Liability

Members are not personally liable for the debts of the company. They risk only their investment, as if they were shareholders of a corporation. Are the members of the LLC liable in the following case? You be the judge.

You be the Judge

Ridgaway v. Silk

2004 Conn. Super. LEXIS 548
Superior Court of Connecticut, 2004

Facts: Norman Costello and Robert Giordano were members of Silk, LLC, which owned a bar and adult entertainment nightclub in Groton, Connecticut, called Silk Stockings. Anthony Sulls went drinking there one night—and drinking heavily. Although he was obviously drunk, employees at Silk Stockings continued to serve him. Costello and Giordano were working there that night. They both greeted customers (who numbered in the hundreds), supervised employees, and performed "other PR work." When Sulls left the nightclub at 1:45 a.m. with two friends, he drove off the highway at high speed, killing himself and one of his passengers, William Ridgaway, Jr.

Ridgaway's estate sued Costello and Giordano personally. The defendants filed a motion for summary judgment seeking dismissal of the complaint.

You Be the Judge: ***Are Costello and Giordano personally liable to Ridgaway's estate?***

Argument for Costello and Giordano: The defendants did not own Silk Stockings; they were simply members of an LLC that owned the nightclub. The whole point of an LLC is to protect members against personal liability. The assets of Silk, LLC, are at risk, but not the personal assets of Costello and Giordano.

Argument for Ridgaway's Estate: The defendants are not liable for being *members* of Silk, LLC, they are liable for their own misdeeds as *employees* of the LLC. They were both present at Silk Stockings on the night in question, meeting and greeting customers and supervising employees. It is possible that they might actually have served drinks to Sulls, but in any event, they did not adequately supervise and train their employees to prevent them from serving alcohol to someone who was clearly drunk. The world would be an intolerable place to live if employees were free to be as careless as they wished, knowing that they were not liable because they were members of an LLC.

Tax Status

As in a partnership, income flows through the company to the individual members, avoiding the double taxation of a corporation.

Formation

To organize an LLC, you must have a charter and you should have an operating agreement. The charter is short, containing basic information such as name and address. It must be filed with the Secretary of State in the jurisdiction in which it is being formed. An operating agreement sets out the rights and obligations of the owners, who are called "members." If an LLC does not adopt its own operating agreement, LLC statutes provide a default option. However, these standardized provisions may not be what members would choose if they thought about it. Therefore, it is often better for an LLC to prepare its own personalized operating agreement. The Horning case that began this chapter illustrates one of the many things that can go wrong when an LLC does not have an operating agreement.

On this issue, corporations have an advantage over LLCs. Corporations are so familiar that the standard documents (such as a charter, by-laws, and shareholder agreement) are well established and widely available. Lawyers can form a corporation easily, and the Internet offers a host of free forms. This is not the case with LLCs. As yet, the law is so unsettled that standard forms may be dangerous, while customized forms can be expensive. The following case illustrates the importance of a well-drafted operating agreement.

Wyoming.com, LLC v. Lieberman

2005 WY 42; 109 P.3d 883; 2005 Wyo. LEXIS 48
Supreme Court of Wyoming, 2005

Facts: Lieberman was a member of an LLC called Wyoming.com. After he withdrew, he and the other members disagreed about what his membership was worth. Wyoming.com filed a lawsuit asking the court to determine the financial rights and obligations of the parties, if any, upon the withdrawal of a member.

The Supreme Court of Wyoming reached a decision that may have sounded logical but left Lieberman in a sad twilight zone—neither in nor out of the LLC. The court ruled that Lieberman still owned part of the business despite his withdrawal as a member. So far, so good. But neither the LLC statute nor the company's operating agreement required the LLC to pay a member the value of his share. Therefore, neither party had any further rights or obligations. In other words, Lieberman was still an owner, but he was not entitled to any payment. Not quite understanding the implications of this ruling, Lieberman filed a motion seeking financial information about the company. The original trial court denied the request on the theory that since Lieberman had no right to a payout, the company had no obligation to give him financial data.

Issue: ***Does Lieberman have a right to any financial data about Wyoming.com?***

Excerpts from Justice Golden's Decision: [The prior Lieberman case] held that no provision exists either in Wyoming statutes or the operating agreements of Wyoming.com requiring any particular disposition of a member's equity interest upon his withdrawal as a member. Thus, Wyoming.com could not legally force Lieberman to sell his equity interest at any particular value, and Lieberman could not force Wyoming.com to buy his equity interest at any particular value.

This answered the question presented by Wyoming.com in its [lawsuit]. While not explicitly stated in the opinion, with the question answered, nothing remains but to dismiss the [case]. No further proceedings are required to resolve this action. As specifically applied to this case, Lieberman simply retains his equity interest and nothing further is required of either party as a direct result of Lieberman's withdrawal as a member.

Excerpts from Justice Kite's Concurring Decision: I concur with the result reached by the majority in this matter solely because it is mandated by [the prior Lieberman case]. I joined [the] dissenting opinion in that case because I found it more appropriate to allow a minority interest owner in an LLC a mechanism to realize the value of his equity interest. Given the majority's ruling that Mr. Lieberman owns an equity interest, but neither the operating agreement nor the statute provide a method for him to realize the value of that interest, there is nothing left for the district court to order Wyoming.com LLC to do. [The court should consider that] those rights and responsibilities in the context of other forms of business organizations are well developed and may provide guidance in the realm of the LLC.

Flexibility

Unlike S corporations, LLCs can have members that are corporations, partnerships, or nonresident aliens. LLCs can also have different classes of stock. Unlike corporations, LLCs are not required to hold annual meetings or maintain a minute book.

Transferability of Interests

Unless the operating agreement provides otherwise, the members of the LLC must obtain the unanimous permission of the remaining members before transferring their ownership rights. This is yet another reason to have an operating agreement.

LLCs cannot issue stock options, which is potentially a serious problem because options may be an essential lure in attracting and retaining top talent.

Duration

It used to be that LLCs automatically dissolved upon the withdrawal of a member (owing to, for example, death, resignation, or bankruptcy). The current trend in state laws, however, is to permit an LLC to continue in operation even after a member withdraws.

Going Public

Once an LLC goes public, it loses its favorable tax status and is taxed as a corporation, not a partnership.[5] Thus, there is no advantage to using the LLC form of organization for a publicly traded company. And there are some disadvantages: unlike corporations, publicly traded LLCs do not enjoy a well-established set of statutory and case law that is relatively consistent across the many states. For this reason, privately held companies that begin as LLCs usually change to corporations when they go public.

It is worth noting, too, that because of securities laws, it is important for an LLC to have an operating agreement that permits managers the right to convert the LLC into a corporation at the time of a public offering without the consent of the members.[6]

Changing Forms

Some companies that are now corporations might prefer to be LLCs. However, the IRS would consider this change to be a sale of the corporate assets and would levy a tax on the value of these assets. For this reason, few corporations have made the change. However, switching from a partnership to an LLC or from an LLC to a corporation is not considered a sale and does not have the same adverse tax impact.

Piercing the LLC Veil

It has long been the case that, if corporate shareholders do not comply with the technicalities of the law, they may be held personally liable for the debts of the corporation (an issue that will be discussed in more depth in Chapter 33). As the following case illustrates, members of an LLC can also be held liable under the same circumstances.

BLD Products, LTC. v. Technical Plastics of Oregon, LLC

2006 U.S. Dist. LEXIS 89874
United States District Court for the District of Oregon, 2006

Facts: Mark Hardie was the sole member of Technical Plastics of Oregon, LLC (TPO). He operated the business out of an office in his home. Hardie regularly used TPO's accounts to pay such expenses as landscaping and housecleaning. TPO also paid some of Hardie's personal credit card bills, loan payments on his Ford truck, the cost of constructing a deck on his house, his stepson's college bills, and the cost of family vacations to Disneyland, as well as miscellaneous bills from GI Joe's, Wrestler's World, K-Mart, and Mattress World. At the same time, Hardie deposited cash advances from his personal credit cards into the TPO checking account. Hardie did not take a salary from TPO. When TPO filed for bankruptcy, it owed BLD Products approximately $120,000 for goods that it had purchased.

In some cases, a court will "pierce the veil" of a corporation and hold its shareholders personally liable for the debts of the business. BLD argued that the same doctrine should apply to LLCs and the court should hold Hardie personally liable for TPO's debts.

---

[5]26 U.S.C. §7704.

[6]In this way, under Rule 144 (which is discussed in Chapter 36 on securities regulation), members can include the time during which they owned interests in the LLC when calculating their holding period for stock.

BLD filed for summary judgment.

Issues: ***Does the corporate doctrine of piercing the corporate veil apply to LLCs? Should Hardie be personally liable for TPO's debts?***

Excerpts from Judge King's Decision: I conclude that the piercing doctrine may be applied to LLCs under the same circumstances in which it is applied to corporations. We have characterized that formulation [for piercing a corporate veil] as a three-part test:

1. the defendant controlled the debtor corporation;
2. the defendant engaged in improper conduct; and
3. as a result of that improper conduct plaintiff was unable to collect on a debt against the insolvent corporation.

There is no issue that Hardie, as the sole member and manager of TPO, controlled the company. Turning to the second prong of the test, there is substantial evidence of improper conduct, particularly in the nature of commingling of assets and a general disregard of TPO's LLC form and status as a separate legal entity. Hardie frequently and in significant amounts paid his personal expenses from the TPO business account. The amounts are well beyond small dips into petty cash. There is inadequate documentation about how funds flowed between Hardie, as an individual, and TPO. I realize that Hardie elected to be paid in a manner other than by a regular salary but that does not excuse the lack of documentation. Hardie treated TPO and its assets as his personal funds.

That leaves the third prong of the test, whether Hardie's improper conduct resulted in BLD being unable to collect on its approximately $120,000 debt. I cannot determine as a matter of law that the inability to pay the entire $120,000 debt was due to Hardie's improper conduct over the years. Consequently, I grant partial summary judgment that BLD is entitled to pierce the corporate veil, making Hardie personally liable, but that the amount for which Hardie is personally liable will have to be determined by the jury.

Legal Uncertainty

As we have observed, LLCs are a relatively new form of organization without a consistent and widely developed body of law. As a result, members of an LLC may find themselves in the unhappy position of litigating issues of law which, although well established for corporations, are not yet clear for LLCs. Win or lose, lawsuits are expensive in both time and money.

An important area of legal uncertainty involves managers' duties to the members of the organization. For example, it is not clear in many jurisdictions if managers of an LLC have a legal obligation to act in the best interest of members. Delaware courts have recently ruled that an LLC's managers do have a fiduciary duty to its members unless the operating agreement provides otherwise. (In that state, an operating agreement can limit any duty except the requirement of good faith and fair dealing.) However, this uncertainty means that, before becoming a member of an LLC, it is important to understand both state law and the terms of the operating agreement.

Furthermore, when managers of a corporation violate their duty to the organization by, say, approving a merger without sufficient investigation, shareholders are allowed to bring a so-called **derivative lawsuit** in the name of the corporation against the managers. This right was established by common law. It is unclear, however, if members of an LLC have the same right, especially in a state such as New York where the LLC statute does not explicitly authorize derivative lawsuits. The following case resolves this issue, but only for New York state.

Tzolis v. Wolff

884 N.E.2d 1005; 855 N.Y.S.2d 6; 2008 N.Y. LEXIS 226
Court of Appeals of New York, 2008

Facts: Soterios Tzolis owned 25 percent of Smith Pennington Property Co. LLC, which owned a Manhattan hotel. Herbert Wolff managed the LLC. Tzolis alleged that Wolff first leased and then sold the hotel to family and friends at a price below market value. Tzolis filed a derivative suit against Wolff on the grounds that the man had violated his duties to the LLC.

The trial court ruled that members of an LLC had no right to bring a derivative action because the statute had not explicitly permitted such suits. Tzolis appealed.

Issue: ***Do members of an LLC have the right to bring a derivative suit against managers of the company?***

Excerpts from Justice Smith's Decision: The derivative suit has been part of the general corporate law of this state at least since 1832. It was not created by statute, but by case law. [The judge in a 1832 case said:]

> "no injury the stockholders may sustain by a fraudulent breach of trust, can, upon the general principles of equity, be suffered to pass without a remedy. I will never determine that a court cannot lay hold of every such breach of trust. I will never determine that frauds of this kind are out of the reach of courts of law; for an intolerable grievance would follow from such a determination."

We now consider whether to recognize derivative actions on behalf of the LLC, as to which no statutory provision for such an action exists. In addressing the question, we continue to heed the realization: When fiduciaries are faithless to their trust, the victims must not be left wholly without a remedy. [T]o determine that frauds of this kind are out of the reach of courts of law would lead to "an intolerable grievance."

To hold that there is no remedy when corporate fiduciaries use corporate assets to enrich themselves was unacceptable in 1832, and it is still unacceptable today. Derivative suits are not the only possible remedy, but they are the one that has been recognized for most of two centuries, and to abolish them in the LLC context would be a radical step.

[C]ourts have repeatedly recognized derivative suits in the absence of express statutory authorization. In light of this, it could hardly be argued that the mere absence of authorizing language in the Limited Liability Company Law bars the courts from entertaining derivative suits by LLC members.

We therefore hold that members of LLCs may sue derivatively.

In its reasoning, this court relied on corporate law precedents. However, in a recent case also involving derivative actions, a Delaware court did not follow that approach. The Delaware LLC statute clearly provides that *members* can bring derivative actions. That bit of clarity is helpful. But what about *creditors* of an LLC? We know that creditors of a *corporation* have that right. Does the same rule apply to LLCs?

In the case in question, the board of JetDirect Aviation LLC approved four major acquisitions, all the while knowing that its financials were inaccurate. The company ultimately went bankrupt and, thus, was unable to repay a $34 million loan to CML. The lender filed a derivative action against JetDirect's careless board members. But, much to everyone's surprise, two Delaware courts ruled that CML could *not* bring a derivative action because the Delaware LLC statute had not explicitly authorized such lawsuits. CML was simply out of luck. The lower court observed, "[T]here is nothing absurd about different legal principles applying to corporations and LLCs."

CML would not necessarily agree. And the lower court itself acknowledged that commentators had all assumed that such suits were permitted. It turned out they were wrong. This result may make lenders less willing to finance LLCs and therefore render LLCs a less-desirable form of organization.[7] In short, many issues of law that are well established for corporations still reside in foggy territory when it comes to LLCs.

Choices: LLC v. Corporation

When starting a business, which form makes the most sense—LLC or corporation? The tax status of an LLC is a major advantage over a corporation. Although an S corporation has the same tax status as an LLC, it also has all the annoying rules about classes of stock and number of shareholders. Once an LLC is established, it does not have as many housekeeping rules as corporations—it does not, for example, have to make annual filings or hold annual meetings. However, the LLC is not right for everyone. If done properly, an LLC is more expensive to set up than a corporation because it needs to have a thoughtfully crafted

[7] *CML V, LLC v. Bax*, 2011 Del. LEXIS 480 (S. Ct. Del, 2011).

operating agreement. Also, venture capitalists almost always refuse to invest in LLCs, preferring C corporations instead. There are four reasons for this preference: (1) arcane tax issues, (2) C corporations are easier to merge, sell, or take public, (3) corporations can issue stock options, and (4) the general legal uncertainty involving LLCs.

EXAM Strategy

Question: Hortense and Gus are each starting a business. Hortense's business is an Internet startup. Gus will be opening a yarn store. Hortense needs millions of dollars in venture capital and expects to go public soon. Gus has borrowed $10,000 from his girlfriend, which he hopes to pay back soon. Should either of these businesses organize as an LLC?

Strategy: Sole proprietorships may be best for businesses without substantial capital needs and without significant liability issues. Corporations are best for businesses that will need substantial outside capital and expect to go public shortly.

Result: An LLC is not the best choice for either of these businesses. Venture capitalists will insist that Hortense's business be a corporation, especially if it is going public soon. A yarn store has few liability issues, and Gus does not expect to have any outside investors. Hence, a sole proprietorship would be more appropriate for Gus's business.

Benefit Corporations and LLCs

The benefit organization, known as a B corporation or B LLC, is one that has pledged to behave in a socially responsible manner, even as it pursues profits. (Thus, it is *not* a non-profit.) The Benefit company's focus is on the triple bottom line: "people, planet and profits." Currently, a handful of states (such as Maryland, New Jersey, New York, Vermont and Virginia) permit B organizations.

Almost 500 businesses nationwide, including King Arthur Flour Company, Inc. and Seventh Generation, have become Benefit organizations. To obtain B status, shareholders must first give their approval. Then the company has to obtain certification from an independent third party, such as B Lab. Companies with B status must prepare an annual benefit report that includes an assessment of their societal and environmental impact.

General Partnerships

Partnership
An unincorporated association of two or more co-owners who operate a business for profit.

A **partnership** is an unincorporated association of two or more co-owners who carry on a business for profit.[8] Each co-owner is called a *general partner*.

Liability

Each partner is personally liable for the debts of the enterprise whether or not she caused them. Thus, a partner is liable for any injury that another partner or an employee causes while on partnership business as well as for any contract signed on behalf of the partnership.

[8]Uniform Partnership Act §6(1).

This form of organization can be particularly risky if the group of owners is large and the partners do not know each other.

At age 53, Matter feared losing everything he owned.

Daniel Matter knows firsthand about the risks of a partnership. A former partner in the accounting firm Pannell Kerr Foster, he thought he had heard the last of the firm when he resigned his partnership. He was wrong. *Seven* years later, he and 260 other former partners of the California firm were served with a 78-page lawsuit seeking $24 million in damages. The lawsuit alleged that Pannell Kerr had been negligent in preparing financial reports for a bankrupt Tennessee savings and loan. Although Daniel Matter had never worked for that particular client, he was potentially liable because he had been a partner when the audit was done. At age 53, Matter feared losing everything he owned.

Management

As many law, accounting, and consulting firms have grown larger, they have discovered another disadvantage to partnerships: management can be difficult. In theory, all partners in a firm are equal and have an equal right to share in management. When two sisters-in-law form a small accounting firm, they can easily discuss business issues—from hiring a new associate to choosing a photocopy machine. But when the partnership has 1,000 accountants speaking four different languages on three continents, consultation becomes difficult. Although most large firms authorize a management committee to make day-to-day decisions, other partners may still expect to be consulted. One partner in a law firm complained bitterly when all 163 partners were assembled to vote on the style of ceiling tile for the conference room. Yet, to be fair, the managing partner had called for the vote because everyone had complained when he changed the typeface on the firm's stationery without consulting them.

Transfer of Ownership

Financing a partnership may be difficult because the firm cannot sell shares as a corporation does. The capital needs of the partnership must be provided by contributions from partners or by borrowing. Likewise, a partner only has the right to transfer the *value* of her partnership interest, not the interest itself. She cannot, for example, transfer the right to participate in firm management. Take the case of Evan and his mother. She is a partner in the immensely profitable McBain Consulting firm. She dies, leaving him an orphan with no siblings. He overcomes his grief as best he can and goes to her office on the next Monday to take over her job and her partnership. Imagine his surprise when her partners tell him that, as her sole heir, he can inherit the *value* of her partnership but he has no right to be a partner. He is out on the sidewalk within the hour. The partners have promised him a check in the mail.

Dissociation

When a partner quits, that event is called a *dissociation*. A dissociation is a fork in the road: the partnership can either buy out the departing partner(s) and continue in business or wind up the business and terminate the partnership. Most large firms provide in their partnership agreement that, upon dissociation, the business continues.

Formation

Given the disadvantages, why does anyone do business as a partnership? Like sole proprietorships, partnerships are easy to form. Although a partnership should have a written agreement, it is perfectly legal without one. In fact, nothing is required in the way of forms or filings or agreements. If two or more people do business together, sharing management, profits and losses, they have a partnership, whether they know it or not, and are subject to all the rules of partnership law.

A partnership has an important advantage over a sole proprietorship—partners. Sole proprietors are on their own; partners have colleagues to help them and, equally important, to supply capital for the business. Sole proprietorships sometimes turn into partnerships for exactly this reason.

Taxes

As we have seen above, partnerships are not a taxable entity, which means that profits flow through to the owners.

Limited Liability Partnerships

A limited liability partnership (LLP) is a type of general partnership that most states now permit. There is a very important distinction, however, between LLPs and general partnerships: **in an LLP, the partners are not liable for the debts of the partnership.**[9] They are, naturally, liable for their own misdeeds, just as if they were a member of an LLC or a shareholder of a corporation.

To form an LLP, the partners must file a statement of qualification with state officials. LLPs must also file annual reports. The other attributes of a partnership remain the same. Thus, an LLP is not a taxable entity, and it has the right to choose its duration (that is, it can, but does not have to, survive the dissociation of a member).

Although an LLP can be much more advantageous for partners than a general partnership, it is absolutely crucial to comply with all the technicalities of the LLP statute. Otherwise, partners lose protection against personal liability. Note the sad result for Michael Gaus and John West, who formed a Texas LLP. Unfortunately, they did not renew the LLP registration each year, as the statute required. Four years after its initial registration, the partnership entered into a lease. When the partners ultimately stopped paying rent and abandoned the premises, they were both were held personally liable for the rent because the LLP registration had expired. As the court pointed out, the statute did not contain a "substantial compliance" section, nor did it contain a grace period for filing a renewal application. In short, close only counts in horseshoes and hand grenades, not in LLPs.

Limited Partnerships and Limited Liability Limited Partnerships

Although limited partnerships and limited liability limited partnerships sound confusingly similar to limited liability partnerships and general partnerships, like many siblings, they operate very differently. And truth to tell, limited partnerships and limited liability limited partnerships are relatively rare—they are generally used only for estate planning purposes (usually, to reduce estate taxes) and for highly sophisticated investment vehicles. You

[9]UPA §306(c).

should be aware of their existence, but you may not see them very often in your business life. Here are the major features:

Structure

Limited partnerships must have at least one *limited* partner and one *general* partner.

Liability

Limited partners are not *personally* liable, but general partners are. Like corporate shareholders, limited partners risk only their investment in the partnership (which is called their "capital contribution"). In contrast, general partners of the limited partnership are personally liable for the debts of the organization.

However, the revised version of the Uniform Limited Partnership Act permits a limited partnership, in its certificate of formation and partnership agreement, simply to declare itself a *limited liability* limited partnership.[10] **In a limited liability limited partnership, the general partner is not personally liable for the debts of the partnership.** This provision effectively removes the major disadvantage of limited partnerships. Although, at this writing, fewer than half the states have actually passed the revised version of the Uniform Limited Partnership Act, this revision would seem to indicate the trend for the future.

Taxes

Limited partnerships are not taxable entities. Income is taxed only once before landing in a partner's pocket.

Formation

The general partners must file a **certificate of limited partnership** with their Secretary of State. Although most limited partnerships do have a partnership agreement, it is not required.

Management

General partners have the right to manage a limited partnership. Limited partners are essentially passive investors with few management rights beyond the right to be informed about the partnership business. Limited partnership agreements can, however, expand the rights of limited partners.

Transfer of Ownership

Limited partners have the right to transfer the *value* of their partnership interest, but they can sell or give away the interest itself only if the partnership agreement permits.

Duration

Unless the partnership agreement provides otherwise, limited partnerships enjoy perpetual existence—they continue even as partners come and go.

EXAM Strategy

Question: In which one or more of the following forms of organization is it true that none of the partners are liable for the debts of the partnership?

[10]ULPA §102(9).

1. General partnership
2. Limited liability partnership
3. Limited partnership
4. Limited liability limited partnership

Strategy: All these partnerships sound similar, but they are in fact very different, so it is important to keep them straight!

Result: In a general partnership, all the partners are liable. In a limited liability partnership, none are liable. In a limited partnership, the general partners are liable. In a limited liability limited partnership, none of the partners are liable. The correct answers are 2. and 4.

Professional Corporations

Traditionally, most professionals (such as lawyers and doctors) were not permitted to incorporate their businesses, so they organized as partnerships. Now professionals are allowed to incorporate, but in a special way. These organizations are called "professional corporations" or "PCs." **PCs provide more liability protection than a general partnership.** If a member of a PC commits malpractice, the corporation's assets are at risk, but not the personal assets of the innocent members. If Drs. Sharp, Payne, and Graves form a *partnership*, all the partners will be personally liable when Dr. Payne accidentally leaves her scalpel inside a patient. If the three doctors have formed a *PC* instead, Dr. Payne's Aspen condo and the assets of the PC will be at risk, but not the personal assets of the two other doctors.

Generally, the shareholders of a PC are not personally liable for the contract debts of the organization, such as leases or bank loans. Thus, if Sharp, Payne, & Graves, P.C. is unable to pay its rent, the landlord cannot recover from the personal assets of any of the doctors. As partners, the doctors would be personally liable.

PCs have some limitations. First, all shareholders of the corporation must be members of the same profession. For Sharp, Payne, & Graves, P.C., that means all shareholders must be licensed physicians. Other valued employees cannot own stock. Second, like other corporations, the required legal technicalities for forming and maintaining a PC are expensive and time-consuming. Third, tax issues can be complicated. A PC is a separate taxable entity, like any other corporation. It must pay tax on its profits, and then its shareholders pay tax on any dividends they receive. *Salaries*, however, are deductible from firm profits. Thus, the PC can avoid paying taxes on its profits by paying out all the profits as salary. But any profits remaining in firm coffers *at the end of the year* are taxable. To avoid tax, PCs must be careful to calculate their profits accurately and pay them out before year's end. This chore can be time-consuming, and any error may cause unnecessary tax liability.

Joint Ventures

Imax Corp. decided that it would like to partner with cinema operators—it would supply its big screens in return for a share of the box office revenue. The arrangement that Imax is describing is not like the other partnerships we have discussed in this chapter—it is a joint venture. A **joint venture** is a partnership for a limited purpose. Imax and the cinema operators would not merge; they would simply work together. Each organization retains its own identity. Imax would be liable to an electrician whom the cinema operator had hired to install an Imax screen, but not to the cinema's popcorn supplier.

Joint venture
A partnership for a limited purpose.

FRANCHISES

This chapter has presented an overview of the various forms of organization. Franchises are not, strictly speaking, a separate form of organization. They are included here because they represent an important option for entrepreneurs. The United States has nearly half a million franchised businesses, which employ almost 8 million people. Total sales are $1.3 trillion a year. Well-known franchises include Hampton Hotels, McDonald's, and Supercuts. Most franchisors and franchisees are corporations, although they could legally choose to be any of the forms discussed in this chapter.

Buying a franchise is a compromise between starting one's own business as an entrepreneur and working for someone else as an employee. Franchisees are free to choose which franchise to buy, where to locate it, and how to staff it. But they are not completely on their own. They are buying an established business with the kinks worked out. In case the owner has never boiled water before, the McDonald's operations manual explains everything from how to set the temperature controls on the stove, to the number of seconds that fries must cook, to the length of time they can be held in the rack before being discarded. And a well-known name like McDonald's or Subway ought, by itself, to bring customers through the door.

© Andy Z./Shutterstock.com

If you have been to an IMAX movie, you may have benefited from a joint venture between IMAX and cinema operators.

There is, however, a fine line between being helpful and being oppressive. Franchisees sometimes complain that franchisor control is too tight—tips on cooking fries might be appreciated, but rules on how often to sweep the floor are not. Sometimes franchisors, in their zeal to maintain standards, prohibit innovation that appeals to regional tastes. Just because spicy biscuits are not popular in New England does not mean they should be banned in the South.

Franchises can be very costly to acquire, anywhere from several thousand dollars to many millions. That fee is usually payable up front, whether or not a sandwich or burger is ever sold. On top of the up-front fee, franchisees also typically pay an annual fee that is a percentage of *gross sales revenues,* not *profit.* Sometimes the fee seems to eat up all the profits. Franchisees also complain when they are forced to buy supplies from headquarters. In theory, the franchisors can purchase hamburger meat and paper plates more cheaply in bulk and also maintain quality controls. On the other hand, the franchisees are a captive audience, and they sometimes allege that headquarters has little incentive to keep prices low. Indeed, some franchisors make most of their profit from the products they sell to their store owners. Often, the franchise agreement permits the company to change the terms of the agreement by raising fees or expenses. Franchisees also grumble when they are forced to contribute to expensive "co-op advertising" that benefits all the outlets in the region. The sandwich franchise Quiznos recently spent $100 million to settle litigation with potential franchisees, who claimed that the company took their fees without finding a store location for them, and some existing store owners, who complained that the company forced them to buy *everything* (including soap in the bathrooms and the piped-in music) from the company at inflated prices.

All franchisors must comply with the Federal Trade Commission's (FTC) Franchise Rule. In addition, some states also impose their own franchise requirements. Under FTC rules, a franchisor must deliver to a potential purchaser a so-called Franchise Disclosure Document (FDD) at least 14 calendar days before any contract is signed or money is paid. The FDD must provide information on:

- The history of the franchisor and its key executives
- Litigation with franchisees
- Bankruptcy filings by the company and its officers and directors
- Costs to buy and operate a franchise
- Restrictions, if any, on suppliers, products, and customers
- Territory – any limitations (in either the real or virtual worlds) on where the franchisee can sell or any restrictions on other franchisees selling in the same territory
- Business continuity – under what circumstances can the franchisor fire the franchisee and the franchisee's rights to renew or sell the franchise
- Franchisor's training program
- Required advertising expenses
- A list of current franchisees and those that have left in the prior three years (a lot of either may be a bad sign)
- A report on prior owners of stores that the franchisor has reaquired
- Earnings information is not required; but if disclosed, the franchisor must reveal the basis for this information
- Audited financials for the franchisor
- A sample set of the contracts that a franchisee is expected to sign

The purpose of the FDD is to ensure that the franchisor discloses all relevant facts. It is not a guarantee of quality because the FTC does not investigate to make sure that the information is accurate. After the fact, if the FTC discovers the franchisor has violated the rules, it may sue on the franchisee's behalf. (The franchisee does not have the right to bring suit personally against someone who violates

"Be cool, Cat."

FTC franchise rules, but it may be able to sue under state law.)

Suppose you obtain an FDD for "Shrinking Cats," a franchise that offers psychiatric services for neurotic felines. The company has lost money on all the outlets it operates itself; it has sold only three franchises, two of which have gone out of business; and all the required contracts are ridiculously favorable to the franchisor. Nevertheless, the FTC will still permit sales as long as the franchisor discloses all the information required in the FDD.

As the following case illustrates, the franchisor has much of the power in a franchise relationship.

National Franchisee Association v. Burger King Corporation

2010 U.S. Dist. LEXIS 123065
United States District Court for the Southern District of Florida, 2010

Facts: The Burger King Corporation (BKC) would not allow franchisees to have it their way. Instead, BKC forced them to sell the double-cheeseburger (DCB) and, later, the Buck Double (the DCB minus one slice of cheese) for no more than $1.00. Franchisees alleged that, because this price was below their cost, they were losing money on every double cheeseburger they sold. The National Franchisee Association (NFA), to which 75 percent of BKC's individual franchisees belonged, filed suit alleging that (1) BKC did not have the right to set maximum prices; and (2) that even if BKC had such a right, it had violated its obligation under the franchise agreement to act in good faith.

The court dismissed the first claim because the franchise agreement unambiguously permitted BKC to set whatever prices it wanted. But the court allowed the NFA to proceed with the second claim. BKC filed a motion to dismiss.

Issue: ***Was BKC acting in good faith when it forced franchisees to sell items below cost?***

Excerpts from Judge Moore's Decision: The motive of BKC in exercising its discretion to set prices under the contract is key. [B]ad faith involves a subterfuge or evasion of contractual duties. [T]here are at least two ways a plaintiff can go about raising a claim of bad faith. Plaintiffs can allege facts identifying defendant's improper ulterior motive(s). For example, if a franchisee had evidence that a franchisor had a secret agenda to take over the franchise and operate it as a company-owned business, and was deliberately setting prices to weaken the targeted franchisee, such a plaintiff could raise a claim of bad faith by alleging the existence of that plan.

It is more likely, however, that plaintiffs will lack direct evidence of dishonesty. In these cases, plaintiffs must allege some facts tending to show that no reasonable person could have thought that the steps taken by the defendant were a reasonable means of carrying out the contract's defined purposes. If no reasonable person would have exercised discretion as defendant had, the natural inference is that defendant must have had some hidden improper motive.

[T]he magnitude of the injury claimed by plaintiff is of central importance. [A]n inference of bad faith may arise when the defendant exercises discretion in such a manner as to effectively destroy whatever benefits the plaintiff could have reasonably expected under the contract. The logic is that the measure with such severe results could not have been within the contemplation of the parties.

[N]one of the facts alleged by plaintiffs are sufficient to support a claim of bad faith. Plaintiffs rely principally on their allegation that franchisees could not produce and sell DCB or Buck Doubles at a cost less than $1.00, and therefore that franchisees suffer a loss on each of these items sold. There are a variety of legitimate reasons why a firm selling multiple products may choose to set the price of a single product below cost. Among other things, such a strategy might help build goodwill and customer loyalty, hold or shift customer traffic away from competitors, or serve as loss leaders to generate increased sales on other higher margin products.

The issue is not whether such a strategy was wise or ultimately successful or mistaken. In the absence of some other evidence of improper motive, the question is whether it was so irrational and capricious that no reasonable person would have made such a decision. There is nothing about the pricing decision that suggests BKC was doing anything other than seeking to promote the performance of its franchisees. Nothing about this action suggests bad faith.

[T]o the extent plaintiffs seek to raise a claim of bad faith by pointing to the injuries allegedly caused them by

BKC's decision, plaintiffs must allege that the damage to their overall business was so severe as to deprive them of their reasonable expectations under the contract. Plaintiffs come nowhere close to alleging such an impact. Significantly, nowhere do plaintiffs claim that their overall business has been appreciably impaired. Nor do they allege that their overall businesses are no longer profitable or that their competitive positions or economic viability going forward are threatened.

For the foregoing reasons, it is ORDERED AND ADJUDGED that Defendant's Motion to Dismiss is GRANTED.

Chapter Conclusion

The process of starting a business is immensely time-consuming. Eighteen-hour days are the norm. Not surprisingly, entrepreneurs are sometimes reluctant to spend their valuable time on legal issues that, after all, do not contribute directly to the bottom line. No customer buys more fried chicken because the franchise is a limited liability company instead of a corporation. Wise entrepreneurs know, however, that careful attention to legal issues is an essential component of success. The form of organization affects everything from taxes to liability to management control. The idea for the business may come first, but legal considerations occupy a close second place.

Exam Review

	Separate Taxable Entity	Personal Liability for Owners	Ease of Formation	Transferable Interests (Easily Bought and Sold)	Perpetual Existence	Other Features
Sole Proprietorship	No	Yes	Very easy	No, can only sell entire business	No	
Corporation	Yes	No	Difficult	Yes	Yes	
Close Corporation	Yes, for C corporation No, for S corporation	No	Difficult	Transfer restrictions	Yes	Protection of minority shareholders. No board of directors required
S Corporation	No	No	Difficult	Transfer restrictions	Yes	Only 100 shareholders. Only one class of stock. Shareholders must be individuals, estates, trusts, charities, or pension funds and be citizens or residents of the United States. All shareholders must agree to S status
Limited Liability Company	No	No	Difficult	Yes, if the operating agreement permits	Varies by state, but generally, yes	No limit on the number of shareholders, the number of classes of stock, or the type of shareholder

General Partnership	No	Yes	Easy	No	Depends on the partnership agreement	Management can be difficult
Limited Liability Partnership	No	No	Difficult	No	Depends on the partnership agreement	
Limited Partnership	No	Yes, for general partner No, for limited partners	Difficult	Yes (for limited partners), if partnership agreement permits	Yes	
~~Limited Liability Limited Partnership~~	No	No	Difficult	Yes (for limited partners), if partnership agreement permits	Yes	
Professional Corporation	Yes	No	Difficult	Shareholders must all be members of same profession	Yes, as long as it has shareholders	Complex tax issues
Joint Venture	No	Yes	Easy	No	No	Partnership for a limited purpose
Franchise	All these issues depend on the form of organization chosen by participants.					Established business. Name recognition. Management assistance. Loss of control. Fees may be high

Multiple-Choice Questions

1. A sole proprietorship:

(a) Must file a tax return

(b) Requires no formal steps for its creation

(c) Must register with the Secretary of State

(d) May sell stock

(e) Provides limited liability to the owner

2. CPA Question: Assuming all other requirements are met, a corporation may elect to be treated as an S corporation under the Internal Revenue Code if it has:

(a) Both common and preferred stockholders

(b) A partnership as a stockholder

(c) 100 or fewer stockholders

(d) The consent of a majority of the stockholders

Strategy: Review the list of requirements for an S corporation. (See the "Result" at the end of this section.)

3. A limited liability company:

(a) Is regulated by a well-established body of law

(b) Pays taxes on its income

(c) May issue stock options

(d) Must register with state authorities

(e) Protects the owners from personal liability for their own misdeeds

4. CPA QUESTION A joint venture is a(n):

(a) Association limited to no more than two persons in business for profit

(b) Enterprise of numerous co-owners in a nonprofit undertaking

(c) Corporate enterprise for a single undertaking of limited duration

(d) Association of persons engaged as co-owners in a single undertaking for profit

5. A limited liability partnership:

(a) Has ownership interests that cannot be transferred

(b) Protects the partners from liability for the debts of the partnership

(c) Must pay taxes on its income

(d) Requires no formal steps for its creation

(e) Permits a limited number of partners

2. Result: An S corporation can have only one class of stock. A partnership cannot be a stockholder, and all the shareholders must consent to S corporation status. C is the correct answer.

Essay Questions

EXAM Strategy

1. Question: Alan Dershowitz, a law professor famous for his wealthy clients (O. J. Simpson, among others), joined with other lawyers to open a kosher delicatessen, Maven's Court. Dershowitz met with greater success at the bar than in the kitchen—the deli failed after barely a year in business. One supplier sued for overdue bills. What form of organization would have been the best choice for Maven's Court?

Strategy: A sole proprietorship would not have worked because there was more than one owner. A partnership would have been a disaster because of unlimited liability. They could have met all the requirements of an S corporation or an LLC. (See the "Result" at the end of this section.)

2. Question: Mrs. Meadows opened a biscuit shop called The Biscuit Bakery. The business was not incorporated. Whenever she ordered supplies, she was careful to sign the contract in the name of the business, not personally: The Biscuit Bakery by Daisy Meadows. Unfortunately, she had no money to pay her flour bill. When the vendor threatened to sue her, Mrs. Meadows told him that he could only sue the business because all the contracts were in the business's name. Will Mrs. Meadows lose her dough?

Strategy: The first step is to figure out what type of organization her business is. Then recall what liability protection that organization offers. (See the "Result" at the end of this section.)

3. **YOU BE THE JUDGE WRITING PROBLEM** Cellwave was a limited partnership that applied to the Federal Communications Commission (FCC) for a license to operate cellular telephone systems. After the FCC awarded the license, it discovered that, although all the limited partners had signed the limited partnership agreement, Cellwave had never filed its limited partnership certificate with the Secretary of State in Delaware. The FCC dismissed Cellwave's application on the grounds that the partnership did not exist when the application was filed. Did the FCC have the right to dismiss Cellwave's application? **Argument for Cellwave:** The limited partnership was effectively in existence as soon as the limited partners signed the agreement. The Secretary of State could not refuse to accept the certificate for filing; that was a mere formality. **Argument for the FCC:** When Cellwave applied for a license, it did not exist legally. Formalities matter.

4. Kristine bought a Rocky Mountain Chocolate Factory franchise. Her franchise agreement required her to purchase a cash register that cost $3,000, with an annual maintenance fee of $773. The agreement also provided that Rocky Mountain could change to a more expensive system. Within a few months after signing the agreement, Kristine learned that she would have to buy a new cash register that cost $20,000, with annual maintenance fees of $2,000. Does Kristine have to buy this new cash register? Did Rocky Mountain act in bad faith?

5. What is the difference between close corporations and S corporations?

1. Result: Maven's Court would have chosen an LLC or an S corporation.

2. Result: The Biscuit Bakery was a sole proprietorship. No matter how Mrs. Meadows signed the contracts, she is still personally liable for the debts of the business.

Discussion Questions

1. **ETHICS** Lee McNeely told Hardee's officials that he was interested in purchasing multiple restaurants in Arkansas. A Hardee's officer assured him that any of the company-owned stores in Arkansas would be available for purchase. However,

the company urged him to open a new store in Maumelle and sent him a letter estimating first-year sales at around $800,000. McNeely built the Maumelle restaurant, but gross sales the first year were only $508,000. When McNeely asked to buy an existing restaurant, a Hardee's officer refused, informing him that Hardee's rarely sold company-owned restaurants. The disclosure document contained no misstatements, but McNeely brought suit alleging fraud in the sale of the Maumelle franchise. Does McNeely have a valid claim against Hardee's? Apart from the legal issues, did Hardee's officers behave ethically? What Life Principles were they applying?

2. Leonard, an attorney, was negligent in his representation of Anthony. In settlement of Anthony's claim against him, Leonard signed a promissory note for $10,400 on behalf of his law firm, an LLC. When the law firm did not pay, Anthony filed suit against Leonard personally for payment of the note. Is a member personally liable for the debt of an LLC that was caused by his own negligence?

3. Think of a business concept that would be appropriate for each of the following: a sole proprietorship, a corporation, and a limited liability company.

4. As you will see in Chapter 33, Facebook began life as a corporation, not an LLC. Why did the founder, Mark Zuckerberg, make that decision?

5. Corporations developed to encourage investors to contribute the capital needed to create large-scale manufacturing enterprises. But LLCs are often start-ups or other small businesses. Why do their members deserve limited liability? And is it fair that LLCs do not have to pay income taxes?

CHAPTER 32

© Evan Meyer/Shutterstock.com

Partnerships

Chase stood at the edge of a meadow near the top of the Porcupine Mountains in the Upper Peninsula of Michigan. The sun glistened off apple blossoms, birds called to each other, and the Lake of the Clouds stretched out to the horizon below. Chase had never been happier. As an architect, he believed in designing "green" houses that blended with nature. Sharing his vision, Danielle had hired him to create a house for this perfect location. The large budget would allow Chase to realize many of his architectural and environmental beliefs. But he needed help—a landscape designer and a decorator who could work with the spectacular setting and his splendid design.

Bailey and Chase began to suspect they were in trouble.

Bailey was Chase's choice for the interior design; she could create the sleek, warm look he sought using only natural products. With Zack's landscape plan, the house would appear to be a natural part of the site. At their first meeting, all three designers committed to the project and rapidly agreed to a deal: Chase would receive 50 percent of the profits, Bailey and Zack 25 percent each. All three would have veto rights over the work of the other two. As the meeting ended, Chase poured glasses of sparkling water. "Here's to our new partnership. We'll build the most beautiful and most environmentally responsible house in America," he said, rising to his feet. The three raised a toast to their success.

The honeymoon lasted only a few weeks. Chase wanted solar panels over the entire roof so that the house could be completely off grid, but Bailey thought the panels were ugly—she insisted on slate instead. When Bailey suggested consulting the owner, Chase blew up. "What do owners know?" he demanded. Zack sided with Bailey on that issue. But then both Chase and Bailey disagreed with Zack, who wanted to relocate the house to save some specimen trees. "Reduce solar efficiency to save a few ratty old trees?" Chase asked incredulously. Outvoted, Zack quit in disgust. Bailey and Chase began to suspect they were in trouble.

Their apprehension proved all too well founded. Outraged that her house was not finished on time, Danielle sued the three designers. When Chase protested that it was not *his* fault Zack quit, Danielle snarled into the phone, "I don't know and I don't care whose fault it is. All I know is that my house isn't ready. I'll see you and your partners in court!" Meanwhile, Zack was last spotted recuperating on Bora Bora, far from the reach of the U.S. legal system.

The plight of this threesome illustrates common partnership problems. Although Chase, Bailey, and Zack never signed an agreement or filed a form, they nonetheless had formed a partnership. Not only did they refer to themselves as partners, but they intended to share profits and co-manage the business. The partnership is liable to Danielle for any damages the delay caused. If the partnership does not have enough assets to pay, each of the partners is personally liable—even if the delay was totally Zack's fault. When Zack left before finishing the project, he wrongfully dissociated from the partnership. Chase and Bailey must pay him the value of his share of the partnership, but they can subtract from that total any damages he caused. If the damages are more than the value of his partnership share, he owes them money. But his former partners must pay Danielle, whether or not they can actually recover from Zack in Bora Bora.

Introduction

Partnerships have two important advantages: they do not pay taxes and they are easy to form.[1] Many professionals, such as accountants and lawyers, traditionally favored this form of organization. Some of the rules can be complex, however, and, like any relationship, a partnership requires careful tending.

Traditionally, partnerships were regulated by common law, but a lack of consistency among the states became troublesome as interstate commerce grew. To solve this problem, the National Conference of Commissioners on Uniform State Laws proposed the Uniform Partnership Act (UPA) in 1914. Since then there have been several revisions, the most recent in 1997. More than two-thirds of the states have now passed the latest revision, so we base our discussion on that version of the law.

Although the UPA has made life easier, common law still plays an important role in regulating partnerships. To some degree, that is always true with statutes. No matter how well written they are, the courts are called upon to interpret some provisions. In addition, the UPA directs courts to apply common law to resolve any issue that it does not cover. Finally, many of the rules in the UPA are so-called **default rules**, meaning that they apply unless the partners reach a different agreement. When partners write their own rules, they must sometimes ask the courts to interpret ambiguous provisions.

Default rules
Rules that govern a partnership unless the partners agree otherwise.

Creating a Partnership

Some legal relationships are carefully delineated. By and large, people know whether or not they are married. Similarly, people usually know if they have formed a corporation. Partnerships are trickier, more like living together than getting married. It can be difficult to tell if a

[1]These issues are discussed at greater length in Chapter 31, on starting a business. Although the partnership itself does not pay taxes, each partner must pay taxes on his share of the partnership's profits.

live-in relationship—or a partnership—really exists. The UPA does not *require* partnerships to prepare a written agreement or make a formal filing. However, the UPA does *permit* a partnership to file a statement with the local Secretary of State that contains basic information about the partnership.[2]

Factors that Matter

How can you tell if you have a partnership? According to the UPA, **the association of two or more persons to carry on as co-owners a business for profit forms a partnership, whether or not the persons intend to form a partnership.**[3]

Note that a partnership is an association of two or more people. If only one person is involved in the business, it is a sole proprietorship, not a partnership.

What factors do the courts consider in determining whether a partnership exists?

- **Sharing profits.** No matter what their arrangement, if two people do not share the profits of their business, they are not partners. Period. However, just because they do share in the profits does not necessarily make them partners. In other words, sharing profits is a necessary but not sufficient condition for being partners.
- **Sharing losses.** Although landlords, employees, and even creditors may share in business profits, usually no one other than a partner is willing to sign on for a share of the losses. Sharing losses is strong evidence of a partnership.
- **Management of the business.** If participants are not involved in management, the courts will generally not consider them to be partners.
- **Oral or written agreement.** The law does not require a formal agreement, either written or oral. Nor is a formal agreement enough on its own to create a partnership. In a partnership, actions speak louder than words. If the people act like partners, then the law will treat them as such. If they do not act like partners, then nothing they say is enough, on its own, to create a partnership. Note, however, that in a close case, referring to yourselves as partners may help sway a court, but it is not enough *by itself* to create a partnership.
- **Charitable businesses.** Because charitable businesses do not technically make profits, they cannot be a partnership. When Aaron and Elijah agree to run the annual jamboree at their children's school, they expect to clear $35,000 after expenses, but they are not partners because their fund-raising has a charitable purpose.

Now let's apply these rules to real examples. Kevin and Brenda formed an electrical contracting business. The business did so well that Kevin's first wife, Cynthia, asked the court to increase his child support payments. Kevin argued that because he and Brenda were partners, he was entitled to only half of the business's profits. Therefore, his child support should not be increased.

Cynthia claimed that Kevin and Brenda were *not* partners because Kevin had reported all the income from the business on his personal tax return, while Brenda had reported none. Kevin had even put "sole proprietorship" in bold letters on the top of his return. No written partnership agreement existed. Kevin and Brenda never informed their accountant that they were a partnership. When Kevin answered interrogatories for Cynthia's lawsuit, he stated that he was sole owner and that Brenda worked for him. Nonetheless, the court held

[2]UPA §105.

[3]UPA §202(a).

that Brenda and Kevin were partners because Brenda helped manage the business and shared in its profits.[4]

In contrast, when Nancy Green borrowed money from Joseph DiFebo to make a down payment on four houses, they agreed that they were partners. Although Green bought the properties in her name alone, the two signed this document:

> Nancy R. Green and Joseph A. DiFebo are equal partners in the following Wilmington, Delaware, properties: 807 Pine Street, 427 East 3rd St., 611 East 7th Street, 613 East 7th Street.
>
> On the death of Nancy R. Green, her half-interest is left to her daughters, Kelly R. Green and Stacy R. Green. On the death of Joseph A. DiFebo, his half-interest is left to his daughters, Amy DiFebo and Beth Durham.
>
> If Nancy R. Green survives Joseph A. DiFebo, she makes all decisions on the above properties.

DiFebo did some repair work on the buildings but never asked Green for a share of the rentals. When the city condemned one of the properties, Green refused to give DiFebo half the proceeds. DiFebo testified that, in his mind, the money he transferred to Green established a partnership between them. Green testified that at no time did she consider their arrangement to be a partnership.

The court was less concerned about what the *agreement said* than how the *parties acted*. Although they had called themselves "equal partners," they did not share profits. DiFebo said he had not taken his share of the profits because he did not want his wife to find out about his arrangements (financial and otherwise) with Green. Ruling that their contract was a will, not a partnership agreement, the court denied DiFebo's claim.[5]

The following case illustrates the adage that a lawyer who represents himself has a fool for a client. Were they partners? You be the judge.

[4]*In re Marriage of Cynthia Hassiepen*, 269 Ill. App. 3d 559, 646 N.E.2d 1348, 1995 Ill. App. LEXIS 101 (1995).
[5]*Green v. Schagrin*, 1989 Del. Super. LEXIS 295 (1989).

You be the Judge

NADEL V. STARKMAN

2010 N.J. Super. Unpub. LEXIS 2542
Superior Court of New Jersey, Appellate Division, 2010

Facts: Morris Starkman hired Raymond Nadel just after he graduated from law school. At the beginning, Nadel was clearly an associate, not a partner, but after some years working together, the two men signed an agreement that changed their relationship—although to what is not clear. The agreement clarified many important issues (such as Nadel's vacation time), but it failed to resolve the most crucial question: was Nadel now a partner?

The agreement offered some hints to answering this question, but unfortunately the clues pointed in different directions. It stated that:

- The practice had "heretofore" been owned solely by Starkman;
- Nadel had an "interest in the firm";
- The firm would continue to be owned solely by Starkman, who had the right to make all management decisions;
- Starkman was the sole owner and Nadel was an independent contractor;
- Nadel would receive a percentage of the firm's net income, and he was guaranteed a minimum income each year;
- The firm would pay for Nadel's benefits, but not Starkman's.

Other relevant facts:

- The firm never filed a partnership tax return;

- Its checking accounts remained solely in Starkman's name and were entitled "Morris Starkman, Attorney at Law";
- Nadel never had authority to sign checks, and none of the checks bore his name;
- The firm's signage, letterhead, and advertisements all used the name Starkman & Nadel.

Later, Starkman decided that the firm should become a limited liability company (LLC). The agreement he prepared stated that he would own 99 percent to Nadel's 1 percent. It also stated that Nadel was an employee. Nadel refused to sign the agreement. At trial, Starkman testified that Nadel had refused to sign because he wanted a pension plan and a severance package. Nadel maintained that he had not been willing to give up his partnership interest.

The agreement had referred to the two men's "excellent relationship," but that did not last long. Starkman soon began looking for Nadel's replacement. (He waited to send the termination letter until Nadel was on vacation, which probably did not help their relationship.) Starkman formed a partnership with David Rochman, while Nadel filed suit, asking the court to determine the reasonable value of his ownership interest in the firm.

At trial, Rochman (who had since parted ways with Starkman) and others testified that Starkman had told them that Nadel was his partner and he owed the man a substantial buyout. The trial judge believed Nadel, while finding Starkman evasive and dishonest. She ruled that the two men had intended to form a partnership and had indeed done so. Starkman appealed.

You Be the Judge: ***Were Starkman and Nadel partners?***

Argument for Nadel: There was substantial evidence of a partnership, both in the agreement itself and in the two men's behavior. The agreement provided for the sharing of net profits, which is an important indicator of a partnership. Also, it implied Nadel was a partner when it referred to his "interest in the firm" and stated that the practice was "heretofore" owned solely by Starkman. As for the provision in the agreement that referred to Starkman as the sole owner, that simply meant that he was the managing partner. In any event, if the agreement was unclear, any ambiguity should be interpreted against Starkman because he is the one who drafted it.

As for behavior, the trial judge found that the parties *intended* to create a partnership and that Nadel refused to convert the business to an LLC because he would not give up his partnership interest. Starkman repeatedly referred to the business as a partnership and admitted to other people that he owed Nadel a substantial buyout.

Argument for Starkman: Both the agreement and the two men's behavior provide overwhelming evidence that there was *no* partnership. The agreement does not refer to itself as a partnership agreement. It clearly stated that Nadel was an independent contractor rather than a partner. The agreement did not grant Nadel the right to make management decisions. It did make provisions for his benefits and vacation time, but not Starkman's. These provisions indicated he was an employee, not a partner.

As for behavior, Nadel did not share in the firm's losses and the firm did not file a partnership tax return. (Presumably two lawyers would have known enough to file the appropriate tax return.)

Partnership by Estoppel

Raymond Nadel wanted to be Morris Starkman's partner so that he could share in the profits of the enterprise. *Partnership by estoppel* is concerned with the opposite situation—a person does not want to be considered a partner because he wishes to avoid the *liability* of the partnership. The twist is that partnership by estoppel applies in situations where the participants are *not,* in fact, partners but are held to be liable as if they were.

Partnership by estoppel applies if:

- **Participants tell other people that they are partners (even though they are not), or they allow other people to say, without contradiction, that they are partners;**
- **A third party relies on this assertion; and**
- **The third party suffers harm.**

Dr. William Martin was held liable under a theory of partnership by estoppel because he told a patient that he and Dr. John Maceluch were partners (although they were not); the patient relied on this statement and made appointments to see Dr. Maceluch; and she was harmed by Dr. Maceluch's malpractice. He refused to come to the hospital when she was in labor, and as a result, her child was born with brain damage. Although Dr. Martin was out of the country at the time, he was also liable.[6]

Dr. Martin could have avoided this problem by being very careful *not* to refer to Dr. Maceluch as his partner. Presumably, he used the word "partner" to reassure the patient. Instead of "partner," he could have said "colleague," "associate," or "assistant." Dr. Martin should also have been careful to correct anyone who referred to Dr. Maceluch as his partner.

Note that even if the court determined that Raymond Nadel and Morris Starkman were *not* partners, Nadel could still be liable to a third party who had been harmed by the firm if Starkman had told that person that Nadel was a partner. In short, Nadel could end up with all of the downside but none of the upside of being a partner.

Relationship between Partners and Outsiders

Under the UPA, **the rules governing the liability of partners to outsiders are *mandatory*.** Partners may not change them. **In contrast, most of the rules governing the relationship *among* partners are *default* provisions**, meaning that the partners can change these rules if they desire.[7]

In the relationship between partners and outsiders, two questions arise: When is the partnership liable to outsiders? If the partnership is liable, who must pay the debt?

Liability of the Partnership to Outsiders

Under the UPA, **every partner is an agent of the partnership for the purpose of its business.**[8]

Authority

Partnership liability is based on the rules of agency law, discussed in Chapter 28. As an agent, a partner has three types of authority:

- **Actual authority.** A partnership is liable for any act of a partner that it authorized. Suppose Tamika and Daniel have formed the TD partnership to buy and sell used books. They decide that they would be willing to pay up to $100 for any first-edition *Harry Potter* books. When Daniel agrees to pay $75 to a customer who brings in such a book, the partnership is liable.
- **Implied authority.** A partnership is liable for any act of a partner that is reasonably necessary to carry out an authorized transaction. If Daniel spends $20 to take a taxi to meet a potential customer, the partnership must reimburse him.
- **Apparent authority.** A partnership is liable for an unauthorized act of a partner if the partner *appears* to be carrying on the business of the partnership or even business of the same type. Without Daniel's knowledge, Tamika promises to pay a large sum for Jane's record collection. Jane is a regular customer of the TD partnership and simply assumes that Tamika has authority to act. The TD partnership is liable because buying used records is the same kind of business as buying used books.

---

[6] *Haught v. Maceluch*, 681 F.2d 290, 1982 U.S. App. LEXIS 17123 (5th Cir. 1982).
[7] The exceptions are listed in UPA §103.
[8] UPA §301(1).

This issue frequently arises when a partnership breaks up but fails to notify customers. If Tamika and Daniel terminate their partnership but do not tell Jane, both of the former partners are liable on any deal Tamika enters into with Jane, as long as the transaction reasonably relates to the TD business.

Ratification

As with every agency relationship, partners can ratify unauthorized acts. **If the partnership accepts the benefit of the unauthorized transaction or fails to repudiate it, the partnership has ratified it.** Once ratified, these actions are as valid as if they had been authorized from the beginning. Thus, Daniel exceeds his authority when he offers Matthew $1,000 for any Stephen King first edition. Tamika is outraged, but she never tells Matthew that the deal is no good. After scouring the city, Matthew finds a first edition of *Misery*. The partnership must pay for the book, no matter how miserable it makes Tamika.

Information

As agent, a partner has a duty to pass on all relevant information to the partnership. Whether or not a partner actually fulfills this obligation, the partnership is treated as if it had been notified. Under the UPA, **whatever one partner knows, the partnership is deemed to know**. Under the terms of TD's storefront lease, the landlord must give 90 days' notice if he does not want to renew. He gives notice to Tamika, who forgets to tell Daniel. The notice is nonetheless valid, and the landlord has every right to evict the partnership. If someone is going to suffer harm because of Tamika's mistake, in all fairness, it should be the partnership, which had the bad judgment to take on an unreliable partner.

Tort Liability

A partnership is responsible for the *intentional* and *negligent* torts of a partner that occur *in the ordinary course* of the partnership's business or with the *actual* authority of the partners. When Daniel tells a customer that a book is a valuable, first-edition Tom Clancy when it really is a worthless Book of the Month Club edition, the partnership is liable for this intentional misrepresentation because it occurred in the ordinary course of the partnership's business. But if Daniel gets in a fight at a bar on Saturday night, the partnership is not liable because that had nothing to do with the partnership's business.

Paying the Debts of the Partnership

The basic rule of partnership liability is simply stated: **all partners are personally liable for all debts of the partnership**. All of a partner's assets are at risk. This rule applies whether or not the individual partner was in any way responsible for the debts. Thus, for example, when the accounting firm Laventhol & Horwath went bankrupt, the partners were personally liable, and some had to sell their houses to pay the partnership's debts.

Joint and Several Liability

Partners have *joint and several* liability for partnership obligations. Joint and several liability means that a creditor can sue the partnership and the partners together, or in separate lawsuits, or in any combination. The partnership and the partners are all individually liable for the full amount of the debt, but obviously the creditor cannot keep collecting after he has already received the total amount owed. **Also note that, even if creditors have a judgment against an individual partner, they cannot go after that partner's assets until all the partnership's assets are exhausted.**[9]

[9]UPA §307.

Letitia, one of the world's wealthiest people, enters into a partnership with penniless Harry to drill for oil on her land. While driving on partnership business, Harry crashes into Gus, seriously injuring him. Gus can sue any combination of the partnership, Letitia, and Harry for the full amount, even though Letitia was 2,000 miles away on her Caribbean island when the accident occurred and she had many times cautioned Harry to drive carefully. Even if Gus obtains a judgment against Letitia, however, he cannot recover against her while the partnership still has assets. So, for all practical purposes, he must try to collect first against the partnership. If the partnership is bankrupt and he manages to collect the full amount from Letitia, he cannot then try to recover against Harry. (As we will see in a minute, Letitia may be able to recover from Harry some portion of what she paid Gus.)

Letitia is not wild about Harry's behavior, so she insists that he agree in writing to share all liabilities of the partnership 50/50. Unfortunately for Letitia, the liability rule is *mandatory,* not a default provision, so her agreement with Harry has absolutely no impact on the rights of Gus or any other creditor. He can still recover from Letitia for all debts of the partnership. She can always try to recover from Harry, but he is penniless, so good luck.

Liability of Incoming Partners

A partner is personally liable only for obligations the partnership incurred while he was a partner. His liability for debts incurred before he became partner is limited to his investment in the partnership.[10] Does this rule make sense? Why should an incoming partner be liable in any way for debts the partnership incurred before he became a partner? These issues haunted the investment bank Goldman Sachs when the Englishman Robert Maxwell drowned. Long known as an international wheeler-dealer, Maxwell stole money from his companies' pension plans to pay for the purchase of newspapers and publishing houses around the world. He drowned after falling—or jumping—over the side of his yacht late one evening. After his death, investigators discovered that more than $1 billion was missing from his various enterprises. The looted pension plans sued Goldman, which settled the lawsuits for $250 million. That was the simple part. The more complicated issue was how to divide this liability among the Goldman partners. Current partners argued that the liability should be borne by those who were Goldman partners when the Maxwell transactions occurred. But the ex-partners balked at having to pay as much as $4 million apiece for a settlement they had not agreed to or even had a chance to vote on.

He drowned after falling—or jumping—over the side of his yacht late one evening.

In a sense, the UPA supports both of these positions. Goldman's ex-partners were personally liable for debts incurred while they were members of the firm. However, current partners were also liable, up to the amount of their investment in the partnership, for debts incurred even before they joined.

EXAM Strategy

Question: Mark and Shania are students who also have a business on the side selling baskets of fruit and vegetables that are cut to look like flowers. They advertise that all ingredients are organic. One day, Mark is in a hurry, and instead of driving across town to the organic food co-op, he purchases ingredients from the closest grocery

[10] UPA §306.

store, Unsafeway. Hannibal has a chemical allergy, so when he eats fruit from Mark's basket, he becomes ill. He sues Mark and Shania and is awarded $10,000 in damages. Is Shania personally liable?

Strategy: First decide if Mark and Shania have a partnership. If so, is the partnership liable for Mark's actions? Is Shania liable for the debts of the partnership that were incurred by Mark?

Result: Although Mark and Shania are students, they also run a business for profit and therefore, are partners for purposes of that business. The partnership is liable for Mark's actions because he was authorized to act. Hannibal must first try to recover the judgment from the partnership. Only if the partnership has no assets can he recover from Mark or Shania individually. At that point, Hannibal has the right to recover from Shania, even though she personally did nothing wrong.

Relationship Among Partners

The rules governing the relationship between partners and outsiders are mandatory; the partners cannot change them. In contrast, the rules regulating the relationship among partners are more flexible—the partners can alter many of them by agreement. If these rules can be changed, why are they in the UPA at all? Partnerships are often formed casually. Sometimes the partners themselves do not even realize they have a partnership. In situations such as these, the default rules apply. Also, some partnerships may not want to undertake the effort and expense of preparing their own agreement. For them, the off-the-rack rules work well enough, and they do not need a custom-tailored version.

Financial Rights

Sharing Profits

Partners share profits equally unless they agree otherwise. This basic rule applies no matter how much money, time, or effort an individual partner contributes to the partnership. After graduation, Dawn convinces her friends, Niels and Sonya, to return with her to Jackson, Mississippi, to open a coffee bar. Niels and Sonya each contribute $15,000. Dawn has nothing to contribute financially. But she does know Jackson. When Dawn's Coffee Bar opens for business, she attracts sellout crowds. Meanwhile, Niels and Sonya are working 20-hour days, first renovating the building and then serving customers. Dawn rarely sees the dawn, or even noon. Niels and Sonya have contributed more time and money and may have done more for the bar's success, but they must share profits equally with Dawn unless the three agreed otherwise.

© kgelati/Shutterstock.com

What is Dawn's share of the profits?

Sharing Losses

Partners share losses according to their share of profits unless they agree otherwise. If Dawn's Coffee Bar fizzles after the first few months of success, then Dawn is responsible for one-third of the losses because she received one-third of the profits. It is too late for her to argue that it was not her fault the business failed.

Payment for Work Done

Partners are not entitled to any payment beyond their share of profits unless they agree otherwise. Niels and Sonya have no right to a greater share of the profits in return for their extra work. It is simply too difficult for the courts to evaluate each partner's contributions. ("Sonya didn't get to work until 9:15." "That's not true, I was there at 8:45, but you didn't see me because I was out back washing your dirty dishes....") This rule may seem arbitrary, but at least it is easy to enforce. The only exception, which we will see later, is that partners are entitled to remuneration for services performed in winding up the partnership.

In the following case, the father made a number of mistakes—he died without a will and left his business without a written partnership agreement. The result was the last thing he would ever have wanted: all-out war among his children.

BANKER V. ESTATE OF BANKER

911 N.Y.S.2d 691; 2010 N.Y. Misc. LEXIS 1145
Supreme Court of New York, Delaware County, 2010

Facts: Father Banker owned Peaceful Valley Campground (which more accurately should have been called Angry Family Battleground). Peaceful Valley (PV) operated as both a campground, with cabins and an RV site. When Father Banker died without a will, each of his four sons inherited roughly 10 percent, while his widow got the rest. One son, Arnold, bought out his mother's share, so he owned roughly two-thirds.

Because the four brothers had made no other arrangement, PV operated as a partnership. Arnold was the only brother who worked in the business. He lived year-round in a house on the campground, where he was on call 24 hours a day during the seven-month camping season. He dealt with routine camp business (including reservations and maintenance), as well as emergencies. Off-season, he made repairs and did office work.

The partnership paid Arnold a salary of about $25,000 a year. It also paid his live-in girlfriend, Linda Romeo, about $10,000 a year for office work and cleaning. In addition, PV paid some of Arnold's personal expenses. The other brothers had not agreed to these payments.

The brothers objected to payments from PV to Arnold, alleging that, as a partner, Arnold had no right to payment for the work he performed.

Issue: ***Was Arnold entitled to any payment in addition to his share of partnership profits?***

Excerpts from Justice Peckham's Decision: The personal expenses of Arnold alleged to have been paid from the partnership include meals and lodging, a truck, furniture and fixtures, and sunglasses. The meals and lodging were trips related to campground business. The furniture and fixtures were actually two additional cabins for the campground. The truck was purchased for use at the campground hauling materials and supplies and also canoes the camp rents out. The sunglasses were for Arnold's use working around the camp. [T]he objection to these expenses is denied.

There is no written partnership agreement and no proof was introduced that the partners ever agreed to Arnold's salary. [W]hen there is no written partnership agreement, the New York Partnership Law effectively becomes the partnership agreement. Under the Partnership Law of New York, consent by all the partners was needed [for a partner to receive] compensation for services rendered to the partnership. No such consent was given by the three minority partners in the Peaceful Valley partnership. No consent having been given, the payment of a salary violated the partnership agreement and the law and must be refunded.

The work Ms. Romeo performed is the same type of work done by Arnold and could have been done by him. The other partners did not agree to hire Ms. Romeo, nor to the payments made to her. [Arnold must repay these amounts.]

Partnership Property

All partnership property belongs to the partnership as a whole, not to the individual partners. A partner has no right to use or sell property except for the benefit of the partnership. Suppose that the partnership owns the building that houses their coffee bar. Upstairs, above the bar, are three apartments. "Wow! This is great," says Niels, "I get the front unit." Does Niels have the right to live in one of the three apartments? After all, Dawn and Sonya can have the other two. Although the arrangement sounds fair, in fact, Niels has no right to live there unless the other partners agree.

Right to Transfer a Partnership Interest

A partnership is a personal relationship built on trust. Therefore, a partner can no more sell his partnership share to a stranger than a spouse can come home one night and announce, "I'm leaving the marriage but, don't worry, I've found a substitute." **Without the approval of the other partners, a partner cannot sell her share; she can only transfer her right to receive profits and losses. A new partner can only be admitted to a partnership by unanimous consent of the other partners.**[11] It would be unfair to force partners to work with, or face unlimited liability for, someone they do not consider trustworthy. Sonya gets in serious debt to a fellow gambler, Nathan Detroit. Fearful that Nathan will ruin her manicure if she does not pay her debt, she agrees to give him her share of the partnership, which is her only asset. He knows a lot about coffee, and she is sure he will do fine as a partner. Although Niels and Dawn feel sorry for Sonya's predicament, they refuse to admit Nathan as a partner. Without their permission, Sonya has no right to transfer ownership rights or management authority to Nathan. Niels and Dawn cannot be forced to work with someone they do not want to touch with a 10-foot pole. However, Sonya can transfer to Nathan the right to receive her share of the partnership's profits.

What if Sonya refuses to assign to Nathan her right to receive profits from the partnership? **Creditors can attach partnership profits through a charging order.** A **charging order** is simply a court order granting a third party the right to receive a share of partnership profits.

Similar rules apply when a partner dies. A partner's heirs have no right to specific partnership property; they do not become partners themselves, nor do they have any say in partnership management. They do have a right to receive the value of a partnership share. In large, sophisticated partnerships, the partnership agreement will usually short-circuit arguments by establishing in advance how to calculate the value of a share.

Management Rights

Right to Manage

Each and every partner has equal rights in the management and conduct of the business unless the partners agree otherwise. In a large partnership, with hundreds of partners, too many cooks can definitely spoil the firm's profitability. That is why large partnerships are almost always run by one or a few partners who are designated as managing partners or members of the executive committee. Some firms are run almost dictatorially by the "rainmaker"—the partner who brings in the most business. Nonetheless, even in an autocratic firm, the atmosphere tends to be less hierarchical than in a corporation, where employees are accustomed to the concept of having a boss. Whatever the reality, partners by and large like to think of themselves as being the equal of every other partner.

Right to Bind the Partnership

As we have discussed, partners are agents of the partnership and have the power to bind the partnership through actual, implied, or apparent authority. The partnership is liable to third parties for a partner's actions. **If these actions are not authorized by the partnership, the partner still has the *power* to bind the partnership, but not the *right*.** In this case, the partnership is liable to the third party, and the partner is liable to the partnership. If the

[11]UPA §401(i).

partner has both the *power* and the *right,* he is not personally liable to the partnership no matter how harmful his actions.

A partner is authorized to bind the partnership for any transaction within the ordinary course of its business unless the partner knows that the other partners would disapprove. Dawn decides she would rather buy coffee from Hadley than from the regular supplier in New York. She has the authority to switch suppliers unless she knows that Sonya and Niels would object because Hadley's coffee is not free trade. If Dawn signs a contract with Hadley, knowing that her partners disapprove, the partnership is liable to Hadley, but Dawn is liable to the partnership.

Right to Vote

Unless the partners agree otherwise, all partners have an equal vote, regardless of their contributions to the partnership. For ordinary partnership affairs, the majority has the right to make a decision. To amend the partnership agreement or to make decisions outside the ordinary course of business, the vote must be unanimous. What happens when Dawn wants to introduce organic teas, over Niels's dead body? The partners vote. Since this is an ordinary partnership matter, the majority rules. If Dawn can get Sonya on her side, she will win approval for the healthy teas. It makes no difference that Dawn never contributed any cash to the partnership; she has the right to vote.

This is the default rule, but many partnerships change it by agreement. Accounting and law firms, for instance, often award partners a certain number of points each year based on how much business they bring in or how hard they work. The more points, the higher their compensation and the more their votes count. Some firms, run by a particularly powerful partner, may effectively have only one vote—his. The managing partner of a large law firm once said, "This partnership has a one-man, one-vote rule, and I'm the one man."

Right to Know

It is difficult to manage an enterprise without adequate information. **Therefore, the UPA grants each partner the right to inspect and copy the partnership's books and records.** This right is unconditional and does not depend upon the partner's purpose or motive. However, books and records are not enough, by themselves, to keep a partner fully informed. Therefore, the UPA requires all partners and the partnership to volunteer any information that might reasonably be necessary for other partners to exercise their rights. All partners and the partnership also have a duty to supply any other information that a partner reasonably requests. These rules are mandatory; the partners may not change them by agreement among themselves.

Management Duties

Partners have the right to manage the partnership. In addition, they also have duties to the partnership and the other partners. These duties are mandatory; the partners may not waive them.

Duties of Care

Partners are liable to the partnership for gross negligence, reckless conduct, intentional misconduct, or a knowing violation of the law. Partners are not liable for ordinary negligence.[12] As you remember from earlier in this chapter, a partnership is liable for the intentional and negligent torts of a partner that occur in the ordinary course of business. But, as you have just learned, the partner is not liable to the partnership for ordinary negligence. These two rules intersect in the following case.

---

[12]UPA §404.

Moren v. Jax Restaurant

679 N.W.2d 165, 2004 Minn. App. LEXIS 459
Court of Appeals of Minnesota, 2004

Facts: Jax was a pizza restaurant in Foley, Minnesota, owned by two sisters: Nicole Moren and Amy Benedetti. They operated it as a partnership. One afternoon, Moren ended her regular shift at 4:00 p.m. and left to pick up her two-year-old son, Remington, from day care. When her sister called her to say that one of the cooks had not come to work, Moren returned to the restaurant with Remington. Moren's husband said he would pick the child up in about 20 minutes.

Because Moren did not want Remington running around the restaurant, she brought him into the kitchen with her, set him on top of the counter, and began rolling out pizza dough using the dough-pressing machine. As she was making pizzas, Remington reached his hand into the dough press. His hand was crushed, causing permanent injuries. His father brought suit on Remington's behalf against the partnership for negligence. The partnership, in its turn, sued Moren, arguing that she had to reimburse the partnership for any payments to Remington. The district court granted summary judgment to Moren. The restaurant appealed.

Issue: ***Is Moren liable to the partnership for her own negligence?***

Excerpts from Judge Crippen's Decision: The partnership [argues] that its obligation to compensate Remington is diminished in proportion to the predominating negligence of Moren as a mother, although it is responsible for her conduct as a business owner. Under Minnesota's Uniform Partnership Act of 1994 (UPA), a partnership is liable for loss or injury caused to a person as a result of a wrongful act or omission, or other actionable conduct, of a partner acting in the ordinary course of business of the partnership or with authority of the partnership. [Moreover], a partnership [must] indemnify a partner for liabilities incurred by the partner in the ordinary course of the business of the partnership. Thus, under the plain language of the UPA, a partner has a right to indemnity from the partnership, but the partnership's claim of indemnity from a partner is not authorized or required.

The district court correctly concluded that Nicole Moren's conduct was in the ordinary course of business of the partnership and, as a result, indemnity by the partner to the partnership was inappropriate. It is undisputed that one of the cooks scheduled to work that evening did not come in, and that Moren's partner asked her to help in the kitchen. It also is undisputed that Moren was making pizzas for the partnership when her son was injured. Because her conduct at the time of the injury was in the ordinary course of business of the partnership, under the UPA, her conduct bound the partnership and it owes indemnity to her for her negligence.

[The restaurant] also claims that because Nicole Moren's action of bringing Remington into the kitchen was partly motivated by personal reasons, her conduct was outside the ordinary course of business. Even if the predominant motive of the partner was to benefit himself or third persons, such does not prevent the concurrent business purpose from being within the scope of the partnership. [W]e conclude that the conduct of Nicole Moren was no less in the ordinary course of business because it also served personal purposes. It is undisputed that Moren was acting for the benefit of the partnership by making pizzas when her son was injured, and even though she was simultaneously acting in her role as a mother, her conduct remained in the ordinary course of the partnership business.

Affirmed.

Duty of Loyalty

Partners have a limited fiduciary duty to their partnership.

Competing with the Partnership. **Each partner must turn over to the partnership all earnings from any activity that is related to the partnership's business.** Cara, Max, and Brooke are partners in a Beverly Hills law firm. While Cara is vacationing near Santa Fe, a guest in the next-door hacienda is arrested in the middle of the night for drunk driving. Cara goes down to the police station and persuades the police officer to release the guest. Her new client gratefully insists on paying her $5,000 for her efforts. Cara figures the fee will go a long way toward paying the cost of her vacation. Cara figures wrong. She must turn the fee over to the partnership because she earned it doing the kind of work that the partnership does. It is irrelevant that she was on vacation.

Taking a Business Opportunity. **A partner may not take an opportunity away from the partnership unless the other partners consent.** Suppose that Beverly Hills needs a lawyer to serve as city counsel and offers the post to Max. He cannot take the job himself without the firm's permission. If he violates this duty, the partnership is entitled to the value of the opportunity he has taken.

Using Partnership Property. **A partner must turn over to the partnership any profit he earns from use of partnership property without the consent of the partners.** The partnership's office is in an old, beautifully restored historic building. Max runs a party-planning service on the side—MAXimum Fun. He occasionally holds parties on the weekends in the partnership's elegant foyer without telling Brooke and Cara. When they find out, they are maximum angry, and for good reason—Max has violated his duty to the partnership.

© Corbis Bridge / Alamy

Does Max get to keep the profit from these parties?

Conflict of Interest. **A partner has a conflict of interest whenever the partnership does business with him, a member of his family, or a business partly or fully owned by him. In that case, the partner must turn all profits over to the partnership.** Suppose that Max hires MAXimum Fun to put on the firm's 10th-anniversary celebration. Unless the other partners consent in advance, Max must turn over to the partnership any profits he earns from the party.

In the following case, one partner bought partnership property at a public auction. Is that a conflict of interest?

Marsh v. Gentry

642 S.W.2d 574, 1982 Ky. LEXIS 315
Supreme Court of Kentucky, 1982

Facts: Tom Gentry and John Marsh were partners in a business that bought and sold racehorses. The partnership paid $155,000 for Champagne Woman, who subsequently had a foal named Excitable Lady. The partners decided to sell Champagne Woman at the annual Keeneland auction, the world's premier thoroughbred horse auction. On the day of the auction, Gentry decided to bid on the horse personally, without telling Marsh. Gentry bought Champagne Woman for $135,000. Later, he told Marsh that someone from California had approached him about buying Excitable Lady. Marsh agreed to the sale. Although he repeatedly asked Gentry the name of the purchaser, Gentry refused to tell him. Not until 11 months later, when Excitable Lady won a race at Churchill Downs, did Marsh learn that Gentry had been the purchaser. Marsh became the Excitable Man.

Issue: ***Did Gentry violate his fiduciary duty when he bought partnership property without telling his partner?***

Excerpts from Justice O'Hara's Decision: Admittedly, at an auction sale, the specific identity of a purchaser cannot be ascertained before the sale, but [Kentucky partnership law] required a full disclosure by Gentry to Marsh that he would be a prospective purchaser.

As to the private sale of Excitable Lady, Marsh consented to a sale from the partnership, at a specified price, to the prospective purchaser in California. Even though Marsh obtained the stipulated purchase price, a partner has an absolute right to know when his partner is the purchaser. Partners scrutinize buyouts by their partners in an entirely different light than an ordinary third party sale. This distinction is vividly made without contradiction when Marsh later indicated that he would not have consented to either sale had he known that Gentry was the purchaser. Under these facts, it is obvious that Gentry failed to disclose all that he knew concerning the sales, including his desire to purchase partnership property.

[P]artners, in their relations with other partners, [must] maintain a higher degree of good faith due to the partnership agreement. The requirement of full disclosure among partners as to partnership business cannot be escaped.

Finally, Gentry maintains that it is an accepted practice at auction sales of thoroughbreds for one partner to secretly bid on partnership stock to accomplish a buyout. We would emphatically state, however, for the benefit of those engaged in such practices, that where an "accepted business practice" conflicts with existing law, the law, whether statutory or court ordered, is controlling. To hold otherwise would be chaotic.

Good Faith and Fair Dealing

Partners have an obligation of good faith and fair dealing to each other and to the partnership. They must deal with each other *fairly* and *without coercion.* Behavior that would be acceptable in an arm's-length transaction may be unacceptable between partners. Hartz Mountain Industries, Inc., was the managing partner of a real estate business in northern New Jersey. Eugene Heller was Hartz's partner. According to the partnership agreement, when Heller left the partnership, Hartz would have the properties appraised and buy Heller's share. Hartz had the right to choose the appraiser. Over Heller's objection, Hartz chose Robert DiFalco. Hartz's own internal appraisals valued the properties at more than $214 million, but DiFalco produced an appraisal of $133 million—a slight discrepancy of more than $80 million.

The court found that, while Hartz had technically complied with the partnership agreement, it had breached its obligation of good faith and fair dealing. Courts generally pay a great deal of respect to appraisals, especially when both parties have agreed in advance to the appraisal process. But the court did not accept the appraisal in this case because Hartz had violated its duty to Heller by choosing such an unreliable appraiser.[13]

EXAM Strategy

Question: Tom is a bully. He and Penelope start a test prep business. The partnership agreement specifies that Penelope is entitled to 30 percent of the profits, but that Tom is the managing partner with the right to run the day-to-day affairs of the business. Because students love Penelope's gentle demeanor, the business flourishes. A large university offers the partnership a contract to provide test prep services to all of its students. Tom decides to take that business himself without telling Penelope. He also reduces her income from the partnership. She asks for data on the partnership's profitability, but Tom refuses to give it to her. He also moves the business into a shabbier, cheaper building that Penelope hates. What rights does Penelope have?

[13] *Heller v. Hartz Mountain Industries, Inc.*, 270 N.J. Super. 143, 636 A.2d 599, 1993 N.J. Super. LEXIS 903 (N.J. Super. Ct. Law Div. 1993).

Strategy: The partnership agreement determines most of the rights between partners, but some rights are mandatory and cannot be changed by the partners.

Result: Tom does have the right to move the partnership into a different building, but he cannot take the opportunity to provide services to the university without telling Penelope. She is entitled to see the books and records of the partnership.

Terminating a Partnership

Partnership at will
A partnership with no fixed duration. Any of the partners may leave at any time, for any reason.

Term partnership
A partnership in which the partners agree in advance how long it will last.

The rules on termination depend, in part, on the type of partnership. If the partners have not agreed how long their partnership will last, they have a **partnership at will**, and any of them may leave at any time, for any reason. Taylor, Jay, and Gabriela are partners in the Donut Partnership, which owns a racehorse by the name of Speedy Donut. They see their business as a lark, to last as long as they are having fun, so they make no decision about its duration. When Taylor decamps after only two months, leaving Jay and Gabriela holding the feedbag, they have no legal right to complain.

With a **term partnership**, the partners have agreed in advance how long it will last. At the end of the specified term, the partnership automatically ends. If Taylor, Jay, and Gabriela agree to sell Speedy Donut and end their business relationship in five years, or if they agree the partnership will end when Speedy Donut runs in the Kentucky Derby, they have a term partnership.

Dissociation

Dissociation
When a partner leaves the partnership.

A partnership begins with an association of two or more people. Appropriately, the end of a partnership begins with a *dissociation*. A **dissociation** occurs when a partner quits. However, a dissociation does not inevitably lead to the termination of the partnership business. A dissociation is a fork in the road: **when one or more partners dissociate, the partnership can either buy out the departing partner(s) and continue in business or wind up the business and terminate the partnership**. Exhibit 32.1 illustrates the dissociation process under the UPA.

Rightful versus Wrongful Dissociation

A partnership is a personal relationship built on trust. As we have seen, all partners are agents for the partnership, and each partner is personally liable for its debts. The actions of one partner can profoundly affect the financial health of every other partner. Under these circumstances, courts will not force someone to remain in a partnership, no matter what the partnership agreement says, any more than they will force a couple to stay married because of their vows at the altar. Partners can always dissociate, but like any divorcing spouse, they may have to pay damages for the harm that their departure causes. As courts are wont to say: **a partner always has the power to leave a partnership but may not have the right**.

Rightful Dissociation. A rightful dissociation occurs if:

- *A partner in a partnership at will serves notice that he intends to withdraw.*
- *The partners agree in advance on an event that causes dissociation.* Jay plans to attend business school in three years, so the partnership agreement provides that he will be automatically dissociated from the partnership at that point.

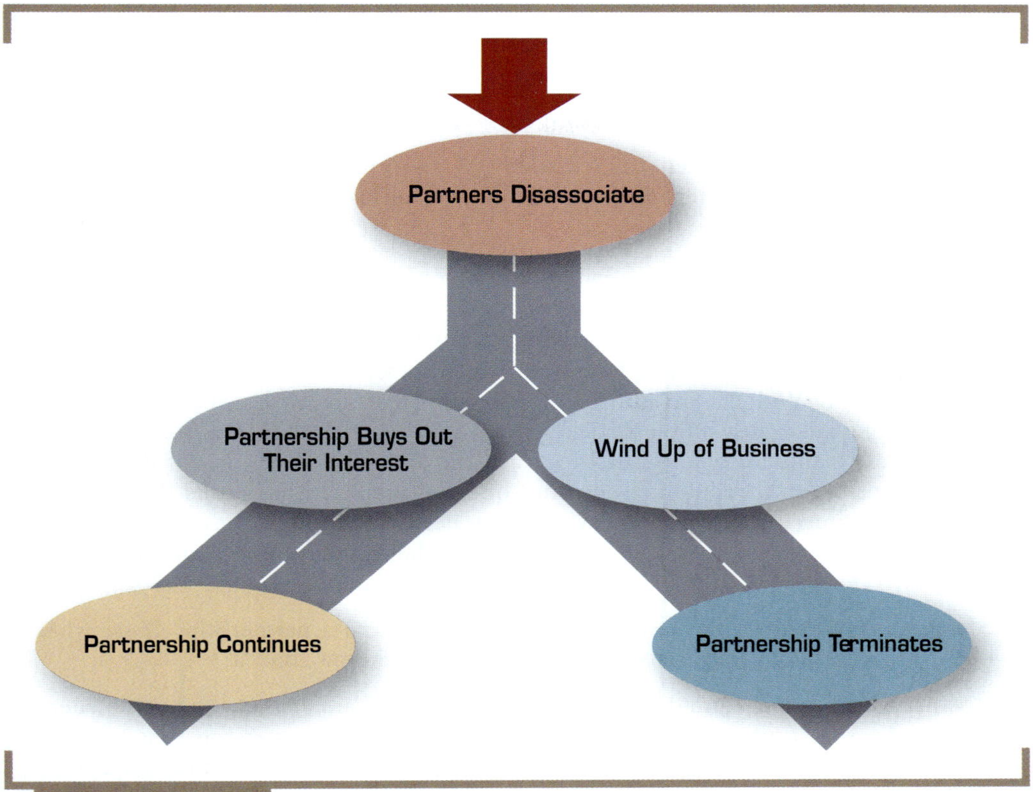

EXHIBIT 32.1

- *A partner dies or becomes incompetent.*
- *A partner is expelled by the other partners.* Partnership agreements can establish a process for expelling a partner. Often, under such agreements, the partnership does not even have to give a reason for expulsion. If a certain percentage of the partners (say, 75 percent) vote against someone, she is out. However, in the absence of such a provision in the partnership agreement, the UPA permits the expulsion of a partner only if (1) it is illegal to carry on the business with her or (2) she has transferred her partnership interest.

Even lawyers sometimes forget the law. The prestigious law firm of Cadwalader, Wickersham, & Taft fired a partner in its New York office. However, the partnership agreement said nothing about expulsion. A court upheld the firing but awarded the former partner $3 million in damages. In short, the law firm had the power, but not the right, to expel a partner. Unlike employees of a corporation, partners cannot be fired unless their partnership agreement specifically allows for it.

Wrongful Dissociation. A wrongful dissociation occurs if:

- *A partner violates the partnership agreement.* The Donut Partnership agreement prohibits racetrack betting. When Taylor wins the Pick Six, he is automatically dissociated.
- *A partner in a term partnership withdraws before the end of the term.* The Donut Partnership is supposed to last five years, but Jay withdraws after five months.
- *A court expels a partner in a term partnership because her behavior is harmful.* A court has the right to expel a partner who engages in wrongful conduct that harms the

partnership or violates the partnership agreement in a serious way. Gabriela drugs the favored Speedy Donut so that she can win a bet on a long shot in the race. A court could expel her, and that would constitute a wrongful dissociation.

- *A partner in a term partnership becomes bankrupt.*

Once a partner is dissociated, the remaining partners must decide how to proceed; they can either continue the partnership as an ongoing business or terminate it.

EXAM Strategy

Question: In their spare time, Maisy and Roland like to build widgets for Facebook.com. (Widgets are software applications that permit Facebook users to do cool things like post bumper stickers on their pages.) Under Facebook rules, Maisy and Roland are paid a small fee each time someone uses one of their applications. After this sideline becomes quite profitable, Maisy tells Roland that she is going to start building widgets on her own without him—she thinks she is more creative than Roland. Does Maisy have the right to exclude Roland?

Strategy: There are three questions to answer: Is there a partnership? If so, what kind of partnership? Does Maisy have the right to withdraw from it?

Result: Maisy and Roland do have a partnership—they are carrying on as co-owners of a business for profit. It does not matter that the word "partnership" has never passed their lips. Because there is no partnership agreement, they have a partnership at will. With this form of partnership, Maisy can withdraw at any time for any reason.

Continuation of the Partnership Business

If a partner is dissociated from the partnership, the other partners can continue the business, but they must buy out the ex-partner.[14] Most large firms provide in their partnership agreement that, upon dissociation, the business continues.

Financial Settlement

If the partnership decides to continue, it must pay the ex-partner the value of her share of the business. This value is equal to her share of the proceeds if (1) the partnership were sold as an ongoing business or (2) the partnership's assets were liquidated, whichever calculation is greater. For example, if Gabriela is adjudged incompetent by a court, she is automatically dissociated from the Donut Partnership. At that point, Speedy Donut is worth $500,000 and the partnership has debts of $50,000, for a total value of $450,000. Gabriela is entitled to at least a one-third share—$150,000. If, however, the partnership is worth $600,000 as an ongoing business, Gabriela is entitled to $200,000.

Now the plot thickens. If Gabriela's dissociation was *wrongful,* the partnership can subtract any damages she caused from the amount it owes her. A court expels Gabriela

[14]If the ex-partner's dissociation was rightful, she can vote in this decision. If her dissociation was wrongful, she has no right to vote.

from the partnership because she drugged Speedy Donut. His recovery is slow and he is unable to race for months, costing the partnership $100,000. Taylor and Jay could subtract that $100,000 from the $200,000 they owe her, so she ultimately receives a check for only $100,000. If her bad acts caused more than $200,000 in damage, she owes them money.

Liability of the Dissociated Partner to Outsiders for Debts Incurred *before* Dissociation

A dissociated partner is liable to outsiders for debts incurred during her term as a partner, but the partnership must indemnify her for these debts. After Gabriela departs, a bank sues the partnership for failure to repay its loan. Although Gabriela is no longer a partner, she was one when the partnership borrowed the money. As we have seen, the bank may be able to recover from her. If it does, however, the partnership must indemnify her, that is, the partnership must reimburse her for any amounts she pays the bank. This outcome is only fair because, when the partnership purchased her share, it reduced the payment to reflect liabilities such as this.

Liability of the Dissociated Partner to Outsiders for Debts Incurred *after* Dissociation

A dissociated partner is liable to outsiders for the debts of the partnership incurred within two years after she leaves, but only if the creditor reasonably believes she is still a partner. The partnership must indemnify her for these debts. If Taylor and Jay buy an expensive saddle on credit from their regular supplier, Gabriela is also liable unless the saddler knows she is dissociated. The partnership would have to reimburse her (if it has enough funds). To protect herself, however, Gabriela can file a statement of dissociation with the Secretary of State. Although the saddler rarely spends his free afternoons perusing the public records, he is deemed to have notice of this filing 90 days after Gabriela makes it.

Liability of the Dissociated Partner to the Partnership

If the ex-partner harms the partnership after she leaves, she is liable for the damage she causes. If Gabriela lets a feed supplier believe that she is still a partner and then buys feed on credit, the partnership may be liable for her charges. If so, she must reimburse the partnership.

Termination of the Partnership Business

When a partner is dissociated, the partnership may choose to terminate the business rather than continue it. **Ending a partnership business involves three steps: dissolution, winding up, and termination.**

Dissolution

Unless the partners agree otherwise, a partnership dissolves under the following circumstances:

- *In a partnership at will, when a partner notifies the partnership that he intends to withdraw and the remaining partners cannot agree unanimously to continue the business.*
- *In a term partnership, when:*
    - *A partner is dissociated before the end of the term and half of the remaining partners vote to wind up the partnership business.* When Jay dies, he is dissociated from the partnership. If Gabriela votes to wind up the business, the partnership is dissolved.
    - *All the partners agree to dissolve.* Although the Donut Partnership is supposed to last five years, Taylor, Jay, and Gabriela can agree among themselves to wind up the

business whenever they want. If Speedy Donut is a cream puff on the racetrack, they can decide to dissolve their partnership and sell the pastry.

- *The term expires or the partnership achieves its goal.* If Speedy Donut runs in the Derby, the Donut Partnership automatically dissolves.

- *In any partnership, when:*
  - *An event occurs which the partners had agreed would cause dissolution.* The Donut Partnership agreement provided that the partnership would dissolve if Speedy Donut failed to win a race in any 12-month period. When Speedy Donut goes winless, the partnership dissolves.
  - *The partnership business becomes illegal.* If horse racing is banned, the Donut Partnership automatically dissolves.
  - *A court determines that the partnership is unlikely to succeed.* If the partners simply cannot get along or they cannot make a profit, any partner has the right to ask a court to dissolve the partnership. If Taylor and Jay quarrel over everything and are unable to reach agreement on anything, a court is likely to agree to dissolve the partnership.

Note that even if one of these events occurs, partners can always decide (by unanimous vote) to continue a partnership. Indeed, even after the winding-up process begins, the partners can change their minds and continue the business.

Winding Up

During the winding-up process, all debts of the partnership are paid, and the remaining proceeds are distributed to the partners.

Who Does It? Unless the partnership agreement provides otherwise, any partner who has not wrongfully dissociated has the right to oversee the winding up.

Are They Paid? Partners are entitled to reasonable compensation for their work in winding up the partnership.

What Do They Do? The winding-up process can be complex and take as long as several years to complete. The partners in charge can either sell the entire business as a whole, sell the individual assets of the business, distribute specific assets to the partners, or some combination of these options. They have the right to complete unfinished transactions and do whatever is necessary to wind up the business, but they do not have the right to take on new business.

If Taylor is winding up the Donut Partnership, he can sell Speedy Donut outright, buy feed for him until the sale, sue to recover any winnings that have not been paid, and settle partnership debts. But can he enter the horse in additional races? In a similar case, a court permitted the partner in charge of winding up a racing business to pay entrance fees for races even though the horses would, in all likelihood, be sold before the races. The court assumed that buyers would pay more for horses that were eligible to race in upcoming events.[15]

The partnership is bound by the acts of the partners in charge of winding up. As the following case illustrates, this rule can sometimes lead to unhappy results.

---

[15] *Central Trust & S. Deposit Co. v. Respass*, 112 Ky. 606, 66 S.W. 421 (1902).

Jefferson Insurance Co. v. Curle

771 S.W.2d 424, 1989 Tenn. App. LEXIS 30
Tennessee Court of Appeals, 1989

Facts: Michael Curle and Steven Shelley were partners doing business under the name C & S Roofing. When the partnership dissolved, Curle agreed to complete one unfinished project (the Bishop house) and left Shelley to wind up the other partnership business. Shelley canceled the partnership's general liability insurance policy without telling Curle. While painting the Bishop house, Dennis Whitsett fell through a hole in the roof that the partnership had left covered only with tar paper. When Whitsett sought to recover from the partnership for his serious injuries, Curle and Shelley asked the insurance company to pay the claim.

The trial court found the policy canceled as to Steven Shelley, individually, but in full force and effect as to the partnership and Michael Curle, individually. The insurance company appealed.

Issue: ***Was the partnership bound by Shelley's decision during the winding-up process to cancel the policy, even though he had not told Curle?***

Excerpts from Judge McLemore's Decision: [The Tennessee Partnership Act] clearly states: "After dissolution a partner can bind the partnership ... by any act appropriate for winding up partnership affairs or completing transactions unfinished at dissolution." The liquidating partner owes a continuing fiduciary duty to the other partners and has an obligation to act equitably toward them. However, these obligations run between partners and do not absolve any partner from being bound by the liquidating partner's actions in winding up partnership affairs. In the present case, we hold Shelley's cancellation of the partnership insurance policy and collection of unused premiums to be within his authority in winding up the partnership's affairs.

For the foregoing reasons, the judgment of the trial court holding the policy canceled as to Steven Shelley, individually, is affirmed, but that portion of the judgment holding that the policy is in full force and effect as to C & S Roofing, a partnership, and Michael Curle, individually, is reversed; and we hold that the policy is canceled as to all insureds and, thus, provides no coverage to any of the defendants for the accident alleged by Dennis Whitsett.

Who Is Liable If a Partner Takes on New Business? During the winding-up process, the partners continue to be liable for the debts of the partnership that were incurred before dissolution. But what if a partner oversteps her bounds during the winding-up process and takes on new business? All of the other partners are liable unless they have filed a statement of dissolution with the Secretary of State. This statement is effective 90 days after it is filed.

How Are Partnership Proceeds Distributed? During the winding-up process, the assets of the partnership are paid out in the following order:

- First, to creditors of the partnership, including creditors who are partners. Suppose that the Donut Partnership has assets of $30,000. It owes $20,000 each to the feed supplier, the stabler, and Jay, for a total of $60,000. It will pay $10,000 to each of the three creditors—Jay is treated exactly like the outsiders.
- Second, any leftover funds (or obligations) are distributed to the partners. Unless the partnership agreement provides otherwise, partners share equally in profits—and losses. In this example, the Donut Partnership had only enough assets to pay half its $60,000 debt. Each partner would then contribute $10,000 to pay the amount still owing. Jay's payment would be a wash—he owes $10,000, but he is also entitled to be paid $10,000.

Termination

After the sometimes lengthy and complex winding up, the actual termination of a partnership is anticlimactic. Termination happens automatically once the winding up is finished. The partnership is not required to do anything official; it can go out of the world even more quietly and simply than it came in.

Chapter Conclusion

In some ways, a partnership is an old-fashioned form of organization. From the late 1770s until the mid-19th century, virtually all businesses were partnerships. Then corporations gained in popularity, and now new forms have arisen such as limited liability companies and limited liability partnerships (both discussed in Chapter 31). These new forms of organization have many of the advantages of a partnership without the disadvantage of unlimited liability.

It is no surprise that to protect their partners from personal liability, many accounting firms, law firms, brokerage houses, advertising agencies, and investment banks that were originally partnerships have changed their form of organization to one of the newer options. But many organizations continue to act like partnerships even though they have changed their official form of organization. And, before the partnership baby gets thrown out with the liability bathwater, it is worth noting that many organizations—law, accounting, and investment banking firms, to name a few—have been highly successful as partnerships. The lack of hierarchy in partnerships encourages collaboration while the lure of ownership motivates employees.

Partnership law is important for another reason. As we have seen in this chapter, partnerships are often formed inadvertently by people who do not realize they are in such a relationship until a dispute arises. It is useful to know in advance the kind of behavior that will create a partnership and understand the consequences.

Exam Review

1. **FORMING A PARTNERSHIP** In determining whether a partnership exists, a court will consider whether the parties:

   - Share the profits of the business,
   - Share the losses of the business,
   - Share management of the business, and
   - Have an oral or written partnership agreement (pp. 788–792)

EXAM Strategy

Question: Suppose that in the chapter's opening vignette, Chase, Bailey, and Zack signed a document stating, "The undersigned expressly agree that they are not partners." If they continued to work together on the house, sharing the profits and the management, would they have been partners?

Strategy: Remember that in the case of partnerships, actions speak louder than words. (See the "Result" at the end of this section.)

2. **PARTNERSHIP BY ESTOPPEL** If someone is not a member of a partnership, she will nonetheless be considered a partner by estoppel if (1) she tells other people she is a partner or allows other people to say, without contradiction, that she is a partner; (2) a third party relies on this assertion; and (3) the third party suffers harm. (pp. 791–792)

Question: Helen parked her new Chevrolet in the parking lot at the airport in Springfield, Ohio. Bryan was giving flying lessons to Edward. Bryan told Edward to taxi a plane off the runway. Edward, standing on the ground next to the plane, cranked up the engine. The throttle was set too far open, so the plane began to move. Edward chased the plane on foot, grabbed its left wing, and swung the airplane in a semicircle, crashing it into Helen's car. Bryan operated his flying business under the name Bryan-Carl Air Service. Bryan and Carl were not partners, but Helen sued them both on a theory of partnership by estoppel. She argued that they had used a name for their business that sounded like a partnership. She had never heard of their business until the collision. Is Carl liable to Helen as a partner by estoppel?

Strategy: These elements are required for partnership by estoppel: the participants must have held themselves out as partners even though they are not; a third party must have relied on that representation and suffered harm. (See the "Result" at the end of this section.)

3. **PARTNERS AS AGENTS** Every partner is an agent of the partnership for the purpose of its business. A partnership is responsible for the intentional and negligent torts of a partner that occur in the ordinary course of the partnership's business or with the actual, implied or apparent authority of the other partners. (pp. 792–793)

Question: While Warren Lyon was representing Betty Cook in divorce proceedings, she inherited $60,000. Lyon suggested Cook invest her money in a corporation of which he was president. Although he promised her a substantial return, the company went bankrupt shortly thereafter. Lyon was a partner in a law firm. The firm was not in the business of giving investment advice, it did not know that Lyon was giving such advice, nor did it receive any fee from Cook for the "investment service." Is the law firm liable for Cook's loss?

Strategy: Was Lyon acting within the ordinary course of the partnership's business? Was he acting with actual, implied or apparent authority? (See the "Result" at the end of this section.)

4. **A PARTNER'S LIABILITY FOR THE DEBTS OF THE PARTNERSHIP** All partners are personally liable for all debts of the partnership incurred while they were members of the partnership. Partners have joint and several liability for partnership obligations. A partner's liability for debts incurred before she became a partner is limited to her investment in the partnership. (pp. 793–795)

5. **DEFAULT RULES AMONG PARTNERS** Unless they agree otherwise, partners:

- Share profits equally,
- Share losses according to their share of profits,
- Are not entitled to any payment beyond their share of profits, even if they perform work for the partnership,
- Have no right to use or sell specific partnership property except for the benefit of the partnership,
- Each have an equal vote, regardless of their contributions to the partnership, and
- Each have an equal right in the management of the business. (pp. 795–798)

6. **TRANSFERRING A PARTNERSHIP SHARE** Without the approval of the other partners, a partner cannot sell her share. She can only transfer the right to receive profits and losses. A new partner can be admitted to a partnership only by unanimous consent of the other partners. (p. 797)

7. **CREDITORS' RIGHTS** Creditors can attach partnership profits through a charging order. (p. 797)

8. **A PARTNER'S LIABILITY TO THE PARTNERSHIP** Partners are liable to the partnership for any damages resulting from their gross negligence, reckless conduct, intentional misconduct, or a knowing violation of the law. Partners are not liable to the partnership for ordinary negligence. (pp. 793–795)

9. **OUTSIDE EARNINGS** Each partner must turn over to the partnership all earnings from any activity that is related to the partnership's business. (pp. 799–800)

10. **PARTNERSHIP OPPORTUNITY** A partner may not take an opportunity away from the partnership unless the other partners consent. (p. 800)

11. **CONFLICT OF INTEREST** A partner has a conflict of interest whenever the partnership does business with him, a member of his family, or a business partly or fully owned by him. The partner must turn all profits over to the partnership. (p. 800)

12. **A PARTNER'S OBLIGATION TO THE PARTNERSHIP** Partners have an obligation of good faith and fair dealing to each other and to the partnership. (pp. 798–802)

13. **DISSOCIATION** A dissociation occurs when a partner leaves the partnership. (pp. 802–805)

14. **AFTER DISSOCIATION** When one or more partners dissociate, the partnership can either buy out the departing partner(s) and continue in business or wind up the business and terminate the partnership. (pp. 804–805)

15. **THE RIGHT TO WITHDRAW** A partner always has the power to leave a partnership but may not have the right. (p. 805)

16. **PARTNERSHIP AT WILL** If partners do not have an agreement about the duration of their partnership, it is called a partnership at will, and any of them can leave at any time for any reason. (p. 805)

17. TERM PARTNERSHIP With a term partnership, the partners have agreed in advance how long the partnership will last. (p. 806)

18. DISSOCIATED PARTNER A dissociated partner is liable to outsiders for debts incurred during her term as a partner, but the partnership must indemnify her for these debts. A dissociated partner is liable for the debts of the partnership incurred within two years after she leaves, but only if the creditor reasonably believes she is still a partner. The partnership must indemnify her for these debts. (pp. 805–806)

19. ENDING A PARTNERSHIP If the partners decide to end the partnership business, they must take three steps: dissolution, winding up, and termination. (pp. 805–806)

20. THE WINDING-UP PROCESS During the winding-up process, the partners have the right to complete unfinished transactions and do whatever is necessary to terminate the business. They do not have the right to take on new business. The assets of the partnership are paid out:

- First, to creditors of the partnership, including creditors who are partners.
- Second, to partners. (pp. 806–807)

1. Result: The document would have had no impact. So long as they act like partners, they are partners.

2. Result: Two of the three elements are there—Brian and Carl held themselves out as partners and Helen suffered harm. But Carl was not a partner by estoppel because, before the accident, Helen did not know that Carl had held himself out as Bryan's partner. She had not *relied on* their representation.

3. Result: The firm was not in the investment advisory business, so Lyon was not acting within the ordinary course of business. He did not have actual authority, but he might have had apparent authority, in which case the firm would be liable.

Multiple-Choice Questions

1. CPA QUESTION Which of the following is not necessary to create a partnership?

(a) Execution of a written partnership agreement
(b) Agreement to share ownership of the partnership
(c) Intention of conducting a business for profit
(d) Intention of creating a relationship recognized as a partnership

2. If a partner dissociates, he is entitled to:

(a) Force the termination of the partnership
(b) Receive indemnification from liability for present partnership debt
(c) Receive indemnification from damages he caused the partnership
(d) Receive only his share of the value of the partnership assets when it ultimately liquidates

3. **CPA QUESTION** Cobb, Inc., a partner in TLC Partnership, assigns its partnership interest to Bean, who is not made a partner. After the assignment, Bean asserts the right to (1) participate in the management of TLC and (2) Cobb's share of TLC's partnership profits. Bean is correct as to which of these rights?
   (a) 1 only
   (b) 2 only
   (c) 1 and 2
   (d) Neither 1 nor 2

4. **CPA QUESTION** Ted Fein, a partner in the ABC Partnership, wishes to withdraw from the partnership and sell his interest to Gold. All of the other partners in ABC have agreed to admit Gold as a partner and to hold Fein harmless for the past, present, and future liabilities of ABC. A provision in the original partnership agreement states that the partnership will continue upon the death or withdrawal of one or more of the partners. As a result of Fein's withdrawal and Gold's admission to the partnership, Gold:
   (a) Is personally liable for partnership liabilities arising before and after his admission as a partner
   (b) Has the right to participate in the management of ABC
   (c) Acquired only the right to receive Fein's share of the profits of ABC
   (d) Must contribute cash or property to ABC in order to be admitted with the same rights as the other partners

5. Blackriver Partnership is in the process of winding up. It has three partners: Jason, Keira, and Lancelot. The partnership has assets of $90,000, but debts of $60,000, including $30,000 it owes to Jason. Who gets what?
   (a) Each partner receives $10,000.
   (b) Each partner receives $30,000.
   (c) Jason receives $30,000 and the other two get $10,000 each.
   (d) Jason receives $40,000 and the other two get $10,000 each.

Essay Questions

1. **ETHICS** Arthur, John, and George formed a partnership to drill and maintain cesspools for two years. After less than two months, John and George sent a letter to Arthur, informing him that they were dissolving the partnership. Arthur sued the two other men, asking the court to declare that the partnership still existed and he had the right to continue in the business. Do John and George have the power to dissolve a term partnership before the end of the term? Aside from the legal issue, is it fair to Arthur for the court to allow his two partners to walk away from their partnership? He had counted on a two-year commitment; they gave only two months.

2. **YOU BE THE JUDGE WRITING PROBLEM** Herbert, an artist, entered into an agreement with Randy for the reproduction and distribution of his paintings. Herbert was to receive 50 percent of the gross sales revenues. Randy was responsible for all losses and for management of the business. Before leaving on a trip to Israel,

where he feared he might be in some danger, Randy signed a partnership agreement with Herbert stating that they jointly owned the business. Shortly after Randy returned from the trip, the two men terminated their business relationship, and Herbert revoked his authorization for the sale of prints. When Randy continued selling the prints, Herbert filed suit. Randy argued that the two had formed a partnership and that he was authorized to sell assets of the partnership. Were Herbert and Randy partners? **Argument for Herbert:** A partnership agreement does not create a partnership. Randy alone managed the business. Herbert shared only revenues, not profits or losses. **Argument for Randy:** Herbert and Randy both provided services to the business: Randy paid for the printing, and Herbert did the artwork. These two men signed a partnership agreement, and they obviously intended to be partners.

3. Seventy-Three Land, Inc., sued Maxlar Partners for the balance due on a note made by the partnership. Max, a partner, asked the court to dismiss the claim against him personally because the plaintiff had not first tried to collect against the partnership. Does Max have a valid claim?

4. Pedro and Juan have a business selling ties with fraternity insignia. Pedro finds out that an online shirt business is for sale. It sounds like a great idea—customers send in their measurements and get back a custom-made shirt at a price no higher than an off-the-rack shirt at the local department store. Does Pedro have to let Juan in on the great opportunity?

5. Brothers Sydney and Ashley were partners in a real estate partnership in Pennsylvania. They received identical salaries. Sydney moved to Florida to establish residency so that he could obtain a divorce there. His lawyer told him not to return to Pennsylvania until he had resolved his marital problems. After Sydney had been gone almost a year, Ashley decided to increase his own salary to compensate for the additional work he was doing. Does Ashley have the right to pay himself more if he is doing more work?

Discussion Questions

1. Mike Love and Brian Wilson were members of the Beach Boys. In the 1960s, they wrote songs together. The copyrights for these songs were later sold to Rondor, which paid the two men royalties when the songs were played. In 2004, Wilson re-recorded some of these songs on a CD called *Good Vibrations*. This CD was distributed in the United Kingdom by the newspaper *The Mail on Sunday*. Love sued Wilson, arguing that the two men had a partnership and Wilson had violated the partnership agreement by re-recording the songs without Love's permission. Did Mike Love and Brian Wilson have a partnership?

2. Dutch, Bill, and Heidi were equal partners in a lawn care business. Bill and Heidi wanted to borrow money from the bank to buy more trucks and expand the business. Dutch was dead set against the idea. When the matter came to a vote, Bill and Heidi voted in favor, Dutch against. Dutch was so annoyed that he told the bank not to lend the money and, further, that he would not be responsible for repaying the loan. The bank loaned the money, the business failed, and the bank sued all three partners. Is Dutch liable on the loan?

3. Carrie and Laura started a business together to sell bridesmaid dresses online. Carrie spent months preparing the financials and meeting with potential investors while Laura designed dresses and found suppliers. Once Carrie was finished with the financials and had identified some potential investors, Laura announced that she preferred to work with Scott and Carrie was out of the business. What rights does Carrie have?

4. Is it fair that partners are not entitled to be paid for work they do for the partnership? What about poor Arnold in the Peaceful Valley case—he was on call 24/7 and his girlfriend was cleaning the latrines, but they were not entitled to be paid.

5. Is there any good reason to be in a partnership? If so, for what sort of business would it make sense?

CHAPTER 33

LIFE AND DEATH OF A CORPORATION

© Evan Meyer/Shutterstock.com

On July 26, 2004, Mark Zuckerberg signed a certificate of incorporation for his company, which he called TheFacebook, Inc. At 11:34 a.m. on July 29, 2004, that certificate was filed with the Secretary of State for Delaware, and TheFacebook began its life as a corporation. Zuckerberg had started this social networking Internet site the previous February in his dorm room at Harvard. By December 2004, TheFacebook had almost 1 million users. By the beginning of 2006, the company was estimated to be worth between $750 million and $2 billion. Today, TheFacebook is valued at more than $50 billion. As Zuckerberg built his company, what did he need to know about the law?

Zuckerberg started TheFacebook in his dorm room at Harvard. Within 10 months, it had almost 1 million users.

Most of the country's largest businesses, and many of its small ones, are corporations. In this chapter, you will learn how to form a corporation and also how to avoid traps that await the unwary entrepreneur before and after a business is formed. Finally, you will learn how to dissolve a corporation.

Before the Corporation Is Formed

TheFacebook operated for five months before it was incorporated. During this period, Zuckerberg needed to be careful to avoid liability as a promoter.

Promoter's Liability

The promoter is the person who creates the corporation. It is his idea; he raises the capital, hires the lawyers, calls the shots. Mark Zuckerberg was TheFacebook's promoter. Sometimes, promoters are so eager to get their business going that they sign contracts on behalf of the corporation before it is legally formed. Zuckerberg had moved company headquarters to Palo Alto, California before the certificate of incorporation was filed. Suppose that he finds the perfect location for his headquarters. He is eager to sign the lease before someone else snatches the opportunity away, but TheFacebook does not yet legally exist—it is not incorporated. What would happen if he signed the lease anyway?

© AP Photo/Paul Sakuma

Within a few years, Mark Zuckerberg went from college student to Silicon Valley billionaire.

- **The promoter is personally liable on any contract signed before the corporation is formed.** If Zuckerberg signs the lease before TheFacebook, Inc., legally exists, he is personally liable for the rent due.
- **The corporation is not liable on any contracts signed *before* incorporation unless it *adopts* the contract *after* incorporation.** What does **adoption** mean? Either the board of directors takes a formal vote saying, "We hereby adopt this contract," or they act as if they had adopted it. If TheFacebook uses the space Zuckerberg rented, it has adopted the contract. But Zuckerberg is still on the hook.
- **Even if the corporation adopts the contract, the promoter is still liable until the third party (in this case, the landlord) agrees to a *novation.*** A **novation** creates a *new* contract. Even if TheFacebook adopts the contract, Zuckerberg is still personally liable to the landlord until the landlord signs a new contract with him and TheFacebook explicitly stating that only the corporation is liable, not Zuckerberg.

Novation
A new contract.

Like many sets of rules, this one has an exception:

- **If it is clear that the parties did not intend the promoter to be liable, then he is released from liability once the corporation adopts the contract.** To protect himself, Zuckerberg would want the lease to state that TheFacebook is not yet formed but will be liable when it is formed, and that he is not personally liable for rental payments once TheFacebook adopts the contract.

EXAM Strategy

Question: Dr. Warfield hired Wolfe, a young carpenter, to build his house. A week or so after they signed the contract, Wolfe filed Articles of Incorporation for Wolfe Construction, Inc. Warfield made payments to the corporation. Unfortunately, the work on the house was shoddy—the architect said he did not know whether to blow up the house or try to salvage what was there. Warfield sued Wolfe and Wolfe Construction, Inc. for damages. Wolfe argued that if he was liable as a promoter, then the corporation must be absolved and that, conversely, if the corporation was held liable he, as an individual, must not be. Who is liable to Warfield? Does it matter if Wolfe signed the contract in his own name or in the name of the corporation?

Strategy: Wolfe's argument is wrong—Warfield does not have to choose between suing him individually or suing the corporation. He can certainly sue both.

Result: Wolfe is personally liable on any contract signed before the corporation is filed, no matter whose name is on the contract. The corporation is liable only if it adopts the contract. Did it do so here? The fact that the corporation cashed checks that were made out to it means that the corporation is also liable. So Warfield can sue both Wolfe and the corporation.

Defective Incorporation

A promoter is liable on contracts signed before the corporation exists. What happens, though, if the promoter makes some reasonable effort to incorporate but does not succeed? In these situations, the law can be reasonably tolerant. (Remember, however, that litigation is extremely painful and it is far, far better simply to comply with all the rules from the start.)

De Jure Corporation

"De jure" is Latin for "by law." **A *de jure* corporation means that the promoter has substantially complied with the requirements for incorporation but has made some minor error.** He has perhaps misspelled the name of the corporation's registered agent (more about the registered agent later). In this case, no one, not even the state, can challenge the validity of the corporation.

De Facto Corporation

"De facto" is Latin for "in fact." **A *de facto* corporation means that the promoter has made a good faith effort to incorporate and has actually used the corporation to conduct business.** In this case, the state can challenge the validity of the corporation, but a third party cannot. Suppose that Mark Zuckerberg fills out the incorporation form and files it, but the Secretary of State does not stamp it for weeks. In the meantime, Zuckerberg signs a lease for TheFacebook. In many states, no stamp means no corporation. Nonetheless, Zuckerberg has a *de facto* corporation because he made a reasonable effort to incorporate and has used the corporation to conduct business. The landlord cannot challenge the validity of the corporation and claim that Zuckerberg is personally liable on the lease. Only the corporation is liable.

Corporation by Estoppel

A corporation by estoppel means that, if a party enters into a contract *believing* in good faith that the corporation exists, he cannot later take advantage of the fact that it does not. Suppose that Zuckerberg's attorney tells him that TheFacebook, Inc., has been formed, but in fact he never even attempted to incorporate it. In the meantime, Zuckerberg buys many Apple computers in TheFacebook's name. Under the theory of corporation by estoppel, Zuckerberg is *not* personally liable even though the corporation does not exist. Both he and Apple thought he was buying on behalf of the corporation. Why should Apple receive a windfall, and why should Zuckerberg be penalized, simply because his lawyer made a mistake? This rule works both ways: If a bank loans money to TheFacebook, Inc., Zuckerberg cannot refuse to pay it back simply because TheFacebook does not yet exist. At the time Zuckerberg received the loan, he believed the corporation had been formed.

In the following case, a contract is so unclear, the courts have to step in. What is the proper legal result? Is that the most reasonable outcome?

You be the Judge

GS Petroleum, Inc. v. R and S Fuel, Inc.

2009 Del. Super. LEXIS 200
Superior Court of Delaware, 2009

Facts: On March 13, GS Petroleum (GS) signed an agreement to sell a Shell gas station to R and S Fuel, Inc. (Fuel). On April 2, Fuel opened a corporate bank account and began writing checks on it. On April 15, Fuel took possession of the Shell station. Later, it took out insurance in the company's name. Unfortunately, what Fuel did not do was pay the money it owed under the contract.

So far, this looks like just a breach of contract case. But there is one more fact that greatly complicates this simple picture: Fuel did not actually come into existence until March 27, two weeks after the contract was signed. The introduction to the contract stated that it was "entered by and between R and S Fuel, Inc., and GS Petroleum, Inc." The signature lines at the end looked like this:

Richard Simpson
R And S Fuel Inc.
Buyer
Susan Stamm and Richard Simpson

GS filed suit for $124,000 against the corporation but also personally against Richard Simpson and Susan Stamm. The two individuals filed a motion for summary judgment.

You Be the Judge: ***Were Simpson and Stamm personally liable for the debts of Fuel?***

Argument for GS: The corporation did not exist when the contract was signed, so someone else has to be liable. Simpson and Stamm were the promoters, their names appear on the contract, and Simpson actually signed it. No corporate title is attached to his name on the signature line, which indicates he was signing as an individual, not a corporate officer. And when Simpson signed the contract, he was acting as Stamm's agent. So she is liable, too.

The defendants argue that the business was a *de facto* corporation, but they need to read this textbook more carefully. To qualify, they must have made a good faith effort to comply with corporate law, but here they had not bothered to file the forms with the Secretary of State. That is not a good faith effort.

While they are reviewing the text, Simpson and Stamm should also note that even if Fuel adopted the contract, they are still liable until the parties sign a novation. That did not happen here. And no provision of the contract explicitly or impliedly released the two defendants.

To find Simpson and Stamm liable is the only fair result. Someone is going to be out a lot of money. It should be the people responsible for losing that money, not the innocent party who sold them a perfectly good business.

Argument for Simpson and Stamm: It is true that Simpson's signature line did not list a corporate title, but that was simply an oversight. He was clearly signing for the corporation. As for Stamm, she cannot be liable for an agreement she did not sign.

Promoters who sign an agreement on behalf of a corporation are only liable if the parties *intended* that result. GS entered into this agreement with a corporation. Note that the document states it is an agreement with just Fuel; not Fuel, Simpson, and Stamm. Everyone understood that to be the case. GS has not alleged that Fuel was a sham corporation. Even before the corporate documents were filed, Simpson and Stamm ran the business as a corporation. They opened a bank account in the company's name, they used only business checks, and they bought insurance in the corporate name. If GS wanted the two individuals to be liable, the document should have said so.

Also, R and S Fuel was a *de facto* corporation at the time the agreement was signed. Simpson and Stamm were in the process of organizing it, they were making a good faith effort, and they were using the corporation to conduct business. In the case of a *de facto* corporation, third parties such as GS have no right to challenge its validity.

INCORPORATION PROCESS

The mechanics of incorporation are easy: simply download the form and mail or fax it to the Secretary of State for your state. But do not let this easy process fool you; the incorporation document needs to be completed with some care. The corporate charter defines the corporation, including everything from the company's name to the number of shares it will issue and the liability of its directors. States use different terms to refer to a charter; some call it the "articles of incorporation," others use "articles of organization," and still others say "certificate" instead of "articles." All of these terms mean the same thing. Similarly, some states use the term "shareholders," and others use "stockholders;" they are both the same.

There is no federal corporation code, which means that a company can incorporate only under state law, not federal law. No matter where a company actually does business, it may incorporate in any state. This decision is important because the organization must live by the laws of whichever state it chooses for incorporation. To encourage similarity among state corporation statutes, the American Bar Association drafted the Model Business Corporation Act as a guide. Many states do use the Act as a model, although Delaware does not. In discussing corporate law in this and the following chapters, we will give examples from both the Model Act and specific states, especially Delaware. Why Delaware? Despite its small size, it has a disproportionate influence on corporate law. More than half of all public companies are incorporated there, including 60 percent of Fortune 500 companies.

Where to Incorporate?

Traditionally, companies incorporated either in their home state or in Delaware. They typically must pay filing fees and franchise taxes in their state of incorporation, as well as in any state in which they do business. To avoid this double set of fees, a business that will be operating primarily in one state would probably select that state for incorporation rather than Delaware. But if a company is going to do business in several states, it might consider choosing Delaware.

Delaware has not always been a popular choice for corporations. In the early 1900s, New Jersey held the position that Delaware does today. When Woodrow Wilson became governor (on his way to the White House), he toughened New Jersey's laws. Looking for a state with a more hospitable environment, companies found one across the Delaware River. What is good for business is good for Delaware, too. Each year, it collects substantial filing fees and taxes from companies that, for the most part, conduct little business in the state.

Delaware offers corporations several advantages:

- *Laws that favor management.* Delaware laws offer flexibility. For example, if the shareholders want to take a vote in writing instead of holding a meeting, many other states require the vote to be unanimous; Delaware requires only a majority to agree. The Delaware legislature also tries to keep up to date by changing its code to reflect new developments in corporate law. For example, it was one of the first states to eliminate a rigid format for corporate charters.
- *An efficient court system.* Delaware has a special court (called "Chancery Court") that hears nothing but business cases and has judges who are experts in corporate law. In other states, judges who practiced in fields such as criminal law or divorce also hear corporate cases.[1] In an emergency involving, say, a hostile takeover, Delaware judges will hear cases and reach decisions on short notice. This preferential treatment is typically not available in other states.

---

[1]When Pennzoil sued Texaco in Texas over a breach of contract, the judge who tried the case was experienced in hearing divorce cases. Many lawyers felt that his ignorance of corporate matters contributed to the jury's Texas-sized verdict—$11 *billion.*

- *An established body of precedent.* Because so many businesses incorporate in the state, its courts hear a vast number of corporate cases, creating a large body of precedent. Thus lawyers feel they can more easily predict the outcome of a case in Delaware than in a state where few corporate disputes are tried.

The financial bonanza that Delaware realizes from its incorporation business has not gone unnoticed by other states. New York, Ohio, Pennsylvania, and, ironically, New Jersey have all modified their corporate laws to attract incorporation business. Large companies in the western part of the country often choose Nevada as their home state because of its attractive laws. Of course, management—not shareholders—chooses the state of incorporation and pays the state fees. Some commentators argue that states are so eager to attract corporate revenue that their laws unfairly favor management over shareholders. They refer to this competition as the "race to the bottom."[2] However, some recent studies indicate that, when a company reincorporates in Delaware, its stock price does not go down. Evidently, financial markets do not perceive shareholders to be at a disadvantage in Delaware.

Once a company has decided *where* to incorporate, the next step is to prepare and file the charter. The charter must always be filed with the Secretary of State; some jurisdictions also require that it be filed in a county office. Some states supply a form to be completed. Delaware and the Model Act require that certain information be included, but the incorporators can list it any way they want. The incorporators may also include some optional provisions.

Charter's Required Provisions

Name

The Model Act imposes two requirements in selecting a name. First, all corporations must use one of the following words in their name: "corporation," "incorporated," "company," or "limited." Delaware also accepts some additional terms, such as "association" or "institute." Both the Model Act and Delaware permit abbreviations (such as "inc." or "corp.") or equivalent terms in another language (such as "S.A.," which is the French abbreviation for corporation).

Second, under both the Model Act and Delaware law, a new corporate name must be different from that of any corporation that already exists in that state. If your name is Freddy du Pont, you cannot name your corporation "Freddy du Pont, Inc.," because Delaware already has a company named E. I. du Pont de Nemours and Company. It does not matter that Freddy du Pont is your real name or that the existing company is a large chemical business while you want to open a video arcade. The names are too similar. In addition, some states ban improper names. For example, Pennsylvania refused to accept "I Choose Hell Productions" because its statute prohibits names that "constitute blasphemy, profane cursing or swearing, or that profane the Lord's name." The state did accept ICH Productions. Zuckerberg chose "TheFacebook" because that was what Harvard students called their freshman directory.

What if you wake from a deep sleep late one night with the perfect corporate name in your head, but the charter is not quite ready for filing? In Delaware, you can reserve a name for 120 days for a fee of $75. That takes care of Delaware, but you know your corporation will soon be going national. How can you protect your name in other states? The Model Act also permits the advance registration of a corporate name. Alternatively, you can form a "nameholder" organization: a corporation that incurs minimum annual fees because it is inactive but does reserve its name.

---

[2]When Delaware passed its corporation law in 1899, the *American Law Review* attacked its pro-management bias as an effort by a "little community of truck-farmers and clam diggers ... determined to get her little, tiny, sweet, round, baby hand into the grab bag." Quoted in the *Economist* October 25, 2003, p. 55.

All this bother and expense discourage most start-ups from reserving their names nationwide. If they later expand into another state where someone else is already using their name, they either buy the name back or use a different name in that jurisdiction. The problem multiplies if they want to register their name overseas as well. When Steven Spielberg, Jeffrey Katzenberg, and David Geffen launched their Hollywood studio, DreamWorks SKG, they spent nearly $500,000 to clear rights to the name in 108 countries around the world. (Of course, that was a small drop in the $2 billion bucket they raised from investors.)

Address and Registered Agent

A company must have an official address in the state in which it is incorporated so that the Secretary of State knows where to contact it—and so that anyone who wants to sue the corporation can serve the complaint in the state. Since most companies incorporated in Delaware do not actually have an office there, they hire a registered agent to serve as their official presence in the state.

Incorporators

The incorporator signs the charter and delivers it to the Secretary of State for filing. The incorporator is not required to buy stock, nor does he necessarily have any future relationship with the company. Often, the lawyer who prepares the charter serves as incorporator. If no lawyer is involved, typically the promoter is also the incorporator. That is what happened with TheFacebook—Mark Zuckerberg served as the incorporator. The incorporator incurs liability only if he knows that something in the charter is not true when he signs it.

Purpose

The corporation is required to give its purpose for existence. In the 19th century, when corporations were a new concept, states thought it important to keep tight control over them. Under the ***ultra vires* doctrine**, a corporation cannot undertake any transaction unless its charter permits it. Corporate officers understandably chafed at this restriction. To avoid problems of *ultra vires*, most companies now use a very broad purpose clause such as TheFacebook's:

Ultra vires doctrine
A corporation cannot undertake a transaction unless permitted to do so by its charter.

> The purpose of the Corporation is to engage in any lawful act or activity for which corporations may be organized under the General Corporation Law of Delaware.

Essentially, the only way to violate this purpose clause is to commit an illegal act.

Stock

The charter must provide three items of information about the company's stock.

Par Value. The concept of par value was designed to protect investors. Originally, par value was supposed to be close to market price. A company could not issue stock at a price less than par, which meant that it could not sell to insiders at a sweetheart price well below market value. (Once the stock was *issued*, it could be *traded* at any price.) In modern times, par value does not relate to market value; it is usually some nominal figure such as 1¢ or $1 per share. Companies can dispense with the concept altogether and issue stock that has no par value. When making this decision, the company should check the state's filing fees because they may be based on the par value of the company's stock. TheFacebook stock has a par value of $0.0001 (one-hundredth of one cent) per share.

Number of Shares. Before stock can be sold, it must first be authorized in the charter. The corporation can authorize as many shares as the incorporators choose, but the more shares, the higher the filing fee. After incorporation, a company can add authorized shares by simply amending its charter and paying the additional fee. TheFacebook charter authorizes the creation of 10,000,000 shares.

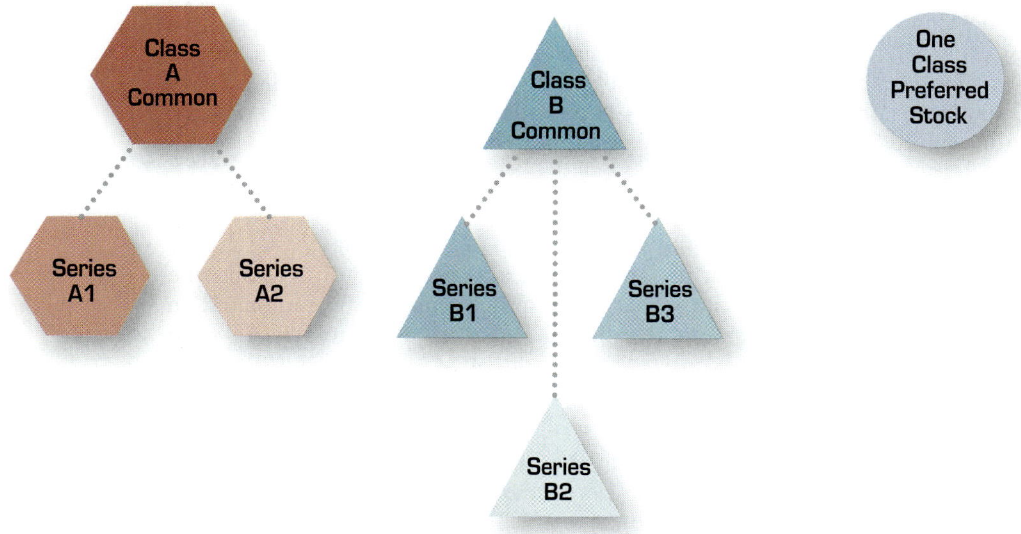

EXHIBIT 33.1

Authorized and unissued
Stock that has been authorized, but not yet sold.

Authorized and issued
Stock has been authorized and sold; another word for it is outstanding.

Treasury stock
Stock that a company has sold, but later bought back.

Stock that has been authorized but not yet sold is called **authorized and unissued**. Stock that has been sold is termed **authorized and issued** or **outstanding**. Stock that the company has sold but later bought back is **treasury stock**.

Classes and Series. Different shareholders often make different contributions to a company. Some may be involved in management, while others may simply contribute financially. Early investors may feel that they are entitled to more control than those who come along later (and who perhaps take less risk). Corporate structure can be infinitely flexible in defining the rights of these various shareholders. Stock can be divided into categories called **classes**, and these classes can be further divided into subcategories called **series**. All stock in a series has the same rights, and all series in a class are fundamentally the same, except for minor distinctions. For example, in a class of preferred stock, all shareholders may be entitled to a dividend, but the amount of the dividend may vary by series. Different classes of stock, however, may have very different rights—a class of preferred stock is different from a class of common stock. Exhibit 33.1 illustrates the concept of class and series. Defining the rights of a class or series of stock is like baking a cake—the stock can contain virtually any combination of the following ingredients (although the result may not be to everyone's taste):

- *Dividend rights.* The charter establishes whether the shareholder is entitled to dividends and, if so, in what amount. No matter what the charter says, the corporation may not pay dividends unless it is solvent, that is, unless it has enough assets to pay its debts.
- *Voting rights.* Shareholders are usually entitled to elect directors and vote on charter amendments, among other issues, but these rights can vary among different series and classes of stock. When Ford Motor Co. went public in 1956, it issued Class B common stock to members of the Ford family. This class of stock holds about 40 percent of the voting power and, thereby, effectively controls the company. Not surprisingly, the chairman of the company has often been named "Ford." TheFacebook recently amended its charter to create two classes of stock with different voting rights, presumably so that Zuckerberg can maintain control after the company goes public.

- *Liquidation rights.* The charter specifies the order in which classes of stockholders will be paid upon dissolution of the company. This provision is important if there are not enough assets to pay everyone.
- *Preemptive rights.* If a corporation later issues additional shares of its stock, the original shareholders will own a smaller percentage of the company. For example, if a company has 10 shareholders, each owning 1 share, and it later issues another 10 shares to others, each of the old shareholders will then own 5 percent of the company instead of 10 percent. To prevent this **dilution**, some companies grant preemptive rights: the old shareholders have the right to acquire enough new stock to prevent their share of the company from being diminished. In our example, each old shareholder would be entitled to buy enough new shares to keep their ownership at 10 percent. Of course, they are not required to buy this stock.
- *Conversion rights.* Some classes of stock may have the right to convert into shares of a different class. For example, if a company does not meet its financial projections, nonvoting stock may have the right to convert into voting stock.
- *Redemption rights.* Similarly, the shareholders of some classes of stock may have the right to force a company to buy their stock back if, for example, the company does not meet its financial goals.

These are the ingredients for any class or series of stock. Some stock comes prepackaged like a cake mix. "Preferred" and "common" stock are two classic types.

Owners of **preferred stock** have preference on dividends and also, typically, in liquidation. If a class of preferred stock is entitled to dividends, then it must receive its dividends before common stockholders are paid theirs. If holders of **cumulative preferred** stock miss their dividend one year, common shareholders cannot receive a dividend until the cumulative preferred shareholders have been paid all that they are owed, no matter how long that takes. Alternatively, holders of **non-cumulative preferred** stock lose an annual dividend for good if the company cannot afford it in the year it is due. When a company dissolves, preferred stockholders typically have the right to receive their share of corporate assets before common shareholders. Exhibit 33.2 illustrates the order of payment for dividends. Preferred stock can have any combination of other ingredients, such

Preferred stock
The owners of preferred stock have preference on dividends and also, typically, in liquidation.

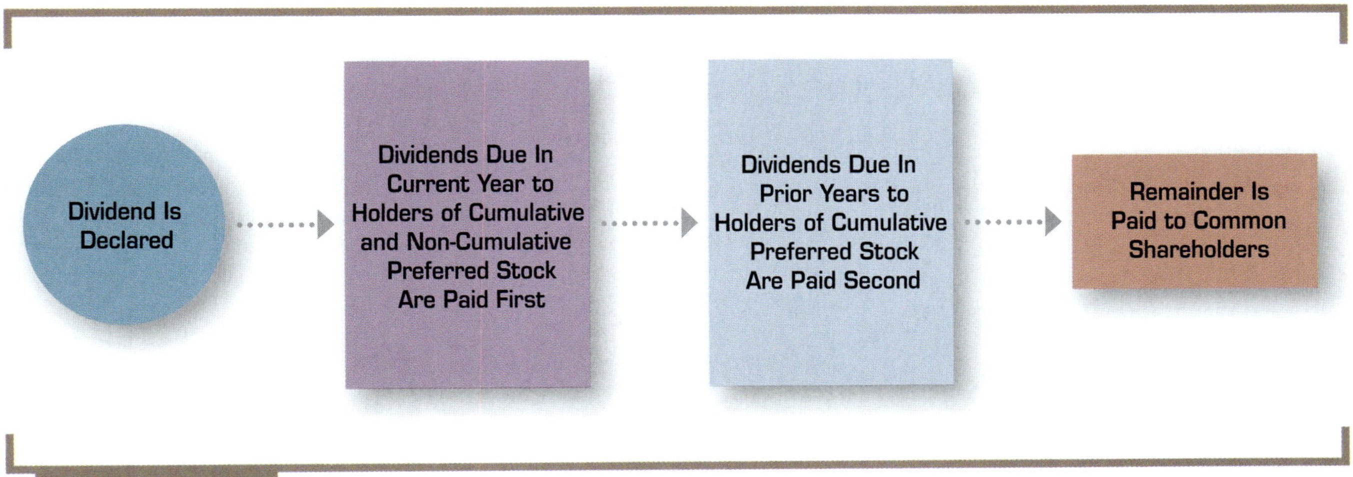

EXHIBIT 33.2

as preemptive rights or conversion rights. Sometimes preferred shareholders have voting rights, but usually they do not.

***Common stock* is last in line for any corporate payouts, including dividends and liquidation payments.** If the company is liquidated, creditors of the company and preferred shareholders are typically paid before common shareholders. But being a common shareholder is not all bad news—common shareholders often have most of the voting rights. They also have greater profit potential; preferred stock typically has a limit on the size of dividends, common does not. If the business does well, common stock will often increase in value faster than preferred stock.

Venture capitalists (professional investors who are in the business of financing companies) often choose a type of stock called **participating preferred stock**, which permits them to have their cake and eat it, too. Upon liquidation of the company, these shareholders are paid first, receiving whatever they paid for the stock plus accrued dividends. Then they are treated as if they had converted their preferred shares into common stock, so they get to share the rest of the proceeds with common shareholders.

Charter's Optional Provisions

Many corporations add optional provisions to their charters. Bear in mind, however, that once a provision is in the charter, it can be changed only by a vote of the shareholders and the filing of an amendment with the Secretary of State. This process can be cumbersome and expensive. Therefore, when in doubt, it is usually a good idea not to include extra provisions in the charter. Nonetheless, some provisions are so important that they belong there, despite the effort and expense required to change them.

Director Liability

Although incorporation protects shareholders against personal liability for the debts of the company, anyone involved in the management of the business can be personally liable for his own wrongdoing. For example, shareholders may sue directors for making an unprofitable decision. The potential liability in such a lawsuit is enormous. Even if the director is found not liable, the legal fees can be devastating.

Under most state statutes, a corporation may include in its charter a provision that protects directors from personal liability to the corporation or its shareholders for anything other than egregious misbehavior involving, for example, bad faith or intentional misconduct.[3] These provisions are called **exculpatory clauses**. TheFacebook charter has an exculpatory clause stating:

Exculpatory clause
A provision that protects directors from personal liability to the corporation and its shareholders for anything other than egregious misbehavior.

> To the fullest extent permitted by the Delaware General Corporation Law…a director of the Corporation shall not be personally liable to the Corporation or its stockholders for monetary damages for breach of fiduciary duty as a director.

Indemnification
Requires a company to pay the legal fees of directors who are sued for actions taken on behalf of the company.

Corporations also typically add an **indemnification** provision to their charter that requires the company to pay the legal fees of directors who are sued for any actions taken on behalf of the company. Without these protective provisions, companies would be unable to hire directors.

The following case illustrates the power of an exculpatory clause. Note that the directors are not liable even for acts of gross negligence.

[3]See, for example, 8 Del. C. §102(7).

Rodriguez v. Loudeye Corporation

2008 Wash. App. LEXIS 767
Court of Appeals of Washington, 2008

Facts: Loudeye Corporation provided digital music for cell phones and other consumer electronics. It was headquartered in Seattle, Washington, but incorporated in Delaware (where it did not have any offices). As permitted under Delaware law, Loudeye's charter had an exculpatory clause protecting directors from liability. Such provisions were unenforceable under Washington law.

Loudeye's directors decided to sell the company because it was not generating enough revenue to compete effectively. Nokia offered a price that was three times market value. After extensive negotiations with Nokia and an unsuccessful search for other buyers, Loudeye's board accepted Nokia's bid.

A Loudeye shareholder named Eli Rodriguez filed suit against five members of the board of directors, alleging that the directors had breached their fiduciary duties by failing to obtain the best price. He thought the board should have conducted a formal auction. He also alleged that the board had conflicts of interest and had approved the sale because they would receive special financial benefits (such as severance payments and stock options).

The Loudeye directors filed a motion to dismiss, alleging that the exculpatory clause in the company's charter protected them from liability. Rodriguez argued that Washington law should apply and, therefore, the clause was invalid. He also argued that, even if the exculpatory clause was valid, it did not apply in this case. The trial court granted the motion to dismiss and Rodriguez appealed.

Issues: ***Which state law applies to a company that is headquartered in Washington but incorporated in Delaware? Does the exculpatory clause in the Loudeye charter protect its directors from liability?***

Excerpts from Judge Agid's Decision: Shareholder claims involving a corporation's internal affairs are governed by the law of the state in which the corporation was incorporated. Thus, because Loudeye is a Delaware corporation, Delaware law applies here.

[T]o the extent these allegations describe gross negligence in the sale of the corporation, their conduct is not actionable. [O]nly if there are allegations establishing that the director's conduct is motivated by an actual intent to do harm, or occurs when directors consciously and intentionally disregard their responsibilities, and is conduct so far beyond the bounds of reasonable judgment that it seems essentially inexplicable on any ground other than bad faith [are the directors liable].

[A]s the directors point out, [that] situation typically is when the directors in the acquired corporation also have interests in the acquiring corporation or when directors seek to entrench themselves in their positions of control. But neither situation is present here. The complaint therefore fails to state a claim.

We affirm the trial court's dismissal of the complaint.

Cumulative Voting

For sheer drama, few corporate battles have exceeded the fight between the elephant, Gulf Oil, and the flea, Mesa Petroleum. When T. Boone Pickens, the CEO of Mesa, announced that Gulf Oil was badly managed, he was picking on the sixth-largest oil company in America. Pickens nominated himself to be Gulf's savior. His plan was to buy enough of the company's shares so that he could elect himself to the board of directors. Pickens's goal was possible only because Gulf was incorporated in Pennsylvania, a state that then had cumulative voting.

For sheer drama, few corporate battles have exceeded the fight between the elephant, Gulf Oil, and the flea, Mesa Petroleum.

At the time, Gulf Oil had 15 directors, all elected annually. Under a *regular* voting system, the 15 people who receive the most votes are awarded the seats. If Pickens owned one share, he could vote for as many as 15 *different* candidates, but he could not pool his votes; that is, he could not cast multiple votes for any one candidate. Thus, he could only vote for himself to be director once. To be sure of getting elected to the board, he would have to buy half of Gulf's shares, plus one. Gulf had 165 million shares outstanding, so Pickens would have to buy 82,500,001 shares. Once he had bought that many shares, he could elect *all* the directors because he would own a majority of the company's stock. As Gulf's stock was trading at around $40 per share, Pickens would have had to invest more than $3 billion ($3,300,000,040) to achieve his goal.

Under a cumulative voting system, however, Pickens is allowed to pool his shares and vote them all for the same person (in this case, himself). How many shares would Pickens have to own to elect himself to the board? This is the formula:

$$\text{Number of shares needed to elect one director} = \frac{\text{Number of shares outstanding}}{\text{Number of directors being elected} + 1} + 1$$

This is how the formula worked in Pickens's case, where x stands for the number of shares he needed to elect one director:

$$x = \frac{165,000,000}{15 + 1} + 1$$

$$x = 10,312,501$$

This 10 million shares is a lot less than the 82 million he needed under a regular voting system. At a price per share of $40, Pickens would have to invest roughly $400 million ($412,500,040) under a cumulative voting system, compared with $3 billion under a regular system.

In a desperate effort to prevent Pickens from being elected to its board of directors, Gulf called a special meeting of shareholders to change its state of incorporation from Pennsylvania to Delaware and eliminate cumulative voting. (Delaware and the Model Act both permit, but do not require, it.) For months, both sides ran full-page advertisements in newspapers across the country to persuade shareholders. Gulf spent $9 million and Mesa $8 million on the fight alone, not counting money spent buying Gulf shares. In the end, Gulf won the battle but lost the war. It won the shareholder vote by a small margin, but the company was so weakened by this fight that it sold out to Chevron Oil shortly thereafter. The fight so frightened other companies that many changed their state of organization to Delaware. Pennsylvania then changed its statue to be like Delaware's.

After Incorporation

Once the charter has been filed (and the filing fee paid), the corporation legally exists, but work is not done yet. The shareholders must still complete a few additional tasks.

Directors and Officers

Once the corporation is organized, the incorporators elect the first set of directors. Thereafter, shareholders elect directors. Under the Model Act, a corporation is required to have at least one director unless (1) *all* the shareholders sign an agreement that eliminates the board, or (2) the corporation has 50 or fewer shareholders. To elect directors, the shareholders may hold a meeting, or, in the more typical case for a small company, they elect directors by **written consent**. (In most states and under the Model Act, all the shareholders must sign, but in Delaware, a majority is sufficient.) A typical written consent looks like this:

Classic American Novels, Inc.
Written Consent

The undersigned shareholders of Classic American Novels, Inc., a corporation organized and existing under the General Corporation Law of the State of Wherever, hereby agree that the following action shall be taken with full force and effect as if voted at a validly called and held meeting of the shareholders of the corporation:

Agreed: That the following people are elected to serve as directors for one year, or until their successors have been duly elected and qualified:

Herman Melville
Louisa May Alcott
Mark Twain

Dated: ______________ Signed: ______________________
Willa Cather

Dated: ______________ Signed: ______________________
Nathaniel Hawthorne

Dated: ______________ Signed: ______________________
Harriet Beecher Stowe

Once the incorporators or shareholders have chosen the directors, the directors must elect the officers of the corporation. They can use a consent form, if they wish. The Model Act is flexible. It simply requires a corporation to have whatever officers are described in the bylaws. The same person can hold more than one office. Exhibit 33.3 illustrates the election process in corporations.

The written consents and any records of actual meetings are kept in a **minute book**, which is the official record of the corporation. Entrepreneurs sometimes feel they are too busy to bother with all these details, but if a corporation is ever sold, the lawyers for the buyers will *insist* on a well-organized and complete minute book. In one case, a company that was seeking a $100,000 bank loan could not find all of its minutes. Many of its early shareholders and directors were not available to reauthorize prior deeds. In the end, the company had to merge itself into a newly created corporation so it could start fresh with a new set of corporate records. The company spent $10,000 on this task, a large chunk out of the $100,000 loan.

Minute book
A book that contains a summary of a company's official actions.

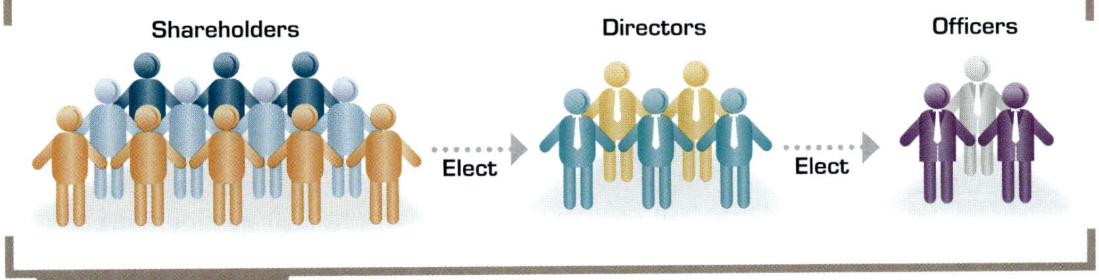

EXHIBIT 33.3

Bylaws

Bylaws
A document that specifies the organizational rules of a corporation or other organization, such as the date of the annual meeting and the required number of directors.

Quorum
The percentage of stock that must be represented for a meeting to count.

The **bylaws** list all the "housekeeping" details for the corporation. For example, bylaws set the date of the annual shareholders' meeting, define what a **quorum** is (i.e., what percentage of stock must be represented for a meeting to count), indicate how many directors there will be, give titles to officers, fix the procedure for calling a special meeting of the shareholders or directors, and establish the fiscal (i.e., tax) year of the corporation. When there is a choice, it is usually better to place provisions in the bylaws rather than the charter, because the bylaws are easier to change. Under the Model Act, directors can amend the bylaws without calling a meeting of the shareholders or paying a filing fee. TheFacebook charter provides that "....the Board of Directors of the Corporation is expressly authorized to make, amend, or repeal Bylaws of the Corporation."

The shareholders can always override the directors if they want, but they rarely do. In the following case, the directors' ignorance of company bylaws led to disaster.

IN RE BIGMAR

2002 Del. Ch. LEXIS 45
Court of Chancery, Delaware, 2002

Facts: Bigmar was a Delaware corporation that manufactured and marketed pharmaceuticals in Europe. While trying to raise additional capital, the company's founder, John Tramontana, met Cynthia May. She lied to him about her education, wealth, and connections in the investment community. Unfortunately, he believed her. The upshot was that May became Bigmar's president and a director of the company. She soon took control of the company's financial records and refused to give Tramontana any information (always a bad sign).[4] When Bigmar ran out of money, Tramontana sent May an email asking for her resignation. She did not respond. (Also a bad sign.)

The company was in desperate financial shape, but Tramontana managed to find a bank willing to buy $1 million of Bigmar stock. He called a special meeting of the board of directors to approve the sale of shares and to fire May. The meeting was to take place by telephone. To establish a quorum necessary for the meeting to be valid, at least five of the nine directors had to take part. May and her three allies on the board refused to participate.

Tramontana testified that, at the appointed time, he met with two directors in his office. They used a speaker feature on a cell phone that Tramontana borrowed from Danilo Graticola to call two other directors, one of whom was in Heathrow Airport in London. The five directors unanimously resolved to issue the stock to the bank. The meeting then adjourned so that they could consult counsel. It was reconvened the next day, at which time they voted to fire May.

The following day, the bank transferred $1 million to Bigmar. Tramontana instructed the company's transfer agent to send stock certificates to the bank, but May contradicted his order. Tramontana and May went to court to determine if the director's meeting was valid and the bank entitled to the shares.

Issue: ***Was the meeting of the Bigmar board of directors valid?***

Excerpts from Judge Jacobs's Decision: Ms. May attacks the validity of the meeting(s) [claiming that] no meeting at which a quorum of directors was present ever took place.

There is evidence that the meeting(s) did occur. Minutes of the meetings were prepared, and all but one of the Tramontana directors gave sworn testimony that the meeting(s) took place exactly as the minutes recite. Ordinarily that would be sufficient, but this is not an ordinary case, for several reasons.

First, the minutes were prepared by counsel, who was not present at the meetings and who simply reduced to writing what Mr. Tramontana told him had occurred. Second, there is no independent documentation or testimony of any third party witness that corroborates the directors'

[4]She did, however, send him this email: I wish for GOd's sake that you would GROW [UP] just a little...you've F the banking up here in Sweden so I can't get the money that I made [arrangements] for...damn idiot...take a shower and clean your ears out...you can't follow a straight line without having your ego and little hissy fits...Get off the playground...before the big boys beat you up...

testimony. Moreover, any notes taken at the meeting(s) were destroyed. Further, many of the telephone records whose production was requested were not produced, and the records that were produced either fail to corroborate the Tramontana directors' testimony,[5] or those documents are inconsistent with that testimony.[6]

Third, for the directors' testimony to be accepted, the Court would have to "buy into" a scenario that (to put it charitably) is most improbable. Although Mr. Tramontana had a speaker phone in his office, he testified that he decided to conduct the board meeting on Mr. Graticola's borrowed cell phone. His explanation for that unusual decision was that Mr. Graticola had described his new cell phone's technology in glowing terms and Mr. Tramontana elected to use the telephone to ingratiate his company with Graticola. [T]he story does have some plausibility, however slight. But even that minimal plausibility vanishes when one is told that the same identical scenario occurred a second time, at the adjourned meeting. I find this scenario too implausible for even a gullible factfinder to swallow. Accordingly, the Court is unable to determine that those directors' meetings were validly convened and conducted.

Although the analysis could stop here, that would leave the Court (and perhaps a reader of this Opinion) with a sense of dissatisfaction because Mr. Tramontana's testimony leaves unanswered questions. In purely human terms, this issue was most difficult and perplexing for the Court.

It is plausible, and the available evidence does indicate, that Mr. Tramontana attempted to assemble all of his colleagues for a telephonic meeting. [But one director] was unavailable, as he was en route from London to Ireland at that time. Because a quorum required the attendance of five directors, [this director's] unavailability meant that the telephonic meeting failed for lack of a quorum. Mr. Tramontana believed, nonetheless, that the problem could be solved by obtaining from himself and his colleagues' individual written consent resolutions taking the actions recited in the minutes. Unfortunately (and unbeknownst to Mr. Tramontana), Bigmar's by-laws required that any director action by written consent must be unanimous. [When] Mr. Tramontana learned of that unanimity requirement, [he] decided to [say] that a quorum of five directors was present and that a board meeting was held.

I am persuaded that [Mr. Tramontana and his colleagues acted] in the good-faith belief that unless the issuance of the shares to the Bank was upheld, the Company would fall into the hands of Ms. May, who was incapable of saving the Company. I think it plausible that they believed that at worst, they failed to observe a highly technical legal requirement that, on balance, was too insignificant to justify the ruination of the Company.

The principles of corporate governance, such as those violated here, exist precisely because those procedures enable courts and parties to distinguish between acts that lawfully bind the corporation and its constituents, from those that do not. The directors may have believed in good faith that they had no alternative but to testify as they did, but good faith is not sufficient to validate a procedurally invalid proceeding.

Shareholder Agreements

The shareholders of a start-up company often work together intensively. If a shareholder sells her stock to someone who does not share the same vision, conflict is inevitable. To avoid this situation, shareholders of start-ups often sign a shareholder agreement granting a right of first refusal on the company's stock. In a typical agreement, if a shareholder wants to sell, she must first offer the stock to the company at the same price that the outsider has offered. If, after 30 days, the company has not agreed to buy the stock, she must then offer it to the other shareholders. Only if they also refuse to buy it within 30 days can she then sell it to an outsider at the same price that she offered to the company and shareholders.

[5][The] cell phone bills for the [director who is supposed to have received a call in the London airport] do not show any incoming calls to him at Heathrow Airport at 3:00 p.m., London time, which is when the meeting is said to have started. Since [his] cell phone provider was located in Ireland where he lived, [this director] would have incurred a roaming charge for any calls received outside of Ireland, and the roaming charge would have been reflected on his cell phone bill.

[6]For example, Mr. Tramontana's telephone records show that he made an 11-minute telephone call to Mr. Graticola's cell phone number at 7:12 p.m.—a time that Mr. Tramontana claimed to have had Mr. Graticola's cell phone in his possession.

Similarly, if a shareholder dies, his estate may be required to offer the stock to the company or other shareholders. In the case of death, it is more difficult to determine the market value of the stock, so the shareholder agreement often provides a formula for making this determination.

Sometimes shareholder agreements focus not on who owns the company but how their stock is voted. For example, Craig O. McCaw was willing to sell a majority interest in Cellular One to Affiliated Publications, but he was not willing to give up control of the company. After all, he had single-handedly built it into the largest cell phone company in the United States. His solution? McCaw and Affiliated entered into a shareholder agreement requiring Affiliated to vote its stock in Cellular One as McCaw directed. Affiliated trusted McCaw's business acumen enough to want him to continue running the company even though he was only a minority shareholder. This same goal can be achieved by means of a so-called voting trust.

Issuing Debt

Most start-up companies begin with some combination of equity and debt. Equity (i.e., stock) is described in the charter; debt is not. Authorizing debt is often one of the first steps a new company takes. There are several types of debt:

Bonds
Long-term secured debt.

Debentures
Long-term unsecured debt.

Notes
When issued by a company, short-term debt, typically payable within five years.

- **Bonds** are long-term debt secured by some of the company's assets. If the company is unable to pay the debt, creditors have a right to specific assets, such as accounts receivable or inventory.
- **Debentures** are long-term *unsecured* debt. If the company cannot meet its obligations, the debenture holders are paid after bondholders, but before stockholders.
- **Notes** are short-term debt, typically payable within five years. They may be either secured or unsecured.

Foreign Corporations

A company is called a *domestic* corporation in the state where it incorporates and a *foreign* corporation everywhere else.

Ned has sworn that he will never again suffer through a bitter Chicago winter. No, he is not relocating; he has invented a new fabric that looks like fur. It is better than real fur, though, because it breathes, repels water, and is washable. He knows that his business will soon be a national success.

Ned, like many entrepreneurs before him, incorporates Fabulous Fake Furs, Inc. (FFF), in Delaware. He is still, however, living in Chicago (where he now *adores* the winter). Company headquarters are down the street from his condominium. The main manufacturing facility is in Texas, with warehouses in Minnesota and New York. A sales staff calls on all the major department stores and online merchants across the country.

Ned has obligations to the state of Delaware because he incorporated there—he must pay taxes and annual fees. But what about the other states where he is doing business? Someone had to pay to build the roads and educate the workforce in these states. Must he contribute, too? The states certainly think so. They require a foreign corporation that is doing business within their borders to register with them and obtain a "certificate of authority." This registration process is called **qualifying to do business**.

Qualifying to do business
Registering a corporation in a state in which it is not organized but in which it has an ongoing presence.

What constitutes "doing business"? **Opening an office or establishing any other ongoing presence counts as doing business.** Clearly, FFF must register in Illinois, Texas, Minnesota, and New York because it has a permanent presence in these states. Typically, the following activities do *not* count as doing business: holding meetings, opening a bank account, soliciting sales orders, or any isolated transaction. If FFF's directors hold a meeting in Alaska, Ned attends a trade show in Wisconsin, or a sales rep takes an order at a store in California, these activities do not constitute doing business, and FFF does not have to register in these states.

To qualify, a company must file corporate documents with the state, list a registered agent, and pay annual fees and taxes on income generated in that jurisdiction. As a general rule, of course, companies would prefer not to register. Some states fine any companies they catch doing business without registering. Under the Model Act, a company that is doing business without qualifying cannot bring a lawsuit in that state until it registers (and pays back fees, taxes, and penalties). But note that, if the company is not actually doing business, then it may file suit without qualifying first. And whether or not it has qualified, a company can always *defend* against a lawsuit.

EXAM Strategy

Question: You are about to form a corporation. What do you have to do before filling out the form? Which provisions are boilerplate and, therefore, do not require special effort on your part?

Strategy: Review the description of required and optional charter provisions.

Result: Before filling out the form, you need to choose a name and check to make sure it is available. If you are incorporating someplace where you do not have an office, you will also have to hire a registered agent. You do not have to decide the purpose of the corporation; standard boilerplate works here. Unless you will have outside investors from the beginning, you do not have to think a lot about your capital structure—that is, the number and par value of your shares. Just authorize as many shares as you can for the base filing fee, and choose a nominal par value. It makes sense to add an exculpatory clause to protect your directors from liability, especially if you are going to be one. There is no need for cumulative voting at this stage.

Death of the Corporation

Sometimes, business ideas are not successful and the corporation fails. This death can be voluntary (the shareholders elect to terminate the corporation) or forced (by court order). Sometimes, a court takes a step that is much more damaging to shareholders than simply dissolving the corporation—it removes the shareholders' limited liability.

Piercing the Corporate Veil

One of the major purposes of a corporation is to protect its owners—the shareholders—from personal liability for the debts of the organization. Sometimes, however, a court will **pierce the corporate veil**; that is, the court will hold shareholders personally liable for the debts of the corporation. Courts generally pierce a corporate veil in four circumstances:

Pierce the corporate veil
A court holds shareholders personally liable for the debts of the corporation.

- *Failure to observe formalities.* If an organization does not act like a corporation, it will not be treated like one. It must, for example, hold required shareholders' and directors' meetings (or sign consents), keep a minute book as a record of these meetings, and make all the required state filings. Even a corporation with only one shareholder must comply with these formalities. Sole shareholders usually just sign a written consent in lieu of a meeting. In addition, as we saw in the *GS Petroleum* case, officers must be careful to sign all corporate documents with a corporate title, not as an individual. Otherwise, creditors may well be in doubt about whether they were dealing with an individual or a corporation. An officer should sign like this:

Classic American Novels, Inc.
By: Stephen Crane
Stephen Crane, President

If he signs simply "Stephen Crane," creditors may successfully claim that he is personally liable.

- *Commingling of assets.* Nothing makes a court more willing to pierce a corporate veil than evidence that shareholders have mixed their assets with those of the corporation. Sometimes, for example, shareholders use corporate assets to pay their personal debts or even mix corporate and personal funds in one bank account. If shareholders commingle assets, it is genuinely difficult for creditors to determine which assets belong to whom. This confusion is generally resolved in favor of the creditors—*all* assets are deemed to belong to the corporation.

- *Inadequate capitalization.* If the founders of a corporation do not raise enough capital (either through debt or equity) to give the business a fighting chance of paying its debts, courts may require shareholders to pay corporate obligations. Therefore, if the corporation does not have sufficient capital, it needs to buy insurance, particularly to protect against tort liability. Judges are likelier to hold shareholders liable if the alternative is to send an injured tort victim away empty-handed. For example, Oriental Fireworks Co. had hundreds of thousands of dollars in annual sales but only $13,000 in assets. The company did not bother to obtain any liability insurance, keep a minute book, or defend lawsuits. There was no need because the company had no money. But then a court pierced the corporate veil and found the owner of the company personally liable.[7]

- *Fraud.* Corporations cannot be used to shelter fraud. Imagine that a con artist forms a corporation entitled Brooklyn Bridge, Inc. He then sells shares in the organization by convincing "investors," aka "victims," that the company really does own the famous New York landmark. If he is caught, the victims can go after his personal assets, even though the fraud was committed in the name of a corporation.

The following case is a good example of when a court should pierce the corporate veil.

If the owner of this amusement park fails to purchase adequate insurance, its shareholders may be personally liable.

[7] *Rice v. Oriental Fireworks Co.*, 75 Or. App. 627, 707 P.2d 1250, 1985 Ore. App. LEXIS 3928.

Brooks v. Becker

2005 Va. Cir. LEXIS 13
Circuit Court of Fairfax County, Virginia, 2005

Facts: Ronald Becker was the sole shareholder, officer, and director of Becker Interiors. Becker and his partner, Robert LaPointe, used approximately $300,000 of Becker Interiors' funds to renovate their residence, pay their personal credit card bills, and invest in another company of which Becker was president. Becker sold a corporate car for $73,700 and deposited those funds into his personal account, along with the corporation's income tax refund check of $12,850.

Becker Interiors supervised the major renovation of a house in McLean, Virginia. The company hired Stephen Brooks as a subcontractor on the project. When the company refused to pay Brooks, he filed suit, winning a judgment against the company for $54,597.09. But it turned out that Becker Interiors had no assets.

Brooks then sued Ronald Becker in an attempt to pierce the corporate veil and hold Becker personally liable for the debts of the corporation.

Issues: ***Can Brooks pierce the corporate veil? Is Becker personally liable for the debts of the corporation?***

Excerpts from Judge Roush's Decision: The decision to ignore the separate existence of a corporate entity and impose personal liability upon shareholders for debts of the corporation is an extraordinary act to be taken only when necessary to promote justice. Disregarding the corporate entity is usually warranted only under the extraordinary circumstances where: the shareholder sought to be held personally liable has controlled or used the corporation to evade a personal obligation, to perpetrate fraud or a crime, to commit an injustice, or to gain an unfair advantage. Piercing the corporate veil is justified when the unity of interest and ownership is such that the separate personalities of the corporation and the individual no longer exist and to adhere to that separateness would work an injustice.

In this case, the evidence convinces the court that the extraordinary remedy of piercing the corporate veil should be granted. Becker knowingly violated his duties as an officer, director, and shareholder of Becker Interiors and treated the corporation's funds as his personal piggy bank. His testimony that the corporate expenditures on his personal residence were a legitimate business expense because he wanted to use the residence as a showcase of his work was simply not credible. Nor did the court believe Becker's testimony that he commingled his personal funds with the corporation's funds on the advice of his accountant. The court found more credible Becker's later testimony that his accountant was "mystified" by his comingling of funds between his personal and corporate accounts.

Accordingly, the court will enter judgment against Becker in the amount of $54,597.09.

EXAM Strategy

Question: Jose is an employee and shareholder of Birdsong, a company that sells farm equipment. Jose shows Marta how to use the hay baler she has just bought from the company. He also gives her an instructional pamphlet that Birdsong had prepared. Unfortunately, Jose's advice is wrong, and so is the pamphlet's. Marta is injured while using the baler. It turns out that Birdsong's charter was revoked for failure to make the required annual filings with the Arkansas Secretary of State. In all other ways, Birdsong operated as a corporation. Is Birdsong liable to Marta? Is Jose personally liable to her?

Strategy: In theory, Jose could be liable as a shareholder because the charter of the corporation had been revoked or if the corporate veil was pierced. In addition, he could be personally liable for his own wrongdoing.

Result: Birdsong is liable for its carelessness in preparing the pamphlet. Although Birdsong was not technically a corporation, it has operated as one. Therefore, under the theory of corporation by estoppel, Jose is not liable. Nor has Birdsong done anything to warrant its veil being pierced. Jose is, however, liable for his own negligence. Therefore, he is liable for the bad advice he gave Marta.

Termination

Terminating a corporation is a three-step process:

- *Vote.* The directors recommend to the shareholders that the corporation be dissolved, and a majority of the shareholders agree.
- *Filing.* The corporation files "Articles of Dissolution" with the Secretary of State.
- *Winding up.* The officers of the corporation pay its debts and distribute the remaining property to shareholders. When the winding up is completed, the corporation ceases to exist.

The Secretary of State may dissolve a corporation that violates state law by, for example, failing to pay the required annual fees. Indeed, many corporations, particularly small ones, do not bother with the formal dissolution process. They simply cease paying their annual fees and let the Secretary of State act. A court may dissolve a corporation if it is insolvent or if its directors and shareholders cannot resolve conflict over how the corporation should be managed. The court will then appoint a receiver to oversee the winding up.

Chapter Conclusion

Virtually every businessperson will, at some point, work for a corporation or own shares in one. Indeed, corporations are so important that we devote three chapters to them. Although they are an exceedingly useful form of organization, they are also exceedingly formal. State corporation codes contain precise rules that must be followed to the letter. To do otherwise is to court disaster.

Exam Review

1. **PROMOTERS** Promoters are personally liable for contracts they sign before the corporation is formed unless the corporation and the third party agree to a novation. (p. 816)

Question: Ajouelo signed an employment contract with Wilkerson. The contract stated: "Whatever company, partnership, or corporation that Wilkerson may form for the purpose of manufacturing shall succeed Wilkerson and exercise the rights and assume all of Wilkerson's obligations as fixed by this contract." Two months later, Wilkerson formed Auto-Soler Co. Ajouelo entered into a new contract with Auto-Soler that provided that the company was liable for Wilkerson's obligations under the old contract. Neither Wilkerson nor the company ever paid Ajouelo. He sued Wilkerson personally. Does Wilkerson have any obligations to Ajouelo?

Strategy: A promoter is not liable for a contract he signed on behalf of a yet-to-be-formed corporation if the third party (in this case, Wilkinson) agrees to a novation. (See the "Result" at the end of this section.)

2. **STATE OF INCORPORATION** Companies generally incorporate in the state in which they will be doing business. However, if they intend to operate in several states, they may choose to incorporate in a jurisdiction known for its favorable corporate laws, such as Delaware or Nevada. (pp. 816–817)

3. **THE CHARTER**

Required Provisions A corporate charter must generally include the company's name, address, registered agent, purpose, and a description of its stock. The charter must be signed by at least one incorporator. (pp. 820–824)
Optional Provisions A company's charter may include a number of optional provisions, such as cumulative voting and indemnification for officers and directors. (pp. 824–826)

Question: Does par value matter? Did it ever?

Strategy: There are a lot of terms in this chapter, but it is a good idea to remember what they mean because you are likely to hear them again in your life as a businessperson. (See the "Result" at the end of this section.)

Question: At this writing, TheFacebook, Inc. is estimated to have 2.2 billion shares outstanding and four directors. Without cumulative voting, how many shares would you have to purchase to be sure of electing yourself to the board? If the company's charter required cumulative voting, how many shares would you have to buy to achieve this goal? What if there were 15 directors?

Strategy: The formula is

$$\text{Number of shares needed to elect one director} = \frac{\text{Number of shares outstanding}}{\text{Number of directors being elected} + 1} + 1$$

(See the "Result" at the end of this section.)

4. **FOREIGN CORPORATION** A corporation must register in every state in which it is doing business. (pp. 830–831)

5. **PIERCING THE CORPORATE VEIL** A court may, under certain circumstances, pierce the corporate veil and hold shareholders personally liable for the debts of the corporation. (pp. 831–834)

6. **TERMINATION** Termination of a corporation is a three-step process requiring a shareholder vote, the filing of "Articles of Dissolution," and the winding up of the enterprise's business. (p. 834)

1. Result: Wilkerson may have had an ethical obligation to Ajouelo but not a legal one. The court held that the second contract was a novation, which ended Wilkerson's obligations under the first contract.

3. Result: *First question:* The original purpose of par value was to protect shareholders from unscrupulous managers who wanted to issue stock at below market value. Now, it has no purpose other than as the basis for state filing fees. The only issue is that you want to set it low enough that it does not trigger a higher-than-necessary fee.
Second question: Without cumulative voting, you would have to buy 1 share more than 1.1 billion shares. With four directors, you would have to buy 1 share more than 440 million. With 15 directors, you would have to buy 1 share more than 137.5 million.

Multiple-Choice Questions

1. **CPA QUESTION** Generally, a corporation's articles of incorporation must include all of the following **except** the:
   (a) Name of the corporation's registered agent
   (b) Name of each incorporator
   (c) Number of authorized shares
   (d) Quorum requirements

2. **CPA QUESTION** Destiny Manufacturing, Inc., is incorporated under the laws of Nevada. Its principal place of business is in California, and it has permanent sales offices in several other states. Under the circumstances, which of the following is correct?
   (a) California may validly demand that Destiny incorporate under the laws of the state of California.
   (b) Destiny must obtain a certificate of authority to transact business in California and the other states in which it does business.
   (c) Destiny is a foreign corporation in California, but *not* in the other states.
   (d) California may prevent Destiny from operating as a corporation if the laws of California differ regarding organization and conduct of the corporation's internal affairs.

3. **CPA QUESTION** A corporate stockholder is entitled to which of the following rights?
   (a) Elect officers
   (b) Receive annual dividends
   (c) Approve dissolution
   (d) Prevent corporate borrowing

4. Participating preferred stockholders:
   (a) only receive payment after other preferred shareholders have been paid
   (b) only receive payment after common shareholders have been paid
   (c) are treated like both a preferred shareholder and a common shareholder
   (d) receive all their payments before all other shareholders

5. Debentures are:
   (a) long-term secured debt
   (b) short-term secured debt
   (c) long-term unsecured debt
   (d) short-term unsecured debt

6. If the terms of a company's charter and bylaws conflict, which governs?
   (a) The charter governs.
   (b) The bylaw governs.
   (c) They are both invalid.
   (d) Shareholders must vote to determine which is valid.

Essay Questions

1. In the *GS Petroleum* case earlier in this chapter, what should the signature line have looked like?

2. Michael incorporated Erin Homes, Inc., to manufacture mobile homes. He issued himself a stock certificate for 100 shares for which he made no payment. He and his wife served as officers and directors of the organization, but, during the eight years of its existence, the corporation held only one meeting. Erin always had its own checking account, and all proceeds from the sales of mobile homes were deposited there. It filed federal income tax returns each year using its own federal identification number. John and Thelma paid $17,500 to purchase a mobile home from Erin, but the company never delivered it to them. John and Thelma sued Erin Homes and Michael, individually. Should the court "pierce the corporate veil" and hold Michael personally liable?

3. The Resolution Trust Corp. (RTC) sued the directors of the Commonwealth Savings Association seeking to recover from them personally $200 million that the bank lost in bad real estate loans. The directors approved the loans after state and federal regulatory agencies had issued reports criticizing the bank's loan practices. The directors failed to implement policies and procedures to prevent problems with the loan portfolio and failed to monitor loan officers adequately. There was no evidence that the directors knowingly committed illegal acts or acts outside their authority. Under Texas law, the RTC could recover for the directors' negligence only if their acts were *ultra vires*. Were these acts *ultra vires?*

4. Waste Management, Inc., the country's largest waste hauler, changed its name to WMX Technologies, Inc. Similarly, U.S. Steel changed its moniker to USX Corp. and

American Airlines became AMR Corp. What legal steps would be necessary for these companies to protect their new corporate names?

5. Dickens, Inc. is a bookstore incorporated in Nevada. From its warehouse in Montana, it ships books to all 50 states. The company's owner lives in New York, and its web designer lives in California. Where is Dickens a domestic corporation? Where must it qualify to do business?

Discussion Questions

1. In the *Loudeye* case, the court ruled that if the charter has an exculpatory clause, directors are not liable unless they are grossly negligent, motivated by an actual intent to do harm, or intentionally disregard their responsibilities. Is that a reasonable standard?

2. **ETHICS** In the *Bigmar* case, the court clearly believed that the directors had lied on the witness stand. Should the directors have been charged with perjury? Did they do the right thing when they lied on the stand to protect their company from the evil Ms. May?

3. Angelica is planning to start a home security business in McGehee, Arkansas. She plans to start modestly but hopes to expand her business within 5 years to neighboring towns and, perhaps, within 10 years to neighboring states. Her inclination is to incorporate her business in Delaware. Is her inclination correct?

4. States compete for lucrative filing fees by passing corporate statutes that favor management. One proposed solution to this problem would be a federal system of corporate registration. Is this a good idea? What are the impediments to such as system?

5. Ford Motor Co. and TheFacebook, Inc. have both created dual classes of stock so that the founders can continue to control their company even after it goes public. Should corporate laws permit this? Should some shareholders be more equal than others? If the founders want to control a company, why shouldn't they buy enough regular stock to do so?

CHAPTER 34

Corporate Management

© Evan Meyer/Shutterstock.com

Rick says: Bob and I own a bar and restaurant in Nevada. It's a pretty good business, but what really brings in the bucks is the keno game in the lounge. Keno is like bingo, only you get to choose the numbers you play. Here is the weird thing—there is absolutely *no* skill involved, but people just *love* to play the game. It is a license to print money. It's as if the folks just want to hand us their cash. We have each pulled in 4 *million* big ones since we bought this business.

It's true that I don't spend as much time at the restaurant as Rick does, but then again, my girlfriend isn't the "manager" there.

You'd think that amount of money would be enough to get Bob's attention, but he acts like the business just runs itself. He can barely be bothered to show up. So I've set up a meeting with city officials, hoping to convince them to put the keno contract up for bid. I'll get the contract in my own name and cut Bob out. He's nothing but dead weight.

Bob says: Whine, whine, whine. Something must be going right with our business; we've made four million bucks, for Pete's sake. It's true that I don't spend as much time at the restaurant as Rick does, but then again, my girlfriend isn't the "manager" there. What Rick's doing there doesn't really count as work. Also, any time he asks me to do something, I'm all over it. I don't know what he's so hot and bothered about.

What obligations does Rick have to the business he owns with Bob? In a similar case later in the chapter—*Anderson v. Bellino*—the court ruled that Rick could not take the keno contract away from their jointly owned corporation. Read on to see why.

Stakeholder
Anyone who is affected by the activities of a corporation, such as employees, customers, creditors, suppliers, shareholders, and neighbors.

Corporations are complicated creatures with many different interest groups: shareholders, officers, directors, and **stakeholders**, such as the community, employees, suppliers, creditors, and customers. Business life was not always so complicated. Before the Industrial Revolution in the 18th and 19th centuries, a business owner typically supplied both capital and management. However, the cash needs of the great manufacturing enterprises spawned by the Industrial Revolution were larger than any small group of individuals could supply. To find capital, firms sought outside investors, who often had neither the knowledge nor the desire to manage the enterprise. Investors without management skills complemented managers without capital. (Throughout these corporation chapters, the term "manager" includes both directors and officers.)

Modern businesses still have the same vast need for capital and the same division between managers and investors. Because shareholders are too numerous and too uninformed to manage the enterprises they own, they elect directors to manage for them. The directors set policy and then appoint officers to implement corporate goals. The Model Business Corporation Act describes the directors' role thus: "All corporate powers shall be exercised by or under the authority of, and the business and affairs of the corporation managed by or under the direction of, its board of directors…."[1]

Directors have the authority to manage the corporate business, but they also have important responsibilities to shareholders and stakeholders. However, the interests of these various groups often conflict. In the 2000s, the world faced two financial crises which were caused, in part, by corporate executives who engaged in highly risky activities that left them wealthy and their shareholders broke. Because of abuses by managers that in some cases included outright fraud, Congress and other regulators have tried to rebalance the power among managers, shareholders, and stakeholders. Part of their goal has been to enhance shareholder oversight of the companies they own. These two chapters are about this balance of rights and responsibilities.

Managers Versus Shareholders: The Fundamental Conflict

The following newspaper excerpt illustrates the natural conflict between managers and shareholders:

> The mood here in reaction to the sale of *The Los Angeles Times* to the Tribune Company may have been best summed up by Mark H. Willes, the company's chairman, when he left the board meeting that approved the transaction late Sunday evening. Mr. Willes burst into tears and wept openly, according to several people who saw him. The sale of the paper and its parent, the Times Mirror Company, would make Mr. Willes an immensely wealthy man. And it would earn tens of thousands of dollars, in some instances more, for each of the reporters, editors and many other employees of the Times Mirror Company who hold stock and stock options.
>
> But for many people in this city, both in *The Los Angeles Times* newsroom and outside, the deal felt humiliating, they said, as if something precious had been stolen away. "There is a feeling that yesterday, a part of this city's soul was *The Los Angeles Times*," said Geoffrey Cowan, dean of the Annenberg School of Communications at the University of Southern California. "I'm not sure how much that is true tomorrow." He added, "There is a loss of identity."

---

[1]A committee of the American Bar Association drafted the Model Business Corporation Act to serve as a guideline for states to use when enacting a corporate code. More than half the states have now adopted some version of it. The corporate statutes of Delaware also serve as a model for other states.

> Within the newsroom, many people expressed anger that the Chandler family, which has controlled the company for decades, had sold the company to an outsider, in spite of assurances in recent years that it never would. "The Chandler family long ago lost interest in running a newspaper and they're just interested in the profits," said Ken Reich, a columnist who has worked at *The Los Angeles Times* for 35 years.[2]

This episode illustrates the ongoing debate over corporate governance in America. Managers serve at least three masters: themselves, shareholders, and other stakeholders. These masters have conflicting goals:

- **Managers** want two things: first, to keep their jobs, and second, to build an institution that will survive them. Mark Willes, chairman of *The Los Angeles Times*, wept when his company was sold despite the immense wealth he received from the sale. To him, the job was what mattered.
- **Shareholders** want a high stock price, *right now*, not five years from now. As owners, the members of the Chandler family cared more about their own profits than they did about the newspaper and its important role in the life of the city.
- **Stakeholders**, those who work for the *Los Angeles Times*, read it, sell it ink, or own the food shop across the street from its plant want the newspaper to stay in business. The speaker of the California State Assembly lamented the sale because the paper had been a booster for the whole city of Los Angeles. (Generally, managers are not included in the stakeholder category because their interests may be different from those of lower-level employees.)

Did the Chandler family have a legal or ethical obligation to consider the impact of this sale on the managers and stakeholders? Or should everyone simply accept that shareholders—and their profits—come first? Would it have been fair to shareholders if the managers had vetoed the sale? These are the difficult issues of corporate governance that companies face. Only one thing is clear: managers cannot please all the stakeholders all the time.

The courts have generally held that **managers have a fiduciary duty to act in the best interests of the corporation's shareholders**. Since shareholders are primarily concerned about their return on investment, managers must *maximize shareholder value*, which means providing shareholders with the highest possible financial return from dividends and stock price. However, reality is more complicated than this simple rule indicates. It is often difficult to determine which strategy will best maximize shareholder value. And what about *stakeholders*? Must managers totally ignore their interests? In the following landmark case, the court explicitly permits the board to consider the interests of stakeholders over those of some shareholders. Commentators have described this case as "the most innovative and promising case in our corporation law."

---

[2]James Sterngold, "In Los Angeles, Tears and a Feeling of Loss," p. C16. From *The New York Times*, March 14, 2000.

Landmark Case

Unocal Corp. v. Mesa Petroleum Co.

493 A.2d 946, 1985 Del. LEXIS 482
Supreme Court of Delaware, 1985

Facts: Mesa Petroleum Co. offered to purchase 64 million shares of Unocal's stock at a cash price of $54 per share. Upon merger of the two companies, Mesa planned to exchange the remaining Unocal shares for "junk bonds" that Mesa (but no one else, including the court) valued at $54 per share. Unocal's investment bankers advised the board of directors that the Mesa proposal was wholly inadequate and that an offer of over $60 per share would have been reasonable. The board rejected the Mesa offer and then made its own competing offer of $72 per share to all shareholders except Mesa. (This type of offer is called a "selective exchange offer.") The board's offer effectively preempted Mesa because no shareholder would accept the $54 Mesa offer when the $72 Unocal offer was also available. The Delaware court issued a preliminary injunction against Unocal's offer unless it included Mesa.

Issues: ***Could Unocal make an offer to buy stock from all shareholders except Mesa? In making this offer, did Unocal have the right to consider the interests of other stakeholders?***

Excerpts from Justice Moore's Decision: In the board's exercise of corporate power to forestall a takeover bid, our analysis begins with the basic principle that corporate directors have a fiduciary duty to act in the best interests of the corporation's stockholders. The restriction placed upon a selective stock repurchase is that the directors may not have acted solely or primarily out of a desire to perpetuate themselves in office. This entails an analysis by the directors of the nature of the takeover bid and its effect on the corporate enterprise. Examples of such concerns may include inadequacy of the price offered, nature and timing of the offer, questions of illegality, the impact on "constituencies" other than shareholders (i.e., creditors, customers, employees, and perhaps even the community generally), the risk of nonconsummation, and the quality of securities being offered in the exchange. While not a controlling factor, it also seems to us that a board may reasonably consider the basic stockholder interests at stake, including those of short term speculators, whose actions may have fueled the coercive aspect of the offer at the expense of the long-term investor.

In adopting the selective exchange offer, the board stated that its objective was either to defeat the inadequate Mesa offer or, should the offer still succeed, provide its stockholders with $72 a share. We find that both purposes are valid. However, such efforts would have been thwarted by Mesa's participation in the exchange offer. First, if Mesa could tender its shares, Unocal would effectively be subsidizing the former's continuing effort to buy Unocal stock at $54 per share. Second, Mesa could not, by definition, fit within the class of shareholders being protected from its own coercive and inadequate tender offer. Thus, we are satisfied that the selective exchange offer is reasonably related to the threats posed.

The decision of the Court of Chancery is therefore *reversed*, and the preliminary injunction is *vacated*.

Devil's Advocate In this case, the court says that the board cannot act with the primary goal of keeping itself in office. One could argue, however, that that is precisely what the board did. It *said* that it was concerned about stakeholders but, conveniently, stakeholder interests coincided precisely with its own. When forced to choose between shareholders, who in fact *own the company,* and stakeholders, why should the board be allowed to choose stakeholders? This choice seems particularly tainted given the board's conflict of interest.

A number of states have adopted statutes that codify the *Unocal* decision. These statutes permit directors, when making a decision, to consider, for example, "both the short-term and long-term best interests of the corporation, taking into account, and weighing as the directors deem appropriate, the effects thereof on the corporation's shareholders and the other corporate constituent groups...."[3] The next section looks more closely at directors' responsibilities to their various constituencies.

Resolving the Conflict: The Business Judgment Rule

Officers and directors have a fiduciary duty to act in the best interests of their stockholders, but under the **business judgment rule,** the courts allow managers great leeway in carrying out this responsibility. The business judgment rule is a common law concept that has achieved national acceptance. It is a fundamental principle of corporate law. To be protected by the business judgment rule, managers must act in good faith:

Duty of Loyalty	1. Without a conflict of interest
Duty of Care	2. With the care that an ordinarily prudent person would take in a similar situation, and 3. In a manner they reasonably believe to be in the best interests of the corporation.

The business judgment rule is two shields in one: it protects both the manager and her decision. **If a manager has complied with the rule, a court will not hold her personally liable for any harm her decision has caused the company, nor will the court rescind her decision.** If the manager violates the business judgment rule, then she has the burden of proving that her decision was entirely fair to the shareholders. If it was not entirely fair, she may be held personally liable and the decision can be rescinded.

The business judgment rule accomplishes three goals:

- *It permits directors to do their job.* Business is risky. No one can guarantee perfect decision making all the time. If directors were afraid they would be liable for every decision that led to a loss, they would never make a decision, or at least not a risky one.
- *It keeps judges out of corporate management.* Shareholders would generally prefer that their investments be overseen by experienced corporate managers, not judges. Without the business judgment rule, judges would be tempted, if not required, to second-guess managers' decisions.
- *It encourages directors to serve.* No one in his right mind would serve as a director if he knew that every decision was open to attack in the courtroom. Even if the company pays the legal bills, who wants to spend years in litigation?

Analysis of the business judgment rule is typically divided into two parts. The obligation of a manager to act without a conflict of interest is called the **duty of loyalty.** The requirements that a manager act with care and in the best interests of the corporation are referred to as the **duty of care.**

Duty of loyalty
The obligation of a manager to act without a conflict of interest.

Duty of care
The requirement that a manager act with care and in the best interests of the corporation.

Duty of Loyalty

The duty of loyalty prohibits managers from making a decision that benefits them at the expense of the corporation.

[3]Indiana Code §23-1-35-1.

Duty of loyalty is violated in the event of:

• Self-Dealing

Self-dealing means that a manager makes a decision benefiting either himself or another company with which he has a relationship. While working at the Blue Moon restaurant, Zeke signs a contract on behalf of the restaurant to purchase bread from Rising Sun Bakery. Unbeknownst to anyone at Blue Moon, he is a part owner of Rising Sun. Zeke has engaged in self-dealing, which is a violation of the duty of loyalty.

Once a manager engages in self-dealing, the business judgment rule no longer applies. This does not mean the manager is automatically liable to the corporation or that his decision is automatically void. All it means is that the court will no longer presume that the transaction was acceptable. Instead, the court will scrutinize the deal more carefully. A self-dealing transaction is valid in any one of the following situations:

- **The disinterested members of the board of directors approve the transaction.** Disinterested directors are those who do not themselves benefit from the transaction.
- **The disinterested shareholders approve it.** The transaction is valid if the shareholders who do not benefit from it are willing to approve it.
- **The transaction was entirely fair to the corporation.** In determining fairness, the courts will consider whether the price was reasonable and the impact of the transaction on the corporation.

Exhibit 34.1 illustrates the rules on self-dealing.

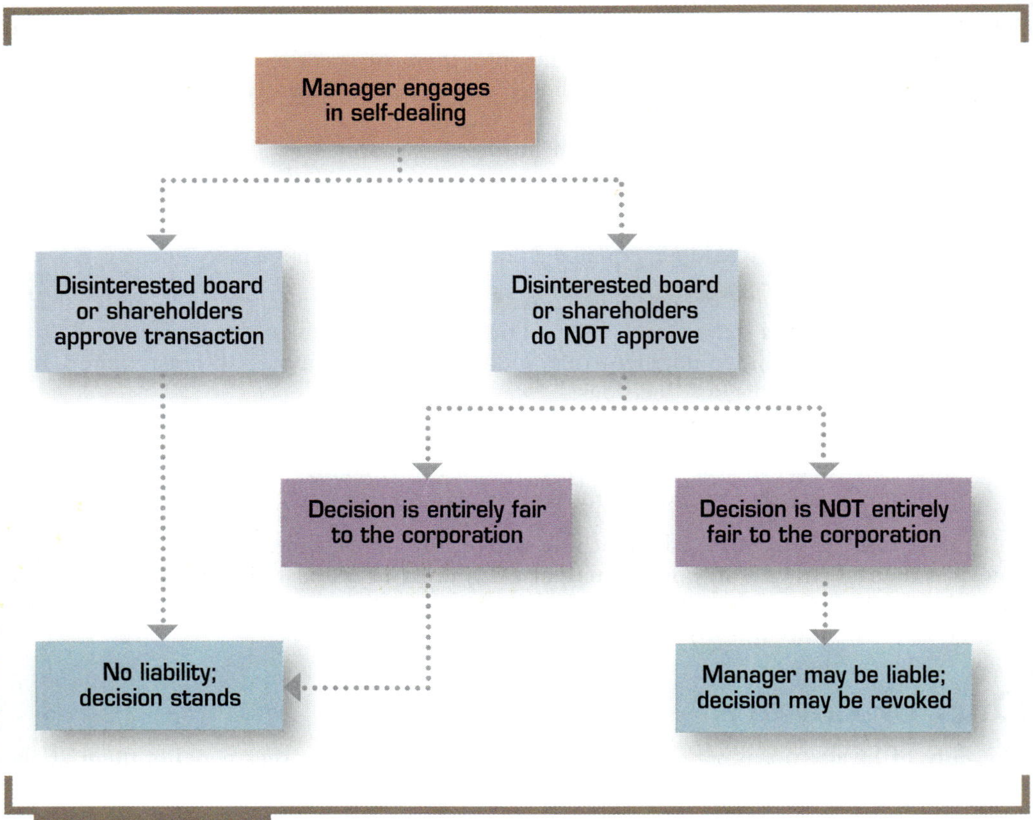

EXHIBIT 34.1

Corporate officers, especially in family businesses, sometimes forget that they do not have the right to do whatever they want. The following case illustrates the business judgment rule and also the enduring principle that litigation is a very sad method for resolving family disputes.

Lippman v. Shaffer

15 Misc. 3d 705; 836 N.Y.S.2d 766; 2006 N.Y. Misc. LEXIS 4212
Supreme Court of New York, 2006

Facts: Years ago, Harry Lippman purchased Despatch Industries, Inc., which manufactured hardware for cabinets. His son, James, worked for the company. Later, James's son, Wade, and son-in-law, Alan Shaffer, also went on the company payroll. Both young men signed identical employment contracts. After Wade and James had a falling out, Wade resigned from the company. The Despatch board agreed to pay $1.3 million to both Wade and Alan. Company tax returns referred to these as "severance" payments, although Alan continued to work for the company and receive a salary.

Wade filed suit against Alan and Despatch, alleging that the payments to Alan were improper and should be returned. The defendants argued that the payments were protected by the business judgment rule. Wade filed a motion for summary judgment.

Issue: ***Were the payments to Alan protected by the business judgment rule?***

Excerpts from Judge Fisher's Decision: Generally, the actions of directors are protected by the business judgment rule, which bars judicial inquiry into actions of corporate directors taken in good faith and in the exercise of honest judgment in the lawful and legitimate furtherance of corporate purposes. As such, the business judgment rule prevents a court from second-guessing corporate decision making.

[T]he business judgment rule is not applicable when the directors have an interest in the challenged transaction. Directors are self-interested in a challenged transaction where they will receive a direct financial benefit from the transaction which is different from the benefit to shareholders generally.

The court's first inquiry is whether the business judgment rule applies. Here, it does not. Plaintiffs have established that there was no contractual or other legitimate reason to give [Alan] the equivalent of the so-called severance payments made to Wade because the severance terms of [Alan's] employment contract covering such payments were not then triggered. To avoid liability, the board will have to demonstrate entire fairness by presenting evidence of the manner by which it otherwise discharged all of its fiduciary duties.

The difficulty in defendants' position lies in the undisputed fact that no events had transpired to trigger any severance payments to [Alan] under the agreements. [Alan] states the following rationale for the payments: "Whatever Wade got, I would get. Whatever I got, Wade would get." Inasmuch as severance payments were contractually due to Wade, but not to [Alan, his] payments may only be described as a gift of corporate assets and therefore he got more than Wade got, to the tune of $ 1.3 million.

[Wade's motion for summary judgment is granted.]

Corporate Opportunity

The self-dealing rules prevent managers from *forcing* their companies into unfair deals. The corporate opportunity doctrine is the reverse—it prohibits managers from *excluding* their company from favorable deals. **Managers are in violation of the corporate opportunity doctrine if they compete against the corporation without its consent.**

Long ago, Charles Guth was president of Loft, Inc., which operated a chain of candy stores. These stores sold Coca-Cola. Guth purchased the Pepsi-Cola Company personally, without offering the opportunity to Loft. The Delaware court found that Guth had violated the corporate opportunity doctrine and ordered him to transfer all his shares in PepsiCo to Loft.[4] That was in 1939 and Pepsi-Cola was bankrupt; today, PepsiCo, Inc., is worth more than $100 billion.

[4]*Guth v. Loft*, 5 A.2d 503, 23 Del. Ch. 255, 1939 Del. LEXIS 13 (Del. 1939).

If a manager suspects that company officers would be displeased to learn about his new sideline, that is an indication he is skating on thin ice.

If a manager first offers an opportunity to disinterested directors or shareholders, and they turn it down, the manager then has the right to take advantage of the opportunity himself. (Remember that "disinterested directors or shareholders" are those who do not personally benefit from the transaction.) Sometimes, however, either through oversight or ignorance, managers do not seek permission in advance. To avoid violating the corporate opportunity doctrine, the manager must show after the fact that the company would have been unable to benefit from the opportunity. For example, Cellular Information Systems, Inc., had just emerged from bankruptcy proceedings when one of its directors learned that a cell-phone license covering part of Michigan was for sale. The director purchased the license himself, and the company sued. The court found the director not liable because the company could not have afforded to purchase the license itself.[5]

A manager will often find it difficult to prove that the company could not have used an opportunity itself. However, these disputes are easy to avoid—the manager must simply ask permission first. Certainly, if a manager suspects that company officers would be displeased to learn about his new sideline, that is an indication that he is skating on thin ice.

In the following case, the manager felt that he had a good reason for taking a corporate opportunity. Unfortunately, the court disagreed.

Anderson v. Bellino

265 Neb. 577, 658 N.W.2d 645, 2003 Neb. LEXIS 49
Supreme Court of Nebraska, 2003

Facts: Richard Bellino and Robert Anderson formed LaVista Lottery, Inc. (Lottery) to operate a restaurant, lounge, and keno game in LaVista, Nevada. They each owned 50 percent of the stock of Lottery, and both were officers and directors.

During the next nine years, Lottery grossed more than $100 million. Bellino and Anderson each received over $4 million in salary and dividends. Although Bellino and Anderson were both involved in Lottery, Bellino spent more time, in part because of his personal relationship with Lottery's lounge manager. During this period, Bellino did not complain to Anderson about his lack of involvement in Lottery, and Anderson never refused to do anything that Bellino asked him to do.

Resentful of Anderson's work ethic, Bellino set up a meeting with LaVista's city administrator. Until that meeting, the city had been satisfied with Lottery's performance. But after the meeting, the administrator recommended to the city council that the keno contract be put up for competitive bid. Bellino incorporated LaVista Keno, Inc. (Keno) to bid on the contract.

Bellino wrote to Anderson complaining that he (Bellino) was doing too much work for Lottery at too little pay. (Evidently, $4 million is not as much as it used to be.) Therefore, Bellino intended to resign from Lottery and bid on the city contract himself. Anderson offered to do more work or whatever Bellino wanted, but Bellino refused any effort at reconciliation. He then submitted a bid on behalf of Keno. At the time he submitted the bid, Bellino was still an officer of Lottery, as well as a director and a 50 percent shareholder. Anderson also bid on the contract on behalf of Lottery. The city awarded the new contract to Keno.

Anderson and Lottery filed suit against Bellino and Keno, alleging that they had usurped a corporate opportunity. The lower court found for Anderson and Lottery. It ordered Bellino to pay $644,992.63 but provided that Bellino could receive a credit of $172,514.63 against the judgment if Bellino transferred the stock of Keno to Lottery and persuaded the city to relicense the keno contract from Keno to Lottery.

[5] *Broz v. Cellular Information Systems, Inc.*, 673 A.2d 148, 1996 Del. LEXIS 105.

Issues: ***Did Bellino usurp a corporate opportunity? Is he liable to Lottery?***

Excerpts from Justice Miller-Lerman's Decision: Bellino and Keno claim that if a corporate opportunity existed, it was limited to the opportunity to bid for the keno contract, that Bellino did nothing to impede Lottery from bidding for the keno contract by merely submitting a competing bid, and that, therefore, Bellino did not usurp a corporate opportunity.

Contrary to the arguments asserted by Bellino and Keno, the corporate opportunity was not the right to bid; the bidding process was merely the "preliminary step" by which Lottery sought to acquire the opportunity embodied in the award of the keno contract. The facts thus establish that the keno contract was a corporate opportunity for Lottery.

When discussing a corporate officer or director's fiduciary duty to the corporation, we have stated:

> Although an officer or a director of a corporation is not necessarily precluded from entering into a separate business because it is in competition with the corporation, his fiduciary relationship to the corporation and its stockholders is such that if he does so he must prove that he did so in good faith and did not act in such a manner as to cause or contribute to the injury or damage of the corporation, or deprive it of business; if he fails in this proof, there has been a breach of that fiduciary trust or relationship.

The evidence is uncontroverted that Bellino's successful bid for the LaVista keno contract deprived Lottery of its only source of business. Bellino, through Keno, should not have competed with Lottery for the LaVista keno contract.

We affirm the district court's order.

EXAM Strategy

Question: Otto signed a lease with Landlord on a storefront in Georgetown, in Washington, D.C. He convinced his nephew Nick to start a furniture store in the space. Otto and Nick formed a corporation to operate the store. Otto owned 51 percent and Nick 49 percent of the company's stock. Otto signed a lease between himself and the store at a price that was 20 percent higher than the rent Otto was paying Landlord. Otto purchased a warehouse and then rented it to the corporation at a fair market rent. Nick sued, alleging that the two leases were not valid. Were they?

Strategy: Under the business judgment rule, the courts will not second-guess a corporate action. However, if a manager engages in self-dealing, the business judgment rule does not apply.

Result: Otto violated the duty of loyalty twice. The lease for the storefront was self-dealing—it directly benefited him. When he purchased the warehouse, he took a corporate opportunity that he should have offered first to the company. He is personally liable for any damages to the corporation. The company also has the right to cancel both leases and to purchase the warehouse from him.

Duty of Care

In addition to the *duty of loyalty*, managers also owe a *duty of care.* **The duty of care requires officers and directors to act in the best interests of the corporation and to use the same care that an ordinarily prudent person would in a similar situation.** An ordinarily prudent person would have a rational business purpose, avoid illegal behavior, and make informed decisions. Officers and directors of corporations must do no less.

Rational Business Purpose

Courts generally agree in principle that directors and officers are liable to shareholders for decisions that have no rational business purpose. In practice, however, these same courts have been extremely supportive of managerial decisions, looking hard to find some justification. For years, the Chicago Cubs baseball team was the only major American professional sports team whose home field did not have lights. Cubs fans could only take themselves out to the ball game during the day. A shareholder sued on the grounds that the Cubs' revenues were peanuts and Cracker Jack compared with those generated by other teams that played at night. The Cubs defended their decision on the grounds that a large night crowd would cause the neighborhood to deteriorate, depressing the value of Wrigley Field (which was not owned by the Cubs). The court rooted for the home team and found that the Cubs' excuse was a "rational purpose" and a legitimate exercise of the business judgment rule.[6]

If a decision does not have a rational business purpose, the managers are liable and the decision can be rescinded. If a court decides that there is a rational business purpose, both the manager and the decision are protected.

Legality

Courts are generally unsympathetic to managers who engage in illegal behavior, even if their goal is to help the company. For example, the managing director of an amusement park in New York used corporate funds to purchase the silence of people who threatened to complain that the park was illegally operating on Sunday. The court ordered the director to repay the money he had spent on bribes, even though the company had earned large profits on Sundays.[7]

Informed Decision

Generally, courts will protect managers who make an *informed* decision, even if the decision ultimately harms the company. Making an informed decision means carefully investigating the facts. However, even if the decision is uninformed, the directors will not be held liable if the decision was entirely fair to the shareholders. The board of Technicolor, Inc., agreed to sell the film processing company, knowing little about the terms of the deal and without seeking other bidders. The directors simply knew that the sales price was higher than the appraised value of the company. Five years later, the buyer sold the company for a $750 million profit. The former shareholders sued, alleging that the directors had made an uninformed decision. The state supreme court held that, because the directors had been so careless, they had to prove that the price and the process by which it had been determined were both fair.[8]

Exhibit 34.2 provides an overview of the duty of care.

---

[6] *Shlensky v. Wrigley*, 95 Ill. App. 2d 173, 237 N.E.2d 776, 1968 Ill. App. LEXIS 1107 (Ill. App. Ct. 1968).
[7] *Roth v. Robertson*, 64 Misc. 343, 118 N.Y.S. 351, 1909 N.Y. Misc. LEXIS 279 (N.Y. 1909).
[8] The state supreme court sent the case back to the lower court to determine whether the deal had been fair to the shareholders. *Cede & Co., Inc. v. Technicolor, Inc.*, 634 A.2d 345, 1993 Del. LEXIS 398 (Del. 1993). The lower court ultimately decided that the transaction had indeed been fair. *Cinerama, Inc. v. Technicolor, Inc.*, 663 A.2d 1134, 1994 Del. Ch. LEXIS 178 (Del. Ch. 1994). The state supreme court, however, disagreeing with the valuation method used by the trial court, reversed that decision and remanded it once again to the trial court for further proceedings. *Cede & Co. v. Technicolor*, 684A.2d 289, 1996 Del. LEXIS 386 (Del. 1996). Yet again, in 2000, the Delaware Supreme Court (somewhat apologetically) overruled the trial court and returned the case for another trial. *Cede & Co. v. Technicolor, Inc.*, 758 A.2d 485, 2000 Del. LEXIS 283 (Del. 2000). The results from this trial were again appealed. Finally, in 2005, the Supreme Court of Delaware upheld most of the trial court rulings and remanded with simple instructions to change the interest rate it used to calculate damages. *Cede & Co. v. Technicolor, Inc.*, 2005 Del. LEXIS 177 (Del. 2005). The original sale of stock took place in 1983. This has been the longest case in the 200-year history of the Delaware Court of Chancery.

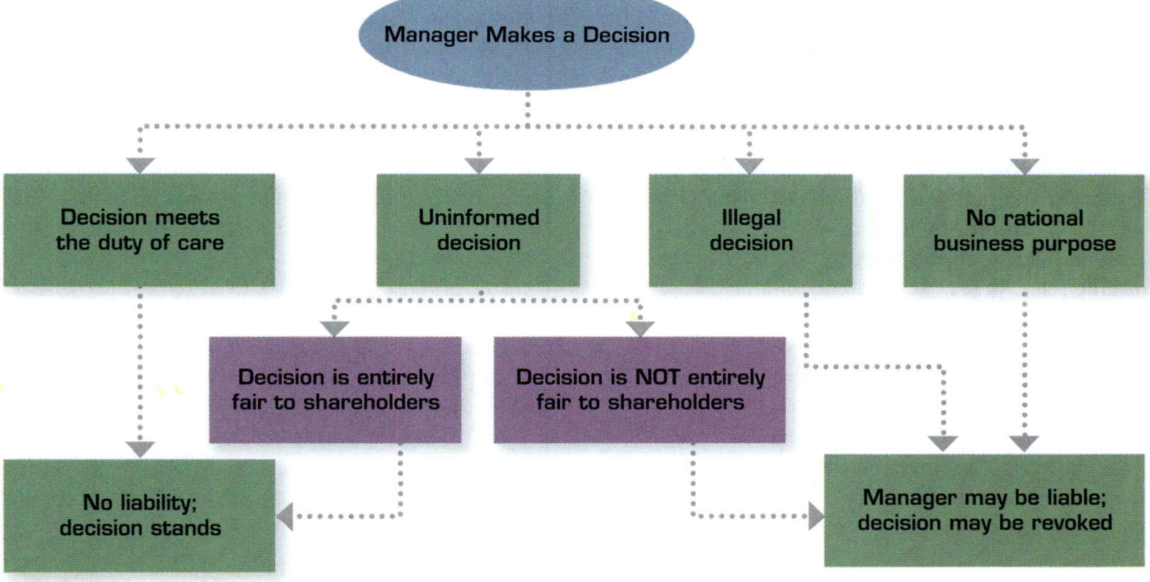

EXHIBIT 34.2

In the following case, the board of directors failed to hold meetings. Were their decisions informed?

RSL Communications v. Bildirici

2006 U.S. Dist. LEXIS 67548
United States District Court for the Southern District of New York, 2006

Facts: Ronald S. Lauder founded RSL Ltd., a multinational telecommunications corporation. RSL Plc was a subsidiary of RSL Ltd. The subsidiary began by issuing $1.4 billion of bonds. A few years later, in July, Lauder provided it with a $100 million line of credit. The company's board of directors did not hold a meeting to approve the Lauder loan. In August, RSL Plc drew down $25 million from that loan. The following March, the company's directors held their first board meeting in a year. Five days later, RSL Plc filed for bankruptcy.

The issue before the court is whether the members of the board of directors of RSL Plc breached their duty of care to the company when they failed to hold a board meeting for a year at a time when the company was in a precarious financial position.

Issue: ***Did the directors of RCL Plc violate their duty of care to the corporation?***

Excerpts from Judge Karas's Decision: Under New York law, a director shall perform his duties as a director, in good faith and with that degree of care which an ordinarily prudent person in a like position would use under similar circumstances. It is well settled that the duty of due care requires that a director's decision be made on the basis of reasonable diligence in gathering and considering material information.

When faced with allegations of misconduct, a defendant director may raise the business judgment rule as an absolute defense. [U]nder Delaware law the business judgment rule applies even where conclusions were stupid or irrational, as long as the process employed was either rational or employed in a *good faith* effort to advance corporate interests.

Although the standard of review for business judgments is deferential, to receive the protection of the business judgment rule, a director must show an exercise of judgment, not simply the existence of a business decision. Directors' fiduciary duties require them to do more than passively rubber-stamp the decisions of the active managers. Thus, where the directors' methodologies and procedures are so restricted in scope, so shallow in execution, or otherwise so *pro forma* or halfhearted as to constitute a pretext or a sham, inquiry into their acts is not shielded by the business judgment rule. The Directors may not seek the protection of the business judgment rule on the ground that they made no decisions and took no actions.

It is undisputed that the Defendants did not hold board meetings on behalf of RSL Plc during the time period relevant to this action. Despite this, RSL Plc still operated and took actions such as drawing down $25 million from the Lauder loan, apparently at the direction of RSL Ltd. However, no independent board discussions regarding the propriety of this and other business decisions were held on behalf of RSL Plc by its board of directors.

Indeed, the law does not tolerate inaction of the sort Defendants are alleged to have engaged in, as Defendants allegedly failed to consider any information they had regarding the company's financial health and allegedly failed to make a business judgment as a board regarding any financial decision on behalf of RSL Plc.

Defendants point to cases which hold that small, closely held corporations with directors frequently in close contact with one another may dispense with formalities such as board meetings when making business decisions. However, RSL Plc is not a small corporation, as it accrued more than $1.4 billion in debt. Further, while it is clear that some of RSL Plc's board members had some contact during the period in question, [there were no] behind-the-scenes meetings where the business of RSL Plc was discussed by these members, let alone an agreement not to have a board meeting.

Defendants argue that they were fully informed regarding RSL Plc's financial matters because some Defendants were also board members of RSL Ltd., and that in that capacity, they exercised judgment on behalf of RSL Ltd, the parent of RSL Plc. This argument is unpersuasive. [I]ndividuals who act in a dual capacity as directors of two corporations, one of whom is parent and the other subsidiary, owe the same duty of good management to both corporations.

EXAM Strategy

Question: You are the CEO of a software company. You will only allow your engineers to create software for Apple computers, not for PCs, because you think Apple is cooler. Some of your shareholders disagree with this policy. Is your decision protected by the business judgment rule?

Strategy: Remember that you owe a duty of care to the corporation. This means that you must have a rational business purpose for your decision.

Result: The courts are very generous in defining a rational business purpose. They would probably uphold your decision as long as it was not in some way personally benefitting you, e.g., as long as you are not a major shareholder of Apple.

More Conflict: Takeovers

The business judgment rule is an important guideline for officers and directors in the routine management of corporations. The business judgment rule also plays a crucial role in corporate takeover battles. But the business judgment rule is not, by itself, sufficient for resolving all the issues that arise in these battles. Therefore, both Congress and many state legislatures have passed statutes that define the roles of the various combatants in hostile takeovers. Thus, the law of takeovers is rooted in both common and statutory law.

There are three ways to acquire control of a company:

- **Buy the company's assets.** Such a sale must be approved by both the shareholders and the board of directors of the acquired company.

- **Merge with the company.** In a merger, one company absorbs another. The acquired company ceases to exist. A merger must be approved by the shareholders and the board of directors of the target.
- **Buy stock from the shareholders.** This method is called a **tender offer** because the acquirer asks shareholders to "tender," or offer their stock for sale. As long as shareholders tender enough stock, the acquirer gains control. Typically, the bidder makes an offer (at a price above market value). This offer is usually contingent—that is, if a certain percentage of the shareholders do not tender, the offer terminates automatically. Although an acquisition can proceed without the approval of the board of the target company, resistance from the board can hinder the deal and even torpedo it. We will discuss shortly some of the weapons available to the target board. A tender offer is called a **hostile takeover** if the board of the target resists.

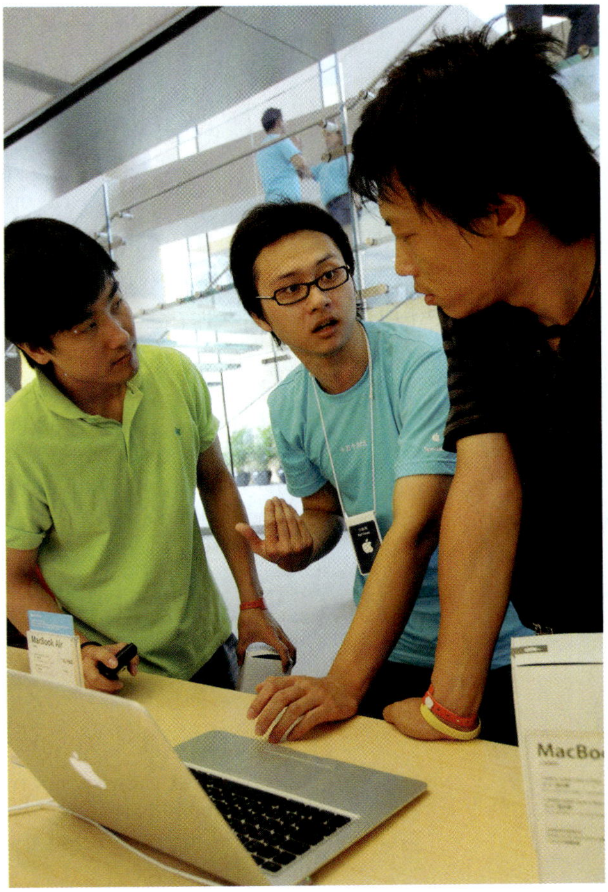

©Imaginechina/Corbis

Apple may be cooler but is that reason enough to refuse to write software for PCs?

Two scenarios are common in hostile takeovers:

- The target has assets that the bidder genuinely wants.
- A speculator plans to acquire control and then resell all or part of the company at a profit. Speculators, sometimes called **corporate raiders**, often say that they are acquiring stock in a company because it is undervalued; their ostensible goal is to improve management and raise stock prices. In practice, however, oftentimes another bidder comes along who buys their stock at a higher price; the raiders dismember the company and sell its parts; or the target company buys its own stock back at a higher-than-market price. (Management is willing to pay a premium price to keep the company intact and their jobs safe.)

In the beginning, state and federal governments barely regulated tender offers at all. Over time, targets began to ask Congress and their state legislatures to umpire these increasingly rancorous battles. Both states and the federal government have stepped into the ring as referees, generally more on the side of the target than of the bidder.[9]

Tender offer
A public offer to buy a block of stock directly from shareholders.

Hostile takeover
An outsider buys a company in the face of opposition from the target company's board of directors.

Federal Regulation of Tender Offers: The Williams Act

The Williams Act applies only if the target company's stock is publicly traded. **Under the Williams Act:**

- Any individual or group who together acquire more than 5 percent of a company's stock must file a public disclosure document (called a "Schedule 13D") with the Securities and Exchange Commission (SEC).

[9]R. Morck, A. Schleifer, and R.W. Vishny, "Management Ownership and Market Valuation: An Empirical Analysis," Working Paper No. 23, Institute for Financial Research, Faculty of Business, University of Alberta, quoted in P.-O. Bjuggren, "Ownership and Efficiency in Companies Listed on Stockholm Stock Exchange 1985," in M. Faure and R. Van den Bergh, *Essays in Law and Economics* (MAKLU, Antwerp, 1985).

- On the day a tender offer begins, a bidder must file a disclosure statement with the SEC;
- A bidder must keep a tender offer open for at least 20 business days initially, and for at least 10 business days after any substantial change in the terms of the offer;
- Any shareholder may withdraw acceptance of the tender offer at any time while the offer is still open;
- If the bidder raises the price offered, all selling shareholders must be paid the higher price, regardless of when they tendered; and
- If the stockholders tender more shares than the bidder wants to buy, it must purchase shares *pro rata* (in other words, it must buy the same proportion from everyone, *not* first come, first served).

Observe that the Williams Act regulates only the behavior of the *bidder*, not that of the *target company*. After Congress passed the Act, the number of tender offers declined and the average premium over market price increased. But target companies did not rely merely on the Williams Act to protect against the threat of takeovers. They were busy formulating other defenses.

State Regulation of Takeovers

A company's response to a takeover attempt is largely governed by state law, both common and statutory.

Common Law of Takeovers

To protect themselves from hostile takeovers, companies adopt defensive measures known as **antitakeover devices** or **shark repellents**. (The acquiring shareholder in a hostile takeover is sometimes referred to as a "shark.") Common shark repellents include the following:

- **Asset lockup.** The target sells off the assets that the shark most wants. Suppose that Ingrid is the CEO of Casablanca, Inc., a successful film production company that owns a vast and valuable library of old films. Turner has indicated that he may want to acquire Casablanca because he covets its library. Ingrid tries to pass the bait to someone else, either by selling the film library or by giving someone else the option to buy it.
- **Greenmail.** The target buys back the shark's stock at a premium price. Ingrid suspects that Turner is not really interested in owning Casablanca stock; he simply wants to turn a quick profit. Ingrid offers to buy back Turner's stock at a price 30 percent higher than he paid for it.
- **Shareholder rights plan ("poison pill").** When an outside shareholder acquires more than a certain percentage of company stock, a rights plan dilutes the value of these shares.[10] Now Ingrid becomes truly creative. She gets Casablanca to issue a special share of preferred stock to each current shareholder.[11] If a shark purchases more than

---

[10]In a recent case, a Delaware court explicitly permitted a poison pill that applied to outside shareholders but not the chairman of the company. *Yucaipa Am. Alliance Fund II, L.P. v. Riggio*, 1 A.3d 310; 2010 Del. Ch. LEXIS 172.

[11]Although in theory, the shareholders must approve the issuance of a new class of stock, some companies have so-called *blank check preferred stock* in their charters. When this stock is authorized, its rights and other characteristics are left blank, to be filled in by the board of directors upon issuance. It is like an unloaded gun that can be armed by the board whenever a shark threatens.

20 percent of Casablanca's stock and subsequently merges with Casablanca, this preferred stock can be converted into 10 shares of the acquiring company. Thus, for each share of Casablanca that Turner buys, he also has to give away 10 of his own shares, making the takeover much more expensive for him. No wonder these, and other similar tactics, are called "poison pills;" they could certainly prove fatal to a shark.

Target companies are often afraid of sharks.

- **Chewable poison pills.** These pills are exactly like a poison pill except that they expire automatically if a cash tender offer is made for 100 percent of the company's stock, at a price at least, say, 25 percent above market value. Chewable poison pills were adopted in response to complaints by institutional shareholders that regular pills are nothing more than protection for incompetent managers. A chewable pill would give Ingrid plenty of clout when negotiating with outsiders but limit her ability to turn down an offer that is clearly in the shareholders' best interest.
- **Dead-hand poison pills.** A dead-hand poison pill can be removed only by vote of the directors who installed the pill or by their handpicked successors. In this way, the decision is in the "dead hands" of the prior board. Without a dead-hand poison pill, Turner could dismantle Casablanca's shark repellents by electing some of his supporters to the board. Dead-hand poison pills are invalid in some states, but if Casablanca is incorporated in a state that does permit this defense, Turner's nominees to the board would not be able to remove the company's poison pill.
- **Staggered board of directors.** With a typical board of directors, all directors run for election each year, with the result that the entire board can be voted out at the same time. With a staggered board, only a portion of the directors are elected each year. Therefore, replacing the entire board takes some years to accomplish. Casablanca has a staggered board, in which each director serves a three-year term and only 4 of the 12 directors are elected each year. If Turner takes over the company, he will not gain control of the board for two years, and it will be three before he can replace all the directors.
- **Supermajority voting.** Ordinarily, shareholders can approve charter amendments by a majority vote, but some companies require a higher percentage to approve important changes. If Ingrid wants to make a takeover more difficult, she can ask shareholders to amend Casablanca's charter to require a *supermajority* vote of, say, 80 percent to approve a merger. Thus, Turner will not be able to merge his company with Casablanca unless he buys 80 percent of Casablanca.
- **White knight.** A white knight is another company that rescues the target from a hostile takeover. Because Turner has publicly criticized Ingrid's management of Casablanca, she despises him and would prefer to sell to *anyone* else. She locates another buyer who she hopes will retain her management team.

Management typically cannot use poison pills, staggered boards of directors, supermajority voting, and white knights without shareholder approval. (Although management could issue stock under a poison pill plan, the stock would first have to be authorized by the shareholders.) Shareholder approval is not required to implement the other shark repellents.

As a general rule, Delaware courts defer to boards of directors, allowing them great latitude in fighting off takeovers. (Not all states are as protective.) Like so much in corporate law, a balancing act is involved: the courts need to allow the board of a target company enough time to communicate with shareholders, search for alternatives, and force a higher price from the bidder, while at the same time allowing shareholders enough power to sell the company if they desire. Perhaps for this reason, legal rules on antitakeover devices are complex and sometimes seem to depend on the specific details of a particular case. But these are the general guidelines:

- **When establishing takeover defenses, shareholder welfare must be the board's primary concern.** The directors may institute shark repellents, but they must do so to ensure that bids are high, not to protect their own jobs. A poison pill is acceptable if it gives management enough bargaining power to negotiate a high price for shareholders, but not if it makes a takeover impossible.
- **If it is clear that the company will ultimately be sold, the board must auction the company to the highest bidder; it cannot give preferential treatment to a lower bidder.** The board cannot sell the company to a white knight at a lower price than someone else has offered, no matter how much management might personally dislike the shark.

In the following case, a bidder tried a new approach to winning a hostile takeover. Should the court permit this action? You be the judge.

You be the Judge

Airgas, Inc. v. Air Products and Chemicals, Inc.

8 A.3d 1182; 2010 Del. LEXIS 585
Supreme Court of Delaware, 2010

Facts: Air Products and Chemicals, Inc. (Air Products) launched a tender offer to acquire 100 percent of the shares of Airgas, Inc. (Airgas). The Airgas board of directors rejected these bids because they were lower than the market price. Airgas's charter provided for a staggered board of nine directors—at each annual meeting, three would run for election.

At Airgas's annual meeting in September, shareholders elected three of Air Products's nominees to the board. Air Products also proposed a bylaw (the January Bylaw) that switched Airgas's annual meeting to January rather than September. This change would mean that the next annual meeting would be in only four months. Air Products's plan was to vote out three more directors in January, which would have the effect of reducing their terms by eight months. Shareholders approved this amendment with a 51 percent vote in favor. Because not all shareholders voted, the favorable vote actually constituted only 45.8 percent of the outstanding shares. To amend the Airgas charter and eliminate the staggered board would have taken a 67 percent vote of the shareholders who cast ballots.

Airgas filed suit, alleging that the January Bylaw was invalid because it was a back-door method of eliminating the staggered board without a 67 percent vote of the shareholders. (A bylaw is invalid if it conflicts with the charter.) The lower court upheld the January Bylaw, and Airgas appealed.

You Be the Judge: ***Was the January Bylaw valid?***

Argument for Air Products: Airgas's charter provides that directors serve terms that expire at "the annual meeting of stockholders held in the third year following the year of their election." The January Bylaw complies with this charter provision as written because the January meeting will take place "in the third year after the directors' election." Nowhere does the charter say that directors have to serve three full years. If Airgas wins this case, corporations in Delaware will have to calculate the dates of their annual meetings with mathematical precision.

Moreover, 51 percent of the shares at the annual meeting voted in favor of the January Bylaw. If it was unfair or against the best interests of shareholders, they could have voted against it. Why should the court thwart the shareholders' intent?

Argument for Airgas: In 25 years, Airgas has never held its annual meeting earlier than July 28. We are not arguing that Airgas has to wait exactly 365 days to schedule its next annual meeting, but it should delay at least 11 months. Moreover, the company's fiscal year ends on March 31, so if the meeting were to be held in January, Airgas would not have new financial results to report to its shareholders.

The charter term is ambiguous—does it mean that directors have to serve into the start of the third year, or do they have to serve three full years? Regardless of what the actual language says, the *intent* is clear—directors are meant to serve three years. Air Products has found a loophole that violates the spirit of the charter provision and frustrates the purpose of staggered boards, which is to provide stability. The court should not allow Air Products to avoid the clear intent of the charter so that it can acquire a company at less than market value.

It is true that that 51 percent of the shares *at the meeting* voted in favor of the January Bylaw, but this was only 45.8 percent of the shares outstanding. That is not even a majority, never mind the 67 percent vote required to amend the charter. Moreover, if the January Bylaw is upheld, effectively three of the board members will be removed without cause. Under the charter, removal without cause also requires a 67 percent vote.

EXAM Strategy

Question: You are the CEO of Bubble Gum, Inc., a publicly traded company. Pink Co. has just made an offer to buy Bubble. Pink is particularly interested in Bubble's farmland, on which grows the corn for the sweetener used in the gum. You despise the CEO of Pink and know if Pink takes over the company, you will be fired. Your friend at ChewCo says his company would be interested in buying Bubble, but at a lower price than Pink is willing to pay. You are convinced that the company is better off long-term with ChewCo. What can you do immediately to protect Bubble from Pink?

Strategy: Shark repellents that require shareholder approval will not work because you do not have time to call a shareholders' meeting. Remember that your primary duty is to your shareholders.

Result: You cannot simply agree to a sale to ChewCo—once it is clear that the company will be sold, you must auction it to the highest bidder. You could try an asset lockup—selling off the company's farmland. Perhaps that would discourage Pink from making the purchase.

State Antitakeover Statutes

In fighting takeover battles, companies have also found support in state governments because legislators fear the impact on the local economy if a major employer leaves. When the Belzberg family threatened a hostile takeover of auto parts manufacturer Arvin Industries, the Indiana legislature quickly passed a tough antitakeover bill that had been drafted by Arvin's own lawyers. Shortly thereafter, Arvin and the Belzbergs settled. Arvin was not only the second-largest employer in Columbus, Indiana, it was an all-purpose fairy godmother. Among its charitable activities, it built two new schools, subsidized the salary of the school superintendent, and opened a summer camp. Columbus residents were delighted that Arvin survived the takeover attempt, but company shareholders might have preferred a bidding war for their stock. After all, shareholders do not necessarily care if the children of

Columbus spend their summers at leafy Camp Grenada or sleazy Mall City. Once again, the interests of these two corporate constituencies clash.

Most states have now passed laws to deter hostile takeovers. Among the common varieties are the following:

- **Statutes that automatically impede hostile takeovers.** These statutes, for instance, might ban hostile mergers for five years after the acquirer buys 10 percent of a company. Or investors who acquire as much as 20 percent of a company lose their voting rights unless the other shareholders move to reinstate the rights (not likely!). These provisions do not apply to bids that have been approved by the board of directors of the target company. In many states, such as Delaware, the board can opt out of the statute altogether and refuse to accept its protection.
- **Statutes that authorize companies to fight off hostile takeovers.** These statutes typically permit management, when responding to a hostile takeover, to consider the welfare of company stakeholders, such as the community, customers, suppliers, and employees. Some even go so far as to allow management to consider the regional or national economy. Since takeovers are almost always harmful to these other constituencies, company management has a ready excuse for fighting the takeover.

Most of these statutes do not totally eliminate hostile takeovers. A determined, well-financed bidder can still be successful. But these state statutes do tip the playing field in favor of management. Research indicates that takeover battles are much more profitable to the shareholders of targets than to bidders.

Ethics Supporters of these state statutes argue that large, publicly traded corporations owe a duty to all of their constituencies. The loss of a large corporate presence can be immensely disruptive to a community. Perhaps a state should have the right to prevent economic upheaval within its borders.

Opponents contend that shareholders own the company and their interests ought to be paramount. Antitakeover legislation entrenches management and prevents shareholders from obtaining the premium that accompanies a takeover. Opponents also argue that, if other *stake*holders are so concerned with the well-being of the company, let them put their money where their mouths are and buy stock. And if current managers cannot offer shareholders as high a stock price as an outside raider, they ought to be replaced.

Delaware companies can choose not to accept the protection of the antitakeover statute. What is the ethical choice for directors?

Chapter Conclusion

Managers of corporations have a fiduciary duty to shareholders and are charged with running the organization for their benefit. The law, whether federal or state, common or statutory, grants managers great freedom in deciding how to promote the shareholders' interest. In the takeover arena, lawmakers have given managers considerable leeway in defending their organizations from outside attack.

Exam Review

1. **FIDUCIARY DUTY** Officers and directors have a fiduciary duty to act in the best interests of the shareholders of the corporation. (p. 841)

2. **BUSINESS JUDGMENT RULE** If managers comply with the business judgment rule, a court will not hold them personally liable for any harm their decisions cause the company, nor will the court rescind the decision. (pp. 843–850)

Question: Employees of Exxon Corp. paid some $59 million in corporate funds as bribes to Italian political parties to secure special favors and other illegal commitments. The board of directors decided not to sue the employees who had committed the illegal acts. Were these decisions protected by the business judgment rule?

Strategy: Two decisions are at issue here: illegal payments and the decision not to sue. (See the "Result" at the end of this section.)

3. **DUTY OF LOYALTY** Managers may not enter into an agreement on behalf of their corporation that benefits them personally unless the disinterested directors or shareholders have first approved it. If the manager does not seek the necessary approval, the business judgment rule no longer applies, and the manager will be liable unless the transaction was entirely fair to the corporation. (pp. 843–847)

4. **CORPORATE OPPORTUNITY** Under the duty of loyalty, managers may not take advantage of an opportunity that rightfully belongs to the corporation. (pp. 845–846)

Question: Vern owned 32 percent of Coast Oyster Co. and served as president and director. Coast was struggling to pay its debts, so Vern suggested that the company sell some of its oyster beds to Keypoint Co. After the sale, officers at Coast discovered that Vern owned 50 percent of Keypoint. They demanded that he give the Keypoint stock to Coast. Did Vern violate his duty to Coast?

Strategy: Here, Vern has violated the duty of loyalty not once, but twice. (See the "Result" at the end of this section.)

5. **DUTY OF CARE** Under the duty of care, managers must make legal, informed decisions that have a rational business purpose. (pp. 847–850)

6. **WILLIAMS ACT** The Williams Act regulates the activities of a bidder in a tender offer for stock in a publicly traded corporation. (pp. 851–852)

7. **TAKEOVER DEFENSES** Under common law, shareholder welfare must be the board's primary concern when establishing takeover defenses. If it is clear that the company will ultimately be sold, the board must auction the company to the highest bidder; it cannot give preferential treatment to a lower bidder. (pp. 852–855)

EXAM Strategy

Question: The board of Harmony, Inc., is concerned that the company may be the target of a hostile takeover. It has decided to adopt antitakeover devices. Which one of the following statements is *false*?

a. Harmony may divest one of its divisions, as long as it does so at fair market value.

b. Harmony may adopt a poison pill, as long as the purpose is to give management enough bargaining power to negotiate a high price for shareholders.

c. If it becomes clear that Harmony is going to be sold, the directors have an obligation to auction the company off to the highest bidder, no matter how loathsome the directors find the bidder to be.

d. If Harmony offers to buy back any of its stock, it must treat its shareholders equally.

Strategy: Apply the principle established in the *Unocal* case earlier in the chapter. (See the "Result" at the end of this section.)

8. **STATE STATUTES** Many states have passed antitakeover statutes that render hostile takeovers more difficult for the bidder. (pp. 855–856)

2. Result: The business judgment rule would not protect the underlying illegal payments, but it did protect the decision not to sue. In other words, anyone who *made* an illegal payment had violated the business judgment rule, but the people who had decided not to pursue the violators had not themselves breached the business judgment rule because they had not violated the duty of care or the duty of loyalty.

4. Result: If the shareholders and directors did not know of Vern's interest in Keypoint, they could not evaluate the contract properly. Vern should have told them. Also, by purchasing stock in Keypoint, Vern took a corporate opportunity. He had to turn over any profits he had earned on the transaction, as well as his stock in Keypoint.

7. Result: In the *Unocal* case, the court permitted the company to exclude one shareholder from its buyback offer. D is the correct answer.

MULTIPLE-CHOICE QUESTIONS

1. If a manager engages in self-dealing, which of the following answers will *NOT* protect him from a finding that he violated the business judgment rule:

(a) The disinterested members of the board approved the transaction.
(b) The transaction was of minor importance to the company.
(c) The disinterested shareholders approved the transaction.
(d) The transaction was entirely fair to the corporation.

2. In the *Lippman* case involving a payout to the son and son-in-law:

(a) The son-in-law was entitled to the payment because he represented the daughter's interest in the company.

(b) The son-in-law was entitled to the payment because he had the same employment contract as the son.

(c) The son-in-law was entitled to the payment because the business judgment rule protects decisions by corporate directors.

(d) The son-in-law was not entitled to the payment.

3. The duty of care:

(a) Is not a requirement of the business judgment rule

(b) Protects directors who make an uninformed decision if it was entirely fair to the company

(c) Protects a decision that has a rational business purpose, even if the activity was illegal

(d) Will not protect directors who make a decision that harms the company

4. Under the Williams Act:

(a) If shareholders offer more stock than the bidder wants, it must purchase shares *pro rata*.

(b) Target companies must reveal the names of any shareholders who acquire more than 5 percent of its stock.

(c) A bidder must file a disclosure statement at least 24 hours before the tender offer begins.

(d) Once a shareholder has accepted a tender offer, she cannot withdraw it.

5. Takeovers are *NOT* regulated by:

(a) Federal statute

(b) Federal common law

(c) State statutes

(d) State common law

Essay Questions

1. YOU BE THE JUDGE WRITING PROBLEM Asher and Stephen formed a corporation named "Ampersand" to produce plays. Both men were employed by the corporation. Stephen decided to write *Philly's Beat,* focusing on the history of rock and roll in Philadelphia. As the play went into production, however, the two men quarreled over Asher's repeated absences from work and the company's serious financial difficulties. Stephen resigned from Ampersand and formed another corporation to produce the play. Did the opportunity to produce *Philly's Beat* belong to Ampersand? **Argument for Stephen:** Ampersand was formed for the purpose of producing plays, not writing them. When Stephen wrote *Philly's Beat,* he was not competing against Ampersand. Furthermore, Ampersand could not afford to produce the play even if it had had the opportunity. **Argument for**

Asher: Ampersand was in the business of producing plays, and it wanted *Philly's Beat*. Ampersand was perfectly able to afford the cost of production—until Stephen resigned.

2. Both Viacom and Paramount owned a diverse group of entertainment businesses. QVC was a televised shopping channel. The Paramount board of directors accepted a merger offer from Viacom at a price of $69 per share. QVC and Viacom then entered a bidding war for Paramount. QVC ultimately made the highest offer, at $90 per share. The Paramount board rejected QVC's bid on the grounds that a Viacom merger would be more in keeping with Paramount's business strategy. Does a board of directors have the right to reject a high bidder on the belief that the low bidder would be better for the company?

3. Eve bought defective ball bearings from Saginaw Corp. Alfred was the sole shareholder of the company and also its landlord. After Alfred sold all of Saginaw's assets, he withheld enough money to cover the rent that Saginaw owed him. As a result, Saginaw had no money to pay Eve. Does Eve have a claim against Alfred?

4. Ulrick and Birger started an air taxi service in Berlin, Germany, under the name Berlinair, Inc. Birger was approached by a group of travel agents who were interested in hiring an air charter business to take German tourists on vacation. Birger formed Air Berlin Charter Co. (ABC) and was its sole owner. On behalf of ABC, he entered into a contract with the Berlin travel agents. Birger concealed his negotiations from Ulrick, even though he used Berlinair working time, staff, money, and facilities. Birger defended his behavior on the grounds that Berlinair could not afford to enter into a contract with the travel agents. Has Birger violated the corporate opportunity doctrine?

5. Wallace, Inc. adopted a poison pill. Five years later, Moore Corp. offered to buy all Wallace's stock for $56 a share, which was 27 percent over the existing market price. However, the offer was contingent upon the Wallace board eliminating the poison pill. Wallace consulted with its investment banker, which advised the company that the offer was inadequate but did not indicate what the shares were really worth. Moore then raised its offer price to $60 per share, and again the bankers opined that the offer was inadequate. Both the board and its banker believed that Wallace's recently adopted corporate strategy would lead to an increased stock price. Indeed, the company's recent financial results had been better than expected. Despite these improved results, more than 73 percent of Wallace shareholders offered their shares to Moore. When Wallace refused to remove the poison pill, Moore filed suit. Was the board's refusal to remove the poison pill a violation of the business judgment rule?

Discussion Questions

1. Some companies adopt a staggered board of directors as an antitakeover defense. How does a staggered board affect cumulative voting?

2. Congressional Airlines was highly profitable operating flights between Washington, D.C., and New York City. The directors approved a plan to offer flights from Washington to Boston. This decision turned out to be a major mistake, and the

airline ultimately went bankrupt. Under what circumstances would shareholders be successful in bringing suit against the directors?

3. **ETHICS** Ronald O. Perelman, chairman of the board and CEO of Pantry Pride, met with his counterpart at Revlon, Michel C. Bergerac, to discuss a friendly acquisition of Revlon by Pantry Pride. Revlon rebuffed Pantry Pride's overtures, perhaps in part because Bergerac did not like Perelman. The Revlon board of directors agreed to sell the company to Forstmann Little & Co. at a price of $56 per share. Pantry Pride announced that it would engage in fractional bidding to top any Forstmann offer by a slightly higher one. To discourage Pantry Pride, the Revlon board granted Forstmann the right to purchase Revlon's Vision Care and National Health Laboratories divisions at a price some $100–$175 million below their value. Was the board within its rights in selling off these two divisions? Do the shareholders of Revlon have the right to prevent a sale of the company to Forstmann at a price lower than Pantry Pride offered? Is it ethical for a board to base a takeover decision on personal animosity? What are a board's ethical obligations to shareholders?

4. An appraiser valued a subsidiary of Signal Co. at between $230 million and $260 million. Six months later, Burmah Oil offered to buy the subsidiary at $480 million, giving Signal only three days to respond. The board of directors accepted the offer without obtaining an updated valuation of the subsidiary or determining if other companies would offer a higher price. Members of the board were sophisticated, with a great deal of experience in the oil industry. A Signal Co. shareholder sued to prevent the sale. Is the Signal board protected by the business judgment rule?

5. Courts have tended to be protective of managers who fight against hostile takeovers, even if the bidder is offering a price much higher than the market value of the shares. Why? Do the courts have the balance right when resolving disputes between these two groups?

CHAPTER 35

SHAREHOLDERS

© Evan Meyer/Shutterstock.com

In little more than a decade, Enron Corp. transformed itself from a modest pipeline company into a $65 billion global energy business. Enron's officers earned fabulous wealth and became major celebrities. But no sooner had the ink dried on newspaper and magazine articles lauding the Enron business model when suddenly, shockingly, the company collapsed into bankruptcy court. What happened to Enron?

Enron had become, in essence, an energy trading enterprise that required a lot of cash. To obtain the cash, it created subsidiaries that held substantial sums in safe investments. Enron borrowed money that was secured by these subsidiaries, but—and here is the catch—it excluded this debt from its financial statements. The income from energy sales appeared as revenue for Enron, but the debt to support this income was off the books. None of these "special" arrangements was disclosed clearly to shareholders.

Moreover, compensation for top executives was tied directly to the company's stock price. So managers had a powerful incentive to raise the stock price in any way possible, legal or not. Stock manipulation and questionable accounting practices became standard operating procedure at the firm. The company would, for example, book as current revenues its (optimistic) assessment of what future revenues might be for new deals.

Managers had a powerful incentive to raise the stock price in any way possible, legal or not.

After a few stock analysts began to ask tough questions, Enron restated its earnings by nearly $600 million, which caused investors to lose confidence. Enron stock entered a death spiral into bankruptcy, destroying the net worth (and the dreams) of many employees and shareholders. It turned out, however, that not all employees suffered dramatic financial losses—the top executives had sold hundreds of millions of dollars in stock before the collapse, even as they were exhorting other employees and shareholders to continue buying.

Outrage and uproar ensued. Inquiring minds wanted to know: Why did the law fail to protect Enron shareholders? Why did the impressive board of directors miss—or ignore—obvious signs of trouble? At the same time, other prominent companies confessed to shady accounting practices: Xerox Corp., Merrill Lynch, and Lucent, among others. The CEO of investment bank Goldman Sachs said, "I cannot think of a time when business overall has been held in less repute."

What is the solution to this raft of corporate wrongdoing? Some commentators claim that there are simply a few bad apples in the executive orchard. More pessimistic commentators argue that wholesale changes are needed in the regulation of public companies. After reading this chapter, you decide.

INTRODUCTION

Shareholders technically own the companies in which they invest, but their power over these enterprises is very limited. As Chapter 34 revealed, **directors, not shareholders, have the right to manage the corporate business**. In this chapter, we look at shareholder rights—what control do they exercise over the enterprises they own?

The topic of shareholder rights is a contentious, controversial topic. In this century, we have already experienced two financial meltdowns—one at the beginning of the 2000s and one at the end—that starkly revealed the different incentives faced by shareholders and managers. Too often, managers earned exorbitant compensation from highly risky, short-term decisions that in the longer run left shareholders holding an empty bag. If CEOs made a risky decision that paid off, they profited enormously. If the decision failed, they might be fired, but even then they were likely to have received generous compensation all along. On the way out the door, many also got severance payments that left them wealthy beyond most people's dreams. For example, in the two years before investment banks Bear Stearns Companies, Inc. and Lehman Brothers Holdings, Inc. failed, their top five executives took home \$1.4 billion and \$1 billion respectively, even as their shareholders were left with nothing.

Even worse, investigations after the fact revealed that too many managers had gamed compensation plans, stacked the boards of their companies with their friends, and ignored shareholder interests. Compliant boards had been little more than rubber stamps, approving whatever the officers wanted. In anger and frustration, shareholders, Congress, the Securities and Exchange Commission (SEC), and stock exchanges undertook an unprecedented effort to rebalance corporate power. Yet these changes are little more than a shot in the dark, without compelling evidence that they will enhance financial stability or improve shareholder results.

A note before we begin: at one time, corporate stock was primarily owned by individuals. But now, institutional investors—pension plans, mutual funds, insurance companies, banks, foundations, and university endowments—own more than 50 percent of all shares publicly traded in the United States.[1] Institutional investors, with enormous sums to invest,

[1]Shareholders play a very different role in privately held companies than in publicly traded corporations. Not only do privately held corporations have fewer shareholders, but these owners take a more active role in management, often serving as a director, officer, or employee. A public corporation is one that (1) has completed a public offering under the Securities Act of 1933, or (2) has securities traded on a national exchange, or (3) has at least 500 shareholders and total assets that exceed \$10 million. For a discussion of public corporations, see Chapter 36, on securities law.

have little choice but to buy the stocks of large companies. If they are unhappy with management, it is difficult for them to do the "Wall Street walk"—that is, sell their shares—because a sale of their large stock holdings would depress the market price. And where would they invest the proceeds? Institutional investors cannot all profit simply by trading shares among themselves. For better or worse, the fate of fund managers hangs on the success of these large companies.

Rights of Shareholders

If you own a car, you expect to be able to drive it whenever you want. If you own it with four of your friends, you may not be able to use it every Saturday night, but you will get to drive it *sometimes*, even if only on Sunday mornings. Of course, you will also be responsible for changing the oil sometimes, too. Owning stock in a corporation is different. As an owner, you have no right to use any *specific* asset of the corporation. If you own stock in Starbucks Corp., your share of stock plus $6.25 entitles you to a triple grande soy vanilla latte, the same as everyone else. By the same token, if the pipes freeze and the local Starbucks store floods, the manager has no right to call you, as a shareholder, to help clean up the mess. **As a shareholder, you have neither the *right* nor the *obligation* to manage the day-to-day business of the enterprise.** So what rights do you have?

Right to Information

A company's obligation to provide shareholders with information depends on whether it is publicly or privately held. Privately held companies are regulated by state law, while publicly traded enterprises must also meet SEC standards. More than half the states have adopted as state law some version of the Model Business Corporation Act (Model Act), which requires only limited disclosure.[2] In contrast, the SEC requires companies to provide shareholders with extensive information.

Even if a corporation is not required to volunteer information, shareholders have the right to obtain certain data upon request. **Under the Model Act, shareholders acting in good faith and with a proper purpose have the right to inspect and copy the corporation's minute book, accounting records, and shareholder lists.** A **proper purpose** is one that aids the shareholder in managing and protecting her investment. If Celeste receives an offer to sell her shares in a bakery called Devil Desserts, Inc., she may want to look carefully at the company's accounting records to determine the value of her stock. Or, if she is convinced the directors are mismanaging the company, she might demand a list of shareholders so that she can ask them to join her in a lawsuit. This purpose is proper—though the company may not like it—and the company is required to give her the list. If, however, Celeste wants to use the shareholder list as a potential source for her new business selling exercise equipment, the company could legitimately turn her down. The following case is typical: the court must decide if the shareholder is acting in his role as owner or competitor.

[2]A committee of the American Bar Association drafted the Model Business Corporation Act to serve as a guideline for states to use when enacting a corporate code. The corporate statutes of Delaware also serve as a model for some states.

You be the Judge

Chopra v. Helio Solutions, Inc.

2007 Cal. App. Unpub. LEXIS 5909
Court of Appeal of California, 2007

Facts: Paul Chopra was a minority shareholder and former director of Helio Solutions, Inc. Both he and Helio were in the business of reselling Sun Microsystems hardware and software. Chopra suspected that (1) some of Helio's majority shareholders had purchased a building and leased it to Helio at an excessive rent; (2) the company had broken a lease so that it could rent this building; (3) some shareholders had used assets of the corporation to secure a personal loan; (4) Helio had permitted ex-employees to take away substantial business; and (5) the company had not collected a $1 million debt it was owed. In addition, he wanted to know if Helio was planning to issue stock and thereby dilute his ownership. Finally, he felt that his dividend of $1,952.55 was unreasonably low, given that Helio had $88 million in revenue.

Chopra hired a forensic accountant to help him investigate Helio's finances. At the accountant's request, Chopra asked Helio for these documents:

1. Articles of incorporation;
2. Minutes for meetings of the board of directors and shareholders;
3. All financial statements;
4. All tax returns;
5. The general ledger with accompanying journals;
6. Income and balance sheets;
7. Schedule of accounts payable and received and inventory;
8. Depreciation schedule for fixed assets;
9. Supporting documents, including bank loans, lines of credit, accrued payroll liabilities, sales tax liabilities, other receivables, loans to officers and owners, significant prepayments or deposits, and equipment lease agreements;
10. Monthly bank statements;
11. Company credit card statements;
12. Compensation records;
13. The following contracts: life insurance policies for officers and/or stockholders, pension plan and profit sharing plans, stock purchase plans, equipment and building leases, employment and bonus agreements for owners or key employees, covenants not to compete, loan agreements and credit information, documents connected with the company's real property, option grants, and each owner's curriculum vitae;
14. A list of patents held by the company;
15. Budget projections for the current year;
16. Company brochures and/or marketing information;
17. A list of key management personnel with job titles;
18. An overview of company positions and objectives for each department manager; and
19. Information regarding contingencies and lawsuits.

Helio Solutions gave Chopra items 1–6 but refused to turn over the other material. He filed suit.

You Be the Judge: ***Which of these documents must a company provide to its shareholders?***

Argument for Chopra: All these documents are necessary for assessing the value of Chopra's investment in the company and determining whether his interests as a minority shareholder are being protected. For example, without employee agreements and compensation information, he cannot assess the current corporate financial situation, value the business, determine if the business is being properly managed, or discover whether the majority shareholders or directors are improperly diverting corporate funds for their own benefit. He needs the contracts and agreements related to equipment and building leases to determine whether the majority shareholders had purchased a building and leased it to Helio at an excessive rate.

Argument for Helio: Chopra is simply on a fishing expedition to find information that would help him compete against Helio. It seems as if he wants to use Helio's budget projections and managerial objectives so that he can beat them to the punch on some of their new initiatives. Many of the requests relate to specific shareholders rather than to the company. Complying with these requests would be unreasonably burdensome to Helio. It would take weeks of work to pull these documents together and photocopy them. Shareholders have some rights to corporate information, but they are not entitled to unlimited access to corporate confidences and secrets.

Right to Vote

A corporation must have at least one class of stock with voting rights. Typically, common shareholders have the right to vote and preferred shareholders do not, but there are many exceptions to this rule.

Shareholder Meetings

Annual shareholder meetings are the norm for publicly traded companies. Although technically not all states require public companies to hold an annual meeting of shareholders, the New York Stock Exchange (NYSE) requires companies listed with it to do so. Companies whose stock is not publicly traded can either hold an annual meeting or use written consents from their shareholders. (Written consents are discussed in Chapter 33.) Under the Model Act, the board of directors and shareholders owning at least 10 percent of the company's stock each have the right to call a *special* meeting to vote on an emergency issue that cannot wait until the next annual meeting—for example, to conclude a merger or sell off substantial assets.

Everyone who owns stock on the **record date** must be sent notice of a meeting, whether it is an annual or a special meeting. The record date can be any day that is no more than 70 days before the meeting. The votes taken at a shareholder meeting are not valid unless a **quorum** is present, meaning that shareholders owning a certain percentage of the shares are represented, either in person or by proxy.

Quorum
The percentage of voters who must be present for a meeting to count.

Companies are permitted to hold shareholder meetings online rather than in person. Many companies do both, conducting a live meeting with virtual access. In 2010, Symantec Corporation became the first Fortune 500 company to eliminate the in-person meeting and hold a virtual-only version. Unfortunately, the company used this opportunity to limit rather than expand access. It broadcast only in audio, not video, which meant that participants had no opportunity to read body language or even know that three directors were absent. In the question-and-answer period, management read and answered only two questions from shareholders, without providing an opportunity for follow-up questions. Nor did they reveal who had asked the questions or even what questions they had chosen not to answer.

Proxy
The person whom a shareholder appoints to vote for her at a meeting of the corporation. Also, the document a shareholder signs appointing this substitute voter.

Ethics Symantec's actions in holding a virtual shareholder meeting were legal. If you had been a shareholder and had attended the meeting in cyberspace, would you have been satisfied with the company's virtual format?

© REUTERS/Tim Shaffer

A traditional shareholder meeting looks like this. Is a virtual meeting a reasonable substitute?

Proxies

Under common law, shareholders could cast a vote only by attending the shareholders' meeting. Such a rule in a publicly traded corporation would effectively disfranchise many shareholders who have neither the time nor the interest to travel around the country attending meetings. Modern statutory law permits shareholders to appoint someone else to vote for them. Confusingly, both this person and the card the shareholder signs to appoint the substitute voter are called a **proxy**.

Under the Model Act, a proxy is valid for only 11 months unless the form provides for a longer period. For public corporations, however, SEC rules specify that a proxy is valid only for the next meeting. After that, it automatically expires. Under both state and federal law, the shareholder can generally revoke a proxy at any time.

Under SEC rules, companies are not required to solicit proxies, but virtually all of them do because that is the only practical way to obtain a quorum. Along with the proxy, the company must also give shareholders a **proxy statement** and an **annual report**. The proxy statement provides information on everything from management compensation to a list of directors who miss too many meetings. The annual report contains detailed financial data. Under SEC rules, companies are required to post all of this information on their website. They must then mail to shareholders either hard copies of all the information, including ballots, or a card telling shareholders how to view the materials and vote online. But shareholders always have the right to request hard-copy versions.

Annual report
A document that the SEC requires public companies to provide to their shareholders each year.

Even if a company decides not to solicit proxies for a shareholder meeting, it cannot avoid its obligation to communicate with its shareholders. The SEC requires public companies, whether or not they solicit proxies, to give shareholders all the information required in a proxy statement and an annual report.

Shareholder Proposals

Shareholders who oppose a company policy may use the proxy process to challenge that policy. **Under SEC rules, any shareholder who has continuously owned for one year at least 1 percent of the company or $2,000 of stock can require that one proposal be placed in the company's proxy statement to be voted on at the shareholder meeting.**

If a company refuses to include a shareholder proposal in its proxy material, shareholders can appeal to the SEC. These are the major SEC regulations on shareholder resolutions:[3]

- *The proposal cannot relate to the ordinary business operations of the corporation.* For example, the SEC used to routinely exclude all proposals that asked a board of directors to develop a succession plan for the CEO, on the theory that this request related to the management of the workforce, which is part of the ordinary business operations of a company. But the SEC recently overruled itself and decided that succession planning is an important board function that raises significant policy issues. Now these proposals are permitted in proxy statements.

- *The proposal must relate to operations accounting for at least 5 percent of total assets, gross sales, or net earnings.* AT&T refused to include in its proxy statement an anti-Israel proposal from a white supremacy group on the grounds that the company's business with Israel accounted for less than 1 percent of sales.

- *The proposal cannot interfere with the company's proxy solicitation.* Management can exclude more than one proposal on the same topic and proposals that were voted down decisively in the past.

- *The proposal cannot require the company to violate a federal or state law.* Bell & Howell excluded a shareholder proposal that called for the company to hire qualified women because the proposal might require the company to violate federal and state antidiscrimination laws.

- *The shareholder cannot use a proposal to seek satisfaction of a personal grievance against the company.* Lee Data Corp. excluded a proposal requested by an employee/shareholder who had been fired for sexual harassment. The goal of his proposal was to embarrass the company and provide fodder for his lawsuit.

Traditionally, many shareholder proposals had a social policy agenda: cut greenhouse gases, withdraw from Myanmar, or ban genetically modified ingredients, for example. Now, many relate to corporate-governance issues: permit secret ballots, adopt cumulative voting,

[3]Rule 14a-8.

or repeal takeover defenses. Prior to 1985, only *two* proposals had been approved—*ever*. In recent years, shareholders of the 100 largest American companies have approved 20 percent of the corporate governance resolutions, but none of the social policy proposals.

Note, however, that even if a proposal meets SEC standards *and* is approved by a majority of shareholders, the company may not necessarily implement it. Resolutions are binding on a company only if they are within the narrow realm of shareholder power. For example, because shareholders have the right to amend company bylaws, such proposals are binding. But a shareholder vote that requires the board to take action is not binding because the board that has the right to manage the company, not the shareholders. Thus, even though the SEC requires companies to allow a vote on proposals about succession planning, the board still does not *have* to develop a succession plan, even if a majority of shareholders vote in favor. Most proposals are *non-binding*, and companies implement fewer than half of those that their shareholders approve.

Frustrated at this unresponsive behavior by boards, shareholders have begun to withhold their vote from any director who fails to support a successful shareholder proposal. Even this threat has not yet had a significant impact on board response to shareholder proposals.

Ironically, companies sometimes implement shareholder proposals that have not received support from a majority of the shareholders. The pressure of shareholder proposals is credited with inducing many American companies to withdraw from South Africa when its government had apartheid laws. Other companies implement shareholder proposals without even putting them up for a vote. Indeed, a substantial number of shareholder proposals are now withdrawn before a vote because the company is willing to negotiate and accommodate. For instance, Colgate-Palmolive Co. agreed to a proposal by institutional investors to permit secret ballots at shareholder meetings.

EXAM Strategy

Question: Shareholders of Beazer Homes USA asked for a proposal requiring disclosure about the construction company's risks in the mortgage market. This was a time when many companies were struggling with bad loans to home buyers. Beazer asked the SEC for permission to exclude this proposal from its proxy statement. What did the SEC rule?

Strategy: The SEC allows companies to exclude proposals that relate to the ordinary business operations of the company.

Result: The SEC ruled that Beazer Homes was required to include the mortgage proposal because these risks directly affected the value of the company in a time of extraordinary challenges in this industry. Shortly thereafter, Beazer announced that it would stop originating mortgages.

Election and Removal of Directors

The process of electing directors to the board of a publicly traded company is different from what most people think. At this writing, shareholders do *not* have the right to use the company's proxy statement to propose nominees for director. Instead, the nominating committee of the board of directors produces a slate of directors, with one name per opening. Typically, the names are approved by the CEO. This slate is then placed in the proxy statement and sent to shareholders, whose only choice is to vote in favor of a nominee or to withhold their vote (i.e., not vote at all). If shareholders want to vote for someone who was not selected by the company, they have to nominate their own slate, prepare and distribute a proxy statement to other shareholders, and then communicate why their slate is superior, all the while fighting against the company's almost unlimited financial resources. This process is complex, expensive, and disruptive to the company. Not surprisingly, only a few shareholder groups undertake this effort each year. Recent research does indicate, however, that companies with a director elected through proxy contests outperform their peers in both the short and long run.[4]

This traditional corporate voting method is called **plurality voting**. A successful candidate does not need to receive a majority vote; he must simply receive more than any competitor. Since there are no competitors, one vote is sufficient (and that vote could be his own). Even if a large number of shareholders withhold their votes, the nominee may be embarrassed, but as long as he receives that one vote, he is elected. Thus, for example, in the waning years of Michael Eisner's rule at Disney Enterprises Inc., shareholders withheld 43 percent of their votes from him. But that vote of no confidence did not cause the board to fire him, nor did he immediately resign.

Plurality voting
To be elected, a candidate only needs to receive more votes than her opponent, not a majority of the votes cast.

Congress, other regulators, and major shareholders are now reforming corporate democracy in an effort to rebalance the relationship between managers and shareholders.

Independent Directors. Congress began its reform effort by passing the Sarbanes-Oxley Act (SOX), which applies to all publicly traded corporations in the United States, as well as to all foreign companies listed on a U.S. stock exchange. Among other provisions, SOX stipulates that **all members of a board's audit committee must be independent, and at least one of these members must be a financial expert. Independent directors** are those who are not employees of the company and, therefore, presumably not in the pocket of the CEO.

Independent directors
Members of the board of directors who are not employees of the company. Also known as outside directors.

Likewise, the NYSE and NASDAQ require that, for companies listed on these exchanges:

- Independent directors must comprise a majority of the board;
- They must meet regularly on their own without **inside directors**, that is, members of the board who are also employees of the corporation;
- Only independent directors can serve on audit, compensation, or nominating committees; and
- Audit committees must have at least three directors who are financially literate.

Inside directors
Members of the board of directors who are also employees of the corporation.

The effectiveness of these reforms, however, is uncertain. One study found that 45 percent of directors who are technically "independent" have friendship ties to the CEO. And, as the second eBay case in this chapter illustrates, even independent directors are often financially beholden to the CEO. At a minimum, the CEO is more likely to fire them from their lucrative directorships than shareholders are, so their incentives are often more aligned with the CEO. Also, some commentators argue that because independent directors do not work full time for the company, they know *less* about what is really going on and have to rely *more* on company executives.

What happens to independent directors who fail to carry out their watchdog responsibilities? Unless they personally commit fraud, the answer is: not much. After all, if the SEC were aggressive about going after independent directors, few people would be willing to serve in that role. Even if they are sued, the corporation or its insurance company usually pays the damages. For the first time, however, the SEC has brought suit against three independent directors. As friends and neighbors of the CEO at DHB Industries, Inc. they actively assisted him in a cover-up of wrong-doing.

[4]The Investor Responsibility Research Center Institute. See *http://www.irrcinstitute.org/pdf/PR_5_25_09.pdf*.

Shareholder Activists. Proxy advisors, such as Institutional Shareholder Services, Inc. (ISS), are a new development in corporate democracy. They advise institutional investors on how to vote their shares. Proxy advisors and hedge funds (which often own substantial stockholdings) wield significant power. ISS alone can affect up to 20 to 40 percent of the vote at a company. Corporate managers argue that this is too much power—that activists may well have an agenda that is contrary to that of other shareholders, and that they support corporate governance initiatives without proof of effectiveness. In any event, boards have become more responsive to the demands of shareholder activists and, as a result, are more likely to replace executives who perform badly, either in their corporate or personal lives. For example, the board of Hewlett-Packard fired CEO Mark Hurd for a combination of reasons that included his fudging of expense reports to hide his relationship with someone who accused him of sexual harassment, and, perhaps worst of all, bad press.

Majority voting systems. Because of pressure from shareholder activists, two-thirds of the S&P 500 (large companies) now refuse to seat a director if fewer than half of the shares that vote tick off her name on the ballot. However, among smaller companies—those in the Russell 3000 Index—three-quarters still permit plurality voting, where one vote is often sufficient to insure election.[5]

Proxy access. By a 3-2 vote of the commissioners, the SEC approved proxy access rules that required companies to include in their proxy material the names of board nominees selected by large shareholders (that is, those who had owned 3 percent of the company for three years). But when business groups sued the SEC to prevent implementation, a federal appeals court invalidated the proxy access rule on the grounds that the SEC had not followed required procedures in adopting it. The SEC elected not to appeal this decision.[6] However, proxy access survives in a weakened form because the SEC amended Rule 14a-8 so that shareholders can now make proposals which would change company bylaws to permit proxy access. This two-step process is more complicated, and less likely to succeed, than the one-step version the SEC originally proposed. Also, such proposals are binding on the company only if state law permits. Such a proposal could be binding in Delaware.

The effectiveness of this rule change is uncertain. At this stage, it has not changed the reality that for most companies, shareholders have little say on board nominations.

Compensation for Officers and Directors—The Problem

Given the control that the CEO has over the selection process for the board of directors, it is not surprising that when the board sets the CEO's compensation, the results can sometimes appear to unfairly favor the CEO over the shareholders whose money is being used to pay him. After all, the CEO can easily replace stingy directors. Between 2001 and 2003, public companies spent 9.8 percent of their net income on compensation for top executives. In 1975, the top 100 CEOs earned 39 times as much as the average worker. By 2005, that ratio was over 400. See Exhibit 35.1 for an illustration of this trend.

The ratio in Japan is 11 to 1; in Britain, it is 22 to 1. Or, to look at it another way, the average salary of the CEO of a Fortune 500 company in 1960 was twice that of the president of the United States. In 2006, the ratio was 30 to 1.

Here are some examples of executive compensation that particularly agitated shareholders:

- Michael Eisner was the head of Walt Disney Corporation for 20 years. At the beginning of his tenure, the company did very well, and few complained when he was exceedingly well paid. But for the final *13* years, he earned $800 million

---

[5]The S&P 500 is composed of 500 leading companies in the most important U.S. industries, while the Russell 3000 is made up of the largest 3000 companies in the United States, representing 98 percent of the investable U.S. equity market.

[6]*Business Roundtable v. SEC*, 2011 U.S. App. LEXIS 14988 (D.C. Cir, 2011).

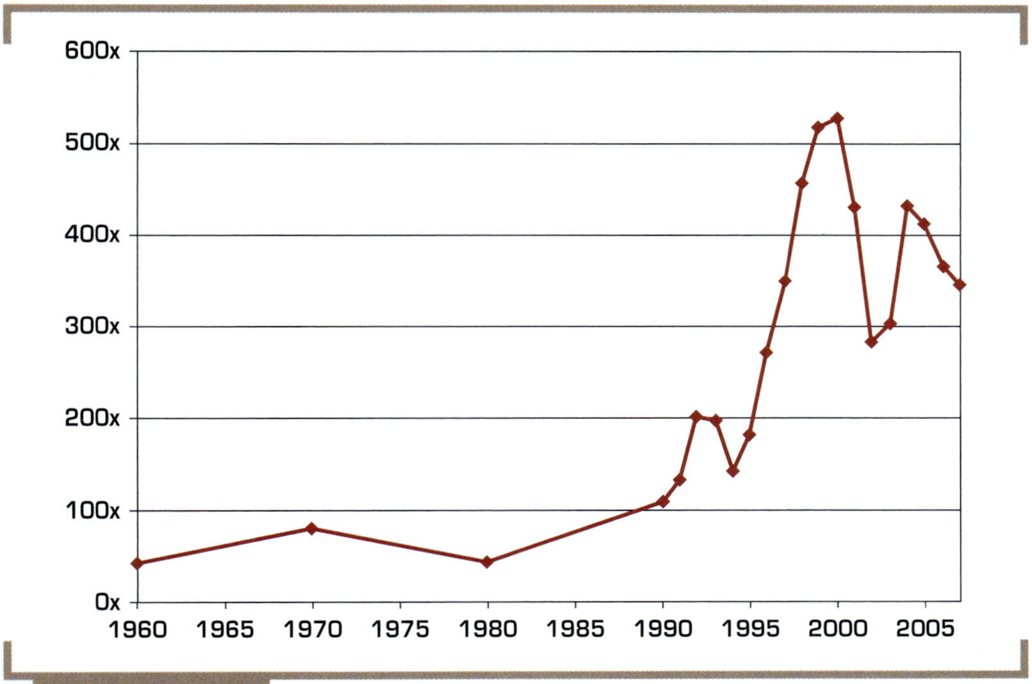

EXHIBIT 35.1 CEOs' pay as a multiple of the average worker's pay, 1960-2007
Source: *Executive Excess 2008*, the 15th Annual CEO Compensation Survey from the Institute for Policy Studies and United for a Fair Economy.[7]

while the stock performed worse than government bonds (a much less risky investment).

- The CEO of Fannie Mae earned $90 million during a time when the company's accounting system was so flawed that it overstated its earnings by $11 billion.
- Executives whose companies survived the 2008 financial crisis only because of taxpayer bailouts still received enormous bonuses. For example, taxpayers spent $180 billion to save American International Group, Inc., even as the company awarded bonuses of $165 million.

To many investors, sky-high executive salaries have become the symbol of all that is wrong with corporate governance. In many companies, salaries are the least of the compensation. Executives also received:

Stock options. Concerned about escalating executive salaries, shareholder activists began advocating "pay-for-performance" plans. The theory was that if executives received stock options instead of cash salaries, their incentives would be more closely aligned with those of shareholders. It was a good theory, but in practice, it did not work as intended.

---

[7]Prepared by Professor G. William Miller, University of California at Santa Cruz, *http://sociology.ucsc.edu/whorulesamerica/power/wealth.html*.

Stock options became a "heads, I win; tails, you lose" game. When stock prices soared in a bull market, options became unexpectedly valuable. In some cases, managers were richly rewarded even when their company had underperformed the (rising) market. However, when stock prices fell, boards lowered the price of the options.

Also, companies played games with options. After the 9/11 terrorist attack, the stock market was closed for four days. When it reopened, stocks took a bigger plunge than they had in any week since Nazi Germany invaded France at the beginning of World War II. In what appeared to be an unseemly exploitation of a national tragedy, 186 companies granted stock options to 511 executives during those few weeks. That is more than twice the number of companies that usually issued stock options in September.[8] These grants, if questionable, were at least legal; not so the backdated options that more than 2,000 companies appear to have issued their executives. In granting options, companies claimed that they had been issued on an earlier date, when the stock price was lower. This practice is fraud.

Termination, retirement plans, and death benefits. Most public companies provide their top executives with generous termination payments, no matter whether the person dies or is fired. Indeed, many CEO employment contracts provide that employees are entitled to severance pay unless fired for committing a particular type of felony. Dying also pays. For example, Nabor Industries Ltd. agreed to pay its 78-year-old CEO $263 million when he dies. The CEO of the Shaw Group was entitled to $17 million if he did not compete with the company after he dies. Yes, you read that right—he was to be paid for not competing after death.

Lavish perks. Executives had long received perks such as country club memberships and cars, but the roster of options expanded. One of the most popular perks was use of the corporate jet. One study found a high correlation between the use of the company plane and membership in far-flung golf clubs. Unfortunately, the correlation is inverse: the more companies spent on private jets, the worse their stock performed.

No wonder that executive compensation became a hot topic for shareholder proposals. Why did executive pay become so lavish?

Directors, not Shareholders, Set Executive Compensation. Directors set the CEO's compensation, but shareholders are the ones who pay the money. People tend to spend someone else's money more generously than their own. Also, directors and the CEO are often friends. Imagine if you got to decide how much your friend could spend dining out, knowing that someone else, whom you had never met, would have to pay the bill. It would be easy to be generous.

Shareholders Bear the Risk. Once again, executive compensation is a "heads I win; tails you lose" game. As we discussed at the beginning of the chapter, if CEOs make a risky decision that pays off, they typically profit enormously. Even if the decision turns out badly, they are often well paid anyway.

Benchmarking Games. Compensation is rarely linked closely to individual performance but instead to overall industry or stock market performance, which is defined in a way to favor executives. Two-thirds of the largest 1,000 U.S. companies report that they performed better than their peers.[9] That is, in part, because benchmarks can be manipulated.

---

[8]Charles Forelle, James Bandler, and Mark Maremont, "Executive Pay: The 9/11 Factor," *The Wall Street Journal,* July 15, 2006, p. A1.

[9]Kevin J. Murphy, "Politics, Economics and Executive Compensation," reported in Lucian Bebchuk and Jesse Fried, *Pay without Performance,* Harvard University Press, 2004, p. 71.

For example, Tootsie Roll Industries Inc., with $500 million in sales, benchmarked against Kraft Foods Inc., with $42.2 billion in earnings. Indeed, every company Tootsie Roll benchmarked against had higher revenues.

Campbell Soup used one set of benchmark companies to determine executive compensation but another set to evaluate its total shareholder return. In all fairness, it seems that Campbell ought to be consistent—presumably only one set of companies is the right comparison group.

The CEO Gets All the Credit. Compensation committees sometimes act as if the CEO and (maybe) a few other top executives are solely responsible for a company's success. Although there is much talk about "pay for performance," the reality is that luck can be as important a determinant of executive compensation as good performance.[10] After James Kilts became CEO of Gillette Co., the stock price went up 61 percent. He had added $20 billion in shareholder value, and therefore, to many, it seemed only fair when he was rewarded with a $153 million payout. But was it? About half the increase in Gillette revenues during the time that Kilts was running the show were attributable to currency fluctuations. A cheaper dollar increased revenue overseas. If the dollar had moved in the opposite direction, there might not have been any increase in revenue.

The Busier the Directors, the Higher the Executive Pay. Generally, executives are more likely to be overpaid if directors serve on many boards. These directors may be too busy to pay attention to such details. Also, trophy directors may be afraid that if they offend a chief executive at one company, word will get around, jeopardizing their position on other boards.

Most Executives Are Above Average. Of course, not everyone can be above average, but most directors believe that their executives are. No one wants to admit to hiring incompetents. Suppose that you are on a company's compensation committee and have data about industry averages. If your executives are above average in performance, you should pay them above-average salaries. If they are not above average, you should fire them, which few boards want to do, except in the face of disaster. If *you* raise salaries, the industry average also rises. Thus, the next company that sets compensation has an even higher bar to jump. For example, Colgate-Palmolive awarded 2 million stock options to its CEO on the understanding that he would receive no further grants for five years. Three years later, however, when consultants found that the CEO's compensation had fallen below the median, the company immediately awarded him an additional 2.6 million options.

Compensation Consultants Often Have Conflicts of Interest. Many companies hire compensation consultants to offer advice on executive pay. These same consultants may also provide other services to the company—such as human resource management—for which the fees can be substantial. The consultants have every incentive to suggest generous packages. In any event, it is not their money.

To make matters even worse for shareholders, lavish compensation does not appear to improve a business's success. A study of the 58 companies that were most generous to their CEOs found that, on average, these companies significantly underperformed both the market generally and their industry in particular.[11]

---

[10]See, for example, Marianne Bertrand and Sendhil Mullainathan, "Are CEOs Rewarded for Luck? The Ones Without Principals Are," *The Quarterly Journal of Economics*, August 2001.

[11]Reed Abelson, "Who Profits If the Boss Is Overfed?" *New York Times*, June 20, 1999, Business Section, p. 9.

Corporate executives are not the only people to earn fabulous salaries. Some athletes earn even more than CEOs. What is the difference between athletes and executives (besides a hook shot)? Athletes' salaries are indeed negotiated at arm's length with the team owner who will actually be paying the bill. This negotiation process means that (1) athletes' pay is not camouflaged; (2) they do not receive enormous severance packages on their way out the door; and (3) their retirement pay ranges from modest to nonexistent.[12] Also, an athlete's performance is transparent and easy to measure.

Compensation for Officers and Directors—A Solution?

The federal government has begun to respond to these perceived abuses.

Proxy Rules. The SEC began this process by amending its proxy rules to require more information about executive compensation. A proxy statement must now include a summary table setting out the full amount of compensation for the five highest-earning executives. The company must explain, for example, why option grants were approved and how much retirement benefits are worth. Companies must also disclose if the pay package increases the risk of large losses. The goal of this provision is to discourage companies from offering pay plans that reward executives for taking excessive risks.

SOX. Under SOX:

- A company cannot make personal loans to its directors or officers.
- If a company has to restate its earnings, the SEC has the right to demand that the CEO and CFO reimburse the company for any bonus or profits they received from selling company stock within a year of the release of the flawed financials. This is a so-called clawback provision. (See bizlawupdate.com for an article about how this clawback provision is working.)

Dodd-Frank. In 2010, Congress passed the Dodd-Frank Wall Street Reform and Consumer Protection Act. Dodd-Frank:

- Requires that compensation committees for all companies listed on a stock exchange must be composed solely of independent directors.
- Strengthens the clawback provisions of SOX and extends it to three years.
- Requires so-called "say-on-pay." At least once every three years, companies must take a *non-binding* shareholder vote on executive compensation (that is, for executive officers, but not for directors). In 2010, for the first time ever, shareholders voted against an executive pay plan—54 percent of Motorola's shareholders opposed CEO Sanjay Jha's compensation. The board had promised him 3 percent of the company if the plan to split Motorola in two succeeded, or a guaranteed payment if it did not. This vote was non-binding, and the company made no promise to respond.
- At least once every six years, companies must take a *non-binding* shareholder vote on how often to hold the say-on-pay vote—once a year, every two years, or every three years.
- In the event of a merger or sale of all company assets, shareholders have the right to a *non-binding* vote on so-called golden parachutes—special payments to executives because of the transaction.

---

[12]Some of the material in this section on executive compensation is drawn from Lucian Bebchuk and Jesse Fried, *Pay without Performance*, Harvard University Press, 2004.

- Companies must disclose the relationship between financial performance and the executive compensation they actually paid.
- Companies must disclose the CEO's compensation and the median compensation of all other company employees, as well as the ratio of these two numbers.

Even with these new protections in place, shareholder influence over executive compensation is far from guaranteed. Note that the shareholder resolutions are nonbinding. And there is little shareholders can do to challenge executive compensation in the courts. To be successful, shareholders must prove that the board violated the business judgment rule, either by making a decision that was *grossly uninformed* or by setting an amount so high that it had *no relation* to the value of the services performed and was really a gift.[13] As the following case indicates, courts tend to be unsympathetic to this line of argument.

BREHM V. EISNER

2006 Del. LEXIS 307
Supreme Court of Delaware, 2006

Facts: Michael Ovitz founded Creative Artists Agency (CAA), the premier talent agency in Hollywood. As a partner at this agency, he earned between $20 and $25 million per year. He was also a longtime friend of Michael Eisner, chairman and CEO of the Walt Disney Company. Ovitz lacked experience managing a diversified public company, but Disney hired him to be its president with the hope that he could improve the company's talent relationships and increase foreign revenues. Upon the advice of Graef Crystal, a compensation consultant, the board approved Ovitz's contract.

After 14 months, all parties agreed that the experiment had failed, so Ovitz left Disney—but not empty-handed. Under his contract, he was entitled to $130 million in severance pay.[14]

Shareholders of Disney sued the board, alleging that it had violated the business judgment rule and that such a large payout was a waste of corporate assets. The trial court held for Disney, and the shareholders appealed.

Issues: ***Did Disney directors have the right to pay $130 million to an employee who had worked unsuccessfully at the company for only 14 months?***

Excerpts from Justice Jacobs's Decision: [T]he compensation committee [of the Board of Directors] was informed of the material facts relating to the payout. If measured in terms of the documentation that would have been generated if "best practices" had been followed, that record leaves much to be desired. [But, the] committee reasonably believed that the analysis of the terms of the [contract] was within Crystal's professional or expert competence, and the committee relied on the information, opinions, reports, and statements made by Crystal. Furthermore, Crystal appears to have been selected with reasonable care, especially in light of his previous engagements with the company.

[The purpose of the business judgment rule] is to protect directors who rely in good faith upon information presented to them from various sources, including any other person as to matters the member reasonably believes are within such person's professional or expert competence and who has been selected with reasonable care by and on behalf of the corporation. For these reasons, we uphold the Chancellor's [that is, the trial court's] determination that the compensation committee members did not breach their fiduciary duty of care.

The shareholders claim the payment of the severance amount to Ovitz constituted waste. A claim of waste will arise only in the rare, unconscionable case where directors irrationally squander or give away corporate assets.

[The shareholders] claim that provisions of the [contract] were wasteful because they incentivized Ovitz to perform poorly in order to obtain payment. The approval

[13]The business judgment rule is discussed at length in Chapter 34.

[14]As Ira Gershwin put it, "Nice work if you can get it, and if you get it—won't you tell me how?"

of the [contract] had a rational business purpose: to induce Ovitz to leave CAA, at what would otherwise be a considerable cost to him, in order to join Disney. To suggest that at the time he entered into the [contract,] Ovitz would engineer an early departure at the cost of his extraordinary reputation in the entertainment industry and his historical friendship with Eisner is not only fanciful but also without proof in the record.

For the reasons stated above, the judgment of the Chancellor is affirmed.

Fundamental Corporate Changes

A corporation must seek shareholder approval before undergoing any of the following fundamental changes:

- **Mergers.** As a general rule, one corporation cannot merge with another unless a majority of both sets of shareholders approve. This rule is always true for shareholders of the *acquired* company because they are always affected by the merger. But when an elephant acquires a peanut, it makes little sense for the elephant to vote. So, shareholders of the *acquiring* company vote only if the merger will have a major impact on their company.
- **Sale of assets.** Generally, shareholders are not asked to approve the sale of corporate assets. After all, one could hardly ask shareholders of the Coca-Cola Company to approve the sale of every bottle of Coke at every grocery store in the country. But shareholders must approve any sale that involves "all or substantially all" of the company's assets.
- **Dissolution.** A corporation cannot *voluntarily* dissolve without shareholder approval. However, as discussed in Chapter 33, the state or a court can *involuntarily* dissolve a corporation regardless of shareholder views.
- **Amendments to the charter.** Directors propose amendments to the charter, but these amendments are not valid unless approved by shareholders.
- **Amendments to the bylaws.** Both directors and shareholders have the right to amend the bylaws.

Right to Dissent

If a private corporation (i.e., one whose stock is not publicly traded) decides to undertake a fundamental change, the Model Act and many state laws require the company to buy back the stock of any shareholders who object to this decision. This process is referred to as **dissenters' rights**, and the company must pay "fair value" for the stock. Fundamental changes include a merger or a sale of most of the company's assets. Devil Desserts, Inc., manufactures sinfully rich chocolate delights. The board of directors is now considering a merger with Angel Treats Ltd., a company that sells low-fat, low-calorie (and in shareholder Celeste's opinion, low-taste) desserts. Celeste fully expects the value of the company to plummet after the merger, but her fellow shareholders support the board's decision. In a public company, Celeste could simply sell her stock, but Devil is a private corporation, and there is no market for its stock. She has the right to dissent because a merger is a fundamental change.

Right to Protection from Other Shareholders

Anyone who owns enough stock to control a corporation has a fiduciary duty to minority shareholders (those with less than a controlling interest). The courts have long recognized that minority shareholders are entitled to extra protection because it is easy (perhaps even natural) for controlling shareholders to take advantage of them. In the following case, craigslist adopted a rights plan (which, as you may remember from the prior chapter, is also called a poison pill). But the pill was too bitter for eBay to swallow.

eBay Domestic Holdings, Inc. v. Newmark

2010 Del. Ch. LEXIS 187
Court of Chancery of Delaware, 2010

Facts: The company craigslist, Inc., owned the most popular website in the country for classified ads. It had just two shareholders—Craig Newmark and Jim Buckmaster—and only 34 employees. eBay, Inc. was a publicly traded company that operated online auction sites worldwide. It employed over 16,000 people. eBay bought a minority interest in craigslist, with the goal of ultimately acquiring the company or, failing that, learning the "secret sauce" of craigslist's success. It turned out, though, that craigslist and eBay were not a good match because they had entirely different cultures and approaches to business. While craigslist focused on enhancing its user community rather than maximizing its profits or expanding its business model, eBay's primary focus was to increase profitability and market share.

Without undergoing any premarital discussions in which these divergent goals might have been revealed, eBay purchased 28.4 percent of craigslist's shares. Under the explicit terms of the deal, it had the right to compete with craigslist. Craig and Jim said that if eBay was able to offer customers a better experience, then it should be allowed to do so.

As eBay gradually realized that Craig and Jim would never sell out to them, at least in this lifetime, it launched a competing classifieds website at **www.Kijiji.com**. In this process, it used nonpublic information about craigslist that it garnered, without Craig and Jim's knowledge, from its relationship with the company. That "betrayal" further inflamed the situation. As other people have discovered, agreeing in theory to an open marriage is very different from experiencing it in practice. Jim and Craig were furious about eBay's foray into online classifieds. They asked for a divorce, but eBay refused to sell its stock.

Craig and Jim, in their role as directors, responded by adopting a rights plan that restricted eBay's ability to buy more shares of craigslist or sell its existing shares to third parties. They also eliminated its right to choose one board member. In response, eBay filed suit, alleging that this rights plan violated craigslist's fidcuciary rights to eBay as a minority shareholder.

Issue: ***Did Craig, Jim, and craiglist violate their fiduciary duty to the minority shareholder?***

Excerpts from Chancellor Chandler's Decision: All directors of Delaware corporations are fiduciaries of the corporations' stockholders. Similarly, controlling stockholders are fiduciaries of their corporations' minority stockholders.

[In a situation such as this,] directors must (1) identify the proper corporate objectives served by their actions; and (2) justify their actions as reasonable in relationship to those objectives. Thus, the two main issues I confront are: First, did Jim and Craig properly and reasonably perceive a threat to craigslist's corporate policy and effectiveness? Second, if they did, is the Rights Plan a proportional response to that threat?

Jim and Craig contend that they identified a threat to craigslist and its corporate policies that will materialize after they both die and their craigslist shares are distributed to their heirs. To prevent this unwanted potential future reality, Jim and Craig have adopted the Rights Plan *now* so that their vision of craigslist's culture can bind *future* fiduciaries and stockholders from beyond the grave. Having given new meaning to the concept of a "dead-hand pill," Jim and Craig ask this Court to validate their attempt to use a pill to shape the future of the space-time continuum.

Ultimately, defendants failed to prove that craigslist possesses a palpable, distinctive, and advantageous culture that sufficiently promotes stockholder value to support the indefinite implementation of a poison pill. Jim and Craig did not make any serious attempt to prove that the craigslist culture, which rejects any attempt to further monetize its services, translates into increased profitability for stockholders.

I am sure that part of the reason craigslist is so popular is because it offers a free service that is also extremely useful. It may be that offering free classifieds is an essential component of a successful online classifieds venture. After all, by offering free classifieds, craigslist is able to attract such a large community of users that real estate brokers in New York City gladly pay fees to list apartment rentals in order to access the vast community of craigslist users. Giving away services to attract business is a sales tactic, however, not a corporate culture. To the extent business measures like loss-leading products, money-back coupons, or putting products on sale are cultural artifacts, they reflect the American capitalist culture, not something unique to craigslist.

The defendants also failed to prove at trial that when adopting the Rights Plan, they concluded in good faith that there was a sufficient connection between the craigslist "culture" (however amorphous and intangible it might be) and the promotion of stockholder value. Jim and Craig simply disliked the possibility that the Grim Reaper someday will catch up with them and that a company like eBay might, in the future, purchase a controlling interest in craigslist. They considered this possible future state unpalatable, not because of how it affects the value of the entity for its stockholders, but rather because of their own personal preferences. Jim and Craig therefore failed to prove at trial that they acted in the good faith pursuit of a proper *corporate* purpose when they deployed the Rights Plan.

I personally appreciate and admire Jim's and Craig's desire to be of service to communities. The corporate form in which craigslist operates, however, is not an appropriate vehicle for purely philanthropic ends, at least not when there are other stockholders interested in realizing a return on their investment. If Jim and Craig were the only stockholders affected by their decisions, then there would be no one to object. eBay, however, holds a significant stake in craigslist, and Jim and Craig's actions affect others besides themselves.

As long as Jim and Craig have control, they can maintain the craigslist "culture" regardless of whether eBay sells some or all of its shares. The Rights Plan therefore does not have a reasonable connection to Jim and Craig's professed goal. It therefore falls outside the range of reasonableness.

I rescind the Rights Plan in its entirety.

Ordinary Business Transactions

Minority shareholders have the right to overturn an ordinary business transaction between the corporation and a controlling shareholder unless the corporation can show that the transaction is fair to the minority shareholders. The Sinclair Oil Co. owned 97 percent of Sinclair Venezuelan Oil Co. (Sinven). Sinven's minority shareholders complained that Sinclair

- Forced Sinven to pay dividends so large that the subsidiary faced bankruptcy
- Hired other, wholly owned, subsidiaries but not Sinven, and
- Refused to force its other subsidiaries to abide by their contracts with Sinven; for instance, a Sinclair subsidiary signed a contract with Sinven to buy crude oil but failed to purchase the required amount.[15]

The court ruled that the dividend policy was fair to the minority shareholders because they received the dividends, too. Sinclair was not under any obligation to hire Sinven. But Sinclair did have to ensure that other subsidiaries complied with their Sinven contracts.

Excluding Minority Shareholders

Controlling shareholders must include minority shareholders in any favorable arrangements that they make for their own stock. A successful savings and loan (S&L) had stock that, in theory, was worth $2,400 a share but, in reality, it rarely traded because of the high price. The controlling shareholder could have split the stock so that shareholders received 100 shares worth $24 each. Instead, he concocted a shrewd plan whereby he and his friends (who together owned 85 percent of the stock) exchanged their S&L stock for shares in a new corporation. Stock of the new company sold well, but there was still

---

[15] *Sinclair Oil Corp. v. Levien,* 280 A.2d 717, 1971 Del. LEXIS 225 (Del. 1971).

virtually no market for the remaining S&L shares. The court held that the controlling shareholders could not exclude the minority without a compelling business purpose, which did not exist in this case.[16]

Expelling Shareholders

There is an old saying that you can choose your friends, but not your family. Can you choose your fellow shareholders? Sometimes, relations between shareholders become so bitter that the majority attempts to expel a minority owner. **Many states prohibit a company from expelling shareholders unless the firm pays a fair price for the minority stock and the expulsion has a legitimate business purpose.** Delaware has an even higher standard—the transaction must be "entirely fair." This standard requires that both the price and the process of approval be fair. Theodore Lerner owned 70 shares in the family real estate company, Lawrence Lerner only 25. When Lawrence sued Theodore for mismanagement, Theodore amended the charter to reclassify each share of stock into 1/35th of a share and to buy out any fractional shares. Lawrence ended up with 5/7ths of a share, which the company purchased. The court, however, halted the squeeze-out because it had no legitimate business purpose.[17]

Sometimes, relations between shareholders become so bitter that the majority attempts to expel a minority owner.

Right to Monitor

As owners of an enterprise, shareholders play a relatively passive role. Primarily, they have the right to *monitor,* meaning the right to receive information and the right to vote on proposals put to them by the board. Shareholders do not, by and large, have the right to *initiate* corporate changes.

EXAM Strategy

Question: The five Brown children were all owners of the Roundup Ranch, Inc., in Montana. Peter owned 51 percent of the corporation; the rest was evenly divided among his four siblings. Because coal companies were encroaching on Roundup, Peter traded the Montana ranch for equivalent land in New Mexico. His siblings were not happy—their only interest in owning the ranch had been to maintain a connection with their family homestead. What could they do?

Strategy: Because Peter owned a majority of the shares, he had the right to sell the ranch. But because he is undertaking a fundamental change, his siblings do have some rights.

Result: The siblings have the right to dissent—that is, to require the company to buy back their stock, which is what the unhappy siblings required the unhappier Peter to do.

---

[16] *Jones v. H. F. Ahmanson & Co.*, 1 Cal. 3d 93, 460 P.2d 464, 1969 Cal. LEXIS 195 (1969).
[17] *Lerner v. Lerner*, 306 Md. 771, 511 A.2d 501 (Md. App. 1986).

ENFORCING SHAREHOLDER RIGHTS

Shareholders in serious conflict with management have two different mechanisms for enforcing their rights: a derivative lawsuit or a direct lawsuit.

Derivative Lawsuits

A derivative lawsuit is brought by *shareholders* to remedy a wrong to the *corporation*. The suit is brought in the name of the corporation, and all proceeds of the litigation go to the corporation. For example, as you saw in the earlier case, shareholders of Disney were upset when the board of directors approved a $130 million severance package for Michael Ovitz, who had served as Disney's president for a rocky 14 months. Shareholders wanted to sue the directors for having approved this compensation plan. But they had no right to sue on their *own* behalf because it was the *company* that had been harmed. Any injury to the shareholders was indirect. Thus, only the corporation could sue. And who would authorize a suit against the directors on behalf of the corporation? The directors, of course. Because the directors are unlikely to sue themselves, the law permits derivative actions, by which shareholders can sue managers who have violated their duty to the corporation. Because damages go to the *corporation*, the individual shareholders benefit only to the extent that the settlement causes their stock to rise in value.

The same rule applies if an outsider harms the corporation. If Disney decided not to sue a customer that refused to pay its bill, the shareholders could do so, but only in a derivative action, that is, only in the name of the corporation. Once again, any recovery goes to the corporation.

Litigation is tremendously expensive. How can shareholders afford to sue if they are not entitled to damages? A corporation that loses a derivative suit must pay the legal fees of the victorious shareholders. Most derivative lawsuits are litigated by lawyers eager to earn these fees. (Losing shareholders are not required to pay the corporation's legal fees.[18]) Most derivative lawsuits are initiated by lawyers who seek out shareholders and persuade them to sue. Without this incentive, few shareholders would bring derivative suits and much corporate wrongdoing would go unpunished. As we have seen, shareholders have limited power; derivative lawsuits are a means of protecting their rights.

Most derivative suits are brought in Delaware, so this discussion is based on Delaware law. Most other corporate statutes are similar to those of Delaware.

Making Demand

Before bringing suit, shareholders must first "make demand" on the board of directors. In other words, they must notify the board that the corporation has been wronged and ask the board to bring suit in the name of the corporation directly. There is one crucial exception to this rule: shareholders are not required to make demand if it would *clearly be futile* because a majority of the directors either have a conflict of interest or were careless when making the decision. In the following case, the court ruled that making demand on eBay would be futile.

---

[18]Under the Private Securities Litigation Reform Act, class action plaintiffs in suits brought under the securities laws must pay the corporation's legal expenses if the court determines that the suit was frivolous or abusive. 104 Pub. L. No. 67, 109 Stat. 737.

In Re eBay, Inc. Shareholders Litigation

2004 Del. Ch. LEXIS 4
Court of Chancery of Delaware, 2004

Facts: Pierre M. Omidyar and Jeffrey Skoll founded eBay, Inc., a company that hosts an online auction site. Later, Robert C. Kagle and Margaret C. Whitman joined the eBay board. Whitman also became president and CEO. Goldman Sachs Group Inc. twice served as lead underwriter when eBay sold shares to the public. Then Whitman became a director of Goldman. Afterwards, Goldman served as eBay's financial advisor when it acquired PayPal, Inc.

During this period in which Goldman engaged in three major transactions with eBay, the investment bank also served as underwriter for a substantial number of technology companies that went public. Many investors wanted to buy stock in these initial public offerings (IPOs) because an immediate and large profit was virtually guaranteed. Often stock prices doubled or tripled on the day of the offering. Goldman allowed Omidyar, Skoll, Kagle, and Whitman, all directors of eBay, to buy shares in hundreds of its IPOs, effectively giving them millions of dollars in profits. The following chart reveals the percentage of eBay shares that each director owned and the number of Goldman IPOs in which he or she was allowed to invest:

Director	Percentage of eBay shares owned	Number of IPOs in which director took part
Omidyar	>23%	40
Skoll	13%	75
Whitman	3.3%	>100
Kagle	Not disclosed in case	25

In each case, the eBay directors sold the stock immediately, and did earn millions of dollars in total profit.

eBay shareholders sued, alleging that Goldman had effectively bribed the defendants to continue giving business to the bank. The lawsuit was brought as a derivative action in the name of eBay. The plaintiffs alleged that demand was futile because the directors had a conflict of interest.

The board of directors of eBay had seven members: Omidyar, Kagle, Whitman, Philippe Bourguignon, Scott D. Cook, Dawn G. Lepore, and Howard D. Schultz. (At the time of the lawsuit, Skoll was no longer a director.) The court determined that the three defendants had a conflict of interest because they were the targets of the lawsuit. It was obvious they would not vote for eBay to pursue the litigation. If one of the remaining four directors also had a conflict, then that would constitute a majority and demand would be excused. The shareholders could then proceed with the lawsuit.

Issues: ***Did a majority of the board of directors have a conflict of interest? Was demand on the board futile?***

Excerpts from Chancellor Chandler's Decision: Plaintiffs allege that Cook, Lepore, Schultz, and Bourguignon have received huge financial benefits as a result of their positions as eBay directors and, furthermore, that they owe their positions on the board to Omidyar, Whitman, Kagle, and Skoll.

[I]n 1998, when Cook joined eBay's board, it awarded him 900,000 [stock] options. In 1998, eBay adopted a director's stock option plan pursuant to which each non-employee director was to be awarded 30,000 options each year. [T]he stock options are worth potentially millions of dollars.

© AP Photo/Paul Sakuma

Was it right for Meg Whitman to buy stock in Goldman IPOs?

I need not address each of the four outside directors, as I agree with plaintiffs that the allegations of the complaint are sufficient to raise a reasonable doubt as to Cook's independence from the eBay insider directors who accepted Goldman Sachs' IPO allocations.

First, Whitman, Omidyar, Kagle, and Skoll (and their affiliates) own about one-half of eBay's outstanding common stock. As a result, these eBay officers and directors effectively have the ability to control eBay and to direct its affairs and business, including the election of directors and the approval of significant corporate transactions.

Second, a significant number of options have not yet vested and will never vest unless the outside directors remain directors of eBay. ["Vested" means that the owner is allowed to keep the options, even if he leaves the company.] Given that the value of the options for Cook (and allegedly for the other outside directors) potentially run into the millions of dollars, one cannot conclude realistically that Cook would be able to objectively and impartially consider a demand to bring litigation against those to whom he is beholden for his current position and future position on eBay's board. With the specific allegations of the complaint in mind, I conclude that plaintiffs have adequately demonstrated that demand on eBay's board should be excused as futile.

Ethics The activities described in this case were standard operating procedure at the time. Yet, these defendants were *billionaires.* Why would they engage in behavior that was potentially damaging to their reputation and to their company? Would you have done the same? Why or why not?

If Demand Is Required

If shareholders are required to make demand, the board has three choices:

1. It can agree with the shareholders and file suit on behalf of the corporation. In this case, the shareholders cannot bring their own derivative action. Although technically, the board is required to put the interests of the corporation first, it is, shall we say, very unlikely that a board will decide to file suit.
2. The board can reject the demand (or fail to respond). To proceed with their suit in this case, the plaintiffs must convince the court that the board has violated the business judgment rule because it had a conflict of interest or was careless in rejecting the demand. Again, this is a low-probability event.
3. The board can appoint a Special Litigation Committee (SLC). The SLC is typically comprised of at least two independent directors (usually those elected after the disputed activity occurred). If the SLC determines that the lawsuit is without merit, then the court must generally dismiss the case unless the shareholders can show the rejection was uninformed or not in good faith. There does not appear to be a single case in which an SLC recommended that litigation continue or a court overturned the decision of an SLC.

Exhibit 35.2 illustrates the course of derivative litigation. The most important issue is whether a court will require demand. Shareholders know that if they make demand, the directors will appoint an SLC, which will then kill the suit. Therefore, shareholders typically file suit without making demand and wait for the company to go to court to ask that the suit be dismissed unless demand is made. If the court indeed requires demand, the shareholders know they have lost and typically withdraw the case. If, however, the shareholders can convince the court that demand is not required, the shareholders have won and the parties settle.

More Fortune 500 companies are incorporated in Delaware than in any other state, making its corporate law the most influential in the nation. The Model Act has, however, deviated from Delaware law by proposing that demand be required in *all* derivative cases. This approach essentially ignores the possibility that demand might be futile.

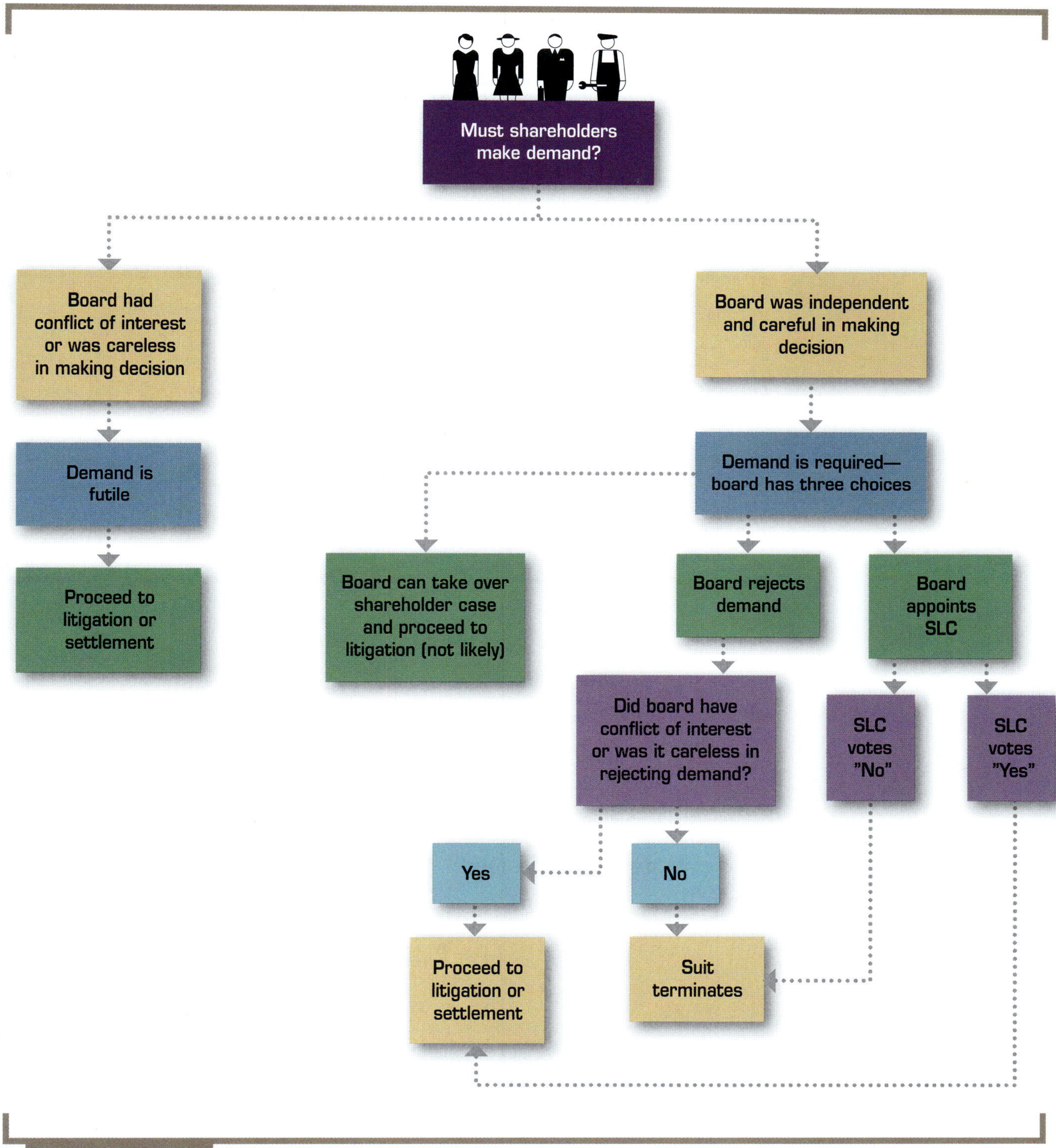
Must shareholders make demand?
Board had conflict of interest or was careless in making decision
Demand is futile
Proceed to litigation or settlement
Board was independent and careful in making decision
Demand is required—board has three choices
Board can take over shareholder case and proceed to litigation (not likely)
Board rejects demand
Board appoints SLC
Did board have conflict of interest or was it careless in rejecting demand?
SLC votes "No"
SLC votes "Yes"
Yes
No
Proceed to litigation or settlement
Suit terminates

EXHIBIT 35.2

(shareholders)

Direct Lawsuits = shareholders own rights

Shareholders are permitted to sue the corporation directly only if their own rights have been harmed. If, for example, the corporation denies shareholders the right to inspect its books and records or to hold a shareholder meeting, they may sue in their own name and keep any damages awarded. The corporation is not required to pay the shareholders' legal fees; winning shareholders can use part of any damage award for this purpose. With a direct action, shareholders are more likely to get their day in court because they are not required to make demand first.

The following table displays some of the important distinguishing features of derivative suits and direct actions:

Features	Derivative Action	Direct Action
Enforces the Rights of:	The corporation	The shareholder(s)
Damages Are Paid to:	The corporation	The shareholder(s)
Procedural Requirements	• Plaintiffs make demand on the board unless clearly futile. • If demand is futile, plaintiffs proceed with the case. • If demand is made, either the board or the SLC can terminate the case.	The same as regular litigation

EXAM Strategy

Question: Shareholders of Hewlett-Packard Co. were outraged that the board of directors paid CEO Carleton Fiorina $40 million after it fired her. The shareholders filed suit directly. Do the shareholders have the right to bring this suit on their own behalf against the board of directors?

Strategy: Shareholders can bring suit directly only if they have been personally harmed. If the harm is to the corporation, then shareholders must bring a derivative action in the name of the company.

Result: In this case, the harm was to the corporation. The shareholders were harmed only indirectly, when the price of their stock went down. A derivative action was their only option.

Chapter Conclusion

Two major financial collapses in the first decade of this century led to harsher scrutiny of corporate governance. The sight of huge payouts to top executives, even as their companies fell in heaps around them, spurred shareholder—and governmental—anger. We are now engaged in a great experiment—what can shareholders do, with and without government aid, to improve corporate accountability and performance? What is the right balance of power between shareholders and managers?

Regulatory changes and shareholder power have led to some concrete results. At the beginning of this century, about half of publicly traded companies combined the position of CEO and chairman of the board of directors. For most companies, those two jobs are now separate. CEOs now serve an average of 6.3 years, down from 8.1 years a decade ago. More independent directors, who take their independence more seriously, populate boards.

But corporate governance is not an end in itself—its goal is to improve performance. It is early days yet, but so far there is no compelling evidence of a significant relationship between good corporate governance and improved financial results.

In the end, it may be that the answer lies, at least in part, in the character of corporate leaders. In analyzing Enron and its aftermath, a *Wall Street Journal* article concluded: "[N]ot one of the instances of egregious abuse of shareholder interest could have occurred if the CEO had simply said, 'No!' It takes a person of character to know what lines you don't cross."[19]

Exam Review

1. **DIRECTORS** Directors, not shareholders, have the right to manage the corporate business. (p. 863)

2. **THE SEC** The Securities and Exchange Commission regulates the relationship between publicly held corporations and their shareholders. The SEC plays a less active role in privately held corporations. (p. 863)

3. **SHAREHOLDER RIGHTS** Shareholders have the right to:
   - Receive annual financial statements (if their company is publicly traded),
   - Inspect and copy the corporation's records (for a proper purpose),
   - Elect and remove directors, and
   - Approve fundamental corporate changes, such as a merger or a major sale of assets. (pp. 864–879)

Question: The board of directors of Finalco Group, Inc., decided to sell most of the company's assets to Western Savings. Shortly after the proposed sale was announced, Finalco's largest shareholder said he opposed the transaction. Does Finalco need his approval for the sale?

Strategy: Shareholders have the right to approve fundamental corporate changes. Was this a fundamental change? (See the "Result" at the end of this section.)

[19]David Wessel, "Why the Bad Guys of the Boardroom Emerged en Masse," *Wall Street Journal*, June 20, 2002, p. A1.

4. **PROXIES** Virtually all publicly held companies solicit proxies from their shareholders. A proxy authorizes someone else to vote in place of the shareholder. (pp. 866–867)

5. **SHAREHOLDER PROPOSALS** Under certain circumstances, public companies must include shareholder proposals in the proxy statement. (pp. 867–868)

EXAM Strategy

Question: An institutional investor wanted A&P, the grocery store chain, to permit large shareholders to place comments about the company's financial performance in its proxy statement. Which would be a better strategy for achieving this goal: a shareholder proposal or an amendment to the company's bylaws?

Strategy: Shareholder proposals are treated differently from bylaw amendments. Which one is more likely to affect the behavior of the company? (See the "Result" at the end of this section.)

6. **INDEPENDENT DIRECTORS** Under SOX, all members of a board's audit committee must be independent. For companies listed on the NYSE or NASDAQ, independent directors must comprise a majority of the board and only independent directors can serve on audit, compensation, or nominating committees. (p. 869)

7. **EXECUTIVE COMPENSATION**

- Under SOX, a company cannot make personal loans to its directors or officers. If a company has to restate its earnings, its CEO and CFO must reimburse the company for any bonus or profits they received from selling company stock within a year of the release of the flawed financials.
- Dodd-Frank requires shareholder "say-on-pay." In addition, companies must disclose the CEO's compensation and the median compensation of all other company employees, as well as the ratio of these two numbers. (pp. 870–876)

8. **DISSENTERS' RIGHTS** A shareholder who objects to a fundamental change in the corporation can insist that her shares be bought out at fair value. (p. 876)

9. **RIGHTS AND OBLIGATIONS OF CONTROLLING SHAREHOLDERS** Controlling shareholders:

- May not enter into unfair business transactions with the corporation,
- Have a fiduciary duty to minority shareholders,
- May not exclude minority shareholders from beneficial arrangements involving stock, and
- Are prohibited from expelling minority shareholders unless the expulsion is done for a legitimate business purpose. (pp. 876–879)

10. **DERIVATIVE LAWSUITS** A derivative lawsuit is brought by shareholders to remedy a wrong to the corporation. The suit is brought in the name of the corporation, and all proceeds of the litigation go to the corporation. (pp. 880–883)

Question: Daniel Cowin was a minority shareholder of Bresler & Reiner, Inc., a public company that developed real estate in Washington, D.C. He alleged numerous instances of corporate mismanagement, fraud, self-dealing, and breach of fiduciary duty by the board of directors. He sought damages for the diminished value of his stock. Could Cowin bring this suit as a direct action, or must it be a derivative suit?

Strategy: If the wrong was to the corporation, then Cowin must bring a derivative lawsuit. He can bring a direct action only if the harm was to him personally. (See the "Result" at the end of this section.)

3. Result: Yes, it was a sale of most of the company's assets. The board could not proceed without the approval of the owners of a majority of shares.

5. Result: A shareholder proposal is not binding on the company. Even if the shareholders approved a proposal, A&P would be under no obligation to carry it out. A bylaw amendment, on the other hand, would be binding on the company.

10. Result: The court ruled that the injury had fallen equally on all the shareholders, and therefore, a derivative suit was appropriate.

Multiple-Choice Questions

1. The president of R. Hoe & Co., Inc., refused to call a special meeting of the shareholders although 55 percent of them requested it. One purpose of the meeting was to demand that the former president be reinstated. Do shareholders have the right to make these two requests?
   (a) Yes to both.
   (b) No to both.
   (c) The shareholders have the right to call a meeting, but not to reinstate the president.
   (d) The shareholders have the right to reinstate the president, but not to call a meeting.

2. Under SOX and Dodd-Frank:
   (a) Companies are prohibited from making personal loans to directors and officers.
   (b) If a company restates its earnings, the five top executives must reimburse the company for any income they have received during that period.

(c) All directors must be independent.
(d) Shareholders have the right to strike down golden parachutes.

3. A company is allowed to hold its annual meeting online:
(a) If a majority of its shareholders approve
(b) If it also hold a live meeting for shareholders who want to attend in person
(c) If it simulcasts a video of the meeting
(d) Any way it wants, as long as shareholders are notified

4. To be elected to a board of a publicly traded company, a candidate must:
(a) Receive a majority of the votes cast
(b) Receive a majority vote of the shares outstanding
(c) Receive a plurality of the votes cast
(d) Receive a plurality of the shares outstanding

5. If directors and officers cause harm to their company:
(a) Shareholders have the right to file suit against them and recover damages.
(b) Shareholders have the right to file suit against them and recover damages only if the board permits the suit.
(c) Shareholders have the right to file suit against them and recover damages only if the board permits the suit or a court deems the demand futile.
(d) Shareholders do not have the right to file suit against them.

Essay Questions

1. William H. Sullivan, Jr., purchased all the voting shares of the New England Patriots Football Club, Inc. (the Old Patriots). He organized a new corporation called the New Patriots Football Club, Inc. The boards of directors of the two companies agreed to merge. After the merger, the nonvoting stock in the Old Patriots was to be exchanged for cash. Do minority shareholders of the Old Patriots have the right to prevent the merger? If so, under what theory?

2. **ETHICS** Edgar Bronfman, Jr., dropped out of high school to go to Hollywood and write songs and produce movies. Eventually, he left Hollywood to work in the family business—the Bronfmans owned 36 percent of Seagram Co., a liquor and beverage conglomerate. Promoted to president of the company at the age of 32, Bronfman seized a second chance to live his dream. Seagram received 70 percent of its earnings from its 24 percent ownership of DuPont Co. Bronfman sold this stock *at less than market value* to purchase (at an inflated price) 80 percent of MCA, a movie and music company that had been a financial disaster for its prior owners. Some observers thought Bronfman had gone Hollywood, others that he had gone crazy. After the deal was announced, the price of Seagram shares fell 18 percent. Was there anything Seagram shareholders could do to prevent what to them was not a dream but a nightmare? Apart from legal issues, was Bronfman's decision ethical? What ethical obligations does he owe Seagram's shareholders?

3. **YOU BE THE JUDGE WRITING PROBLEM** Two shareholders of Bruce Co., Harry and Yolan Gilbert, were fighting management for control of the company. They asked for permission to inspect Bruce's stockholder list so that they could either solicit support for their slate of directors at the upcoming stockholder meeting, attempt to buy additional stock from other stockholders, or both. Bruce's board refused to allow the Gilberts to see the shareholder list on the grounds that the Gilberts owned another corporation that competed with Bruce. Do the Gilberts have the right to see Bruce's shareholder list? **Argument for the Gilberts:** If shareholders of a company have a proper purpose, they are entitled to inspect shareholder lists. Soliciting votes and buying stock are both proper purposes. **Argument for Bruce:** The Gilberts are simply offering a pretext. They could use this information to compete against the company. No shareholder has the right to cause harm.

4. When Classic Corp. went public at $12 a share, its waterbed business was floating along nicely—the company had annual sales of $23 million and turned a hefty profit. The company then sprang a leak and suffered through many years of losses. Isaac, who owned 64 percent of the stock, decided to take the company private again (by buying shareholders' stock) at a price of 20 *cents* a share. Classic hired two financial advisers who opined that the buyout price was fair. The board of directors voted in favor of the sale and then scheduled a special shareholder meeting to vote on the buyout. Do the minority shareholders have any rights?

5. Shareholders lost their gamble when they bought stock of Jackpot Enterprises, Inc. Fed up with management, a shareholder asked the company to include a proposal in the proxy statement that would require the board of directors to sell or merge the company. Must Jackpot include this proposal in its proxy statement?

Discussion Questions

1. Pfizer Inc. paid $2.3 billion to settle civil and criminal charges alleging that it had illegally marketed 13 of its most important drugs. This settlement made history, but not in a good way. It was both the largest criminal fine and the largest settlement of civil health care fraud charges *ever* paid. Shareholders filed a derivative suit against the Pfizer board and top executives. Defendants responded with a motion to dismiss on the grounds that shareholders had not made demand on the board. Is demand necessary?

2. **ETHICS** After a recent annual meeting, Cisco Systems reported the results of the votes on both management and shareholder proposals. The company reported the results of its own proposals as a simple ratio of those in favor divided by the total number of votes cast. But for shareholder proposals, it reported the percentage as a ratio of those in favor divided by all outstanding shares. As a result, it reported the favorable vote for one shareholder proposal as 19 percent when, in fact, 34 percent of the votes cast supported this proposal. Is Cisco behaving ethically?

3. For several years, CSK Auto, Inc., fraudulently reported inflated earnings. During this period, Maynard Jenkins was CEO. He was not involved in the fraud, however, and was never charged with a crime. Nonetheless, using a SOX provision, the SEC sought

to claw back some of his earnings during this period. Should Jenkins be financially responsible for fraud that occurred on his watch, even though he did not participate?

4. Prior to the DuPont Co.'s annual shareholder meeting, Friends of the Earth Oceanic Society submitted a proposal requiring the company to (1) accelerate its phaseout of the production of chlorofluorocarbons and halons, (2) present to shareholders a report detailing research and development efforts to find environmentally sound substitutes, and (3) report to shareholders on marketing plans to sell those substitutes. Must DuPont include this proposal in its proxy material for the annual meeting?

5. Would the following initiatives improve corporate governance? Can you think of others that would?

a. Shareholder proposals: require the board of directors to implement shareholder proposals that receive a majority vote,

b. Proxy access: as proposed by the SEC,

c. Majority vote: prohibit boards of directors from seating directors who fail to receive a majority vote of shares cast,

d. Compensation: base compensation on the company's growth in earnings compared with those of its competitors, not just increases in earnings (that might be caused by a general market rise).

CHAPTER 36

Securities Regulation

In 1926, America was gripped by a fever of stock market speculation. "Playing the market" became a national mania. The most engrossing news on any day's front page was the market. Up and up it soared. The cause of this psychological virus is uncertain, but the focus of the infection was the New York Stock Exchange (NYSE). Between 1926 and 1929, annual volume more than doubled.

Much of this feverish trading was done on margin. Customers put down only 10 or 20 percent of a stock's purchase price and then borrowed the rest from their broker. This easy-payment plan excited the gambling instinct of unwary amateurs and professional speculators alike. By September 1929, the volume of these margin loans was equal to about half the entire public debt of the United States.

From the peak of the bull market in September to the debacle of October 29, over $32 billion of equity value simply vanished from the earth.

On September 4, 1929, stock prices began to soften, and for the next month, they slid gently. Over the weekend of October 19, brokers sent out thousands of margin calls, asking customers to pay down loans that now exceeded the value of their stock. If customers failed to pay, brokers dumped their stock on the market, causing prices to fall further and brokers to make more margin calls. Soon there was a mad scramble of selling as prices plunged in wild disorder. Tens of thousands of investors across the country were wiped out as the value of their stock fell below what they had borrowed to buy it. On Tuesday, October 29, 1929, the speculative boom completely collapsed. That day, 4 million shares were traded, a record that stood for 30 years. From the peak of the bull market in September to the debacle of October 29, over $32 billion of equity value simply vanished from the earth.

The stock market crash spawned the Great Depression—the most pervasive, persistent, and destructive economic crisis the nation has ever faced. Retail trade fell by one-half, automobile production by two-thirds, steel by three-quarters. In 1933, more businesses failed than in any other year in history. Surviving businesses responded to the crisis by cutting dividends, reducing inventories, laying off workers, slashing wages, and canceling capital investments.

Unemployment statistics were the most poignant of all. In 1932, one in every five people in the labor force was out of a job, more than twice the highest level reached in the most recent U.S. recession. And this was at a time before widespread unemployment benefits. Millions of others were underemployed, working only two or three days a week for wages that could not support a family. Distress cut across all economic and social classes. Bankers, insurance agents, architects, and lawyers joined the throng of unemployed. Articles such as the following were common in newspapers across the land:

> *New York, Jan. 6, 1933 (AP)*—After vainly trying to get a stay of dispossession until Jan. 15 from his apartment in Brooklyn, yesterday, Peter J. Cornell, 48 years old, a former roofing contractor out of work and penniless, fell dead in the arms of his wife. A doctor gave the cause of his death as heart disease, and the police said it had at least partly been caused by the bitter disappointment of a long day's fruitless attempt to prevent himself and his family being put out on the streets.[1]

INTRODUCTION

At the time of the great stock market crash, only state, not federal law, regulated securities (such as stocks and bonds). Congress recognized that the country needed a national securities system if it was to avoid another such catastrophe. In 1933, Congress passed the Securities Act of 1933 (1933 Act) to regulate the issuance of new securities. The next year, it passed the Securities Exchange Act of 1934 (1934 Act) to regulate companies with publicly traded securities. The 1934 Act also established the Securities and Exchange Commission (SEC), the regulatory agency that oversees the securities industry.

The Securities and Exchange Commission

The SEC creates law in three different ways:

- **Rules.** The securities statutes are often little more than general guides. Through its rules, the SEC fills in the crucial details.
- **Releases.** These are informal pronouncements from the SEC on current issues. Releases often operate as two-way communications. When the SEC issues a release to announce a proposed change in the rules, it also asks for comments on the proposal.
- **No-action letters.** Anyone who is in doubt about whether a particular transaction complies with the securities laws can ask the SEC directly. The response is called a no-action letter because it states that "the staff will recommend that the Commission take no action" if the transaction is done in a specified manner.

In addition to creating laws, the SEC has the power to enforce them. It can bring **cease and desist orders** against those who violate the securities laws, and it can also levy fines or

---

[1]The material in this section is adapted from Cabell Phillips, *From the Crash to the Blitz* (Toronto: Macmillan, 1969).

confiscate profits from illegal transactions. Those accused of wrongdoing can appeal these sanctions to the courts. The SEC does not have the authority to bring a criminal action; it refers criminal cases to the Justice Department.

What Is a Security?

Both the 1933 and the 1934 Acts regulate securities. The official definition of a security includes stock, bonds, treasury stock, notes, debentures, evidence of indebtedness, certificates of interest or participation in any profit-sharing agreement, and 17 other equivalents. Courts have interpreted this definition to mean that a **security** is any transaction in which the buyer (1) invests money in a common enterprise and (2) expects to earn a profit predominantly from the efforts of others.

Security
Any transaction in which the buyer invests money in a common enterprise and expects to earn a profit predominantly from the efforts of others.

This definition covers investments that are not necessarily *called* securities. For example, they may be called orange trees. W. J. Howey Co. owned large citrus groves in Florida. It sold these trees to investors, most of whom were from out of state and knew nothing about farming. Purchasers were expected to hire someone to take care of their trees—someone like Howey-in the-Hills, Inc., a related company that just happened to be in the service business. Customers were free to hire any service company, but 85 percent of the acreage was covered by service contracts with Howey-in-the-Hills. The court held that Howey was selling a security (no matter how orange or tart), because the purchaser was investing in a common enterprise (the orange grove) expecting to earn a profit from Howey's farmwork.

Other courts have interpreted the term "security" to include animal breeding arrangements (chinchillas, silver foxes, or beavers, take your pick); condominium purchases in which the developer promises the owner a certain level of income from rentals; and even investments in whiskey.

Securities Act of 1933

The 1933 Act requires that before offering or selling securities, the issuer must register the securities with the SEC unless the securities qualify for an exemption. An **issuer** is the company that sells the stock initially. Registering securities with the SEC in a public offering is a major undertaking, but the 1933 Act exempts some securities and also some particular types of securities transactions from the full-blown registration requirements of a public offering.

Issuer
A company that sells its own stock.

It is also important to remember that **when an issuer registers securities, the SEC does not investigate the quality of the offering.** Permission from the SEC to sell securities does not mean that the company has a good product or will be successful. SEC approval simply means that, on the surface, the company has provided all required information about itself and its major products. The guiding principle of the federal securities laws is that investors can make a reasoned decision on whether to buy or sell securities if they have full and accurate information about a company and the security it is selling. For example, the Green Bay Packers football team sold an offering of stock to finance stadium improvements. The prospectus admitted:

> IT IS VIRTUALLY IMPOSSIBLE that any investor will ever make a profit on the stock purchase. The company will pay no dividends, and the shares cannot be sold.

This does not sound like a stock you want in your retirement fund; on the other hand, the SEC will not prevent Green Bay from selling it, or you from buying it, so long as you understand what the risks are.

Companies must deliver certain documents to investors and also file them with the SEC. Almost all filings with the SEC must be made electronically, using the Electronic Data Gathering, Analysis, and Retrieval (EDGAR) system. Once filed with the SEC, this information is available online (at **http://www.sec.gov**).

General Exemption

Before offering securities for sale, the issuer must determine whether they are exempt from registration under the 1933 Act. Typically, exemptions are based on two factors: the type of security and the type of transaction.

Exempt Securities

The 1933 Act exempts some types of securities from registration because they (1) are inherently low-risk, (2) are regulated by other statutes, or (3) are not really investments. The following securities are exempt from registration:

- **Government securities,** which include any security issued or guaranteed by federal or state government;
- **Bank securities,** which include any security issued or guaranteed by a bank;
- **Short-term notes,** which are high-quality negotiable notes or drafts that are due within nine months of issuance and are not sold to the general public;
- **Nonprofit issues,** which include any security issued by a nonprofit religious, educational, or charitable organization; and
- **Insurance policies and annuity contracts,** which are governed by insurance regulations.

Exempt Transactions

Section 4(2) of the 1933 Act exempts from registration "transactions by an issuer not involving any public offering." These are simple words to define a complex problem. In effect, this language means that an issuer is not required to register securities that are sold in a private offering; that is, an offering with only a few investors or a relatively small amount of money involved. In private offerings, the full-blown disclosure of a public offering is neither necessary nor appropriate. For instance, a group of sophisticated investors who know an industry well do not need full disclosure. Or, if the amount at stake is relatively small, it would not make economic sense for the issuer to incur the heavy expense of a public offering.

There is an important distinction between exempt *securities* and exempt *transactions*. Exempt *securities* are always exempt, throughout their lives, no matter how many times they are sold. Stock sold in an exempt *transaction* is exempt only that one time, not necessarily in any subsequent sale. Suppose that County Bank sells stock to the public. Under the 1933 Act, the bank is never required to register these securities, no matter how many times they are sold. On the other hand, suppose that Tumbleweed, Inc., a quilt maker, sells $5 million worth of stock in a private offering that is exempt from registration. Shamika buys 100 shares of this stock. Seven years later, the company decides to sell stock in a public offering that must be registered. As part of this public offering, Shamika sells her 100 shares. This time, the shares must be registered because they are being sold in a *public offering*.

Most small companies use private, not public, offerings to raise capital. There are three different types of private offerings—intrastate, Regulation D, and Regulation A—each with its own set of rules.

The first time this quilt maker sold shares in her company, they were exempt from registration. They will not necessarily be exempt in subsequent sales.

Intrastate Offering Exemption

Under SEC Rule 147, an issuer is not required to register securities that are *offered* and *sold* only to residents of the state in which the issuer is incorporated and does business. This exemption was designed to provide local financing for local businesses. To qualify under Rule 147, 80 percent of the issuer's revenues and assets must be in-state, and it must also intend to spend 80 percent of the offering's proceeds in-state. Neither the issuer nor any purchaser can sell the securities outside the state for nine months after the offering.

Rule 147 is a **safe harbor**—if an issuer totally complies with it, the offering definitely qualifies as intrastate. But even if the issuer does not comply absolutely with the rule, the SEC or the courts may still consider the offering to be intrastate; however, the issuer cannot be sure in advance how the decision will come out. Sonic was a Utah corporation that sold stock to Utah residents. *Seven* months later, the company sold stock to an Illinois company. Although Sonic violated Rule 147 by making the second sale too early, the court held that the company had nonetheless qualified for an intrastate offering because it had not intended, at the time of the original offering, to sell stock outside Utah.[2] A safe harbor is less dangerous, but a voyage outside its boundaries does not necessarily end in disaster.

Safe Harbor
A set of requirements that, if met, indicate *automatic* compliance with a law.

Regulation D

Regulation D is far and away the most popular route for private offerings. Tens of thousands of these offerings take place each year. Three different types of private offerings can be made under Regulation D (often referred to as Reg D) using Rules 504, 505, and 506. To understand Reg D, there are several important definitions you need to know:

- **Accredited investors** are institutions (such as banks and insurance companies) or wealthy individuals. To qualify, individuals must have a net worth (not counting their home) of more than $1 million or an annual income of more than $200,000.
- **Sophisticated investors** Are *unsophisticated* investors people who do not care for opera? No, they are investors who are unable to assess the risks of an offering themselves.
- **Restricted stock** means the securities must be purchased for investment purposes. As a general rule, the buyer cannot resell, either publicly or privately, for one year.

Accredited investors
Institutions (such as banks and insurance companies) or wealthy individuals. To qualify, individuals must have a net worth (not counting their home) of more than $1 million or an annual income of more than $200,000).

Sophisticated investor
Someone who is able to assess the risk of an offering.

Restricted stock
Securities purchased strictly for investment purposes.

Rule 504. Under this rule (known as the "seed capital" rule), you may either:

- Sell up to $1 million in restricted stock privately to anyone during each 12-month period; or,
- Sell up to $1 million in non-restricted stock with public advertising if the transaction is registered under a state law with appropriate disclosure requirements; or,
- Sell up to $1 million in non-restricted stock with public advertising if the transaction is exempted under a state law and sales are limited to accredited investors.

Rule 505. You may sell up to $5 million of stock during each 12-month period, subject to the following restrictions:

- You may sell to an unlimited number of accredited investors, but to only 35 unaccredited investors.
- You may not advertise the stock publicly.

[2] *Busch v. Carpenter*, 827 F.2d 653, 1987 U.S. App. LEXIS 11034 (10th Cir. 1987).

- You need not provide information to accredited investors but must make disclosure to unaccredited investors, including a certified balance sheet. This requirement is a high hurdle because the disclosure requirements, although less demanding than for a public offering, are nonetheless burdensome.
- Stock purchased under this rule is restricted.

Rule 506. You may sell an unlimited amount of stock, subject to the following restrictions:

- You may sell to an unlimited number of accredited investors, but to only 35 unaccredited investors.
- You may not advertise the stock publicly.
- You need not provide information to accredited investors but must make disclosure to unaccredited investors, including a certified balance sheet.
- Stock purchased under this rule is restricted.
- One further wrinkle: if an unaccredited purchaser is unsophisticated, he must have a **purchaser representative** to help him evaluate the investment.

The following table sets out the menu of choices under Reg D:

	Maximum Value of Securities Sold in a 12-Month Period	Maximum Number of Investors	Disclosure Required:	Is Public Advertising Permitted?	Are Securities Restricted?
Rule 504 Option 1:	$1 million	Unlimited	None	No	Yes
Option 2:	$1 million	Unlimited	Appropriate state disclosure	Yes	No
Option 3:	$1 million, provided offering is exempt under state law	Unlimited accredited investors	None	Yes	No
Rule 505	$5 million	No limit on accredited investors; no more than 35 unaccredited investors	Only for unaccredited investors	No	Yes
Rule 506	No limit	No limit on accredited investors; no more than 35 unaccredited investors, who must either be sophisticated or have a purchaser representative	Only for unaccredited investors	No	Yes

Regulation A

Although an offering under Regulation A (Reg A) is *called* a private offering, it really is a small public offering. **Reg A permits an issuer to sell up to $5 million of securities *publicly* in any 12-month period.** The issuer must give each purchaser an offering circular that provides the same disclosure required for unaccredited investors under Reg D. Stock sold in a Reg A offering is not restricted.

The following table compares a public offering, Reg A, and Reg D:

	Initial Public Offering	**Regulation A**	**Regulation D**
Maximum Value of Securities Sold	No limit	$5 million	$1 million, $5 million, or no limit, depending on the rule
Public Solicitation of Purchasers	Permitted	Permitted	Permitted only under Rule 504
Suitability Requirements for Purchasers	No requirements	No requirements	Must determine if investors are accredited or sophisticated
Disclosure Requirements	Elaborate registration statement, audited financials	Offering circular that is less detailed than a registration statement, unaudited financials	Rule 504: may require disclosure under state law Rules 505 and 506: none for accredited investors, the same requirements as Reg A for unaccredited investors
Resale of Securities	Permitted	Permitted	Sometimes permitted under Rule 504, otherwise not permitted for one year

Direct Public Offerings

Traditionally, a small company either sold stock to people it knew well or hired an investment banker to place the securities with a wider public. But now, instead of going through Wall Street, many companies trying to raise capital for the first time sell stock to the public themselves through a direct public offering (DPO). In a DPO, the issuer typically sells shares to its stakeholders: customers, employees, suppliers, or the community. The issuer makes a DPO offering under Rule 147, Reg D, or Reg A.

Selling stock to the public without the help of an investment bank can be challenging. Thanksgiving Coffee Co. used both modern technology and old-fashioned methods. It advertised on its website but also placed ads on bags of coffee beans, in its catalogs, and in notices to suppliers. The company raised $1.25 million.

The advantages of a DPO are:

- It is much cheaper and faster than a regular public offering done through an underwriter.
- It can be an effective marketing tool—shareholders tend to become even more loyal customers.
- The Internet provides an easy and inexpensive mechanism for reaching potential investors.

The downsides of a DPO are:

- There is a limit to how much a company can raise in this way.
- Company officers typically do not have as much expertise about the securities markets as securities lawyers, investment bankers, and other professionals do.
- Each investor must receive written information about the company. The cost of this disclosure can be prohibitive when dealing with many small investors. Mailing a $10 disclosure document to hundreds of investors who only want to buy $50 worth of stock each may not be an efficient means of raising money.
- Although shareholders are warned that they should view their purchases as long-term investments, some will inevitably want to sell their shares. Setting up a system to permit these trades can be tricky and time-consuming.

EXAM Strategy

Question: As a pitcher for the Cleveland Indians farm team, Randy Newsom had dreams of glory but a paycheck that was a nightmare—$8,000 for the season. Newsom came up with a clever solution: he set up a website that offered fans the opportunity to buy a share of his future. For only $20, the buyer was entitled to .002 percent of his career pay. Any problems with this plan?

Strategy: Remember that even orange trees can be securities.

Result: Newsom was selling securities: buyers were investing in him, hoping that they could earn a profit from his efforts. He had neither registered the securities nor qualified for an exemption, so his plan was illegal.

Public Offerings

When a company wishes to raise significant amounts of capital from a large number of people, it has to do a public offering. A company's first public sale of securities is called **an initial public offering** or an **IPO.** Because companies are now more successful in raising money privately, the number of IPOs has declined from an annual average of around 500 in the 1990s to a current average of about 130. Any public sale of securities after the IPO is called a **secondary offering**. This is the process an issuer follows for either type of sale:

Initial public offering (IPO)
A company's first public sale of securities.

Secondary offering
Any public sale of securities by a company after the initial public offering.

Firm commitment underwriting
The underwriter buys stock from the issuer and sells it to the public.

Best efforts underwriting
The underwriter does not buy the stock from the issuer but instead acts as the issuer's agent in selling the securities.

1. *Underwriting.* For a public offering, companies hire an investment bank to serve as underwriter. In a **firm commitment underwriting**, the underwriter buys the stock from the issuer and resells it to the public. The underwriter bears the risk that the stock may sell at a lower price than expected. In a **best efforts underwriting**, the underwriter does not buy the stock but instead acts as the company's agent in selling it. If the stock sells at a low price, the company, not the underwriter, is the loser.

2. *Registration statement.* The **registration statement** has two purposes: to notify the SEC that a sale of securities is pending and to disclose information to prospective purchasers. The registration statement typically must include detailed information about the issuer and its business, a description of the stock, the proposed use of the proceeds from the offering, and two years of audited balance sheets and income statements. But the amount of required disclosure depends on the issuer—more disclosure is required for an IPO than for an offering by a so-called "well-known seasoned issuer." Preparing a registration statement is neither quick nor inexpensive— a typical IPO recently cost $8 million.

3. *Prospectus.* Typically, buyers never see the registration statement; they are given the **prospectus** instead. (The prospectus is included in the registration statement that is sent to the SEC.) The prospectus includes the important disclosures about the company, while the registration statement includes additional information that is of interest to the SEC but not to the typical investor, such as the names and addresses of the lawyers for the issuer and underwriter. All investors must receive a copy of the prospectus before purchasing the stock.

4. *Sales effort.* Even before the final registration statement and prospectus are completed, the investment bank begins its sales effort. It cannot actually make sales during this period, but it can solicit offers. The SEC closely regulates an issuer's sales effort to make sure that no one is unduly hyping the stock. For example, the SEC delayed an offering of stock by Google Inc. after *Playboy* magazine published an interview with its founders.

5. *Going effective.* Once its review of the preliminary registration statement is complete, the SEC sends the issuer a **comment letter**, listing changes that must be made to the registration statement. An issuer almost always amends the registration statement at least once, and sometimes more than once. Remember that the SEC does not assess the value of the stock or the merit of the investment. Its role is to ensure that the company has disclosed enough to enable investors to make an informed decision. After the SEC has approved a final registration statement (which includes, of course, the final prospectus), the issuer and underwriter agree on a price for the stock and the date to **go effective;** that is, to begin the sale.

In the following case, eToys sued its underwriter, Goldman Sachs, for underpricing its stock offering. Should Goldman be liable? You be the judge.

You be the Judge

EBC I, Inc. v. Goldman Sachs & Co.

2005 N.Y. LEXIS 1178
Court of Appeals of New York, 2005

Facts: Goldman Sachs was the lead underwriter for eToys' initial public offering. In the IPO, eToys agreed to sell 8,320,000 shares of its stock to Goldman at a price of $18.65 per share, for resale to the public at $20. (Goldman had the option to buy an additional 1,248,000 shares at the same price.) The bank's potential profit was $1.35 per share, for a maximum of $12,916,800.

On the first day of the offering, the price of eToys' stock rose as high as $85 and closed at $76.56. Within a year, however, the price had fallen below $20. eToys ultimately filed for bankruptcy protection.

In its lawsuit, eToys alleged that Goldman made side deals with other clients, allowing them to purchase shares in eToys' offering in exchange for kickbacks to Goldman of a portion of their profits on the stock. This arrangement would have created an incentive for Goldman to underprice the stock. eToys also alleged that Goldman had a fiduciary duty to eToys that it violated by not disclosing this conflict of interest.

Goldman filed a motion to dismiss, denying that it had a fiduciary relationship to eToys.

You Be the Judge: ***Did Goldman have a fiduciary duty to eToys? Did it violate this duty?***

Argument for eToys: A fiduciary relationship exists between two parties if one of them is under a duty to act for or to give advice for the benefit of the other. eToys hired Goldman for its expertise and paid handsomely for its advice about many aspects of going public. The company would never have relied on this advice had it known about the side deals with other clients—deals that could harm eToys.

eToys trusted Goldman, the bank betrayed that trust, and eToys suffered an enormous financial penalty as a result.

Argument for Goldman Sachs: This is a simple case: eToys sold stock, Goldman bought it. Goldman negotiated the best price it could. If eToys was unhappy with this deal, it had no one to blame but itself.

If eToys expected Goldman to act as a fiduciary, the agreement should have said so explicitly. The company always knew that its interests were different from Goldman's. eToys sought the highest price; Goldman had to ensure that it could resell the shares at a profit. The lower the price to eToys, the lower the risk to Goldman. Goldman took a substantial risk buying this stock, and in this case, the risk paid off. That does not always happen.

eToys was a sophisticated company with sophisticated advisors. Its stockholders included well-known venture-capital firms. Its largest single stockholder, Idealab, was an incubator for successful technology companies. eToys' law firm—the Venture Law Group, P.C.—specialized in representing high-tech companies. During one year, this law firm was fourth on the list of firms that handled the most initial public offerings for technology companies.

In short, the offering price was not "set" by Goldman; it was negotiated by two sophisticated parties.

Sales of Restricted Securities

The SEC wants to ensure that the public sale of stock takes place in an orderly manner. Therefore, it imposes some restrictions on the sale of stock even after a company has gone public. **Rule 144 limits the resale of two types of securities issued by public companies: *control securities* and *restricted securities*.**

A **restricted security** is any stock purchased from the issuer in a private offering (such as Reg D). If the issuer is private (that is, not subject to the reporting requirements of the 1934 Act), these restricted securities cannot be sold for one year. But, once the company goes public, the holding period on restricted securities shrinks to six months from the date of purchase. After six months, these restricted securities can be sold freely unless they are also control securities, in which case those restrictions still apply.

Control security
Stock held by any shareholder who owns more than 10 percent of a class of stock or by any officer or director of the company.

A **control security** is stock held by any shareholder who owns more than 10 percent of a class of stock or by any officer or director of the company. In any three-month period, such an insider can sell only an amount of stock equal to the average weekly trading volume for the prior four weeks or 1 percent of the number of shares outstanding, whichever is greater. The purpose of this rule is to protect other investors from precipitous declines in stock price. If company insiders sold all of their stock in one day, the price would plunge, causing losses to the other shareholders.

EXAM Strategy

Question: You are the CEO of Calmm.com, Inc. The company's board has decided to sell $2 million in stock. You have 40 wealthy friends who would like to invest a total of $1 million. What would be the best way to raise these funds? Would a public offering work?

Strategy: Review the options for both private and public offerings.

Result: A public offering is not a good idea—it would cost millions. Rule 504 is not suitable because it would limit you to raising only $1 million. Under Rule 505, you could sell to all your wealthy friends (if they are accredited investors), and as many as 35 unaccredited investors. Rule 506 is more complicated (and therefore more expensive), so Rule 505 would be a better choice.

Liability Under the 1933 Act

Liability for Selling Unregistered Securities

Section 12(a)(1) of the 1933 Act imposes liability on anyone who sells a security that is neither registered nor exempt. The purchaser of the security can demand rescission—a return of his money (plus interest) in exchange for the stock—or, if he no longer owns the stock, he can ask for damages.

Fraud

Under Section 12(a)(2) of the 1933 Act, **the seller of a security is liable for making any material misstatement or omission, either oral or written, in connection with the offer or sale of a security.** This provision applies to offerings that are *public* or *private* and *registered* or *unregistered* if there is some use of interstate commerce, such as mail, telephone (even for an *intra*state call), or check (that clears). It is difficult to imagine a securities transaction that does not involve interstate commerce. Both the SEC and any purchasers of the stock can sue the issuer.

Criminal Liability

Under Section 24 of the 1933 Act, the Justice Department can prosecute anyone who willfully violates the Act.

Liability for the Registration Statement

Section 11 of the 1933 Act establishes the penalties for any errors in a registration statement. **If a final registration statement contains a material misstatement or omission, the purchaser of the security can recover from everyone who signed the registration statement.** This list of signatories includes the issuer, its directors, and chief officers; experts (such as auditors, engineers, or lawyers); and the underwriters. Everyone who signed the registration statement is jointly and severally liable for any error, except the experts, who are liable only for misstatements in the part of the registration statement for which they were responsible.[3] Thus, an auditor is liable for misstatements in the financials but not, say, for omissions about the CEO's criminal past.

Damages. To prevail under Section 11, the plaintiff need only prove that there was a material misstatement or omission and that she lost money. **Material** means important enough to affect an investor's decision. The plaintiff does not have to prove that she relied on (or even *read*) the registration statement, that she bought the stock from the issuer, or that the defendant was negligent. The plaintiff can recover the difference between what she paid for the stock and its value on the date of the lawsuit.

Material
Important enough to affect an investor's decision.

Suppose that Pet Detective, Inc., does an IPO at $10 per share. A week later, Ace Investora buys 1,000 shares at $10 each. He knows nothing about the company, but he likes the name. This stock turns out to be a dog—Pet Detective has only 2 agencies, not the 200 stated in the registration statement. After Investora sells the stock at 10 cents a share, he can sue under Section 11 for $9,900.

Due Diligence. All is not hopeless, however, for those who have signed the registration statement. If the statement contains a material misstatement or omission, the company is liable and has no defense. But everyone else who signed the registration statement can avoid liability by showing that he investigated the registration statement as thoroughly as a "prudent person in the management of his own property." This investigation is called **due diligence**. Its importance cannot be overstated. The SEC does not conduct its own investigation to ensure that the registration statement is accurate. It can only ensure that, on the surface, the issuer has supplied all relevant information. If an issuer chooses to lie, the SEC has no way of knowing. It is the job of the underwriters to check the accuracy of the filing. Thus, underwriters typically spend weeks visiting the company, reading all its corporate documents (including minutes back to the beginning), and calling its bankers, customers, suppliers, and competitors to ensure that the registration statement is accurate and no skeletons have been overlooked.

Due diligence
An investigation of the registration statement by someone who signs it.

When Section 11 was first passed, investment bankers were outraged. Some predicted that this liability provision would cause capital in America to dry up, that grass would grow on Wall Street. In fact, the first case under Section 11 arose 35 years and 27,000 registration statements later. In this case—*Escott v. Barchris Construction Corp.*—the registration statement was profoundly flawed.[4] The underwriter failed to read the minutes of the executive committee meetings that revealed the company to be in serious financial condition. Much of the company's alleged backlog of orders was from nonexistent corporations. Proceeds of the offering were earmarked to pay off debt, not to buy new plant

---

[3]Joint and several liability means that all members of a group are liable. The plaintiff can sue them as a group or anyone of them individually for the full amount owing. The plaintiff cannot recover more than the total amount of the damages owing, however.

[4]283 F. Supp. 643, 1968 U.S. Dist. LEXIS 3853 (S.D.N.Y. 1968).

and equipment as the registration statement had indicated. The company's directors, underwriters, and underwriters' counsel were held liable.

SECURITIES EXCHANGE ACT OF 1934

Most buyers do not purchase new securities from the issuer in an initial public offering. Rather they buy stock that is publicly traded in the open market. This stock is, in a sense, *secondhand* because others, perhaps many others, have already owned it. The purpose of the 1934 Act is to maintain the integrity of this secondary market.

General Provisions of the 1934 Act

Registration Requirements

As we have seen, the 1933 Act requires an issuer to register securities before selling them. That is a onetime effort for the company. The 1933 Act does not require the issuer to provide shareholders with any additional information in later years. Suppose that an automobile company registered and sold securities for the first time in 1946. Purchasers of those securities knew a lot about the firm—in 1946. But how can current investors assess the company? The 1934 Act plugs this hole. It requires issuers with publicly traded stock to continue to make information available to the public so that current—and potential—shareholders can evaluate the company. It is often said that the 1933 Act registers securities and the 1934 Act registers companies.

Under the 1934 Act, an issuer must register with the SEC if (1) it completes a public offering under the 1933 Act, or (2) its securities are traded on a national exchange (such as the NYSE), or (3) it has at least 500 shareholders *and* total assets that exceed $10 million. A company can *de*register if its number of shareholders falls below 300 or if it has fewer than 500 shareholders and assets of less than $10 million.

Disclosure Requirements—Section 13

Reporting Company
A company registered under the 1934 Act.

Like the 1933 Act, the 1934 Act focuses on disclosure. The difference is that the 1933 Act requires onetime disclosure when a company sells stock to the public. The 1934 Act requires ***ongoing,*** regular disclosure for any company with a class of stock that is publicly traded. Companies that register under the 1934 Act are called **reporting companies. Section 13 requires reporting companies to file the following documents:**

- An initial, detailed information statement when the company first registers (similar to the filing required under the 1933 Act);
- Annual reports on Form 10-K, containing audited financial statements, a detailed analysis of the company's performance, and information about officers and directors;
- Quarterly reports on Form 10-Q, which are less detailed than 10-Ks and contain unaudited financials; and
- Form 8-K to report any significant developments, such as bankruptcy, a change in control, a purchase or sale of significant assets, the resignation of a director as a result of a policy dispute, a change in fiscal year, or a change in auditing firms.

In response to corporate scandals, Congress passed the Sarbanes-Oxley Act of 2002 (SOX). It requires each company's CEO and CFO to certify that:

- The information in the quarterly and annual reports is true;
- The company has effective internal controls; and

- The officers have informed the company's audit committee and its auditors of any concerns that they have about the internal control system.

A reporting company must send its annual report to shareholders. All annual reports and other 1934 Act filings are available on the SEC website.

New Developments: The Facebook Problem

The SEC faces a new challenge in regulating private companies. Traditionally, companies went public when a small number of investors could no longer provide sufficient capital. But some young, sought-after companies in California, such as Facebook, Twitter, and Zynga, have the opposite problem—so many people want to buy their stock that they may be forced to go public.

Most of these companies' stock is owned by venture capitalists who originally bought stock in a private offering or employees who were granted stock options as part of their compensation. Now that the stock is so valuable, these shareholders want to cash out. Private exchanges (such as SecondMarket and SharesPost) have developed to help shareholders sell their stock to the many willing buyers.

As private companies, these businesses are not required to make any ongoing financial disclosure. Lots of investors are willing to buy anyway. But once an enterprise has 500 shareholders (and $10 million in assets), it becomes a public company and must comply with the disclosure requirements of the 1934 Act. However, going public carries some serious burdens: it costs at least $5 million a year to comply with SEC regulations, and public shareholders sometimes pressure companies to take a short-term view—they want profits now.

Should Facebook (and other enterprises like it) be forced to go public even though investors are willing to buy stock without the financial disclosure required of public companies? The SEC and Facebook have already reached one compromise—shareholders who own restricted stock do not count towards the 500 limit. For its part, Facebook no longer allows current employees to sell stock and, indeed, now gives new employees "restricted units" that convert into stock when the company goes public.

At this writing, the SEC has notified Congress that it is reviewing all the regulations that govern private sales of stock, and, in particular, it will consider:

- Raising the limit on the number of shareholders in a private company above 499.
- Permitting private companies greater leeway in advertising stock sales.
- Permitting the use of so-called crowd-funding methods for raising capital. (Crowd-funding is a method in which business owners use the Internet to raise small amounts of money from small investments—say, $100,000 raised by selling shares at $100 each.)

Those in favor of these reforms argue that they will encourage investment and job growth, while opponents fear that reduced disclosure will facilitate fraud.

Proxy Requirements—Section 14

As discussed in Chapter 35, most shareholders of public corporations do not attend annual shareholder meetings. Instead, the company solicits their proxies, permitting them to vote by mail rather than in person. If a company solicits proxies, it is required to supply shareholders with a proxy statement that is intended to give them enough information to make informed decisions about the company. The proxy statement contains detailed information about officers and directors, including their experience, relationship with the company, and compensation. (The annual report provides financial information.) Proxy statements must also be filed with the SEC. Proxy contests and shareholder proposals are discussed in Chapter 35.

Under SEC rules, a company is not *required* to solicit proxies from shareholders, but if it does not, it is unlikely to obtain the quorum needed for the meeting to be held. In any event, a company cannot avoid its responsibility to inform shareholders. Whether or not it solicits proxies, it is still required to furnish shareholders with an information statement that contains essentially the same material as a proxy statement.

Short-Swing Trading—Section 16

During congressional hearings after the 1929 stock market crash, witnesses testified that insiders had manipulated the stock market. For example, insiders would buy a large block of stock, announce a substantial dividend, and then divest before the dividend was reduced. Section 16 was designed to prevent corporate insiders—officers, directors, and shareholders who own more than 10 percent of the company—from taking unfair advantage of privileged information to manipulate the market.

Section 16 takes a two-pronged approach:

- First, insiders must **report** their trades within two business days. This report must also reveal their total stock holdings in the company. The filings must be made to the SEC electronically, and both the SEC and the company are required to post them on their respective websites within one business day after the report is made.
- Second, insiders must **turn over to the corporation** any profits they make from the purchase and sale or sale and purchase of company securities in a six-month period. Section 16 is a strict liability provision. It applies even if the insider did not actually take advantage of secret information or try to manipulate the market; if she bought and sold or sold and bought stock in a six-month period, she is liable.

Suppose that Manuela buys 20,000 shares of her company's stock in June at $10 a share. In September, her (uninsured) winter house in Florida is destroyed by a hurricane. To raise money for rebuilding, she sells the stock at $12 per share, making a profit of $40,000. But she has violated Section 16 and must turn over the profit to her company.

Liability Under the 1934 Act

Section 18

Under Section 18, anyone who makes a false or misleading statement in a filing under the 1934 Act is liable to buyers or sellers who (1) acted in reliance on the statement and (2) can prove that the price at which they bought or sold was affected by the false filing. Section 18 applies to all filings under the 1934 Act, including proxy statements and annual reports. For example, a court ruled that plaintiffs could bring suit against the directors and officers of a pharmaceutical company that manufactured a contraceptive device called the Dalkon Shield. In its annual report filed with the SEC, the company emphasized the safety, reliability, and efficiency of the Dalkon Shield, failing to reveal that in fact, there was substantial evidence that the device was less effective and more harmful than it had disclosed. Indeed, seven women had died from using the Dalkon Shield, and many others were rendered infertile.[5]

Section 10(b)

Section 18 applies only to *filings* under the 1934 Act. What happens if a company executive makes a false public *statement* about the company, or writes an untrue statement somewhere other than in a filing? In one case, a corporate officer bought up shares of his company's stock even as he made pessimistic public statements about the company. That is the type of behavior that Section 10(b) is designed to prevent. **Section 10(b) prohibits**

[5] *Ross v. A. H. Robins Co.*, 607 F.2d 545, (2d Cir, 1979).

fraud in connection with the purchase and sale of any security, whether or not the security is registered under the 1934 Act.

The SEC adopted Rule 10b-5 to clarify Section 10(b), but the rule is still a relatively vague, catch-all provision designed to fill any holes left by other sections of the securities laws.[6] Interpretation has largely been left to the courts, which generally have interpreted Rule 10b-5 as follows:

- **A misstatement or omission of a material fact.** Anyone who fails to disclose material information, or makes incomplete or inaccurate disclosure, is liable.
- **The term "material"** has the same meaning as under the 1933 Act: important enough to affect an investor's decision. For example, a company repeatedly and falsely denied that it was involved in merger negotiations. It was liable even though the negotiations had only been in a preliminary stage.[7]
- **Scienter.** This is a legal term meaning *willfully, knowingly, or recklessly*. To be liable under Rule 10b-5, the defendant must have (1) known (or been reckless in not knowing) that the statement was inaccurate and (2) intended for the plaintiff to rely on the statement. Negligence is not enough. A group of shareholders sued the accounting firm Ernst & Ernst because it had failed to discover, during the course of an audit, that a company's chief executive was stealing funds. According to the shareholders, the auditors should have discovered that the executive refused to allow anyone else to open his mail and, therefore, should have been suspicious of wrongdoing. The court found Ernst & Ernst not liable. Although it may have been negligent, it had not *intentionally* or even *recklessly* facilitated fraud.[8]
- **Purchase or sale.** Rule 10b-5 covers both buyers and sellers. It does not include, however, someone who failed to purchase stock because of a material misstatement. In the case of the company executive who spread negative rumors about his company while he bought stock, those who sold because of his false rumors could sue under Rule 10b-5, but not those who simply failed to buy.
- **Reliance.** To bring suit, a plaintiff must show that she relied on the misstatement or omission. In the case of open-market trades, reliance is difficult to prove, so the courts are willing to assume it.
- **Economic loss.** The plaintiffs must suffer a loss in the value of their investment. For example, a couple sold their pharmaceutical business to another company in exchange for stock of the purchaser. Some time later, they discovered that the purchaser had lied about its financial condition. However, the court held that the couple could not recover because by the time they sold their stock in the purchaser, it was worth substantially more than when they acquired it. Thus, they had not suffered an economic loss.
- **Loss causation.** The economic loss must have been caused by the misstatement of a material fact. For example, a group of investors bought stock in Dura

[6]Rule 10b-5 prohibits any person, in connection with a purchase or sale of any security, from (1) employing any device, scheme, or artifice to defraud; (2) making any untrue statement of a material fact or omitting to state a material fact necessary in order to make the statements made, in light of the circumstances under which they were made, not misleading; or (3) engaging in any act, practice, or course of business that operates or would operate as a fraud or deceit upon any person.

[7]*Basic Inc. v. Levinson*, 485 U.S. 224, 108 S. Ct. 978, 1988 U.S. LEXIS 1197 (1988).

[8]*Ernst & Ernst v. Hochfelder*, 425 U.S. 185, 96 S. Ct. 1375, 1976 U.S. LEXIS 2 (1976).

> Pharmaceuticals. They alleged that, when making the purchase, they had relied on statements by company executives that (1) its drug sales would be profitable and (2) the Food and Drug Administration would approve its new asthma spray device. Neither of these statements turned out to be true, and the company's stock price fell. Plaintiffs argued that, if it had not been for the misrepresentations, the stock price would have been lower when they purchased stock and then would not have fallen as far (or at all) when the truth came out.

The Supreme Court ruled, however, that the plaintiffs could not recover because there was no proof that the misstatements had *caused* the decline in stock price. The price drop could have been the result of other factors, such as changes in the industry or in the economy as a whole.[9]

Both the 1933 Act and the 1934 Act specify that misstatements and omissions create liability only if they are material. In the following case, a unanimous Supreme Court provided guidance on what "material" means.

MATRIXX INITIATIVES, INC. V. SIRACUSANO

2011 U.S. LEXIS 2416
Supreme Court of the United States, 2011

Facts: Zicam Cold Remedy was a nasal spray (or gel) that accounted for 70 percent of Matrixx's sales revenue. Its active ingredient was zinc gluconate. Matrixx began receiving reports that some Zicam users had developed anosmia (that is, they had lost their sense of smell). The company learned for the first time that some studies had linked the use of zinc sulfate to the loss of smell.

Matrixx then found out that two doctors were planning to make a presentation at a conference about patients who had developed anosmia after Zicam use. Matrixx sent them a letter warning them that they did not have permission to use the name of Matrixx or its products. The doctors deleted references to Zicam.

Nine people filed suit against Matrixx, alleging that Zicam had damaged their sense of smell. Matrixx then issued statements that Zicam was poised for growth and that revenues would increase by more than 80 percent. In its 10-Q filing with the SEC, Matrixx warned of the potential "'material adverse effect' that could result from product liability claims, "whether or not proven to be valid." It did not disclose, however, that plaintiffs had already sued Matrixx.

After the Food and Drug Administration (FDA) announced that it was investigating Zicam, Matrixx's stock price fell. Matrixx issued a press release stating:

> Matrixx believes statements alleging that Zicam products caused anosmia (loss of smell) are completely unfounded and misleading. In no clinical trial of zinc gluconate gel products has there been a single report of lost or diminished olfactory function (sense of smell). A multitude of environmental and biologic influences are known to affect the sense of smell. Chief among them is the common cold. As a result, the population most likely to use cold remedy products is already at increased risk of developing anosmia.

The day after this press release, Matrixx stock price bounced back. Shortly thereafter, however, the TV show *Good Morning America* reported that more than a dozen patients had suffered from anosmia after using Zicam and that some had filed lawsuits against Matrixx. The company's stock price plummeted.

A group of shareholders filed suit, alleging that Matrixx had violated Section 10(b) and Rule 10b-5. The trial court granted Matrixx's motion to dismiss on the grounds that, without a statistical correlation between the use of Zicam and anosmia, the reported incidents were not material. The Court of Appeals reversed. The Supreme Court granted *certiorari*.

---

[9]*Dura Pharmaceuticals, Inc. v. Broudo*, 125 S. Ct. 1627, 2005 U.S. LEXIS 3478 (2005).

Issues: ***Was Matrixx required to disclose allegations of harm for which there was not statistical correlation? Did Matrixx violate §10(b) and Rule 10b-5?***

Excerpts from Justice Sotomayor's Decision, writing for a unanimous court: To prevail on a §10(b) claim, a plaintiff must show that the defendant made a statement that was *misleading* as to a *material* fact. [T]his materiality requirement is satisfied when there is a substantial likelihood that the disclosure of the omitted fact would have been viewed by the reasonable investor as having significantly altered the "total mix" of information made available.

[M]edical researchers consider multiple factors in assessing causation. A lack of statistically significant data does not mean that medical experts have no reliable basis for inferring a causal link between a drug and adverse events. Not only does the FDA rely on a wide range of evidence of causation, it sometimes acts on the basis of evidence that suggests, but does not prove, causation. For example, the FDA requires manufacturers of over-the-counter drugs to revise their labeling to include a warning as soon as there is reasonable evidence of an association of a serious hazard with a drug; a causal relationship need not have been proved.

Given that medical professionals and regulators act on the basis of evidence of causation that is not statistically significant, it stands to reason that in certain cases, reasonable investors would as well. As a result, assessing the materiality of adverse event reports is a fact-specific inquiry that requires consideration of the source, content, and context of the reports.

Application of [the] "total mix" standard does not mean that pharmaceutical manufacturers must disclose all reports of adverse events. Adverse event reports are daily events in the pharmaceutical industry. The fact that a user of a drug has suffered an adverse event, standing alone, does not mean that the drug caused that event. Something more is needed, but that something more is not limited to statistical significance.

Moreover, it bears emphasis that §10(b) and Rule 10b-5(b) do not create an affirmative duty to disclose any and all material information. Disclosure is required under these provisions only when necessary to make statements made, in the light of the circumstances under which they were made, not misleading. Even with respect to information that a reasonable investor might consider material, companies can control what they have to disclose under these provisions by controlling what they say to the market.

[W]e conclude that respondents have adequately pleaded materiality. Matrixx received information that plausibly indicated a reliable causal link between Zicam and anosmia. Importantly, Zicam Cold Remedy accounted for 70 percent of Matrixx's sales.

It is substantially likely that a reasonable investor would have viewed this information as having significantly altered the "total mix" of information made available. Matrixx told the market that revenues were going to rise 50 and then 80 percent. [H]owever, Matrixx had information indicating a significant risk to its leading revenue-generating product.

For the reasons stated, the judgment of the Court of Appeals for the Ninth Circuit is

Affirmed.

Ethics Matrixx learned that its products were potentially causing a loss of smell, which is no minor matter. People with anosmia cannot properly taste food, so they often lose interest in eating, which can lead to malnutrition and depression. Was it ethical for the company to prohibit doctors from presenting information about Zicam at a conference? Did the company have an ethical obligation to alert the public to this issue? What about its obligation to its shareholders?

In the case of large frauds, where many people lose lots of money, the company at the heart of the wrongdoing is often bankrupt, so plaintiffs scramble to find other deep pockets from which to recover their losses. One approach they have tried is to go after those who did not commit the fraud themselves, but who aided and abetted it. Section 10(b) is often their weapon of choice. However, the Supreme Court is unsympathetic to this approach. Athough this time, the Supreme Court was divided 5-3, with one justice not taking part.

Stoneridge Investment Partners, LLC v. Scientific-Atlanta, Inc.

28 S. Ct. 761; 2008 U.S. LEXIS 1091
Supreme Court of the United States, 2008

Facts: Charter Communications, Inc., a cable operator, engaged in a variety of fraudulent practices to pump up its financial statements so they would meet Wall Street expectations. When these efforts fell short, Charter approached two of its suppliers—Scientific-Atlanta and Motorola—for help in furthering the fraud. These two companies supplied Charter with the digital cable converter (set-top) boxes that Charter furnished its customers. Charter arranged to overpay the suppliers $20 for each set-top box it purchased, with the understanding that they would return the overpayment by purchasing advertising from Charter. These transactions had no economic purpose other than inflating Charter's revenue and operating cash flow numbers by $17 million. They violated generally accepted accounting principles. The plan was successful—Charter did manage to fool its auditors.

The inflated numbers were included in financial statements filed with the SEC and reported to the public. Purchasers of Charter stock sued the two suppliers, alleging that they had violated Section 10(b) and Rule 10b-5. The District Court granted defendants' motion to dismiss. The U.S. Court of Appeals for the Eighth Circuit affirmed. The Supreme Court granted *certiorari*.

Issue: ***Is someone who aids and abets a violation of Section 10(b) liable under the statute?***

Excerpts from Justice Kennedy's Decision: Reliance by the plaintiff upon the defendant's deceptive acts is an essential element of the §10(b) cause of action. [In this case, no] member of the investing public had knowledge, either actual or presumed, of [defendants'] deceptive acts during the relevant times. Petitioner, as a result, cannot show reliance upon any of [defendants'] actions except in an indirect chain that we find too remote for liability.

It is true that a dynamic, free economy presupposes a high degree of integrity in all of its parts. Were the implied cause of action to be extended to the practices described here, however, there would be a risk that the federal power would be used to invite litigation beyond the immediate sphere of securities litigation and in areas already governed by functioning and effective state-law guarantees. Section 10(b) does not incorporate common-law fraud into federal law.

[E]xtensive discovery and the potential for uncertainty and disruption in a lawsuit allow plaintiffs with weak claims to extort settlements from innocent companies. Adoption of petitioner's approach would expose a new class of defendants to these risks. [C]ontracting parties might find it necessary to protect against these threats, raising the costs of doing business. Overseas firms with no other exposure to our securities laws could be deterred from doing business here. This, in turn, may raise the cost of being a publicly traded company under our law and shift securities offerings away from domestic capital markets.

Here respondents were acting in concert with Charter in the ordinary course as suppliers, not in the investment sphere. Charter was free to do as it chose in preparing its books, conferring with its auditor, and preparing and then issuing its financial statements. In these circumstances, the investors cannot be said to have relied upon any of [defendants'] deceptive acts in the decision to purchase or sell securities; and as the requisite reliance cannot be shown, respondents have no liability to petitioner. The judgment of the Court of Appeals is affirmed.

Devil's Advocate If the suppliers had not taken part in Charter's scheme, the company would not have been able to release fake numbers or fool its auditors. The suppliers knew exactly what they were doing and what the result would be. The court argues that holding the suppliers liable would harm domestic capital markets. But rampant fraud would also harm capital markets. The Court refers to this scheme as "unconventional." That is a nice word for deliberate, intentional fraud.

The Private Securities Litigation Reform Act of 1995

The Private Securities Litigation Reform Act modifies many existing laws, including the 1934 Act. Its amendment to the 1934 Act was intended to discourage fraud suits by shareholders. Under this amendment, companies are liable to shareholders for so-called forward-looking statements (that is, financial projections or statements about future plans) *only if* (1) the company fails to include a warning that the predictions may not come to pass, *and* (2) the shareholders can show that company executives knew the predictions were false. Suppose a pharmaceutical company predicts that a new drug will generate billions in sales, but two years later, the drug is a total failure. Before this statute, shareholders would have had a strong case, but now the company would not be liable as long as it had disclosed, at the time of making the prediction, reasons why the drug might not be a success. Even if the company failed to mention these reasons, it would be liable only if executives knew the prediction to be false when they made it.

Insider Trading

The day before Merck & Co. announced its takeover of Schering-Plough, the price of Schering stock rose by 8 percent. A lucky guess on the part of traders? Federal investigators think not. That was one of the incidents they probed during a three-year investigation into insider trading in the hedge fund industry. The probe became public when one of the principals of a research company sent this email to firm clients:

> Today two fresh-faced eager beavers from the FBI showed up unannounced (obviously) on my doorstep, thoroughly convinced that my clients have been trading on copious insider information. (They obviously have been recording my cell phone conversations for quite some time, with what motivation I have no idea.) We obviously beg to differ, so have therefore declined the young gentleman's gracious offer to wear a wire and therefore ensnare you in their devious web.

It turns out that other people were not so reluctant to secretly tape record conversations. This evidence was used to build cases against employees of more than three dozen companies (including the man who sent the email). The group are alleged to have earned tens of millions of dollars in illegal profits. They potentially face years in prison and millions of dollars in fines.

Insider trading is a crime punishable by fines and imprisonment. So now you know that insider trading is dangerous, but exactly what is it? That question is not easy to answer. As noted, Rule 10b-5 is a vaguely worded rule that generally prohibits fraud. The language of the rule never explicitly mentions insider trading, but courts have interpreted it to prohibit this activity. Although the courts are nominally *interpreting* the rule, in fact, they are more or less fashioning this crime out of whole cloth. Insider trading has been described as "the judicial oak that has grown from little more than a legislative acorn." The SEC has argued many times that anyone in possession of nonpublic material information must disclose it or refrain from trading. But in the following Landmark Case, the most famous on the topic of insider trading, the Supreme Court rejected the SEC's view.

They potentially face years in prison and millions of dollars in fines.

Landmark Case

Chiarella v. United States

445 U.S. 222; 1980 U.S. LEXIS 88
Supreme Court of the United States, 1980

Facts: Chiarella was a printer at Pandick Press, a company that printed the documents used to announce corporate takeover bids. For security reasons, the first drafts of these documents disguised the names of the companies involved. Chiarella used other information in the early drafts to figure out the identities of five target companies. He then secretly bought shares in these companies, selling them at a profit once the takeover was announced and the names revealed.

In the end, however, this scheme did not turn out to be profitable for Chiarella. When the SEC figured out what he had done, it brought civil charges against him. To settle those charges, he agreed to turn over his profits to the sellers of the shares. Then Pandick Press fired him, he was convicted of criminal violations of Section10(b) and Rule 10b-5, he was sentenced to a year in prison, and the Court of Appeals affirmed his conviction. But the Supreme Court granted *certiorari*.

Issue: ***Did Chiarella violate securities laws when he traded on secret information that he acquired in his job as a printer?***

Excerpts from Justice Powell's Decision[10]: [S]ilence in connection with the purchase or sale of securities may operate as a fraud actionable under §10(b). But such liability is premised upon a duty to disclose arising from a relationship of trust and confidence between parties to a transaction. Application of a duty to disclose prior to trading guarantees that corporate insiders, who have an obligation to place the shareholder's welfare before their own, will not benefit personally through fraudulent use of material, nonpublic information.

In this case, the defendant was convicted of violating §10(b) although he was not a corporate insider and he received no confidential information from the target company. Moreover, the "market information" upon which he relied did not concern the earning power or operations of the target company, but only the plans of the acquiring company. Defendant's use of that information was not a fraud under §10(b) unless he was subject to an affirmative duty to disclose it before trading.

In effect, the trial court instructed the jury that defendant owed a duty to everyone; to all sellers, indeed, to the market as a whole. The Court of Appeals' decision rested solely upon its belief that the federal securities laws have "created a system providing equal access to information necessary for reasoned and intelligent investment decisions." The use by anyone of material information not generally available is fraudulent, this theory suggests, because such information gives certain buyers or sellers an unfair advantage over less informed buyers and sellers.

This reasoning suffers from two defects. First, not every instance of financial unfairness constitutes fraudulent activity under §10(b). Second, the element required to make silence fraudulent—a duty to disclose—is absent in this case. No duty could arise from defendant's relationship with the sellers of the target company's securities, for defendant had no prior dealings with them. He was not their agent, he was not a fiduciary, he was not a person in whom the sellers had placed their trust and confidence. He was, in fact, a complete stranger who dealt with the sellers only through impersonal market transactions.

We cannot affirm defendant's conviction without recognizing a general duty between all participants in market transactions to forgo actions based on material, nonpublic information. Formulation of such a broad duty should not be undertaken absent some explicit evidence of congressional intent. [N]o such evidence emerges from the language or legislative history of §10(b). We hold that a duty to disclose under §10(b) does not arise from the mere possession of nonpublic market information. The judgment of the Court of Appeals is

Reversed.

[10]For ease of reading, we have substituted "defendant" for "petitioner."

Instead of the SEC's simple proposal, we have instead a much more complex set of rules:

- **Strangers.** As we saw in the landmark *Chiarella* case, **someone who trades on inside information is liable only if he breaches a fiduciary duty.** Suppose that, while looking in a dumpster, Harry finds correspondence indicating that MediSearch, Inc., will shortly announce a major breakthrough in the treatment of AIDS. Harry buys the stock, which promptly quadruples in value. Harry will be dining at the Ritz, not in the dumpster or in federal prison, because he has no fiduciary duty to MediSearch.

- **Fiduciaries.** Anyone who works for a company is a fiduciary. **A fiduciary violates Rule 10b-5 if she trades stock of her company while in possession of nonpublic material information.** If the director of research for MediSearch learns of the promising new treatment for AIDS and buys stock in the company before the information is public, she has violated Rule 10b-5. This rule applies not only to employees who work for the company, but also to **constructive insiders**—others who receive confidential information while they have an indirect employment relationship, such as employees of the company's auditors or law firm. Thus, if a lawyer who works at the firm that is patenting MediSearch's new discovery buys stock before the information is public, she has violated Rule 10b-5.

Constructive insider
Anyone who receives confidential information while in an indirect employment relationship with a company, such as employees of the company's auditors or law firm.

- ***Possession* versus *use* of information.** Suppose that an insider sells stock just after learning that her company is about to report lower earnings, but before this information is public. When challenged by the SEC, she argues that she sold her stock for other reasons—say, to buy a new house, or set her son up in business. To deal with this type of situation, the SEC issued **Rule 10b5-1, which provides that an insider violates Rule 10b-5 if she trades while in possession of material, nonpublic information unless she has committed in advance to a plan to sell those securities.** Thus, if an insider knows that she will want to sell stock to pay college tuition, she can establish such a sales plan in advance. (And, then, despite any change in circumstances, she must sell according to the plan.) She will then not be liable for the sales, no matter what inside information she ultimately learns.

- **Tippers.** What about people who do not trade themselves, but pass on information to someone who does? **Insiders who pass on nonpublic, material information are liable under Rule 10b-5, even if they do not trade themselves, so long as (1) they know the information is confidential and (2) they expect some personal gain.** Personal gain is loosely defined. Essentially, any gift to a friend counts as personal gain. W. Paul Thayer was a corporate director, deputy secretary of defense, and former fighter pilot ace who gave stock tips to his girlfriend in lieu of paying her rent. That counted as personal gain, and he spent a year and a half in prison.

- **Tippees. Those who receive tips—tippees—are liable for trading on inside information, even if they do not have a fiduciary relationship to the company, so long as (1) they know the information is confidential, (2) they know that it came from an insider who was violating his fiduciary duty, and (3) the insider expected some personal gain.** Barry Switzer, then head football coach at the University of Oklahoma, went to a track meet to see his son compete. While sunbathing on the bleachers, he overheard someone talking about a company that was going to be acquired. Switzer bought the stock but was acquitted of insider trading charges because the insider had not breached his fiduciary duty. He had not tipped anyone on purpose—he had simply been careless. Also, Switzer did not know that the insider was breaching a fiduciary duty, and the insider expected no personal gain.[11]

[11] *SEC v. Switzer*, 590 F. Supp. 756, 1984 U.S. Dist. LEXIS 15303 (W.D. Okla. 1984).

- **Takeovers.** Frustrated by its lack of success under Rule 10b-5, the SEC adopted Rule 14e-3. **This rule prohibits trading on inside information during a tender offer if the trader knows the information was obtained from either the bidder or the target company.** The trader or tipper need not have violated a fiduciary duty.
- **Misappropriation.** In an effort to tighten the insider trading noose further, the SEC developed a new theory—misappropriation. Under this theory, **a person is liable if he trades in securities (1) for personal profit, (2) using confidential information, and (3) in breach of a fiduciary duty to the source of the information.** This theory applies even if that source was not the company whose stock was traded. For example, James O'Hagan was a lawyer in a firm that represented a company attempting to take over Pillsbury Co. Although O'Hagan did not work on the case, he heard about it and then bought stock in Pillsbury. After the takeover attempt was publicly announced, O'Hagan sold his stock in Pillsbury at profit of more than $4.3 million.[12] The Supreme Court ruled that O'Hagan had violated insider trading laws. While it was true that he had no fiduciary duty to Pillsbury, he did owe one to his law firm, which was the source of the information. According to the court, what he had done was the same thing as embezzlement.[13]

When he revealed confidential information, was he expecting personal gain?

After the *O'Hagan* case established the principle of misappropriation, it was still not clear how this rule applied to family members. If a wife told her husband that her company was about to be taken over and he then sold company stock as a result, was he in violation of 10b-5? Did he have a fiduciary duty to her? Rule 10b-5-2 establishes that anyone who receives non-public, material information from a spouse, parent, child or sibling has a fiduciary duty unless the trader can prove that he did not have a duty of trust or confidence to the family member in question.

EXAM Strategy

Question: Paul was an investment banker who sometimes bragged about deals he was working on. One night he told a bartender, Ryanne, about an upcoming deal, without revealing his connection to it. Ryanne bought stock in the company Paul had mentioned. Both were prosecuted for insider trading. Ryanne was acquitted but Paul was convicted, even though Ryanne was the one who made money. How is that possible?

Strategy: Note that there are different standards for tippers and tippees.

Result: Paul is liable if he knew the information was confidential and he expected some personal gain. A gift counts as personal gain. (The courts have an expansive definition of

[12]O'Hagan used the profits that he gained through this trading to conceal his previous embezzlement of client funds. There is a moral here.

[13]*United States v. O'Hagan*, 521 U.S. 642, 117 S. Ct. 2199, 1997 U.S. LEXIS 4033.

"gift"—practically anything counts. Here, the information could be interpreted as a tip to the bartender.) Ryanne was not liable because she did not know the information was confidential and that it came from an insider who was violating his fiduciary duty.

Why is insider trading a crime? Who is harmed? After all, if you buy or sell stock in a company, presumably you are reasonably content with the price or you would not have traded. Insider trading is illegal because:

- It offends our fundamental sense of fairness. No one wants to be in a poker game with marked cards.
- Investors will lose confidence in the market if they feel that insiders have an unfair advantage.
- Investment banks typically "make a market" in stocks, meaning that they hold extra shares so that orders can be filled smoothly. If an insider buys stock because she knows the company is about to sign an important contract, she earns the profit on that information at the expense of the market maker who sold her the stock. These market makers expect to earn a certain profit. If they do not earn it from normal stock appreciation, they simply raise the commission they charge for being a market maker. As a result, everyone who buys and sells stock pays a slightly higher price because insider trading skims off some of the profits.

Sarbanes-Oxley

The Sarbanes-Oxley Act (SOX) is an amendment to the 1934 Act that applies to all U.S companies reporting under the 1934 Act, as well as to all foreign companies listed on a U.S. stock exchange. In addition to the provisions we discussed earlier, SOX:

- Requires companies to disclose if they have an ethics code and, if they do not, why not.
- Imposes fines and imprisonment on anyone who interferes with a federal investigation into fraud.
- Permits an employee who blows the whistle on a securities law violation to sue the company if it retaliates against the employee. SOX also makes it a crime to retaliate against someone who blows the whistle on any federal offense.
- Establishes a new Public Accounting Oversight Board to oversee the auditing of reporting companies.

Dodd-Frank

The Dodd-Frank Wall Street Reform and Consumer Protection Act amends the 1934 Act to provide a reward system for whistleblowers. Dodd-Frank also establishes a requirement that reporting companies tell the SEC and post on their websites information about their use of "conflict minerals" (such as tin, tungsten, and gold). A conflict mineral is one that is being used to finance the war in the Democratic Republic of the Congo or a neighboring country.

In addition, energy mining companies must disclose payments they make to other governments for oil, gas, and mineral rights. The goal of this provision is to provide information to the citizens of foreign countries about how much revenue their governments are receiving so that they can hold officials responsible for misspending.

Blue Sky Laws

At the end of the 19th century, years before the great stock market crash, states had already begun to regulate the sale of securities. These statutes are called **blue sky laws** (because crooks were willing to sell naive investors a "piece of the great blue sky"). Currently, all states and the District of Columbia have blue sky laws.

Exemption from State Regulation

To make life easier for issuers of stock, Congress passed the **National Securities Markets Improvement Act (NSMIA) of 1996.** Essentially, states may no longer regulate offerings of securities that are:

- Traded on a national exchange,
- Exempt under Rule 506, or
- Sold to a **qualified purchaser.**[14]

State Regulation

Any securities offerings not covered by the NSMIA must comply with state securities laws. Easier said than done. The 50 states have exhibited great creativity in crafting their securities laws and, as a result, have caused many headaches for issuers of securities. To begin, the 1933 Act is primarily concerned with disclosure, but many state statutes focus on the quality of the investment and require a so-called *merit review*. For example, in 1981, the Massachusetts securities commissioner refused to allow Apple Computer Co. to sell its initial public offering in Massachusetts because he believed the stock, selling at 92 times earnings, was too risky. He "protected" Massachusetts residents from this investment.

Typically, states take one of the following approaches to securities offerings:

- *Registration by notification*. Some states permit issuers with an established track record simply to file a notice before offering their securities.
- *Registration by coordination*. Some states permit issuers that have registered with the SEC simply to file copies of the federal registration statement (and perhaps some additional documents) with the state.
- *Registration by qualification*. Some states require issuers to undergo a full-blown registration, complete with a merit review.

Facilitating State Regulation

All is not bleak, however. There are three options that ease the process of complying with state securities requirements.

Coordinated Equity Review (CER)

For offerings over $5 million that are registered with the SEC, the issuer might be able to take advantage of the **Coordinated Equity Review (CER)** program. Under this program, the issuer files in every state in which it wants to sell securities, but it only has to deal with Pennsylvania, which takes responsibility for coordinating the comments from all other states. The process is simpler, but state officials still have the right to conduct a merit review.

[14]The SEC was supposed to define this term in 1996, but it has not yet done so. What's the rush?

Small Company Offering Registration (SCOR)

Most states permit a so-called **small company offering registration (SCOR)** for use in offerings of up to $1 million over any 12-month period. The issuer has the right to advertise publicly (even on the Internet) and can sell any amount of securities to any number of investors (as long as the total offering does not exceed $1 million). The relatively simple form (U-7) is in a question-and-answer format. It is designed to be filled out by company executives without the assistance of lawyers or accountants who are securities experts. Any company using a SCOR form can request a coordinated review from the states in which it has filed. Under this system, a designated lead state takes responsibility for coordinating the process with all other states. The result is a faster, simpler process. States do have the right to conduct a merit review, although it tends to be less burdensome than the usual merit examination. SCOR registration is designed to be used with Rule 147, Rule 504, and Reg A.

Uniform Limited Offering Exemption

Under the **Uniform Limited Offering Exemption,** most states largely exempt from registration any offerings under Rule 505.

The moral of the story? Securities offerings are exceedingly complex and require professional supervision. Do not attempt this at home!

Chapter Conclusion

The 1929 stock market crash and the Great Depression that followed were an economic catastrophe for the United States. The Securities Act of 1933 and the Securities Exchange Act of 1934 were designed to prevent such disasters from ever occurring again. Whether or not they achieve that goal, they undoubtedly enhance the reliability and stability of the securities markets.

Exam Review

1. **SECURITY** A security is any transaction in which the buyer invests money in a common enterprise and expects to earn a profit predominantly from the efforts of others. (p. 893)

Question: Jonah bought 12 paintings from Theo's Art Gallery at a total cost of $1 million. Theo told Jonah that the paintings were a safe investment that could only go up in value. The gallery permitted any purchaser to trade in a painting in return for any other artwork the gallery owned. In the trade-in, the purchaser would get credit for the amount of the original painting and then pay the difference if the new painting was worth more. When Jonah's paintings did not increase in value, he sued Theo for a violation of the securities laws. Were these paintings securities?

Strategy: Are all three elements of a security present here? (See the "Result" at the end of this section.)

2. REGISTRATION Before any offer or sale, an issuer must register securities with the SEC unless the securities qualify for an exemption. (p. 893)

3. EXEMPTIONS These securities are exempt from the registration requirement: government securities, bank securities, short-term notes, nonprofit issues, insurance policies, and annuity contracts. (pp. 894–898)

4. SECURITIES OFFERINGS The following table compares the different types of securities offerings:

	Public Offering	Intrastate Offering	Regulation A	Regulation D: Rule 504	Regulation D: Rule 505	Regulation D: Rule 506
Maximum Value of Securities Sold	Unlimited	Unlimited	\$5 million	\$1 million	\$5 million	Unlimited
Public Solicitation of Purchasers	Permitted	Permitted	Permitted	Sometimes permitted	Not permitted	Not permitted
Suitability Requirements for Purchasers	No requirements	Must reside in issuer's state	No requirements	May be limited to accredited investors	No limit on accredited investors; no more than 35 unaccredited investors	No limit on accredited investors; no more than 35 unaccredited investors who, if unsophisticated, must have a purchaser representative
Disclosure Requirements	Elaborate registration statement; audited financials	None	Offering circular that is less detailed than a registration statement	May be required under state law	Same requirements as Reg A for unaccredited investors; no disclosure to accredited investors	Same requirements as Reg A for unaccredited investors; no disclosure to accredited investors
Resale of Securities	Permitted	Permitted, but may not be made out of state for nine months	Permitted	Sometimes permitted	Not permitted for one year	Not permitted for one year

EXAM Strategy

CPA Question: Hamilton Corp. makes a \$4.5 million securities offering under Rule 505 of Regulation D of the Securities Act of 1933. Under this regulation, Hamilton is:

a. Required to provide full financial information to accredited investors only

b. Allowed to make the offering through a general solicitation

c. Limited to selling to no more than 35 nonaccredited investors

d. Allowed to sell to an unlimited number of investors, both accredited and nonaccredited

Strategy: The answer is not (a) because accredited investors are never entitled to *more* disclosure than other investors. The answer is not (b) because Rule 505 does not permit a general solicitation. The answer is not (d) because Rule 505 is limited to only 35 unaccredited investors. (See the "Result" at the end of this section.)

5. **LIABILITY UNDER THE 1933 ACT** If a final registration statement contains a material misstatement or omission, the purchaser of a security offered under that statement can recover from everyone who signed it. (pp. 900–902)

6. **THE 1934 ACT** The 1934 Act requires public companies to make regular filings with the SEC. (pp. 902–908)

7. **SECTION 16** Under Section 16, insiders who buy and sell or sell and buy company stock within a six-month period must turn over to the corporation any profits from the trades. They must also disclose any trades they make in company stock. (p. 904)

Question: You are the president of Turbocharge, Inc., a publicly traded company. You have been buying stock recently because you think the company's product—a more efficient hybrid engine—is very promising. One day, you show up at work and find your desk in the hallway. The CEO has fired you. In a huff, you sell all your company stock. The only silver lining to your cloud is that you make a large profit. Or is this a silver lining?

Strategy: You can be in violation of Section 16 even if you did not have any inside information when you trade. (See the "Result" at the end of this section.)

8. **SECTION 10(B)** Section 10(b) prohibits fraud in connection with the purchase and sale of any security, whether or not the issuer is registered under the 1934 Act. (pp. 904–908)

9. **INSIDER TRADING** Section 10(b) also prohibits insider trading. (pp. 909–913)

10. **SOX** Sarbanes Oxley:

    - imposes fines and imprisonment on anyone who interferes with a federal investigation into fraud.
    - permits an employee who blows the whistle on a securities law violation to sue the company if it retaliates against the employee. SOX also makes it a crime to retaliate against someone who blows the whistle on any federal offense. (p. 913)

11. **DODD-FRANK** The Dodd-Frank Act

    - provides a reward system for whistleblowers, and
    - requires that reporting companies tell the SEC and post on their websites information about their use of conflict minerals. (p. 913)

12. **THE NSMIA** The National Securities Markets Improvement Act prohibits states from regulating securities offerings that are:
    - traded on a national exchange,
    - exempt under Rule 506, or
    - sold to "qualified purchasers." (p. 914)

13. **BLUE SKY LAWS** Any securities offerings not covered by the NSMIA must comply with state securities laws, which are varied and complex. (pp. 914–915)

1. Result: The paintings were not securities because there was no "common enterprise." The investors did not pool funds or share profits with other investors.

4. Result: The answer is (c).

7. Result: You are in violation of Section 16. Even though you acted without any bad intent, you must turn over all your profits to the company.

Multiple-Choice Questions

1. **CPA QUESTION** When a common stock offering requires registration under the Securities Act of 1933:
   (a) The registration statement is automatically effective when filed with the SEC.
   (b) The issuer would act unlawfully if it were to sell the common stock without providing the investor with a prospectus.
   (c) The SEC will determine the investment value of the common stock before approving the offering.
   (d) The issuer may make sales 10 days after filing the registration statement.

2. **CPA QUESTION** Pace Corp. previously issued 300,000 shares of its common stock. The shares are now actively traded on a national securities exchange. The original offering was exempt from registration under the Securities Act of 1933. Pace has $2.5 million in assets and 425 shareholders. With regard to the Securities Exchange Act of 1934, Pace is:
   (a) Required to file a registration statement because its assets exceed $2 million in value
   (b) Required to file a registration statement even though it has fewer than 500 shareholders
   (c) Not required to file a registration statement because the original offering of its stock was exempt from registration
   (d) Not required to file a registration statement unless insiders own at least 5 percent of its outstanding shares of stock

3. Lily would like to raise money for her video game start-up by advertising the shares on her website, but without substantial financial disclosure. What should she do?

(a) Nothing. If she is going to solicit purchasers publicly, she must undertake an IPO.

(b) Use Rule 504 to sell up to $1 million in stock to accredited investors, and make sure the offering is exempt under state law.

(c) Use Rule 504 to sell up to $1 million in stock to any purchasers and register the stock under a state law.

(d) Use Rule 505 sell up to $5 million in stock to an unlimited number of accredited investors and no more than 35 unaccredited investors.

4. If a publicly traded company wishes to issue more stock, it will undertake a(n)____________. If the underwriter buys the stock and resells it to the public, that is a ____________ underwriting. Before buying the stock, investors must receive a copy of the ____________.

(a) IPO, best efforts, registration statement

(b) IPO, firm commitment, registration statement

(c) Secondary offering, best efforts, prospectus

(d) Secondary offering, firm commitment, prospectus

5. Three months ago, Noah bought stock under Rule 506 in TreesNFlowers, Inc. He has lost interest in the company and would like to sell the stock. Which of the following statements is true:

(a) He can sell the stock now, so long as he sells it to an accredited investor.

(b) He can sell the stock now, so long as the company grants permission.

(c) He must hold on to the stock for at least nine months.

(d) He could sell the stock in three months, but only if the company goes public in the meantime.

Essay Questions

1. A railroad's employees noticed that a lot of people in suits were touring the rail yard. The CFO asked for a list of all trains owned by the company. Workers began speculating that the company might be sold and they would all lose their jobs. The company's code of conduct made it illegal to disseminate material nonpublic information. Two employees—an engineer and a trainman—bought stock in the railroad. When the railroad did indeed change hands, they were able to sell their stock for $1 million profit. Are the employees liable under insider trading rules?

2. Fluor, an engineering and construction company, was awarded a $1 billion project to build a coal gasification plant in South Africa. Fluor signed an agreement with a South African client that prohibited them both from announcing the agreement until March 10. Accordingly, Fluor denied all rumors that a major transaction was pending. Between March 3 and March 6, the State Teachers Retirement Board pension fund sold 288,257 shares of Fluor stock. After the contract was announced, the stock price went up. Did Fluor violate Rule 10b-5?

3. Do you love ice cream? Here is an opportunity for you! For only $800, you can buy a cow from Berkshire Ice Cream. The company gets milk from the cow, and you get to share in the profits from the sale of ice cream. Just last month, Berkshire mailed $32,000 worth of checks to investors, who are expecting a 20 percent annual rate of return. Are there any problems with this plan?

4. **ETHICS** ETS Payphones, Inc., sold pay phones to the public. The company then leased back the pay phones from the purchaser, promising a guaranteed 14 percent annual return on their investment. Although ETS's marketing materials trumpeted the "incomparable pay phone" as "an exciting business opportunity," the pay phones did not generate enough revenue for ETS to make the required payments. The SEC sued, alleging that ETS had been selling unregistered securities. Were the pay phone contracts securities under the 1933 Act? These allegedly "guaranteed" investments are particularly attractive to older and less-sophisticated investors. Was it ethical to pitch a high-risk investment to vulnerable investors who were unable to assess the risks accurately?

5. Suppose that, while waiting in line at the grocery store, you overhear a stranger saying that the FDA is going to approve a new drug tomorrow—one that will be a huge success for Alpha Pharmaceuticals. Is it legal for you to buy stock in Alpha?

Discussion Questions

1. Federal security laws are based on the assumption that investors are knowledgeable enough to assess the quality of a stock, so long as the issuer provides adequate disclosure. Many states take a different approach—they refuse to permit the sale of securities that they deem to be of poor quality. Should securities laws protect investors in this way?

2. **ETHICS** David Sokol worked at Berkshire Hathaway for legendary investor Warren Buffett, who is renowned not only for his investment skills but also his ethics. Bankers suggested to both Sokol and the CEO of Lubrizol that the company might be a good buy for Berkshire. Sokol then found out that the CEO of Lubrizol planned to ask his board for permission to approach Berkshire about a possible acquisition. Sokol purchased $10 million worth of Lubrizol stock before recommending Lubrizol to Buffett. Sokol mentioned to Buffett "in passing" that he owned shares of Lubrizol. Buffett did not ask any questions about the timing or amount of Sokol's purchases. Sokol made a $3 million profit when Berkshire acquired Lubrizol. Did Sokol violate insider trading laws? Did he behave ethically? What about Buffett?

3. Refco Inc. failed to disclose in SEC filings that millions of dollars of its accounts receivables were uncollectible. Two months after its IPO, the company went bankrupt. Shareholders filed suit against the company's law firm, alleging that it was liable under Section 10(b) for drafting Refco's SEC filings that contained these material omissions. Is the law firm liable? Should it be? Is this a stronger or weaker case than *Stoneridge*?

4. Facebook, Inc. is valued at more than $50 billion, and yet, because it is still privately held, it is not required to make any disclosure about its finances. Once the number of

its shareholders reaches 500, it will be deemed a public company and will be required to make significant (and expensive) financial disclosure. Should the SEC change its rules so that these reporting requirements are not triggered until companies have more than 500 shareholders? Which is more important—to minimize the disclosure burden on companies or to protect investors who are willing to buy stock even without financial disclosure?

5. Do you agree with the court's decision in the *Stoneridge* case?

6. The SEC believes that anyone in possession of nonpublic material information about a company should be required to disclose it before trading on the stock of that enterprise. Instead, the courts have developed a more complex set of rules. Do you agree with the SEC or the courts on this issue?

CHAPTER 37

BANKRUPTCY

© Evan Meyer/Shutterstock.com

Three bankruptcy stories:

1. Tim's account: "First, there was Christmas. Was I really not going to buy my eight-year-old the Xbox he'd been begging for? Then my daughter's basketball team qualified for the nationals at Disney World. She's a talented player, and if she sticks with it, maybe she'll get a college scholarship. The kids had never been to Disney World. How could we say no? Then my car died. And I didn't get a bonus this year. Next thing you know, we had $27,000 in credit card debt. Then we had some uninsured medical bills. We were seriously underwater. There was just no way we could pay all that money back."

We were seriously underwater. There was just no way we could pay all that money back.

2. Kristen was a talented gardener and had always loved flowers. Sometimes she did the flowers for friends' weddings. When the guy who owned the local flower shop wanted to retire, it seemed a great opportunity to buy the business. She had lots of good ideas for improving it. First, she renovated the space so that people could hold parties there. She hired staff to keep the shop open longer hours. Everything went really well. Then the recession hit, and people cut back on nonessentials like flowers. How could she pay her loans?

3. General Motors (GM), once a symbol of American business, filed for bankruptcy in 2009. At the time, its liabilities were $90 billion more than its assets. It also had 325,000 employees and even more stakeholders: retired employees, car owners, suppliers, investors, and communities in which it operated and its employees lived and paid taxes. GM emerged from bankruptcy 40 days later with fewer brands, factories, and workers, but ready to do business. The next year, the company was profitable.

Bankruptcy law always has been and always will be controversial. Typically, in other countries, the goal of bankruptcy law is to protect creditors and punish debtors, even sending debtors to prison. Indeed, many of America's first settlers fled England to escape debtors' prison. As if to compensate for Europe's harsh regimes, American bankruptcy laws were traditionally more lenient toward debtors.[1]

The General Motors example illustrates the good news about American bankruptcy. It is efficient (40 days!) and effective at reviving ailing companies. Everyone—investors, employees, the country—benefits from GM's survival. And although Kristen's flower shop did not survive, bankruptcy laws will protect her so that she is not afraid to try entrepreneurship again.[2] New businesses fail more often than not, but they are nonetheless important engines of growth for our country. We all benefit from the jobs they create and the taxes they pay.

Tim represents the bad news in bankruptcy laws. Unfortunately, he is often the type of person who first comes to mind when people think about bankrupts. And people do not like Tim very much. They think: why should he be rewarded for his irresponsibility, when I get stuck paying all my bills? But a more difficult bankruptcy process will probably not discourage Tim. He is the kind of guy who cares a lot about current pleasures and little about future pain. No matter what bankruptcy laws we have, he will not say no to Disney World. Should the laws become too onerous, businesses will fail, entrepreneurs will be discouraged, and the Tims of the world will continue to spend more than they should.

But maybe America has too much of a good thing. This nation has the highest bankruptcy rate in the world. In the most recent year, there was one bankruptcy filing for every 200 Americans.[3] Clearly, bankruptcy laws play a vital role in our economy. They have the potential to resuscitate failing companies while encouraging entrepreneurship. At the same time, it is important not to enable irresponsible spendthrifts. Do American bankruptcy laws reach the right balance?

Overview of the Bankruptcy Code

The federal Bankruptcy Code (the Code) is divided into eight chapters. All chapters except one have odd numbers. Chapters 1, 3, and 5 are administrative rules that generally apply to all types of bankruptcy proceedings. These chapters, for example, define terms and establish the rules of the bankruptcy court. Chapters 7, 9, 11, 12, and 13 are substantive rules for different types of bankruptcies. All of these substantive chapters have one of two objectives—rehabilitation or liquidation.

Rehabilitation

The objective of Chapters 11 and 13 is to rehabilitate the debtor. Many debtors can return to financial health provided they have the time and breathing space to work out their problems. These chapters hold creditors at bay while the debtor develops a payment plan. In return for retaining some of their assets, debtors typically promise to pay creditors a portion of their future earnings.

---

[1]Bankruptcy law was so important to the drafters of the Constitution that they specifically listed it as one of the subjects that Congress had the right to regulate (Article 1, Section 8).

[2]See, for example, Seung-Hyun Lee, Yasuhiro Yamakawa, Mike W. Peng, and Jay B. Barney, "How do bankruptcy laws affect entrepreneurship development around the world?" in the *Journal of Business Venturing*, JBV-05559, 2010.

[3]Some of these filings are by businesses, although that percentage is small. In the last 15 years, more than 95 percent of all bankruptcy filings have been by consumers.

Liquidation

When debtors are unable to develop a feasible plan for rehabilitation under Chapter 11 or 13, Chapter 7 provides for liquidation (also known as a **straight bankruptcy**). Most of the debtor's assets are distributed to creditors, but the debtor has no obligation to share future earnings.

Straight bankruptcy
Also known as liquidation, this form of bankruptcy mandates that the bankrupt's assets be distributed to creditors but the debtor has no obligation to share future earnings.

Chapter Description

The following options are available under the Bankruptcy Code:

Number	Topic	Description
Chapter 7	Liquidation	The bankrupt's assets are sold to pay creditors. If the debtor owns a business, it terminates. The creditors have no right to the debtor's future earnings.
Chapter 11	Reorganization	This chapter is designed for businesses and wealthy individuals. Businesses continue in operation, and creditors receive a portion of the debtor's current assets and future earnings.
Chapter 13	Consumer reorganization	Chapter 13 offers reorganization for the typical consumer. Creditors usually receive a portion of the individual's current assets and future earnings.

In liquidation, most of the debtor's assets are distributed to creditors.

Debtors are sometimes eligible to file under more than one chapter. No choice is irrevocable because both debtors and creditors have the right to ask the court to convert a case from one chapter to another at any time during the proceedings. For example, if creditors have asked for liquidation under Chapter 7, a bankrupt consumer may request rehabilitation under Chapter 13.

Goals

The Bankruptcy Code has three primary goals:

- *To preserve as much of the debtor's property as possible.* In keeping with this goal, the Code requires debtors to disclose all of their assets and prohibits them from transferring assets immediately before a bankruptcy filing.
- *To divide the debtor's assets fairly between the debtor and creditors.* On the one hand, creditors are entitled to payment. On the other hand, debtors are often so deeply in debt that full payment is virtually impossible in any reasonable period of time. The Code tries to balance the creditors' right to be paid with the debtors' desire to get on with their lives, unburdened by prior debts.
- *To divide the debtor's assets fairly among creditors.* Creditors rarely receive all they are owed, but at least they are treated fairly, according to established rules. Creditors do not benefit from simply being the first to file or from any other gamesmanship.

Chapter 7 Liquidation

All bankruptcy cases proceed in a roughly similar pattern, regardless of chapter. We use Chapter 7 as a template to illustrate common features of all bankruptcy cases. Later on, the discussions of the other chapters will indicate how they differ from Chapter 7.

Filing a Petition

Any individual, partnership, corporation, or other business organization that lives, conducts business, or owns property in the United States can file under the Code. (Chapter 13, however, is available only to individuals.) The traditional term for someone who could not pay his debts was **bankrupt,** but the Code uses the term **debtor** instead. We use both terms interchangeably.

Debtor
Someone who cannot pay his debts and files for protection under the Bankruptcy Code.

A case begins with the filing of a bankruptcy petition in federal district court. The district court typically refers bankruptcy cases to a specialized bankruptcy judge. Either party can appeal the decision of the bankruptcy judge back to the district court and, from there, to the federal appeals court.

Debtors may go willingly into the bankruptcy process by filing a **voluntary petition,** or they may be dragged into court by creditors who file an **involuntary petition**. Originally, when the goal of bankruptcy laws was to protect creditors, voluntary petitions did not exist; all petitions were involuntary. Because the bankruptcy process is now viewed as being favorable to debtors, the vast majority of bankruptcy filings in this country are voluntary petitions.

Voluntary petition
Filed by a debtor to initiate a bankruptcy case.

Involuntary petition
Filed by creditors to initiate a bankruptcy case.

Voluntary Petition

Any debtor (whether a business or an individual) has the right to file for bankruptcy. It is not necessary that the debtor's liabilities exceed assets. Debtors sometimes file a bankruptcy petition because cash flow is so tight they cannot pay their debts, even though they are not technically insolvent. However, *individuals* must meet two requirements before filing:

- Within 180 days before the filing, an individual debtor must undergo credit counseling with an approved agency.
- Individual debtors may only file under Chapter 7 if they earn less than the median income in their state *or* they cannot afford to pay back at least $7,025 over five years.[4] Generally, all other debtors must file under Chapter 11 or Chapter 13. (These Chapters require the bankrupt to repay some debt.)

[4]In some circumstances, debtors with income higher than $7,025 may still be eligible to file under Chapter 7, but the formula is highly complex and more than most readers want to know. The formula is available at 11 USC Section 707(b)(2)(A). Also, you can google "bapcpa means test" and then click on the Department of Justice website. The dollar amounts are updated every three years. You can find them by googling "federal register bankruptcy revision of dollar amounts."

The voluntary petition must include the following documents:

Document	Description
Petition	Begins the case. Easy to fill out, it requires checking a few boxes and typing in little more than name, address, and Social Security number.
List of Creditors	The names and addresses of all creditors.
Schedule of Assets and Liabilities	A list of the debtor's assets and debts.
Claim of Exemptions	A list of all assets that the debtor is entitled to keep.
Schedule of Income and Expenditures	The debtor's job, income, and expenses.
Statement of Financial Affairs	A summary of the debtor's financial history and current financial condition. In particular, the debtor must list any recent payments to creditors and any other property held by someone else for the debtor.

Involuntary Petition

Creditors may force a debtor into bankruptcy by filing an involuntary petition. The creditors' goal is to preserve as much of the debtor's assets as possible and to ensure that all creditors receive a fair share. Naturally, the Code sets strict limits—debtors cannot be forced into bankruptcy every time they miss a credit card payment. **An involuntary petition must meet all of the following requirements:**

- The debtor must owe at least $14,425 in unsecured claims to the creditors who file.[5]
- If the debtor has at least 12 creditors, 3 or more must sign the petition. If the debtor has fewer than 12 creditors, any one of them may file a petition.
- The creditors must allege either that a custodian for the debtor's property has been appointed in the prior 120 days or that the debtor has generally not been paying debts that are due.

What does "a custodian for the debtor's property" mean? *State* laws sometimes permit the appointment of a custodian to protect a debtor's assets. The Code allows creditors to pull a case out from under state law and into federal bankruptcy court by filing an involuntary petition. In the event that a debtor objects to an involuntary petition, the bankruptcy court must hold a trial to determine whether the creditors have met the Code's requirements.

Order for relief

An official acknowledgment that a debtor is under the jurisdiction of the bankruptcy court.

Once a voluntary petition is filed or an involuntary petition approved, the bankruptcy court issues an **order for relief**. This order is an official acknowledgment that the debtor is under the jurisdiction of the court, and it is, in a sense, the start of the whole bankruptcy process. An involuntary debtor must now make all the filings that accompany a voluntary petition.

[5]In Chapter 24, on secured transactions, we discuss the difference between secured and unsecured claims at some length. A secured claim is one in which the creditor has the right to foreclose on a specific piece of the debtor's property (known as **collateral**) if the debtor fails to pay the debt when due. For example, if Lee borrows money from GMAC Finance to buy a car, the company has the right to repossess the car if Lee fails to repay the loan. GMAC's loan is **secured**. An **unsecured** loan has no collateral. If the debtor fails to repay, the creditor can make a general claim against the debtor but has no right to foreclose on a particular item of the debtor's property.

Trustee

The trustee is responsible for gathering the bankrupt's assets and dividing them among creditors. This is a critical role in a bankruptcy case. Trustees are typically lawyers or CPAs, but any generally competent person can serve. Creditors have the right to elect the trustee, but often they do not bother. If the creditors do not elect a trustee, then the **U.S. Trustee** appoints one. Each region of the country has a U.S. Trustee selected by the U.S. attorney general. Besides appointing trustees as necessary, this U.S. Trustee oversees the administration of bankruptcy law in the region.

The U.S. Trustee
Oversees the administration of bankruptcy law in a region.

Creditors

After the court issues an order for relief, the U.S. Trustee calls a meeting of all of the creditors. At the meeting, the bankrupt must answer (under oath) any question the creditors pose about his financial situation. If the creditors want to elect a trustee, they do so at this meeting.

After the meeting of creditors, unsecured creditors must submit a ***proof of claim***. This document is a simple form stating the name of the creditor and the amount of the claim. The trustee and the debtor also have the right to file on behalf of a creditor. But if a claim is not filed, the creditor loses any right to be paid. The trustee, debtor, or any creditor can object to a claim on the grounds that the debtor does not really owe that money. The court then holds a hearing to determine the validity of the claim.

Proof of claim
A form stating the name of an unsecured creditor and the amount of the claim against the debtor.

Secured creditors do not file proofs of claim unless the claim exceeds the value of their collateral. In this case, they are unsecured creditors for the excess amount and must file a proof of claim for it. Suppose that Deborah borrows $750,000 from Morton in return for a mortgage on her house. If she does not repay the debt, he can foreclose. Unfortunately, property values plummet, and by the time Deborah files a voluntary petition in bankruptcy, the house is worth only $500,000. Morton is a secured creditor for $500,000 and need file no proof of claim for that amount. But he is an unsecured creditor for $250,000 and will lose his right to this excess amount unless he files a proof of claim for it.

Automatic Stay

A fox chased by hounds has no time to make rational long-term decisions. What that fox needs is a safe burrow. Similarly, it is difficult for debtors to make sound financial decisions when hounded night and day by creditors shouting, "Pay me! Pay me!" The Code is designed to give debtors enough breathing space to sort out their affairs sensibly. An automatic stay is a safe burrow for the bankrupt. It goes into effect as soon as the petition is filed. An **automatic stay** prohibits creditors from collecting debts that the bankrupt incurred before the petition was filed. Creditors may not sue a bankrupt to obtain payment, nor may they take other steps, outside of court, to pressure the debtor for payment. The following case illustrates how persistent creditors can be.

Automatic stay
Prohibits creditors from collecting debts that the bankrupt incurred before the petition was filed.

JACKSON V. HOLIDAY FURNITURE

309 B.R. 33, 2004 Bankr. LEXIS 548
United States Bankruptcy Court for the Western District of Missouri, 2004

Facts: In April, Cora and Frank Jackson purchased a recliner chair on credit from Dan Holiday Furniture. They made payments until November. That month, they filed for protection under the Bankruptcy Code. Dan Holiday received a notice of the bankruptcy. This notice stated that the store must stop all efforts to collect on the Jacksons' debt.

Despite this notice, a Dan Holiday collector telephoned the Jacksons' house 10 times between November 15 and December 1 and left a card in their door threatening repossession of the chair. On December 1, Frank (without Cora's knowledge) went to Dan Holiday to pay the $230 owed for November and December. He told the store owner about the bankruptcy filing but allegedly added that he and his wife wanted to continue making payments directly to Dan Holiday.

In early January, employees at Dan Holiday learned that Frank had died the month before. Nevertheless, after Cora failed to make the payment for the month of January, a collector telephoned her house 26 times between January 14 and February 19. The store owner's sister left the following message on Cora's answering machine:

> Hello. This is Judy over at Dan Holiday Furniture. And this is the last time I am going to call you. If you do not call me, I will be at your house. And I expect you to call me today. If there is a problem, I need to speak to you about it. You need to call me. We need to get this thing going. You are a January and February payment behind. And if you think you are going to get away with it, you've got another thing coming.

When Cora returned home on February 18, she found seven bright yellow slips of paper in her doorjamb stating that a Dan Holiday truck had stopped by to repossess her furniture. The cards read: "OUR TRUCK was here to **REPOSSESS** Your furniture (sic). 241-6933 Dan Holiday Furn. & Appl. Co."

The threat to send a truck was merely a ruse designed to frighten Cora. In truth, Dan Holiday did not really want the recliner back. The owner just wanted to talk directly with Cora about making payments.

Also on February 18, Dan Holiday sent Cora a letter stating that she had 24 hours to bring her account current or else **"Repossession** Will Be Made and **Legal Action Will Be Taken."** That same day, Cora's bankruptcy attorney contacted Dan Holiday. Thereafter, all collection activity ceased.

Issues: ***Did Dan Holiday violate the automatic stay provisions of the Bankruptcy Code? What is the penalty for a violation?***

Excerpts from Judge Venters's Decision:[6] The automatic stay prohibits the commencement or continuation of any action against the debtor that arose before the commencement of the bankruptcy case and forbids any act by a pre-petition creditor to obtain possession of property of the bankruptcy estate. An individual injured by a creditor's violation of the automatic stay shall recover actual damages, including costs and attorneys' fees, and in appropriate circumstances, may recover punitive damages.

In this case, there is no question that Dan Holiday repeatedly violated the automatic stay. [T]he Court finds that the Jacksons suffered financial damages in the amount of $230.00, which represents the coerced payments that Dan Holiday received from Frank Jackson on December 1.

The Court finds that punitive damages are warranted in this case based on Dan Holiday's egregious, intentional violations of the automatic stay. Dan Holiday's conduct was remarkably bad in that, after it had actual knowledge of the Jacksons' bankruptcy, and after coercing payments from the Jacksons covering the months of November and December, it made no less than twenty-six telephone calls to the Jacksons' household in January and February. Dan Holiday's continued collection efforts were in flagrant violation of the protections Congress afforded to debtors under the automatic stay.

In this matter, the Court is somewhat hampered in assessing punitive damages by the lack of evidence concerning the ability of Dan Holiday to pay. [An owner] testified that Dan Holiday was a family-owned business that has been in existence for 52 years, and the Court assumes that it is a relatively small business. Under the circumstances of this case, the Court believes that an appropriate penalty would be $100.00 for each illegal contact with the Jacksons after December 1, when it is crystal clear that Dan Holiday had actual knowledge of the Jacksons' bankruptcy filing, for a total of $2,800.00. The Court believes that this penalty will be sufficient to sting the pocketbook of Dan Holiday and impress upon Dan Holiday and its owners and employees the importance of debtor protections under the Bankruptcy Code, as well as to deter further transgressions.

The Court also will award the Jacksons their attorneys' fees and costs in the amount of $1,142.42, an amount the Court considers eminently fair and reasonable under the circumstances of this case.

Bankruptcy Estate

Bankruptcy estate
The new legal entity created when a debtor files a bankruptcy petition. The debtor's existing assets pass into the estate.

The filing of the bankruptcy petition creates a new legal entity separate from the debtor—the **bankruptcy estate**. All of the bankrupt's assets pass to the estate except exempt property and new property that the debtor acquires after the petition is filed.

[6]For readability's sake, we refer to the plaintiffs as "the Jacksons," not "debtors," as the court did.

Exempt Property

Unpaid creditors may be angry, but generally they do not want the debtor to starve to death. **The Code permits *individual* debtors (but not organizations) to keep some property for themselves.** This exempt property saves the debtor from destitution during the bankruptcy process and provides the foundation for a new life once the process is over.

In this one area of bankruptcy law, the Code defers to state law. Although the Code lists various types of exempt property, it permits states to opt out of the federal system and define a different set of exemptions. A majority of states have indeed opted out of the Code, and for their residents, the Code exemptions are irrelevant. Alternatively, some states allow the debtor to choose between state or federal exemptions.

Under the *federal* Code, a debtor is allowed to exempt only $21,625 of the value of her home. If the house is worth more than that, the trustee sells it and returns $21,625 of the proceeds to the debtor. Most *states* exempt items such as the debtor's home, household goods, cars, work tools, disability and pension benefits, alimony, and health aids. Indeed, some states set no limit on the value of exempt property. Both Florida and Texas, for example, permit debtors to keep homes of unlimited value and a certain amount of land. (Texas also allows debtors to hang on to two firearms; athletic and sporting equipment; two horses, mules or donkeys and a saddle, blanket, and bridle for each; up to a total value of $60,000 per family.) Not surprisingly, these generous exemptions sometimes lead to abuses. Therefore, the Code provides that debtors can take advantage of state exemptions only if they have lived in that state for two years prior to the bankruptcy. And they can exempt only $146,450 of any house that was acquired during the 40 months before the bankruptcy.

Voidable Preferences

A major goal of the bankruptcy system is to divide the debtor's assets fairly among creditors. It would not be fair, or in keeping with this goal, if debtors were permitted to pay off some of their creditors immediately before filing a bankruptcy petition. These transfers are called **preferences** because they give unfair preferential treatment to some creditors. The trustee has the right to void such preferences.

Preference
When a debtor unfairly pays creditors immediately before filing a bankruptcy petition.

Preferences can take two forms: payments and liens. A *payment* simply means that the debtor gives a creditor cash that would otherwise end up in the bankruptcy estate. A *lien* means a security interest in the debtor's property. In bankruptcy proceedings, secured creditors are more likely to be paid than unsecured creditors. If the debtor grants a security interest in specific property, he vaults that creditor out of the great unwashed mass of unsecured creditors and into the elite company of secured creditors. If it happens immediately before the petition is filed, it is unfair to other unsecured creditors.

The trustee can void any transfer (whether payment or lien) that meets all of the following requirements:

- The transfer was to a creditor of the bankrupt.
- It was to pay an existing debt.
- The creditor received more from the transfer than she would have received during the bankruptcy process.
- The debtor's liabilities exceeded assets at the time of the transfer.
- The transfer took place in the 90-day period before the filing of the petition.

Don Farrall/Photodisc/Getty Images

The debtor who hides assets from the approaching storm of bankruptcy is making a fraudulent transfer.

Insider
Family members of an individual debtor, officers and directors of a corporation, or partners of a partnership.

In addition, the trustee can void a transfer to an insider that occurs in the *year* preceding the filing of the petition. **Insiders** are family members of an individual, officers and directors of a corporation, or partners of a partnership.

Fraudulent Transfers

Suppose that a debtor sees bankruptcy approaching across the horizon like a tornado. He knows that, once the storm hits and he files a petition, everything he owns except a few items of exempt property will become part of the bankruptcy estate. Before that happens, he may be tempted to give some of his property to friends or family to shelter it from the tornado. If he succumbs to temptation, however, he is committing a fraudulent transfer.

A transfer is fraudulent if it is made within the year before a petition is filed and its purpose is to hinder, delay, or defraud creditors. The trustee can void any fraudulent transfer. The debtor has committed a crime and may be prosecuted.

Not all payments by a debtor prior to filing are considered voidable preferences or fraudulent transfers. **A trustee cannot void pre-petition payments made *in the ordinary course.*** In a business context, that means a trustee cannot void payments from, say, a grocery store to its regular cookie supplier. For consumers, the trustee cannot void payments below $600 or other routine payments, say, to the electric or water company. In these situations, the bankrupt is clearly not trying to cheat creditors. Even the insolvent are allowed to shower with the lights on.

Even the insolvent are allowed to shower with the lights on.

EXAM Strategy

Question: Eddie and Lola appeared to be happily married. But then Eddie's business failed, and he owed millions. Suddenly, Lola announced that she wanted a divorce. Eddie immediately agreed to transfer all of the couple's remaining assets to her as part of the divorce settlement. Are you suspicious? Is there a problem?

Strategy: Was this a voidable preference or a fraudulent transfer? What difference does it make?

Result: In a voidable preference, the debtor makes an unfair transfer to a creditor. In a fraudulent transfer, the bankrupt's goal is to hold on to assets himself. In a case similar to this one, the court ruled that the transfer was fraudulent because Eddie intended to shield his assets from all creditors.

Payment of Claims

Imagine a crowded delicatessen on a Saturday evening. People are pushing and shoving because they know there is not enough food for everyone; some customers will go home hungry. The delicatessen could simply serve whoever pushes to the front of the line, or it could establish a number system to ensure that the most deserving customers are served first—longtime patrons or those who called ahead. The Code has, in essence, adopted a number system to prevent a free-for-all fight over the bankrupt's assets. Indeed, one of the Code's primary goals is to ensure that creditors are paid in the proper order, not according to who pushes to the front of the line.

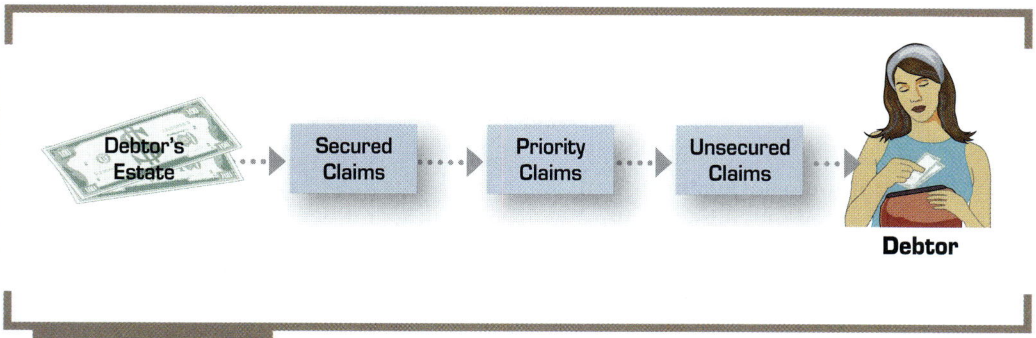

EXHIBIT 37.1

All claims are placed in one of three classes: (1) secured claims, (2) priority claims, and (3) unsecured claims. The second class—priority claims—has seven subcategories; the third class—unsecured claims—has three. **The trustee pays the bankruptcy estate to the various classes of claims in order of rank.** A higher class is paid in full before the next class receives any payment at all. In the case of *priority* claims, each *subcategory* is paid in order, with the higher subcategory receiving full payment before the next subcategory receives anything. If there are not enough funds to pay an entire subcategory, all claimants in that group receive a *pro rata* share. The rule is different for unsecured claims. All categories of *unsecured* claims are treated the same, and if there are not enough funds to pay the *entire* class, everyone in the class shares *pro rata*. If, for example, there is only enough money to pay 10 percent of the claims owing to unsecured creditors, then each creditor receives 10 percent of her claim. In bankruptcy parlance, this is referred to as "getting 10 cents on the dollar." The debtor is entitled to any funds remaining after all claims have been paid. The payment order is shown in Exhibit 37.1.

Secured Claims

Creditors whose loans are secured by specific collateral are paid first. Secured claims are fundamentally different from all other claims because they are paid by selling a specific asset, not out of the general funds of the estate. Sometimes, however, collateral is not valuable enough to pay off the entire secured debt. In this case, the creditor must wait in line with the unsecured creditors for the balance. Deborah (whom we met earlier in the section entitled "Creditors") borrowed $750,000 from Morton, secured by a mortgage on her house. By the time she files a voluntary petition, the house is worth only $500,000. Morton is a secured creditor for $500,000 and is paid that amount as soon as the trustee sells the house. But Morton is an unsecured creditor for $250,000 and will only receive this amount if the estate has enough funds to pay the unsecured creditors.

Priority Claims

There are seven subcategories of priority claims. Each category is paid in order, with the first group receiving full payment before the next group receives anything.

- *Alimony and child support.* The trustee must first pay any claims for alimony and child support. However, if the trustee is administering assets that could pay these support claims, then the trustee's fees are paid first.
- *Administrative expenses.* These include fees to the trustee, lawyers, and accountants.
- *Gap expenses.* If creditors file an involuntary petition, the debtor will continue to operate her business until the order for relief. Any expenses she incurs in the ordinary course of her business during this so-called **gap period** are paid now.

Gap period
The period between the time that a creditor files an involuntary petition and the court issues the order for relief.

- *Payments to employees.* The trustee now pays back wages to the debtor's employees for work performed during the 180 days prior to the date of the petition. The trustee, however, can pay no more than $11,725 to each employee. Any other wages become unsecured claims.
- *Employee benefit plans.* The trustee pays what the debtor owes to employee pension, health, or life insurance plans for work performed during the 180 days prior to the date of the petition. The total payment for wages and benefits under this and the prior paragraph cannot exceed $11,725 times the number of employees.
- *Consumer deposits.* Any individual who has put down a deposit with the bankrupt for consumer goods is entitled to a refund of up to $2,600. If Stewart puts down a $3,000 deposit on a Miata sports car, he is entitled to a refund of $2,600 when the Trustie Car Lot goes bankrupt.
- *Taxes.* The trustee pays the debtor's income taxes for the three years prior to filing and property taxes for one prior year.
- *Intoxication injuries.* The trustee next pays the claims of anyone injured by a bankrupt who was driving a vehicle while drunk or on drugs.

Unsecured Claims

Last, and frequently very much least, the trustee pays unsecured claims. All three of these unsecured subcategories have an equal claim and must be paid together.

- *Secured claims that exceed the value of the available collateral.* If funds permit, the trustee pays Morton the $250,000 that his collateral did not cover.
- *Priority claims that exceed the priority limits.* The trustee now pays employees, Stewart, and the tax authorities who were not paid in full the first time around because their claims exceeded the priority limits.
- *All other unsecured claims.* Unsecured creditors have now reached the delicatessen counter. They can only hope that some food remains.

Discharge

Fresh start
After the termination of a bankruptcy case, creditors cannot make a claim against the debtor for money owed before the initial bankruptcy petition was filed.

Discharge
The debtor no longer has an obligation to pay a debt.

Filing a bankruptcy petition is embarrassing, time-consuming, and disruptive. It can affect the debtor's credit rating for years, making the simplest car loan a challenge. To encourage debtors to file for bankruptcy despite the pain involved, the Code offers a powerful incentive: the **fresh start**. Once a bankruptcy estate has been distributed to creditors, they cannot make a claim against the debtor for money owed before the filing, *whether or not they actually received any payment.* These pre-petition debts are **discharged**. All is forgiven, if not forgotten.

Discharge is an essential part of bankruptcy law. Without it, debtors would have little incentive to take part. To avoid abuses, however, the Code limits both the type of debts that can be discharged and the circumstances under which discharge can take place. In addition, a debtor must complete an approved course on financial management before receiving a discharge.

Debts That Cannot Be Discharged

The following debts are *never* discharged, and the debtor remains liable in full until they are paid:

- Income taxes for the three years prior to filing and property taxes for the prior year.
- Money obtained fraudulently. Kenneth Smith ran a home repair business that fleeced senior citizens by making unnecessary repairs. Three months after he was found

liable for fraud, he filed a voluntary petition in bankruptcy. The court held that his liability on the fraud claim could not be discharged.[7]

- Any loan of more than $600 that a consumer uses to purchase luxury goods within 90 days before the order for relief is granted.
- Cash advances on a credit card totaling more than $875 that an individual debtor takes out within 70 days before the order for relief.
- Debts omitted from the Schedule of Assets and Liabilities that the debtor filed with the petition, if the creditor did not know about the bankruptcy and therefore did not file a proof of claim.
- Money that the debtor stole or obtained through a violation of fiduciary duty.
- Money owed for alimony or child support.
- Debts stemming from intentional and malicious injury.
- Fines and penalties owed to the government.
- Liability for injuries caused by the debtor while operating a vehicle under the influence of drugs or alcohol. (Yet another reason why friends don't let friends drive drunk.)
- Liability for breach of duty to a bank. During the 1980s, a record number of savings and loans failed because their officers had made too many risky loans (in some cases to friends and family). This provision, added to the Code in 1990, was designed to prevent these officers from declaring bankruptcy to avoid their liability to bank shareholders.
- Debts stemming from a violation of securities laws.
- Student loans can be discharged only if repayment would cause undue hardship. As the following case illustrates, proving undue hardship is difficult.

In Re Stern

288 B.R. 36; 2002 Bankr. LEXIS 1609
United States Bankruptcy Court for the Northern District of New York, 2002

Facts: James Stern took out student loans to attend Bates College and Syracuse College of Law. Afterward, he had difficulty finding a job as a lawyer, so he opened his own practice. Both he and his wife earned less than $20,000 a year.

A client sued Stern for malpractice. Although Stern won, his malpractice premiums increased so much that he could no longer afford the insurance. Believing that his debt and default on his student loans made him unemployable as a lawyer, he moved with his wife to her native country, France. Unfortunately, he did not speak French and, therefore, could not obtain a job, even as a street sweeper. His wife's total income over six months in France was $2,200. Even more unfortunately, their expenses in France were higher than in the United States.

Stern owed $147,000 in student loans: $56,000 in principal and $91,000 in interest. He calculated that paying this debt would cost $1,167 per month over 30 years. He asked the court to discharge these student loans on grounds of undue hardship. As he put it, "I'm never going to be able to get a house, I'm never going to be able to have a car, and I won't—you know, I want to have kids. I want to be responsible, and I can't—I can't possibly pay this amount and have a life, not with what I expect I'll be able to earn."

[7] *In re Smith,* 848 F.2d 813, 1988 U.S. App. LEXIS 8037 (7th Cir. 1988).

Issue: *Is Stern entitled to a discharge of his student loans on grounds of undue hardship?*

Excerpts from Judge Gerling's Decision:[8] [E]ducational loans are different from most loans. They are made without business considerations, without security, without cosigners, and rely for repayment solely on the debtor's future increased income resulting from the education. In this sense, the loan is viewed as a mortgage on the debtor's future.

[To obtain a discharge,] Stern must prove more than his present inability to pay his student loan obligations. He must also establish that his current financial hardship is likely to be long-term. In this case, Stern possesses both a bachelor's degree and a Juris Doctorate. Stern apparently has decided that he no longer wishes to pursue a legal career. He is certainly well within his rights to make such a choice. Nevertheless, [b]orrowers under the various guaranteed student loan programs are obligated to repay their loans even if they are unable to obtain employment in their chosen field of study.

The Court finds disturbing Stern's failure to maximize his income and minimize his expenses. He and his wife have elected to relocate to France, where Stern admitted that the cost of living is higher. Nor is there any evidence that he ever made any effort to obtain employment in the United States in order to enhance his earnings, whether it be in business, government, or in a private law firm in Syracuse or elsewhere. Instead, he opted to move to a country where he acknowledges he cannot even get a job as a street sweeper because of his inability to speak the language.

Obviously, Stern would prefer to be in a position that would allow him to allocate those monies [he owes] to a mortgage on a home or to the raising of children. Those are certainly commendable goals; but the fact that they may not be attainable at this time because of the student loans and Stern's, as well as his wife's, current employment situation, does not meet the fundamental standard from which "undue hardship" is measured and does not provide a basis for granting Stern [even] a partial discharge at this time.

While Stern and his wife have experienced some "bumps in the road," the direction they take in the future appears very much in their control based on their age, health, and education. Indeed, it is the very education that he obtained as a result of the student loans at both the undergraduate and graduate levels, which, arguably, should ultimately allow him to pursue employment opportunities not available to others who were unable to pursue higher education for whatever reason. While Stern testified that he no longer wishes to continue in the legal profession, certainly, there are other career opportunities available to him by virtue of his education, training, and experience.

Circumstances That Prevent Debts from Being Discharged

Apart from identifying the *kinds* of debts that cannot be discharged, the Code also prohibits the discharge of debts under the following *circumstances:*

- *Business organizations.* Under Chapter 7 (but *not* the other Chapters), only the debts of individuals can be discharged, not those of business organizations. Once its assets have been distributed, the organization must cease operation. If it continues in business, it is responsible for all pre-petition debts. Shortly after E. G. Sprinkler Corp. entered into an agreement with its union employees, it filed for bankruptcy under Chapter 7. Its debts were discharged, and the company began operation again. A court ordered it to pay its obligations to the employees because, once the company resumed business, it was responsible for all of its pre-filing debts.[9]
- *Revocation.* A court can revoke a discharge within one year if it discovers the debtor engaged in fraud or concealment.
- *Dishonesty or bad faith behavior.* The court may deny discharge altogether if the debtor has, for example, made fraudulent transfers, hidden assets, falsified records, disobeyed court orders, refused to testify, or otherwise acted in bad faith. For

[8]Although the court refers to Stern as "Debtor," we use his surname.

[9]*In re Goodman*, 873 F.2d 598, 1989 U.S. App. LEXIS 5472 (2d Cir. 1989).

instance, a court denied discharge under Chapter 7 to a couple who failed to list 15 pounds of marijuana on their Schedule of Assets and Liabilities. The court was unsympathetic to their arguments that a listing of this asset might have caused larger problems than merely being in debt.[10]

- *Repeated filings for bankruptcy.* Congress feared that some debtors, attracted by the lure of a fresh start, would make a habit of bankruptcy. Therefore, a debtor who has received a discharge under Chapter 7 or 11 cannot receive another discharge under Chapter 7 for at least eight years after the prior filing. And a debtor who received a prior discharge under Chapter 13 cannot in most cases receive one under Chapter 7 for at least six years.

Ethics Banks and credit card companies lobbied Congress hard for the prohibition against repeated bankruptcy filings. They argued that irresponsible consumers run up debt and then blithely walk away. You might think that, if this were true, lenders would avoid customers with a history of bankruptcy. Research indicates, though, that lenders actually *target* those consumers, repeatedly sending them offers to borrow money. The reason is simple: these consumers are much more likely to take cash advances, which carry very high interest rates. And this is one audience that *must* repay its loans for the simple reason that these borrowers cannot declare bankruptcy again.[11] Is this strategy ethical?

EXAM Strategy

Question: Someone stole a truck full of cigarettes. Zeke found the vehicle abandoned at a truck stop. Not being a thoughtful fellow, he took the truck and sold it with its cargo. Although Tobacco Company never found out who stole the truck originally, it did discover Zeke's role. A court ordered Zeke to pay Tobacco $50,000. He also owed his wife $25,000 in child support. Unfortunately, he only had $20,000 in assets. After he files for bankruptcy, who will get paid what?

Strategy: There are two issues: the order in which the debts are paid and whether they will be discharged.

Result: Child support is a priority claim, so that will be paid first. In a similar case, the court refused to discharge the claim over the theft of the truck, ruling that that was an intentional and malicious injury. Nor will a court discharge the child support claim. So Zeke will be on the hook for both debts, but the child support must be paid first.

[10] *In re Tripp*, 224 B.R. 95, 1998 Bankr. LEXIS 1108 (1998).

[11] See Katherine M. Porter, "Bankrupt Profits: The Credit Industry's Business Model for Postbankruptcy Lending," University of Iowa Legal Studies Research Paper No. 07-26, Iowa Law Review, Vol. 94, 2008. This paper is available by googling "ssrn katherine porter bankrupt profits".

Reaffirmation

Reaffirm
To promise to pay a debt even after it is discharged.

Sometimes debtors are willing to **reaffirm** a debt, meaning they promise to pay even after discharge. They may want to reaffirm a secured debt to avoid losing the collateral. For example, a debtor who has taken out a loan secured by a car may reaffirm that debt so that the finance company will not repossess it. Sometimes debtors reaffirm because they feel guilty or want to maintain a good relationship with the creditor. They may have borrowed from a family member or an important supplier. Because discharge is a fundamental pillar of the bankruptcy process, creditors are not permitted to unfairly pressure the bankrupt. To be valid, the reaffirmation must:

- Not violate common law standards for fraud, duress, or unconscionability. If creditors force a bankrupt into reaffirming a debt, the reaffirmation is invalid.
- Have been filed in court before the discharge is granted.
- Include the detailed disclosure statement required by the statute (Section 524).
- Be approved by the court if the debtor is not represented by an attorney or if, as a result of the reaffirmed debt, the bankrupt's expenses exceed his income.

In the following case, the debtor sought to reaffirm the loan on his truck. He may have been afraid that if he did not, the lender would repossess it, leaving him stranded. It is hard to get around Dallas without a car. Should the court permit the reaffirmation?

In Re: Grisham

436 B.R. 896; 2010 Bankr. LEXIS 2907
United States Bankruptcy Court for the Northern District of Texas, 2010

Facts: Two months before filing for bankruptcy, William Grisham bought a Dodge truck (Nitro-V6 Utility 4D SLT 2WD). At the time of his bankruptcy filing, the vehicle was worth $16,000, but he owed $17,500 on it. The annual interest rate was 17.5 percent, the monthly payments were $400, and the payment schedule was almost 6 years. In addition, Grisham owed:

$29,000 to the IRS
$75,000 in alimony
$100,000 in student loans
$70,000 in unsecured debt
$274,000 total in addition to the truck

Grisham sought to reaffirm the truck loan. Should the court allow him to do so?

Issue: ***Would reaffirmation of this debt create an undue hardship for the debtor?***

Excerpts from Judge Jernigan's Decision: [F]rom the outset, this court was concerned that the Debtor wished to reaffirm debt on personal property in which there is no equity. [T]he Debtor describes himself as "retired/unemployed." The Debtor's only source of income is $1,928 per month of social security income and $1,698 per month of unemployment benefits—the latter of which will soon expire. The Debtor owns no real property and testified that he currently resides rent-free at a relative's home. The Debtor's monthly net income, after deducting his living expenses, is a negative $1,091.

While the monthly payments on the vehicle are not eye-popping, for this Debtor, in his current situation, it is unduly burdensome. In particular, this Debtor is burdened with several obligations that will likely survive his discharge in bankruptcy (large IRS debt; large alimony; and large student loan debt). Finally, the court heard no compelling testimony to justify why the Debtor purchased his vehicle right before filing bankruptcy (sometimes this may be defensible and sometimes not). In summary, the court will not stamp its seal of approval on the Debtor's reaffirmation of the debt. To do so would create a hardship on this Debtor and does not otherwise seem justified.

Bankruptcy is about "fresh starts" and new beginnings. It is about belt-tightening and shedding past bad habits. Too often, a reaffirmation agreement will reveal that someone just does not comprehend this and wants to go forward in a manner that will impair his fresh start and perpetuate bad habits from the past.

The court realizes that this is sometimes complicated. [T]here are probably situations in which a vehicle-lender will repossess the debtor's vehicle post-discharge, even when the debtor is making regular and timely contractual payments for the car post-discharge—for the simple reason that the debtor did not "reaffirm." Thus, the court can understand why a debtor and his counsel might see the wisdom of entering into a reaffirmation agreement, even if they can envision the court may never approve it because of the negative math. Perhaps they imagine that this will help the debtor with the car lender post-discharge, if they at least tried to get the reaffirmation agreement approved with the court. Moreover, perhaps the debtor genuinely needs a car and worries that, absent an attempt at a reaffirmation agreement, he will surely lose the car post-discharge and may not be able to purchase (*i.e.*, obtain financing) for another vehicle in the near future.

The court realizes that we are in a world where car lenders may not always act like economically rational animals. And, the court appreciates that car lenders may sometimes have their own economic pressures with which to contend. But, again, the fresh start is the overriding purpose of a chapter 7 bankruptcy case. Many reaffirmation agreements presented to the court are the farthest thing from a "fresh start" that one could ever imagine. Many times it is time to say "good riddance" to the car. And many times—maybe, just maybe—a car lender will see the wisdom of renegotiating a car loan if reaffirmation is denied.

Accordingly,

IT IS ORDERED that the Reaffirmation Agreement is disapproved.

Chapter 11 Reorganization

For a business, the goal of a Chapter 7 bankruptcy is euthanasia—putting it out of its misery by shutting it down and distributing its assets to creditors. Chapter 11 has a much more complicated and ambitious goal—resuscitating a business so that it can ultimately emerge as a viable economic concern, as General Motors did. Keeping a business in operation benefits virtually all company stakeholders: employees, customers, creditors, shareholders, and the community.

Both individuals and businesses can use Chapter 11. Businesses usually prefer Chapter 11 over Chapter 7 because Chapter 11 does not require them to dissolve at the end, as Chapter 7 does. The threat of death creates a powerful incentive to try rehabilitation under Chapter 11. Individuals, however, tend to prefer Chapter 13 because it is specifically designed for them.

A Chapter 11 proceeding follows many of the same steps as Chapter 7: a petition (either voluntary or involuntary), order for relief, meeting of creditors, proofs of claim, and an automatic stay. There are, however, some significant differences.

Debtor in Possession

Chapter 11 does not require a trustee. The bankrupt is called the **debtor in possession** and, in essence, serves as trustee. The debtor in possession has two jobs: to operate the business and to develop a plan of reorganization. A trustee is chosen only if the debtor is incompetent or uncooperative. In that case, the creditors can elect the trustee, but if they do not choose to do so, the U.S. Trustee appoints one.

Debtor in possession
The debtor acts as trustee in a Chapter 11 bankruptcy.

Creditors' Committee

In a Chapter 11 case, the creditors' committee is important because typically, there is no neutral trustee to watch over their interests. The committee generally protects the interests of its constituency and may play a role in developing the plan of reorganization. Moreover, the Bankruptcy Code requires the committee to communicate diligently with all creditors. The U.S. Trustee typically appoints the seven largest *un*secured creditors to the committee. However, the court may require the U.S. Trustee to appoint some small-business creditors as well. Secured creditors do not serve because their interests require less protection. If the debtor is a corporation, the U.S. Trustee may also appoint a committee of shareholders. The Code refers to the **claims** of creditors and the **interests** of shareholders.

Plan of Reorganization

Once the bankruptcy petition is filed, an automatic stay goes into effect to provide the debtor with temporary relief from creditors. The next stage is to develop a plan of reorganization that provides for the payment of debts and the continuation of the business. For the first 120 days (which the court can extend up to 18 months), the debtor has the exclusive right to propose a plan. If the debtor fails to file a plan, or if the court rejects it, then creditors and shareholders can develop their own plan.

Confirmation of the Plan

Anyone who proposes a plan of reorganization must also prepare a **disclosure statement** to be mailed out with the plan. The purpose of this statement is to provide creditors and shareholders with enough information to make an informed judgment. The statement describes the company's business, explains the plan, calculates the company's liquidation value, and assesses the likelihood that the debtor can be rehabilitated. The court must approve a disclosure statement before it is sent to creditors and shareholders.

All the creditors and shareholders have the right to vote on the plan of reorganization. In preparation for the vote, each creditor and shareholder is assigned to a class. Everyone in a class has similar claims or interests. Chapter 11 classifies claims in the same way as Chapter 7: (1) secured claims, (2) priority claims, and (3) unsecured claims. Each secured claim is usually in its own class because each one is secured by different collateral. Shareholders are also divided into classes depending upon their interests. For example, holders of preferred stock are in a different class from common shareholders.

Creditors and shareholders receive a ballot with their disclosure statement to vote for or against the plan of reorganization. After the vote, the bankruptcy court holds a **confirmation hearing** to determine whether it should accept the plan. **The court will approve a plan if a majority *of each class* votes in favor of it *and* if the "yes" votes hold at least two-thirds of the total debt in that class.**

Even if some classes vote against the plan, the court can still confirm it under what is called a **cramdown** (as in "the plan is crammed down the creditors' throats"). The court will not impose a cramdown unless, in its view, the plan is feasible and fair. If the court rejects the plan of reorganization, the creditors must develop a new one. In the following case, the court did impose a cramdown.

In Re Fox

2000 Bankr. LEXIS 1713
United States Bankruptcy Court, District of Kansas, 2000

Facts: Donald Fox founded Midland Fumigant, Inc., a company in the business of fumigating stored wheat, corn, and other grain. In a prior case, a competitor, United Phosphorus, Ltd., obtained a verdict of $2 million against Midland and Fox for fraud.

Unable to pay the judgment, Fox filed a voluntary petition under Chapter 11 of the Bankruptcy Code. His plan of reorganization envisioned that he would use revenues from Midland to pay off his creditors in full over five years, with interest. To ensure that the plan of reorganization was feasible, Fox hired CPA Kirk Wiesner to analyze Midland's financial statements and prepare projections of its income and expenses. Wiesner also reviewed Midland's operations, business, products, and the industry. He concluded that the plan's projections were conservative and could be met easily.

Midland had six classes of creditors. All of the classes accepted the plan except the two classes in which United was a member. The bankruptcy judge noted that United had an incentive to oppose Midland's reorganization because this business was highly competitive and, if Midland were to cease operations, United would be able to raise its prices substantially.

Issues: ***Was Fox's plan of reorganization feasible and fair? Should the court impose a cramdown?***

Excerpts from Judge Robinson's Decision: Debtor has proposed a plan which pays all creditors in full, with interest. United, the only objecting creditor, will be paid in full [within 16 months]. Debtor has provided a reasonable and orderly repayment of his debts. Debtor's desire and intent to provide a mechanism for him to retain his business interests and assets is consistent with the purposes of the Bankruptcy Code. The plan may satisfy [the Code] even though the plan may not be one which the creditors would themselves design.

United contends that the Plan is not feasible because the projections of Midland's income and expenses are unreliable. The purpose [of the Bankruptcy Code] is to prevent confirmation of visionary schemes that promise creditors and equity security holders more than the debtor can possibly attain after confirmation.

Will the reorganized debtor emerge from bankruptcy solvent and with a reasonable prospect of success? Debtor's expert, Kirk Wiesner, analyzed Midland's financial statements, and determined that Midland would have sufficient income and cash flow during the life of Debtor's Plan, to make the anticipated distributions and loans that will fund Debtor's Plan. Based on Wiesner's Projections, which proved conservative in [the past], when Midland's actual income doubled the projected income, the Court concludes that Midland will have a continuing ability to distribute and loan funds to the Debtor as contemplated.

The Plan has a reasonable assurance of success and is not likely to be followed by liquidation, or the need for further financial reorganization. As such, the Debtor's Plan meets the feasibility requirement. The Court further notes that the United States Trustee has filed a statement in support of confirmation of the Plan.

[T]he Court finds that the Debtor's Plan is fair and equitable and, as a result, the fact that [two] Classes did not accept the Plan does not preclude confirmation.

The Debtor's Plan is confirmed over the objection of United and over the dissenting votes of [two] Classes for the reasons stated.

Discharge

A confirmed plan of reorganization is binding on the debtor, creditors, and shareholders. **The debtor now owns the assets in the bankrupt estate, free of all obligations except those listed in the plan.** Under a typical plan of reorganization, the debtor gives some current assets to creditors and also promises to pay them a portion of future earnings. In contrast, the Chapter 7 debtor typically relinquishes all assets (except exempt property) to creditors but then has no obligation to turn over future income. Exhibit 37.2 illustrates the steps in a Chapter 11 bankruptcy.

Small-Business Bankruptcy

Out of concern that the lengthy procedure in Chapter 11 was harming the creditors of small businesses, in 2005 Congress included provisions designed to speed up the process for businesses with less than $2 million in debt. After the order for relief, the bankrupt has the exclusive right to file a plan for 180 days. Both a plan and a disclosure statement must be filed within 300 days. The court must confirm or reject the plan within 45 days after its filing. If these deadlines are not met, the case can be converted to Chapter 7 or dismissed.

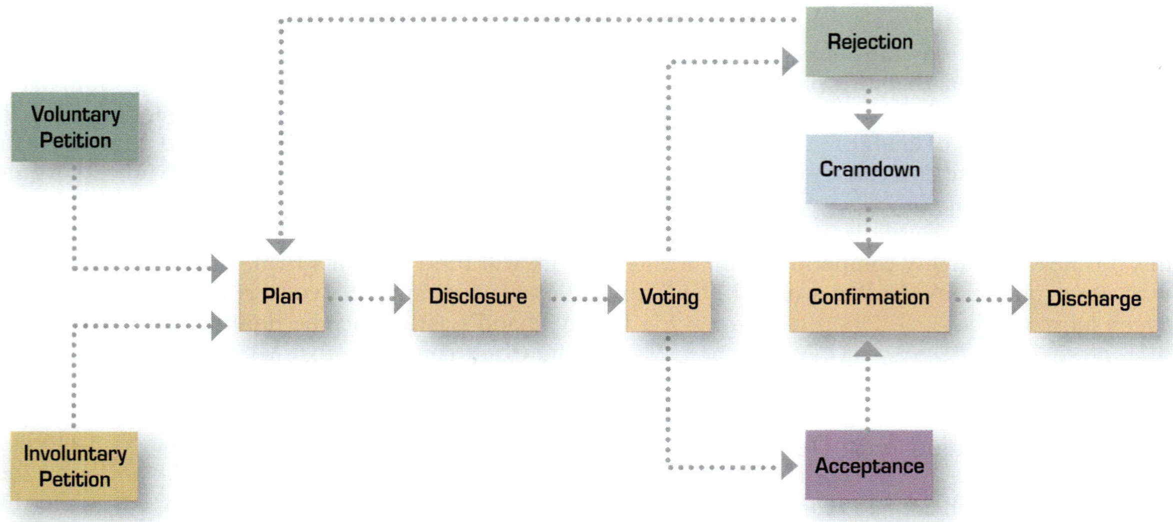

EXHIBIT 37.2

Chapter 13 Consumer Reorganizations

The purpose of Chapter 13 is to rehabilitate an individual debtor. It is not available at all to businesses or to individuals with more than $360,475 in unsecured debts or $1,081,400 in secured debts. Under Chapter 13, the bankrupt consumer typically keeps most of her assets in exchange for a promise to repay some of her debts using future income. Therefore, to be eligible, the debtor must have a regular source of income. Individuals usually choose this chapter because it is easier and cheaper than Chapters 7 and 11. Consequently, more money is retained for both creditors and debtor.

As you read at the beginning of the chapter, debtors can convert from one chapter to another as they wish. In this case, the trustees objected to a conversion. The case went all the way to the Supreme Court, which split 5-4. How would you have voted?

You be the Judge

Marrama v. Citizens Bank of Massachusetts

127 S. Ct. 1105; 2007 U.S. LEXIS 2651
Supreme Court of the United States, 2007

Facts: When Robert Marrama filed a voluntary petition under Chapter 7, he lied. Although he disclosed that he was the sole beneficiary of a trust that owned a house in Maine, he listed its value as zero. Marrama also denied that he had transferred any property during the prior year. Neither statement was true: the Maine property was valuable (how many houses are worth zero?), and he had given it for free to the trust seven months prior to filing for bankruptcy protection. Marrama also lied when he claimed that he was not entitled to a tax refund. In fact, he knew that a check for $8,700 from the Internal Revenue Service was in the mail.

Once Marrama found out that the bankruptcy trustees were going after the Maine property, he filed a notice to convert his Chapter 7 bankruptcy to Chapter 13. The trustee and creditors objected. They contended that because Marrama had acted in bad faith when he tried to conceal the Maine property from his creditors, he should not be permitted to convert. The bankruptcy court and the appeals court agreed. The Supreme Court granted *certiorari*.

You Be The Judge: ***Can a bankruptcy court refuse to allow a debtor to convert from Chapter 7 to Chapter 13?***

Argument for Marrama: Under the Bankruptcy Code, a Chapter 7 debtor may convert a case, with only two restrictions. First, the bankrupt can convert only once. Second, the debtor must meet the conditions that would have been required for him to file under the new chapter in the first place. Nothing in the Code suggests that a bankruptcy judge has the right to prohibit a conversion because of the debtor's bad faith.

If a debtor acts in bad faith, the court has other remedies: it can convert the case back to a Chapter 7 liquidation; it can refuse to approve the plan of payment; or it can charge the debtor with perjury. That is the law, whether the trustee and creditors like it or not.

Argument for the Bankruptcy Trustee: A bankruptcy court has the unquestioned right to dismiss a Chapter 13 petition if the debtor demonstrates bad faith. There seems no logical reason why a court would have the right to dismiss a case for bad faith but not the right to prohibit a filing under Chapter 13 to begin with. In both cases, the court is simply saying that the individual does not qualify as a debtor under Chapter 13. That individual is not a member of the class of honest but unfortunate debtors whom the bankruptcy laws were enacted to protect.

EXAM Strategy

Question: Why did Marrama first file under Chapter 7 and then try to switch to Chapter 13 after he was caught lying?

Strategy: This question is a good test of your understanding of the advantages and disadvantages of the different chapters. For help in answering this question, you might want to look at the chart at the end of the chapter. Remember that Chapter 7 is a liquidation provision—it takes more of the bankrupt's money upfront but then discharges his debts and gives him a fresh start for the future. Chapter 13 does not take as many assets during the bankruptcy process but may attach all the debtor's disposable income for the next five years.

Result: Marrama filed under Chapter 7 in the hope that he could hold on to his house while all his debts were discharged. Once that plan failed, he tried to switch to Chapter 13 in the hope that he could keep the house and give up his disposable income instead. This case illustrates the different emphases of Chapters 7 and 13.

A bankruptcy under Chapter 13 generally follows the same course as Chapter 11: the debtor files a petition, creditors submit proofs of claim, the court imposes an automatic stay, the debtor files a plan, and the court confirms the plan. But there are some differences.

Beginning a Chapter 13 Case

To initiate a Chapter 13 case, the debtor must file a voluntary petition. **Creditors cannot use an involuntary petition to force a debtor into Chapter 13.** In all Chapter 13 cases, the U.S. Trustee appoints a trustee to supervise the debtor, although the debtor remains in possession of the bankruptcy estate. The trustee also serves as a central clearinghouse for the debtor's payments to creditors. The debtor pays the trustee who, in turn, transmits these funds to creditors. For this service, the trustee is allowed up to 10 percent of the payments.

Plan of Payment

The debtor must file a plan of payment within 15 days after filing the voluntary petition. Only the debtor can file a plan; the creditors have no right to file their own version. Under the plan, the debtor must (1) commit some future earnings to pay off debts, (2) promise to pay all secured and priority claims in full, and (3) treat all remaining classes equally. If the plan does not provide for the debtor to pay off creditors in full, then all of the debtor's disposable income for the next five years must go to creditors.

Within 30 days after filing the plan of payment, the debtor must begin making payments to the trustee under the plan. The trustee holds these payments until the plan is confirmed and then transmits them to creditors. The debtor continues to make payments to the trustee until the plan has been fully implemented. If the plan is rejected, the trustee returns the payments to the debtor.

Only the bankruptcy court has the authority to confirm or reject a plan of payment. Creditors have no right to vote on it. However, to confirm a plan, the court must ensure that:

- The creditors have the opportunity to voice their objections at a hearing;
- All of the unsecured creditors receive at least as much as they would have if the bankruptcy estate had been liquidated under Chapter 7;
- The plan is feasible and the bankrupt will be able to make the promised payments;
- The plan does not extend beyond three years without good reason and in no event lasts longer than five years; and
- The debtor is acting in good faith, making a reasonable effort to pay obligations.

Discharge

Once confirmed, a plan is binding on all creditors whether they like it or not. **The debtor is washed clean of all pre-petition debts except those provided for in the plan, but, unlike Chapter 7 , the debts are not *permanently* discharged.** If the debtor violates the plan, all of the debts are revived, and the court may either dismss the case or convert it to a liquidation proceeding under Chapter 7. The debts become permanently discharged only when the bankrupt fully complies with the plan.

Note, however, that any debtor who has received a discharge under Chapter 7 or 11 within the prior four years, or under Chapter 13 within the prior two years, is not eligible under Chapter 13.

If the debtor's circumstances change, the debtor, the trustee, or unsecured creditors can ask the court to modify the plan. Most such requests come from debtors whose income has declined. However, if the debtor's income rises, the creditors or the trustee can ask that payments increase, too.

Chapter Conclusion

Whenever an individual or organization incurs more debts than it can pay in a timely fashion, everyone loses. The debtor loses control of his assets and the creditors lose money. Bankruptcy laws cannot create assets where there are none (or not enough), but they can ensure that the debtor's assets, however limited, are fairly divided between the debtor and creditors. Any bankruptcy system that accomplishes this goal must be deemed a success. Is the U.S. Bankruptcy Code fair?

Exam Review

This chart sets out the important elements of each bankruptcy chapter.

	Chapter 7	Chapter 11	Chapter 13
Objective	Liquidation	Reorganization	Consumer reorganization
Who May Use It	Individual or organization	Individual or organization	Individual
Type of Petition	Voluntary or involuntary	Voluntary or involuntary	Only voluntary
Administration of Bankruptcy Estate	Trustee	Debtor in possession (trustee selected only if debtor is unable to serve)	Trustee
Selection of Trustee	Creditors have right to elect trustee; otherwise, U.S. Trustee makes appointment	Usually no trustee	Appointed by U.S. Trustee
Participation in Formulation of Plan	No plan is filed	Both creditors and debtor can propose plans	Only debtor can propose a plan
Creditor Approval of Plan	Creditors do not vote	Creditors vote on plan, but court may approve plan without the creditors' support	Creditors do not vote on plan
Impact on Debtor's Post-petition Income	Not affected; debtor keeps all future earnings	Must contribute toward payment of pre-petition debts	Must contribute toward payment of pre-petition debts

1. Question: Mark Milbank's custom furniture business was unsuccessful, so he repeatedly borrowed money from his wife and her father. He promised that the loans would enable him to spend more time with his family. Instead, he spent more time in bed with his next-door neighbor. After the divorce, his ex-wife and her father demanded repayment of the loans. Milbank filed for protection under Chapter 13. What could his ex-wife and her father do to help their chances of being repaid?

Strategy: First ask yourself what kind of creditor they are: secured or unsecured. Then think about what creditors can do to get special treatment. (See the "Result" at the end of this section.)

EXAM Strategy

2. After a jury ordered actor Kim Basinger to pay $8 million for violating a movie contract, she filed for bankruptcy protection, claiming $5 million in assets and $11 million in liabilities. Under which Chapter should she file? Why?

Strategy: Look at the requirements for each Chapter. Was Basinger eligible for Chapter 13? What would be the advantages and disadvantages of Chapters 7 and 11? (See the "Result" at the end of this section.)

1. Result: The father and the ex-wife were unsecured creditors who, as a class, come last on the priority list. The court granted their request not to discharge their loans on the grounds that Milbank had acted in bad faith.

2. Result: Basinger was not eligible to file under Chapter 13 because she had debts of $11 million. She first filed under Chapter 11 in a effort to retain some of her assets, but then her creditors would not approve her plan of reorganization, so she converted to liquidation under Chapter 7.

Multiple-Choice Questions

1. **CPA QUESTION** A voluntary petition filed under the liquidation provisions of Chapter 7 of the federal Bankruptcy Code:
   (a) Is not available to a corporation unless it has previously filed a petition under the reorganization provisions of Chapter 11 of the Code
   (b) Automatically stays collection actions against the debtor **except** by secured creditors
   (c) Will be dismissed unless the debtor has 12 or more unsecured creditors whose claims total at least $5,000
   (d) Does **not** require the debtor to show that the debtor's liabilities exceed the fair market value of assets

2. **CPA QUESTION** Decal Corp. incurred substantial operating losses for the past three years. Unable to meet its current obligations, Decal filed a petition of reorganization under Chapter 11 of the federal Bankruptcy Code. Which of the following statements is correct?
   (a) A creditors' committee, if appointed, will consist of unsecured creditors.
   (b) The court must appoint a trustee to manage Decal's affairs.
   (c) Decal may continue in business only with the approval of a trustee.
   (d) The creditors' committee must select a trustee to manage Decal's affairs.

3. **CPA QUESTION** Unger owes a total of $50,000 to eight unsecured creditors and one fully secured creditor. Quincy is one of the unsecured creditors and is owed $6,000. Quincy has filed a petition against Unger under the liquidation provisions of Chapter 7 of the federal Bankruptcy Code. Unger has been unable to pay debts as

they become due. Unger's liabilities exceed Unger's assets. Unger has filed papers opposing the bankruptcy petition. Which of the following statements regarding Quincy's petition is correct?

(a) It will be dismissed because the secured creditor failed to join in the filing of the petition.

(b) It will be dismissed because three unsecured creditors must join in the filing of the petition.

(c) It will be granted because Unger's liabilities exceed Unger's assets.

(d) It will be granted because Unger is unable to pay Unger's debts as they become due.

4. Dale is in bankruptcy proceedings under Chapter 13. Which of the following statements is true?

(a) His debtors must have filed an involuntary petition.

(b) His unsecured creditors will be worse off than if he had filed under Chapter 7.

(c) All of his debts are discharged as soon as the court approves his plan.

(d) His creditors have an opportunity to voice objections to his plan.

5. Grass Co. is in bankruptcy proceedings under Chapter 11. _______ serves as trustee. In the case of _______ the court can approve a plan of reorganization over the objections of the creditors.

(a) The debtor in possession, a cramdown

(b) A person appointed by the U.S. Trustee, fraud

(c) The head of the creditors' committee, reaffirmation

(d) The U.S. Trustee, voidable preference

Essay Questions

1. James, the owner of an auto parts store, told his employee, Rickey, to clean and paint some tires in the basement. Highly flammable gasoline fumes accumulated in the poorly ventilated space. James threw a firecracker into the basement as a joke, intending only to startle Rickey. Sparks from the firecracker caused an explosion and fire that severely burned him. Rickey filed a personal injury suit against James for $1 million. Is this debt dischargeable under Chapter 7?

2. Mary Price went for a consultation about a surgical procedure to remove abdominal fat. When Robert Britton met with her, he wore a name tag that identified him as a doctor, and was addressed as "doctor" by the nurse. Britton then examined Price, touching her stomach and showing her where the incision would be made. It turned out that Britton was the office manager, not a doctor. Although a doctor actually performed the surgery on Price, Britton was present. It turned out that the doctor left a tube in Price's body at the site of the incision. The area became infected, requiring corrective surgery. A jury awarded Price $275,000 in damages in a suit against Britton. He subsequently filed a Chapter 7 bankruptcy petition. Is this judgment dischargeable in bankruptcy court?

3. **YOU BE THE JUDGE WRITING PROBLEM** Lydia D'Ettore received a degree in computer programming at the DeVry Institute of Technology, with a grade point average of 2.51. To finance her education, she borrowed $20,516.52 from a federal student loan program. After graduation, she could not find a job in her field, so she went to work as a clerk at an annual salary of $12,500. D'Ettore and her daughter lived with her parents free of charge. After setting aside $50 a month in savings and paying bills that included $233 for a new car (a Suzuki Samurai) and $50 for jewelry from Zales, her disposable income was $125 per month. D'Ettore asked the bankruptcy court to discharge the debts she owed DeVry for her education. Did the debts to the DeVry Institute impose an undue hardship on D'Ettore? **Argument for D'Ettore:** Lydia D'Ettore lives at home with her parents. Even so, her disposable income is a meager $125 a month. She would have to spend every single penny of her disposable income for nearly 15 years to pay back her $20,500 debt to DeVry. That would be an undue hardship. **Argument for the Creditors:** The U.S. government guaranteed D'Ettore's loan. Therefore, if the court discharges it, the American taxpayer will have to pay the bill. Why should taxpayers subsidize an irresponsible student? D'Ettore must also stop buying new cars and jewelry. And why should the government pay her debts while she saves money every month?

4. Dr. Ibrahim Khan caused an automobile accident in which a fellow physician, Dolly Yusufji, became a quadriplegic. Khan signed a contract for the lifetime support of Yusufji. When he refused to make payments under the contract, she sued him and obtained a judgment for $1,205,400. Khan filed a Chapter 11 petition. At the time of the bankruptcy hearing, five years after the accident, Khan had not paid Yusufji anything. She was dependent on a motorized wheelchair; he drove a Rolls-Royce. Is Khan's debt dischargeable under Chapter 11?

5. After filing for bankruptcy, Yvonne Brown sought permission of the court to reaffirm a $6,000 debt to her credit union. The debt was unsecured, and she was under no obligation to pay it. The credit union had published the following notice in its newsletter:

   > If you are thinking about filing bankruptcy, THINK about the long-term implications. This action, filing bankruptcy, closes the door on TOMORROW. Having no credit means no ability to purchase cars, houses, credit cards. Look into the future—no loans for the education of your children.

   Should the court approve Brown's reaffirmation?

Discussion Questions

1. **ETHICS** On November 5, Hawes, Inc., a small subcontractor, opened an account with Basic Corp., a supplier of construction materials. Hawes promised to pay its bills within 30 days of purchase. Although Hawes purchased a substantial quantity of goods on credit from Basic, it made few payments on the accounts until the following March, when it paid Basic over $21,000. On May 14, Hawes filed a voluntary petition under Chapter 7. Does the bankruptcy trustee have a right to recover this payment? Is it fair to Hawes's other creditors if Basic is allowed to keep the $21,000 payment?

2. Look on the web for your state's rules on exempt property. Compared with other states and the federal government, is your state generous or stingy with exemptions?

In considering a new bankruptcy statute, Congress struggled mightily over whether or not to permit state exemptions at all. Is it fair for exemptions to vary by state? Why should someone in one state fare better than his her neighbor across the state line?

3. Some states permit debtors an unlimited exemption on their homes. Is it fair for bankrupts to be allowed to keep multimillion dollar homes while their creditors remain unpaid? But other states allow as little as $5,000. Should bankrupts be thrown out on the street? What amount is fair?

4. What about the rules regarding repeated bankruptcy filings? Debtors cannot obtain a discharge under Chapter 7 within eight years of a prior filing. Under Chapter 13, no discharge is available within four years of a prior Chapter 7 or 11 filing and within two years of a prior Chapter 13 filing. Are these rules too onerous, too lenient, or just right?

5. A bankrupt who owns a house has the option of either paying the mortgage or losing his home. The only advantage of bankruptcy is that his debt to the bank is discharged. The U.S. House of Representatives passed a bill permitting a bankruptcy judge to adjust the terms of mortgages to aid debtors in holding onto their houses. Proponents argued that this change in the law would reduce foreclosures and stabilize the national housing market. Opponents said that it was not fair to reward homeowners for being irresponsible. How would you vote if you were in the Senate?

6. In the *Grisham* case, the debtor had virtually no income but owed about $200,000 in debts that could not be discharged. What kind of fresh start is that? Should limits be placed on the total debt that cannot be discharged? Is the list of non-dischargeable debts appropriate?

UNIT 8

piterimages

Property and Cyberlaw

CHAPTER 41

CYBERLAW

© Steve Allen/Jupiterimages

Garrett always said that his computer was his best friend. He was online all the time, g-chatting with his friends, listening to music, doing research for his courses, and, okay, maybe playing a few games now and again. Occasionally, the computer could be annoying. It would crash once in a while, trashing part of a paper before he saved it. And there was the time that a copy of an email he sent Lizzie complaining about Caroline somehow ended up in Caroline's inbox. He was pretty irritated when the White Sox tickets he bought in an online auction turned out to be for a Little League team. And he was tired of all the spam advertising pornographic websites. But these things happen and, despite the petty annoyances, his computer was an important part of his life.

Then one day, Garrett received a panicked text message from a teammate on the college wrestling squad telling him to click on a certain website pronto to see someone they knew. Garrett eagerly clicked on the website and discovered, to his horror, that *he* was featured—in the nude. The website was selling DVDs showing him and other members of the wrestling team in the locker room in various states of undress. Other DVDs, from other locker and shower rooms, were for sale, too, showing football players and wrestlers from dozens of universities. The DVDs had titles like "Straight Off the Mat" and "Voyeur Time." No longer trusting technology, Garrett pulled on his running shoes and dashed over to the office of his business law professor.

Garrett eagerly clicked on the website and discovered, to his horror, that he was featured—in the nude.

Computers and the Internet—cyberspace—together comprise one of the great technological developments of modern times.[1] And its importance and impact continue to grow. Beginning in December 2010, the world watched the "Arab Spring"—popular uprisings throughout the Middle East that brought down governments in Tunisia, Egypt, and Libya, and challenged leaders throughout the area. These movements were organized and fueled by the Internet. In response, threatened governments fought back by trying to limit access to the Internet generally and social media sites in particular. In Syria, police demanded the Facebook passwords of suspected protest organizers. Meanwhile, in England, a different type of protest challenged a court ruling. A married soccer player obtained an injunction prohibiting newspapers from revealing his alleged affair, or even the existence of the injunction. Within days, Ryan Giggs and his affair was one of the top topics on Twitter.

Cyberspace is a disruptive technology which, depending on your perspective, can fight repression or undermine legitimate laws. It has brought change to every aspect of our lives—how we make friends, buy things, obtain news, campaign for election, start revolutions, challenge the status quo.

Inevitably, new technologies create the need for new law. In the 13th century, England was one of the first countries to develop passable roads. Like the Internet, these roadways greatly enhanced communication, creating social and business opportunities, but also enabled new crimes. Good roads meant that bad guys could sneak out of town without paying their bills. Parliament responded with laws to facilitate the collection of out-of-town debts. Similarly, while the Internet has opened up enormous opportunities in both our business and personal lives, it has also created the need for new laws, both to pave the way for these opportunities and to limit their dangers.

The process of lawmaking never stops. Judges sit and legislatures meet—all in an effort to create better rules and a better society. However, in an established area of law, such as contracts, the basic structure changes little. Cyberlaw is different because it is still very much in its infancy. Not only are new laws being created almost daily, but whole areas of regulation are, as yet, unpaved roads. Although the process of rule making has progressed well, much debate still surrounds cyberspace law and much work remains to be done. This chapter focuses on the existing rules and also discusses the areas of regulation that are still incomplete and being debated.

Cyberlaw affects many areas of our lives. This chapter, however, deals with issues that are unique to the cyberworld, such as online privacy, spam, and cybercrimes.

Before beginning the chapter in earnest, let's return briefly to Garrett, the wrestler. What recourse does Garrett have for his Internet injuries? The nude video incident happened at Illinois State University and seven other colleges. Approximately 30 athletes filed suit against GTE and PSINet for selling the videos online, but the two web hosts were found not to be liable under the Communications Decency Act because they had not produced the videos themselves—they had simply permitted the sale of someone else's content. What about Garrett's other computer injuries? Lizzie was not being a good friend, but it was perfectly legal for her to forward Garrett's email to Caroline. The seller of the White Sox tickets violated both federal and state fraud statutes. The federal CAN-SPAM Act regulates spam—unsolicited commercial email—but a lawsuit is a slow and awkward tool for killing such a flourishing weed.

---

[1]The term "Internet" means "the international computer network of both Federal and non-Federal interoperable packet switched data networks," according to 47 U.S. Section 230 (f)(1). It began in the 1960s as a project to link military contractors and universities. Now, it is a giant network that connects smaller groups of linked computer networks. The World Wide Web was created in 1991 by Tim Berners-Lee as a subnetwork of the Internet. It is a decentralized collection of documents containing text, pictures, and sound. Users can move from document to document using links that form a "web" of information.

PRIVACY

The Internet has vastly increased our ability to communicate quickly and widely. In the pre-Internet era, setting up a meeting required days of phone tag. Intraoffice memos were typed, photocopied, and then hand-delivered by messengers. Catalog orders were sent via regular mail, a slow, inefficient, and costly method. As wonderful as cybercommunication can be, though, it is not without its dangers.

Tracking Tools

Consumers enter the most personal data—credit card numbers, bank accounts, lists of friends, medical information, product preferences—on the Internet. Because our interactions with a computer often take place in isolation (sitting alone at home, at work or in a cafe), the experience *feels* private. It is anything but. In effect, the Internet provides a very large window through which the government, employers, businesses, and criminals can find out more than they should about you and your money, habits, beliefs, and health. Even email has its dangers: who has not been embarrassed by an email that ended up in the wrong mailbox?

The most troubling aspect of these Internet privacy issues is that consumers are often unaware of who has access to what personal information, how it is being used, and with what consequences. As a result, a privacy discussion seems abstract. But the reality is that the Internet provides many opportunities for good guys and bad to secretly gather information for their own purposes, both good and bad.

It used to be that marketers geared their ads to specific websites, but now they target individual consumers. The 50 most popular websites in America (which account for 40 percent of all page views) install thousands of tracking tools on the computers of people who visit their sites. Called "behavioral targeting," these tools not only collect data on *all* the websites someone visits, they also record keystrokes to keep track of whatever information the consumer has entered online. These tools are placed on computers without notice or warning to the consumer. In a recent report, **Dictionary.com** was the worst offender, placing over 200 tools on the computers of unaware visitors. On the other hand, **Wikipedia.org** is one highly popular site that installs none.[2] To take another example of privacy issues, as part of its Street View program that provides photographs of streets around the world, Google (accidentally, it says) captured data from home Wi-Fi networks.

Once the trackers have gathered financial, health, and other personal information, they sell it to data-gathering companies that build profiles which, while technically anonymous, can include so much personal information that it is possible to identify individuals. How many times have you revealed your ZIP code, birth date, and gender on the Internet? Those three pieces of information are usually enough to identify an individual's name and address. The profiles are then sold to advertisers on stock market-like exchanges. Now that cell phones have GPS tracking devices and readers use electronic books, where you have been and what you are reading is also available. In a recent Dilbert cartoon, the boss refers to a smart phone as an "employee locator device."

Suppose, for example, that you look online at puppies in shelters. You may find that the next time you go to your gmail account, there will be dog ads. One company markets a databank with the names of 150 million registered voters. Anyone can buy a list of voters that is sliced and diced however they want (say, Republicans between the ages of 45 and 60 with Hispanic surnames and incomes greater than $50,000 who live in Kansas City). Puppy ads seem harmless, or even beneficial, but if marketers can put together a databank of

[2]Julia Angwin and Tom McGinty, "Sites Feed Personal Details to New Tracking Industry," *The Wall Street Journal*, July 30, 2010.

Hispanic Republican voters, they can also find out who has visited a website for recovering alcoholics or unrecovered gamblers or Nazi sympathizers. Or who uses antidepressants or reads socialist writings. Do you want all this information available to anyone who is willing to pay for it? What if employers buy information about job candidates so that they can refuse to hire someone with health issues?

In short, Internet users are inadvertently providing intensely personal data to unknown people for unknown uses. The problem is likely to grow. The newest web language, HTML5, permits tracking software to store larger amounts of data. Also, software developers have created tracking tools that are harder to delete. Every browser uses a different deletion system, which makes life even more complicated for the concerned consumer.

Many commentators argue that without significant changes in the law, our privacy will be obliterated. But, so far, consumers have been relatively unconcerned. They tend to be unaware of the dangers, and they appreciate the benefits—for example, this tracking software can be used to store passwords so that when you log on to **Amazon.com**, the site recognizes you and lets you in without your having to enter your email address and password. Consumers can also benefit from targeted advertisements—long-distance runners may like seeing ads for running shoes, not cigarettes. Industry representatives argue that without the revenue from ads, many Internet sites would not be free to consumers. As a result, privacy on the Internet is very much like the weather—everyone talks about it, but (so far) no one has done much about it. But this you should believe: highly personal information about *you* has been collected without your knowledge or approval.

Regulation of Online Privacy

There is a wide range of possible sources of laws and regulations to protect online privacy, but they are in an early, and relatively ineffective, stage of development.

Self-Regulation

In an effort to forestall government regulation, several marketing trade groups issued their own report, "Self-Regulatory Principles for Online Behavioral Advertising." These principles require websites that use tracking tools to provide notice of data collection that is "clear, prominent, and conveniently located." In addition, the websites must permit consumers to opt out of tracking with only a few clicks. However, we have been unable to find a single website that complies with these principles, even among the companies that sponsored the report.

Members of Congress have filed many bills to regulate online privacy. So intense, however, is the debate between industry and consumer advocates that no consensus—and little law—has emerged. There is, however, some applicable government regulation.

The First Amendment

How would you like to be called a cockroach, mega-scumbag, and crook in front of thousands of people? Or be accused of having a fake medical degree, fat thighs, and poor feminine hygiene? What would you think if your ex-wife told 55,000 people that your insensitivity made her so sick she was throwing up every day? **The First Amendment to the Constitution protects free speech,** and that includes these postings—and worse—which have appeared on Internet message boards and blogs. As upsetting as they may be, they are protected as free speech under the First Amendment so long as the poster is not violating some other law. In these cases, the plaintiffs argued that the statements were defamatory but the courts disagreed, ruling that they were simply opinions.

Explaining its ruling in one of the cases, the court said:

> Users [of the Internet] are able to engage freely in informal debate and criticism, leading many to substitute gossip for accurate reporting and often to adopt a provocative, even combative tone. Hyperbole and exaggeration are common, and 'venting' is at least as common as careful and

considered argumentation. Some commentators have likened cyberspace to a frontier society free from the conventions and constraints that limit discourse in the real world.

It hardly need be said that this [court does not] condone [these] rude and childish posts; indeed, [the] intemperate, insulting, and often disgusting remarks understandably offended plaintiff and possibly many other readers. Nevertheless, the fact that society may find speech offensive is not a sufficient reason for suppressing it. Indeed, if it is the speaker's opinion that gives offense, that consequence is a reason for according it constitutional protection.[3]

In the following case, a teacher received hostile emails. Should the First Amendment protect the anonymous person who sent them?

[3] *Krinsky v. Doe,* 6159 Cal. App. 4th 1154, 2008 Cal. App. LEXIS 180.

You be the Judge

Juzwiak v. John/Jane Doe

415 N.J. Super. 442; 2 A.3d 428; 2010 N.J. Super. LEXIS 154
Superior Court of New Jersey, Appellate Division, 2010

Facts: Juzwiak was a tenured teacher at Hightstown High School in New Jersey. He received three emails from someone who signed himself "Josh," with the address, "Josh Hartnett **jharthat@yahoo.com**." The teacher did not know anyone of that name. These emails said:

1. Subject line: "Hopefully you will be gone permanently"

   Text: "We are all praying for that. Josh"
2. Subject line: "I hear Friday is 'D' day for you"

   Text: "I certainly hope so. You don't deserve to be allowed to teach anymore. Not just in Hightstown but anywhere. If Hightstown bids you farewell I will make it my lifes [sic] work to ensure that wherever you look for work they know what you have done."
3. Subject line: "Mr. Juzwiak in the Hightstown/East Windsor School System."

   Text: It has been brought to my attention and I am sure many of you know that Mr. J is reapplying for his position as a teacher in this town. It has further been pointed out that certain people are soliciting supporters for him. This is tantamount to supporting the devil himself. I am not asking anyone to speak out against Mr. J but I urge you to then be silent as we can not continue to allow the children of this school system nor the parents to be subjected to his evil ways. Thank you. Josh

It seems that this third email was sent to other people, but it was not clear to whom.

Because Juzwiak did not know who "Josh" was, he filed a complaint against "John/Jane Doe," seeking damages for intentional infliction of emotional distress. As part of the lawsuit, he served a subpoena on Yahoo!, asking it to reveal "Josh's" identity. When Yahoo! notified "Josh" of the lawsuit, he asked the court to quash the subpoena.

In a court hearing, Juzwiak testified that the threatening emails had severely disrupted his life, causing deep anger and depression as well as insomnia that had impaired his ability to concentrate and function effectively. In addition, this emotional stress had exacerbated his back problems and caused him to lose 20 pounds. Although he had already been taking antidepressants, a psychiatrist prescribed four additional drugs for depression, anxiety, and insomnia, which were not effective in reducing his symptoms. Juzwiak also stated that he had thoughts of hurting himself and the entire episode had consumed his life for several months.

When the trial court refused to issue the subpoena against Yahoo!, Juzwiak appealed.

You Be the Judge: ***Should the trial court have issued the subpoena? Which interest is more important: "Josh's" First Amendment right to free speech or Juzwiak's protection from harassing emails?***

Argument for "Josh": Free speech is the first, and most important, right in the Bill of Rights. To ensure a vibrant marketplace of ideas, the First Amendment protects not only open but also anonymous speech. Sometimes speakers must be allowed to withhold their identities to protect themselves from harassment and persecution.

Nothing in these messages was a realistic threat to the teacher's safety. "Hopefully you will be gone permanently" could easily mean "Hope you will move out of town." Juzwiak reported these emails to the police, but they took no action. Presumably they would have done so if there had been any real threat.

Nor did these emails constitute an intentional infliction of emotional distress. They were not so extreme and outrageous as to be utterly intolerable in a civilized community. "Josh" did not accuse Juzwiak of vile or criminal acts. The language was not obscene or profane. In short, if Juzwiak is going to teach high school, he needs to develop a thicker skin and a better sense of humor.

Argument for Juzwiak: The right to speak anonymously is not absolute. *"Josh"* requires protection from harassment? That is an absurd argument.

These emails contained death threats: "Hopefully you will be gone permanently" and "I hear Friday is 'D' day for you." Juzwiak was frightened enough to go to the police. He suffered serious physical and emotional harm. These emails are not entitled to the protection of the First Amendment.

Furthermore, the emails constituted intentional infliction of emotional distress. They were extreme and outrageous conduct designed to cause harm. They achieved their goal.

In balancing the rights in this case, why would the court protect "Josh," who has set out to cause harm, over the innocent teacher?

The Fourth Amendment

The Fourth Amendment to the Constitution prohibits unreasonable searches and seizures by the government. In enforcing this provision of the Constitution, the courts ask: did the person being searched have a legitimate expectation of privacy in the place searched or the item seized? If yes, then the government must obtain a warrant from a court before conducting the search. (For more on this topic, investigate Chapter 8, on crime.) The Fourth Amendment applies to computers.

The architecture professor in the following case would have benefited from a course in business law, and perhaps in computer science, too.

United States of America v. Angevine

281 F.3d 1130, 2002 U.S. App. LEXIS 2746
United States Court of Appeals for the Tenth Circuit, 2002

Facts: Professor Eric Angevine taught architecture at Oklahoma State University. The university provided him with a computer that was linked to the university network, and through it to the Internet. Professor Angevine used this computer to download more than 3,000 pornographic images of young boys. After viewing the images and printing some of them, he deleted the files. Tipped off by Professor Angevine's wife, police officers seized the computer without first obtaining a search warrant. They then turned the machine over to a police computer expert, who retrieved the pornographic files that the professor had deleted.

The Oklahoma State University computer policy stated that:

- The contents of all storage media owned or stored on university computing facilities are the property of the university.
- Employees cannot use university computers to access obscene material.
- The university reserves the right to view or scan any file or software stored on a computer or passing

through the network and will do so periodically to audit the use of university resources. The university cannot guarantee confidentiality of stored data.

- System administrators keep logs of file names that may indicate why a particular data file is being erased, when it was erased, and what user identification has erased it.

The trial court held that federal agents did not need a warrant to search Professor Angevine's office computer because he had no expectation of privacy. He was sentenced to 51 months in prison for "knowing possession of child pornography." The professor appealed.

Issue: ***Did Professor Angevine have a reasonable expectation of privacy in his office computer?***

Excerpts from Judge Brorby's Decision: Oklahoma State University policies and procedures prevent its employees from reasonably expecting privacy in data downloaded from the Internet onto University computers. The University computer-use policy reserved the right to randomly audit Internet use and to monitor specific individuals suspected of misusing University computers. The policy explicitly cautions computer users that information flowing through the University network is not confidential either in transit or in storage on a University computer. These office practices and procedures should have warned reasonable employees not to access child pornography with University computers.

While Professor Angevine did attempt to erase the child pornography, the University computer policy warned system administrators kept file logs recording when and by whom files were deleted. Moreover, given his transmission of the pornographic data through a monitored University network, deleting the files alone was not sufficient to establish a reasonable expectation of privacy.

We hold Professor Angevine could not have an objectively reasonable expectation of privacy.

This case involved someone who transmitted information through an electronic system owned by his employer. What happens if a suspect in a crime sends emails through a system that he personally pays for? Does he have a reasonable expectation of privacy? The following case answers these questions.

United States of America v. Warshak

631 F.3d 266; 2010 U.S. App. LEXIS 25415
United States Court of Appeals for the Sixth Circuit, 2010

Facts: Steven Warshak owned Berkeley Premium Nutraceuticals, Inc., a company that sold herbal supplements. The company had only been modestly successful until it began to market Enzyte, a supplement that promised to increase masculine endowment. At its peak, Berkeley had annual sales of around $250 million.

As is the case with all such products, Enzyte was a fraud. Advertisements quoted surveys that had never been conducted and doctors who did not exist. As a result, customers typically did not buy the product a second time. Warshak had a solution to this problem—an auto-ship program. A man would order a free sample, providing his credit card to pay for the shipping. Berkeley would then automatically send him more product, and, of course, charge his credit card.

Without obtaining a search warrant first, a federal prosecutor asked Warshak's Internet service provider (ISP) for copies of his emails. Based on the evidence contained in these 25,000 emails, Warshak was convicted of mail, wire, and bank fraud and sentenced to 25 years in prison. He appealed on the grounds that the government had violated the Fourth Amendment by obtaining emails without a search warrant. He argued that he had had a reasonable expectation of privacy.

Issue: ***Did Warshak have a reasonable expectation of privacy in his emails?***

Excerpts from Justice Boggs's Decision: Warshak plainly manifested an expectation that his emails would be shielded from outside scrutiny. [H]is entire business and personal life was contained within the emails seized. Given the often sensitive and sometimes damning substance of his emails, we think it highly unlikely that Warshak expected them to be made public, for people seldom unfurl their dirty laundry in plain view. Therefore, we conclude that Warshak had a subjective expectation of privacy in the contents of his emails.

The next question is whether society is prepared to recognize that expectation as reasonable. This question is one of grave import and enduring consequence, given the prominent role that email has assumed in modern communication. Since the advent of email, the telephone call and the letter have waned in importance, and an explosion of Internet-based communication has taken place. People are now able to send sensitive and intimate information, instantaneously, to friends, family, and colleagues half a world away. Lovers exchange sweet nothings, and businessmen swap ambitious plans, all with the click of a mouse button. Commerce has also taken hold in email. Online purchases are often documented in email accounts, and email is frequently used to remind patients and clients of imminent appointments.

In short, "account" is an apt word for the conglomeration of stored messages that comprises an email account, as it provides an account of its owner's life. By obtaining access to someone's email, government agents gain the ability to peer deeply into his activities.

[T]he Fourth Amendment must keep pace with the inexorable march of technological progress, or its guarantees will wither and perish. While a letter is in the mail, the police may not intercept it and examine its contents unless they first obtain a warrant based on probable cause. If we accept that an email is analogous to a letter or a phone call, it is manifest that agents of the government cannot compel a commercial ISP to turn over the contents of an email without triggering the Fourth Amendment. Emails must pass through an ISP's servers to reach their intended recipient. Thus, the ISP is the functional equivalent of a post office or a telephone company. [T]he police may not storm the post office and intercept a letter, and they are likewise forbidden from using the phone system to make a clandestine recording of a telephone call—unless they get a warrant, that is. It only stands to reason that, if government agents compel an ISP to surrender the contents of a subscriber's emails, those agents have thereby conducted a Fourth Amendment search, which necessitates compliance with the warrant requirement.

Accordingly, we hold that a subscriber enjoys a reasonable expectation of privacy in the contents of emails that are stored with, or sent or received through, a commercial ISP. The government may not compel a commercial ISP to turn over the contents of a subscriber's emails without first obtaining a warrant based on probable cause.

As the *Warshak* court observes, electronic communications—email, text messages, instant messaging—have for many people taken the place of letters and telephone calls. So it is important to know your privacy rights. **Although the courts are feeling their way in this new territory, at this writing, for criminal cases:**

1. If your employer has a reasonably articulated policy notifying you that it has the right to access and read electronic communications on a system that it provides, then you do not have a reasonable expectation of privacy when using that system. The police need not obtain a search warrant before reading your messages.

2. You do have a reasonable right to privacy on a system that you provide for yourself, so the police must obtain a search warrant before accessing these messages.

Note that both of these Fourth Amendment cases involve criminal defendants. However, Fourth Amendment protections also apply to *government* workers in civil cases. For example, when a police officer persistently exceeded his monthly quota of text messages, his superior accessed these communications to determine if they were work-related. It turned out that they were mostly sexually suggestive texts sent to the married officer's mistress. After the officer was disciplined, he filed suit alleging that the department had violated his Fourth Amendment rights. The Supreme Court held that a government employer has the right to review its employee's electronic communications for a work-related purpose, if the search was "justified at its inception" and if "the measures adopted are reasonably related to the objectives of the search and not excessively intrusive in light of the circumstances giving rise to the search."[4]

[4]*City of Ontario v. Quon*, 130 S. Ct. 2619; 2010 U.S. LEXIS 4972 (S.Ct. 2010).

The FTC

Section 5 of the FTC Act prohibits unfair and deceptive acts or practices. The Federal Trade Commission (FTC) applies this statute to online privacy policies. It does not require websites to have a privacy policy, but if they do have one, they must comply with it, and it cannot be deceptive. For example, Sears paid consumers who visited **sears.com** and **kmart.com** websites $10 to become members of the "My SHC Community" and participate in "exciting, engaging, and on-going interactions—always on your terms and always by your choice." As part of this process, consumers downloaded "research" software that tracked their online browsing. Only at the end of a lengthy user agreement did Sears reveal the full extent of the data collected, that it could include the contents of shopping carts, online bank statements, drug prescription records, DVD rental records, and some personal email information. In a consent decree with the FTC, Sears agreed to stop collecting data from consumers who downloaded the software and to destroy all data it had previously collected.

The FTC also brought action against Twitter after hackers gained access through its administrative system to Twitter accounts. Twitter had allowed any employee access to the administrative system, which was protected by an easy-to-guess password. The hackers reset passwords and sent fake tweets. For example, an unauthorized person sent a tweet from President-elect Barack Obama's Twitter account offering free gasoline to users who took an Internet poll (which seems benign compared with what the hacker could have said, but still not a good situation). The FTC found that Twitter had engaged in deceptive acts because its (lack of) security practices had violated the company's promise to users that it would protect their information from unauthorized access. As part of the settlement, Twitter agreed to strengthen its security practices.

In addition to cases the FTC has brought against individual companies, it also issued a report entitled "Self-Regulatory Principles for Online Behavioral Advertising." As the name implies, these rules are voluntary. They provide that companies should clearly disclose the information that they collect and also offer consumers an easy-to-use, easy-to-find method for opting out. However, we have not found a website that complies with this policy. The FTC has been working on a binding privacy policy for years, with no result yet.

One more cyberlaw issue: imagine that you are reading a blog that favorably reviews a new Microsoft product. Before clicking on the Buy button, would you want to know that Microsoft had given the blogger a free computer? The FTC thinks you should. Under FTC rules, bloggers face fines as high as $1,000 if they do not disclose all compensation they receive (either in cash or free products) for writing product reviews. Moreover, celebrities must disclose their relationships with advertisers when making endorsements outside of traditional ads, such as on talk shows or in social media.

Electronic Communications Privacy Act of 1986

The Electronic Communications Privacy Act of 1986 (ECPA) is a federal statute that prohibits unauthorized interception of, access to, or disclosure of wire and electronic communications. The definition of electronic communication includes email and transmissions from pagers and cell phones. Violators are subject to both criminal and civil penalties. An action does not violate the ECPA if it is unintentional or if either party consents. Also, the USA Patriot Act, passed after the September 11th attacks, has broadened the *government's* right to monitor electronic communications.

Under the ECPA:

1. **Any intended recipient of an electronic communication has the right to disclose it.** Thus, if you sound off in an email to a friend about your boss, the (erstwhile) friend may legally forward that email to the boss or anyone else.

2. **Internet service providers (ISPs) are generally prohibited from disclosing electronic messages to anyone other than the addressee,** unless this disclosure is necessary for the performance of their service or for the protection of their own rights or property.
3. **An employer has the right to monitor workers' electronic communications if (1) the employee consents, (2) the monitoring occurs in the ordinary course of business, or (3) in the case of email, if the employer provides the computer system.**[5] Note that an employer has the right to monitor electronic communication even if it does not relate to work activities.

One lesson from the ECPA: email is not private, and it is dangerous. Although the *Warshak* court ruled that defendants have an expectation of privacy in emails they have sent over a system that they provide for themselves, that simply means the police must first obtain a search warrant before accessing emails, which is not that difficult. To get a search warrant, the police just need probable cause that they will find evidence of a crime in the place to be searched.

The majority of employers monitor their employees' email. In the event of litigation, the opposing party can access all emails—even messages that have in theory been deleted. Many people who should have known better have been caught in the email trap. Merrill Lynch stock analyst Henry Blodget praised stocks to the public even as he was referring to them in emails as a "piece of s***." He has been banned for life from the securities industry. Then there was Harry Stonecipher, the CEO of Boeing, who sent explicit emails to the employee with whom he was having an extramarital affair. When copies of the emails were sent to the board of directors, he was fired. In the following case, two important principles are at stake. Which one should win?

[5]The ECPA provides that, under certain circumstances, the police can access email without a warrant, but the *Warshak* court declared that provision unconstitutional.

You be the Judge

Scott v. Beth Israel Medical Center Inc.

847 N.Y.S.2d 436; 2007 N.Y. Misc. LEXIS 7114
Supreme Court of New York, 2007

Facts: Beth Israel Medical Center (BI)'s email policy stated:

> All information and documents created, received, saved, or sent on the Medical Center's computer or communications systems are the property of the Medical Center. Employees have no personal privacy right in any material created, received, saved, or sent using Medical Center communication or computer systems. The Medical Center reserves the right to access and disclose such material at any time without prior notice.

Dr. Norman Scott was head of the orthopedics department at BI. His contract with the hospital provided for $14 million in severance pay if he was fired without cause. BI did fire him, and the question was whether it was for cause or not. In preparation for a lawsuit against BI, Scott used the hospital's computer system to send emails to his lawyer. Each of these emails included the following notice:

> This message is intended only for the use of the Addressee and may contain information that is privileged and confidential.

If you are not the intended recipient, you are hereby notified that any dissemination of this communication is strictly prohibited. If you have received this communication in error, please erase all copies of the message and its attachments and notify us immediately.

BI obtained copies of all of Scott's emails. It notified him that it had copies of the emails to his lawyer. No one at BI had read the emails yet, but they intended to do so. Communications between a client and lawyer are generally protected, but a client waives this privilege if he publicly discloses the information. When Scott requested that the emails be returned to him unread, BI refused. Scott filed a motion seeking the return of the documents.

You Be the Judge: ***Did Scott have a right to privacy in emails he sent to his lawyer using the BI system?***

Argument for Scott: Despite BI's policy, all the emails Scott sent asserted that they were confidential. That should be enough to protect them. The attorney-client privilege is a foundation of our legal system. It is absolutely crucial for justice that clients be able to communicate with their lawyers in confidence. In a test between a core principle such as attorney-client privilege and a private entity's email policy, the privilege must win. The hospital should not be allowed to read Scott's emails.

Argument for BI: Scott was aware of BI's policy and knew that emails were the property of the hospital. Therefore, when he sent the emails, he was disclosing them publicly. If the communications were that important, he should have made a greater effort to protect them. BI has the right to read them.

Children's Online Privacy Protection Act of 1998

The Children's Online Privacy Protection Act of 1998 (COPPA) prohibits Internet operators from collecting information from children under 13 without parental permission. It also requires sites to disclose how they will use any information they acquire. Enforcement is in the hands of the FTC. The website for Mrs. Fields cookies offered birthday coupons for free cookies to children under 13. Although the company did not share information with outsiders, it did collect personal information without parental consent from 84,000 children. This information included names, home addresses, and birth dates. Mrs. Fields paid a penalty of $100,000 and agreed not to violate the law again.

But first you have to give me some personal information.

State Regulation

An exhaustive list of state laws is beyond the scope of this book, but be aware that some states have passed their own online privacy laws. To take some examples, the constitution of the state of California confers the right to privacy. Further, the California Online Privacy Act of 2003 requires any website that collects personal information from California residents to post a privacy policy conspicuously and then abide by its terms. Connecticut, Nebraska, and Pennsylvania also regulate online privacy policies.

Two states, Minnesota and Nevada, require ISPs to obtain their customers' consent before providing information about them. Connecticut and Delaware require employers to notify their workers before monitoring emails or Internet usage.

European Law

The European Convention on Human Rights declares, "Everyone has the right to respect for his private and family life, his home, and his correspondence." The European Union's e-Privacy Directive requires an opt-in system, under which tracking tools cannot be used unless the consumer is told how the tools will be used and then specifically grants permission for their use. However, this directive may be interpreted to mean that consumers have granted permission for tracking tools if they fail to change the default privacy settings on their web browsers. At this writing, European nations are just beginning to implement the e-Privacy Directive, so it may be some time before the impact of these rules is clear.

In theory, even companies outside Europe will have to comply with European rules if they interact with European customers. Recently, European agencies insisted that Google, Microsoft, and Yahoo! enhance their protection of users' search histories; and a court in Italy held that Google had violated that country's privacy laws by posting a video of students bullying an autistic boy. Stay tuned.

Spyware

Is your computer running sluggishly? Does it crash frequently? Has the home page on your web browser suddenly changed without your consent? Is there a program in your systems tray that you do not recognize? You might have **spyware** on your computer.

Spyware
A computer program that enters a user's computer without permission and monitors and reports the user's activities.

Congress has considered legislation to control spyware but has not taken final action. California has enacted the Consumer Protection Against Computer Spyware Act, which makes spyware illegal.

Spam

Spam is officially known as *unsolicited commercial email (UCE)* or *unsolicited bulk email (UBE)*. Whatever it is called, it is one of the most annoying aspects of email. It has been estimated that 90 percent of email is spam. And roughly half of these messages were fraudulent—either in content (promoting a scam) or in packaging (the headers or return address are false). Aside from the annoyance factor, bulk email adds to the cost of connecting to the Internet as ISPs increase server capacity to handle the millions of spam emails.

The Controlling the Assault of Non-Solicited Pornography and Marketing Act (CAN-SPAM) is a federal statute that does not prohibit spam but instead regulates it. This statute applies to virtually all promotional emails, whether or not the sender has a preexisting relationship with the recipient. Under this statute, commercial email:

- May not have deceptive headings (From, To, Reply To, Subject),
- Must offer an opt-out system permitting the recipient to unsubscribe (and must honor those requests promptly),
- Must clearly indicate that the email is an advertisement,
- Must provide a valid physical return address (not a post office box), and
- Must clearly indicate the nature of pornographic messages.

A company can avoid these requirements by obtaining advance permission from the recipients.

CAN-SPAM seems to have had little impact on the quantity of spam (although it has made opt-out provisions more common in legitimate commercial emails). More effective have been the tools developed by online security firms and governments that prevent as much as 98 percent of spam from reaching your email inbox.

But spammers have found other outlets. They post messages in the comment sections of websites and on social media sites such as Facebook and Twitter. Their goal is to entice you to click on a link that may take you to a website that sells foolproof "investments" or that simply steals bank information from your computer. If that link seems to come from a Facebook friend or someone whom you follow on Twitter, it seems more reliable. A recent study found that 8 percent of links sent via Twitter are fraudulent, but they are 20 times more likely to be clicked than those in spam email.[6]

EXAM Strategy

Question: **Cruise.com** operated a website selling cruise vacations. It sent unsolicited email advertisements—dubbed "E-deals"—to prospective customers. Eleven of these "E-deals" went to **inbox@webguy.net**. Each message offered the recipient an opportunity to be removed from the mailing list by clicking on a line of text or by writing to a specific postal address. Has **Cruise.com** violated the CAN-SPAM Act?

Strategy: Remember that this Act does not prohibit all unsolicited emails.

Result: **Cruise.com** was not in violation because it offered the recipients a way to unsubscribe. Also, it provided a valid physical return address.

Internet Service Providers and Web Hosts: Communications Decency Act of 1996

ISPs are companies, such as Earthlink, that provide connection to the Internet. Web hosts post web pages on the Internet. Both play important roles in cyberspace. As the legal structure that supports the Internet develops, so have legal issues involving these players.

The Internet is an enormously powerful tool for disseminating information. But what if some of this information happens to be false or in violation of our privacy rights? Is an ISP liable for transmitting it to the world? In 1995, a trial judge in New York held that an ISP, Prodigy Services Company, was potentially liable for defamatory statements that an unidentified person posted on one of its bulletin boards.[7] The message alleged that the president of an investment bank had committed "criminal and fraudulent acts." It was not only a false statement—it was posted on the most widely read financial computer bulletin board in the country. Although one can only feel sympathy for the target of this slur, the decision nonetheless alarmed many observers who argued that there was no way ISPs could review every piece of information that hurtles through their portals. The next year, Congress overruled the Prodigy case by passing the Communications Decency Act of 1996 (CDA).[8] **Under the CDA, ISPs and web hosts are not liable for information that is**

---

[6]"Long life spam," *The Economist*, November 20, 2010, p. 67.

[7]*Stratton Oakmont, Inc. v. Prodigy Services Company*, 1995 N.Y. Misc. LEXIS 229.

[8]47 U.S.C. 230.

provided by someone else. Only content providers are liable. The following case lays out the arguments in favor of the CDA, but also illustrates some of the costs of the statute (and of the Internet).

Carafano v. Metrosplash.com, Inc.[9]

339 F.3d 1119, 2003 U.S. App. LEXIS 16548
United States Court of Appeals for the Ninth Circuit, 2003

Facts: **Matchmaker.com** is an Internet dating service that permits members to post profiles of themselves and to view the profiles of other members. Matchmaker reviews photos for impropriety before posting them but does not examine the profiles.

Christianne Carafano is an actor who uses the stage name Chase Masterson. She has appeared in numerous films and television shows, such as *Star Trek: Deep Space Nine* and *General Hospital.* Without her knowledge, someone in Berlin posted a profile of her in the Los Angeles section of Matchmaker. In answer to the question "Main source of current events?" the person posting the profile put "*Playboy Playgirl*" and for "Why did you call?" responded "Looking for a one-night stand." In addition, the essays indicated that she was looking for a "hard and dominant" man with "a strong sexual appetite" and that she "liked sort of being controlled by a man, in and out of bed." Pictures of the actor taken off the Internet were included with the profile. The profile also provided her home address and an email address, which, when contacted, produced an automatic email reply stating, "You think you are the right one? Proof it!!" [sic], and providing Carafano's home address and telephone number.

Unaware of the improper posting, Carafano began receiving sexually explicit messages on her home voice mail, as well as a sexually explicit fax that threatened her and her son. She received numerous phone calls, letters, and email from male fans, expressing concern that she had given out her address and phone number (but simultaneously indicating an interest in meeting her). Feeling unsafe, Carafano and her son moved out of their home for several months.

One Saturday a week or two after the profile was first posted, Carafano's assistant, Siouxzan Perry, learned of the false profile through a message from "Jeff." Acting on Carafano's instructions, Perry contacted Matchmaker, demanding that the profile be removed immediately. The Matchmaker employee did not remove it then because Perry herself had not posted it, but on Monday morning, the company blocked the profile from public view and then deleted it the following day.

Carafano filed suit against Matchmaker alleging invasion of privacy, misappropriation of the right of publicity, defamation, and negligence. The district court rejected Matchmaker's argument for immunity under the CDA on the grounds that the company provided part of the profile content.

Issue: ***Does the CDA protect Matchmaker from liability?***

Excerpts from Judge Thomas's Decision: Through [the CDA], Congress granted most Internet services immunity from liability for publishing false or defamatory material so long as the information was provided by another party. As a result, Internet publishers are treated differently from corresponding publishers in print, television, and radio. Congress enacted this provision for two basic policy reasons: to promote the free exchange of information and ideas over the Internet and to encourage voluntary monitoring for offensive or obscene material.

Interactive computer services have millions of users. It would be impossible for service providers to screen each of their millions of postings for possible problems. Faced with potential liability for each message republished by their services, interactive computer service providers might choose to severely restrict the number and type of messages posted. Congress considered the weight of the speech interests implicated and chose to immunize service providers to avoid any such restrictive effect. Under [the CDA], therefore, so long as a third party willingly provides the essential published content, the interactive service provider receives full immunity regardless of the specific editing or selection process.

The fact that some of the content [in Carafano's fake profile] was formulated in response to Matchmaker's questionnaire does not [make Matchmaker liable]. Doubtless, the questionnaire facilitated the expression of information

[9]**Matchmaker.com**, Inc. changed its legal name to **Metrosplash.com**, Inc. but continued to do business as **Matchmaker.com**.

by individual users. However, the selection of the content was left exclusively to the user. Matchmaker cannot be considered an "information content provider" under the statute because no profile has any content until a user actively creates it.

Further, even assuming Matchmaker could be considered an information content provider, the statute would still bar Carafano's claims unless Matchmaker created or developed the particular information at issue. In this case, critical information about Carafano's home address and the email address that revealed her phone number were transmitted unaltered to profile viewers. Thus, Matchmaker did not play a significant role in creating, developing, or "transforming" the relevant information.

Thus, despite the serious and utterly deplorable consequences that occurred in this case, we conclude that Congress intended that service providers such as Matchmaker be afforded immunity from suit.

Note that the CDA does not protect web hosts or ISPs that engage in wrongdoing. For example, Bright Builders, Inc, hosted **copycatclubs.com**, a website that, as you might guess, sold counterfeit golf clubs. The court held that Bright Builders was liable despite the CDA because it participated in the design, building, marketing, and support of **copycatclubs.com**. It even helped locate the counterfeit clubs that the website sold.[10] Ultimately, a jury returned a verdict of $770,750 against Bright Builders.

Also, the CDA does not protect web hosts and ISPs from contract liability. For example, after Cynthia Barnes broke up with her boyfriend, he created a profile of her on a Yahoo! website. He then spitefully posted nude photos of the two of them taken without her knowledge, together with her addresses and phone numbers at home and at work. He also suggested that she was interested in sex with random strangers. Many men were willing to oblige. For months, Yahoo! did not even respond to Barnes's request to remove the profile. Not until a TV show prepared to run a story about the incident did the company's director of communications contact Barnes to promise that the profile would be removed immediately. Still Yahoo! took no action until two months later, when Barnes sued. The appeals court ruled that Barnes could bring a contract claim against Yahoo! under a theory of promissory estoppel–that she had relied on the company's promise.[11]

EXAM Strategy

Question: Someone posted an anonymous review on **TripAdvisor.com** alleging that the owner of a restaurant had entertained a prostitute there. The allegation was false. TripAdvisor refused to investigate or remove the review. Does the restaurant owner have a valid claim against the website?

Strategy: Remember that web hosts are liable only if they have engaged in wrongdoing.

Result: As a web host, TripAdvisor is not liable for content. It would be liable only if it promised to take down the review and then did not.

[10] *Roger Cleveland Golf Co. v. Price*, 2010 U.S. Dist. LEXIS 128044.

[11] *Barnes v. Yahoo!, Inc.*, 570 F.3d 1096 (9th Cir., 2008). Promissory estoppel is discussed at greater length in Chapter 10.

Crime on the Internet

Despite its great benefits, the Internet has also opened new frontiers in crime for the dishonest and unscrupulous.

Hacking

During the 2008 presidential campaign, college student David Kernell guessed Sarah Palin's email password, accessed her personal Yahoo! account, and published the content of some of her emails. To many, his actions seemed like an amusing prank. The joke turned out not to be so funny when Kernell was sentenced to one year in prison.

Hacking
Gaining unauthorized access to a computer system.

Gaining unauthorized access to a computer system is called **hacking**. It is a major crime. The Federal Bureau of Investigation ranks cybercrime as its third-highest priority, right behind terrorism and spying. The Pentagon reports that hackers make more than 250,000 attempts annually on its computers. The goal of hackers is varied; some do it for little more than the thrill of the challenge. The objective for other hackers may be industrial espionage, extortion, theft of credit card information, or revenge for perceived slights. Kernell hoped to prevent Palin from being elected vice president.

Hacking is a crime under the federal Computer Fraud and Abuse Act of 1986 (CFAA).[12] This statute applies to any computer, cell phone, iPod, or other gadget attached to the Internet. **The CFAA prohibits:**

- Accessing a computer without authorization and obtaining information from it,
- Computer espionage,
- Theft of financial information,
- Theft of information from the U.S. government,
- Theft from a computer,
- Computer fraud,
- Intentional, reckless, and negligent damage to a computer,
- Trafficking in computer passwords, and
- Computer extortion.

The CFAA also provides for civil remedies so that someone who has been harmed by a hacker can personally recover damages from the wrongdoer. Employers have begun to use the CFAA to bring civil cases against former employees who take company information with them when they go to work for a competitor. At this writing, the courts are inconsistent on the issue of whether such an activity constitutes "unauthorized access" and is, therefore, a violation of the CFAA. Also, database owners sometimes claim that an unauthorized user who "shares" the login credentials of a legitimate purchaser has violated the CFAA. Because the courts have split on these issues, the outcome of such a case depends on geography.[13]

There are two problems with the CFAA. First, while the statute prohibits the use of a virus to harm a computer, it does not ban the creation of viruses that someone else could use for

[12] 18 U.S.C. Section 1030.

[13] See, for example, *Int'l Airport Centers LLC v. Citrin*, 440 F 3d 418 (7th Cir., 2006); *Lasco Foods, Inc. v. Hall & Shaw Sales*, 600 F. Supp. 2d 1045 (E. Dist. Mo, 2009); *Orbit One Communications Inc. v. Numerex Corp*, 692 F. Supp. 2d 373 (S.D.N.Y. 2010); *State Analysis Inc. v. American Financial Services Assoc*, 621 F. Supp. 2d 309 (E.D. Va., 2009); and *AtPac Inc. v. Aptitude Solutions Inc.*, 730 F. Supp. 2d 1174, (E.D. CA, 2010).

hacking. Thus, it is legal for websites to sell source code for viruses—codes that even beginners can use destructively.

Second, the CFAA applies only to U.S. criminals. Because the Internet is truly international, cybercriminals do not always fall within the jurisdiction of American laws. For example, a computer virus called ILOVEYOU caused an estimated $7 billion worth of damage worldwide. Although the perpetrator would have been subject to prosecution under the CFAA in the United States, he lived in the Philippines, which did not have laws prohibiting cybercrime. Nor could the suspect be extradited automatically to the United States because the extradition treaty only applied if both nations had the same law. The Philippines ultimately dropped all charges against the suspect.

Is this the real deal, or a cheap imitation?

Fraud

Fraud is a growth business on the Internet. The Internet's anonymity and speed facilitate fraud, and computers help criminals identify and contact victims. Common scams include advance fee scams,[14] the sale of merchandise that is either defective or nonexistent, the so-called Nigerian letter scam,[15] billing for services that are touted as "free," fake scholarship search services, romance fraud (you meet someone online who wants to visit you but needs money for travel expenses), and credit card scams (for a fee, you can get a credit card, even with a poor credit rating). One of the new scams involves *over*payment. You are renting out a house, selling a pet, or accepting a job, and "by accident," you are sent too much money. You wire the excess back, only to find out that the initial check or funds transfer was no good.

Fraud is the deception of another person for the purpose of obtaining money or property from him. It can be prosecuted under state law or the Computer Fraud and Abuse Act. In addition, federal mail and wire fraud statutes prohibit the use of mail or wire communication in furtherance of a fraudulent scheme.[16] The FTC can bring civil cases under Section 5 of the FTC Act. (Chapter 8, on crime, discusses fraud.)

Auctions

Internet auctions are the number one source of consumer complaints about online fraud. Wrongdoers either sell goods they do not own, provide defective goods, or offer fakes. In a recent case—which will not reduce the amount of auction fraud—a court held that eBay, the Internet auction site, was not liable to Tiffany & Company for the counterfeit Tiffany products sold on the site. The jewelry company had sued after discovering that most items advertised on eBay as Tiffany products were, in fact, fakes. The court held that eBay's only legal obligation was to remove products once told that they were counterfeit.[17]

---

[14]As in, "If you are willing to pay a fee in advance, then you will have access to (pick your choice) favorable financing, lottery winnings from overseas, attractive investment opportunities that will make you rich."

[15]Victims receive an email from someone alleging to be a Nigerian government official who has stolen money from the government. He needs some place safe to park the money for a short time. The official promises that, if the victim will permit her account to be used for this purpose, she will be allowed to keep a percentage of the stolen money. Instead, of course, once the "official" has the victim's bank information, he cleans out the account.

[16]U.S.C. Sections 1341–1346.

[17]*Tiffany Inc. v. eBay, Inc.*, 600 F.3d 93, 2010 U.S. App. LEXIS 6735 (2nd Cir., 2010) and, on remand, 2010 U.S. Dist. LEXIS 96596 (S.D.N.Y, 2010).

Shilling
When a seller at auction either bids on his own goods or agrees to cross-bid with a group of other sellers.

Shilling is an increasingly popular online auction fraud. **Shilling means that a seller either bids on his own goods or agrees to cross-bid with a group of other sellers.** Shilling is prohibited because the owner drives up the price of his own item by bidding on it. Thus, for example, Kenneth Walton, a San Francisco lawyer, put up for auction on eBay an abstract painting purportedly by famous artist Richard Diebenkorn. A bidder offered $135,805 before eBay withdrew the item in response to charges that Walton had placed a bid on the painting himself and had also engaged in cross-bidding with a group of other eBay users. Although Walton claimed that he had placed the bids for friends, he ultimately pleaded guilty to charges of federal wire and mail fraud. He was sentenced to almost four years in prison and paid almost $100,000 in restitution to those who overpaid for the items he bid on.

To date, eBay has generally responded to shillers by suspending them. Shillers are also subject to suit under general anti-fraud statutes. In addition, some states explicitly prohibit shilling.[18]

Identity Theft

Identity theft is one of the scariest crimes against property. Thieves steal the victim's social security number and other personal information such as bank account numbers and mother's maiden name, which they use to obtain loans and credit cards. The money owed is never repaid, leaving victims to prove that they were not responsible for the debts. The thieves may even commit (additional) crimes under their new identities. Meanwhile, the victim may find himself unable to obtain a credit card, loan, or job. One victim spent several nights in jail after he was arrested for a crime that his alter ego had committed.

Although identity fraud existed before computers, the Internet has made it much easier. For example, consumer activists were able to purchase the social security numbers of the director of the CIA, the Attorney General of the United States, and other top administration officials. The cost? Only $26 each. No surprise then that 8 million Americans are victims of this crime each year.

A number of federal statutes deal with identity theft or its consequences. **The Identity Theft and Assumption Deterrence Act of 1998 prohibits the use of false identification to commit fraud or other crime and it also permits the victim to seek restitution in court.**[19] The Truth in Lending Act limits liability on a stolen credit card to $50. The Social Security Protection Act of 2010 prohibits government agencies from printing social security numbers on checks.

A number of states have also passed identity theft statutes. Almost every state now requires companies to notify consumers when their personal information has been stolen. Many states also restrict the use and disclosure of social security numbers.

What can you do to prevent the theft of your identity?

1. Check your credit reports at least once a year. (Consumers are entitled by law to one free credit report every year from each of the three major reporting agencies. You can order these reports at **https://www.annualcreditreport.com**.)

2. Place a freeze on your credit report so that anyone who is about to issue a loan or credit card will double-check with you first.

3. If you suspect that your identity has been stolen, contact the FTC at 877-IDTHEFT, 877-438-4338, or google "ftc identity theft" to get to the FTC's identity theft site. Also, file a police report immediately and keep a copy to show creditors. Notify the three credit agencies.

---

[18]For example, New Mexico law provides that "It shall be unlawful to employ shills or puffers at any such auction sale or to offer or to make or to procure to be offered or made any false bid or offer any false bid to buy or pretend to buy any article sold or offered for sale." N.M. Stat. Section 61-16-14.

[19]18 U.S. Section 1028.

Phishing

Phishing
A fraudster sends a message directing the recipient to enter personal information on a website that is an illegal imitation of a legitimate site.

Have you ever received an instant message from a Facebook friend saying, "Hey, what's up?" with a link to an IQ test? This instant message is not from a friend, but rather from a fraudster hoping to lure the recipient into revealing her personal information. In this case, people who clicked on the link were told that they had to provide their cell phone number to get the test results. Next thing they knew, they had been signed up for some expensive cell phone service. This scam is part of one of the most rapidly growing areas of Internet fraud: **phishing. In this crime, a fraudster sends a message directing the recipient to enter personal information on a website that is an illegal imitation of a legitimate site.**

In a traditional phishing scam, large numbers of generic emails are sprayed over the Internet asking millions of people to log on to, say, a fake bank site. But the latest development—called **spear phishing**—involves personalized messages sent from someone the victim knows. For example, your sister asks for your social security number so she can add you as a beneficiary to her life insurance policy. In reality, this email has come from a fraudster who hacked into her Facebook account to gain access to her lists of friends and family.[20] Even "Like" buttons can be "clickjacked" to take unwary users to bogus sites.

Prosecutors can bring criminal charges against phishers for fraud. The companies whose websites have been copied can sue these criminals for fraud, trademark infringement, false advertising, and cybersquatting (discussed further in Chapter 42, on intellectual property).

No reputable company will ask customers to respond to an email with personal information. When in doubt, close the suspicious email, relaunch your web browser, and then go to the company's main website. If the legitimate company needs information from you, it will so indicate on the site.

EXAM Strategy

Question: TruePrint sent emails to thousands of consumers, advertising its business card service. The subject line said, "FREE GIFT!" Consumers who opened the email, were then asked to click on a link, which led to a web page that asked for personal information. After filling in the information and clicking a "Continue" button, they landed on a second web page. In the fine print at the bottom of this page was the following statement: "Printing is free. Pay only for shipping and processing. Please see our Free Offer Details for more information." Finally, at the end of the process on the next web page, consumers learned that shipping the free gift would cost $5.67, payable by credit card or check. The email did not make any reference to TruePrint. Has TruePrint violated the law?

Strategy: Indeed, TruePrint has violated two laws.

Result: First, it has advertised a "free gift" when, in fact, the gift costs $5.67. That is fraud. Second, it has violated the CAN-SPAM act because the subject line of the email is untrue—the gift is not free. It has further violated CAN-SPAM by its failure to provide TruePrint's valid physical return address.

[20]To prevent your Facebook account from being hijacked, be careful when accessing it over a public network (such as in a hotel or airport), where fraudsters might be able to capture your password. If you text "otp" to 32665, you will receive a password that can be used only once (a "one-time password"). Fraudsters thus cannot use this password to access your account.

Chapter Conclusion

The Internet has changed our lives in ways that were inconceivable a generation ago, and the law is rushing to catch up. Courts will apply some old laws in new ways and, as legislators and courts learn from experience, new laws will be enacted.

Inevitably, the law of cyberspace will become increasingly international. What does Europe accomplish by regulating Internet privacy if its citizens spend a good portion of their time on American websites? What will the FTC do if scam artists or spammers operate offshore? Effective regulation of cyberspace will require cooperation among nations and between government and industry.

Exam Review

1. **THE FIRST AMENDMENT** The First Amendment to the Constitution protects speech on the Internet so long as the speech does not violate some other law. (pp. 1037–1039)

2. **THE FOURTH AMENDMENT** The Fourth Amendment to the Constitution prohibits unreasonable searches and seizures by the government. This provision applies to computers. (pp. 1039–1041)

3. **REASONABLE EXPECTATION OF PRIVACY** If your employer has a reasonably articulated policy notifying you that it has the right to access and read electronic communications on a system that it provides, then you do not have a reasonable expectation of privacy when using that system. You do have a reasonable right to privacy on a system that you provide for yourself. (pp. 1039–1040)

Question: Three travel agents use fictitious accounts to steal millions of frequent flyer miles. Must the police obtain a warrant before searching their email accounts?

Strategy: The answer depends on what type of email account the agents used.

4. **THE FTC ACT** Section 5 of the FTC Act prohibits unfair and deceptive practices. The FTC does not require websites to have a privacy policy, but if they do have one, it cannot be deceptive and they must comply with it. (p. 1042)

5. **THE ECPA** The Electronic Communications Privacy Act of 1986 is a federal statute that prohibits unauthorized interception or disclosure of wire and electronic communications. However, it permits an employer to monitor workers' electronic communications if (1) the employee consents, (2) the monitoring occurs in the ordinary course of business, or (3) the employer provides the computer system (in the case of email). (pp. 1042–1044)

6. **COPPA** The Children's Online Privacy Protection Act of 1998 prohibits Internet operators from collecting information from children under 13 without parental permission. It also requires sites to disclose how they will use any information they acquire. (p. 1044)

7. **E-PRIVACY DIRECTIVE** The European Union's e-Privacy Directive requires an opt-in system under which tracking tools cannot be used unless the consumer is told how the tools will be used and then specifically grants permission for their use. (pp. 1044–1045)

8. **CAN-SPAM** The Controlling the Assault of Non-Solicited Pornography and Marketing Act (CAN-SPAM) is a federal statute that does not prohibit spam but instead regulates it. Under this statute, commercial email:
   - May not have deceptive headings (From, To, Reply To, Subject),
   - Must offer an opt-out system permitting the recipient to unsubscribe (and must honor those requests promptly),
   - Must clearly indicate that the email is an advertisement,
   - Must provide a valid physical return address (not a post office box), and
   - Must clearly indicate the nature of pornographic messages. (p. 1045)

9. **THE CDA** Under the Communications Decency Act of 1996, ISPs and web hosts are not liable for information that is provided by someone else. (pp. 1046–1048)

EXAM Strategy

Question: Ton Cremers was the director of security at Amsterdam's famous Rijksmuseum and the operator of the Museum Security Network (the Network) website. Robert Smith, a handyman working for Ellen Batzel in North Carolina, sent an email to the Network alleging that Batzel was the granddaughter of Heinrich Himmler (one of Hitler's henchmen) and that she had art that Himmler had stolen. These allegations were completely untrue. Cremers posted Smith's email on the Network's website and sent it to the Network's subscribers. Cremers exercised some editorial discretion in choosing which emails to send to subscribers, generally omitting any that were unrelated to stolen art. Is Cremers liable to Batzel for the harm that this inaccurate information caused?

Strategy: Cremers is liable only if he is a content provider. (See the "Result" at the end of this section.)

10. **THE CFAA** Hacking is a crime under the federal Computer Fraud and Abuse Act of 1986. The CFAA prohibits:
    - Accessing a computer without authorization and obtaining information from it,
    - Computer espionage,
    - Theft of financial information,
    - Theft of information from the U.S. government,

- Theft from a computer,
- Computer fraud,
- Intentional, reckless, and negligent damage to a computer,
- Trafficking in computer passwords, and
- Computer extortion. (pp. 1049–1050)

Question: To demonstrate the inadequacies of existing computer security systems, Cornell student Robert Morris created a computer virus. His plan, however, went awry, as plans sometimes do. He thought his virus would be relatively harmless, but it ran amok, crashing scores of computers at universities, military sites, and medical research sites. Has he committed a crime, or is he liable only for civil penalties? Does it matter that he did not intend to cause damage?

Strategy: Review the provisions of the CFAA. (See the "Result" at the end of this section.)

11. **FRAUD** Fraud is the deception of another person for the purpose of obtaining money or property from him. (pp. 1050–1052)

12. **IDENTITY THEFT** The Identity Theft and Assumption Deterrence Act of 1998 prohibits the use of false identification to commit fraud or other crime. (p. 1051)

3. Result: If their employer owns the email system, the agents have no expectation of privacy and the police do not need a search warrant. If, however, they are sending emails over a system they are paying for themselves, then the police do need a warrant.

9. Result: The court found that Cremers was not liable under the CDA.

10. Result: Morris was convicted of a crime under the CFAA. He intended to trespass on a computer, so it did not matter that he had no intent to cause harm.

Multiple-Choice Questions

1. Beth sent fraudulent emails through both her account at work and her personal account at home. Although Beth had never read her employer's handbook, it said the company had the right to access work emails. The police ________ obtain a search warrant before reading her work emails. They ________ obtain a search warrant before reading the emails from her personal account.
   (a) need to, need to
   (b) need not, need not
   (c) need to, need not
   (d) need not, need to

2. Because Blaine Blogger reviews movies on his blog, cinemas allow him in for free. Nellie Newspaper Reporter also gets free admission to movies. Blaine ________ disclose on his blog that he receives free tickets. Nellie ________ disclose in her articles that she receives free tickets.
   (a) must, must
   (b) need not, need not
   (c) must, need not
   (d) need not, must

3. An employer has the right to monitor workers' electronic communications if
   (a) The employee consents.
   (b) The monitoring occurs in the ordinary course of business.
   (c) The employer provides the computer system.
   (d) All of the above
   (e) None of the above

4. Spiro Spammer sends millions of emails a day asking people to donate to his college tuition fund. Oddly enough, many people do. Everything in the emails is accurate (including his 1.9 GPA). Which of the following statements is true?
   (a) Spiro has violated the CAN-SPAM Act because he has sent unsolicited commercial emails.
   (b) Spiro has violated the CAN-SPAM Act if he has not offered recipients an opportunity to unsubscribe.
   (c) Spiro has violated the CAN-SPAM Act because he is asking for money.
   (d) Spiro has violated the CAN-SPAM Act unless the recipients have granted permission to him to send these emails.

5. Sushila suspects that her boyfriend is being unfaithful. While he is asleep, she takes his iPod out from under his pillow and goes through all his playlists. Then she finds what she has been looking for: Plum's Playlist. It is full of romantic songs. Sushila sends Plum an email that says, "You are the most evil person in the universe!" Which law has Sushila violated?
   (a) The First Amendment
   (b) The CDA
   (c) The ECPA
   (d) The CFAA
   (e) None

Essay Questions

1. **ETHICS** Chitika, Inc., provided online tracking tools on websites. When consumers clicked the "opt-out" button, indicating that they did not want to be tracked, they were not—for 10 days. After that, the software would resume tracking. Is there a legal problem with Chitika's system? An ethical problem? What Life Principles were operating here?

2. **YOU BE THE JUDGE WRITING PROBLEM** Jerome Schneider wrote several books on how to avoid taxes. These books were sold on **Amazon.com**. Amazon permits visitors to post comments about items for sale. Amazon's policy suggests that these comments should be civil (e.g., no profanity or spiteful remarks). The comments about Schneider's books were not so kind. One person alleged Schneider was a felon. When Schneider complained, an Amazon representative agreed that some of the postings violated its guidelines and promised that they would be removed within one to two business days. Two days later, the posting had not been removed. Schneider filed suit. **Argument for Schneider:** Amazon has editorial discretion over the posted comments. It both establishes guidelines and then monitors the comments to ensure that they comply with the guidelines. These activities make Amazon an information content provider, not protected by the Communications Decency Act. Also, Amazon violated its promise to take down the content. **Argument for Amazon:** The right to edit material is not the same thing as creating the material in the first place.

3. Over the course of 10 months, Joseph Melle sent more than 60 million unsolicited email advertisements to AOL members. What charges could be brought against him? Would you need more information before deciding?

4. What can you do to protect your privacy online? Draw up a concrete list of steps that you might reasonably consider. Are there some actions that you would not be willing to take because they are not worth it to you?

5. Craig Hare offered computers and related equipment for sale on various Internet auction websites. He accepted payment but not responsibility—he never shipped the goods. Which government agencies might bring charges against him?

Discussion Questions

1. Marina Stengart used her company laptop to communicate with her lawyer via her personal, password-protected, web-based email account. The company's policy stated:

   > E-mail and voice mail messages, internet use and communication, and computer files are considered part of the company's business and client records. Such communications are not to be considered private or personal to any individual employee. Occasional personal use is permitted; however, the system should not be used to solicit for outside business ventures, charitable organizations, or for any political or religious purpose, unless authorized by the Director of Human Resources.

   After she filed an employment lawsuit against her employer, the company hired an expert to access her emails that had been automatically stored on the laptop. Are these emails protected by the attorney-client privilege? How does this case compare with *Scott v. Beth Israel* earlier in the chapter?

2. **Roommates.com** operated a website designed to match people renting spare rooms with those looking for a place to live. Before subscribers could search listings or post housing opportunities on Roommate's website, they had to create profiles, a process that required them to answer a series of questions that included the subscriber's sex, sexual orientation, and whether he would bring children to a household. The site also

encouraged subscribers to provide "Additional Comments," describing themselves and their desired roommate in an open-ended essay. Here are some typical ads:

- "I am not looking for Muslims."
- "Not acceptable: freaks, geeks, prostitutes (male or female), druggies, pet cobras, drama queens, or mortgage brokers."
- "Must be a black gay male!"
- We are 3 Christian females who Love our Lord Jesus Christ.... We have weekly bible studies and bi-weekly times of fellowship."

Many of the ads violated the Fair Housing Act. Is **Roommates.com** liable?

3. **ETHICS** Matt Drudge published a report on his website (**http://www.drudgereport.com**) that White House aide Sidney Blumenthal "has a spousal abuse past that has been effectively covered up.... There are court records of Blumenthal's violence against his wife." The *Drudge Report* is an electronic publication focusing on Hollywood and Washington gossip. AOL paid Drudge $3,000 a month to make the *Drudge Report* available to AOL subscribers. Drudge emailed his reports to AOL, which then posted them. Before posting, however, AOL had the right to edit content. Drudge ultimately retracted his allegations against Blumenthal, who sued AOL. He alleged that under the Communications Decency Act of 1996, AOL was a "content provider" because it paid Drudge and edited what he wrote. Do you agree? Putting liability aside, what moral obligation did AOL have to its members? To Blumenthal? Should AOL be liable for content it bought and provided to its members?

4. Lori Drew created a fake MySpace profile, pretending to be a teenage boy. Through that boy's identity, she bullied 13-year-old Megan Meier. The girl killed herself shortly after receiving a message saying, "The world would be a better place without you." MySpace requires all users to agree to its terms of service which require "truthful and accurate" information. Has Drew violated the CFAA?

5. Tracking tools provide benefits to consumers but they also carry risks. Should Congress regulate them? If so, what should the law provide?

INTELLECTUAL PROPERTY

Cooper is a producer at a small indie film company in Los Angeles. He puts together packages that have a script, a director, and actors. He then finds investors who pay to make the movie and distributors who purchase the right to release it in cinemas, on TV, and on DVD. (Although most people think that box office results are what count, the reality is that, historically, over half of most movies' revenue came from home entertainment options such as DVD rentals and sales.)

Cooper is pretty excited about two packages he has put together: one stars established actor Robert de Niro, and the other features an up-and-coming director working with movie star Clive Owen. But his excitement has turned to disappointment—shockingly, he cannot find anyone willing to invest in either movie. Cooper hears the same thing from everyone: "DVD sales are way down, so we know we won't get the payback we used to. We can't afford to invest in as many movies."

On a flight to New York in search of investors, Cooper finds himself sitting next to a man who is watching a movie on his computer. Cooper knows this movie has not even been released to DVD yet. Clearly, the man has downloaded it from an illegal website. Cooper slowly crushes the plastic cup in his hand. What's wrong with that guy? Doesn't he know that movies cost money to make? Doesn't he realize people like him are killing an industry?

On a flight to New York in search of investors, Cooper finds himself sitting next to a man who is watching a movie on his computer.... Clearly, the man has downloaded it from an illegal website.

Introduction

For much of history, land was the most valuable form of property. It was the primary source of wealth and social status. Today, intellectual property is a major source of wealth. New ideas—for manufacturing processes, computer programs, medicines, books—bring both affluence and influence.

Although both can be valuable assets, land and intellectual property are fundamentally different. The value of land lies in the owner's right to exclude, to prevent others from entering it. Intellectual property, however, has little economic value unless others use it. This ability to share intellectual property is both good news and bad. On the one hand, the owner can produce and sell unlimited copies of, say, a software program, but on the other hand, the owner has no easy way to determine if someone is using the program for free. The high cost of developing intellectual property, combined with the low cost of reproducing it, makes it particularly vulnerable to theft.

Because intellectual property is nonexclusive, many people see no problem with using it for free. But when consumers take intellectual property—movies, songs, and books—without paying for it, they ensure that fewer of these items will be produced.

Some commentators suggest that the United States has been a technological leader partly because its laws have always provided strong protection for intellectual property. The Constitution provided for patent protection early in the country's history.

The conflict between those who have intellectual property and those who want to use it has taken on a global dimension. Developing countries argue that American intellectual property laws increase the price of medicines, such as AIDS drugs and vaccines, that could save more lives if only they were cheaper and, therefore, more readily available. "Patents kill" is their slogan. The United States responds that without patent protection, there would be no innovation, no miracle drugs.

But even U.S. drug companies admit that patents can sometimes stifle innovation. The pharmaceutical company Bristol-Meyers Squibb says that it cannot conduct research on many cancer-fighting drugs because of patents held by its competitors. Information technology firms make a similar complaint. In a study of the American semiconductor business, researchers found that more patents did not necessarily mean more innovation. Instead, some companies were simply more aggressive about patenting every possible aspect of their research. Nor was there any evidence that innovation increased as patent rights were enhanced.

The role of intellectual property law is to balance the rights of those who create intellectual property and those who would enjoy it. And as this chapter reveals, such a balancing act is no easy feat.

Patents

Patent
A grant by the government permitting the inventor exclusive use of an invention for a specified period.

A **patent** is a grant by the government permitting the inventor exclusive use of an invention for 20 years from the date of filing (or 14 years from the date of issuance in the case of design patents). During this period, no one may make, use, or sell the invention without permission. In return, the inventor publicly discloses information about the invention that anyone can use upon expiration of the patent.

Types of Patents

There are three types of patents: utility patents, design patents, and plant patents.

Utility Patent

Whenever people use the word "patent" by itself, they are referring to a utility patent. This type of patent is available to those who invent (or significantly improve) any of the following:

Type of Invention	Example
Mechanical invention	A hydraulic jack used to lift heavy aircraft
Electrical invention	A prewired, portable wall panel for use in large, open-plan offices
Chemical invention	The chemical 2-chloroethylphosphonic acid used as a plant growth regulator
Process	A method for applying a chemical compound to an established plant such as rice in order to inhibit the growth of weeds selectively; the application can be patented separately from the actual chemical
Machine	A device that enables a helicopter pilot to control all flight functions (pitch, roll, and heave) with one hand
Composition of matter	A sludge used as an explosive at construction sites; the patent specifies the water content, the density, and the types of solids contained in the mixture

What about an electronic signal—is that patentable? An inventor filed a patent application for a method of encoding additional information on electronic signals emitted from digital audio files. The process was very useful, but the court ruled that it was not patentable because the signal is not a mechanical, electrical, or chemical invention, a process, a machine, or the composition of matter.[1]

A patent is not available solely for an idea, but only for its tangible application. Thus patents are not available for laws of nature, scientific principles, mathematical algorithms, or formulas such as $a^2 + b^2 = c^2$.

Business Method Patents. In recent years, so-called "business method patents" have been controversial. These patents involve a particular way of doing business that often includes data processing or mathematical calculations. Business method patents have been particularly common in e-commerce. For example, Amazon.com patented its One-Click method of instant ordering. The company then obtained an injunction to prevent barnesandnoble.com from using its Express Lane service that was similar to One-Click. The judge directed barnesandnoble.com to add another step to its ordering process. The Patent and Trademark Office (PTO) affirmed the Amazon patent, which will expire in 2017.

Facebook has been granted a patent on a process that "dynamically provides a news feed about a user of a social network." Most social media sites, such as LinkedIn, Twitter, and Flickr, use some version of this technology. At this writing, two important issues are unknown: the exact scope of the patent and how aggressive Facebook will be in enforcing it.

It would be very helpful if the courts provided more clarity—and certainty—about the scope and enforceability of business method patents. In a recent case, *Bilski v. Kappos*, the Supreme Court ruled that business methods are *generally* patentable, even as it held that the *particular* patent in the case (a method for hedging risk in commodities trading) was too abstract to be acceptable.[2] In the same case, the Supreme Court encouraged lower courts to

[1] *In re Nuijten*, 500 F.3d 1346; 2007 U.S. App. LEXIS 22426.

[2] 2010 U.S. LEXIS 5521 (S.Ct. 2010).

narrow the scope of business method patents, but did not offer guidance as to what these limits should be. For the time being, it seems that inventors will continue to apply for business method patents while waiting for lower courts to develop standards that meet the approval of the Supreme Court. This could be a lengthy wait—in the *Bilski* case, 13 years elapsed from the filing of the patent application until the Supreme Court decision.

However, in 2011 Congress passed the America Invents Act (AIA). Under this statute, anyone who has been charged with infringement of certain *financial service* business method patents has the right (from 2012 to 2020) to challenge the validity of that patent.

Patents on Living Organisms. In 1980, the Supreme Court ruled that living organisms could be patented.[3] That case involved genetically engineered bacteria that was used to treat oil spills. The bacteria could be patented because it was different from anything found in nature and was also useful.

As a result of this ruling, the PTO began issuing patents on human genetic material. A total of 20 percent of all genes were patented, and the companies that owned these patents were valued at billions of dollars. Then, in 2010, a federal district court ruled that genes could not be patented. The patent at issue in this case allowed laboratories to isolate DNA that contained certain genes and then test them for mutations associated with breast and ovarian cancer. However, a federal appeals court overruled the district court, holding that the genes could be patented (but, in this case, not the process by which the genes were compared).[4] It seems likely that the Supreme Court will weigh in on this dispute.

Braun patented the appearance not the function, of this blender.

Design Patent

A design patent protects the appearance, not the function, of an item. It is granted to anyone who invents a new, original, and ornamental design for an article. For example, Braun, Inc., patented the look of its handheld electric blenders. Design patents last 14 years from the date of issuance, not 20 years from the date of filing.

Plant Patent

Anyone who creates a new type of plant can patent it, provided that the inventor is able to reproduce it asexually—through grafting, for instance, rather than by planting its seeds. For example, one company patented its unique heather plant.

Requirements for a Patent

To receive a patent, an invention must be:

- **Novel**. An invention is not patentable if it (1) is known or has already been used in this country, (2) has been described in a publication here or overseas, or (3) is otherwise available to the public. For example, an inventor discovered a new use for existing chemical compounds but was not permitted to patent it because the compounds had already been described in prior publications, though the new uses had not.[5]
- **Nonobvious**. An invention is not patentable if it is obvious to a person with ordinary skill in that particular area. An inventor was

[3] *Diamond v. Chakrabarty*, 447 U.S. 303 (S. Ct. 1980).
[4] *Ass'n for Molecular Pathology v. United States PTO*, 2011 U.S. App. LEXIS 15649, 99 U.S.P.Q.2D (BNA) 1398. (Fed, Cir., 2011).
[5] *In re Schoenwald*, 964 F.2d 1122, 1992 U.S. App. LEXIS 10181 (Fed. Cir. 1992).

not allowed to patent a waterflush system designed to remove cow manure from the floor of a barn because it was obvious.[6]

- **Useful**. To be patented, an invention must be useful. It need not necessarily be commercially valuable, but it must have some current use. Being merely of scientific interest is not enough. Thus, a company was denied a patent for a novel process for making steroids because they had no therapeutic value.[7]

EXAM Strategy

Question: In 1572, during the reign of Queen Elizabeth I of England, a patent application was filed for a knife with a bone handle rather than a wooden one. Would this patent be granted under current U.S. law?

Strategy: Was a bone handle novel, nonobvious, and useful?

Result: It was useful—no splinters from a bone handle. It was novel—no one had ever done it before. But the patent was denied because it was obvious.

Patent Application and Issuance

To obtain a patent, the inventor must file a complex application with the PTO. If a patent examiner determines that the application meets all legal requirements, the PTO will issue the patent. If an examiner denies a patent application for any reason, the inventor can appeal that decision to the Patent Trial and Appeal Board in the PTO and from there to the Court of Appeals for the Federal Circuit in Washington.[8]

Under the AIA, third parties have the right to submit so-called "prior art"—that is, evidence that the invention is not novel. Even after a patent has been granted, third parties have limited rights to challenge its validity.

Priority Between Two Inventors

When two people invent the same product, who is entitled to a patent—the first to invent or the first to file an application? Until 2013, the person who invents and puts the invention into practice has priority over the first filer. But in 2013, the AIA changes the law so that the first person to *file* a patent application has priority. Because inventors will now be applying earlier than they have done in the past, this statute makes it easier for them to amend their applications. The AIA brings the United States into conformity with most of the rest of the world.

Prior Sale

An inventor must apply for a patent within one year of selling the product commercially. The purpose of this rule is to encourage prompt disclosure of inventions. It prevents someone from inventing a product, selling it for years, and then obtaining a 20-year monopoly with a patent.

---

[6] *Sakraida v. Ag Pro, Inc.*, 425 U.S. 273, 96 S. Ct. 1532, 1976 U.S. LEXIS 146 (1976).

[7] *Brenner v. Manson*, 383 U.S. 519, 86 S. Ct. 1033, 1966 U.S. LEXIS 2907 (1966).

[8] Recall from Chapter 3 that the Court of Appeals for the Federal Circuit is the 13th United States Court of Appeals. It hears appeals from specialized trial courts.

Provisional Patent Application

Inventors who are unable to assess the market value of their ideas sometimes hesitate to file a patent application because the process is expensive and cumbersome. A successful application can cost tens of thousands of dollars because the PTO charges a separate fee for each step of the process. Thus, for example, an inventor must pay a fee each time a patent examiner raises a legitimate question that requires an amendment to the application. Even if the examiner is wrong, the applicant may have to pay a fee even to file a disagreement. Thus, an inventor may struggle to raise sufficient funds in the one-year filing window to pay for the patent process. However, the AIA now permits the PTO to charge lower fees to individuals or small entities.

In addition, the PTO permits inventors to make a simpler, shorter filing called a **provisional patent application (PPA)**. This application provides a provable date of filing. Once filed, the application sits dormant for a year, giving the inventors an opportunity to show their ideas to potential investors without incurring the full expense of a patent application. PPA protection lasts only one year. To maintain protection after that time, the inventor must file a nonprovisional patent application.

Duration of a Patent

Patents are valid for 20 years from the date of *filing* the application (except design patents, which are valid for 14 years from date of *issuance*). In the last 15 years, the number of patent applications has increased from 950 a day to 2,000. And the typical patent application is longer and more complicated. As a result, more than 1 million applications are now pending. Approval of a patent can take anywhere from 3 to 6 years from the date of filing. These delays mean that patent holders effectively receive much less than 20 years of protection (although in the case of exceptional delays, it is possible to request an extension). They also threaten the ability of American inventors to attract investors, monetize their inventions, and compete with foreign businesses.

Infringement

A patent holder has the exclusive right to use the invention during the term of the patent. A holder can prohibit others from using any product that is substantially the same, license the product to others for a fee, and recover damages from anyone who uses the product without permission.

Patent Trolls

As we have seen, the patent office must deal with a growing caseload. As a result, the examiners typically spend less than 25 hours reviewing each application. Applicants are not required to demonstrate that the invention is novel, and often the examiner neither knows nor has the time to research the issue. Thus, patents are sometimes issued for inventions that are not really new.

Traditionally, this issue was not that important because companies with overlapping patents did not litigate who the real inventor was. They were too busy developing products to sell. But then came **patent trolls**. They do not make or market products—they simply buy portfolios of patents for the purpose of bringing patent infringement claims against companies already using the technology. Typically, patent trolls request an injunction to prevent the use of the technology during litigation, potentially harming a multimillion-dollar product over a patent worth much less. Because the trolls are not using the technology themselves, they do not have to worry about a cross-injunction against them. Oftentimes, patent trolls are simply hoping that even legitimate users will pay them to go away. In a recent report, the FTC found that these practices "can deter innovation by raising costs and risks without making a technological contribution."[9] In response to criticism, patent trolls argue that they are encouraging innovation by making patents more valuable.

Patent troll
Someone who buys a portfolio of patents for the purpose of making patent infringement claims.

[9] U.S. Fed. Trade Comm'n, *The Evolving IP Marketplace: Aligning Patent Notice and Remedies with Competition* (March 7, 2011).

Some hedge funds have entered the patent troll business. In addition, a company owned by Paul Allen, one of Microsoft's founders, recently began filing suit against companies that are using technology that his research lab allegedly invented prior to 2005. These suits have been filed against most of the major players in Silicon Valley—Apple, eBay, Facebook, Google, and Netflix—for their use of technology that improves users' online experience. (Such as suggestions for related reading and pop-up ads or stock quotes.) The technology at issue is key to these companies.

Ethics Is the patent troll business ethical? Under what circumstances would you be willing to engage in this practice? Paul Allen is wealthy beyond most people's dreams. Why would he be involved in this litigation? What is your Life Principle in this case?

International Patent Treaties

About half of all patent applications are filed in more than one country. This process used to be a logistical nightmare because almost every country had its own unique filing procedures and standards. Companies were reluctant to develop products based on technology that they were not sure they actually owned. Several treaties now facilitate this process, although it is still not the one-stop (or one-click) effort that inventors desire. These treaties were drafted by the World Intellectual Property Organization (WIPO) of the United Nations.

The Paris Convention for the Protection of Industrial Property (Paris Convention) requires each member country to grant to citizens of other member countries the same rights under patent law as its own citizens enjoy. Thus, the patent office in each member country must accept and recognize all patent and trademark applications filed with it by anyone who lives in any member country. For example, the French patent office cannot refuse to accept an application from an American, so long as the American has complied with French law. Under this treaty, inventors who file in one country have up to one year to file elsewhere and still maintain patent protection.

The Patent Law Treaty requires that countries use the same standards for the form and content of patent applications (whether submitted on paper or electronically). This treaty reduces the procedural conflicts over issues such as translations and fees.

The **Patent Cooperation Treaty** (PCT) is a step toward providing more coordinated patent review across many countries. Inventors who pay a fee and file a so-called PCT patent application are granted patent protection in the 143 PCT countries for up to 30 months. During this time, they can decide how many countries they actually want to file in. (Inventors have one year of protection under the Paris Convention; this treaty grants an additional 18 months.)

Once a PCT application is filed, one of the major patent offices prepares an "international search report"

© Susan S. Samuelson

WIPO headquarters in Geneva, Switzerland.

and issues a nonbinding opinion on whether the invention is patentable. This report, while nonbinding, helps applicants assess the patentability of their inventions and provides persuasive evidence to national patent offices. Inventors who wish to proceed internationally must then have the report translated and file it with applications and fees in whichever countries they want a patent.

The United States PTO has bilateral agreements with 16 other patent offices under a so-called **Patent Prosecution Highway**. Under this system, once a patent is approved by one country, it goes to the head of the line for patent examination in the other country.

In addition to these treaties, any country that joins the World Trade Organization (WTO) must agree to trade-related aspects of intellectual property rights (TRIPS). This agreement does not create an international patent system, but it does require all participants to meet minimum standards for the protection of intellectual property. How individual countries achieve that goal is left to them.

Finally, the European Union is in the process of developing a single European patent that would require only one application.

COPYRIGHTS

The holder of a copyright owns the *particular tangible expression* of an idea, but not the underlying idea or method of operation. Abner Doubleday could have copyrighted a book setting out his particular version of the rules of baseball, but he could not have copyrighted the rules themselves, nor could he have required players to pay him a royalty. Similarly, the inventor of double-entry bookkeeping could copyright a pamphlet explaining his system, but not the system itself.

Unlike patents, the ideas underlying copyrighted material need not be novel. For example, three movies—*Like Father Like Son, Vice Versa, and Freaky Friday*—are about a parent and child who switch bodies. The movies all have the same plot, but there is no copyright violation because their *expressions* of the basic idea are different.

The Copyright Act protects literature, music, drama, choreography, pictures, sculpture, movies, recordings, architectural works, and computer databases, and computer programs "to the extent that they incorporate authorship in the programmer's expression of original ideas, as distinguished from the ideas themselves."

A work is copyrighted *automatically* once it is in tangible form. For example, once a songwriter puts notes on paper, the work is copyrighted without further ado. But if she whistles a happy tune without writing it down, the song is not copyrighted, and anyone else can use it without permission. Registration with the Copyright Office of the Library of Congress is necessary only if the holder wishes to bring suit to enforce the copyright. Although authors still routinely place the copyright symbol (©) on their works, such a precaution is not necessary in the United States. However, some lawyers still recommend using the copyright symbol because other countries recognize it. Also, the penalties for intentional copyright infringement are heavier than for unintentional violations, and the presence of a copyright notice is evidence that the infringer's actions were intentional.

In the following case, you can imagine the author's frustration when a celebrity stole her thunder and her sales by writing a book on the very same topic. But did the celebrity violate copyright law? This case also anticipates our discussion of trademarks.

Lapine v. Seinfeld

375 Fed. Appx. 81; 2010 U.S. App. Lexis 8778
United States Court of Appeals for the Second Circuit, 2010

Facts: Missy Chase Lapine wrote a book called *The Sneaky Chef: Simple Strategies for Hiding Healthy Foods in Kids' Favorite Meals*, which was about how to disguise vegetables so that children would eat them. Her strategy was to add pureed vegetables to food that children like, such as macaroni and cheese. (We are not making this up.) Four months later, Jessica Seinfeld, wife of comedian Jerry Seinfeld, published a book entitled *Deceptively Delicious: Simple Secrets To Get Your Kids Eating Good Food*, which featured recipes involving pureed vegetables in (guess what?) macaroni and cheese and other kid-friendly foods.

Lapine filed suit against Seinfeld, alleging violation of her copyright in the content of the book, as well as her trademark in the name and cover design. The district court granted Seinfeld's motion for summary judgment, and Lapine appealed.

Issue: ***Did Seinfeld violate Lapine's copyright and trademark in* The Sneaky Chef?**

Excerpts from the Decision of the Court:

1. Copyright Infringement
   Plaintiffs assert that the two works are substantially similar in their unique and innovative expression of the idea of sneaking vegetables into children's food by means of a cookbook containing comprehensive instructions for making and storing a variety of vegetable purees in advance, and then using the purees in specially created recipes for children's favorite foods. We are not persuaded.

Stockpiling vegetable purees for covert use in children's food is an idea that cannot be copyrighted. In no case does copyright protection for an original work of authorship extend to any idea, procedure, process, system, method of operation, concept, principle, or discovery, regardless of the form in which it is described, explained, illustrated, or embodied in such work. It is a fundamental principle of our copyright doctrine that ideas, concepts, and processes are not protected from copying.

Further, to the extent the two works have general and abstract similarities—including their vaguely similar titles and inclusion of illustrations of prepared dishes, health advice, personal narrative, descriptions of how to make purees, instructions for preparing dishes, and language about children's healthy eating—the district court correctly concluded that these elements do not raise a fact issue for trial because they are "scenes a faire," or unprotectible elements that follow naturally from the work's theme rather than from the author's creativity.

AP Photo

Rob Loud/Getty Images

Did Seinfeld (on the right) violate Lapine's copyright?

Our independent comparison of the two cookbooks confirms that the total concept and feel of *Deceptively Delicious* is very different from that of *The Sneaky Chef*. *Deceptively Delicious* lacks the extensive discussion of child behavior, food philosophy, and parenting that pervades *The Sneaky Chef*. Unlike *The Sneaky Chef*, which uses primarily black, gray, and shades of brownish orange, *Deceptively Delicious* employs bright colors and more photographs. While *The Sneaky Chef* assumes greater familiarity with cooking, recommends thirteen methods for hiding healthy foods, and provides recipes for multiple-ingredient purees, *Deceptively Delicious* instructs readers about only single-ingredient purees and contains more basic instructions.

Plaintiffs correctly note that no plagiarist can excuse the wrong by showing how much of her work she did not pirate. Like the district court, we nevertheless conclude as a matter of law that the two cookbooks lack the substantial similarity required to support an inference of copyright infringement.

2. Trademark Infringement
Having considered the overall impression on a consumer and the context in which the competing marks are displayed, we reach the same conclusion as the district court: the marks are not confusingly similar. Defendants' depictions of a winking woman holding brownies near carrots or simply "shushing" are very different from plaintiffs' considerably less detailed and less colorful image of a female chef winking and "shushing" while holding carrots behind her back. Further, defendants' use of the famous "Seinfeld" name reduces any likelihood of confusion regarding the marks. In sum, like the district court, we conclude that dissimilarity of the marks is dispositive.

Copyright Term

More than 300 years ago, on April 10, 1710, Queen Anne of England approved the first copyright statute. Called the Statute of Anne, it provided copyright protection for 14 years, which could be extended by another 14 years if the copyright owner was still alive when the first term expired. Many credit the Statute of Anne with greatly expanding the burst of intellectual activity that we now refer to as the Enlightenment.

American law adopted these same time limits, which stayed in effect until the 20th century. Since then, copyright holders have fought aggressively to lengthen the copyright period. These efforts have been led by the Walt Disney Company, which wants to protect its rights in Mickey Mouse. Today, a copyright is valid until 70 years after the death of the work's only or last living author, or, in the case of works owned by a corporation, the copyright lasts 95 years from publication or 120 years from creation, whichever is shorter. Once a copyright expires, anyone may use the material. Mark Twain died in 1910, so anyone may now publish *Tom Sawyer* without permission and without paying a copyright fee.

Infringement

Anyone who uses copyrighted material without permission is violating the Copyright Act. **To prove a violation, the plaintiff must present evidence that the work was original** and that either:

- The infringer actually copied the work, or
- The infringer had access to the original and the two works are substantially similar.

A court may (1) prohibit the infringer from committing further violations, (2) order destruction of the infringing material, and (3) require the infringer to pay damages, profits earned, and attorney's fees. Damages can be substantial. In a recent case, a jury ordered SAP to pay Oracle $1.3 *billion* for copyright infringement of Oracle's software.

First Sale Doctrine

Suppose you buy a CD that, in the end, you do not like. Under the ***first sale doctrine,*** you have the legal right to sell that CD. **The first sale doctrine permits a person who owns a lawfully made copy of a copyrighted work to sell or otherwise dispose of the copy**. Note, however, that the first sale doctrine does not permit the owner to *make a copy and sell it.* If you listen to a CD and then decide to sell it, that is legal. But it is not legal to copy the CD onto your iPod and then sell the original or any copy of it.

Fair Use

Because the period of copyright protection is so long, it has become even more important to uphold the exceptions to the law. Bear in mind that the point of copyright laws is to encourage creative work. A writer who can control, and profit from, artistic work will be inclined to produce more. If enforced oppressively, however, the copyright laws could stifle creativity by denying access to copyrighted work. **The fair use doctrine** permits limited use of copyrighted material without permission of the author for purposes such as criticism, comment, news reporting, scholarship, or research. Courts generally do not permit a use that will decrease revenues from the original work by, say, competing with it. A reviewer is permitted, for example, to quote from a book without the author's permission, but could not reproduce so much that the review was competing with the book itself.

Fair use doctrine
Permits limited use of copyrighted material without permission of the author for purposes such as criticism, comment, news reporting, scholarship, or research.

Fair use has become a highly controversial issue in this age of the Internet. For example, Universal Music demanded that YouTube remove a home video of a toddler dancing to a Prince song. A director making a documentary on torture was denied permission to use a short clip showing torture on the TV show *24.* Then J. K. Rowling, the author of the *Harry Potter* series of books, sued to prevent the publication of the *Harry Potter Lexicon*, an unauthorized reference guide to the books that contained direct quotations, paraphrases, and plot summaries. The court ruled that although such a guide can be fair use, this one was not because the author had copied too much of Rowling's distinctive original language.[10]

Also under the fair use doctrine, faculty members are permitted to photocopy and distribute copyrighted materials to students, so long as the materials are brief and the teacher's action is spontaneous. If, over his breakfast coffee one morning, Professor Learned spots a terrific article in *Mad Magazine* that perfectly illustrates a point he intends to make in class that day, the fair use doctrine permits him to photocopy the page and distribute it to his class. However, under a misinterpretation of the fair use doctrine, some faculty had been in the habit of routinely preparing lengthy course packets of copyrighted material without permission of the authors. In *Basic Books, Inc. v. Kinkos Graphic Corp.*,[11] a federal court held that this practice violated the copyright laws because the material was more than one short passage and because it was sold to students. Now, when professors put together course packets, they (or the copy shop) must obtain permission and pay a royalty for the use of copyrighted material. Likewise, it is illegal for students to make photocopies of a classmate's course packet or textbook.

Parody

Parody has a long history in the United States—some of our most cherished songs have been based on parodies. Before Francis Scott Key wrote the words to "The Star-Spangled Banner," other lyrics that mocked colonial governors had been set to the same music. (The tune was well known as a drinking song.)

---

[10] *Warner Bros. Entertainment Inc. v. RDR Books*, 575 F. Supp. 2d 513; 2008 U.S. Dist. LEXIS 67771, (S.D.N.Y., 2008).

[11] 758 F. Supp. 1522, 1991 U.S. Dist. LEXIS 3804 (S.D.N.Y. 1991). A federal appeals court reached the same result in *Princeton University Press v. Michigan Document Services, Inc.*, 99 F.3d 1381, 1996 U.S. App. LEXIS 29132 (6th Cir. 1996).

I wish you good luck on your journey to deny our First Amendment rights.

Because of the political and social commentary that is inherent in many parodies, courts have long granted them special respect. In a case involving a 2 Live Crew parody of the song "Pretty Woman," the Supreme Court decided in favor of 2 Live Crew, holding that **parody is a fair use of copyrighted material so long as the use of the original is not excessive.**[12] The parody may copy enough to remind the audience of the original work, but not so much that the parody harms the market for the original.

The following email exchange between Richard Saperstein, a movie producer, and Tom Strickler, a talent agent, which zapped around Hollywood, illustrates the importance of the 2 Live Crew case (to which Strickler refers).

> [From Saperstein to Strickler:]
> Tom—
> Please give me a call about a spec script Elia Infascelli-Smith has gone out with called $40,000 MAN. As you know, along with Universal, we control the rights to SIX MILLION DOLLAR MAN. My understanding is this spec includes characters we own.
> Best—Richard
>
> [Strickler's response:]
> Richard:
> Good news. As you may know, The United States Supreme Court has affirmed the right of Parody as an unassailable First Amendment Right. This has enabled you to make movies like *Scream* and *Scary Movie*, in which you parody many films which Dimension does not own or control.
> The script is a parody, and if you have any problems, I suggest you hire a Constitutional lawyer and file a brief with the US Supreme Court. This will be an uphill battle—the court voted 9 to 0 when this last hit the docket and those stubborn justices all believe in Stare Decisis.
> And if you succeed at the Supreme Court—you will have to stop making *Scream* and *Scary Movie*.
> This will take about 5 to 7 years … and lawyers are an expensive breed, but I wish you good luck on your journey to deny our First Amendment rights.
> All the best,
> Tom

Digital Music and Movies

One of the major challenges for legal institutions in regulating copyrights is simply that modern intellectual property is so easy to copy. Many consumers are in the habit of violating the law by downloading copyrighted material—music, movies and books—for free. They seem to believe that if it is easy to steal something, then the theft is somehow acceptable. In one survey of adolescents aged 12 to 17, 75 percent agreed with the statement, "file-sharing is so easy to do, it's unrealistic to expect people not to do it."[13]

The entertainment world used to turn a blind eye, but illegal downloading is threatening the viability of recording companies, movie studios, and publishers. The statistics are compelling: in 2008, 40 *billion* songs were downloaded illegally, which is as much as 95 percent of all downloaded music! In the first decade of this century, music sales at American

[12] *Campbell v. Acuff-Rose Music, Inc.*, 510 U.S. 569, 114 S. Ct. 1164, 1994 U.S. LEXIS 2052 (1994).
[13] *http://pewinternet.org/Reports/2009/9-The-State-of-Music-Online-Ten-Years-After-Napster/The-State-of-Music-Online-Ten-Years-After-Napster.aspx?view=all#footnote25* or google *"pew 10 years after napster"*.

record labels declined by 58 percent. Without profitable record labels, who will find and promote new stars? As we saw in the opening scenario, which is a true story, this type of theft is having a profound effect on entertainment and publishing. But it is not just "big companies" that suffer—it is also the artists, musicians, actors, and writers, most of whom are not wealthy rock stars.

Government and industry are striking back. The Prioritizing Resources and Organization for Intellectual Property Act (Pro-IP) permits law enforcement officials to confiscate any equipment used to steal copyrighted material. In addition, the Recording Industry Association of America (RIAA) developed a strategy of aggressively suing those who download music illegally. Then a coalition of entertainment businesses sued two companies that distributed the software used by many consumers to violate copyright law. So important was this issue that the Supreme Court waded into these murky waters.

METRO-GOLDWYN-MAYER STUDIOS, INC. v. GROKSTER, LTD.

125 S. Ct. 2764, 2005 U.S. Lexis 5212
Supreme Court of the United States, 2005

Facts: Grokster, Ltd., and StreamCast Networks, Inc., distributed free software that allowed computer users to share electronic files through peer-to-peer networks, so called because users' computers communicated directly with each other, not through central servers. The Grokster and StreamCast software could be used for legal purposes. Indeed, peer-to-peer networks were utilized by universities, government agencies, corporations, libraries, and individuals, among others. Even the briefs in this very case could be downloaded legally with the StreamCast software.

Nonetheless, nearly 90 percent of the files available for download through Grokster or StreamCast were copyrighted. Billions of files were shared each month—the probable scope of copyright infringement was staggering. The two companies encouraged the illegal uses of their software. For example, the chief technology officer of StreamCast said that "the goal is to get in trouble with the law and get sued. It's the best way to get in the news."

A group of copyright holders (MGM and others) sued Grokster and StreamCast, alleging that they were violating the copyright law by knowingly and intentionally distributing their software to users who would reproduce and distribute copyrighted works illegally. Both parties moved for summary judgment. The trial court held for Grokster and StreamCast; the appeals court affirmed. The Supreme Court granted *certiorari*.

Issue: ***Were Grokster and StreamCast violating copyright law?***

Excerpts from Justice Souter's Decision: The more artistic protection is favored, the more technological innovation may be discouraged; the administration of copyright law is an exercise in managing the trade-off. [T]he indications are that the ease of copying songs or movies using software like Grokster's is fostering disdain for copyright protection. When a widely shared service or product is used to commit infringement, it may be impossible to enforce rights in the protected work effectively against all direct infringers, the only practical alternative being to go against the distributor of the copying device. We hold that one who distributes a device with the object of promoting its use to infringe copyright, as shown by clear expression or other affirmative steps taken to foster infringement, is liable for the resulting acts of infringement by third parties.

We are, of course, mindful of the need to keep from trenching on regular commerce or discouraging the development of technologies with lawful and unlawful potential. Accordingly, mere knowledge of infringing potential or of actual infringing uses would not be enough here to subject a distributor to liability. The inducement rule, instead, premises liability on purposeful, culpable expression and conduct, and thus does nothing to compromise legitimate commerce or discourage innovation having a lawful promise.

Grokster distributed an electronic newsletter containing links to articles promoting its software's ability to access popular copyrighted music. And both companies communicated a clear message by responding affirmatively to requests for help in locating and playing copyrighted materials. [N]either company attempted to develop filtering tools or other mechanisms to diminish the infringing activity using their software. It is useful to recall that StreamCast and Grokster make money by selling advertising space, by directing ads to the screens of computers employing their software. As the record shows, the more the software is used, the more ads are sent out and the greater the advertising revenue becomes. Since the extent of the software's use determines the gain to the distributors, the commercial sense of their enterprise turns on high-volume use, which the record shows is infringing. The unlawful objective is unmistakable.

In addition to intent to bring about infringement and distribution of a device suitable for infringing use, [MGM must show] evidence of actual infringement by recipients of the software. As the account of the facts indicates, there is evidence of infringement on a gigantic scale.

On remand, reconsideration of MGM's motion for summary judgment will be in order.

The No Electronic Theft Act

Enacted in 1997, the **No Electronic Theft Act** is intended to deter the downloading of copyrighted material. It provides for criminal penalties for the reproduction or distribution of copyrighted material that has a retail value greater than $1,000, even if the offender has no profit motive. Thus, for instance, if a student photocopied for 10 of her friends a textbook that is worth $150, she could be subject to criminal penalties, including a prison term of one year. Originally, the Justice Department did not enforce this statute, but it has now begun to do so, particularly against those who set up networks to trade games, movies, and music.

The Family Entertainment and Copyright Act

Under the **Family Entertainment and Copyright Act,** it is a criminal offense to use a camcorder to film a movie in the theater. This statute also establishes criminal penalties for willful copyright infringement that involves distributing software, music, or film on a computer network.

The Digital Millennium Copyright Act

The good news is that Mary Schmich wrote an influential article in the *Chicago Tribune*. The bad news is that people deleted her name, attributed the article to Kurt Vonnegut, and sent it around the world via email. Tom Tomorrow's cartoon was syndicated to 100 newspapers, but by the time the last papers received it, the cartoon had already gone zapping around cyberspace. Because his name had been deleted from the original, some editors thought he had plagiarized it.

In response to such incidents, Congress passed the **Digital Millennium Copyright Act** (DMCA), which provides that:

- **It is illegal to delete copyright information, such as the name of the author or the title of the article**. It is also illegal to distribute false copyright information. Thus, anyone who emailed Schmich's article without her name on it, or who claimed it was his own work, would be violating the law.
- **It is illegal to circumvent encryption or scrambling devices that protect copyrighted works**. For example, some software programs are designed so that they can only be copied once. Anyone who overrides this protective device to make another copy is violating the law. (The statute does permit purchasers of copyrighted software to make one backup copy.) If you buy a Disney DVD that prevents you from fast-forwarding through commercials, you are violating the DMCA if you figure out how to do it anyway.
- **It is illegal to distribute tools and technologies used to circumvent encryption devices.** If you tell others how to fast-forward through the Disney commercials, you have violated the statute.

- **Online service providers (OSPs) are not liable for posting copyrighted material so long as they are unaware that the material is illegal and they remove it promptly after receiving notice that it violates copyright law.** This type of provision is called a safe harbor.

EXAM Strategy

Question: Many of the videos posted on YouTube are copyrighted material, including thousands of hours of shows owned by Viacom, such as *The Colbert Report* and *The Daily Show*. Viacom sued YouTube for violating its copyrights. Among the evidence Viacom presented was an email from one YouTube founder to another, saying, "... please stop putting stolen videos on the site. We're going to have a tough time defending the fact that we're not liable for the copyrighted material on the site because we didn't put it up when one of the co-founders is blatantly stealing content from other sites and trying to get everyone to see it."[14] YouTube presented evidence that it had responded within one day to Viacom's "takedown notice." Is YouTube liable?

Strategy: Viacom argued that YouTube was well aware that much of its content was illegal. YouTube responded that it met the requirements of the Safe Harbor provision.

Result: The court found for YouTube. General awareness that many postings infringed copyrights did not impose a duty for YouTube to monitor its videos. Its only requirement was to respond when notified of infringement. YouTube did just that in this case.[15]

International Copyright Treaties

The Berne Convention requires member countries to provide automatic copyright protection to any works created in another member country. The protection does not expire until 50 years after the death of the author.[16] The WIPO Copyright Treaty and the WIPO Performances and Phonograms Treaty add computer programs, movies, and music to the list of copyrightable materials.

In 2004, Congress enacted a law that permits the president to appoint a copyright law enforcement officer charged with the responsibility for stopping copyright infringement overseas. Also, for the first time, Congress funded the National Intellectual Property Law Enforcement Coordination Council, which was established to protect American intellectual property internationally.

---

[14]Quoted in "Federal Judge Hands Google Victory in Viacom's $1 Billion Suit Over YouTube Content" by Michael Liedtke on Law.com, June 24, 2010.

[15]*Viacom Int'l, Inc. v. YouTube, Inc.*, 718 F. Supp. 2d 514 (S.D.N.Y., 2010).

[16]Under U.S. law, copyrights last 70 years. The United States must grant works created in other signatory countries a copyright that lasts either 50 years or the length of time granted in that country, whichever is longer, but in no case longer than 70 years.

TRADEMARKS

Trademark
Any combination of words and symbols that a business uses to identify its products or services and distinguish them from others.

A **trademark** is any combination of words and symbols that a business uses to identify its products or services and distinguish them from others. Trademarks are important to both consumers and businesses. Consumers use trademarks to distinguish between competing products. People who feel that Nike shoes fit their feet best can rely on the Nike trademark to know they are buying the shoe they want. A business with a high-quality product can use a trademark to develop a loyal base of customers who are able to distinguish its product from another.

Types of Marks

There are four different types of marks:

- **Trademarks** are affixed to *goods* in interstate commerce.
- **Service marks** are used to identify *services*, not products. Fitness First, Burger King, and Weight Watchers are service marks. In this chapter, the terms "trademark" and "mark" are used to refer to both trademarks and service marks.
- **Certification marks** are words or symbols used by a person or organization to attest that products and services produced by others meet certain standards. The Good Housekeeping Seal of Approval means that the Good Housekeeping organization has determined that a product meets its standards.
- **Collective marks** are used to identify members of an organization. The Lions Club, the Girl Scouts of America, and the Masons are examples of collective marks.

Ownership and Registration

Under common law, the first person to use a mark in trade owns it. Registration with the federal government is not necessary. However, under the federal Lanham Act, the owner of a mark may register it on the Lanham Act Principal Register. A trademark owner may use the symbol ™ at any time, even before registering it, but not until the mark is registered can the symbol ® be placed next to it. Registration has several advantages:

- Even if a mark has been used in only one or two states, registration makes it valid nationally.
- Registration notifies the public that a mark is in use because anyone who applies for registration first searches the Public Register to ensure that no one else has rights to the mark.
- Five years after registration, a mark becomes virtually incontestable because most challenges are barred.
- The damages available under the Lanham Act are higher than under common law.
- The holder of a registered trademark generally has the right to use it as an Internet domain name.

Under the Lanham Act, the owner files an application with the PTO. The PTO will accept an application only if the owner has already used the mark attached to a product in interstate commerce or promises to use the mark within six months after the filing. In addition, the applicant must be the *first* to use the mark in interstate commerce. Initially, the trademark is valid for 10 years, but the owner can renew it for an unlimited number of 10-year terms as long as the mark is still in use.

Valid Trademarks

Words (Reebok), symbols (Microsoft's flying window logo), phrases (Nike's "Just do it"), shapes (Apple's iPod), sounds (NBC's three chimes), colors (Owens Corning's pink insulation), and even scents (plumeria blossoms on sewing thread) can be trademarked. **To be valid, a trademark must be distinctive**—that is, the mark must clearly distinguish one product from another. There are five basic categories of distinctive marks:

- **Fanciful marks** are made-up words such as Kodak or Saucony.
- **Arbitrary marks** use existing words that do *not* describe the product—Prince tennis racquets, for example. No one really thinks that these racquets are designed by or for royalty.
- **Suggestive marks** *indirectly* describe the product's function. "Greyhound" implies that the bus line is swift, and "Coppertone" suggests what customers will look like after applying the product.
- Marks with **secondary meaning** cannot, by themselves, be trademarked unless they have been used for so long that they are now associated with the product in the public's mind. When a film company released a movie called *Ape*, it used as an illustration a picture that looked like a scene from *King Kong*—a gigantic gorilla astride the World Trade Center in New York City. The court held that the movie posters of *King Kong* had acquired a secondary meaning in the mind of the public, so the *Ape* producers were forced to change their poster.[17]
- **Trade dress** is the image and overall appearance of a business or product. It may include size, shape, color, or texture. The Supreme Court held that a Mexican restaurant was entitled to protection under the Lanham Act for the shape and general appearance of the exterior of its building as well as the decor, menu, servers' uniforms, and other features reflecting the total image of the restaurant.[18]

The following categories *cannot* be trademarked:

- **Similar to an existing mark.** To avoid confusion, the PTO will not grant a trademark that is similar to one already in existence on a similar product. Once the PTO had granted a trademark for "Pledge" furniture polish, it refused to trademark "Promise" for the same product. "Chat noir" and "black cat" were also too similar because one is simply a translation of the other. Houghton-Mifflin Co. successfully sued to prevent a punk rock band from calling itself Furious George because the name is too similar to Curious George, the star of a series of children's books.
- **Generic trademarks.** No one is permitted to trademark an item's ordinary name—"shoe" or "book," for example.

Is Furious George too similar to Curious George?

© Susan Van Etten

[17] *Paramount Pictures Corp. v. Worldwide Entertainment Corp.*, 2 Media L. Rep. 1311, 195 U.S.P.Q. (BNA) 539, 1977 U.S. Dist. LEXIS 17931 (S.D.N.Y. 1977).

[18] *Two Pesos, Inc. v. Taco Cabana, Inc.*, 505 U.S. 763, 112 S. Ct. 2753, 1992 U.S. LEXIS 4533 (1992).

Sometimes, however, a word begins as a trademark and later becomes a generic name. Zipper, escalator, aspirin, linoleum, thermos, yo-yo, band-aid, ping-pong, and nylon all started out as trademarks but became generic. Once a name is generic, the owner loses the trademark because the name can no longer be used to distinguish one product from another—all products are called the same thing. That is why Xerox Corp. encourages people to say, "I'll photocopy this document," rather than "I'll xerox it." Jeep, Rollerblade, and TiVo are names that began as trademarks and may now be generic. What about "app store"? Microsoft has sued Apple, disputing its right to trademark this term. Meanwhile, Facebook has trademarked, "face," "book," "like," "wall," and "poke." The goal is not to prevent consumers from using these terms but rather to warn off other companies.

- **Descriptive marks**. Words cannot be trademarked if they simply describe the product—such as "low-fat," "green," or "crunchy." Descriptive words can, however, be trademarked if they do *not* describe that particular product because they then become distinctive rather than descriptive. "Blue Diamond" is an acceptable trademark for nuts so long as the nuts are neither blue nor diamond-shaped.
- **Names.** The PTO generally will not grant a trademark in a surname because other people are already using it and have the right to continue. No one could register "Jefferson" as a trademark. However, a surname can be used as part of a longer title—"Jefferson Home Tours," for instance. Similarly, no one can register a geographical name such as "Boston" unless it is also associated with another word, such as "Boston Ale."
- **Deceptive marks**. The PTO will not register a mark that is deceptive. It refused to register a trademark with the words "National Collection and Credit Control" and an eagle superimposed on a map of the United States because this trademark gave the false impression that the organization was an official government agency.
- **Scandalous or immoral trademarks**. The PTO refused to register a mark that featured a nude man and woman embracing. In upholding the PTO's decision, the court was unsympathetic to arguments that this was the perfect trademark for a newsletter on sex.[19] This author once had a client who wanted to apply for a trademark for marijuana: "Sweet Mary Jane, she never lets you down." However, the client was unwilling to admit to affixing the name to his product and shipping it in interstate commerce. Now, medical marijuana is legal in 16 states but the PTO refuses to register marijuana trademarks.

Infringement

To win an infringement suit, the trademark owner must show that the defendant's trademark is likely to deceive customers about who has made the goods or provided the services. As we saw in the *Seinfeld* case, the court ruled there was no trademark infringement because consumers would not be confused by the names or covers of the two books.

In the event of infringement, the rightful owner is entitled to (1) an injunction prohibiting further violations, (2) destruction of the infringing material, (3) up to three times actual damages, (4) any profits the infringer earned on the product, and (5) attorney's fees.

What about a perfume for dogs? Would a reasonable consumer confuse Pucci with Gucci, Bono Sports with Ralph Lauren Polo Sports, or Miss Claybone for Liz Claiborne? None of these companies challenged the parody use of their names for a dog perfume. But Tommy Hilfiger Licensing, Inc. did not see the humor in the name Timmy Holedigger. The court,

[19]*In re McGinley*, 660 F.2d 481, 211 U.S.P.Q. (BNA) 668, 1981 CCPA LEXIS 177 (C.C.P.A. 1981).

however, advised Hilfiger "to chill," pointing out that there was no evidence of actual confusion.[20] On the other hand, auction website eBay did prevent a seller of perfumes from using the name Perfumebay. The court ruled that the use of "ebay" confused consumers.[21]

The following case raises an issue of confusion in cyberspace. Once again, the Internet is challenging intellectual property laws that were not conceived with this technology in mind.

[20] *Tommy Hilfiger Licensing, Inc. v. Nature Labs, LLC,* 221 F. Supp. 2d 410; 2002 U.S. Dist. LEXIS 14841 (2002).

[21] *Perfumebay.com Inc. v. eBay Inc.*, 506 F.3d 1165, 2007 U.S. App. LEXIS 25726.

You be the Judge

Network Automation, Inc. v. Advanced Systems Concepts, Inc.

2011 U.S. App. Lexis 4488
United States Court of Appeals for the Ninth Circuit, 2011

Facts: Network Automation and Advanced Systems Concepts both sold job scheduling and management software, and both advertised on the Internet. Network sold its software under the trademarked name Auto-Mate, while Systems used the trademark ActiveBatch. Customers paid between $995 and $10,995 to use these software programs.

Google AdWords is a program that sells "keywords," which are search terms that trigger the display of a sponsor's advertisement. When a user enters a keyword, Google displays the links generated by its own algorithm in the main part of the page, along with advertisements in a separate "Sponsored Links" section next to or above the objective results. Multiple advertisers can purchase the same keyword.

Although ActiveBatch was Systems's trademark, Network purchased it as a keyword. This purchase meant that anyone who googled "ActiveBatch" would see a web page where the top results were links to Systems' own website and various articles about the product. But in the "Sponsored Sites" section of the page, users would see the following ad:

> Job Scheduler
> Windows Job Scheduling + Much More. Easy to Deploy, Scalable. D/L Trial *www.NetworkAutomation.com*

Sometimes, they would also see an equivalent ad for Systems' software—the real ActiveBatch.

Systems alleged that this use of ActiveBatch was a violation of its trademark on the word. The trial court issued an injunction prohibiting Network's purchase of the Google keyword. Network appealed.

You Be the Judge: ***Has Network violated Systems's trademark by purchasing it as a Google keyword?***

Argument for Systems: Network and Systems are direct competitors. Their two products—AutoMate and ActiveBatch—perform the same functions and are both advertised on the Internet. Network is deliberately confusing customers about whose product ActiveBatch really is.

When consumers use the Internet, they tend not to read carefully—they just click away. Few customers analyze the web address of an ad to make sure they are going to the right website. Indeed, customers may not even be aware of who owns ActiveBatch. The Network ad certainly does not reveal that Systems owns this software. Customers could easily assume that whatever web address comes up belongs to the rightful owner.

When customers search for a generic term, they know that they will encounter links from a variety of sources, but when they look for a trade name, their expectation is that they will only be linked to that specific product. For this reason, the use of another company's trade name can create tremendous confusion.

Network has bought the right to use Systems's trademark as a ruse to fool potential customers. This subterfuge is exactly the sort of behavior that trademark laws are designed to prevent.

Argument for Network: Today, most consumers are sophisticated about the Internet. They skip from site to site, ready to hit the Back button whenever they are not satisfied with a site's contents. They fully expect to find some sites that are not what they imagine based on a glance at the domain name or search engine summary. Consumers do not form any firm expectations about the sponsorship of a website until they have seen the landing page—if then.

Even if Systems's arguments were true for consumer purchases, the typical customer for this software is a sophisticated businessperson buying an expensive product. These purchasers are likely to be very careful and will not be confused by Google ads. Also, they will probably understand the mechanics of Internet search engines and the nature of sponsored links.

In the end, Network's intent was not to confuse consumers but rather to allow them to compare its product to ActiveBatch. That goal is a completely appropriate use of a trademark.

Federal Trademark Dilution Act of 1995

Before Congress passed the Federal Trademark Dilution Act of 1995 (FTDA), a trademark owner could win an infringement lawsuit only by proving that consumers would be deceived about who had really made the product. **This statute prevents others from using a trademark in a way that (1) dilutes its value, even though consumers are not confused about the origin of the product; or (2) tarnishes it by association with unwholesome goods or services**. For example, Barbie's Playhouse was a website with a font and colors similar to those used by Mattel for its copyrighted Barbie doll. Also, the doll at the bottom of the website looked like a Barbie doll. The court found that Barbie's Playhouse had violated the FTDA.[22]

Domain Names

Over 130 million Internet addresses, known as *domain names*, are currently active, so it is often difficult to find a distinctive name for a new business. Domain names can be immensely valuable as they are an important component of doing business. Suppose you want to buy a new pair of jeans. Without thinking twice, you type in **http://www.jcrew.com** and there you are, ready to order. What if that address took you to a different site altogether, say, the personal site of one Jackie Crew? The store might lose out on a sale. Companies not only want to own their own domain name, they want to prevent complaint sites such as **http://www.untied.com** (about United Airlines), **http://www.ihatestarbucks.com**, or the always popular variation on the "sucks" theme, such as **http://macdonaldssucks.com**. Generic domain names can be valuable, too. Shopping.com paid $750,000 to acquire its domain name from the previous (lucky) owner.

Cybersquatting. Who has the right to a domain name? In the beginning, the National Science Foundation, which maintained the Internet, granted Network Solutions, Inc. (NSI), a private company, the right to allocate domain names. NSI charged no fee for domain names and the rule was "first come, first served." Then so-called cybersquatters began to register domain names, not to use, but to sell to others. Someone, for example, tried to sell the name "Bill Gates" for $1 million.

In response to complaints, NSI began suspending any domain name that was challenged by the holder of a registered trademark. For instance, NSI would not allow Princeton Review to keep kaplan.com, which Princeton had acquired simply to inconvenience its arch rival in the test preparation business. Congress then passed the **Anticybersquatting Consumer Protection Act (ACPA), which permits both trademark owners and famous people to sue anyone who registers their name as a domain name in "bad faith."** The rightful owner of a trademark is entitled to damages of up to $100,000. Verizon was awarded damages of $33.15 million against OnlineNIC Inc., which had registered 663 domain names that were confusingly similar to Verizon trademarks.

---

[22]*Mattel, Inc. v. Jcom, Inc.*, 1998 U.S. Dist. LEXIS 16195.

ICANN. As both the value and the number of domain names soared, the U.S. government transferred management of the Internet, including the allocation of names, to a private, nonprofit, international organization, the Internet Corporation for Assigned Names and Numbers (ICANN). Disputes over domain names can be decided by arbitration under ICANN's Uniform Domain Name Dispute Resolution Policy (UDRP) rather than by litigation under the ACPA. For example, Jay Leno used the ICANN process to win a cybersquatting case against someone who was using thejaylenoshow.com to attract viewers to his own real estate website.

To bring a UDRP case, the complainant (i.e., the plaintiff) must allege that:

- The domain name creates confusion because it is similar to a registered trademark.
- The respondent (i.e., the defendant) has no legitimate reason to use the domain name.
- The respondent registered the domain name in bad faith. If the respondent is a competitor of the complainant and has acquired the domain name to disrupt the complainant's business (à la Princeton Review), that is evidence of bad faith. So is an attempt by the respondent to sell the name to the complainant.

If the complainant wins, it is entitled either to take over the domain name or to cancel it. For example, in a dispute over wal-martsucks.com, the WIPO arbitrator ordered that the name be transferred to Wal-Mart. The respondent had demonstrated his bad faith by attempting to sell the name for $530,000. In a similar case, however, the WIPO arbitrator found for a respondent who had registered Wallmartcanadasucks.com. In this case, the respondent had not tried to sell the name and was using the website to criticize Wal-Mart. As the arbitrator stated in his opinion: "Posting defamatory material on a website would not justify revocation of a domain name. The Policy should not be used to shut down robust debate and criticism." Either party has the option before or after an ICANN arbitration to litigate the issue in court.

At this writing, the courts have also held that criticism sites do not violate the ACPA so long as they do not have a bad faith intent to make a profit. The sites do not violate trademark law unless they create consumer confusion.[23]

Theft of domain name. In this crowded world, few people are the first to do anything. David Goncalves achieved this distinction in an unfortunate way—he became the first person in the United States to be convicted of stealing a domain name. After hacking into the files of a domain name registrar, he transferred to himself ownership of P2P.com. He then sold this name for $111,211 to professional basketball player Mark Madsen, who was running a business that bought and sold domain names. P2P could be a valuable name for someone who wanted to operate a peer-to-peer network. Goncalves was convicted under a state fraud statute as well as the Computer Fraud and Abuse Act (which we discussed in Chapter 41, on cyberlaw).

Trademarking a domain name. Our discussion thus far has been about registering a trademark as a domain name. Sometimes businesses want to do the opposite—trademark a domain name. The PTO will issue such a trademark only for services offered via the Internet. Thus, it trademarked "eBay" for "on-line trading services in which seller posts items to be auctioned and bidding is done electronically." The PTO will not trademark a domain name that is merely an address and does not identify the service provided.

---

[23]See, for example, *Career Agents Network, Inc. v. careeragentsnetwork.biz*, 2010 U.S. Dist. LEXIS 17263 (E.D.MI, 2010).

International Trademark Treaties

Under the **Paris Convention**, if someone registers a trademark in one country, then he has a grace period of six months, during which he can file in any other country using the same original filing date. Under the **Madrid Agreement**, any trademark registered with the international registry is valid in all signatory countries. (The United States is a signatory.) The **Trademark Law Treaty** simplifies and harmonizes the process of applying for trademarks around the world. Now, a U.S. firm seeking international trademark protection need only file one application, in English, with the PTO, which sends the application to the WIPO, which transmits it to each country in which the applicant would like trademark protection.

EXAM Strategy

Question: Jerry Falwell was a nationally known Baptist minister. You can read about him on falwell.com. You can also read about him at fallwell.com—a site critical of his views on homosexuality. This site has a disclaimer indicating that it is not affiliated with Reverend Falwell. The minister sued fallwell.com, alleging a violation of trademark law and the anti-cybersquatting statute. Was there a violation?

Strategy: To win a trademark claim, the reverend had to show that there was some confusion between the two sites. To win the cybersquatting claim, he had to show bad faith on the part of fallwell.com.

Result: The reverend lost on both counts. The court ruled that there was no confusion— fallwell.com had a clear disclaimer. Also, there was no indication of bad faith. The court was reluctant to censor political commentary.

Trade Secrets

Trade secret
A formula, device, process, method, or compilation of information that, when used in business, gives the owner an advantage over competitors.

What do the formulas for Coke and motor oil have in common with computer circuitry, a machine for making adhesive tape, and a procedure for applying hair dye? They are all trade secrets. **A trade secret is a formula, device, process, method, or compilation of information that, when used in business, gives the owner an advantage over competitors who do not know it**. In determining if information is a trade secret, courts consider:

- How difficult (and expensive) was the information to obtain? Was it readily available from other sources?
- Does the information create an important competitive advantage?
- Did the company make a reasonable effort to protect it?

It has been estimated that the theft of trade secrets costs U.S. businesses $100 billion a year. In response, most states have now adopted the **Uniform Trade Secrets Act (UTSA)**. Anyone who misappropriates a trade secret is liable to the owner for (1) actual damages, (2) unjust enrichment, or (3) a reasonable royalty. If the misappropriation was willful or malicious, the court may award attorney's fees and double damages. A jury awarded Avery Dennison Corp. $40 million in damages from a competitor that had misappropriated secret information about the adhesives used in self-stick stamps.

Although a company can patent some types of trade secrets, it may be reluctant to do so because patent registration requires that the formula be disclosed publicly. In addition, patent protection expires after 20 years. Some types of trade secrets cannot be patented—customer lists, business plans, manufacturing processes, and marketing strategies.

The following case deals with a typical issue: how much information can employees take with them when they start their own, competing business?

Pollack v. Skinsmart Dermatology and Aesthetic Center P.C.

2004 Pa. Dist. & Cnty. Dec. Lexis 214
Common Pleas Court of Philadelphia County, Pennsylvania, 2004

Facts: Dr. Andrew Pollack owned the Philadelphia Institute of Dermatology (PID), a dermatology practice. Drs. Toby Shawe and Samy Badawy worked for PID as independent contractors, receiving a certain percentage of the revenues from each patient they treated. Natalie Wilson was Dr. Pollack's medical assistant.

Pollack tentatively agreed to sell the practice to Shawe and Badawy. But instead of buying his practice, the two doctors decided to start their own, which they called Skinsmart. They executed a lease for the Skinsmart office space, offered Wilson a job, and instructed PID staff members to make copies of their appointment books and printouts of the patient list. Then they abruptly resigned from PID. Wilson called PID patients to reschedule procedures at Skinsmart. The two doctors also called patients and sent out a mailing to patients and referring physicians to tell them about Skinsmart.

Pollack filed suit, alleging that the two doctors had misappropriated trade secrets.

Issue: ***Did Shawe and Badawy misappropriate trade secrets from PID?***

Excerpts from Judge Cohen's Decision: The right of a business person to be protected against unfair competition stemming from the usurpation of his or her trade secrets must be balanced against the right of an individual to the unhampered pursuit of the occupations and livelihoods for which he or she is best suited. For this reason, to qualify for protection, the information must be the particular secrets of the complaining employer, not general secrets of the trade in which he is engaged.

Against this backdrop, it is clear the patient list is a trade secret, worthy of protection. As conceded by defendants, the confidentiality of patient information ensures that it remain unknown to those outside the practice and makes the patient list valuable. Through the substantial efforts of plaintiff, the patient list was compiled over numerous years, and contained 20,000 names with related information. PID spent money for computers, software, and employees to keep and maintain the patient list. Within the offices of PID, the information was not universally known or accessible. Not every staff member, including the practicing physicians, could pull the records. Wilson did not have access to them and the doctors relied on other PID employees to access the patient list. These same factors demonstrate that plaintiff sought to protect the secrecy of the information.

The plaintiff must demonstrate that the trade secret has value and importance to him and his business. As noted above, defendants acknowledge the value of the patient list to PID's practice. In addition, plaintiff relied upon the patient list as the core component of his practice.

To have the rights to the use of the trade secret, the plaintiff needs to show he either discovered or owned the trade secret. Plaintiff compiled the patient list over numerous years. The patient list was maintained on PID's computers by PID's employees. Plaintiff's tax returns show that PID was owned solely by plaintiff. These facts establish plaintiff's ownership of the patient list.

Summary judgment is granted on the issue of liability against defendants Shawe, Badawy, and Wilson.

Only civil penalties are available under the Uniform Trade Secrets Act. To safeguard national security and maintain the nation's industrial and economic edge, Congress passed the **Economic Espionage Act of 1996, which makes it a *criminal* offense to steal (or attempt to steal) trade secrets for the benefit of someone other than the owner, including for the**

benefit of any foreign government. Xiaodong Sheldon Meng was convicted of violating this statute after he was caught stealing computer code used in military weapons. He had committed the theft on behalf of the government of China. Meng was sentenced to 24 months in prison. Timothy Kissane received the same sentence for stealing computer source code from an employer. He planned to sell it to the company's competitors.

Chapter Conclusion

Intellectual property takes many different forms. It can be an Internet domain name, a software program, a cartoon character, a formula for motor oil, or a process for making drugs. Because of its great variety, intellectual property can be difficult to protect. Yet, for many individuals and companies, intellectual property is the most valuable asset they will ever own. As its economic value increases, so does the need to understand the rules of intellectual property law.

EXAM REVIEW

	Patent	**Copyright**	**Trademark**	**Trade Secrets**
Protects:	Mechanical, electrical, chemical inventions; processes; machines; composition of matter; designs; plants	The tangible expression of an idea, but not the idea itself	Words and symbols that a business uses to identify its products or services	A formula, device, process, method, or compilation of information that, when used in business, gives the owner an advantage over competitors who do not know it
Requirements for Legal Protection:	Application approved by PTO	An item is automatically copyrighted once it is in tangible form	Use is the only requirement; registration is not necessary but does offer some benefits	Must be kept confidential
Duration:	20 years after the application is filed (14 years from date of issuance for a design patent)	70 years after the death of the work's only or last living author or, for a corporation, 95 years from publication or 120 years from creation	Valid for 10 years but the owner can renew for an unlimited number of terms as long as the mark is still being used	As long as it is kept confidential

Multiple-Choice Questions

1. Thomas's English muffins wanted to protect the method by which it makes muffins with air pockets—what it calls "nooks and crannies." What would be the best way to achieve this goal?

(a) Patent

(b) Copyright

(c) Trademark

(d) Trade secret

(e) This method cannot be protected.

2. VitaminWater has become such a success that other companies are also now selling similar (but not identical) flavored colored water. Some competitors bottle their drinks in a similar bell-shaped bottle with a two-toned label that has a horizontal color band. What is the best infringement claim for VitaminWater to make against these competitors?

(a) Patent

(b) Copyright

(c) Trademark

(d) Trade secret

(e) There is no good claim

3. Faber-Castell began manufacturing pencils in 1761. Although pencils and erasers had both existed for some time, the company did not begin putting erasers on the ends of its pencils until the 1870s. The company was sued by an inventor who had previously patented this idea. The case went to the Supreme Court. Who won the case?

(a) The patent holder, because no one had ever put an erase on a pencil before

(b) The patent holder, because the PTO had approved his patent

(c) Faber-Castell, because the pencil with an eraser was not novel

(d) Faber-Castell, because the pencil with an eraser was not useful

4. If you buy a DVD, you have the legal right to:

(a) Watch it as many times as you want and then give it away.

(b) Copy it to your computer and then give it to a friend.

(c) Copy it to your computer and sell it on eBay.

(d) All of the above.

(e) a and b only.

5. A couple thought of a clever name for an automobile. They wanted to protect this name so that they could ultimately sell it to a car manufacturer. What would be the best method to obtain this goal?

(a) Patent

(b) Copyright

(c) Trademark

(d) Trade secret

(e) This name cannot be protected.

Essay Questions

1. In the documentary movie *Expelled: No Intelligence Allowed,* there was a 15-second clip of "Imagine," a song by John Lennon. The purpose of the scene was to criticize the song's message. His wife and sons, who held the copyright, sued to block this use of the song. Under what theory did the movie makers argue that they had the right to use this music? Did they win?

2. **ETHICS** After Edward Miller left his job as a salesperson at the New England Insurance Agency, Inc., he took some of his New England customers to his new employer. At New England, the customer lists had been kept in file cabinets. Although the company did not restrict access to these files, it claimed there was a "You do not peruse my files and I do not peruse yours" understanding. The lists were not marked "confidential" or "not to be disclosed." Did Miller steal New England's trade secrets? Whether or not he violated the law, was it ethical for him to use this information at his new job? What is your Life Principle?

3. Rebecca Reyher wrote (and copyrighted) a children's book entitled *My Mother Is the Most Beautiful Woman in the World.* The story was based on a Russian folk tale told to her by her own mother. Years later, the children's TV show *Sesame Street* televised a skit entitled "The Most Beautiful Woman in the World." The *Sesame Street* version took place in a different locale and had fewer frills, but the sequence of events in both stories was identical. Has *Sesame Street* infringed Reyher's copyright?

4. Roger Schlafly applied for a patent for two prime numbers. (A prime number cannot be evenly divided by any number other than itself and 1. Examples of primes are 2, 3, 5, 7, 11, and 13.) Schlafly's numbers are a bit longer—one is 150 digits, the other is 300. His numbers, when used together, can help perform the type of mathematical operation necessary for exchanging coded messages by computer. Should the PTO issue this patent?

5. Frank B. McMahon wrote one of the first psychology textbooks to feature a light, easily readable style. He also included many colloquialisms and examples that appealed to a youthful student market. Charles G. Morris wrote a psychology textbook that copied McMahon's style. Has Morris infringed McMahon's copyright?

6. Victoria's Secret, a well-known lingerie company, found out that a man named Victor Moseley was running a small store in Kentucky named "Victor's Little Secret." Moseley's shop sold clocks, patches, temporary tattoos, stuffed animals, coffee mugs, leather biker wallets, Zippo lighters, diet formula, jigsaw puzzles, handcuffs, hosiery, greeting cards, incense burners, car air fresheners, sunglasses, jewelry, candles, and adult novelties. Women's lingerie represented about 5 percent of its sales. Does Victoria's Secret have a valid intellectual property claim?

7. Question: DatagraphiX manufactured and sold computer graphics equipment that allowed users to transfer large volumes of information directly from computers to microfilm. Customers were required to keep maintenance documentation on site for the DatagraphiX service personnel. The service manual carried this legend: "No other use, direct or indirect, of this document or of any information derived there from is authorized. No copies of any part of this document shall be made without written approval by DatagraphiX." In addition, on every page of the maintenance manual, the company placed warnings that the information was proprietary and not to be duplicated. Frederick J. Lennen left DatagraphiX to start his own company that serviced DatagraphiX equipment. Can DatagraphiX prevent Lennen from using its manuals?

Strategy: With trade secrets, the key is that the owner has made a reasonable effort to protect them. (See the "Result" at the end of this section.)

8. Question: "Hey, Paula," a pop hit that spent months on the music charts, was back on the radio 30 years later, but in a form the song's author never intended. Talk-show host Rush Limbaugh played a version with the same music as the original but with lyrics that poked fun at President Bill Clinton's alleged sexual misconduct with Paula Jones. Has Limbaugh violated the author's copyright?

Strategy: Although this example may look like a copyright violation, it falls under an exception. (See the "Result" at the end of this section.)

9. Question: Research Corp. applied for a patent for a so-called halftoning technique that uses a mathematical formula to enable monitors and printers with limited color options to simulate a wider range of colors. Is this technique patentable?

Strategy: Are these inventors attempting to patent a mathematical algorithm or formula? (See the "Result" at the end of this section.)

7. Result: The court held that these manuals were DatagraphiX's trade secrets.

8. Result: Parody (especially about politics!) is a fair use of copyrighted material so long as use of the original is not excessive.

9. Result: The trial court ruled that this patent application was invalid because it was too abstract. But the appellate court overruled, holding that, although the patent used mathematical algorithms, the inventors were patenting the process not the algorithms. It upheld the patent.[24]

[24] *Research Corporation Technologies, Inc., v. Microsoft Corporation*, 627 F.3d 859; 2010 U.S. App. LEXIS 24984; 97 U.S.P.Q.2D (BNA) 1274, (Fed. Cir., 2010).

Discussion Questions

1. **ETHICS** Virtually any TV show, movie, or song can be downloaded for free on the Internet. Most of this material is copyrighted and was very expensive to produce. Most of it is also available for a fee through such legitimate sites as iTunes. What is your ethical obligation? Should you pay $1.99 to download an episode of *American Idol* from iTunes or take it for free from an illegal site? What is your Life Principle?

2. For much of history, the copyright term was limited to 28 years. Now it is as long as 120 years. What is a fair copyright term? Some commentators argue that because so much intellectual property is stolen, owners need longer protection. Do you agree with this argument?

3. Do you agree with the court that the band Furious George violated the copyright of Curious George?

4. Should Amazon be able to patent the One-Click method of ordering? What about Facebook's patent on a process that "dynamically provides a news feed about a user of a social network"? Were these inventions really novel and nonobvious? What should the standard be for business method patents?

5. Fredrik Colting wrote a book entitled *60 Years Later: Coming Through the Rye*, a riff on J. D. Salinger's famous *Catcher in the Rye*. Colting's book imagined how Salinger's protagonist, Holden Caulfield, would view life as a 76-year old. Alice Randall wrote a novel entitled *The Wind Done Gone*, which retells the Civil War novel *Gone with the Wind* from the perspective of Scarlett O'Hara's (imagined) black half-sister. Both Colting and Randall were sued and both alleged fair use. Should they win?

6. The Susan G. Komen breast cancer charity trademarked the term "for the cure." It has brought suit against other charities that use the term, as in "run for the cure" or "kites for the cure." It also sues charities that use the same shade of pink that it has long used on its ribbons. Should Komen be able to trademark "for the cure" and the color pink?

7. Should a wildflower garden be eligible for intellectual property protection?

CHAPTER 43

REAL PROPERTY AND LANDLORD-TENANT LAW

Some men have staked claims to land for its oil, others for its gold. But Paul Termarco and Gene Murdoch are staking their claim to an island using ... hot dogs. Their quest to market frankfurters in the New Jersey wilderness has made their children blush with embarrassment, their wives shrug in bewilderment, and strangers burst into laughter.

Paul Termarco and Gene Murdoch are staking their claim to an island using ... hot dogs.

But for three years, the two friends from West Milford have sold chili dogs, cheese dogs, and the ever traditional, hold-everything-but-the-mustard hot dogs from a tiny island in Greenwood Lake. Now it seems as though everyone knows about "Hot Dog Island."

"People love it," said Termarco. "They say, 'Thank you for being here.' I always say, 'No. Thank *you*.'" The personalized service and the inexpensive prices (hot dogs cost $1.75; chili dogs, cheese dogs, and sauerkraut, $2) have cultivated a base of regulars. "I think it's great. It's better than going to a restaurant for two hours and spending a lot of money," said Joan Vaillant, who frequently jet skis to the island for hot dogs slathered in mustard.

At two-eighths of an acre, the island's craggy rocks, scrubby bushes, and ash trees are difficult to spot. Termarco doesn't mind. "Not everyone can say they own an island," he boasted. Termarco and Murdoch decided to claim the slip of land after chatting with a local restaurateur a few years ago. Termarco had just finished suggesting that the man expand his lakeside business to the island when Murdoch kicked his friend under the table.

"We left thinking, 'We can do this ourselves,'" said Murdoch, who rushed to the township offices the following day to see who owned the island.

Property records showed that the state owned the lake and lake floor, but nobody owned the island. An attorney told them about the law of adverse possession written in the

1820's. If Murdoch and Termarco could show that they used the island for five years, it would be theirs. As crazy as the scheme sounded, Murdoch figured it was worth trying.[1]

Can two friends acquire an island simply by *pretending* they own it? Yes. As we will see, the law of adverse possession permits people to obtain title to land by using it, if they meet certain stringent criteria. We examine the rules later in the chapter and decide how likely Murdoch and Termarco are to succeed. For now, the lesson is that real property law can provide surprises—and profit.

NATURE OF REAL PROPERTY

Property falls into three categories: real, personal, and intellectual. Real property, which is the focus of this chapter, consists of the following:

- **Land.** Land is the most common and important form of real property. In England, land was historically the greatest source of wealth and social status, far more important than industrial or commercial enterprises. As a result, the law of real property has been of paramount importance for nearly 1,000 years, developing very gradually to reflect changing conditions. Some real property terms sound medieval for the simple reason that they *are* medieval. By contrast, the common law of torts and contracts is comparatively new.

  Real property usually also includes anything underground (subsurface right), and some amount of airspace above land (air rights).
- **Buildings.** Buildings are real property. Houses, office buildings, apartment complexes, and factories all fall in this category.
- **Plant life.** Plant life growing on land is real property whether the plants are naturally occurring, such as trees, or cultivated crops. When a landowner sells his property, plant life is automatically included in the sale unless the parties agree otherwise. A landowner may also sell the plant life separately if he wishes. A sale of the plant life alone, without the land, is a sale of goods. (Goods, as you may recall, are movable things.) If Douglas agrees to sell all of the fir trees on his property, this sale of goods will be governed by the Uniform Commercial Code (UCC), regardless of whether Douglas or the buyer is obligated to cut the trees.[2]
- **Fixtures.** Fixtures are goods that have become attached to real property. A house (which is real property) contains many fixtures. The furnace and heating ducts were goods when they were manufactured and when they were sold to the builder because they were movable. But when the builder attached them to the house, the items became fixtures. By contrast, neither the refrigerator nor the grand piano is a fixture.

When an owner sells real property, the buyer normally obtains the fixtures unless the parties specify otherwise. Sometimes it is difficult to determine whether something is a fixture. The general rule is this: **an object is a fixture if a reasonable person would consider**

---

[1]Leslie Haggin, "Pair Stake Their Claim to Hot Dog Island," *Record* (Bergen, N.J.), Sep. 5, 1994, p. A12. Excerpted with permission of *The Record*, Hackensack, N.J.
[2]UCC §2-107(2).

the item to be a permanent part of the property, taking into account attachment, adaptation, and other objective manifestations of permanence:

- *Attachment.* If an object is attached to property in such a way that removing it would damage the property, it is probably a fixture. Heating ducts could be removed from a house, but only by ripping open walls and floors, so they are fixtures.
- *Adaptation.* Something that is made or adapted *especially for attachment* to the particular property is probably a fixture, such as custom-made bookshelves fitted in a library.
- *Other manifestations of permanence.* If the owner of the property clearly intends the item to remain permanently, it is probably a fixture. Suppose a homeowner constructs a large concrete platform in his backyard, then buys a heavy metal shed and bolts it to the platform. His preparatory work indicates that he expects the shed to remain permanently, and a court would likely declare it a fixture.

For many, beef is a dietary fixture. Is the cattle scale a fixture?

FREEMAN V. BARRS

237 S.W.3d 285
Missouri Court of Appeals, 2007

Facts: Mary Ann Barrs paid $3.5 million to Francis Freeman for 4,000 acres of ranch land, including a covered "pole-barn," which had open sides, a large cattle scale, and an enclosed veterinarian's office. The parties used a form contract, which stated that all fixtures were included with the sale. The document offered space for the parties to specify items that were included or excluded with the sale, but neither party listed the cattle scale as either in or out of the deal. After the agreement went through, Barrs and Freeman got into a beef over who owned the scale. The trial judge grilled numerous witnesses and ultimately weighed in on the side of Barrs, declaring the scale a fixture that belonged to the real estate. Broiling, Freeman appealed.

Issue: ***Was the cattle scale a fixture?***

Excerpts from Judge Parrish's Decision: Steve McFadden, the president of Sooner Scale, Inc., the maker of the scale, testified that he had designed the present scale. The scale was designed to be portable, and 70% of the scales he sold were installed in the present manner. He further stated that he could move the present scales by cutting away a welded metal fence and lifting the scale with heavy machinery, [a] process he often performs. McFadden further stated that the removal of the fence would take approximately one hour with use of a cutting torch, and thereafter the scale could be moved within fifteen minutes.

Characterization of an item as a fixture depends upon the finding of three elements: annexation to the realty, adaptation to the use to which the realty is devoted, and intent of the annexor that the object become a permanent accession to the freehold. The latter two elements, adaptation and intent, are more important in determining whether a chattel became a fixture than the method by which the chattel is affixed to a freehold.

Annexation. The scale was purchased by plaintiff to "start selling cattle from the ranch and not sending them to the sale barn to keep the price up a little." The scale weighs approximately 6,500 pounds. A fence and gates within the structure had to be cut off in order to install the scale. A concrete slab was poured in the structure for placement of the scale. The scale was placed on pipes on the ground and pushed with a tractor across the pipes onto the slab. Concrete ramps were installed on two sides of the scale and fencing was constructed to direct cattle onto the scale. The metal posts for the fence were set in the concrete. The scale has remained in place since its installation.

Adaptation. Ray Stone had been ranch manager for plaintiff. At the time of trial he had an agreement with defendant that permitted him to run cattle on the property. He "just kind of saw after the place" for her. He told the court that the scale was integral to a cattle-working facility. The scale was used to weigh cattle for sale and to determine required dosages of medicine administered to cattle.

Intent. The manufacturer sold peripheral items that permitted the scale to be moved. This included a trailer and an inverter. Plaintiff did not buy that equipment. Ray Stone told the court that the scale was purchased "to be stationary whether it was portable or not."

This court concludes that the scale was a fixture; that, therefore, the sale of the real estate on which it was situate included the sale of the scale. A 6,500-pound scale placed on a specially sized concrete pad and surrounded by metal pole fencing set in the concrete is annexed to the real estate on which the concrete pad is poured. The permanency of the installation is emphasized by the fact the facility is covered and has a veterinary office in which the printer for the scale may be operated. The scale was put in place to facilitate the cattle operation on the premises. It had been used for that purpose since its purchase. Its adaptation for that purpose enhanced the operation of the cattle ranch.

Affirmed.

Estates in Real Property

Use and ownership of real estate can take many different legal forms. A person may own property outright, having the unrestricted use of the land and an unlimited right to sell it. Such a person owns a **fee simple absolute**. However, someone may also own a lesser interest in real property. The different rights that someone can hold in real property are known as **estates** or **interests.** Both terms simply indicate specified rights in property.

Fee simple absolute
Full ownership privileges in a property.

Concurrent Estates

When two or more people own real property at the same time, they have **concurrent estates**. The most common forms of concurrent estates are tenancy in common, joint tenancy, and tenancy by the entirety.

Concurrent estate
Two or more people owning property at the same time.

Tenancy in Common

The most common form of concurrent estate is **tenancy in common**. Suppose Patricia owns a house. Patricia agrees to sell her house to Quincy and Rebecca. When she **conveys** the deed, that is, transfers the deed, "to Quincy and Rebecca," those two now have a tenancy in common. This kind of estate can also be created in a will. If Patricia had died still owning the house, and left it in her will to "Sam and Tracy," then Sam and Tracy would have a tenancy in common. Tenancy in common is the "default setting" when multiple people acquire property. Co-owners are automatically considered tenants in common unless another type of interest (joint tenancy, tenancy by the entirety) is specified.

Tenancy in common
Two or more people holding equal interest in a property, but with no right of survivorship.

A tenancy in common might have 2 owners, or 22, or any number. The tenants in common do not own a particular section of the property; they own an equal interest in the entire property. Quincy and Rebecca each own a 50 percent interest in the entire house.

Any co-tenant may convey her interest in the property to another person. Thus, if Rebecca moves 1,000 miles away, she may sell her 50 percent interest in the house to Sidney. Further, when a co-tenant dies, her interest in the property passes to her heirs, along with all of her other assets.

Partition Since any tenant in common has the power to convey her interest, some people may find themselves sharing ownership with others they do not know or, worse, dislike. What to do? Partition, or division of the property among the co-tenants. Any co-tenant is entitled to demand partition of the property. If the various co-tenants cannot agree on a fair division, a co-tenant may request a court to do it. **All co-tenants have an absolute right to partition.**

A court will normally attempt a **partition by kind,** meaning that it actually divides the land equally among the co-tenants. If three co-tenants own a 300-acre farm and the court can divide the land so that the three sections are of roughly equal value, it will perform a partition in kind, even if one or two of the co-tenants oppose partition. If partition by kind is impossible because there is no fair way to divide the property, the court will order the real estate sold and the proceeds divided equally.

Image Source/Jupiterimages

Partition by kind might be the best way to divide a piece of property like this vineyard.

Joint Tenancy

Joint tenancy is similar to tenancy in common but is used less frequently. The parties, called joint tenants, again own a percentage of the entire property and also have the absolute right of partition. The primary difference is that a **joint tenancy** includes the right of survivorship. This means that when one joint tenant dies, his interest in the property passes to *the surviving joint tenants.* Recall that a tenant in common, by contrast, has the power to leave his interest in the real estate to his heirs. Because a joint tenant cannot leave the property to his heirs, courts do not favor this form of ownership. The law presumes that a concurrent estate is a tenancy in common; a court will interpret an estate as a joint tenancy only if the parties creating it clearly intended that result.

Joint tenancy
Two or more people holding equal interest in a property, with the right of survivorship.

Joint tenancy has one other curious feature. Although joint tenants may not convey their interest by will, they may do so during their lifetime. If Frank and George own vacation property as joint tenants, Frank has the power to sell his interest to Harry. But as soon as he does so, the joint tenancy is **severed,** that is, broken. Harry and George are now tenants in common, and the right of survivorship is destroyed.

But when does a severance officially take place? The answer was of critical importance in the following case.

Jackson v. Estate of Green

771 N.W.2d 675
Supreme Court of Michigan, 2009

Facts: Green and Jackson owned land as joint tenants. Green filed a petition asking a court to partition the parcels, but he died while the partition was still pending.

The lower courts found that because the partition was not complete at the time of Green's death, the land reverted to Jackson.

Green's estate appealed.

Issue: ***Does filing for the partition of a joint tenancy terminate survivorship rights?***

Excerpts from Justice Corrigan's Decision: We agree with the Court of Appeals that defendant's interest in the parcel of land automatically reverted to plaintiff when defendant died. Thus, defendant's estate has no interest in the property, and even if defendant's partition action survived his death under Michigan's survival statute, nothing remains to partition.

The principal characteristic of the joint tenancy is the right of survivorship. Upon the death of one joint tenant, the surviving tenant or tenants take the whole estate. An ordinary joint tenancy may be severed, and the right of survivorship thereby destroyed, by an act of the parties, conveyance by either party, or levy and sale on an execution against one of the parties.

A party can sever a joint tenancy by compelling a partition. Until an order of partition has been entered, however, a partition has not been compelled and, thus, the joint tenancy has not been severed. It is not the filing of the partition action which terminates the joint tenancy, but only the judgment in such action which has that effect.

This rule is based on two related concepts: First, the theory of survivorship—that at the moment of death, ownership vests exclusively in the surviving joint tenant or tenants—and second, the doctrine that severance of the joint tenancy does not occur until the partition suit reaches final judgment.

Accordingly, we would hold that the filing of the partition action did not sever the joint tenancy because an order effectuating a partition had not entered at the time of defendant's death. Therefore, regardless whether defendant's partition action survived his death under the survival statute, his interest in the parcel of land did not.

Affirmed.

Exhibit 43.1 illustrates tenancy in common and joint tenancy.

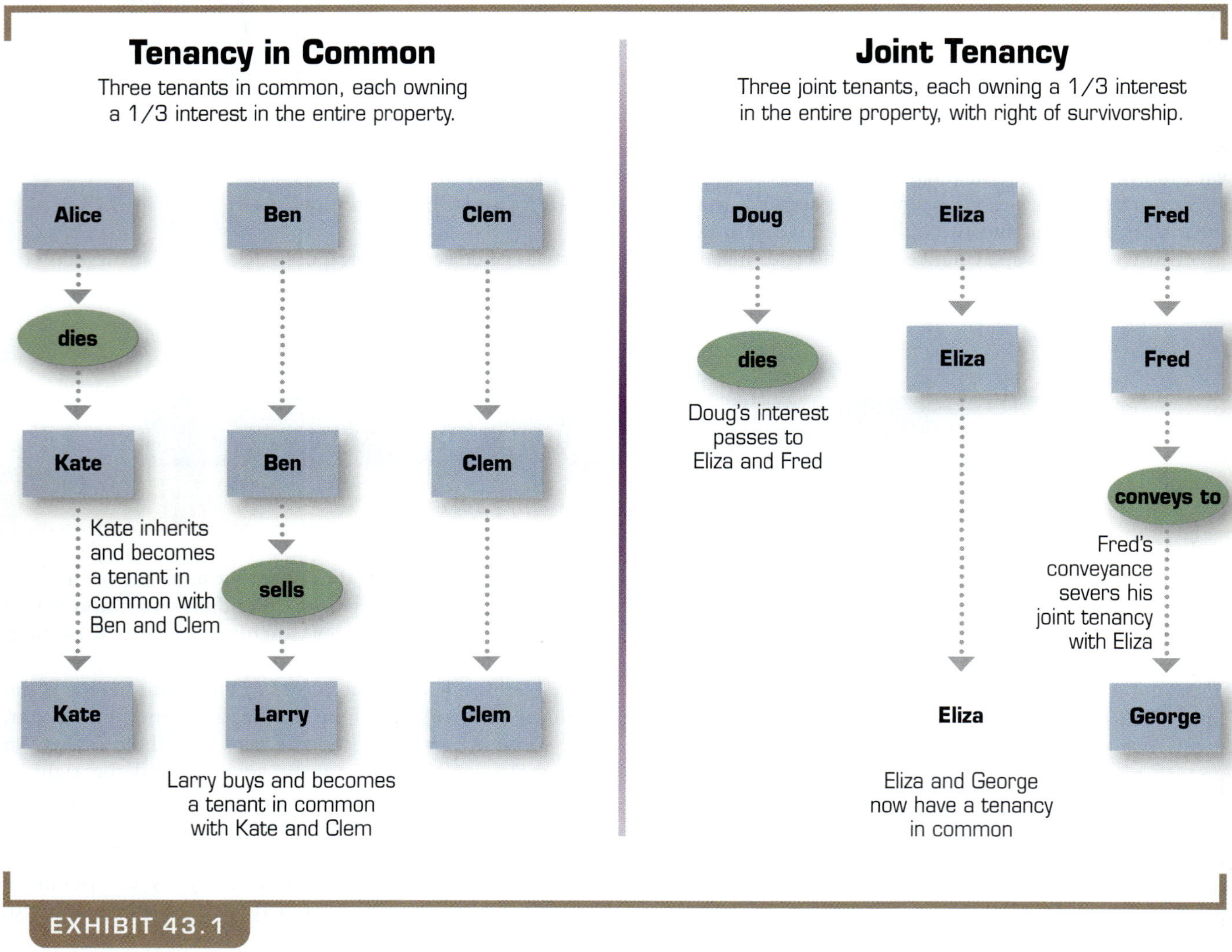

EXHIBIT 43.1

EXAM Strategy

Question: Thomas, aged 80, has spent a lifetime accumulating unspoiled land in Oregon. He owns 16,000 acres, which he plans to leave to his five children. He is not so crazy about his grandchildren. Thomas cringes at the problems the grandchildren would cause if some of them inherited an interest in the land and became part-owners along with Thomas's own children. Should Thomas leave his land to his children as tenants in common or joint tenants?

Strategy: When a co-tenant dies, her interest in property passes to her heirs. When a joint tenant dies, his interest in the property passes to the surviving joint tenants.

Result: Thomas is better off leaving the land to his children as joint tenants. That way, when one of his children dies, that child's interest in the land will go to Thomas's surviving children, not to his grandchildren. (There are other approaches Thomas could take, such as creation of a trust, and they are discussed in Chapter 45, on planning for the future.)

Tenancy by the Entirety This form of ownership exists in slightly over half of the states. **The husband and wife each own the entire property, and they both have a right of survivorship.** So when the husband dies, his one-half interest in the property automatically passes to his wife. Neither party has a right to convey his or her interest. If the parties wish to sell their interests, they must do so together. An advantage of this is that no creditor may seize the property based on a debt incurred by only one spouse. If a husband goes bankrupt, creditors may not take his house if he and his wife own it as tenants by the entirety. Divorce terminates a tenancy by the entirety and leaves the two parties as tenants in common.

Community Property French and Spanish settlers brought **community property** law to the South and West, and nine states still use this form of ownership for a married couple.[3] This system allows the husband and wife to maintain separate ownership of assets they bring to the marriage or inherit. Those assets are called **separate property.** They remain the private property of each spouse during the marriage. Either spouse may convey separate property to another person during the marriage and may leave the separate property to anyone he or she wishes. But income or assets that either party *earns* during the marriage are considered **community property, which must be equally shared** during the marriage, regardless of who earns it. Neither party may convey community property without the consent of the other. When a spouse dies, one-half of the community property goes to the surviving spouse, and the other half goes to the heirs of the deceased.

Suppose Margarita marries Jean Claude in Texas, a community property state. At the time of the marriage, Jean Claude owns a ranch but Margarita owns nothing. Jean Claude's ranch is separate property. He is free to convey it to someone else during his lifetime, and at his death, he may leave it to anyone he wishes. During the marriage, Margarita inherits a Renoir painting worth $3 million; it is separate property, which she may freely dispose of. While married, Jean Claude earns $6,000 per year, translating children's poetry. Margarita earns $900,000 producing gory television shows. The income is community property, and each spouse is entitled to $453,000 per year.

---

[3]Arizona, California, Idaho, Louisiana, Nevada, New Mexico, Texas, and Washington all have a community property law, while Wisconsin's system is a variation of the same principle.

Future Interests

Life estate
Ownership of property for the lifetime of a particular person.

A property owner may convey less than all of his rights to another person. For example, if Andrew has a fee simple absolute in Serenity Farm, he may convey a **life estate** to Claire, meaning that Claire gets the property only for her life. The remaining rights in the land are called *future interests.*

We look at two future interests: a reversion and a remainder.

Reversion

Reversion
The right of an owner (or her heirs) to property upon the death of a life tenant.

If Andrew conveys Serenity Farm "to Claire for her life," Claire has a life estate in the property. Andrew has a **reversion**, meaning that upon Claire's death, the property automatically returns to him or to his heirs. The significance of a future interest is this: even though Claire may live for 50 more years, Andrew may convey his reversion at any time. The right to own Serenity Farm upon Claire's death is a valuable right, and Andrew may sell the reversion. Once a sale is made, however, the buyer has to bide his time until Claire's death, but when she dies, the land is his.

Remainder

Suppose Andrew conveys Tranquility Farm "to Douglas for life, and then to Ernie." Douglas has a life estate and Ernie has a **remainder.** A remainder has exactly the same value as a reversion. The difference is that when the life tenant dies, the property goes to a named third person, not to the original owner.

Example: Andrew owns a fee simple absolute in property and ...	What was conveyed?	What future interest remains?
Conveys the property "to Betty."	Sale of the entire estate	None
Conveys the property "to Claire for her life."	Life estate	Andrew has a reversion. The property reverts to him or his heirs upon Claire's death.
Conveys the property "to Douglas for his life and then to Ernie."	Life estate	Ernie has a remainder and Andrew has nothing.

Nonpossessory Interests

All of the estates and interests that we have examined thus far focused on one thing: possession of the land. Now we look at interests that *never* involve possession. These interests may be very valuable, even though the holder never lives on the land.

Easements

The Alabama Power Co. drove a flatbed truck over land owned by Thomas Burgess, damaging the property. The power company did this to reach its power lines and wooden transmission poles. Burgess had never given Alabama Power permission to enter his land, and he sued for the damage that the heavy trucks caused. He recovered—nothing. Alabama Power had an *easement* to use Burgess's land.

Easement
The right to enter land belonging to another and make limited use of it.

An **easement** gives one person the right to enter land belonging to another and make a limited use of it, without taking anything away. Burgess had bought his land from a man named Denton, who years earlier had sold an easement to Alabama Power. The easement gave the power company the right to construct several transmission poles on one section of Denton's land and to use reasonable means to reach the poles. Alabama Power owned that easement forever, and when Burgess bought the land, he took it subject to the easement. Alabama Power drove its trucks across a section of land where the power company had never gone before, and the easement did not explicitly give the company this right. But the court found that the company had no other way to reach its poles, and therefore, the easement allowed this use. Burgess is stuck with his uninvited guest as long as he owns the land.[4]

There are two kinds of easements. The first, an **easement appurtenant,** benefits its owner in the use of *another parcel of land.* Suppose Madeline buys vacation land that is near a lake but without waterfront access. Wade owns lakefront land, and he sells Madeline an easement, allowing her to cross his property, on foot or in a car, to reach the water. This is an easement appurtenant since it benefits its owner (Madeline) in the use of her land. Madeline's land is the **dominant tenement;** that is, the property that benefits from the easement. Wade's parcel is the **servient tenement,** the land that is burdened by the easement. Typically, the dominant tenement is adjacent to the servient, but it need not be.

An easement appurtenant *runs with the land,* meaning that if the owner of the dominant tenement sells her land, the buyer acquires the easement as well. However, the owner may *not* sell an easement by itself to someone else. If Madeline sells her property to Jason, he acquires the right to waltz across Wade's land. But Madeline has no right to sell only the easement to Jason while retaining her property.

The second kind of easement, an **easement in gross,** benefits its owner, but *not in the use of other land.* The Alabama Power Co. had an easement in gross in Burgess's land. The company had the right to install power lines across the property and use reasonable means to reach them. However, this right did not benefit any other property owned by the company, so it was an easement in gross. Most easements in gross *may* be sold. If Alabama Power no longer needed its power lines on Burgess's land, it could sell its easement to another company, for example, a cable television company.[5]

Creation of Easements

Grant or Reservation Property owners normally create easements in one of two ways. A **grant** occurs when a landowner expressly intends to convey an easement to someone else. This is how Alabama Power acquired its easement. The company offered to buy the right to use the land, and Denton agreed to sell. The parties signed an agreement and *recorded* the easement, meaning they placed it on file in the land registry, so that interested parties were on notice. When Burgess bought the land from Denton, he knew (or should have known) about the easement.

A **reservation** occurs when an owner sells land but keeps some right to enter the property. A farmer might sell 40 acres to a developer but reserve an easement giving him the right to drive his equipment across a specified strip of the land.

Implication or Necessity Easements are less frequently created in these two ways. An **easement by implication** arises when an owner subdivides land in a way that *clearly implies* the creation of an easement in favor of the new parcels. Suppose Jason owns

---

[4] *Burgess v. Alabama Power Co.*, 658 So. 2d 435, 1995 Ala. LEXIS 119 (Ala. 1995).

[5] A related nonpossessory estate—and one that can benefit society and posterity—is a **conservation easement,** in which a property owner agrees to forbid certain development on her property, forever.

lakefront property with a boat ramp. He subdivides his land and sells several parcels that do not reach the lake, promising all purchasers use of the boat ramp. This subdivision clearly implies the right to cross Jason's land to use the boat ramp since there is no other access. The new owners have an easement by implication.

An **easement by necessity** arises when the dominant tenement *absolutely must* make use of other property. Yolanda leases a ninth-floor apartment to Darrin. Darrin has an easement by necessity to use the stairs and elevators since he has no other method of reaching his apartment, short of skydiving.

Prescription Joseph Leto bought undeveloped land in 1946 and used it on weekends for family gatherings, picnicking, and nature walks. He reached his property by using a jeep trail that crossed land he did not own, land eventually purchased by Digital Equipment Corp. (DEC). Leto continued to use the trail for nearly 30 years, until DEC sued to keep him off its property. Neither DEC nor the previous owner had ever given Leto permission to use the land. Did Leto have an easement? Yes, he had an **easement by prescription.**[6] An easement by prescription may arise when someone makes use of property belonging to another, if his use is:

- Open and notorious,
- Adverse to the owner, and
- Continuous and uninterrupted for the number of years required by local statute.

The theory of easement by prescription is that landowners must take some initiative to protect their property rights. If they fail to do so, they may lose certain rights in their land (or, as we will see in the section on adverse possession later in this chapter, they may lose the land altogether). But someone seeking an easement by prescription must satisfy each element. His use of the property must be open and notorious, so that a reasonable landowner would be aware of what is happening and have a chance to stop it. The use must be adverse to the owner, meaning without the owner's permission. A landowner who *permits* another to cross his land nullifies any possibility of easement by implication. Finally, the use must continue without interruption for as long as required by the state statute, which is often 7 years but may be more or less in a particular state. Joseph Leto continued his use of the trail for nearly 30 years, much longer than the local statute required. Once he acquired the easement by prescription, it was potentially his forever, and when DEC acquired the land, it did so subject to Leto's easement.

During the 19th century, many railroads obtained easements to lay down rails, and, by 1900, trains ran on over 300,000 miles of track throughout the country. Today, railroads use less than half that much track. What happens to the thousands of miles of unused land? Some state laws, and some contracts, require property to revert to the owner when an easement is abandoned. Yet federal, state, and local governments have turned many miles of unused track into trails for hiking and biking. Many environmentalists strongly support this "rails to trails" conversion. Some property owners believe that their reversionary rights are being violated and demand compensation. Local governments point out that they continue to shore up and maintain the original rail bank for possible future train use, and that the easements are therefore not abandoned.

Profit

Profit
The right to enter land belonging to another and take something from it.

A **profit** gives one person the right to enter land belonging to another and take something away. You own 100 acres of vacation property, and suddenly a mining company informs you that the land contains valuable nickel deposits. You may choose to sell a profit to the mining

[6] *Digital Equipment Corp. v. Leto,* Mass. Lawyers Weekly No. 14-008-94 (Mass. Land Court 1994).

company, allowing it to enter your land and take away the nickel. You receive cash up front, and the company earns money from the sale of the mineral. The rules about creating and transferring easements apply to profits as well.

License

A **license** gives the holder temporary permission to enter another's property. Unlike an easement or profit, a license is a *temporary* right. When you attend a basketball game by buying a ticket, the basketball team that sells you the ticket is the licensor and you are the licensee. You are entitled to enter the licensor's premises, namely the basketball arena, and to remain during the game, though the club can revoke the license if you behave unacceptably.

License
The right to enter land belonging to another temporarily.

Mortgage

Generally, in order to buy a house, a prospective owner must borrow money. The bank or other lender will require security before it hands over its money, and the most common form of security for a real estate loan is a mortgage. A **mortgage** is a security interest in real property. The homeowner who borrows money is the **mortgagor** because she is *giving* the mortgage to the lender. The lender, in turn, is the **mortgagee**, the party acquiring a security interest. The mortgagee in most cases obtains a **lien** on the house, meaning the right to foreclose on the property if the mortgagor fails to pay back the money borrowed. A mortgagee forecloses by taking legal possession of the property, auctioning it to the highest bidder, and using the proceeds to pay off the loan.

Mortgage
A security interest in real property.

Mortgagor
An owner who gives a security interest in property in order to obtain a loan.

Mortgagee
The party acquiring a security interest in property.

Adverse Possession

You may recall Paul Termarco and Gene Murdoch, who opened this chapter by trying to sell you—and all the world—a hot dog from an island in the middle of a New Jersey lake. As we mentioned then, Termarco and Murdoch had their sights set on more than mustard and relish: they hoped that by using the island *as if* they owned it, they *would* own it. They were relying on the doctrine of adverse possession. This old rule of law is analogous to easement by prescription, which we analyzed earlier. Under certain conditions, easement by prescription permits a person who makes use of land continuously to establish an easement for that use. Adverse possession goes even further, allowing someone to take title to land if she meets certain tests.

In most states, to gain ownership of land by adverse possession, the user must prove:

- Entry and exclusive possession,
- Open and notorious possession,
- A claim adverse to the owner, and
- Continuous possession for a statutory period.

Entry and Exclusive Possession

The user must take physical possession of the land and must be the only one to do so. If the owner is still occupying the land, or if other members of the public share its use, there can be no adverse possession.

Open and Notorious Possession

The user's presence must be visible and generally known in the area, so that the owner is on notice that his title is contested. This ensures that the owner can protect his property by ejecting the user. Someone making secret use of the land gives the owner no opportunity to do this, and hence acquires no rights in the land.

A Claim Adverse to the Owner

The user must clearly assert that the land is his. He does not need to register a deed or take other legal steps, but he must act as though he is the sole owner. If the user occupies the land with the owner's permission, there is no adverse claim and the user acquires no rights in the property. To succeed, the user must protect his possession of the land against all others the way any normal landowner would. This may mean erecting a home if the area is residential, or fencing property that is used to graze cattle, or posting "No Trespassing" signs in a wilderness area.

Must the user *believe* he has a title, or only act as though he does? The states are divided on this question. Many states focus only on the adverse *acts* of the user: it is sufficient if his conduct indicates he is the sole owner, regardless of what he thinks. This is the modern trend. But other states require a mistaken *belief* that the user has title to the land. For example, some states require that the user demonstrate "color of title," meaning that he has some document that *he believed* gave him good title to the land, though in reality it never did.

Continuous Possession for the Statutory Period

State statutes on adverse possession prescribe a period of years for continuous use of the land. Originally, most states required about 20 years to gain adverse possession, but the trend has been to shorten this period. Many states now demand 10 years, and a few require only 5 years' use. The reason for shortening the period is to reward those who *make use* of land. Even within a single state, statutes may prescribe various periods for different types of land. For example, adverse possession in a wilderness area may require more than 20 years' possession.

Regardless of the length of time required, the use must be continuous. In a residential area, the user would have to occupy the land year round for the prescribed period. In a wilderness area generally used only in the summer, a user could gain ownership by seasonal use.

A user may be able to meet the statutory period by **tacking,** which permits her to add on to her years of occupancy any years certain predecessors were in possession. The predecessors must have been in *privity* with the current user, meaning there was some legal relationship. Suppose that for 12 years, Martha adversely possesses land owned by Jake. Martha then moves, selling her interest in the land to Nancy, who occupies the land for 9 years. The total of 21 years is sufficient for adverse possession in any state, and Nancy now owns the land.

Sailing back to Hot Dog Island, how did Murdoch and Termarco fare? They certainly entered on the land and established themselves as the exclusive occupants. Their use has been open and notorious, allowing anyone who claimed ownership to take steps to eject them from the property. Their actions have been adverse to anyone else's claim. If the two hot dog entrepreneurs have grilled those dogs for the full statutory period, they should take title to the island.[7]

In the following case, the couple claiming adverse possession must do without friendly hot dog sellers because they have taken up residence in a ghost town.

[7]Unfortunately, there are no press accounts to inform us of the island's current status.

Ray v. Beacon Hudson Mountain Corp.

88 N.Y.2d 154, 666 N.E.2d 532, 1996 N.Y. LEXIS 676
Court of Appeals of New York, 1996

Facts: In 1931, Rose Ray purchased a cottage in a mountaintop resort town in the Adirondacks, at the same time agreeing to rent the land on which the structure stood. The long-term lease required her to pay the real estate taxes and provided that when the tenancy ended, the landlord would buy back the cottage at fair market value. In 1960, the landlord terminated the lease of everyone in the town, so Ray and all other residents packed up and left. She died in 1962, without ever getting a penny for the cottage. The next year, Mt. Beacon Incline Lands, Inc., bought all rights to the abandoned 156-acre resort.

Robert and Margaret Ray, the son and daughter-in-law of Rose Ray, reentered the cottage and began to use it one month per year, every summer from 1963 to 1988. They paid taxes, insured the property, installed utilities, and posted "No Trespassing" signs.

In 1978, Beacon Hudson bought the resort in a tax foreclosure sale. Finally, in 1988, the Rays filed suit, claiming title to the cottage by adverse possession. Beacon Hudson counterclaimed, seeking to eject the Rays. The trial court ruled for the couple. The appellate court reversed, stating that the Rays had been absent too frequently to achieve adverse possession. The Rays appealed to New York's highest court.

Issue: ***Did the Rays acquire title by adverse possession?***

Excerpts from Judge Titone's Decision: The element of continuity will be defeated where the adverse possessor interrupts the period of possession by abandoning the premises. However, the hostile claimant's actual possession of the property need not be constant to satisfy the "continuity" element of the claim. Rather, the requirement of continuous possession is satisfied when the adverse claimant's acts of possessing the property are consistent with acts of possession that ordinary owners of like properties would undertake.

Here, defendant claims that plaintiffs' possession of the property was not continuous because they were physically present there for only one month out of the summer season. However, this argument fails to take into consideration plaintiffs' other acts of dominion and control over the premises that are indicative of their actual possession of an estate in land. Here, plaintiffs' installation of utilities and overall preservation of the cottage, a permanent and substantial structure, in a veritable ghost town, for the duration of the statutory period demonstrates continuous, actual occupation of land by improvement. Thus, plaintiffs' actual summertime use for a full month each season, coupled with their repeated acts of repelling trespassers, improving, posting, padlocking, and securing of the property in their absences throughout the statutory period, demonstrated their continuous dominion and control over, and thus possession of, the property.

Such seasonal presence, coupled with plaintiffs' preservation of the premises for the statutory period of 10 years—which was made more obvious by the fact that all neighboring structures had collapsed due to vandalism and abandonment—was sufficient to place the record owner on notice of their hostile and exclusive claim of ownership.

[The appellate court is reversed and the Rays obtain title by adverse possession.]

Land Use Regulation

Nuisance Law

A **nuisance** is an unprivileged interference with a person's use and enjoyment of her property. Offensive noise, odors, or smoke often give rise to nuisance claims. Courts typically balance the utility of the act that is causing the problem against the harm done to neighboring property owners. If a suburban homeowner begins to raise pigs in her backyard, the neighbors may find the bouquet offensive; a court will probably issue an **abatement,** that is, an order requiring the homeowner to eliminate the nuisance.

Community members can use the old doctrine of nuisance for more serious problems than pigs. An apartment building in Berkeley, California, became widely known as a drug house, and the neighbors suffered. Here is how two of the neighbors described their lives:

> I have been confronted by the drug dealers, drug customers, and prostitutes that frequent and work around and from 1615–1617 Russell Street. Weekly I have lost many hours of sleep from the cars that burn rubber after each drug buy in the middle of the night.
>
> Because of this illegal activity, my child is unable to use our front yard, and I even have to check the back yard since it has been intruded upon from time to time by people running from the police. He is learning to count by how many gunshots he hears and can't understand why he can't even enjoy our rose garden.

These were but two of the affidavits written by neighbors of a 36-unit building owned by Albert Lew. Month after month neighbors complained to Lew that his tenants were destroying the neighborhood. But Lew refused to evict the drug dealers or take any serious steps to limit the crime. So the neighbors used the law of nuisance to restore their community.

Sixty-six neighbors of the drug house each filed a small claims case against Lew, claiming that he was permitting a nuisance to exist on his property. The neighbors won their small claims cases, but Lew appealed, as he had a right to, for a new trial in Superior Court. A sergeant testified that he had been to the building over 250 times during two years. Residents testified about how frightening life had become. The Superior Court awarded damages of $218,325 to the neighbors and the court of appeals affirmed the award, holding that neighbors injured by a nuisance may seek an abatement and damages. As Lew discovered, the law of nuisance can be a powerful weapon for creating a better neighborhood.[8]

Zoning

Zoning statutes are state laws that permit local communities to regulate building and land use. The local communities, whether cities, towns, or counties, then pass zoning ordinances that control many aspects of land development. For example, a town's zoning ordinance may divide the community into an industrial zone where factories may be built, a commercial zone in which stores of a certain size are allowed, and several residential zones in which only houses may be constructed. Within the residential zones, there may be further divisions, for example, permitting two-family houses in certain areas and requiring larger lots in others.

An owner prohibited by an ordinance from erecting a certain kind of building, or adding on to his present building, may seek a **variance** from the zoning board, meaning an exception granted for special reasons unique to the property. Whether a board will grant a variance generally depends upon the type of the proposed building, the nature of the community, the reason the owner claims he is harmed by the ordinance, and the reaction of neighbors.

Ethics Many people abhor "adult" businesses, such as strip clubs and pornography shops. Urban experts agree that a large number of these concerns in a neighborhood often causes crime to increase and property values to drop. Nonetheless, many people patronize such businesses, which can earn a good profit. Should a city have the right to restrict adult businesses? New York City officials determined that the number of sex

[8] *Lew v. Superior Court,* 20 Cal. App. 4th 866, 1993 Cal. App. LEXIS 1198 (Cal. Ct. App. 1993).

shops had grown steadily for two decades and that their presence harmed various neighborhoods. With the support of community groups, the city passed a zoning ordinance that prohibited adult businesses from all residential neighborhoods, from some commercial districts, *and* from being within 500 feet of schools, houses of worship, day-care centers, or other sex shops (to avoid clustering). Owners and patrons of these shops protested, claiming that the city was unfairly denying the public access to a form of entertainment that it obviously desired. Is the New York City zoning ordinance reasonable?

Eminent Domain

Eminent domain is the power of the government to take private property for public use. A government may need land to construct a highway, airport, university, or public housing. All levels of government—federal, state, and local—have this power. But the Fifth Amendment of the United States Constitution states: ". . . nor shall private property be taken for public use, without just compensation." The Supreme Court has held that this clause, the Takings Clause, applies not only to the federal government but also to state and local governments. So, although all levels of government have the power to take property, they must pay the owner a fair price.

Eminent domain
The power of the government to take private property for public use.

A "fair price" generally means the reasonable market value of the land. Generally, if the property owner refuses the government's offer, the government will file suit seeking **condemnation** of the land, that is, a court order specifying what compensation is just and awarding title to the government.

A related issue concerns local governments requiring property owners to *dedicate* some of their land to public use in exchange for zoning permission to build or expand on their own property. For example, if a store owner wishes to expand his store, a town might grant zoning permission only if the owner dedicates a different part of his property for use as a public bike path. The Supreme Court has recently diminished the power of local governments to require such dedication.[9]

Landlord-Tenant Law

Apartments are certainly a type of real property, and many students are keenly interested in renters' rights. We now turn our attention to landlord-tenant law.

A freehold estate is the right to possess real property and use it in any lawful manner. What we think of as "owning" land is in fact a freehold estate. **When an owner of a freehold estate allows another person temporary, exclusive possession of the property, the parties have created a landlord-tenant relationship.** The freehold owner is the **landlord**, and the person allowed to possess the property is the **tenant**. The landlord has conveyed a leasehold interest to the tenant, meaning the right to temporary possession. Courts also use the word *tenancy* to describe the tenant's right to possession.

Landlord
The owner of a freehold estate who allows another person temporarily to live on his property.

Tenant
A person given temporary possession of the landlord's property.

A leasehold may be commercial or residential. In a commercial tenancy, the owner of a building may rent retail space to a merchant, offices to a business, or industrial space to a manufacturer. When someone rents an apartment or house, he has a residential leasehold.

[9] The Supreme Court's ruling came in *Dolan v. City of Tigard*, 512 U.S. 374, 114 S. Ct. 2309, 1994 U.S. LEXIS 4836 (1994), which we discuss in more detail in Chapter 5, on constitutional law.

Three Legal Areas Combined

Property law influences landlord-tenant cases because the landlord is conveying rights in real property to the tenant. She is also keeping a **reversionary interest** in the property, meaning the right to possess the property when the lease ends. Contract law plays a role because the basic agreement between the landlord and tenant is a contract. A **lease** is a contract that creates a landlord-tenant relationship. And negligence law increasingly determines the liability of landlord and tenant when there is an injury to a person or property. Many states have combined these three legal issues into landlord-tenant statutes.

Lease
An agreement in which an owner gives a tenant the right to use property.

Lease

The statute of frauds generally requires that a lease be in writing. Some states will enforce an oral lease if it is for a short term, such as one year or less, but even when an oral lease is permitted, it is wiser for the parties to put their agreement in writing because a written lease avoids many misunderstandings. At a minimum, a lease must state the names of the parties, the premises being leased, the duration of the agreement, and the rent. But a well-drafted lease generally includes many provisions, called *covenants* and *conditions*. A **covenant** is simply a promise by either the landlord or the tenant to do something or refrain from doing something. For example, most leases include a covenant concerning the tenant's payment of a security deposit and the landlord's return of the deposit, a covenant describing how the tenant may use the premises, and several covenants about who must maintain and repair the property. Generally, tenants may be fined but not evicted for violating lease covenants. A **condition** is similar to a covenant, but it allows for a landlord to evict a tenant if there is a violation. In many states, conditions in leases must be clearly labeled as "conditions" or "evictable offenses."

Types of Tenancy

There are four types of tenancy: a tenancy for years, a periodic tenancy, a tenancy at will, and a tenancy at sufferance. The most important feature distinguishing one from the other is how each tenancy terminates. In some cases, a tenancy terminates automatically, while in others, one party must take certain steps to end the agreement.

Tenancy for Years

Tenancy for years
A lease for a stated, fixed period.

Any lease for a stated, fixed period is a **tenancy for years**. If a landlord rents a summer apartment for the months of June, July, and August of next year, that is a tenancy for years. A company that rents retail space in a mall beginning January 1, 2012, and ending December 31, 2015, also has a tenancy for years. A tenancy for years terminates automatically when the agreed period ends.

Periodic Tenancy

Periodic tenancy
A lease for a fixed period, automatically renewable unless terminated.

A **periodic tenancy** is created for a fixed period and then automatically continues for additional periods until either party notifies the other of termination. This is probably the most common variety of tenancy, and the parties may create one in either of two ways. Suppose a landlord agrees to rent you an apartment "from month to month, rent payable on the first." That is a periodic tenancy. The tenancy automatically renews itself every month unless either party gives adequate notice to the other that she wishes to terminate. A periodic tenancy could also be for one-year periods—in which case it automatically renews for an additional year if neither party terminates—or for any other period.

The parties also create a periodic tenancy if, when a *tenancy for years* expires, the tenant continues to pay rent and the landlord accepts it. Ariadne agrees to rent property called Naxos for three years, with rent payable once per month. When the three years are up, the tenancy for years expires automatically. Ariadne continues to pay the monthly rent, however, and the landlord accepts her checks. The parties have created a periodic tenancy.

What is the period? If the tenant is renting *commercial property*, the new periodic tenancy is for the same period as the old tenancy for years, up to a maximum of one year. In other words, if Naxos is an office building, Ariadne's new periodic tenancy is for one year (since her original lease was for more than a year). Once the landlord accepts a single monthly rental check, both he and Ariadne are bound for the full year. In many states, if the property is *residential*, the new periodic tenancy is month-to-month. If Naxos is a vacation house, either party can end the lease with 30 days' notice. A landlord's notice terminating a tenancy is often called a **notice to quit**.

Notice to quit
A landlord's notice terminating a tenancy.

Tenancy at Will

A **tenancy at will** has no fixed duration and may be terminated by either party at any time. Tenancies at will are unusual tenancies.[10] Typically, the agreement is vague, with no specified rental period and with payment, perhaps, to be made in kind. The parties might agree, for example, that a tenant farmer could use a portion of his crop as rent. Since either party can end the agreement at any time, it provides no security for either landlord or tenant.

Tenancy at will
A tenancy with no fixed duration, which may be terminated by either party at any time.

Tenancy at Sufferance

A **tenancy at sufferance** occurs when a tenant remains on the premises, against the wishes of the landlord, after the expiration of a true tenancy. Thus, a tenancy at sufferance is not a true tenancy because the tenant is staying without the landlord's agreement. The landlord has the option of seeking to evict the tenant or of forcing the tenant to pay a *use and occupancy fee* for as long as she stays. These distinctions are technical but important.

Tenancy at sufferance
A tenancy that exists without the permission of the landlord, after the expiration of a true tenancy.

In the following case, all parties acknowledged that the tenant refused to pay rent. But it was the landlord's failure to understand different types of tenancy that proved more important and led to a surprising result.

Elwell v. Minor

2006 WL 1920562
Connecticut Superior Court, 2006

Facts: Winfield Elwell orally agreed to rent an apartment in Vernon, Connecticut, to Lucille Minor on a month-to-month basis. The rent was $575. Four years later, Elwell increased the rent to $625, and the next year to $650, taking effect that September. Minor tendered $625 and included a letter explaining that she did not want to pay the increased rent for September or October but that she would pay the increase in later months. Elwell rejected the payment. Minor then tendered the check a second time, and Elwell again returned it.

[10]The courts of some states, annoyingly, use the term "tenancy at will" for what are, in reality, periodic tenancies. They do this to bewilder law students and even lawyers, a goal at which they are quite successful. This text uses tenancy at will in its more widely known sense, meaning a tenancy terminable at any time.

Elwell told Minor to pay $650 or vacate. She did neither, so Elwell began eviction proceedings (called "summary process") by serving on Minor a Notice to Quit for nonpayment of rent. After additional negotiations failed, Elwell served a second Notice to Quit. At trial, Minor argued that nonpayment of *rent* was an improper grounds for evicting a tenant at sufferance. She asked the court to dismiss the case.

Issue: ***May a landlord evict a tenant at sufferance for nonpayment of rent?***

Excerpts from Judge White's Decision: During the month of September, Minor and Elwell corresponded extensively. In her letters, Minor refused to pay the increased rental amount which Elwell demanded. She gave reasons why she did not want to pay $650 instead of $625 and even attempted to negotiate postponing the rent increase until later months. Elwell rejected Minor's efforts by returning the checks that she tendered and continuing to insist on a $650 rental amount. These communications reveal a definite dispute between the parties which precludes the formation of a new one-month lease.

Because Minor remained in possession of the premises without a new monthly contract, she should be treated as a holdover occupying the apartment without the legal right to do so [in other words, as a tenant at sufferance]. In this case, the defendant was not a tenant at will, because such a tenancy exists only when the occupation of the property is with the landlord's consent, continuing during the tenancy. Elwell also served Minor with the first notice to quit for nonpayment of rent expressing his intention to terminate the lease. Once the lease terminated, Minor became a tenant at sufferance.

Nonpayment of rent is not a proper ground for the eviction of a tenant at sufferance because a tenant at sufferance is not required to pay rent, but only use and occupancy. When two parties enter into a month-to-month lease, they do not ordinarily designate a definite date when the lease, by its own terms, will expire. Instead the parties establish a tenancy at will which the tenant may terminate by moving out and the landlord may terminate by serving a notice to quit. Such a lease could never expire by lapse of time because there is no term defining the temporal existence of the lease. So, the law treats a month-to-month lease as a series of individual leases which expire at the end of the month and are ordinarily renewed each month by implication. Once the agreement expires by operation of law, the tenant's obligation to pay rent transforms into an obligation to pay a reasonable sum for the use and occupancy of the premises. Without an obligation to pay rent there can be no summary process for nonpayment of rent.

The proper statutory basis for pursuing summary process against a tenant who failed to pay a reasonable sum for use and occupancy would be that the tenant originally had the right or privilege to occupy the premises but such right or privilege has terminated. Elwell's second notice to quit cites improper grounds for the eviction of a tenant at sufferance. The notice to quit is defective and deprives this court of subject matter jurisdiction in this summary process action. This action is dismissed.

Landlord's Duties

Duty to Deliver Possession

The landlord's first important duty is to deliver possession of the premises at the beginning of the tenancy, that is, to make the rented space available to the tenant. In most cases, this presents no problems and the new tenant moves in. But what happens if the previous tenant has refused to leave when the new tenancy begins?

The **"English rule"** obligates the landlord to remove the previous tenant in time for the new tenant to take possession. The majority of American states enforce this rule. If the old tenant is still in possession when the new tenant arrives, the landlord has breached the lease. The new tenant has two alternative remedies. She may terminate the lease and sue the landlord for costs she incurs obtaining other accommodations. Or she may affirm the lease, refuse to pay rent for the period in which she cannot take possession, sue for the cost of other accommodations, and then take possession when the old tenant is finally evicted.

The **"American rule"** is more favorable to the landlord. (Although called the American rule, this is in fact the minority rule in this country—anything to keep you off balance.) This rule holds that the landlord has no duty to deliver actual possession of the premises. If the previous tenant remains in possession, the landlord has not breached the lease. Under this rule, the new tenant generally has the power to act as a landlord toward the old tenant. The new tenant may evict the old tenant and recover damages caused by her delay in leaving. Alternatively, the new tenant may treat the holdover as a tenant at will for a new rental period and may charge the normal rent for that period.

Quiet Enjoyment

All tenants are entitled to quiet enjoyment of the premises, meaning the right to use the property without the interference of the landlord. Most leases expressly state this covenant of quiet enjoyment. And if a lease includes no such covenant, the law implies the right of quiet enjoyment anyway, so all tenants are protected. If a landlord interferes with the tenant's quiet enjoyment, he has breached the lease, entitling the tenant to damages.

The most common interference with quiet enjoyment is an **eviction**, meaning some act that forces the tenant to abandon the premises. Of course, some evictions are legal, as when a tenant fails to pay the rent. But some evictions are illegal. There are two types of eviction: actual and constructive.

Eviction
An act that forces a tenant to abandon the property.

Actual Eviction

If a landlord prevents the tenant from possessing the premises, he has actually evicted her. Suppose a landlord decides that a group of students are "troublemakers." Without going through lawful eviction procedures in court, the landlord simply waits until the students are out of the apartment and changes all the locks. By denying the students access to the premises, the landlord has actually evicted them and has breached their right of quiet enjoyment. He is liable for all expenses they suffer, such as retrieving their possessions, the cost of alternate housing, and moving expenses. In some states, he may be liable for punitive damages for failing to go through proper eviction procedures.

Even a partial eviction is an interference with quiet enjoyment. Suppose Louise rents an apartment with a storage room. If the landlord places his own goods in the storage room, he has partially evicted Louise because a tenant is entitled to the *exclusive* possession of the premises. In all states, Louise would be allowed to deduct from her rent the value of the storage space, and in many states, she would not be obligated to pay any rent for the apartment as long as the landlord continued the partial eviction.

Constructive Eviction

If a landlord substantially interferes with the tenant's use and enjoyment of the premises, he has constructively evicted her. Courts construe certain behavior as the equivalent of an eviction. In these cases, the landlord has not actually prevented the tenant from *possessing* the premises but has instead interfered so greatly with her *use and enjoyment* that the law regards the landlord's actions as equivalent to an eviction. Suppose the heating system in an apartment house in Juneau, Alaska, fails during January. The landlord, an avid sled dog racer, tells the tenants he is too busy to fix the problem. If the tenants move out, the landlord has constructively evicted them and is liable for all expenses they suffer.

To claim a constructive eviction, the tenant must vacate the premises. The tenant must also prove that the interference was sufficiently serious and lasted long enough that she was forced to move out. A lack of hot water for two days is not fatal, but lack of any water for two weeks creates a constructive eviction.

Other Interference

A landlord's conduct may interfere with quiet enjoyment even when it is not so harmful as to force a constructive eviction. Suppose a landlord, living in the ground-floor unit, gives trumpet lessons in his apartment six nights a week until 1:00 a.m., producing such a cacophony that a group of students living upstairs can neither study nor sleep. If the students continue to live in the apartment because they cannot afford a better place, there has been no constructive eviction. But the landlord's conduct interferes with the tenants' quiet enjoyment, and the students are entitled to damages.

Duty to Maintain Premises

Historically, the common law placed no burden on the landlord to repair and maintain the premises. This made sense because rental property had traditionally been farmland. Buildings, such as a house or barn, were far less important than the land itself, and no one expected the landlord to fix a leaking roof. Today, the vast majority of rental property is used for housing or business purposes. Space in a building is frequently all that a tenant is renting, and the condition of the building is of paramount importance. Most states have changed the common law rule and placed various obligations on the landlord to maintain the property.

In most states, a landlord has a duty to deliver the premises in a habitable condition and a continuing duty to maintain the habitable condition. This duty overlaps with the quiet enjoyment obligation, but it is not identical. The tenant's right to quiet enjoyment focuses primarily on the tenant's *ability to use* the rented property. The landlord's duty to maintain the property focuses on whether the property *meets a particular legal standard.* The required standard may be stated in the lease, created by a state statute, or implied by law.

A landlord's duty to maintain the premises may be stated in the lease, created by statute, or implied by law.

Lease

The lease itself generally obligates the landlord to maintain the exterior of any buildings and the common areas. If a lease does not do so, state law may imply the obligation.

Building Codes

Many state and local governments have passed building codes, which mandate minimum standards for commercial and/or residential property. The codes are likely to be stricter for residential property and may demand such things as minimum room size, sufficient hot water, secure locks, proper working kitchens and bathrooms, absence of insects and rodents, and other basics of decent housing. Generally, all rental property must comply with the building code, whether the lease mentions the code or not.

Implied Warranty of Habitability

Students Maria Ivanow, Thomas Tecza, and Kenneth Gearin rented a house from Les and Martha Vanlandingham. The monthly rent was $900. But the roommates failed to pay any rent for the final five months of the tenancy. After they moved out, the Vanlandinghams sued. How much did the landlords recover? Nothing. The landlords had breached the implied warranty of habitability.

The implied warranty of habitability requires that a landlord meet all standards set by the local building code, or that the premises be fit for human habitation. Most states, though not all, *imply* this warranty of habitability, meaning that the landlord must meet this standard whether the lease includes it or not. In some states, the implied warranty means that the premises must at least satisfy the local building code. Other states require property that is "fit for human habitation," which means that a landlord might comply with the building code, yet still fail the implied warranty of habitability if the rental property is unfit to live in.

The Vanlandinghams breached the implied warranty. The students had complained repeatedly about a variety of problems. The washer and dryer, which were included in the lease, frequently failed. A severe roof leak caused water damage in one of the bedrooms. Defective pipes flooded the bathroom. The refrigerator frequently malfunctioned, and the roommates repaired it several times. The basement often flooded, and when it was dry, rats and opossums lived in it. The heat sometimes failed.

The basement often flooded, and when it was dry, rats and opossums lived in it.

In warranty of habitability cases, a court normally considers the severity of the problems and their duration. If the defective conditions seriously interfere with the tenancy, the court declares the implied warranty breached and orders a **rent abatement;** that is, a reduction in the rent owed. The longer the defects continued and the greater their severity, the more the rent is abated. In the case of Maria Ivanow and friends, the court abated the rent 50 percent. The students had already paid more than the abated rent to the landlord, so they owed nothing for the last five months.[11]

Duty to Return Security Deposit

Most landlords require tenants to pay a security deposit, in case the tenant damages the premises. In many states, a landlord must either return the security deposit soon after the tenant has moved out or notify the tenant of the damage and the cost of the repairs. In addition, landlords are often obligated to credit tenants with interest earned on the deposit. In many states, a landlord who fails to return the deposit in a timely fashion can be forced to pay double or even triple damages to the tenant, a question raised in the following dispute.

MISHKIN V. YOUNG

107 P.3d 393, 2005 WL 452168
Supreme Court of Colorado, 2005

Facts: A Colorado statute required a landlord either to return a security deposit or provide an accounting of why money was being withheld. The landlord had to do this within one month of the tenant's surrender of the property, or up to 60 days if the lease permitted. If the landlord failed to refund the money, the tenant, after giving seven days' notice, could sue for treble damages. The landlord could avoid the treble damages by refunding the deposit within those seven days.

Marc Mishkin leased an apartment from Dean Young, paying a security deposit of $1,625. The lease stated that the deposit would be returned no later than 45 days after the tenant moved out. After Mishkin left, Young did not return the money. Forty-eight days after leaving, Mishkin sent a demand for the deposit, notifying Young that in seven days, he would sue for treble damages. Six days later, Young gave Mishkin a statement detailing $1,574.60 worth of property damage along with a check for $50.40.

[11] *Vanlandingham v. Ivanow*, 246 Ill. App. 3d 348, 615 N.E.2d 1361, 1993 Ill. App. LEXIS 985 (Ill. Ct. App. 1993).

Mishkin sued. The trial court ruled that Young was entitled to withhold the money because of the damages. Mishkin appealed. The appellate court ruled that the Colorado statute required the landlord to return the full security deposit within the seven-day period. Young appealed.

Issue: ***May a landlord avoid the treble damages by accounting for the security deposit within seven days of the tenant's notice to sue?***

Excerpts from Justice Kourlis's Decision: [Earlier] cases implicitly indicate that a landlord's failure to account for a security deposit as required by subsection (1) [of the statute] constitutes a forfeiture of all rights to withhold any portion of the deposit and subjects the landlord to treble damages. A landlord may avoid treble damages only by returning the entire security deposit during the seven days following a tenant's demand notice. An accounting during this seven-day period does not protect a landlord from treble damages because this period is beyond the statutory deadline of subsection (1) and the landlord has already forfeited all rights to retain the deposit. The purpose of the seven-day notice provision is to give landlords one last week to avoid treble damages by returning the security deposit. It does not give landlords a second chance to account for the deposit. The money actually belongs to the tenant; it was only security for the landlord, who has by unilateral action forfeited all right to retain any of it. Therefore, we now make explicit what has been implicit in our prior rulings: We hold that a landlord may not avoid treble damages by accounting for a security deposit during the seven-day period following a tenant's demand notice.

Contrary to the landlord's contention, our interpretation does not render the remaining provisions of the Act meaningless. Subsection (2) [which states that the landlord forfeits the entire deposit if he fails to return the money or account for it within the statutory period] performs a critical function by encouraging most landlords to expeditiously account for their tenants' security deposits. Yet the case may arise where a landlord finds forfeiture an insufficient inducement to account for the withholding of a tenant's security deposit. In such situations, the prospect of treble damages provided for by subsection (3) proves instrumental. Not only do treble damages act as a formidable deterrent to landlords who might otherwise wrongfully withhold a tenant's security deposit, but they also give tenants an enticing legal remedy where the alternative is to forgo a relatively small but often vital sum of money.

[Affirmed.]

Final Word on Security Deposits The discussion and case both concerned residential leases, where security deposits are almost inevitable. Note that, in a commercial lease, the tenant may have less statutory protection but more bargaining power. A financially sound company might negotiate a lease with no security deposit or perhaps offer a letter of credit for security instead of cash. The interest saved over several years could be substantial.

Tenant's Duties

Duty to Pay Rent

Rent
Compensation paid by a tenant to a landlord.

Rent is the compensation the tenant pays the landlord for use of the premises, and paying the rent is the tenant's foremost obligation. The lease normally specifies the amount of rent and when it must be paid. Typically, the landlord requires that rent be paid at the beginning of each rental period, whether that is monthly, annually, or otherwise.

Escalator clause
A lease clause allowing the landlord to raise the rent for specified reasons.

Both parties must be certain they understand whether the rent includes utilities such as heat and hot water. Some states mandate that the landlord pay certain utilities, such as water. Many leases include an **escalator clause**, permitting the landlord to raise the rent during the course of the lease if his expenses increase for specified reasons. For example, a tax escalator clause allows the landlord to raise the rent if his real estate taxes go up. Any escalator clause should state the percentage of the increase that the landlord may pass on to the tenant.

Landlord's Remedies for Nonpayment of Rent

If the tenant fails to pay rent on time, the landlord has several remedies. She is entitled to apply the security deposit to the unpaid rent. She may also sue the tenant for nonpayment of rent, demanding the unpaid sums, cost of collection, and interest. Finally, the landlord may evict a tenant who has failed to pay rent.

State statutes prescribe the steps a landlord must take to evict a tenant for nonpayment. Typically, the landlord must serve a termination notice on the tenant and wait for a court hearing. At the hearing, the landlord must prove that the tenant has failed to pay rent on time. If the tenant has no excuse for the nonpayment, the court grants an order evicting him. The order authorizes a sheriff to remove the tenant's goods and place them in storage, at the tenant's expense. However, if the tenant was withholding rent because of unlivable conditions, the court may refuse to evict.

EXAM Strategy

Question: Leo rents an apartment from Donna for $900 per month, both parties signing a lease. After six months, Leo complains about defects, including bugs, inadequate heat, and window leaks. He asks Donna to fix the problems, but she responds that the heat is fine and that Leo caused the insects and leaks. Leo begins to send in only $700 for the monthly rent. Donna repeatedly phones Leo, asking for the remaining rent. When he refuses to pay, she waits until he leaves for the day, then has a moving company place his belongings in storage. She changes the locks, making it impossible for him to re-enter. Leo sues. What is the likely outcome?

Strategy: A landlord is entitled to begin proper eviction proceedings against a tenant who has not paid rent. However, the landlord must follow specified steps, including a termination notice and a court hearing. Review the consequences for actual eviction, described in the section "Quiet Enjoyment."

Result: Donna has ignored the legal procedures for evicting a tenant. Instead, she engaged in *actual eviction*, which is quick, and in the short term, effective. However, by breaking the law, Donna has ensured that Leo will win his lawsuit. He is entitled to possession of the apartment, as well as damages for rent he may have been forced to pay elsewhere, injury to his possessions, and the cost of retrieving them. He may receive punitive damages as well. Bad strategy, Donna.

Duty to Mitigate

Pickwick & Perkins, Ltd., was a store in the Burlington Square Mall in Burlington, Vermont. Pickwick had a five-year lease but abandoned the space almost two years early and ceased paying rent. The landlord waited approximately eight months before renting the space to a new tenant and then sued, seeking the unpaid rent. Pickwick defended on the grounds that Burlington had failed to **mitigate damages,** that is, to keep its losses to a minimum by promptly seeking another tenant. Burlington argued that it had no legal obligation to mitigate. Burlington's position accurately reflected the common law rule, which permitted the landlord to let the property lie vacant and allow the damages to add up. But the common law evolves over time, and this time, the Vermont Supreme Court changed the rule. The judges pointed out that, historically, a lease was a conveyance of an estate, and property law had never required mitigation. However, the court asserted, a lease is now regarded as both a contract and a conveyance. Under contract law, the nonbreaching party must make a reasonable effort to minimize losses, and that same rule applies, said the court, to a landlord. Burlington lost. The Vermont ruling is typical of current decisions, although some courts still do not require mitigation.[12]

Duty to Use Premises for Proper Purpose

A lease normally lists what a tenant may do in the premises and prohibits other activities. For example, a residential lease allows the tenant to use the property for normal living purposes, but not for any retail, commercial, or industrial purpose. A commercial lease might allow a tenant to operate a retail clothing store but not a restaurant. A landlord may evict a tenant who violates the lease by using the premises for prohibited purposes.

A tenant may not use the premises for any illegal activity, such as gambling or selling drugs. The law itself implies this condition in every lease, so a tenant who engages in illegal acts on the leased property is subject to eviction, regardless of whether the lease mentions such conduct.

Duty Not to Damage Premises

A tenant is liable to the landlord for any significant damage he causes to the property. The tenant is not liable for normal wear and tear. If, however, he knocks a hole in a wall or damages the plumbing, the landlord may collect the cost of repairs, either by using the security deposit or by suing, if necessary. A landlord may also seek to evict a tenant for serious damage to the property.

A tenant is permitted to make reasonable changes in the leased property so that he can use it as intended. Someone leasing an apartment is permitted to hang pictures on the wall. But a tenant leasing commercial space should make certain that the lease specifies the alterations he can make and whether he is obligated to return the premises to their original condition at the end of the lease.

Recall that a **fixture** is an item of personal property that is permanently attached to real estate. A furnace is a fixture, as are custom cabinets installed in a kitchen. The common law rule held that all fixtures belonged to the landlord. The contemporary trend, though, is the opposite. In commercial leases, it is common for tenants to install expensive equipment as part of their business, for example, commercial ovens in a restaurant. These are called **trade fixtures.** Most states permit commercial tenants to remove trade fixtures, provided the tenant restores the property to its original condition. In residential leases, some states still prohibit the tenant from removing a fixture, but courts today are likelier to permit removal, provided the tenant does not harm the premises in the process.

Duty Not to Disturb Other Tenants

Most leases, commercial and residential, include a covenant that the tenant will not disturb other tenants in the building. A landlord may evict a tenant who unreasonably disturbs others. The test is *reasonableness.* A landlord does not have the right to evict a residential tenant for giving one loud party but may evict a tenant who repeatedly plays loud music late at night and disturbs the quiet enjoyment of other tenants.

---

[12]*O'Brien v. Black,* 162 Vt. 448, 648 A.2d 1374, 1994 Vt. LEXIS 89 (1994).

INJURIES

You invite a friend to dinner in your rented home, but after the meal, she slips and falls, seriously injuring her back. Are you liable? Is the landlord?

Tenant's Liability

A tenant is generally liable for injuries occurring within the premises she is leasing, whether that is an apartment, a store, or otherwise. If a tenant permits grease to accumulate on a kitchen floor and a guest slips and falls, the tenant is liable. If a merchant negligently installs display shelving that tips onto a customer, the merchant pays for the harm. Generally, a tenant is not liable for injuries occurring in common areas over which she has no control, such as exterior walkways. If a tenant's dinner guest falls because the building's common stairway has loose steps, the landlord is probably liable.

Landlord's Liability

Common Law Rules

Historically, the common law held a landlord responsible for injuries on the premises only in a limited number of circumstances, which we will describe. In reading these common law rules, be aware that many states have changed them, dramatically increasing the landlord's liability.

Latent Defects If the landlord knows of a dangerous condition on the property and realizes the tenant will not notice it, the landlord is liable for any injuries. For example, if a landlord knows that a porch railing is weak and fails to inform the tenant, the landlord is responsible if the tenant plunges off the porch. But notice that, under the common law, if the landlord notifies the tenant of the latent defect, he is no longer liable.

Common Areas The landlord is usually responsible for maintaining the common areas, and along with this obligation may go liability for torts. As we saw above, if your guest falls downstairs in a common hallway because the stairs were defective, the landlord is probably liable.

Negligent Repairs Even in areas where the landlord has no duty to make repairs, if he volunteers to do so and does the work badly, he is responsible for resulting harm.

Public Use If the premises are to be used for a public purpose, such as a store or office, the landlord is generally obligated to repair any dangerous defects, although the tenant is probably liable as well. The purpose of this stricter rule is to ensure that the general public can safely visit commercial establishments. If a landlord realizes that the plate glass in a store's door is loose, he must promptly repair it or suffer liability for any injuries.

Modern Trend

Increasingly, state legislatures and courts are discarding the common law classifications described above and holding landlords liable under the normal rules of negligence law. **In many states, a landlord must use reasonable care to maintain safe premises and is liable for foreseeable harm.** For example, the common law rule merely required a landlord to notify a tenant of a latent defect, such as a defective porch railing. Most states now have building codes that require a landlord to maintain structural elements such as railings in safe condition. States further imply a warranty of habitability, which mandates reasonably safe living conditions. So, in many states, a landlord is no longer saved from negligence suits merely by giving notice of defects—he has to fix them.

Exculpatory Clauses

Exculpatory clause
A lease clause that relieves a landlord of liability for injuries.

You have found an apartment you can afford, in the right neighborhood, and the landlord presents you with a lease to sign. You notice an **exculpatory clause**, which states that the landlord is *not* liable for any injuries that occur on the rented premises, whether to you or your guests, regardless of the cause. You feel uncomfortable about the clause because it seems to suggest that the landlord can ignore serious defects and still escape liability. Should you sign the lease?

Today, **exculpatory clauses are generally void in residential leases.** Courts dislike such clauses because the parties typically have unequal bargaining power, and the goal of the law is to encourage safe housing managed by responsible landlords. So courts in many states simply ignore exculpatory clauses and apply normal rules of negligence to determine whether or not a landlord is liable for an injury. However, this is not universally the case; in some states, a court may still enforce an exculpatory clause in a residential lease. A concerned tenant should learn the local law before signing such a lease.

Chapter Conclusion

Real property law is ancient but forceful. Although real property today is not the dominant source of wealth that it was in medieval England, it is still the greatest asset that most people will ever possess—and is worth understanding.

When property is rented, a special relationship exists between landlord and tenant. Each has numerous obligations to the other. The current trend is clearly for expanded landlord liability, but how far that will continue is impossible to divine.

Exam Review

1. **REAL PROPERTY; FIXTURES** Real property includes land, buildings, air and subsurface rights, plant life, and fixtures. A fixture is any good that has become attached to other real property, such as land. (pp. 1088–1090)

EXAM Strategy

Question: Paul and Shelly Higgins had two wood stoves in their home. Each rested on, but was not attached to, a built-in brick platform. The downstairs wood stove was connected to the chimney flue and was used as part of the main heating system for the house. The upstairs stove, in the master bedroom, was purely decorative. It had no stovepipe connecting it to the chimney. The Higginses sold their house to Jack Everitt, and neither party said anything about the two stoves. Is Everitt entitled to either stove? Both stoves?

Strategy: An object is a fixture if a reasonable person would consider the item to be a permanent part of the property, taking into account attachment, adaptation, and other objective manifestations of permanence. (See the "Result" at the end of this section.)

2. **CONCURRENT ESTATES** When two or more people own real property at the same time, they have a concurrent estate. In both a tenancy in common and a joint tenancy, all owners have a share in the entire property. The primary difference is that joint tenants have the right of survivorship, meaning that when a joint tenant dies, his interest passes to the other joint tenants. A tenant in common has the power to leave her estate to her heirs. (pp. 1090–1093)

Question: Howard Geib, Walker McKinney, and John D. McKinney owned two vacation properties as joint tenants with right of survivorship. The parties were not getting along well, and Geib petitioned the court to partition the properties. The trial court ruled that the fairest way to do this was to sell both properties and divide the proceeds. The two McKinneys appealed, claiming that a partition by sale was improper because it would destroy their right of survivorship. Comment.

Strategy: Do joint tenants have a right to partition? Are there any limits on that right? (See the "Result" at the end of this section.)

3. **FUTURE INTERESTS** Future interests are presently existing nonpossessory rights that may or may not develop later. (p. 1094)

4. **ADVERSE POSSESSION** Adverse possession permits the user of land to gain title if he can prove entry and exclusive possession, open and notorious possession, a claim adverse to the owner, and continuous possession for the required statutory period. (pp. 1097–1099)

5. **GOVERNMENT REGULATION** Nuisance law, zoning ordinances, and eminent domain all permit a government to regulate property and in some cases to take it for public use. (pp. 1099–1101)

6. **LANDLORD-TENANT** When an owner of a freehold estate allows another person temporary, exclusive possession of the property, the parties have created a landlord-tenant relationship. (pp. 1101–1102)

7. **TENANCIES** Any lease for a stated, fixed period is a tenancy for years. A periodic tenancy is created for a fixed period and then automatically continues for additional periods until either party notifies the other of termination. A tenancy at will has no fixed duration and may be terminated by either party at any time. A tenancy at sufferance occurs when a tenant remains, against the wishes of the landlord, after the expiration of a true tenancy. (pp. 1102–1104)

8. **QUIET ENJOYMENT** All tenants are entitled to the quiet enjoyment of the premises, without the interference of the landlord. (pp. 1105–1106)

9. **SECURITY DEPOSITS**. Landlords may require tenants to post a deposit that can be used to pay for repairs if a tenant damages the property. But many landlords fail to promptly return security deposits to tenants who leave no damage behind. In those cases, tenants are often able to sue for as much as three times their security deposit. (pp. 1107–1108)

10. **RENT** The tenant is obligated to pay the rent, and the landlord may evict for nonpayment. The modern trend is to require a landlord to mitigate damages caused by a tenant who abandons the premises before the lease expires. (pp. 1108–1109)

EXAM Strategy

Question: Loren Andreo leased retail space in his shopping plaza to Tropical Isle Pet Shop for five years, at a monthly rent of $2,100. Tropical Isle vacated the premises 18 months early, turned in the key to Andreo, and acknowledged liability for the unpaid rent. Andreo placed a "for rent" sign in the store window and spoke to a commercial real estate broker about the space. But he did not enter into a formal listing agreement with the broker, or take any other steps to rent the space, for about nine months. With approximately nine months remaining on the unused part of Tropical's lease, Andreo hired a commercial broker to rent the space. He also sued Tropical for 18 months' rent. Comment.

Strategy: When a tenant abandons leased property early, the landlord is obligated to mitigate damages. Did Andreo? (See the "Result" at the end of this section.)

11. **DAMAGE** A tenant is liable to the landlord for any significant damage he causes to the property. (p. 1110)

12. **DISTURBANCES** A tenant must not disturb other tenants. (p. 1110)

EXAM Strategy

Question: Doris Rowley rented space from the city of Mobile, Alabama, to run the Back Porch Restaurant. Her lease prohibited assignment or subletting without the landlord's permission. Rowley's business became unprofitable, and she asked the city's real estate officer for permission to assign her lease. She told the officer that she had "someone who would accept if the lease was assigned." Rowley provided no other information about the assignee. The city refused permission. Rowley repeated her requests several times without success, and finally she sued. Rowley alleged that the city had unreasonably withheld permission to assign and had caused her serious financial losses as a result. Comment.

Strategy: A landlord may not unreasonably refuse permission to assign a lease. Was the city's refusal unreasonable? (See the "Result" at the end of this section.)

13. **PERSONAL INJURY** At common law, a landlord had very limited liability for injuries on the premises, but today many courts require a landlord to use reasonable care and hold her liable for foreseeable harm. (pp. 1111–1112)

1. Result: A buyer normally takes all fixtures. The downstairs stove was permanently attached to the house and used as part of the heating system. The owner who installed it *intended* that it remain, and it was a fixture; Everitt got it. The upstairs stove was not permanently attached and was not a fixture; the sellers could take it with them.

2. Result: The McKinneys lost. Any co-tenant (including a joint tenant) has an absolute right to partition. Difficulties in partitioning are irrelevant.

10. Result: For about nine months, Andreo made no serious effort to lease the store. The court rejected his rent claim for that period, permitting him to recover unpaid money only for the period he made a genuine effort to lease the space.

12. Result: A landlord is allowed to evaluate a prospective assignee, including its financial stability and intended use of the property. Mobile could not do that because Rowley provided no information about the proposed assignee. Mobile wins.

Multiple-Choice Questions

1. Quick, Onyx, and Nash were deeded a piece of land as tenants in common. The deed provided that Quick owned one-half the property and Onyx and Nash owned one-quarter each. If Nash dies, the property will be owned as follows:

(a) Quick 1⁄2, Onyx 1⁄2

(b) Quick 5⁄8, Onyx 3⁄8

(c) Quick 1⁄3, Onyx 1⁄3, Nash's heirs 1⁄3

(d) Quick 1⁄2, Onyx 1⁄4, Nash's heirs 1⁄4

2. Which of the following forms of tenancy will be created if a tenant stays in possession of leased premises without the landlord's consent, after the tenant's one-year written lease expires?

(a) Tenancy at will

(b) Tenancy for years

(c) Periodic tendency

(d) Tenancy at sufferance

3. To be enforceable, a long-term residential real estate lease must:

(a) Require the tenant to obtain liability insurance

(b) Define the tenant's duty to mitigate

(c) Be in writing

(d) Specify a due date for rent

(e) All of the above

4. A tenant renting an apartment under a three-year written lease that does not contain any specific restrictions may be evicted for:

(a) Counterfeiting money in the apartment

(b) Keeping a dog in the apartment

(c) Failing to maintain a liability insurance policy on the apartment

(d) Making structural repairs to the apartment

5. A tenant's personal property will become a fixture and belong to the landlord if its removal would:
   (a) Increase the value of the personal property
   (b) Cause a material change to the personal property
   (c) Result in substantial harm to the landlord's property
   (d) Change the use of the landlord's property back to its prior use

Essay Questions

1. In 1944, W. E. Collins conveyed land to the Church of God of Prophecy. The deed said: "This deed is made with the full understanding that should the property fail to be used for the Church of God, it is to be null and void and property to revert to W. E. Collins or heirs." In the late 1980s, the church wished to move to another property and sought a judicial ruling that it had the right to sell the land. The trial court ruled that the church owned a fee simple absolute and had the right to sell the property. Comment.

2. Nome 2000, a partnership, owned a large tract of wilderness land in Alaska. The Fagerstrom family had used the property for camping and holidays since about 1944. In 1966, Charles and Peggy Fagerstrom marked off an area for a cabin and brought material to build the cabin, but never did so. In about 1970, they built a picnic area on the land, and in about 1974, they placed a camper trailer on the land, where it remained until the lawsuit. In 1987, Nome 2000 sued to eject the Fagerstroms from the land. The Fagerstroms had used the land only during the summer months. No one lived in the area during the winter months, when it was virtually uninhabitable. Has the family adversely possessed the land from Nome 2000?

3. **YOU BE THE JUDGE WRITING PROBLEM** Frank Deluca and his son David owned the Sportsman's Pub on Fountain Street in Providence, Rhode Island. The Delucas applied to the city for a license to employ topless dancers in the pub. Did the city have the power to deny the Delucas' request? **Argument for the Delucas:** Our pub is perfectly legal. Further, no law in Rhode Island prohibits topless dancing. We are morally and legally entitled to present this entertainment. The city should not use some phony moralizing to deny customers what they want. **Argument for Providence:** This section of Providence is zoned to prohibit topless dancing, just as it is zoned to bar manufacturing. There are other parts of town where the Delucas can open one of their sleazy clubs if they want to, but we are entitled to deny a permit in this area.

4. Kenmart Realty sued to evict Mr. and Ms. Alghalabio for nonpayment of rent and sought the unpaid monies, totaling several thousand dollars. In defense, the Alghalabios claimed that their apartment was infested with rats. They testified that there were numerous rat holes in the walls of the living room, bedroom, and kitchen, that there were rat droppings all over the apartment, and that on one occasion, they saw their toddler holding a live rat. They testified that the landlord had refused numerous requests to exterminate. Please rule on the landlord's suit.

5. Lisa Preece rented an apartment from Turman Realty, paying a $300 security deposit. Georgia law states: "Any landlord who fails to return any part of a security deposit which is required to be returned to a tenant pursuant to this article shall be liable to the tenant in the amount of three times the sum improperly withheld plus reasonable attorney's fees." When Preece moved out, Turman did not return her security deposit, and she sued for triple damages plus attorney's fees, totaling $1,800. Turman offered evidence that its failure to return the deposit was inadvertent and that it had procedures reasonably designed to avoid such errors. Is Preece entitled to triple damages? Attorney's fees?

Discussion Questions

1. The Estates is a suburb outside of Los Angeles. Local zoning ordinances require that lots be "at least 1 acre in size." Al owns a 1-acre lot in The Estates which has never been developed. He needs cash and wants to sell the property.

   Al finds a potential buyer who offers him $100,000 for the acre. But he also finds a pair of interested buyers who each offer him $75,000 for half of his acre. Al is furious that he cannot divide his acre and sell it to two buyers. "I need that extra $50,000," he rants. "It's my land, and I should be able to do what I want with it!"

   Do you sympathize with Al, or do you think the zoning restriction is reasonable?

2. Donny Delt and Sammy Sigma are students and roommates. They lease a house in a neighborhood near campus. Few students live on the block.

   The students do not have large parties, but they often have friends over at night. The friends sometimes play high-volume music in their cars and sometimes speak loudly when going to and from their cars. Also, departing late-night guests often leave beer cans and fast-food wrappers in the street.

   Neighbors complain about being awakened in the wee hours of the morning. They are considering filing a nuisance lawsuit against Donny and Sammy. Would such an action be reasonable? Do you think Donny and Sammy are creating a nuisance? If so, why? If not, where is the line—what amount of late-night noise does amount to a nuisance?

3. In 1966, Arketex Ceramic Corp. sold land in rural Indiana to Malcolm Aukerman. The deed described the southern boundary as the section line between sections 11 and 14 of the land. Farther south than this section line stood a dilapidated fence running east to west. Aukerman and Arketex both believed that this fence was the actual southern boundary of his new land, though in fact it lay on Arketex's property.

   Aukerman installed a new electrified fence, cleared the land on "his" side of the new fence, and began to graze cattle there. In 1974, Harold Clark bought the land that bordered Aukerman's fence, assuming that the fence was the correct boundary. In 1989, Clark had his land surveyed and discovered that the true property line lay north of the electric fence. Aukerman filed suit, seeking a court order that he had acquired the disputed land by adverse possession. The statutory period in Indiana is 20 years. Who wins? Who *ought* to win? Does adverse possession make sense as a social policy? Why or why not?

4. Imagine that you sign a lease and that you are to move into your new apartment on August 15. When you arrive, the previous tenant has not moved out. In fact, he has no intention of moving out. Compare the English and the American rules. Should the landlord be in charge of getting rid of the old tenant, or should you have the obligation to evict him?

5. When landlords wrongfully withhold security deposits, they can often be sued for three times the amount of the security deposit. Is this reasonable? Should a landlord have to pay $3,000 for a $1,000 debt? What if you fail to pay a rent on time? Should you have to pay three times the amount of your normal rent? If your answers to these two questions are different, why?

CHAPTER 44

PERSONAL PROPERTY AND BAILMENT

© Steve Allen/Jupiterimages

"My only child is a no-good thief," Riley murmurs sadly to his visitors. "He has always treated me contemptuously. Now he's been sentenced to five years for stealing from a children's charity. He is my only heir, but why should I leave him everything?"

My only child is a no-good thief. He is my only heir, but why should I leave him everything?

Riley continues talking to his three guests: a bishop, a rabbi, and Earnest, a Boy Scout leader. "I have $500,000 in stocks and bonds in my bank deposit box. Tomorrow morning, I'm going to go down to the bank, take out all the papers, and hand them over to the Boy Scouts so that other kids won't turn out so bad." Everyone applauds his generosity, and they photograph Riley and Earnest shaking hands. But the following morning, on his way to the bank, Riley is struck by an ambulance and killed. A dispute arises over the money. The three witnesses assure the court that Riley was on his way to give the money to the Boy Scouts. From prison, the ne'er-do-well son demands the money as Riley's sole heir. Who wins? Personal property law holds the answer.

Personal property
All tangible property other than real property.

Personal property means all tangible property other than real property. In Chapter 43, we saw that real property is land and things firmly attached to it, such as buildings, crops, and minerals. All other physical objects are personal property—a bus, a toothbrush, a share of stock.

In this chapter, we look at several ways in which personal property can be acquired. In the section on gifts, we learn that Riley's no-good son gets the money. Riley intended to give the stocks and bonds to the Boy Scouts the following day, but he never completed a valid gift because he failed to *deliver* the papers. We will then turn to disputes over found property. And finally, we examine bailments, which occur when the owner of personal property permits another to possess it.

GIFTS

Gift
A voluntary transfer of property from one person to another, without consideration.

Donor
A person who gives property away.

Donee
A person who receives a gift of property.

A **gift** is a voluntary transfer of property from one person to another without any consideration. Recall from Chapter 12 that, for consideration to exist, parties must normally make an exchange. But a gift is a one-way transaction, without anything given in return. The person who gives property away is the **donor**, and the one who receives it is the **donee**.

A gift involves three elements:

- The donor *intends to transfer* ownership of the property to the donee immediately.
- The donor *delivers* the property to the donee.
- The donee *accepts* the property.

If all three elements are met, the donee becomes the legal owner of the property. If the donor later says, "I've changed my mind, give that back!" the donee is free to refuse.

Intention to Transfer Ownership

The donor must intend to transfer ownership to the property right away, immediately giving up all control of the item. Notice the two important parts of this element. First, the donor's intention must be to *transfer ownership;* that is, to give title to the donee. Merely proving that the owner handed you property does not guarantee that you have received a gift; if the owner only intended that you *use* the item, there is no gift, and she can demand it back.

Second, the donor must also intend the property to transfer *immediately.* A promise to make a gift in the future is unenforceable. Promises about future behavior are governed by contract law, and a contract is unenforceable without consideration. If Sarah hands Lenny the keys to a $600,000 yacht and says, "Lenny, it's yours," then it *is* his, since Sarah intends to transfer ownership right away. But if Sarah says to Max, "Next week, I'm going to give you my yacht," Max has not received a gift because Sarah did not intend an immediate transfer. Nor does Max have an enforceable contract since there is no consideration for Sarah's promise.

A *revocable gift* is governed by a special rule, and it is actually not a gift at all. Suppose Harold tells his daughter Faith, "The mule is yours from now on, but if you start acting stupid again, I'm taking her back." Harold has retained some control over the animal, which means he has not intended to transfer ownership. There is no gift, and no transfer of ownership. Harold still owns the mule.

When Dominic Tenaglia's automobile broke down, his brother Nick generously offered to give him a replacement car. Nick delivered a Chevrolet to Dominic, and both brothers understood that the car was a gift. Nick wrote "gift" on the car's certificate of title, but he did not immediately give the certificate to Dominic. A week later, while Dominic was driving the Chevrolet, he was involved in an accident. Both brothers had insurance, through different insurers, for cars they owned. The two companies disputed which one was liable for Dominic's accident. The court determined that Nick's company was still liable for any damage caused by the Chevrolet. Nick had presented the car to Dominic but had not relinquished *all* control over it. Ownership of a car is unlike ownership of a computer or a sweater because it requires possession of the certificate of title. Because Nick still had the certificate at the time of the accident, he had the power to take back the Chevrolet whenever he wanted. He had not made a valid gift of the automobile, and Dominic's insurer won the case.[1]

Delivery

Physical Delivery

The donor must deliver the property to the donee. Generally, this involves physical delivery—a handoff, if you will. If Anna hands Eddie a Rembrandt drawing, saying "I want you to have this forever," she has satisfied the delivery requirement. In the chapter opening, Riley promised to give half a million dollars to the Boy Scouts the following day. But he never delivered the stocks and bonds, so there was no gift. The Boy Scouts received nothing, and all of the money became part of Riley's estate, to be inherited by his unworthy son.

Constructive Delivery

Physical delivery is the most common and the surest way to make a gift, but it is not always necessary. **A donor makes constructive delivery by transferring ownership without a physical delivery.** Most courts permit constructive delivery only when physical delivery is impossible or extremely inconvenient. Suppose Anna wants to give her niece Jen a blimp, which is parked in a hangar at the airport. The blimp will not fit through the doorway of Jen's dorm. Instead of flying the aircraft to the university, Anna may simply deliver to Jen the certificate of title and the keys to the blimp. When she has done that, Jen owns the aircraft.

Delivery to an Agent

A donor might deliver the property to an agent, either someone working for him or for the donee. Assume that Randolph says to Mortimer, "Old boy, I should like for you to have my Rolls Royce." If Randolph gives the keys and the title to his own butler, there is no gift. By definition, the agent works for the donor, and thus the donor still has control and ownership of the property. But if the donor delivers the property to the donee's agent, the gift is made. So, If Randolph delivers the car to Mortimer's butler, then Mortimer owns the car.

Property Already in Donee's Possession

Sometimes a donor decides to give property to a donee who already has possession of it. In that case, no delivery is required, and the donee need only demonstrate that the donor intended to transfer present *ownership*. Larry lends a grand piano to Leslie for the summer. At the end of the summer, Larry announces that she can keep the instrument. As long as Larry clearly intends that Leslie gets ownership of the piano, the gift is completed.

Inter Vivos Gifts and Gifts *Causa Mortis*

A gift can be either *inter vivos* or *causa mortis*. An ***inter vivos* gift** means a gift made "during life," that is, when the donor is not under any fear of impending death. The vast majority of gifts are *inter vivos*, involving a healthy donor and donee. Shirley, age 30 and in good health, gives Terry an eraser for his birthday. This is an *inter vivos* gift, which is absolute. The gift becomes final upon delivery, and the donor may *not* revoke it. If Shirley and Terry have a fight the next day, Shirley has no power to erase her eraser gift.

***Inter vivos* gift**
A gift made during the donor's life, with no fear of impending death.

A **gift *causa mortis*** is one made in contemplation of approaching death. The gift is valid if the donor dies as expected, but it is revoked if he recovers. Suppose Lenny's doctors have told him he will probably die of a liver ailment within a month. Lenny calls Jane to his bedside and hands her a fistful of cash, saying, "I'm dying, this money is yours." Jane sheds a tear, then

Gift *causa mortis*
A gift made in contemplation of approaching death.

[1]*Motorists Mutual Insurance Co. v. State Farm Mutual Automobile Insurance Co.*, 1990 Ohio App. LEXIS 3027 (Ohio Ct. App. 1990).

sprints to the bank. If Lenny dies of the liver ailment within a few weeks, Jane gets to keep the money. The law permits the gift *causa mortis* to act as a kind of substitute for a will since the donor's delivery of the property clearly indicates his intentions. But note that this kind of gift is revocable. Since a gift *causa mortis* is conditional (upon the donor's death), the donor has the right to revoke it at any time before he dies. If Lenny telephones Jane the next day and says that he has changed his mind, he gets the money back. Further, if the donor recovers and does not die as expected, the gift is automatically revoked.

Acceptance

The donee must accept the gift. This rarely leads to disputes, but if a donee should refuse a gift and then change her mind, she is out of luck. Her repudiation of the donor's offer means there is no gift, and she has no rights in the property.

EXAM Strategy

Question: Julie does good deeds for countless people, and many are deeply grateful. On Monday, Wilson tells Julie, "You are a wonderful person, and I have a present for you. I am giving you this baseball, which was the 500th home run hit by one of the great players of all time." He hands her the ball, which is worth nearly half a million dollars.

Julie's good fortune continues on Tuesday, when another friend, Cassandra, tells Julie, "I only have a few weeks to live. I want you to have this signed first edition of *Ulysses*. It is priceless, and it is yours." The book is worth about $200,000. On Wednesday, Wilson and Cassandra decide they have been foolhardy, and both demand that Julie return the items. Must she do so?

Strategy: Both of these donors are attempting to revoke their gifts. An *inter vivos* gift cannot be revoked, but a gift *causa mortis* can be. To answer the question, you must know what kind of gifts these were.

Result: A gift *causa mortis* is one made in fear of approaching death, and this rule applies to Cassandra. Such a gift is revocable any time before the donor dies, so Cassandra gets her book back. A gift *inter vivos* is one made without any such fear of death. Most gifts fall in this category, and they are irrevocable. Wilson was not anticipating his demise, so his was a gift *inter vivos*. Julie keeps the baseball.

The following case offers a combination of love, alcohol, and diamonds—always a volatile mix.

You be the Judge

ALBINGER V. HARRIS
2002 Mont. 118, 2002 WL 1226858
Montana Supreme Court, 2002

Facts: Michelle Harris and Michael Albinger lived together, on and off, for three years. Their roller-coaster relationship was marred by alcohol abuse and violence. When they announced their engagement, Albinger gave Harris a $29,000 diamond ring, but the couple broke off their wedding plans because of emotional and physical turmoil. Harris returned the ring. Later, they reconciled and resumed their marriage plans, and Albinger gave his fiancée the ring again. This cycle repeated several times over the three years. Each time they broke off their relationship, Harris returned the ring to Albinger, and each time they made up, he gave it back to her.

On one occasion, Albinger held a knife over Harris as she lay in bed, threatening to chop off her finger if she didn't remove the ring. He beat her and forcibly removed the ring. Criminal charges were brought but then dropped when, inevitably, the couple reconciled. Another time, Albinger told her to "take the car, the horse, the dog, and the ring and get the hell out." Finally, mercifully, they ended their stormy affair, and Harris moved to Kentucky—keeping the ring.

Albinger sued for the value of the ring. The trial court found that the ring was a conditional gift, made in contemplation of marriage, and ordered Harris to pay its full value. She appealed. The Montana Supreme Court had to decide, in a case of first impression, whether an engagement ring was given in contemplation of marriage. (In Montana, and many states, neither party to a broken engagement may sue for breach of contract.)

You Be the Judge: ***Who owns the ring?***

Argument for Harris: The main problem with calling the ring a "conditional gift" is that there is no such thing. The elements of a gift are intent, delivery, and acceptance, and Harris has proven all three. A gift is not a contract, nor is it a loan. Once a gift has been accepted, the donor has no more rights in the property and may not demand its return. Hundreds of years of litigation have resulted in only one exception to this rule—a gift *causa mortis*—and despite some cynical claims to the contrary, marriage is not death. If this court carves a new exception to the long-standing rule, other unhappy donors will dream up more "conditions" that supposedly entitle them to their property. What is more, to create a special rule for engagement rings would be blatant gender bias because the exception would only benefit men. This court should stick to settled law and permit the recipient of a gift to keep it.

Argument for Albinger: The symbolism of an engagement ring is not exactly news. For decades, Americans have given rings—frequently diamond—in contemplation of marriage. All parties understand why the gift is made and what is expected if the engagement is called off: the ring must be returned. Albinger's *intent,* to focus on one element, was conditional—and Michelle Harris understood that. Each time the couple separated, she gave the ring back. She knew that she could wear this beautiful ring in anticipation of their marriage, but that custom and decency required its return if the wedding was off. She knew it, that is, until greed got the better of her and she fled to Kentucky, attempting to profit at the expense of Albinger's generosity. We are not asking for new law, but for confirmation of what everyone has known for generations: there is no wedding ring when there is no wedding.

The following table distinguishes between a contract and a gift:

A Contract and a Gift Distinguished

A Contract:	
Lou: I will pay you $2,000 to paint the house, if you promise to finish by July 3.	Abby: I agree to paint the house by July 3, for $2,000.
Lou and Abby have a contract. Each promise is consideration in support of the other promise. Lou and Abby can each enforce the other's promise.	
A Gift:	
Lou hands Phil two opera tickets, saying: I want you to have these two tickets to *Rigoletto."*	Phil says, "Hey, thanks."
This is a valid *inter vivos* gift. Lou intended to transfer ownership immediately and delivered the property to Phil, who now owns the tickets.	
Neither Contract nor Gift:	
Lou: You're a great guy. Next week, I'm going to give you two tickets to *Rigoletto.*	Jason: Hey, thanks.
There is no gift because Lou did not intend to transfer ownership immediately, and he did not deliver the tickets. There is no contract because Jason has given no consideration to support Lou's promise.	

Found Property

Dejected and ashamed, you walk to the university with your head hung low, knowing that your failure to study means you will fare poorly on today's quiz concerning *found property*. Suddenly, there is a gleam of light, not in your mind (which is vacant), but right there on the sidewalk. You stoop to pick it up—a ring! You stop in at the local jewelry shop, where you learn the ruby marvel is worth just over $7,000. Dazzled and delighted, you walk into the classroom and take the test. Question 1 reads: "A student discovers a ruby ring while walking to class. May the student keep the ring?" You have no idea what the answer is and you cannot concentrate anyway. So you write the two safest words in the law: "It depends." That is a fine start, but to learn the full answer, read on.

The law of found property has bewitched the courts of this country for nearly two centuries. Judges have made valiant attempts to base their rulings on principles of sound public policy, but the results have been confusing and contradictory. **The primary goal of the common law has been to get found property back to its proper owner, if possible.** The finder must make a good faith effort to locate the owner of the property and return the goods to him. In some states, the finder is obligated to notify the police of what she has found and entrust the property to them until the owner can be located or until a stated period has passed. **A second policy has been to reward the finder if no owner can be located.** But courts are loath to encourage trespassing, so finders who discover personal property on someone else's land generally cannot keep it. Those basic policies yield various outcomes, depending on the nature of the property. In the end, the law recognizes four kinds of found property:

- **Abandoned property** is something that the owner has knowingly discarded because she no longer wants it. A vase thrown into a garbage can is abandoned. Generally, a finder is permitted to keep abandoned property. But because the owner loses all rights in abandoned property, a court never *presumes* abandonment. The finder must prove that the owner intended to relinquish all rights.
- **Lost property** is something accidentally given up. A ring that falls off a finger into the street is lost property. Usually, the finder of lost property has rights superior to all the world except the true owner. If the true owner comes forward, he gets his property back; otherwise, the finder may keep it. However, if the finder has discovered the item on land belonging to another, the landowner is probably entitled to keep it.
- **Mislaid property** is something the owner has intentionally placed somewhere and then forgotten. A book deliberately placed on a bus seat by an owner who forgets to take it with her is mislaid property. Generally, the finder gets no rights in property that has simply been mislaid. If the true owner cannot be located, the mislaid item belongs to the owner of the premises where the item was found.
- **Treasure trove** is coins or currency concealed by an owner so long ago that it is likely the owner has died. A sackful of gold coins minted in 1860, found under the roots of a 150-year-old tree, is treasure trove. The finder can generally keep treasure trove.

Finding statutes
Laws that govern found property. Also known as estray statutes.

Many states have enacted laws, called **finding statutes** or **estray statutes**, governing found property. In some cases, the legislation incorporates the common law principles outlined above, but in other states, the new law modifies the old rules. A New York statute, for example, has removed the distinction between lost and mislaid property and now generally permits the finder to keep what he has discovered, regardless of where he found it. The finder is, however, required to turn over the property either to the police or the owner of the premises where the item was found. If the true owner is not located during a stated period, the finder is then entitled to whatever he found.

The following case has contributed significantly to modern legal ideas on found property. It may seem to come from a Charles Dickens novel, but it actually happened. A villainous goldsmith sought to take advantage of a poor chimney sweep's boy. Would he get away with it? Read on.

Landmark Case

Armorie v. Delamirie

93 ER 664 Middlesex, 1722

Facts: Before Parliament banned the practice in 1840, many English chimney sweeps forced young children to climb the narrow flues and do the cleaning. Armorie was one such boy. But fortune smiled on him, and he found a jeweled ring. To discover its value, he carried the ring to a local goldsmith.

Armorie handed the ring to the goldsmith's apprentice, who removed the jewels from the ring and pretended to weigh it. He called out to the goldsmith that the ring was worth three halfpence. The goldsmith then offered that amount to Armorie.

Not being a fool, Armorie refused the offer and demanded that the ring be returned. The apprentice gave him the ring, but without the jewels.

Issue: ***Did the chimney sweep have a legal right to retain possession of the found jewels?***

Excerpts from Justice Pratt's Decision: The finder of a jewel, though he does not by such finding acquire an absolute property or ownership, has such a property as will enable him to keep it against all but the rightful owner. As to the value of the jewel, the Chief Justice directed the jury that unless the defendant did produce the jewel, and shew it not to be of the finest water, they should presume the strongest against him, and make the value of the best jewels the measure of their damages: which they accordingly did.

Accession

Accession occurs when one person uses labor, materials, or both to add value to personal property belonging to another. This generally occurs by agreement. Suppose Leasing Corp. agrees to lease a truck to Delivery Co., for use in its business. The contract may permit Delivery to modify the truck's storage space to meet its special needs. If so, the agreement should also state whether Delivery has to return the truck to its original condition at the end of the lease and whether Delivery is entitled to any payment for improvements made.

Accession
Occurs when one person uses labor, materials, or both to add value to personal property belonging to another person.

Sometimes one party makes accessions without agreement. If the improvements can be "undone" without damage to the property, then the improver must do that. For example, if Delivery Co. simply bolts a few shelves into the truck, it should remove them before returning the truck. Problems arise when the improvements cannot be removed without damaging the property. Assuming the property has become more valuable, must the owner pay the improver for the work done? It normally depends upon whether the improver acted wrongfully, or merely made a mistake.

Wrongful Accessions

If the improver knows he is making accessions without authority, the owner may generally take the improved property without paying for the work done. Suppose the lease between Leasing Corp. and Delivery Co. states that Delivery may not modify the truck without written permission. Delivery goes ahead anyway and reconfigures the truck to meet its needs. Even if the work substantially increases the truck's value, Leasing Corp. probably owes nothing for the accessions.

Mistaken Accessions

If the improver mistakenly believes he is entitled to add accessions, the owner probably has to pay for the increased value. Suppose that, based on its previous leases with Leasing Corp., Delivery Co. believes it has the right to modify its new truck, though in fact it has no such permission. If the modifications increase the value of the vehicle, Leasing probably has to pay for the accessions.

Bailment

Bailment
The rightful possession of goods by one who is not the owner, usually by mutual agreement between the bailor and bailee.

Involuntary bailment
A bailment that occurs without an agreement between the bailor and bailee.

A **bailment** is the rightful possession of goods by someone who is not the owner. The one who delivers the goods is the **bailor** and the one in possession is the **bailee.** Bailments are common. Suppose you are going out of town for the weekend and loan your motorcycle to Stan. You are the bailor, and your friend is the bailee. When you check your suitcase with the airline, you are again the bailor and the airline is the bailee. If you rent a car at your destination, you become the bailee while the rental agency is the bailor. In each case, someone other than the true owner has rightful, temporary possession of personal property.

Parties generally create a bailment by agreement. In each of the examples above, the parties agreed to the bailment. In two cases, the agreement included payment, which is common but not essential. When you buy your airline ticket, you pay for your ticket, and the price includes the airline's agreement, as bailee, to transport your suitcase. When you rent a car, you pay the bailor for the privilege of using it. By loaning your motorcycle, you engage in a bailment without either party paying compensation.

A bailment without any agreement is called a **constructive,** or involuntary, **bailment**. Suppose you find a wristwatch in your house that you know belongs to a friend. As we saw in the section above, you are obligated to return the watch to the true owner, and until you do so, you are the bailee, liable for harm to the property. This is called a constructive bailment because, with no agreement between the parties, the law is *construing* a bailment.

Karl Weatherly/Getty Images

When you loan your motorcycle to Stan, you are the bailor and Stan is the bailee.

Control

To create a bailment, the bailee must assume physical control of an item with intent to possess. A bailee may be liable for loss or damage to the property, and so it is not fair to hold him liable unless he has taken physical control of the goods, intending to possess them.

Disputes about whether someone has taken control often arise in parking lot cases. When a car is damaged or stolen, the lot's owner may try to avoid liability by claiming it lacked control of the parked auto and therefore was not a bailee. If the lot is a "park and lock" facility, where the car's owner retains the key and the lot owner exercises *no control at all,* there is probably no bailment and no liability for damage.

By contrast, when a driver leaves her keys with a parking attendant, the lot clearly is exercising control of the auto, and the parties have created a bailment. The lot is probably liable for loss or damage in that case.

EXAM Strategy

Question: Jack arrives at Airport Hotel's valet parking area in a Ferrari, just as Kim drives up in her Smart Car. A valet drives Kim's car away, but the supervisor asks Jack to park the Ferrari himself, in the hotel's lot across the street. Jack parks as instructed, locking the Ferrari and keeping the keys. During the night, both vehicles are stolen. The owners sue for the value of their vehicles—about $10,000 for Kim's Smart Car and $350,000 for Jack's Ferrari. Each owner will win if there was a bailment but lose if there was not. Can either or both prove a bailment?

Strategy: To create a bailment, the bailee must assume physical control with intent to possess.

Result: When the valet drove Kim's car away, the hotel assumed control with intent to possess. The parties created a bailment, and the hotel is liable. But Jack loses. The hotel never had physical control of the Ferrari. Employees did not park the vehicle, and Jack kept the keys. Jack's was a "park and lock" case, with no bailment.

Rights of the Bailee

The bailee's primary right is possession of the property. **Anyone who interferes with the bailee's rightful possession is liable to her.** Suppose that, after you loan your motorcycle to Stan, Mel sees Stan park the bike, realizes Stan isn't the owner, rides the motorcycle away, and locks it up until you return. Mel is liable to Stan for any damages Stan suffered while deprived of transportation.

Even a bailor is liable if he wrongfully takes back property from a bailee. If a car agency rents Francine a car for a three-day weekend but then repossesses it for use elsewhere, it is liable to her for any damages, even though it owns the car. The bailor must abide by the agreement.

If you store your furniture in a warehouse, the storage company is your bailee, but it has no right to curl up in your bed.

The bailee is typically, though not always, permitted to use the property. Obviously, a customer is permitted to drive a car rented from an agency. When a farmer loans his tractor to a neighbor, the bailee is entitled to use the machine for normal farm purposes. But some bailees have no authority to use the goods. If you store your furniture in a warehouse, the storage company is your bailee, but it has no right to curl up in your bed. The bailee may be entitled to compensation. This depends upon the agreement. If Owner leaves a power boat at the boatyard for repairs, the boatyard, a bailee, is entitled to payment for the work it does. As with any contract, the exact compensation should be clearly agreed upon before any work begins. If there is no agreement, the boatyard will probably receive the reasonable value of its services.

Duties of the Bailee

The bailee is strictly liable to redeliver the goods on time to the bailor, or to whomever the bailor designates. Strict liability means there are virtually no exceptions. Rudy stores his $6,000 drum set with Melissa's Warehouse while he is on vacation. Blake arrives at the warehouse and shows a forged letter, supposedly from Rudy, granting Blake permission to remove the drums. If Melissa permits Blake to take the drums, she will owe Rudy $6,000, even if the forgery was a high-quality job.

Due Care

The bailee is obligated to exercise due care. **The level of care required depends upon who receives the benefit of the bailment.** There are three possibilities:

- *Sole benefit of bailee.* If the bailment is for the sole benefit of the bailee, the bailee is required to use **extraordinary care** with the property. Generally, in these cases, the bailor loans something for free to the bailee. Since the bailee is paying nothing for the use of the goods, most courts consider her the only one to benefit from the bailment. If your neighbor loans you a power lawn mower, the bailment is probably for your sole benefit. You are liable if you are even slightly inattentive in handling the lawn mower and can expect to pay for virtually any harm done.
- *Mutual benefit.* When the bailment is for the mutual benefit of bailor and bailee, the bailee must use **ordinary care** with the property. Ordinary care is what a reasonably prudent person would use under the circumstances. When you rent a car, you benefit from the use of the car, and the agency profits from the fee you pay. When the airline hauls your suitcase to your destination, both parties benefit. Most bailments benefit both parties, and courts decide the majority of bailment disputes under this standard.
- *Sole benefit of bailor.* When the bailment benefits only the bailor, the bailee must use only **slight care.** This kind of bailment is called a **gratuitous bailment,** and the bailee is liable only for **gross negligence.** Sheila enters a pie-eating contest and asks you to hold her $14,000 diamond engagement ring while she competes. You put the ring in your pocket. Sheila wins the $20 first prize, but the ring has disappeared. This was a gratuitous bailment, and you are not liable to Sheila unless she can prove gross negligence on your part. If the ring dropped from your pocket or was stolen, you are not liable. If you used the ring to play catch with friends, you are liable.

Burden of Proof

In an ordinary negligence case, the plaintiff has the burden of proof to demonstrate that the defendant was negligent and caused the harm alleged. In bailment cases, the burden of proof is reversed. **Once the bailor has proven the existence of a bailment and loss or harm to the goods, a presumption of negligence arises, and the burden shifts to the bailee to prove adequate care.** This is a major change from ordinary negligence cases. Georgina's car is struck by another auto. If Georgina sues for negligence, it is her burden to prove that the defendant was driving unreasonably and caused the harm. By comparison, assume that Georgina rents Chance her sailboat for a month. At the end of the month, Chance announces that the boat is at the bottom of Lake Michigan. If Georgina sues Chance, she only needs to demonstrate that the parties had a bailment and that Chance failed to return the boat. The burden then shifts to Chance to prove that the boat was lost through no fault of his own. If Chance cannot meet that burden, Georgina recovers the full value of the boat.

The following case raises many of the issues in this section. Long before his time as president, Abraham Lincoln was a lawyer who argued more than 150 cases before the Supreme Court of Illinois. The case for Weedman is modeled after the arguments that a young Lincoln actually made.

You be the Judge

Johnson v. Weedman

5 Ill. 495
Supreme Court of Illinois, 1843

Facts: Johnson left his horse with Weedman, paying him to board and feed the animal. Johnson did not grant Weedman permission to ride the horse. Nonetheless, Weedman took the horse for a 15-mile ride.

Later that day, the horse died. However, the trial court found that Weedman had not abused the animal and that the ride had not caused the horse's death. The court did not grant damages to Johnson, and Johnson appealed.

You Be the Judge: ***Should Weedman pay for Johnson's dead horse?***

Argument for Johnson: Your honor, Weedman was in possession of my client's horse only to feed him and see to his basic needs. My client did not give him permission to take the horse out of the pasture. Weedman made personal use of my client's property when he took a 15-mile ride that was in no way necessary. The trial court's finding that Weedman did not abuse the horse during the ride is irrelevant. My client must be compensated for the loss of his animal.

Argument for Weedman: My client had a legal right to possession of the horse. Riding the horse was not a substantial abuse of his rights as bailee. The horse was returned to the pasture in good condition. It was not abandoned and was not devalued in any way by the ride. The plaintiff is therefore not entitled to any compensation. The coincidental death of the horse does not change that fact.

Exculpatory Clauses

Bailees often use exculpatory clauses in an effort to limit their liability. Recall that an **exculpatory clause** is any part of a contract that attempts to relieve one of the parties of future liability. Exculpatory clauses are commonly employed in parking garages, coat check locations in restaurants, warehouses, suitcase lockers, and so forth. An exculpatory clause at a coat check counter might state that the restaurant is not responsible for any loss or damage to the customer's coat, for example. Are such clauses valid? That depends upon several factors.

Exculpatory clause
A contract clause that attempts to relieve one of the parties from future liability.

If the bailor is a corporation and it has bargaining power roughly equal to the bailee's, a court will probably enforce an exculpatory clause. If a manufacturer agrees to park five of its aircraft in a hangar owned by Hannah Corp., and Hannah's storage contract states that it is not responsible for any losses caused by fire, flood, or hurricane, then Hannah is probably protected when fire destroys the manufacturer's planes. Both parties are businesses, and the law assumes they should live with whatever agreement they bargained for. However, even if the parties have equal bargaining power, an exculpatory clause is generally unenforceable if it attempts to exclude an intentional tort or reckless behavior.

When the bailor is a consumer, the exculpatory clause stands on shaky ground because judges generally presume the parties have unequal bargaining power. Courts look to see whether the clause was clearly written and easily visible.

EXAM Strategy

Question: A producer shot a low-budget horror movie and then delivered 10 reels of negative film to Filmprocess Corp, for processing. Filmprocess lost the reels. The producer sued for $5 million, the cost of production. Filmprocess based its defense on an exculpatory clause in the parties' contract, which stated that the producer accepted the full risk of loss for any film delivered to Filmprocess and that the producer would insure against such loss. Who will win the lawsuit?

Strategy: The producer delivered its film to Filmprocess. What relationship did that create? A bailment is the rightful possession of goods by one who is not the owner. The parties have created a bailment. Are exculpatory clauses enforced in bailments? If the bailor is a corporation and it has bargaining power roughly equal to the bailee's, a court will probably enforce a bailment exculpatory clause, except in cases of intentional tort or gross negligence.

Result: The producer will lose its claim for $5 million. Both parties were corporations, with roughly equal bargaining power, and the exculpatory clause is valid. There was no intentional tort or gross negligence, so the clause will be enforced.

The following case arises in a familiar setting and indicates the wide reach of bailment principles.

Tannenbaum v. New York Dry Cleaning, Inc.

2001 N.Y. Slip Op. 40076 (U), 2001 WL 913272
Civil Court of the City of New York, 2001

Facts: When Rob Tannenbaum picked up his $160 shirt at the dry cleaners, he found it badly torn. He sued, claiming negligence. New York Cleaners denied causing the tearing. In addition, the cleaner claimed that even if the company damaged the shirt, an exculpatory clause on the back of the ticket limited its liability to 10 times the cleaning fee of $2, or $20.

Issues: ***Was the cleaner negligent? If so, did the exculpatory clause limit the company's liability?***

Excerpts from Judge Samuels' Decision: To the customer, it doesn't seem reasonable that he should be able to recover only $20 for the destruction of the $160 shirt he took to the dry cleaner to be laundered.

The Limitation Clause reads as follows:

> In laundering, we cannot guarantee against color loss, and shrinkage; or against damage to weak and tender fabrics. The company's liability with respect to any lost article shall not exceed 10 times our charge for processing it.

The foregoing is printed in gray type, against a light yellow background, and is significantly more difficult for a person with good eyesight to read than the text on the front of the claim ticket.

This case is clearly one of bailment for hire. When a bailee is unable to return the bailed item, or (as here) returns it in damaged condition, a rebuttable presumption arises that the loss of, or damage to, the item is attributable to the bailee's negligence.

At trial, Defendant denied that the Shirt had been damaged while in its care, but did not offer, in the alternative, any explanation negating the presumption of negligence. Accordingly, Defendant is liable for negligence, unless its disclaimer is effective.

New York law has long disfavored exculpatory clauses that relieve a party to a contract from liability for the consequences of its own negligence. The law's disfavor has been expressed in strict requirements that the disclaimer of liability for negligence be made explicit and be communicated in such a way as to ensure that the party who is to be bound by the disclaimer has knowingly accepted such disclaimer.

It appears that Defendant sought to enjoy the protections of a disclaimer without alarming its customers by causing them actually to contemplate the Limitation Clause. Defendant offered no evidence that it had taken any steps to call Claimant's attention to its terms beyond giving him the Claim Ticket. [T]he Court finds that Claimant was not aware of, and did not assent to be bound by, the Limitation Clause.

Claimant is awarded judgment in the amount of $160, plus interest and costs.

Rights and Duties of the Bailor

The bailor's rights and duties are the reverse of the bailee's. The bailor is entitled to the return of his property on the agreed-upon date. He is also entitled to receive the property in good condition and to recover damages for harm to the property if the bailee failed to use adequate care.

Liability for Defects

Depending upon the type of bailment, the bailor is potentially liable for known or even unknown defects in the property. **If the bailment is for the sole benefit of the bailee, the bailor must notify the bailee of any known defects.** Suppose Megan lends her stepladder to Dave. The top rung is loose and Megan knows it, but she forgets to tell Dave. The top rung crumbles, and Dave falls onto his girlfriend's iguana. Megan is liable to Dave and the girlfriend unless the defect in the ladder was obvious. Notice that Megan's liability is not only to the bailee, but also to any others injured by the defects. Megan would not be liable if she had notified Dave of the defective rung.

In a mutual-benefit bailment, the bailor is liable not only for known defects but also for unknown defects that the bailor could have discovered with reasonable diligence. Suppose RentaLot rents a power sander to Dan. RentaLot does not realize that the sander has faulty wiring, but a reasonable inspection would have revealed the problem. When Dan suffers a serious shock from the defect, RentaLot is liable to him, even though it was unaware of the problem.

If the bailor is in the business of renting property, the bailment is probably subject to implied warranties. As we saw in Chapter 22 on product liability, the Uniform Commercial Code creates various implied warranties for goods sold or leased by a merchant. Recall that a merchant is someone in the business of selling or leasing that type of goods. A car rental company is a merchant with respect to its cars, so it rents the autos subject to implied warranties that they are fit for their normal purposes. Because these warranties are implied by law, they normally exist whether the parties say anything about them or not. Bailors may attempt to limit these implied warranties by provisions in the bailment agreement, but courts disfavor such limitations, especially when the bailee is a consumer.

Common Carriers and Contract Carriers

A carrier is a company that transports goods for others. It is a bailee of every shipment entrusted to it. There are two kinds of carriers: common carriers and contract carriers. The distinction is important because each type of company has a different level of liability.

Common carrier
A company that transports goods and makes its services regularly available to the general public.

A **common carrier** makes its services available on a regular basis to the general public. For example, a trucking company located in St. Louis that is willing to haul freight for anyone, to any destination in the country, is a common carrier. **Generally, a common carrier is strictly liable for harm to the bailor's goods.** Common carriers are governed by a statute known as the Carmack Amendment.[2] Under this law, a bailor needs only to establish that it delivered property to the carrier in good condition and that the cargo arrived damaged. The carrier is then liable unless it can show that it was not negligent *and* that the loss was caused by an act of God (such as a hurricane), an act of a public enemy (a nation at war with the United States), an act of the bailor itself (for example, by packaging the goods improperly), an act of a public authority (for example, a state inspector forcing a delay), or the inherent nature of the goods (such as fruit that spoiled naturally). These defenses are difficult to prove, and in most cases, a common carrier is liable for harm to the property.

A common carrier is, however, allowed to limit its liability by contract. For example, a common carrier might offer the bailor the choice of two shipping rates: a low rate, with a

[2]49 U.S.C. §11707.

In some states, there is a limit on a hotel's liability.

Contract carrier
A company that transports goods for particular customers.

maximum liability, say, of $10,000, or a higher shipping rate, with full liability for any harm to the goods. In that case, if the bailor chooses the lower rate, the limitation on liability is enforceable. Even if the bailor proves a loss of $300,000, the carrier owes merely $10,000.

A **contract carrier** does not make its services available to the general public but engages in continuing agreements with particular customers. Assume that Steel Curtain Shipping is a trucking company in Pittsburgh that hauls cargo to California for two or three steel producers and carries manufactured goods from California to Pennsylvania and New York for a few West Coast companies. Steel Curtain is a contract carrier. **A contract carrier does not incur strict liability.** The normal bailment rules apply, and a contract carrier can escape liability by demonstrating that it exercised due care of the property.

Innkeepers

Hotels, motels, and inns frequently act as bailees of their guests' property. Most states have special innkeeper statutes that regulate liability.

Hotel patrons often assume that anything they bring to a hotel is safe. But some state innkeeper statutes impose an absolute limit on a hotel's liability. Other statutes require guests to leave valuables in the inn's safe deposit box. And even that may not be enough to protect them fully. For example, a state statute might require the guest to register the nature and value of the goods with the hotel. These statutes are designed to limit risk—but of course, some people *like* risk. In the following case, a high-stakes gambler placed a large bet ... on his hotel dresser.

GNOC Corp. v. Powers

2006 WL 560687 N.J. Superior Court, Appellate Division, 2006

Facts: David Powers liked to wager. He and a friend arrived at the Hilton Casino in Atlantic City for a two-day stay. It was Powers' fourth visit to the hotel. They checked in at the front desk and received electronic room keys. Clearly visible signs, posted there and in each room, notified guests that the hotel was not responsible "for valuables or other property left in room," and that the hotel had a safe for valuables.

Powers won $76,000, which he converted into $25,000 cash, 10 gray chips worth $5,000 each, and 1 white $1,000 chip. He and his friend retired to their rooms. During the night, both Powers and his friend had various room service deliveries. Sometime before he went to bed, Powers placed his cash, chips, and a money clip on the dresser. At 4:19 a.m., the front desk issued a second key to Powers's room to an unknown person. Powers awoke to discover that his cash, chips, and clip were gone.

Powers ended up $25,000 in debt to the casino, and when he refused to pay, the hotel sued. Powers claimed that the Hilton owed him $76,000 for the stolen merchandise. The trial judge ruled in favor of the Hilton based on New Jersey's innkeeper statute, which states:

> If the proprietor of any hotel shall provide a safe or other depository in the hotel's office or in another convenient place, for the safekeeping of *any valuables belonging to guests* of the hotel, and shall place, in a conspicuous position in the room or rooms occupied by each guest, a notice stating the fact that a safe is provided in which valuables may be deposited, and any guest shall neglect to deliver valuables to the person in charge of the safe, the proprietor shall not be liable in any sum for the loss of valuables sustained by that guest, by theft or otherwise. . . . "Valuables" *includes* money, bank notes, bonds, precious stones, jewelry, ornaments [etc] and *any other articles of similar value.*

Powers appealed.

Issue: ***Did the innkeeper statute protect the hotel?***

Excerpts from the ***Per Curiam*** **decision:** It is defendant's contention that because casino chips are not specifically enumerated in [the innkeeper statute] and are not items of value as they are merely an accounting mechanism to evidence a debt owed by the casino, [the statute] does not apply to them. Further, he asserts that the chips do not "belong to guests," pointing to [a related statute] which provides:

> Each gaming chip and plaque is solely evidence of a debt that the issuing casino licensee owes to the person legally in possession of the gaming chip or plaque, and *shall remain in the property of the issuing casino licensee.*

To be sure, casino chips are not specifically listed as one of the enumerated items in the definition of "valuables." But the list is not exhaustive, as it is preceded by the word "includes" and followed by the words "any other articles of similar value." Included under the statutory definition of valuables are "money, bank notes, bonds, securities, checks, business papers, documents." As the motion judge observed: "While the statute may not say casino chips, it does have in there the things that have, like chips, no intrinsic value of their own [but] are evidence of either value or debt." And too, although the hotel owns the chips, while they are in the possession of the guest they belong to that guest until redeemed for cash.

So too, defendant's reliance upon [an earlier case called *Heinz*] is misplaced. *Heinz* concerned strict compliance with the statutorily required notice. Here, defendant concedes that the Hilton complied with the statutory notice requirements. Where, as here, a hotel is in strict compliance with the notice requirements, the Act operates as a bar to plaintiff's recovery.

Affirmed.

Chapter Conclusion

Personal property law plays an almost daily role in all of our lives. The manager of a dry cleaning company, the finder of lost property, and a bank officer who rents safe deposit boxes must all realize that they could incur substantial liability for personal property, whether they intend to accept that obligation or not. Understanding personal property law can be worth a lot of chips—but do not leave them lying around your hotel room.

EXAM REVIEW

1. **GIFTS** A gift is a voluntary transfer of property from one person to another without consideration. The elements of a gift are intention to transfer ownership immediately, delivery, and acceptance. (pp. 1120–1123)

2. **FOUND PROPERTY** The finder of property must attempt to locate the true owner unless the property was abandoned. State estray statutes have made some changes in the common law, but the following principles generally govern:

   - Abandoned property—the finder may keep it.
   - Lost property—the finder generally has rights superior to everyone but the true owner, except that if she found it on land belonging to another, the property owner generally is entitled to it.
   - Mislaid property—generally, the finder has no rights in the property.
   - Treasure trove—generally, the finder may keep it. (pp. 1124–1125)

EXAM Strategy

Question: The government accused Carlo Francia and another person of stealing a purse belonging to Frances Bainlardi. A policeman saw Francia sorting through the contents of the purse, which included a photo identification of Bainlardi. Francia kept some items, such as cash, while discarding others. At trial, Francia claimed that he had thought the purse was lost or abandoned. Besides the fact that Francia's accomplice was holding burglary tools, what is the weakness in Francia's defense?

Strategy: The finder of property must attempt to locate the true owner unless the property was abandoned. Is there any likelihood that the purse was abandoned? If it was not abandoned, did Francia attempt to locate the owner? (See the "Result" at the end of this section.)

3. **ACCESSION** Accession occurs when one person uses labor, materials, or both to add value to personal property belonging to another. If the improver knows he is making accessions without authority, the owner may generally take the improved property without compensating for the work done. If the improver mistakenly believes that he is entitled to add accessions, the owner probably has to pay for the increased value. (pp. 1125–1126)

4. **BAILMENT** A bailment is the rightful possession of goods by one who is not the owner. The one who delivers the goods is the bailor, and the one in possession is the bailee. To create a bailment, the bailee must assume physical control with intent to possess. (pp. 1127–1133)

5. **BAILEE'S RIGHTS** The bailee is always entitled to possess the property, is frequently allowed to use it, and may be entitled to compensation. (p. 1127)

6. **REDELIVERY** The bailee is strictly liable to redeliver the goods to the bailor. (pp. 1127–1128)

EXAM Strategy

Question: Shannon borrows Marty's car, but when she returns the auto, she hands the keys to Scott, who claims he is Marty's brother. Scott offers a driver's license and passport to reassure Shannon. Scott is actually a con artist. Marty sues Shannon. Outcome?

a. Marty will win.

b. Marty will win only if a *reasonable person* would have spotted the fraud.

c. Marty will win only if he in fact has no brother named Scott.

d. Marty will lose because Scott offered reasonable identification.

Strategy: Make sure you know the standard a bailee must meet for redelivering goods. (See the "Result" at the end of this section.)

7. **BAILEE'S DUTY OF CARE** The bailee is obligated to exercise due care. The level of care required depends upon who receives the benefit of the bailment: if the bailee is the sole beneficiary, she must use extraordinary care; if the parties mutually benefit, the bailee must use ordinary care; and if the bailor is the sole beneficiary of the bailment, the bailee must use only slight care. (p. 1128)

8. PRESUMPTION OF NEGLIGENCE Once the bailor has proven the existence of a bailment and loss, a presumption of negligence arises, and the burden shifts to the bailee to prove adequate care. (pp. 1128–1129)

Question: Lonny Joe owned two rare 1955 Ford Thunderbird automobiles, one red and one green, both in mint condition. He stored the cars in his garage. His friend Stephanie wanted to use the red car in a music video, so Lonny Joe rented it to her for two days, for $300 per day. When she returned the red car, Lonny Joe discovered a long scratch along one side. That same day, he noticed a long scratch along the side of the green car. He sued Stephanie for harm to the red car. Lonny Joe sued an electrician for damage to the green car, claiming that the scratch occurred while the electrician was fixing a heater in the garage. Explain the different burdens of proof in the two cases.

Strategy: In an ordinary negligence case, the plaintiff must prove all elements by a preponderance of the evidence. However, in a bailment, a *presumption* of negligence arises. To answer this question, you need to know whether Lonny Joe established a bailment with either or both defendants. (See the "Result" at the end of this section.)

9. EXCULPATORY CLAUSES Exculpatory clauses, seeking to relieve a bailee of liability for damage to the goods, may be enforced between two corporations of equal bargaining power but are seldom enforced against a consumer. (pp. 1129–1130)

10. DEFECTS The bailor must keep the property in suitable repair, free of any hidden defects. If the bailor is in the business of renting property, the bailment is probably subject to implied warranties. (p. 1131)

11. COMMON CARRIERS Generally, a common carrier is strictly liable for harm to the bailor's goods. A contract carrier incurs only normal bailment liability. (pp. 1131–1132)

12. INNKEEPERS The liability of an innkeeper is regulated by state statute. A guest intending to store valuables with an innkeeper must follow the statute to the letter. (pp. 1132–1133)

2. Result: Abandoned property is something that the owner has knowingly discarded because she no longer wants it. The burden is on the finder to prove that the property was abandoned, which will be impossible in this case since no one would throw away cash and credit cards. Because the purse contained photo identification, Francia could easily have located its owner. He made no attempt to do so, and his defense is unpersuasive.

6. Result: The bailee is strictly liable to redeliver the goods to the bailor. There are no excuses. The "reasonable person" standard does not apply. The correct answer is (a).

8. Result: Lonny Joe had no bailment with the electrician because the electrician never assumed control of the car. To win that case, Lonny Joe must prove that the electrician behaved unreasonably and caused the scratch. However, when Lonny Joe rented Stephanie the red car, the parties created a bailment, and the law *presumes* Stephanie caused the damage unless she can prove otherwise. That is a hard burden, and Stephanie will likely lose.

Multiple-Choice Questions

1. Which of the following requirements must be met to create a bailment?

I. Delivery of personal property to the intended bailee

II. Possession by the intended bailee

(a) I only

(b) II only

(c) Both I and II

(d) None of the above

2. Consider the following:

I. A house (value: $150,000)

II. A giant high-definition television in the house (value: $4,999)

III. The land that the house sits upon (value: $30,000)

IV. An old car in the house's garage (value: $5,001)

How many of these items are personal property?

(a) All four of them

(b) Three of them

(c) Two of them

(d) One of them

(e) None of them

3. Holding out an envelope, Alan says, "Ben, I'm giving you these opera tickets." Without taking the envelope, Ben replies, "Why would I want opera tickets? Loser." Alan leaves, crestfallen. Later that day, a girl whom Ben has liked for some time says, "I sure wish I were going to the opera tonight." Ben scrambles, calls Alan, and says, "Alan, old buddy, I accept your gift of the opera tickets. I'm on my way over to pick them up."

Does Ben have a legal right to the tickets?

(a) Yes, because Alan intended to transfer ownership

(b) Yes, because offers to give gifts cannot be revoked

(c) No, because no consideration was given

(d) No, because Ben did not accept the gift when offered

4. Gina has season tickets to Cardinals games. One Monday, she promises to give her tickets to Friday's game to Ed, a friend who works across town. On Tuesday, Gina hands the tickets to Al, an administrative assistant. An hour later, when Al still has the tickets and has not given them to Ed, Gina returns. "Sorry," she says, "but my cousins are coming to town this weekend. I'll need those tickets back." Gina is entitled to get the tickets back if Al works for…

(a) Gina

(b) Ed

(c) Both A and B

(d) None of the above

5. Craig finds a rare 1955 double-date penny, worth $4,000, on a city sidewalk outside a coin collectors' convention. The penny is ___________ property. If the true owner cannot be found, then the penny will belong to ___________.
   (a) lost, Craig
   (b) lost, the city
   (c) abandoned, Craig
   (d) abandoned, the city
   (e) mislaid, Craig

Essay Questions

1. During her second year at the Juilliard School of Music in New York City, Ann Rylands had a chance to borrow for one month a rare Guadagnini violin made in 1768. She returned the violin to the owner in Philadelphia, but then she telephoned her father to ask if he would buy it for her. He borrowed money from his pension fund and paid the owner. Ann traveled to Philadelphia to pick up the violin. She had exclusive possession of the violin for the next 20 years, using it in her professional career. Unfortunately, she became an alcoholic, and during one period when she was in a treatment center, she entrusted the violin to her mother for safekeeping. At about that time, her father died. When Ann was released from the center, she requested return of the violin, but her mother refused. Who owns the violin?

2. Ronald Armstead worked for First American Bank as a courier. His duties included making deliveries between the bank's branches in Washington, D.C. Armstead parked the bank's station wagon near the entrance of one branch in violation of a sign saying: "No Parking—Rush Hour Zone." In the rear luggage section of the station wagon were four locked bank dispatch bags containing checks and other valuable documents. Armstead had received tickets for illegal parking at this spot on five occasions. Shortly after Armstead entered the bank, a tow truck arrived and its operator prepared to tow the station wagon. Transportation Management, Inc., operated the towing service on behalf of the District of Columbia. Armstead ran out to the vehicle and told the tow truck operator that he was prepared to drive the vehicle away immediately. But the operator drove away with the station wagon in tow. One-and-a-half hours later, a bank employee paid for the car's release, but one dispatch bag, containing documents worth $107,000, was missing. First American sued Transportation Management and the District of Columbia. The defendants sought summary judgment, claiming they *could not* be liable. Were they correct?

3. During the Great Depression of the 1930s, the federal government's Works Progress Administration hired artists to create public works of art. The goal was to provide employment and beautify the nation. The artist James Daugherty painted six murals on the walls of the public high school in Stamford, Connecticut. During the 1970s, the city began to restore its high school. The architect and school officials agreed that the Daugherty murals should be preserved. They arranged for the construction workers to remove the murals to prevent harm. By accident, the workers rolled them up and placed them near the trash dumpsters for disposal. A student found the murals and took them home, and later notified the federal government's General Services Administration (GSA) of his find. The GSA arranged to transport the murals to an art

restorer named Hiram Hoelzer for storage and eventual restoration, when funds could be arranged. Over *19 years* went by before anyone notified the Stamford School system where the murals were. In the meantime, neither the GSA nor anyone else paid Hoelzer for the storage or restoration. By 1989, the murals were valued at $1.25 million by Sotheby's, an art auction house. Hoelzer filed suit, seeking a declaration that the murals had been abandoned. Were they abandoned? What difference would that make when determining ownership?

4. Marjan International Corp. sells handmade Oriental rugs. V. K. Putman, Inc., is a Montana trucking company. Marjan delivered valuable rugs to Putman for shipment from New York City to Tacoma, Washington. Unfortunately, there were several delays in transit. The truck driver encountered snowstorms and closed roads. His truck also overheated and required repairs in a garage. Before the driver resumed the trip, he stopped to pick up and load other goods. When the truck finally arrived in Tacoma, two bales of rugs were missing. Marjan sued on the grounds that Putman was a common carrier, but Putman claimed it was a contract carrier. What difference does it make whether Putman was a common carrier or a contract carrier, and how is that determined?

5. **YOU BE THE JUDGE WRITING PROBLEM** Eileen Murphy often cared for her elderly neighbor, Thomas Kenney. He paid her $25 per day for her help and once gave her a bank certificate of deposit worth $25,000. She spent the money. Murphy alleged that shortly before his death, Kenney gave her a large block of shares in three corporations. He called his broker, intending to instruct him to transfer the shares to Murphy's name, but the broker was ill and unavailable. So Kenney told Murphy to write her name on the shares and keep them, which she did. Two weeks later, Kenney died. When Murphy presented the shares to Kenney's broker to transfer ownership to her, the broker refused because Kenney had never endorsed the shares as the law requires—that is, signed them over to Murphy. Was Murphy entitled to the $25,000? To the shares? **Argument for Murphy:** The purpose of the law is to do what a donor intended, and it is obvious that Kenney intended Murphy to have the $25,000 and the shares. Why else would he have given them to her? A greedy estate should not be allowed to interfere with the deceased's intentions. **Argument for the Estate:** Murphy is not entitled to the $25,000 because we have no way of knowing what Kenney's intentions were when he gave her the money. She is not entitled to the shares of stock because Kenney's failure to endorse them over to her meant he never *delivered* them, and that is an essential element of a gift.

Discussion Questions

1. Consider revocable gifts. The example early in the chapter was, "The mule is yours from now on, but if you ever start acting stupid again, I'm taking her back." In such a case, the giver still owns the mule and can take it back at any time. Is this reasonable? Should stating a condition "cancel" a gift, or should the gift recipient in this example own the mule?

2. Is it sensible to distinguish between *inter vivos* gifts and gifts *causa mortis*? Should someone "on his deathbed" be able to change his mind so easily?

3. In the case of a gratuitous bailment, the bailee is liable only if he is grossly negligent. Is this good policy? If you agree to watch someone's property, shouldn't you be required to be careful even if you are not being paid?

4. Common carriers are not usually liable when property is damaged, but they are not liable for "acts of God"—floods, hurricanes, and the like. Is this fair? If you send a friend an important item via UPS and the UPS truck is hit by a tornado, who should pay for the lost item? Isn't UPS in a better financial position to pay for the loss? (In the end, they might well offer to pay for the loss, but they would not be legally *required* to do so.)

5. Dan checks into a nice beachfront hotel. He does not want to expose his $10,000 Patek Phillipe wristwatch to salt water, so he leaves it in the dresser in the room. When he returns from the beach, the watch is gone. He is shocked to learn that the hotel is not legally responsible for the value of his watch. Is the law reasonable in such cases? *Should* the hotel be liable? Why or why not?

CHAPTER 45

PLANNING FOR THE FUTURE: WILLS, TRUSTS, AND INSURANCE

© Steve Allen/Jupiterimages

Emily and Nick had been friends since childhood. In high school, they were teammates on the cross-country squad; in college, they often commiserated over tough courses and difficult romances. After college, Emily went to business school, and from there to a hedge fund. Nick followed his lifelong dream of becoming a high school teacher. But they still kept in touch and were members of the same running club. They even purchased houses near each other. When an old estate went on the market, Emily bought the manor house, Nick the gatekeeper's cottage.

By age 45, Nick was married with two children. Although his salary was modest, he saved carefully, purchased enough life insurance to replace his income if he died prematurely, and signed a will that would divide his assets in an orderly way. To pay the premiums on his life insurance, his family gave up resort vacations and went to visit their families instead.

To pay the premiums on his life insurance, his family gave up resort vacations.

"Boring!" thought Emily. "I can't believe you spend so much on life insurance," she scolded Nick. "You can't afford it." For her part, Emily was making a fortune each and every year. She had been divorced once, was currently separated from her second husband, had one child by each marriage, and was involved in a passionate affair with her personal trainer. Her husband was living in the house with their child, while Emily resided with her boyfriend in a fancy condo she owned downtown. She took lavish vacations, bought expensive jewelry and artwork, and kept intending to write a will. She earned so much money, she figured she did not need life insurance.

One bright fall day, Emily and Nick were driving in Emily's new Viper sports car to a road race. She was so busy showing Nick all the gadgets that she did not notice when the truck in front of them stopped suddenly. Her car plowed into the truck, killing them both instantly.

Nick's widow was devastated. But because of Nick's careful planning, she was able to keep her house and maintain her family's lifestyle. Emily's extended family did not fare so well. The ex-spouse, estranged spouse, children, and boyfriend spent years and hundreds of thousands of dollars squabbling and ultimately litigating the rights to her money, the house, the downtown condo, and the rest of her estate. Her hedge fund went out of business and was unable to pay her pension or even her salary for the last year. Because her ex-spouse and her husband were no longer receiving support from her, they had to sell their houses and move the children to new school districts. For children who were already suffering from the loss of their mother, this was an added emotional blow.

Bad things happen to good people (and good businesses). This chapter is about mitigating the risks of these bad things by planning for the future. Virtually everyone should have a will, and absolutely everyone should make careful, considered decisions on how much and what kinds of insurance coverage they need.

Introduction to Estate Planning

There is one immutable law of the universe: "you can't take it with you." Regardless of your fame or wealth, eventually you and your material goods will part. But you *can* control where your assets go after your death. Or you can decide not to bother with an estate plan and leave all in chaos behind you.

Definitions

Like many areas of the law, estate planning uses its own terminology:

- **Estate planning.** The process of giving away property after (or in anticipation of) death.
- **Estate.** The legal entity that holds title to assets after the owner dies and before the property is distributed.
- **Decedent.** The person who has died.
- **Testator** or **testatrix.** Someone who has signed a valid will. **Testatrix** is the female version (from the Latin).
- **Intestate.** To die without a will.
- **Heir.** Technically, the term *heir* refers to someone who inherits from a decedent who died intestate. **Devisee** means someone who inherits under a will. However, common parlance and many courts use *heir* to refer to anyone who inherits property, and we follow that usage in this chapter.

- **Probate.** The process of carrying out the terms of a will.
- **Executor** or **executrix.** A personal representative *chosen by the decedent* to carry out the terms of the will. An **executrix** is a female executor.
- **Administrator** or **administratrix.** A personal representative appointed *by the probate court* to oversee the probate process for someone who has died intestate (or without appointing an executor). As you can guess, an **administratrix** is a female administrator.
- **Grantor or settlor.** Someone who creates a trust.
- **Donor.** Someone who makes a gift or creates a trust.

Throughout this chapter, we use the masculine and feminine versions of *testator, executor,* and *administrator* interchangeably. These are dated terms that reflect a sexist era when men and women had different legal rights. It would be more progressive to bury these words in the same graveyard as *authoress* and *poetess,* but courts and lawyers still use them, and so must we.

Purpose

Estate planning has two primary goals: to ensure that property is distributed as the owner desires and to minimize estate taxes. Although tax issues are beyond the scope of this chapter, they are an important element of estate planning, often affecting not only how people transfer their property but, in some cases, to whom. For instance, wealthy people may give money to charity, at least in part, to minimize the taxes on the rest of their estate. In the *Paradee* case discussed later in this chapter, grandparents set up an insurance trust as a means of passing money tax-free to their grandchild.

Probate Law

The federal government and many states levy estate taxes (although traditionally, state taxes have been much lower). But only the states, and not the federal government, have probate codes to regulate the creation and implementation of wills and trusts. These codes vary from state to state. This chapter, therefore, speaks only of general trends among the states. Certainly, anyone who is preparing a will must consult the laws of the relevant state. To make probate law more consistent, the National Conference of Commissioners on Uniform State Laws issued a Uniform Probate Code (UPC). However, fewer than half of the states have adopted it.

Wills

Will
A legal document that disposes of the testator's property after death.

A will is a legal document that disposes of the testator's property after death. It can, in most instances, be revoked or altered at any time until death. Virtually every adult, even those with only modest assets, should have a will to:

- Ensure that their assets (modest though they may be) are distributed in accordance with their wishes.
- Select a personal representative to oversee the estate. If the decedent does not name an executor in a will, the court will appoint an administrator. Generally, people prefer to have a friend, rather than a court, in charge of their property.
- Avoid unnecessary expenses. Those who die intestate often leave behind issues for lawyers to resolve. A properly drafted will can also reduce the estate tax bill.

- Provide guardians for minor children. If parents do not appoint a guardian before they die, a court will. Presumably, the parents are best able to make this choice.

The following examples suggest another purpose for a will: to say what you really think.[1]

> I give to the Lieutenant-General Cromwell one of my words ... which he must want, seeing that he hath never kept any of his own.
>
> —Philip, fifth Earl of Pembroke, seventeenth century

> Seeing that I had the misfortune to be married to the aforesaid Elizabeth, who, ever since our union, has tormented me in every possible way; that not content with making game of all my remonstrances, she has done all she could to render my life miserable; that Heaven seems to have sent her into the world solely to drive me out of it; that the strength of Samson, the genius of Homer, the prudence of Augustus, the skill of Pyrrhus, the patience of Job, the philosophy of Socrates, the subtlety of Hannibal, the vigilance of Hermogenes, would not suffice to subdue the perversity of her character ... weighing seriously all these considerations ... I bequeath, to my said wife Elizabeth, the sum of one shilling.
>
> —John George, 1791

> I leave Parson Chavasse (Maggy's husband) the snuff box I got from the Sarnia Militia, as a small token of gratitude for the service he has done my family in taking a sister that no man of taste would have taken.
>
> —William Dunlop, Canada, 1842

> Before anything else is to be done, 50 cents is to be paid to my son-in-law to enable him to buy for himself a good stout rope with which to hang himself, and thus rid mankind of one of the most infamous scoundrels that ever roamed this broad land or dwelt outside of a penitentiary.
>
> —Garvey B. White, 1908

Requirements for a Valid Will

Generally speaking, a person may leave his assets to whomever he wants. However, the testatrix must be:

- Of **legal age** (which is 18).
- Of **sound mind.** That is, she must be able to understand what a will is, more or less what she owns, who her relatives are, and how she is disposing of her property.
- Acting without **undue influence.** Undue influence means that one person has enough power over another to force him to do something against his free will.

Legal Technicalities

A testator must comply with the legal requirements for executing a will: it must be in writing, and the testator must sign it or direct someone else to sign it for him, if he is too weak. Generally, two witnesses must also sign the will. Under the 2008 amendment to the UPC, a notarized will does not require any witnesses, but only a few states have passed this amendment. No one named in a will should also serve as a witness because, in many states, a witness may not inherit under a will. The importance of abiding by the legal technicalities cannot be overstated. No matter what the testator's intent, courts generally do not enforce a will unless each requirement of the law has been fully met. As we have observed before, close only counts in horseshoes and hand grenades.

---

[1]Jeff Stryker, "They Couldn't Resist: Oh, One Last Thing ...," *New York Times*, May 21, 2000, §4, p. 7.

Holographic Will

Holographic will
A will that is handwritten and signed by the testator, but not witnessed.

Some states recognize a **holographic will:** a will that is handwritten and signed by the testatrix, but not witnessed. Note that a holographic *must* be written in a testator's own handwriting—it cannot be typed. Suppose Rowena is on a plane that suffers engine trouble. For 15 minutes, the pilot struggles to control the plane. Despite his efforts, it crashes, killing everyone aboard. During those 15 minutes, Rowena writes on a Post-it note, "This is my last will and testament. I leave all my assets to the National Gallery of Art in Washington, D.C." She signs her name, but her fellow passengers are too frantic to witness it. This note is found in the wreckage of the plane. Her previous will, signed and witnessed in a lawyer's office, left everything to her beau, Ivan. If Rowena resides in one of the majority of states that accepts a holographic will, then Ivan is out of luck and the National Gallery will inherit all. One court has, indeed, accepted as a will a handwritten Post-it note that had not been witnessed.

Nuncupative Will

Some states will also accept a nuncupative will. This is the formal term for an oral will. For a nuncupative will to be valid, the testatrix must know she is dying, there must be three witnesses, and these witnesses must know that they are listening to her will. Suppose that Rowena survives the airplane crash for a few hours. Instead of writing a will on the plane, she whispers to a nurse in the hospital, "I'd like all my property to go to the Angell Memorial Cat Hospital." This oral will is valid if there are two other witnesses and Rowena also says, "I'm dying. Please witness my oral will." The cat hospital, however, is only entitled to her personal property. Nuncupative wills cannot be used to dispose of real estate. Ivan would inherit her farm.

Spouse's Share

Forced share
The percentage of a decedent's estate that a spouse is entitled to claim under state law. Also known as a **statutory share.**

A spouse is entitled to a **forced share** of the decedent's estate (unless she waives that right by written contract). In community property states, a spouse can override the will and claim one-half of all marital property acquired during the marriage, except property that the testator inherited or received as a gift.[2] Although this rule sounds easy and fair, implementation can be troublesome. If a couple has been married for many years and has substantial assets, it can be very difficult to sort out what is and is not community property. Suppose that the testatrix inherited a million dollars 20 years before her death. She and her husband both earned sizable incomes during their careers. How can a court tell what money bought which asset? Anyone in a situation such as this should keep detailed records.

In most non–community property states, a spouse can override the will and claim some percentage of the decedent's probate estate (again, unless he has waived that right by written contract). The Uniform Probate Code (UPC), provides a complex formula that depends on how long the couple was married and what percentage of marital assets each held.

Children's Share

Parents are not required to leave assets to their children. They may disinherit their children for any reason.[3] In most states, this is true even if the children are minors whom the testator was obligated to support while alive.

---

[2]Arizona, California, Idaho, Louisiana, Nevada, New Mexico, Texas, and Washington all have community property law; Wisconsin's system is a variation of the same principle.

[3]The only exception to this rule is Louisiana, whose laws are based on the French model.

However, the law presumes that a **pretermitted child** (that is, a child left nothing in the parent's will) was omitted by accident unless the parent clearly indicates in the will that he has omitted the child on purpose. To do so, he must either leave her some nominal amount, such as $1, or specifically write in the will that the omission was intentional: "I am making no bequest to my daughter because she has chosen a religion of which I disapprove."

Pretermitted child
A child who is left nothing under the parent's will.

If a pretermitted child is left out by accident, she is generally entitled to the same share she would have received if her parent had died intestate, that is, without a will. Does this rule make sense? How likely is it that a parent with sufficient mental capacity to make a valid will would *forget* a child? Do you think the father in the following case simply forgot?

Issue
A person's direct descendants, such as children and grandchildren.

In re Estate of Josiah James Treloar, Jr.

151 N.H. 460; 859 A.2d 1162; 2004 N.H. LEXIS 177
Supreme Court of New Hampshire, 2004

Facts: Josiah James Treloar, Jr.'s first will left his estate to his wife unless she died before he did, in which case one piece of land was to go to his daughter Evelyn, another to his son, Rodney, and the rest of his estate was to be divided equally among Evelyn, Rodney, and another daughter, Beverly.

After his daughter Evelyn died, Josiah executed a new will. To help his lawyer in preparing this document, Josiah gave him a copy of the old will with handwritten changes, including Evelyn's name crossed out. The new will left the estate to Rodney and Beverly equally. Evelyn's children and her husband, Leon, got nothing, although Leon, was named as executor. Josiah referred to Leon as "my son-in-law."

Under New Hampshire law, all **issue** (including children and grandchildren) can qualify as pretermitted heirs. The law assumes that if the testator does not leave anything to his issue or does not refer to them in his will, it is because he has forgotten them. They are therefore entitled to a share of his estate. If Josiah had mentioned Evelyn, then the assumption would be that he had not forgotten her or her children. Evelyn's children argued that they were entitled to a share of Josiah's estate because he had not left her or them out on purpose. Josiah's attorney was serving as executor (not Leon). When he refused to pay the children, they sued.

Issue: ***Are Evelyn's children entitled to a share of Josiah's estate?***

Excerpts from Justice Galway's Decision:[4] The purpose of the statute [on pretermitted heirs] is to prevent a mistake or unintended failure by the testator to remember the natural object of his or her bounty. This rule of law is conclusive unless there is evidence in the will itself that the omission was intentional. To be a pretermitted heir, the child must not be named in the will, referred to in the will, or be a devisee or legatee under the will.

The executor asserts that, although the will names neither Evelyn nor her children, there are sufficient indirect references to Evelyn to satisfy the statute. The executor first argues that the reference in the will to revoking "all prior wills and testamentary instruments" coupled with evidence of the prior will, which specifically named Evelyn, and the testator's handwritten changes to it, demonstrate that he had Evelyn in mind when he prepared the will.

The court's task is not to investigate the circumstances to divine the intent of the testator; rather, it is to review the language contained within the four corners of the will for a determination of whether the testator named or referred to Evelyn's children. We disagree with the executor that we must read the wills together. [The new] will stands on its own.

The executor next argues that the reference to Leon as the testator's "son-in-law" showed that he had Evelyn in mind when he drafted the [new] will. [T]he testator did

[4]For readability, we use the term "Evelyn's children" instead of "respondents" and "executor" instead of "petitioner."

not use his daughter's name. Nor did he use the phrase "son-in-law" in a bequest. Rather, he used the phrase "son-in-law" to identify the individual he wished to appoint as his executor.

Even if the will indirectly referred to Evelyn, these indirect references would not satisfy the statute for the purposes of disinheriting Evelyn's children. [T]he naming of one person, however closely related to another, without more, is no reference to that other. It is well established that there must be a reference in the will to the child himself. It is not sufficient to infer that the child was not forgotten because a sibling or other relative was remembered in the will.

For all of the above reasons, we conclude that Evelyn's children are pretermitted heirs.

As we have observed before, the laws regarding wills are very precise. It seems highly unlikely that Josiah remembered his son-in-law but forgot the daughter to whom the son-in-law had been married. No matter—the will did not meet the requirements of the statute, so Evelyn's children were in luck.

In drafting a will, lawyers almost always use the term **issue** instead of children. *Issue* means all direct descendants, such as children, grandchildren, great-grandchildren, and so on. If the will leaves property to "my children" and one child dies before the testator, the child's children would not inherit their parent's share. But if the will says "to my issue" and one child dies first, her children will inherit her share.

Per stirpes
Each branch of the family receives an equal share.

Per capita
Each heir receives the same amount.

The will must also indicate whether issue are to inherit per stirpes or per capita. **Per stirpes** means that each *branch* of the family receives an equal share. Each child of the decedent receives the same amount, and, if a child has already died, her heirs inherit her share. **Per capita** means that each *heir* receives the same amount. If the children have died, then each grandchild inherits the same amount. Suppose that Gwendolyn has two children, Lance and Arthur. Lance has one child, Arthur has four. Both sons predecease their mother. If Gwendolyn's will says "per stirpes," Lance's child will inherit her father's entire share, which is half of Gwendolyn's estate. Arthur's four children will share their father's portion, so each will receive one-eighth (¼ × ½). If Gwendolyn's will says, "per capita," each of her grandchildren will inherit one-fifth of her estate. Although it might sound fairer to give all grandchildren the same inheritance, most people choose a per stirpes distribution on the theory that they are treating their *children* equally. The following chart illustrates the difference between per stirpes and per capita.

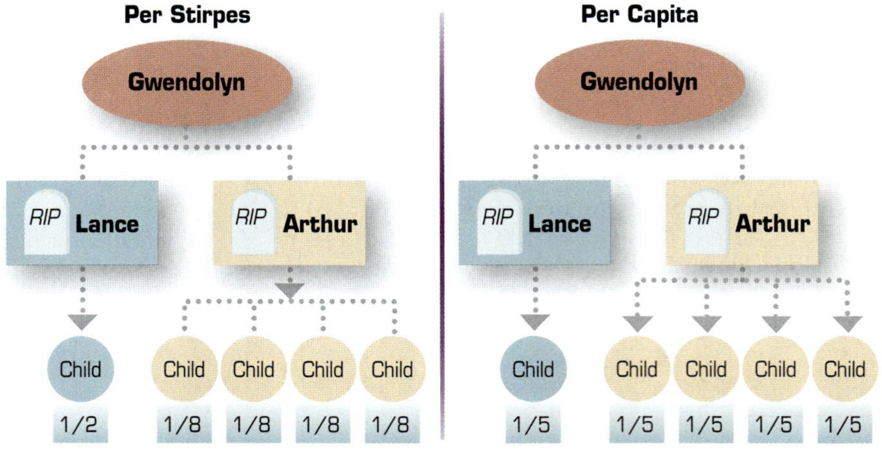

Amending a Will

A testator can generally revoke or alter a will at any time prior to death. In most states, he can revoke a will by destroying it, putting an *X* through it, writing "revoked" (or some synonym) on it, or signing a new will. He can also execute an amendment—called a **codicil**—to change specific terms of the will while keeping the rest of it intact. A codicil must meet all the requirements of a will, such as two witnesses. Suppose that Uncle Herman, who has a long and elaborate will, now wants his sterling silver Swiss Army knife to go to Cousin Larry rather than Niece Shannon. Instead of redoing his whole will, he can ask his lawyer to draw up a codicil changing only that one provision.

Codicil
An amendment to a will.

A change in family situation may also revoke part or all of a will automatically. Under the UPC, divorce or annulment cancels the ex-spouse's inheritance under a will. In some states, marriage, divorce, or the birth of a child revokes a will unless the instrument was clearly executed with that event in mind. A testatrix can state in the will, for instance, that she is making it in anticipation of her marriage.

Intestacy

When singer John Denver died unexpectedly in a plane accident, he had had several marriages, children, and platinum albums. His estate was worth $20 million. What he did not have was a will, as is the case with 60 percent of Americans. When someone dies intestate, the law steps in and determines how to distribute the decedent's property. Although, in theory, intestacy laws are supposed to be based on what most people would prefer, in practice, they are not. The vast majority of married people, for instance, leave all their assets to their surviving spouse. Most intestacy laws do not. In some states, if a married person dies intestate, some portion of her property (one-half or two-thirds) goes to her spouse, and the remainder to her issue (including grandchildren). Few people would actually want grandchildren to take a share of their estate in preference to their spouse. In other states, the decedent's estate is shared among her issue, her spouse, and her parents. If she has no issue, her spouse shares the estate with her parents. The moral of the story? As the late great law professor A. James Casner used to say, "Only a fool would die without a will."

Power of Attorney

A **power of attorney** is a document that permits the **attorney-in-fact** to act for the principal. (An attorney-in-fact need not be a lawyer.) Typically, a power of attorney expires if the principal revokes it, becomes incapacitated, or dies. But a **durable** power is valid even if the principal can no longer make decisions for herself. An **immediate power** becomes effective when signed; a **springing power** is effective at some time in the future, typically when the principal becomes incompetent and is no longer able to manage his affairs.

Lawyers generally recommend that their clients execute a durable power of attorney, particularly if they are elderly or in poor health. The power of attorney permits the client not only to choose an attorney-in-fact, but also to give advance instructions, such as "loan money to my son, Billy, if ever he needs it." If a client becomes incompetent and has no power of attorney, a court will appoint a guardian. As a general rule, it is better to make choices yourself rather than leave them to a court.

Probate

The testatrix cannot implement the terms of the will from beyond the grave, so she appoints an executor for this task. Typically, the executor is a family member, lawyer, or close friend. If the decedent does not select an executor, the probate court appoints an administrator to fulfill the same functions. The executor (or the administrator) has important responsibilities and, in a large estate, may spend a significant amount of time carrying out his functions. He has a fiduciary duty to the estate and is potentially liable to the heirs for any mistakes—from bad investment choices to errors in property valuation. Both the executor and the administrator are entitled to reasonable compensation—typically between 1 and 5 percent of the estate's value, although family members and friends often waive the fee.

Property Not Transferred by Will

A will does not control the distribution of joint property, retirement benefits, or life insurance. As explained in Chapter 43, property that is held in a joint tenancy automatically passes to the surviving owner, regardless of provisions in the decedent's will. This form of ownership is often used by family members—spouses or parents and children—as a simple method of transferring ownership without a will. Pension plans, other retirement benefits, and life insurance are also excluded from the decedent's estate and pass to whomever is named as beneficiary.

Anatomical Gifts

As immunosuppressant drugs improve, doctors are increasingly successful at transplanting human organs. The demand for these organs—hearts, corneas, kidneys, livers, pituitary glands, skin—is much greater than the supply. **The Uniform Anatomical Gift Act (UAGA) allows an individual to indicate her desire to be a donor either by putting a provision in her will or by signing an organ donation card in the presence of two witnesses.** Alternatively, DonateLives is an iPhone app that allows users to register as organ donors. The UAGA also provides that, unless a decedent has affirmatively indicated her desire not to be a donor, family members have the right to make a gift of her organs after death.

Living Wills

At the age of 32, Nancy Cruzan was in a devastating car accident. Lying facedown in a ditch, she stopped breathing for 14 minutes. Medics revived her, but she remained in a deep coma, unable to interact with her surroundings, although she did seem to feel pain. For seven years, she lay in a fetal position in a hospital bed. Her hands were so twisted that her nails cut her wrists. No one in her situation had ever recovered, but if she were fed, she could live 25 years. Cruzan's parents asked a court for permission to stop feeding her.

Ultimately, the Supreme Court upheld a Missouri law that family members cannot choose to discontinue treatment for an incompetent person unless there is clear and convincing evidence the patient would have made that choice herself.[5] After the Supreme Court decision, the probate court in Missouri heard new witnesses testify that Cruzan had said she would not want to live "like a vegetable." The lower court considered this clear and convincing evidence about Cruzan's wishes and granted the family permission to withhold feeding.

Living will
In the event that a person is unable to make medical decisions, this document indicates her preferences and may also appoint someone else to makes these decisions for her. Also known as an **advance directive.**

Health care proxy
Someone who has authority to make health care decisions for a person who is incompetent.

Spurred by the *Cruzan* case, many people executed so-called **living wills** or **advance directives.** Living wills permit adults to refuse medical treatment that would unreasonably prolong their lives, such as artificial feeding, cardiac resuscitation, or mechanical respiration. In addition, a living will can be used to appoint a **health care proxy** to make decisions for a person who has become incompetent. Concerned that living wills are not detailed enough, the Center for Ethics in Health Care developed POLST (Physician Orders for Life-Sustaining Treatment). These forms provide more detailed instructions on specific interventions.

Experts estimate that more than 75 percent of the population will not be capable of making their own medical decisions at the end of their lives. What happens if their family members disagree about what to do? A living will can resolve those disputes. Terri Schiavo was only 26 years old when her heart stopped beating one evening, causing brain damage that put her in a persistent vegetative state. Her husband said she would not have wanted to live

[5] *Cruzan v. Director, Missouri Department of Health*, 497 U.S. 261, 1990 U.S. LEXIS 3301 (1990).

that way and asked to have her feeding tube removed; her parents disagreed and fought him through the courts. Even Congress intervened to try to keep the tube in place. Her husband ultimately prevailed and the tube was removed, but only after 15 years of litigation and public uproar. If Schiavo had had a living will, her family would have had more privacy, fewer legal bills, and, perhaps, greater peace.

If Schiavo had had a living will, her family would have had more privacy, fewer legal bills, and, perhaps, greater peace.

Doctors are permitted to shorten a patient's life by withholding medical treatment. Can they go the next step and prescribe medication to end the life of a terminal patient who is suffering intolerably? Montana, Oregon, and Washington are the only states that specifically allow doctors to prescribe a fatal dose of drugs to a dying patient. In Oregon and Washington, about 50 terminally ill people die from **assisted suicide** each year.

Assisted suicide
The process of hastening death for a terminally ill patient at the request of the patient.

EXAM Strategy

Question: Tim's will leaves all his money to his cat, Princess Ida. After he dies, his widow and children claim that they are entitled to a share of his estate. Is this true? Will Princess Ida be living like royalty?

Strategy: The answer is different for his wife and children.

Result: Tim's wife is entitled to a share of his assets unless she signed a contract waiving that right. His children are entitled to a share of his assets unless he clearly indicated in his will that he intended to leave them out.

TRUSTS

Trusts are an increasingly popular method for managing assets, both during life and after death. In the United States, over a trillion dollars are held in personal trusts. A **trust** is an entity that separates legal and beneficial ownership. It involves three people: the grantor (also called the settlor or donor), who creates and funds it; the trustee, who manages the assets; and the beneficiary, who receives the financial proceeds. The trustee technically owns the property, but she must use it for the good of the beneficiary. In other words, the trustee holds **legal** title, while the beneficiary holds **equitable** title. A grantor can create a trust during her lifetime or after her death through her will. **There are four requirements for establishing a trust:**

Trust
An entity that separates the legal and beneficial ownership of assets.

- **Legal capacity.** As with any contract, the grantor must be of legal age and sound mind.
- **Trustee.** The grantor must appoint at least one trustee (who may be the grantor himself). The trust does not end if the appointed trustee dies or resigns. Either the trust instrument provides for successor trustees or a court can appoint one.
- **Beneficiary.** A trust must have specific beneficiaries, although it need not list them by name. It can instead list a class, such as "living children of the grantors."
- **Trust property.** The grantor must transfer specific assets to the trust, although these assets can be nominal. A grantor might, for instance, establish a trust with $10 and then add other assets later.

The Uniform Trust Code (UTC) establishes consistent laws on the creation and administration of trusts. About half the states have passed some version of this code.

Advantages and Disadvantages

Why do people use trusts? These are among the advantages:

- **Control.** The grantor can control her assets after her death. In the trust document, she can direct the trustees to follow a specific investment strategy, and she can determine how much income the beneficiaries receive. As an example, suppose the grantor has a husband and children. She wants to provide her husband with adequate income after her death, but she does not want him to spend so lavishly that nothing is left for the children. Nor does she want him to spend all her money on his second wife. The grantor could create a trust in her will that allows her husband to spend the income and, upon his death, gives the principal to their children.
- **Caring for children.** Minor children cannot legally manage property on their own, so parents or grandparents often establish trusts to take care of these assets until the children grow up.
- **Tax savings.** Although tax issues are beyond the scope of this chapter, it is worth noting that trusts can reduce estate taxes. For example, many married couples use a **marital trust** and parents or grandparents can establish **generation-skipping trusts** to reduce the estate tax bill.
- **Privacy.** A will is filed in probate court and becomes a matter of public record. Anyone can obtain a copy of it. Some companies are even in the business of providing copies to celebrity hounds. Jacqueline Kennedy Onassis's will is particularly popular. Trusts, however, are private documents and are not available to the public.
- **Probate.** Because a will must go through the often-lengthy probate process, the heirs may not receive assets for some time. Assets that are put into a trust *before the grantor dies* do not go through probate; the beneficiaries have immediate access to them.
- **Protecting against creditors.** A few states now permit so-called asset protection trusts. These trusts permit someone to place all his assets in a trust. He can spend trust funds himself, but his creditors have no right to the assets. For example, Hartwell has an unfortunate alcohol and drug problem, but he is no fool. When he inherited millions on his 21st birthday, he placed them all in an asset protection trust. Later he married, had children, and got divorced. He also was in a car accident that caused the death of a young investment banker. Both his wife and the banker's husband sued him, looking for financial support. But they are both out of luck. His assets are protected from all creditors.

Ethics Is an asset protection trust fair? Why would states permit their citizens to hide money from legitimate creditors? The short answer: to attract trust business from out of state. Trusts generate billions of dollars in fees each year. If you were a state legislator, how would you vote when this legislation came up for approval? If you had substantial assets, would you put them in such a trust? What Life Principles apply here?

The major *disadvantage* of a trust is expense. Although it is always possible for the grantor to establish a trust himself with the aid of software or form books, trusts are complex instruments with many potential pitfalls. Do-it-yourself trusts are a recipe for disaster. In addition to the legal fees required to establish a trust, the trustees may have to be paid. Professional trustees typically charge an annual fee of about 1 percent of the trust's assets. Family members usually do not expect payment. Trusts can also save some money, however, because the grantor will have fewer assets to probate, and therefore the executor's fees will be lower.

Types of Trusts

Depending upon the goal in establishing a trust, a grantor has two choices.

Living Trust

Also known as an *inter vivos trust,* a **living trust** is established while the grantor is still alive. In the typical living trust, the grantor serves as trustee during his lifetime. He maintains total control over the assets and avoids a trustee's fee. If the grantor becomes disabled or dies, the successor trustee, who is named in the trust instrument, takes over automatically. All of the assets stay in the trust and avoid probate. Most (but not all) living trusts are **revocable**, meaning that the grantor can terminate or change the trust at any time.

Living trust
A trust established while the grantor is still alive.

Revocable trust
A trust that can be terminated or changed at any time.

Testamentary Trust

A **testamentary trust** is created by a will. It goes into effect when the grantor dies. Naturally, it is **irrevocable** because the grantor is dead. The grantor's property must first go through probate on its way to the trust. Living trusts are particularly popular with older people because they want to ensure that their assets will be properly managed if they become disabled. Younger people typically opt for a testamentary trust because the probability they will become disabled any time soon is remote. Also they want to avoid the effort of transferring their assets to the trust while they are still alive.

Testamentary trust
A trust that goes into effect when a grantor dies.

Trust Administration

The primary obligation of trustees is to carry out the terms of the trust. They may exercise any powers expressly granted to them in the trust instrument and any implied powers reasonably necessary to implement the terms of the trust, unless that power has been specifically prohibited. **In carrying out the terms of the trust, the trustees have a fiduciary duty to the beneficiary.** This fiduciary duty includes:

- **A duty of loyalty.** In managing the trust, the trustees must put the interests of the beneficiaries first. They must disclose any relevant information to the beneficiaries. They may not commingle their own assets with those of the trust, do business with the trust (unless expressly permitted by the terms of the trust), or favor one beneficiary over another.
- **A duty of care.** The trustee must act as a reasonable person would when managing the assets of *another*. (This is a higher standard than requiring a trustee to act as a reasonable person would when managing his *own* affairs.) The trustee must make careful investments, keep accurate records, and collect debts owed the trust.

A trustee is liable to the beneficiaries of the trust if she breaches her duty. The following case provides an excellent example of a trustee who violated her fiduciary duty. The bad trustee was not only liable for violating *her* duty but also for aiding *someone else's* misbehavior.

Paradee v. Paradee

2010 Del. Ch. LEXIS 212
Court of Chancery of Delaware, 2010

Facts: Charles Paradee, Sr. (Senior) had a son, Charles Jr. (Junior), and a grandson, Charles III (who was called Trey). Senior's first wife died. When he was 71 years old, he married Eleanor, age 54. Junior and Eleanor grew to despise each other, thereby ending the relationship between Junior and Senior. But Senior maintained a loving relationship with Trey.

To provide for Trey, Senior created an irrevocable trust. He gave the Trust $366,000, which it used to buy an insurance policy on the lives of Senior and Eleanor. Once both of them died, Trey would receive $1.7 million. Eugene Sterling, the life insurance agent who sold the policy to the Trust, was the initial trustee, but Trey had the right to become trustee when he turned 30.

Senior began to slip mentally. He and Eleanor sent Sterling a letter instructing him to revoke the Trust. But the family lawyer, Joanna Reiver, told Eleanor that, oddly enough, irrevocable trusts are irrevocable. It turned out, however, that the trustee did have the right to loan its assets. Although lawyers told Sterling that any loan had to be on the same terms as an arms-length transaction, Sterling ignored this advice. He borrowed money from the insurance company, with the policy as security. He then loaned this money to Senior and Eleanor on terms that were highly favorable to them. If the Trust did not pay the interest it owed to the insurance company, the policy would lapse.

Senior died. At that point, the Trust had the right to call the loan, but Sterling made no effort to collect it. Trey turned 30, but Sterling did not tell him that he was entitled to be trustee. When Sterling died, Eleanor appointed herself as trustee. She stopped paying interest to the Trust, which meant that it could not pay what it owed to the insurance company, and the policy lapsed.

When Trey finally found out about the trust, he filed suit against Eleanor alleging that she had violated her fiduciary duties and that she had also aided and abetted Sterling in the violation of his.

Issue: ***Did Eleanor violate her fiduciary duty? Is she liable for aiding and abetting Sterling?***

Excerpts from Judge Laster's Decision[6]: Reiver testified at trial about Eleanor's motive in allowing the Policy to lapse: "I think that she did not want Trey to be in a position where he would be better off on her death, and know about it, and be in control of it." Eleanor consciously, intentionally, and vengefully refused to take any action to protect or preserve the Policy because she did not want Trey to benefit.

To prevail on a claim for aiding and abetting a breach of fiduciary duty, Trey had to prove (1) the existence of a fiduciary relationship; (2) that the fiduciary breached his duty; (3) that the non-fiduciary defendant knowingly participated in the breach; and (4) damages resulting from the concerted action of the fiduciary and the non-fiduciary.

At the time he made the Trust Loan, Sterling was Trustee and a fiduciary for the Trust. Instead of evaluating what was in the best interests of the Trust, he evaluated whether he could please his longtime clients, the Paradees. Sterling should have asked himself whether the Trust Loan was good for the Trust. He chose instead to ask whether there was a plausible reason to think the Trust Loan could be extended without harming the Trust. As Sterling stated in his letter to Reiver, "I can find no reason not to loan out a portion of the Policy value." He should have examined the Trust Loan from precisely the opposite point of view: whether there was any reason *to* loan a portion of the Policy value. If Sterling had considered what was best for the Trust, he would have refused the Paradees' request. There was no upside to the Trust in loaning funds to the Paradees.

It is bedrock law that the conduct of one who knowingly joins with a fiduciary in breaching a fiduciary obligation is equally culpable. Eleanor induced Sterling to breach his fiduciary duties by taking advantage of his primary loyalty to the Paradees. She is liable to the same extent as Sterling would have been, had he not passed away.

[Eleanor does] not dispute that once she became Trustee after Sterling's death, [she] should have informed Trey about the Trust and should have used Trust assets to maintain the Policy.

For the loss of the Policy, I award damages of [what the policy would have been worth if it had not lapsed]. Trey asks that [Eleanor] be ordered to pay his attorneys' fees and expenses. Having intentionally destroyed the Trust's value, Eleanor must bear the cost of remedying her breaches of fiduciary duty.

[6]For ease of reading, we refer to Trey by name rather than as "petitioner."

By the time Trey found out about the trust, Sterling was dead and thus no longer liable. But he was the trustee who had caused the most harm (by making the loan). If Eleanor had not been liable for aiding and abetting Sterling, Trey would not have been able to recover the full amount lost.

Termination

A trust ends upon the occurrence of any of these events:

- On the date indicated by the grantor.
- If the trust is revocable, when revoked by the grantor. Even if the trust is irrevocable, the grantor and all the beneficiaries can agree to revoke it.
- When the purpose of the trust has been fulfilled. If the grantor established the trust to pay college tuition for his grandchildren, the trust ends when the last grandchild graduates.

Even if one of these events does not occur, the **Rule Against Perpetuities** provides that a trust must end within 21 years of the death of some named person who is alive when the trust is created. For centuries, the Rule Against Perpetuities has been the law in England and the United States. However, nearly half the states now permit trusts that last forever—so-called **dynasty** or **perpetual trusts.** These trusts avoid estate taxes and generally allow donors to control their money forever. Whether or not eternal control is a good idea is best left to psychology texts.

Perpetual trust
A trust that lasts forever. Also known as a **dynasty trust.**

EXAM Strategy

Question: Maddie set up a trust for her children, with Field as trustee. Field decided to sell a piece of trust real estate to his wife without obtaining an appraisal, attempting to market the property, or consulting a real estate agent. Maddie was furious and ordered him not to make the sale. Can she stop him? Would she have to go to court?

Strategy: The answer depends upon what type of trust she has established.

Result: If the trust is revocable, Maddie can simply terminate it and take the property back. If it is irrevocable, she could still prevent the sale by going to court because Field has violated the duties he owes to the beneficiaries. He has violated the duty of loyalty by selling trust property to his wife. He has violated the duty of care by failing to act as a reasonable seller would.

INTRODUCTION TO INSURANCE

No matter how careful our behavior, we are all subject to risk—from automobile accidents, injury, illness, fires, early death, and other catastrophes. No wonder that, from the earliest times, people have sought insurance against these unpredictable and unpreventable dangers.

Insurance has its own terminology, so it is important to begin by defining key terms:

- **Person.** An individual, corporation, partnership, or any other legal entity.
- **Insurance.** A contract in which one person, in return for a fee, agrees to guarantee another against loss caused by a specific type of danger.

- **Insurer.** The person who issues the insurance policy and serves as guarantor.
- **Insured.** The person whose loss is the subject of the insurance policy.
- **Owner.** The person who enters into the insurance contract and pays the premiums.
- **Premium.** The consideration that the owner pays under the policy.
- **Beneficiary.** The person who receives the proceeds from the insurance policy.

The beneficiary, the insured, and the owner can be, but are not necessarily, the same person. If a homeowner buys fire insurance for her house, she is the insured, the owner, and the beneficiary because she bought the policy and receives the proceeds if her house burns down. If a mother buys a life insurance policy on her son that is payable to his children in the event of his death, then the mother is the owner, the son is the insured, and the grandchildren are the beneficiaries.

Before beginning a study of insurance law, it is important to understand the economics of the insurance industry. Suppose that you have recently purchased a $500,000 house. The probability your house will burn down in the next year is 1 in 1,000. That is a low risk, but the consequences would be devastating, especially since you could not afford to rebuild. Instead of bearing that risk yourself, you take out a fire insurance policy. You pay an insurance company $1,200 in return for a promise that, if your house burns down in the next 12 months, the company will pay you $500,000. The insurance company sells the same policy to 1,000 similar homeowners, expecting that on average one of these houses will burn down. If all 1,000 policyholders pay $1,200, the insurance company takes in $1.2 million each year, but expects to pay out only $500,000. It will put some money aside in case two houses burn down, or even worse, a major forest fire guts a whole tract of houses. It must also pay overhead expenses, such as marketing and administration. And, of course, shareholders expect profits.

Insurance Contract

An insurance policy must meet all the common law requirements for a contract. There must be an offer, acceptance, and consideration. The owner must have legal capacity; that is, he must be an adult of sound mind. Fraud, duress, and undue influence invalidate a policy. In theory, insurance contracts need not be in writing because the Statute of Frauds does not apply to any contract that can be performed within one year, and it is possible that the house may burn down or the car may crash within a year. Some states, however, specifically require insurance contracts to be in writing.

Offer and Acceptance

The purchaser of a policy makes an offer by delivering an application and a premium to the insurer. The insurance company then has the option of either accepting or rejecting the offer. **It can accept by oral notice, by written notice, or by delivery of the policy. It also has a fourth option—a written binder.** A *binder* is a short document acknowledging receipt of the application and premium. It indicates that a policy is *temporarily* in effect, but it does not constitute final acceptance. The insurer still has the right to reject the offer once it has examined the application carefully. Kyle buys a house on April 1 and wants insurance right away. The insurance company issues a binder to him the same day. If Kyle's house burns down on April 2, the insurer must pay, even though it has not yet issued the final policy. If, however, there is no fire, but on April 2, the company decides Kyle is a bad risk, it has the right to reject his application at that time.

Limiting Claims by the Insured

Insurance policies can sometimes look like a quick way to make easy money. More than one person suffering from overwhelming financial pressure has insured a building to the hilt and then burned it down for the insurance money. Unbelievably, more than one parent has killed a child to collect the proceeds of a life insurance policy. Therefore, the law has created a number of rules to protect insurance companies from fraud and bad faith on the part of insureds.

Insurable Interest

Insurable interest
Someone would suffer a loss if the insured event occurs.

An insurance contract is not valid unless the owner has an insurable interest in the subject matter of the policy. To understand why an insurable interest is important, read this tragic story. To celebrate their engagement, Deana Wild and James Coates took a sightseeing trip along the California coast with Coates's mother, Virginia Rearden. They seemed to be just one big happy family. Tragically, Wild slipped while walking along the edge of a cliff at Big Sur and fell to her death. That would have been the end of the story except that, the day before, Rearden had taken out a $35,000 life insurance policy on Wild, naming Coates and Rearden as beneficiaries. When the insurance company investigated, it learned that Coates was married to someone else. Therefore, he could not be Wild's fiance, and neither he nor Rearden had an insurable interest in Wild. It also turned out that Rearden had taken out the policy without Wild's knowledge. Ultimately, a jury determined that Rearden had pushed Wild over the cliff and convicted her of first degree murder. She was sentenced to life in prison without parole.

These are the rules on insurable interest:

- **Definition.** A person has an **insurable interest** if she would be harmed by the danger that she has insured against. If Jessica takes out a fire insurance policy on her own barn, she will presumably be reluctant to burn it down. However, if she buys a policy on Nathan's barn, she will not mind—she may even be delighted—when fire sweeps through the building. It is a small step to saying that she might even burn the barn down herself.
- **Amount of loss.** The insurable interest can be no greater than the actual amount of loss suffered. If the barn is worth $50,000, but Jessica insures it (and pays premiums) for $100,000, she will recover only $50,000 when it burns down. The goal is to make sure that Jessica does not profit from the policy.
- **Life insurance.** A person always has an insurable interest in his own life and the life of his spouse or fiancee. Parents and minor children also have an insurable interest in each other. Creditors have a legitimate interest in someone who owes them money. For some states, the standard is that you have an insurable interest in someone if the person is worth more to you alive than dead.
- **Work relationships.** Business partners, employers, and employees have an insurable interest in each other if they would suffer some financial harm from the death of the insured. For example, companies sometimes buy **key person life insurance** on their officers as compensation if they were to die.

Virginia Rearden pushed Deana Wild to her death from a Big Sur cliff. If the insurance company had known that Rearden did not have an insurable interest in Wild, the company would have refused to issue the policy, and Wild might not have died.

Material
Important to the insurer's decision to issue a policy or set a premium amount.

Misrepresentation

Insurers have the right to void a policy if, during the application process, the insured makes a material misstatement or conceals a material fact. The policy is voidable whether the misstatement was oral or in writing, and in many states, whether it was intentional or unintentional. **Material** means that the misstatement or omission affected the insurer's decision to issue the policy or set a premium amount. Note that a lie can void a policy even if it does not relate to the actual loss.

For example, John Cummings tested positive for cocaine during a visit to a hospital for treatment of a gunshot wound to his chest. When he applied for life insurance six months later, he said on the application that, in the prior five years, he had not used any controlled drugs without a prescription by a physician. He also specifically denied using cocaine. A year later, Cummings died of a gunshot wound to his head. (He truly should have upgraded his circle of friends.) In investigating his death, the insurance company obtained medical records from the hospital which revealed the cocaine use. Of course, the insurance company refused to pay on the policy. His beneficiary sued, but the court ruled that a misrepresentation can be material even if it is not related to the actual cause of death. If the company had known about his drug use, it would not have issued the policy or it would have demanded a higher premium. Cummings's policy was void.[7]

Bad Faith by the Insurer

Insurance policies often contain a *covenant of good faith and fair dealing*. Even if the policy itself does not *explicitly* include such a provision, an increasing number of courts (but not all) *imply* this covenant. An insurance company can violate the covenant of good faith and fair dealing by (1) fraudulently inducing someone to buy a policy, (2) refusing to pay a valid claim, or (3) refusing to accept a reasonable settlement offer that has been made to an insured. When an insurance company violates the covenant of good faith and fair dealing, it becomes liable for both compensatory and punitive damages.

Fraud

In recent years, a number of insurance companies have paid serious damages to settle fraud charges involving the sale of life insurance. The companies trained their salespeople to tell elderly customers that a new policy was better when, in fact, it was much worse. State Farm Insurance agreed to pay its customers $200 million to settle such a suit. Officials in Florida ordered Prudential Insurance Company of America to pay as much as $2 billion in damages after they determined that, for more than a decade, the company had deliberately cheated its customers. Prudential also trained agents to target the elderly.

Ethics Presumably, the agents knew that defrauding elderly people was wrong. Why did they do it? How could you protect yourself from being in that situation?

Refusing to Pay a Valid Claim

Perhaps because juries feel sympathy for those who must deal with an immovable bureaucracy, damage awards are often sizeable when an insurance company has refused to pay a legitimate claim. For example, a jury in Ohio entered a $13 million verdict against Buckeye Union Insurance Co. for its bad faith refusal to pay a claim. An Ohio sheriff stopped the

[7] *Cummings v. American General Life Insurance Co.*, 2008 U.S. Dist. LEXIS 37157 (Fed. Dist. Ct. 2008).

automobile of 19-year-old Eugene Leber. As the sheriff approached Leber's car, he slipped on ice and his gun discharged. By incredibly bad luck, the bullet struck Leber, permanently paralyzing him from the rib cage down. The insurance company recognized that it was liable under the policy, but it nonetheless fought the case for *16* years.

Consumers complain that insurance companies often "lowball"—that is, they make an unreasonably low offer to settle a claim. Some insurance companies even set claims quotas that limit how much their adjusters can pay out each year, regardless of the merits of each individual claim. If juries continue to award multimillion-dollar verdicts, insurance companies may decide simply to pay the claims.

In the following case, the insurance company ultimately paid the claim, but not fast enough to satisfy the jury.

Goodson v. American Standard Insurance Company of Wisconsin

89 P.3d 409, 2004 Colo. LEXIS 388
Supreme Court of Colorado, 2004

Facts: Dawn Goodson and her two children were in an automobile accident while driving a car owned by Chet Weber. He was insured by American Standard Insurance Company of Wisconsin.

To treat injuries that she and her children suffered in the accident, Goodson sought care from a chiropractor. She submitted these bills, totaling about $8,000, to American Standard. The insurance company offered a number of erroneous reasons why it should not pay the claims: that the chiropractor was not a member of American Standard's preferred provider organization, that Weber's policy was not in effect at the time of the accident, and that Goodson and her children needed to undergo an independent medical evaluation to determine whether their injuries were related to the accident and whether their medical treatment was reasonable and necessary. In the end, American Standard did pay Goodson's bills, but it took 18 months to do so.

Goodson filed suit against American Standard, alleging that it had engaged in a bad faith breach of the insurance contract. Although the company's delay in payment had not actually cost Goodson any money, it had caused her substantial emotional distress. The jury awarded Goodson and her children $75,000 in actual damages and an additional $75,000 in punitive damages. The appeals court overturned the verdict. Goodson appealed to the state Supreme Court.

Issue: ***Can Goodson recover damages for emotional distress without showing any economic loss caused by American Standard's delay in paying her claim?***

Excerpts from Justice Hobbs's Decision: To establish that the insurer breached its duties of good faith and fair dealing, the insured must show that a reasonable insurer under the circumstances would have paid or otherwise settled the claim. Compensatory damages for economic and non-economic losses are available to make the insured whole and, where appropriate, punitive damages are available to punish the insurer and deter wrongful conduct by other insurers. Non-economic losses recognized under the rubric of compensatory damages include emotional distress; pain and suffering; inconvenience; fear and anxiety; and impairment of the quality of life. To recover punitive damages, the insured must establish that the insurer's breach was accompanied by circumstances of fraud, malice, or willful and wanton conduct. A punitive damages award cannot exceed the amount of actual damages and, in certain situations, may be increased or decreased by the court.

Goodson proved to the jury that she suffered emotional distress as a result of this delay. The anxiety, fear, stress, and uncertainty she experienced occurred as a result of her worry about whether she would be financially responsible for her medical bills, which American Standard refused to pay. An insured purchases insurance in the first place so as not to suffer such anxiety, fear, stress, and uncertainty. The fact that an insurer finally pays in full does not erase the distress caused by the bad faith conduct.

Accordingly, we reverse the court of appeals and remand the case to that court with instructions to reinstate the trial court's judgment entered on the jury verdict.

Refusing to Accept a Settlement Offer

An insurer also violates the covenant of good faith and fair dealing when it wrongfully refuses to settle a claim. Suppose that Dmitri has a $100,000 automobile insurance policy. After he injures Tanya in a car accident, she sues him for $5 million. As provided in the policy, Dmitri's insurance company defends him against Tanya's claim. She offers to settle for $100,000, but the insurance company refuses because it only has $100,000 at risk anyway. It may get lucky with the jury. Instead, a jury comes in with a $2 million verdict. The insurance company is only liable for $100,000, but Dmitri must pay $1.9 million. A court might well find that the insurance company had violated its covenant of good faith and fair dealing.

EXAM Strategy

Question: Geoff takes out renter's insurance with Fastball Insurance Co. On the application where it asks if he has any pets, he fills in "poodle." Although he does not know it, his "poodle" is really a Portuguese water dog. The two breeds look a lot alike. A month later, his apartment is robbed. Fastball investigates and discovers that Geoff does not have a poodle after all. It denies his claim. Geoff files suit. What result?

Strategy: There are two issues here: Was Geoff's answer on the application a *material* misstatement? Was Fastball's denial in bad faith?

Result: Geoff's misrepresentation was not material—the difference between these two breeds of dog would not have affected liability on the renter's policy. If he had said he had an attack dog such as a Doberman, perhaps the premium would have been lower because the dog would scare off intruders (or higher because the dog would also attack friends and neighbors), but poodles and Portuguese water dogs are equally friendly. Fastball would be liable for refusing to pay the claim.

Types of Insurance

Insurance is available for virtually any risk. Bruce Springsteen insured his voice and Jamie Lee Curtis her legs. When Kerry Wallace shaved her head to promote the *Star Trek* films, she bought insurance in case her hair failed to grow back. Food critic Egon Ronay insured his taste buds. And an amateur dramatics group took out insurance to protect against the risk that a member of the audience might die laughing. Most people, however, get by with six different types of insurance: property, life, health, disability, liability, and automobile.

Property Insurance

Property insurance
Covers physical damage to real estate, personal property, or inventory from causes such as fire, smoke, lightning, wind, riot, vandalism, or theft.

Property insurance (also known as **casualty insurance**) covers physical damage to real estate, personal property (boats, furnishings), or inventory from causes such as fire, smoke, lightning, wind, riot, vandalism, or theft.

Life Insurance

Life insurance
Provides for payments to a beneficiary upon the death of the insured.

Life insurance is really death insurance—it provides for payments to a beneficiary upon the death of the insured. The purpose is to replace at least some of the insured's income so that her family will not be financially devastated.

Term Insurance

Term insurance is the simplest, cheapest life insurance option. It is purchased for a specific period, such as 1, 5, or 20 years. If the insured dies during the period of the policy, the insurance company pays the policy amount to the beneficiary. If the owner stops paying premiums, the policy terminates and the beneficiary receives nothing. As the probability of death rises with age, so do the premiums. A $200,000 10-year term policy on a 25-year-old nonsmoking woman in good health costs as little as $95 annually; at age 60, the same policy costs about $400. Term insurance is the best choice for a person who simply wants to protect his family by replacing his income if he dies young.

Whole Life Insurance

Whole life or **straight life** insurance is designed to cover the insured for his entire life. A portion of the premiums pays for insurance, and the remainder goes into savings. This savings portion is called the **cash value** of the policy. The company pays dividends on this cash value and typically, after some years, the dividends are large enough to cover the premium so that the owner does not have to pay any more. The cash value accrues without being taxed until the policy is cashed in. The owner can borrow against the cash value, in many cases at a below-market rate. In addition, if the owner cancels the policy, the insurance company will pay her the policy's cash value. When the owner purchases the policy, the company typically sets a premium that stays constant over the life of the policy. A healthy 25-year-old non-smoking woman pays annual premiums of roughly $1,900 per year on a $200,000 policy.

The advantage of a whole life policy is that it forces people to save. It also has some significant disadvantages:

- The investment returns from the savings portion of whole life insurance have traditionally been mediocre. Mutual funds may offer better investment opportunities.
- A significant portion of the premium for the first year goes to pay overhead and commissions. Agents have a great incentive to sell whole life policies, rather than term, because their commissions are much higher.
- Unless the customer holds a policy for about 20 years, it will typically generate little cash value. Half of all whole life policyholders drop their policies in the first seven or eight years. At that point, the policy has generated little more than commissions for the agent.
- Whole life insurance provides the same amount of insurance throughout the insured's life. In contrast, most people need more insurance when they have young children and less as they approach retirement age.

Universal Life

Universal life insurance is a flexible combination of whole life and term. The owner can adjust the premiums over the life of the policy and also adjust the allocation of the premiums between insurance and savings. The options are complex and often difficult for the customer to understand.

Annuities

As life expectancy has increased, people have begun to worry as much about supporting themselves in their old age as they do about dying young. **Annuities** are the reverse of life insurance—they make payments *until* death, whereas life insurance pays *after* death. In the basic annuity contract, the owner makes a lump-sum payment to an insurance company in return for a fixed annual income for the rest of her life, no matter how long she lives. If she dies tomorrow, the insurance company makes a huge profit. If she lives to be 95, the company loses money. But whatever happens, she knows she will have an income until the day she dies.

Annuity
Payment to a beneficiary during his lifetime.

In a **deferred annuity contract,** the owner makes a lump-sum payment but receives no income until some later date, say, in 10 or 20 years when he retires. From that date forward, he will receive payments for the rest of his life.

Health Insurance

Traditional health insurance plans are **pay for service.** The insurer pays for virtually any treatment that any doctor orders. The good news under this system is that policyholders have the largest possible choice of doctor and treatment. The bad news is that doctors and patients have an incentive to overspend on health care because the insurance company picks up the tab. It has been estimated that as many as one-third of the medical procedures performed in pay for service plans have little medical justification, which in the end is not good for the patient.

Instead of, or in addition to, pay for service plans, many insurers offer **managed care plans.** There are many variations on this theme, but they all work to limit treatment choices. In some plans, the patient has a primary care physician who must approve all visits to specialists. In **health maintenance organizations,** known as **HMOs,** the patient can be treated only by doctors in the organization unless there is some extraordinary need for an outside specialist.

Neither type of plan is perfect. In pay for service plans, doctors have an incentive to overtreat. In managed care plans, they may have an incentive to undertreat. For example, a recent study revealed that managed care plans tend to treat mental illness primarily with drugs. A combination of drugs and therapy tends to be more successful, but it is also more expensive.

Disability Insurance

Disability insurance
Replaces the insured's income if he becomes unable to work because of illness or injury.

Disability insurance replaces the insured's income if he becomes unable to work because of illness or injury. Perhaps you are thinking, "That will never happen to me." In fact, the average person is seven times more likely to be disabled for at least 90 days than she is to die before age 65. A significant percentage of all mortgage foreclosures are caused by an owner's disability. Everyone should have disability insurance to replace between 60 and 75 percent of their income. (There is no need for 100 percent replacement because expenses while unemployed are lower.) Many employers provide disability protection.

Liability Insurance

Liability insurance
Reimburses the insured for any liability she incurs by accidentally harming someone else.

Most insurance—property, life, health, disability—is designed to reimburse the insured (or her family) for any harm she suffers. **Liability insurance** is different. **Its purpose is to reimburse the insured for any liability she incurs by (accidentally) harming someone else.** This type of insurance covers tort claims by:

- Those injured on property owned by the insured—the mail carrier who slips and falls on the front sidewalk, or the parents of the child who drowns in the pool,
- Those injured by the insured away from home or business—the jogger crushed by an insured who loses control of his rollerblades, and
- Those whose property is damaged by the insured—the owner whose stone wall is pulverized by the insured's swerving car.

These are the types of claims covered in a *personal* liability policy. *Business* liability policies may also protect against other sorts of claims:

- Professional malpractice on the part of an accountant, architect, doctor, engineer, or lawyer.
- Product liability for any injuries caused by the company's products.

- Employment practices liability insurance to protect employers against claims of sexual harassment, discrimination, and wrongful termination on the part of an employee. Note that this insurance typically does not protect the person who actually commits the wrongdoing—the sexual harasser, for instance—but it does protect the innocent insureds, such as the company itself.

The following case explores the boundaries of liability policies.

You be the Judge

Metropolitan Property and Casualty Insurance Company v. Marshall

2010 NY Slip Op 51149U; 2010 N.Y. Misc. LEXIS 2824
Supreme Court of New York, 2010

Facts: Jacqueline Marshall's son, Evan, lived in a psychiatric facility. The hospital gave him a weekend pass to visit his mother. While at his mother's house, he murdered Denise Fox, decapitating and dismembering her and depositing her body in his mother's garbage cans. He pleaded guilty and was sentenced to 30 years to life.

Fox's family sued Jacqueline Marshall, alleging that she was negligent in not notifying the neighbors that her son was out on a weekend pass, and not telling them that he had a basement room in which he liked to dismember mannequins and watch violent pornography. Marshall said that she did not even know the hospital had issued a pass to her son.

Marshall had a homeowners liability policy with Metropolitan Property. Ordinarily, if an insured is sued, the insurance company represents her at trial. But instead, Metropolitan asked a court to rule that Marshall's policy did not cover this murder and the company did not have to represent her in the case brought by Fox's family.

Marshall's policy:

- Covered damages caused by an accident,
- Defined an accident as an event that is "unexpected, unusual, and unforeseeable," and
- Excluded coverage for an intentional act committed by an insured or at the direction of the insured.

Metropolitan refused coverage on the grounds that Evan's acts were intentional, not accidental.

You Be the Judge: ***Was Fox's murder an accident for purposes of the policy? Is Marshall covered by her insurance policy?***

Argument for Metropolitan: Newspapers described this murder as "one of the most gruesome murders in Long Island history." This crime was the opposite of an accident; it was cold-blooded and deliberate.

Insurance policies are not intended to protect against this type of behavior. Indeed, it would be bad public policy if they did. As a society, we want people to be held responsible for murders and not have insurance companies pay their liabilities. Besides, the policy clearly states that it does not apply to any intentional act.

Argument for Marshall: Jacqueline Marshall did not murder Denise Fox; her son did. The intentional act was his, not hers. If he had been the insured, the policy would not apply, but such was not the case.

Clearly, this murder was unexpected—the psychiatric hospital would never have released Evan if the doctors had known how dangerous he was. From Marshall's perspective, it was an accident. Nothing could have been more "unexpected, unusual, and unforeseeable."

Automobile Insurance

An automobile insurance policy is a combination of several different types of coverage that, depending on state law, are either mandatory or optional. These are the basic types of coverage:

- **Collision** covers the cost of repairing or replacing a car that is damaged in an accident.
- **Comprehensive** covers fire, theft, and vandalism—but not collision.

- **Liability** covers harm that the owner causes to other people or their property—such as their bodies, cars, or stone walls. Most states require drivers to carry liability insurance.
- **Uninsured motorist** covers the owner and anyone else in the car who is injured by an uninsured motorist.

Chapter Conclusion

Life is a risky business. Cars crash, people die, houses burn. So what can we do? Sign a will, buy insurance, and get on with our lives, knowing that we have prepared as best we can.

Exam Review

1. **WILL** A legal document that disposes of the testator's property after death. (pp. 1142–1149)

2. **HOLOGRAPHIC WILL** A will that is handwritten and signed by the testator but not witnessed. (p. 1144)

3. **NUNCUPATIVE WILL** The formal term for an oral will. (p. 1144)

EXAM Strategy

Question: If you were in an emergency situation and desperately wanted to prepare a new will, under what circumstances would a holographic will be preferable to the nuncupative option?

Strategy: The two types of wills have different requirements for witnesses. (See the "Result" at the end of this section.)

4. **SURVIVING SPOUSE AND CHILDREN** A spouse is entitled to a certain share of the decedent's estate. Children have no automatic right to share in a parent's estate so long as the parent indicates in his will that the pretermitted children have been left out on purpose. (pp. 1144–1146)

EXAM Strategy

Question: Josh was a crotchety fellow, often at odds with his family. In his will, he left his son an autographed copy of his book, *A Guide to Federal Prisons.* He completely omitted his daughter, instead leaving the rest of his substantial estate to the Society for the Assistance of Convicted Felons. Which child fared better?

Strategy: Pretermitted children fare differently from those named in the will. (See the "Result" at the end of this section.)

5. **PER STIRPES V. PER CAPITA** In a will, a per stirpes distribution means that each *branch* of the family receives an equal share. Per capita means that each *heir* receives the same amount. (p. 1146)

6. **REVOCATION OF A WILL** A testator may generally revoke or alter a will at any time prior to death. (p. 1147)

7. **INTESTACY** Sixty percent of Americans die intestate—that is, without a will. In this event, the law determines how the decedent's property will be distributed. (p. 1147)

8. **PROPERTY NOT COVERED BY A WILL** A will does not control the distribution of joint property, life insurance, or retirement benefits. (p. 1148)

9. **LIVING WILL** A living will permits an adult to refuse medical treatment that would prolong life. (pp. 1148–1149)

10. **TRUST** A trust is an entity that separates legal and beneficial ownership. (pp. 1149–1153)

11. **TRUSTEE'S DUTY** In carrying out the terms of a trust, the trustee has a fiduciary duty to the beneficiary. (pp. 1151–1153)

12. **CONTRACT** An insurance policy must meet all the common law requirements for a contract—offer, acceptance, and consideration. (pp. 1154–1158)

13. **INSURABLE INTEREST** A person has an insurable interest if she would be harmed by the danger that she has insured against. (p. 1155)

14. **MATERIAL MISREPRESENTATION** Insurers have the right to void a policy if the insured makes a material misstatement or conceals a material fact. (p. 1156)

Question: When Mark applied for life insurance with Farmstead, he indicated on the application that he had not received any traffic tickets in the preceding five years. In fact, he had received several such citations for driving while intoxicated. Two years later, Mark was shot to death. When Farmstead discovered the traffic tickets, it denied coverage to his beneficiary. Was Farmstead in the right?

Strategy: A misrepresentation is material if it affects the insurer's decision to issue a policy or set a premium amount. (See the "Result" at the end of this section.)

15. **BAD FAITH BY INSURER** Many courts have held that insurance policies contain a covenant of good faith and fair dealing and have found insurance companies liable for compensatory and punitive damages if they commit fraud, refuse to pay legitimate claims in a timely manner, or wrongfully refuse to settle a claim. (pp. 1156–1158)

16. **PROPERTY INSURANCE** Property insurance covers physical damage to real estate, personal property (boats, furnishings), or inventory from causes such as fire, smoke, lightning, wind, riot, vandalism, or theft. (p. 1158)

17. **ANNUITIES** Annuities are the reverse of life insurance policies; they make payments *until* death. (pp. 1159–1160)

18. **HEALTH INSURANCE** Health insurance is available in pay for service plans, managed care plans, or HMOs. (p. 1160)

19. **DISABILITY INSURANCE** Disability insurance replaces the insured's income if he becomes unable to work because of illness or injury. (p. 1160)

20. **LIABILITY INSURANCE** Liability insurance reimburses the insured for any liability that she incurs by accidentally harming someone else. (pp. 1160–1161)

3. Result: A holographic will does not require witnesses, a nuncupative will requires three.

4. Result: Because the son was not totally omitted from the will, he is entitled to nothing more than the book, while the daughter who received nothing under the will gets more than her brother—she receives whatever share she would be entitled to if Josh had died intestate.

14. Result: If Mark had told the truth, Farmstead still would have issued the policy, but the premium would have been higher. It can refuse to pay the claim, even though the issue that he lied about was not a factor in his death.

MULTIPLE-CHOICE QUESTIONS

1. **CPA QUESTION** A decedent's will provided that the estate was to be divided among the decedent's issue per capita and not per stirpes. If there are two surviving children and three grandchildren who are children of a predeceased child at the time the will is probated, how will the estate be divided?

   (a) 1⁄2 to each surviving child

   (b) 1⁄3 to each surviving child and 1⁄9 to each grandchild

   (c) 1⁄4 to each surviving child and 1⁄6 to each grandchild

   (d) 1⁄5 to each surviving child and grandchild

2. **CPA QUESTION** A personal representative of an estate would breach her fiduciary duties if she:

   (a) Combined personal funds with funds of the estate so that both could purchase Treasury bills

   (b) Represented the estate in a lawsuit brought against it by a disgruntled relative of the decedent

   (c) Distributed property in satisfaction of the decedent's debts

   (d) Engaged a non-CPA to prepare the records for the estate's final accounting

3. Blake tells his client that there are five good reasons to set up a trust. Which of the following is *not* a good reason?

(a) To pay his grandchildren's college tuition if they go to the same college he attended

(b) To save money, since a trust is cheaper than a will

(c) To make sure the money is properly invested

(d) To avoid probate

(e) To safeguard his privacy

4. A(n) ________ power of attorney becomes effective when signed. A(n) ________ power of attorney becomes effective at a later date. A(n) ________ power of attorney is valid even if the principal becomes incapacitated.

(a) durable, springing, immediate

(b) springing, durable, durable

(c) immediate, springing, durable

(d) immediate, durable, durable

5. If Chip buys an insurance policy covering his daughter Sarah's apartment, then ________ is the insured, ________ is the beneficiary, and ________ is the owner.

(a) Sarah, Sarah, Sarah,

(b) Chip, Chip, Chip

(c) Sarah, Chip, Chip

(d) Sarah, Sarah, Chip

Essay Questions

1. If your grandparents were to die leaving a large estate, and all of their children were also dead, would you prefer a per stirpes or per capita distribution?

2. **YOU BE THE JUDGE WRITING PROBLEM** Linda and Eddie had two children before they were divorced. Under the terms of their divorce, Eddie became the owner of their house. When he died suddenly, their children inherited the property. Linda moved into the house with the children and began paying the mortgage that was in Eddie's name. She also took out fire insurance. When the house burned down, the insurance company refused to pay the policy because she did not have an insurable interest. Do you agree? **Argument for the Insurance Company:** Linda did not own the house; therefore, she had no insurable interest. **Argument for Linda:** She was harmed when the house burned down because she and her children had no place to live. She was paying the mortgage, so she also had a financial interest.

3. Dannie Harvey sued her employer, O. R. Whitaker, for sexual harassment, discrimination, and defamation. Whitaker counterclaimed for libel and slander, requesting $1 million in punitive damages. Both Whitaker and Harvey were insured by Allstate under identical homeowner's policies. This policy explicitly promised to defend Harvey against the exact claim Whitaker had made against her. Harvey's

Allstate agent, however, told her that she was not covered. Because the agent kept all copies of Harvey's insurance policies in his office, she took him at his word. She had no choice but to defend against the claim on her own. Whitaker mounted an exceedingly hostile litigation attack, taking 80 depositions. After a year, Allstate agreed to defend Harvey. However, instead of hiring the lawyer who had been representing her, it chose another lawyer who had no expertise in this type of case and was a close friend of Whitaker's attorney. Harvey's new lawyer refused to meet her or to attend any depositions. Harvey and Whitaker finally settled. Whitaker had spent $1 million in legal fees, Harvey $169,000, and Allstate $2,513. Does Harvey have a claim against Allstate?

4. Clyde received a letter from his automobile insurance company notifying him that it would not renew his policy that was set to expire on February 28. Clyde did not obtain another policy, and, in a burst of astonishingly bad luck, on March 1, at 2:30 a.m., he struck another vehicle, killing two men. Later that day, Clyde applied for insurance coverage. As part of this application, he indicated that he had not been involved in any accident in the last three years. The new policy was effective as of 12:01 a.m. on March 1. Will the estates of the two dead men be able to recover under this policy?

5. Da-Keen is the trustee of a trust that was established by his parents to pay his children's college tuition. One of his children is going to Princeton, where the tuition is more than $50,000. Another child is attending a state university, where the tuition is one-tenth of Princeton's. He is paying both of these tuition bills. In addition, he has used trust assets to buy bonds issued by Harvard, the college he attended. Has Da-Keen violated his fiduciary duty?

Discussion Questions

1. Suzy Tomlinson, 74, met a tragic end—she drowned, fully clothed, in her bathtub after a night out partying with 36-year-old J. B. Carlson. He had taken her home at 1 a.m. and was the last person to see her alive. The two were not only party buddies; Suzy was on the board of directors of a company J. B. had started. Her family was stunned to find out that she had a $15 million life insurance policy, with the proceeds payable to a company J. B. controlled. He said it was a key person policy. He wanted to protect the company if she died because she had frequently introduced him to potential investors. Is the life insurance policy valid?

2. Should you have a will? Do you have one?

3. Is an asset protection trust fair? Should wealthy people be able to avoid paying their liabilities? What about perpetual trusts that avoid estate taxes forever? If you were a state legislator, how would you vote when this legislation came up for approval? If you had substantial assets, would you put them in such a trust? What Life Principles apply here?

4. Billionaire Warren Buffett said that children should inherit enough money so that they can do anything, but not so much that they can do nothing. Is it good for people to inherit money? How much? At what age? How much would you like to leave your children?

5. **ETHICS** Donna and Carl Nichols each bought term life insurance from Prudential Insurance Company of America. These policies contained a provision stating that if the insured became disabled, the premiums did not have to be paid and the policy would still stay in effect. This term is called a "waiver of premium." Carl became totally disabled, and his premiums were waived. Some years later, two Prudential sales managers convinced the Nicholses to convert their term life insurance policies into whole life insurance policies. They promised that, once Carl made the conversion, he would only have to pay premiums on the new policy for a six-month waiting period. They even wrote "WP to be included in this policy" on the application form. "WP" stood for waiver of premium benefit. Only after the new policy was issued did the Nicholses learn that Prudential would not waive the premium. The Nicholses had exchanged a policy on which they owed nothing further for a policy on which they now had to pay premiums that they could not afford. Do the Nicholses have a claim against Prudential? Regardless of the legal outcome, did Prudential have an ethical obligation to the Nicholses?

APPENDIX A

The Constitution of the United States

Preamble

We the People of the United States, in Order to form a more perfect Union, establish Justice, insure domestic Tranquility, provide for the common defense, promote the general Welfare, and secure the Blessings of Liberty to ourselves and our Posterity, do ordain and establish this Constitution for the United States of America.

ARTICLE I

Section 1.

All legislative Powers herein granted shall be vested in a Congress of the United States, which shall consist of a Senate and House of Representatives.

Section 2.

The House of Representatives shall be composed of Members chosen every second Year by the People of the several States, and the Electors in each State shall have the Qualifications requisite for Electors of the most numerous Branch of the State Legislature.

No Person shall be a Representative who shall not have attained to the Age of twenty five Years, and been seven Years a Citizen of the United States, and who shall not, when elected, be an Inhabitant of that State in which he shall be chosen.

Representatives and direct Taxes shall be apportioned among the several States which may be included within this Union, according to their respective Numbers, which shall be determined by adding to the whole Number of free Persons, including those bound to Service for a Term of Years, and excluding Indians not taxed, three fifths of all other Persons. The actual Enumeration shall be made within three Years after the first Meeting of the Congress of the United States, and within every subsequent Term of ten Years, in such Manner as they shall by Law direct. The number of Representatives shall not exceed one for every thirty Thousand, but each State shall have at Least one Representative; and until such enumeration shall be made, the State of New Hampshire shall be entitled to chuse three, Massachusetts eight, Rhode Island and Providence Plantations one, Connecticut five, New-York six, New Jersey four, Pennsylvania eight, Delaware one, Maryland six, Virginia ten, North Carolina five, South Carolina five, and Georgia three.

When vacancies happen in the Representation from any State, the Executive Authority thereof shall issue Writs of Election to fill such vacancies.

The House of Representatives shall chuse their Speaker and other Officers; and shall have the sole Power of Impeachment.

Section 3.

The Senate of the United States shall be composed of two Senators from each State, chosen by the Legislature thereof, for six Years; and each Senator shall have one Vote.

Immediately after they shall be assembled in Consequence of the first Election, they shall be divided as equally as may be into three Classes. The Seats of the Senators of the first Class shall be vacated at the Expiration of the second Year, of the second Class at the Expiration of the fourth Year, and of the third Class at the Expiration of the sixth Year, so that one third may be chosen every second Year; and if Vacancies happen by Resignation or otherwise, during the Recess of the Legislature of any State, the Executive thereof may make temporary Appointments until the next Meeting of the Legislature, which shall then fill such Vacancies.

No Person shall be a Senator who shall not have attained to the Age of thirty Years, and been nine Years a Citizen of the United States, and who shall not, when elected, be an Inhabitant of that State for which he shall be chosen.

The Vice President of the United States shall be President of the Senate, but shall have no Vote, unless they be equally divided.

The Senate shall chuse their other Officers, and also a President pro tempore, in the Absence of the Vice President, or when he shall exercise the Office of President of the United States.

The Senate shall have the sole power to try all Impeachments. When sitting for that Purpose, they shall be an Oath or Affirmation. When the President of the United States is tried, the Chief Justice shall preside: And no Person shall be convicted without the Concurrence of two thirds of the Members present.

Judgment in Cases of Impeachment shall not extend further than to removal from Office, and disqualification to hold and enjoy any Office of honor, Trust or Profit under the United States: but the Party convicted shall nevertheless be liable and subject to Indictment, Trial, Judgment and Punishment, according to Law.

Section 4.

The Times, Places and Manner of holding Elections for Senators and Representatives, shall be prescribed in each State by the Legislature thereof: but the Congress may at any time by Law make or alter such Regulations, except as to the Places of chusing Senators.

The Congress shall assemble at least once in every Year, and such Meeting shall be on the first Monday in December, unless they shall by Law appoint a different Day.

Section 5.

Each House shall be the Judge of the Elections, Returns and Qualifications of its own Members, and a Majority of each shall constitute a Quorum to do Business; but a smaller Number may adjourn from day to day, and may be authorized to compel the Attendance of absent Members, in such Manner, and under such Penalties as each House may provide.

Each House may determine the Rules of its Proceedings, punish its Members for disorderly Behaviour, and, with the Concurrence of two thirds, expel a Member.

Each House shall keep a Journal of its Proceedings, and from time to time publish the same, excepting such Parts as may in their Judgment require Secrecy; and the Yeas and Nays of the Members of either House on any question shall, at the Desire of one fifth of those Present, be entered on the Journal.

Neither House, during the Session of Congress, shall, without the Consent of the other, adjourn for more than three days, nor to any other Place than that in which the two Houses shall be sitting.

Section 6.

The Senators and Representatives shall receive a Compensation for their Services, to be ascertained by Law, and paid out of the Treasury of the United States. They shall in all Cases, except Treason, Felony and Breach of the Peace, be privileged from Arrest during their Attendance at the Session of their respective Houses, and in going to and returning from the same; and for any Speech or Debate in either House, they shall not be questioned in any other Place.

No Senator or Representative shall, during the Time for which he was elected, be appointed to any civil Office under the Authority of the United States, which shall have been created, or the Emoluments whereof shall have been encreased during such time; and no Person holding any Office under the United States, shall be a Member of either House during his Continuance in Office.

Section 7.

All Bills for raising Revenue shall originate in the House of Representatives; but the Senate may propose or concur with Amendments as on other Bills.

Every Bill which shall have passed the House of Representatives and the Senate, shall, before it become a Law, be presented to the President of the United States; If he approve he shall sign it, but if not he shall return it, with his Objections to that House in which it shall have originated, who shall enter the Objections at large on their Journal, and proceed to reconsider it. If after such Reconsideration two thirds of that House shall agree to pass the Bill, it shall be sent, together with the Objections, to the other House, by which it shall likewise be reconsidered, and if approved by two thirds of that House, it shall become a Law. But in all such Cases the Votes of both Houses shall be determined by Yeas and Nays, and the Names of the Persons voting for and against the Bill shall be entered on the Journal of each House respectively. If any Bill shall not be returned by the President within ten Days (Sundays excepted) after it shall have been presented to him, the Same shall be a Law, in like Manner as if he had signed it, unless the Congress by their Adjournment prevent its Return, in which Case it shall not be a Law.

Every Order, Resolution, or Vote to which the Concurrence of the Senate and House of Representatives may be necessary (except on a question of Adjournment) shall be presented to the President of the United States; and before the Same shall take Effect, shall be approved by him, or being disapproved by him, shall be repassed by two thirds of the Senate and House of Representatives, according to the Rules and Limitations prescribed in the Case of a Bill.

Section 8.

The Congress shall have Power to lay and collect Taxes, Duties, Imposts and Excises, to pay the Debts and provide for the common Defence and general Welfare of the United States; but all Duties, Imposts and Excises shall be uniform throughout the United States;

To borrow Money on the credit of the United States;

To regulate Commerce with foreign Nations, and among the several States, and with the Indian Tribes;

To establish an uniform Rule of Naturalization, and uniform Laws on the subject of Bankruptcies throughout the United States;

To coin Money, regulate the Value thereof, and of foreign Coin, and fix the Standard of Weights and Measures;

To provide for the Punishment of counterfeiting the Securities and current Coin of the United States;

To establish Post Offices and post Roads;

To promote the Progress of Science and useful Arts, by securing for limited Times to Authors and Inventors the exclusive Right to their respective Writings and Discoveries;

To constitute Tribunals inferior to the Supreme Court;

To define and punish Piracies and Felonies committed on the high Seas, and Offenses against the Law of Nations;

To declare War, grant Letters of Marque and Reprisal, and make Rules concerning Captures on Land and Water;

To raise and support Armies, but no Appropriation of Money to that Use shall be for a longer Term than two Years;

To provide and maintain a Navy;

To make Rules for the Government and Regulation of the land and naval Forces;

To provide for calling forth the Militia to execute the Laws of the Union, suppress Insurrections and repel Invasions;

To provide for organizing, arming, and disciplining, the Militia, and for governing such Part of them as may be employed in the Service of the United States, reserving to the States respectively, the Appointment of the Officers, and the Authority of training the Militia according to the discipline described by Congress;

To exercise exclusive Legislation in all Cases whatsoever, over such District (not exceeding ten Miles square) as may, by Cession of particular States, and the Acceptance of Congress, become the Seat of the Government of the United States, and to exercise like Authority over all Places purchased by the Consent of the Legislature of the State in which the Same shall be, for the Erection of Forts, Magazines, Arsenals, dock-Yards, and other needful Buildings;—And

To make all Laws which shall be necessary and proper for carrying into Execution the foregoing Powers, and all other Powers vested by this Constitution in the Government of the United States, or in any Department or Officer thereof.

Section 9.

The Migration or Importation of such Persons as any of the States now existing shall think proper to admit, shall not be prohibited by the Congress prior to the Year one thousand eight hundred and eight, but a Tax or Duty may be imposed on such Importation, not exceeding ten dollars for each Person.

The Privilege of the Writ of Habeas Corpus shall not be suspended, unless when in Cases of Rebellion or Invasion the public Safety may require it.

No Bill of Attainder or ex post facto Law shall be passed.

No Capitation, or other direct, Tax shall be laid, unless in Proportion to the Census or Enumeration herein before directed to be taken.

No Tax or Duty shall be laid on Articles exported from any State.

No Preference shall be given by any Regulation of Commerce or Revenue to the Ports of one State over those of another; nor shall Vessels bound to, or from, one State, be obliged to enter, clear, or pay Duties in another.

No Money shall be drawn from the Treasury, but in Consequence of Appropriations made by Laws; and a regular Statement and Account of the Receipts and Expenditures of all public Money shall be published from time to time.

No Title of Nobility shall be granted by the United States: And no Person holding any Office of Profit or Trust under them, shall, without the Consent of the Congress, accept of any present, Emolument, Office, or Title, of any kind whatever, from any King, Prince, or foreign State.

Section 10.

No State shall enter into any Treaty, Alliance, or Confederation; grant Letters of Marque and Reprisal; coin Money; emit Bills of Credit; make any Thing but gold and silver Coin a Tender in Payment of Debts; pass any Bill of Attainder, ex post facto Law, or Law impairing the Obligation of Contracts, or grant any Title of Nobility.

No State shall, without the Consent of the Congress, lay any Imposts or Duties on Imports or Exports, except what may be absolutely necessary for executing its inspection Laws: and the net Produce of all Duties and Imposts, laid by any State on Imports or Exports, shall be for the Use of the Treasury of the United States; and all such Laws shall be subject to the Revision and Controul of the Congress.

No State shall, without the Consent of Congress, lay any Duty of Tonnage, keep Troops, or Ships of War in time of Peace, enter into any Agreement or Compact with another State, or with a foreign Power, or engage in War, unless actually invaded, or in such imminent Danger as will not admit of delay.

ARTICLE II

Section 1.

The executive Power shall be vested in a President of the United States of America. He shall hold his Office during the Term of four Years, and, together with the Vice President, chosen for the same Term, be elected, as follows:

Each State shall appoint, in such Manner as the Legislature thereof may direct, a Number of Electors, equal to the whole Number of Senators and Representatives to which the State may be entitled in the Congress: but no Senator or Representative, or Person holding an Office of Trust or Profit under the United States, shall be appointed an Elector.

The Electors shall meet in their respective States, and vote by Ballot for two Persons, of whom one at least shall not be an Inhabitant of the same State with themselves. And they shall make a list of all the Persons voted for, and of the Number of Votes for each; which List they shall sign and certify, and transmit sealed to the Seat of the Government of the United States, directed to the President of the Senate. The President of the Senate shall, in the presence of the Senate and House of Representatives, open all the Certificates, and the Votes shall be counted. The Person having the greatest Number of Votes shall be the President, if such Number be a Majority of the whole Number of Electors appointed; and if there be more than one who have such Majority, and have an equal Number of Votes, then the House of Representatives shall immediately chuse by Ballot one of them for President; and if no Person have a Majority, then from the five highest on the List the said House shall in like Manner chuse the President. But in chusing the President, the Votes shall be taken by States, the Representation from each State having one Vote; A quorum for this Purpose shall consist of a Member or Members from two thirds of the States, and a Majority of all the States shall be necessary to a Choice. In every Case, after the Choice of the President, the Person having the greatest Number of Votes of the Electors shall be the Vice President. But if there should remain two or more who have equal Votes, the Senate shall chuse from them by Ballot the Vice President.

The Congress may determine the Time of Chusing the Electors, and the Day on which they shall give their Votes; which Day shall be the same throughout the United States.

No Person except a natural born Citizen, or a Citizen of the United States, at the time of the Adoption of this Constitution, shall be eligible to the Office of President; neither shall any Person be eligible to that Office who shall not have attained to the Age of thirty five Years, and been fourteen Years a Resident within the United States.

In Case of the Removal of the President from Office, or of his Death, Resignation, or Inability to discharge the Powers and Duties of the said Office, the Same shall devolve on the Vice President, and the Congress may by Law provide for the Case of Removal, Death, Resignation or Inability, both of the President and Vice President, declaring what Officer shall then act as President, and such Officer shall act accordingly, until the Disability be removed, or a President shall be elected.

The President shall, at stated Times, receive for his Services, a Compensation, which shall neither be encreased nor diminished during the Period for which he shall have been elected, and he shall not receive within that Period any other Emolument from the United States, or any of them.

Before he enter on the Execution of his Office, he shall take the following Oath or Affirmation:—"I do solemnly swear (or affirm) that I will faithfully execute the Office of President of the United States, and will to the best of my Ability, preserve, protect and defend the Constitution of the United States."

Section 2.

The President shall be Commander in Chief of the Army and Navy of the United States, and of the Militia of the several States, when called into the actual Service of the United States; he may require the Opinion, in writing, of the principal Officer in each of the executive Departments, upon any Subject relating to the Duties of their respective Offices, and he shall have Power to grant Reprieves and Pardons for Offenses against the United States, except in Cases of Impeachment.

He shall have Power, by and with the Advice and Consent of the Senate, to make Treaties, providing two thirds of the Senators present concur; and he shall nominate, and by and with the Advice and Consent of the Senate, shall appoint Ambassadors, other public Ministers and Consuls, Judges of the supreme Court, and all other Officers of the United States, whose Appointments are not herein otherwise provided for, and which shall be established by Law: but the Congress may by Law vest the Appointment of such inferior Officers, as they think proper, in the President alone, in the Courts of Law, or in the Heads of Departments.

The President shall have Power to fill up all Vacancies that may happen during the Recess of the Senate, by granting Commissions which shall expire at the End of their next Session.

Section 3.

He shall from time to time give to the Congress Information of the State of the Union, and recommend to their Consideration such Measures as he shall judge necessary and expedient; he may, on extraordinary Occasions, convene both Houses, or either of them, and in Case of Disagreement between them, with Respect to the Time of Adjournment, he may adjourn them to such Time as he shall think proper, he shall receive Ambassadors and other public Ministers; he shall take Care that the Laws be faithfully executed, and shall Commission all the Offices of the United States.

Section 4.

The President, Vice President and all civil Officers of the United States, shall be removed from Office on Impeachment for, and Conviction of, Treason, Bribery, or other high Crimes and Misdemeanors.

ARTICLE III

Section 1.

The judicial Power of the United States, shall be vested in one supreme Court, and in such inferior Courts as the Congress may from time to time ordain and establish. The Judges, both of the supreme and inferior Courts, shall hold their Offices during good Behaviour, and shall, at Times, receive for their Services, a Compensation, which shall not be diminished during their Continuance in Office.

Section 2.

The judicial Power shall extend to all Cases, in Law and Equity, arising under this Constitution, the Laws of the United States, and Treaties made, or which shall be made, under their Authority;—to all Cases affecting Ambassadors, other public Ministers and Consuls;—to all Cases of admiralty and maritime Jurisdiction;—to Controversies to which the United States shall be a Party;—to controversies between two or more States;—between a State and Citizens of another State;—between Citizens of different States;—between Citizens of the same State claiming Lands under Grants of different States; and between a State, or the Citizens thereof, and foreign States, Citizens or Subjects.

In all Cases affecting Ambassadors, other public Ministers and Consuls, and those in which a State shall be Party, the supreme Court shall have original Jurisdiction. In all the other Cases before mentioned, the supreme Court shall have appellate Jurisdiction, both as to Law and Fact, with such Exceptions, and under such Regulations as the Congress shall make.

The Trial of all Crimes, except in Cases of Impeachment, shall be by Jury; and such Trial shall be held in the State where the said Crimes shall have been committed; but when not committed within any State, the Trial shall be at such Place or Places as the Congress may by Law have directed.

Section 3.

Treason against the United States, shall consist only in levying War against them, or in adhering to their Enemies, giving them Aid and Comfort. No Person shall be convicted of Treason unless on the Testimony of two Witnesses to the same overt Act, or on Confession in open Court.

The Congress shall have Power to declare the Punishment of Treason, but no Attainder of Treason shall work Corruption of Blood, or Forfeiture except during the Life of the Person attainted.

ARTICLE IV

Section 1.

Full Faith and Credit shall be given in each State to the public Acts, Records, and judicial Proceedings of every other State. And the Congress may by general Laws prescribe the Manner in which such Acts, Records and Proceedings shall be proved, and the Effect thereof.

Section 2.

The Citizens of each State shall be entitled to all Privileges and Immunities of Citizens in the several States.

A Person charged in any State with Treason, Felony, or other Crime, who shall flee from Justice, and be found in another State, shall on Demand of the executive Authority of the State from which he fled, be delivered up, to be removed to the State having Jurisdiction of the Crime.

No Person held to Service or Labour in one State, under the Laws thereof, escaping into another, shall, in Consequence of any Law or Regulation therein, be discharged from such Service or Labour, but shall be delivered up on Claim of the Party to whom such Service or Labour may be due.

Section 3.

New States may be admitted by the Congress into this Union; but no new State shall be formed or erected within the Jurisdiction of any other State; nor any State be formed by the Junction of two or more States, or Parts of States, without the Consent of the Legislatures of the States concerned as well as the Congress.

The Congress shall have Power to dispose of and make all needful Rules and Regulations respecting the Territory or other Property belonging to the United States; and nothing in this Constitution shall be so construed as to Prejudice any Claims of the United States, or of any particular State.

Section 4.

The United States shall guarantee to every State in this Union a Republican Form of Government, and shall protect each of them against Invasion; and on Application of the Legislature, or of the Executive (when the Legislature cannot be convened) against domestic Violence.

ARTICLE V

The Congress, whenever two thirds of both Houses shall deem it necessary, shall propose Amendments to this Constitution, or, on the Application of the Legislatures of two thirds of the several States, shall call a Convention for proposing Amendments, which, in either Case, shall be valid to all Intents and Purposes, as Part of this Constitution, when ratified by the Legislatures of three fourths of the several States, or by Conventions in three fourths thereof, as the one or the other Mode of Ratification may be proposed by the Congress; Provided that no Amendment which may be made prior to the Year One thousand eight hundred and eight shall in any Manner affect the first and fourth Clauses in the Ninth Section of the first Article; and that no State, without its Consent, shall be deprived of its equal Suffrage in the Senate.

ARTICLE VI

All Debts contracted and Engagements entered into, before the Adoption of this Constitution, shall be as valid against the United States under this Constitution, as under the Confederation.

This Constitution, and the Laws of the United States which shall be made in Pursuance thereof; and all Treaties made, or which shall be made, under the Authority of the United States, shall be the supreme Law of the Land; and the Judges in every State shall be bound thereby, any Thing in the Constitution or Laws of any State to the Contrary notwithstanding.

The Senators and Representatives before mentioned, and the Members of the several State Legislatures, and all executive and judicial Officers, both of the United States and of the Several States, shall be bound by Oath or Affirmation, to support this Constitution; but no religious Test shall ever be required as a Qualification to any Office or public Trust under the United States.

ARTICLE VII

The Ratification of the Conventions of nine States, shall be sufficient for the Establishment of this Constitution between the States so ratifying the Same.

Amendment I [1791].

Congress shall make no law respecting an establishment of religion, or prohibiting the free exercise thereof; or abridging the freedom of speech, or the press; or the right of the people peaceably to assemble, and to petition the Government for a redress of grievances.

Amendment II [1791].

A well regulated Militia, being necessary to the security for a free State, the right of the people to keep and bear Arms, shall not be infringed.

Amendment III [1791].

No Soldier shall, in time of peace be quartered in any house, without the consent of the Owner, nor in time of war, but in a manner to be prescribed by law.

Amendment IV [1791].

The right of the people to be secure in their persons, houses, papers, and effects, against unreasonable searches and seizures, shall not be violated, and no Warrants shall issue, but upon probable cause, supported by Oath or Affirmation, and particularly describing the place to be searched, and the persons or things to be seized.

Amendment V [1791].

No person shall be held to answer for a capital, or otherwise infamous crime, unless on a presentment or indictment of a Grand Jury, except in cases arising in the land or naval forces, or in the Militia, when in actual service in time of War or public danger;

nor shall any person be subject for the same offense to be twice put in jeopardy of life or limb; nor shall be compelled in any criminal case to be a witness against himself, nor be deprived of life, liberty, or property, without due process of law; nor shall private property be taken for public use, without just compensation.

Amendment VI [1791].

In all criminal prosecutions, the accused shall enjoy the right to a speedy and public trial, by an impartial jury of the State and district wherein the crime shall have been committed, which district shall have been previously ascertained by law, and to be informed of the nature and cause of the accusation; to be confronted with the Witnesses against him; to have compulsory process for obtaining witnesses in his favor, and to have the Assistance of counsel for his defence.

Amendment VII [1791].

In suits at common law, where the value in controversy shall exceed twenty dollars, the right of trial by jury shall be preserved, and no fact tried by a jury, shall be otherwise re-examined in any Court of the United States, than according to the rules of the common law.

Amendment VIII [1791].

Excessive bail shall not be required, no excessive fines imposed, nor cruel and unusual punishments inflicted.

Amendment IX [1791].

The enumeration in the Constitution, of certain rights, shall not be construed to deny or disparage others retained by the people.

Amendment X [1791].

The powers not delegated to the United States by the Constitution, nor prohibited by it to the States, are reserved to the States respectively, or to the people.

Amendment XI [1798].

The judicial power of the United States shall not be construed to extend to any suit in law or equity, commenced or prosecuted against one of the United States by Citizens of another State, or by Citizens or Subjects of any Foreign State.

Amendment XII [1804].

The Electors shall meet in their respective states and vote by ballot for President and Vice-President, one of whom, at least, shall not be an inhabitant of the same state with themselves; they shall name in their ballots the person voted for as President, and in distinct ballots the person voted for as Vice-President, and they shall make distinct lists of all persons voted for as President, and of all persons voted for as Vice-President, and of the number of votes for each, which lists they shall sign and certify, and transmit sealed to the seat of the government of the United States, directed to the President of the Senate;—The President of the Senate shall, in the presence of the Senate and House of Representatives, open all the certificates and the votes shall then be counted;—The person having the greatest number of votes for President, shall be the President, if such number be a majority of the whole number of Electors appointed; and if no person have such majority, then from the persons having the highest numbers not exceeding three on the list of those voted for as President, the House of Representatives shall choose immediately, by ballot, the President. But in choosing the President, the votes shall be taken by states, the representation from each state having one vote; a quorum for this purpose shall consist of a member or members from two-thirds of the states, and a majority of all the states shall be necessary to a choice. And if the House of Representatives shall not choose a President whenever the right of choice shall devolve upon them, before the fourth day of March next following, then the Vice-President shall act as President, as in the case of the death or other constitutional disability of the President. The person having the greatest number of votes as Vice-President, shall be the Vice-President, if such number be a majority of the whole number of Electors appointed, and if no person have a majority, then from the two highest numbers on the list, the Senate shall choose the Vice-President; a quorum for the purpose shall consist of two-thirds of the whole number of Senators, and a majority of the whole number shall be necessary to a choice. But no person constitutionally ineligible to the office of President shall be eligible to that of the Vice-President of the United States.

Amendment XIII [1865].

Section 1. Neither slavery nor involuntary servitude, except as a punishment for crime whereof the party shall have been duly convicted, shall exist within the United States, or any place subject to their jurisdiction.

Section 2. Congress shall have power to enforce this article by appropriate legislation.

Amendment XIV [1868].

Section 1. All persons born or naturalized in the United States, and subject to the jurisdiction thereof, are citizens of the United States and of the State wherein they reside. No State shall make or enforce any law which shall abridge the privileges or immunities of citizens of the United States; nor shall any State deprive any person of life, liberty, or property, without due process of law; nor deny to any person within its jurisdiction the equal protection of the laws.

Section 2. Representatives shall be appointed among the several States according to their respective numbers, counting the whole number of persons in each State, excluding Indians not taxed. But when the right to vote at any election for the choice of electors for President and Vice President of the United States, Representatives in Congress, the Executive and Judicial officers of a State, or the members of the Legislature thereof, is denied to any of the male inhabitants of such State, being twenty-one years of age, and citizens of the United States, or in any way abridged, except for participation in rebellion, or other crime, the basis of representation therein shall be reduced in the proportion which the number of such male citizens shall bear the whole number of male citizens twenty-one years of age in such State.

Section 3. No person shall be a Senator or Representative in Congress, or elector of President and Vice President, or hold any office, civil or military, under the United States, or under any State, who, having previously taken an oath, as a member of Congress, or as an officer of the United States, or as a member of any State legislature, or as an executive or judicial officer of any State, to support the Constitution of the United States, shall have engaged in insurrection or rebellion against the same, or given aid or comfort to the enemies thereof. But Congress may by a vote of two-thirds of each House, remove such disability.

Section 4. The validity of the public debt of the United States, authorized by law, including debts incurred for payment of pensions and bounties for services in suppressing insurrection or rebellion, shall not be questioned. But neither the United States nor any State shall assume or pay any debt or obligation incurred in aid of insurrection of rebellion against the United States, or any claim for the loss or emancipation of any slave; but all such debts, obligations and claims shall be held illegal and void.

Section 5. The Congress shall have power to enforce, by appropriate legislation, the provisions of this article.

Amendment XV [1870].

Section 1. The right of citizens of the United States to vote shall not be denied or abridged by the United States or by any State on account of race, color, or previous condition of servitude.

Section 2. The Congress shall have power to enforce this article by appropriate legislation.

Amendment XVI [1913].

The Congress shall have power to lay and collect taxes on incomes, from whatever source derived, without apportionment among the several States, and without regard to any census or enumeration.

Amendment XVII [1913].

The Senate of the United States shall be composed of two Senators from each State, elected by the people thereof, for six years; and each Senator shall have one vote. The electors in each State shall have the qualifications requisite for electors of the most numerous branch of the State legislatures.

When vacancies happen in the representation of any State in the Senate, the executive authority of each State shall issue writs of election to fill such vacancies; *Provided,* That the legislature of any State may empower the executive thereof to make temporary appointments until the people fill the vacancies by election as the legislature may direct.

This amendment shall not be construed as to affect the election or term of any Senator chosen before it becomes valid as part of the Constitution.

Amendment XVIII [1919].

Section 1. After one year from the ratification of this article the manufacture, sale, or transportation of intoxicating liquors within, the importation thereof into, or the exportation thereof from the United States and all territory subject to the jurisdiction thereof for beverage purposes is hereby prohibited.

Section 2. The Congress and the several States shall have concurrent power to enforce this article by appropriate legislation.

Section 3. This article shall be inoperative unless it shall have been ratified as an amendment to the Constitution by the legislatures of the several States, as provided in the Constitution, within seven years from the date of the submission hereof to the States by the Congress.

Amendment XIX [1920].

The right of citizens of the United States to vote shall not be denied or abridged by the United States or by any State on account of sex.

Congress shall have power to enforce this article by appropriate legislation.

Amendment XX [1933].

Section 1. The terms of the President and Vice President shall end at noon on the 20th day of January, and the terms of Senators and Representatives at noon on the 3d day of January, of the years in which such terms would have ended if this article had not been ratified; and the terms of their successors shall then begin.

Section 2. The Congress shall assemble at least once in every year, and such meeting shall begin at noon on the 3d day of January, unless they shall by law appoint a different day.

Section 3. If, at the time fixed for the beginning of the term of the President, the President elect shall have died, the Vice President elect shall become President. If a President shall not have been chosen before the time fixed for the beginning of his term, or if the President elect shall have failed to qualify, then the Vice President elect shall act as President until a President shall have qualified; and the Congress may by law provide for the case wherein neither a President elect nor a Vice President elect shall have qualified, declaring who shall then act as President, or the manner in which one who is to act shall be selected, and such person shall act accordingly until a President or Vice President shall have qualified.

Section 4. The Congress may by law provide for the case of the death of any of the persons from whom the House of Representatives may choose a President whenever the right of choice shall have devolved upon them, and for the case of the death of any of the persons from whom the Senate may choose a Vice President whenever the right of choice shall have devolved upon them.

Section 5. Sections 1 and 2 shall take effect on the 15th day of October following the ratification of this article.

Section 6. This article shall be inoperative unless it shall have been ratified as an amendment to the Constitution by the legislatures of three-fourths of the several States within seven years from the date of its submission.

Amendment XXI [1933].

Section 1. The eighteenth article of amendment to the Constitution of the United States is hereby repealed.

Section 2. The transportation or importation into any State, Territory, or possession of the United States for delivery or use therein of intoxicating liquors, in violation of the laws thereof, is hereby prohibited.

Section 3. This article shall be inoperative unless it shall have been ratified as an amendment to the Constitution by conventions in the several States, as provided in the Constitution, within seven years from the date of the submission hereof to the States by the Congress.

Amendment XXII [1951].

Section 1. No person shall be elected to the office of the President more than twice, and no person who has held the office of President, or acted as President, for more than two years of a term to which some other person was elected President shall be elected to the office of the President more than once. But this Article shall not apply to any person holding the office of President when this Article was proposed by the Congress, and shall not prevent any person who may be holding the office of President, or acting as President, during the term within which this Article becomes operative from holding the office of President, or acting as President during the remainder of such term.

Section 2. This article shall be inoperative unless it shall have been ratified as an amendment to the Constitution by the legislatures of three-fourths of the several States within seven years from the date of its submission to the States by the Congress.

Amendment XXIII [1961].

Section 1. The District constituting the seat of Government of the United States shall appoint in such manner as the Congress may direct:

A number of electors of President and Vice President equal to the whole number of Senators and Representatives in Congress to which the District would be entitled if it were a State, but in no event more than the least populous State; they shall be in addition to those appointed by the States, but they shall be considered, for the purposes of the election of President and Vice President, to be electors appointed by a State; and they shall meet in the District and perform such duties as provided by the twelfth article of amendment.

Section 2. The Congress shall have power to enforce this article by appropriate legislation.

Amendment XXIV [1964].

Section 1. The right of citizens of the United States to vote in any primary or other election for President or Vice President, for electors for President or Vice President, or for Senator or Representative in Congress, shall not be denied or abridged by the United States or any State by reason of failure to pay any poll tax or other tax.

Section 2. The Congress shall have power to enforce this article by appropriate legislation.

Amendment XXV [1967].

Section 1. In case of the removal of the President from office or of his death or resignation, the Vice President shall become President.

Section 2. Whenever there is a vacancy in the office of the Vice President, the President shall nominate a Vice President who shall take office upon confirmation by a majority vote of both Houses of Congress.

Section 3. Whenever the President transmits to the President pro tempore of the Senate and the Speaker of the House of Representatives his written declaration that he is unable to discharge the powers and duties of his office, and until he transmits to them a written declaration to the contrary, such powers and duties shall be discharged by the Vice President as Acting President.

Section 4. Whenever the Vice President and a majority of either the principal officers of the executive departments or of such other body as Congress may by law provide, transmit to the President pro tempore of the Senate and the Speaker of the House of Representatives their written declaration that the President is unable to discharge the powers and duties of his office, the Vice President shall immediately assume the powers and duties of the office as Acting President.

Thereafter, when the President transmits to the President pro tempore of the Senate and the Speaker of the House of Representatives his written declaration that no inability exists, he shall resume the powers and duties of his office unless the Vice President and a majority of either the principal officers of the executive department or of such other body as Congress may by law provide, transmit within four days to the President pro tempore of the Senate and the Speaker of the House of Representatives their written declaration that the President is unable to discharge the powers and duties of his office. Thereupon Congress shall decide the issue, assembling within forty-eight hours for that purpose if not in session. If the Congress, within twenty-one days after receipt of the latter written declaration, or, if Congress is not in session, within twenty-one days after Congress is required to assemble, determines by two-thirds vote of both Houses that the President is unable to discharge the powers and duties of his office, the Vice President shall continue to discharge the same as Acting President; otherwise, the President shall resume the powers and duties of his office.

Amendment XXVI [1971].

Section 1. The right of citizens of the United States, who are eighteen years of age or older, to vote shall not be denied or abridged by the United States or by any State on account of age.

Section 2. The Congress shall have power to enforce this article by appropriate legislation.

Amendment XXVII [1992].

No law, varying the compensation for the services of the Senators and Representatives, shall take effect, until an election of Representatives shall have intervened.

APPENDIX B

Uniform Commercial Code (Selected Provisions)

The code consists of the following articles:

Art.

1. General provisions
2. Sales

2A. Leases

3. Negotiable instruments
4. Bank deposits and collections

4A. Fund transfers

5. Letters of credit
6. Repealer of Article 6—Bulk Transfers and [Revised] Article 6—Bulk sales
7. Warehouse Receipts, Bills of Lading and Other Documents of Title
8. Investment Securities
9. Secured Transactions
10. Effective Date and Repealer
11. Effective Date and Transmission provisions

ARTICLE I

GENERAL PROVISIONS

PART 1 Short Title, Construction, Application and Subject Matter of the Act

§ 1-101. Short Title.

This Act shall be known and may be cited as Uniform Commercial Code.

§ 1-102. Purposes; Rules of Construction; Variation by Agreement.

(1) This Act shall be liberally construed and applied to promote its underlying purposes and policies.

(2) Underlying purposes and policies of this Act are

(a) to simplify, clarify and modernize the law governing commercial transactions;

(b) to permit the continued expansion of commercial practices through custom, usage and agreement of the parties;

(c) to make uniform the law among the various jurisdictions.

(3) The effect of provisions of this Act may be varied by agreement, except as otherwise provided in this Act and except that the obligations of good faith, diligence, reasonableness and care prescribed by this Act may not be disclaimed by agreement but the parties may by agreement determine the standards by which the performance of such obligations is to be measured if such standards are not manifestly unreasonable.

(4) The presence in certain provisions of this Act of the words "unless otherwise agreed" or words of similar import does not imply that the effect of other provisions may not be varied by agreement under subsection (3).

(5) In this Act unless the context otherwise requires

(a) words in the singular number include the plural, and in the plural include the singular;

(b) words of the masculine gender include the feminine and the neuter, and when the sense so indicates words of the neuter gender may refer to any gender.

§ 1-103. Supplementary General Principles of Law Applicable.

Unless displaced by the particular provisions of this Act, the principles of law and equity, including the law merchant and the law relative to capacity to contract, principal and agent, estoppel, fraud, misrepresentation, duress, coercion, mistake, bankruptcy, or other validating or invalidating cause shall supplement its provisions.

§ 1-104. Construction Against Implicit Repeal.

This Act being a general act intended as a unified coverage of its subject matter, no part of it shall be deemed to be impliedly repealed by subsequent legislation if such construction can reasonably be avoided.

§ 1-105. Territorial Application of the Act; Parties' Power to Choose Applicable Law.

(1) Except as provided hereafter in this section, when a transaction bears a reasonable relation to this state and also to

another state or nation the parties may agree that the law either of this state or of such other state or nation shall govern their rights and duties. Failing such agreement this Act applies to transactions bearing an appropriate relation to this state.

(2) Where one of the following provisions of this Act specifies the applicable law, that provision governs and a contrary agreement is effective only to the extent permitted by the law (including the conflict of laws rules) so specified:

Rights of creditors against sold goods. Section 2–402.

Applicability of the Article on Leases. Sections 2A–105 and 2A–106.

Applicability of the Article on Bank Deposits and Collections. Section 4–102.

Governing law in the Article on Funds Transfers. Section 4A–507.

Letters of Credit, Section 5–116.

Bulk sales subject to the Article on Bulk Sales. Section 6–103.

Applicability of the Article on Investment Securities. Section 8–106.

Law governing perfection, the effect of perfection or nonperfection, and the priority of security interests and agricultural liens. Sections 9–301 through 9–307.

As amended in 1972, 1987, 1988, 1989, 1994, 1995, and 1999.

§ 1–106. Remedies to Be Liberally Administered.

(1) The remedies provided by this Act shall be liberally administered to the end that the aggrieved party may be put in as good a position as if the other party had fully performed but neither consequential or special nor penal damages may be had except as specifically provided in this Act or by other rule of law.

(2) Any right or obligation declared by this Act is enforceable by action unless the provision declaring it specifies a different and limited effect.

§ 1–107. Waiver or Renunciation of Claim or Right After Breach.

Any claim or right arising out of an alleged breach can be discharged in whole or in part without consideration by a written waiver or renunciation signed and delivered by the aggrieved party.

§ 1–108. Severability.

If any provision or clause of this Act or application thereof to any person or circumstances is held invalid, such invalidity shall not affect other provisions or applications of the Act which can be given effect without the invalid provision or application, and to this end the provisions of this Act are declared to be severable.

§ 1–109. Section Captions.

Section captions are parts of this Act.

PART 2 General Definitions and Principles of Interpretation

§ 1–201. General Definitions.

Subject to additional definitions contained in the subsequent Articles of this Act which are applicable to specific Articles or Parts thereof, and unless the context otherwise requires, in this Act:

(1) "Action" in the sense of a judicial proceeding includes recoupment, counterclaim, set-off, suit in equity and any other proceedings in which rights are determined.

(2) "Aggrieved party" means a party entitled to resort to a remedy.

(3) "Agreement" means the bargain of the parties in fact as found in their language or by implication from other circumstances including course of dealing or usage of trade or course of performance as provided in this Act (Sections 1–205 and 2–208). Whether an agreement has legal consequences is determined by the provisions of this Act, if applicable; otherwise by the law of contracts (Section 1–103). (Compare "Contract".)

(4) "Bank" means any person engaged in the business of banking.

(5) "Bearer" means the person in possession of an instrument, document of title, or certificated security payable to bearer or indorsed in blank.

(6) "Bill of lading" means a document evidencing the receipt of goods for shipment issued by a person engaged in the business of transporting or forwarding goods, and includes an airbill. "Airbill" means a document serving for air transportation as a bill of lading does for marine or rail transportation, and includes an air consignment note or air waybill.

(7) "Branch" includes a separately incorporated foreign branch of a bank.

(8) "Burden of establishing" a fact means the burden of persuading the triers of fact that the existence of the fact is more probable than its non-existence.

(9) "Buyer in ordinary course of business" means a person that buys goods in good faith, without knowledge that the sale violates the rights of another person in the goods, and in the ordinary course from a person, other than a pawnbroker, in the business of selling goods of that kind. A person buys goods in the ordinary course if the sale to the person comports with the usual or customary practices in the kind of business in which the seller is engaged or with the seller's own usual or customary practices. A person that sells oil, gas, or other minerals at the wellhead or minehead is a person in the business of selling goods of that kind. A buyer in ordinary course of business may buy for cash, by exchange of other property, or on secured or unsecured credit, and may acquire goods or documents of title

under a pre-existing contract for sale. Only a buyer that takes possession of the goods or has a right to recover the goods from the seller under Article 2 may be a buyer in ordinary course of business. A person that acquires goods in a transfer in bulk or as security for or in total or partial satisfaction of a money debt is not a buyer in ordinary course of business.

(10) "Conspicuous": A term or clause is conspicuous when it is so written that a reasonable person against whom it is to operate ought to have noticed it. A printed heading in capitals (as: NON-NEGOTIABLE BILL OF LADING) is conspicuous. Language in the body of a form is "conspicuous" if it is in larger or other contrasting type or color. But in a telegram any stated term is "conspicuous". Whether a term or clause is "conspicuous" or not is for decision by the court.

(11) "Contract" means the total legal obligation which results from the parties' agreement as affected by this Act and any other applicable rules of law. (Compare "Agreement".)

(12) "Creditor" includes a general creditor, a secured creditor, a lien creditor and any representative of creditors, including an assignee for the benefit of creditors, a trustee in bankruptcy, a receiver in equity and an executor or administrator of an insolvent debtor's or assignor's estate.

(13) "Defendant" includes a person in the position of defendant in a cross-action or counterclaim.

(14) "Delivery" with respect to instruments, documents of title, chattel paper, or certificated securities means voluntary transfer of possession.

(15) "Document of title" includes bill of lading, dock warrant, dock receipt, warehouse receipt or order for the delivery of goods, and also any other document which in the regular course of business or financing is treated as adequately evidencing that the person in possession of it is entitled to receive, hold and dispose of the document and the goods it covers. To be a document of title a document must purport to be issued by or addressed to a bailee and purport to cover goods in the bailee's possession which are either identified or are fungible portions of an identified mass.

(16) "Fault" means wrongful act, omission or breach.

(17) "Fungible" with respect to goods or securities means goods or securities of which any unit is, by nature or usage of trade, the equivalent of any other like unit. Goods which are not fungible shall be deemed fungible for the purposes of this Act to the extent that under a particular agreement or document unlike units are treated as equivalents.

(18) "Genuine" means free of forgery or counterfeiting.

(19) "Good faith" means honesty in fact in the conduct or transaction concerned.

(20) "Holder" with respect to a negotiable instrument, means the person in possession if the instrument is payable to bearer or, in the cases of an instrument payable to an identified person, if the identified person is in possession. "Holder" with respect to a document of title means the person in possession if the goods are deliverable to bearer or to the order of the person in possession.

(21) To "honor" is to pay or to accept and pay, or where a credit so engages to purchase or discount a draft complying with the terms of the credit.

(22) "Insolvency proceedings" includes any assignment for the benefit of creditors or other proceedings intended to liquidate or rehabilitate the estate of the person involved.

(23) A person is "insolvent" who either has ceased to pay his debts in the ordinary course of business or cannot pay his debts as they become due or is insolvent within the meaning of the federal bankruptcy law.

(24) "Money" means a medium of exchange authorized or adopted by a domestic or foreign government and includes a monetary unit of account established by an intergovernmental organization or by agreement between two or more nations.

(25) A person has "notice" of a fact when

(a) he has actual knowledge of it; or

(b) he has received a notice or notification of it; or

(c) from all the facts and circumstances known to him at the time in question he has reason to know that it exists.

A person "knows" or has "knowledge" of a fact when he has actual knowledge of it. "Discover" or "learn" or a word or phrase of similar import refers to knowledge rather than to reason to know. The time and circumstances under which a notice or notification may cease to be effective are not determined by this Act.

(26) A person "notifies" or "gives" a notice or notification to another by taking such steps as may be reasonably required to inform the other in ordinary course whether or not such other actually comes to know of it. A person "receives" a notice or notification when

(a) it comes to his attention; or

(b) it is duly delivered at the place of business through which the contract was made or at any other place held out by him as the place for receipt of such communications.

(27) Notice, knowledge or a notice or notification received by an organization is effective for a particular transaction from the time when it is brought to the attention of the individual conducting that transaction, and in any event from the time when it would have been brought to his attention if the organization had exercised due diligence. An organization exercises due diligence if it maintains reasonable routines for communicating significant information to the person conducting the transaction and there is reasonable compliance with the routines. Due diligence does not require an individual acting for the organization to communicate information unless such communication is part of his regular duties or unless he has reason to know of the transaction and that the transaction would be materially affected by the information.

(28) "Organization" includes a corporation, government or governmental subdivision or agency, business trust, estate, trust, partnership or association, two or more persons having a joint or common interest, or any other legal or commercial entity.

(29) "Party", as distinct from "third party", means a person who has engaged in a transaction or made an agreement within this Act.

(30) "Person" includes an individual or an organization (See Section 1–102).

(31) "Presumption" or "presumed" means that the trier of fact must find the existence of the fact presumed unless and until evidence is introduced which would support a finding of its non-existence.

(32) "Purchase" includes taking by sale, discount, negotiation, mortgage, pledge, lien, issue or re-issue, gift or any other voluntary transaction creating an interest in property.

(33) "Purchaser" means a person who takes by purchase.

(34) "Remedy" means any remedial right to which an aggrieved party is entitled with or without resort to a tribunal.

(35) "Representative" includes an agent, an officer of a corporation or association, and a trustee, executor or administrator of an estate, or any other person empowered to act for another.

(36) "Rights" includes remedies.

(37) "Security interest" means an interest in personal property or fixtures which secures payment or performance of an obligation. The term also includes any interest of a consignor and a buyer of accounts, chattel paper, a payment intangible, or a promissory note in a transaction that is subject to Article 9. The special property interest of a buyer of goods on identification of those goods to a contract for sale under Section 2–401 is not a "security interest", but a buyer may also acquire a "security interest" by complying with Article 9. Except as otherwise provided in Section 2–505, the right of a seller or lessor of goods under Article 2 or 2A to retain or acquire possession of the goods is not a "security interest", but a seller or lessor may also acquire a "security interest" by complying with Article 9. The retention or reservation of title by a seller of goods notwithstanding shipment or delivery to the buyer (Section 2–401) is limited in effect to a reservation of a "security interest".

Whether a transaction creates a lease or security interest is determined by the facts of each case; however, a transaction creates a security interest if the consideration the lessee is to pay the lessor for the right to possession and use of the goods is an obligation for the term of the lease not subject to termination by the lessee, and

(a) the original term of the lease is equal to or greater than the remaining economic life of the goods,

(b) the lessee is bound to renew the lease for the remaining economic life of the goods or is bound to become the owner of the goods,

(c) the lessee has an option to renew the lease for the remaining economic life of the goods for no additional consideration or nominal additional consideration upon compliance with the lease agreement, or

(d) the lessee has an option to become the owner of the goods for no additional consideration or nominal additional consideration upon compliance with the lease agreement.

A transaction does not create a security interest merely because it provides that

(a) the present value of the consideration the lessee is obligated to pay the lessor for the right to possession and use of the goods is substantially equal to or is greater than the fair market value of the goods at the time the lease is entered into,

(b) the lessee assumes risk of loss of the goods, or agrees to pay taxes, insurance, filing, recording, or registration fees, or service or maintenance costs with respect to the goods,

(c) the lessee has an option to renew the lease or to become the owner of the goods,

(d) the lessee has an option to renew the lease for a fixed rent that is equal to or greater than the reasonably predictable fair market rent for the use of the goods for the term of the renewal at the time the option is to be performed, or

(e) the lessee has an option to become the owner of the goods for a fixed price that is equal to or greater than the reasonably predictable fair market value of the goods at the time the option is to be performed.

For purposes of this subsection (37):

(x) Additional consideration is not nominal if (i) when the option to renew the lease is granted to the lessee the rent is stated to be the fair market rent for the use of the goods for the term of the renewal determined at the time the option is to be performed, or (ii) when the option to become the owner of the goods is granted to the lessee the price is stated to be the fair market value of the goods determined at the time the option is to be performed. Additional consideration is nominal if it is less than the lessee's reasonably predictable cost of performing under the lease agreement if the option is not exercised;

(y) "Reasonably predictable" and "remaining economic life of the goods" are to be determined with reference to the facts and circumstances at the time the transaction is entered into; and

(z) "Present value" means the amount as of a date certain of one or more sums payable in the future, discounted to the date certain. The discount is determined by the interest rate specified by the parties if the rate is not manifestly unreasonable at the time the transaction is entered into; otherwise, the discount is determined by a commercially reasonable rate that takes into account the facts and circumstances of each case at the time the transaction was entered into.

(38) "Send" in connection with any writing or notice means to deposit in the mail or deliver for transmission by any other usual means of communication with postage or cost of transmission provided for and properly addressed and in the case of an instrument to an address specified thereon or otherwise agreed, or if there be none to any address reasonable under the circumstances. The receipt of any writing or notice within the time at which it would have arrived if properly sent has the effect of a proper sending.

(39) "Signed" includes any symbol executed or adopted by a party with present intention to authenticate a writing.

(40) "Surety" includes guarantor.

(41) "Telegram" includes a message transmitted by radio, teletype, cable, any mechanical method of transmission, or the like.

(42) "Term" means that portion of an agreement which relates to a particular matter.

(43) "Unauthorized" signature means one made without actual, implied or apparent authority and includes a forgery.

(44) "Value". Except as otherwise provided with respect to negotiable instruments and bank collections (Sections 3–303, 4–210 and 4–211) a person gives "value" for rights if he acquires them

(a) in return for a binding commitment to extend credit or for the extension of immediately available credit whether or not drawn upon and whether or not a chargeback is provided for in the event of difficulties in collection; or

(b) as security for or in total or partial satisfaction of a pre-existing claim; or

(c) by accepting delivery pursuant to a preexisting contract for purchase; or

(d) generally, in return for any consideration sufficient to support a simple contract.

(45) "Warehouse receipt" means a receipt issued by a person engaged in the business of storing goods for hire.

(46) "Written" or "writing" includes printing, typewriting or any other intentional reduction to tangible form.

§ 1–202. Prima Facie Evidence by Third Party Documents.

A document in due form purporting to be a bill of lading, policy or certificate of insurance, official weigher's or inspector's certificate, consular invoice, or any other document authorized or required by the contract to be issued by a third party shall be prima facie evidence of its own authenticity and genuineness and of the facts stated in the document by the third party.

§ 1–203. Obligation of Good Faith.

Every contract or duty within this Act imposes an obligation of good faith in its performance or enforcement.

§ 1–204. Time; Reasonable Time; "Seasonably".

(1) Whenever this Act requires any action to be taken within a reasonable time, any time which is not manifestly unreasonable may be fixed by agreement.

(2) What is a reasonable time for taking any action depends on the nature, purpose and circumstances of such action.

(3) An action is taken "seasonably" when it is taken at or within the time agreed or if no time is agreed at or within a reasonable time.

§ 1–205. Course of Dealing and Usage of Trade.

(1) A course of dealing is a sequence of previous conduct between the parties to a particular transaction which is fairly to be regarded as establishing a common basis of understanding for interpreting their expressions and other conduct.

(2) A usage of trade is any practice or method of dealing having such regularity of observance in a place, vocation or trade as to justify an expectation that it will be observed with respect to the transaction in question. The existence and scope of such a usage are to be proved as facts. If it is established that such a usage is embodied in a written trade code or similar writing the interpretation of the writing is for the court.

(3) A course of dealing between parties and any usage of trade in the vocation or trade in which they are engaged or of which they are or should be aware give particular meaning to and supplement or qualify terms of an agreement.

(4) The express terms of an agreement and an applicable course of dealing or usage of trade shall be construed wherever reasonable as consistent with each other; but when such construction is unreasonable express terms control both course of dealing and usage of trade and course of dealing controls usage trade.

(5) An applicable usage of trade in the place where any part of performance is to occur shall be used in interpreting the agreement as to that part of the performance.

(6) Evidence of a relevant usage of trade offered by one party is not admissible unless and until he has given the other party such notice as the court finds sufficient to prevent unfair surprise to the latter.

§ 1–206. Statute of Frauds for Kinds of Personal Property Not Otherwise Covered.

(1) Except in the cases described in subsection (2) of this section a contract for the sale of personal property is not enforceable by way of action or defense beyond five thousand dollars in amount or value of remedy unless there is some writing which indicates that a contract for sale has been made between the parties at a defined or stated price, reasonably identifies the subject matter, and is signed by the party against whom enforcement is sought or by his authorized agent.

(2) Subsection (1) of this section does not apply to contracts for the sale of goods (Section 2–201) nor of securities (Section 8–113) nor to security agreements (Section 9–203).

As amended in 1994.

§ 1–207. Performance or Acceptance Under Reservation of Rights.

(1) A party who with explicit reservation of rights performs or promises performance or assents to performance in a manner demanded or offered by the other party does not thereby prejudice the rights reserved. Such words as "without prejudice", "under protest" or the like are sufficient.

(2) Subsection (1) does not apply to an accord and satisfaction.

As amended in 1990.

§ 1–208. Option to Accelerate at Will.

A term providing that one party or his successor in interest may accelerate payment or performance or require collateral or additional collateral "at will" or "when he deems himself insecure" or in words of similar import shall be construed to mean that he shall have power to do so only if he in good faith believes that the prospect of payment or performance is impaired. The burden of establishing lack of good faith is on the party against whom the power has been exercised.

§ 1-209. Subordinated Obligations.

An obligation may be issued as subordinated to payment of another obligation of the person obligated, or a creditor may subordinate his right to payment of an obligation by agreement with either the person obligated or another creditor of the person obligated. Such a subordination does not create a security interest as against either the common debtor or a subordinated creditor. This section shall be construed as declaring the law as it existed prior to the enactment of this section and not as modifying it. Added 1966.

Note: *This new section is proposed as an optional provision to make it clear that a subordination agreement does not create a security interest unless so intended.*

ARTICLE II
SALES

PART 1 Short Title, General Construction and Subject Matter

§ 2-101. Short Title.

This Article shall be known and may be cited as Uniform Commercial Code—Sales.

§ 2-102. Scope; Certain Security and Other Transactions Excluded From This Article.

Unless the context otherwise requires, this Article applies to transactions in goods; it does not apply to any transaction which although in the form of an unconditional contract to sell or present sale is intended to operate only as a security transaction nor does this Article impair or repeal any statute regulating sales to consumers, farmers or other specified classes of buyers.

§ 2-103. Definitions and Index of Definitions.

(1) In this Article unless the context otherwise requires

(a) "Buyer" means a person who buys or contracts to buy goods.

(b) "Good faith" in the case of a merchant means honesty in fact and the observance of reasonable commercial standards of fair dealing in the trade.

(c) "Receipt" of goods means taking physical possession of them.

(d) "Seller" means a person who sells or contracts to sell goods.

(2) Other definitions applying to this Article or to specified Parts thereof, and the sections in which they appear are:

"Acceptance". Section 2–606.
"Banker's credit". Section 2–325.
"Between merchants". Section 2–104.
"Cancellation". Section 2–106(4).
"Commercial unit". Section 2–105.
"Confirmed credit". Section 2–325.
"Conforming to contract". Section 2–106.
"Contract for sale". Section 2–106.
"Cover". Section 2–712.
"Entrusting". Section 2–403.
"Financing agency". Section 2–104.
"Future goods". Section 2–105.
"Goods". Section 2–105.
"Identification". Section 2–501.
"Installment contract". Section 2–612.
"Letter of Credit". Section 2–325.
"Lot". Section 2–105
"Merchant". Section 2–104.
"Overseas". Section 2–323.
"Person in position of seller". Section 2–707.
"Present sale". Section 2–106.
"Sale". Section 2–106.
"Sale on approval". Section 2–326.
"Sale or return". Section 2–326.
"Termination". Section 2–106.

(3) The following definitions in other Articles apply to this Article:

"Check". Section 3–104.
"Consignee". Section 7–102.
"Consignor". Section 7–102.
"Consumer goods". Section 9–109.
"Dishonor". Section 3–507.
"Draft". Section 3–104.

(4) In addition Article 1 contains general definitions and principles of construction and interpretation applicable throughout this Article.

As amended in 1994 and 1999.

§ 2-104. Definitions: "Merchant"; "Between Merchants"; "Financing Agency".

(1) "Merchant" means a person who deals in goods of the kind or otherwise by his occupation holds himself out as having knowledge or skill peculiar to the practices or goods involved in the transaction or to whom such knowledge or skill may be attributed by his employment of an agent or broker or other intermediary who by his occupation holds himself out as having such knowledge or skill.

(2) "Financing agency" means a bank, finance company or other person who in the ordinary course of business makes advances against goods or documents of title or who by arrangement with either the seller or the buyer intervenes in ordinary course to

make or collect payment due or claimed under the contract for sale, as by purchasing or paying the seller's draft or making advances against it or by merely taking it for collection whether or not documents of title accompany the draft. "Financing agency" includes also a bank or other person who similarly intervenes between persons who are in the position of seller and buyer in respect to the goods (Section 2–707).

(3) "Between merchants" means in any transaction with respect to which both parties are chargeable with the knowledge or skill of merchants.

§ 2–105. Definitions: Transferability; "Goods"; "Future" Goods; "Lot"; "Commercial Unit".

(1) "Goods" means all things (including specially manufactured goods) which are movable at the time of identification to the contract for sale other than the money in which the price is to be paid, investment securities (Article 8) and things in action. "Goods" also includes the unborn young of animals and growing crops and other identified things attached to realty as described in the section on goods to be severed from realty (Section 2–107).

(2) Goods must be both existing and identified before any interest in them can pass. Goods which are not both existing and identified are "future" goods. A purported present sale of future goods or of any interest therein operates as a contract to sell.

(3) There may be a sale of a part interest in existing identified goods.

(4) An undivided share in an identified bulk of fungible goods is sufficiently identified to be sold although the quantity of the bulk is not determined. Any agreed proportion of such a bulk or any quantity thereof agreed upon by number, weight or other measure may to the extent of the seller's interest in the bulk be sold to the buyer who then becomes an owner in common.

(5) "Lot" means a parcel or a single article which is the subject matter of a separate sale or delivery, whether or not it is sufficient to perform the contract.

(6) "Commercial unit" means such a unit of goods as by commercial usage is a single whole for purposes of sale and division of which materially impairs its character or value on the market or in use. A commercial unit may be a single article (as a machine) or a set of articles (as a suite of furniture or an assortment of sizes) or a quantity (as a bale, gross, or carload) or any other unit treated in use or in the relevant market as a single whole.

§ 2–106. Definitions: "Contract"; "Agreement"; "Contract for Sale"; "Sale"; "Present Sale"; "Conforming" to Contract; "Termination"; "Cancellation".

(1) In this Article unless the context otherwise requires "contract" and "agreement" are limited to those relating to the present or future sale of goods. "Contract for sale" includes both a present sale of goods and a contract to sell goods at a future time. A "sale" consists in the passing of title from the seller to the buyer for a price (Section 2–401). A "present sale" means a sale which is accomplished by the making of the contract.

(2) Goods or conduct including any part of a performance are "conforming" or conform to the contract when they are in accordance with the obligations under the contract.

(3) "Termination" occurs when either party pursuant to a power created by agreement or law puts an end to the contract otherwise than for its breach. On "termination" all obligations which are still executory on both sides are discharged but any right based on prior breach or performance survives.

(4) "Cancellation" occurs when either party puts an end to the contract for breach by the other and its effect is the same as that of "termination" except that the cancelling party also retains any remedy for breach of the whole contract or any unperformed balance.

§ 2–107. Goods to Be Severed From Realty: Recording.

(1) A contract for the sale of minerals or the like (including oil and gas) or a structure or its materials to be removed from realty is a contract for the sale of goods within this Article if they are to be severed by the seller but until severance a purported present sale thereof which is not effective as a transfer of an interest in land is effective only as a contract to sell.

(2) A contract for the sale apart from the land of growing crops or other things attached to realty and capable of severance without material harm thereto but not described in subsection (1) or of timber to be cut is a contract for the sale of goods within this Article whether the subject matter is to be severed by the buyer or by the seller even though it forms part of the realty at the time of contracting, and the parties can by identification effect a present sale before severance.

(3) The provisions of this section are subject to any third party rights provided by the law relating to realty records, and the contract for sale may be executed and recorded as a document transferring an interest in land and shall then constitute notice to third parties of the buyer's rights under the contract for sale.

As amended in 1972.

PART 2 Form, Formation and Readjustment of Contract

§ 2–201. Formal Requirements; Statute of Frauds.

(1) Except as otherwise provided in this section a contract for the sale of goods for the price of $500 or more is not enforceable by way of action or defense unless there is some writing sufficient to indicate that a contract for sale has been made between the parties and signed by the party against whom enforcement is sought or by his authorized agent or broker. A writing is not insufficient because it omits or incorrectly states a term agreed upon but the contract is not enforceable under this paragraph beyond the quantity of goods shown in such writing.

(2) Between merchants if within a reasonable time a writing in confirmation of the contract and sufficient against the sender is received and the party receiving it has reason to know its contents, it satisfies the requirements of subsection (1) against such party unless written notice of objection to its contents is given within ten days after it is received.

(3) A contract which does not satisfy the requirements of subsection (1) but which is valid in other respects is enforceable

(a) if the goods are to be specially manufactured for the buyer and are not suitable for sale to others in the ordinary course of the seller's business and the seller, before notice of repudiation is received and under circumstances which reasonably indicate that the goods are for the buyer, has made either a substantial beginning of their manufacture or commitments for their procurement; or

(b) if the party against whom enforcement is sought admits in his pleading, testimony or otherwise in court that a contract for sale was made, but the contract is not enforceable under this provision beyond the quantity of goods admitted; or

(c) with respect to goods for which payment has been made and accepted or which have been received and accepted (Sec. 2–606).

§ 2-202. Final Written Expression: Parol or Extrinsic Evidence.

Terms with respect to which the confirmatory memoranda of the parties agree or which are otherwise set forth in a writing intended by the parties as a final expression of their agreement with respect to such terms as are included therein may not be contradicted by evidence of any prior agreement or of a contemporaneous oral agreement but may be explained or supplemented

(a) by course of dealing or usage of trade (Section 1–205) or by course of performance (Section 2–208); and

(b) by evidence of consistent additional terms unless the court finds the writing to have been intended also as a complete and exclusive statement of the terms of the agreement.

§ 2-203. Seals Inoperative.

The affixing of a seal to a writing evidencing a contract for sale or an offer to buy or sell goods does not constitute the writing a sealed instrument and the law with respect to sealed instruments does not apply to such a contract or offer.

§ 2-204. Formation in General.

(1) A contract for sale of goods may be made in any manner sufficient to show agreement, including conduct by both parties which recognizes the existence of such a contract.

(2) An agreement sufficient to constitute a contract for sale may be found even though the moment of its making is undetermined.

(3) Even though one or more terms are left open a contract for sale does not fail for indefiniteness if the parties have intended to make a contract and there is a reasonably certain basis for giving an appropriate remedy.

§ 2-205. Firm Offers.

An offer by a merchant to buy or sell goods in a signed writing which by its terms gives assurance that it will be held open is not revocable, for lack of consideration, during the time stated or if no time is stated for a reasonable time, but in no event may such period of irrevocability exceed three months; but any such term of assurance on a form supplied by the offeree must be separately signed by the offeror.

§ 2-206. Offer and Acceptance in Formation of Contract.

(1) Unless other unambiguously indicated by the language or circumstances

(a) an offer to make a contract shall be construed as inviting acceptance in any manner and by any medium reasonable in the circumstances;

(b) an order or other offer to buy goods for prompt or current shipment shall be construed as inviting acceptance either by a prompt promise to ship or by the prompt or current shipment of conforming or nonconforming goods, but such a shipment of non-conforming goods does not constitute an acceptance if the seller seasonably notifies the buyer that the shipment is offered only as an accommodation to the buyer.

(2) Where the beginning of a requested performance is a reasonable mode of acceptance an offeror who is not notified of acceptance within a reasonable time may treat the offer as having lapsed before acceptance.

§ 2-207. Additional Terms in Acceptance or Confirmation.

(1) A definite and seasonable expression of acceptance or a written confirmation which is sent within a reasonable time operates as an acceptance even though it states terms additional to or different from those offered or agreed upon, unless acceptance is expressly made conditional on assent to the additional or different terms.

(2) The additional terms are to be construed as proposals for addition to the contract. Between merchants such terms become part of the contract unless:

(a) the offer expressly limits acceptance to the terms of the offer;

(b) they materially alter it; or

(c) notification of objection to them has already been given or is given within a reasonable time after notice of them is received.

(3) Conduct by both parties which recognizes the existence of a contract is sufficient to establish a contract for sale although the writings of the parties do not otherwise establish a contract. In such case the terms of the particular contract consist of those

terms on which the writings of the parties agree, together with any supplementary terms incorporated under any other provisions of this Act.

§ 2-208. Course of Performance or Practical Construction.

(1) Where the contract for sale involves repeated occasions for performance by either party with knowledge of the nature of the performance and opportunity for objection to it by the other, any course of performance accepted or acquiesced in without objection shall be relevant to determine the meaning of the agreement.

(2) The express terms of the agreement and any such course of performance, as well as any course of dealing and usage of trade, shall be construed whenever reasonable as consistent with each other; but when such construction is unreasonable, express terms shall control course of performance and course of performance shall control both course of dealing and usage of trade (Section 1–205).

(3) Subject to the provisions of the next section on modification and waiver, such course of performance shall be relevant to show a waiver or modification of any term inconsistent with such course of performance.

§ 2-209. Modification, Rescission and Waiver.

(1) An agreement modifying a contract within this Article needs no consideration to be binding.

(2) A signed agreement which excludes modification or rescission except by a signed writing cannot be otherwise modified or rescinded, but except as between merchants such a requirement on a form supplied by the merchant must be separately signed by the other party.

(3) The requirements of the statute of frauds section of this Article (Section 2–201) must be satisfied if the contract as modified is within its provisions.

(4) Although an attempt at modification or rescission does not satisfy the requirements of subsection (2) or (3) it can operate as a waiver.

(5) A party who has made a waiver affecting an executory portion of the contract may retract the waiver by reasonable notification received by the other party that strict performance will be required of any term waived, unless the retraction would be unjust in view of a material change of position in reliance on the waiver.

§ 2-210. Delegation of Performance; Assignment of Rights.

(1) A party may perform his duty through a delegate unless otherwise agreed or unless the other party has a substantial interest in having his original promisor perform or control the acts required by the contract. No delegation of performance relieves the party delegating of any duty to perform or any liability for breach.

(2) Except as otherwise provided in Section 9–406, unless otherwise agreed, all rights of either seller or buyer can be assigned except where the assignment would materially change the duty of the other party, or increase materially the burden or risk imposed on him by his contract, or impair materially his chance of obtaining return performance. A right to damages for breach of the whole contract or a right arising out of the assignor's due performance of his entire obligation can be assigned despite agreement otherwise.

(3) The creation, attachment, perfection, or enforcement of a security interest in the seller's interest under a contract is not a transfer that materially changes the duty of or increases materially the burden or risk imposed on the buyer or impairs materially the buyer's chance of obtaining return performance within the purview of subsection (2) unless, and then only to the extent that, enforcement actually results in a delegation of material performance of the seller. Even in that event, the creation, attachment, perfection, and enforcement of the security interest remain effective, but (i) the seller is liable to the buyer for damages caused by the delegation to the extent that the damages could not reasonably by prevented by the buyer, and (ii) a court having jurisdiction may grant other appropriate relief, including cancellation of the contract for sale or an injunction against enforcement of the security interest or consummation of the enforcement.

(4) Unless the circumstances indicate the contrary a prohibition of assignment of "the contract" is to be construed as barring only the delegation to the assigness of the assignor's performance.

(5) An assignment of "the contract" or of "all my rights under the contract" or an assignment in similar general terms is an assignment of rights and unless the language or the circumstances (as in an assignment for security) indicate the contrary, it is a delegation of performance of the duties of the assignor and its acceptance by the assignee constitutes a promise by him to perform those duties. This promise is enforceable by either the assignor or the other party to the original contract.

(6) The other party may treat any assignment which delegates performance as creating reasonable grounds for insecurity and may without prejudice to his rights against the assignor demand assurances from the assignee (Section 2–609).

As amended in 1999.

PART 3 General Obligation and Construction of Contract

§ 2-301. General Obligations of Parties.

The obligation of the seller is to transfer and deliver and that of the buyer is to accept and pay in accordance with the contract.

§ 2-302. Unconscionable Contract or Clause.

(1) If the court as a matter of law finds the contract or any clause of the contract to have been unconscionable at the time it was made the court may refuse to enforce the contract, or it may enforce the remainder of the contract without the

unconscionable clause, or it may so limit the application of any unconscionable clause as to avoid any unconscionable result.

(2) When it is claimed or appears to the court that the contract or any clause thereof may be unconscionable the parties shall be afforded a reasonable opportunity to present evidence as to its commercial setting, purpose and effect to aid the court in making the determination.

§ 2-303. Allocations or Division of Risks.

Where this Article allocates a risk or a burden as between the parties "unless otherwise agreed", the agreement may not only shift the allocation but may also divide the risk or burden.

§ 2-304. Price Payable in Money, Goods, Realty, or Otherwise.

(1) The price can be made payable in money or otherwise. If it is payable in whole or in part in goods each party is a seller of the goods which he is to transfer.

(2) Even though all or part of the price is payable in an interest in realty the transfer of the goods and the seller's obligations with reference to them are subject to this Article, but not the transfer of the interest in realty or the transferor's obligations in connection therewith.

§ 2-305. Open Price Term.

(1) The parties if they so intend can conclude a contract for sale even though the price is not settled. In such a case the price is a reasonable price at the time for delivery if

(a) nothing is said as to price; or

(b) the price is left to be agreed by the parties and they fail to agree; or

(c) the price is to be fixed in terms of some agreed market or other standard as set or recorded by a third person or agency and it is not so set or recorded.

(2) A price to be fixed by the seller or by the buyer means a price for him to fix in good faith.

(3) When a price left to be fixed otherwise than by agreement of the parties fails to be fixed through fault of one party the other may at his option treat the contract as cancelled or himself fix a reasonable price.

(4) Where, however, the parties intend not to be bound unless the price be fixed or agreed and it is not fixed or agreed there is no contract. In such a case the buyer must return any goods already received or if unable so to do must pay their reasonable value at the time of delivery and the seller must return any portion of the price paid on account.

§ 2-306. Output, Requirements and Exclusive Dealings.

(1) A term which measures the quantity by the output of the seller or the requirements of the buyer means such actual output or requirements as may occur in good faith, except that no quantity unreasonably disproportionate to any stated estimate or in the absence of a stated estimate to any normal or otherwise comparable prior output or requirements may be tendered or demanded.

(2) A lawful agreement by either the seller or the buyer for exclusive dealing in the kind of goods concerned imposes unless otherwise agreed an obligation by the seller to use best efforts to supply the goods and by the buyer to use best efforts to promote their sale.

§ 2-307. Delivery in Single Lot or Several Lots.

Unless otherwise agreed all goods called for by a contract for sale must be tendered in a single delivery and payment is due only on such tender but where the circumstances give either party the right to make or demand delivery in lots the price if it can be apportioned may be demanded for each lot.

§ 2-308. Absence of Specified Place for Delivery.

Unless otherwise agreed

(a) the place for delivery of goods is the seller's place of business or if he has none his residence; but

(b) in a contract for sale of identified goods which to the knowledge of the parties at the time of contracting are in some other place, that place is the place for their delivery; and

(c) documents of title may be delivered through customary banking channels.

§ 2-309. Absence of Specific Time Provisions; Notice of Termination.

(1) The time for shipment or delivery or any other action under a contract if not provided in this Article or agreed upon shall be a reasonable time.

(2) Where the contract provides for successive performances but is indefinite in duration it is valid for a reasonable time but unless otherwise agreed may be terminated at any time by either party.

(3) Termination of a contract by one party except on the happening of an agreed event requires that reasonable notification be received by the other party and an agreement dispensing with notification is invalid if its operation would be unconscionable.

§ 2-310. Open Time for Payment or Running of Credit; Authority to Ship Under Reservation.

Unless otherwise agreed

(a) payment is due at the time and place at which the buyer is to receive the goods even though the place of shipment is the place of delivery; and

(b) if the seller is authorized to send the goods he may ship them under reservation, and may tender the documents of title, but the buyer may inspect the goods after their arrival before payment is due unless such inspection is inconsistent with the terms of the contract (Section 2–513); and

(c) if delivery is authorized and made by way of documents of title otherwise than by subsection (b) then payment is due at the time and place at which the buyer is to receive the documents regardless of where the goods are to be received; and

(d) where the seller is required or authorized to ship the goods on credit the credit period runs from the time of shipment but post-dating the invoice or delaying its dispatch will correspondingly delay the starting of the credit period.

§ 2–311. Options and Cooperation Respecting Performance.

(1) An agreement for sale which is otherwise sufficiently definite (subsection (3) of Section 2–204) to be a contract is not made invalid by the fact that it leaves particulars of performance to be specified by one of the parties. Any such specification must be made in good faith and within limits set by commercial reasonableness.

(2) Unless otherwise agreed specifications relating to assortment of the goods are at the buyer's option and except as otherwise provided in subsections (1)(c) and (3) of Section 2–319 specifications or arrangements relating to shipment are at the seller's option.

(3) Where such specification would materially affect the other party's performance but is not seasonably made or where one party's cooperation is necessary to the agreed performance of the other but is not seasonably forthcoming, the other party in addition to all other remedies

(a) is excused for any resulting delay in his own performance; and

(b) may also either proceed to perform in any reasonable manner or after the time for a material part of his own performance treat the failure to specify or to cooperate as a breach by failure to deliver or accept the goods.

§ 2–312. Warranty of Title and Against Infringement; Buyer's Obligation Against Infringement.

(1) Subject to subsection (2) there is in a contract for sale a warranty by the seller that

(a) the title conveyed shall be good, and its transfer rightful; and

(b) the goods shall be delivered free from any security interest or other lien or encumbrance of which the buyer at the time of contracting has no knowledge.

(2) A warranty under subsection (1) will be excluded or modified only by specific language or by circumstances which give the buyer reason to know that the person selling does not claim title in himself or that he is purporting to sell only such right or title as he or a third person may have.

(3) Unless otherwise agreed a seller who is a merchant regularly dealing in goods of the kind warrants that the goods shall be delivered free of the rightful claim of any third person by way of infringement or the like but a buyer who furnishes specifications to the seller must hold the seller harmless against any such claim which arises out of compliance with the specifications.

§ 2–313. Express Warranties by Affirmation, Promise, Description, Sample.

(1) Express warranties by the seller are created as follows:

(a) Any affirmation of fact or promise made by the seller to the buyer which relates to the goods and becomes part of the basis of the bargain creates an express warranty that the goods shall conform to the affirmation or promise.

(b) Any description of the goods which is made part of the basis of the bargain creates an express warranty that the goods shall conform to the description.

(c) Any sample or model which is made part of the basis of the bargain creates an express warranty that the whole of the goods shall conform to the sample or model.

(2) It is not necessary to the creation of an express warranty that the seller use formal words such as "warrant" or "guarantee" or that he have a specific intention to make a warranty, but an affirmation merely of the value of the goods or a statement purporting to be merely the seller's opinion or commendation of the goods does not create a warranty.

§ 2–314. Implied Warranty: Merchantability; Usage of Trade.

(1) Unless excluded or modified (Section 2–316), a warranty that the goods shall be merchantable is implied in a contract for their sale if the seller is a merchant with respect to goods of that kind. Under this section the serving for value of food or drink to be consumed either on the premises or elsewhere is a sale.

(2) Goods to be merchantable must be at least such as

(a) pass without objection in the trade under the contract description; and

(b) in the case of fungible goods, are of fair average quality within the description; and

(c) are fit for the ordinary purposes for which such goods are used; and

(d) run, within the variations permitted by the agreement, of even kind, quality and quantity within each unit and among all units involved; and

(e) are adequately contained, packaged, and labeled as the agreement may require; and

(f) conform to the promises or affirmations of fact made on the container or label if any.

(3) Unless excluded or modified (Section 2–316) other implied warranties may arise from course of dealing or usage of trade.

§ 2-315. Implied Warranty: Fitness for Particular Purpose.

Where the seller at the time of contracting has reason to know any particular purpose for which the goods are required and that the buyer is relying on the seller's skill or judgment to select or furnish suitable goods, there is unless excluded or modified under the next section an implied warranty that the goods shall be fit for such purpose.

§ 2-316. Exclusion or Modification of Warranties.

(1) Words or conduct relevant to the creation of an express warranty and words or conduct tending to negate or limit warranty shall be construed wherever reasonable as consistent with each other; but subject to the provisions of this Article on parol or extrinsic evidence (Section 2–202) negation or limitation is inoperative to the extent that such construction is unreasonable.

(2) Subject to subsection (3), to exclude or modify the implied warranty of merchantability or any part of it the language must mention merchantability and in case of a writing must be conspicuous, and to exclude or modify any implied warranty of fitness the exclusion must be by a writing and conspicuous. Language to exclude all implied warranties of fitness is sufficient if it states, for example, that "There are no warranties which extend beyond the description on the face hereof."

(3) Notwithstanding subsection (2)

(a) unless the circumstances indicate otherwise, all implied warranties are excluded by expressions like "as is", "with all faults" or other language which in common understanding calls the buyer's attention to the exclusion of warranties and makes plain that there is no implied warranty; and

(b) when the buyer before entering into the contract has examined the goods or the sample or model as fully as he desired or has refused to examine the goods there is no implied warranty with regard to defects which an examination ought in the circumstances to have revealed to him; and

(c) an implied warranty can also be excluded or modified by course of dealing or course of performance or usage of trade.

(4) Remedies for breach of warranty can be limited in accordance with the provisions of this Article on liquidation or limitation of damages and on contractual modification of remedy (Sections 2–718 and 2–719).

§ 2-317. Cumulation and Conflict of Warranties Express or Implied.

Warranties whether express or implied shall be construed as consistent with each other and as cumulative, but if such construction is unreasonable the intention of the parties shall determine which warranty is dominant. In ascertaining that intention the following rules apply:

(a) Exact or technical specifications displace an inconsistent sample or model or general language of description.

(b) A sample from an existing bulk displaces inconsistent general language of description.

(c) Express warranties displace inconsistent implied warranties other than an implied warranty of fitness for a particular purpose.

§ 2-318. Third Party Beneficiaries of Warranties Express or Implied.

Note: If this Act is introduced in the Congress of the United States this section should be omitted. (States to select one alternative.)

Alternative A A seller's warranty whether express or implied extends to any natural person who is in the family or household of his buyer or who is a guest in his home if it is reasonable to expect that such person may use, consume or be affected by the goods and who is injured in person by breach of the warranty. A seller may not exclude or limit the operation of this section.

Alternative B A seller's warranty whether express or implied extends to any natural person who may reasonably be expected to use, consume or be affected by the goods and who is injured in person by breach of the warranty. A seller may not exclude or limit the operation of this section.

Alternative C A seller's warranty whether express or implied extends to any person who may reasonably be expected to use, consume or be affected by the goods and who is injured by breach of the warranty. A seller may not exclude or limit the operation of this section with respect to injury to the person of an individual to whom the warranty extends.

As amended 1966.

§ 2-319. F.O.B. and F.A.S. Terms.

(1) Unless otherwise agreed the term F.O.B. (which means "free on board") at a named place, even though used only in connection with the stated price, is a delivery term under which

(a) when the term is F.O.B. the place of shipment, the seller must at that place ship the goods in the manner provided in this Article (Section 2–504) and bear the expense and risk of putting them into the possession of the carrier; or

(b) when the term is F.O.B. the place of destination, the seller must at his own expense and risk transport the goods to that place and there tender delivery of them in the manner provided in this Article (Section 2–503);

(c) when under either (a) or (b) the term is also F.O.B. vessel, car or other vehicle, the seller must in addition at his own expense and risk load the goods on board. If the term is F.O.B. vessel the buyer must name the vessel and in an appropriate case the seller must comply with the provisions of this Article on the form of bill of lading (Section 2–323).

(2) Unless otherwise agreed the term F.A.S. vessel (which means "free alongside") at a named port, even though used only in connection with the stated price, is a delivery term under which the seller must

(a) at his own expense and risk deliver the goods alongside the vessel in the manner usual in that port or on a dock designated and provided by the buyer; and

(b) obtain and tender a receipt for the goods in exchange for which the carrier is under a duty to issue a bill of lading.

(3) Unless otherwise agreed in any case falling within subsection (1)(a) or (c) or subsection (2) the buyer must seasonably give any needed instructions for making delivery, including when the term is F.A.S. or F.O.B. the loading berth of the vessel and in an appropriate case its name and sailing date. The seller may treat the failure of needed instructions as a failure of cooperation under this Article (Section 2–311). He may also at his option move the goods in any reasonable manner preparatory to delivery or shipment.

(4) Under the term F.O.B. vessel or F.A.S. unless otherwise agreed the buyer must make payment against tender of the required documents and the seller may not tender nor the buyer demand delivery of the goods in substitution for the documents.

§ 2–320. C.I.F. and C. & F. Terms.

(1) The term C.I.F. means that the price includes in a lump sum the cost of the goods and the insurance and freight to the named destination. The term C. & F. or C.F. means that the price so includes cost and freight to the named destination.

(2) Unless otherwise agreed and even though used only in connection with the stated price and destination, the term C.I.F. destination or its equivalent requires the seller at his own expense and risk to

(a) put the goods into the possession of a carrier at the port for shipment and obtain a negotiable bill or bills of lading covering the entire transportation to the named destination; and

(b) load the goods and obtain a receipt from the carrier (which may be contained in the bill of lading) showing that the freight has been paid or provided for; and

(c) obtain a policy or certificate of insurance, including any war risk insurance, of a kind and on terms then current at the port of shipment in the usual amount, in the currency of the contract, shown to cover the same goods covered by the bill of lading and providing for payment of loss to the order of the buyer or for the account of whom it may concern; but the seller may add to the price the amount of the premium for any such war risk insurance; and

(d) prepare an invoice of the goods and procure any other documents required to effect shipment or to comply with the contract; and

(e) forward and tender with commercial promptness all the documents in due form and with any indorsement necessary to perfect the buyer's rights.

(3) Unless otherwise agreed the term C. & F. or its equivalent has the same effect and imposes upon the seller the same obligations and risks as a C.I.F. term except the obligation as to insurance.

(4) Under the term C.I.F. or C. & F. unless otherwise agreed the buyer must make payment against tender of the required documents and the seller may not tender nor the buyer demand delivery of the goods in substitution for the documents.

§ 2–321. C.I.F. or C. & F.: "Net Landed Weights"; "Payment on Arrival"; Warranty of Condition on Arrival.

Under a contract containing a term C.I.F. or C. & F.

(1) Where the price is based on or is to be adjusted according to "net landed weights", "delivered weights", "out turn" quantity or quality or the like, unless otherwise agreed the seller must reasonably estimate the price. The payment due on tender of the documents called for by the contract is the amount so estimated, but after final adjustment of the price a settlement must be made with commercial promptness.

(2) An agreement described in subsection (1) or any warranty of quality or condition of the goods on arrival places upon the seller the risk of ordinary deterioration, shrinkage and the like in transportation but has no effect on the place or time of identification to the contract for sale or delivery or on the passing of the risk of loss.

(3) Unless otherwise agreed where the contract provides for payment on or after arrival of the goods the seller must before payment allow such preliminary inspection as is feasible; but if the goods are lost delivery of the documents and payment are due when the goods should have arrived.

§ 2–322. Delivery "Ex-Ship".

(1) Unless otherwise agreed a term for delivery of goods "ex-ship" (which means from the carrying vessel) or in equivalent language is not restricted to a particular ship and requires delivery from a ship which has reached a place at the named port of destination where goods of the kind are usually discharged.

(2) Under such a term unless otherwise agreed

(a) the seller must discharge all liens arising out of the carriage and furnish the buyer with a direction which puts the carrier under a duty to deliver the goods; and

(b) the risk of loss does not pass to the buyer until the goods leave the ship's tackle or are otherwise properly unloaded.

§ 2–323. Form of Bill of Lading Required in Overseas Shipment; "Overseas".

(1) Where the contract contemplates overseas shipment and contains a term C.I.F. or C. & F. or F.O.B. vessel, the seller unless otherwise agreed must obtain a negotiable bill of lading stating that the goods have been loaded on board or, in the case of a term C.I.F. or C. & F., received for shipment.

(2) Where in a case within subsection (1) a bill of lading has been issued in a set of parts, unless otherwise agreed if the documents are not to be sent from abroad the buyer may demand tender of

the full set; otherwise only one part of the bill of lading need be tendered. Even if the agreement expressly requires a full set

(a) due tender of a single part is acceptable within the provisions of this Article on cure of improper delivery (subsection (1) of Section 2–508); and

(b) even though the full set is demanded, if the documents are sent from abroad the person tendering an incomplete set may nevertheless require payment upon furnishing an indemnity which the buyer in good faith deems adequate.

(3) A shipment by water or by air or a contract contemplating such shipment is "overseas" insofar as by usage of trade or agreement it is subject to the commercial, financing or shipping practices characteristic of international deep water commerce.

§ 2-324. "No Arrival, No Sale" Term.

Under a term "no arrival, no sale" or terms of like meaning, unless otherwise agreed,

(a) the seller must properly ship conforming goods and if they arrive by any means he must tender them on arrival but he assumes no obligation that the goods will arrive unless he has caused the non-arrival; and

(b) where without fault of the seller the goods are in part lost or have so deteriorated as no longer to conform to the contract or arrive after the contract time, the buyer may proceed as if there had been casualty to identified goods (Section 2–613).

§ 2-325. "Letter of Credit" Term; "Confirmed Credit".

(1) Failure of the buyer seasonably to furnish an agreed letter of credit is a breach of the contract for sale.

(2) The delivery to seller of a proper letter of credit suspends the buyer's obligation to pay. If the letter of credit is dishonored, the seller may on seasonable notification to the buyer require payment directly from him.

(3) Unless otherwise agreed the term "letter of credit" or "banker's credit" in a contract for sale means an irrevocable credit issued by a financing agency of good repute and, where the shipment is overseas, of good international repute. The term "confirmed credit" means that the credit must also carry the direct obligation of such an agency which does business in the seller's financial market.

§ 2-326. Sale on Approval and Sale or Return; Rights of Creditors.

(1) Unless otherwise agreed, if delivered goods may be returned by the buyer even though they conform to the contract, the transaction is

(a) a "sale on approval" if the goods are delivered primarily for use, and

(b) a "sale or return" if the goods are delivered primarily for resale.

(2) Goods held on approval are not subject to the claims of the buyer's creditors until acceptance; goods held on sale or return are subject to such claims while in the buyer's possession.

(3) Any "or return" term of a contract for sale is to be treated as a separate contract for sale within the statute of frauds section of this Article (Section 2–201) and as contradicting the sale aspect of the contract within the provisions of this Article or on parol or extrinsic evidence (Section 2–202).

As amended in 1999.

§ 2-327. Special Incidents of Sale on Approval and Sale or Return.

(1) Under a sale on approval unless otherwise agreed

(a) although the goods are identified to the contract the risk of loss and the title do not pass to the buyer until acceptance; and

(b) use of the goods consistent with the purpose of trial is not acceptance but failure seasonably to notify the seller of election to return the goods is acceptance, and if the goods conform to the contract acceptance of any part is acceptance of the whole; and

(c) after due notification of election to return, the return is at the seller's risk and expense but a merchant buyer must follow any reasonable instructions.

(2) Under a sale or return unless otherwise agreed

(a) the option to return extends to the whole or any commercial unit of the goods while in substantially their original condition, but must be exercised seasonably; and

(b) the return is at the buyer's risk and expense.

§ 2-328. Sale by Auction.

(1) In a sale by auction if goods are put up in lots each lot is the subject of a separate sale.

(2) A sale by auction is complete when the auctioneer so announces by the fall of the hammer or in other customary manner. Where a bid is made while the hammer is falling in acceptance of a prior bid the auctioneer may in his discretion reopen the bidding or declare the goods sold under the bid on which the hammer was falling.

(3) Such a sale is with reserve unless the goods are in explicit terms put up without reserve. In an auction with reserve the auctioneer may withdraw the goods at any time until he announces completion of the sale. In an auction without reserve, after the auctioneer calls for bids on an article or lot, that article or lot cannot be withdrawn unless no bid is made within a reasonable time. In either case a bidder may retract his bid until the auctioneer's announcement of completion of the sale, but a bidder's retraction does not revive any previous bid.

(4) If the auctioneer knowingly receives a bid on the seller's behalf or the seller makes or procures such as bid, and notice has not been given that liberty for such bidding is reserved, the buyer may at his option avoid the sale or take the goods at the price of the last good faith bid prior to the completion of the sale. This subsection shall not apply to any bid at a forced sale.

PART 4 Title, Creditors and Good Faith Purchasers

§ 2–401. Passing of Title; Reservation for Security; Limited Application of This Section.

Each provision of this Article with regard to the rights, obligations and remedies of the seller, the buyer, purchasers or other third parties applies irrespective of title to the goods except where the provision refers to such title. Insofar as situations are not covered by the other provisions of this Article and matters concerning title became material the following rules apply:

(1) Title to goods cannot pass under a contract for sale prior to their identification to the contract (Section 2–501), and unless otherwise explicitly agreed the buyer acquires by their identification a special property as limited by this Act. Any retention or reservation by the seller of the title (property) in goods shipped or delivered to the buyer is limited in effect to a reservation of a security interest. Subject to these provisions and to the provisions of the Article on Secured Transactions (Article 9), title to goods passes from the seller to the buyer in any manner and on any conditions explicitly agreed on by the parties.

(2) Unless otherwise explicitly agreed title passes to the buyer at the time and place at which the seller completes his performance with reference to the physical delivery of the goods, despite any reservation of a security interest and even though a document of title is to be delivered at a different time or place; and in particular and despite any reservation of a security interest by the bill of lading

(a) if the contract requires or authorizes the seller to send the goods to the buyer but does not require him to deliver them at destination, title passes to the buyer at the time and place of shipment; but

(b) if the contract requires delivery at destination, title passes on tender there.

(3) Unless otherwise explicitly agreed where delivery is to be made without moving the goods,

(a) if the seller is to deliver a document of title, title passes at the time when and the place where he delivers such documents; or

(b) if the goods are at the time of contracting already identified and no documents are to be delivered, title passes at the time and place of contracting.

(4) A rejection or other refusal by the buyer to receive or retain the goods, whether or not justified, or a justified revocation of acceptance revests title to the goods in the seller. Such revesting occurs by operation of law and is not a "sale".

§ 2–402. Rights of Seller's Creditors Against Sold Goods.

(1) Except as provided in subsections (2) and (3), rights of unsecured creditors of the seller with respect to goods which have been identified to a contract for sale are subject to the buyer's rights to recover the goods under this Article (Sections 2–502 and 2–716).

(2) A creditor of the seller may treat a sale or an identification of goods to a contract for sale as void if as against him a retention of possession by the seller is fraudulent under any rule of law of the state where the goods are situated, except that retention of possession in good faith and current course of trade by a merchant-seller for a commercially reasonable time after a sale or identification is not fraudulent.

(3) Nothing in this Article shall be deemed to impair the rights of creditors of the seller

(a) under the provisions of the Article on Secured Transactions (Article 9); or

(b) where identification to the contract or delivery is made not in current course of trade but in satisfaction of or as security for a pre-existing claim for money, security or the like and is made under circumstances which under any rule of law of the state where the goods are situated would apart from this Article constitute the transaction a fraudulent transfer or voidable preference.

§ 2–403. Power to Transfer; Good Faith Purchase of Goods; "Entrusting".

(1) A purchaser of goods acquires all title which his transferor had or had power to transfer except that a purchaser of a limited interest acquires rights only to the extent of the interest purchased. A person with voidable title has power to transfer a good title to a good faith purchaser for value. When goods have been delivered under a transaction of purchase the purchaser has such power even though

(a) the transferor was deceived as to the identity of the purchaser, or

(b) the delivery was in exchange for a check which is later dishonored, or

(c) it was agreed that the transaction was to be a "cash sale", or

(d) the delivery was procured through fraud punishable as larcenous under the criminal law.

(2) Any entrusting of possession of goods to a merchant who deals in goods of that kind gives him power to transfer all rights of the entruster to a buyer in ordinary course of business.

(3) "Entrusting" includes any delivery and any acquiescence in retention of possession regardless of any condition expressed between the parties to the delivery or acquiescence and regardless of whether the procurement of the entrusting or the possessor's disposition of the goods have been such as to be larcenous under the criminal law.

(4) The rights of other purchasers of goods and of lien creditors are governed by the Articles on Secured Transactions (Article 9), Bulk Transfers (Article 6) and Documents of Title (Article 7).

As amended in 1988.

PART 5 Performance

§ 2-501. Insurable Interest in Goods; Manner of Identification of Goods.

(1) The buyer obtains a special property and an insurable interest in goods by identification of existing goods as goods to which the contract refers even though the goods so identified are non-conforming and he has an option to return or reject them. Such identification can be made at any time and in any manner explicitly agreed to by the parties. In the absence of explicit agreement identification occurs

(a) when the contract is made if it is for the sale of goods already existing and identified;

(b) if the contract is for the sale of future goods other than those described in paragraph (c), when goods are shipped, marked or otherwise designated by the seller as goods to which the contract refers;

(c) when the crops are planted or otherwise become growing crops or the young are conceived if the contract is for the sale of unborn young to be born within twelve months after contracting or for the sale of crops to be harvested within twelve months or the next normal harvest season after contracting whichever is longer.

(2) The seller retains an insurable interest in goods so long as title to or any security interest in the goods remains in him and where the identification is by the seller alone he may until default or insolvency or notification to the buyer that the identification is final substitute other goods for those identified.

(3) Nothing in this section impairs any insurable interest recognized under any other statute or rule of law.

§ 2-502. Buyer's Right to Goods on Seller's Insolvency.

(1) Subject to subsections (2) and (3) and even though the goods have not been shipped a buyer who has paid a part or all of the price of goods in which he has a special property under the provisions of the immediately preceding section may on making and keeping good a tender of any unpaid portion of their price recover them from the seller if:

(a) in the case of goods bought for personal, family, or household purposes, the seller repudiates or fails to deliver as required by the contract; or

(b) in all cases, the seller becomes insolvent within ten days after receipt of the first installment on their price.

(2) The buyer's right to recover the goods under subsection (1)(a) vests upon acquisition of a special property, even if the seller had not then repudiated or failed to deliver.

(3) If the identification creating his special property has been made by the buyer he acquires the right to recover the goods only if they conform to the contract for sale.

As amended in 1999.

§ 2-503. Manner of Seller's Tender of Delivery.

(1) Tender of delivery requires that the seller put and hold conforming goods at the buyer's disposition and give the buyer any notification reasonably necessary to enable him to take delivery. The manner, time and place for tender are determined by the agreement and this Article, and in particular

(a) tender must be at a reasonable hour, and if it is of goods they must be kept available for the period reasonably necessary to enable the buyer to take possession; but

(b) unless otherwise agreed the buyer must furnish facilities reasonably suited to the receipt of the goods.

(2) Where the case is within the next section respecting shipment tender requires that the seller comply with its provisions.

(3) Where the seller is required to deliver at a particular destination tender requires that he comply with subsection (1) and also in any appropriate case tender documents as described in subsections (4) and (5) of this section.

(4) Where goods are in the possession of a bailee and are to be delivered without being moved

(a) tender requires that the seller either tender a negotiable document of title covering such goods or procure acknowledgment by the bailee of the buyer's right to possession of the goods; but

(b) tender to the buyer of a non-negotiable document of title or of a written direction to the bailee to deliver is sufficient tender unless the buyer seasonably objects, and receipt by the bailee of notification of the buyer's rights fixes those rights as against the bailee and all third persons; but risk of loss of the goods and of any failure by the bailee to honor the non-negotiable document of title or to obey the direction remains on the seller until the buyer has had a reasonable time to present the document or direction, and a refusal by the bailee to honor the document or to obey the direction defeats the tender.

(5) Where the contract requires the seller to deliver documents

(a) he must tender all such documents in correct form, except as provided in this Article with respect to bills of lading in a set (subsection (2) of Section 2–323); and

(b) tender through customary banking channels is sufficient and dishonor of a draft accompanying the documents constitutes non-acceptance or rejection.

§ 2-504. Shipment by Seller.

Where the seller is required or authorized to send the goods to the buyer and the contract does not require him to deliver them at a particular destination, then unless otherwise agreed he must

(a) put the goods in the possession of such a carrier and make such a contract for their transportation as may be reasonable having regard to the nature of the goods and other circumstances of the case; and

(b) obtain and promptly deliver or tender in due form any document necessary to enable the buyer to obtain possession of the goods or otherwise required by the agreement or by usage of trade; and

(c) promptly notify the buyer of the shipment.

Failure to notify the buyer under paragraph (c) or to make a proper contract under paragraph (a) is a ground for rejection only if material delay or loss ensues.

§ 2–505. Seller's Shipment under Reservation.

(1) Where the seller has identified goods to the contract by or before shipment:

(a) his procurement of a negotiable bill of lading to his own order or otherwise reserves in him a security interest in the goods. His procurement of the bill to the order of a financing agency or of the buyer indicates in addition only the seller's expectation of transferring that interest to the person named.

(b) a non-negotiable bill of lading to himself or his nominee reserves possession of the goods as security but except in a case of conditional delivery (subsection (2) of Section 2–507) a non-negotiable bill of lading naming the buyer as consignee reserves no security interest even though the seller retains possession of the bill of lading.

(2) When shipment by the seller with reservation of a security interest is in violation of the contract for sale it constitutes an improper contract for transportation within the preceding section but impairs neither the rights given to the buyer by shipment and identification of the goods to the contract nor the seller's powers as a holder of a negotiable document.

§ 2–506. Rights of Financing Agency.

(1) A financing agency by paying or purchasing for value a draft which relates to a shipment of goods acquires to the extent of the payment or purchase and in addition to its own rights under the draft and any document of title securing it any rights of the shipper in the goods including the right to stop delivery and the shipper's right to have the draft honored by the buyer.

(2) The right to reimbursement of a financing agency which has in good faith honored or purchased the draft under commitment to or authority from the buyer is not impaired by subsequent discovery of defects with reference to any relevant document which was apparently regular on its face.

§ 2–507. Effect of Seller's Tender; Delivery on Condition.

(1) Tender of delivery is a condition to the buyer's duty to accept the goods and, unless otherwise agreed, to his duty to pay for them. Tender entitles the seller to acceptance of the goods and to payment according to the contract.

(2) Where payment is due and demanded on the delivery to the buyer of goods or documents of title, his right as against the seller to retain or dispose of them is conditional upon his making the payment due.

§ 2–508. Cure by Seller of Improper Tender or Delivery; Replacement.

(1) Where any tender or delivery by the seller is rejected because non-conforming and the time for performance has not yet expired, the seller may seasonably notify the buyer of his intention to cure and may then within the contract time make a conforming delivery.

(2) Where the buyer rejects a non-conforming tender which the seller had reasonable grounds to believe would be acceptable with or without money allowance the seller may if he seasonably notifies the buyer have a further reasonable time to substitute a conforming tender.

§ 2–509. Risk of Loss in the Absence of Breach.

(1) Where the contract requires or authorizes the seller to ship the goods by carrier

(a) if it does not require him to deliver them at a particular destination, the risk of loss passes to the buyer when the goods are duly delivered to the carrier even though the shipment is under reservation (Section 2–505); but

(b) if it does require him to deliver them at a particular destination and the goods are there duly tendered while in the possession of the carrier, the risk of loss passes to the buyer when the goods are there duly so tendered as to enable the buyer to take delivery.

(2) Where the goods are held by a bailee to be delivered without being moved, the risk of loss passes to the buyer

(a) on his receipt of a negotiable document of title covering the goods; or

(b) on acknowledgment by the bailee of the buyer's right to possession of the goods; or

(c) after his receipt of a non-negotiable document of title or other written direction to deliver, as provided in subsection (4) (b) of Section 2–503.

(3) In any case not within subsection (1) or (2), the risk of loss passes to the buyer on his receipt of the goods if the seller is a merchant; otherwise the risk passes to the buyer on tender of delivery.

(4) The provisions of this section are subject to contrary agreement of the parties and to the provisions of this Article on sale on approval (Section 2–327) and on effect of breach on risk of loss (Section 2–510).

§ 2–510. Effect of Breach on Risk of Loss.

(1) Where a tender or delivery of goods so fails to conform to the contract as to give a right of rejection the risk of their loss remains on the seller until cure or acceptance.

(2) Where the buyer rightfully revokes acceptance he may to the extent of any deficiency in his effective insurance

coverage treat the risk of loss as having rested on the seller from the beginning.

(3) Where the buyer as to conforming goods already identified to the contract for sale repudiates or is otherwise in breach before risk of their loss has passed to him, the seller may to the extent of any deficiency in his effective insurance coverage treat the risk of loss as resting on the buyer for a commercially reasonable time.

§ 2-511. Tender of Payment by Buyer; Payment by Check.

(1) Unless otherwise agreed tender of payment is a condition to the seller's duty to tender and complete any delivery.

(2) Tender of payment is sufficient when made by any means or in any manner current in the ordinary course of business unless the seller demands payment in legal tender and gives any extension of time reasonably necessary to procure it.

(3) Subject to the provisions of this Act on the effect of an instrument on an obligation (Section 3–310), payment by check is conditional and is defeated as between the parties by dishonor of the check on due presentment.

As amended in 1994.

§ 2-512. Payment by Buyer Before Inspection.

(1) Where the contract requires payment before inspection non-conformity of the goods does not excuse the buyer from so making payment unless

(a) the non-conformity appears without inspection; or

(b) despite tender of the required documents the circumstances would justify injunction against honor under this Act (Section 5–109(b)).

(2) Payment pursuant to subsection (1) does not constitute an acceptance of goods or impair the buyer's right to inspect or any of his remedies.

As amended in 1995.

§ 2-513. Buyer's Right to Inspection of Goods.

(1) Unless otherwise agreed and subject to subsection (3), where goods are tendered or delivered or identified to the contract for sale, the buyer has a right before payment or acceptance to inspect them at any reasonable place and time and in any reasonable manner. When the seller is required or authorized to send the goods to the buyer, the inspection may be after their arrival.

(2) Expenses of inspection must be borne by the buyer but may be recovered from the seller if the goods do not conform and are rejected.

(3) Unless otherwise agreed and subject to the provisions of this Article on C.I.F. contracts (subsection (3) of Section 2–321), the buyer is not entitled to inspect the goods before payment of the price when the contract provides

(a) for delivery "C.O.D." or on other like terms; or

(b) for payment against documents of title, except where such payment is due only after the goods are to become available for inspection.

(4) A place or method of inspection fixed by the parties is presumed to be exclusive but unless otherwise expressly agreed it does not postpone identification or shift the place for delivery or for passing the risk of loss. If compliance becomes impossible, inspection shall be as provided in this section unless the place or method fixed was clearly intended as an indispensable condition failure of which avoids the contract.

§ 2-514. When Documents Deliverable on Acceptance; When on Payment.

Unless otherwise agreed documents against which a draft is drawn are to be delivered to the drawee on acceptance of the draft if it is payable more than three days after presentment; otherwise, only on payment.

§ 2-515. Preserving Evidence of Goods in Dispute.

In furtherance of the adjustment of any claim or dispute

(a) either party on reasonable notification to the other and for the purpose of ascertaining the facts and preserving evidence has the right to inspect, test and sample the goods including such of them as may be in the possession or control of the other; and

(b) the parties may agree to a third party inspection or survey to determine the conformity or condition of the goods and may agree that the findings shall be binding upon them in any subsequent litigation or adjustment.

PART 6 Breach, Repudiation and Excuse

§ 2-601. Buyer's Rights on Improper Delivery.

Subject to the provisions of this Article on breach in installment contracts (Section 2–612) and unless otherwise agreed under the sections on contractual limitations of remedy (Sections 2–718 and 2–719), if the goods or the tender of delivery fail in any respect to conform to the contract, the buyer may

(a) reject the whole; or

(b) accept the whole; or

(c) accept any commercial unit or units and reject the rest.

§ 2-602. Manner and Effect of Rightful Rejection.

(1) Rejection of goods must be within a reasonable time after their delivery or tender. It is ineffective unless the buyer seasonably notifies the seller.

(2) Subject to the provisions of the two following sections on rejected goods (Sections 2–603 and 2–604),

(a) after rejection any exercise of ownership by the buyer with respect to any commercial unit is wrongful as against the seller; and

(b) if the buyer has before rejection taken physical possession of goods in which he does not have a security interest under the provisions of this Article (subsection (3) of Section 2–711), he is under a duty after rejection to hold them with reasonable care at the seller's disposition for a time sufficient to permit the seller to remove them; but

(c) the buyer has no further obligations with regard to goods rightfully rejected.

(3) The seller's rights with respect to goods wrongfully rejected are governed by the provisions of this Article on Seller's remedies in general (Section 2–703).

§ 2–603. Merchant Buyer's Duties as to Rightfully Rejected Goods.

(1) Subject to any security interest in the buyer (subsection (3) of Section 2–711), when the seller has no agent or place of business at the market of rejection a merchant buyer is under a duty after rejection of goods in his possession or control to follow any reasonable instructions received from the seller with respect to the goods and in the absence of such instructions to make reasonable efforts to sell them for the seller's account if they are perishable or threaten to decline in value speedily. Instructions are not reasonable if on demand indemnity for expenses is not forthcoming.

(2) When the buyer sells goods under subsection (1), he is entitled to reimbursement from the seller or out of the proceeds for reasonable expenses of caring for and selling them, and if the expenses include no selling commission then to such commission as is usual in the trade or if there is none to a reasonable sum not exceeding ten per cent on the gross proceeds.

(3) In complying with this section the buyer is held only to good faith and good faith conduct hereunder is neither acceptance nor conversion nor the basis of an action for damages.

§ 2–604. Buyer's Options as to Salvage of Rightfully Rejected Goods.

Subject to the provisions of the immediately preceding section on perishables if the seller gives no instructions within a reasonable time after notification of rejection the buyer may store the rejected goods for the seller's account or reship them to him or resell them for the seller's account with reimbursement as provided in the preceding section. Such action is not acceptance or conversion.

§ 2–605. Waiver of Buyer's Objections by Failure to Particularize.

(1) The buyer's failure to state in connection with rejection a particular defect which is ascertainable by reasonable inspection precludes him from relying on the unstated defect to justify rejection or to establish breach

(a) where the seller could have cured it if stated seasonably; or

(b) between merchants when the seller has after rejection made a request in writing for a full and final written statement of all defects on which the buyer proposes to rely.

(2) Payment against documents made without reservation of rights precludes recovery of the payment for defects apparent on the face of the documents.

§ 2–606. What Constitutes Acceptance of Goods.

(1) Acceptance of goods occurs when the buyer

(a) after a reasonable opportunity to inspect the goods signifies to the seller that the goods are conforming or that he will take or retain them in spite of their nonconformity; or

(b) fails to make an effective rejection (subsection (1) of Section 2–602), but such acceptance does not occur until the buyer has had a reasonable opportunity to inspect them; or

(c) does any act inconsistent with the seller's ownership; but if such act is wrongful as against the seller it is an acceptance only if ratified by him.

(2) Acceptance of a part of any commercial unit is acceptance of that entire unit.

§ 2–607. Effect of Acceptance; Notice of Breach; Burden of Establishing Breach After Acceptance; Notice of Claim or Litigation to Person Answerable Over.

(1) The buyer must pay at the contract rate for any goods accepted.

(2) Acceptance of goods by the buyer precludes rejection of the goods accepted and if made with knowledge of a non-conformity cannot be revoked because of it unless the acceptance was on the reasonable assumption that the non-conformity would be seasonably cured but acceptance does not of itself impair any other remedy provided by this Article for non-conformity.

(3) Where a tender has been accepted

(a) the buyer must within a reasonable time after he discovers or should have discovered any breach notify the seller of breach or be barred from any remedy; and

(b) if the claim is one for infringement or the like (subsection (3) of Section 2–312) and the buyer is sued as a result of such a breach he must so notify the seller within a reasonable time after he receives notice of the litigation or be barred from any remedy over for liability established by the litigation.

(4) The burden is on the buyer to establish any breach with respect to the goods accepted.

(5) Where the buyer is sued for breach of a warranty or other obligation for which his seller is answerable over

(a) he may give his seller written notice of the litigation. If the notice states that the seller may come in and defend and that if the seller does not do so he will be bound in any action against him by his buyer by any determination of fact common to the two litigations, then unless the seller after seasonable receipt of the notice does come in and defend he is so bound.

(b) if the claim is one for infringement or the like (subsection (3) of Section 2–312) the original seller may demand in writing that his buyer turn over to him control of the litigation including settlement or else be barred from any remedy over and if he also agrees to bear all expense and to satisfy any adverse judgment, then unless the buyer after seasonable receipt of the demand does turn over control the buyer is so barred.

(6) The provisions of subsections (3), (4) and (5) apply to any obligation of a buyer to hold the seller harmless against infringement or the like (subsection (3) of Section 2–312).

§ 2-608. Revocation of Acceptance in Whole or in Part.

(1) The buyer may revoke his acceptance of a lot or commercial unit whose non-conformity substantially impairs its value to him if he has accepted it

(a) on the reasonable assumption that its nonconformity would be cured and it has not been seasonably cured; or

(b) without discovery of such non-conformity if his acceptance was reasonably induced either by the difficulty of discovery before acceptance or by the seller's assurances.

(2) Revocation of acceptance must occur within a reasonable time after the buyer discovers or should have discovered the ground for it and before any substantial change in condition of the goods which is not caused by their own defects. It is not effective until the buyer notifies the seller of it.

(3) A buyer who so revokes has the same rights and duties with regard to the goods involved as if he had rejected them.

§ 2-609. Right to Adequate Assurance of Performance.

(1) A contract for sale imposes an obligation on each party that the other's expectation of receiving due performance will not be impaired. When reasonable grounds for insecurity arise with respect to the performance of either party the other may in writing demand adequate assurance of due performance and until he receives such assurance may if commercially reasonable suspend any performance for which he has not already received the agreed return.

(2) Between merchants the reasonableness of grounds for insecurity and the adequacy of any assurance offered shall be determined according to commercial standards.

(3) Acceptance of any improper delivery or payment does not prejudice the party's right to demand adequate assurance of future performance.

(4) After receipt of a justified demand failure to provide within a reasonable time not exceeding thirty days such assurance of due performance as is adequate under the circumstances of the particular case is a repudiation of the contract.

§ 2-610. Anticipatory Repudiation.

When either party repudiates the contract with respect to a performance not yet due the loss of which will substantially impair the value of the contract to the other, the aggrieved party may

(a) for a commercially reasonable time await performance by the repudiating party; or

(b) resort to any remedy for breach (Section 2–703 or Section 2–711), even though he has notified the repudiating party that he would await the latter's performance and has urged retraction; and

(c) in either case suspend his own performance or proceed in accordance with the provisions of this Article on the seller's right to identify goods to the contract notwithstanding breach or to salvage unfinished goods (Section 2–704).

§ 2-611. Retraction of Anticipatory Repudiation.

(1) Until the repudiating party's next performance is due he can retract his repudiation unless the aggrieved party has since the repudiation cancelled or materially changed his position or otherwise indicated that he considers the repudiation final.

(2) Retraction may be by any method which clearly indicates to the aggrieved party that the repudiating party intends to perform, but must include any assurance justifiably demanded under the provisions of this Article (Section 2–609).

(3) Retraction reinstates the repudiating party's rights under the contract with due excuse and allowance to the aggrieved party for any delay occasioned by the repudiation.

§ 2-612. "Installment Contract"; Breach.

(1) An "installment contract" is one which requires or authorizes the delivery of goods in separate lots to be separately accepted, even though the contract contains a clause "each delivery is a separate contract" or its equivalent.

(2) The buyer may reject any installment which is non-conforming if the non-conformity substantially impairs the value of that installment and cannot be cured or if the non-conformity is a defect in the required documents; but if the non-conformity does not fall within subsection (3) and the seller gives adequate assurance of its cure the buyer must accept that installment.

(3) Whenever non-conformity or default with respect to one or more installments substantially impairs the value of the whole contract there is a breach of the whole. But the aggrieved party reinstates the contract if he accepts a non-conforming installment without seasonably notifying of cancellation or if he brings an action with respect only to past installments or demands performance as to future installments.

§ 2-613. Casualty to Identified Goods.

Where the contract requires for its performance goods identified when the contract is made, and the goods suffer casualty without fault of either party before the risk of loss passes to the buyer, or in a proper case under a "no arrival, no sale" term (Section 2–324) then

(a) if the loss is total the contract is avoided; and

(b) if the loss is partial or the goods have so deteriorated as no longer to conform to the contract the buyer may nevertheless demand inspection and at his option either treat the contract as voided or accept the goods with due allowance from the contract price for the deterioration or the deficiency in quantity but without further right against the seller.

§ 2-614. Substituted Performance.

(1) Where without fault of either party the agreed berthing, loading, or unloading facilities fail or an agreed type of carrier becomes unavailable or the agreed manner of delivery otherwise becomes commercially impracticable but a commercially reasonable substitute is available, such substitute performance must be tendered and accepted.

(2) If the agreed means or manner of payment fails because of domestic or foreign governmental regulation, the seller may withhold or stop delivery unless the buyer provides a means or manner of payment which is commercially a substantial equivalent. If delivery has already been taken, payment by the means or in the manner provided by the regulation discharges the buyer's obligation unless the regulation is discriminatory, oppressive or predatory.

§ 2-615. Excuse by Failure of Presupposed Conditions.

Except so far as a seller may have assumed a greater obligation and subject to the preceding section on substituted performance:

(a) Delay in delivery or non-delivery in whole or in part by a seller who complies with paragraphs (b) and (c) is not a breach of his duty under a contract for sale if performance as agreed has been made impracticable by the occurrence of a contingency the nonoccurrence of which was a basic assumption on which the contract was made or by compliance in good faith with any applicable foreign or domestic governmental regulation or order whether or not it later proves to be invalid.

(b) Where the causes mentioned in paragraph (a) affect only a part of the seller's capacity to perform, he must allocate production and deliveries among his customers but may at his option include regular customers not then under contract as well as his own requirements for further manufacture. He may so allocate in any manner which is fair and reasonable.

(c) The seller must notify the buyer seasonably that there will be delay or non-delivery and, when allocation is required under paragraph (b), of the estimated quota thus made available for the buyer.

§ 2-616. Procedure on Notice Claiming Excuse.

(1) Where the buyer receives notification of a material or indefinite delay or an allocation justified under the preceding section he may by written notification to the seller as to any delivery concerned, and where the prospective deficiency substantially impairs the value of the whole contract under the provisions of this Article relating to breach of installment contracts (Section 2–612), then also as to the whole,

(a) terminate and thereby discharge any unexecuted portion of the contract; or

(b) modify the contract by agreeing to take his available quota in substitution.

(2) If after receipt of such notification from the seller the buyer fails so to modify the contract within a reasonable time not exceeding thirty days the contract lapses with respect to any deliveries affected.

(3) The provisions of this section may not be negated by agreement except in so far as the seller has assumed a greater obligation under the preceding section.

PART 7 Remedies

§ 2-701. Remedies for Breach of Collateral Contracts Not Impaired.

Remedies for breach of any obligation or promise collateral or ancillary to a contract for sale are not impaired by the provisions of this Article.

§ 2-702. Seller's Remedies on Discovery of Buyer's Insolvency.

(1) Where the seller discovers the buyer to be insolvent he may refuse delivery except for cash including payment for all goods theretofore delivered under the contract, and stop delivery under this Article (Section 2–705).

(2) Where the seller discovers that the buyer has received goods on credit while insolvent he may reclaim the goods upon demand made within ten days after the receipt, but if misrepresentation of solvency has been made to the particular seller in writing within three months before delivery the ten day limitation does not apply. Except as provided in this subsection the seller may not base a right to reclaim goods on the buyer's fraudulent or innocent misrepresentation of solvency or of intent to pay.

(3) The seller's right to reclaim under subsection (2) is subject to the rights of a buyer in ordinary course or other good faith purchaser under this Article (Section 2–403). Successful reclamation of goods excludes all other remedies with respect to them.

§ 2-703. Seller's Remedies in General.

Where the buyer wrongfully rejects or revokes acceptance of goods or fails to make a payment due on or before delivery or repudiates with respect to a part or the whole, then with respect to any goods directly affected and, if the breach is of the whole contract (Section 2–612), then also with respect to the whole undelivered balance, the aggrieved seller may

(a) withhold delivery of such goods;

(b) stop delivery by any bailee as hereafter provided (Section 2–705);

(c) proceed under the next section respecting goods still unidentified to the contract;

(d) resell and recover damages as hereafter provided (Section 2–706);

(e) recover damages for non-acceptance (Section 2–708) or in a proper case the price (Section 2–709);

(f) cancel.

§ 2–704. Seller's Right to Identify Goods to the Contract Notwithstanding Breach or to Salvage Unfinished Goods.

(1) An aggrieved seller under the preceding section may

(a) identify to the contract conforming goods not already identified if at the time he learned of the breach they are in his possession or control;

(b) treat as the subject of resale goods which have demonstrably been intended for the particular contract even though those goods are unfinished.

(2) Where the goods are unfinished an aggrieved seller may in the exercise of reasonable commercial judgment for the purposes of avoiding loss and of effective realization either complete the manufacture and wholly identify the goods to the contract or cease manufacture and resell for scrap or salvage value or proceed in any other reasonable manner.

§ 2–705. Seller's Stoppage of Delivery in Transit or Otherwise.

(1) The seller may stop delivery of goods in the possession of a carrier or other bailee when he discovers the buyer to be insolvent (Section 2–702) and may stop delivery of carload, truckload, planeload or larger shipments of express or freight when the buyer repudiates or fails to make a payment due before delivery or if for any other reason the seller has a right to withhold or reclaim the goods.

(2) As against such buyer the seller may stop delivery until

(a) receipt of the goods by the buyer; or

(b) acknowledgment to the buyer by any bailee of the goods except a carrier that the bailee holds the goods for the buyer; or

(c) such acknowledgment to the buyer by a carrier by reshipment or as warehouseman; or

(d) negotiation to the buyer of any negotiable document of title covering the goods.

(3) (a) To stop delivery the seller must so notify as to enable the bailee by reasonable diligence to prevent delivery of the goods.

(b) After such notification the bailee must hold and deliver the goods according to the directions of the seller but the seller is liable to the bailee for any ensuing charges or damages.

(c) If a negotiable document of title has been issued for goods the bailee is not obliged to obey a notification to stop until surrender of the document.

(d) A carrier who has issued a non-negotiable bill of lading is not obliged to obey a notification to stop received from a person other than the consignor.

§ 2–706. Seller's Resale Including Contract for Resale.

(1) Under the conditions stated in Section 2–703 on seller's remedies, the seller may resell the goods concerned or the undelivered balance thereof. Where the resale is made in good faith and in a commercially reasonable manner the seller may recover the difference between the resale price and the contract price together with any incidental damages allowed under the provisions of this Article (Section 2–710), but less expenses saved in consequence of the buyer's breach.

(2) Except as otherwise provided in subsection (3) or unless otherwise agreed resale may be at public or private sale including sale by way of one or more contracts to sell or of identification to an existing contract of the seller. Sale may be as a unit or in parcels and at any time and place and on any terms but every aspect of the sale including the method, manner, time, place and terms must be commercially reasonable. The resale must be reasonably identified as referring to the broken contract, but it is not necessary that the goods be in existence or that any or all of them have been identified to the contract before the breach.

(3) Where the resale is at private sale the seller must give the buyer reasonable notification of his intention to resell.

(4) Where the resale is at public sale

(a) only identified goods can be sold except where there is a recognized market for a public sale of futures in goods of the kind; and

(b) it must be made at a usual place or market for public sale if one is reasonably available and except in the case of goods which are perishable or threaten to decline in value speedily the seller must give the buyer reasonable notice of the time and place of the resale; and

(c) if the goods are not to be within the view of those attending the sale the notification of sale must state the place where the goods are located and provide for their reasonable inspection by prospective bidders; and

(d) the seller may buy.

(5) A purchaser who buys in good faith at a resale takes the goods free of any rights of the original buyer even though the seller fails to comply with one or more of the requirements of this section.

(6) The seller is not accountable to the buyer for any profit made on any resale. A person in the position of a seller (Section 2–707) or a buyer who has rightfully rejected or justifiably revoked acceptance must account for any excess over the amount of his security interest, as hereinafter defined (subsection (3) of Section 2–711).

§ 2-707. "Person in the Position of a Seller".

(1) A "person in the position of a seller" includes as against a principal an agent who has paid or become responsible for the price of goods on behalf of his principal or anyone who otherwise holds a security interest or other right in goods similar to that of a seller.

(2) A person in the position of a seller may as provided in this Article withhold or stop delivery (Section 2–705) and resell (Section 2–706) and recover incidental damages (Section 2–710).

§ 2-708. Seller's Damages for Non-Acceptance or Repudiation.

(1) Subject to subsection (2) and to the provisions of this Article with respect to proof of market price (Section 2–723), the measure of damages for non-acceptance or repudiation by the buyer is the difference between the market price at the time and place for tender and the unpaid contract price together with any incidental damages provided in this Article (Section 2–710), but less expenses saved in consequence of the buyer's breach.

(2) If the measure of damages provided in subsection (1) is inadequate to put the seller in as good a position as performance would have done then the measure of damages is the profit (including reasonable overhead) which the seller would have made from full performance by the buyer, together with any incidental damages provided in this Article (Section 2–710), due allowance for costs reasonably incurred and due credit for payments or proceeds of resale.

§ 2-709. Action for the Price.

(1) When the buyer fails to pay the price as it becomes due the seller may recover, together with any incidental damages under the next section, the price

(a) of goods accepted or of conforming goods lost or damaged within a commercially reasonable time after risk of their loss has passed to the buyer; and

(b) of goods identified to the contract if the seller is unable after reasonable effort to resell them at a reasonable price or the circumstances reasonably indicate that such effort will be unavailing.

(2) Where the seller sues for the price he must hold for the buyer any goods which have been identified to the contract and are still in his control except that if resale becomes possible he may resell them at any time prior to the collection of the judgment. The net proceeds of any such resale must be credited to the buyer and payment of the judgment entitles him to any goods not resold.

(3) After the buyer has wrongfully rejected or revoked acceptance of the goods or has failed to make a payment due or has repudiated (Section 2–610), a seller who is held not entitled to the price under this section shall nevertheless be awarded damages for non-acceptance under the preceding section.

§ 2-710. Seller's Incidental Damages.

Incidental damages to an aggrieved seller include any commercially reasonable charges, expenses or commissions incurred in stopping delivery, in the transportation, care and custody of goods after the buyer's breach, in connection with return or resale of the goods or otherwise resulting from the breach.

§ 2-711. Buyer's Remedies in General; Buyer's Security Interest in Rejected Goods.

(1) Where the seller fails to make delivery or repudiates or the buyer rightfully rejects or justifiably revokes acceptance then with respect to any goods involved, and with respect to the whole if the breach goes to the whole contract (Section 2–612), the buyer may cancel and whether or not he has done so may in addition to recovering so much of the price as has been paid

(a) "cover" and have damages under the next section as to all the goods affected whether or not they have been identified to the contract; or

(b) recover damages for non-delivery as provided in this Article (Section 2–713).

(2) Where the seller fails to deliver or repudiates the buyer may also

(a) if the goods have been identified recover them as provided in this Article (Section 2–502); or

(b) in a proper case obtain specific performance or replevy the goods as provided in this Article (Section 2–716).

(3) On rightful rejection or justifiable revocation of acceptance a buyer has a security interest in goods in his possession or control for any payments made on their price and any expenses reasonably incurred in their inspection, receipt, transportation, care and custody and may hold such goods and resell them in like manner as an aggrieved seller (Section 2–706).

§ 2-712. "Cover"; Buyer's Procurement of Substitute Goods.

(1) After a breach within the preceding section the buyer may "cover" by making in good faith and without unreasonable delay any reasonable purchase of or contract to purchase goods in substitution for those due from the seller.

(2) The buyer may recover from the seller as damages the difference between the cost of cover and the contract price together with any incidental or consequential damages as hereinafter defined (Section 2–715), but less expenses saved in consequence of the seller's breach.

(3) Failure of the buyer to effect cover within this section does not bar him from any other remedy.

§ 2–713. Buyer's Damages for Non-Delivery or Repudiation.

(1) Subject to the provisions of this Article with respect to proof of market price (Section 2–723), the measure of damages for non-delivery or repudiation by the seller is the difference between the market price at the time when the buyer learned of the breach and the contract price together with any incidental and consequential damages provided in this Article (Section 2–715), but less expenses saved in consequence of the seller's breach.

(2) Market price is to be determined as of the place for tender or, in cases of rejection after arrival or revocation of acceptance, as of the place of arrival.

§ 2–714. Buyer's Damages for Breach in Regard to Accepted Goods.

(1) Where the buyer has accepted goods and given notification (subsection (3) of Section 2–607) he may recover as damages for any non-conformity of tender the loss resulting in the ordinary course of events from the seller's breach as determined in any manner which is reasonable.

(2) The measure of damages for breach of warranty is the difference at the time and place of acceptance between the value of the goods accepted and the value they would have had if they had been as warranted, unless special circumstances show proximate damages of a different amount.

(3) In a proper case any incidental and consequential damages under the next section may also be recovered.

§ 2–715. Buyer's Incidental and Consequential Damages.

(1) Incidental damages resulting from the seller's breach include expenses reasonably incurred in inspection, receipt, transportation and care and custody of goods rightfully rejected, any commercially reasonable charges, expenses or commissions in connection with effecting cover and any other reasonable expense incident to the delay or other breach.

(2) Consequential damages resulting from the seller's breach include

(a) any loss resulting from general or particular requirements and needs of which the seller at the time of contracting had reason to know and which could not reasonably be prevented by cover or otherwise; and

(b) injury to person or property proximately resulting from any breach of warranty.

§ 2–716. Buyer's Right to Specific Performance or Replevin.

(1) Specific performance may be decreed where the goods are unique or in other proper circumstances.

(2) The decree for specific performance may include such terms and conditions as to payment of the price, damages, or other relief as the court may deem just.

(3) The buyer has a right of replevin for goods identified to the contract if after reasonable effort he is unable to effect cover for such goods or the circumstances reasonably indicate that such effort will be unavailing or if the goods have been shipped under reservation and satisfaction of the security interest in them has been made or tendered. In the case of goods bought for personal, family, or household purposes, the buyer's right of replevin vests upon acquisition of a special property, even if the seller had not then repudiated or failed to deliver.

As amended in 1999.

§ 2–717. Deduction of Damages From the Price.

The buyer on notifying the seller of his intention to do so may deduct all or any part of the damages resulting from any breach of the contract from any part of the price still due under the same contract.

§ 2–718. Liquidation or Limitation of Damages; Deposits.

(1) Damages for breach by either party may be liquidated in the agreement but only at an amount which is reasonable in the light of the anticipated or actual harm caused by the breach, the difficulties of proof of loss, and the inconvenience or nonfeasibility of otherwise obtaining an adequate remedy. A term fixing unreasonably large liquidated damages is void as a penalty.

(2) Where the seller justifiably withholds delivery of goods because of the buyer's breach, the buyer is entitled to restitution of any amount by which the sum of his payments exceeds

(a) the amount to which the seller is entitled by virtue of terms liquidating the seller's damages in accordance with subsection (1), or

(b) in the absence of such terms, twenty per cent of the value of the total performance for which the buyer is obligated under the contract or $500, whichever is smaller.

(3) The buyer's right to restitution under subsection (2) is subject to offset to the extent that the seller establishes

(a) a right to recover damages under the provisions of this Article other than subsection (1), and

(b) the amount or value of any benefits received by the buyer directly or indirectly by reason of the contract.

(4) Where a seller has received payment in goods their reasonable value or the proceeds of their resale shall be treated as payments for the purposes of subsection (2); but if the seller has notice of the buyer's breach before reselling goods received in part performance, his resale is subject to the conditions laid down in this Article on resale by an aggrieved seller (Section 2–706).

§ 2–719. Contractual Modification or Limitation of Remedy.

(1) Subject to the provisions of subsections (2) and (3) of this section and of the preceding section on liquidation and limitation of damages,

(a) the agreement may provide for remedies in addition to or in substitution for those provided in this Article and may limit or alter the measure of damages recoverable under this Article, as by limiting the buyer's remedies to return of the goods and repayment of the price or to repair and replacement of nonconforming goods or parts; and

(b) resort to a remedy as provided is optional unless the remedy is expressly agreed to be exclusive, in which case it is the sole remedy.

(2) Where circumstances cause an exclusive or limited remedy to fail of its essential purpose, remedy may be had as provided in this Act.

(3) Consequential damages may be limited or excluded unless the limitation or exclusion is unconscionable. Limitation of consequential damages for injury to the person in the case of consumer goods is prima facie unconscionable but limitation of damages where the loss is commercial is not.

§ 2–720. Effect of "Cancellation" or "Rescission" on Claims for Antecedent Breach.

Unless the contrary intention clearly appears, expressions of "cancellation" or "rescission" of the contract or the like shall not be construed as a renunciation or discharge of any claim in damages for an antecedent breach.

§ 2–721. Remedies for Fraud.

Remedies for material misrepresentation or fraud include all remedies available under this Article for non-fraudulent breach. Neither rescission or a claim for rescission of the contract for sale nor rejection or return of the goods shall bar or be deemed inconsistent with a claim for damages or other remedy.

§ 2–722. Who Can Sue Third Parties for Injury to Goods.

Where a third party so deals with goods which have been identified to a contract for sale as to cause actionable injury to a party to that contract

(a) a right of action against the third party is in either party to the contract for sale who has title to or a security interest or a special property or an insurable interest in the goods; and if the goods have been destroyed or converted a right of action is also in the party who either bore the risk of loss under the contract for sale or has since the injury assumed that risk as against the other;

(b) if at the time of the injury the party plaintiff did not bear the risk of loss as against the other party to the contract for sale and there is no arrangement between them for disposition of the recovery, his suit or settlement is, subject to his own interest, as a fiduciary for the other party to the contract;

(c) either party may with the consent of the other sue for the benefit of whom it may concern.

§ 2–723. Proof of Market Price: Time and Place.

(1) If an action based on anticipatory repudiation comes to trial before the time for performance with respect to some or all of the goods, any damages based on market price (Section 2–708 or Section 2–713) shall be determined according to the price of such goods prevailing at the time when the aggrieved party learned of the repudiation.

(2) If evidence of a price prevailing at the times or places described in this Article is not readily available the price prevailing within any reasonable time before or after the time described or at any other place which in commercial judgment or under usage of trade would serve as a reasonable substitute for the one described may be used, making any proper allowance for the cost of transporting the goods to or from such other place.

(3) Evidence of a relevant price prevailing at a time or place other than the one described in this Article offered by one party is not admissible unless and until he has given the other party such notice as the court finds sufficient to prevent unfair surprise.

§ 2–724. Admissibility of Market Quotations.

Whenever the prevailing price or value of any goods regularly bought and sold in any established commodity market is in issue, reports in official publications or trade journals or in newspapers or periodicals of general circulation published as the reports of such market shall be admissible in evidence. The circumstances of the preparation of such a report may be shown to affect its weight but not its admissibility.

§ 2–725. Statute of Limitations in Contracts for Sale.

(1) An action for breach of any contract for sale must be commenced within four years after the cause of action has accrued. By the original agreement the parties may reduce the period of limitation to not less than one year but may not extend it.

(2) A cause of action accrues when the breach occurs, regardless of the aggrieved party's lack of knowledge of the breach. A breach of warranty occurs when tender of delivery is made, except that where a warranty explicitly extends to future performance of the goods and discovery of the breach must await the time of such performance the cause of action accrues when the breach is or should have been discovered.

(3) Where an action commenced within the time limited by subsection (1) is so terminated as to leave available a remedy by another action for the same breach such other action may be commenced after the expiration of the time limited and within six months after the termination of the first action unless the termination resulted from voluntary discontinuance or from dismissal for failure or neglect to prosecute.

(4) This section does not alter the law on tolling of the statute of limitations nor does it apply to causes of action which have accrued before this Act becomes effective.

ARTICLE II

AMENDMENTS (EXCERPTS)[1]

PART 1 Short Title, General Construction and Subject Matter

§ 2-103. Definitions and Index of Definitions.

* * * *

(1) In this article unless the context otherwise requires

* * * *

(b) "Conspicuous", with reference to a term, means so written, displayed, or presented that a reasonable person against which it is to operate ought to have noticed it. A term in an electronic record intended to evoke a response by an electronic agent is conspicuous if it is presented in a form that would enable a reasonably configured electronic agent to take it into account or react to it without review of the record by an individual. Whether a term is "conspicuous" or not is a decision for the court. Conspicuous terms include the following:

(i) for a person:

(A) a heading in capitals equal to or greater in size than the surrounding text, or in contrasting type, font, or color to the surrounding text of the same or lesser size;

(B) language in the body of a record or display in larger type than the surrounding text, or in contrasting type, font, or color to the surrounding text of the same size, or set off from surrounding text of the same size by symbols or other marks that call attention to the language; and

(ii) for a person or an electronic agent, a term that is so placed in a record or display that the person or electronic agent cannot proceed without taking action with respect to the particular term.

(c) "Consumer" means an individual who buys or contracts to buy goods that, at the time of contracting, are intended by the individual to be used primarily for personal, family, or household purposes.

(d) "Consumer contract" means a contract between a merchant seller and a consumer.

* * * *

(j) "Good faith" means honesty in fact and the observance of reasonable commercial standards of fair dealing.

(k) "Goods" means all things that are movable at the time of identification to a contract for sale. The term includes future goods, specially manufactured goods, the unborn young of animals, growing crops, and other identified things attached to realty as described in Section 2-107. The term does not include information, the money in which the price is to be paid, investment securities under Article 8, the subject matter of foreign exchange transactions, and choses in action.

* * * *

(m) "Record" means information that is inscribed on a tangible medium or that is stored in an electronic or other medium and is retrievable in perceivable form.

(n) "Remedial promise" means a promise by the seller to repair or replace the goods or to refund all or part of the price upon the happening of a specified event.

* * * *

(p) "Sign" means, with present intent to authenticate or adopt a record,

(i) to execute or adopt a tangible symbol; or

(ii) to attach to or logically associate with the record an electronic sound, symbol, or process.

* * * *

PART 2 Form, Formation, Terms and Readjustment of Contract; Electronic Contracting

§ 2-201. Formal Requirements; Statute of Frauds.

(1) A contract for the sale of goods for the price of $5,000 or more is not enforceable by way of action or defense unless there is some record sufficient to indicate that a contract for sale has been made between the parties and signed by the party against whom which enforcement is sought or by the party's authorized agent or broker. A record is not insufficient because it omits or incorrectly states a term agreed upon but the contract is not enforceable under this subsection beyond the quantity of goods shown in the record.

(2) Between merchants if within a reasonable time a record in confirmation of the contract and sufficient against the sender is received and the party receiving it has reason to know its contents, it satisfies the requirements of subsection (1) against such party the recipient unless notice of objection to its contents is given in a record within 10 days after it is received.

(3) A contract which does not satisfy the requirements of subsection (1) but which is valid in other respects is enforceable

(a) if the goods are to be specially manufactured for the buyer and are not suitable for sale to others in the ordinary course of the seller's business and the seller, before notice of repudiation is received and under circumstances which reasonably indicate that the goods are for the buyer, has made either a substantial beginning of their manufacture or commitments for their procurement; or

(b) if the party against whom which enforcement is sought admits in the party's pleading, or in the party's testimony or otherwise under oath that a contract for sale was made, but the contract is not enforceable under this paragraph beyond the quantity of goods admitted; or

(c) with respect to goods for which payment has been made and accepted or which have been received and accepted (Sec. 2–606).

(4) A contract that is enforceable under this section is not rendered unenforceable merely because it is not capable of being performed within one year or any other applicable period after its making.

* * * *

§ 2–207. Terms of Contract; Effect of Confirmation.

If (i) conduct by both parties recognizes the existence of a contract although their records do not otherwise establish a contract, (ii) a contract is formed by an offer and acceptance, or (iii) a contract formed in any manner is confirmed by a record that contains terms additional to or different from those in the contract being confirmed, the terms of the contract, subject to Section 2–202, are:

(a) terms that appear in the records of both parties;

(b) terms, whether in a record or not, to which both parties agree; and

(c) terms supplied or incorporated under any provision of this Act.

* * * *

PART 3 General Obligation and Construction of Contract

* * * *

§ 2–312. Warranty of Title and Against Infringement; Buyer's Obligation Against Infringement.

(1) Subject to subsection (2) there is in a contract for sale a warranty by the seller that

(a) the title conveyed shall be good, good and its transfer rightful and shall not, because of any colorable claim to or interest in the goods, unreasonably expose the buyer to litigation; and

(b) the goods shall be delivered free from any security interest or other lien or encumbrance of which the buyer at the time of contracting has no knowledge.

(2) Unless otherwise agreed a seller that is a merchant regularly dealing in goods of the kind warrants that the goods shall be delivered free of the rightful claim of any third person by way of infringement or the like but a buyer that furnishes specifications to the seller must hold the seller harmless against any such claim that arises out of compliance with the specifications.

(3) A warranty under this section may be disclaimed or modified only by specific language or by circumstances that give the buyer reason to know that the seller does not claim title, that the seller is purporting to sell only the right or title as the seller or a third person may have, or that the seller is selling subject to any claims of infringement or the like.

§ 2–313. Express Warranties by Affirmation, Promise, Description, Sample; Remedial Promise.

(1) In this section, "immediate buyer" means a buyer that enters into a contract with the seller.

* * * *

(4) Any remedial promise made by the seller to the immediate buyer creates an obligation that the promise will be performed upon the happening of the specified event.

§ 2–313A. Obligation to Remote Purchaser Created by Record Packaged with or Accompanying Goods.

(1) This section applies only to new goods and goods sold or leased as new goods in a transaction of purchase in the normal chain of distribution. In this section:

(a) "Immediate buyer" means a buyer that enters into a contract with the seller.

(b) "Remote purchaser" means a person that buys or leases goods from an immediate buyer or other person in the normal chain of distribution.

(2) If a seller in a record packaged with or accompanying the goods makes an affirmation of fact or promise that relates to the goods, provides a description that relates to the goods, or makes a remedial promise, and the seller reasonably expects the record to be, and the record is, furnished to the remote purchaser, the seller has an obligation to the remote purchaser that:

(a) the goods will conform to the affirmation of fact, promise or description unless a reasonable person in the position of the remote purchaser would not believe that the affirmation of fact, promise or description created an obligation; and

(b) the seller will perform the remedial promise.

(3) It is not necessary to the creation of an obligation under this section that the seller use formal words such as "warrant" or "guarantee" or that the seller have a specific intention to undertake an obligation, but an affirmation merely of the value of the goods or a statement purporting to be merely the seller's opinion or commendation of the goods does not create an obligation.

(4) The following rules apply to the remedies for breach of an obligation created under this section:

(a) The seller may modify or limit the remedies available to the remote purchaser if the modification or limitation is furnished to the remote purchaser no later than the time of purchase or if the modification or limitation is contained in the record that contains the affirmation of fact, promise or description.

(b) Subject to a modification or limitation of remedy, a seller in breach is liable for incidental or consequential damages under Section 2–715, but the seller is not liable for lost profits.

(c) The remote purchaser may recover as damages for breach of a seller's obligation arising under subsection (2) the loss resulting in the ordinary course of events as determined in any manner that is reasonable.

(5) An obligation that is not a remedial promise is breached if the goods did not conform to the affirmation of fact, promise or description creating the obligation when the goods left the seller's control.

§ 2-313B. Obligation to Remote Purchaser Created by Communication to the Public.

(1) This section applies only to new goods and goods sold or leased as new goods in a transaction of purchase in the normal chain of distribution. In this section:

(a) "Immediate buyer" means a buyer that enters into a contract with the seller.

(b) "Remote purchaser" means a person that buys or leases goods from an immediate buyer or other person in the normal chain of distribution.

(2) If a seller in advertising or a similar communication to the public makes an affirmation of fact or promise that relates to the goods, provides a description that relates to the goods, or makes a remedial promise, and the remote purchaser enters into a transaction of purchase with knowledge of and with the expectation that the goods will conform to the affirmation of fact, promise, or description, or that the seller will perform the remedial promise, the seller has an obligation to the remote purchaser that:

(a) the goods will conform to the affirmation of fact, promise or description unless a reasonable person in the position of the remote purchaser would not believe that the affirmation of fact, promise or description created an obligation; and

(b) the seller will perform the remedial promise.

(3) It is not necessary to the creation of an obligation under this section that the seller use formal words such as "warrant" or "guarantee" or that the seller have a specific intention to undertake an obligation, but an affirmation merely of the value of the goods or a statement purporting to be merely the seller's opinion or commendation of the goods does not create an obligation.

(4) The following rules apply to the remedies for breach of an obligation created under this section:

(a) The seller may modify or limit the remedies available to the remote purchaser if the modification or limitation is furnished to the remote purchaser no later than the time of purchase. The modification or limitation may be furnished as part of the communication that contains the affirmation of fact, promise or description.

(b) Subject to a modification or limitation of remedy, a seller in breach is liable for incidental or consequential damages under Section 2–715, but the seller is not liable for lost profits.

(c) The remote purchaser may recover as damages for breach of a seller's obligation arising under subsection (2) the loss resulting in the ordinary course of events as determined in any manner that is reasonable.

(5) An obligation that is not a remedial promise is breached if the goods did not conform to the affirmation of fact, promise or description creating the obligation when the goods left the seller's control.

* * * *

§ 2-316. Exclusion or Modification of Warranties.

* * * *

(2) Subject to subsection (3), to exclude or modify the implied warranty of merchantability or any part of it in a consumer contract the language must be in a record, be conspicuous and state "The seller undertakes no responsibility for the quality of the goods except as otherwise provided in this contract," and in any other contract the language must mention merchantability and in case of a record must be conspicuous. Subject to subsection (3), to exclude or modify the implied warranty of fitness the exclusion must be in a record and be conspicuous. Language to exclude all implied warranties of fitness in a consumer contract must state "The seller assumes no responsibility that the goods will be fit for any particular purpose for which you may be buying these goods, except as otherwise provided in the contract," and in any other contract the language is sufficient if it states, for example, that "There are no warranties which extend beyond the description on the face hereof." Language that satisfies the requirements of this subsection for the exclusion and modification of a warranty in a consumer contract also satisfies the requirements for any other contract.

(3) Notwithstanding subsection (2):

(a) unless the circumstances indicate otherwise, all implied warranties are excluded by expressions like "as is", "with all faults" or other language which in common understanding calls the buyer's attention to the exclusion of warranties, makes plain that there is no implied warranty, and in a consumer contract evidenced by a record is set forth conspicuously in the record; and

(b) when the buyer before entering into the contract has examined the goods or the sample or model as fully as desired or has refused to examine the goods after a demand by the seller there is no implied warranty with regard to defects which an examination ought in the circumstances to have revealed to the buyer; and

(c) an implied warranty can also be excluded or modified by course of dealing or course of performance or usage of trade.

* * * *

§ 2-318. Third Party Beneficiaries of Warranties Express or Implied.

(1) In this section:

(a) "Immediate buyer" means a buyer that enters into a contract with the seller.

(b) "Remote purchaser" means a person that buys or leases goods from an immediate buyer or other person in the normal chain of distribution.

Alternative A to subsection (2) (2) A seller's warranty whether express or implied to an immediate buyer, a seller's remedial promise to an immediate buyer, or a seller's obligation to a remote purchaser under Section 2–313A or 2–313B extends to any natural person who is in the family or household of the immediate buyer or the remote purchaser or who is a guest in the home of either if it is reasonable to expect that the person may use, consume or be affected by the goods and who is injured in person by breach of the warranty, remedial promise or obligation. A seller may not exclude or limit the operation of this section.

Alternative B to subsection (2) (2) A seller's warranty whether express or implied to an immediate buyer, a seller's remedial promise to an immediate buyer, or a seller's obligation to a remote purchaser under Section 2–313A or 2–313B extends to any natural person who may reasonably be expected to use, consume or be affected by the goods and who is injured in person by breach of the warranty, remedial promise or obligation. A seller may not exclude or limit the operation of this section.

Alternative C to subsection (2) (2) A seller's warranty whether express or implied to an immediate buyer, a seller's remedial promise to an immediate buyer, or a seller's obligation to a remote purchaser under Section 2–313A or 2–313B extends to any person that may reasonably be expected to use, consume or be affected by the goods and that is injured by breach of the warranty, remedial promise or obligation. A seller may not exclude or limit the operation of this section with respect to injury to the person of an individual to whom the warranty, remedial promise or obligation extends.

* * * *

PART 5 Performance

* * * *

§ 2–502. Buyer's Right to Goods on Seller's Insolvency.

(1) Subject to subsections (2) and (3) and even though the goods have not been shipped a buyer who that has paid a part or all of the price of goods in which the buyer has a special property under the provisions of the immediately preceding section may on making and keeping good a tender of any unpaid portion of their price recover them from the seller if:

(a) in the case of goods bought by a consumer, the seller repudiates or fails to deliver as required by the contract; or

(b) in all cases, the seller becomes insolvent within ten days after receipt of the first installment on their price.

(2) The buyer's right to recover the goods under subsection (1) vests upon acquisition of a special property, even if the seller had not then repudiated or failed to deliver.

(3) If the identification creating the special property has been made by the buyer, the buyer acquires the right to recover the goods only if they conform to the contract for sale.

* * * *

§ 2–508. Cure by Seller of Improper Tender or Delivery; Replacement.

(1) Where the buyer rejects goods or a tender of delivery under Section 2–601 or 2–612 or except in a consumer contract justifiably revokes acceptance under Section 2–608(1)(b) and the agreed time for performance has not expired, a seller that has performed in good faith, upon seasonable notice to the buyer and at the seller's own expense, may cure the breach of contract by making a conforming tender of delivery within the agreed time. The seller shall compensate the buyer for all of the buyer's reasonable expenses caused by the seller's breach of contract and subsequent cure.

(2) Where the buyer rejects goods or a tender of delivery under Section 2–601 or 2–612 or except in a consumer contract justifiably revokes acceptance under Section 2–608(1)(b) and the agreed time for performance has expired, a seller that has performed in good faith, upon seasonable notice to the buyer and at the seller's own expense, may cure the breach of contract, if the cure is appropriate and timely under the circumstances, by making a tender of conforming goods. The seller shall compensate the buyer for all of the buyer's reasonable expenses caused by the seller's breach of contract and subsequent cure.

§ 2–509. Risk of Loss in the Absence of Breach.

(1) Where the contract requires or authorizes the seller to ship the goods by carrier

(a) if it does not require the seller to deliver them at a particular destination, the risk of loss passes to the buyer when the goods are delivered to the carrier even though the shipment is under reservation (Section 2–505); but

(b) if it does require the seller to deliver them at a particular destination and the goods are there tendered while in the possession of the carrier, the risk of loss passes to the buyer when the goods are there so tendered as to enable the buyer to take delivery.

(2) Where the goods are held by a bailee to be delivered without being moved, the risk of loss passes to the buyer

(a) on the buyer's receipt of a negotiable document of title covering the goods; or

(b) on acknowledgment by the bailee to the buyer of the buyer's right to possession of the goods; or

(c) after the buyer's receipt of a non-negotiable document of title or other direction to deliver in a record, as provided in subsection (4)(b) of Section 2–503.

(3) In any case not within subsection (1) or (2), the risk of loss passes to the buyer on the buyer's receipt of the goods.

* * * *

§ 2-513. Buyer's Right to Inspection of Goods.

* * * *

(3) Unless otherwise agreed, the buyer is not entitled to inspect the goods before payment of the price when the contract provides

(a) for delivery on terms that under applicable course of performance, course of dealing, or usage of trade are interpreted to preclude inspection before payment; or

(b) for payment against documents of title, except where such payment is due only after the goods are to become available for inspection.

* * * *

PART 6 Breach, Repudiation and Excuse

* * * *

§ 2-605. Waiver of Buyer's Objections by Failure to Particularize.

(1) The buyer's failure to state in connection with rejection a particular defect or in connection with revocation of acceptance a defect that justifies revocation precludes the buyer from relying on the unstated defect to justify rejection or revocation of acceptance if the defect is ascertainable by reasonable inspection

(a) where the seller had a right to cure the defect and could have cured it if stated seasonably; or

(b) between merchants when the seller has after rejection made a request in a record for a full and final statement in record form of all defects on which the buyer proposes to rely.

(2) A buyer's payment against documents tendered to the buyer made without reservation of rights precludes recovery of the payment for defects apparent on the face of the documents.

* * * *

§ 2-607. Effect of Acceptance; Notice of Breach; Burden of Establishing Breach After Acceptance; Notice of Claim or Litigation to Person Answerable Over.

(3) Where a tender has been accepted

(a) the buyer must within a reasonable time after the buyer discovers or should have discovered any breach notify the seller; however, failure to give timely notice bars the buyer from a remedy only to the extent that the seller is prejudiced by the failure and

(b) if the claim is one for infringement or the like (subsection (3) of Section 2–312) and the buyer is sued as a result of such a breach the buyer must so notify the seller within a reasonable time after the buyer receives notice of the litigation or be barred from any remedy over for liability established by the litigation.

* * * *

§ 2-608. Revocation of Acceptance in Whole or in Part.

* * * *

(4) If a buyer uses the goods after a rightful rejection or justifiable revocation of acceptance, the following rules apply:

(a) Any use by the buyer that is unreasonable under the circumstances is wrongful as against the seller and is an acceptance only if ratified by the seller.

(b) Any use of the goods that is reasonable under the circumstances is not wrongful as against the seller and is not an acceptance, but in an appropriate case the buyer shall be obligated to the seller for the value of the use to the buyer.

* * * *

§ 2-612. "Installment Contract"; Breach.

* * * *

(2) The buyer may reject any installment which is -non-conforming if the non-conformity substantially impairs the value of that installment to the buyer or if the non-conformity is a defect in the required documents; but if the non-conformity does not fall within subsection (3) and the seller gives adequate assurance of its cure the buyer must accept that installment.

(3) Whenever non-conformity or default with respect to one or more installments substantially impairs the value of the whole contract there is a breach of the whole. But the aggrieved party reinstates the contract if the party accepts a non-conforming installment without seasonably notifying of cancellation or if the party brings an action with respect only to past installments or demands performance as to future installments.

* * * *

PART 7 Remedies

§ 2-702. Seller's Remedies on Discovery of Buyer's Insolvency.

* * * *

(2) Where the seller discovers that the buyer has received goods on credit while insolvent the seller may reclaim the goods upon demand made within a reasonable time after the buyer's receipt of the goods. Except as provided in this subsection the seller may not base a right to reclaim goods on the buyer's fraudulent or innocent misrepresentation of solvency or of intent to pay.

* * * *

§ 2-705. Seller's Stoppage of Delivery in Transit or Otherwise.

(1) The seller may stop delivery of goods in the possession of a carrier or other bailee when the seller discovers the buyer to be insolvent (Section 2–702) or when the buyer repudiates or fails to make a payment due before delivery or if for any other reason the seller has a right to withhold or reclaim the goods.

* * * *

§ 2-706. Seller's Resale Including Contract for Resale.

(1) In an appropriate case involving breach by the buyer, the seller may resell the goods concerned or the undelivered balance thereof. Where the resale is made in good faith and in a commercially reasonable manner the seller may recover the difference between the contract price and the resale price together with any incidental or consequential damages allowed under the provisions of this Article (Section 2–710), but less expenses saved in consequence of the buyer's breach.

* * * *

§ 2-708. Seller's Damages for Non-Acceptance or Repudiation.

(1) Subject to subsection (2) and to the provisions of this Article with respect to proof of market price (Section 2–723)

(a) the measure of damages for non-acceptance by the buyer is the difference between the contract price and the market price at the time and place for tender together with any incidental or consequential damages provided in this Article (Section 2–710), but less expenses saved in consequence of the buyer's breach; and

(b) the measure of damages for repudiation by the buyer is the difference between the contract price and the market price at the place for tender at the expiration of a commercially reasonable time after the seller learned of the repudiation, but no later than the time stated in paragraph (a), together with any incidental or consequential damages provided in this Article (Section 2–710), but less expenses saved in consequence of the buyer's breach.

(2) If the measure of damages provided in subsection (1) or in Section 2–706 is inadequate to put the seller in as good a position as performance would have done then the measure of damages is the profit (including reasonable overhead) which the seller would have made from full performance by the buyer, together with any incidental or consequential damages provided in this Article (Section 2–710).

§ 2-709. Action for the Price.

(1) When the buyer fails to pay the price as it becomes due the seller may recover, together with any incidental or consequential damages under the next section, the price

(a) of goods accepted or of conforming goods lost or damaged within a commercially reasonable time after risk of their loss has passed to the buyer; and

(b) of goods identified to the contract if the seller is unable after reasonable effort to resell them at a reasonable price or the circumstances reasonably indicate that such effort will be unavailing.

* * * *

* * * *

* * * *

§ 2-710. Seller's Incidental and Consequential Damages.

(1) Incidental damages to an aggrieved seller include any commercially reasonable charges, expenses or commissions incurred in stopping delivery, in the transportation, care and custody of goods after the buyer's breach, in connection with return or resale of the goods or otherwise resulting from the breach.

(2) Consequential damages resulting from the buyer's breach include any loss resulting from general or particular requirements and needs of which the buyer at the time of contracting had reason to know and which could not reasonably be prevented by resale or otherwise.

(3) In a consumer contract, a seller may not recover consequential damages from a consumer.

* * * *

§ 2-713. Buyer's Damages for Non-Delivery or Repudiation.

(1) Subject to the provisions of this Article with respect to proof of market price (Section 2–723), if the seller wrongfully fails to deliver or repudiates or the buyer rightfully rejects or justifiably revokes acceptance

(a) the measure of damages in the case of wrongful failure to deliver by the seller or rightful rejection or justifiable revocation of acceptance by the buyer is the difference between the market price at the time for tender under the contract and the contract price together with any incidental or consequential damages provided in this Article (Section 2–715), but less expenses saved in consequence of the seller's breach; and

(b) the measure of damages for repudiation by the seller is the difference between the market price at the expiration of a commercially reasonable time after the buyer learned of the repudiation, but no later than the time stated in paragraph (a), and the contract price together with any incidental or consequential damages provided in this Article (Section 2–715), but less expenses saved in consequence of the seller's breach.

* * * *

§ 2-725. Statute of Limitations in Contracts for Sale.

(1) Except as otherwise provided in this section, an action for breach of any contract for sale must be commenced within the later of four years after the right of action has accrued under subsection (2) or (3) or one year after the breach was or should have been discovered, but no longer than five years after the right of action accrued. By the original agreement the parties may reduce the period of limitation to not less than one year but may not extend it; however, in a consumer contract, the period of limitation may not be reduced.

(2) Except as otherwise provided in subsection (3), the following rules apply:

(a) Except as otherwise provided in this subsection, a right of action for breach of a contract accrues when the breach occurs, even if the aggrieved party did not have knowledge of the breach.

(b) For breach of a contract by repudiation, a right of action accrues at the earlier of when the aggrieved party elects to treat the repudiation as a breach or when a commercially reasonable time for awaiting performance has expired.

(c) For breach of a remedial promise, a right of action accrues when the remedial promise is not performed when due.

(d) In an action by a buyer against a person that is answerable over to the buyer for a claim asserted against the buyer, the buyer's right of action against the person answerable over accrues at the time the claim was originally asserted against the buyer.

(3) If a breach of a warranty arising under Section 2–312, 2–313 (2), 2–314, or 2–315, or a breach of an obligation other than a remedial promise arising under Section 2–313A or 2–313B, is claimed the following rules apply:

(a) Except as otherwise provided in paragraph (c), a right of action for breach of a warranty arising under Section 2–313(2), 2–314 or 2–315 accrues when the seller has tendered delivery to the immediate buyer, as defined in Section 2–313, and has completed performance of any agreed installation or assembly of the goods.

(b) Except as otherwise provided in paragraph (c), a right of action for breach of an obligation other than a remedial promise arising under Section 2–313A or 2–313B accrues when the remote purchaser, as defined in sections 2–313A and 2–313B, receives the goods.

(c) Where a warranty arising under Section 2–313(2) or an obligation other than a remedial promise arising under 2–313A or 2–313B explicitly extends to future performance of the goods and discovery of the breach must await the time for performance the right of action accrues when the immediate buyer as defined in Section 2–313 or the remote purchaser as defined in Sections 2–313A and 2–313B discovers or should have discovered the breach.

(d) A right of action for breach of warranty arising under Section 2–312 accrues when the aggrieved party discovers or should have discovered the breach. However, an action for breach of the warranty of non-infringement may not be commenced more than six years after tender of delivery of the goods to the aggrieved party.

* * * *

ARTICLE IIA
LEASES

PART 1 General Provisions

§ 2A-101. Short Title.

This Article shall be known and may be cited as the Uniform Commercial Code—Leases.

§ 2A-102. Scope.

This Article applies to any transaction, regardless of form, that creates a lease.

§ 2A-103. Definitions and Index of Definitions.

(1) In this Article unless the context otherwise requires:

(a) "Buyer in ordinary course of business" means a person who in good faith and without knowledge that the sale to him [or her] is in violation of the ownership rights or security interest or leasehold interest of a third party in the goods buys in ordinary course from a person in the business of selling goods of that kind but does not include a pawnbroker. "Buying" may be for cash or by exchange of other property or on secured or unsecured credit and includes receiving goods or documents of title under a pre-existing contract for sale but does not include a transfer in bulk or as security for or in total or partial satisfaction of a money debt.

(b) "Cancellation" occurs when either party puts an end to the lease contract for default by the other party.

(c) "Commercial unit" means such a unit of goods as by commercial usage is a single whole for purposes of lease and division of which materially impairs its character or value on the market or in use. A commercial unit may be a single article, as a machine, or a set of articles, as a suite of furniture or a line of machinery, or a quantity, as a gross or carload, or any other unit treated in use or in the relevant market as a single whole.

(d) "Conforming" goods or performance under a lease contract means goods or performance that are in accordance with the obligations under the lease contract.

(e) "Consumer lease" means a lease that a lessor regularly engaged in the business of leasing or selling makes to a lessee who is an individual and who takes under the lease primarily for a personal, family, or household purpose [, if the total payments to be made under the lease contract, excluding payments for options to renew or buy, do not exceed $______].

(f) "Fault" means wrongful act, omission, breach, or default.

(g) "Finance lease" means a lease with respect to which:

(i) the lessor does not select, manufacture or supply the goods;

(ii) the lessor acquires the goods or the right to possession and use of the goods in connection with the lease; and

(iii) one of the following occurs:

(A) the lessee receives a copy of the contract by which the lessor acquired the goods or the right to possession and use of the goods before signing the lease contract;

(B) the lessee's approval of the contract by which the lessor acquired the goods or the right to possession and use of the goods is a condition to effectiveness of the lease contract;

(C) the lessee, before signing the lease contract, receives an accurate and complete statement designating the promises and warranties, and any disclaimers of warranties, limitations or modifications of remedies, or liquidated damages, including those of a third party, such as the manufacturer of the goods, provided to the lessor by the person supplying the goods in connection with or as part of the contract by which the lessor acquired the goods or the right to possession and use of the goods; or

(D) if the lease is not a consumer lease, the lessor, before the lessee signs the lease contract, informs the lessee in writing (a) of the identity of the person supplying the goods to the lessor, unless the lessee has selected that person and directed the lessor to acquire the goods or the right to possession and use of the goods from that person, (b) that the lessee is entitled under this Article to any promises and warranties, including those of any third party, provided to the lessor by the person supplying the goods in connection with or as part of the contract by which the lessor acquired the goods or the right to possession and use of the goods, and (c) that the lessee may communicate with the person supplying the goods to the lessor and receive an accurate and complete statement of those promises and warranties, including any disclaimers and limitations of them or of remedies.

(h) "Goods" means all things that are movable at the time of identification to the lease contract, or are fixtures (Section 2A–309), but the term does not include money, documents, instruments, accounts, chattel paper, general intangibles, or minerals or the like, including oil and gas, before extraction. The term also includes the unborn young of animals.

(i) "Installment lease contract" means a lease contract that authorizes or requires the delivery of goods in separate lots to be separately accepted, even though the lease contract contains a clause "each delivery is a separate lease" or its equivalent.

(j) "Lease" means a transfer of the right to possession and use of goods for a term in return for consideration, but a sale, including a sale on approval or a sale or return, or retention or creation of a security interest is not a lease. Unless the context clearly indicates otherwise, the term includes a sublease.

(k) "Lease agreement" means the bargain, with respect to the lease, of the lessor and the lessee in fact as found in their language or by implication from other circumstances including course of dealing or usage of trade or course of performance as provided in this Article. Unless the context clearly indicates otherwise, the term includes a sublease agreement.

(l) "Lease contract" means the total legal obligation that results from the lease agreement as affected by this Article and any other applicable rules of law. Unless the context clearly indicates -otherwise, the term includes a sublease contract.

(m) "Leasehold interest" means the interest of the lessor or the lessee under a lease contract.

(n) "Lessee" means a person who acquires the right to possession and use of goods under a lease. Unless the context clearly indicates otherwise, the term includes a sublessee.

(o) "Lessee in ordinary course of business" means a person who in good faith and without knowledge that the lease to him [or her] is in violation of the ownership rights or security interest or leasehold interest of a third party in the goods, leases in ordinary course from a person in the business of selling or leasing goods of that kind but does not include a pawnbroker. "Leasing" may be for cash or by exchange of other property or on secured or unsecured credit and includes receiving goods or documents of title under a pre-existing lease contract but does not include a transfer in bulk or as security for or in total or partial satisfaction of a money debt.

(p) "Lessor" means a person who transfers the right to possession and use of goods under a lease. Unless the context clearly indicates otherwise, the term includes a sublessor.

(q) "Lessor's residual interest" means the lessor's interest in the goods after expiration, termination, or cancellation of the lease contract.

(r) "Lien" means a charge against or interest in goods to secure payment of a debt or performance of an obligation, but the term does not include a security interest.

(s) "Lot" means a parcel or a single article that is the subject matter of a separate lease or delivery, whether or not it is sufficient to perform the lease contract.

(t) "Merchant lessee" means a lessee that is a merchant with respect to goods of the kind subject to the lease.

(u) "Present value" means the amount as of a date certain of one or more sums payable in the future, discounted to the date certain. The discount is determined by the interest rate specified by the parties if the rate was not manifestly unreasonable at the time the transaction was entered into; otherwise, the discount is determined by a commercially reasonable rate that takes into account the facts and circumstances of each case at the time the transaction was entered into.

(v) "Purchase" includes taking by sale, lease, mortgage, security interest, pledge, gift, or any other voluntary transaction creating an interest in goods.

(w) "Sublease" means a lease of goods the right to possession and use of which was acquired by the lessor as a lessee under an existing lease.

(x) "Supplier" means a person from whom a lessor buys or leases goods to be leased under a finance lease.

(y) "Supply contract" means a contract under which a lessor buys or leases goods to be leased.

(z) "Termination" occurs when either party pursuant to a power created by agreement or law puts an end to the lease contract otherwise than for default.

(2) Other definitions applying to this Article and the sections in which they appear are:

"Accessions". Section 2A–310(1).
"Construction mortgage". Section 2A–309(1)(d).
"Encumbrance". Section 2A–309(1)(e).
"Fixtures". Section 2A–309(1)(a).
"Fixture filing". Section 2A–309(1)(b).
"Purchase money lease". Section 2A–309(1)(c).

(3) The following definitions in other Articles apply to this Article:

"Accounts". Section 9–106.
"Between merchants". Section 2–104(3).
"Buyer". Section 2–103(1)(a).
"Chattel paper". Section 9–105(1)(b).
"Consumer goods". Section 9–109(1).
"Document". Section 9–105(1)(f).
"Entrusting". Section 2–403(3).
"General intangibles". Section 9–106.
"Good faith". Section 2–103(1)(b).
"Instrument". Section 9–105(1)(i).
"Merchant". Section 2–104(1).
"Mortgage". Section 9–105(1)(j).
"Pursuant to commitment". Section 9–105(1)(k).
"Receipt". Section 2–103(1)(c).
"Sale". Section 2–106(1).
"Sale on approval". Section 2–326.
"Sale or return". Section 2–326.
"Seller". Section 2–103(1)(d).

(4) In addition Article 1 contains general definitions and principles of construction and interpretation applicable throughout this Article.

As amended in 1990 and 1999.

§ 2A–104. Leases Subject to Other Law.

(1) A lease, although subject to this Article, is also subject to any applicable:

(a) certificate of title statute of this State: (list any certificate of title statutes covering automobiles, trailers, mobile homes, boats, farm tractors, and the like);

(b) certificate of title statute of another jurisdiction (Section 2A–105); or

(c) consumer protection statute of this State, or final consumer protection decision of a court of this State existing on the effective date of this Article.

(2) In case of conflict between this Article, other than Sections 2A–105, 2A–304(3), and 2A–305(3), and a statute or decision referred to in subsection (1), the statute or decision controls.

(3) Failure to comply with an applicable law has only the effect specified therein.

As amended in 1990.

§ 2A–105. Territorial Application of Article to Goods Covered by Certificate of Title.

Subject to the provisions of Sections 2A–304(3) and 2A–305(3), with respect to goods covered by a certificate of title issued under a statute of this State or of another jurisdiction, compliance and the effect of compliance or noncompliance with a certificate of title statute are governed by the law (including the conflict of laws rules) of the jurisdiction issuing the certificate until the earlier of (a) surrender of the certificate, or (b) four months after the goods are removed from that jurisdiction and thereafter until a new - certificate of title is issued by another jurisdiction.

§ 2A–106. Limitation on Power of Parties to Consumer Lease to Choose Applicable Law and Judicial Forum.

(1) If the law chosen by the parties to a consumer lease is that of a jurisdiction other than a jurisdiction in which the lessee resides at the time the lease agreement becomes enforceable or within 30 days thereafter or in which the goods are to be used, the choice is not enforceable.

(2) If the judicial forum chosen by the parties to a consumer lease is a forum that would not otherwise have jurisdiction over the lessee, the choice is not enforceable.

§ 2A–107. Waiver or Renunciation of Claim or Right After Default.

Any claim or right arising out of an alleged default or breach of warranty may be discharged in whole or in part without consideration by a written waiver or renunciation signed and delivered by the aggrieved party.

§ 2A–108. Unconscionability.

(1) If the court as a matter of law finds a lease contract or any clause of a lease contract to have been unconscionable at the time it was made the court may refuse to enforce the lease contract, or it may enforce the remainder of the lease contract without the unconscionable clause, or it may so limit the application of any unconscionable clause as to avoid any unconscionable result.

(2) With respect to a consumer lease, if the court as a matter of law finds that a lease contract or any clause of a lease contract has been induced by unconscionable conduct or that unconscionable conduct has occurred in the collection of a claim arising from a lease contract, the court may grant appropriate relief.

(3) Before making a finding of unconscionability under subsection (1) or (2), the court, on its own motion or that of a party, shall afford the parties a reasonable opportunity to present evidence as to the setting, purpose, and effect of the lease contract or clause thereof, or of the conduct.

(4) In an action in which the lessee claims unconscionability with respect to a consumer lease:

(a) If the court finds unconscionability under subsection (1) or (2), the court shall award reasonable attorney's fees to the lessee.

(b) If the court does not find unconscionability and the lessee claiming unconscionability has brought or maintained an action he [or she] knew to be groundless, the court shall award reasonable attorney's fees to the party against whom the claim is made.

(c) In determining attorney's fees, the amount of the recovery on behalf of the claimant under subsections (1) and (2) is not controlling.

§ 2A-109. Option to Accelerate at Will.

(1) A term providing that one party or his [or her] successor in interest may accelerate payment or performance or require collateral or additional collateral "at will" or "when he [or she] deems himself [or herself] insecure" or in words of similar import must be construed to mean that he [or she] has power to do so only if he [or she] in good faith believes that the prospect of payment or performance is impaired.

(2) With respect to a consumer lease, the burden of establishing good faith under subsection (1) is on the party who exercised the power; otherwise the burden of establishing lack of good faith is on the party against whom the power has been exercised.

PART 2 Formation and Construction of Lease Contract

§ 2A-201. Statute of Frauds.

(1) A lease contract is not enforceable by way of action or defense unless:

(a) the total payments to be made under the lease contract, excluding payments for options to renew or buy, are less than $1,000; or

(b) there is a writing, signed by the party against whom enforcement is sought or by that party's authorized agent, sufficient to indicate that a lease contract has been made between the parties and to describe the goods leased and the lease term.

(2) Any description of leased goods or of the lease term is sufficient and satisfies subsection (1)(b), whether or not it is specific, if it reasonably identifies what is described.

(3) A writing is not insufficient because it omits or incorrectly states a term agreed upon, but the lease contract is not enforceable under subsection (1)(b) beyond the lease term and the quantity of goods shown in the writing.

(4) A lease contract that does not satisfy the requirements of subsection (1), but which is valid in other respects, is enforceable:

(a) if the goods are to be specially manufactured or obtained for the lessee and are not suitable for lease or sale to others in the ordinary course of the lessor's business, and the lessor, before notice of repudiation is received and under circumstances that reasonably indicate that the goods are for the lessee, has made either a substantial beginning of their manufacture or commitments for their procurement;

(b) if the party against whom enforcement is sought admits in that party's pleading, testimony or otherwise in court that a lease contract was made, but the lease contract is not enforceable under this provision beyond the quantity of goods admitted; or

(c) with respect to goods that have been received and accepted by the lessee.

(5) The lease term under a lease contract referred to in subsection (4) is:

(a) if there is a writing signed by the party against whom enforcement is sought or by that party's authorized agent specifying the lease term, the term so specified;

(b) if the party against whom enforcement is sought admits in that party's pleading, testimony, or otherwise in court a lease term, the term so admitted; or

(c) a reasonable lease term.

§ 2A-202. Final Written Expression: Parol or Extrinsic Evidence.

Terms with respect to which the confirmatory memoranda of the parties agree or which are otherwise set forth in a writing intended by the parties as a final expression of their agreement with respect to such terms as are included therein may not be contradicted by evidence of any prior agreement or of a contemporaneous oral agreement but may be explained or supplemented:

(a) by course of dealing or usage of trade or by course of performance; and

(b) by evidence of consistent additional terms unless the court finds the writing to have been intended also as a complete and exclusive statement of the terms of the agreement.

§ 2A-203. Seals Inoperative.

The affixing of a seal to a writing evidencing a lease contract or an offer to enter into a lease contract does not render the writing a sealed instrument and the law with respect to sealed instruments does not apply to the lease contract or offer.

§ 2A-204. Formation in General.

(1) A lease contract may be made in any manner sufficient to show agreement, including conduct by both parties which recognizes the existence of a lease contract.

(2) An agreement sufficient to constitute a lease contract may be found although the moment of its making is undetermined.

(3) Although one or more terms are left open, a lease contract does not fail for indefiniteness if the parties have intended to make a lease contract and there is a reasonably certain basis for giving an appropriate remedy.

§ 2A-205. Firm Offers.

An offer by a merchant to lease goods to or from another person in a signed writing that by its terms gives assurance it will be held open is not revocable, for lack of consideration, during the time stated or, if no time is stated, for a reasonable time, but in no event may the period of irrevocability exceed 3 months. Any such term of assurance on a form supplied by the offeree must be separately signed by the offeror.

§ 2A-206. Offer and Acceptance in Formation of Lease Contract.

(1) Unless otherwise unambiguously indicated by the language or circumstances, an offer to make a lease contract must be construed as inviting acceptance in any manner and by any medium reasonable in the circumstances.

(2) If the beginning of a requested performance is a reasonable mode of acceptance, an offeror who is not notified of acceptance within a reasonable time may treat the offer as having lapsed before acceptance.

§ 2A-207. Course of Performance or Practical Construction.

(1) If a lease contract involves repeated occasions for performance by either party with knowledge of the nature of the performance and opportunity for objection to it by the other, any course of performance accepted or acquiesced in without objection is relevant to determine the meaning of the lease agreement.

(2) The express terms of a lease agreement and any course of performance, as well as any course of dealing and usage of trade, must be construed whenever reasonable as consistent with each other; but if that construction is unreasonable, express terms control course of performance, course of performance controls both course of dealing and usage of trade, and course of dealing - controls usage of trade.

(3) Subject to the provisions of Section 2A–208 on modification and waiver, course of performance is relevant to show a waiver or modification of any term inconsistent with the course of performance.

§ 2A-208. Modification, Rescission and Waiver.

(1) An agreement modifying a lease contract needs no consideration to be binding.

(2) A signed lease agreement that excludes modification or rescission except by a signed writing may not be otherwise modified or rescinded, but, except as between merchants, such a requirement on a form supplied by a merchant must be separately signed by the other party.

(3) Although an attempt at modification or rescission does not satisfy the requirements of subsection (2), it may operate as a waiver.

(4) A party who has made a waiver affecting an executory portion of a lease contract may retract the waiver by reasonable notification received by the other party that strict performance will be required of any term waived, unless the retraction would be unjust in view of a material change of position in reliance on the waiver.

§ 2A-209. Lessee under Finance Lease as Beneficiary of Supply Contract.

(1) The benefit of the supplier's promises to the lessor under the supply contract and of all warranties, whether express or implied, including those of any third party provided in connection with or as part of the supply contract, extends to the lessee to the extent of the lessee's leasehold interest under a finance lease related to the supply contract, but is subject to the terms warranty and of the supply contract and all defenses or claims arising therefrom.

(2) The extension of the benefit of supplier's promises and of warranties to the lessee (Section 2A–209(1)) does not: (i) modify the rights and obligations of the parties to the supply contract, whether arising therefrom or otherwise, or (ii) impose any duty or liability under the supply contract on the lessee.

(3) Any modification or rescission of the supply contract by the supplier and the lessor is effective between the supplier and the lessee unless, before the modification or rescission, the supplier has received notice that the lessee has entered into a finance lease related to the supply contract. If the modification or rescission is effective between the supplier and the lessee, the lessor is deemed to have assumed, in addition to the obligations of the lessor to the lessee under the lease contract, promises of the supplier to the lessor and warranties that were so modified or rescinded as they existed and were available to the lessee before modification or rescission.

(4) In addition to the extension of the benefit of the supplier's promises and of warranties to the lessee under subsection (1), the lessee retains all rights that the lessee may have against the supplier which arise from an agreement between the lessee and the supplier or under other law.

As amended in 1990.

§ 2A-210. Express Warranties.

(1) Express warranties by the lessor are created as follows:

(a) Any affirmation of fact or promise made by the lessor to the lessee which relates to the goods and becomes part of the basis of the bargain creates an express warranty that the goods will conform to the affirmation or promise.

(b) Any description of the goods which is made part of the basis of the bargain creates an express warranty that the goods will conform to the description.

(c) Any sample or model that is made part of the basis of the bargain creates an express warranty that the whole of the goods will conform to the sample or model.

(2) It is not necessary to the creation of an express warranty that the lessor use formal words, such as "warrant" or "guarantee," or that the lessor have a specific intention to make a warranty, but an affirmation merely of the value of the goods or a statement purporting to be merely the lessor's opinion or commendation of the goods does not create a warranty.

§ 2A-211. Warranties Against Interference and Against Infringement; Lessee's Obligation Against Infringement.

(1) There is in a lease contract a warranty that for the lease term no person holds a claim to or interest in the goods that arose from an act or omission of the lessor, other than a claim by way of infringement or the like, which will interfere with the lessee's enjoyment of its leasehold interest.

(2) Except in a finance lease there is in a lease contract by a lessor who is a merchant regularly dealing in goods of the kind a warranty that the goods are delivered free of the rightful claim of any person by way of infringement or the like.

(3) A lessee who furnishes specifications to a lessor or a supplier shall hold the lessor and the supplier harmless against any claim by way of infringement or the like that arises out of compliance with the specifications.

§ 2A–212. Implied Warranty of Merchantability.

(1) Except in a finance lease, a warranty that the goods will be merchantable is implied in a lease contract if the lessor is a merchant with respect to goods of that kind.

(2) Goods to be merchantable must be at least such as

(a) pass without objection in the trade under the description in the lease agreement;

(b) in the case of fungible goods, are of fair average quality within the description;

(c) are fit for the ordinary purposes for which goods of that type are used;

(d) run, within the variation permitted by the lease agreement, of even kind, quality, and quantity within each unit and among all units involved;

(e) are adequately contained, packaged, and labeled as the lease agreement may require; and

(f) conform to any promises or affirmations of fact made on the container or label.

(3) Other implied warranties may arise from course of dealing or usage of trade.

§ 2A–213. Implied Warranty of Fitness for Particular Purpose.

Except in a finance of lease, if the lessor at the time the lease contract is made has reason to know of any particular purpose for which the goods are required and that the lessee is relying on the lessor's skill or judgment to select or furnish suitable goods, there is in the lease contract an implied warranty that the goods will be fit for that purpose.

§ 2A–214. Exclusion or Modification of Warranties.

(1) Words or conduct relevant to the creation of an express warranty and words or conduct tending to negate or limit a warranty must be construed wherever reasonable as consistent with each other; but, subject to the provisions of Section 2A–202 on parol or extrinsic evidence, negation or limitation is inoperative to the extent that the construction is unreasonable.

(2) Subject to subsection (3), to exclude or modify the implied warranty of merchantability or any part of it the language must mention "merchantability", be by a writing, and be conspicuous. Subject to subsection (3), to exclude or modify any implied warranty of fitness the exclusion must be by a writing and be conspicuous. Language to exclude all implied warranties of fitness is sufficient if it is in writing, is conspicuous and states, for example, "There is no warranty that the goods will be fit for a particular purpose".

(3) Notwithstanding subsection (2), but subject to subsection (4),

(a) unless the circumstances indicate otherwise, all implied warranties are excluded by expressions like "as is" or "with all faults" or by other language that in common understanding calls the lessee's attention to the exclusion of warranties and makes plain that there is no implied warranty, if in writing and conspicuous;

(b) if the lessee before entering into the lease contract has examined the goods or the sample or model as fully as desired or has refused to examine the goods, there is no implied warranty with regard to defects that an examination ought in the circumstances to have revealed; and

(c) an implied warranty may also be excluded or modified by course of dealing, course of performance, or usage of trade.

(4) To exclude or modify a warranty against interference or against infringement (Section 2A–211) or any part of it, the language must be specific, be by a writing, and be conspicuous, unless the circumstances, including course of performance, course of dealing, or usage of trade, give the lessee reason to know that the goods are being leased subject to a claim or interest of any person.

§ 2A–215. Cumulation and Conflict of Warranties Express or Implied.

Warranties, whether express or implied, must be construed as consistent with each other and as cumulative, but if that construction is unreasonable, the intention of the parties determines which warranty is dominant. In ascertaining that intention the following rules apply:

(a) Exact or technical specifications displace an inconsistent sample or model or general language of description.

(b) A sample from an existing bulk displaces inconsistent general language of description.

(c) Express warranties displace inconsistent implied warranties other than an implied warranty of fitness for a particular purpose.

§ 2A–216. Third-Party Beneficiaries of Express and Implied Warranties.

Alternative A A warranty to or for the benefit of a lessee under this Article, whether express or implied, extends to any natural person who is in the family or household of the lessee or who is a guest in the lessee's home if it is reasonable to expect that such person may use, consume, or be affected by the goods and who is injured in person by breach of the warranty. This section does not displace principles of law and equity that extend a warranty to or for the benefit of a lessee to other persons. The operation of this section may not be excluded, modified, or limited, but an exclusion, modification, or limitation of the warranty, including any with respect to rights and remedies, effective against the lessee is also effective against any beneficiary designated under this section.

Alternative B A warranty to or for the benefit of a lessee under this Article, whether express or implied, extends to any natural person who may reasonably be expected to use, consume, or be affected by the goods and who is injured in person by breach of the warranty. This section does not displace principles of law and equity that extend a warranty to or for the benefit of a lessee to other persons. The operation of this section may not be excluded, modified, or limited, but an exclusion, modification, or limitation of the warranty, including any with respect to rights and remedies, effective against the lessee is also effective against the beneficiary designated under this section.

Alternative C A warranty to or for the benefit of a lessee under this Article, whether express or implied, extends to any person who may reasonably be expected to use, consume, or be affected by the goods and who is injured by breach of the warranty. The operation of this section may not be excluded, modified, or limited with respect to injury to the person of an individual to whom the warranty extends, but an exclusion, modification, or limitation of the warranty, including any with respect to rights and remedies, effective against the lessee is also effective against the beneficiary designated under this section.

§ 2A-217. Identification.

Identification of goods as goods to which a lease contract refers may be made at any time and in any manner explicitly agreed to by the parties. In the absence of explicit agreement, identification occurs:

(a) when the lease contract is made if the lease contract is for a lease of goods that are existing and identified;

(b) when the goods are shipped, marked, or otherwise designated by the lessor as goods to which the lease contract refers, if the lease contract is for a lease of goods that are not existing and identified; or

(c) when the young are conceived, if the lease contract is for a lease of unborn young of animals.

§ 2A-218. Insurance and Proceeds.

(1) A lessee obtains an insurable interest when existing goods are identified to the lease contract even though the goods identified are nonconforming and the lessee has an option to reject them.

(2) If a lessee has an insurable interest only by reason of the lessor's identification of the goods, the lessor, until default or insolvency or notification to the lessee that identification is final, may substitute other goods for those identified.

(3) Notwithstanding a lessee's insurable interest under subsections (1) and (2), the lessor retains an insurable interest until an option to buy has been exercised by the lessee and risk of loss has passed to the lessee.

(4) Nothing in this section impairs any insurable interest recognized under any other statute or rule of law.

(5) The parties by agreement may determine that one or more parties have an obligation to obtain and pay for insurance covering the goods and by agreement may determine the beneficiary of the proceeds of the insurance.

§ 2A-219. Risk of Loss.

(1) Except in the case of a finance lease, risk of loss is retained by the lessor and does not pass to the lessee. In the case of a finance lease, risk of loss passes to the lessee.

(2) Subject to the provisions of this Article on the effect of default on risk of loss (Section 2A–220), if risk of loss is to pass to the lessee and the time of passage is not stated, the following rules apply:

(a) If the lease contract requires or authorizes the goods to be shipped by carrier

(i) and it does not require delivery at a particular destination, the risk of loss passes to the lessee when the goods are duly delivered to the carrier; but

(ii) if it does require delivery at a particular destination and the goods are there duly tendered while in the possession of the carrier, the risk of loss passes to the lessee when the goods are there duly so tendered as to enable the lessee to take delivery.

(b) If the goods are held by a bailee to be delivered without being moved, the risk of loss passes to the lessee on acknowledgment by the bailee of the lessee's right to possession of the goods.

(c) In any case not within subsection (a) or (b), the risk of loss passes to the lessee on the lessee's receipt of the goods if the lessor, or, in the case of a finance lease, the supplier, is a merchant; otherwise the risk passes to the lessee on tender of delivery.

§ 2A-220. Effect of Default on Risk of Loss.

(1) Where risk of loss is to pass to the lessee and the time of passage is not stated:

(a) If a tender or delivery of goods so fails to conform to the lease contract as to give a right of rejection, the risk of their loss remains with the lessor, or, in the case of a finance lease, the supplier, until cure or acceptance.

(b) If the lessee rightfully revokes acceptance, he [or she], to the extent of any deficiency in his [or her] effective insurance coverage, may treat the risk of loss as having remained with the lessor from the beginning.

(2) Whether or not risk of loss is to pass to the lessee, if the lessee as to conforming goods already identified to a lease contract repudiates or is otherwise in default under the lease contract, the lessor, or, in the case of a finance lease, the supplier, to the extent of any deficiency in his [or her] effective insurance coverage may treat the risk of loss as resting on the lessee for a commercially reasonable time.

§ 2A-221. Casualty to Identified Goods.

If a lease contract requires goods identified when the lease contract is made, and the goods suffer casualty without fault of the lessee, the lessor or the supplier before delivery, or the goods suffer casualty before risk of loss passes to the lessee pursuant to the lease agreement or Section 2A–219, then:

(a) if the loss is total, the lease contract is avoided; and

(b) if the loss is partial or the goods have so deteriorated as to no longer conform to the lease contract, the lessee may nevertheless demand inspection and at his [or her] option either treat the lease contract as avoided or, except in a finance lease that is not a consumer lease, accept the goods with due allowance from the rent payable for the balance of the lease term for the deterioration or the deficiency in quantity but without further right against the lessor.

PART 3 Effect of Lease Contract

§ 2A-301. Enforceability of Lease Contract.

Except as otherwise provided in this Article, a lease contract is effective and enforceable according to its terms between the parties, against purchasers of the goods and against creditors of the parties.

§ 2A-302. Title to and Possession of Goods.

Except as otherwise provided in this Article, each provision of this Article applies whether the lessor or a third party has title to the goods, and whether the lessor, the lessee, or a third party has possession of the goods, notwithstanding any statute or rule of law that possession or the absence of possession is fraudulent.

§ 2A-303. Alienability of Party's Interest Under Lease Contract or of Lessor's Residual Interest in Goods; Delegation of Performance; Transfer of Rights.

(1) As used in this section, "creation of a security interest" includes the sale of a lease contract that is subject to Article 9, Secured Transactions, by reason of Section 9–109(a)(3).

(2) Except as provided in subsections (3) and Section 9–407, a provision in a lease agreement which (i) prohibits the voluntary or involuntary transfer, including a transfer by sale, sublease, creation or enforcement of a security interest, or attachment, levy, or other judicial process, of an interest of a party under the lease contract or of the lessor's residual interest in the goods, or (ii) makes such a transfer an event of default, gives rise to the rights and remedies provided in subsection (4), but a transfer that is prohibited or is an event of default under the lease agreement is otherwise effective.

(3) A provision in a lease agreement which (i) prohibits a transfer of a right to damages for default with respect to the whole lease contract or of a right to payment arising out of the transferor's due performance of the transferor's entire obligation, or (ii) makes such a transfer an event of default, is not enforceable, and such a transfer is not a transfer that materially impairs the propsect of obtaining return performance by, materially changes the duty of, or materially increases the burden or risk imposed on, the other party to the lease contract within the purview of subsection (4).

(4) Subject to subsection (3) and Section 9–407:

(a) if a transfer is made which is made an event of default under a lease agreement, the party to the lease contract not making the transfer, unless that party waives the default or otherwise agrees, has the rights and remedies described in Section 2A–501(2);

(b) if paragraph (a) is not applicable and if a transfer is made that (i) is prohibited under a lease agreement or (ii) materially impairs the prospect of obtaining return performance by, materially changes the duty of, or materially increases the burden or risk imposed on, the other party to the lease contract, unless the party not making the transfer agrees at any time to the transfer in the lease contract or otherwise, then, except as limited by contract, (i) the transferor is liable to the party not making the transfer for damages caused by the transfer to the extent that the damages could not reasonably be prevented by the party not making the transfer and (ii) a court having jurisdiction may grant other appropriate relief, including cancellation of the lease contract or an injunction against the transfer.

(5) A transfer of "the lease" or of "all my rights under the lease", or a transfer in similar general terms, is a transfer of rights and, unless the language or the circumstances, as in a transfer for security, indicate the contrary, the transfer is a delegation of duties by the transferor to the transferee. Acceptance by the transferee constitutes a promise by the transferee to perform those duties. The promise is enforceable by either the transferor or the other party to the lease contract.

(6) Unless otherwise agreed by the lessor and the lessee, a delegation of performance does not relieve the transferor as against the other party of any duty to perform or of any liability for default.

(7) In a consumer lease, to prohibit the transfer of an interest of a party under the lease contract or to make a transfer an event of default, the language must be specific, by a writing, and conspicuous.

As amended in 1990 and 1999.

§ 2A-304. Subsequent Lease of Goods by Lessor.

(1) Subject to Section 2A–303, a subsequent lessee from a lessor of goods under an existing lease contract obtains, to the extent of the leasehold interest transferred, the leasehold interest in the goods that the lessor had or had power to transfer, and except as provided in subsection (2) and Section 2A–527(4), takes subject to the existing lease contract. A lessor with voidable title has power to transfer a good leasehold interest to a good faith subsequent lessee for value, but only to the extent set forth in the preceding sentence. If goods have been delivered under a transaction of purchase the lessor has that power even though:

(a) the lessor's transferor was deceived as to the identity of the lessor;

(b) the delivery was in exchange for a check which is later dishonored;

(c) it was agreed that the transaction was to be a "cash sale"; or

(d) the delivery was procured through fraud punishable as larcenous under the criminal law.

(2) A subsequent lessee in the ordinary course of business from a lessor who is a merchant dealing in goods of that kind to whom the goods were entrusted by the existing lessee of that lessor before the interest of the subsequent lessee became enforceable against that lessor obtains, to the extent of the leasehold interest transferred, all of that lessor's and the existing lessee's rights to the goods, and takes free of the existing lease contract.

(3) A subsequent lessee from the lessor of goods that are subject to an existing lease contract and are covered by a certificate of title issued under a statute of this State or of another jurisdiction takes no greater rights than those provided both by this section and by the certificate of title statute.

As amended in 1990.

§ 2A-305. Sale or Sublease of Goods by Lessee.

(1) Subject to the provisions of Section 2A–303, a buyer or sublessee from the lessee of goods under an existing lease contract obtains, to the extent of the interest transferred, the leasehold interest in the goods that the lessee had or had power to transfer, and except as provided in subsection (2) and Section 2A–511(4), takes subject to the existing lease contract. A lessee with a voidable leasehold interest has power to transfer a good leasehold interest to a good faith buyer for value or a good faith sublessee for value, but only to the extent set forth in the preceding sentence. When goods have been delivered under a transaction of lease the lessee has that power even though:

(a) the lessor was deceived as to the identity of the lessee;

(b) the delivery was in exchange for a check which is later dishonored; or

(c) the delivery was procured through fraud punishable as larcenous under the criminal law.

(2) A buyer in the ordinary course of business or a sublessee in the ordinary course of business from a lessee who is a merchant dealing in goods of that kind to whom the goods were entrusted by the lessor obtains, to the extent of the interest transferred, all of the lessor's and lessee's rights to the goods, and takes free of the existing lease contract.

(3) A buyer or sublessee from the lessee of goods that are subject to an existing lease contract and are covered by a certificate of title issued under a statute of this State or of another jurisdiction takes no greater rights than those provided both by this section and by the certificate of title statute.

§ 2A-306. Priority of Certain Liens Arising by Operation of Law.

If a person in the ordinary course of his [or her] business furnishes services or materials with respect to goods subject to a lease contract, a lien upon those goods in the possession of that person given by statute or rule of law for those materials or services takes priority over any interest of the lessor or lessee under the lease contract or this Article unless the lien is created by statute and the statute provides otherwise or unless the lien is created by rule of law and the rule of law provides otherwise.

§ 2A-307. Priority of Liens Arising by Attachment or Levy on, Security Interests in, and Other Claims to Goods.

(1) Except as otherwise provided in Section 2A–306, a creditor of a lessee takes subject to the lease contract.

(2) Except as otherwise provided in subsection (3) and in Sections 2A–306 and 2A–308, a creditor of a lessor takes subject to the lease contract unless the creditor holds a lien that attached to the goods before the lease contract became enforceable.

(3) Except as otherwise provided in Sections 9–317, 9–321, and 9–323, a lessee takes a leasehold interest subject to a security interest held by a creditor of the lessor.

As amended in 1990 and 1999.

§ 2A-308. Special Rights of Creditors.

(1) A creditor of a lessor in possession of goods subject to a lease contract may treat the lease contract as void if as against the creditor retention of possession by the lessor is fraudulent under any statute or rule of law, but retention of possession in good faith and current course of trade by the lessor for a commercially reasonable time after the lease contract becomes enforceable is not fraudulent.

(2) Nothing in this Article impairs the rights of creditors of a lessor if the lease contract (a) becomes enforceable, not in current course of trade but in satisfaction of or as security for a pre-existing claim for money, security, or the like, and (b) is made under circumstances which under any statute or rule of law apart from this Article would constitute the transaction a fraudulent transfer or voidable preference.

(3) A creditor of a seller may treat a sale or an identification of goods to a contract for sale as void if as against the creditor retention of possession by the seller is fraudulent under any statute or rule of law, but retention of possession of the goods pursuant to a lease contract entered into by the seller as lessee and the buyer as lessor in connection with the sale or identification of the goods is not fraudulent if the buyer bought for value and in good faith.

§ 2A-309. Lessor's and Lessee's Rights When Goods Become Fixtures.

(1) In this section:

(a) goods are "fixtures" when they become so related to particular real estate that an interest in them arises under real estate law;

(b) a "fixture filing" is the filing, in the office where a mortgage on the real estate would be filed or recorded, of a financing statement covering goods that are or are to become fixtures and conforming to the requirements of Section 9–502(a) and (b);

(c) a lease is a "purchase money lease" unless the lessee has possession or use of the goods or the right to possession or use of the goods before the lease agreement is enforceable;

(d) a mortgage is a "construction mortgage" to the extent it secures an obligation incurred for the construction of an improvement on land including the acquisition cost of the land, if the recorded writing so indicates; and

(e) "encumbrance" includes real estate mortgages and other liens on real estate and all other rights in real estate that are not ownership interests.

(2) Under this Article a lease may be of goods that are fixtures or may continue in goods that become fixtures, but no lease exists under this Article of ordinary building materials incorporated into an improvement on land.

(3) This Article does not prevent creation of a lease of fixtures pursuant to real estate law.

(4) The perfected interest of a lessor of fixtures has priority over a conflicting interest of an encumbrancer or owner of the real estate if:

(a) the lease is a purchase money lease, the conflicting interest of the encumbrancer or owner arises before the goods become fixtures, the interest of the lessor is perfected by a fixture filing before the goods become fixtures or within ten days thereafter, and the lessee has an interest of record in the real estate or is in possession of the real estate; or

(b) the interest of the lessor is perfected by a fixture filing before the interest of the encumbrancer or owner is of record, the lessor's interest has priority over any conflicting interest of a predecessor in title of the encumbrancer or owner, and the lessee has an interest of record in the real estate or is in possession of the real estate.

(5) The interest of a lessor of fixtures, whether or not perfected, has priority over the conflicting interest of an encumbrancer or owner of the real estate if:

(a) the fixtures are readily removable factory or office machines, readily removable equipment that is not primarily used or leased for use in the operation of the real estate, or readily removable replacements of domestic appliances that are goods subject to a consumer lease, and before the goods become fixtures the lease contract is enforceable; or

(b) the conflicting interest is a lien on the real estate obtained by legal or equitable proceedings after the lease contract is enforceable; or

(c) the encumbrancer or owner has consented in writing to the lease or has disclaimed an interest in the goods as fixtures; or

(d) the lessee has a right to remove the goods as against the encumbrancer or owner. If the lessee's right to remove terminates, the priority of the interest of the lessor continues for a reasonable time.

(6) Notwithstanding paragraph (4)(a) but otherwise subject to subsections (4) and (5), the interest of a lessor of fixtures, including the lessor's residual interest, is subordinate to the conflicting interest of an encumbrancer of the real estate under a construction mortgage recorded before the goods become fixtures if the goods become fixtures before the completion of the construction. To the extent given to refinance a construction mortgage, the conflicting interest of an encumbrancer of the real estate under a mortgage has this priority to the same extent as the encumbrancer of the real estate under the construction mortgage.

(7) In cases not within the preceding subsections, priority between the interest of a lessor of fixtures, including the lessor's residual interest, and the conflicting interest of an encumbrancer or owner of the real estate who is not the lessee is determined by the priority rules governing conflicting interests in real estate.

(8) If the interest of a lessor of fixtures, including the lessor's residual interest, has priority over all conflicting interests of all owners and encumbrancers of the real estate, the lessor or the lessee may (i) on default, expiration, termination, or cancellation of the lease agreement but subject to the agreement and this Article, or (ii) if necessary to enforce other rights and remedies of the lessor or lessee under this Article, remove the goods from the real estate, free and clear of all conflicting interests of all owners and encumbrancers of the real estate, but the lessor or lessee must reimburse any encumbrancer or owner of the real estate who is not the lessee and who has not otherwise agreed for the cost of repair of any physical injury, but not for any diminution in value of the real estate caused by the absence of the goods removed or by any necessity of replacing them. A person entitled to reimbursement may refuse permission to remove until the party seeking removal gives adequate security for the performance of this obligation.

(9) Even though the lease agreement does not create a security interest, the interest of a lessor of fixtures, including the lessor's residual interest, is perfected by filing a financing statement as a fixture filing for leased goods that are or are to become fixtures in accordance with the relevant provisions of the Article on Secured Transactions (Article 9).

As amended in 1990 and 1999.

§ 2A–310. Lessor's and Lessee's Rights When Goods Become Accessions.

(1) Goods are "accessions" when they are installed in or affixed to other goods.

(2) The interest of a lessor or a lessee under a lease contract entered into before the goods became accessions is superior to all interests in the whole except as stated in subsection (4).

(3) The interest of a lessor or a lessee under a lease contract entered into at the time or after the goods became accessions is superior to all subsequently acquired interests in the whole except as stated in subsection (4) but is subordinate to interests in the whole existing at the time the lease contract was made unless the holders of such interests in the whole have in writing consented to the lease or disclaimed an interest in the goods as part of the whole.

(4) The interest of a lessor or a lessee under a lease contract described in subsection (2) or (3) is subordinate to the interest of

(a) a buyer in the ordinary course of business or a lessee in the ordinary course of business of any interest in the whole acquired after the goods became accessions; or

(b) a creditor with a security interest in the whole perfected before the lease contract was made to the extent that the creditor makes subsequent advances without knowledge of the lease contract.

(5) When under subsections (2) or (3) and (4) a lessor or a lessee of accessions holds an interest that is superior to all interests in the whole, the lessor or the lessee may (a) on default, expiration, termination, or cancellation of the lease contract by the other party but subject to the provisions of the lease contract and this Article, or (b) if necessary to enforce his [or her] other rights and remedies under this Article, remove the goods from the whole, free and clear of all interests in the whole, but he [or she] must reimburse any holder of an interest in the whole who is not the lessee and who has not otherwise agreed for the cost of repair of any physical injury but not for any diminution in value of the whole caused by the absence of the goods removed or by any necessity for replacing them. A person entitled to reimbursement may refuse permission to remove until the party seeking removal gives adequate security for the performance of this obligation.

§ 2A–311. Priority Subject to Subordination.

Nothing in this Article prevents subordination by agreement by any person entitled to priority.

As added in 1990.

PART 4 Performance of Lease Contract: Repudiated, Substituted and Excused

§ 2A–401. Insecurity: Adequate Assurance of Performance.

(1) A lease contract imposes an obligation on each party that the other's expectation of receiving due performance will not be impaired.

(2) If reasonable grounds for insecurity arise with respect to the performance of either party, the insecure party may demand in writing adequate assurance of due performance. Until the insecure party receives that assurance, if commercially reasonable the insecure party may suspend any performance for which he [or she] has not already received the agreed return.

(3) A repudiation of the lease contract occurs if assurance of due performance adequate under the circumstances of the particular case is not provided to the insecure party within a reasonable time, not to exceed 30 days after receipt of a demand by the other party.

(4) Between merchants, the reasonableness of grounds for insecurity and the adequacy of any assurance offered must be determined according to commercial standards.

(5) Acceptance of any nonconforming delivery or payment does not prejudice the aggrieved party's right to demand adequate assurance of future performance.

§ 2A–402. Anticipatory Repudiation.

If either party repudiates a lease contract with respect to a performance not yet due under the lease contract, the loss of which performance will substantially impair the value of the lease contract to the other, the aggrieved party may:

(a) for a commercially reasonable time, await retraction of repudiation and performance by the repudiating party;

(b) make demand pursuant to Section 2A–401 and await assurance of future performance adequate under the circumstances of the particular case; or

(c) resort to any right or remedy upon default under the lease contract or this Article, even though the aggrieved party has notified the repudiating party that the aggrieved party would await the repudiating party's performance and assurance and has urged retraction. In addition, whether or not the aggrieved party is pursuing one of the foregoing remedies, the aggrieved party may suspend performance or, if the aggrieved party is the lessor, proceed in accordance with the provisions of this Article on the lessor's right to identify goods to the lease contract notwithstanding default or to salvage unfinished goods (Section 2A–524).

§ 2A–403. Retraction of Anticipatory Repudiation.

(1) Until the repudiating party's next performance is due, the repudiating party can retract the repudiation unless, since the repudiation, the aggrieved party has cancelled the lease contract or materially changed the aggrieved party's position or otherwise indicated that the aggrieved party considers the repudiation final.

(2) Retraction may be by any method that clearly indicates to the aggrieved party that the repudiating party intends to perform under the lease contract and includes any assurance demanded under Section 2A–401.

(3) Retraction reinstates a repudiating party's rights under a lease contract with due excuse and allowance to the aggrieved party for any delay occasioned by the repudiation.

§ 2A–404. Substituted Performance.

(1) If without fault of the lessee, the lessor and the supplier, the agreed berthing, loading, or unloading facilities fail or the agreed type of carrier becomes unavailable or the agreed manner of delivery otherwise becomes commercially impracticable, but a commercially reasonable substitute is available, the substitute performance must be tendered and accepted.

(2) If the agreed means or manner of payment fails because of domestic or foreign governmental regulation:

(a) the lessor may withhold or stop delivery or cause the supplier to withhold or stop delivery unless the lessee provides a means or manner of payment that is commercially a substantial equivalent; and

(b) if delivery has already been taken, payment by the means or in the manner provided by the regulation discharges the lessee's obligation unless the regulation is discriminatory, oppressive, or predatory.

§ 2A–405. Excused Performance.

Subject to Section 2A–404 on substituted performance, the following rules apply:

(a) Delay in delivery or nondelivery in whole or in part by a lessor or a supplier who complies with paragraphs (b) and (c) is not a default under the lease contract if performance as agreed has been made impracticable by the occurrence of a contingency the nonoccurrence of which was a basic assumption on which the lease contract was made or by compliance in good faith with any applicable foreign or domestic governmental regulation or order, whether or not the regulation or order later proves to be invalid.

(b) If the causes mentioned in paragraph (a) affect only part of the lessor's or the supplier's capacity to perform, he [or she] shall allocate production and deliveries among his [or her] customers but at his [or her] option may include regular customers not then under contract for sale or lease as well as his [or her] own requirements for further manufacture. He [or she] may so allocate in any manner that is fair and reasonable.

(c) The lessor seasonably shall notify the lessee and in the case of a finance lease the supplier seasonably shall notify the lessor and the lessee, if known, that there will be delay or nondelivery and, if allocation is required under paragraph (b), of the estimated quota thus made available for the lessee.

§ 2A–406. Procedure on Excused Performance.

(1) If the lessee receives notification of a material or indefinite delay or an allocation justified under Section 2A–405, the lessee may by written notification to the lessor as to any goods involved, and with respect to all of the goods if under an installment lease contract the value of the whole lease contract is substantially impaired (Section 2A–510):

(a) terminate the lease contract (Section 2A–505(2)); or

(b) except in a finance lease that is not a consumer lease, modify the lease contract by accepting the available quota in substitution, with due allowance from the rent payable for the balance of the lease term for the deficiency but without further right against the lessor.

(2) If, after receipt of a notification from the lessor under Section 2A–405, the lessee fails so to modify the lease agreement within a reasonable time not exceeding 30 days, the lease contract lapses with respect to any deliveries affected.

§ 2A–407. Irrevocable Promises: Finance Leases.

(1) In the case of a finance lease that is not a consumer lease the lessee's promises under the lease contract become irrevocable and independent upon the lessee's acceptance of the goods.

(2) A promise that has become irrevocable and independent under subsection (1):

(a) is effective and enforceable between the parties, and by or against third parties including assignees of the parties, and

(b) is not subject to cancellation, termination, modification, repudiation, excuse, or substitution without the consent of the party to whom the promise runs.

(3) This section does not affect the validity under any other law of a covenant in any lease contract making the lessee's promises irrevocable and independent upon the lessee's acceptance of the goods.

As amended in 1990.

PART 5 Default

A. In General

§ 2A–501. Default: Procedure.

(1) Whether the lessor or the lessee is in default under a lease contract is determined by the lease agreement and this Article.

(2) If the lessor or the lessee is in default under the lease contract, the party seeking enforcement has rights and remedies as provided in this Article and, except as limited by this Article, as provided in the lease agreement.

(3) If the lessor or the lessee is in default under the lease contract, the party seeking enforcement may reduce the party's claim to judgment, or otherwise enforce the lease contract by self-help or any available judicial procedure or nonjudicial procedure, including administrative proceeding, arbitration, or the like, in accordance with this Article.

(4) Except as otherwise provided in Section 1–106(1) or this Article or the lease agreement, the rights and remedies referred to in subsections (2) and (3) are cumulative.

(5) If the lease agreement covers both real property and goods, the party seeking enforcement may proceed under this Part as to the goods, or under other applicable law as to both the real property and the goods in accordance with that party's rights and remedies in respect of the real property, in which case this Part does not apply.

As amended in 1990.

§ 2A–502. Notice After Default.

Except as otherwise provided in this Article or the lease agreement, the lessor or lessee in default under the lease contract is not entitled to notice of default or notice of enforcement from the other party to the lease agreement.

§ 2A–503. Modification or Impairment of Rights and Remedies.

(1) Except as otherwise provided in this Article, the lease agreement may include rights and remedies for default in

addition to or in substitution for those provided in this Article and may limit or alter the measure of damages recoverable under this Article.

(2) Resort to a remedy provided under this Article or in the lease agreement is optional unless the remedy is expressly agreed to be exclusive. If circumstances cause an exclusive or limited remedy to fail of its essential purpose, or provision for an exclusive remedy is unconscionable, remedy may be had as provided in this Article.

(3) Consequential damages may be liquidated under Section 2A–504, or may otherwise be limited, altered, or excluded unless the limitation, alteration, or exclusion is unconscionable. Limitation, alteration, or exclusion of consequential damages for injury to the person in the case of consumer goods is prima facie unconscionable but limitation, alteration, or exclusion of damages where the loss is commercial is not prima facie unconscionable.

(4) Rights and remedies on default by the lessor or the lessee with respect to any obligation or promise collateral or ancillary to the lease contract are not impaired by this Article.

As amended in 1990.

§ 2A–504. Liquidation of Damages.

(1) Damages payable by either party for default, or any other act or omission, including indemnity for loss or diminution of anticipated tax benefits or loss or damage to lessor's residual interest, may be liquidated in the lease agreement but only at an amount or by a formula that is reasonable in light of the then anticipated harm caused by the default or other act or omission.

(2) If the lease agreement provides for liquidation of damages, and such provision does not comply with subsection (1), or such provision is an exclusive or limited remedy that circumstances cause to fail of its essential purpose, remedy may be had as provided in this Article.

(3) If the lessor justifiably withholds or stops delivery of goods because of the lessee's default or insolvency (Section 2A–525 or 2A–526), the lessee is entitled to restitution of any amount by which the sum of his [or her] payments exceeds:

(a) the amount to which the lessor is entitled by virtue of terms liquidating the lessor's damages in accordance with subsection (1); or

(b) in the absence of those terms, 20 percent of the then present value of the total rent the lessee was obligated to pay for the balance of the lease term, or, in the case of a consumer lease, the lesser of such amount or $500.

(4) A lessee's right to restitution under subsection (3) is subject to offset to the extent the lessor establishes:

(a) a right to recover damages under the provisions of this Article other than subsection (1); and

(b) the amount or value of any benefits received by the lessee directly or indirectly by reason of the lease contract.

§ 2A–505. Cancellation and Termination and Effect of Cancellation, Termination, Rescission, or Fraud on Rights and Remedies.

(1) On cancellation of the lease contract, all obligations that are still executory on both sides are discharged, but any right based on prior default or performance survives, and the cancelling party also retains any remedy for default of the whole lease contract or any unperformed balance.

(2) On termination of the lease contract, all obligations that are still executory on both sides are discharged but any right based on prior default or performance survives.

(3) Unless the contrary intention clearly appears, expressions of "cancellation," "rescission," or the like of the lease contract may not be construed as a renunciation or discharge of any claim in damages for an antecedent default.

(4) Rights and remedies for material misrepresentation or fraud include all rights and remedies available under this Article for default.

(5) Neither rescission nor a claim for rescission of the lease contract nor rejection or return of the goods may bar or be deemed inconsistent with a claim for damages or other right or remedy.

§ 2A–506. Statute of Limitations.

(1) An action for default under a lease contract, including breach of warranty or indemnity, must be commenced within 4 years after the cause of action accrued. By the original lease contract the parties may reduce the period of limitation to not less than one year.

(2) A cause of action for default accrues when the act or omission on which the default or breach of warranty is based is or should have been discovered by the aggrieved party, or when the default occurs, whichever is later. A cause of action for indemnity accrues when the act or omission on which the claim for indemnity is based is or should have been discovered by the indemnified party, whichever is later.

(3) If an action commenced within the time limited by subsection (1) is so terminated as to leave available a remedy by another action for the same default or breach of warranty or indemnity, the other action may be commenced after the expiration of the time limited and within 6 months after the termination of the first action unless the termination resulted from voluntary discontinuance or from dismissal for failure or neglect to prosecute.

(4) This section does not alter the law on tolling of the statute of limitations nor does it apply to causes of action that have accrued before this Article becomes effective.

§ 2A–507. Proof of Market Rent: Time and Place.

(1) Damages based on market rent (Section 2A–519 or 2A–528) are determined according to the rent for the use of the goods concerned for a lease term identical to the remaining lease term of the original lease agreement and prevailing at the times specified in Sections 2A–519 and 2A–528.

(2) If evidence of rent for the use of the goods concerned for a lease term identical to the remaining lease term of the original lease agreement and prevailing at the times or places described in this Article is not readily available, the rent prevailing within any reasonable time before or after the time described or at any other place or for a different lease term which in commercial judgment or under usage of trade would serve as a reasonable substitute for the one described may be used, making any proper allowance for the difference, including the cost of transporting the goods to or from the other place.

(3) Evidence of a relevant rent prevailing at a time or place or for a lease term other than the one described in this Article offered by one party is not admissible unless and until he [or she] has given the other party notice the court finds sufficient to prevent unfair surprise.

(4) If the prevailing rent or value of any goods regularly leased in any established market is in issue, reports in official publications or trade journals or in newspapers or periodicals of general circulation published as the reports of that market are admissible in evidence. The circumstances of the preparation of the report may be shown to affect its weight but not its admissibility.

As amended in 1990.

B. Default by Lessor

§ 2A-508. Lessee's Remedies.

(1) If a lessor fails to deliver the goods in conformity to the lease contract (Section 2A–509) or repudiates the lease contract (Section 2A–402), or a lessee rightfully rejects the goods (Section 2A–509) or justifiably revokes acceptance of the goods (Section 2A–517), then with respect to any goods involved, and with respect to all of the goods if under an installment lease contract the value of the whole lease contract is substantially impaired (Section 2A–510), the lessor is in default under the lease contract and the lessee may:

(a) cancel the lease contract (Section 2A–505(1));

(b) recover so much of the rent and security as has been paid and is just under the circumstances;

(c) cover and recover damages as to all goods affected whether or not they have been identified to the lease contract (Sections 2A–518 and 2A–520), or recover damages for nondelivery (Sections 2A–519 and 2A–520);

(d) exercise any other rights or pursue any other remedies provided in the lease contract.

(2) If a lessor fails to deliver the goods in conformity to the lease contract or repudiates the lease contract, the lessee may also:

(a) if the goods have been identified, recover them (Section 2A–522); or

(b) in a proper case, obtain specific performance or replevy the goods (Section 2A–521).

(3) If a lessor is otherwise in default under a lease contract, the lessee may exercise the rights and pursue the remedies provided in the lease contract, which may include a right to cancel the lease, and in Section 2A–519(3).

(4) If a lessor has breached a warranty, whether express or implied, the lessee may recover damages (Section 2A–519(4)).

(5) On rightful rejection or justifiable revocation of acceptance, a lessee has a security interest in goods in the lessee's possession or control for any rent and security that has been paid and any expenses reasonably incurred in their inspection, receipt, transportation, and care and custody and may hold those goods and dispose of them in good faith and in a commercially reasonable manner, subject to Section 2A–527(5).

(6) Subject to the provisions of Section 2A–407, a lessee, on notifying the lessor of the lessee's intention to do so, may deduct all or any part of the damages resulting from any default under the lease contract from any part of the rent still due under the same lease contract.

As amended in 1990.

§ 2A-509. Lessee's Rights on Improper Delivery; Rightful Rejection.

(1) Subject to the provisions of Section 2A–510 on default in installment lease contracts, if the goods or the tender or delivery fail in any respect to conform to the lease contract, the lessee may reject or accept the goods or accept any commercial unit or units and reject the rest of the goods.

(2) Rejection of goods is ineffective unless it is within a reasonable time after tender or delivery of the goods and the lessee seasonably notifies the lessor.

§ 2A-510. Installment Lease Contracts: Rejection and Default.

(1) Under an installment lease contract a lessee may reject any delivery that is nonconforming if the nonconformity substantially impairs the value of that delivery and cannot be cured or the nonconformity is a defect in the required documents; but if the nonconformity does not fall within subsection (2) and the lessor or the supplier gives adequate assurance of its cure, the lessee must accept that delivery.

(2) Whenever nonconformity or default with respect to one or more deliveries substantially impairs the value of the installment lease contract as a whole there is a default with respect to the whole. But, the aggrieved party reinstates the installment lease contract as a whole if the aggrieved party accepts a nonconforming delivery without seasonably notifying of cancellation or brings an action with respect only to past deliveries or demands performance as to future deliveries.

§ 2A-511. Merchant Lessee's Duties as to Rightfully Rejected Goods.

(1) Subject to any security interest of a lessee (Section 2A–508(5)), if a lessor or a supplier has no agent or place of business at the market of rejection, a merchant lessee, after rejection of goods in his [or her] possession or control, shall follow any

reasonable instructions received from the lessor or the supplier with respect to the goods. In the absence of those instructions, a merchant lessee shall make reasonable efforts to sell, lease, or otherwise dispose of the goods for the lessor's account if they threaten to decline in value speedily. Instructions are not reasonable if on demand indemnity for expenses is not forthcoming.

(2) If a merchant lessee (subsection (1)) or any other lessee (Section 2A–512) disposes of goods, he [or she] is entitled to reimbursement either from the lessor or the supplier or out of the proceeds for reasonable expenses of caring for and disposing of the goods and, if the expenses include no disposition commission, to such commission as is usual in the trade, or if there is none, to a reasonable sum not exceeding 10 percent of the gross proceeds.

(3) In complying with this section or Section 2A–512, the lessee is held only to good faith. Good faith conduct hereunder is neither acceptance or conversion nor the basis of an action for damages.

(4) A purchaser who purchases in good faith from a lessee pursuant to this section or Section 2A–512 takes the goods free of any rights of the lessor and the supplier even though the lessee fails to comply with one or more of the requirements of this Article.

§ 2A–512. Lessee's Duties as to Rightfully Rejected Goods.

(1) Except as otherwise provided with respect to goods that threaten to decline in value speedily (Section 2A–511) and subject to any security interest of a lessee (Section 2A–508(5)):

(a) the lessee, after rejection of goods in the lessee's possession, shall hold them with reasonable care at the lessor's or the supplier's disposition for a reasonable time after the lessee's seasonable notification of rejection;

(b) if the lessor or the supplier gives no instructions within a reasonable time after notification of rejection, the lessee may store the rejected goods for the lessor's or the supplier's account or ship them to the lessor or the supplier or dispose of them for the lessor's or the supplier's account with reimbursement in the manner provided in Section 2A–511; but

(c) the lessee has no further obligations with regard to goods rightfully rejected.

(2) Action by the lessee pursuant to subsection (1) is not acceptance or conversion.

§ 2A–513. Cure by Lessor of Improper Tender or Delivery; Replacement.

(1) If any tender or delivery by the lessor or the supplier is rejected because nonconforming and the time for performance has not yet expired, the lessor or the supplier may seasonably notify the lessee of the lessor's or the supplier's intention to cure and may then make a conforming delivery within the time provided in the lease contract.

(2) If the lessee rejects a nonconforming tender that the lessor or the supplier had reasonable grounds to believe would be acceptable with or without money allowance, the lessor or the supplier may have a further reasonable time to substitute a conforming tender if he [or she] seasonably notifies the lessee.

§ 2A–514. Waiver of Lessee's Objections.

(1) In rejecting goods, a lessee's failure to state a particular defect that is ascertainable by reasonable inspection precludes the lessee from relying on the defect to justify rejection or to establish default:

(a) if, stated seasonably, the lessor or the supplier could have cured it (Section 2A–513); or

(b) between merchants if the lessor or the supplier after rejection has made a request in writing for a full and final written statement of all defects on which the lessee proposes to rely.

(2) A lessee's failure to reserve rights when paying rent or other consideration against documents precludes recovery of the payment for defects apparent on the face of the documents.

§ 2A–515. Acceptance of Goods.

(1) Acceptance of goods occurs after the lessee has had a reasonable opportunity to inspect the goods and

(a) the lessee signifies or acts with respect to the goods in a manner that signifies to the lessor or the supplier that the goods are conforming or that the lessee will take or retain them in spite of their nonconformity; or

(b) the lessee fails to make an effective rejection of the goods (Section 2A–509(2)).

(2) Acceptance of a part of any commercial unit is acceptance of that entire unit.

§ 2A–516. Effect of Acceptance of Goods; Notice of Default; Burden of Establishing Default after Acceptance; Notice of Claim or Litigation to Person Answerable Over.

(1) A lessee must pay rent for any goods accepted in accordance with the lease contract, with due allowance for goods rightfully rejected or not delivered.

(2) A lessee's acceptance of goods precludes rejection of the goods accepted. In the case of a finance lease, if made with knowledge of a nonconformity, acceptance cannot be revoked because of it. In any other case, if made with knowledge of a nonconformity, acceptance cannot be revoked because of it unless the acceptance was on the reasonable assumption that the nonconformity would be seasonably cured. Acceptance does not of itself impair any other remedy provided by this Article or the lease agreement for nonconformity.

(3) If a tender has been accepted:

(a) within a reasonable time after the lessee discovers or should have discovered any default, the lessee shall notify the lessor and the supplier, if any, or be barred from any remedy against the party notified;

(b) except in the case of a consumer lease, within a reasonable time after the lessee receives notice of litigation for infringement or the like (Section 2A–211) the lessee shall notify the lessor or be barred from any remedy over for liability established by the litigation; and

(c) the burden is on the lessee to establish any default.

(4) If a lessee is sued for breach of a warranty or other obligation for which a lessor or a supplier is answerable over the following apply:

(a) The lessee may give the lessor or the supplier, or both, written notice of the litigation. If the notice states that the person notified may come in and defend and that if the person notified does not do so that person will be bound in any action against that person by the lessee by any determination of fact common to the two litigations, then unless the person notified after seasonable receipt of the notice does come in and defend that person is so bound.

(b) The lessor or the supplier may demand in writing that the lessee turn over control of the litigation including settlement if the claim is one for infringement or the like (Section 2A–211) or else be barred from any remedy over. If the demand states that the lessor or the supplier agrees to bear all expense and to satisfy any adverse judgment, then unless the lessee after seasonable receipt of the demand does turn over control the lessee is so barred.

(5) Subsections (3) and (4) apply to any obligation of a lessee to hold the lessor or the supplier harmless against infringement or the like (Section 2A–211).

As amended in 1990.

§ 2A–517. Revocation of Acceptance of Goods.

(1) A lessee may revoke acceptance of a lot or commercial unit whose nonconformity substantially impairs its value to the lessee if the lessee has accepted it:

(a) except in the case of a finance lease, on the reasonable assumption that its nonconformity would be cured and it has not been seasonably cured; or

(b) without discovery of the nonconformity if the lessee's acceptance was reasonably induced either by the lessor's assurances or, except in the case of a finance lease, by the difficulty of discovery before acceptance.

(2) Except in the case of a finance lease that is not a consumer lease, a lessee may revoke acceptance of a lot or commercial unit if the lessor defaults under the lease contract and the default substantially impairs the value of that lot or commercial unit to the lessee.

(3) If the lease agreement so provides, the lessee may revoke acceptance of a lot or commercial unit because of other defaults by the lessor.

(4) Revocation of acceptance must occur within a reasonable time after the lessee discovers or should have discovered the ground for it and before any substantial change in condition of the goods which is not caused by the nonconformity. Revocation is not effective until the lessee notifies the lessor.

(5) A lessee who so revokes has the same rights and duties with regard to the goods involved as if the lessee had rejected them.

As amended in 1990.

§ 2A–518. Cover; Substitute Goods.

(1) After a default by a lessor under the lease contract of the type described in Section 2A–508(1), or, if agreed, after other default by the lessor, the lessee may cover by making any purchase or lease of or contract to purchase or lease goods in substitution for those due from the lessor.

(2) Except as otherwise provided with respect to damages liquidated in the lease agreement (Section 2A–504) or otherwise determined pursuant to agreement of the parties (Sections 1–102(3) and 2A–503), if a lessee's cover is by lease agreement substantially similar to the original lease agreement and the new lease agreement is made in good faith and in a commercially reasonable manner, the lessee may recover from the lessor as damages (i) the present value, as of the date of the commencement of the term of the new lease agreement, of the rent under the new lease agreement applicable to that period of the new lease term which is comparable to the then remaining term of the original lease agreement minus the present value as of the same date of the total rent for the then remaining lease term of the original lease agreement, and (ii) any incidental or consequential damages, less expenses saved in consequence of the lessor's default.

(3) If a lessee's cover is by lease agreement that for any reason does not qualify for treatment under subsection (2), or is by purchase or otherwise, the lessee may recover from the lessor as if the lessee had elected not to cover and Section 2A–519 governs.

As amended in 1990.

§ 2A–519. Lessee's Damages for Non-Delivery, Repudiation, Default, and Breach of Warranty in Regard to Accepted Goods.

(1) Except as otherwise provided with respect to damages liquidated in the lease agreement (Section 2A–504) or otherwise determined pursuant to agreement of the parties (Sections 1–102(3) and 2A–503), if a lessee elects not to cover or a lessee elects to cover and the cover is by lease agreement that for any reason does not qualify for treatment under Section 2A–518(2), or is by purchase or otherwise, the measure of damages for non-delivery or repudiation by the lessor or for rejection or revocation of acceptance by the lessee is the present value, as of the date of the default, of the then market rent minus the present value as of the same date of the original rent, computed for the remaining lease term of the original lease

agreement, together with incidental and consequential damages, less expenses saved in consequence of the lessor's default.

(2) Market rent is to be determined as of the place for tender or, in cases of rejection after arrival or revocation of acceptance, as of the place of arrival.

(3) Except as otherwise agreed, if the lessee has accepted goods and given notification (Section 2A–516(3)), the measure of damages for non-conforming tender or delivery or other default by a lessor is the loss resulting in the ordinary course of events from the lessor's default as determined in any manner that is reasonable together with incidental and consequential damages, less expenses saved in consequence of the lessor's default.

(4) Except as otherwise agreed, the measure of damages for breach of warranty is the present value at the time and place of acceptance of the difference between the value of the use of the goods accepted and the value if they had been as warranted for the lease term, unless special circumstances show proximate damages of a different amount, together with incidental and consequential damages, less expenses saved in consequence of the lessor's default or breach of warranty.

As amended in 1990.

§ 2A–520. Lessee's Incidental and Consequential Damages.

(1) Incidental damages resulting from a lessor's default include expenses reasonably incurred in inspection, receipt, transportation, and care and custody of goods rightfully rejected or goods the acceptance of which is justifiably revoked, any commercially reasonable charges, expenses or commissions in connection with effecting cover, and any other reasonable expense incident to the default.

(2) Consequential damages resulting from a lessor's default include:

(a) any loss resulting from general or particular requirements and needs of which the lessor at the time of contracting had reason to know and which could not reasonably be prevented by cover or otherwise; and

(b) injury to person or property proximately resulting from any breach of warranty.

§ 2A–521. Lessee's Right to Specific Performance or Replevin.

(1) Specific performance may be decreed if the goods are unique or in other proper circumstances.

(2) A decree for specific performance may include any terms and conditions as to payment of the rent, damages, or other relief that the court deems just.

(3) A lessee has a right of replevin, detinue, sequestration, claim and delivery, or the like for goods identified to the lease contract if after reasonable effort the lessee is unable to effect cover for those goods or the circumstances reasonably indicate that the effort will be unavailing.

§ 2A–522. Lessee's Right to Goods on Lessor's Insolvency.

(1) Subject to subsection (2) and even though the goods have not been shipped, a lessee who has paid a part or all of the rent and security for goods identified to a lease contract (Section 2A–217) on making and keeping good a tender of any unpaid portion of the rent and security due under the lease contract may recover the goods identified from the lessor if the lessor becomes insolvent within 10 days after receipt of the first installment of rent and security.

(2) A lessee acquires the right to recover goods identified to a lease contract only if they conform to the lease contract.

C. Default by Lessee

§ 2A–523. Lessor's Remedies.

(1) If a lessee wrongfully rejects or revokes acceptance of goods or fails to make a payment when due or repudiates with respect to a part or the whole, then, with respect to any goods involved, and with respect to all of the goods if under an installment lease contract the value of the whole lease contract is substantially impaired (Section 2A–510), the lessee is in default under the lease contract and the lessor may:

(a) cancel the lease contract (Section 2A–505(1));

(b) proceed respecting goods not identified to the lease contract (Section 2A–524);

(c) withhold delivery of the goods and take possession of goods previously delivered (Section 2A–525);

(d) stop delivery of the goods by any bailee (Section 2A–526);

(e) dispose of the goods and recover damages (Section 2A–527), or retain the goods and recover damages (Section 2A–528), or in a proper case recover rent (Section 2A–529)

(f) exercise any other rights or pursue any other remedies provided in the lease contract.

(2) If a lessor does not fully exercise a right or obtain a remedy to which the lessor is entitled under subsection (1), the lessor may recover the loss resulting in the ordinary course of events from the lessee's default as determined in any reasonable manner, together with incidental damages, less expenses saved in consequence of the lessee's default.

(3) If a lessee is otherwise in default under a lease contract, the lessor may exercise the rights and pursue the remedies provided in the lease contract, which may include a right to cancel the lease. In addition, unless otherwise provided in the lease contract:

(a) if the default substantially impairs the value of the lease contract to the lessor, the lessor may exercise the rights and pursue the remedies provided in subsections (1) or (2); or

(b) if the default does not substantially impair the value of the lease contract to the lessor, the lessor may recover as provided in subsection (2).

As amended in 1990.

§ 2A–524. Lessor's Right to Identify Goods to Lease Contract.

(1) After default by the lessee under the lease contract of the type described in Section 2A–523(1) or 2A–523(3)(a) or, if agreed, after other default by the lessee, the lessor may:

(a) identify to the lease contract conforming goods not already identified if at the time the lessor learned of the default they were in the lessor's or the supplier's possession or control; and

(b) dispose of goods (Section 2A–527(1)) that demonstrably have been intended for the particular lease contract even though those goods are unfinished.

(2) If the goods are unfinished, in the exercise of reasonable commercial judgment for the purposes of avoiding loss and of effective realization, an aggrieved lessor or the supplier may either complete manufacture and wholly identify the goods to the lease contract or cease manufacture and lease, sell, or otherwise dispose of the goods for scrap or salvage value or proceed in any other reasonable manner.

As amended in 1990.

§ 2A–525. Lessor's Right to Possession of Goods.

(1) If a lessor discovers the lessee to be insolvent, the lessor may refuse to deliver the goods.

(2) After a default by the lessee under the lease contract of the type described in Section 2A–523(1) or 2A–523(3)(a) or, if agreed, after other default by the lessee, the lessor has the right to take possession of the goods. If the lease contract so provides, the lessor may require the lessee to assemble the goods and make them available to the lessor at a place to be designated by the lessor which is reasonably convenient to both parties. Without removal, the lessor may render unusable any goods employed in trade or business, and may dispose of goods on the lessee's premises (Section 2A–527).

(3) The lessor may proceed under subsection (2) without judicial process if that can be done without breach of the peace or the lessor may proceed by action.

As amended in 1990.

§ 2A–526. Lessor's Stoppage of Delivery in Transit or Otherwise.

(1) A lessor may stop delivery of goods in the possession of a carrier or other bailee if the lessor discovers the lessee to be insolvent and may stop delivery of carload, truckload, planeload, or larger shipments of express or freight if the lessee repudiates or fails to make a payment due before delivery, whether for rent, security or otherwise under the lease contract, or for any other reason the lessor has a right to withhold or take possession of the goods.

(2) In pursuing its remedies under subsection (1), the lessor may stop delivery until

(a) receipt of the goods by the lessee;

(b) acknowledgment to the lessee by any bailee of the goods, except a carrier, that the bailee holds the goods for the lessee; or

(c) such an acknowledgment to the lessee by a carrier via reshipment or as warehouseman.

(3) (a) To stop delivery, a lessor shall so notify as to enable the bailee by reasonable diligence to prevent delivery of the goods.

(b) After notification, the bailee shall hold and deliver the goods according to the directions of the lessor, but the lessor is liable to the bailee for any ensuing charges or damages.

(c) A carrier who has issued a nonnegotiable bill of lading is not obliged to obey a notification to stop received from a person other than the consignor.

§ 2A–527. Lessor's Rights to Dispose of Goods.

(1) After a default by a lessee under the lease contract of the type described in Section 2A–523(1) or 2A–523(3)(a) or after the lessor refuses to deliver or takes possession of goods (Section 2A–525 or 2A–526), or, if agreed, after other default by a lessee, the lessor may dispose of the goods concerned or the undelivered balance thereof by lease, sale, or otherwise.

(2) Except as otherwise provided with respect to damages liquidated in the lease agreement (Section 2A–504) or otherwise determined pursuant to agreement of the parties (Sections 1–102(3) and 2A–503), if the disposition is by lease agreement substantially similar to the original lease agreement and the new lease agreement is made in good faith and in a commercially reasonable manner, the lessor may recover from the lessee as damages (i) accrued and unpaid rent as of the date of the commencement of the term of the new lease agreement, (ii) the present value, as of the same date, of the total rent for the then remaining lease term of the original lease agreement minus the present value, as of the same date, of the rent under the new lease agreement applicable to that period of the new lease term which is comparable to the then remaining term of the original lease agreement, and (iii) any incidental damages allowed under Section 2A–530, less expenses saved in consequence of the lessee's default.

(3) If the lessor's disposition is by lease agreement that for any reason does not qualify for treatment under subsection (2), or is by sale or otherwise, the lessor may recover from the lessee as if the lessor had elected not to dispose of the goods and Section 2A–528 governs.

(4) A subsequent buyer or lessee who buys or leases from the lessor in good faith for value as a result of a disposition under this section takes the goods free of the original lease contract and any rights of the original lessee even though the lessor fails to comply with one or more of the requirements of this Article.

(5) The lessor is not accountable to the lessee for any profit made on any disposition. A lessee who has rightfully rejected or justifiably revoked acceptance shall account to the lessor for any excess over the amount of the lessee's security interest (Section 2A–508(5)).

As amended in 1990.

§ 2A–528. Lessor's Damages for Non-acceptance, Failure to Pay, Repudiation, or Other Default.

(1) Except as otherwise provided with respect to damages liquidated in the lease agreement (Section 2A–504) or otherwise determined pursuant to agreement of the parties (Section 1–102(3) and 2A–503), if a lessor elects to retain the goods or a lessor elects to dispose of the goods and the disposition is by lease agreement that for any reason does not qualify for treatment under Section 2A–527(2), or is by sale or otherwise, the lessor may recover from the lessee as damages for a default of the type described in Section 2A–523(1) or 2A–523(3)(a), or if agreed, for other default of the lessee, (i) accrued and unpaid rent as of the date of the default if the lessee has never taken possession of the goods, or, if the lessee has taken possession of the goods, as of the date the lessor repossesses the goods or an earlier date on which the lessee makes a tender of the goods to the lessor, (ii) the present value as of the date determined under clause (i) of the total rent for the then remaining lease term of the original lease agreement minus the present value as of the same date of the market rent as the place where the goods are located computed for the same lease term, and (iii) any incidental damages allowed under Section 2A–530, less expenses saved in consequence of the lessee's default.

(2) If the measure of damages provided in subsection (1) is inadequate to put a lessor in as good a position as performance would have, the measure of damages is the present value of the profit, including reasonable overhead, the lessor would have made from full performance by the lessee, together with any incidental damages allowed under Section 2A–530, due allowance for costs reasonably incurred and due credit for payments or proceeds of disposition.

As amended in 1990.

§ 2A–529. Lessor's Action for the Rent.

(1) After default by the lessee under the lease contract of the type described in Section 2A–523(1) or 2A–523(3)(a) or, if agreed, after other default by the lessee, if the lessor complies with subsection (2), the lessor may recover from the lessee as damages:

(a) for goods accepted by the lessee and not repossessed by or tendered to the lessor, and for conforming goods lost or damaged within a commercially reasonable time after risk of loss passes to the lessee (Section 2A–219), (i) accrued and unpaid rent as of the date of entry of judgment in favor of the lessor (ii) the present value as of the same date of the rent for the then remaining lease term of the lease agreement, and (iii) any incidental damages allowed under Section 2A–530, less expenses saved in consequence of the lessee's default; and

(b) for goods identified to the lease contract if the lessor is unable after reasonable effort to dispose of them at a reasonable price or the circumstances reasonably indicate that effort will be unavailing, (i) accrued and unpaid rent as of the date of entry of judgment in favor of the lessor, (ii) the present value as of the same date of the rent for the then remaining lease term of the lease agreement, and (iii) any incidental damages allowed under Section 2A–530, less expenses saved in consequence of the lessee's default.

(2) Except as provided in subsection (3), the lessor shall hold for the lessee for the remaining lease term of the lease agreement any goods that have been identified to the lease contract and are in the lessor's control.

(3) The lessor may dispose of the goods at any time before collection of the judgment for damages obtained pursuant to subsection (1). If the disposition is before the end of the remaining lease term of the lease agreement, the lessor's recovery against the lessee for damages is governed by Section 2A–527 or Section 2A–528, and the lessor will cause an appropriate credit to be provided against a judgment for damages to the extent that the amount of the judgment exceeds the recovery available pursuant to Section 2A–527 or 2A–528.

(4) Payment of the judgment for damages obtained pursuant to subsection (1) entitles the lessee to the use and possession of the goods not then disposed of for the remaining lease term of and in accordance with the lease agreement.

(5) After default by the lessee under the lease contract of the type described in Section 2A–523(1) or Section 2A–523(3)(a) or, if agreed, after other default by the lessee, a lessor who is held not entitled to rent under this section must nevertheless be awarded damages for non-acceptance under Sections 2A–527 and 2A–528.

As amended in 1990.

§ 2A–530. Lessor's Incidental Damages.

Incidental damages to an aggrieved lessor include any commercially reasonable charges, expenses, or commissions incurred in stopping delivery, in the transportation, care and custody of goods after the lessee's default, in connection with return or disposition of the goods, or otherwise resulting from the default.

§ 2A–531. Standing to Sue Third Parties for Injury to Goods.

(1) If a third party so deals with goods that have been identified to a lease contract as to cause actionable injury to a party to the lease contract (a) the lessor has a right of action against the third party, and (b) the lessee also has a right of action against the third party if the lessee:

(i) has a security interest in the goods;

(ii) has an insurable interest in the goods; or

(iii) bears the risk of loss under the lease contract or has since the injury assumed that risk as against the lessor and the goods have been converted or destroyed.

(2) If at the time of the injury the party plaintiff did not bear the risk of loss as against the other party to the lease contract and there is no arrangement between them for disposition of the recovery,

his [or her] suit or settlement, subject to his [or her] own interest, is as a fiduciary for the other party to the lease contract.

(3) Either party with the consent of the other may sue for the benefit of whom it may concern.

§ 2A-532. Lessor's Rights to Residual Interest.

In addition to any other recovery permitted by this Article or other law, the lessor may recover from the lessee an amount that will fully compensate the lessor for any loss of or damage to the lessor's residual interest in the goods caused by the default of the lessee.

As added in 1990.

REVISED ARTICLE III NEGOTIABLE INSTRUMENTS

PART 1 General Provisions and Definitions

§ 3-101. Short Title.

This Article may be cited as Uniform Commercial Code–Negotiable Instruments.

§ 3-102. Subject Matter.

(a) This Article applies to negotiable instruments. It does not apply to money, to payment orders governed by Article 4A, or to securities governed by Article 8.

(b) If there is conflict between this Article and Article 4 or 9, Articles 4 and 9 govern.

(c) Regulations of the Board of Governors of the Federal Reserve System and operating circulars of the Federal Reserve Banks supersede any inconsistent provision of this Article to the extent of the inconsistency.

§ 3-103. Definitions.

(a) In this Article:

(1) "Acceptor" means a drawee who has accepted a draft.

(2) "Drawee" means a person ordered in a draft to make payment.

(3) "Drawer" means a person who signs or is identified in a draft as a person ordering payment.

(4) "Good faith" means honesty in fact and the observance of reasonable commercial standards of fair dealing.

(5) "Maker" means a person who signs or is identified in a note as a person undertaking to pay.

(6) "Order" means a written instruction to pay money signed by the person giving the instruction. The instruction may be addressed to any person, including the person giving the instruction, or to one or more persons jointly or in the alternative but not in succession. An authorization to pay is not an order unless the person authorized to pay is also instructed to pay.

(7) "Ordinary care" in the case of a person engaged in business means observance of reasonable commercial standards, prevailing in the area in which the person is located, with respect to the business in which the person is engaged. In the case of a bank that takes an instrument for processing for collection or payment by automated means, reasonable commercial standards do not require the bank to examine the instrument if the failure to examine does not violate the bank's prescribed procedures and the bank's procedures do not vary unreasonably from general banking usage not disapproved by this Article or Article 4.

(8) "Party" means a party to an instrument.

(9) "Promise" means a written undertaking to pay money signed by the person undertaking to pay. An acknowledgment of an obligation by the obligor is not a promise unless the obligor also undertakes to pay the obligation.

(10) "Prove" with respect to a fact means to meet the burden of establishing the fact (Section 1–201(8)).

(11) "Remitter" means a person who purchases an instrument from its issuer if the instrument is payable to an identified person other than the purchaser.

(b) [Other definitions' section references deleted.]

(c) [Other definitions' section references deleted.]

(d) In addition, Article 1 contains general definitions and principles of construction and interpretation applicable throughout this Article.

§ 3-104. Negotiable Instrument.

(a) Except as provided in subsections (c)and (d), "negotiable instrument" means an unconditional promise or order to pay a fixed amount of money, with or without interest or other charges described in the promise or order, if it:

(1) is payable to bearer or to order at the time it is issued or first comes into possession of a holder;

(2) is payable on demand or at a definite time; and

(3) does not state any other undertaking or instruction by the person promising or ordering payment to do any act in addition to the payment of money, but the promise or order may contain (i) an undertaking or power to give, maintain, or protect collateral to secure payment, (ii) an authorization or power to the holder to confess judgment or realize on or dispose of collateral, or (iii) a waiver of the benefit of any law intended for the advantage or protection of an obligor.

(b) "Instrument" means a negotiable instrument.

(c) An order that meets all of the requirements of subsection (a), except paragraph (1), and otherwise falls within the definition of "check" in subsection (f) is a negotiable instrument and a check.

(d) A promise or order other than a check is not an instrument if, at the time it is issued or first comes into possession of a holder, it contains a conspicuous statement, however expressed, to the effect that the promise or order is not negotiable or is not an instrument governed by this Article.

(e) An instrument is a "note" if it is a promise and is a "draft" if it is an order. If an instrument falls within the definition of both "note" and "draft," a person entitled to enforce the instrument may treat it as either.

(f) "Check" means (i) a draft, other than a documentary draft, payable on demand and drawn on a bank or (ii) a cashier's check or teller's check. An instrument may be a check even though it is described on its face by another term, such as "money order."

(g) "Cashier's check" means a draft with respect to which the drawer and drawee are the same bank or branches of the same bank.

(h) "Teller's check" means a draft drawn by a bank (i) on anoth- er bank, or (ii) payable at or through a bank.

(i) "Traveler's check" means an instrument that (i) is payable on demand, (ii) is drawn on or payable at or through a bank, (iii) is designated by the term "traveler's check" or by a substantially similar term, and (iv) requires, as a condition to payment, a countersignature by a person whose specimen signature appears on the instrument.

(j) "Certificate of deposit" means an instrument containing an acknowledgment by a bank that a sum of money has been received by the bank and a promise by the bank to repay the sum of money. A certificate of deposit is a note of the bank.

§ 3–105. Issue of Instrument.

(a) "Issue" means the first delivery of an instrument by the maker or drawer, whether to a holder or nonholder, for the purpose of giving rights on the instrument to any person.

(b) An unissued instrument, or an unissued incomplete instrument that is completed, is binding on the maker or drawer, but nonissuance is a defense. An instrument that is conditionally issued or is issued for a special purpose is binding on the maker or drawer, but failure of the condition or special purpose to be fulfilled is a defense.

(c) "Issuer" applies to issued and unissued instruments and means a maker or drawer of an instrument.

§ 3–106. Unconditional Promise or Order.

(a) Except as provided in this section, for the purposes of Section 3–104(a), a promise or order is unconditional unless it states (i) an express condition to payment, (ii) that the promise or order is subject to or governed by another writing, or (iii) that rights or obligations with respect to the promise or order are stated in another writing. A reference to another writing does not of itself make the promise or order conditional.

(b) A promise or order is not made conditional (i) by a reference to another writing for a statement of rights with respect to collateral, prepayment, or acceleration, or (ii) because payment is limited to resort to a particular fund or source.

(c) If a promise or order requires, as a condition to payment, a countersignature by a person whose specimen signature appears on the promise or order, the condition does not make the promise or order conditional for the purposes of Section 3–104(a). If the person whose specimen signature appears on an instrument fails to countersign the instrument, the failure to countersign is a defense to the obligation of the issuer, but the failure does not prevent a transferee of the instrument from becoming a holder of the instrument.

(d) If a promise or order at the time it is issued or first comes into possession of a holder contains a statement, required by applicable statutory or administrative law, to the effect that the rights of a holder or transferee are subject to claims or defenses that the issuer could assert against the original payee, the promise or order is not thereby made conditional for the purposes of Section 3–104(a); but if the promise or order is an instrument, there cannot be a holder in due course of the instrument.

§ 3–107. Instrument Payable in Foreign Money.

Unless the instrument otherwise provides, an instrument that states the amount payable in foreign money may be paid in the foreign money or in an equivalent amount in dollars calculated by using the current bank-offered spot rate at the place of payment for the purchase of dollars on the day on which the instrument is paid.

§ 3–108. Payable on Demand or at Definite Time.

(a) A promise or order is "payable on demand" if it (i) states that it is payable on demand or at sight, or otherwise indicates that it is payable at the will of the holder, or (ii) does not state any time of payment.

(b) A promise or order is "payable at a definite time" if it is payable on elapse of a definite period of time after sight or acceptance or at a fixed date or dates or at a time or times readily ascertainable at the time the promise or order is issued, subject to rights of (i) prepayment, (ii) acceleration, (iii) extension at the option of the holder, or (iv) extension to a further definite time at the option of the maker or acceptor or automatically upon or after a specified act or event.

(c) If an instrument, payable at a fixed date, is also payable upon demand made before the fixed date, the instrument is payable on demand until the fixed date and, if demand for payment is not made before that date, becomes payable at a definite time on the fixed date.

§ 3–109. Payable to Bearer or to Order.

(a) A promise or order is payable to bearer if it:

(1) states that it is payable to bearer or to the order of bearer or otherwise indicates that the person in possession of the promise or order is entitled to payment;

(2) does not state a payee; or

(3) states that it is payable to or to the order of cash or otherwise indicates that it is not payable to an identified person.

(b) A promise or order that is not payable to bearer is payable to order if it is payable (i) to the order of an identified person or (ii) to an identified person or order. A promise or order that is payable to order is payable to the identified person.

(c) An instrument payable to bearer may become payable to an identified person if it is specially indorsed pursuant to Section 3–205(a). An instrument payable to an identified person may become payable to bearer if it is indorsed in blank pursuant to Section 3–205(b).

§ 3–110. Identification of Person to Whom Instrument Is Payable.

(a) The person to whom an instrument is initially payable is determined by the intent of the person, whether or not authorized, signing as, or in the name or behalf of, the issuer of the instrument. The instrument is payable to the person intended by the signer even if that person is identified in the instrument by a name or other identification that is not that of the intended person. If more than one person signs in the name or behalf of the issuer of an instrument and all the signers do not intend the same person as payee, the instrument is payable to any person intended by one or more of the signers.

(b) If the signature of the issuer of an instrument is made by automated means, such as a check-writing machine, the payee of the instrument is determined by the intent of the person who supplied the name or identification of the payee, whether or not authorized to do so.

(c) A person to whom an instrument is payable may be identified in any way, including by name, identifying number, office, or account number. For the purpose of determining the holder of an instrument, the following rules apply:

(1) If an instrument is payable to an account and the account is identified only by number, the instrument is payable to the person to whom the account is payable. If an instrument is payable to an account identified by number and by the name of a person, the instrument is payable to the named person, whether or not that person is the owner of the account identified by number.

(2) If an instrument is payable to:

(i) a trust, an estate, or a person described as trustee or representative of a trust or estate, the instrument is payable to the trustee, the representative, or a successor of either, whether or not the beneficiary or estate is also named;

(ii) a person described as agent or similar representative of a named or identified person, the instrument is payable to the represented person, the representative, or a successor of the representative;

(iii) a fund or organization that is not a legal entity, the instrument is payable to a representative of the members of the fund or organization; or

(iv) an office or to a person described as holding an office, the instrument is payable to the named person, the incumbent of the office, or a successor to the incumbent.

(d) If an instrument is payable to two or more persons alternatively, it is payable to any of them and may be negotiated, discharged, or enforced by any or all of them in possession of the instrument. If an instrument is payable to two or more persons not alternatively, it is payable to all of them and may be negotiated, discharged, or enforced only by all of them. If an instrument payable to two or more persons is ambiguous as to whether it is payable to the persons alternatively, the instrument is payable to the persons alternatively.

§ 3–111. Place of Payment.

Except as otherwise provided for items in Article 4, an instrument is payable at the place of payment stated in the instrument. If no place of payment is stated, an instrument is payable at the address of the drawee or maker stated in the instrument. If no address is stated, the place of payment is the place of business of the drawee or maker. If a drawee or maker has more than one place of business, the place of payment is any place of business of the drawee or maker chosen by the person entitled to enforce the instrument. If the drawee or maker has no place of business, the place of payment is the residence of the drawee or maker.

§ 3–112. Interest.

(a) Unless otherwise provided in the instrument, (i) an instrument is not payable with interest, and (ii) interest on an interest-bearing instrument is payable from the date of the instrument.

(b) Interest may be stated in an instrument as a fixed or variable amount of money or it may be expressed as a fixed or variable rate or rates. The amount or rate of interest may be stated or described in the instrument in any manner and may require reference to information not contained in the instrument. If an instrument provides for interest, but the amount of interest payable cannot be ascertained from the description, interest is payable at the judgment rate in effect at the place of payment of the instrument and at the time interest first accrues.

§ 3–113. Date of Instrument.

(a) An instrument may be antedated or postdated. The date stated determines the time of payment if the instrument is payable at a fixed period after date. Except as provided in Section 4–401(c), an instrument payable on demand is not payable before the date of the instrument.

(b) If an instrument is undated, its date is the date of its issue or, in the case of an unissued instrument, the date it first comes into possession of a holder.

§ 3–114. Contradictory Terms of Instrument.

If an instrument contains contradictory terms, typewritten terms prevail over printed terms, handwritten terms prevail over both, and words prevail over numbers.

§ 3–115. Incomplete Instrument.

(a) "Incomplete instrument" means a signed writing, whether or not issued by the signer, the contents of which show at the time of signing that it is incomplete but that the signer intended it to be completed by the addition of words or numbers.

(b) Subject to subsection (c), if an incomplete instrument is an instrument under Section 3–104, it may be enforced according to its terms if it is not completed, or according to its terms as augmented by completion. If an incomplete instrument is not an instrument under Section 3–104, but, after completion, the requirements of Section 3–104 are met, the instrument may be enforced according to its terms as augmented by completion.

(c) If words or numbers are added to an incomplete instrument without authority of the signer, there is an alteration of the incomplete instrument under Section 3–407.

(d) The burden of establishing that words or numbers were added to an incomplete instrument without authority of the signer is on the person asserting the lack of authority.

§ 3–116. Joint and Several Liability; Contribution.

(a) Except as otherwise provided in the instrument, two or more persons who have the same liability on an instrument as makers, drawers, acceptors, indorsers who indorse as joint payees, or anomalous indorsers are jointly and severally liable in the capacity in which they sign.

(b) Except as provided in Section 3–419(e) or by agreement of the affected parties, a party having joint and several liability who pays the instrument is entitled to receive from any party having the same joint and several liability contribution in accordance with applicable law.

(c) Discharge of one party having joint and several liability by a person entitled to enforce the instrument does not affect the right under subsection (b) of a party having the same joint and several liability to receive contribution from the party discharged.

§ 3–117. Other Agreements Affecting Instrument.

Subject to applicable law regarding exclusion of proof of contemporaneous or previous agreements, the obligation of a party to an instrument to pay the instrument may be modified, supplemented, or nullified by a separate agreement of the obligor and a person entitled to enforce the instrument, if the instrument is issued or the obligation is incurred in reliance on the agreement or as part of the same transaction giving rise to the agreement. To the extent an obligation is modified, supplemented, or nullified by an agreement under this section, the agreement is a defense to the obligation.

§ 3–118. Statute of Limitations.

(a) Except as provided in subsection (e), an action to enforce the obligation of a party to pay a note payable at a definite time must be commenced within six years after the due date or dates stated in the note or, if a due date is accelerated, within six years after the accelerated due date.

(b) Except as provided in subsection (d) or (e), if demand for payment is made to the maker of a note payable on demand, an action to enforce the obligation of a party to pay the note must be commenced within six years after the demand. If no demand for payment is made to the maker, an action to enforce the note is barred if neither principal nor interest on the note has been paid for a continuous period of 10 years.

(c) Except as provided in subsection (d), an action to enforce the obligation of a party to an unaccepted draft to pay the draft must be commenced within three years after dishonor of the draft or 10 years after the date of the draft, whichever period expires first.

(d) An action to enforce the obligation of the acceptor of a certified check or the issuer of a teller's check, cashier's check, or traveler's check must be commenced within three years after demand for payment is made to the acceptor or issuer, as the case may be.

(e) An action to enforce the obligation of a party to a certificate of deposit to pay the instrument must be commenced within six years after demand for payment is made to the maker, but if the instrument states a due date and the maker is not required to pay before that date, the six-year period begins when a demand for payment is in effect and the due date has passed.

(f) An action to enforce the obligation of a party to pay an accepted draft, other than a certified check, must be commenced (i) within six years after the due date or dates stated in the draft or acceptance if the obligation of the acceptor is payable at a definite time, or (ii) within six years after the date of the acceptance if the obligation of the acceptor is payable on demand.

(g) Unless governed by other law regarding claims for indemnity or contribution, an action (i) for conversion of an instrument, for money had and received, or like action based on conversion, (ii) for breach of warranty, or (iii) to enforce an obligation, duty, or right arising under this Article and not governed by this section must be commenced within three years after the [cause of action] accrues.

§ 3–119. Notice of Right to Defend Action.

In an action for breach of an obligation for which a third person is answerable over pursuant to this Article or Article 4, the defendant may give the third person written notice of the litigation, and the person notified may then give similar notice to any other person who is answerable over. If the notice states (i) that the person notified may come in and defend and (ii) that failure to do so will bind the person notified in an action later brought by the person giving the notice as to any determination of fact common to the two litigations, the person notified is so bound unless after seasonable receipt of the notice the person notified does come in and defend.

PART 2 Negotiation, Transfer, and Indorsement

§ 3–201. Negotiation.

(a) "Negotiation" means a transfer of possession, whether voluntary or involuntary, of an instrument by a person other than the issuer to a person who thereby becomes its holder.

(b) Except for negotiation by a remitter, if an instrument is payable to an identified person, negotiation requires transfer of possession of the instrument and its indorsement by the holder. If an instrument is payable to bearer, it may be negotiated by transfer of possession alone.

§ 3–202. Negotiation Subject to Rescission.

(a) Negotiation is effective even if obtained (i) from an infant, a corporation exceeding its powers, or a person without capacity, (ii) by fraud, duress, or mistake, or (iii) in breach of duty or as part of an illegal transaction.

(b) To the extent permitted by other law, negotiation may be rescinded or may be subject to other remedies, but those remedies may not be asserted against a subsequent holder in due course or a person paying the instrument in good faith and without knowledge of facts that are a basis for rescission or other remedy.

§ 3–203. Transfer of Instrument; Rights Acquired by Transfer.

(a) An instrument is transferred when it is delivered by a person other than its issuer for the purpose of giving to the person receiving delivery the right to enforce the instrument.

(b) Transfer of an instrument, whether or not the transfer is a negotiation, vests in the transferee any right of the transferor to enforce the instrument, including any right as a holder in due course, but the transferee cannot acquire rights of a holder in due course by a transfer, directly or indirectly, from a holder in due course if the transferee engaged in fraud or illegality affecting the instrument.

(c) Unless otherwise agreed, if an instrument is transferred for value and the transferee does not become a holder because of lack of indorsement by the transferor, the transferee has a specifically enforceable right to the unqualified indorsement of the transferor, but negotiation of the instrument does not occur until the indorsement is made.

(d) If a transferor purports to transfer less than the entire instrument, negotiation of the instrument does not occur. The transferee obtains no rights under this Article and has only the rights of a partial assignee.

§ 3–204. Indorsement.

(a) "Indorsement" means a signature, other than that of a signer as maker, drawer, or acceptor, that alone or accompanied by other words is made on an instrument for the purpose of (i) negotiating the instrument, (ii) restricting payment of the instrument, or (iii) incurring indorser's liability on the instrument, but regardless of the intent of the signer, a signature and its accompanying words is an indorsement unless the accompanying words, terms of the instrument, place of the signature, or other circumstances unambiguously indicate that the signature was made for a purpose other than indorsement. For the purpose of determining whether a signature is made on an instrument, a paper affixed to the instrument is a part of the instrument.

(b) "Indorser" means a person who makes an indorsement.

(c) For the purpose of determining whether the transferee of an instrument is a holder, an indorsement that transfers a security interest in the instrument is effective as an unqualified indorsement of the instrument.

(d) If an instrument is payable to a holder under a name that is not the name of the holder, indorsement may be made by the holder in the name stated in the instrument or in the holder's name or both, but signature in both names may be required by a person paying or taking the instrument for value or collection.

§ 3–205. Special Indorsement; Blank Indorsement; Anomalous Indorsement.

(a) If an indorsement is made by the holder of an instrument, whether payable to an identified person or payable to bearer, and the indorsement identifies a person to whom it makes the instrument payable, it is a "special indorsement." When specially indorsed, an instrument becomes payable to the identified person and may be negotiated only by the indorsement of that person. The principles stated in Section 3–110 apply to special indorsements.

(b) If an indorsement is made by the holder of an instrument and it is not a special indorsement, it is a "blank indorsement." When indorsed in blank, an instrument becomes payable to bearer and may be negotiated by transfer of possession alone until specially indorsed.

(c) The holder may convert a blank indorsement that consists only of a signature into a special indorsement by writing, above the signature of the indorser, words identifying the person to whom the instrument is made payable.

(d) "Anomalous indorsement" means an indorsement made by a person who is not the holder of the instrument. An anomalous indorsement does not affect the manner in which the instrument may be negotiated.

§ 3–206. Restrictive Indorsement.

(a) An indorsement limiting payment to a particular person or otherwise prohibiting further transfer or negotiation of the instrument is not effective to prevent further transfer or negotiation of the instrument.

(b) An indorsement stating a condition to the right of the indorsee to receive payment does not affect the right of the indorsee to enforce the instrument. A person paying the instrument or taking it for value or collection may disregard the condition, and the rights and liabilities of that person are not affected by whether the condition has been fulfilled.

(c) If an instrument bears an indorsement (i) described in Section 4–201(b), or (ii) in blank or to a particular bank using the words "for deposit," "for collection," or other words indicating a purpose of having the instrument collected by a bank for the indorser or for a particular account, the following rules apply:

(1) A person, other than a bank, who purchases the instrument when so indorsed converts the instrument unless the amount paid for the instrument is received by the indorser or applied consistently with the indorsement.

(2) A depositary bank that purchases the instrument or takes it for collection when so indorsed converts the instrument unless the amount paid by the bank with respect to the instrument is received by the indorser or applied consistently with the indorsement.

(3) A payor bank that is also the depositary bank or that takes the instrument for immediate payment over the counter from a person other than a collecting bank converts the instrument unless the proceeds of the instrument are received by the indorser or applied consistently with the indorsement.

(4) Except as otherwise provided in paragraph (3), a payor bank or intermediary bank may disregard the indorsement and is not liable if the proceeds of the instrument are not received by the indorser or applied consistently with the indorsement.

(d) Except for an indorsement covered by subsection (c), if an instrument bears an indorsement using words to the effect that payment is to be made to the indorsee as agent, trustee, or other fiduciary for the benefit of the indorser or another person, the following rules apply:

(1) Unless there is notice of breach of fiduciary duty as provided in Section 3–307, a person who purchases the instrument from the indorsee or takes the instrument from the indorsee for collection or payment may pay the proceeds of payment or the value given for the instrument to the indorsee without regard to whether the indorsee violates a fiduciary duty to the indorser.

(2) A subsequent transferee of the instrument or person who pays the instrument is neither given notice nor otherwise affected by the restriction in the indorsement unless the transferee or payor knows that the fiduciary dealt with the instrument or its proceeds in breach of fiduciary duty.

(e) The presence on an instrument of an indorsement to which this section applies does not prevent a purchaser of the instrument from becoming a holder in due course of the instrument unless the purchaser is a converter under subsection (c) or has notice or knowledge of breach of fiduciary duty as stated in subsection (d).

(f) In an action to enforce the obligation of a party to pay the instrument, the obligor has a defense if payment would violate an indorsement to which this section applies and the payment is not permitted by this section.

§ 3-207. Reacquisition.

Reacquisition of an instrument occurs if it is transferred to a former holder, by negotiation or otherwise. A former holder who reacquires the instrument may cancel indorsements made after the reacquirer first became a holder of the instrument. If the cancellation causes the instrument to be payable to the reacquirer or to bearer, the reacquirer may negotiate the instrument. An indorser whose indorsement is canceled is discharged, and the discharge is effective against any subsequent holder.

PART 3 Enforcement of Instruments

§ 3-301. Person Entitled to Enforce Instrument.

"Person entitled to enforce" an instrument means (i) the holder of the instrument, (ii) a nonholder in possession of the instrument who has the rights of a holder, or (iii) a person not in possession of the instrument who is entitled to enforce the instrument pursuant to Section 3–309 or 3–418(d). A person may be a person entitled to enforce the instrument even though the person is not the owner of the instrument or is in wrongful possession of the instrument.

§ 3-302. Holder in Due Course.

(a) Subject to subsection (c) and Section 3–106(d), "holder in due course" means the holder of an instrument if:

(1) the instrument when issued or negotiated to the holder does not bear such apparent evidence of forgery or alteration or is not otherwise so irregular or incomplete as to call into question its authenticity; and

(2) the holder took the instrument (i) for value, (ii) in good faith, (iii) without notice that the instrument is overdue or has been dishonored or that there is an uncured default with respect to payment of another instrument issued as part of the same series, (iv) without notice that the instrument contains an unauthorized signature or has been altered, (v) without notice of any claim to the instrument described in Section 3–306, and (vi) without notice that any party has a defense or claim in recoupment described in Section 3–305(a).

(b) Notice of discharge of a party, other than discharge in an insolvency proceeding, is not notice of a defense under subsection (a), but discharge is effective against a person who became a holder in due course with notice of the discharge. Public filing or recording of a document does not of itself constitute notice of a defense, claim in recoupment, or claim to the instrument.

(c) Except to the extent a transferor or predecessor in interest has rights as a holder in due course, a person does not acquire rights of a holder in due course of an instrument taken (i) by legal process or by purchase in an execution, bankruptcy, or creditor's sale or similar proceeding, (ii) by purchase as part of a bulk transaction not in ordinary course of business of the transferor, or (iii) as the successor in interest to an estate or other organization.

(d) If, under Section 3–303(a)(1), the promise of performance that is the consideration for an instrument has been partially performed, the holder may assert rights as a holder in due course of the instrument only to the fraction of the amount payable under the instrument equal to the value of the partial performance divided by the value of the promised performance.

(e) If (i) the person entitled to enforce an instrument has only a security interest in the instrument and (ii) the person obliged to pay the instrument has a defense, claim in recoupment, or claim to the instrument that may be asserted against the person who granted the security interest, the person entitled to enforce the instrument may assert rights as a holder in due course only to an amount payable under the instrument which, at the time of enforcement of the instrument, does not exceed the amount of the unpaid obligation secured.

(f) To be effective, notice must be received at a time and in a manner that gives a reasonable opportunity to act on it.

(g) This section is subject to any law limiting status as a holder in due course in particular classes of transactions.

§ 3-303. Value and Consideration.

(a) An instrument is issued or transferred for value if:

(1) the instrument is issued or transferred for a promise of performance, to the extent the promise has been performed;

(2) the transferee acquires a security interest or other lien in the instrument other than a lien obtained by judicial proceeding;

(3) the instrument is issued or transferred as payment of, or as security for, an antecedent claim against any person, whether or not the claim is due;

(4) the instrument is issued or transferred in exchange for a negotiable instrument; or

(5) the instrument is issued or transferred in exchange for the incurring of an irrevocable obligation to a third party by the person taking the instrument.

(b) "Consideration" means any consideration sufficient to support a simple contract. The drawer or maker of an instrument has a defense if the instrument is issued without consideration. If an instrument is issued for a promise of performance, the issuer has a defense to the extent performance of the promise is due and the promise has not been performed. If an instrument is issued for value as stated in subsection (a), the instrument is also issued for consideration.

§ 3-304. Overdue Instrument.

(a) An instrument payable on demand becomes overdue at the earliest of the following times:

(1) on the day after the day demand for payment is duly made;

(2) if the instrument is a check, 90 days after its date; or

(3) if the instrument is not a check, when the instrument has been outstanding for a period of time after its date which is unreasonably long under the circumstances of the particular case in light of the nature of the instrument and usage of the trade.

(b) With respect to an instrument payable at a definite time the following rules apply:

(1) If the principal is payable in installments and a due date has not been accelerated, the instrument becomes overdue upon default under the instrument for nonpayment of an installment, and the instrument remains overdue until the default is cured.

(2) If the principal is not payable in installments and the due date has not been accelerated, the instrument becomes overdue on the day after the due date.

(3) If a due date with respect to principal has been accelerated, the instrument becomes overdue on the day after the accelerated due date.

(c) Unless the due date of principal has been accelerated, an instrument does not become overdue if there is default in payment of interest but no default in payment of principal.

§ 3-305. Defenses and Claims in Recoupment.

(a) Except as stated in subsection (b), the right to enforce the obligation of a party to pay an instrument is subject to the following:

(1) a defense of the obligor based on (i) infancy of the obligor to the extent it is a defense to a simple contract, (ii) duress, lack of legal capacity, or illegality of the transaction which, under other law, nullifies the obligation of the obligor, (iii) fraud that induced the obligor to sign the instrument with neither knowledge nor reasonable opportunity to learn of its character or its essential terms, or (iv) discharge of the obligor in insolvency proceedings;

(2) a defense of the obligor stated in another section of this Article or a defense of the obligor that would be available if the person entitled to enforce the instrument were enforcing a right to payment under a simple contract; and

(3) a claim in recoupment of the obligor against the original payee of the instrument if the claim arose from the transaction that gave rise to the instrument; but the claim of the obligor may be asserted against a transferee of the instrument only to reduce the amount owing on the instrument at the time the action is brought.

(b) The right of a holder in due course to enforce the obligation of a party to pay the instrument is subject to defenses of the obligor stated in subsection (a)(1), but is not subject to defenses of the obligor stated in subsection (a)(2) or claims in recoupment stated in subsection (a)(3) against a person other than the holder.

(c) Except as stated in subsection (d), in an action to enforce the obligation of a party to pay the instrument, the obligor may not assert against the person entitled to enforce the instrument a defense, claim in recoupment, or claim to the instrument (Section 3–306) of another person, but the other person's claim to the instrument may be asserted by the obligor if the other person is joined in the action and personally asserts the claim against the person entitled to enforce the instrument. An obligor is not obliged to pay the instrument if the person seeking enforcement of the instrument does not have rights of a holder in due course and the obligor proves that the instrument is a lost or stolen instrument.

(d) In an action to enforce the obligation of an accommodation party to pay an instrument, the accommodation party may assert against the person entitled to enforce the instrument any defense or claim in recoupment under subsection (a) that the accommodated party could assert against the person entitled to enforce the instrument, except the defenses of discharge in insolvency proceedings, infancy, and lack of legal capacity.

§ 3–306. Claims to an Instrument.

A person taking an instrument, other than a person having rights of a holder in due course, is subject to a claim of a property or possessory right in the instrument or its proceeds, including a claim to rescind a negotiation and to recover the instrument or its proceeds. A person having rights of a holder in due course takes free of the claim to the instrument.

§ 3–307. Notice of Breach of Fiduciary Duty.

(a) In this section:

(1) "Fiduciary" means an agent, trustee, partner, corporate officer or director, or other representative owing a fiduciary duty with respect to an instrument.

(2) "Represented person" means the principal, beneficiary, partnership, corporation, or other person to whom the duty stated in paragraph (1) is owed.

(b) If (i) an instrument is taken from a fiduciary for payment or collection or for value, (ii) the taker has knowledge of the fiduciary status of the fiduciary, and (iii) the represented person makes a claim to the instrument or its proceeds on the basis that the transaction of the fiduciary is a breach of fiduciary duty, the following rules apply:

(1) Notice of breach of fiduciary duty by the fiduciary is notice of the claim of the represented person.

(2) In the case of an instrument payable to the represented person or the fiduciary as such, the taker has notice of the breach of fiduciary duty if the instrument is (i) taken in payment of or as security for a debt known by the taker to be the personal debt of the fiduciary, (ii) taken in a transaction known by the taker to be for the personal benefit of the fiduciary, or (iii) deposited to an account other than an account of the fiduciary, as such, or an account of the represented person.

(3) If an instrument is issued by the represented person or the fiduciary as such, and made payable to the fiduciary personally, the taker does not have notice of the breach of fiduciary duty unless the taker knows of the breach of fiduciary duty.

(4) If an instrument is issued by the represented person or the fiduciary as such, to the taker as payee, the taker has notice of the breach of fiduciary duty if the instrument is (i) taken in payment of or as security for a debt known by the taker to be the personal debt of the fiduciary, (ii) taken in a transaction known by the taker to be for the personal benefit of the fiduciary, or (iii) deposited to an account other than an account of the fiduciary, as such, or an account of the represented person.

§ 3–308. Proof of Signatures and Status as Holder in Due Course.

(a) In an action with respect to an instrument, the authenticity of, and authority to make, each signature on the instrument is admitted unless specifically denied in the pleadings. If the validity of a signature is denied in the pleadings, the burden of establishing validity is on the person claiming validity, but the signature is presumed to be authentic and authorized unless the action is to enforce the liability of the purported signer and the signer is dead or incompetent at the time of trial of the issue of validity of the signature. If an action to enforce the instrument is brought against a person as the undisclosed principal of a person who signed the instrument as a party to the instrument, the plaintiff has the burden of establishing that the defendant is liable on the instrument as a represented person under Section 3–402(a).

(b) If the validity of signatures is admitted or proved and there is compliance with subsection (a), a plaintiff producing the instrument is entitled to payment if the plaintiff proves entitlement to enforce the instrument under Section 3–301, unless the defendant proves a defense or claim in recoupment. If a defense or claim in recoupment is proved, the right to payment of the plaintiff is subject to the defense or claim, except to the extent the plaintiff proves that the plaintiff has rights of a holder in due course which are not subject to the defense or claim.

§ 3–309. Enforcement of Lost, Destroyed, or Stolen Instrument.

(a) A person not in possession of an instrument is entitled to enforce the instrument if (i) the person was in possession of the instrument and entitled to enforce it when loss of possession occurred, (ii) the loss of possession was not the result of a transfer by the person or a lawful seizure, and (iii) the person cannot reasonably obtain possession of the instrument because the instrument was destroyed, its whereabouts cannot be determined, or it is in the wrongful possession of an unknown person or a person that cannot be found or is not amenable to service of process.

(b) A person seeking enforcement of an instrument under subsection (a) must prove the terms of the instrument and the person's right to enforce the instrument. If that proof is made, Section 3–308 applies to the case as if the person seeking enforcement had produced the instrument. The court may not enter judgment in favor of the person seeking enforcement unless it finds that the person required to pay the instrument is adequately protected against loss that might occur by reason of a claim by another person to enforce the instrument. Adequate protection may be provided by any reasonable means.

§ 3–310. Effect of Instrument on Obligation for Which Taken.

(a) Unless otherwise agreed, if a certified check, cashier's check, or teller's check is taken for an obligation, the obligation is discharged to the same extent discharge would result if an amount of money equal to the amount of the instrument were taken in payment of the obligation. Discharge of the obligation does not affect any liability that the obligor may have as an indorser of the instrument.

(b) Unless otherwise agreed and except as provided in subsection (a), if a note or an uncertified check is taken for an obligation, the obligation is suspended to the same extent the obligation would be discharged if an amount of money equal to the amount of the instrument were taken, and the following rules apply:

(1) In the case of an uncertified check, suspension of the obligation continues until dishonor of the check or until it is paid or certified. Payment or certification of the check results in discharge of the obligation to the extent of the amount of the check.

(2) In the case of a note, suspension of the obligation continues until dishonor of the note or until it is paid. Payment of the note results in discharge of the obligation to the extent of the payment.

(3) Except as provided in paragraph (4), if the check or note is dishonored and the obligee of the obligation for which the instrument was taken is the person entitled to enforce the instrument, the obligee may enforce either the instrument or the obligation. In the case of an instrument of a third person which is negotiated to the obligee by the obligor, discharge of the obligor on the instrument also discharges the obligation.

(4) If the person entitled to enforce the instrument taken for an obligation is a person other than the obligee, the obligee may not enforce the obligation to the extent the obligation is suspended. If the obligee is the person entitled to enforce the instrument but no longer has possession of it because it was lost, stolen, or destroyed, the obligation may not be enforced to the extent of the amount payable on the instrument, and to that extent the obligee's rights against the obligor are limited to enforcement of the instrument.

(c) If an instrument other than one described in subsection (a) or (b) is taken for an obligation, the effect is (i) that stated in subsection (a) if the instrument is one on which a bank is liable as maker or acceptor, or (ii) that stated in subsection (b) in any other case.

§ 3-311. Accord and Satisfaction by Use of Instrument.

(a) If a person against whom a claim is asserted proves that (i) that person in good faith tendered an instrument to the claimant as full satisfaction of the claim, (ii) the amount of the claim was unliquidated or subject to a bona fide dispute, and (iii) the claimant obtained payment of the instrument, the following subsections apply.

(b) Unless subsection (c) applies, the claim is discharged if the person against whom the claim is asserted proves that the instrument or an accompanying written communication contained a conspicuous statement to the effect that the instrument was tendered as full satisfaction of the claim.

(c) Subject to subsection (d), a claim is not discharged under subsection (b) if either of the following applies:

(1) The claimant, if an organization, proves that (i) within a reasonable time before the tender, the claimant sent a conspicuous statement to the person against whom the claim is asserted that communications concerning disputed debts, including an instrument tendered as full satisfaction of a debt, are to be sent to a designated person, office, or place, and (ii) the instrument or accompanying communication was not received by that designated person, office, or place.

(2) The claimant, whether or not an organization, proves that within 90 days after payment of the instrument, the claimant tendered repayment of the amount of the instrument to the person against whom the claim is asserted. This paragraph does not apply if the claimant is an organization that sent a statement complying with paragraph (1)(i).

(d) A claim is discharged if the person against whom the claim is asserted proves that within a reasonable time before collection of the instrument was initiated, the claimant, or an agent of the claimant having direct responsibility with respect to the disputed obligation, knew that the instrument was tendered in full satisfaction of the claim.

§ 3-312. Lost, Destroyed, or Stolen Cashier's Check, Teller's Check, or Certified Check.*

(a) In this section:

(1) "Check" means a cashier's check, teller's check, or certified check.

(2) "Claimant" means a person who claims the right to receive the amount of a cashier's check, teller's check, or certified check that was lost, destroyed, or stolen.

(3) "Declaration of loss" means a written statement, made under penalty of perjury, to the effect that (i) the declarer lost possession of a check, (ii) the declarer is the drawer or payee of the check, in the case of a certified check, or the remitter or payee of the check, in the case of a cashier's check or teller's check, (iii) the loss of possession was not the result of a transfer by the declarer or a lawful seizure, and (iv) the declarer cannot reasonably obtain possession of the check because the check was destroyed, its whereabouts cannot be determined, or it is in the wrongful possession of an unknown person or a person that cannot be found or is not amenable to service of process.

(4) "Obligated bank" means the issuer of a cashier's check or teller's check or the acceptor of a certified check.

(b) A claimant may assert a claim to the amount of a check by a communication to the obligated bank describing the check with reasonable certainty and requesting payment of the amount of the check, if (i) the claimant is the drawer or payee of a certified check or the remitter or payee of a cashier's check or teller's check, (ii) the communication contains or is accompanied by a declaration of loss of the claimant with respect to the check, (iii) the communication is received at a time and in a manner affording the bank a reasonable time to act on it before the check is paid, and (iv) the claimant provides reasonable identification if requested by the obligated bank. Delivery of a declaration of loss is a warranty of the truth of the statements made in the declaration. If a claim is asserted in compliance with this subsection, the following rules apply:

(1) The claim becomes enforceable at the later of (i) the time the claim is asserted, or (ii) the 90th day following the date of the check, in the case of a cashier's check or teller's check, or the 90th day following the date of the acceptance, in the case of a certified check.

(2) Until the claim becomes enforceable, it has no legal effect and the obligated bank may pay the check or, in the case of a teller's check, may permit the drawee to pay the check. Payment to a person entitled to enforce the check discharges all liability of the obligated bank with respect to the check.

(3) If the claim becomes enforceable before the check is presented for payment, the obligated bank is not obliged to pay the check.

(4) When the claim becomes enforceable, the obligated bank becomes obliged to pay the amount of the check to the claimant if payment of the check has not been made to a person entitled to enforce the check. Subject to Section 4–302(a)(1), payment to the claimant discharges all liability of the obligated bank with respect to the check.

(c) If the obligated bank pays the amount of a check to a claimant under subsection (b)(4) and the check is presented for payment by a person having rights of a holder in due course, the claimant is obliged to (i) refund the payment to the obligated bank if the check is paid, or (ii) pay the amount of the check to the person having rights of a holder in due course if the check is dishonored.

(d) If a claimant has the right to assert a claim under subsection (b) and is also a person entitled to enforce a cashier's check, teller's check, or certified check which is lost, destroyed, or stolen, the claimant may assert rights with respect to the check either under this section or Section 3–309.

Added in 1991.

PART 4 Liability of Parties

§ 3–401. Signature.

(a) A person is not liable on an instrument unless (i) the person signed the instrument, or (ii) the person is represented by an agent or representative who signed the instrument and the signature is binding on the represented person under Section 3–402.

(b) A signature may be made (i) manually or by means of a device or machine, and (ii) by the use of any name, including a trade or assumed name, or by a word, mark, or symbol executed or adopted by a person with present intention to authenticate a writing.

§ 3–402. Signature by Representative.

(a) If a person acting, or purporting to act, as a representative signs an instrument by signing either the name of the represented person or the name of the signer, the represented person is bound by the signature to the same extent the represented person would be bound if the signature were on a simple contract. If the represented person is bound, the signature of the representative is the "authorized signature of the represented person" and the represented person is liable on the instrument, whether or not identified in the instrument.

(b) If a representative signs the name of the representative to an instrument and the signature is an authorized signature of the represented person, the following rules apply:

(1) If the form of the signature shows unambiguously that the signature is made on behalf of the represented person who is identified in the instrument, the representative is not liable on the instrument.

(2) Subject to subsection (c), if (i) the form of the signature does not show unambiguously that the signature is made in a representative capacity or (ii) the represented person is not identified in the instrument, the representative is liable on the instrument to a holder in due course that took the instrument without notice that the representative was not intended to be liable on the instrument. With respect to any other person, the representative is liable on the instrument unless the representative proves that the original parties did not intend the representative to be liable on the instrument.

(c) If a representative signs the name of the representative as drawer of a check without indication of the representative status and the check is payable from an account of the represented person who is identified on the check, the signer is not liable on the check if the signature is an authorized signature of the represented person.

§ 3–403. Unauthorized Signature.

(a) Unless otherwise provided in this Article or Article 4, an unauthorized signature is ineffective except as the signature of the unauthorized signer in favor of a person who in good faith pays the instrument or takes it for value. An unauthorized signature may be ratified for all purposes of this Article.

(b) If the signature of more than one person is required to constitute the authorized signature of an organization, the signature of the organization is unauthorized if one of the required signatures is lacking.

(c) The civil or criminal liability of a person who makes an unauthorized signature is not affected by any provision of this Article which makes the unauthorized signature effective for the purposes of this Article.

§ 3–404. Impostors; Fictitious Payees.

(a) If an impostor, by use of the mails or otherwise, induces the issuer of an instrument to issue the instrument to the impostor, or to a person acting in concert with the impostor, by impersonating the payee of the instrument or a person authorized to act for the payee, an indorsement of the instrument by any person in the name of the payee is effective as the indorsement of the payee in favor of a person who, in good faith, pays the instrument or takes it for value or for collection.

(b) If (i) a person whose intent determines to whom an instrument is payable (Section 3–110(a) or (b)) does not intend the person identified as payee to have any interest in the instrument, or (ii) the person identified as payee of an instrument is a fictitious person, the following rules apply until the instrument is negotiated by special indorsement:

(1) Any person in possession of the instrument is its holder.
(2) An indorsement by any person in the name of the payee stated in the instrument is effective as the indorsement of the payee in favor of a person who, in good faith, pays the instrument or takes it for value or for collection.

(c) Under subsection (a) or (b), an indorsement is made in the name of a payee if (i) it is made in a name substantially similar to that of the payee or (ii) the instrument, whether or not indorsed, is deposited in a depositary bank to an account in a name substantially similar to that of the payee.

(d) With respect to an instrument to which subsection (a) or (b) applies, if a person paying the instrument or taking it for value or for collection fails to exercise ordinary care in paying or taking the instrument and that failure substantially contributes to loss resulting from payment of the instrument, the person bearing the loss may recover from the person failing to exercise ordinary care to the extent the failure to exercise ordinary care contributed to the loss.

§ 3–405. Employer's Responsibility for Fraudulent Indorsement by Employee.

(a) In this section:

(1) "Employee" includes an independent contractor and employee of an independent contractor retained by the employer.
(2) "Fraudulent indorsement" means (i) in the case of an instrument payable to the employer, a forged indorsement purporting to be that of the employer, or (ii) in the case of an instrument with respect to which the employer is the issuer, a forged indorsement purporting to be that of the person identified as payee.
(3) "Responsibility" with respect to instruments means authority (i) to sign or indorse instruments on behalf of the employer, (ii) to process instruments received by the employer for bookkeeping purposes, for deposit to an account, or for other disposition, (iii) to prepare or process instruments for issue in the name of the employer, (iv) to supply information determining the names or addresses of payees of instruments to be issued in the name of the employer, (v) to control the disposition of instruments to be issued in the name of the employer, or (vi) to act otherwise with respect to instruments in a responsible capacity. "Responsibility" does not include authority that merely allows an employee to have access to instruments or blank or incomplete instrument forms that are being stored or transported or are part of incoming or outgoing mail, or similar access.

(b) For the purpose of determining the rights and liabilities of a person who, in good faith, pays an instrument or takes it for value or for collection, if an employer entrusted an employee with responsibility with respect to the instrument and the employee or a person acting in concert with the employee makes a fraudulent indorsement of the instrument, the indorsement is effective as the indorsement of the person to whom the instrument is payable if it is made in the name of that person. If the person paying the instrument or taking it for value or for collection fails to exercise ordinary care in paying or taking the instrument and that failure substantially contributes to loss resulting from the fraud, the person bearing the loss may recover from the person failing to exercise ordinary care to the extent the failure to exercise ordinary care contributed to the loss.

(c) Under subsection (b), an indorsement is made in the name of the person to whom an instrument is payable if (i) it is made in a name substantially similar to the name of that person or (ii) the instrument, whether or not indorsed, is deposited in a depositary bank to an account in a name substantially similar to the name of that person.

§ 3–406. Negligence Contributing to Forged Signature or Alteration of Instrument.

(a) A person whose failure to exercise ordinary care substantially contributes to an alteration of an instrument or to the making of a forged signature on an instrument is precluded from asserting the alteration or the forgery against a person who, in good faith, pays the instrument or takes it for value or for collection.

(b) Under subsection (a), if the person asserting the preclusion fails to exercise ordinary care in paying or taking the instrument and that failure substantially contributes to loss, the loss is allocated between the person precluded and the person asserting the preclusion according to the extent to which the failure of each to exercise ordinary care contributed to the loss.

(c) Under subsection (a), the burden of proving failure to exercise ordinary care is on the person asserting the preclusion. Under subsection (b), the burden of proving failure to exercise ordinary care is on the person precluded.

§ 3–407. Alteration.

(a) "Alteration" means (i) an unauthorized change in an instrument that purports to modify in any respect the obligation of a party, or (ii) an unauthorized addition of words or numbers or other change to an incomplete instrument relating to the obligation of a party.

(b) Except as provided in subsection (c), an alteration fraudulently made discharges a party whose obligation is affected by the alteration unless that party assents or is precluded from asserting the alteration. No other alteration discharges a party, and the instrument may be enforced according to its original terms.

(c) A payor bank or drawee paying a fraudulently altered instrument or a person taking it for value, in good faith and without notice of the alteration, may enforce rights with respect to the instrument (i) according to its original terms, or (ii) in the case of an incomplete instrument altered by unauthorized completion, according to its terms as completed.

§ 3–408. Drawee Not Liable on Unaccepted Draft.

A check or other draft does not of itself operate as an assignment of funds in the hands of the drawee available for its payment, and the drawee is not liable on the instrument until the drawee accepts it.

§ 3–409. Acceptance of Draft; Certified Check.

(a) "Acceptance" means the drawee's signed agreement to pay a draft as presented. It must be written on the draft and may consist of the drawee's signature alone. Acceptance may be made at any time and becomes effective when notification pursuant to instructions is given or the accepted draft is delivered for the purpose of giving rights on the acceptance to any person.

(b) A draft may be accepted although it has not been signed by the drawer, is otherwise incomplete, is overdue, or has been dishonored.

(c) If a draft is payable at a fixed period after sight and the acceptor fails to date the acceptance, the holder may complete the acceptance by supplying a date in good faith.

(d) "Certified check" means a check accepted by the bank on which it is drawn. Acceptance may be made as stated in subsection (a) or by a writing on the check which indicates that the check is certified. The drawee of a check has no obligation to certify the check, and refusal to certify is not dishonor of the check.

§ 3–410. Acceptance Varying Draft.

(a) If the terms of a drawee's acceptance vary from the terms of the draft as presented, the holder may refuse the acceptance and treat the draft as dishonored. In that case, the drawee may cancel the acceptance.

(b) The terms of a draft are not varied by an acceptance to pay at a particular bank or place in the United States, unless the acceptance states that the draft is to be paid only at that bank or place.

(c) If the holder assents to an acceptance varying the terms of a draft, the obligation of each drawer and indorser that does not expressly assent to the acceptance is discharged.

§ 3–411. Refusal to Pay Cashier's Checks, Teller's Checks, and Certified Checks.

(a) In this section, "obligated bank" means the acceptor of a certified check or the issuer of a cashier's check or teller's check bought from the issuer.

(b) If the obligated bank wrongfully (i) refuses to pay a cashier's check or certified check, (ii) stops payment of a teller's check, or (iii) refuses to pay a dishonored teller's check, the person asserting the right to enforce the check is entitled to compensation for expenses and loss of interest resulting from the nonpayment and may recover consequential damages if the obligated bank refuses to pay after receiving notice of particular circumstances giving rise to the damages.

(c) Expenses or consequential damages under subsection (b) are not recoverable if the refusal of the obligated bank to pay occurs because (i) the bank suspends payments, (ii) the obligated bank asserts a claim or defense of the bank that it has reasonable grounds to believe is available against the person entitled to enforce the instrument, (iii) the obligated bank has a reasonable doubt whether the person demanding payment is the person entitled to enforce the instrument, or (iv) payment is prohibited by law.

§ 3–412. Obligation of Issuer of Note or Cashier's Check.

The issuer of a note or cashier's check or other draft drawn on the drawer is obliged to pay the instrument (i) according to its terms at the time it was issued or, if not issued, at the time it first came into possession of a holder, or (ii) if the issuer signed an incomplete instrument, according to its terms when completed, to the extent stated in Sections 3–115 and 3–407. The obligation is owed to a person entitled to enforce the instrument or to an indorser who paid the instrument under Section 3–415.

§ 3–413. Obligation of Acceptor.

(a) The acceptor of a draft is obliged to pay the draft (i) according to its terms at the time it was accepted, even though the acceptance states that the draft is payable "as originally drawn" or equivalent terms, (ii) if the acceptance varies the terms of the draft, according to the terms of the draft as varied, or (iii) if the acceptance is of a draft that is an incomplete instrument, according to its terms when completed, to the extent stated in Sections 3–115 and 3–407. The obligation is owed to a person entitled to enforce the draft or to the drawer or an indorser who paid the draft under Section 3–414 or 3–415.

(b) If the certification of a check or other acceptance of a draft states the amount certified or accepted, the obligation of the acceptor is that amount. If (i) the certification or acceptance does not state an amount, (ii) the amount of the instrument is subsequently raised, and (iii) the instrument is then negotiated to a holder in due course, the obligation of the acceptor is the amount of the instrument at the time it was taken by the holder in due course.

§ 3–414. Obligation of Drawer.

(a) This section does not apply to cashier's checks or other drafts drawn on the drawer.

(b) If an unaccepted draft is dishonored, the drawer is obliged to pay the draft (i) according to its terms at the time it was issued or, if not issued, at the time it first came into possession of a holder, or (ii) if the drawer signed an incomplete instrument, according to its terms when completed, to the extent stated in Sections 3–115 and 3–407. The obligation is owed to a person entitled to enforce the draft or to an indorser who paid the draft under Section 3–415.

(c) If a draft is accepted by a bank, the drawer is discharged, regardless of when or by whom acceptance was obtained.

(d) If a draft is accepted and the acceptor is not a bank, the obligation of the drawer to pay the draft if the draft is dishonored by the acceptor is the same as the obligation of an indorser under Section 3–415(a) and (c).

(e) If a draft states that it is drawn "without recourse" or otherwise disclaims liability of the drawer to pay the draft, the drawer is not liable under subsection (b) to pay the draft if the draft is not a check. A disclaimer of the liability stated in subsection (b) is not effective if the draft is a check.

(f) If (i) a check is not presented for payment or given to a depositary bank for collection within 30 days after its date, (ii) the drawee suspends payments after expiration of the 30-day period without paying the check, and (iii) because of the suspension of payments, the drawer is deprived of funds maintained with the drawee to cover payment of the check, the drawer to the extent deprived of funds may discharge its obligation to pay the check by assigning to the person entitled to enforce the check the rights of the drawer against the drawee with respect to the funds.

§ 3–415. Obligation of Indorser.

(a) Subject to subsections (b), (c), and (d) and to Section 3–419(d), if an instrument is dishonored, an indorser is obliged to pay the amount due on the instrument (i) according to the terms of the instrument at the time it was indorsed, or (ii) if the indorser indorsed an incomplete instrument, according to its terms when completed, to the extent stated in Sections 3–115 and 3–407. The obligation of the indorser is owed to a person entitled to enforce the instrument or to a subsequent indorser who paid the instrument under this section.

(b) If an indorsement states that it is made "without recourse" or otherwise disclaims liability of the indorser, the indorser is not liable under subsection (a) to pay the instrument.

(c) If notice of dishonor of an instrument is required by Section 3–503 and notice of dishonor complying with that section is not given to an indorser, the liability of the indorser under subsection (a) is discharged.

(d) If a draft is accepted by a bank after an indorsement is made, the liability of the indorser under subsection (a) is discharged.

(e) If an indorser of a check is liable under subsection (a) and the check is not presented for payment, or given to a depositary bank for collection, within 30 days after the day the indorsement was made, the liability of the indorser under subsection (a) is discharged.

As amended in 1993.

§ 3–416. Transfer Warranties.

(a) A person who transfers an instrument for consideration warrants to the transferee and, if the transfer is by indorsement, to any subsequent transferee that:

(1) the warrantor is a person entitled to enforce the instrument;
(2) all signatures on the instrument are authentic and authorized;
(3) the instrument has not been altered;
(4) the instrument is not subject to a defense or claim in recoupment of any party which can be asserted against the warrantor; and
(5) the warrantor has no knowledge of any insolvency proceeding commenced with respect to the maker or acceptor or, in the case of an unaccepted draft, the drawer.

(b) A person to whom the warranties under subsection (a) are made and who took the instrument in good faith may recover from the warrantor as damages for breach of warranty an amount equal to the loss suffered as a result of the breach, but not more than the amount of the instrument plus expenses and loss of interest incurred as a result of the breach.

(c) The warranties stated in subsection (a) cannot be disclaimed with respect to checks. Unless notice of a claim for breach of warranty is given to the warrantor within 30 days after the claimant has reason to know of the breach and the identity of the warrantor, the liability of the warrantor under subsection (b) is discharged to the extent of any loss caused by the delay in giving notice of the claim.

(d) A [cause of action] for breach of warranty under this section accrues when the claimant has reason to know of the breach.

§ 3–417. Presentment Warranties.

(a) If an unaccepted draft is presented to the drawee for payment or acceptance and the drawee pays or accepts the draft, (i) the person obtaining payment or acceptance, at the time of presentment, and (ii) a previous transferor of the draft, at the time of transfer, warrant to the drawee making payment or accepting the draft in good faith that:

(1) the warrantor is, or was, at the time the warrantor transferred the draft, a person entitled to enforce the draft or authorized to obtain payment or acceptance of the draft on behalf of a person entitled to enforce the draft;
(2) the draft has not been altered; and
(3) the warrantor has no knowledge that the signature of the drawer of the draft is unauthorized.

(b) A drawee making payment may recover from any warrantor damages for breach of warranty equal to the amount paid by the drawee less the amount the drawee received or is entitled to receive from the drawer because of the payment. In addition, the drawee is entitled to compensation for expenses and loss of interest resulting from the breach. The right of the drawee to recover damages under this subsection is not affected by any failure of the drawee to exercise ordinary care in making payment. If the drawee accepts the draft, breach of warranty is a defense to the obligation of the acceptor. If the acceptor makes payment with respect to the draft, the acceptor is entitled to recover from any warrantor for breach of warranty the amounts stated in this subsection.

(c) If a drawee asserts a claim for breach of warranty under subsection (a) based on an unauthorized indorsement of the draft or an alteration of the draft, the warrantor may defend by proving that the indorsement is effective under Section 3–404 or 3–405 or the drawer is precluded under Section 3–406 or 4–406 from asserting against the drawee the unauthorized indorsement or alteration.

(d) If (i) a dishonored draft is presented for payment to the drawer or an indorser or (ii) any other instrument is presented for payment to a party obliged to pay the instrument, and (iii) payment is received, the following rules apply:

(1) The person obtaining payment and a prior transferor of the instrument warrant to the person making payment in good faith that the warrantor is, or was, at the time the warrantor transferred the instrument, a person entitled to enforce the instrument or authorized to obtain payment on behalf of a person entitled to enforce the instrument.
(2) The person making payment may recover from any warrantor for breach of warranty an amount equal to the amount paid plus expenses and loss of interest resulting from the breach.

(e) The warranties stated in subsections (a) and (d) cannot be disclaimed with respect to checks. Unless notice of a claim for breach of warranty is given to the warrantor within 30 days after the claimant has reason to know of the breach and the identity of the warrantor, the liability of the warrantor under subsection (b) or (d) is discharged to the extent of any loss caused by the delay in giving notice of the claim.

(f) A [cause of action] for breach of warranty under this section accrues when the claimant has reason to know of the breach.

§ 3–418. Payment or Acceptance by Mistake.

(a) Except as provided in subsection (c), if the drawee of a draft pays or accepts the draft and the drawee acted on the mistaken belief that (i) payment of the draft had not been stopped pursuant to Section 4–403 or (ii) the signature of the drawer of the draft was authorized, the drawee may recover the amount of the draft from the person to whom or for whose benefit payment was made or, in the case of acceptance, may revoke the acceptance. Rights of the drawee under this subsection are not affected by failure of the drawee to exercise ordinary care in paying or accepting the draft.

(b) Except as provided in subsection (c), if an instrument has been paid or accepted by mistake and the case is not covered by subsection (a), the person paying or accepting may, to the extent permitted by the law governing mistake and restitution, (i) recover the payment from the person to whom or for whose benefit payment was made or (ii) in the case of acceptance, may revoke the acceptance.

(c) The remedies provided by subsection (a) or (b) may not be asserted against a person who took the instrument in good faith and for value or who in good faith changed position in reliance on the payment or acceptance. This subsection does not limit remedies provided by Section 3–417 or 4–407.

(d) Notwithstanding Section 4–215, if an instrument is paid or accepted by mistake and the payor or acceptor recovers payment or revokes acceptance under subsection (a) or (b), the instrument is deemed not to have been paid or accepted and is treated as dishonored, and the person from whom payment is recovered has rights as a person entitled to enforce the dishonored instrument.

§ 3–419. Instruments Signed for Accommodation.

(a) If an instrument is issued for value given for the benefit of a party to the instrument ("accommodated party") and another party to the instrument ("accommodation party") signs the instrument for the purpose of incurring liability on the instrument without being a direct beneficiary of the value given for the instrument, the instrument is signed by the accommodation party "for accommodation."

(b) An accommodation party may sign the instrument as maker, drawer, acceptor, or indorser and, subject to subsection (d), is obliged to pay the instrument in the capacity in which the accommodation party signs. The obligation of an accommodation party may be enforced notwithstanding any statute of frauds and whether or not the accommodation party receives consideration for the accommodation.

(c) A person signing an instrument is presumed to be an accommodation party and there is notice that the instrument is signed for accommodation if the signature is an anomalous indorsement or is accompanied by words indicating that the signer is acting as surety or guarantor with respect to the obligation of another party to the instrument. Except as provided in Section 3–605, the obligation of an accommodation party to pay the instrument is not affected by the fact that the person enforcing the obligation had notice when the instrument was taken by that person that the accommodation party signed the instrument for accommodation.

(d) If the signature of a party to an instrument is accompanied by words indicating unambiguously that the party is guaranteeing collection rather than payment of the obligation of another party to the instrument, the signer is obliged to pay the amount due on the instrument to a person entitled to enforce the instrument only if (i) execution of judgment against the other party has been returned unsatisfied, (ii) the other party is insolvent or in an insolvency proceeding, (iii) the other party cannot be served with process, or (iv) it is otherwise apparent that payment cannot be obtained from the other party.

(e) An accommodation party who pays the instrument is entitled to reimbursement from the accommodated party and is entitled to enforce the instrument against the accommodated party. An accommodated party who pays the instrument has no right of recourse against, and is not entitled to contribution from, an accommodation party.

§ 3–420. Conversion of Instrument.

(a) The law applicable to conversion of personal property applies to instruments. An instrument is also converted if it is taken by transfer, other than a negotiation, from a person not entitled to enforce the instrument or a bank makes or obtains payment with respect to the instrument for a person not entitled to enforce the instrument or receive payment. An action for conversion of an instrument may not be brought by (i) the issuer or acceptor of the instrument or (ii) a payee or indorsee who did not receive delivery of the instrument either directly or through delivery to an agent or a co-payee.

(b) In an action under subsection (a), the measure of liability is presumed to be the amount payable on the instrument, but recovery may not exceed the amount of the plaintiff's interest in the instrument.

(c) A representative, other than a depositary bank, who has in good faith dealt with an instrument or its proceeds on behalf of one who was not the person entitled to enforce the instrument is not liable in conversion to that person beyond the amount of any proceeds that it has not paid out.

PART 5 Dishonor

§ 3–501. Presentment.

(a) "Presentment" means a demand made by or on behalf of a person entitled to enforce an instrument (i) to pay the instrument made to the drawee or a party obliged to pay the instrument or, in the case of a note or accepted draft payable at a bank, to the bank, or (ii) to accept a draft made to the drawee.

(b) The following rules are subject to Article 4, agreement of the parties, and clearing-house rules and the like:

(1) Presentment may be made at the place of payment of the instrument and must be made at the place of payment if the instrument is payable at a bank in the United States; may be made by any commercially reasonable means, including an oral, written, or electronic communication; is effective when the demand for payment or acceptance is received by the person to whom presentment is made; and is effective if made to any one of two or more makers, acceptors, drawees, or other payors.

(2) Upon demand of the person to whom presentment is made, the person making presentment must (i) exhibit the instrument, (ii) give reasonable identification and, if presentment is made on behalf of another person, reasonable evidence of authority to do so, and (…) sign a receipt on the instrument for any payment made or surrender the instrument if full payment is made.

(3) Without dishonoring the instrument, the party to whom presentment is made may (i) return the instrument for lack of a necessary indorsement, or (ii) refuse payment or acceptance for failure of the presentment to comply with the terms of the instrument, an agreement of the parties, or other applicable law or rule.

(4) The party to whom presentment is made may treat presentment as occurring on the next business day after the day of presentment if the party to whom presentment is made has established a cut-off hour not earlier than 2 P.M. for the receipt and processing of instruments presented for payment or acceptance and presentment is made after the cut-off hour.

§ 3–502. Dishonor.

(a) Dishonor of a note is governed by the following rules:

(1) If the note is payable on demand, the note is dishonored if presentment is duly made to the maker and the note is not paid on the day of presentment.

(2) If the note is not payable on demand and is payable at or through a bank or the terms of the note require presentment, the note is dishonored if presentment is duly made and the note is not paid on the day it becomes payable or the day of presentment, whichever is later.

(3) If the note is not payable on demand and paragraph (2) does not apply, the note is dishonored if it is not paid on the day it becomes payable.

(b) Dishonor of an unaccepted draft other than a documentary draft is governed by the following rules:

(1) If a check is duly presented for payment to the payor bank otherwise than for immediate payment over the counter, the check is dishonored if the payor bank makes timely return of the check or sends timely notice of dishonor or nonpayment under Section 4–301 or 4–302, or becomes accountable for the amount of the check under Section 4–302.

(2) If a draft is payable on demand and paragraph (1) does not apply, the draft is dishonored if presentment for payment is duly made to the drawee and the draft is not paid on the day of presentment.

(3) If a draft is payable on a date stated in the draft, the draft is dishonored if (i) presentment for payment is duly made to the drawee and payment is not made on the day the draft becomes payable or the day of presentment, whichever is later, or (ii) presentment for acceptance is duly made before the day the draft becomes payable and the draft is not accepted on the day of presentment.

(4) If a draft is payable on elapse of a period of time after sight or acceptance, the draft is dishonored if presentment for acceptance is duly made and the draft is not accepted on the day of presentment.

(c) Dishonor of an unaccepted documentary draft occurs according to the rules stated in subsection (b)(2), (3), and (4), except that payment or acceptance may be delayed without dishonor until no later than the close of the third business day of the drawee following the day on which payment or acceptance is required by those paragraphs.

(d) Dishonor of an accepted draft is governed by the following rules:

(1) If the draft is payable on demand, the draft is dishonored if presentment for payment is duly made to the acceptor and the draft is not paid on the day of presentment.

(2) If the draft is not payable on demand, the draft is dishonored if presentment for payment is duly made to the acceptor and

payment is not made on the day it becomes payable or the day of presentment, whichever is later.

(e) In any case in which presentment is otherwise required for dishonor under this section and presentment is excused under Section 3–504, dishonor occurs without presentment if the instrument is not duly accepted or paid.

(f) If a draft is dishonored because timely acceptance of the draft was not made and the person entitled to demand acceptance consents to a late acceptance, from the time of acceptance the draft is treated as never having been dishonored.

§ 3–503. Notice of Dishonor.

(a) The obligation of an indorser stated in Section 3–415(a) and the obligation of a drawer stated in Section 3–414(d) may not be enforced unless (i) the indorser or drawer is given notice of dishonor of the instrument complying with this section or (ii) notice of dishonor is excused under Section 3–504(b).

(b) Notice of dishonor may be given by any person; may be given by any commercially reasonable means, including an oral, written, or electronic communication; and is sufficient if it reasonably identifies the instrument and indicates that the instrument has been dishonored or has not been paid or accepted. Return of an instrument given to a bank for collection is sufficient notice of dishonor.

(c) Subject to Section 3–504(c), with respect to an instrument taken for collection by a collecting bank, notice of dishonor must be given (i) by the bank before midnight of the next banking day following the banking day on which the bank receives notice of dishonor of the instrument, or (ii) by any other person within 30 days following the day on which the person receives notice of dishonor. With respect to any other instrument, notice of dishonor must be given within 30 days following the day on which dishonor occurs.

§ 3–504. Excused Presentment and Notice of Dishonor.

(a) Presentment for payment or acceptance of an instrument is excused if (i) the person entitled to present the instrument cannot with reasonable diligence make presentment, (ii) the maker or acceptor has repudiated an obligation to pay the instrument or is dead or in insolvency proceedings, (iii) by the terms of the instrument presentment is not necessary to enforce the obligation of indorsers or the drawer, (iv) the drawer or indorser whose obligation is being enforced has waived presentment or otherwise has no reason to expect or right to require that the instrument be paid or accepted, or (v) the drawer instructed the drawee not to pay or accept the draft or the drawee was not obligated to the drawer to pay the draft.

(b) Notice of dishonor is excused if (i) by the terms of the instrument notice of dishonor is not necessary to enforce the obligation of a party to pay the instrument, or (ii) the party whose obligation is being enforced waived notice of dishonor. A waiver of presentment is also a waiver of notice of dishonor.

(c) Delay in giving notice of dishonor is excused if the delay was caused by circumstances beyond the control of the person giving the notice and the person giving the notice exercised reasonable diligence after the cause of the delay ceased to operate.

§ 3–505. Evidence of Dishonor.

(a) The following are admissible as evidence and create a presumption of dishonor and of any notice of dishonor stated:

(1) a document regular in form as provided in subsection (b) which purports to be a protest;

(2) a purported stamp or writing of the drawee, payor bank, or presenting bank on or accompanying the instrument stating that acceptance or payment has been refused unless reasons for the refusal are stated and the reasons are not consistent with dishonor;

(3) a book or record of the drawee, payor bank, or collecting bank, kept in the usual course of business which shows dishonor, even if there is no evidence of who made the entry.

(b) A protest is a certificate of dishonor made by a United States consul or vice consul, or a notary public or other person authorized to administer oaths by the law of the place where dishonor occurs. It may be made upon information satisfactory to that person. The protest must identify the instrument and certify either that presentment has been made or, if not made, the reason why it was not made, and that the instrument has been dishonored by nonacceptance or nonpayment. The protest may also certify that notice of dishonor has been given to some or all parties.

PART 6 Discharge and Payment

§ 3–601. Discharge and Effect of Discharge.

(a) The obligation of a party to pay the instrument is discharged as stated in this Article or by an act or agreement with the party which would discharge an obligation to pay money under a simple contract.

(b) Discharge of the obligation of a party is not effective against a person acquiring rights of a holder in due course of the instrument without notice of the discharge.

§ 3–602. Payment.

(a) Subject to subsection (b), an instrument is paid to the extent payment is made (i) by or on behalf of a party obliged to pay the instrument, and (ii) to a person entitled to enforce the instrument. To the extent of the payment, the obligation of the party obliged to pay the instrument is discharged even though payment is made with knowledge of a claim to the instrument under Section 3–306 by another person.

(b) The obligation of a party to pay the instrument is not discharged under subsection (a) if:

(1) a claim to the instrument under Section 3–306 is enforceable against the party receiving payment and (i) payment is made

with knowledge by the payor that payment is prohibited by injunction or similar process of a court of competent jurisdiction, or (ii) in the case of an instrument other than a cashier's check, teller's check, or certified check, the party making payment accepted, from the person having a claim to the instrument, indemnity against loss resulting from refusal to pay the person entitled to enforce the instrument; or

(2) the person making payment knows that the instrument is a stolen instrument and pays a person it knows is in wrongful possession of the instrument.

§ 3–603. Tender of Payment.

(a) If tender of payment of an obligation to pay an instrument is made to a person entitled to enforce the instrument, the effect of tender is governed by principles of law applicable to tender of payment under a simple contract.

(b) If tender of payment of an obligation to pay an instrument is made to a person entitled to enforce the instrument and the tender is refused, there is discharge, to the extent of the amount of the tender, of the obligation of an indorser or accommodation party having a right of recourse with respect to the obligation to which the tender relates.

(c) If tender of payment of an amount due on an instrument is made to a person entitled to enforce the instrument, the obligation of the obligor to pay interest after the due date on the amount tendered is discharged. If presentment is required with respect to an instrument and the obligor is able and ready to pay on the due date at every place of payment stated in the instrument, the obligor is deemed to have made tender of payment on the due date to the person entitled to enforce the instrument.

§ 3–604. Discharge by Cancellation or Renunciation.

(a) A person entitled to enforce an instrument, with or without consideration, may discharge the obligation of a party to pay the instrument (i) by an intentional voluntary act, such as surrender of the instrument to the party, destruction, mutilation, or cancellation of the instrument, cancellation or striking out of the party's signature, or the addition of words to the instrument indicating discharge, or (ii) by agreeing not to sue or otherwise renouncing rights against the party by a signed writing.

(b) Cancellation or striking out of an indorsement pursuant to subsection (a) does not affect the status and rights of a party derived from the indorsement.

§ 3–605. Discharge of Indorsers and Accommodation Parties.

(a) In this section, the term "indorser" includes a drawer having the obligation described in Section 3–414(d).

(b) Discharge, under Section 3–604, of the obligation of a party to pay an instrument does not discharge the obligation of an indorser or accommodation party having a right of recourse against the discharged party.

(c) If a person entitled to enforce an instrument agrees, with or without consideration, to an extension of the due date of the obligation of a party to pay the instrument, the extension discharges an indorser or accommodation party having a right of recourse against the party whose obligation is extended to the extent the indorser or accommodation party proves that the extension caused loss to the indorser or accommodation party with respect to the right of recourse.

(d) If a person entitled to enforce an instrument agrees, with or without consideration, to a material modification of the obligation of a party other than an extension of the due date, the modification discharges the obligation of an indorser or accommodation party having a right of recourse against the person whose obligation is modified to the extent the modification causes loss to the indorser or accommodation party with respect to the right of recourse. The loss suffered by the indorser or accommodation party as a result of the modification is equal to the amount of the right of recourse unless the person enforcing the instrument proves that no loss was caused by the modification or that the loss caused by the modification was an amount less than the amount of the right of recourse.

(e) If the obligation of a party to pay an instrument is secured by an interest in collateral and a person entitled to enforce the instrument impairs the value of the interest in collateral, the obligation of an indorser or accommodation party having a right of recourse against the obligor is discharged to the extent of the impairment. The value of an interest in collateral is impaired to the extent (i) the value of the interest is reduced to an amount less than the amount of the right of recourse of the party asserting discharge, or (ii) the reduction in value of the interest causes an increase in the amount by which the amount of the right of recourse exceeds the value of the interest. The burden of proving impairment is on the party asserting discharge.

(f) If the obligation of a party is secured by an interest in collateral not provided by an accommodation party and a person entitled to enforce the instrument impairs the value of the interest in collateral, the obligation of any party who is jointly and severally liable with respect to the secured obligation is discharged to the extent the impairment causes the party asserting discharge to pay more than that party would have been obliged to pay, taking into account rights of contribution, if impairment had not occurred. If the party asserting discharge is an accommodation party not entitled to discharge under subsection (e), the party is deemed to have a right to contribution based on joint and several liability rather than a right to reimbursement. The burden of proving impairment is on the party asserting discharge.

(g) Under subsection (e) or (f), impairing value of an interest in collateral includes (i) failure to obtain or maintain perfection or recordation of the interest in collateral, (ii) release of collateral without substitution of collateral of equal value, (iii) failure to perform a duty to preserve the value of collateral owed, under Article 9 or other law, to a debtor or surety or other person secondarily liable, or (iv) failure to comply with applicable law in disposing of collateral.

(h) An accommodation party is not discharged under subsection (c), (d), or (e) unless the person entitled to enforce the instrument knows of the accommodation or has notice under Section 3–419(c) that the instrument was signed for accommodation.

(i) A party is not discharged under this section if (i) the party asserting discharge consents to the event or conduct that is the basis of the discharge, or (ii) the instrument or a separate agreement of the party provides for waiver of discharge under this section either specifically or by general language indicating that parties waive defenses based on suretyship or impairment of collateral.

ADDENDUM TO REVISED ARTICLE III

Notes to Legislative Counsel

1. If revised Article 3 is adopted in your state, the reference in Section 2–511 to Section 3–802 should be changed to Section 3–310.

2. If revised Article 3 is adopted in your state and the Uniform Fiduciaries Act is also in effect in your state, you may want to consider amending Uniform Fiduciaries Act § 9 to conform to Section 3–307(b)(2)(iii) and (4)(iii). See Official Comment 3 to Section 3–307.

REVISED ARTICLE IV

BANK DEPOSITS AND COLLECTIONS

PART 1 General Provisions and Definitions

§ 4–101. Short Title.

This Article may be cited as Uniform Commercial Code—Bank Deposits and Collections.

As amended in 1990.

§ 4–102. Applicability.

(a) To the extent that items within this Article are also within Articles 3 and 8, they are subject to those Articles. If there is conflict, this Article governs Article 3, but Article 8 governs this Article.

(b) The liability of a bank for action or non-action with respect to an item handled by it for purposes of presentment, payment, or collection is governed by the law of the place where the bank is located. In the case of action or non-action by or at a branch or separate office of a bank, its liability is governed by the law of the place where the branch or separate office is located.

§ 4–103. Variation by Agreement; Measure of Damages; Action Constituting Ordinary Care.

(a) The effect of the provisions of this Article may be varied by agreement, but the parties to the agreement cannot disclaim a bank's responsibility for its lack of good faith or failure to exercise ordinary care or limit the measure of damages for the lack or failure. However, the parties may determine by agreement the standards by which the bank's responsibility is to be measured if those standards are not manifestly unreasonable.

(b) Federal Reserve regulations and operating circulars, clearing-house rules, and the like have the effect of agreements under subsection (a), whether or not specifically assented to by all parties interested in items handled.

(c) Action or non-action approved by this Article or pursuant to Federal Reserve regulations or operating circulars is the exercise of ordinary care and, in the absence of special instructions, action or non-action consistent with clearing-house rules and the like or with a general banking usage not disapproved by this Article, is prima facie the exercise of ordinary care.

(d) The specification or approval of certain procedures by this Article is not disapproval of other procedures that may be reasonable under the circumstances.

(e) The measure of damages for failure to exercise ordinary care in handling an item is the amount of the item reduced by an amount that could not have been realized by the exercise of ordinary care. If there is also bad faith it includes any other damages the party suffered as a proximate consequence.

As amended in 1990.

§ 4–104. Definitions and Index of Definitions.

(a) In this Article, unless the context otherwise requires:

(1) "Account" means any deposit or credit account with a bank, including a demand, time, savings, passbook, share draft, or like account, other than an account evidenced by a certificate of deposit;

(2) "Afternoon" means the period of a day between noon and midnight;

(3) "Banking day" means the part of a day on which a bank is open to the public for carrying on substantially all of its banking functions;

(4) "Clearing house" means an association of banks or other payors regularly clearing items;

(5) "Customer" means a person having an account with a bank or for whom a bank has agreed to collect items, including a bank that maintains an account at another bank;

(6) "Documentary draft" means a draft to be presented for acceptance or payment if specified documents, certificated securities (Section 8–102) or instructions for uncertificated securities (Section 8–102), or other certificates, statements, or the like are to be received by the drawee or other payor before acceptance or payment of the draft;

(7) "Draft" means a draft as defined in Section 3–104 or an item, other than an instrument, that is an order;

(8) "Drawee" means a person ordered in a draft to make payment;

(9) "Item" means an instrument or a promise or order to pay money handled by a bank for collection or payment. The term does not include a payment order governed by Article 4A or a credit or debit card slip;

(10) "Midnight deadline" with respect to a bank is midnight on its next banking day following the banking day on which it receives the relevant item or notice or from which the time for taking action commences to run, whichever is later;

(11) "Settle" means to pay in cash, by clearing-house settlement, in a charge or credit or by remittance, or otherwise as agreed. A settlement may be either provisional or final;

(12) "Suspends payments" with respect to a bank means that it has been closed by order of the supervisory authorities, that a public officer has been appointed to take it over, or that it ceases or refuses to make payments in the ordinary course of business.

(b) [Other definitions' section references deleted.]

(c) [Other definitions' section references deleted.]

(d) In addition, Article 1 contains general definitions and principles of construction and interpretation applicable throughout this Article.

§ 4–105. "Bank"; "Depositary Bank"; "Payor Bank"; "Intermediary Bank"; "Collecting Bank"; "Presenting Bank".

In this Article:

(1) "Bank" means a person engaged in the business of banking, including a savings bank, savings and loan association, credit union, or trust company;

(2) "Depositary bank" means the first bank to take an item even though it is also the payor bank, unless the item is presented for immediate payment over the counter;

(3) "Payor bank" means a bank that is the drawee of a draft;

(4) "Intermediary bank" means a bank to which an item is transferred in course of collection except the depositary or payor bank;

(5) "Collecting bank" means a bank handling an item for collection except the payor bank;

(6) "Presenting bank" means a bank presenting an item except a payor bank.

§ 4–106. Payable Through or Payable at Bank: Collecting Bank.

(a) If an item states that it is "payable through" a bank identified in the item, (i) the item designates the bank as a collecting bank and does not by itself authorize the bank to pay the item, and (ii) the item may be presented for payment only by or through the bank.

Alternative A (b) If an item states that it is "payable at" a bank identified in the item, the item is equivalent to a draft drawn on the bank.

Alternative B (b) If an item states that it is "payable at" a bank identified in the item, (i) the item designates the bank as a collecting bank and does not by itself authorize the bank to pay the item, and (ii) the item may be presented for payment only by or through the bank.

(c) If a draft names a nonbank drawee and it is unclear whether a bank named in the draft is a co-drawee or a collecting bank, the bank is a collecting bank.

As added in 1990.

§ 4–107. Separate Office of Bank.

A branch or separate office of a bank is a separate bank for the purpose of computing the time within which and determining the place at or to which action may be taken or notices or orders shall be given under this Article and under Article 3.

As amended in 1962 and 1990.

§ 4–108. Time of Receipt of Items.

(a) For the purpose of allowing time to process items, prove balances, and make the necessary entries on its books to determine its position for the day, a bank may fix an afternoon hour of 2 P.M. or later as a cutoff hour for the handling of money and items and the making of entries on its books.

(b) An item or deposit of money received on any day after a cutoff hour so fixed or after the close of the banking day may be treated as being received at the opening of the next banking day.

As amended in 1990.

§ 4–109. Delays.

(a) Unless otherwise instructed, a collecting bank in a good faith effort to secure payment of a specific item drawn on a payor other than a bank, and with or without the approval of any person involved, may waive, modify, or extend time limits imposed or permitted by this [act] for a period not exceeding two additional banking days without discharge of drawers or indorsers or liability to its transferor or a prior party.

(b) Delay by a collecting bank or payor bank beyond time limits prescribed or permitted by this [act] or by instructions is excused if (i) the delay is caused by interruption of communication or computer facilities, suspension of payments by another bank, war, emergency conditions, failure of equipment, or other circumstances beyond the control of the bank, and (ii) the bank exercises such diligence as the circumstances require.

§ 4-110. Electronic Presentment.

(a) "Agreement for electronic presentment" means an agreement, clearing-house rule, or Federal Reserve regulation or operating circular, providing that presentment of an item may be made by transmission of an image of an item or information describing the item ("presentment notice") rather than delivery of the item itself. The agreement may provide for procedures governing retention, presentment, payment, dishonor, and other matters concerning items subject to the agreement.

(b) Presentment of an item pursuant to an agreement for presentment is made when the presentment notice is received.

(c) If presentment is made by presentment notice, a reference to "item" or "check" in this Article means the presentment notice unless the context otherwise indicates.

As added in 1990.

§ 4-111. Statute of Limitations.

An action to enforce an obligation, duty, or right arising under this Article must be commenced within three years after the [cause of action] accrues.

As added in 1990.

PART 2 Collection of Items: Depositary and Collecting Banks

§ 4-201. Status of Collecting Bank as Agent and Provisional Status of Credits; Applicability of Article; Item Indorsed "Pay Any Bank".

(a) Unless a contrary intent clearly appears and before the time that a settlement given by a collecting bank for an item is or becomes final, the bank, with respect to an item, is an agent or sub-agent of the owner of the item and any settlement given for the item is provisional. This provision applies regardless of the form of indorsement or lack of indorsement and even though credit given for the item is subject to immediate withdrawal as of right or is in fact withdrawn; but the continuance of ownership of an item by its owner and any rights of the owner to proceeds of the item are subject to rights of a collecting bank, such as those resulting from outstanding advances on the item and rights of recoupment or setoff. If an item is handled by banks for purposes of presentment, payment, collection, or return, the relevant provisions of this Article apply even though action of the parties clearly establishes that a particular bank has purchased the item and is the owner of it.

(b) After an item has been indorsed with the words "pay any bank" or the like, only a bank may acquire the rights of a holder until the item has been:

(1) returned to the customer initiating collection; or

(2) specially indorsed by a bank to a person who is not a bank.

As amended in 1990.

§ 4-202. Responsibility for Collection or Return; When Action Timely.

(a) A collecting bank must exercise ordinary care in:

(1) presenting an item or sending it for presentment;

(2) sending notice of dishonor or nonpayment or returning an item other than a documentary draft to the bank's transferor after learning that the item has not been paid or accepted, as the case may be;

(3) settling for an item when the bank receives final settlement; and

(4) notifying its transferor of any loss or delay in transit within a reasonable time after discovery thereof.

(b) A collecting bank exercises ordinary care under subsection (a) by taking proper action before its midnight deadline following receipt of an item, notice, or settlement. Taking proper action within a reasonably longer time may constitute the exercise of ordinary care, but the bank has the burden of establishing timeliness.

(c) Subject to subsection (a)(1), a bank is not liable for the insolvency, neglect, misconduct, mistake, or default of another bank or person or for loss or destruction of an item in the possession of others or in transit.

As amended in 1990.

§ 4-203. Effect of Instructions.

Subject to Article 3 concerning conversion of instruments (Section 3–420) and restrictive indorsements (Section 3–206), only a collecting bank's transferor can give instructions that affect the bank or constitute notice to it, and a collecting bank is not liable to prior parties for any action taken pursuant to the instructions or in accordance with any agreement with its transferor.

§ 4-204. Methods of Sending and Presenting; Sending Directly to Payor Bank.

(a) A collecting bank shall send items by a reasonably prompt method, taking into consideration relevant instructions, the nature of the item, the number of those items on hand, the cost of collection involved, and the method generally used by it or others to present those items.

(b) A collecting bank may send:

(1) an item directly to the payor bank;

(2) an item to a nonbank payor if authorized by its transferor; and

(3) an item other than documentary drafts to a nonbank payor, if authorized by Federal Reserve regulation or operating circular, clearing-house rule, or the like.

(c) Presentment may be made by a presenting bank at a place where the payor bank or other payor has requested that presentment be made.

As amended in 1990.

§ 4–205. Depositary Bank Holder of Unindorsed Item.

If a customer delivers an item to a depositary bank for collection:

(1) the depositary bank becomes a holder of the item at the time it receives the item for collection if the customer at the time of delivery was a holder of the item, whether or not the customer indorses the item, and, if the bank satisfies the other requirements of Section 3–302, it is a holder in due course; and

(2) the depositary bank warrants to collecting banks, the payor bank or other payor, and the drawer that the amount of the item was paid to the customer or deposited to the customer's account.

As amended in 1990.

§ 4–206. Transfer Between Banks.

Any agreed method that identifies the transferor bank is sufficient for the item's further transfer to another bank.

As amended in 1990.

§ 4–207. Transfer Warranties.

(a) A customer or collecting bank that transfers an item and receives a settlement or other consideration warrants to the transferee and to any subsequent collecting bank that:

(1) the warrantor is a person entitled to enforce the item;

(2) all signatures on the item are authentic and authorized;

(3) the item has not been altered;

(4) the item is not subject to a defense or claim in recoupment (Section 3–305(a)) of any party that can be asserted against the warrantor; and

(5) the warrantor has no knowledge of any insolvency proceeding commenced with respect to the maker or acceptor or, in the case of an unaccepted draft, the drawer.

(b) If an item is dishonored, a customer or collecting bank transferring the item and receiving settlement or other consideration is obliged to pay the amount due on the item (i) according to the terms of the item at the time it was transferred, or (ii) if the transfer was of an incomplete item, according to its terms when completed as stated in Sections 3–115 and 3–407. The obligation of a transferor is owed to the transferee and to any subsequent collecting bank that takes the item in good faith. A transferor cannot disclaim its obligation under this subsection by an indorsement stating that it is made "without recourse" or otherwise disclaiming liability.

(c) A person to whom the warranties under subsection (a) are made and who took the item in good faith may recover from the warrantor as damages for breach of warranty an amount equal to the loss suffered as a result of the breach, but not more than the amount of the item plus expenses and loss of interest incurred as a result of the breach.

(d) The warranties stated in subsection (a) cannot be disclaimed with respect to checks. Unless notice of a claim for breach of warranty is given to the warrantor within 30 days after the claimant has reason to know of the breach and the identity of the warrantor, the warrantor is discharged to the extent of any loss caused by the delay in giving notice of the claim.

(e) A cause of action for breach of warranty under this section accrues when the claimant has reason to know of the breach.

As amended in 1990.

§ 4–208. Presentment Warranties.

(a) If an unaccepted draft is presented to the drawee for payment or acceptance and the drawee pays or accepts the draft, (i) the person obtaining payment or acceptance, at the time of presentment, and (ii) a previous transferor of the draft, at the time of transfer, warrant to the drawee that pays or accepts the draft in good faith that:

(1) the warrantor is, or was, at the time the warrantor transferred the draft, a person entitled to enforce the draft or authorized to obtain payment or acceptance of the draft on behalf of a person entitled to enforce the draft;

(2) the draft has not been altered; and

(3) the warrantor has no knowledge that the signature of the purported drawer of the draft is unauthorized.

(b) A drawee making payment may recover from a warrantor damages for breach of warranty equal to the amount paid by the drawee less the amount the drawee received or is entitled to receive from the drawer because of the payment. In addition, the drawee is entitled to compensation for expenses and loss of interest resulting from the breach. The right of the drawee to recover damages under this subsection is not affected by any failure of the drawee to exercise ordinary care in making payment. If the drawee accepts the draft (i) breach of warranty is a defense to the obligation of the acceptor, and (ii) if the acceptor makes payment with respect to the draft, the acceptor is entitled to recover from a warrantor for breach of warranty the amounts stated in this subsection.

(c) If a drawee asserts a claim for breach of warranty under subsection (a) based on an unauthorized indorsement of the draft or an alteration of the draft, the warrantor may defend by proving that the indorsement is effective under Section 3–404 or 3–405 or the drawer is precluded under Section 3–406 or 4–406 from asserting against the drawee the unauthorized indorsement or alteration.

(d) If (i) a dishonored draft is presented for payment to the drawer or an indorser or (ii) any other item is presented for payment to a party obliged to pay the item, and the item is paid, the person obtaining payment and a prior transferor of the item warrant to the person making payment in good faith that the warrantor is, or was, at the time the warrantor transferred the item, a person entitled to enforce the item or authorized to obtain payment on behalf of a person entitled to enforce the item. The person making payment may recover from any warrantor for breach of warranty an amount equal to the amount paid plus expenses and loss of interest resulting from the breach.

(e) The warranties stated in subsections (a) and (d) cannot be disclaimed with respect to checks. Unless notice of a claim for breach of warranty is given to the warrantor within 30 days after the claimant has reason to know of the breach and the identity of the warrantor, the warrantor is discharged to the extent of any loss caused by the delay in giving notice of the claim.

(f) A cause of action for breach of warranty under this section accrues when the claimant has reason to know of the breach.

As amended in 1990.

§ 4–209. Encoding and Retention Warranties.

(a) A person who encodes information on or with respect to an item after issue warrants to any subsequent collecting bank and to the payor bank or other payor that the information is correctly encoded. If the customer of a depositary bank encodes, that bank also makes the warranty.

(b) A person who undertakes to retain an item pursuant to an agreement for electronic presentment warrants to any subsequent collecting bank and to the payor bank or other payor that retention and presentment of the item comply with the agreement. If a customer of a depositary bank undertakes to retain an item, that bank also makes this warranty.

(c) A person to whom warranties are made under this section and who took the item in good faith may recover from the warrantor as damages for breach of warranty an amount equal to the loss suffered as a result of the breach, plus expenses and loss of interest incurred as a result of the breach.

As added in 1990.

§ 4–210. Security Interest of Collecting Bank in Items, Accompanying Documents and Proceeds.

(a) A collecting bank has a security interest in an item and any accompanying documents or the proceeds of either:

(1) in case of an item deposited in an account, to the extent to which credit given for the item has been withdrawn or applied;

(2) in case of an item for which it has given credit available for withdrawal as of right, to the extent of the credit given, whether or not the credit is drawn upon or there is a right of charge-back; or

(3) if it makes an advance on or against the item.

(b) If credit given for several items received at one time or pursuant to a single agreement is withdrawn or applied in part, the security interest remains upon all the items, any accompanying documents or the proceeds of either. For the purpose of this section, credits first given are first withdrawn.

(c) Receipt by a collecting bank of a final settlement for an item is a realization on its security interest in the item, accompanying documents, and proceeds. So long as the bank does not receive final settlement for the item or give up possession of the item or accompanying documents for purposes other than collection, the security interest continues to that extent and is subject to Article 9, but:

(1) no security agreement is necessary to make the security interest enforceable (Section 9–203(1)(a));

(2) no filing is required to perfect the security interest; and

(3) the security interest has priority over conflicting perfected security interests in the item, accompanying documents, or proceeds.

As amended in 1990 and 1999.

§ 4–211. When Bank Gives Value for Purposes of Holder in Due Course.

For purposes of determining its status as a holder in due course, a bank has given value to the extent it has a security interest in an item, if the bank otherwise complies with the requirements of Section 3–302 on what constitutes a holder in due course.

As amended in 1990.

§ 4–212. Presentment by Notice of Item Not Payable by, Through, or at Bank; Liability of Drawer or Indorser.

(a) Unless otherwise instructed, a collecting bank may present an item not payable by, through, or at a bank by sending to the party to accept or pay a written notice that the bank holds the item for acceptance or payment. The notice must be sent in time to be received on or before the day when presentment is due and the bank must meet any requirement of the party to accept or pay under Section 3–501 by the close of the bank's next banking day after it knows of the requirement.

(b) If presentment is made by notice and payment, acceptance, or request for compliance with a requirement under Section 3–501 is not received by the close of business on the day after maturity or, in the case of demand items, by the close of business on the third banking day after notice was sent, the presenting bank may treat the item as dishonored and charge any drawer or indorser by sending it notice of the facts.

As amended in 1990.

§ 4–213. Medium and Time of Settlement by Bank.

(a) With respect to settlement by a bank, the medium and time of settlement may be prescribed by Federal Reserve regulations or circulars, clearing-house rules, and the like, or agreement. In the absence of such prescription:

(1) the medium of settlement is cash or credit to an account in a Federal Reserve bank of or specified by the person to receive settlement; and

(2) the time of settlement is:

(i) with respect to tender of settlement by cash, a cashier's check, or teller's check, when the cash or check is sent or delivered;

(ii) with respect to tender of settlement by credit in an account in a Federal Reserve Bank, when the credit is made;

(iii) with respect to tender of settlement by a credit or debit to an account in a bank, when the credit or debit is made or, in the case of tender of settlement by authority to charge an account, when the authority is sent or delivered; or

(iv) with respect to tender of settlement by a funds transfer, when payment is made pursuant to Section 4A–406(a) to the person receiving settlement.

(b) If the tender of settlement is not by a medium authorized by subsection (a) or the time of settlement is not fixed by subsection (a), no settlement occurs until the tender of settlement is accepted by the person receiving settlement.

(c) If settlement for an item is made by cashier's check or teller's check and the person receiving settlement, before its midnight deadline:

(1) presents or forwards the check for collection, settlement is final when the check is finally paid; or

(2) fails to present or forward the check for collection, settlement is final at the midnight deadline of the person receiving settlement.

(d) If settlement for an item is made by giving authority to charge the account of the bank giving settlement in the bank receiving settlement, settlement is final when the charge is made by the bank receiving settlement if there are funds available in the account for the amount of the item.

As amended in 1990.

§ 4–214. Right of Charge-Back or Refund; Liability of Collecting Bank: Return of Item.

(a) If a collecting bank has made provisional settlement with its customer for an item and fails by reason of dishonor, suspension of payments by a bank, or otherwise to receive settlement for the item which is or becomes final, the bank may revoke the settlement given by it, charge back the amount of any credit given for the item to its customer's account, or obtain refund from its customer, whether or not it is able to return the item, if by its midnight deadline or within a longer reasonable time after it learns the facts it returns the item or sends notification of the facts. If the return or notice is delayed beyond the bank's midnight deadline or a longer reasonable time after it learns the facts, the bank may revoke the settlement, charge back the credit, or obtain refund from its customer, but it is liable for any loss resulting from the delay. These rights to revoke, charge back, and obtain refund terminate if and when a settlement for the item received by the bank is or becomes final.

(b) A collecting bank returns an item when it is sent or delivered to the bank's customer or transferor or pursuant to its instructions.

(c) A depositary bank that is also the payor may charge back the amount of an item to its customer's account or obtain refund in accordance with the section governing return of an item received by a payor bank for credit on its books (Section 4–301).

(d) The right to charge back is not affected by:

(1) previous use of a credit given for the item; or

(2) failure by any bank to exercise ordinary care with respect to the item, but a bank so failing remains liable.

(e) A failure to charge back or claim refund does not affect other rights of the bank against the customer or any other party.

(f) If credit is given in dollars as the equivalent of the value of an item payable in foreign money, the dollar amount of any charge-back or refund must be calculated on the basis of the bank-offered spot rate for the foreign money prevailing on the day when the person entitled to the charge-back or refund learns that it will not receive payment in ordinary course.

As amended in 1990.

§ 4–215. Final Payment of Item by Payor Bank; When Provisional Debits and Credits Become Final; When Certain Credits Become Available for Withdrawal.

(a) An item is finally paid by a payor bank when the bank has first done any of the following:

(1) paid the item in cash;

(2) settled for the item without having a right to revoke the settlement under statute, clearing-house rule, or agreement; or

(3) made a provisional settlement for the item and failed to revoke the settlement in the time and manner permitted by statute, clearing-house rule, or agreement.

(b) If provisional settlement for an item does not become final, the item is not finally paid.

(c) If provisional settlement for an item between the presenting and payor banks is made through a clearing house or by debits or credits in an account between them, then to the extent that provisional debits or credits for the item are entered in accounts between the presenting and payor banks or between the presenting and successive prior collecting banks seriatim, they become final upon final payment of the item by the payor bank.

(d) If a collecting bank receives a settlement for an item which is or becomes final, the bank is accountable to its customer for the amount of the item and any provisional credit given for the item in an account with its customer becomes final.

(e) Subject to (i) applicable law stating a time for availability of funds and (ii) any right of the bank to apply the credit to an obligation of the customer, credit given by a bank for an item in a customer's account becomes available for withdrawal as of right:

(1) if the bank has received a provisional settlement for the item, when the settlement becomes final and the bank has had a reasonable time to receive return of the item and the item has not been received within that time;

(2) if the bank is both the depositary bank and the payor bank, and the item is finally paid, at the opening of the bank's second banking day following receipt of the item.

(f) Subject to applicable law stating a time for availability of funds and any right of a bank to apply a deposit to an obligation of the depositor, a deposit of money becomes available for withdrawal as of right at the opening of the bank's next banking day after receipt of the deposit.

As amended in 1990.

§ 4–216. Insolvency and Preference.

(a) If an item is in or comes into the possession of a payor or collecting bank that suspends payment and the item has not been finally paid, the item must be returned by the receiver, trustee, or agent in charge of the closed bank to the presenting bank or the closed bank's customer.

(b) If a payor bank finally pays an item and suspends payments without making a settlement for the item with its customer or the presenting bank which settlement is or becomes final, the owner of the item has a preferred claim against the payor bank.

(c) If a payor bank gives or a collecting bank gives or receives a provisional settlement for an item and thereafter suspends payments, the suspension does not prevent or interfere with the settlement's becoming final if the finality occurs automatically upon the lapse of certain time or the happening of certain events.

(d) If a collecting bank receives from subsequent parties settlement for an item, which settlement is or becomes final and the bank suspends payments without making a settlement for the item with its customer which settlement is or becomes final, the owner of the item has a preferred claim against the collecting bank.

As amended in 1990.

PART 3 Collection of Items: Payor Banks

§ 4–301. Deferred Posting; Recovery of Payment by Return of Items; Time of Dishonor; Return of Items by Payor Bank.

(a) If a payor bank settles for a demand item other than a documentary draft presented otherwise than for immediate payment over the counter before midnight of the banking day of receipt, the payor bank may revoke the settlement and recover the settlement if, before it has made final payment and before its midnight deadline, it

(1) returns the item; or

(2) sends written notice of dishonor or nonpayment if the item is unavailable for return.

(b) If a demand item is received by a payor bank for credit on its books, it may return the item or send notice of dishonor and may revoke any credit given or recover the amount thereof withdrawn by its customer, if it acts within the time limit and in the manner specified in subsection (a).

(c) Unless previous notice of dishonor has been sent, an item is dishonored at the time when for purposes of dishonor it is returned or notice sent in accordance with this section.

(d) An item is returned:

(1) as to an item presented through a clearing house, when it is delivered to the presenting or last collecting bank or to the clearing house or is sent or delivered in accordance with clearing-house rules; or

(2) in all other cases, when it is sent or delivered to the bank's customer or transferor or pursuant to instructions.

As amended in 1990.

§ 4–302. Payor Bank's Responsibility for Late Return of Item.

(a) If an item is presented to and received by a payor bank, the bank is accountable for the amount of:

(1) a demand item, other than a documentary draft, whether properly payable or not, if the bank, in any case in which it is not also the depositary bank, retains the item beyond midnight of the banking day of receipt without settling for it or, whether or not it is also the depositary bank, does not pay or return the item or send notice of dishonor until after its midnight deadline; or

(2) any other properly payable item unless, within the time allowed for acceptance or payment of that item, the bank either accepts or pays the item or returns it and accompanying documents.

(b) The liability of a payor bank to pay an item pursuant to subsection (a) is subject to defenses based on breach of a presentment warranty (Section 4–208) or proof that the person seeking enforcement of the liability presented or transferred the item for the purpose of defrauding the payor bank.

As amended in 1990.

§ 4–303. When Items Subject to Notice, Stop-Payment Order, Legal Process, or Setoff; Order in Which Items May Be Charged or Certified.

(a) Any knowledge, notice, or stop-payment order received by, legal process served upon, or setoff exercised by a payor bank comes too late to terminate, suspend, or modify the bank's right or duty to pay an item or to charge its customer's account for the item if the knowledge, notice, stop-payment order, or legal process is received or served and a reasonable time for the bank to act thereon expires or the setoff is exercised after the earliest of the following:

(1) the bank accepts or certifies the item;

(2) the bank pays the item in cash;

(3) the bank settles for the item without having a right to revoke the settlement under statute, clearing-house rule, or agreement;

(4) the bank becomes accountable for the amount of the item under Section 4–302 dealing with the payor bank's responsibility for late return of items; or

(5) with respect to checks, a cutoff hour no earlier than one hour after the opening of the next banking day after the banking day on which the bank received the check and no later than the close of that next banking day or, if no cutoff hour is fixed, the close of the next banking day after the banking day on which the bank received the check.

(b) Subject to subsection (a), items may be accepted, paid, certified, or charged to the indicated account of its customer in any order.

As amended in 1990.

PART 4 Relationship Between Payor Bank and Its Customer

§ 4–401. When Bank May Charge Customer's Account.

(a) A bank may charge against the account of a customer an item that is properly payable from the account even though the charge creates an overdraft. An item is properly payable if it is authorized by the customer and is in accordance with any agreement between the customer and bank.

(b) A customer is not liable for the amount of an overdraft if the customer neither signed the item nor benefited from the proceeds of the item.

(c) A bank may charge against the account of a customer a check that is otherwise properly payable from the account, even though payment was made before the date of the check, unless the customer has given notice to the bank of the postdating describing the check with reasonable certainty. The notice is effective for the period stated in Section 4–403(b) for stop-payment orders, and must be received at such time and in such manner as to afford the bank a reasonable opportunity to act on it before the bank takes any action with respect to the check described in Section 4–303. If a bank charges against the account of a customer a check before the date stated in the notice of postdating, the bank is liable for damages for the loss resulting from its act. The loss may include damages for dishonor of subsequent items under Section 4–402.

(d) A bank that in good faith makes payment to a holder may charge the indicated account of its customer according to:

(1) the original terms of the altered item; or

(2) the terms of the completed item, even though the bank knows the item has been completed unless the bank has notice that the completion was improper.

As amended in 1990.

§ 4–402. Bank's Liability to Customer for Wrongful Dishonor; Time of Determining Insufficiency of Account.

(a) Except as otherwise provided in this Article, a payor bank wrongfully dishonors an item if it dishonors an item that is properly payable, but a bank may dishonor an item that would create an overdraft unless it has agreed to pay the overdraft.

(b) A payor bank is liable to its customer for damages proximately caused by the wrongful dishonor of an item. Liability is limited to actual damages proved and may include damages for an arrest or prosecution of the customer or other consequential damages. Whether any consequential damages are proximately caused by the wrongful dishonor is a question of fact to be determined in each case.

(c) A payor bank's determination of the customer's account balance on which a decision to dishonor for insufficiency of available funds is based may be made at any time between the time the item is received by the payor bank and the time that the payor bank returns the item or gives notice in lieu of return, and no more than one determination need be made. If, at the election of the payor bank, a subsequent balance determination is made for the purpose of reevaluating the bank's decision to dishonor the item, the account balance at that time is determinative of whether a dishonor for insufficiency of available funds is wrongful.

As amended in 1990.

§ 4–403. Customer's Right to Stop Payment; Burden of Proof of Loss.

(a) A customer or any person authorized to draw on the account if there is more than one person may stop payment of any item drawn on the customer's account or close the account by an order to the bank describing the item or account with reasonable certainty received at a time and in a manner that affords the bank a reasonable opportunity to act on it before any action by the bank with respect to the item described in Section 4–303. If the signature of more than one person is required to draw on an account, any of these persons may stop payment or close the account.

(b) A stop-payment order is effective for six months, but it lapses after 14 calendar days if the original order was oral and was not confirmed in writing within that period. A stop-payment order may be renewed for additional six-month periods by a writing given to the bank within a period during which the stop-payment order is effective.

(c) The burden of establishing the fact and amount of loss resulting from the payment of an item contrary to a stop-payment order or order to close an account is on the customer.

The loss from payment of an item contrary to a stop-payment order may include damages for dishonor of subsequent items under Section 4–402.

As amended in 1990.

§ 4–404. Bank Not Obliged to Pay Check More Than Six Months Old.

A bank is under no obligation to a customer having a checking account to pay a check, other than a certified check, which is presented more than six months after its date, but it may charge its customer's account for a payment made thereafter in good faith.

§ 4–405. Death or Incompetence of Customer.

(a) A payor or collecting bank's authority to accept, pay, or collect an item or to account for proceeds of its collection, if otherwise effective, is not rendered ineffective by incompetence of a customer of either bank existing at the time the item is issued or its collection is undertaken if the bank does not know of an adjudication of incompetence. Neither death nor incompetence of a customer revokes the authority to accept, pay, collect, or account until the bank knows of the fact of death or of an adjudication of incompetence and has reasonable opportunity to act on it.

(b) Even with knowledge, a bank may for 10 days after the date of death pay or certify checks drawn on or before the date unless ordered to stop payment by a person claiming an interest in the account.

As amended in 1990.

§ 4–406. Customer's Duty to Discover and Report Unauthorized Signature or Alteration.

(a) A bank that sends or makes available to a customer a statement of account showing payment of items for the account shall either return or make available to the customer the items paid or provide information in the statement of account sufficient to allow the customer reasonably to identify the items paid. The statement of account provides sufficient information if the item is described by item number, amount, and date of payment.

(b) If the items are not returned to the customer, the person retaining the items shall either retain the items or, if the items are destroyed, maintain the capacity to furnish legible copies of the items until the expiration of seven years after receipt of the items. A customer may request an item from the bank that paid the item, and that bank must provide in a reasonable time either the item or, if the item has been destroyed or is not otherwise obtainable, a legible copy of the item.

(c) If a bank sends or makes available a statement of account or items pursuant to subsection (a), the customer must exercise reasonable promptness in examining the statement or the items to determine whether any payment was not authorized because of an alteration of an item or because a purported signature by or on behalf of the customer was not authorized. If, based on the statement or items provided, the customer should reasonably have discovered the unauthorized payment, the customer must promptly notify the bank of the relevant facts.

(d) If the bank proves that the customer failed, with respect to an item, to comply with the duties imposed on the customer by subsection (c), the customer is precluded from asserting against the bank:

(1) the customer's unauthorized signature or any alteration on the item, if the bank also proves that it suffered a loss by reason of the failure; and

(2) the customer's unauthorized signature or alteration by the same wrongdoer on any other item paid in good faith by the bank if the payment was made before the bank received notice from the customer of the unauthorized signature or alteration and after the customer had been afforded a reasonable period of time, not exceeding 30 days, in which to examine the item or statement of account and notify the bank.

(e) If subsection (d) applies and the customer proves that the bank failed to exercise ordinary care in paying the item and that the failure substantially contributed to loss, the loss is allocated between the customer precluded and the bank asserting the preclusion according to the extent to which the failure of the customer to comply with subsection (c) and the failure of the bank to exercise ordinary care contributed to the loss. If the customer proves that the bank did not pay the item in good faith, the preclusion under subsection (d) does not apply.

(f) Without regard to care or lack of care of either the customer or the bank, a customer who does not within one year after the statement or items are made available to the customer (subsection (a)) discover and report the customer's unauthorized signature on or any alteration on the item is precluded from asserting against the bank the unauthorized signature or alteration. If there is a preclusion under this subsection, the payor bank may not recover for breach or warranty under Section 4–208 with respect to the unauthorized signature or alteration to which the preclusion applies.

As amended in 1990.

§ 4–407. Payor Bank's Right to Subrogation on Improper Payment.

If a payor has paid an item over the order of the drawer or maker to stop payment, or after an account has been closed, or otherwise under circumstances giving a basis for objection by the drawer or maker, to prevent unjust enrichment and only to the extent necessary to prevent loss to the bank by reason of its payment of the item, the payor bank is subrogated to the rights

(1) of any holder in due course on the item against the drawer or maker;

(2) of the payee or any other holder of the item against the drawer or maker either on the item or under the transaction out of which the item arose; and

(3) of the drawer or maker against the payee or any other holder of the item with respect to the transaction out of which the item arose.

As amended in 1990.

PART 5 Collection of Documentary Drafts

§ 4–501. Handling of Documentary Drafts; Duty to Send for Presentment and to Notify Customer of Dishonor.

A bank that takes a documentary draft for collection shall present or send the draft and accompanying documents for presentment and, upon learning that the draft has not been paid or accepted in due course, shall seasonably notify its customer of the fact even though it may have discounted or bought the draft or extended credit available for withdrawal as of right.

As amended in 1990.

§ 4–502. Presentment of "On Arrival" Drafts.

If a draft or the relevant instructions require presentment "on arrival", "when goods arrive" or the like, the collecting bank need not present until in its judgment a reasonable time for arrival of the goods has expired. Refusal to pay or accept because the goods have not arrived is not dishonor; the bank must notify its transferor of the refusal but need not present the draft again until it is instructed to do so or learns of the arrival of the goods.

§ 4–503. Responsibility of Presenting Bank for Documents and Goods; Report of Reasons for Dishonor; Referee in Case of Need.

Unless otherwise instructed and except as provided in Article 5, a bank presenting a documentary draft:

(1) must deliver the documents to the drawee on acceptance of the draft if it is payable more than three days after presentment, otherwise, only on payment; and

(2) upon dishonor, either in the case of presentment for acceptance or presentment for payment, may seek and follow instructions from any referee in case of need designated in the draft or, if the presenting bank does not choose to utilize the referee's services, it must use diligence and good faith to ascertain the reason for dishonor, must notify its transferor of the dishonor and of the results of its effort to ascertain the reasons therefor, and must request instructions.

However, the presenting bank is under no obligation with respect to goods represented by the documents except to follow any reasonable instructions seasonably received; it has a right to reimbursement for any expense incurred in following instructions and to prepayment of or indemnity for those expenses.

As amended in 1990.

§ 4–504. Privilege of Presenting Bank to Deal With Goods; Security Interest for Expenses.

(a) A presenting bank that, following the dishonor of a documentary draft, has seasonably requested instructions but does not receive them within a reasonable time may store, sell, or otherwise deal with the goods in any reasonable manner.

(b) For its reasonable expenses incurred by action under subsection (a) the presenting bank has a lien upon the goods or their proceeds, which may be foreclosed in the same manner as an unpaid seller's lien.

As amended in 1990.

REVISED ARTICLE IX SECURED TRANSACTIONS

PART 1 General Provisions

[Subpart 1. Short Title, Definitions, and General Concepts]

§ 9–101. Short Title.

This article may be cited as Uniform Commercial Code—Secured Transactions.

§ 9–102. Definitions and Index of Definitions.

(a) In this article:

(1) "Accession" means goods that are physically united with other goods in such a manner that the identity of the original goods is not lost.

(2) "Account", except as used in "account for", means a right to payment of a monetary obligation, whether or not earned by performance, (i) for property that has been or is to be sold, leased, licensed, assigned, or otherwise disposed of, (ii) for services rendered or to be rendered, (iii) for a policy of insurance issued or to be issued, (iv) for a secondary obligation incurred or to be incurred, (v) for energy provided or to be provided, (vi) for the use or hire of a vessel under a charter or other contract, (vii) arising out of the use of a credit or charge card or information contained on or for use with the card, or (viii) as winnings in a lottery or other game of chance operated or sponsored by a State, governmental unit of a State, or person licensed or authorized to operate the game by a State or governmental unit of a State. The term includes health-care insurance receivables. The term does not include (i) rights to payment evidenced by chattel paper or an instrument, (ii) commercial tort claims, (iii) deposit accounts, (iv) investment property, (v) letter-of-credit rights or letters of credit, or (vi) rights to payment for money or funds advanced or

sold, other than rights arising out of the use of a credit or charge card or information contained on or for use with the card.

(3) "Account debtor" means a person obligated on an account, chattel paper, or general intangible. The term does not include persons obligated to pay a negotiable instrument, even if the instrument constitutes part of chattel paper.

(4) "Accounting", except as used in "accounting for", means a record:

(A) authenticated by a secured party;

(B) indicating the aggregate unpaid secured obligations as of a date not more than 35 days earlier or 35 days later than the date of the record; and

(C) identifying the components of the obligations in reasonable detail.

(5) "Agricultural lien" means an interest, other than a security interest, in farm products:

(A) which secures payment or performance of an obligation for:

(i) goods or services furnished in connection with a debtor's farming operation; or

(ii) rent on real property leased by a debtor in connection with its farming operation;

(B) which is created by statute in favor of a person that:

(i) in the ordinary course of its business furnished goods or services to a debtor in connection with a debtor's farming operation; or

(ii) leased real property to a debtor in connection with the debtor's farming operation; and

(C) whose effectiveness does not depend on the person's possession of the personal property.

(6) "As-extracted collateral" means:

(A) oil, gas, or other minerals that are subject to a security interest that:

(i) is created by a debtor having an interest in the minerals before extraction; and

(ii) attaches to the minerals as extracted; or

(B) accounts arising out of the sale at the wellhead or minehead of oil, gas, or other minerals in which the debtor had an interest before extraction.

(7) "Authenticate" means:

(A) to sign; or

(B) to execute or otherwise adopt a symbol, or encrypt or similarly process a record in whole or in part, with the present intent of the authenticating person to identify the person and adopt or accept a record.

(8) "Bank" means an organization that is engaged in the business of banking. The term includes savings banks, savings and loan associations, credit unions, and trust companies.

(9) "Cash proceeds" means proceeds that are money, checks, deposit accounts, or the like.

(10) "Certificate of title" means a certificate of title with respect to which a statute provides for the security interest in question to be indicated on the certificate as a condition or result of the security interest's obtaining priority over the rights of a lien creditor with respect to the collateral.

(11) "Chattel paper" means a record or records that evidence both a monetary obligation and a security interest in specific goods, a security interest in specific goods and software used in the goods, a security interest in specific goods and license of software used in the goods, a lease of specific goods, or a lease of specific goods and license of software used in the goods. In this paragraph, "monetary obligation" means a monetary obligation secured by the goods or owed under a lease of the goods and includes a monetary obligation with respect to software used in the goods. The term does not include (i) charters or other contracts involving the use or hire of a vessel or (ii) records that evidence a right to payment arising out of the use of a credit or charge card or information contained on or for use with the card. If a transaction is evidenced by records that include an instrument or series of instruments, the group of records taken together constitutes chattel paper.

(12) "Collateral" means the property subject to a security interest or agricultural lien. The term includes:

(A) proceeds to which a security interest attaches;

(B) accounts, chattel paper, payment intangibles, and promissory notes that have been sold; and

(C) goods that are the subject of a consignment.

(13) "Commercial tort claim" means a claim arising in tort with respect to which:

(A) the claimant is an organization; or

(B) the claimant is an individual and the claim:

(i) arose in the course of the claimant's business or profession; and

(ii) does not include damages arising out of personal injury to or the death of an individual.

(14) "Commodity account" means an account maintained by a commodity intermediary in which a commodity contract is carried for a commodity customer.

(15) "Commodity contract" means a commodity futures contract, an option on a commodity futures contract, a commodity option, or another contract if the contract or option is:

(A) traded on or subject to the rules of a board of trade that has been designated as a contract market for such a contract pursuant to federal commodities laws; or

(B) traded on a foreign commodity board of trade, exchange, or market, and is carried on the books of a commodity intermediary for a commodity customer.

(16) "Commodity customer" means a person for which a commodity intermediary carries a commodity contract on its books.

(17) "Commodity intermediary" means a person that:

(A) is registered as a futures commission merchant under federal commodities law; or

(B) in the ordinary course of its business provides clearance or settlement services for a board of trade that has been designated as a contract market pursuant to federal commodities law.

(18) "Communicate" means:

(A) to send a written or other tangible record;

(B) to transmit a record by any means agreed upon by the persons sending and receiving the record; or

(C) in the case of transmission of a record to or by a filing office, to transmit a record by any means prescribed by filing-office rule.

(19) "Consignee" means a merchant to which goods are delivered in a consignment.

(20) "Consignment" means a transaction, regardless of its form, in which a person delivers goods to a merchant for the purpose of sale and:

(A) the merchant:

(i) deals in goods of that kind under a name other than the name of the person making delivery;

(ii) is not an auctioneer; and

(iii) is not generally known by its creditors to be substantially engaged in selling the goods of others;

(B) with respect to each delivery, the aggregate value of the goods is $1,000 or more at the time of delivery;

(C) the goods are not consumer goods immediately before delivery; and

(D) the transaction does not create a security interest that secures an obligation.

(21) "Consignor" means a person that delivers goods to a consignee in a consignment.

(22) "Consumer debtor" means a debtor in a consumer transaction.

(23) "Consumer goods" means goods that are used or bought for use primarily for personal, family, or household purposes.

(24) "Consumer goods transaction" means a consumer transaction in which:

(A) an individual incurs an obligation primarily for personal, family, or household purposes; and

(B) a security interest in consumer goods secures the obligation.

(25) "Consumer obligor" means an obligor who is an individual and who incurred the obligation as part of a transaction entered into primarily for personal, family, or household purposes.

(26) "Consumer transaction" means a transaction in which (i) an individual incurs an obligation primarily for personal, family, or household purposes, (ii) a security interest secures the obligation, and (iii) the collateral is held or acquired primarily for personal, family, or household purposes. The term includes consumer-goods transactions.

(27) "Continuation statement" means an amendment of a financing statement which:

(A) identifies, by its file number, the initial financing statement to which it relates; and

(B) indicates that it is a continuation statement for, or that it is filed to continue the effectiveness of, the identified financing statement.

(28) "Debtor" means:

(A) a person having an interest, other than a security interest or other lien, in the collateral, whether or not the person is an obligor;

(B) a seller of accounts, chattel paper, payment intangibles, or promissory notes; or

(C) a consignee.

(29) "Deposit account" means a demand, time, savings, passbook, or similar account maintained with a bank. The term does not include investment property or accounts evidenced by an instrument.

(30) "Document" means a document of title or a receipt of the type described in Section 7–201(2).

(31) "Electronic chattel paper" means chattel paper evidenced by a record or records consisting of information stored in an electronic medium.

(32) "Encumbrance" means a right, other than an ownership interest, in real property. The term includes mortgages and other liens on real property.

(33) "Equipment" means goods other than inventory, farm products, or consumer goods.

(34) "Farm products" means goods, other than standing timber, with respect to which the debtor is engaged in a farming operation and which are:

(A) crops grown, growing, or to be grown, including:

(i) crops produced on trees, vines, and bushes; and

(ii) aquatic goods produced in aquacultural operations;

(B) livestock, born or unborn, including aquatic goods produced in aquacultural operations;

(C) supplies used or produced in a farming operation; or

(D) products of crops or livestock in their unmanufactured states.

(35) "Farming operation" means raising, cultivating, propagating, fattening, grazing, or any other farming, livestock, or aquacultural operation.

(36) "File number" means the number assigned to an initial financing statement pursuant to Section 9–519(a).

(37) "Filing office" means an office designated in Section 9–501 as the place to file a financing statement.

(38) "Filing-office rule" means a rule adopted pursuant to Section 9–526.

(39) "Financing statement" means a record or records composed of an initial financing statement and any filed record relating to the initial financing statement.

(40) "Fixture filing" means the filing of a financing statement covering goods that are or are to become fixtures and satisfying Section 9–502(a) and (b). The term includes the filing of a

financing statement covering goods of a transmitting utility which are or are to become fixtures.

(41) "Fixtures" means goods that have become so related to particular real property that an interest in them arises under real property law.

(42) "General intangible" means any personal property, including things in action, other than accounts, chattel paper, commercial tort claims, deposit accounts, documents, goods, instruments, investment property, letter-of-credit rights, letters of credit, money, and oil, gas, or other minerals before extraction. The term includes payment intangibles and software.

(43) "Good faith" means honesty in fact and the observance of reasonable commercial standards of fair dealing.

(44) "Goods" means all things that are movable when a security interest attaches. The term includes (i) fixtures, (ii) standing timber that is to be cut and removed under a conveyance or contract for sale, (iii) the unborn young of animals, (iv) crops grown, growing, or to be grown, even if the crops are produced on trees, vines, or bushes, and (v) manufactured homes. The term also includes a computer program embedded in goods and any supporting information provided in connection with a transaction relating to the program if (i) the program is associated with the goods in such a manner that it customarily is considered part of the goods, or (ii) by becoming the owner of the goods, a person acquires a right to use the program in connection with the goods. The term does not include a computer program embedded in goods that consist solely of the medium in which the program is embedded. The term also does not include accounts, chattel paper, commercial tort claims, deposit accounts, documents, general intangibles, instruments, investment property, letter-of-credit rights, letters of credit, money, or oil, gas, or other minerals before extraction.

(45) "Governmental unit" means a subdivision, agency, department, county, parish, municipality, or other unit of the government of the United States, a State, or a foreign country. The term includes an organization having a separate corporate existence if the organization is eligible to issue debt on which interest is exempt from income taxation under the laws of the United States.

(46) "Health-care-insurance receivable" means an interest in or claim under a policy of insurance which is a right to payment of a monetary obligation for health-care goods or servies provided.

(47) "Instrument" means a negotiable instrument or any other writing that evidences a right to the payment of a monetary obligation, is not itself a security agreement or lease, and is of a type that in ordinary course of business is transferred by delivery with any necessary indorsement or assignment. The term does not include (i) investment property, (ii) letters of credit, or (iii) writings that evidence a right to payment arising out of the use of a credit or charge card or information contained on or for use with the card.

(48) "Inventory" means goods, other than farm products, which:

(A) are leased by a person as lessor;

(B) are held by a person for sale or lease or to be furnished under a contract of service;

(C) are furnished by a person under a contract of service; or

(D) consist of raw materials, work in process, or materials used or consumed in a business.

(49) "Investment property" means a security, whether certificated or uncertificated, security entitlement, securities account, commodity contract, or commodity account.

(50) "Jurisdiction of organization", with respect to a registered organization, means the jurisdiction under whose law the organization is organized.

(51) "Letter-of-credit right" means a right to payment or performance under a letter of credit, whether or not the beneficiary has demanded or is at the time entitled to demand payment or performance. The term does not include the right of a beneficiary to demand payment or performance under a letter of credit.

(52) "Lien creditor" means:

(A) a creditor that has acquired a lien on the property involved by attachment, levy, or the like;

(B) an assignee for benefit of creditors from the time of assignment;

(C) a trustee in bankruptcy from the date of the filing of the petition; or

(D) a receiver in equity from the time of appointment.

(53) "Manufactured home" means a structure, transportable in one or more sections, which, in the traveling mode, is eight body feet or more in width or 40 body feet or more in length, or, when erected on site, is 320 or more square feet, and which is built on a permanent chassis and designed to be used as a dwelling with or without a permanent foundation when connected to the required utilities, and includes the plumbing, heating, air-conditioning, and electrical systems contained therein. The term includes any structure that meets all of the requirements of this paragraph except the size requirements and with respect to which the manufacturer voluntarily files a certification required by the United States Secretary of Housing and Urban Development and complies with the standards established under Title 42 of the United States Code.

(54) "Manufactured-home transaction" means a secured transaction:

(A) that creates a purchase-money security interest in a manufactured home, other than a manufactured home held as inventory; or

(B) in which a manufactured home, other than a manufactured home held as inventory, is the primary collateral.

(55) "Mortgage" means a consensual interest in real property, including fixtures, which secures payment or performance of an obligation.

(56) "New debtor" means a person that becomes bound as debtor under Section 9–203(d) by a security agreement previously entered into by another person.

(57) "New value" means (i) money, (ii) money's worth in property, services, or new credit, or (iii) release by a transferee of an interest in property previously transferred to the transferee.

The term does not include an obligation substituted for another obligation.

(58) "Noncash proceeds" means proceeds other than cash proceeds.

(59) "Obligor" means a person that, with respect to an obligation secured by a security interest in or an agricultural lien on the collateral, (i) owes payment or other performance of the obligation, (ii) has provided property other than the collateral to secure payment or other performance of the obligation, or (iii) is otherwise accountable in whole or in part for payment or other performance of the obligation. The term does not include issuers or nominated persons under a letter of credit.

(60) "Original debtor", except as used in Section 9–310(c), means a person that, as debtor, entered into a security agreement to which a new debtor has become bound under Section 9–203(d).

(61) "Payment intangible" means a general intangible under which the account debtor's principal obligation is a monetary obligation.

(62) "Person related to", with respect to an individual, means:

(A) the spouse of the individual;

(B) a brother, brother-in-law, sister, or sister-in-law of the individual;

(C) an ancestor or lineal descendant of the individual or the individual's spouse; or

(D) any other relative, by blood or marriage, of the individual or the individual's spouse who shares the same home with the individual.

(63) "Person related to", with respect to an organization, means:

(A) a person directly or indirectly controlling, controlled by, or under common control with the organization;

(B) an officer or director of, or a person performing similar functions with respect to, the organization;

(C) an officer or director of, or a person performing similar functions with respect to, a person described in subparagraph (A);

(D) the spouse of an individual described in subparagraph (A), (B), or (C); or

(E) an individual who is related by blood or marriage to an individual described in subparagraph (A), (B), (C), or (D) and shares the same home with the individual.

(64) "Proceeds", except as used in Section 9–609(b), means the following property:

(A) whatever is acquired upon the sale, lease, license, exchange, or other disposition of collateral;

(B) whatever is collected on, or distributed on account of, collateral;

(C) rights arising out of collateral;

(D) to the extent of the value of collateral, claims arising out of the loss, nonconformity, or interference with the use of, defects or infringement of rights in, or damage to, the collateral; or (E) to the extent of the value of collateral and to the extent payable to the debtor or the secured party, insurance payable by reason of the loss or nonconformity of, defects or infringement of rights in, or damage to, the collateral.

(65) "Promissory note" means an instrument that evidences a promise to pay a monetary obligation, does not evidence an order to pay, and does not contain an acknowledgment by a bank that the bank has received for deposit a sum of money or funds.

(66) "Proposal" means a record authenticated by a secured party which includes the terms on which the secured party is willing to accept collateral in full or partial satisfaction of the obligation it secures pursuant to Sections 9–620, 9–621, and 9–622.

(67) "Public-finance transaction" means a secured transaction in connection with which:

(A) debt securities are issued;

(B) all or a portion of the securities issued have an initial stated maturity of at least 20 years; and

(C) the debtor, obligor, secured party, account debtor or other person obligated on collateral, assignor or assignee of a secured obligation, or assignor or assignee of a security interest is a State or a governmental unit of a State.

(68) "Pursuant to commitment", with respect to an advance made or other value given by a secured party, means pursuant to the secured party's obligation, whether or not a subsequent event of default or other event not within the secured party's control has relieved or may relieve the secured party from its obligation.

(69) "Record", except as used in "for record", "of record", "record or legal title", and "record owner", means information that is inscribed on a tangible medium or which is stored in an electronic or other medium and is retrievable in perceivable form.

(70) "Registered organization" means an organization organized solely under the law of a single State or the United States and as to which the State or the United States must maintain a public record showing the organization to have been organized.

(71) "Secondary obligor" means an obligor to the extent that:

(A) the obligor's obligation is secondary; or

(B) the obligor has a right of recourse with respect to an obligation secured by collateral against the debtor, another obligor, or property of either.

(72) "Secured party" means:

(A) a person in whose favor a security interest is created or provided for under a security agreement, whether or not any obligation to be secured is outstanding;

(B) a person that holds an agricultural lien;

(C) a consignor;

(D) a person to which accounts, chattel paper, payment intangibles, or promissory notes have been sold;

(E) a trustee, indenture trustee, agent, collateral agent, or other representative in whose favor a security interest or agricultural lien is created or provided for; or

(F) a person that holds a security interest arising under Section 2–401, 2–505, 2–711(3), 2A–508(5), 4–210, or 5–118.

(73) "Security agreement" means an agreement that creates or provides for a security interest.

(74) "Send", in connection with a record or notification, means:

(A) to deposit in the mail, deliver for transmission, or transmit by any other usual means of communication, with postage or cost of transmission provided for, addressed to any address reasonable under the circumstances; or

(B) to cause the record or notification to be received within the timce that it would have been received if properly sent under subparagraph (A).

(75) "Software" means a computer program and any supporting information provided in connection with a transaction relating to the program. The term does not include a computer program that is included in the definition of goods.

(76) "State" means a State of the United States, the District of Columbia, Puerto Rico, the United States Virgin Islands, or any territory or insular possession subject to the jurisdiction of the United States.

(77) "Supporting obligation" means a letter-of-credit right or secondary obligation that supports the payment or performance of an account, chattel paper, a document, a general intangible, an instrument, or investment property.

(78) "Tangible chattel paper" means chattel paper evidenced by a record or records consisting of information that is inscribed on a tangible medium.

(79) "Termination statement" means an amendment of a financing statement which:

(A) identifies, by its file number, the initial financing statement to which it relates; and

(B) indicates either that it is a termination statement or that the identified financing statement is no longer effective.

(80) "Transmitting utility" means a person primarily engaged in the business of:

(A) operating a railroad, subway, street railway, or trolley bus;

(B) transmitting communications electrically, electromagnetically, or by light;

(C) transmitting goods by pipeline or sewer; or

(D) transmitting or producing and transmitting electricity, steam, gas, or water.

(b) The following definitions in other articles apply to this article:

"Applicant." Section 5–102

"Beneficiary." Section 5–102

"Broker." Section 8–102

"Certificated security." Section 8–102

"Check." Section 3–104

"Clearing corporation." Section 8–102

"Contract for sale." Section 2–106

"Customer." Section 4–104

"Entitlement holder." Section 8–102

"Financial asset." Section 8–102

"Holder in due course." Section 3–302

"Issuer" (with respect to a letter of credit or letter-of-credit right). Section 5–102

"Issuer" (with respect to a security). Section 8–201

"Lease." Section 2A–103

"Lease agreement." Section 2A–103

"Lease contract." Section 2A–103

"Leasehold interest." Section 2A–103

"Lessee." Section 2A–103

"Lessee in ordinary course of business." Section 2A–103

"Lessor." Section 2A–103

"Lessor's residual interest." Section 2A–103

"Letter of credit." Section 5–102

"Merchant." Section 2–104

"Negotiable instrument." Section 3–104

"Nominated person." Section 5–102

"Note." Section 3–104

"Proceeds of a letter of credit." Section 5–114

"Prove." Section 3–103

"Sale." Section 2–106

"Securities account." Section 8–501

"Securities intermediary." Section 8–102

"Security." Section 8–102

"Security certificate." Section 8–102

"Security entitlement." Section 8–102

"Uncertificated security." Section 8–102

(c) Article 1 contains general definitions and principles of construction and interpretation applicable throughout this article.

Amended in 1999 and 2000.

§ 9–103. Purchase-Money Security Interest; Application of Payments; Burden of Establishing.

(a) In this section:

(1) "purchase-money collateral" means goods or software that secures a purchase-money obligation incurred with respect to that collateral; and

(2) "purchase-money obligation" means an obligation of an obligor incurred as all or part of the price of the collateral or for value given to enable the debtor to acquire rights in or the use of the collateral if the value is in fact so used.

(b) A security interest in goods is a purchase-money security interest:

(1) to the extent that the goods are purchase-money collateral with respect to that security interest;

(2) if the security interest is in inventory that is or was purchase-money collateral, also to the extent that the security interest secures a purchase-money obligation incurred with respect to other inventory in which the secured party holds or held a purchase-money security interest; and

(3) also to the extent that the security interest secures a purchase-money obligation incurred with respect to software in which the secured party holds or held a purchase-money security interest.

(c) A security interest in software is a purchase-money security interest to the extent that the security interest also secures a purchase-money obligation incurred with respect to goods in which the secured party holds or held a purchase-money security interest if:

(1) the debtor acquired its interest in the software in an integrated transaction in which it acquired an interest in the goods; and

(2) the debtor acquired its interest in the software for the principal purpose of using the software in the goods.

(d) The security interest of a consignor in goods that are the subject of a consignment is a purchase-money security interest in inventory.

(e) In a transaction other than a consumer-goods transaction, if the extent to which a security interest is a purchase-money security interest depends on the application of a payment to a particular obligation, the payment must be applied:

(1) in accordance with any reasonable method of application to which the parties agree;

(2) in the absence of the parties' agreement to a reasonable method, in accordance with any intention of the obligor manifested at or before the time of payment; or

(3) in the absence of an agreement to a reasonable method and a timely manifestation of the obligor's intention, in the following order:

(A) to obligations that are not secured; and

(B) if more than one obligation is secured, to obligations secured by purchase-money security interests in the order in which those obligations were incurred.

(f) In a transaction other than a consumer-goods transaction, a purchase-money security interest does not lose its status as such, even if:

(1) the purchase-money collateral also secures an obligation that is not a purchase-money obligation;

(2) collateral that is not purchase-money collateral also secures the purchase-money obligation; or

(3) the purchase-money obligation has been renewed, refinanced, consolidated, or restructured.

(g) In a transaction other than a consumer-goods transaction, a secured party claiming a purchase-money security interest has the burden of establishing the extent to which the security interest is a purchase-money security interest.

(h) The limitation of the rules in subsections (e), (f), and (g) to transactions other than consumer-goods transactions is intended to leave to the court the determination of the proper rules in consumer-goods transactions. The court may not infer from that limitation the nature of the proper rule in consumer-goods transactions and may continue to apply established approaches.

§ 9–104. Control of Deposit Account.

(a) A secured party has control of a deposit account if:

(1) the secured party is the bank with which the deposit account is maintained;

(2) the debtor, secured party, and bank have agreed in an authenticated record that the bank will comply with instructions originated by the secured party directing disposition of the funds in the deposit account without further consent by the debtor; or

(3) the secured party becomes the bank's customer with respect to the deposit account.

(b) A secured party that has satisfied subsection (a) has control, even if the debtor retains the right to direct the disposition of funds from the deposit account.

§ 9–105. Control of Electronic Chattel Paper.

A secured party has control of electronic chattel paper if the record or records comprising the chattel paper are created, stored, and assigned in such a manner that:

(1) a single authoritative copy of the record or records exists which is unique, identifiable and, except as otherwise provided in paragraphs (4), (5), and (6), unalterable;

(2) the authoritative copy identifies the secured party as the assignee of the record or records;

(3) the authoritative copy is communicated to and maintained by the secured party or its designated custodian;

(4) copies or revisions that add or change an identified assignee of the authoritative copy can be made only with the participation of the secured party;

(5) each copy of the authoritative copy and any copy of a copy is readily identifiable as a copy that is not the authoritative copy; and

(6) any revision of the authoritative copy is readily identifiable as an authorized or unauthorized revision.

§ 9–106. Control of Investment Property.

(a) A person has control of a certificated security, uncertificated security, or security entitlement as provided in Section 8–106.

(b) A secured party has control of a commodity contract if:

(1) the secured party is the commodity intermediary with which the commodity contract is carried; or

(2) the commodity customer, secured party, and commodity intermediary have agreed that the commodity intermediary will apply any value distributed on account of the commodity contract as directed by the secured party without further consent by the commodity customer.

(c) A secured party having control of all security entitlements or commodity contracts carried in a securities account or commodity account has control over the securities account or commodity account.

§ 9–107. Control of Letter-of-Credit Right.

A secured party has control of a letter-of-credit right to the extent of any right to payment or performance by the issuer or any nominated person if the issuer or nominated person has consented to an assignment of proceeds of the letter of credit under Section 5–114(c) or otherwise applicable law or practice.

§ 9–108. Sufficiency of Description.

(a) Except as otherwise provided in subsections (c), (d), and (e), a description of personal or real property is sufficient, whether or not it is specific, if it reasonably identifies what is described.

(b) Except as otherwise provided in subsection (d), a description of collateral reasonably identifies the collateral if it identifies the collateral by:

(1) specific listing;

(2) category;

(3) except as otherwise provided in subsection (e), a type of collateral defined in [the Uniform Commercial Code];

(4) quantity;

(5) computational or allocational formula or procedure; or

(6) except as otherwise provided in subsection (c), any other method, if the identity of the collateral is objectively determinable.

(c) A description of collateral as "all the debtor's assets" or "all the debtor's personal property" or using words of similar import does not reasonably identify the collateral.

(d) Except as otherwise provided in subsection (e), a description of a security entitlement, securities account, or commodity account is sufficient if it describes:

(1) the collateral by those terms or as investment property; or

(2) the underlying financial asset or commodity contract.

(e) A description only by type of collateral defined in [the Uniform Commercial Code] is an insufficient description of:

(1) a commercial tort claim; or

(2) in a consumer transaction, consumer goods, a security entitlement, a securities account, or a commodity account.

[Subpart 2. Applicability of Article]

§ 9–109. Scope.

(a) Except as otherwise provided in subsections (c) and (d), this article applies to:

(1) a transaction, regardless of its form, that creates a security interest in personal property or fixtures by contract;

(2) an agricultural lien;

(3) a sale of accounts, chattel paper, payment intangibles, or promissory notes;

(4) a consignment;

(5) a security interest arising under Section 2–401, 2–505, 2–711 (3), or 2A–508(5), as provided in Section 9–110; and

(6) a security interest arising under Section 4–210 or 5–118.

(b) The application of this article to a security interest in a secured obligation is not affected by the fact that the obligation is itself secured by a transaction or interest to which this article does not apply.

(c) This article does not apply to the extent that:

(1) a statute, regulation, or treaty of the United States preempts this article;

(2) another statute of this State expressly governs the creation, perfection, priority, or enforcement of a security interest created by this State or a governmental unit of this State;

(3) a statute of another State, a foreign country, or a governmental unit of another State or a foreign country, other than a statute generally applicable to security interests, expressly governs creation, perfection, priority, or enforcement of a security interest created by the State, country, or governmental unit; or

(4) the rights of a transferee beneficiary or nominated person under a letter of credit are independent and superior under Section 5–114.

(d) This article does not apply to:

(1) a landlord's lien, other than an agricultural lien;

(2) a lien, other than an agricultural lien, given by statute or other rule of law for services or materials, but Section 9–333 applies with respect to priority of the lien;

(3) an assignment of a claim for wages, salary, or other compensation of an employee;

(4) a sale of accounts, chattel paper, payment intangibles, or promissory notes as part of a sale of the business out of which they arose;

(5) an assignment of accounts, chattel paper, payment intangibles, or promissory notes which is for the purpose of collection only;

(6) an assignment of a right to payment under a contract to an assignee that is also obligated to perform under the contract;

(7) an assignment of a single account, payment intangible, or promissory note to an assignee in full or partial satisfaction of a preexisting indebtedness;

(8) a transfer of an interest in or an assignment of a claim under a policy of insurance, other than an assignment by or to a health-care provider of a health-care-insurance receivable and any subsequent assignment of the right to payment, but Sections 9–315 and 9–322 apply with respect to proceeds and priorities in proceeds;

(9) an assignment of a right represented by a judgment, other than a judgment taken on a right to payment that was collateral;

(10) a right of recoupment or set-off, but:

(A) Section 9–340 applies with respect to the effectiveness of rights of recoupment or set-off against deposit accounts; and

(B) Section 9–404 applies with respect to defenses or claims of an account debtor;

(11) the creation or transfer of an interest in or lien on real property, including a lease or rents thereunder, except to the extent that provision is made for:

(A) liens on real property in Sections 9–203 and 9–308;

(B) fixtures in Section 9–334;

(C) fixture filings in Sections 9–501, 9–502, 9–512, 9–516, and 9–519; and

(D) security agreements covering personal and real property in Section 9–604;

(12) an assignment of a claim arising in tort, other than a commercial tort claim, but Sections 9–315 and 9–322 apply with respect to proceeds and priorities in proceeds; or

(13) an assignment of a deposit account in a consumer transaction, but Sections 9–315 and 9–322 apply with respect to proceeds and priorities in proceeds.

§ 9–110. Security Interests Arising under Article 2 or 2A.

A security interest arising under Section 2–401, 2–505, 2–711(3), or 2A–508(5) is subject to this article. However, until the debtor obtains possession of the goods:

(1) the security interest is enforceable, even if Section 9–203(b)(3) has not been satisfied;

(2) filing is not required to perfect the security interest;

(3) the rights of the secured party after default by the debtor are governed by Article 2 or 2A; and

(4) the security interest has priority over a conflicting security interest created by the debtor.

PART 2 Effectiveness of Security Agreement; Attachment of Security Interest; Rights of Parties to Security Agreement

[Subpart 1. Effectiveness and Attachment]

§ 9–201. General Effectiveness of Security Agreement.

(a) Except as otherwise provided in [the Uniform Commercial Code], a security agreement is effective according to its terms between the parties, against purchasers of the collateral, and against creditors.

(b) A transaction subject to this article is subject to any applicable rule of law which establishes a different rule for consumers and [insert reference to (i) any other statute or regulation that regulates the rates, charges, agreements, and practices for loans, credit sales, or other extensions of credit and (ii) any consumer-protection statute or regulation].

(c) In case of conflict between this article and a rule of law, statute, or regulation described in subsection (b), the rule of law, statute, or regulation controls. Failure to comply with a statute or regulation described in subsection (b) has only the effect the statute or regulation specifies.

(d) This article does not:

(1) validate any rate, charge, agreement, or practice that violates a rule of law, statute, or regulation described in subsection (b); or

(2) extend the application of the rule of law, statute, or regulation to a transaction not otherwise subject to it.

§ 9–202. Title to Collateral Immaterial.

Except as otherwise provided with respect to consignments or sales of accounts, chattel paper, payment intangibles, or promissory notes, the provisions of this article with regard to rights and obligations apply whether title to collateral is in the secured party or the debtor.

§ 9–203. Attachment and Enforceability of Security Interest; Proceeds; Supporting Obligations; Formal Requisites.

(a) A security interest attaches to collateral when it becomes enforceable against the debtor with respect to the collateral, unless an agreement expressly postpones the time of attachment.

(b) Except as otherwise provided in subsections (c) through (i), a security interest is enforceable against the debtor and third parties with respect to the collateral only if:

(1) value has been given;

(2) the debtor has rights in the collateral or the power to transfer rights in the collateral to a secured party; and

(3) one of the following conditions is met:

(A) the debtor has authenticated a security agreement that provides a description of the collateral and, if the security interest covers timber to be cut, a description of the land concerned;

(B) the collateral is not a certificated security and is in the possession of the secured party under Section 9–313 pursuant to the debtor's security agreement;

(C) the collateral is a certificated security in registered form and the security certificate has been delivered to the secured party under Section 8–301 pursuant to the debtor's security agreement; or

(D) the collateral is deposit accounts, electronic chattel paper, investment property, or letter-of-credit rights, and the secured party has control under Section 9–104, 9–105, 9–106, or 9–107 pursuant to the debtor's security agreement.

(c) Subsection (b) is subject to Section 4–210 on the security interest of a collecting bank, Section 5–118 on the security interest of a letter-of-credit issuer or nominated person, Section 9–110 on a security interest arising under Article 2 or 2A, and Section 9–206 on security interests in investment property.

(d) A person becomes bound as debtor by a security agreement entered into by another person if, by operation of law other than this article or by contract:

(1) the security agreement becomes effective to create a security interest in the person's property; or

(2) the person becomes generally obligated for the obligations of the other person, including the obligation secured under the security agreement, and acquires or succeeds to all or substantially all of the assets of the other person.

(e) If a new debtor becomes bound as debtor by a security agreement entered into by another person:

(1) the agreement satisfies subsection (b)(3) with respect to existing or after-acquired property of the new debtor to the extent the property is described in the agreement; and

(2) another agreement is not necessary to make a security interest in the property enforceable.

(f) The attachment of a security interest in collateral gives the secured party the rights to proceeds provided by Section 9–315 and is also attachment of a security interest in a supporting obligation for the collateral.

(g) The attachment of a security interest in a right to payment or performance secured by a security interest or other lien on personal or real property is also attachment of a security interest in the security interest, mortgage, or other lien.

(h) The attachment of a security interest in a securities account is also attachment of a security interest in the security entitlements carried in the securities account.

(i) The attachment of a security interest in a commodity account is also attachment of a security interest in the commodity contracts carried in the commodity account.

§ 9–204. After-Acquired Property; Future Advances.

(a) Except as otherwise provided in subsection (b), a security agreement may create or provide for a security interest in after-acquired collateral.

(b) A security interest does not attach under a term constituting an after-acquired property clause to:

(1) consumer goods, other than an accession when given as additional security, unless the debtor acquires rights in them within 10 days after the secured party gives value; or

(2) a commercial tort claim.

(c) A security agreement may provide that collateral secures, or that accounts, chattel paper, payment intangibles, or promissory notes are sold in connection with, future advances or other value, whether or not the advances or value are given pursuant to commitment.

§ 9–205. Use or Disposition of Collateral Permissible.

(a) A security interest is not invalid or fraudulent against creditors solely because:

(1) the debtor has the right or ability to:

(A) use, commingle, or dispose of all or part of the collateral, including returned or repossessed goods;

(B) collect, compromise, enforce, or otherwise deal with collateral;

(C) accept the return of collateral or make repossessions; or

(D) use, commingle, or dispose of proceeds; or

(2) the secured party fails to require the debtor to account for proceeds or replace collateral.

(b) This section does not relax the requirements of possession if attachment, perfection, or enforcement of a security interest depends upon possession of the collateral by the secured party.

§ 9–206. Security Interest Arising in Purchase or Delivery of Financial Asset.

(a) A security interest in favor of a securities intermediary attaches to a person's security entitlement if:

(1) the person buys a financial asset through the securities intermediary in a transaction in which the person is obligated to

pay the purchase price to the securities intermediary at the time of the purchase; and

(2) the securities intermediary credits the financial asset to the buyer's securities account before the buyer pays the securities intermediary.

(b) The security interest described in subsection (a) secures the person's obligation to pay for the financial asset.

(c) A security interest in favor of a person that delivers a certificated security or other financial asset represented by a writing attaches to the security or other financial asset if:

(1) the security or other financial asset:

(A) in the ordinary course of business is transferred by delivery with any necessary indorsement or assignment; and

(B) is delivered under an agreement between persons in the business of dealing with such securities or financial assets; and

(2) the agreement calls for delivery against payment.

(d) The security interest described in subsection (c) secures the obligation to make payment for the delivery.

[Subpart 2. Rights and Duties]

§ 9–207. Rights and Duties of Secured Party Having Possession or Control of Collateral.

(a) Except as otherwise provided in subsection (d), a secured party shall use reasonable care in the custody and preservation of collateral in the secured party's possession. In the case of chattel paper or an instrument, reasonable care includes taking necessary steps to preserve rights against prior parties unless otherwise agreed.

(b) Except as otherwise provided in subsection (d), if a secured party has possession of collateral:

(1) reasonable expenses, including the cost of insurance and payment of taxes or other charges, incurred in the custody, preservation, use, or operation of the collateral are chargeable to the debtor and are secured by the collateral;

(2) the risk of accidental loss or damage is on the debtor to the extent of a deficiency in any effective insurance coverage;

(3) the secured party shall keep the collateral identifiable, but fungible collateral may be commingled; and

(4) the secured party may use or operate the collateral:

(A) for the purpose of preserving the collateral or its value;

(B) as permitted by an order of a court having competent jurisdiction; or

(C) except in the case of consumer goods, in the manner and to the extent agreed by the debtor.

(c) Except as otherwise provided in subsection (d), a secured party having possession of collateral or control of collateral under Section 9–104, 9–105, 9–106, or 9–107:

(1) may hold as additional security any proceeds, except money or funds, received from the collateral;

(2) shall apply money or funds received from the collateral to reduce the secured obligation, unless remitted to the debtor; and

(3) may create a security interest in the collateral.

(d) If the secured party is a buyer of accounts, chattel paper, payment intangibles, or promissory notes or a consignor:

(1) subsection (a) does not apply unless the secured party is entitled under an agreement:

(A) to charge back uncollected collateral; or

(B) otherwise to full or limited recourse against the debtor or a secondary obligor based on the nonpayment or other default of an account debtor or other obligor on the collateral; and

(2) subsections (b) and (c) do not apply.

§ 9–208. Additional Duties of Secured Party Having Control of Collateral.

(a) This section applies to cases in which there is no outstanding secured obligation and the secured party is not committed to make advances, incur obligations, or otherwise give value.

(b) Within 10 days after receiving an authenticated demand by the debtor:

(1) a secured party having control of a deposit account under Section 9–104(a)(2) shall send to the bank with which the deposit account is maintained an authenticated statement that releases the bank from any further obligation to comply with instructions originated by the secured party;

(2) a secured party having control of a deposit account under Section 9–104(a)(3) shall:

(A) pay the debtor the balance on deposit in the deposit account; or

(B) transfer the balance on deposit into a deposit account in the debtor's name;

(3) a secured party, other than a buyer, having control of electronic chattel paper under Section 9–105 shall:

(A) communicate the authoritative copy of the electronic chattel paper to the debtor or its designated custodian;

(B) if the debtor designates a custodian that is the designated custodian with which the authoritative copy of the electronic chattel paper is maintained for the secured party, communicate to the custodian an authenticated record releasing the designated custodian from any further obligation to comply with instructions originated by the secured party and instructing the custodian to comply with instructions originated by the debtor; and

(C) take appropriate action to enable the debtor or its designated custodian to make copies of or revisions to the authoritative copy which add or change an identified assignee of the authoritative copy without the consent of the secured party;

(4) a secured party having control of investment property under Section 8–106(d)(2) or 9–106(b) shall send to the securities intermediary or commodity intermediary with which the security entitlement or commodity contract is maintained an authenticated record that releases the securities intermediary or commodity intermediary from any further obligation to comply with entitlement orders or directions originated by the secured party; and

(5) a secured party having control of a letter-of-credit right under Section 9–107 shall send to each person having an unfulfilled obligation to pay or deliver proceeds of the letter of credit to the secured party an authenticated release from any further obligation to pay or deliver proceeds of the letter of credit to the secured party.

§ 9-209. Duties of Secured Party If Account Debtor Has Been Notified of Assignment.

(a) Except as otherwise provided in subsection (c), this section applies if:

(1) there is no outstanding secured obligation; and

(2) the secured party is not committed to make advances, incur obligations, or otherwise give value.

(b) Within 10 days after receiving an authenticated demand by the debtor, a secured party shall send to an account debtor that has received notification of an assignment to the secured party as assignee under Section 9–406(a) an authenticated record that releases the account debtor from any further obligation to the secured party.

(c) This section does not apply to an assignment constituting the sale of an account, chattel paper, or payment intangible.

§ 9-210. Request for Accounting; Request Regarding List of Collateral or Statement of Account.

(a) In this section:

(1) "Request" means a record of a type described in paragraph (2), (3), or (4).

(2) "Request for an accounting" means a record authenticated by a debtor requesting that the recipient provide an accounting of the unpaid obligations secured by collateral and reasonably identifying the transaction or relationship that is the subject of the request.

(3) "Request regarding a list of collateral" means a record authenticated by a debtor requesting that the recipient approve or correct a list of what the debtor believes to be the collateral securing an obligation and reasonably identifying the transaction or relationship that is the subject of the request.

(4) "Request regarding a statement of account" means a record authenticated by a debtor requesting that the recipient approve or correct a statement indicating what the debtor believes to be the aggregate amount of unpaid obligations secured by collateral as of a specified date and reasonably identifying the transaction or relationship that is the subject of the request.

(b) Subject to subsections (c), (d), (e), and (f), a secured party, other than a buyer of accounts, chattel paper, payment intangibles, or promissory notes or a consignor, shall comply with a request within 14 days after receipt:

(1) in the case of a request for an accounting, by authenticating and sending to the debtor an accounting; and

(2) in the case of a request regarding a list of collateral or a request regarding a statement of account, by authenticating and sending to the debtor an approval or correction.

(c) A secured party that claims a security interest in all of a particular type of collateral owned by the debtor may comply with a request regarding a list of collateral by sending to the debtor an authenticated record including a statement to that effect within 14 days after receipt.

(d) A person that receives a request regarding a list of collateral, claims no interest in the collateral when it receives the request, and claimed an interest in the collateral at an earlier time shall comply with the request within 14 days after receipt by sending to the debtor an authenticated record:

(1) disclaiming any interest in the collateral; and

(2) if known to the recipient, providing the name and mailing address of any assignee of or successor to the recipient's interest in the collateral.

(e) A person that receives a request for an accounting or a request regarding a statement of account, claims no interest in the obligations when it receives the request, and claimed an interest in the obligations at an earlier time shall comply with the request within 14 days after receipt by sending to the debtor an authenticated record:

(1) disclaiming any interest in the obligations; and

(2) if known to the recipient, providing the name and mailing address of any assignee of or successor to the recipient's interest in the obligations.

(f) A debtor is entitled without charge to one response to a request under this section during any six-month period. The secured party may require payment of a charge not exceeding $25 for each additional response.

As amended in 1999.

PART 3 Perfection and Priority

[Subpart 1. Law Governing Perfection and Priority]

§ 9–301. Law Governing Perfection and Priority of Security Interests.

Except as otherwise provided in Sections 9–303 through 9–306, the following rules determine the law governing perfection, the effect of perfection or nonperfection, and the priority of a security interest in collateral:

(1) Except as otherwise provided in this section, while a debtor is located in a jurisdiction, the local law of that jurisdiction governs perfection, the effect of perfection or nonperfection, and the priority of a security interest in collateral.

(2) While collateral is located in a jurisdiction, the local law of that jurisdiction governs perfection, the effect of perfection or nonperfection, and the priority of a possessory security interest in that collateral.

(3) Except as otherwise provided in paragraph (4), while negotiable documents, goods, instruments, money, or tangible chattel paper is located in a jurisdiction, the local law of that jurisdiction governs:

(A) perfection of a security interest in the goods by filing a fixture filing;

(B) perfection of a security interest in timber to be cut; and

(C) the effect of perfection or nonperfection and the priority of a nonpossessory security interest in the collateral.

(4) The local law of the jurisdiction in which the wellhead or minehead is located governs perfection, the effect of perfection or nonperfection, and the priority of a security interest in as-extracted collateral.

§ 9–302. Law Governing Perfection and Priority of Agricultural Liens.

While farm products are located in a jurisdiction, the local law of that jurisdiction governs perfection, the effect of perfection or nonperfection, and the priority of an agricultural lien on the farm products.

§ 9–303. Law Governing Perfection and Priority of Security Interests in Goods Covered by a Certificate of Title.

(a) This section applies to goods covered by a certificate of title, even if there is no other relationship between the jurisdiction under whose certificate of title the goods are covered and the goods or the debtor.

(b) Goods become covered by a certificate of title when a valid application for the certificate of title and the applicable fee are delivered to the appropriate authority. Goods cease to be covered by a certificate of title at the earlier of the time the certificate of title ceases to be effective under the law of the issuing jurisdiction or the time the goods become covered subsequently by a certificate of title issued by another jurisdiction.

(c) The local law of the jurisdiction under whose certificate of title the goods are covered governs perfection, the effect of perfection or nonperfection, and the priority of a security interest in goods covered by a certificate of title from the time the goods become covered by the certificate of title until the goods cease to be covered by the certificate of title.

§ 9–304. Law Governing Perfection and Priority of Security Interests in Deposit Accounts.

(a) The local law of a bank's jurisdiction governs perfection, the effect of perfection or nonperfection, and the priority of a security interest in a deposit account maintained with that bank.

(b) The following rules determine a bank's jurisdiction for purposes of this part:

(1) If an agreement between the bank and the debtor governing the deposit account expressly provides that a particular jurisdiction is the bank's jurisdiction for purposes of this part, this article, or [the Uniform Commercial Code], that jurisdiction is the bank's jurisdiction.

(2) If paragraph (1) does not apply and an agreement between the bank and its customer governing the deposit account expressly provides that the agreement is governed by the law of a particular jurisdiction, that jurisdiction is the bank's jurisdiction.

(3) If neither paragraph (1) nor paragraph (2) applies and an agreement between the bank and its customer governing the deposit account expressly provides that the deposit account is maintained at an office in a particular jurisdiction, that jurisdiction is the bank's jurisdiction.

(4) If none of the preceding paragraphs applies, the bank's jurisdiction is the jurisdiction in which the office identified in an account statement as the office serving the customer's account is located.

(5) If none of the preceding paragraphs applies, the bank's jurisdiction is the jurisdiction in which the chief executive office of the bank is located.

§ 9–305. Law Governing Perfection and Priority of Security Interests in Investment Property.

(a) Except as otherwise provided in subsection (c), the following rules apply:

(1) While a security certificate is located in a jurisdiction, the local law of that jurisdiction governs perfection, the

effect of perfection or nonperfection, and the priority of a security interest in the certificated security represented thereby.

(2) The local law of the issuer's jurisdiction as specified in Section 8–110(d) governs perfection, the effect of perfection or nonperfection, and the priority of a security interest in an uncertificated security.

(3) The local law of the securities intermediary's jurisdiction as specified in Section 8–110(e) governs perfection, the effect of perfection or nonperfection, and the priority of a security interest in a security entitlement or securities account.

(4) The local law of the commodity intermediary's jurisdiction governs perfection, the effect of perfection or nonperfection, and the priority of a security interest in a commodity contract or commodity account.

(b) The following rules determine a commodity intermediary's jurisdiction for purposes of this part:

(1) If an agreement between the commodity intermediary and commodity customer governing the commodity account expressly provides that a particular jurisdiction is the commodity intermediary's jurisdiction for purposes of this part, this article, or [the Uniform Commercial Code], that jurisdiction is the commodity intermediary's jurisdiction.

(2) If paragraph (1) does not apply and an agreement between the commodity intermediary and commodity customer governing the commodity account expressly provides that the agreement is governed by the law of a particular jurisdiction, that jurisdiction is the commodity intermediary's jurisdiction.

(3) If neither paragraph (1) nor paragraph (2) applies and an agreement between the commodity intermediary and commodity customer governing the commodity account expressly provides that the commodity account is maintained at an office in a particular jurisdiction, that jurisdiction is the commodity intermediary's jurisdiction.

(4) If none of the preceding paragraphs applies, the commodity intermediary's jurisdiction is the jurisdiction in which the office identified in an account statement as the office serving the commodity customer's account is located.

(5) If none of the preceding paragraphs applies, the commodity intermediary's jurisdiction is the jurisdiction in which the chief executive office of the commodity intermediary is located.

(c) The local law of the jurisdiction in which the debtor is located governs:

(1) perfection of a security interest in investment property by filing;

(2) automatic perfection of a security interest in investment property created by a broker or securities intermediary; and

(3) automatic perfection of a security interest in a commodity contract or commodity account created by a commodity intermediary.

§ 9–306. Law Governing Perfection and Priority of Security Interests in Letter-of-Credit Rights.

(a) Subject to subsection (c), the local law of the issuer's jurisdiction or a nominated person's jurisdiction governs perfection, the effect of perfection or nonperfection, and the priority of a security interest in a letter-of-credit right if the issuer's jurisdiction or nominated person's jurisdiction is a State.

(b) For purposes of this part, an issuer's jurisdiction or nominated person's jurisdiction is the jurisdiction whose law governs the liability of the issuer or nominated person with respect to the letter-of-credit right as provided in Section 5–116.

(c) This section does not apply to a security interest that is perfected only under Section 9–308(d).

§ 9–307. Location of Debtor.

(a) In this section, "place of business" means a place where a debtor conducts its affairs.

(b) Except as otherwise provided in this section, the following rules determine a debtor's location:

(1) A debtor who is an individual is located at the individual's principal residence.

(2) A debtor that is an organization and has only one place of business is located at its place of business.

(3) A debtor that is an organization and has more than one place of business is located at its chief executive office.

(c) Subsection (b) applies only if a debtor's residence, place of business, or chief executive office, as applicable, is located in a jurisdiction whose law generally requires information concerning the existence of a nonpossessory security interest to be made generally available in a filing, recording, or registration system as a condition or result of the security interest's obtaining priority over the rights of a lien creditor with respect to the collateral. If subsection (b) does not apply, the debtor is located in the District of Columbia.

(d) A person that ceases to exist, have a residence, or have a place of business continues to be located in the jurisdiction specified by subsections (b) and (c).

(e) A registered organization that is organized under the law of a State is located in that State.

(f) Except as otherwise provided in subsection (i), a registered organization that is organized under the law of the United Statesand a branch or agency of a bank that is not organized under the law of the United States or a State are located:

(1) in the State that the law of the United States designates, if the law designates a State of location;

(2) in the State that the registered organization, branch, or agency designates, if the law of the United States authorizes the

registered organization, branch, or agency to designate its State of location; or

(3) in the District of Columbia, if neither paragraph (1) nor paragraph (2) applies.

(g) A registered organization continues to be located in the jurisdiction specified by subsection (e) or (f) notwithstanding:

(1) the suspension, revocation, forfeiture, or lapse of the registered organization's status as such in its jurisdiction of organization; or

(2) the dissolution, winding up, or cancellation of the existence of the registered organization.

(h) The United States is located in the District of Columbia.

(i) A branch or agency of a bank that is not organized under the law of the United States or a State is located in the State in which the branch or agency is licensed, if all branches and agencies of the bank are licensed in only one State.

(j) A foreign air carrier under the Federal Aviation Act of 1958, as amended, is located at the designated office of the agent upon which service of process may be made on behalf of the carrier.

(k) This section applies only for purposes of this part.

[Subpart 2. Perfection]

§ 9–308. When Security Interest or Agricultural Lien Is Perfected; Continuity of Perfection.

(a) Except as otherwise provided in this section and Section 9–309, a security interest is perfected if it has attached and all of the applicable requirements for perfection in Sections 9–310 through 9–316 have been satisfied. A security interest is perfected when it attaches if the applicable requirements are satisfied before the security interest attaches.

(b) An agricultural lien is perfected if it has become effective and all of the applicable requirements for perfection in Section 9–310 have been satisfied. An agricultural lien is perfected when it becomes effective if the applicable requirements are satisfied before the agricultural lien becomes effective.

(c) A security interest or agricultural lien is perfected continuously if it is originally perfected by one method under this article and is later perfected by another method under this article, without an intermediate period when it was unperfected.

(d) Perfection of a security interest in collateral also perfects a security interest in a supporting obligation for the collateral.

(e) Perfection of a security interest in a right to payment or performance also perfects a security interest in a security interest, mortgage, or other lien on personal or real property securing the right.

(f) Perfection of a security interest in a securities account also perfects a security interest in the security entitlements carried in the securities account.

(g) Perfection of a security interest in a commodity account also perfects a security interest in the commodity contracts carried in the commodity account.

Legislative Note: Any statute conflicting with subsection (e) must be made expressly subject to that subsection.

§ 9–309. Security Interest Perfected upon Attachment.

The following security interests are perfected when they attach:

(1) a purchase-money security interest in consumer goods, except as otherwise provided in Section 9–311(b) with respect to consumer goods that are subject to a statute or treaty described in Section 9–311(a);

(2) an assignment of accounts or payment intangibles which does not by itself or in conjunction with other assignments to the same assignee transfer a significant part of the assignor's outstanding accounts or payment intangibles;

(3) a sale of a payment intangible;

(4) a sale of a promissory note;

(5) a security interest created by the assignment of a health-care-insurance receivable to the provider of the health-care goods or services;

(6) a security interest arising under Section 2–401, 2–505, 2–711 (3), or 2A–508(5), until the debtor obtains possession of the collateral;

(7) a security interest of a collecting bank arising under Section 4–210;

(8) a security interest of an issuer or nominated person arising under Section 5–118;

(9) a security interest arising in the delivery of a financial asset under Section 9–206(c);

(10) a security interest in investment property created by a broker or securities intermediary;

(11) a security interest in a commodity contract or a commodity account created by a commodity intermediary;

(12) an assignment for the benefit of all creditors of the transferor and subsequent transfers by the assignee thereunder; and

(13) a security interest created by an assignment of a beneficial interest in a decedent's estate; and

(14) a sale by an individual of an account that is a right to payment of winnings in a lottery or other game of chance.

§ 9–310. When Filing Required to Perfect Security Interest or Agricultural Lien; Security Interests and Agricultural Liens to Which Filing Provisions Do Not Apply.

(a) Except as otherwise provided in subsection (b) and Section 9–312(b), a financing statement must be filed to perfect all security interests and agricultural liens.

(b) The filing of a financing statement is not necessary to perfect a security interest:

(1) that is perfected under Section 9–308(d), (e), (f), or (g);

(2) that is perfected under Section 9–309 when it attaches;

(3) in property subject to a statute, regulation, or treaty described in Section 9–311(a);

(4) in goods in possession of a bailee which is perfected under Section 9–312(d)(1) or (2);

(5) in certificated securities, documents, goods, or instruments which is perfected without filing or possession under Section 9–312(e), (f), or (g);

(6) in collateral in the secured party's possession under Section 9–313;

(7) in a certificated security which is perfected by delivery of the security certificate to the secured party under Section 9–313;

(8) in deposit accounts, electronic chattel paper, investment property, or letter-of-credit rights which is perfected by control under Section 9–314;

(9) in proceeds which is perfected under Section 9–315; or

(10) that is perfected under Section 9–316.

(c) If a secured party assigns a perfected security interest or agricultural lien, a filing under this article is not required to continue the perfected status of the security interest against creditors of and transferees from the original debtor.

§ 9–311. Perfection of Security Interests in Property Subject to Certain Statutes, Regulations, and Treaties.

(a) Except as otherwise provided in subsection (d), the filing of a financing statement is not necessary or effective to perfect a security interest in property subject to:

(1) a statute, regulation, or treaty of the United States whose requirements for a security interest's obtaining priority over the rights of a lien creditor with respect to the property preempt Section 9–310(a);

(2) [list any certificate-of-title statute covering automobiles, trailers, mobile homes, boats, farm tractors, or the like, which provides for a security interest to be indicated on the certificate as a condition or result of perfection, and any non-Uniform Commercial Code central filing statute]; or

(3) a certificate-of-title statute of another jurisdiction which provides for a security interest to be indicated on the certificate as a condition or result of the security interest's obtaining priority over the rights of a lien creditor with respect to the property.

(b) Compliance with the requirements of a statute, regulation, or treaty described in subsection (a) for obtaining priority over the rights of a lien creditor is equivalent to the filing of a financing statement under this article. Except as otherwise provided in subsection (d) and Sections 9–313 and 9–316(d) and (e) for goods covered by a certificate of title, a security interest in property subject to a statute, regulation, or treaty described in subsection (a) may be perfected only by compliance with those requirements, and a security interest so perfected remains perfected notwithstanding a change in the use or transfer of possession of the collateral.

(c) Except as otherwise provided in subsection (d) and Section 9–316(d) and (e), duration and renewal of perfection of a security interest perfected by compliance with the requirements prescribed by a statute, regulation, or treaty described in subsection (a) are governed by the statute, regulation, or treaty. In other respects, the security interest is subject to this article.

(d) During any period in which collateral subject to a statute specified in subsection (a)(2) is inventory held for sale or lease by a person or leased by that person as lessor and that person is in the business of selling goods of that kind, this section does not apply to a security interest in that collateral created by that person.

Legislative Note: This Article contemplates that perfection of a security interest in goods covered by a certificate of title occurs upon receipt by appropriate State officials of a properly tendered application for a certificate of title on which the security interest is to be indicated, without a relation back to an earlier time. States whose certificate-of-title statutes provide for perfection at a different time or contain a relation-back provision should amend the statutes accordingly.

§ 9–312. Perfection of Security Interests in Chattel Paper, Deposit Accounts, Documents, Goods Covered by Documents, Instruments, Investment Property, Letter-of-Credit Rights, and Money; Perfection by Permissive Filing; Temporary Perfection without Filing or Transfer of Possession.

(a) A security interest in chattel paper, negotiable documents, instruments, or investment property may be perfected by filing.

(b) Except as otherwise provided in Section 9–315(c) and (d) for proceeds:

(1) a security interest in a deposit account may be perfected only by control under Section 9–314;

(2) and except as otherwise provided in Section 9–308(d), a security interest in a letter-of-credit right may be perfected only by control under Section 9–314; and

(3) a security interest in money may be perfected only by the secured party's taking possession under Section 9–313.

(c) While goods are in the possession of a bailee that has issued a negotiable document covering the goods:

(1) a security interest in the goods may be perfected by perfecting a security interest in the document; and

(2) a security interest perfected in the document has priority over any security interest that becomes perfected in the goods by another method during that time.

(d) While goods are in the possession of a bailee that has issued a nonnegotiable document covering the goods, a security interest in the goods may be perfected by:

(1) issuance of a document in the name of the secured party;

(2) the bailee's receipt of notification of the secured party's interest; or

(3) filing as to the goods.

(e) A security interest in certificated securities, negotiable documents, or instruments is perfected without filing or the taking of possession for a period of 20 days from the time it attaches to the extent that it arises for new value given under an authenticated security agreement.

(f) A perfected security interest in a negotiable document or goods in possession of a bailee, other than one that has issued a negotiable document for the goods, remains perfected for 20 days without filing if the secured party makes available to the debtor the goods or documents representing the goods for the purpose of:

(1) ultimate sale or exchange; or

(2) loading, unloading, storing, shipping, transshipping, manufacturing, processing, or otherwise dealing with them in a manner preliminary to their sale or exchange.

(g) A perfected security interest in a certificated security or instrument remains perfected for 20 days without filing if the secured party delivers the security certificate or instrument to the debtor for the purpose of:

(1) ultimate sale or exchange; or

(2) presentation, collection, enforcement, renewal, or registration of transfer.

(h) After the 20-day period specified in subsection (e), (f), or (g) expires, perfection depends upon compliance with this article.

§ 9–313. When Possession by or Delivery to Secured Party Perfects Security Interest without Filing.

(a) Except as otherwise provided in subsection (b), a secured party may perfect a security interest in negotiable documents, goods, instruments, money, or tangible chattel paper by taking possession of the collateral. A secured party may perfect a security interest in certificated securities by taking delivery of the certificated securities under Section 8–301.

(b) With respect to goods covered by a certificate of title issued by this State, a secured party may perfect a security interest in the goods by taking possession of the goods only in the circumstances described in Section 9–316(d).

(c) With respect to collateral other than certificated securities and goods covered by a document, a secured party takes possession of collateral in the possession of a person other than the debtor, the secured party, or a lessee of the collateral from the debtor in the ordinary course of the debtor's business, when:

(1) the person in possession authenticates a record acknowledging that it holds possession of the collateral for the secured party's benefit; or

(2) the person takes possession of the collateral after having authenticated a record acknowledging that it will hold possession of collateral for the secured party's benefit.

(d) If perfection of a security interest depends upon possession of the collateral by a secured party, perfection occurs no earlier than the time the secured party takes possession and continues only while the secured party retains possession.

(e) A security interest in a certificated security in registered form is perfected by delivery when delivery of the certificated security occurs under Section 8–301 and remains perfected by delivery until the debtor obtains possession of the security certificate.

(f) A person in possession of collateral is not required to acknowledge that it holds possession for a secured party's benefit.

(g) If a person acknowledges that it holds possession for the secured party's benefit:

(1) the acknowledgment is effective under subsection (c) or Section 8–301(a), even if the acknowledgment violates the rights of a debtor; and

(2) unless the person otherwise agrees or law other than this article otherwise provides, the person does not owe any duty to the secured party and is not required to confirm the acknowledgment to another person.

(h) A secured party having possession of collateral does not relinquish possession by delivering the collateral to a person other than the debtor or a lessee of the collateral from the debtor in the ordinary course of the debtor's business if the person was instructed before the delivery or is instructed contemporaneously with the delivery:

(1) to hold possession of the collateral for the secured party's benefit; or

(2) to redeliver the collateral to the secured party.

(i) A secured party does not relinquish possession, even if a delivery under subsection (h) violates the rights of a debtor. A person to which collateral is delivered under subsection (h) does not owe any duty to the secured party and is not required to confirm the delivery to another person unless the person otherwise agrees or law other than this article otherwise provides.

§ 9-314. Perfection by Control.

(a) A security interest in investment property, deposit accounts, letter-of-credit rights, or electronic chattel paper may be perfected by control of the collateral under Section 9–104, 9–105, 9–106, or 9–107.

(b) A security interest in deposit accounts, electronic chattel paper, or letter-of-credit rights is perfected by control under Section 9–104, 9–105, or 9–107 when the secured party obtains control and remains perfected by control only while the secured party retains control.

(c) A security interest in investment property is perfected by control under Section 9–106 from the time the secured party obtains control and remains perfected by control until:

(1) the secured party does not have control; and

(2) one of the following occurs:

(A) if the collateral is a certificated security, the debtor has or acquires possession of the security certificate;

(B) if the collateral is an uncertificated security, the issuer has registered or registers the debtor as the registered owner; or

(C) if the collateral is a security entitlement, the debtor is or becomes the entitlement holder.

§ 9-315. Secured Party's Rights on Disposition of Collateral and in Proceeds.

(a) Except as otherwise provided in this article and in Section 2–403(2):

(1) a security interest or agricultural lien continues in collateral notwithstanding sale, lease, license, exchange, or other disposition thereof unless the secured party authorized the disposition free of the security interest or agricultural lien; and

(2) a security interest attaches to any identifiable proceeds of collateral.

(b) Proceeds that are commingled with other property are identifiable proceeds:

(1) if the proceeds are goods, to the extent provided by Section 9–336; and

(2) if the proceeds are not goods, to the extent that the secured party identifies the proceeds by a method of tracing, including application of equitable principles, that is permitted under law other than this article with respect to commingled property of the type involved.

(c) A security interest in proceeds is a perfected security interest if the security interest in the original collateral was perfected.

(d) A perfected security interest in proceeds becomes unperfected on the 21st day after the security interest attaches to the proceeds unless:

(1) the following conditions are satisfied:

(A) a filed financing statement covers the original collateral;

(B) the proceeds are collateral in which a security interest may be perfected by filing in the office in which the financing statement has been filed; and

(C) the proceeds are not acquired with cash proceeds;

(2) the proceeds are identifiable cash proceeds; or

(3) the security interest in the proceeds is perfected other than under subsection (c) when the security interest attaches to the proceeds or within 20 days thereafter.

(e) If a filed financing statement covers the original collateral, a security interest in proceeds which remains perfected under subsection (d)(1) becomes unperfected at the later of:

(1) when the effectiveness of the filed financing statement lapses under Section 9–515 or is terminated under Section 9–513; or

(2) the 21st day after the security interest attaches to the proceeds.

§ 9-316. Continued Perfection of Security Interest Following Change in Governing Law.

(a) A security interest perfected pursuant to the law of the jurisdiction designated in Section 9–301(1) or 9–305(c) remains perfected until the earliest of:

(1) the time perfection would have ceased under the law of that jurisdiction;

(2) the expiration of four months after a change of the debtor's location to another jurisdiction; or

(3) the expiration of one year after a transfer of collateral to a person that thereby becomes a debtor and is located in another jurisdiction.

(b) If a security interest described in subsection (a) becomes perfected under the law of the other jurisdiction before the earliest time or event described in that subsection, it remains perfected thereafter. If the security interest does not become perfected under the law of the other jurisdiction before the earliest time or event, it becomes unperfected and is deemed never to have been perfected as against a purchaser of the collateral for value.

(c) A possessory security interest in collateral, other than goods covered by a certificate of title and as-extracted collateral consisting of goods, remains continuously perfected if:

(1) the collateral is located in one jurisdiction and subject to a security interest perfected under the law of that jurisdiction;

(2) thereafter the collateral is brought into another jurisdiction; and

(3) upon entry into the other jurisdiction, the security interest is perfected under the law of the other jurisdiction.

(d) Except as otherwise provided in subsection (e), a security interest in goods covered by a certificate of title which is perfected by any method under the law of another jurisdiction when the goods become covered by a certificate of title from this State remains perfected until the security interest would have become unperfected under the law of the other jurisdiction had the goods not become so covered.

(e) A security interest described in subsection (d) becomes unperfected as against a purchaser of the goods for value and is deemed never to have been perfected as against a purchaser of the goods for value if the applicable requirements for perfection under Section 9–311(b) or 9–313 are not satisfied before the earlier of:

(1) the time the security interest would have become unperfected under the law of the other jurisdiction had the goods not become covered by a certificate of title from this State; or

(2) the expiration of four months after the goods had become so covered.

(f) A security interest in deposit accounts, letter-of-credit rights, or investment property which is perfected under the law of the bank's jurisdiction, the issuer's jurisdiction, a nominated person's jurisdiction, the securities intermediary's jurisdiction, or the commodity intermediary's jurisdiction, as applicable, remains perfected until the earlier of:

(1) the time the security interest would have become unperfected under the law of that jurisdiction; or

(2) the expiration of four months after a change of the applicable jurisdiction to another jurisdiction.

(g) If a security interest described in subsection (f) becomes perfected under the law of the other jurisdiction before the earlier of the time or the end of the period described in that subsection, it remains perfected thereafter. If the security interest does not become perfected under the law of the other jurisdiction before the earlier of that time or the end of that period, it becomes unperfected and is deemed never to have been perfected as against a purchaser of the collateral for value.

[Subpart 3. Priority]

§ 9–317. Interests That Take Priority over or Take Free of Security Interest or Agricultural Lien.

(a) A security interest or agricultural lien is subordinate to the rights of:

(1) a person entitled to priority under Section 9–322; and

(2) except as otherwise provided in subsection (e), a person that becomes a lien creditor before the earlier of the time:

(A) the security interest or agricultural lien is perfected; or

(B) one of the conditions specified in Section 9–203(b)(3) is met and a financing statement covering the collateral is filed.

(b) Except as otherwise provided in subsection (e), a buyer, other than a secured party, of tangible chattel paper, documents, goods, instruments, or a security certificate takes free of a security interest or agricultural lien if the buyer gives value and receives delivery of the collateral without knowledge of the security interest or agricultural lien and before it is perfected.

(c) Except as otherwise provided in subsection (e), a lessee of goods takes free of a security interest or agricultural lien if the lessee gives value and receives delivery of the collateral without knowledge of the security interest or agricultural lien and before it is perfected.

(d) A licensee of a general intangible or a buyer, other than a secured party, of accounts, electronic chattel paper, general intangibles, or investment property other than a certificated security takes free of a security interest if the licensee or buyer gives value without knowledge of the security interest and before it is perfected.

(e) Except as otherwise provided in Sections 9–320 and 9–321, if a person files a financing statement with respect to a purchase-money security interest before or within 20 days after the debtor receives delivery of the collateral, the security interest takes priority over the rights of a buyer, lessee, or lien creditor which arise between the time the security interest attaches and the time of filing.

As amended in 2000.

§ 9–318. No Interest Retained in Right to Payment That Is Sold; Rights and Title of Seller of Account or Chattel Paper with Respect to Creditors and Purchasers.

(a) A debtor that has sold an account, chattel paper, payment intangible, or promissory note does not retain a legal or equitable interest in the collateral sold.

(b) For purposes of determining the rights of creditors of, and purchasers for value of an account or chattel paper from, a debtor that has sold an account or chattel paper, while the buyer's security interest is unperfected, the debtor is deemed to have rights and title to the account or chattel paper identical to those the debtor sold.

§ 9–319. Rights and Title of Consignee with Respect to Creditors and Purchasers.

(a) Except as otherwise provided in subsection (b), for purposes of determining the rights of creditors of, and purchasers for value of goods from, a consignee, while the goods are in the possession of the consignee, the consignee is deemed to have rights and title to the goods identical to those the consignor had or had power to transfer.

(b) For purposes of determining the rights of a creditor of a consignee, law other than this article determines the rights and title of a consignee while goods are in the consignee's possession if, under this part, a perfected security interest held by the consignor would have priority over the rights of the creditor.

§ 9–320. Buyer of Goods.

(a) Except as otherwise provided in subsection (e), a buyer in ordinary course of business, other than a person buying farm products from a person engaged in farming operations, takes free of a security interest created by the buyer's seller, even if the security interest is perfected and the buyer knows of its existence.

(b) Except as otherwise provided in subsection (e), a buyer of goods from a person who used or bought the goods for use primarily for personal, family, or household purposes takes free of a security interest, even if perfected, if the buyer buys:

(1) without knowledge of the security interest;

(2) for value;

(3) primarily for the buyer's personal, family, or household purposes; and

(4) before the filing of a financing statement covering the goods.

(c) To the extent that it affects the priority of a security interest over a buyer of goods under subsection (b), the period of effectiveness of a filing made in the jurisdiction in which the seller is located is governed by Section 9–316(a) and (b).

(d) A buyer in ordinary course of business buying oil, gas, or other minerals at the wellhead or minehead or after extraction takes free of an interest arising out of an encumbrance.

(e) Subsections (a) and (b) do not affect a security interest in goods in the possession of the secured party under Section 9–313.

§ 9–321. Licensee of General Intangible and Lessee of Goods in Ordinary Course of Business.

(a) In this section, "licensee in ordinary course of business" means a person that becomes a licensee of a general intangible in good faith, without knowledge that the license violates the rights of another person in the general intangible, and in the ordinary course from a person in the business of licensing general intangibles of that kind. A person becomes a licensee in the ordinary course if the license to the person comports with the usual or customary practices in the kind of business in which the licensor is engaged or with the licensor's own usual or customary practices.

(b) A licensee in ordinary course of business takes its rights under a nonexclusive license free of a security interest in the general intangible created by the licensor, even if the security interest is perfected and the licensee knows of its existence.

(c) A lessee in ordinary course of business takes its leasehold interest free of a security interest in the goods created by the lessor, even if the security interest is perfected and the lessee knows of its existence.

§ 9–322. Priorities among Conflicting Security Interests in and Agricultural Liens on Same Collateral.

(a) Except as otherwise provided in this section, priority among conflicting security interests and agricultural liens in the same collateral is determined according to the following rules:

(1) Conflicting perfected security interests and agricultural liens rank according to priority in time of filing or perfection. Priority dates from the earlier of the time a filing covering the collateral is first made or the security interest or agricultural lien is first perfected, if there is no period thereafter when there is neither filing nor perfection.

(2) A perfected security interest or agricultural lien has priority over a conflicting unperfected security interest or agricultural lien.

(3) The first security interest or agricultural lien to attach or become effective has priority if conflicting security interests and agricultural liens are unperfected.

(b) For the purposes of subsection (a)(1):

(1) the time of filing or perfection as to a security interest in collateral is also the time of filing or perfection as to a security interest in proceeds; and

(2) the time of filing or perfection as to a security interest in collateral supported by a supporting obligation is also the time of filing or perfection as to a security interest in the supporting obligation.

(c) Except as otherwise provided in subsection (f), a security interest in collateral which qualifies for priority over a conflicting security interest under Section 9–327, 9–328, 9–329, 9–330, or 9–331 also has priority over a conflicting security interest in:

(1) any supporting obligation for the collateral; and

(2) proceeds of the collateral if:

(A) the security interest in proceeds is perfected;

(B) the proceeds are cash proceeds or of the same type as the collateral; and

(C) in the case of proceeds that are proceeds of proceeds, all intervening proceeds are cash proceeds, proceeds of the same type as the collateral, or an account relating to the collateral.

(d) Subject to subsection (e) and except as otherwise provided in subsection (f), if a security interest in chattel paper, deposit accounts, negotiable documents, instruments, investment property, or letter-of-credit rights is perfected by a method other than filing, conflicting perfected security interests in proceeds of the collateral rank according to priority in time of filing.

(e) Subsection (d) applies only if the proceeds of the collateral are not cash proceeds, chattel paper, negotiable documents, instruments, investment property, or letter-of-credit rights.

(f) Subsections (a) through (e) are subject to:

(1) subsection (g) and the other provisions of this part;

(2) Section 4–210 with respect to a security interest of a collecting bank;

(3) Section 5–118 with respect to a security interest of an issuer or nominated person; and

(4) Section 9–110 with respect to a security interest arising under Article 2 or 2A.

(g) A perfected agricultural lien on collateral has priority over a conflicting security interest in or agricultural lien on the same collateral if the statute creating the agricultural lien so provides.

§ 9–323. Future Advances.

(a) Except as otherwise provided in subsection (c), for purposes of determining the priority of a perfected security interest under Section 9–322(a)(1), perfection of the security interest dates from the time an advance is made to the extent that the security interest secures an advance that:

(1) is made while the security interest is perfected only:

(A) under Section 9–309 when it attaches; or

(B) temporarily under Section 9–312(e), (f), or (g); and

(2) is not made pursuant to a commitment entered into before or while the security interest is perfected by a method other than under Section 9–309 or 9–312(e), (f), or (g).

(b) Except as otherwise provided in subsection (c), a security interest is subordinate to the rights of a person that becomes a lien creditor to the extent that the security interest secures an advance made more than 45 days after the person becomes a lien creditor unless the advance is made:

(1) without knowledge of the lien; or

(2) pursuant to a commitment entered into without knowledge of the lien.

(c) Subsections (a) and (b) do not apply to a security interest held by a secured party that is a buyer of accounts, chattel paper, payment intangibles, or promissory notes or a consignor.

(d) Except as otherwise provided in subsection (e), a buyer of goods other than a buyer in ordinary course of business takes free of a security interest to the extent that it secures advances made after the earlier of:

(1) the time the secured party acquires knowledge of the buyer's purchase; or

(2) 45 days after the purchase.

(e) Subsection (d) does not apply if the advance is made pursuant to a commitment entered into without knowledge of the buyer's purchase and before the expiration of the 45-day period.

(f) Except as otherwise provided in subsection (g), a lessee of goods, other than a lessee in ordinary course of business, takes the leasehold interest free of a security interest to the extent that it secures advances made after the earlier of:

(1) the time the secured party acquires knowledge of the lease; or

(2) 45 days after the lease contract becomes enforceable.

(g) Subsection (f) does not apply if the advance is made pursuant to a commitment entered into without knowledge of the lease and before the expiration of the 45-day period.

As amended in 1999.

§ 9–324. Priority of Purchase-Money Security Interests.

(a) Except as otherwise provided in subsection (g), a perfected purchase-money security interest in goods other than inventory or livestock has priority over a conflicting security interest in the same goods, and, except as otherwise provided in Section 9–327, a perfected security interest in its identifiable proceeds also has priority, if the purchase-money security interest is perfected when the debtor receives possession of the collateral or within 20 days thereafter.

(b) Subject to subsection (c) and except as otherwise provided in subsection (g), a perfected purchase-money security interest in inventory has priority over a conflicting security interest in the same inventory, has priority over a conflicting security interest in chattel paper or an instrument constituting proceeds of the inventory and in proceeds of the chattel paper, if so provided in Section 9–330, and, except as otherwise provided in Section 9–327, also has priority in identifiable cash proceeds of the inventory to the extent the identifiable cash proceeds are received on or before the delivery of the inventory to a buyer, if:

(1) the purchase-money security interest is perfected when the debtor receives possession of the inventory;

(2) the purchase-money secured party sends an authenticated notification to the holder of the conflicting security interest;

(3) the holder of the conflicting security interest receives the notification within five years before the debtor receives possession of the inventory; and

(4) the notification states that the person sending the notification has or expects to acquire a purchase-money security interest in inventory of the debtor and describes the inventory.

(c) Subsections (b)(2) through (4) apply only if the holder of the conflicting security interest had filed a financing statement covering the same types of inventory:

(1) if the purchase-money security interest is perfected by filing, before the date of the filing; or

(2) if the purchase-money security interest is temporarily perfected without filing or possession under Section 9–312(f), before the beginning of the 20-day period thereunder.

(d) Subject to subsection (e) and except as otherwise provided in subsection (g), a perfected purchase-money security interest in livestock that are farm products has priority over a conflicting security interest in the same livestock, and, except as otherwise provided in Section 9–327, a perfected security interest in their identifiable proceeds and identifiable products in their unmanufactured states also has priority, if:

(1) the purchase-money security interest is perfected when the debtor receives possession of the livestock;

(2) the purchase-money secured party sends an authenticated notification to the holder of the conflicting security interest;

(3) the holder of the conflicting security interest receives the notification within six months before the debtor receives possession of the livestock; and

(4) the notification states that the person sending the notification has or expects to acquire a purchase-money security interest in livestock of the debtor and describes the livestock.

(e) Subsections (d)(2) through (4) apply only if the holder of the conflicting security interest had filed a financing statement covering the same types of livestock:

(1) if the purchase-money security interest is perfected by filing, before the date of the filing; or

(2) if the purchase-money security interest is temporarily perfected without filing or possession under Section 9–312(f), before the beginning of the 20-day period thereunder.

(f) Except as otherwise provided in subsection (g), a perfected purchase-money security interest in software has priority over a conflicting security interest in the same collateral, and, except as otherwise provided in Section 9–327, a perfected security interest in its identifiable proceeds also has priority, to the extent that the purchase-money security interest in the goods in which the software was acquired for use has priority in the goods and proceeds of the goods under this section.

(g) If more than one security interest qualifies for priority in the same collateral under subsection (a), (b), (d), or (f):

(1) a security interest securing an obligation incurred as all or part of the price of the collateral has priority over a security interest securing an obligation incurred for value given to enable the debtor to acquire rights in or the use of collateral; and

(2) in all other cases, Section 9–322(a) applies to the qualifying security interests.

§ 9-325. Priority of Security Interests in Transferred Collateral.

(a) Except as otherwise provided in subsection (b), a security interest created by a debtor is subordinate to a security interest in the same collateral created by another person if:

(1) the debtor acquired the collateral subject to the security interest created by the other person;

(2) the security interest created by the other person was perfected when the debtor acquired the collateral; and

(3) there is no period thereafter when the security interest is unperfected.

(b) Subsection (a) subordinates a security interest only if the security interest:

(1) otherwise would have priority solely under Section 9–322(a) or 9–324; or

(2) arose solely under Section 2–711(3) or 2A–508(5).

§ 9-326. Priority of Security Interests Created by New Debtor.

(a) Subject to subsection (b), a security interest created by a new debtor which is perfected by a filed financing statement that is effective solely under Section 9–508 in collateral in which a new debtor has or acquires rights is subordinate to a security interest in the same collateral which is perfected other than by a filed financing statement that is effective solely under Section 9–508.

(b) The other provisions of this part determine the priority among conflicting security interests in the same collateral perfected by filed financing statements that are effective solely under Section 9–508. However, if the security agreements to which a new debtor became bound as debtor were not entered into by the same original debtor, the conflicting security interests rank according to priority in time of the new debtor's having become bound.

§ 9-327. Priority of Security Interests in Deposit Account.

The following rules govern priority among conflicting security interests in the same deposit account:

(1) A security interest held by a secured party having control of the deposit account under Section 9–104 has priority over a conflicting security interest held by a secured party that does not have control.

(2) Except as otherwise provided in paragraphs (3) and (4), security interests perfected by control under Section 9–314 rank according to priority in time of obtaining control.

(3) Except as otherwise provided in paragraph (4), a security interest held by the bank with which the deposit account is maintained has priority over a conflicting security interest held by another secured party.

(4) A security interest perfected by control under Section 9–104 (a)(3) has priority over a security interest held by the bank with which the deposit account is maintained.

§ 9-328. Priority of Security Interests in Investment Property.

The following rules govern priority among conflicting security interests in the same investment property:

(1) A security interest held by a secured party having control of investment property under Section 9–106 has priority over a security interest held by a secured party that does not have control of the investment property.

(2) Except as otherwise provided in paragraphs (3) and (4), conflicting security interests held by secured parties each of which has control under Section 9–106 rank according to priority in time of:

(A) if the collateral is a security, obtaining control;

(B) if the collateral is a security entitlement carried in a securities account and:

(i) if the secured party obtained control under Section 8–106(d)(1), the secured party's becoming the person for which the securities account is maintained;

(ii) if the secured party obtained control under Section 8–106(d)(2), the securities intermediary's agreement to comply with the secured party's entitlement orders with respect to security entitlements carried or to be carried in the securities account; or

(iii) if the secured party obtained control through another person under Section 8–106(d)(3), the time on which priority would be based under this paragraph if the other person were the secured party; or

(C) if the collateral is a commodity contract carried with a commodity intermediary, the satisfaction of the requirement for control specified in Section 9–106(b)(2) with respect to commodity contracts carried or to be carried with the commodity intermediary.

(3) A security interest held by a securities intermediary in a security entitlement or a securities account maintained with the securities intermediary has priority over a conflicting security interest held by another secured party.

(4) A security interest held by a commodity intermediary in a commodity contract or a commodity account maintained with the commodity intermediary has priority over a conflicting security interest held by another secured party.

(5) A security interest in a certificated security in registered form which is perfected by taking delivery under Section 9–313(a) and not by control under Section 9–314 has priority over a conflicting security interest perfected by a method other than control.

(6) Conflicting security interests created by a broker, securities intermediary, or commodity intermediary which are perfected without control under Section 9–106 rank equally.

(7) In all other cases, priority among conflicting security interests in investment property is governed by Sections 9–322 and 9–323.

§ 9-329. Priority of Security Interests in Letter-of-Credit Right.

The following rules govern priority among conflicting security interests in the same letter-of-credit right:

(1) A security interest held by a secured party having control of the letter-of-credit right under Section 9–107 has priority to the extent of its control over a conflicting security interest held by a secured party that does not have control.

(2) Security interests perfected by control under Section 9–314 rank according to priority in time of obtaining control.

§ 9-330. Priority of Purchaser of Chattel Paper or Instrument.

(a) A purchaser of chattel paper has priority over a security interest in the chattel paper which is claimed merely as proceeds of inventory subject to a security interest if:

(1) in good faith and in the ordinary course of the purchaser's business, the purchaser gives new value and takes possession of the chattel paper or obtains control of the chattel paper under Section 9–105; and

(2) the chattel paper does not indicate that it has been assigned to an identified assignee other than the purchaser.

(b) A purchaser of chattel paper has priority over a security interest in the chattel paper which is claimed other than merely as proceeds of inventory subject to a security interest if the purchaser gives new value and takes possession of the chattel paper or obtains control of the chattel paper under Section 9–105 in good faith, in the ordinary course of the purchaser's business, and without knowledge that the purchase violates the rights of the secured party.

(c) Except as otherwise provided in Section 9–327, a purchaser having priority in chattel paper under subsection (a) or (b) also has priority in proceeds of the chattel paper to the extent that:

(1) Section 9–322 provides for priority in the proceeds; or

(2) the proceeds consist of the specific goods covered by the chattel paper or cash proceeds of the specific goods, even if the purchaser's security interest in the proceeds is unperfected.

(d) Except as otherwise provided in Section 9–331(a), a purchaser of an instrument has priority over a security interest in the instrument perfected by a method other than possession if the purchaser gives value and takes possession of the instrument in good faith and without knowledge that the purchase violates the rights of the secured party.

(e) For purposes of subsections (a) and (b), the holder of a purchase-money security interest in inventory gives new value for chattel paper constituting proceeds of the inventory.

(f) For purposes of subsections (b) and (d), if chattel paper or an instrument indicates that it has been assigned to an identified secured party other than the purchaser, a purchaser of the chattel paper or instrument has knowledge that the purchase violates the rights of the secured party.

§ 9–331. Priority of Rights of Purchasers of Instruments, Documents, and Securities under Other Articles; Priority of Interests in Financial Assets and Security Entitlements under Article 8.

(a) This article does not limit the rights of a holder in due course of a negotiable instrument, a holder to which a negotiable document of title has been duly negotiated, or a protected purchaser of a security. These holders or purchasers take priority over an earlier security interest, even if perfected, to the extent provided in Articles 3, 7, and 8.

(b) This article does not limit the rights of or impose liability on a person to the extent that the person is protected against the assertion of a claim under Article 8.

(c) Filing under this article does not constitute notice of a claim or defense to the holders, or purchasers, or persons described in subsections (a) and (b).

§ 9–332. Transfer of Money; Transfer of Funds from Deposit Account.

(a) A transferee of money takes the money free of a security interest unless the transferee acts in collusion with the debtor in violating the rights of the secured party.

(b) A transferee of funds from a deposit account takes the funds free of a security interest in the deposit account unless the transferee acts in collusion with the debtor in violating the rights of the secured party.

§ 9–333. Priority of Certain Liens Arising by Operation of Law.

(a) In this section, "possessory lien" means an interest, other than a security interest or an agricultural lien:

(1) which secures payment or performance of an obligation for services or materials furnished with respect to goods by a person in the ordinary course of the person's business;

(2) which is created by statute or rule of law in favor of the person; and

(3) whose effectiveness depends on the person's possession of the goods.

(b) A possessory lien on goods has priority over a security interest in the goods unless the lien is created by a statute that expressly provides otherwise.

§ 9–334. Priority of Security Interests in Fixtures and Crops.

(a) A security interest under this article may be created in goods that are fixtures or may continue in goods that become fixtures. A security interest does not exist under this article in ordinary building materials incorporated into an improvement on land.

(b) This article does not prevent creation of an encumbrance upon fixtures under real property law.

(c) In cases not governed by subsections (d) through (h), a security interest in fixtures is subordinate to a conflicting interest of an encumbrancer or owner of the related real property other than the debtor.

(d) Except as otherwise provided in subsection (h), a perfected security interest in fixtures has priority over a conflicting interest of an encumbrancer or owner of the real property if the debtor has an interest of record in or is in possession of the real property and:

(1) the security interest is a purchase-money security interest;

(2) the interest of the encumbrancer or owner arises before the goods become fixtures; and

(3) the security interest is perfected by a fixture filing before the goods become fixtures or within 20 days thereafter.

(e) A perfected security interest in fixtures has priority over a conflicting interest of an encumbrancer or owner of the real property if:

(1) the debtor has an interest of record in the real property or is in possession of the real property and the security interest:

(A) is perfected by a fixture filing before the interest of the encumbrancer or owner is of record; and

(B) has priority over any conflicting interest of a predecessor in title of the encumbrancer or owner;

(2) before the goods become fixtures, the security interest is perfected by any method permitted by this article and the fixtures are readily removable:

(A) factory or office machines;

(B) equipment that is not primarily used or leased for use in the operation of the real property; or

(C) replacements of domestic appliances that are consumer goods;

(3) the conflicting interest is a lien on the real property obtained by legal or equitable proceedings after the security interest was perfected by any method permitted by this article; or

(4) the security interest is:

(A) created in a manufactured home in a manufactured-home transaction; and

(B) perfected pursuant to a statute described in Section 9–311(a)(2).

(f) A security interest in fixtures, whether or not perfected, has priority over a conflicting interest of an encumbrancer or owner of the real property if:

(1) the encumbrancer or owner has, in an authenticated record, consented to the security interest or disclaimed an interest in the goods as fixtures; or

(2) the debtor has a right to remove the goods as against the encumbrancer or owner.

(g) The priority of the security interest under paragraph (f)(2) continues for a reasonable time if the debtor's right to remove the goods as against the encumbrancer or owner terminates.

(h) A mortgage is a construction mortgage to the extent that it secures an obligation incurred for the construction of an improvement on land, including the acquisition cost of the land, if a recorded record of the mortgage so indicates. Except as otherwise provided in subsections (e) and (f), a security interest in fixtures is subordinate to a construction mortgage if a record of the mortgage is recorded before the goods become fixtures and the goods become fixtures before the completion of the construction. A mortgage has this priority to the same extent as a construction mortgage to the extent that it is given to refinance a construction mortgage.

(i) A perfected security interest in crops growing on real property has priority over a conflicting interest of an encumbrancer or owner of the real property if the debtor has an interest of record in or is in possession of the real property.

(j) Subsection (i) prevails over any inconsistent provisions of the following statutes:

[List here any statutes containing provisions inconsistent with subsection (i).]

Legislative Note: States that amend statutes to remove provisions inconsistent with subsection (i) need not enact subsection (j).

§ 9–335. Accessions.

(a) A security interest may be created in an accession and continues in collateral that becomes an accession.

(b) If a security interest is perfected when the collateral becomes an accession, the security interest remains perfected in the collateral.

(c) Except as otherwise provided in subsection (d), the other provisions of this part determine the priority of a security interest in an accession.

(d) A security interest in an accession is subordinate to a security interest in the whole which is perfected by compliance with the requirements of a certificate-of-title statute under Section 9–311(b).

(e) After default, subject to Part 6, a secured party may remove an accession from other goods if the security interest in the accession has priority over the claims of every person having an interest in the whole.

(f) A secured party that removes an accession from other goods under subsection (e) shall promptly reimburse any holder of a security interest or other lien on, or owner of, the whole or of the other goods, other than the debtor, for the cost of repair of any physical injury to the whole or the other goods. The secured party need not reimburse the holder or owner for any diminution in value of the whole or the other goods caused by the absence of the accession removed or by any necessity for replacing it. A person entitled to reimbursement may refuse permission to remove until the secured party gives adequate assurance for the performance of the obligation to reimburse.

§ 9–336. Commingled Goods.

(a) In this section, "commingled goods" means goods that are physically united with other goods in such a manner that their identity is lost in a product or mass.

(b) A security interest does not exist in commingled goods as such. However, a security interest may attach to a product or mass that results when goods become commingled goods.

(c) If collateral becomes commingled goods, a security interest attaches to the product or mass.

(d) If a security interest in collateral is perfected before the collateral becomes commingled goods, the security interest that attaches to the product or mass under subsection (c) is perfected.

(e) Except as otherwise provided in subsection (f), the other provisions of this part determine the priority of a security interest that attaches to the product or mass under subsection (c).

(f) If more than one security interest attaches to the product or mass under subsection (c), the following rules determine priority:

(1) A security interest that is perfected under subsection (d) has priority over a security interest that is unperfected at the time the collateral becomes commingled goods.

(2) If more than one security interest is perfected under subsection (d), the security interests rank equally in proportion to the value of the collateral at the time it became commingled goods.

§ 9–337. Priority of Security Interests in Goods Covered by Certificate of Title.

If, while a security interest in goods is perfected by any method under the law of another jurisdiction, this State issues a certificate of title that does not show that the goods are subject to the security interest or contain a statement that they may be subject to security interests not shown on the certificate:

(1) a buyer of the goods, other than a person in the business of selling goods of that kind, takes free of the security interest if the buyer gives value and receives delivery of the goods after issuance of the certificate and without knowledge of the security interest; and

(2) the security interest is subordinate to a conflicting security interest in the goods that attaches, and is perfected under Section 9–311(b), after issuance of the certificate and without the conflicting secured party's knowledge of the security interest.

§ 9–338. Priority of Security Interest or Agricultural Lien Perfected by Filed Financing Statement Providing Certain Incorrect Information.

If a security interest or agricultural lien is perfected by a filed financing statement providing information described in Section 9–516(b)(5) which is incorrect at the time the financing statement is filed:

(1) the security interest or agricultural lien is subordinate to a conflicting perfected security interest in the collateral to the extent that the holder of the conflicting security interest gives value in reasonable reliance upon the incorrect information; and

(2) a purchaser, other than a secured party, of the collateral takes free of the security interest or agricultural lien to the extent that, in reasonable reliance upon the incorrect information, the purchaser gives value and, in the case of chattel paper, documents, goods, instruments, or a security certificate, receives delivery of the collateral.

§ 9–339. Priority Subject to Subordination.

This article does not preclude subordination by agreement by a person entitled to priority.

[Subpart 4. Rights of Bank]

§ 9–340. Effectiveness of Right of Recoupment or Set-Off against Deposit Account.

(a) Except as otherwise provided in subsection (c), a bank with which a deposit account is maintained may exercise any right of recoupment or set-off against a secured party that holds a security interest in the deposit account.

(b) Except as otherwise provided in subsection (c), the application of this article to a security interest in a deposit account does not affect a right of recoupment or set-off of the secured party as to a deposit account maintained with the secured party.

(c) The exercise by a bank of a set-off against a deposit account is ineffective against a secured party that holds a security interest in the deposit account which is perfected by control under Section 9–104(a)(3), if the set-off is based on a claim against the debtor.

§ 9–341. Bank's Rights and Duties with Respect to Deposit Account.

Except as otherwise provided in Section 9–340(c), and unless the bank otherwise agrees in an authenticated record, a bank's rights and duties with respect to a deposit account maintained with the bank are not terminated, suspended, or modified by:

(1) the creation, attachment, or perfection of a security interest in the deposit account;

(2) the bank's knowledge of the security interest; or

(3) the bank's receipt of instructions from the secured party.

§ 9-342. Bank's Right to Refuse to Enter into or Disclose Existence of Control Agreement.

This article does not require a bank to enter into an agreement of the kind described in Section 9–104(a)(2), even if its customer so requests or directs. A bank that has entered into such an agreement is not required to confirm the existence of the agreement to another person unless requested to do so by its customer.

PART 4 Rights of Third Parties

§ 9-401. Alienability of Debtor's Rights.

(a) Except as otherwise provided in subsection (b) and Sections 9–406, 9–407, 9–408, and 9–409, whether a debtor's rights in collateral may be voluntarily or involuntarily transferred is governed by law other than this article.

(b) An agreement between the debtor and secured party which prohibits a transfer of the debtor's rights in collateral or makes the transfer a default does not prevent the transfer from taking effect.

§ 9-402. Secured Party Not Obligated on Contract of Debtor or in Tort.

The existence of a security interest, agricultural lien, or authority given to a debtor to dispose of or use collateral, without more, does not subject a secured party to liability in contract or tort for the debtor's acts or omissions.

§ 9-403. Agreement Not to Assert Defenses against Assignee.

(a) In this section, "value" has the meaning provided in Section 3–303(a).

(b) Except as otherwise provided in this section, an agreement between an account debtor and an assignor not to assert against an assignee any claim or defense that the account debtor may have against the assignor is enforceable by an assignee that takes an assignment:

(1) for value;

(2) in good faith;

(3) without notice of a claim of a property or possessory right to the property assigned; and

(4) without notice of a defense or claim in recoupment of the type that may be asserted against a person entitled to enforce a negotiable instrument under Section 3–305(a).

(c) Subsection (b) does not apply to defenses of a type that may be asserted against a holder in due course of a negotiable instrument under Section 3–305(b).

(d) In a consumer transaction, if a record evidences the account debtor's obligation, law other than this article requires that the record include a statement to the effect that the rights of an assignee are subject to claims or defenses that the account debtor could assert against the original obligee, and the record does not include such a statement:

(1) the record has the same effect as if the record included such a statement; and

(2) the account debtor may assert against an assignee those claims and defenses that would have been available if the record included such a statement.

(e) This section is subject to law other than this article which establishes a different rule for an account debtor who is an individual and who incurred the obligation primarily for personal, family, or household purposes.

(f) Except as otherwise provided in subsection (d), this section does not displace law other than this article which gives effect to an agreement by an account debtor not to assert a claim or defense against an assignee.

§ 9-404. Rights Acquired by Assignee; Claims and Defenses against Assignee.

(a) Unless an account debtor has made an enforceable agreement not to assert defenses or claims, and subject to subsections (b) through (e), the rights of an assignee are subject to:

(1) all terms of the agreement between the account debtor and assignor and any defense or claim in recoupment arising from the transaction that gave rise to the contract; and

(2) any other defense or claim of the account debtor against the assignor which accrues before the account debtor receives a notification of the assignment authenticated by the assignor or the assignee.

(b) Subject to subsection (c) and except as otherwise provided in subsection (d), the claim of an account debtor against an assignor may be asserted against an assignee under subsection (a) only to reduce the amount the account debtor owes.

(c) This section is subject to law other than this article which establishes a different rule for an account debtor who is an individual and who incurred the obligation primarily for personal, family, or household purposes.

(d) In a consumer transaction, if a record evidences the account debtor's obligation, law other than this article requires that the record include a statement to the effect that the account debtor's recovery against an assignee with respect to claims and defenses against the assignor may not exceed amounts paid by the account debtor under the record, and the record does not include such a statement, the extent to which a claim of an account debtor against the assignor may be asserted against an assignee is determined as if the record included such a statement.

(e) This section does not apply to an assignment of a health-care-insurance receivable.

§ 9-405. Modification of Assigned Contract.

(a) A modification of or substitution for an assigned contract is effective against an assignee if made in good faith. The assignee acquires corresponding rights under the modified or substituted contract. The assignment may provide that the modification or substitution is a breach of contract by the assignor. This subsection is subject to subsections (b) through (d).

(b) Subsection (a) applies to the extent that:

(1) the right to payment or a part thereof under an assigned contract has not been fully earned by performance; or

(2) the right to payment or a part thereof has been fully earned by performance and the account debtor has not received notification of the assignment under Section 9–406(a).

(c) This section is subject to law other than this article which establishes a different rule for an account debtor who is an individual and who incurred the obligation primarily for personal, family, or household purposes.

(d) This section does not apply to an assignment of a health-care-insurance receivable.

§ 9-406. Discharge of Account Debtor; Notification of Assignment; Identification and Proof of Assignment; Restrictions on Assignment of Accounts, Chattel Paper, Payment Intangibles, and Promissory Notes Ineffective.

(a) Subject to subsections (b) through (i), an account debtor on an account, chattel paper, or a payment intangible may discharge its obligation by paying the assignor until, but not after, the account debtor receives a notification, authenticated by the assignor or the assignee, that the amount due or to become due has been assigned and that payment is to be made to the assignee. After receipt of the notification, the account debtor may discharge its obligation by paying the assignee and may not discharge the obligation by paying the assignor.

(b) Subject to subsection (h), notification is ineffective under subsection (a):

(1) if it does not reasonably identify the rights assigned;

(2) to the extent that an agreement between an account debtor and a seller of a payment intangible limits the account debtor's duty to pay a person other than the seller and the limitation is effective under law other than this article; or

(3) at the option of an account debtor, if the notification notifies the account debtor to make less than the full amount of any installment or other periodic payment to the assignee, even if:

(A) only a portion of the account, chattel paper, or payment intangible has been assigned to that assignee;

(B) a portion has been assigned to another assignee; or

(C) the account debtor knows that the assignment to that assignee is limited.

(c) Subject to subsection (h), if requested by the account debtor, an assignee shall seasonably furnish reasonable proof that the assignment has been made. Unless the assignee complies, the account debtor may discharge its obligation by paying the assignor, even if the account debtor has received a notification under subsection (a).

(d) Except as otherwise provided in subsection (e) and Sections 2A–303 and 9–407, and subject to subsection (h), a term in an agreement between an account debtor and an assignor or in a promissory note is ineffective to the extent that it:

(1) prohibits, restricts, or requires the consent of the account debtor or person obligated on the promissory note to the assignment or transfer of, or the creation, attachment, perfection, or enforcement of a security interest in, the account, chattel paper, payment intangible, or promissory note; or

(2) provides that the assignment or transfer or the creation, attachment, perfection, or enforcement of the security interest may give rise to a default, breach, right of recoupment, claim, defense, termination, right of termination, or remedy under the account, chattel paper, payment intangible, or promissory note.

(e) Subsection (d) does not apply to the sale of a payment intangible or promissory note.

(f) Except as otherwise provided in Sections 2A–303 and 9–407 and subject to subsections (h) and (i), a rule of law, statute, or regulation that prohibits, restricts, or requires the consent of a government, governmental body or official, or account debtor to the assignment or transfer of, or creation of a security interest in, an account or chattel paper is ineffective to the extent that the rule of law, statute, or regulation:

(1) prohibits, restricts, or requires the consent of the government, governmental body or official, or account debtor to the assignment or transfer of, or the creation, attachment, perfection, or enforcement of a security interest in the account or chattel paper; or

(2) provides that the assignment or transfer or the creation, attachment, perfection, or enforcement of the security interest

may give rise to a default, breach, right of recoupment, claim, defense, termination, right of termination, or remedy under the account or chattel paper.

(g) Subject to subsection (h), an account debtor may not waive or vary its option under subsection (b)(3).

(h) This section is subject to law other than this article which establishes a different rule for an account debtor who is an individual and who incurred the obligation primarily for personal, family, or household purposes.

(i) This section does not apply to an assignment of a health-care-insurance receivable.

(j) This section prevails over any inconsistent provisions of the following statutes, rules, and regulations:

[List here any statutes, rules, and regulations containing provisions inconsistent with this section.]

Legislative Note: States that amend statutes, rules, and regulations to remove provisions inconsistent with this section need not enact subsection (j).

As amended in 1999 and 2000.

§ 9–407. Restrictions on Creation or Enforcement of Security Interest in Leasehold Interest or in Lessor's Residual Interest.

(a) Except as otherwise provided in subsection (b), a term in a lease agreement is ineffective to the extent that it:

(1) prohibits, restricts, or requires the consent of a party to the lease to the assignment or transfer of, or the creation, attachment, perfection, or enforcement of a security interest in an interest of a party under the lease contract or in the lessor's residual interest in the goods; or

(2) provides that the assignment or transfer or the creation, attachment, perfection, or enforcement of the security interest may give rise to a default, breach, right of recoupment, claim, defense, termination, right of termination, or remedy under the lease.

(b) Except as otherwise provided in Section 2A–303(7), a term described in subsection (a)(2) is effective to the extent that there is:

(1) a transfer by the lessee of the lessee's right of possession or use of the goods in violation of the term; or

(2) a delegation of a material performance of either party to the lease contract in violation of the term.

(c) The creation, attachment, perfection, or enforcement of a security interest in the lessor's interest under the lease contract or the lessor's residual interest in the goods is not a transfer that materially impairs the lessee's prospect of obtaining return performance or materially changes the duty of or materially increases the burden or risk imposed on the lessee within the purview of Section 2A–303(4) unless, and then only to the extent that, enforcement actually results in a delegation of material performance of the lessor.

As amended in 1999.

§ 9–408. Restrictions on Assignment of Promissory Notes, Health-Care-Insurance Receivables, and Certain General Intangibles Ineffective.

(a) Except as otherwise provided in subsection (b), a term in a promissory note or in an agreement between an account debtor and a debtor which relates to a health-care-insurance receivable or a general intangible, including a contract, permit, license, or franchise, and which term prohibits, restricts, or requires the consent of the person obligated on the promissory note or the account debtor to, the assignment or transfer of, or creation, attachment, or perfection of a security interest in, the promissory note, health-care-insurance receivable, or general intangible, is ineffective to the extent that the term:

(1) would impair the creation, attachment, or perfection of a security interest; or

(2) provides that the assignment or transfer or the creation, attachment, or perfection of the security interest may give rise to a default, breach, right of recoupment, claim, defense, termination, right of termination, or remedy under the promissory note, health-care-insurance receivable, or general intangible.

(b) Subsection (a) applies to a security interest in a payment intangible or promissory note only if the security interest arises out of a sale of the payment intangible or promissory note.

(c) A rule of law, statute, or regulation that prohibits, restricts, or requires the consent of a government, governmental body or official, person obligated on a promissory note, or account debtor to the assignment or transfer of, or creation of a security interest in, a promissory note, health-care-insurance receivable, or general intangible, including a contract, permit, license, or franchise between an account debtor and a debtor, is ineffective to the extent that the rule of law, statute, or regulation:

(1) would impair the creation, attachment, or perfection of a security interest; or

(2) provides that the assignment or transfer or the creation, attachment, or perfection of the security interest may give rise to a default, breach, right of recoupment, claim, defense, termination, right of termination, or remedy under the promissory note, health-care-insurance receivable, or general intangible.

(d) To the extent that a term in a promissory note or in an agreement between an account debtor and a debtor which relates to a health-care-insurance receivable or general intangible or a rule of law, statute, or regulation described in subsection (c) would be effective under law other than this article but is ineffective under subsection (a) or (c), the creation, attachment, or perfection of a security interest in the promissory note, health-care-insurance receivable, or general intangible:

(1) is not enforceable against the person obligated on the promissory note or the account debtor;

(2) does not impose a duty or obligation on the person obligated on the promissory note or the account debtor;

(3) does not require the person obligated on the promissory note or the account debtor to recognize the security interest, pay or render performance to the secured party, or accept payment or performance from the secured party;

(4) does not entitle the secured party to use or assign the debtor's rights under the promissory note, health-care-insurance receivable, or general intangible, including any related information or materials furnished to the debtor in the transaction giving rise to the promissory note, health-care-insurance receivable, or general intangible;

(5) does not entitle the secured party to use, assign, possess, or have access to any trade secrets or confidential information of the person obligated on the promissory note or the account debtor; and

(6) does not entitle the secured party to enforce the security interest in the promissory note, health-care-insurance receivable, or general intangible.

(e) This section prevails over any inconsistent provisions of the following statutes, rules, and regulations:

[List here any statutes, rules, and regulations containing provisions inconsistent with this section.]

Legislative Note: States that amend statutes, rules, and regulations to remove provisions inconsistent with this section need not enact subsection (e).

As amended in 1999.

§ 9-409. Restrictions on Assignment of Letter-of-Credit Rights Ineffective.

(a) A term in a letter of credit or a rule of law, statute, regulation, custom, or practice applicable to the letter of credit which prohibits, restricts, or requires the consent of an applicant, issuer, or nominated person to a beneficiary's assignment of or creation of a security interest in a letter-of-credit right is ineffective to the extent that the term or rule of law, statute, regulation, custom, or practice:

(1) would impair the creation, attachment, or perfection of a security interest in the letter-of-credit right; or

(2) provides that the assignment or the creation, attachment, or perfection of the security interest may give rise to a default, breach, right of recoupment, claim, defense, termination, right of termination, or remedy under the letter-of-credit right.

(b) To the extent that a term in a letter of credit is ineffective under subsection (a) but would be effective under law other than this article or a custom or practice applicable to the letter of credit, to the transfer of a right to draw or otherwise demand performance under the letter of credit, or to the assignment of a right to proceeds of the letter of credit, the creation, attachment, or perfection of a security interest in the letter-of-credit right:

(1) is not enforceable against the applicant, issuer, nominated person, or transferee beneficiary;

(2) imposes no duties or obligations on the applicant, issuer, nominated person, or transferee beneficiary; and

(3) does not require the applicant, issuer, nominated person, or transferee beneficiary to recognize the security interest, pay or render performance to the secured party, or accept payment or other performance from the secured party.

As amended in 1999.

PART 5 Filing

[Subpart 1. Filing Office; Contents and Effectiveness of Financing Statement]

§ 9-501. Filing Office.

(a) Except as otherwise provided in subsection (b), if the local law of this State governs perfection of a security interest or agricultural lien, the office in which to file a financing statement to perfect the security interest or agricultural lien is:

(1) the office designated for the filing or recording of a record of a mortgage on the related real property, if:

(A) the collateral is as-extracted collateral or timber to be cut; or

(B) the financing statement is filed as a fixture filing and the collateral is goods that are or are to become fixtures; or

(2) the office of [ ] [or any office duly authorized by [ ]], in all other cases, including a case in which the collateral is goods that are or are to become fixtures and the financing statement is not filed as a fixture filing.

(b) The office in which to file a financing statement to perfect a security interest in collateral, including fixtures, of a transmitting utility is the office of [ ]. The financing statement also constitutes a fixture filing as to the collateral indicated in the financing statement which is or is to become fixtures.

Legislative Note: The State should designate the filing office where the brackets appear. The filing office may be that of a governmental official (e.g., the Secretary of State) or a private party that maintains the State's filing system.

§ 9–502. Contents of Financing Statement; Record of Mortgage as Financing Statement; Time of Filing Financing Statement.

(a) Subject to subsection (b), a financing statement is sufficient only if it:

(1) provides the name of the debtor;

(2) provides the name of the secured party or a representative of the secured party; and

(3) indicates the collateral covered by the financing statement.

(b) Except as otherwise provided in Section 9–501(b), to be sufficient, a financing statement that covers as-extracted collateral or timber to be cut, or which is filed as a fixture filing and covers goods that are or are to become fixtures, must satisfy subsection (a) and also:

(1) indicate that it covers this type of collateral;

(2) indicate that it is to be filed [for record] in the real property records;

(3) provide a description of the real property to which the collateral is related [sufficient to give constructive notice of a mortgage under the law of this State if the description were contained in a record of the mortgage of the real property]; and

(4) if the debtor does not have an interest of record in the real property, provide the name of a record owner.

(c) A record of a mortgage is effective, from the date of recording, as a financing statement filed as a fixture filing or as a financing statement covering as-extracted collateral or timber to be cut only if:

(1) the record indicates the goods or accounts that it covers;

(2) the goods are or are to become fixtures related to the real property described in the record or the collateral is related to the real property described in the record and is as-extracted collateral or timber to be cut;

(3) the record satisfies the requirements for a financing statement in this section other than an indication that it is to be filed in the real property records; and

(4) the record is [duly] recorded.

(d) A financing statement may be filed before a security agreement is made or a security interest otherwise attaches.

Legislative Note: Language in brackets is optional. Where the State has any special recording system for real property other than the usual grantor-grantee index (as, for instance, a tract system or a title registration or Torrens system) local adaptations of subsection (b) and Section 9–519(d) and (e) may be necessary. See, e.g., Mass. Gen. Laws Chapter 106, Section 9–410.

§ 9–503. Name of Debtor and Secured Party.

(a) A financing statement sufficiently provides the name of the debtor:

(1) if the debtor is a registered organization, only if the financing statement provides the name of the debtor indicated on the public record of the debtor's jurisdiction of organization which shows the debtor to have been organized;

(2) if the debtor is a decedent's estate, only if the financing statement provides the name of the decedent and indicates that the debtor is an estate;

(3) if the debtor is a trust or a trustee acting with respect to property held in trust, only if the financing statement:

(A) provides the name specified for the trust in its organic documents or, if no name is specified, provides the name of the settlor and additional information sufficient to distinguish the debtor from other trusts having one or more of the same settlors; and

(B) indicates, in the debtor's name or otherwise, that the debtor is a trust or is a trustee acting with respect to property held in trust; and

(4) in other cases:

(A) if the debtor has a name, only if it provides the individual or organizational name of the debtor; and

(B) if the debtor does not have a name, only if it provides the names of the partners, members, associates, or other persons comprising the debtor.

(b) A financing statement that provides the name of the debtor in accordance with subsection (a) is not rendered ineffective by the absence of:

(1) a trade name or other name of the debtor; or

(2) unless required under subsection (a)(4)(B), names of partners, members, associates, or other persons comprising the debtor.

(c) A financing statement that provides only the debtor's trade name does not sufficiently provide the name of the debtor.

(d) Failure to indicate the representative capacity of a secured party or representative of a secured party does not affect the sufficiency of a financing statement.

(e) A financing statement may provide the name of more than one debtor and the name of more than one secured party.

§ 9–504. Indication of Collateral.

A financing statement sufficiently indicates the collateral that it covers if the financing statement provides:

(1) a description of the collateral pursuant to Section 9–108; or

(2) an indication that the financing statement covers all assets or all personal property.

As amended in 1999.

§ 9-505. Filing and Compliance with Other Statutes and Treaties for Consignments, Leases, Other Bailments, and Other Transactions.

(a) A consignor, lessor, or other bailor of goods, a licensor, or a buyer of a payment intangible or promissory note may file a financing statement, or may comply with a statute or treaty described in Section 9–311(a), using the terms "consignor", "consignee", "lessor", "lessee", "bailor", "bailee", "licensor", "licensee", "owner", "registered owner", "buyer", "seller", or words of similar import, instead of the terms "secured party" and "debtor".

(b) This part applies to the filing of a financing statement under subsection (a) and, as appropriate, to compliance that is equivalent to filing a financing statement under Section 9–311 (b), but the filing or compliance is not of itself a factor in determining whether the collateral secures an obligation. If it is determined for another reason that the collateral secures an obligation, a security interest held by the consignor, lessor, bailor, licensor, owner, or buyer which attaches to the collateral is perfected by the filing or compliance.

§ 9-506. Effect of Errors or Omissions.

(a) A financing statement substantially satisfying the requirements of this part is effective, even if it has minor errors or omissions, unless the errors or omissions make the financing statement seriously misleading.

(b) Except as otherwise provided in subsection (c), a financing statement that fails sufficiently to provide the name of the debtor in accordance with Section 9–503(a) is seriously misleading.

(c) If a search of the records of the filing office under the debtor's correct name, using the filing office's standard search logic, if any, would disclose a financing statement that fails sufficiently to provide the name of the debtor in accordance with Section 9–503(a), the name provided does not make the financing statement seriously misleading.

(d) For purposes of Section 9–508(b), the "debtor's correct name" in subsection (c) means the correct name of the new debtor.

§ 9-507. Effect of Certain Events on Effectiveness of Financing Statement.

(a) A filed financing statement remains effective with respect to collateral that is sold, exchanged, leased, licensed, or otherwise disposed of and in which a security interest or agricultural lien continues, even if the secured party knows of or consents to the disposition.

(b) Except as otherwise provided in subsection (c) and Section 9–508, a financing statement is not rendered ineffective if, after the financing statement is filed, the information provided in the financing statement becomes seriously misleading under Section 9–506.

(c) If a debtor so changes its name that a filed financing statement becomes seriously misleading under Section 9–506:

(1) the financing statement is effective to perfect a security interest in collateral acquired by the debtor before, or within four months after, the change; and

(2) the financing statement is not effective to perfect a security interest in collateral acquired by the debtor more than four months after the change, unless an amendment to the financing statement which renders the financing statement not seriously misleading is filed within four months after the change.

§ 9-508. Effectiveness of Financing Statement If New Debtor Becomes Bound by Security Agreement.

(a) Except as otherwise provided in this section, a filed financing statement naming an original debtor is effective to perfect a security interest in collateral in which a new debtor has or acquires rights to the extent that the financing statement would have been effective had the original debtor acquired rights in the collateral.

(b) If the difference between the name of the original debtor and that of the new debtor causes a filed financing statement that is effective under subsection (a) to be seriously misleading under Section 9–506:

(1) the financing statement is effective to perfect a security interest in collateral acquired by the new debtor before, and within four months after, the new debtor becomes bound under Section 9B–203(d); and

(2) the financing statement is not effective to perfect a security interest in collateral acquired by the new debtor more than four months after the new debtor becomes bound under Section 9–203(d) unless an initial financing statement providing the name of the new debtor is filed before the expiration of that time.

(c) This section does not apply to collateral as to which a filed financing statement remains effective against the new debtor under Section 9–507(a).

§ 9-509. Persons Entitled to File a Record.

(a) A person may file an initial financing statement, amendment that adds collateral covered by a financing statement, or amendment that adds a debtor to a financing statement only if:

(1) the debtor authorizes the filing in an authenticated record or pursuant to subsection (b) or (c); or

(2) the person holds an agricultural lien that has become effective at the time of filing and the financing statement covers only collateral in which the person holds an agricultural lien.

(b) By authenticating or becoming bound as debtor by a security agreement, a debtor or new debtor authorizes the filing of an initial financing statement, and an amendment, covering:

(1) the collateral described in the security agreement; and

(2) property that becomes collateral under Section 9–315(a)(2), whether or not the security agreement expressly covers proceeds.

(c) By acquiring collateral in which a security interest or agricultural lien continues under Section 9–315(a)(1), a debtor authorizes the filing of an initial financing statement, and an amendment, covering the collateral and property that becomes collateral under Section 9–315(a)(2).

(d) A person may file an amendment other than an amendment that adds collateral covered by a financing statement or an amendment that adds a debtor to a financing statement only if:

(1) the secured party of record authorizes the filing; or

(2) the amendment is a termination statement for a financing statement as to which the secured party of record has failed to file or send a termination statement as required by Section 9–513(a) or (c), the debtor authorizes the filing, and the termination statement indicates that the debtor authorized it to be filed.

(e) If there is more than one secured party of record for a financing statement, each secured party of record may authorize the filing of an amendment under subsection (d).

As amended in 2000.

§ 9-510. Effectiveness of Filed Record.

(a) A filed record is effective only to the extent that it was filed by a person that may file it under Section 9–509.

(b) A record authorized by one secured party of record does not affect the financing statement with respect to another secured party of record.

(c) A continuation statement that is not filed within the six-month period prescribed by Section 9–515(d) is ineffective.

§ 9-511. Secured Party of Record.

(a) A secured party of record with respect to a financing statement is a person whose name is provided as the name of the secured party or a representative of the secured party in an initial financing statement that has been filed. If an initial financing statement is filed under Section 9–514(a), the assignee named in the initial financing statement is the secured party of record with respect to the financing statement.

(b) If an amendment of a financing statement which provides the name of a person as a secured party or a representative of a secured party is filed, the person named in the amendment is a secured party of record. If an amendment is filed under Section 9–514(b), the assignee named in the amendment is a secured party of record.

(c) A person remains a secured party of record until the filing of an amendment of the financing statement which deletes the person.

§ 9-512. Amendment of Financing Statement.

[Alternative A]

(a) Subject to Section 9–509, a person may add or delete collateral covered by, continue or terminate the effectiveness of, or, subject to subsection (e), otherwise amend the information provided in, a financing statement by filing an amendment that:

(1) identifies, by its file number, the initial financing statement to which the amendment relates; and

(2) if the amendment relates to an initial financing statement filed [or recorded] in a filing office described in Section 9–501(a)(1), provides the information specified in Section 9–502(b).

[Alternative B]

(a) Subject to Section 9–509, a person may add or delete collateral covered by, continue or terminate the effectiveness of, or, subject to subsection (e), otherwise amend the information provided in, a financing statement by filing an amendment that:

(1) identifies, by its file number, the initial financing statement to which the amendment relates; and

(2) if the amendment relates to an initial financing statement filed [or recorded] in a filing office described in Section 9–501(a)(1), provides the date [and time] that the initial financing statement was filed [or recorded] and the information specified in Section 9–502(b).

[End of Alternatives]

(b) Except as otherwise provided in Section 9–515, the filing of an amendment does not extend the period of effectiveness of the financing statement.

(c) A financing statement that is amended by an amendment that adds collateral is effective as to the added collateral only from the date of the filing of the amendment.

(d) A financing statement that is amended by an amendment that adds a debtor is effective as to the added debtor only from the date of the filing of the amendment.

(e) An amendment is ineffective to the extent it:

(1) purports to delete all debtors and fails to provide the name of a debtor to be covered by the financing statement; or

(2) purports to delete all secured parties of record and fails to provide the name of a new secured party of record.

Legislative Note: States whose real-estate filing offices require additional information in amendments and cannot search their records by both the name of the debtor and the file number should enact Alternative B to Sections 9–512(a), 9–518(b), 9–519(f), and 9–522(a).

§ 9–513. Termination Statement.

(a) A secured party shall cause the secured party of record for a financing statement to file a termination statement for the financing statement if the financing statement covers consumer goods and:

(1) there is no obligation secured by the collateral covered by the financing statement and no commitment to make an advance, incur an obligation, or otherwise give value; or

(2) the debtor did not authorize the filing of the initial financing statement.

(b) To comply with subsection (a), a secured party shall cause the secured party of record to file the termination statement:

(1) within one month after there is no obligation secured by the collateral covered by the financing statement and no commitment to make an advance, incur an obligation, or otherwise give value; or

(2) if earlier, within 20 days after the secured party receives an authenticated demand from a debtor.

(c) In cases not governed by subsection (a), within 20 days after a secured party receives an authenticated demand from a debtor, the secured party shall cause the secured party of record for a financing statement to send to the debtor a termination statement for the financing statement or file the termination statement in the filing office if:

(1) except in the case of a financing statement covering accounts or chattel paper that has been sold or goods that are the subject of a consignment, there is no obligation secured by the collateral covered by the financing statement and no commitment to make an advance, incur an obligation, or otherwise give value;

(2) the financing statement covers accounts or chattel paper that has been sold but as to which the account debtor or other person obligated has discharged its obligation;

(3) the financing statement covers goods that were the subject of a consignment to the debtor but are not in the debtor's possession; or

(4) the debtor did not authorize the filing of the initial financing statement.

(d) Except as otherwise provided in Section 9–510, upon the filing of a termination statement with the filing office, the financing statement to which the termination statement relates ceases to be effective. Except as otherwise provided in Section 9–510, for purposes of Sections 9–519(g), 9–522(a), and 9–523 (c), the filing with the filing office of a termination statement relating to a financing statement that indicates that the debtor is a transmitting utility also causes the effectiveness of the financing statement to lapse.

As amended in 2000.

§ 9–514. Assignment of Powers of Secured Party of Record.

(a) Except as otherwise provided in subsection (c), an initial financing statement may reflect an assignment of all of the secured party's power to authorize an amendment to the financing statement by providing the name and mailing address of the assignee as the name and address of the secured party.

(b) Except as otherwise provided in subsection (c), a secured party of record may assign of record all or part of its power to authorize an amendment to a financing statement by filing in the filing office an amendment of the financing statement which:

(1) identifies, by its file number, the initial financing statement to which it relates;

(2) provides the name of the assignor; and

(3) provides the name and mailing address of the assignee.

(c) An assignment of record of a security interest in a fixture covered by a record of a mortgage which is effective as a financing statement filed as a fixture filing under Section 9–502(c) may be made only by an assignment of record of the mortgage in the manner provided by law of this State other than [the Uniform Commercial Code].

§ 9–515. Duration and Effectiveness of Financing Statement; Effect of Lapsed Financing Statement.

(a) Except as otherwise provided in subsections (b), (e), (f), and (g), a filed financing statement is effective for a period of five years after the date of filing.

(b) Except as otherwise provided in subsections (e), (f), and (g), an initial financing statement filed in connection with a public-finance transaction or manufactured-home transaction is effective for a period of 30 years after the date of filing if it indicates that it is filed in connection with a public-finance transaction or manufactured-home transaction.

(c) The effectiveness of a filed financing statement lapses on the expiration of the period of its effectiveness unless before the lapse a continuation statement is filed pursuant to subsection (d). Upon lapse, a financing statement ceases to be effective and any security interest or agricultural lien that was perfected by the financing statement becomes unperfected, unless the security interest is perfected otherwise. If the security interest or agricultural lien becomes unperfected upon lapse, it is deemed never to have been perfected as against a purchaser of the collateral for value.

(d) A continuation statement may be filed only within six months before the expiration of the five-year period specified in subsection (a) or the 30-year period specified in subsection (b), whichever is applicable.

(e) Except as otherwise provided in Section 9–510, upon timely filing of a continuation statement, the effectiveness of the initial financing statement continues for a period of five years commencing on the day on which the financing statement would have become ineffective in the absence of the filing. Upon the expiration of the five-year period, the financing statement lapses in the same manner as provided in subsection (c), unless, before the lapse, another continuation statement is filed pursuant to subsection (d). Succeeding continuation statements may be filed in the same manner to continue the effectiveness of the initial financing statement.

(f) If a debtor is a transmitting utility and a filed financing statement so indicates, the financing statement is effective until a termination statement is filed.

(g) A record of a mortgage that is effective as a financing statement filed as a fixture filing under Section 9–502(c) remains effective as a financing statement filed as a fixture filing until the mortgage is released or satisfied of record or its effectiveness otherwise terminates as to the real property.

§ 9–516. What Constitutes Filing; Effectiveness of Filing.

(a) Except as otherwise provided in subsection (b), communication of a record to a filing office and tender of the filing fee or acceptance of the record by the filing office constitutes filing.

(b) Filing does not occur with respect to a record that a filing office refuses to accept because:

(1) the record is not communicated by a method or medium of communication authorized by the filing office;

(2) an amount equal to or greater than the applicable filing fee is not tendered;

(3) the filing office is unable to index the record because:

(A) in the case of an initial financing statement, the record does not provide a name for the debtor;

(B) in the case of an amendment or correction statement, the record:

(i) does not identify the initial financing statement as required by Section 9–512 or 9–518, as applicable; or

(ii) identifies an initial financing statement whose effectiveness has lapsed under Section 9–515;

(C) in the case of an initial financing statement that provides the name of a debtor identified as an individual or an amendment that provides a name of a debtor identified as an individual which was not previously provided in the financing statement to which the record relates, the record does not identify the debtor's last name; or

(D) in the case of a record filed [or recorded] in the filing office described in Section 9–501(a)(1), the record does not provide a sufficient description of the real property to which it relates;

(4) in the case of an initial financing statement or an amendment that adds a secured party of record, the record does not provide a name and mailing address for the secured party of record;

(5) in the case of an initial financing statement or an amendment that provides a name of a debtor which was not previously provided in the financing statement to which the amendment relates, the record does not:

(A) provide a mailing address for the debtor;

(B) indicate whether the debtor is an individual or an organization; or

(C) if the financing statement indicates that the debtor is an organization, provide:

(i) a type of organization for the debtor;

(ii) a jurisdiction of organization for the debtor; or

(iii) an organizational identification number for the debtor or indicate that the debtor has none;

(6) in the case of an assignment reflected in an initial financing statement under Section 9–514(a) or an amendment filed under Section 9–514(b), the record does not provide a name and mailing address for the assignee; or

(7) in the case of a continuation statement, the record is not filed within the six-month period prescribed by Section 9–515(d).

(c) For purposes of subsection (b):

(1) a record does not provide information if the filing office is unable to read or decipher the information; and

(2) a record that does not indicate that it is an amendment or identify an initial financing statement to which it relates, as required by Section 9–512, 9–514, or 9–518, is an initial financing statement.

(d) A record that is communicated to the filing office with tender of the filing fee, but which the filing office refuses to accept for a reason other than one set forth in subsection (b), is effective as a filed record except as against a purchaser of the collateral which gives value in reasonable reliance upon the absence of the record from the files.

§ 9–517. Effect of Indexing Errors.

The failure of the filing office to index a record correctly does not affect the effectiveness of the filed record.

§ 9–518. Claim Concerning Inaccurate or Wrongfully Filed Record.

(a) A person may file in the filing office a correction statement with respect to a record indexed there under the person's name if the person believes that the record is inaccurate or was wrongfully filed.

[Alternative A]

(b) A correction statement must:
(1) identify the record to which it relates by the file number assigned to the initial financing statement to which the record relates;

(2) indicate that it is a correction statement; and

(3) provide the basis for the person's belief that the record is inaccurate and indicate the manner in which the person believes the record should be amended to cure any inaccuracy or provide the basis for the person's belief that the record was wrongfully filed.

[Alternative B]

(b) A correction statement must:
(1) identify the record to which it relates by:

(A) the file number assigned to the initial financing statement to which the record relates; and

(B) if the correction statement relates to a record filed [or recorded] in a filing office described in Section 9–501(a)(1), the date [and time] that the initial financing statement was filed [or recorded] and the information specified in Section 9–502(b);

(2) indicate that it is a correction statement; and

(3) provide the basis for the person's belief that the record is inaccurate and indicate the manner in which the person believes the record should be amended to cure any inaccuracy or provide the basis for the person's belief that the record was wrongfully filed.

[End of Alternatives]

(c) The filing of a correction statement does not affect the effectiveness of an initial financing statement or other filed record.
Legislative Note: States whose real-estate filing offices require additional information in amendments and cannot search their records by both the name of the debtor and the file number should enact Alternative B to Sections 9–512(a), 9–518(b), 9–519(f), and 9–522(a).

[Subpart 2. Duties and Operation of Filing Office]

§ 9-519. Numbering, Maintaining, and Indexing Records; Communicating Information Provided in Records.

(a) For each record filed in a filing office, the filing office shall:

(1) assign a unique number to the filed record;

(2) create a record that bears the number assigned to the filed record and the date and time of filing;

(3) maintain the filed record for public inspection; and

(4) index the filed record in accordance with subsections (c), (d), and (e).

(b) A file number [assigned after January 1, 2002,] must include a digit that:

(1) is mathematically derived from or related to the other digits of the file number; and

(2) aids the filing office in determining whether a number communicated as the file number includes a single-digit or transpositional error.

(c) Except as otherwise provided in subsections (d) and (e), the filing office shall:

(1) index an initial financing statement according to the name of the debtor and index all filed records relating to the initial financing statement in a manner that associates with one another an initial financing statement and all filed records relating to the initial financing statement; and

(2) index a record that provides a name of a debtor which was not previously provided in the financing statement to which the record relates also according to the name that was not previously provided.

(d) If a financing statement is filed as a fixture filing or covers as-extracted collateral or timber to be cut, [it must be filed for record and] the filing office shall index it:

(1) under the names of the debtor and of each owner of record shown on the financing statement as if they were the mortgagors under a mortgage of the real property described; and

(2) to the extent that the law of this State provides for indexing of records of mortgages under the name of the mortgagee, under the name of the secured party as if the secured party were the mortgagee thereunder, or, if indexing is by description, as if the financing statement were a record of a mortgage of the real property described.

(e) If a financing statement is filed as a fixture filing or covers as-extracted collateral or timber to be cut, the filing office shall index an assignment filed under Section 9–514(a) or an amendment filed under Section 9–514(b):

(1) under the name of the assignor as grantor; and

(2) to the extent that the law of this State provides for indexing a record of the assignment of a mortgage under the name of the assignee, under the name of the assignee.

[Alternative A]

(f) The filing office shall maintain a capability:
(1) to retrieve a record by the name of the debtor and by the file number assigned to the initial financing statement to which the record relates; and

(2) to associate and retrieve with one another an initial financing statement and each filed record relating to the initial financing statement.

[Alternative B]

(f) The filing office shall maintain a capability:
(1) to retrieve a record by the name of the debtor and:

(A) if the filing office is described in Section 9–501(a)(1), by the file number assigned to the initial financing statement to which the record relates and the date [and time] that the record was filed [or recorded]; or

(B) if the filing office is described in Section 9–501(a)(2), by the file number assigned to the initial financing statement to which the record relates; and

(2) to associate and retrieve with one another an initial financing statement and each filed record relating to the initial financing statement.

[End of Alternatives]

(g) The filing office may not remove a debtor's name from the index until one year after the effectiveness of a financing statement naming the debtor lapses under Section 9–515 with respect to all secured parties of record.

(h) The filing office shall perform the acts required by subsections (a) through (e) at the time and in the manner prescribed by filing-office rule, but not later than two business days after the filing office receives the record in question.

[(i) Subsection[s] [(b)] [and] [(h)] do[es] not apply to a filing office described in Section 9–501(a)(1).]

Legislative Notes:

1. States whose filing offices currently assign file numbers that include a verification number, commonly known as a "check digit," or can implement this requirement before the effective date of this Article should omit the bracketed language in subsection (b).

2. In States in which writings will not appear in the real property records and indices unless actually recorded the bracketed language in subsection (d) should be used.

3. States whose real-estate filing offices require additional information in amendments and cannot search their records by both the name of the debtor and the file number should enact Alternative B to Sections 9–512 (a), 9–518(b), 9–519(f), and 9–522(a).

4. A State that elects not to require real-estate filing offices to comply with either or both of subsections (b) and (h) may adopt an applicable variation of subsection (i) and add "Except as otherwise provided in subsection (i)," to the appropriate subsection or subsections.

§ 9–520. Acceptance and Refusal to Accept Record.

(a) A filing office shall refuse to accept a record for filing for a reason set forth in Section 9–516(b) and may refuse to accept a record for filing only for a reason set forth in Section 9–516(b).

(b) If a filing office refuses to accept a record for filing, it shall communicate to the person that presented the record the fact of and reason for the refusal and the date and time the record would have been filed had the filing office accepted it. The communication must be made at the time and in the manner prescribed by filing-office rule but [, in the case of a filing office described in Section 9–501(a)(2),] in no event more than two business days after the filing office receives the record.

(c) A filed financing statement satisfying Section 9–502(a) and (b) is effective, even if the filing office is required to refuse to accept it for filing under subsection (a). However, Section 9–338 applies to a filed financing statement providing information described in Section 9–516(b)(5) which is incorrect at the time the financing statement is filed.

(d) If a record communicated to a filing office provides information that relates to more than one debtor, this part applies as to each debtor separately.

Legislative Note: A State that elects not to require real-property filing offices to comply with subsection (b) should include the bracketed language.

§ 9–521. Uniform Form of Written Financing Statement and Amendment.

(a) A filing office that accepts written records may not refuse to accept a written initial financing statement in the following form and format except for a reason set forth in Section 9–516(b):

[NATIONAL UCC FINANCING STATEMENT (FORM UCC1)(REV. 7/29/98)]

[NATIONAL UCC FINANCING STATEMENT ADDENDUM (FORM UCC1Ad)(REV. 07/29/98)]

(b) A filing office that accepts written records may not refuse to accept a written record in the following form and format except for a reason set forth in Section 9–516(b):

[NATIONAL UCC FINANCING STATEMENT AMENDMENT (FORM UCC3)(REV. 07/29/98)]

[NATIONAL UCC FINANCING STATEMENT AMENDMENT ADDENDUM (FORM UCC3Ad)(REV. 07/29/98)]

§ 9–522. Maintenance and Destruction of Records.

[Alternative A]

(a) The filing office shall maintain a record of the information provided in a filed financing statement for at least one year after the effectiveness of the financing statement has lapsed under Section 9–515 with respect to all secured parties of record. The record must be retrievable by using the name of the debtor and by using the file number assigned to the initial financing statement to which the record relates.

[Alternative B]

(a) The filing office shall maintain a record of the information provided in a filed financing statement for at least one year after the effectiveness of the financing statement has lapsed under Section 9–515 with respect to all secured parties of record. The record must be retrievable by using the name of the debtor and:

(1) if the record was filed [or recorded] in the filing office described in Section 9–501(a)(1), by using the file number assigned to the initial financing statement to which the record relates and the date [and time] that the record was filed [or recorded]; or

(2) if the record was filed in the filing office described in Section 9–501(a)(2), by using the file number assigned to the initial financing statement to which the record relates.

[End of Alternatives]

(b) Except to the extent that a statute governing disposition of public records provides otherwise, the filing office immediately may destroy any written record evidencing a financing statement. However, if the filing office destroys a written record, it shall maintain another record of the financing statement which complies with subsection (a).

Legislative Note: States whose real-estate filing offices require additional information in amendments and cannot search their records by both the name of the debtor and the file number should enact Alternative B to Sections 9–512(a), 9–518(b), 9–519(f), and 9–522(a).

§ 9-523. Information from Filing Office; Sale or License of Records.

(a) If a person that files a written record requests an acknowledgment of the filing, the filing office shall send to the person an image of the record showing the number assigned to the record pursuant to Section 9–519(a)(1) and the date and time of the filing of the record. However, if the person furnishes a copy of the record to the filing office, the filing office may instead:

(1) note upon the copy the number assigned to the record pursuant to Section 9–519(a)(1) and the date and time of the filing of the record; and

(2) send the copy to the person.

(b) If a person files a record other than a written record, the filing office shall communicate to the person an acknowledgment that provides:

(1) the information in the record;

(2) the number assigned to the record pursuant to Section 9–519(a)(1); and

(3) the date and time of the filing of the record.

(c) The filing office shall communicate or otherwise make available in a record the following information to any person that requests it:

(1) whether there is on file on a date and time specified by the filing office, but not a date earlier than three business days before the filing office receives the request, any financing statement that:

(A) designates a particular debtor [or, if the request so states, designates a particular debtor at the address specified in the request];

(B) has not lapsed under Section 9–515 with respect to all secured parties of record; and

(C) if the request so states, has lapsed under Section 9–515 and a record of which is maintained by the filing office under Section 9–522(a);

(2) the date and time of filing of each financing statement; and

(3) the information provided in each financing statement.

(d) In complying with its duty under subsection (c), the filing office may communicate information in any medium. However, if requested, the filing office shall communicate information by issuing [its written certificate] [a record that can be admitted into evidence in the courts of this State without extrinsic evidence of its authenticity].

(e) The filing office shall perform the acts required by subsections (a) through (d) at the time and in the manner prescribed by filing-office rule, but not later than two business days after the filing office receives the request.

(f) At least weekly, the [insert appropriate official or governmental agency] [filing office] shall offer to sell or license to the public on a nonexclusive basis, in bulk, copies of all records filed in it under this part, in every medium from time to time available to the filing office.

Legislative Notes:

1. States whose filing office does not offer the additional service of responding to search requests limited to a particular address should omit the bracketed language in subsection (c)(1)(A).

2. A State that elects not to require real-estate filing offices to comply with either or both of subsections (e) and (f) should specify in the appropriate subsection(s) only the filing office described in Section 9–501(a)(2).

§ 9-524. Delay by Filing Office.

Delay by the filing office beyond a time limit prescribed by this part is excused if:

(1) the delay is caused by interruption of communication or computer facilities, war, emergency conditions, failure of equipment, or other circumstances beyond control of the filing office; and

(2) the filing office exercises reasonable diligence under the circumstances.

§ 9-525. Fees.

(a) Except as otherwise provided in subsection (e), the fee for filing and indexing a record under this part, other than an initial financing statement of the kind described in subsection (b), is [the amount specified in subsection (c), if applicable, plus]:

(1) $[X] if the record is communicated in writing and consists of one or two pages;

(2) $[2X] if the record is communicated in writing and consists of more than two pages; and

(3) $[1/2X] if the record is communicated by another medium authorized by filing-office rule.

(b) Except as otherwise provided in subsection (e), the fee for filing and indexing an initial financing statement of the following kind is [the amount specified in subsection (c), if applicable, plus]:

(1) $——— if the financing statement indicates that it is filed in connection with a public-finance transaction;

(2) $——— if the financing statement indicates that it is filed in connection with a manufactured-home transaction.

[Alternative A]

(c) The number of names required to be indexed does not affect the amount of the fee in subsections (a) and (b).

[Alternative B]

(c) Except as otherwise provided in subsection (e), if a record is communicated in writing, the fee for each name more than two required to be indexed is $———.

[End of Alternatives]

(a) The fee for responding to a request for information from the filing office, including for [issuing a certificate showing] [communicating] whether there is on file any financing statement naming a particular debtor, is:

(1) $——— if the request is communicated in writing; and

(2) $——— if the request is communicated by another medium authorized by filing-office rule.

(e) This section does not require a fee with respect to a record of a mortgage which is effective as a financing statement filed as a fixture filing or as a financing statement covering as-extracted collateral or timber to be cut under Section 9–502(c). However, the recording and satisfaction fees that otherwise would be applicable to the record of the mortgage apply.

Legislative Notes:

1. To preserve uniformity, a State that places the provisions of this section together with statutes setting fees for other services should do so without modification.

2. A State should enact subsection (c), Alternative A, and omit the bracketed language in subsections (a) and (b) unless its indexing system entails a substantial additional cost when indexing additional names.

As amended in 2000.

§ 9–526. Filing-Office Rules.

(a) The [insert appropriate governmental official or agency] shall adopt and publish rules to implement this article. The filing-office rules must be[:

(1) consistent with this article[; and

(2) adopted and published in accordance with the [insert any applicable state administrative procedure act]].

(b) To keep the filing-office rules and practices of the filing office in harmony with the rules and practices of filing offices in other jurisdictions that enact substantially this part, and to keep the technology used by the filing office compatible with the technology used by filing offices in other jurisdictions that enact substantially this part, the [insert appropriate governmental official or agency], so far as is consistent with the purposes, policies, and provisions of this article, in adopting, amending, and repealing filing-office rules, shall:

(1) consult with filing offices in other jurisdictions that enact substantially this part; and

(2) consult the most recent version of the Model Rules promulgated by the International Association of Corporate Administrators or any successor organization; and

(3) take into consideration the rules and practices of, and the technology used by, filing offices in other jurisdictions that enact substantially this part.

§ 9–527. Duty to Report.

The [insert appropriate governmental official or agency] shall report [annually on or before ———] to the [Governor and Legislature] on the operation of the filing office. The report must contain a statement of the extent to which:

(1) the filing-office rules are not in harmony with the rules of filing offices in other jurisdictions that enact substantially this part and the reasons for these variations; and

(2) the filing-office rules are not in harmony with the most recent version of the Model Rules promulgated by the International Association of Corporate Administrators, or any successor organization, and the reasons for these variations.

PART 6 Default

[Subpart 1. Default and Enforcement of Security Interest]

§ 9–601. Rights after Default; Judicial Enforcement; Consignor or Buyer of Accounts, Chattel Paper, Payment Intangibles, or Promissory Notes.

(a) After default, a secured party has the rights provided in this part and, except as otherwise provided in Section 9–602, those provided by agreement of the parties. A secured party:

(1) may reduce a claim to judgment, foreclose, or otherwise enforce the claim, security interest, or agricultural lien by any available judicial procedure; and

(2) if the collateral is documents, may proceed either as to the documents or as to the goods they cover.

(b) A secured party in possession of collateral or control of collateral under Section 9–104, 9–105, 9–106, or 9–107 has the rights and duties provided in Section 9–207.

(c) The rights under subsections (a) and (b) are cumulative and may be exercised simultaneously.

(d) Except as otherwise provided in subsection (g) and Section 9–605, after default, a debtor and an obligor have the rights provided in this part and by agreement of the parties.

(e) If a secured party has reduced its claim to judgment, the lien of any levy that may be made upon the collateral by virtue of an execution based upon the judgment relates back to the earliest of:

(1) the date of perfection of the security interest or agricultural lien in the collateral;

(2) the date of filing a financing statement covering the collateral; or

(3) any date specified in a statute under which the agricultural lien was created.

(f) A sale pursuant to an execution is a foreclosure of the security interest or agricultural lien by judicial procedure within the meaning of this section. A secured party may purchase at the sale and thereafter hold the collateral free of any other requirements of this article.

(g) Except as otherwise provided in Section 9–607(c), this part imposes no duties upon a secured party that is a consignor or is a buyer of accounts, chattel paper, payment intangibles, or promissory notes.

§ 9–602. Waiver and Variance of Rights and Duties.

Except as otherwise provided in Section 9–624, to the extent that they give rights to a debtor or obligor and impose duties on a secured party, the debtor or obligor may not waive or vary the rules stated in the following listed sections:

(1) Section 9–207(b)(4)(C), which deals with use and operation of the collateral by the secured party;

(2) Section 9–210, which deals with requests for an accounting and requests concerning a list of collateral and statement of account;

(3) Section 9–607(c), which deals with collection and enforcement of collateral;

(4) Sections 9–608(a) and 9–615(c) to the extent that they deal with application or payment of noncash proceeds of collection, enforcement, or disposition;

(5) Sections 9–608(a) and 9–615(d) to the extent that they require accounting for or payment of surplus proceeds of collateral;

(6) Section 9–609 to the extent that it imposes upon a secured party that takes possession of collateral without judicial process the duty to do so without breach of the peace;

(7) Sections 9–610(b), 9–611, 9–613, and 9–614, which deal with disposition of collateral;

(8) Section 9–615(f), which deals with calculation of a deficiency or surplus when a disposition is made to the secured party, a person related to the secured party, or a secondary obligor;

(9) Section 9–616, which deals with explanation of the calculation of a surplus or deficiency;

(10) Sections 9–620, 9–621, and 9–622, which deal with acceptance of collateral in satisfaction of obligation;

(11) Section 9–623, which deals with redemption of collateral;

(12) Section 9–624, which deals with permissible waivers; and

(13) Sections 9–625 and 9–626, which deal with the secured party's liability for failure to comply with this article.

§ 9–603. Agreement on Standards Concerning Rights and Duties.

(a) The parties may determine by agreement the standards measuring the fulfillment of the rights of a debtor or obligor and the duties of a secured party under a rule stated in Section 9–602 if the standards are not manifestly unreasonable.

(b) Subsection (a) does not apply to the duty under Section 9–609 to refrain from breaching the peace.

§ 9–604. Procedure If Security Agreement Covers Real Property or Fixtures.

(a) If a security agreement covers both personal and real property, a secured party may proceed:

(1) under this part as to the personal property without prejudicing any rights with respect to the real property; or

(2) as to both the personal property and the real property in accordance with the rights with respect to the real property, in which case the other provisions of this part do not apply.

(b) Subject to subsection (c), if a security agreement covers goods that are or become fixtures, a secured party may proceed:

(1) under this part; or

(2) in accordance with the rights with respect to real property, in which case the other provisions of this part do not apply.

(c) Subject to the other provisions of this part, if a secured party holding a security interest in fixtures has priority over all owners and encumbrancers of the real property, the secured party, after default, may remove the collateral from the real property.

(d) A secured party that removes collateral shall promptly reimburse any encumbrancer or owner of the real property, other than the debtor, for the cost of repair of any physical injury caused by the removal. The secured party need not reimburse the encumbrancer or owner for any diminution in value of the real property caused by the absence of the goods removed or by any necessity of replacing them. A person entitled to reimbursement may refuse permission to remove until the secured party gives adequate assurance for the performance of the obligation to reimburse.

§ 9-605. Unknown Debtor or Secondary Obligor.

A secured party does not owe a duty based on its status as secured party:

(1) to a person that is a debtor or obligor, unless the secured party knows:

(A) that the person is a debtor or obligor;

(B) the identity of the person; and

(C) how to communicate with the person; or

(2) to a secured party or lienholder that has filed a financing statement against a person, unless the secured party knows:

(A) that the person is a debtor; and

(B) the identity of the person.

§ 9-606. Time of Default for Agricultural Lien.

For purposes of this part, a default occurs in connection with an agricultural lien at the time the secured party becomes entitled to enforce the lien in accordance with the statute under which it was created.

§ 9-607. Collection and Enforcement by Secured Party.

(a) If so agreed, and in any event after default, a secured party:

(1) may notify an account debtor or other person obligated on collateral to make payment or otherwise render performance to or for the benefit of the secured party;

(2) may take any proceeds to which the secured party is entitled under Section 9–315;

(3) may enforce the obligations of an account debtor or other person obligated on collateral and exercise the rights of the debtor with respect to the obligation of the account debtor or other person obligated on collateral to make payment or otherwise render performance to the debtor, and with respect to any property that secures the obligations of the account debtor or other person obligated on the collateral;

(4) if it holds a security interest in a deposit account perfected by control under Section 9–104(a)(1), may apply the balance of the deposit account to the obligation secured by the deposit account; and

(5) if it holds a security interest in a deposit account perfected by control under Section 9–104(a)(2) or (3), may instruct the bank to pay the balance of the deposit account to or for the benefit of the secured party.

(b) If necessary to enable a secured party to exercise under subsection (a)(3) the right of a debtor to enforce a mortgage nonjudicially, the secured party may record in the office in which a record of the mortgage is recorded:

(1) a copy of the security agreement that creates or provides for a security interest in the obligation secured by the mortgage; and

(2) the secured party's sworn affidavit in recordable form stating that:

(A) a default has occurred; and

(B) the secured party is entitled to enforce the mortgage nonjudicially.

(c) A secured party shall proceed in a commercially reasonable manner if the secured party:

(1) undertakes to collect from or enforce an obligation of an account debtor or other person obligated on collateral; and

(2) is entitled to charge back uncollected collateral or otherwise to full or limited recourse against the debtor or a secondary obligor.

(d) A secured party may deduct from the collections made pursuant to subsection (c) reasonable expenses of collection and enforcement, including reasonable attorney's fees and legal expenses incurred by the secured party.

(e) This section does not determine whether an account debtor, bank, or other person obligated on collateral owes a duty to a secured party.

As amended in 2000.

§ 9-608. Application of Proceeds of Collection or Enforcement; Liability for Deficiency and Right to Surplus.

(a) If a security interest or agricultural lien secures payment or performance of an obligation, the following rules apply:

(1) A secured party shall apply or pay over for application the cash proceeds of collection or enforcement under Section 9–607 in the following order to:

(A) the reasonable expenses of collection and enforcement and, to the extent provided for by agreement and not prohibited by law, reasonable attorney's fees and legal expenses incurred by the secured party;

(B) the satisfaction of obligations secured by the security interest or agricultural lien under which the collection or enforcement is made; and

(C) the satisfaction of obligations secured by any subordinate security interest in or other lien on the collateral subject to the security interest or agricultural lien under which the collection or enforcement is made if the secured party receives an authenticated demand for proceeds before distribution of the proceeds is completed.

(2) If requested by a secured party, a holder of a subordinate security interest or other lien shall furnish reasonable proof of the interest or lien within a reasonable time. Unless the holder complies, the secured party need not comply with the holder's demand under paragraph (1)(C).

(3) A secured party need not apply or pay over for application noncash proceeds of collection and enforcement under Section 9–607 unless the failure to do so would be commercially unreasonable. A secured party that applies or pays over for

application noncash proceeds shall do so in a commercially reasonable manner.

(4) A secured party shall account to and pay a debtor for any surplus, and the obligor is liable for any deficiency.

(b) If the underlying transaction is a sale of accounts, chattel paper, payment intangibles, or promissory notes, the debtor is not entitled to any surplus, and the obligor is not liable for any deficiency.

As amended in 2000.

§ 9–609. Secured Party's Right to Take Possession after Default.

(a) After default, a secured party:

(1) may take possession of the collateral; and

(2) without removal, may render equipment unusable and dispose of collateral on a debtor's premises under Section 9–610.

(b) A secured party may proceed under subsection (a):

(1) pursuant to judicial process; or

(2) without judicial process, if it proceeds without breach of the peace.

(c) If so agreed, and in any event after default, a secured party may require the debtor to assemble the collateral and make it available to the secured party at a place to be designated by the secured party which is reasonably convenient to both parties.

§ 9–610. Disposition of Collateral after Default.

(a) After default, a secured party may sell, lease, license, or otherwise dispose of any or all of the collateral in its present condition or following any commercially reasonable preparation or processing.

(b) Every aspect of a disposition of collateral, including the method, manner, time, place, and other terms, must be commercially reasonable. If commercially reasonable, a secured party may dispose of collateral by public or private proceedings, by one or more contracts, as a unit or in parcels, and at any time and place and on any terms.

(c) A secured party may purchase collateral:

(1) at a public disposition; or

(2) at a private disposition only if the collateral is of a kind that is customarily sold on a recognized market or the subject of widely distributed standard price quotations.

(d) A contract for sale, lease, license, or other disposition includes the warranties relating to title, possession, quiet enjoyment, and the like which by operation of law accompany a voluntary disposition of property of the kind subject to the contract.

(e) A secured party may disclaim or modify warranties under subsection (d):

(1) in a manner that would be effective to disclaim or modify the warranties in a voluntary disposition of property of the kind subject to the contract of disposition; or

(2) by communicating to the purchaser a record evidencing the contract for disposition and including an express disclaimer or modification of the warranties.

(f) A record is sufficient to disclaim warranties under subsection (e) if it indicates "There is no warranty relating to title, possession, quiet enjoyment, or the like in this disposition" or uses words of similar import.

§ 9–611. Notification before Disposition of Collateral.

(a) In this section, "notification date" means the earlier of the date on which:

(1) a secured party sends to the debtor and any secondary obligor an authenticated notification of disposition; or

(2) the debtor and any secondary obligor waive the right to notification.

(b) Except as otherwise provided in subsection (d), a secured party that disposes of collateral under Section 9–610 shall send to the persons specified in subsection (c) a reasonable authenticated notification of disposition.

(c) To comply with subsection (b), the secured party shall send an authenticated notification of disposition to:

(1) the debtor;

(2) any secondary obligor; and

(3) if the collateral is other than consumer goods:

(A) any other person from which the secured party has received, before the notification date, an authenticated notification of a claim of an interest in the collateral;

(B) any other secured party or lienholder that, 10 days before the notification date, held a security interest in or other lien on the collateral perfected by the filing of a financing statement that:

(i) identified the collateral;

(ii) was indexed under the debtor's name as of that date; and

(iii) was filed in the office in which to file a financing statement against the debtor covering the collateral as of that date; and

(C) any other secured party that, 10 days before the notification date, held a security interest in the collateral perfected by compliance with a statute, regulation, or treaty described in Section 9–311(a).

(d) Subsection (b) does not apply if the collateral is perishable or threatens to decline speedily in value or is of a type customarily sold on a recognized market.

(e) A secured party complies with the requirement for notification prescribed by subsection (c)(3)(B) if:

(1) not later than 20 days or earlier than 30 days before the notification date, the secured party requests, in a commercially reasonable manner, information concerning financing statements indexed under the debtor's name in the office indicated in subsection (c)(3)(B); and

(2) before the notification date, the secured party:

(A) did not receive a response to the request for information; or

(B) received a response to the request for information and sent an authenticated notification of disposition to each secured party or other lienholder named in that response whose financing statement covered the collateral.

§ 9–612. Timeliness of Notification before Disposition of Collateral.

(a) Except as otherwise provided in subsection (b), whether a notification is sent within a reasonable time is a question of fact.

(b) In a transaction other than a consumer transaction, a notification of disposition sent after default and 10 days or more before the earliest time of disposition set forth in the notification is sent within a reasonable time before the disposition.

§ 9–613. Contents and Form of Notification before Disposition of Collateral: General.

Except in a consumer-goods transaction, the following rules apply:

(1) The contents of a notification of disposition are sufficient if the notification:

(A) describes the debtor and the secured party;

(B) describes the collateral that is the subject of the intended disposition;

(C) states the method of intended disposition;

(D) states that the debtor is entitled to an accounting of the unpaid indebtedness and states the charge, if any, for an accounting; and

(E) states the time and place of a public disposition or the time after which any other disposition is to be made.

(2) Whether the contents of a notification that lacks any of the information specified in paragraph (1) are nevertheless sufficient is a question of fact.

(3) The contents of a notification providing substantially the information specified in paragraph (1) are sufficient, even if the notification includes:

(A) information not specified by that paragraph; or

(b) minor errors that are not seriously misleading.

(4) A particular phrasing of the notification is not required.

(5) The following form of notification and the form appearing in Section 9–614(3), when completed, each provides sufficient information:

NOTIFICATION OF DISPOSITION OF COLLATERAL

To: [*Name of debtor, obligor, or other person to which the notification is sent*]

From: [*Name, address, and telephone number of secured party*]

Name of Debtor(s): [*Include only if debtor(s) are not an addressee*]

[*For a public disposition:*]

We will sell [or lease or license, *as applicable*] the [*describe collateral*] [to the highest qualified bidder] in public as follows:

Day and Date: _______

Time: _______

Place: _______

[*For a private disposition:*]

We will sell [or lease or license, *as applicable*] the [*describe collateral*] privately sometime after [*day and date*].

You are entitled to an accounting of the unpaid indebted ness secured by the property that we intend to sell [or lease or license as *applicable*] [for a charge of $_______]. You may request an accounting by calling us at [*telephone number*].

[End of Form]

As amended in 2000.

§ 9–614. Contents and Form of Notification before Disposition of Collateral: Consumer-Goods Transaction.

In a consumer-goods transaction, the following rules apply:

(1) A notification of disposition must provide the following information:

(A) the information specified in Section 9–613(1);

(B) a description of any liability for a deficiency of the person to which the notification is sent;

(C) a telephone number from which the amount that must be paid to the secured party to redeem the collateral under Section 9–623 is available; and

(D) a telephone number or mailing address from which additional information concerning the disposition and the obligation secured is available.

(2) A particular phrasing of the notification is not required.

(3) The following form of notification, when completed, provides sufficient information:

[*Name and address of secured party*]

[*Date*]

NOTICE OF OUR PLAN TO SELL PROPERTY

[*Name and address of any obligor who is also a debtor*]

Subject: [*Identification of Transaction*]

We have your [*describe collateral*], because you broke promises in our agreement.

[*For a public disposition:*]

We will sell [*describe collateral*] at public sale. A sale could include a lease or license. The sale will be held as follows:

Date: _______

Time: _______

Place: _______

You may attend the sale and bring bidders if you want.

[*For a private disposition:*]

We will sell [*describe collateral*] at private sale sometime after

[*date*]. A sale could include a lease or license.

The money that we get from the sale (after paying our costs) will reduce the amount you owe. If we get less money than you owe, you [*will or will not, as applicable*] still owe us the difference. If we get more money than you owe, you will get the extra money, unless we must pay it to someone else.

You can get the property back at any time before we sell it by paying us the full amount you owe (not just the past due payments), including our expenses. To learn the exact amount you must pay, call us at [*telephone number*].

If you want us to explain to you in writing how we have figured the amount that you owe us, you may call us at [*telephone number*] [or write us at [*secured party's address*]] and request a written explanation. [We will charge you $_______ for the explanation if we sent you another written explanation of the amount you owe us within the last six months.]

If you need more information about the sale call us at [*telephone number*] [or write us at [*secured party's address*]].

We are sending this notice to the following other people who have an interest in [*describe collateral*] or who owe money under your agreement:

[*Names of all other debtors and obligors, if any*]

[End of Form]

(4) A notification in the form of paragraph (3) is sufficient, even if additional information appears at the end of the form.

(5) A notification in the form of paragraph (3) is sufficient, even if it includes errors in information not required by paragraph (1), unless the error is misleading with respect to rights arising under this article.

(6) If a notification under this section is not in the form of paragraph (3), law other than this article determines the effect of including information not required by paragraph (1).

§ 9-615. Application of Proceeds of Disposition; Liability for Deficiency and Right to Surplus.

(a) A secured party shall apply or pay over for application the cash proceeds of disposition under Section 9–610 in the following order to:

(1) the reasonable expenses of retaking, holding, preparing for disposition, processing, and disposing, and, to the extent provided for by agreement and not prohibited by law, reasonable attorney's fees and legal expenses incurred by the secured party;

(2) the satisfaction of obligations secured by the security interest or agricultural lien under which the disposition is made;

(3) the satisfaction of obligations secured by any subordinate security interest in or other subordinate lien on the collateral if:

(A) the secured party receives from the holder of the subordinate security interest or other lien an authenticated demand for proceeds before distribution of the proceeds is completed; and

(B) in a case in which a consignor has an interest in the collateral, the subordinate security interest or other lien is senior to the interest of the consignor; and

(4) a secured party that is a consignor of the collateral if the secured party receives from the consignor an authenticated demand for proceeds before distribution of the proceeds is completed.

(b) If requested by a secured party, a holder of a subordinate security interest or other lien shall furnish reasonable proof of the interest or lien within a reasonable time. Unless the holder does so, the secured party need not comply with the holder's demand under subsection (a)(3).

(c) A secured party need not apply or pay over for application noncash proceeds of disposition under Section 9–610 unless the failure to do so would be commercially unreasonable. A secured party that applies or pays over for application noncash proceeds shall do so in a commercially reasonable manner.

(d) If the security interest under which a disposition is made secures payment or performance of an obligation, after making the payments and applications required by subsection (a) and permitted by subsection (c):

(1) unless subsection (a)(4) requires the secured party to apply or pay over cash proceeds to a consignor, the secured party shall account to and pay a debtor for any surplus; and

(2) the obligor is liable for any deficiency.

(e) If the underlying transaction is a sale of accounts, chattel paper, payment intangibles, or promissory notes:

(1) the debtor is not entitled to any surplus; and

(2) the obligor is not liable for any deficiency.

(f) The surplus or deficiency following a disposition is calculated based on the amount of proceeds that would have been realized in a disposition complying with this part to a transferee other than the secured party, a person related to the secured party, or a secondary obligor if:

(1) the transferee in the disposition is the secured party, a person related to the secured party, or a secondary obligor; and

(2) the amount of proceeds of the disposition is significantly below the range of proceeds that a complying disposition to a person other than the secured party, a person related to the secured party, or a secondary obligor would have brought.

(g) A secured party that receives cash proceeds of a disposition in good faith and without knowledge that the receipt violates the rights of the holder of a security interest or other lien that is not subordinate to the security interest or agricultural lien under which the disposition is made:

(1) takes the cash proceeds free of the security interest or other lien;

(2) is not obligated to apply the proceeds of the disposition to the satisfaction of obligations secured by the security interest or other lien; and

(3) is not obligated to account to or pay the holder of the security interest or other lien for any surplus.

As amended in 2000.

§ 9-616. Explanation of Calculation of Surplus or Deficiency.

(a) In this section:

(1) "Explanation" means a writing that:

(A) states the amount of the surplus or deficiency;

(B) provides an explanation in accordance with subsection (c) of how the secured party calculated the surplus or deficiency;

(C) states, if applicable, that future debits, credits, charges, including additional credit service charges or interest, rebates, and expenses may affect the amount of the surplus or deficiency; and

(D) provides a telephone number or mailing address from which additional information concerning the transaction is available.

(2) "Request" means a record:

(A) authenticated by a debtor or consumer obligor;

(B) requesting that the recipient provide an explanation; and

(C) sent after disposition of the collateral under Section 9–610.

(b) In a consumer-goods transaction in which the debtor is entitled to a surplus or a consumer obligor is liable for a deficiency under Section 9–615, the secured party shall:

(1) send an explanation to the debtor or consumer obligor, as applicable, after the disposition and:

(A) before or when the secured party accounts to the debtor and pays any surplus or first makes written demand on the consumer obligor after the disposition for payment of the deficiency; and

(B) within 14 days after receipt of a request; or

(2) in the case of a consumer obligor who is liable for a deficiency, within 14 days after receipt of a request, send to the consumer obligor a record waiving the secured party's right to a deficiency.

(c) To comply with subsection (a)(1)(B), a writing must provide the following information in the following order:

(1) the aggregate amount of obligations secured by the security interest under which the disposition was made, and, if the amount reflects a rebate of unearned interest or credit service charge, an indication of that fact, calculated as of a specified date:

(A) if the secured party takes or receives possession of the collateral after default, not more than 35 days before the secured party takes or receives possession; or

(B) if the secured party takes or receives possession of the collateral before default or does not take possession of the collateral, not more than 35 days before the disposition;

(2) the amount of proceeds of the disposition;

(3) the aggregate amount of the obligations after deducting the amount of proceeds;

(4) the amount, in the aggregate or by type, and types of expenses, including expenses of retaking, holding, preparing for disposition, processing, and disposing of the collateral, and attorney's fees secured by the collateral which are known to the secured party and relate to the current disposition;

(5) the amount, in the aggregate or by type, and types of credits, including rebates of interest or credit service charges, to which the obligor is known to be entitled and which are not reflected in the amount in paragraph (1); and

(6) the amount of the surplus or deficiency.

(d) A particular phrasing of the explanation is not required. An explanation complying substantially with the requirements of subsection (a) is sufficient, even if it includes minor errors that are not seriously misleading.

(e) A debtor or consumer obligor is entitled without charge to one response to a request under this section during any six-month period in which the secured party did not send to the debtor or consumer obligor an explanation pursuant to subsection (b)(1). The secured party may require payment of a charge not exceeding $25 for each additional response.

§ 9-617. Rights of Transferee of Collateral.

(a) A secured party's disposition of collateral after default:

(1) transfers to a transferee for value all of the debtor's rights in the collateral;

(2) discharges the security interest under which the disposition is made; and

(3) discharges any subordinate security interest or other subordinate lien [other than liens created under [cite acts or statutes providing for liens, if any, that are not to be discharged]].

(b) A transferee that acts in good faith takes free of the rights and interests described in subsection (a), even if the secured party fails to comply with this article or the requirements of any judicial proceeding.

(c) If a transferee does not take free of the rights and interests described in subsection (a), the transferee takes the collateral subject to:

(1) the debtor's rights in the collateral;

(2) the security interest or agricultural lien under which the disposition is made; and

(3) any other security interest or other lien.

§ 9–618. Rights and Duties of Certain Secondary Obligors.

(a) A secondary obligor acquires the rights and becomes obligated to perform the duties of the secured party after the secondary obligor:

(1) receives an assignment of a secured obligation from the secured party;

(2) receives a transfer of collateral from the secured party and agrees to accept the rights and assume the duties of the secured party; or

(3) is subrogated to the rights of a secured party with respect to collateral.

(b) An assignment, transfer, or subrogation described in subsection (a):

(1) is not a disposition of collateral under Section 9–610; and

(2) relieves the secured party of further duties under this article.

§ 9–619. Transfer of Record or Legal Title.

(a) In this section, "transfer statement" means a record authenticated by a secured party stating:

(1) that the debtor has defaulted in connection with an obligation secured by specified collateral;

(2) that the secured party has exercised its post-default remedies with respect to the collateral;

(3) that, by reason of the exercise, a transferee has acquired the rights of the debtor in the collateral; and

(4) the name and mailing address of the secured party, debtor, and transferee.

(b) A transfer statement entitles the transferee to the transfer of record of all rights of the debtor in the collateral specified in the statement in any official filing, recording, registration, or certificate-of-title system covering the collateral. If a transfer statement is presented with the applicable fee and request form to the official or office responsible for maintaining the system, the official or office shall:

(1) accept the transfer statement;

(2) promptly amend its records to reflect the transfer; and

(3) if applicable, issue a new appropriate certificate of title in the name of the transferee.

(c) A transfer of the record or legal title to collateral to a secured party under subsection (b) or otherwise is not of itself a disposition of collateral under this article and does not of itself relieve the secured party of its duties under this article.

§ 9–620. Acceptance of Collateral in Full or Partial Satisfaction of Obligation; Compulsory Disposition of Collateral.

(a) Except as otherwise provided in subsection (g), a secured party may accept collateral in full or partial satisfaction of the obligation it secures only if:

(1) the debtor consents to the acceptance under subsection (c);

(2) the secured party does not receive, within the time set forth in subsection (d), a notification of objection to the proposal authenticated by:

(A) a person to which the secured party was required to send a proposal under Section 9–621; or

(B) any other person, other than the debtor, holding an interest in the collateral subordinate to the security interest that is the subject of the proposal;

(3) if the collateral is consumer goods, the collateral is not in the possession of the debtor when the debtor consents to the acceptance; and

(4) subsection (e) does not require the secured party to dispose of the collateral or the debtor waives the requirement pursuant to Section 9–624.

(b) A purported or apparent acceptance of collateral under this section is ineffective unless:

(1) the secured party consents to the acceptance in an authenticated record or sends a proposal to the debtor; and

(2) the conditions of subsection (a) are met.

(c) For purposes of this section:

(1) a debtor consents to an acceptance of collateral in partial satisfaction of the obligation it secures only if the debtor agrees to the terms of the acceptance in a record authenticated after default; and

(2) a debtor consents to an acceptance of collateral in full satisfaction of the obligation it secures only if the debtor agrees to the terms of the acceptance in a record authenticated after default or the secured party:

(A) sends to the debtor after default a proposal that is unconditional or subject only to a condition that collateral not in the possession of the secured party be preserved or maintained;

(B) in the proposal, proposes to accept collateral in full satisfaction of the obligation it secures; and

(C) does not receive a notification of objection authenticated by the debtor within 20 days after the proposal is sent.

(d) To be effective under subsection (a)(2), a notification of objection must be received by the secured party:

(1) in the case of a person to which the proposal was sent pursuant to Section 9–621, within 20 days after notification was sent to that person; and

(2) in other cases:

(A) within 20 days after the last notification was sent pursuant to Section 9–621; or

(B) if a notification was not sent, before the debtor consents to the acceptance under subsection (c).

(e) A secured party that has taken possession of collateral shall dispose of the collateral pursuant to Section 9–610 within the time specified in subsection (f) if:

(1) 60 percent of the cash price has been paid in the case of a purchase-money security interest in consumer goods; or

(2) 60 percent of the principal amount of the obligation secured has been paid in the case of a non-purchase-money security interest in consumer goods.

(f) To comply with subsection (e), the secured party shall dispose of the collateral:

(1) within 90 days after taking possession; or

(2) within any longer period to which the debtor and all secondary obligors have agreed in an agreement to that effect entered into and authenticated after default.

(g) In a consumer transaction, a secured party may not accept collateral in partial satisfaction of the obligation it secures.

§ 9–621. Notification of Proposal to Accept Collateral.

(a) A secured party that desires to accept collateral in full or partial satisfaction of the obligation it secures shall send its proposal to:

(1) any person from which the secured party has received, before the debtor consented to the acceptance, an authenticated notification of a claim of an interest in the collateral;

(2) any other secured party or lienholder that, 10 days before the debtor consented to the acceptance, held a security interest in or other lien on the collateral perfected by the filing of a financing statement that:

(A) identified the collateral;

(B) was indexed under the debtor's name as of that date; and

(C) was filed in the office or offices in which to file a financing statement against the debtor covering the collateral as of that date; and

(3) any other secured party that, 10 days before the debtor consented to the acceptance, held a security interest in the collateral perfected by compliance with a statute, regulation, or treaty described in Section 9–311(a).

(b) A secured party that desires to accept collateral in partial satisfaction of the obligation it secures shall send its proposal to any secondary obligor in addition to the persons described in subsection (a).

§ 9–622. Effect of Acceptance of Collateral.

(a) A secured party's acceptance of collateral in full or partial satisfaction of the obligation it secures:

(1) discharges the obligation to the extent consented to by the debtor;

(2) transfers to the secured party all of a debtor's rights in the collateral;

(3) discharges the security interest or agricultural lien that is the subject of the debtor's consent and any subordinate security interest or other subordinate lien; and

(4) terminates any other subordinate interest.

(b) A subordinate interest is discharged or terminated under subsection (a), even if the secured party fails to comply with this article.

§ 9–623. Right to Redeem Collateral.

(a) A debtor, any secondary obligor, or any other secured party or lienholder may redeem collateral.

(b) To redeem collateral, a person shall tender:

(1) fulfillment of all obligations secured by the collateral; and

(2) the reasonable expenses and attorney's fees described in Section 9–615(a)(1).

(c) A redemption may occur at any time before a secured party:

(1) has collected collateral under Section 9–607;

(2) has disposed of collateral or entered into a contract for its disposition under Section 9–610; or

(3) has accepted collateral in full or partial satisfaction of the obligation it secures under Section 9–622.

§ 9–624. Waiver.

(a) A debtor or secondary obligor may waive the right to notification of disposition of collateral under Section 9–611 only by an agreement to that effect entered into and authenticated after default.

(b) A debtor may waive the right to require disposition of collateral under Section 9–620(e) only by an agreement to that effect entered into and authenticated after default.

(c) Except in a consumer-goods transaction, a debtor or secondary obligor may waive the right to redeem collateral under Section 9–623 only by an agreement to that effect entered into and authenticated after default.

[Subpart 2. Noncompliance with Article]

§ 9–625. Remedies for Secured Party's Failure to Comply with Article.

(a) If it is established that a secured party is not proceeding in accordance with this article, a court may order or restrain collection, enforcement, or disposition of collateral on appropriate terms and conditions.

(b) Subject to subsections (c), (d), and (f), a person is liable for damages in the amount of any loss caused by a failure to comply with this article. Loss caused by a failure to comply may include loss resulting from the debtor's inability to obtain, or increased costs of, alternative financing.

(c) Except as otherwise provided in Section 9–628:

(1) a person that, at the time of the failure, was a debtor, was an obligor, or held a security interest in or other lien on the collateral may recover damages under subsection (b) for its loss; and

(2) if the collateral is consumer goods, a person that was a debtor or a secondary obligor at the time a secured party failed to comply with this part may recover for that failure in any event an amount not less than the credit service charge plus 10 percent of the principal amount of the obligation or the time-price differential plus 10 percent of the cash price.

(d) A debtor whose deficiency is eliminated under Section 9–626 may recover damages for the loss of any surplus. However, a debtor or secondary obligor whose deficiency is eliminated or reduced under Section 9–626 may not otherwise recover under subsection (b) for noncompliance with the provisions of this part relating to collection, enforcement, disposition, or acceptance.

(e) In addition to any damages recoverable under subsection (b), the debtor, consumer obligor, or person named as a debtor in a filed record, as applicable, may recover $500 in each case from a person that:

(1) fails to comply with Section 9–208;

(2) fails to comply with Section 9–209;

(3) files a record that the person is not entitled to file under Section 9–509(a);

(4) fails to cause the secured party of record to file or send a termination statement as required by Section 9–513(a) or (c);

(5) fails to comply with Section 9–616(b)(1) and whose failure is part of a pattern, or consistent with a practice, of noncompliance; or

(6) fails to comply with Section 9–616(b)(2).

(f) A debtor or consumer obligor may recover damages under subsection (b) and, in addition, $500 in each case from a person that, without reasonable cause, fails to comply with a request under Section 9–210. A recipient of a request under Section 9–210 which never claimed an interest in the collateral or obligations that are the subject of a request under that section has a reasonable excuse for failure to comply with the request within the meaning of this subsection.

(g) If a secured party fails to comply with a request regarding a list of collateral or a statement of account under Section 9–210, the secured party may claim a security interest only as shown in the list or statement included in the request as against a person that is reasonably misled by the failure.

As amended in 2000.

§ 9–626. Action in Which Deficiency or Surplus Is in Issue.

(a) In an action arising from a transaction, other than a consumer transaction, in which the amount of a deficiency or surplus is in issue, the following rules apply:

(1) A secured party need not prove compliance with the provisions of this part relating to collection, enforcement, disposition, or acceptance unless the debtor or a secondary obligor places the secured party's compliance in issue.

(2) If the secured party's compliance is placed in issue, the secured party has the burden of establishing that the collection, enforcement, disposition, or acceptance was conducted in accordance with this part.

(3) Except as otherwise provided in Section 9–628, if a secured party fails to prove that the collection, enforcement, disposition, or acceptance was conducted in accordance with the provisions of this part relating to collection, enforcement, disposition, or acceptance, the liability of a debtor or a secondary obligor for a deficiency is limited to an amount by which the sum of the secured obligation, expenses, and attorney's fees exceeds the greater of:

(A) the proceeds of the collection, enforcement, disposition, or acceptance; or

(B) the amount of proceeds that would have been realized had the noncomplying secured party proceeded in accordance with the provisions of this part relating to collection, enforcement, disposition, or acceptance.

(4) For purposes of paragraph (3)(B), the amount of proceeds that would have been realized is equal to the sum of the secured obligation, expenses, and attorney's fees unless the secured party proves that the amount is less than that sum.

(5) If a deficiency or surplus is calculated under Section 9–615 (f), the debtor or obligor has the burden of establishing that the amount of proceeds of the disposition is significantly below the range of prices that a complying disposition to a person other than the secured party, a person related to the secured party, or a secondary obligor would have brought.

(b) The limitation of the rules in subsection (a) to transactions other than consumer transactions is intended to leave to the court the determination of the proper rules in consumer transactions. The court may not infer from that limitation the nature of the proper rule in consumer transactions and may continue to apply established approaches.

§ 9–627. Determination of Whether Conduct Was Commercially Reasonable.

(a) The fact that a greater amount could have been obtained by a collection, enforcement, disposition, or acceptance at a different time or in a different method from that selected by the secured party is not of itself sufficient to preclude the secured party from establishing that the collection, enforcement, disposition, or acceptance was made in a commercially reasonable manner.

(b) A disposition of collateral is made in a commercially reasonable manner if the disposition is made:

(1) in the usual manner on any recognized market;

(2) at the price current in any recognized market at the time of the disposition; or

(3) otherwise in conformity with reasonable commercial practices among dealers in the type of property that was the subject of the disposition.

(c) A collection, enforcement, disposition, or acceptance is commercially reasonable if it has been approved:

(1) in a judicial proceeding;

(2) by a bona fide creditors' committee;

(3) by a representative of creditors; or

(4) by an assignee for the benefit of creditors.

(d) Approval under subsection (c) need not be obtained, and lack of approval does not mean that the collection, enforcement, disposition, or acceptance is not commercially reasonable.

§ 9–628. Nonliability and Limitation on Liability of Secured Party; Liability of Secondary Obligor.

(a) Unless a secured party knows that a person is a debtor or obligor, knows the identity of the person, and knows how to communicate with the person:

(1) the secured party is not liable to the person, or to a secured party or lienholder that has filed a financing statement against the person, for failure to comply with this article; and

(2) the secured party's failure to comply with this article does not affect the liability of the person for a deficiency.

(b) A secured party is not liable because of its status as secured party:

(1) to a person that is a debtor or obligor, unless the secured party knows:

(A) that the person is a debtor or obligor;

(B) the identity of the person; and

(C) how to communicate with the person; or

(2) to a secured party or lienholder that has filed a financing statement against a person, unless the secured party knows:

(A) that the person is a debtor; and

(B) the identity of the person.

(c) A secured party is not liable to any person, and a person's liability for a deficiency is not affected, because of any act or omission arising out of the secured party's reasonable belief that a transaction is not a consumer-goods transaction or a consumer transaction or that goods are not consumer goods, if the secured party's belief is based on its reasonable reliance on:

(1) a debtor's representation concerning the purpose for which collateral was to be used, acquired, or held; or

(2) an obligor's representation concerning the purpose for which a secured obligation was incurred.

(d) A secured party is not liable to any person under Section 9–625(c)(2) for its failure to comply with Section 9–616.

(e) A secured party is not liable under Section 9–625(c)(2) more than once with respect to any one secured obligation.

PART 7 Transition

§ 9–701. Effective Date.

This [Act] takes effect on July 1, 2001.

§ 9–702. Savings Clause.

(a) Except as otherwise provided in this part, this [Act] applies to a transaction or lien within its scope, even if the transaction or lien was entered into or created before this [Act] takes effect.

(b) Except as otherwise provided in subsection (c) and Sections 9–703 through 9–709:

(1) transactions and liens that were not governed by [former Article 9], were validly entered into or created before this [Act] takes effect, and would be subject to this [Act] if they had been entered into or created after this [Act] takes effect, and the rights, duties, and interests flowing from those transactions and liens remain valid after this [Act] takes effect; and

(2) the transactions and liens may be terminated, completed, consummated, and enforced as required or permitted by this [Act] or by the law that otherwise would apply if this [Act] had not taken effect.

(c) This [Act] does not affect an action, case, or proceeding commenced before this [Act] takes effect.

As amended in 2000.

§ 9–703. Security Interest Perfected before Effective Date.

(a) A security interest that is enforceable immediately before this [Act] takes effect and would have priority over the rights of a person that becomes a lien creditor at that time is a perfected security interest under this [Act] if, when this [Act] takes effect, the applicable requirements for enforceability and perfection under this [Act] are satisfied without further action.

(b) Except as otherwise provided in Section 9–705, if, immediately before this [Act] takes effect, a security interest is enforceable and would have priority over the rights of a person that becomes a lien creditor at that time, but the applicable requirements for enforceability or perfection under this [Act] are not satisfied when this [Act] takes effect, the security interest:

(1) is a perfected security interest for one year after this [Act] takes effect;

(2) remains enforceable thereafter only if the security interest becomes enforceable under Section 9–203 before the year expires; and

(3) remains perfected thereafter only if the applicable requirements for perfection under this [Act] are satisfied before the year expires.

§ 9–704. Security Interest Unperfected before Effective Date.

A security interest that is enforceable immediately before this [Act] takes effect but which would be subordinate to the rights of a person that becomes a lien creditor at that time:

(1) remains an enforceable security interest for one year after this [Act] takes effect;

(2) remains enforceable thereafter if the security interest becomes enforceable under Section 9–203 when this [Act] takes effect or within one year thereafter; and

(3) becomes perfected:

(A) without further action, when this [Act] takes effect if the applicable requirements for perfection under this [Act] are satisfied before or at that time; or

(B) when the applicable requirements for perfection are satisfied if the requirements are satisfied after that time.

§ 9–705. Effectiveness of Action Taken before Effective Date.

(a) If action, other than the filing of a financing statement, is taken before this [Act] takes effect and the action would have resulted in priority of a security interest over the rights of a person that becomes a lien creditor had the security interest become enforceable before this [Act] takes effect, the action is effective to perfect a security interest that attaches under this [Act] within one year after this [Act] takes effect. An attached security interest becomes unperfected one year after this [Act] takes effect unless the security interest becomes a perfected security interest under this [Act] before the expiration of that period.

(b) The filing of a financing statement before this [Act] takes effect is effective to perfect a security interest to the extent the filing would satisfy the applicable requirements for perfection under this [Act].

(c) This [Act] does not render ineffective an effective financing statement that, before this [Act] takes effect, is filed and satisfies the applicable requirements for perfection under the law of the jurisdiction governing perfection as provided in [former Section 9–103]. However, except as otherwise provided in subsections (d) and (e) and Section 9–706, the financing statement ceases to be effective at the earlier of:

(1) the time the financing statement would have ceased to be effective under the law of the jurisdiction in which it is filed; or

(2) June 30, 2006.

(d) The filing of a continuation statement after this [Act] takes effect does not continue the effectiveness of the financing statement filed before this [Act] takes effect. However, upon the timely filing of a continuation statement after this [Act] takes effect and in accordance with the law of the jurisdiction governing perfection as provided in Part 3, the effectiveness of a financing statement filed in the same office in that jurisdiction before this [Act] takes effect continues for the period provided by the law of that jurisdiction.

(e) Subsection (c)(2) applies to a financing statement that, before this [Act] takes effect, is filed against a transmitting utility and satisfies the applicable requirements for perfection under the law of the jurisdiction governing perfection as provided in [former Section 9–103] only to the extent that Part 3 provides that the law of a jurisdiction other than the jurisdiction in which the financing statement is filed governs perfection of a security interest in collateral covered by the financing statement.

(f) A financing statement that includes a financing statement filed before this [Act] takes effect and a continuation statement filed after this [Act] takes effect is effective only to the extent that it satisfies the requirements of Part 5 for an initial financing statement.

§ 9–706. When Initial Financing Statement Suffices to Continue Effectiveness of Financing Statement.

(a) The filing of an initial financing statement in the office specified in Section 9–501 continues the effectiveness of a financing statement filed before this [Act] takes effect if:

(1) the filing of an initial financing statement in that office would be effective to perfect a security interest under this [Act];

(2) the pre-effective-date financing statement was filed in an office in another State or another office in this State; and

(3) the initial financing statement satisfies subsection (c).

(b) The filing of an initial financing statement under subsection (a) continues the effectiveness of the pre-effective-date financing statement:

(1) if the initial financing statement is filed before this [Act] takes effect, for the period provided in [former Section 9–403] with respect to a financing statement; and

(2) if the initial financing statement is filed after this [Act] takes effect, for the period provided in Section 9–515 with respect to an initial financing statement.

(c) To be effective for purposes of subsection (a), an initial financing statement must:

(1) satisfy the requirements of Part 5 for an initial financing statement;

(2) identify the pre-effective-date financing statement by indicating the office in which the financing statement was filed and providing the dates of filing and file numbers, if any, of the financing statement and of the most recent continuation statement filed with respect to the financing statement; and

(3) indicate that the pre-effective-date financing statement remains effective.

§ 9–707. Amendment of Pre-Effective-Date Financing Statement.

(a) In this section, "Pre-effective-date financing statement" means a financing statement filed before this [Act] takes effect.

(b) After this [Act] takes effect, a person may add or delete collateral covered by, continue or terminate the effectiveness of, or otherwise amend the information provided in, a pre-effective-date financing statement only in accordance with the law of the jurisdiction governing perfection as provided in Part 3. However, the effectiveness of a pre-effective-date financing statement also may be terminated in accordance with the law of the jurisdiction in which the financing statement is filed.

(c) Except as otherwise provided in subsection (d), if the law of this State governs perfection of a security interest, the information in a pre-effective-date financing statement may be amended after this [Act] takes effect only if:

(1) the pre-effective-date financing statement and an amendment are filed in the office specified in Section 9–501;

(2) an amendment is filed in the office specified in Section 9–501 concurrently with, or after the filing in that office of, an initial financing statement that satisfies Section 9–706(c); or

(3) an initial financing statement that provides the information as amended and satisfies Section 9–706(c) is filed in the office specified in Section 9–501.

(d) If the law of this State governs perfection of a security interest, the effectiveness of a pre-effective-date financing statement may be continued only under Section 9–705(d) and (f) or 9–706.

(e) Whether or not the law of this State governs perfection of a security interest, the effectiveness of a pre-effective-date financing statement filed in this State may be terminated after this [Act] takes effect by filing a termination statement in the office in which the pre-effective-date financing statement is filed, unless an initial financing statement that satisfies Section 9–706(c) has been filed in the office specified by the law of the jurisdiction governing perfection as provided in Part 3 as the office in which to file a financing statement.

As amended in 2000.

§ 9–708. Persons Entitled to File Initial Financing Statement or Continuation Statement.

A person may file an initial financing statement or a continuation statement under this part if:

(1) the secured party of record authorizes the filing; and

(2) the filing is necessary under this part:

(A) to continue the effectiveness of a financing statement filed before this [Act] takes effect; or

(B) to perfect or continue the perfection of a security interest.

As amended in 2000.

§ 9–709. Priority.

(a) This [Act] determines the priority of conflicting claims to collateral. However, if the relative priorities of the claims were established before this [Act] takes effect, [former Article 9] determines priority.

(b) For purposes of Section 9–322(a), the priority of a security interest that becomes enforceable under Section 9–203 of this [Act] dates from the time this [Act] takes effect if the security interest is perfected under this [Act] by the filing of a financing statement before this [Act] takes effect which would not have been effective to perfect the security interest under [former Article 9]. This subsection does not apply to conflicting security interests each of which is perfected by the filing of such a financing statement.

A

Abatement An order to the owner of a property to eliminate a nuisance. (Chapter 45)

Absolute privilege Exists in courtrooms and legislative hearings. Anyone speaking there, such as a witness in a court, can say anything and never be sued for defamation. (Chapter 6)

Acceptance Retention of the collateral by a secured party as full or partial satisfaction of a debt. (Chapter 24, 25)

Accepted check A check that the drawee bank has signed. This signature is a promise that the bank will pay the check out of its own funds. (Chapter 26)

Accession The use of labor and/or materials to add value to the personal property of another. (Chapter 44)

Accommodated party Someone who receives a benefit from an accommodation party. (Chapter 26)

Accommodation party Someone who does not benefit from an instrument but agrees to guarantee its payment. (Chapter 26)

Accord and satisfaction An agreement to settle a debt for less than the sum claimed. (Chapter 12)

Accounts Any right to receive payment for goods sold or leased, other than rights covered by chattel paper or instruments. (Chapter 24)

Accredited investor Under the Securities Act of 1933, an accredited investor is an institution (such as a bank or insurance company) or any individual with a net worth of more than $1 million or an annual income of more than $200,000. (Chapter 36)

Acquit To find the defendant not guilty of the crime for which he was tried. (Chapter 8)

Act Any action that a party was not legally required to take in the first place. (Chapter 12)

Act of State doctrine A rule requiring American courts to abstain from cases if a court order would interfere with the ability of the President or Congress to conduct foreign policy. (Chapter 9)

Actual authority An agent is authorized to act for a principal. (Chapter 28)

Ad valorem According to the value of the goods. (Chapter 9)

Additional terms Those terms that raise issues not covered in an offer. (Chapter 20)

Adhesion contract A standard form contract prepared by one party and presented to the other on a "take it or leave it" basis. (Chapter 13)

Adjudicate To hold a formal hearing in a disputed matter and issue an official decision. (Chapter 4)

Administrative law Concerns all agencies, boards, commissions, and other entities created by a federal or state legislature and charged with investigating, regulating, and adjudicating a particular industry or issue. (Chapter 1)

Administrative law judge An agency employee who acts as an impartial decision maker. (Chapter 4)

Administrator A person appointed by the court to oversee the probate process for someone who has died intestate (that is, without a will). (Chapter 45)

Administratrix A female administrator. (Chapter 45)

Adverse possession A means of gaining ownership of land belonging to another by entering upon the property, openly and notoriously, and claiming exclusive use of it for a period of years. (Chapter 43)

Affidavit A written statement signed under oath. (Chapter 8)

Affirm A decision by an appellate court to uphold the judgment of a lower court. (Chapter 1)

Affirmative action A plan introduced in a workplace for the purpose of either remedying the effects of past discrimination or achieving equitable representation of minorities and women. (Chapter 29)

After-acquired property Items that a debtor obtains after making a security agreement with the secured party. (Chapter 24)

Agent A person who acts for a principal. (Chapter 28)

Alternative dispute resolution Any method of resolving a legal conflict other than litigation, such as: negotiation, arbitration, mediation, mini-trials, and summary jury trials. (Chapter 3)

Amendment Any addition to a legal document. The constitutional amendments, the first ten of which are known collectively as the Bill of Rights, secure numerous liberties and protections directly for the people. (Chapter 1)

Annual report Each year, public companies must send their shareholders an annual report that contains detailed financial data. (Chapter 35)

Annuity Payment to a beneficiary during his lifetime. (Chapter 45)

Answer The pleading, filed by the defendant in court and served on the plaintiff, which responds to each allegation in the plaintiff's complaint. (Chapter 3)

Antitrust laws Make it illegal to destroy competition and capture an entire market. (Chapter 9)

Apparent authority A situation in which conduct of a principal causes a third party to believe that the principal consents to have an act done on his behalf by a person purporting to act for him when, in fact, that person is not acting for the principal. (Chapter 29)

Appellant The party who appeals a lower court decision to a higher court. (Chapter 3)

Appellate court Any court in a state or federal system that reviews cases that have already been tried. (Chapter 3)

Appellee The party opposing an appeal from a lower court to a higher court. (Chapter 3)

Arbitration A form of alternative dispute resolution in which the parties hire a neutral third party to hear their respective arguments, receive evidence, and then make a binding decision. (Chapter 30)

Arson Malicious use of fire or explosives to damage or destroy real estate or personal property. (Chapter 8)

Artisan's lien A security interest in personal property. (Chapter 24)

Assault An intentional act that causes the plaintiff to fear an imminent battery. (Chapter 6)

Assignee The party who receives an assignment of contract rights from a party to the contract. (Chapter 16)

Assignment The act by which a party transfers contract rights to a third person. (Chapter 16)

Assignment of rights Transferring contract rights. (Chapter 16)

Assignor The party who assigns contract rights to a third person. (Chapter 16)

Assisted suicide The process of hastening death for a terminally ill patient at the request of this patient. (Chapter 49)

Attachment A court order seizing property of a party to a civil action, so that there will be sufficient assets available to pay the judgment. (Chapter 24)

Authorized and unissued stock Stock that has been approved by the corporation's charter, but has not yet been sold. (Chapter 33)

Authorized and issued stock Stock that has been approved by the corporation's charter and subsequently sold. (Chapter 33)

Automatic stay Prohibits creditors from collecting debts that the bankrupt incurred before the bankruptcy petition was filed. (Chapter 37)

B

Bailee A person who rightfully possesses goods belonging to another. (Chapter 13, 21)

Bailment Giving possession and control of personal property to another person. (Chapter 13, 44)

Bailor One who creates a bailment by delivering goods to another. (Chapter 13, 21)

Bait and switch A practice where sellers advertise products that are not generally available but are being used to draw interested parties in so that they will buy other products. (Chapter 39)

Bankrupt Another term for debtor. (Chapter 37)

Bankruptcy estate The new legal entity created when a debtor files a bankruptcy petition. All of the debtor's existing assets pass into the estate. (Chapter 37)

Battery The intentional touching of another person in a way that is unwanted or offensive. (Chapter 6)

Bearer paper An instrument payable "to bearer." Any holder in due course can demand payment. (Chapter 25)

Best efforts underwriting When the underwriter does not buy the stock but instead acts as the company's agent in selling it. (Chapter 36)

Beyond a reasonable doubt The government's burden in a criminal prosecution. (Chapter 3)

Bilateral contract A binding agreement in which each party has made a promise to the other. (Chapter 10)

Bilateral mistake Occurs when both parties negotiate based on the same factual error. (Chapter 14)

Bill A proposed statute that has been submitted for consideration to Congress or a state legislature. (Chapter 4)

Bill of lading A receipt for goods, given by a carrier such as a ship, that minutely describes the merchandise being shipped. A **negotiable** bill of lading may be transferred to other parties, and entitles any holder to collect the goods. (Chapter 9)

Bill of Rights The first ten amendments to the Constitution. (Chapter 5)

Blue sky laws State securities laws. (Chapter 36)

Bona fide occupational qualification (BFOQ) A job requirement that would otherwise be discriminatory is permitted in situations in which it is *essential* to the position in question. (Chapter 29)

Bona fide purchaser Someone who buys goods in good faith, for value, typically from a seller who has merely voidable title. (Chapter 21)

Bonds Long-term debt secured by some of the issuing company's assets. (Chapter 33)

Brief The written legal argument that an attorney files with an appeal court. (Chapter 3)

Burden of proof The allocation of which party must prove its case. In a civil case, the plaintiff has the burden of proof to persuade the factfinder of every element of her case. In a criminal case, the government has the burden of proof. (Chapter 3)

Business judgment rule A common law rule that protects managers from liability if they are acting without a conflict of interest and make informed decisions that have a rational business purpose. (Chapter 34)

Buyer in ordinary course of business (BIOC) Someone who buys goods in good faith from a seller who routinely deals in such goods. (Chapter 21, 24)

Bylaws A document that specifies the organizational rules of a corporation or other organization, such as the date of the annual meeting and the required number of directors. (Chapter 33)

C

Cap and trade A market-based system for reducing emissions. (Chapter 40)

Capacity The legal ability to enter into a contract. (Chapter 10)

Cashier's check A check that is drawn by a bank on itself. (Chapter 25, 26)

Certificate of deposit An instrument issued by a bank which promises to repay a deposit, with interest, on a specified date. (Chapter 25)

Certified check A check that the drawee bank has signed. This signature is a promise that the bank will pay the check out of its own funds. (Chapter 26)

***Certiorari*, writ of** Formal notice from the United States Supreme Court that it will accept a case for review. (Chapter 3)

Challenge for cause An attorney's request, during *voir dire*, to excuse a prospective juror because of apparent bias. (Chapter 3)

Charging order A court order granting the creditor of a partner the right to receive that partner's share of partnership profits. (Chapter 32)

Chattel paper Any writing that indicates two things: (1) a debtor owes money and (2) a secured party has a security interest in specific goods. The most common chattel paper is a document indicating a consumer sale on credit. (Chapter 24)

Check An instrument in which the drawer orders the drawee bank to pay money to the payee. (Chapter 25)

Check card Another name for a debit card. (Chapter 39)

Check kiting Moving funds between bank accounts to take advantage of the float. (Chapter 26)

Chicago School A theory of antitrust law first developed at the University of Chicago. Adherents to this theory believe that antitrust enforcement should focus on promoting efficiency and should not generally be concerned about the size or number of competitors in any market. (Chapter 38)

Choice of forum provisions Determine the state in which any litigation would take place. (Chapter 19)

Choice of law provisions Determine which state's laws will be used to interpret the contract. (Chapter 19)

CISG See Convention on Contracts for the International Sale of Goods. (Chapter 9)

Civil law The large body of law concerning the rights and duties between parties. It is distinguished from criminal law, which concerns behavior outlawed by a government. (Chapter 1)

Claim in recoupment An issuer subtracts (i.e., "sets off") any other claims he has against the initial payee from the amount he owes on an instrument. (Chapter 25)

Class action A method of litigating a civil lawsuit in which one or more plaintiffs (or occasionally defendants) seek to represent an entire group of people with similar claims against a common opponent. (Chapter 3)

Classification The process by which the Customs Service decides what label to attach to imported merchandise, and therefore what level of tariff to impose. (Chapter 9)

Close corporation A corporation with a small number of shareholders. Its stock is not publicly traded. Also known as a *closely held corporation*. (Chapter 31)

Codicil An amendment to a will. (Chapter 45)

Collateral The property subject to a security interest. (Chapter 24)

Collateral promise A promise to pay the debt of another person, as a favor to the debtor. (Chapter 15)

Collective bargaining Contract negotiations between an employer and a union. (Chapter 30)

Collective bargaining agreement (CBA) A contract between a union and management. (Chapter 30)

Collective bargaining unit The precisely defined group of employees who are represented by a particular union. (Chapter 30)

Commerce clause One of the powers granted by Article I, §8 of the Constitution, it gives Congress exclusive power to regulate international commerce and concurrent power with the states to regulate domestic commerce. (Chapter 5)

Commercial impracticability After the creation of a contract, an entirely unforeseen event occurs which makes enforcement of the contract extraordinarily unfair. (Chapter 17)

Commercial paper Instruments such as checks and promissory notes that contain a promise to pay money. Commercial paper includes both negotiable and non-negotiable instruments. (Chapter 25)

Commercial speech Communication, such as television advertisements, that has the dominant theme of proposing a commercial transaction. (Chapter 5)

Common carrier A transportation company that makes its services available on a regular basis to the general public. (Chapter 49)

Common law Judge-made law, that is, the body of all decisions made by appellate courts over the years. (Chapter 4)

Common stock Certificates that reflect ownership in a corporation. Owners of this equity security are last in line for corporate pay-outs, such as dividends and liquidation proceeds. (Chapter 33)

Comparative negligence A rule of tort law that permits a plaintiff to recover even when the defendant can show that the plaintiff's own conduct contributed in some way to her harm. (Chapter 7)

Compensatory damages The amount of money that the court thinks will restore the plaintiff to the position he was in before the defendant's conduct caused an injury. (Chapter 6)

Complaint A pleading, filed by the plaintiff, providing a short statement of the claim. (Chapter 3)

Compliance program A plan to prevent and detect criminal conduct at all levels of the company. (Chapter 8)

Concerted action Tactics, such as a strike, used by a union to gain a bargaining advantage. (Chapter 30)

Concurrent estate Two or more people owning property at the same time. (Chapter 43)

Conditional promises Promises that a party agrees to perform only if the other side has first done what it promised. (Chapter 19)

Condition A condition is an event that must occur in order for a party to be obligated under a contract. (Chapter 17)

Condition precedent A condition that must occur before a particular contract duty arises. (Chapter 17)

Condition subsequent A condition that must occur after a particular contract duty arises, or the duty will be discharged. (Chapter 17)

Confiscation Expropriation without adequate compensation of property owned by foreigners. (Chapter 9)

Conforming goods Items that satisfy the contract terms. If a contract calls for blue sailboats, then green sailboats are non-conforming. (Chapter 23)

Conscious parallelism When competitors who do not have an explicit agreement nonetheless all make the same competitive decisions. (Chapter 38)

Consent order An agreement entered into by a wrongdoer and an administrative agency (such as the Securities and Exchange Commission or the Federal Trade Commission) in which the wrongdoer agrees not to violate the law in the future. (Chapter 39)

Consequential damages Those resulting from the unique circumstances of *this injured party*. (Chapter 18)

Consideration In contract law, something of legal value that has been bargained for and given in exchange by the parties. (Chapter 12)

Constitution The supreme law of a political entity. The United States Constitution is the highest law in the country. (Chapter 1)

Constructive insider Anyone who receives confidential information while in an indirect employment relationship with a company, such as employees of the company's auditors or law firm. (Chapter 36)

Consumer Any natural person, that is, not a corporation or business. (Chapter 25)

Consumer credit contract A contract in which a consumer borrows money from a lender to purchase goods and services from a seller who is affiliated with the lender. (Chapter 25)

Contract A legally enforceable promise or set of promises. (Chapter 10)

Contract carrier A transportation company that does not make its services available to the general public but engages in continuing agreements with particular customers. (Chapter 44)

Contributory negligence A rule of tort law that permits a negligent defendant to escape liability if she can demonstrate that the plaintiff's own conduct contributed in any way to the plaintiff's harm. (Chapter 7)

Control security Stock owned by any officer or director of the issuer, or by any shareholder who holds more than 10 percent of a class of stock of the issuer. (Chapter 36)

Covenant A promise in a contract. (Chapter 19)

Convention on Contracts for the International Sale of Goods A United Nations sponsored agreement that creates a neutral body of law for sale of goods contracts between companies from different countries. (Chapter 9)

Conversion A tort committed by taking or using someone else's personal property without his permission. (Chapter 6, 26)

Copyright Under federal law, the holder of a copyright owns a particular expression of an idea, but not the idea itself. This ownership right applies to creative activities such as literature, music, drama, and software. (Chapter 42)

Corporation by estoppel Even if a corporation has not actually been formed, courts will sometimes enforce contracts entered into in the belief that the corporation did indeed exist. (Chapter 33)

Compliance program A plan to prevent and detect criminal conduct at all levels of the company. (Chapter 8)

Constructive insider Anyone who has an indirect employment relationship with a company, such as employees of the company's auditors or law firm. (Chapter 36)

Counter-claim A claim made by the defendant against the plaintiff. (Chapter 3)

Cover The buyer's right to obtain substitute goods when a seller has breached a contract. (Chapter 18)

Creditor beneficiary When one party to a contract intends to benefit a third party to whom he owes a debt, that third party is referred to as a creditor beneficiary. (Chapter 16)

Criminal law Rules that permit a government to punish certain behavior by fine or imprisonment. (Chapter 1, 8)

Criminal procedure The process of investigating, interrogating, and trying a criminal defendant. (Chapter 8)

Cross-examination During a hearing, for a lawyer to question an opposing witness. (Chapter 3)

Cure The seller's right to respond to a buyer's rejection of non-conforming goods; the seller accomplishes this by delivering conforming goods before the contract deadline. (Chapter 23)

D

Damages (1) The harm that a plaintiff complains of at trial, such as an injury to her person, or money lost because of a contract breach. (2) Money awarded by a trial court for injury suffered. (Chapter 6)

***De facto* corporation** Occurs when a promoter makes a good faith effort to incorporate (although fails to complete the process entirely) and uses the corporation to conduct business. The state can challenge the validity of the corporation, but a third party cannot. (Chapter 33)

***De jure* corporation** The promoter of the corporation has substantially complied with the requirements for incorporation, but has made some minor error. No one has the right to challenge the validity of the corporation. (Chapter 33)

Debentures Long-term, unsecured debt, typically issued by a corporation. (Chapter 33)

Debtor A person who owes money or some other obligation to another party. (Chapter 24, 37)

Debtor in possession The debtor acts as trustee in a Chapter 11 bankruptcy. (Chapter 37)

Decedent A person who has died. (Chapter 45)

Deed A document that proves ownership of property. (Chapter 43)

Defamation The act of injuring someone's reputation by stating something false about her to a third person. Libel is defamation done either in writing or by broadcast. *Slander* is defamation done orally. (Chapter 6)

Default The failure to perform an obligation, such as the failure to pay money when due. (Chapter 24)

Default judgment Court order awarding one party everything it requested because the opposing party failed to respond in time. (Chapter 3)

Default rules Under the Uniform Partnership Act, these rules govern the relationship among the partners unless the partners explicitly make a different agreement. (Chapter 32)

Defendant The person being sued. (Chapter 1)

Deficiency Having insufficient funds to pay off a debt. (Chapter 24)

Definiteness A doctrine holding that a contract will only be enforced if its terms are sufficiently precise that a court can determine what the parties meant. (Chapter 11)

Delegation The act by which a party to a contract transfers duties to a third person who is not a party to the contract. (Chapter 16)

Delegation of duties A transfer of obligations in a contract. (Chapter 19)

Deponent The person being questioned in a deposition. (Chapter 3)

Deposition A form of discovery in which a party's attorney has the right to ask oral questions of the other party or of a witness. Answers are given under oath. (Chapter 3)

Derivative action A lawsuit brought by shareholders in the name of the corporation to enforce a right of the corporation. (Chapter 35)

Deterrence Using punishment, such as imprisonment, to discourage criminal behavior. (Chapter 8)

Devisee Someone who inherits under a will. (Chapter 45)

Different terms Terms that contradict those in an offer. (Chapter 20)

Direct damages Are those that flow directly from the contract. (Chapter 18)

Direct examination During a hearing, when a lawyer asks questions of his own witness. (Chapter 3)

Directed verdict The decision by a court to instruct a jury that it must find in favor of a particular party because, in the judge's opinion, no reasonable person could disagree on the outcome. (Chapter 3)

Disabled person Someone with a physical or mental impairment that substantially limits a major life activity, or someone who is regarded as having such an impairment. (Chapter 29)

Disability insurance Replaces the insured's income if he becomes unable to work because of illness or injury. (Chapter 45)

Disaffirm To give notice to the other party to a contract that the party giving the notice refuses to be bound by the agreement. (Chapter 14)

Discharge (1) A party to a contract has no more duties. (2) A party to an instrument is released from liability. (Chapter 17, 26, 37)

Disclaimer A statement that a particular warranty does not apply. (Chapter 22)

Discovery A stage in litigation, after all pleadings have been served, in which each party seeks as much relevant information as possible about the opposing party's case. (Chapter 3)

Dishonor An obligor refuses to pay an instrument that is due. (Chapter 26)

Dismiss To terminate a lawsuit, often on procedural grounds, without reaching the merits of the case. (Chapter 3)

Dissociation A dissociation occurs when a partner leaves a partnership. (Chapter 32)

Diversity jurisdiction One of the two main types of civil cases that a United States district court has the power to hear. It involves a lawsuit between citizens of different states, in which at least one party makes a claim for more than $75,000. (Chapter 3)

Domestic corporation A corporation is a domestic corporation in the state in which it was formed. (Chapter 33)

Donee A person who receives a gift. (Chapter 44)

Donee beneficiary When one party to a contract intends to make a gift to a third party, that third party is referred to as a donee beneficiary. (Chapter 16)

Donor A person who makes a gift to another. (Chapter 44)

Double jeopardy A criminal defendant may be prosecuted only once for a particular criminal offense. (Chapter 8)

Draft The drawer of this instrument orders someone else to pay money. Checks are the most common form of draft. The drawer of a check orders a bank to pay money. (Chapter 25)

Dram acts Make businesses liable for serving drinks to intoxicated customers who later cause harm. (Chapter 7)

Drawee The person who pays a draft. In the case of a check, the bank is the drawee. (Chapter 25, 26)

Drawer The person who issues a draft. (Chapter 25)

Due diligence An investigation of the registration statement by someone who signs it. (Chapter 27, 36)

Due process Requires fundamental fairness at all stages of the case. (Chapter 8)

Due Process Clause Part of the Fifth Amendment. *Procedural due process* ensures that before depriving anyone of liberty or property, the government must go through procedures which ensure that the deprivation is fair. *Substantive due process* holds that certain rights, such as privacy, are so fundamental that the government may not eliminate them. (Chapter 5)

Dumping Selling merchandise at one price in the domestic market and at a cheaper, unfair price in an international market. (Chapter 9)

Durable power of attorney An instrument that permits an attorney-in-fact to act for a principal. A durable power is effective until the principal revokes it or dies. It continues in effect even if the principal becomes incapacitated. (Chapter 45)

Duress (1) A criminal defense in which the defendant shows that she committed the wrongful act because a third person threatened her with imminent physical harm. (2) An improper threat made to force another party to enter into a contract. (Chapter 14)

Duty A tax imposed on imported items. (Chapter 9)

Duty of care The requirement that a manager act with care and in the best interests of the corporation. (Chapter 34)

Duty of loyalty The obligation of a manager to act without a conflict of interest. (Chapter 34)

E

Easement The right to enter land belonging to another and make a limited use of it, without taking anything away. (Chapter 43)

Economic loss doctrine A common law rule holding that when an injury is purely economic, and arises from a contract made between two businesses, the injured party may only sue under the UCC. (Chapter 22)

Element A fact that a party to a lawsuit must prove in order to prevail. (Chapter 6)

Embezzlement Fraudulent conversion of property already in the defendant's possession. (Chapter 8)

Eminent domain The power of the government to take private property for public use. (Chapter 5, 43)

Employee at will A worker whose job does not have a specified duration. (Chapter 29)

Enabling legislation A statute authorizing the creation of a new administrative agency and specifying its powers and duties. (Chapter 4)

Engagement letter A written contract by which a client hires an accountant. (Chapter 27)

Entrapment A criminal defense in which the defendant demonstrates that the government induced him to break the law. (Chapter 8)

Equal dignities rule If an agent is empowered to enter into a contract that must be in writing, then the appointment of the agent must also be written. (Chapter 28)

Equal Protection Clause Part of the Fourteenth Amendment, it generally requires the government to treat equally situated people the same. (Chapter 5)

Error of law A mistake made by a trial judge that concerns a legal issue as opposed to a factual matter. Permitting too many leading questions is a legal error; choosing to believe one witness rather than another is a factual matter. (Chapter 3)

Escalator clause A lease clause allowing the landlord to raise the rent for specified reasons. (Chapter 43)

Estate The legal entity that holds title to assets after the owner dies and before the property is distributed. (Chapter 45)

Estoppel Out of fairness, a person is denied the right to assert a claim. (Chapter 28)

Ethics The study of how people ought to act. (Chapter 2)

Eviction An act that forces a tenant to abandon the property. (Chapter 43)

Evidence, rules of Law governing the proof offered during a trial or formal hearing. These rules limit the questions that may be asked of witnesses and the introduction of physical objects. (Chapter 3)

Exclusionary rule In a criminal trial, a ban on the use of evidence obtained in violation of the Constitution. (Chapter 8)

Exclusive dealing contract A contract in which a distributor or retailer agrees with a supplier not to carry the products of any other supplier. (Chapter 38)

Exculpatory clause A contract provision that attempts to release one party from liability in the event the other party is injured. (Chapter 13, 33, 43, 44)

Executed contract A binding agreement in which all parties have fulfilled all obligations. (Chapter 10)

Executive agency An administrative agency within the executive branch of government. (Chapter 4)

Executive order An order by a president or governor, having the full force of law. (Chapter 1)

Executor A person chosen by the decedent to oversee the probate process. (Chapter 15)

Executory contract A binding agreement in which one or more of the parties has not fulfilled its obligations. (Chapter 10)

Executrix A female executor. (Chapter 45)

Exhaustion of remedies A principle of administrative law that no party may appeal an agency action to a court until she has utilized all available appeals within the agency itself. (Chapter 4)

Expectation damages The money required to put one party in the position she would have been in had the other side performed the contract. (Chapter 18)

Expectation interest A remedy in a contract case that puts the injured party in the position he would have been in had both sides fully performed. (Chapter 18)

Expert witness A witness in a court case who has special training or qualifications to discuss a specific issue, and who is generally permitted to state an opinion. (Chapter 3)

Export To transport goods or services out of a country. (Chapter 9)

Express authority Conduct of a principal that, reasonably interpreted, causes the agent to believe that the principal desires him to do a specific act. (Chapter 28)

Express contract A binding agreement in which the parties explicitly state all important terms. (Chapter 10)

Express warranty A guarantee, created by the words or actions of the seller, that goods will meet certain standards. (Chapter 22)

Expropriation A government's seizure of property or companies owned by foreigners. (Chapter 9)

Externality When people do not bear the full cost of their decisions. (Chapter 40)

F

Factfinder The one responsible, during a trial, for deciding what occurred, that is, who did what to whom, when, how, and why. It is either the jury or, in a jury-waived case, the judge. (Chapter 5)

Fair representation, duty of The union's obligation to act on behalf of all members impartially and in good faith. (Chapter 30)

Fair use doctrine Permits limited use of copyrighted material without permission of the author. (Chapter 22)

False imprisonment The intentional restraint of another person without reasonable cause and without her consent. (Chapter 6)

Federal question jurisdiction One of the two main types of civil cases that a United States district court has the power to hear. It involves a federal statute or a constitutional provision. (Chapter 3)

Federal Sentencing Guidelines Detailed rules that judges must follow when sentencing defendants convicted of crimes in federal court. (Chapter 8)

Federalism A form of national government in which power is shared between one central authority and numerous local authorities. (Chapter 1)

Fee simple absolute The greatest possible ownership right in real property, including the right to possess, use, and dispose of the property in any lawful manner. (Chapter 43)

Fee simple defeasible Ownership interest in real property that may terminate upon the occurrence of some limiting event. (Chapter 43)

Felony The most serious crimes, typically those for which the defendant could be imprisoned for more than a year. (Chapter 8)

Fiduciary duty An obligation to behave in a trustworthy and confidential fashion toward the object of that duty. (Chapter 28)

Financing statement A document that a secured party files to give the general public notice that the secured party has a secured interest in the collateral. (Chapter 24)

Finding statutes Laws that govern found property. Also known as estray statutes. (Chapter 44)

Firm commitment underwriting The underwriter buys stock from the issuer and sells it to the public. (Chapter 36)

Firm offer A contract offer that cannot be withdrawn during a stated period. (Chapter 11)

Fixtures Goods that are attached to real estate. (Chapter 24)

Forbearance Refraining from doing something that one has a legal right to do. (Chapter 12)

Force majeure event A disruptive, unexpected occurrence for which neither party is to blame that prevents one or both parties from complying with a contract. (Chapter 19)

Forced share The percentage of a decendent's estate that a spouse is entitled to claim under state law. Also known as statutory share. (Chapter 45)

Foreign corporation A corporation formed in another state. (Chapter 33)

Foreign Sovereign Immunity Act A federal statute that protects other nations from suit in courts of the United States, except under specified circumstances. (Chapter 9)

Formal rulemaking The process whereby an administrative agency notifies the public of a proposed new rule and then permits a formal hearing, with opportunity for evidence and cross-examination, before promulgating the final rule. (Chapter 4)

Founding Fathers The authors of the United States Constitution, who participated in the Constitutional Convention in Philadelphia in 1787. (Chapter 1)

Framers *See* Founding Fathers. (Chapter 5)

Franchise An arrangement in which the franchisee buys from a franchiser the right to establish a business using the franchiser's trade name and selling the franchiser's products. Typically the franchiser also trains the franchisee in the proper operation of the business. (Chapter 31)

Fraud Deception of another person to obtain money or property. (Chapter 6, 8)

Freedom of Information Act (FOIA) A federal statute giving private citizens and corporations access to many of the documents possessed by an administrative agency. (Chapter 4)

Freehold estate The present right to possess property and to use it in any lawful manner. (Chapter 43)

Fresh start After the termination of a bankruptcy case, creditors cannot make a claim against the debtor for money owed before the initial bankruptcy petition was filed. (Chapter 37)

Frustration of purpose After the creation of a contract, an entirely unforeseen event occurs that eliminates the value of the contract for one of the parties. (Chapter 17)

Fully disclosed principal If the third party in an agency relationship knows the identity of the principal, that principal is fully disclosed. (Chapter 28)

Fundamental rights In constitutional law, those rights that are so basic that any governmental interference with them is suspect and likely to be unconstitutional. (Chapter 5)

G

GAAP Generally accepted accounting principles. Rules set by the Financial Accounting Standards Board to be used in preparing financial statements. (Chapter 27)

GAAS Generally accepted auditing standards. Rules set by the American Institute of Certified Public Accountants (AICPA) to be used in conducting audits. (Chapter 27)

Gap-filler provisions UCC rules for supplying missing terms. (Chapter 11)

Gap period The period between the time that creditors file an involuntary petition and the court issues the order for relief. (Chapter 37)

GATT *See* General Agreement on Tariffs and Trade. (Chapter 9)

General Agreement on Tariffs and Trade (GATT) A massive international treaty, negotiated in stages between the 1940s and 1994 and signed by over 130 nations. (Chapter 9)

General intangibles Potential sources of income such as copyrights, patents, trademarks, goodwill and certain other rights to payment. (Chapter 24)

Gift A voluntary transfer of property from one person to another without consideration. (Chapter 44)

Gift *causa mortis* A gift made in contemplation of approaching death. (Chapter 44)

Good faith An honest effort to meet both the spirit and letter of a contract. (Chapter 19)

Goods Anything movable, except for money, securities, and certain legal rights. (Chapter 20, 24)

Grand jury A group of ordinary citizens that decides whether there is probable cause the defendant committed the crime and should be tried. (Chapter 8)

Gratuitous assignment An assignment made as a gift, for no consideration. (Chapter 16)

Greenmail If a company is threatened with a hostile takeover, its board of directors may offer to buy the stock of the attacker at an above-market price with the hope that the attacker will take her profits and leave the company alone. (Chapter 34)

Grievance A formal complaint alleging a contract violation. (Chapter 30)

Guilty A court's finding that a defendant has committed a crime. (Chapter 8)

H

Hacking Gaining unauthorized access to a computer system. (Chapter 41)

Harmless error A ruling made by a trial court which an appeals court determines was legally wrong but not fatal to the decision. (Chapter 3)

Health care proxy Someone who has authority to make health care decisions for a person who is incompetent. (Chapter 45)

Heir Someone who inherits from a decedent who died intestate (that is, without a will). (Chapter 45)

Holder For order paper, anyone in possession of the instrument if it is payable to or indorsed to her. For bearer paper, anyone in possession. (Chapter 25)

Holder in due course Someone who has given value for an instrument, in good faith, without notice of outstanding claims or other defenses. (Chapter 25)

Holographic will A handwritten will that has not been witnessed. (Chapter 45)

Horizontal agreement or merger An agreement or merger between two potential competitors. (Chapter 38)

Hostile takeover An outsider buys a company in the face of opposition from the target company's board of directors. (Chapter 34)

I

Identify In sales law, to designate the specific goods that are the subject of a contract. (Chapter 23)

IFRS "International Financial Reporting Standards" is a new set of international standard accounting rules, used by over 100 countries, currently being proposed for U.S. companies to follow. (Chapter 27)

Illegal contract An agreement that is void because it violates a statute or public policy. (Chapter 13)

Illusory promise An apparent promise that is unenforceable because the promisor makes no firm commitment. (Chapter 12)

Implied authority When a principal directs an agent to undertake a transaction, the agent has the right to do acts that are incidental to it, usually accompany it, or are reasonably necessary to accomplish it. (Chapter 28)

Implied contract A binding agreement created not by explicit language but by the informal words and conduct of the parties. (Chapter 10)

Implied warranty Guarantees created by the Uniform Commercial Code and imposed on the seller of goods. (Chapter 22)

Implied warranty of fitness for a particular purpose If the seller knows that the buyer plans to use the goods for a particular purpose, the seller generally is held to warrant that the goods are in fact fit for that purpose. (Chapter 11)

Implied warranty of habitability A landlord must meet all standards set by the local building code, or otherwise ensure that the premises are fit for human habitation. (Chapter 43)

Implied warranty of merchantability Requires that goods must be of at least average, passable quality in the trade. (Chapter 11)

Import To transport goods or services into a country. (Chapter 9)

Import ban A prohibition of certain goods. (Chapter 9)

In camera "In the judge's chambers," meaning that the judge does something out of view of the jury and the public. (Chapter 3)

Incidental beneficiary Someone who might have benefited from a contract between two others but has no right to enforce that agreement. (Chapter 16)

Incidental damages The relatively minor costs, such as storage and advertising, that the injured party suffered when responding to a contract breach. (Chapter 18)

Incorporator The person who signs a corporate charter. (Chapter 33)

Indemnification A promise to pay someone else's obligations. (Chapter 33)

Independent agency An administrative agency outside the executive branch of government, such as the Interstate Commerce Commission. (Chapter 4)

Independent contractor Someone who undertakes tasks for others and whose work is not closely controlled. (Chapter 28)

Independent directors Members of the board of directors who are not employees of the company. Also known as outside directors. (Chapter 35)

Indictment The government's formal charge that a defendant has committed a crime. (Chapter 8)

Indorser Anyone, other than the issuer or acceptor, who signs an instrument. (Chapter 26)

Indorsement The signature of a payee. (Chapter 25)

Infliction of emotional distress A tort. It can be the *intentional infliction of emotional distress,* meaning that the defendant behaved outrageously and deliberately caused the plaintiff severe psychological injury, or it can be the *negligent infliction of emotional distress,* meaning that the defendant's conduct violated the rules of negligence. (Chapter 6)

Informal rulemaking The process whereby an administrative agency notifies the public of a proposed new rule and permits comment but is then free to promulgate the final rule without a public hearing. (Chapter 4)

Initial public offering (IPO) A company's first public sale of securities. (Chapter 36)

Injunction A court order that a person either do or stop doing something. (Chapter 18)

Inside directors Members of the board of directors who are also officers of the corporation. (Chapter 35)

Insider Family members of an individual debtor, officers and directors of a corporation, or partners of a partnership. (Chapter 33)

Instructions or charge The explanation given by a judge to a jury, outlining the jury's task in deciding a lawsuit and the underlying rules of law the jury should use in reaching its decision. (Chapter 3)

Instruments Drafts, checks, certificates of deposit and notes. (Chapter 24)

Insurable interest A person has an insurable interest if she would be harmed by the danger that she has insured against. (Chapter 45)

Insured A person whose loss is the subject of an insurance policy. (Chapter 45)

Insurer The person who issues an insurance policy. (Chapter 45)

Integrated contract A writing that the parties intend as the complete and final expression of their agreement. (Chapter 15)

Intended beneficiary Someone who may enforce a contract made between two other parties. (Chapter 16)

Intentional infliction of emotional distress An intentional tort in which the harm results from extreme and outrageous conduct that causes serious emotional'harm. (Chapter 6)

Intentional tort An act deliberately performed that violates a legally imposed duty and injures someone. (Chapter 6)

***Inter vivos* gift** A gift made "during life," that is, when the donor is not under any fear of impending death. (Chapter 44)

***Inter vivos* trust** A trust established while the grantor is still living. (Chapter 45)

Interest A legal right in something, such as ownership or a mortgage or a tenancy. (Chapter 18)

Interference with a contract *See* Tortious interference with a contract. (Chapter 6)

Interference with a prospective advantage *See* Tortious interference with a prospective advantage. (Chapter 6)

Internet An international computer network that connects smaller groups of linked computer networks. (Chapter 41)

Interpretive rules A formal statement by an administrative agency expressing its view of what existing statutes or regulations mean. (Chapter 4)

Interrogatory A form of discovery in which one party sends to an opposing party written questions that must be answered under oath. (Chapter 3)

Intestate Without a will. (Chapter 45)

Intrusion A tort if a reasonable person would find the invasion of her private life offensive. (Chapter 6)

Inventory Goods that the seller is holding for sale or lease in the ordinary course of its business. (Chapter 24)

Investigative Reports Discuss character, reputation or lifestyle. They become obsolete in three months. (Chapter 39)

Involuntary bailment A bailment that occurs without an agreement between the bailor and bailee. (Chapter 44)

Involuntary petition Filed by creditors to initiate a bankruptcy case. (Chapter 37)

Invitee Someone who has the right to be on property, such as a customer in a shop. (Chapter 7)

Issue All direct descendants such as children, grandchildren, and so on. (Chapter 45)

Issuer The maker of a promissory note or the drawer of a draft. (Chapter 25, 36)

J

Joint and several liability All members of a group are liable. They can be sued as a group, or any one of them can be sued individually for the full amount owing. (Chapter 27)

Joint liability All members of a group are liable and must be sued together. (Chapter 32)

Joint tenancy Two or more people holding equal interest in a property, with the right of survivorship. (Chapter 43)

Joint venture A partnership for a limited purpose. (Chapter 31)

Judgment *non obstante veredicto* (n.o.v.) "Judgment notwithstanding the verdict." A trial judge overturns the verdict of the jury and enters a judgment in favor of the opposing party. (Chapter 3)

Judgment rate The interest rate that courts use on court-ordered judgments. (Chapter 25)

Judicial activism The willingness shown by certain courts (and not by others) to decide issues of public policy, such as constitutional questions (free speech, equal protection, etc.) and matters of contract fairness (promissory estoppel, unconscionability, etc.). (Chapter 5)

Judicial restraint A court's preference to abstain from adjudicating major social issues and to leave such matters to legislatures. (Chapter 5)

Judicial review The power of the judicial system to examine, interpret, and even nullify actions taken by another branch of government. (Chapter 4)

Jurisdiction The power of a court to hear a particular dispute, civil or criminal, and to make a binding decision. (Chapter 3)

Jurisprudence The study of the purposes and philosophies of the law, as opposed to particular provisions of the law. (Chapter 1)

L

Labor-Management Relations Act Designed to curb union abuses. (Chapter 30)

Landlord The owner of a freehold estate who allows another person temporarily to live on his property. (Chapter 43)

Larceny Taking personal property with the intention of preventing the owner from ever using it. (Chapter 8)

Law merchant The body of rules and customs developed by traders and businesspersons throughout Europe from roughly the fifteenth to the eighteenth century. (Chapter 20)

Lease A contract creating a landlord-tenant relationship. (Chapter 43)

Legal positivism The legal philosophy holding that law is what the sovereign says it is, regardless of its moral content. (Chapter 1)

Legal realism The legal philosophy holding that what really influences law is who makes and enforces it, not what is put in writing. (Chapter 1)

Legal remedy Generally, money damages. It is distinguished from equitable remedy, which includes injunctions and other non-monetary relief. (Chapter 18)

Legislative history Used by courts to interpret the meaning of a statute, this is the record of hearings, speeches, and explanations that accompanied a statute as it made its way from newly proposed bill to final law. (Chapter 4)

Legislative rules Regulations issued by an administrative agency. (Chapter 4)

Letter of credit A commercial device used to guarantee payment in international trade, usually between parties that have not previously worked together. (Chapter 9)

Letter of intent A letter that summarizes negotiating progress. (Chapter 11)

Liability insurance Reimburses the insured for any liability she incurs by accidentally harming someone else. (Chapter 45)

Libel *See* Defamation. (Chapter 6)

License To grant permission to another person (1) to make or sell something or (2) to enter on property. (Chapter 43

Licensee A person who is on the property of another for her own purposes, but with the owner's permission. A social guest is a typical licensee. (Chapter 7)

Lien A security interest created by rule of law, often based on labor that the secured party has expended on the collateral. (Chapter 24)

Life estate An ownership interest in real property entitling the holder to use the property during his lifetime, but which terminates upon his death. (Chapter 43)

Life insurance Provides for payments to a beneficiary upon the death of the insured. (Chapter 45)

Life tenant A person who has the use of a property during his lifetime only. (Chapter 43)

Limited liability company An organization that has the limited liability of a corporation but is not a taxable entity. (Chapter 31)

Limited liability limited partnership In a limited liability limited partnership, the general partner is not personally liable for the debts of the partnership. (Chapter 31)

Limited partnership A partnership with two types of partners: (1) limited partners who have no personal liability for the debts of the enterprise nor any right to manage the business, and (2) general partners who are responsible for management and personally liable for all debts. (Chapter 31)

Liquidated damages A contract clause specifying how much a party must pay upon breach. (Chapter 18)

Liquidated debt The amount of the indebtedness is not in dispute. (Chapter 12)

Litigation The process of resolving disputes through formal court proceedings. (Chapter 3)

Living trust A trust established while the grantor is alive. *See inter vivos* trust. (Chapter 45)

Living will An instrument that permits adults to refuse medical treatment. It can also appoint a health care proxy to make medical decisions for a person who has become incompetent. (Chapter 45)

Local A regional union that represents workers at a particular company. (Chapter 30)

Lockout A management tactic, designed to gain a bargaining advantage, in which the company refuses to allow union members to work (and hence deprives them of their pay). (Chapter 30)

M

Mailbox rule A contract doctrine holding that acceptance is effective upon dispatch, that is, when it is mailed or otherwise taken out of the control of the offeree. (Chapter 11)

Maker The issuer of a promissory note. (Chapter 25)

Marital trust A legal entity created for the purpose of reducing a married couple's estate taxes. (Chapter 45)

Material Important or significant. Information that would affect a person's decision if he knew it. (Chapter 36, 45)

Material breach A violation of a contract that defeats an essential purpose of the agreement. (Chapter 19)

Mechanic's lien A security created when a worker improves real property. (Chapter 24)

Mediation The process of using a neutral person to aid in the settlement of a legal dispute. A mediator's decision is non-binding. (Chapter 3)

Meeting of the minds The parties understood each other and intended to reach an agreement. (Chapter 11)

Merchant Someone who routinely deals in the particulars goods involved, or who appears to have special knowledge or skill in those goods, or who uses agents with special knowledge or skill in those goods. (Chapter 20)

Merchantable The goods are fit for the ordinary purposes for which they are used. (Chapter 22)

Merger An acquisition of one company by another. (Chapter 35)

Minor A person under the age of 18. (Chapter 14)

Minority shareholders Shareholders who do not own enough stock to control their corporation. (Chapter 35)

Minute book Records of shareholder meetings and directors' meetings are kept in the corporation's minute book. (Chapter 33)

Mirror image rule A contract doctrine that requires acceptance to be on exactly the same terms as the offer. (Chapter 11)

Misdemeanor A less serious crime, typically one for which the maximum penalty is incarceration for less than a year, often in a jail, as opposed to a prison. (Chapter 8)

Misrepresentation A factually incorrect statement made during contract negotiations. (Chapter 14)

Mitigation One party acts to minimize its losses when the other party breaches a contract. (Chapter 18)

Modify An appellate court order changing a lower court ruling. (Chapter 3)

Money laundering Taking the profits of criminal acts and either (1) using the money to promote more crime or (2) attempting to conceal the money's source. (Chapter 8)

Monopolization A company acquires or maintains a monopoly through the commission of unacceptably aggressive acts. A violation of §2 of the Sherman Act. (Chapter 38)

Mortgage A security interest in real property. (Chapter 43)

Mortgagee A creditor who obtains a security interest in real property, typically in exchange for money given to the mortgagor to buy the property. (Chapter 43)

Mortgagor A debtor who gives a mortgage (security interest) in real property to a creditor, typically in exchange for money used to buy the property. (Chapter 43)

Motion A formal request that a court take some specified step during litigation. A motion to compel discovery is a request that a trial judge order the other party to respond to discovery. (Chapter 3)

Motion for a protective order A request that the court limit discovery. (Chapter 3)

Multinational enterprise A corporation that is doing business in more than one country simultaneously. (Chapter 9)

N

National Labor Relations Act (NLRA) Ensures the right of workers to form unions and encourages management and unions to bargain collectively. (Chapter 30)

National Labor Relations Board (NLRB) The administrative agency charged with overseeing labor law. (Chapter 30)

Nationalization A government's seizure of property or companies. (Chapter 9)

Natural law The theory that an unjust law is no law at all, and that a rule is only legitimate if based on an immutable morality. (Chapter 1)

Negative or dormant aspect of the Commerce Clause The doctrine that prohibits a state from any action that interferes with or discriminates against interstate commerce. (Chapter 5)

Negligence and strict liability Injuries caused by neglect and oversight rather than by deliberate conduct. (Chapter 6)

Negligence per se Violation of a standard of care set by statute. Driving while intoxicated is illegal; thus, if a drunk driver injures a pedestrian, he has committed negligence per se. (Chapter 7)

Negotiable instrument A type of commercial paper that is freely transferable. (Chapter 25)

Negotiation The transfer of an instrument. To be negotiated, order paper must be indorsed and then delivered to the transferee. For bearer paper, no indorsement is required—it must simply be delivered to the transferee. (Chapter 25)

Nominal damages A token sum, such as one dollar, given to a plaintiff who demonstrates that the defendant breached the contract but cannot prove serious injury. (Chapter 18)

Noncompetition agreement A contract in which one party agrees not to compete with another in a stated type of business. (Chapter 10)

Nonconforming goods Merchandise that differs from that specified in the contract. (Chapter 21)

Non-point source When pollutants are released simultaneously from more than one source. (Chapter 40)

Norris-LaGuardia Act Prohibits federal court injunctions in peaceful labor disputes. (Chapter 40)

North American Free Trade Agreement A commercial association among Canada, the United States, and Mexico designed to eliminate almost all trade barriers. (Chapter 9)

No-strike clause A clause in a CBA that prohibits the union from striking while the CBA is in force. (Chapter 30)

Note An unconditional, written promise that the maker of the instrument will pay a specific amount of money on demand or at a definite time. When issued by a corporation, a note refers to short-term debt, typically payable within five years. (Chapter 33)

Notice to quit A landlord's notice terminating a tenancy. (Chapter 43)

Novation A three-way agreement in which the obligor transfers all rights and duties to a third party. (Chapter 16, 33)

Nuisance An unprivileged interference with a person's use and enjoyment of property. (Chapter 43)

Nuncupative will An oral will. (Chapter 45)

O

Obligee The party to a contract who is entitled to receive performance from the other party. (Chapter 16)

Obligor The party to a contract who is required to do something for the benefit of the other party. (Chapter 16, 24)

Obscenity Constitutional law doctrine holding that some works will receive no First Amendment protection because a court determines they depict sexual matters in an offensive way. (Chapter 5)

Offer In contract law, an act or statement that proposes definite terms and permits the other party to create a contract by accepting those terms. (Chapter 11)

Offeree The party in contract negotiations who receives the first offer. (Chapter 11)

Offeror The party in contract negotiations who makes the first offer. (Chapter 11)

Opinion Because it cannot be proven right or wrong, an opinion is generally a valid defense in defamation cases. (Chapter 6)

Oppression One party uses its superior power to force a contract on the weaker party. (Chapter 13)

Order for relief An official acknowledgment that a debtor is under the jurisdiction of the bankruptcy court. (Chapter 37)

Order paper An instrument that includes the words "pay to the order of" or their equivalent. (Chapter 25)

Output contract An agreement that obligates the seller of goods to sell everything he produces during a stated period to a particular buyer. (Chapter 11)

Outside directors Members of the board of directors who are not employees of the corporation. Also known as independent directors. (Chapter 35)

Override The power of Congress or a state legislature to pass legislation despite a veto by a president or governor. A congressional override requires a two-thirds vote in each house. (Chapter 4)

P

Parol evidence Written or oral evidence, outside the language of a contract, offered by one party to clarify interpretation of the agreement. (Chapter 15)

Parol evidence rule In the case of an integrated contract, neither party may use evidence outside the writing to contradict, vary, or add to its terms. (Chapter 15)

Part performance An exception to the statute of frauds permitting a buyer of real estate to enforce an oral contract if she paid part of the price, entered the property, and made improvements, with the owner's knowledge. (Chapter 15)

Partially disclosed principal If the third party in an agency relationship knows that the agent is acting for a principal, but does not know the identity of the principal, that principal is partially disclosed. (Chapter 28)

Partnership An association of two or more persons to carry on as co-owners of a business for profit. (Chapter 31)

Partnership at will A partnership that has no fixed duration. A partner has the right to resign from the partnership at any time. (Chapter 32)

Partnership by estoppel If a person who is not a partner implies that he is a partner or does not object when other people imply it, he is liable as if he really were a partner. (Chapter 32)

Patent The right to the exclusive use of an invention for 20 years. (Chapter 42)

Patent troll Someone who buys a portfolio of patents for the purpose of making patent infringement claims. (Chapter 42)

Payable on demand The holder of an instrument is entitled to be paid whenever she asks. (Chapter 25)

Payee Someone who is owed money under the terms of an instrument. (Chapter 25)

Per capita Each heir receives the same amount. (Chapter 45)

***Per se* violation of an antitrust law** An automatic breach. Courts will generally not consider mitigating factors. (Chapter 38)

Per stirpes Each branch of the family receives an equal share. (Chapter 45)

Peremptory challenge During *voir dire*, a request by one attorney that a prospective juror be excused for an unstated reason. (Chapter 3)

Perfect tender rule A rule permitting the buyer to reject goods if they fail in any respect to conform to the contract. (Chapter 23)

Perfection A series of steps a secured party must take to protect its rights in collateral against people other than the debtor. (Chapter 24)

Period for years A lease for a fixed period, automatically renewable unless terminated. (Chapter 43)

Periodic tenancy A lease for a fixed period, automatically renewable unless terminated. (Chapter 43)

Perpetual trust A trust that lasts forever. Also known as a dynasty trust. (Chapter 45)

Personal property All property other than real property. (Chapter 44)

Personally identifiable information (PII) Data that identifies a user of a Web site, such as name and address. (Chapter 41)

Personal satisfaction contracts Permit the promisee to make a subjective evaluations of the promisor's performance. (Chapter 17)

Personal services contracts Permits the promisee to make a subjective evaluation of the promisor's performance. (Chapter 17)

Phishing A fraudster sends a message directing the recipient to enter personal information on a website that is an illegal imitation of a legitimate site. (Chapter 41)

Pierce the corporate veil When the court holds shareholders personally liable for the debts of the corporation. (Chapter 33)

Plain meaning rule In statutory interpretation, the premise that words with an ordinary, everyday significance will be so interpreted, unless there is some apparent reason not to. (Chapter 4)

Plaintiff The person who is suing. (Chapter 1)

Plea bargain An agreement in which the defendant pleads guilty to a reduced charge and the prosecution recommends to the judge a relatively lenient sentence. (Chapter 8)

Pleadings The documents that begin a lawsuit: the complaint, the answer, the counter-claim, and reply. (Chapter 3)

Pledge A secured transaction in which a debtor gives collateral to the secured party. (Chapter 24)

Plurality voting To be elected, a candidate only needs to receive more votes than her opponent, not a majority of the votes cast. (Chapter 35)

Point Source A single producer of pollution. (Chapter 40)

Political speech Protected unless it is intended and likely to create imminent lawless action. (Chapter 5)

Positive aspect of the Commerce Clause The power granted to Congress to regulate commerce between the states. (Chapter 5)

Precedent An earlier case that decided the same legal issue as that presently in dispute, and which therefore will control the outcome of the current case. (Chapter 1, 3, 4)

Predatory pricing A violation of §2 of the Sherman Act in which a company lowers its prices below cost to drive competitors out of business. (Chapter 38)

Preemption The doctrine, based on the Supremacy Clause, by which any federal statute takes priority whenever (1) a state statute conflicts or (2) there is no conflict but Congress indicated an intention to control the issue involved. (Chapter 5)

Preference When a debtor unfairly pays creditors immediately before filing a bankruptcy petition. (Chapter 37)

Preferred stock Owners of preferred stock have a right to receive dividends and liquidation proceeds of the company before common shareholders. (Chapter 33)

Preponderance of the evidence The level of proof that a plaintiff must meet to prevail in a civil lawsuit. It means that the plaintiff must offer evidence that, in sum, is slightly more persuasive than the defendant's evidence. (Chapter 3)

Presentment A holder of an instrument makes a demand for payment. (Chapter 26)

Pretermitted child A child omitted from a parent's will. (Chapter 45)

Prima facie "At first sight." A fact or conclusion that is presumed to be true unless someone presents evidence to disprove it. (Chapter 29)

Principal In an agency relationship, the principal is the person for whom the agent is acting. (Chapter 28)

Privacy Act A federal statute prohibiting federal agencies from divulging to other agencies or organizations information about private citizens. (Chapter 4)

Privity The relationship that exists between two parties who make a contract, as opposed to a third party who, though affected by the contract, is not a party to it. (Chapter 21)

Probable cause In a search and seizure case, it means that the information available indicates that it is more likely than not that a search will uncover particular criminal evidence. (Chapter 8)

Probate The process of carrying out the terms of a will. (Chapter 45)

Procedural due process The doctrine which ensures that before the government takes liberty or property, the affected person has a fair chance to oppose the action. (Chapter 5)

Procedural law The rules establishing how the legal system itself is to operate in a particular kind of case. (Chapter 1)

Proceeds Anything that a debtor obtains from the sale or disposition of collateral. Normally, proceeds refers to cash obtained from the sale of the secured property. (Chapter 24)

Production of documents and things A form of discovery in which one party demands that the other furnish original documents or physical things, relating to the suit, for inspection and copying. (Chapter 3)

Product liability The potential responsibility that a manufacturer or seller has for injuries caused by defective goods. (Chapter 22)

Professional corporation A form of organization that permits professionals (such as doctors, lawyers, and accountants) to incorporate. Shareholders are not personally liable for the torts of other shareholders, or for the contract debts of the organization. (Chapter 31)

Profit The right to enter land belonging to another and take something away, such as minerals or timber. (Chapter 43)

Promisee The person to whom a promise is made. (Chapter 16)

Promisor A person who makes a promise. (Chapter 16)

Promissory estoppel A doctrine in which a court may enforce a promise made by the defendant even when there is no contract, if the defendant knew that the plaintiff was likely to rely on the promise, the plaintiff did in fact rely, and enforcement of it is the only way to avoid injustice. (Chapter 10)

Promissory note The maker of the instrument promises to pay a specific amount of money. (Chapter 25)

Promoter The person who creates a corporation by raising capital and undertaking the legal steps necessary for formation. (Chapter 33)

Promulgate To issue a new rule. (Chapter 4)

Proof of claim A form stating the name of an unsecured creditor and the amount of the claim against the debtor. (Chapter 37)

Property insurance Covers physical damage to real estate, personal property, or inventory from causes such as fire, smoke, lightning, wind, riot, vandalism, or theft. (Chapter 45)

Prosecution The government's attempt to convict a defendant of a crime by charging him, trying the case, and forcing him to defend himself. (Chapter 8)

Prospectus Under the Securities Act of 1933, an issuer must provide this document to anyone who purchases a security in a public transaction. The prospectus contains detailed information about the issuer and its business, a description of the stock, and audited financial statements. (Chapter 36)

Protective order A court order limiting one party's discovery. (Chapter 3)

Proxy (1) A person whom the shareholder designates to vote in his place. (2) The written form (typically a card) that the shareholder uses to appoint a designated voter. (Chapter 35)

Proxy statement When a public company seeks proxy votes from its shareholders, it must include a proxy statement. This statement contains information about the company, such as a detailed description of management compensation. (Chapter 35)

Publicly traded corporation A company that (1) has completed a public offering under the Securities Act of 1933, or (2) has securities traded on a national exchange, or (3) has 500 shareholders and $10 million in assets. (Chapter 34)

Punitive damages Money awarded at trial not to compensate the plaintiff for harm but to punish the defendant for conduct that the factfinder considers extreme and outrageous. (Chapter 6)

Purchase money security interest (PMSI) A security interest taken by the person who sells the collateral to the debtor, or by a person who advances money so that the debtor may buy the collateral. (Chapter 24)

Q

Qualified privilege Exists between two people who have a legitimate need to exchange information. (Chapter 29)

Qualifying to do business Registering a corporation in a state in which it is not organized but in which it has an ongoing presence. (Chapter 33)

Quantum meruit "As much as she deserves." The damages awarded in a quasi-contract case. (Chapter 10)

Quasi-contract A legal fiction in which, to avoid injustice, the court awards damages as if a contract had existed, although one did not. (Chapter 10)

Quid pro quo A Latin phrase meaning "this for that." It refers to a form of sexual harassment in which some aspect of a job is made contingent upon sexual activity. (Chapter 39)

Quiet enjoyment A tenant's right to use property without the interference of the landlord. (Chapter 43)

Quorum The number of voters that must be present for a meeting to count. (Chapter 33, 35)

R

Racketeer Influenced and Corrupt Organizations Act (RICO) A powerful federal statute, originally aimed at organized crime, now used in many criminal prosecutions and civil lawsuits. (Chapter 8)

Racketeering acts Any of a long list of specified crimes, such as embezzlement, arson, mail fraud, wire fraud, and so forth. (Chapter 8)

Ratification When someone accepts the benefit of an unauthorized transaction or fails to repudiate it once he has learned of it, he is then bound by it. (Chapter 14)

Reaffirm To promise to pay a debt even after it is discharged. (Chapter 33)

Real property Land, together with certain things associated with it, such as buildings, subsurface rights, air rights, plant life and fixtures. (Chapter 43)

Reasonable Ordinary or usual under the circumstances. (Chapter 19)

Reasonable doubt The level of proof that the government must meet to convict the defendant in a criminal case. The factfinder must be persuaded to a very high degree of certainty that the defendant did what the government alleges. (Chapter 3)

Reciprocal dealing agreement An agreement under which Company *A* will purchase from Company *B* only if Company *B* also buys from Company *A*. These agreements are rule of reason violations of the Sherman Act. (Chapter 38)

Reciprocal promises Promises that are each enforceable independently. (Chapter 19)

Record Information written on paper or stored in an electronic or other medium. (Chapter 26)

Record date To vote at a shareholders meeting, a shareholder must own stock on the record date. (Chapter 36)

Red herring A preliminary prospectus. (Chapter 37)

Redeem To pay the full value of a debt to get the collateral back. (Chapter 24)

Reformation The process by which a court rewrites a contract to ensure its accuracy or viability. (Chapter 18)

Refusal to deal An agreement among competitors that they will not trade with a particular supplier or buyer. Such an agreement is a rule of reason violation of the Sherman Act. (Chapter 38)

Registration statement A document filed with the Securities and Exchange Commission under the Securities Act of 1933 by an issuer seeking to sell securities in a public transaction. (Chapter 36)

Reliance interest A remedy in a contract case that puts the injured party in the position he would have been in had the parties never entered into a contract. (Chapter 18)

Remand The power of an appellate court to return a case to a lower court for additional action. (Chapter 1)

Rent Compensation paid by a tenant to a landlord. (Chapter 43)

Reply A pleading, filed by the plaintiff in response to a defendant's counter-claim. (Chapter 3)

Reporting Company A company registered under the 1934 Act. (Chapter 36)

Repossess A secured party takes collateral because the debtor has defaulted on payments. (Chapter 24)

Representations and warranties Statements of fact about the past or present. (Chapter 19)

Repudiation An indication made by one contracting party to the other that it will not perform. (Chapter 23)

Request for admission A form of discovery in which one party demands that the opposing party either admit or deny particular factual or legal allegations. (Chapter 3)

Requirements contract An agreement that obligates a buyer of specified goods to purchase all of the goods she needs during a stated period from a particular seller. (Chapter 11)

Res ipsa loquitur A doctrine of tort law holding that the facts may imply negligence when the defendant had exclusive control of the thing that caused the harm, the accident would not normally have occurred without negligence, and the plaintiff played no role in causing the injury. (Chapter 7)

Resale price maintenance A *per se* violation of the Sherman Act in which a manufacturer enters into an agreement with retailers about the prices they will charge. (Chapter 38)

Rescind To cancel a contract. (Chapter 14, 17)

Rescission To "undo" a contract and put the parties where they were before they made their agreement. (Chapter 18).

Respondeat superior A rule of agency law holding that a principal is liable when a servant acting within the scope of employment commits a tort that causes physical harm to a person or property. (Chapter 28)

Restitution Restoring an injured party to its original position. (Chapter 8, 14)

Restitution interest A remedy in a contract case that returns to the injured party a benefit that he has conferred on the other party, which it would be unjust to leave with that person. (Chapter 18)

Restricted security Any stock purchased in a private offering (such as one under Regulation D). (Chapter 36)

Restricted stock Securities purchased strictly for investment purposes. (Chapter 36)

Reverse The power of an appellate court to overrule a lower court and grant judgment for the party that had lost in the lower court. (Chapter 3)

Reverse and remand To nullify the lower decision and return the case for reconsideration or retrial. (Chapter 3)

Reversion The right of an owner (or her heirs) to property upon the death of a life tenant. (Chapter 43)

Revocable trust A trust that can be undone or changed at any time. (Chapter 45)

Revocation The act of disavowing a contract offer, so that the offeree no longer has the power to accept. (Chapter 11)

Rider An amendment or addition to a contract. (Chapter 19)

Rule of reason violation An action that breaches the antitrust laws only if it has an anticompetitive impact. (Chapter 38)

Rulemaking The power of an administrative agency to issue regulations. (Chapter 4)

S

S corporation A corporation that is not a taxable entity. (Chapter 31)

Safe Harbor A set of requirements that, if met, indicate *automatic* compliance with a law. (Chapter 36)

Sale on approval A transfer in which a buyer takes goods intending to use them herself, but has the right to return the goods to the seller. (Chapter 21)

Sale or return A transfer in which the buyer takes the goods intending to resell them, but has the right to return the goods to the original owner. (Chapter 21)

Scienter In a case of securities fraud, the plaintiff must prove that the defendant acted willfully, knowingly, or recklessly. (Chapter 36)

Scrivener's error A typo. (Chapter 19)

Secondary boycott Picketing, directed by a union against a company, designed to force that company to stop doing business with the union's employer. (Chapter 30)

Secondary offering Any public sale of securities by a company after the initial public offering. (Chapter 36)

Secured party A person or company that holds a security interest. (Chapter 24)

Security Any purchase in which the buyer invests money in a common enterprise and expects to earn a profit predominantly from the efforts of others. (Chapter 36)

Security agreement A contract in which the debtor gives a security interest to the secured party. (Chapter 24)

Security interest An interest in personal property or fixtures that secures the performance of some obligation. (Chapter 16, 24)

Separation of powers The principle, established by the first three articles of the Constitution, that authority should be divided among the legislative, executive, and judicial branches. (Chapter 5)

Service mark A type of trademark used to identify services, not products. (Chapter 44)

Settlor Someone who creates a trust. (Chapter 45)

Sexual harassment Unwanted sexual advances, comments or touching, sufficiently severe to violate Title VII of the 1964 Civil Rights Act. (Chapter 29)

Shilling A seller at auction either bids on his own goods or agrees to cross-bid with a group of other sellers. (Chapter 41)

Short-swing trading Under §16 of the Securities Exchange Act, insiders must turn over to the corporation any profits they make from the purchase and sale or sale and purchase of company securities in a six-month period. (Chapter 36)

Signatory A person, company, or nation that has signed a legal document, such as a contract, agreement, or treaty. (Chapter 9)

Signature liability The liability of someone who signs an instrument. (Chapter 26)

Sight draft Payable on demand. (Chapter 25)

Single recovery principle A rule of tort litigation that requires a plaintiff to claim all damages, present and future, at the time of trial, not afterwards. (Chapter 6)

Slander *See* Defamation. (Chapter 6)

Sole discretion A party to a contract has the absolute right to make a decision on that issue. (Chapter 19)

Sole proprietorship An unincorporated business owned by a single person. (Chapter 31)

Sophisticated investor Someone who is able to assess the risk of an offering (Chapter 36)

Sovereign The recognized political power, whom citizens obey. (Chapter 1)

Sovereign immunity The right of a national government to be free of lawsuits brought in foreign courts. (Chapter 9)

Spam Unsolicited commercial or bulk e-mail. ("To spam" is to send such e-mail.) (Chapter 41)

Specific deterrence *See* Deterrence. (Chapter 8)

Specific performance A contract remedy requiring the breaching party to perform the contract, by conveying land or some unique asset, rather than by paying money damages. (Chapter 18)

Spyware A computer program that enters a user's computer without permission and monitors and reports the user's activities. (Chapter 41)

Sole proprietorship An unincorporated business owned by one person. (Chapter 31)

Stakeholders Anyone who is affected by the activities of a corporation, such as employees, customers, creditors, suppliers, shareholders, and neighbors. (Chapter 34)

Stare decisis "Let the decision stand." A basic principle of the common law, it means that precedent is usually binding. (Chapter 4)

Statute A law passed by a legislative body, such as Congress. (Chapter 1)

Statute of frauds This law provides that certain contracts are not enforceable unless in writing. (Chapter 15)

Statute of limitations A statute that determines the period within which a particular kind of lawsuit must be filed. (Chapter 17)

Statute of repose A law that places an absolute limit on when a lawsuit may be filed, regardless of when the defect was discovered. (Chapter 22)

Statutory interpretation A court's power to give meaning to new legislation by clarifying ambiguities, providing limits, and ultimately applying it to a specific fact pattern in litigation. (Chapter 4)

Straight bankruptcy Also known as liquidation, this form of bankruptcy mandates that the bankrupt's assets be sold to pay creditors but the creditor has no obligation to share future earnings. (Chapter 37)

Strict liability A tort doctrine holding to a very high standard all those who engage in ultrahazardous activity (e.g., using explosives) or who manufacture certain products. (Chapter 7)

Strict performance Requires one party to perform its obligations precisely, with no deviation from the contract terms. (Chapter 17)

Strike The ultimate weapon of a labor union, it occurs when all or most employees of a particular plant or employer walk off the job and refuse to work. (Chapter 30)

Sublease A tenant's transfer of *some* of his legal interest in a property. (Chapter 43)

Subpoena An order to appear, issued by a court or government body. (Chapter 4)

Subpoena *duces tecum* An order to produce certain documents or things before a court or government body. (Chapter 4)

Subprime loan A loan that has an above-market interest rate because the borrower is high-risk. (Chapter 49)

Subrogated to The bank can substitute for, or take the place of, a party. (Chapter 25)

Substantial performance The promisor performs contract duties well enough to be entitled to his full contract price, minus the value of any defects. (Chapter 17)

Substantive due process *See* Due Process Clause. (Chapter 5)

Substantive law Rules that establish the rights of parties. For example, the prohibition against slander is substantive law, as opposed to procedural law. (Chapter 1)

Summary judgment The power of a trial court to terminate a lawsuit before a trial has begun, on the grounds that no essential facts are in dispute. (Chapter 3)

Supermajority voting Typically, shareholders can approve charter amendments by a majority vote. However, sometimes corporations require more than a majority of shareholders (e.g., 80 percent) to approve certain charter amendments, such as a merger. These provisions are designed to discourage hostile takeovers. (Chapter 34)

Superseding cause An event that interrupts the chain of causation and relieves a defendant from liability based on her own act. (Chapter 7)

Supremacy Clause From Article VI of the Constitution, it declares that federal statutes and treaties take priority over any state law, if there is a conflict between the two or, even absent a conflict, if Congress manifests an intent to preempt the field. (Chapter 5)

Surplus A sum of money greater than the debt incurred. (Chapter 24)

T

Takings Clause Part of the Fifth Amendment, it ensures that when any governmental unit takes private property for public use, it must compensate the owner. (Chapter 5)

Tariff A duty imposed on imported goods by the government of the importing nation. (Chapter 9)

Tenancy at sufferance A tenancy that exists without the permission of the landlord, after the expiration of a true tenancy. (Chapter 43)

Tenancy at will A tenancy with no fixed duration, which may be terminated by either party at any time. (Chapter 43)

Tenancy by the entirety A form of joint ownership available only to married couples. If one member of the couple dies, the property goes automatically to the survivor. Creditors cannot attach the property, nor can one owner sell the property without the other's permission. (Chapter 43)

Tenancy for years A lease for a stated, fixed period. (Chapter 43)

Tenancy in common Two or more people holding equal interest in a property, but with no right of survivorship. (Chapter 43)

Tenant A person given temporary possession of the landlord's property. (Chapter 43)

Tender offer A public offer to buy a block of stock directly from shareholders. (Chapter 34)

Term partnership When the partners agree in advance on the duration of a partnership. (Chapter 32)

Termination statement A document indicating that a secured party no longer claims a security interest in the collateral. (Chapter 24)

Testamentary trust A trust created by the grantor's will. (Chapter 45)

Testator Someone who dies having executed a will. (Chapter 45)

Testatrix A female testator. (Chapter 45)

Third party beneficiary Someone who stands to benefit from a contract to which she is not a party. An *intended* beneficiary may enforce such a contract; an *incidental* beneficiary may not. (Chapter 16)

Three-Fifths Clause A clause in Article 1, section 2 of the United States Constitution, now void and regarded as racist, which required that for purposes of taxation and representation, a slave should be counted as three-fifths of a person. (Chapter 5)

Tied product In a tying arrangement, the product that a buyer must purchase as the condition for being allowed to buy another product. (Chapter 38)

Time draft Payable in the future. (Chapter 25)

Time of the essence clauses Clauses that generally make contract dates strictly enforceable. (Chapter 17)

Tort A civil wrong, committed in violation of a duty that the law imposes. (Chapter 6)

Tortious interference with a contract A tort in which the defendant deliberately impedes an existing contract between the plaintiff and another. (Chapter 6)

Tortious interference with a prospective advantage A tort in which the defendant deliberately obstructs a developing venture or advantage that the plaintiff has created. (Chapter 6)

Tracking When an auditor takes an item of original data and tracks it forward to ensure that it has been properly recorded throughout the bookkeeping process. (Chapter 27)

Trade acceptance A draft drawn by a seller of goods on the buyer and payable to the seller or some third party. (Chapter 25)

Trade secret A formula, device, process, method, or compilation of information that, when used in business, gives the owner an advantage over competitors who do not know it. (Chapter 42)

Trademark Any combination of words and symbols that a business uses to identify its products or services and that federal law will protect. (Chapter 42)

Treasury stock Stock that has been bought back by its issuing corporation. (Chapter 33)

Trespass A tort committed by intentionally entering land that belongs to someone else, or remaining on the land after being asked to leave. (Chapter 6)

Trespasser Anyone on a property without consent. (Chapter 7)

Trial court Any court in a state or federal system that holds formal hearings to determine the facts in a civil or criminal case. (Chapter 3)

Trust An entity that separates legal and beneficial ownership. (Chapter 45)

Tying a product In a tying arrangement, the product offered for sale on the condition that another product be purchased as well. (Chapter 38)

Tying arrangement A violation of the Sherman and Clayton Acts in which a seller requires that two distinct products be purchased together. The seller uses its significant power in the market for the tying product to shut out a substantial part of the market for the tied product. (Chapter 38)

U

Ultra vires An activity that is not permitted by a corporation's charter. (Chapter 33)

Ultrahazardous activity Conduct that is lawful yet unusual and much more likely to cause injury than normal commercial activity. (Chapter 7)

Unconscionable contract An agreement that a court refuses to enforce because it is fundamentally unfair as a result of unequal bargaining power by one party. (Chapter 20)

Undisclosed principal If a third party in an agency relationship does not know that the agent is acting for a principal, that principal is undisclosed. (Chapter 28)

Undue influence One party so dominates the thinking of another party to a contract that the dominant party cannot truly consent to the agreement. (Chapter 14)

Unfair labor practice An act, committed by either a union or an employer, that violates the National Labor Relations Act, such as failing to bargain in good faith. (Chapter 30)

Unilateral contract A binding agreement in which one party has made an offer that the other can accept only by action, not words. (Chapter 10)

Unilateral mistake Occurs when only one party enters a contract under a mistaken assumption. (Chapter 14)

Unliquidated debt A claimed debt that is disputed, either because the parties disagree over whether there is in fact a debt or because they disagree over the amount. (Chapter 12)

U.S. Trustee, The Oversees the administration of bankruptcy law in a region. (Chapter 37)

Usury Charging interest at a rate that exceeds legal limits. (Chapter 13)

Utter To pass on an instrument that one knows to be forged. (Chapter 26)

V

Value The holder has *already* done something in exchange for the instrument. (Chapter 25)

Valuation A process by which the Customs Service determines the fair value of goods being imported, for purposes of imposing a duty. (Chapter 9)

Verdict The decision of the factfinder in a case. (Chapter 3)

Vertical agreement or merger An agreement or merger between two companies at different stages of the production process, such as when a company acquires one of its suppliers or distributors. (Chapter 38)

Veto The power of the president to reject legislation passed by Congress, terminating the bill unless Congress votes by a 2/3 majority to override. (Chapter 4)

Vouching Auditors choose a transaction listed in a company's books and check backwards for original data to support it. (Chapter 27)

Void agreement An agreement that neither party may legally enforce, usually because the purpose of the bargain was illegal or because one of the parties lacked capacity to make it. (Chapter 10)

Voidable contract An agreement that, because of some defect, may be terminated by one party, such as a minor, but not by both parties. (Chapter 10)

Voidable title Limited rights in goods, inferior to those of the owner. (Chapter 21)

Voir dire The process of selecting a jury. Attorneys for the parties and the judge may inquire of prospective jurors whether they are biased or incapable of rendering a fair and impartial verdict. (Chapter 3)

Voluntary petition Filed by a debtor to initiate a bankruptcy case. (Chapter 37)

W

Warrant liability The liability of someone who receives payment on an instrument. (Chapter 26)

Warranty A guarantee that goods will meet certain standards. (Chapter 22)

Warranty of fitness for a particular purpose An assurance under the Uniform Commercial Code that the goods are fit for the special purpose for which the buyer intends them and of which the seller is aware. (Chapter 22)

Warranty of merchantability An assurance under the Uniform Commercial Code that the goods are fit for their ordinary purpose. (Chapter 22)

Whistleblower Someone who discloses wrongful behavior. (Chapter 29)

Will A legal document that disposes of the testator's property after death. (Chapter 45)

Winding up The process whereby the assets of a partnership are sold and the proceeds distributed. (Chapter 32)

World Trade Organization (WTO) Created by GATT to stimulate international commerce and resolve trade disputes. (Chapter 9)

World Wide Web A decentralized collection of documents containing text, pictures and sound that is accessible from Internet sites. It is a sub-network of the Internet. (Chapter 41)

Writ An order from a government compelling someone to do a particular thing. (Chapter 1)

Writ of certiorari A petition asking the Supreme Court to hear a case. (Chapter 3)

Wrongful discharge An employer may not fire a worker for a reason that violates basic social rights, duties or responsibilities. (Chapter 29)

TABLE OF CASES

D

E

F

G

H

I

J

K

L

M

N

O

P

Q

R

S

T

U

V

W

Y

Z

INDEX

A

B

D

E

F

G

Q